Vincent

W9-ASV-220

BARRON'S

Finance & Investment Handbook

Eighth Edition

John Downes, A.B.
Coauthor, *Beating the Dow*
Freelance Financial Writer
Former Vice President, AVCO Financial Services, Inc.
City of New York, Office of the Mayor, Office for Economic Development

Jordan Elliot Goodman, A.B., M.A.
Author, *Master Your Debt*
Author, *Master Your Money Type*
Author, *Everyone's Money Book*
Host, *Answers Radio Show* on www.VoiceAmerica.com
Creator of *Moneyanswers.com* web site
Former Financial Commentator, *Marketplace Morning Report*
Former Wall Street Correspondent, *MONEY Magazine,* Time Warner Inc.
Former Financial Commentator, *NBC News at Sunrise*

© Copyright 2010, 2007, 2003, 1998, 1995, 1990, 1987, 1986 by
Barron's Educational Series, Inc.

All rights reserved.
No part of this publication may be reproduced or
distributed in any form or by any means
without the written permission of the copyright
owner.

All inquiries should be addressed to:
Barron's Educational Series, Inc.
250 Wireless Boulevard
Hauppauge, New York 11788
www.barronseduc.com

Library of Congress Catalog Card No.: 2010031548

ISBN-13: 978-0-7641-6269-5
ISBN-10: 0-7641-6269-1

Library of Congress Cataloging-in-Publication Data

Downes, John, 1936-
    Finance and investment handbook / John Downes, Jordan Elliot
Goodman.—8th ed.
      p. cm.
   Rev. ed. of: Barron's finance & investment handbook. 7th ed. c2007.
Includes bibliographical references and index.
   ISBN-13: 978-0-7641-6269-5
   ISBN-10: 0-7641-6269-1
   1. Finance—Handbooks, manuals, etc. 2. Investments—Handbooks,
manuals, etc. 3. Finance—Dictionaries. 4. Investments—Dictionaries.
I. Goodman, Jordan Elliot. II. Downes, John, 1936- Barron's finance &
investment handbook. III. Title.

HG173.D66 2010
332.67'8—dc22

                                                                    2010031548

PRINTED IN CHINA
9 8 7 6 5 4 3 2 1

CONTENTS

PART I HOW TO INVEST YOUR MONEY:
30 KEY PERSONAL INVESTMENT OPPORTUNITIES

PART II   HOW TO READ AN ANNUAL REPORT

PART III   UNDERSTANDING THE FINANCIAL NEWS

PART IV   DICTIONARY OF FINANCE AND INVESTMENT

PART V   FINANCE AND INVESTMENT READY REFERENCE

APPENDIX

ACKNOWLEDGMENTS

A project as massive as this *Handbook* is clearly the work of more than two people, and to thank all adequately would add considerably to its bulk. There are several individuals and organizations, however, without whose help the project in its present form would not have been feasible at all.

Following is the list of individuals, companies, and organizations whose help in preparation of this book was invaluable.

Accounting Today
A. M. Best Company
American Association of Individual Investors
American Bankers Association
American Council of Life Insurers
American Institute of Certified Public Accountants
American Society of CLU & ChFC (Chartered Life Underwriters)
Associated Credit Bureaus
Board of Trade of The City of New York
The Bond Buyer
Bond Market Association
Boston Stock Exchange
Bowman Communications
Canada Department of Finance
Canadian Bankers Association
Canadian Council of the Federation
Canadian Securities Administrators
Canadian Society of Technical Analysts
Chicago Board of Trade
Chicago Board Options Exchange
Chicago Mercantile Exchange
Cincinnati Stock Exchange
Coffee, Sugar & Cocoa Exchange
Commodity Futures Trading Commission
Conference of State Bank Supervisors
Dow Jones & Company
Employee Benefit Research Institute
Fannie Mae
Federal Reserve Bank of New York
Federal Reserve Board
Federal Trade Commission
Financial Industry Regulatory Authority
FINEX
Frank Russell Company
Futures Industry Association
Goldman Sachs & Company
Health Insurance Institute of America
Hulbert Financial Digest
Insurance Information Institute
Internal Revenue Service

International Petroleum Exchange
International Swaps and Derivatives Association
Institute for Financial Markets
Investment Management Consultants Association
Investment Program Association
Kansas City Board of Trade
Lipper, Inc.
London International Financial Futures Exchange
London Metal Exchange
MidAmerica Commodity Exchange
Minneapolis Grain Exchange
Moneypaper Newsletter
Montreal Exchange/Bourse de Montreal
Mortgage Bankers Association
Municipal Bond Investors Assurance Corporation
Nasdaq Stock Market
National Association of Attorneys General
National Association of Insurance Companies
National Association of Investors Corporation
National Association of Real Estate Investment Trusts
National Association of Realtors
National Association of Variable Annuities
National Credit Union Administration
New York Cotton Exchange
New York Futures Exchange
New York Life Insurance Company
New York Mercantile Exchange
New York Stock Exchange
North American Securities Administrators Association
Office of Thrift Supervision
Options Clearing Corporation
Options Institute
Pacific Exchange
Pension Benefit Guaranty Corporation
Philadelphia Stock Exchange
Securities and Exchange Commission
Securities Industry and Financial Markets Association
SNL Financial LLC
Sydney Futures Exchange
Thomas J. Herzfeld Advisors
Thomson Reuters
Tokyo Stock Exchange
Toronto Stock Exchange
Trimedia Incorporated
U.S. Department of Commerce
U.S. Department of Labor
Value Line Investment Survey
The Weiser Group
Wilshire Associates
Winnipeg Commodity Exchange
World Federation of Exchanges
World Gold Council
Zacks Investment Research

The authors would especially like to thank *Yahoo! Finance* and *The Wall Street Journal* for allowing them to reproduce materials in Part I of this book.

Other people made contributions for which the word acknowledgment doesn't do. Thomas F. Hirsch, Barron's editor for the first two editions, was a full partner in the original project and we value his professional guidance and ongoing friendship. David Rodman of Barron's ably oversaw the 3rd through 7th editions of the *Handbook*. Darrell Buono of Barron's handled an unbelievable amount of editorial work with skill and patience and guided this Eighth Edition to print. Leonard Sloane's tireless work in updating and fact-checking thousands of pieces of information was truly incredible—his efforts and high standards went well beyond the call of duty.

Suzanne and Jason Goodman, Katie Downes, and Annie Downes-Whelan all sacrificed unselfishly at various stages of the project and we are in their debt.

John Downes
Jordan Elliot Goodman

PREFACE TO THE EIGHTH EDITION

This Eighth Edition finds the United States in the early, tentative stages of recovery from what is being called the Great Recession.

When a housing bubble of unprecedented proportions began deflating in 2007, foreclosures on properties of subprime borrowers spread to the mortgage market generally. Banks, investment banks, institutional investors, and other holders of mortgage-backed securities and real estate related derivatives found themselves bloated with "toxic" assets. With their capital severely constricted or eliminated, lenders couldn't make loans, investors facing margin calls were forced to liquidate assets at substantial losses, and individuals confusing HELOCS (home equity lines of credit) with ARMs had to slow their spending on imported consumer goods, assuming they were lucky and not among the 10 percent of the population that lost their jobs.

This credit crunch hobbled foreign economies as well as our own, causing an international recession and a wave of institutional failures that threatened a global economic collapse. Deeming institutions such as Citicorp, Merrill Lynch, and AIG "too big to fail," the U.S. government and Federal Reserve, as well as their international counterparts, stepped in with bailout money and massive economic stimulus programs and precluded Armageddon, at least for the time being.

In the process of replacing its manufacturing-based economy with a service-based economy, the United States went from the world's largest creditor nation to the world's largest debtor nation in the short space of 20 or so years. Facing systemic failure after the Lehman Brothers bankruptcy in 2008, our government's options, as a practical matter, were down to one: borrow even more money from China and other producing countries and continue printing money. Projected annual budget deficits have thus moved from the mid-billions to the trillions of dollars, the national debt has mounted from a pre-crisis level of $8.5 trillion to $13 trillion (not counting Social Security, Medicare, and other "unfunded obligations"), and to the extent we monetize our debt (repay with printed money), we face a choice of high inflation or painful personal sacrifice in the very near future.

What is remarkable is that America's economic fundamentals were seriously deteriorating during a period of unprecedented economic growth and prosperity. The financialization of the American economy became a tradeoff of short-term gain for long-term stability, with modern technology producing financial gimmickry faster than a regulatory establishment could begin to comprehend it, much less address it. Even now, as we appear to be regaining our economic footing thanks to government stimulus that will temporarily exacerbate the fundamental imbalances, our political establishment is resisting the real financial reform that is needed to assure real economic recovery.

Coincidently, the prefaces to the previous seven editions of the *Finance and Investment Handbook* represent in capsule form the 20 odd years of financial history leading to this fix. They are worth rereading, even as they reveal some of the complacency that led us, along with others in the financial marketplace, to occasionally mistake risk for progress.

The *First Edition*, published in 1986, noted that the previous two decades had seen more fundamental changes in finance and investment than any similar period since the Great Depression, which had ushered in massive reforms in the economy and securities markets. Since 1970, deregulation, major tax law revisions, globalization of markets, giant corporate mergers, and, above all, the widespread use of computer and advanced communication technology had altered the world of finance and investments in ways affecting everybody.

Before 1970, investors were typically wealthy people who bought stocks for income and switched to bonds when interest rates exceeded dividends and prospective growth. By the 1970s, mutual funds and other institutional investors became dominant. Acting on behalf of average people, they invested for total returns, capital gains plus dividends in the case of stocks, or capital gains plus interest in the case of bonds. Competition for returns forced a short-term investment focus, assuring volatility. In an effort to reduce or at least redistribute risk, computer technology was used to create a new array of hybrid investments and derivative products. Complex and bewildering investment choices spawned an expanded establishment of investment professionals, specializing in different aspects of the problem and having varying credentials.

The gathering trends of deregulation, globalization, and computerization had a traumatic economic and political backdrop. The Middle East oil embargo in the early 1970s caused skyrocketing oil prices, leading to a combination of runaway inflation and economic stagnation, called stagflation. The years 1973 and 1974 witnessed the worst bear market since 1929. By the early 1980s, inflation had peaked at over 14 percent, the bank prime lending rate had reached a stratospheric 21.5 percent, the economy was in recession, and the Dow Jones Industrial Average, sustained by a group of "all-weather" institutional favorites known as the "Nifty Fifty," was hovering around 1,000, about where it had been 10 years before.

Thus began the "Roaring '80s" and "Reaganomics," marked by controlled but historically high interest rates aimed at ending inflation, by record-setting federal deficits, and by the onset of the longest period of sustained economic growth and stock market gains in American history. Corporate takeovers financed by junk bonds and newly deregulated savings and loan institutions diversifying into speculative real estate investments were, by the mid-1980s, setting the stage for calamity. The *Second Revised Edition*, published in 1987, took account of these developments while noting such landmark new developments as London's Big Bang in 1986 and the historic Tax Reform Act of 1986, which eliminated a confounding maze of tax loopholes and tax shelters, and made economic merits rather than tax advantages the primary criteria for investment decision making.

The Roaring '80s had a bizarre ending and the *Third Revised Edition*, published in 1990, said in part: "The word 'crash,' previously reserved for 1929, was reincarnated to describe the unprecedented and terrifying 508-point drop in the Dow Jones Industrial Average on October 19, 1987, a debacle blamed largely on a computer-age phenomenon known as 'program trading.' Millions turned out for *Wall Street*, a movie inspired by real-life stories of yuppie millionaires who had sadly learned that insider trading meant trading red suspenders for striped pajamas. And in the most expensive financial rescue and restructuring project in history, the government was forced to bail out the depositors in hundreds of savings and loan associations that failed because their managers abused the freedom of deregulation." At the same time, on the global political and economic front, changes were taking place that were literally world-shaking. The Iron Curtain, after 45 years of Cold War, was lifting and there were clear signs that Eastern Bloc countries would be joining the world trade and finance community. Japan had emerged as a leading economic power and the Tokyo stock market, as the '90s approached, was selling at stratospheric levels, with the risk that a major sell-off would send reverberations throughout the world. The dismantling of the Berlin Wall portended a unified Germany as the centerpiece of a European Community scheduled to be completely free of all trade and economic barriers by 1992. More than previous revisions, the *Third Edition* became globally oriented.

The *Fourth Edition* went to press in 1995. With the bull market now 10 years old, the Dow Jones Industrial Average was nearing 5,000, led by high-tech stocks, many already dangerously overvalued. The economy, after a 1991 recession brought on by the Persian Gulf War, was in its fourth year of steady growth with low inflation. The buzz word "Goldilocks economy" implied that the Federal Reserve had finally mastered the art of managing business cycles and keeping the economy, like Goldilocks' porridge, "not too hot, not too cold, just right." Pundits were talking of a "new economy" and a "new paradigm," in which historically excessive stock valuations were justified by assured economic growth and rising corporate profits reflecting productivity gains. (Fed Chairman Alan Greenspan, it should be noted, would soon accuse investors of "irrational exuberance" and remind us that as far as he knew, "the law of business cycles had not been repealed.")

The *Fifth Edition*, published in 1998, noted that the 1990s had brought corporate downsizing and restructuring, massive stock buybacks, strategic mergers on a global scale, and a continuation of strong economic growth, low inflation, and rising stock prices. (The Dow was then around 8,000 on its way to 12,000 by January 2000). We also noted, however, that on the eve of a new millennium, floundering Asian economies and a recession in Japan threatened markets in the United States and challenged the confidence of the new European Monetary Union, with its common currency, the Euro, and its promise of expanded financial markets. The introduction of Roth IRAs, the lowering of long-term capital gains tax rates, and other provisions of the Taxpayer Relief Act of 1997 and the IRS Restructuring and Reform Act of 1998, we noted, acknowledged the increasing importance of self-reliance in personal financial planning.

The *Sixth Edition*, published in 2003, followed the bursting of the "tech bubble," the general stock market decline, and the economic recession that coincided with the turn of the millennium and the inauguration of President George W. Bush. The terrorist attack on the World Trade Center on September 11, 2001 created a general climate of public fear, and the invasion of Iraq—and ongoing unrest and violence there—caused deficits to soar. These factors caused uncertainty in financial markets, where confidence was already shaken after the bankruptcy of Enron Corporation in 2001 decimated the 401(k) retirement plans of employees, and exposed abuses of accounting practices and disclosures, misuse of executive stock options, and violations of rules designed to assure the objectivity of broker research analysts. Enron was followed by a series of debacles caused by abuses of corporate governance at Global Crossing Ltd., WorldCom, Tyco International, and other public companies.

Major legislation covered by the *Sixth Edition* included the Financial Services Modernization Act of 1999 (Gramm-Leach-Bliley Act) that eliminated Glass-Steagall firewalls and put banks, brokers, and insurers into each other's businesses while significantly expanding consumer privacy rights; the Economic Growth and Tax Relief Reconciliation Act of 2001 (EGTRRA), which massively reduced taxes over a 10-year period, liberalized tax-deferred retirement accounts and related educational benefits, and introduced major estate tax reform; the Job Creation and Worker Assistance Act of 2002, designed to stimulate economic recovery in the aftermath of the recession and the September 11 terrorist attacks; and the Sarbanes-Oxley Act of 2002, with its creation of the Public Company Accounting Oversight Board (PCAOB) to protect the interests of investors and further the public interest in the preparation of informative, fair, and independent audit reports.

The *Seventh Edition* added six additional legislative advances, including the Jobs and Growth Tax Relief Reconciliation Act of 2003, the Military Family Tax Relief Act of 2003, the Working Families Tax Relief Act of 2004, the Fair and Accurate Credit Transactions Act of 2004, the Energy Tax Incentives Act of 2005, and the Bankruptcy Abuse Prevention and Consumer Protection Act of 2005. All text affected by these developments has been modified and new commentary added. The Dictionary has been thoroughly updated to take account of these developments, along with other modifications, and new vocabulary created by the continued expansion of electronic trading systems in the United States and proliferating market-based systems. The mutual fund scandals of 2003 and 2004 and a number of investment innovations, such as flexible spending accounts (FSAs), separately managed accounts (SMAs), single stock futures (SSFs), income deposit securities (IDSs), income preferred securities (IPSs), and adaptations of exchange-traded funds (ETFs), are covered. The *Eighth Edition* includes the effects and responses to the 2008 financial crisis.

HOW TO USE THIS *HANDBOOK* EFFECTIVELY

Each section of this *Handbook* is a self-contained entity. At the same time, however, the relevance of the various sections to each other is clear, since the objective of the *Handbook* is to join in one volume the different elements that together make up today's world of finance and investment. Tempting though it was from an editorial standpoint, cross-referencing has been kept to a minimum in the belief that readers would prefer not to be distracted by such editorial devices. At certain points, however, where reliance on the fuller explanation of a term in the *Handbook's* Dictionary of Finance and Investment seemed preferable to a discussion, cross-references to the dictionary are indicated by small capitals (for instance, ABC AGREEMENT). In any case, the dictionary is a source of comprehensive information on terms and concepts used throughout the *Handbook* and should be consulted whenever an aspect of finance and investment is not clear to you. The Table of Contents and especially the Index will also help you locate related information in different parts of the *Handbook* and should be consulted regularly.

*   *   *

Although the *Handbook* was a collaborative effort in every sense of the word, primary responsibility was divided as follows: The sections on investment alternatives and reading financial reports were written by John Downes. The section on reading the financial pages was written by Charles Koshetz and edited by John Downes and Jordan Elliot Goodman. The Dictionary of Finance and Investment was authored coequally by John Downes and Jordan Elliot Goodman. The reference lists and the accompanying explanatory material were compiled, edited, and written by Jordan Elliot Goodman.

John Downes
Jordan Elliot Goodman

PART I

How to Invest Your Money: 30 Key Personal Investment Opportunities

PART I

How to Invest Your Money: 90 Key Personal Investment Opportunities

INTRODUCTION

This section presents 30 basic investment alternatives as they have emerged from the transformative 1970s through the global financial crisis of the late 2000s. It is divided into 30 *basic* alternatives; each discussion, however, includes important variations, which cover the full range of investment choices available to individuals.

The purpose of the section is not to provide advice. Investment decisions must always be made in subjective terms, taking into account one's financial position, risk comfort level, and goals. Rather, the section is designed to set forth in current terms the vital features distinguishing different investments, so you can talk knowledgeably with your investment counselor or, if you are a finance or investment professional, so you can be a better source of advice.

Preceding the discussions of investments is a table showing important characteristics of each investment. The chart is a quick way to learn pertinent facts, but should be used in conjunction with the discussions themselves to make sure you are aware of nuances and exceptions associated with a particular type of investment.

The discussions of investment alternatives begin with short overviews designed to describe the essential features of the investment and, where helpful, provide some historical perspective. These overviews are followed by sections in question-and-answer format designed to present concisely and informatively the basic data needed to evaluate investment alternatives. Let's look at the questions and what they mean. (Remember, if you don't understand a finance or investment term, consult the extensive dictionary in this *Handbook.*)

Buying, Selling, and Holding

How do I buy and sell it? Prior to the 1970s, things were simpler: You bought your stocks and bonds from a broker, your life insurance from an insurance agent, and went to a bank with your savings or your loan request. Then a consolidation trend driven by technology, deregulation, and globalization began that led to a predominance of FINANCIAL SUPERMARKETS offering all these services and more. When an unprecedented bubble in real estate values burst in 2007 and triggered a global credit crisis threatening collapse of the financial system, several troubled financial institutions were deemed too big to fail, essentially meaning too big to exist. In early 2010, after massive federal bailouts and government-arranged "shotgun marriages," institutions emerged that were even bigger and represented even greater systemic risk. Ironic as that seems, it was the only way to avoid a global disaster with the clock ticking. Now that the emergency has been temporarily quieted, reforms are being considered that would reduce the complexity and interconnectedness of that handful of too-big-to-fail institutions and result in a more traditional financial landscape composed of manageable entities with non-conflicting activities subject to appropriate regulation.

While this is being sorted out, however, we can't be absolutely sure who will be buying and selling what, but one thing can be said for certain: You won't sound foolish these days if you ask a bank or broker if a given investment—no matter how specialized—can be bought or sold through his or her firm. DISCOUNT BROKERS are a special breed. They handle a variety of securities, but as a rule function strictly as brokers; some provide research, but do not look to them for investment guidance.

Is there a minimum purchase amount, and what is the price range? This question is aimed at giving you an idea of what it costs to get in the game, which is often more than just the minimum DENOMINATION or UNIT in which an investment is issued. The question cannot always be answered in absolute terms, since broker policies vary in terms of minimum orders and there may be SUITABILITY RULES requiring that you prove a certain financial capacity to take the risks associated with a particular investment. Certain securities trade in ROUND LOTS (for instance, 100 shares of common stock), though it is usually possible to buy ODD LOT quantities (for instance, 35 shares) at a higher commission per unit. In most foreign countries, the term BOARD LOTS is used instead of round lots and common stocks, called ORDINARY SHARES or "ords," tend to be priced in the foreign equivalent of American pennies. Board lots are generally much larger than American round lots and they vary widely.

What fees and charges are involved? Again, we have been specific wherever possible, but with some investments, notably common stocks, commissions are sometimes negotiated, based on the size and nature of the transaction. DISCOUNT BROKERS, which as a rule do not give investment advice but execute trades at rates that are roughly half those of most full-service brokers, also have different rates for different transactions. Online brokers, which are becoming more populous as the Internet expands, offer even deeper discounts than traditional discount brokers for bare-bones service. See the entries for SHARE BROKER and VALUE BROKER in this *Handbook's* dictionary for discussions of different categories of discount broker. You will also frequently see references to DEALER spreads. This term refers to the MARKDOWNS and markups that are deducted from your selling price or added to your buying price when a broker-dealer is operating as a DEALER rather than simply as a BROKER. MARKET MAKERS in thinly traded over-the-counter stocks, bonds, and foreign securities provide bid and offer quotes through PINK SHEETS LLC, a service available to broker-dealers. When Pink Sheet spreads are very wide, which they commonly are, investors can unwittingly pay excessive prices for such securities.

Does it mature, expire, or otherwise terminate? Some investments are issued with a fixed MATURITY DATE, others are not. But even those with a fixed maturity date may be CALLABLE—that is, bought back at the pleasure of the issuer, or as part of a SINKING FUND provision. Others may have PUT OPTIONS, permitting REDEMPTION by the investor before maturity.

Can I sell it quickly? This question has to do with LIQUIDITY, the ability to convert an investment into cash without significant loss of value. Investments normally enjoying high liquidity are those with an active SECONDARY MARKET, in which they are actively traded among other investors subsequent to their original issue. Shares of LISTED SECURITIES have high liquidity. Liquidity can also be provided in other ways: for example, the SPONSOR of a unit investment trust might offer to MAKE A MARKET—to find a buyer to match you as a seller, should the need arise for you to sell.

How is market value determined and how do I keep track of it? MARKET VALUE is the price your investment would fetch in the open market, assuming that it is traded in a SECONDARY MARKET. In these discussions you will often encounter the word VOLATILE, referring to the extent to which the market price of an investment fluctuates independently of the overall market. Professionals use the term SYSTEMATIC RISK or its synonym MARKET RISK when discussing an investment's tendency to rise or fall in price as a result of market forces, as opposed to company-specific factors, which represent NONSYSTEMATIC RISK.

Investment Objectives

Should I buy this if my objective is capital appreciation? The purpose here is to identify investments likely to gain in value—to produce CAPITAL GAINS.

Although APPRECIATION does not refer to capital growth due to factors such as reinvested dividends or compound interest, such factors are noted as a matter of relevance where they exist to a substantial degree. In the same category is appreciation due to ORIGINAL ISSUE DISCOUNT on fixed-income securities, which is considered interest. Other fixed-income investments bought in the market at a DISCOUNT from PAR because rising rates (or other factors) caused lower prices, create appreciation in the sense of capital gains either at REDEMPTION or when resold in the market at a higher price. Prices can also be at a PREMIUM, meaning higher than par value, when speaking of fixed-income investments.

Should I buy this if my objective is income? Here the purpose is to identify investments whose primary feature is providing regular dividend or interest income, as distinguished from alternatives primarily featuring capital gains or other potential values.

To what extent does it protect against inflation? If the value of an investment usually rises at the same or a higher rate than the rate at which INFLATION erodes the purchasing power of the dollar, the investment is inflation-sensitive. Investments vary in the degree of protection they provide—some provide no protection. Although it is probably safe to assume that inflation will prevail for the foreseeable future, an inflation-sensitive asset would decline in value as a function of deflation.

Is it suitable for tax-deferred retirement accounts? Such accounts include INDIVIDUAL RETIREMENT ARRANGEMENTS (IRAs), ROTH IRAS, KEOGH PLANS, 401(K) PLANS, and other pension plans that are TAX-DEFERRED. The question addresses both the legality and, in some cases, the practicality of using a particular investment in such an account. Investments that might be ruled out for an IRA because of the annual maximum per person might be appropriate for an IRA ROLLOVER.

Can I borrow against it? This question considers the general value of an investment as COLLATERAL at a bank or other lending institution, and also the eligibility of an investment for trading in MARGIN ACCOUNTS with brokers under Federal Reserve Board MARGIN REQUIREMENTS. A key consideration is the concept of LEVERAGE, the ability to control a given amount of value with a smaller amount of cash. Borrowing can also be a way of raising cash when an investment is ILLIQUID.

Risk Considerations

How assured can I be of getting my full investment back? Here the discussion concerns safety of PRINCIPAL, which has mainly to do with two types of risk: (1) market or SYSTEMATIC RISK and (2) financial or CREDIT RISK (risk that an issuer will DEFAULT on a contractual obligation or that an EQUITY investment will lose value because of financial difficulty or BANKRUPTCY of an issuer). Insurance considerations and HEDGING, protecting against loss of value through an offsetting position, are also discussed where appropriate.

How assured is my income? Assuming an investment produces income, this question deals with NONSYSTEMATIC RISK and with an issuer's legal obligation to pay income.

Are there any other risks unique to this investment? This question intends only to highlight risks peculiar to a particular investment. It is not meant to imply that any risks not included do not exist.

PERSONAL INVESTMENTS AT A GLANCE

The following chart applies nine key investment criteria to the 30 personal investment alternatives discussed in this section. It is designed simply to answer the question: Is this alternative one I might want to learn more about in view of my own investment objectives? A bullet (●) means that a given characteristic is usually associated, to one degree or another, with a particular alternative. A blank means it is not. A V means that variation within the investment category exists to such an extent that even broad classification would be misleading.

Exceptions abound, and in every case there is a question of degree. In the modern universe of investment alternatives, just about nothing is pure; that fact is indeed what this section of the *Handbook* is all about. So with cognizance of its limitations, use this chart for quick and handy reference and refer to the overviews and questionnaires for more complete understanding.

Investment	Regular Current Income	Capital Appreciation	Tax Benefits	Safety of Principal	Liquidity	Inflation Protection	Leverage*	Future Income or Security	Suitability for IRAs and other Tax-Deferred Accounts
Annuity	●	●	●	●				●	
Bond, Corporate	●	●		●	●	V			●
Closed-End Fund	●	●		V	●	V			●
Collectible		●				●			
Common Stock	●	●		V	●	●	●		●
Convertible Security	●	●		●	●		●		●
Exchange-Traded Funds	●	●	●	V	●	V			●
Foreign Stocks and Bonds	●	●		V	V	●			
Futures Contract on a Commodity		●			●		●		
Futures Contract on an Interest Rate		●			●		●		
Futures Contract on a Stock Index		●			●		●		
Government Agency Security	●	●	●	●	●				●
Life Insurance (Cash Value)		●	●	●		V		●	

Investment								
Money Market Fund	●			●	●		●	●
Mortgage-Backed (Pass-Through) Security	●			●	●		●	●
Municipal Security	●●			●	●		●	●
Mutual Fund (Open-End)	●●			●	>		●	●
Option Contract (Put or Call)	●		●	●				
Option Contract on a Futures Contract (Futures Option)			●	●				
Option Contract on an Interest Rate (Debt Option)	●		●	●				
Option Contract on a Stock Index			●	●				
Option Contract or Futures Contract on a Currency			●	●	>			
Precious Metals	●			●	●		●	
Preferred Stock (Nonconvertible)	●			●	●	●		
Real Estate Investment Trust (REIT and FREIT)	●			●●	●	>	●●	
Real Estate, Physical	>		●	●●	●	●	>	●
Savings Alternatives	●		>	●	●●	>	>	>
Treasury Securities	●●		>	●	●●	>	>	●
Unit Investment Trust	●		>	●	●	>	>	●
Zero-Coupon Security	●	●		●	●			●

* Refers to margin securities and investments wherein large amounts of value can be controlled with small amounts of cash. The general value of investments as loan collateral is covered in the discussions of each of the investment alternatives.

Is it commercially rated? Commercial RATING agencies, such as MOODY'S INVESTORS SERVICE, FITCH RATINGS, and STANDARD & POOR'S CORPORATION, analyze and rate certain securities and their issuers on a continuous basis. Most ratings are designed to indicate a company's financial strength and thus guide investors as to the degree of CREDIT RISK a security represents, though sometimes other factors are rated. Rating changes usually affect market values.

Tax Considerations

What tax advantages (or disadvantages) does it offer? This discussion is designed to present the tax considerations associated with an investment. Obviously, each individual's tax situation is unique and each investor should obtain professional advice to determine whether an investment with certain tax features represents an advantage or disadvantage in his or her particular case.

Economic Considerations

What economic factors most affect buy, hold, and sell decisions? Here again, only the most general economic considerations are covered and what applies in general might not apply to you.

HOW TO INVEST YOUR MONEY: 30 KEY PERSONAL INVESTMENT OPPORTUNITIES

ANNUITY

After getting scant attention during the historic bull market of the '80s and '90s, the annuity became one of Wall Street's hottest products once the dot com bubble burst in 2000 and investors became more concerned with safety. With interest rates plummeting, banks began pitching the products. By the early 2000s, fixed annuities were setting sales records and sales continued strong as market uncertainty persisted. The financial crisis of the late 2000s erased home equity, diminished retirement funds, and left investors facing a prolonged economic slowdown with market instability and potentially high inflation. For many risk-averse investors, annuities seemed more than ever to be the answer.

Annuities come in several varieties, with two basic attractions: (1) tax-deferred capital growth and (2) the option of income for life or a guaranteed period. Among the drawbacks are high penalties (by insurers and the Internal Revenue Service) on premature withdrawal, sometimes onerous fees, and lower investment returns than could usually be realized directly.

Traditionally, annuities provided fixed-income payments for an individual's remaining lifetime in exchange for a lump-sum cash payment. But inflation's negative impact on fixed income annuities combined with increased life expectancy gave rise, in the late 1950s, to the variable annuity, invested in assets, such as stocks, that rise with inflation, thus preserving some purchasing power, although at the price of some market risk.

Annuities are available in two basic types:

Fixed annuities are "fixed" in two ways: (1) The amount you invest earns interest (tax-deferred) at a guaranteed rate (1% to 2% under long-term U.S. government bonds, typically) while your principal is guaranteed not to lose value. (2) When you withdraw or opt to "annuitize" (begin taking monthly income) you receive a guaranteed amount based on your age, sex, and selection of payment options. Inflation protection is, of course, minimal.

Variable annuities, in contrast, are "variable" in two ways: (1) The amount you put in is invested in your choice of a stock, fixed-income bond, or money market account, the value and/or earnings of which vary with market conditions. (2) Market value determines the amount available for withdrawals, or (with actuarial factors) the amount the annuitant is paid from one month to the next. Variable annuities thus offer inflation protection in exchange for market risk (minimized somewhat when switching among funds is permitted).

In general, annuities, with a variety of optional features for both accumulation and payout, are for long-term investors willing to trade liquidity and some degree of return for safety and tax-deferred capital growth, and whose objective is to defer taxability until later (lower tax rate) years and/or to guarantee retirement income.

* * *

What Is an Annuity?

An annuity is a contract between an insurance company and an annuitant whereby the company, in exchange for a single or flexible premium guarantees a fixed or variable payment to the annuitant at a future time. *Immediate annuities* begin paying out as soon as the premium is paid; *deferred annuities,* which may be paid for in a lump sum or in installments, start paying out at a specified date in the future.

Buying, Selling, and Holding

How do I buy and sell it? Insurance brokers, insurance company sales agents, savings institutions, full-service brokers, commercial banks, and other financial service organizations sell annuities.

Is there a minimum purchase amount, and what is the price range? It varies with the plan, but deferred annuities typically have minimums ranging from $1000 to $5000.

What fees and charges are involved? Fees and charges may include front-end load sales charges ranging from 1% to 10% (although there is a trend toward no initial commissions), premium taxes (imposed on the insurance company by some states and passed on to contract holders), annual fees (typically $15 to $30 per year up to a maximum of $1^1/2\%$ of account value), surrender charges or early withdrawal penalties (typically starting at 6% and decreasing to zero over a seven-year period), and other charges. (See Tax Considerations, page 11, for tax penalties).

Does it mature, expire, or otherwise terminate? Yes; both the accumulation period and the payout period are specified in the contract.

Can I sell it quickly? Accumulated cash value (principal payments plus investment earnings) can always be withdrawn, but there may be substantial withdrawal penalties as well as tax penalties.

How is market value determined and how do I keep track of it? Annuities do not have secondary market value, but information concerning account balances is supplied by the insurance company.

Investment Objectives

Should I buy an annuity if my objective is capital appreciation? Not in the sense that you would buy an investment at one price and hope to sell it at a higher price. Annuities are for people seeking guaranteed future income. Of course, payouts increase when variable annuities invested in stocks or other securities having capital gains potential appreciate. Capital gains paid out by annuities are taxed at ordinary income rates, however.

Should I buy this if my objective is income? Income for future guaranteed periods is what annuities are all about.

To what extent does it protect against inflation? Some annuities provide for annual increases in payouts or tie payouts to the Consumer Price Index, but at an extra cost. Variable annuities provide protection when their portfolios are invested in inflation-sensitive securities.

Is it suitable for tax-deferred retirement accounts? Yes, but since annuities have tax-deferred status themselves, it may be wiser to use them as supplements to IRAs, Keoghs, 401(k)s, and other tax-deferred programs.

Can I borrow against it? Yes.

Risk Considerations

How assured can I be of getting back my full investment in an annuity? Insurance companies are heavily regulated and required to maintain reserves, so with highly rated established companies there is low risk of loss due to corporate failure. Most annuities permit early withdrawal of principal, but penalties may apply. Once annuitized (i.e., when payments by the insurance company begin) it becomes a question of how long you live. The insurance company (with the odds in its favor) bets you will die before the annuity is fully paid out.

How assured is my income? Fixed annuities have a guaranteed payout. Variable annuity income fluctuates, but a portion of the payout is often guaranteed. Of course, inflation erodes the purchasing power of payouts.

Are there any other risks unique to this investment? Although heavily regulated, insurance companies are potentially subject to mismanagement and fraud, and policyholders are not themselves covered by federal protection as bank depositors, for example, are covered by the Federal Deposit Insurance Corporation (FDIC).

Is it commercially rated? Yes. Insurance companies are rated by Best's Rating Service.

Tax Considerations

What tax advantages (or disadvantages) does an annuity offer? Earnings on money invested in deferred annuities, including all interest, dividends, and capital gains, accumulate and compound tax-deferred. Portions of payments to annuitants are returns of investor's principal and thus are not subject to income taxes. The rest of the payment, however, is taxed as ordinary income, even the portion representing capital gains that would be taxed at a lower rate if it weren't in an annuity. In variable annuities, you may switch among mutual funds without incurring a capital gains tax liability. Withdrawals of accumulated earnings prior to age $59^{1}/2$ or within 5 years of the purchase date (whichever comes first) are subject to a 10% tax penalty. (An exception is made for life annuities, payable for the lifetimes, or life expectancies, of one or more annuitants.) There is congressional sentiment favorable to tax incentives, such as waiving 50% of the taxes on the first $10,000 of annuity payouts each year, but no such legislation had been enacted as of April 2010.

Economic Considerations

What economic factors most affect buy, hold, and sell decisions? Although factors such as inflationary expectations and anticipated interest rate movements may guide choices among types of annuities, the decision to buy and hold is based on insurance rather than economic considerations. Annuities are appropriate for healthy people without dependents or heirs, who seek assured income for their remaining lives.

BOND, CORPORATE (INTEREST-BEARING)

The traditional attractions of a corporate bond have been (1) higher yield compared to government bonds and (2) relative safety. Whether secured (usually a mortgage bond) or unsecured (called a debenture), it has a higher claim on earnings than equity investments. If the firm goes out of business, bonds also have a higher claim on the assets of the issuer, whose financial well-being is safeguarded by provisions in bond indentures and is closely monitored by the major bond rating services. Interest on corporate bonds is fully taxable.

Much publicized in the 1980s because of their widespread use in financing corporate takeovers were so-called junk bonds, corporate bonds with lower than investment-grade ratings that pay high yields to compensate for high risk. Although issuers could point to the fact that high-yield bonds in general have had a low default record historically, fears that a prolonged recession would put the more heavily leveraged issuers in trouble have caused depressed prices and poor liquidity in the junk bond market at times when the economic outlook was gloomy.

Bonds are contracts between borrowers and lenders in which the issuer (borrower) promises the bondholder (lender) a specified rate of interest and repayment of principal at maturity.

The face, or par, value of a corporate bond is almost always $1000 (the exceptions being baby bonds with pars of $500 or less), but bonds do not necessarily sell at par value. Particularly in the secondary market, bonds are traded at discounts or premiums relative to par in order to bring their stated (coupon) rates in line with market rates. This inverse relationship between bond prices and interest rate movements causes market risk as the term applies to bonds; when market interest rates rise, there is a decline in the price of a bond with a lower fixed interest rate.

Bond prices also vary with the time remaining to maturity. This is because of the time value of money and because time involves risk and risk means higher yield. Bond yields thus normally decrease (and prices increase) as the bond approaches maturity. The concept yield, called DURATION when all its implications are considered, is basic to bond pricing, and it takes into account the price paid for the bond and all cash inflows and their timing.

The safety and value of corporate bonds are also related to credit risk, quite simply the borrower's ability to pay interest and principal when due. The relative financial strength of the issuer, as reflected in the regularly updated rating assigned to its bonds by the major services, influences yield, which is adjusted by changes in the market price.

Concern that hostile takeovers and recapitalizations would weaken the value of existing holdings has inspired protective provisions in bond indenture agreements. Standard & Poor's publishes "Event Risk Covenant Rankings," a system's supplementing its credit ratings, that evaluates such protection. A common provision is the "poison put," which gives bondholders the right to redeem at par if certain designated events occur, such as a hostile takeover, the purchase of a big block of stock, or an excessive dividend payout.

Other considerations influencing corporate bond prices include the existence of call features, which empower the issuer to redeem prior to maturity, often to the disadvantage of the bondholder; call protection periods, which benefit holders; sinking funds, which require the issuer to set aside funds for the retirement of the bonds at maturity; put options giving the investor the right to redeem at specified times prior to maturity; subordinations, which give issues precedence over other issues in liquidation; and guarantees or insurance.

Variable-rate issues, usually called floating-rate notes even though some issues have terms of 30 years, adjust interest rates periodically in line with market rates. These issues generally have lower yields to compensate for the benefit to the holder, but they enjoy greater price stability to the extent the rate adjustments are responsive to market rate movements.

See also the discussions of Convertible Securities and Zero-Coupon Securities.

* * *

What Is a Corporate Bond?

A corporate bond is a debt security of a corporation requiring the issuer to pay the holder the par value at a specified maturity and to make agreed scheduled interest payments.

Buying, Selling, and Holding

How do I buy and sell a corporate bond? Through a securities broker-dealer.

Is there a minimum purchase amount, and what is the price range? Bonds are normally issued with $1000 par values, with baby bonds in smaller denominations. Issuers often have 5-bond minimums and broker-dealers trade in round lots of 10 or 100 units. Odd lots may be available at higher brokerage commissions or dealer spreads.

What fees and charges are involved? A per-bond commission of $2.50 to $20, depending on the broker and negotiations with the customer. However, a minimum charge of $30 is common. New issues involve no charges to the investor.

Does it mature, expire, or otherwise terminate? All bonds have maturity dates, but some may be callable prior to maturity.

Can I sell it quickly? Usually yes. Most major issues are actively traded, but in large amounts. Small lots can be harder to trade and may involve some price sacrifice and higher transaction costs. Some high-yield junk bonds have been hard to sell because of the fear of default.

How is market value determined and how do I keep track of it? The market value of a fixed-income bond is a function of its yield to maturity and prevailing market interest rates. Prices thus decline when interest rates rise and rise when interest rates decline to result in an appropriate competitive yield. A change in the issuer's rating can also cause a change in price as higher (or lower) risk is reflected in the price/yield relationship. Even without a formal rating change, reduced demand can cause lower bond prices; this has been seen in junk bond prices reflecting fears that a recession will cause defaults. Bond prices are quoted in daily newspapers and electronic databases.

Investment Objectives

Should I buy a corporate bond if my objective is capital appreciation? Usually not (unless you're a professional bond trader), although capital appreciation is possible when bonds can be bought at a discount to their par value, bought prior to a drop in market interest rates, or bought at a favorable price because of a decline in the issuer's credit rating.

Should I buy this if my objective is income? Yes; bonds pay interest, usually semiannually. Yields vary with quality. On top-rated bonds, interest rates (or yields if you are trading in the secondary market) are lower than on bonds of less than investment grade, called JUNK BONDS, which pay more and have higher credit risk.

To what extent does it protect against inflation? Although inflationary expectations are built into interest rates, fixed-rate bonds offer no protection against higher inflation. Variable-rate issues offer some protection.

Is it suitable for tax-deferred retirement accounts? Yes.

Can I borrow against it? Yes, subject to Federal Reserve margin rules (convertible bonds only) and brokerage-firm and lending-institution policies.

Risk Considerations

How assured can I be of getting my full investment back? If you hold to maturity, it will depend on the issuer's credit, which is evaluated regularly by the major investor's rating services and reflected in ratings from AAA down to D. If you plan to sell in the secondary market before maturity, you are subject also to market risk, the risk that bond prices will be down as a result of higher interest rates. Sophisticated investors sometimes protect against loss of value due to market risk by hedging, using options and futures available on long-term Treasury securities which are similarly affected by interest rate changes.

How assured is my income? Uninterrupted payment of interest depends on the issuer's financial strength and stability of earnings, factors reflected in its bond rating. Inflation can erode the dollar value of fixed-interest payments.

Are there any other risks unique to this investment? A callable bond can be redeemed by the issuer after a certain period has elapsed. Issuers normally force redemption when interest rates have declined and financing can be obtained more cheaply. Under just those circumstances, however, the investor finds the holding most attractive; the market price is up and the coupon interest rate is higher than the prevailing market interest rate. Look for bonds with call protection (typically 10 years). Event risk, the risk of a deterioration in credit quality owing to takeover-related changes in capitalization, is another consideration. Although issuers considering themselves vulnerable may have indenture provisions to protect bondholders (rated by Standard & Poor's Event Risk Covenant Rankings), such measures can result in early redemption and deprive the holder of a long-term investment.

Is it commercially rated? Yes. Fitch Ratings, Moody's Investors Service, and Standard & Poor's Corporation are the major rating services.

Tax Considerations

What tax advantages (or disadvantages) does a corporate bond offer? None. Bond interest is taxed as ordinary income and realized gains are subject to capital gains tax, except that appreciation resulting from original issue discounts, termed imputed interest, is taxed (as earned) at ordinary income rates.

Economic Considerations

What economic factors most affect buy, hold, or sell decisions? It is best to buy a corporate bond when interest rates are high and the best yields can be obtained. Holding is most attractive when rates are declining, causing an upward move in the market values of fixed-income securities. High inflation erodes the dollar value of fixed interest payments. Poor business conditions over a prolonged period can cause financial weakness and jeopardize a firm's ability to pay.

CLOSED-END FUND

Closed-end funds, so-called because, unlike open-end mutual funds, their sponsoring investment companies do not stand ready to issue and redeem shares on a continuous basis, have a fixed capitalization represented by publicly traded shares that are often listed on the major stock exchanges. Because the net asset value of a closed-end fund varies independently of its own share price, the investment has been compared to a water bed on a boat.

Closed-end funds tend to have specialized portfolios of stocks, bonds, convertibles, or combinations thereof, and may be oriented toward income, capital gains, or a combination of those objectives. Examples are the Korea Fund, which specializes in the stock of Korean firms and is an example of a "single country fund," and ASA Ltd., which invests in South African gold mining stocks. Both are traded on the New York Stock Exchange.

The attraction of a closed-end fund is twofold: (1) Because management is not concerned with continuous buying and selling to accommodate new investors and redemptions, a responsibility of open-end funds that frequently conflicts with ideal market timing, a well-managed closed-end fund can often buy and sell on more favorable terms. (2) Because the popular investor perception is just the opposite— that closed-end funds have less flexibility than open-end funds—shares of closed-end funds can usually be obtained at a discount from net asset value. As a result of these combined factors, annual earnings of closed-end funds sometimes exceed earnings of open-end funds with comparable portfolios.

A special form of closed-end fund is the *dual-purpose fund*. These hybrids have two classes of stock. Preferred shareholders receive all the income from the portfolio—dividends and interest—while common shareholders receive all capital gains realized on the sale of securities in the fund's portfolio. Dual-purpose funds are set up with a specific expiration date, when preferred shares are redeemed at a predetermined price and common shareholders claim the remaining assets, voting either to liquidate or continue the fund on an open-end basis.

Closed-end funds, of which more than 600 are publicly and actively traded, are regulated by the Securities and Exchange Commission.

See also the discussions of Exchange-Traded Portfolios and Mutual Funds.

* * *

What Is a Closed-End Fund?

A closed-end fund is a type of mutual fund that invests in diversified holdings and has a fixed number of shares that are publicly traded.

Buying, Selling, and Holding

How do I buy and sell a closed-end fund? Through a securities broker-dealer.

Is there a minimum purchase amount, and what is the price range? Round-lot 100 share purchases save commissions. Prices vary but many funds sell for $25 or less per share.

What fees and charges are involved? Standard brokerage commissions plus an annual management fee averaging $1/2$% to 1% of the investment.

Does it mature, expire, or otherwise terminate? Funds can be liquidated or converted to open-end funds or operating companies if a majority of shareholders approve. Dual-purpose funds expire, typically in 10 years.

Can I sell it quickly? Usually yes. Most funds offer good liquidity.

How is market value determined and how do I keep track of it? By supply and demand factors affecting shares in the market. Whether shares trade at a premium (rare) or at more or less of a discount (the rule) relative to the net asset value of the fund, can depend on the portfolio, yield, the general market, and factors like year-end tax selling. Some funds have stock buyback programs designed to reduce outstanding shares and increase earnings per share. New issues tend initially to sell at premiums, then to slack off when brokers turn their aggressive sales efforts to other products. *The Wall Street Journal* on Monday and the weekly *Barron's* report the net asset value, price, and discount or premium for the previous week on actively traded funds. Morningstar and other financial websites are readily accessible sources of quotes and other information.

Investment Objectives

Should I buy a closed-end fund if my objective is capital appreciation? Although fund shares rise and fall in the marketplace, influenced, among other factors, by the value of the fund's portfolio, investors seeking to participate in capital gains would select a fund having appreciation as its primary objective— an aggressive stock fund, for example, as opposed to a bond fund, though gains and losses are possible in both. Dual-purpose funds offer two classes of stock, common shareholders benefiting from all the capital gains, preferred shareholders getting all the interest and dividend income. Funds bought at a discount offer the prospect of additional appreciation through increases in fund share prices.

Should I buy this if my objective is income? Yes, especially funds whose objective is income. (See the preceding question.) Some funds offer guaranteed payouts, but it should be recognized that unless the fund generates income equal to the guaranteed payment, it may come out of funds contributed by investors.

To what extent does it protect against inflation? Some portfolios are more inflation-sensitive than others, stocks offering more protection than bonds, for example. Of course, increases in the portfolio benefit investors only when passed on in capital gains distributions or reflected in higher fund share values.

Is it suitable for tax-deferred retirement accounts? Yes.

Can I borrow against it? Yes, subject to Federal Reserve margin requirements and individual lender policies.

Risk Considerations

How assured can I be of getting my full investment back? Fund shares can be just as volatile as other forms of common stock. Professionals use various techniques to hedge funds selling at discounts or premiums or converting to open-end funds. These techniques include purchasing options and selling short other funds, treasury securities and futures, and stocks in the same fund's portfolio. Some funds have "open-ending" provisions, whereby they guarantee that investors can choose to collect the full net asset value of fund shares on a specified future debt; it is important to note, however, that although the net asset value may be higher than the market price, it can be lower than your original investment.

How assured is my income? It depends on the quality of the portfolio and the risk characteristics of the investments comprising it. Funds offering guaranteed payouts may have to liquidate capital to make good.

Are there any other risks unique to this investment? The risk unique to closed-end funds is that the value of fund shares can move independently of the value of the securities comprising the fund's portfolio. If this causes shares to trade at a discount to net asset values, it is bad for holders wishing to sell, although it can be viewed as a buying opportunity. Funds with *managed distributions,* that is, funds where the payouts may represent a combination of portfolio income plus options income or returns of capital, can mislead unwary investors who assume the sizeable distributions represent portfolio income purely. The CEFA website breaks out funds with managed distributions. Investors buying foreign funds to diversify domestic portfolios should make sure the fund's holdings are foreign-based companies and not American multinationals operating in foreign countries.

Is it commercially rated? Funds are not usually rated, but information helpful to investors is provided by Standard & Poor's, Moody's, Morningstar, and other sources.

Tax Considerations

What tax advantages (or disadvantages) does a closed-end fund offer? The tax treatment of closed-end fund shares is the same as for common stock except that capital gains distributions enjoy preferential long-term capital gains treatment regardless of how long the fund has been held.

Economic Considerations

What economic factors most affect buy, hold, or sell decisions? Most experts say to buy when shares can be obtained at a good discount and the stock market seems poised for a rise. Otherwise, decisions should consider the effects of different economic and market scenarios on various types of portfolios, such as bonds, stocks, or convertibles. It is probably wise to avoid new issues, to sell at premiums, to view closed-end funds as long-term investments, and to sell when significant appreciation has occurred.

COLLECTIBLES

Collectibles, the name for a diverse range of physical possessions presumed to gain value with time, have tended to attract investors during periods of high inflation when financial assets become unattractive and economic instability is threatened. In recent years, Internet auctions, such as e-Bay, have increased market liquidity and revived a degree of interest in collectibles as an investment alternative, but most Internet shoppers are looking for bargains and, unless you're talking about van Gogh paintings or Chippendale antiques, realizing full value remains a problem with most collectibles.

There is no universal definition of a collectible. Some experts apply the criteria of rarity, quality, uniqueness, and age, while others put commodities with utilitarian value (like gemstones) or intrinsic value (like coins with gold or silver content) in addition to collector's value in separate categories.

In the broadest definition, however, collectibles are physical assets (not financial or real, in the sense of real estate), that have psychic or utilitarian value for their owners, are unique or in limited supply, and can be expected to increase in value with time and demand. The category thus includes stamps, coins, antiques, gemstones, fine art, photographs, and an almost endless list of other groups and subdivisions ranging from folk art and crafts to baseball cards, comic books, antique automobiles, and miscellaneous collectible junk.

While books have been written on the major categories of collectibles, certain common denominators exist to varying degrees from an investment perspective: often high costs to trade and own; high price volatility; no current income; and undependable or poor liquidity.

These factors plus the opportunity cost of an unproductive investment lead to one conclusion: Collectibles, especially when the relevant group of collectors is solidly in place and in good communication, will probably gain value and outstrip inflation over the long term, but the costs and risks of holding collectibles for investment purposes can be justified only when the assets also provide their owners pleasure or utility.

* * *

What Is a Collectible?

A collectible is a physical asset of a non-real estate and nonfinancial nature that exists in limited supply, usually provides enjoyment or utility to its owner, and is expected to increase in value because of inflation or supply and demand factors such as popularity and rarity.

Buying, Selling, and Holding

How do I buy and sell a collectible? Through dealers, galleries, auctions, online auctions, private owners, flea markets, and catalogs and other collector publications.

Is there a minimum purchase amount, and what is the price range? Minimums and price ranges vary with the collectible and run a gamut from a few pennies to millions of dollars.

What fees and charges are involved? This depends on the collectible, where it is traded, and many other factors, but fees are an important consideration. Costs may include dealer profits (markups), sales taxes, appraisal fees, storage and safe keeping, maintenance, insurance, as well as opportunity cost—the return you would get if your money were invested more productively.

Does it mature, expire, or otherwise terminate? No.

Can I sell it quickly? A collectible varies in liquidity, from one, like a painting or an antique, bought through established dealers standing ready to repurchase at an agreed-on price, to another, salable only through consignment to dealers, auction houses, or Internet auctions.

How is market value determined and how do I keep track of it? Market value is determined by supply and demand. Some collectibles are more vulnerable to fads than others, and the marketplace can be more efficient in one type of collectible than another because it has more dealers and better communication among dealers and collectors. Some major newspapers, like *The New York Times*, carry advertisements for collectibles of various types; most of the main categories of collectibles are served by specialized websites, periodicals or newsletters; and a number of national magazines contain classified sections and even articles aimed at collectors within their fields of interest. Dealers and appraisers are a source of information about market value, but it is important to satisfy oneself as to their objectivity.

Investment Objectives

Should I buy a collectible if my objective is capital appreciation? Yes, but short-term profits depend on a combination of expertise and luck, and long-term appreciation can be affected by fads as well as economic developments.

Should I buy this if my objective is income? No.

To what extent does it protect against inflation? Although there are many risks that can undermine the value of a collectible, if the condition of the collectible remains good and supply and demand factors stay favorable, values will increase with inflation.

Is it suitable for tax-deferred retirement accounts? Collectibles are not legal investments in such accounts unless they are part of portfolios directed by trustees.

Can I borrow against it? That depends on the collectible. Many lenders will accept collectibles as collateral if they are readily marketable.

Risk Considerations

How assured can I be of getting my full investment back? With most collectibles, this has mainly to do with your level of expertise and the amount of time you hold the asset. In the short term, it is likely that costs and commissions will offset whatever small gain might be realized. In the long run, collectibles become more limited in supply and (assuming good quality and condition) more valuable, but only if the demand has continued strong and economic conditions have not eroded purchasing power. Many collectibles are vulnerable to fads, though some bought from well-established and reputable dealers may be sold back at agreed upon prices.

How assured is my income? Collectibles normally provide no income, and are in fact a drain on cash that might otherwise be invested for income.

Are there any other risks unique to this investment? Collectibles are subject to a wide range of unique risks—forgery and other frauds; physical risk, such as deterioration, fire, and theft; "warehouse finds," where a large supply of a previously limited item is suddenly discovered and becomes a drug on the market; the reverse situation, where a large chunk of a given collectible's supply goes "in collection," leaving so little in circulation that diminished interest reduces demand.

Each category has its own special risks and prospective collectors are advised to research them.

Is it commercially rated? No.

Tax Considerations

What tax advantages (or disadvantages) does it offer? Realized capital gains and capital losses are subject to standard rates for capital assets. Other tax advantages may pertain, depending on whether the collecting is done as a hobby or as a for-profit investment activity. Tax advice should be obtained.

Economic Considerations

What economic factors most affect buy, hold, and sell decisions? Collectibles have traditionally been favored by investors in times of inflation, though the value of this investment category as an inflation hedge is tempered by the many risks. The marketability of collectibles is more dependent on good economic conditions than most other investments.

COMMON STOCK

For total return over the long term, no publicly traded investment alternative offers more potential under normal conditions than common stock.

A share of common stock is the basic unit of equity ownership in a corporation. The shareholder is usually entitled to vote in the election of directors and on other important matters and to share in the wealth created by corporate activities, both through the appreciation of share values and the payment of dividends out of the earnings remaining after debt obligations and holders of preferred stock are satisfied. In the event of liquidation of assets, common shareholders divide the assets remaining after creditors and preferred shareholders have been repaid.

In public corporations, shares have market values primarily based on investor expectations of future earnings and dividends. The relationship of this market price to the actual or expected earnings, called the price-earnings ratio or "multiple," is a measure of these expectations. Stock values are also affected by forecasts of business activity in general and by whatever "investor psychology" is produced by the immediate business and economic environment.

Stocks of young, fast-growing companies, particularly those in industries that are cyclical or high technology-oriented, tend to be volatile, to have high price-earnings ratios, and generally to carry a high degree of risk. Called *growth stocks,* they seldom pay dividends, since earnings are reinvested to finance growth. These stocks are often traded on the Nasdaq or on the NYSE AmexEquities (formerly the American Stock Exchange).

At the other end of the spectrum, stocks of old, established firms in mature industries and with histories of regular earnings and dividends tend to be characterized by relative price stability and low multiples. These stocks are usually found listed on the New York Stock Exchange (although there are exceptions) and the cream of the crop are known as blue chips. As a general category, these regular dividend payers are called *income stocks.*

Spanning the growth income continuum is a wide range of common stock investment choices that can be made only in terms of one's personal objectives and risk comfort level. To help in the process is a professional establishment comprised of brokers, investment advisers, and financial planners supported by practitioners of various securities analysis approaches—those trained in fundamental analysis, technical analysis, chartists, and others.

Investors with limited means can gain the advantages of common stock ownership together with the benefits of professional management and portfolio diversification through mutual funds, which are discussed elsewhere in this section.

* * *

What Is Common Stock?

A common stock represents ownership in a corporation, usually carries voting rights, and often earns dividends (paid out at the discretion of the corporation's board of directors).

Buying, Selling, and Holding

How do I buy and sell common stock? Through a securities broker-dealer. Some companies permit direct purchase of shares as part of their dividend reinvestment plans.

Is there a minimum purchase amount, and what is the price range? There is no minimum, but buying in round lots (usually 100 shares) saves extra odd-lot (under 100 shares) charges. Some brokers offer programs allowing odd-lot purchases at regular rates. Stock prices range widely, with the majority under $50.

What fees and charges are involved? The brokerage commission, the principal charge, varies by the value and/or size of transaction. Discount brokers charge less than full-service brokers. Online brokers offering the deepest discounts carry a risk of technical interruptions and may be hiding third market charges. A nominal transfer tax is imposed on sellers by the federal government and several state governments. Interest and other charges may be incurred in margin accounts, in which qualifying stocks can be traded on credit within requirements of the Federal Reserve Board and individual brokerage firms.

Does it mature, expire, or otherwise terminate? No, although tender offers by issuing companies and outside acquirers often give shareholders the opportunity to sell within a set period at a premium over prevailing stock market prices.

Can I sell it quickly? Usually, yes. Shares of publicly held and actively traded companies are highly liquid.

How is market value determined and how do I keep track of it? Market value is basically determined by investor expectations of future earnings and dividend payments, although the value of assets is also important. Prices may also be affected temporarily by large transactions creating bid-offer imbalances, by rumors of various sorts, and by public tender offers. Newspapers and electronic databases show daily prices on stocks traded on exchanges and over the counter.

Investment Objectives

Should I buy common stock if my objective is capital appreciation? Yes, especially growth stocks of younger firms, which tend to reinvest earnings rather than pay dividends as older, established firms do.

Should I buy this if my objective is income? Yes, especially if your objectives also include some capital appreciation and inflation protection. Established companies are more likely to pay dividends regularly than are fast-growing firms that tend to reinvest earnings.

To what extent does it protect against inflation? Over the long run, stocks rise in value and increase dividends with inflation, though they do not protect against hyperinflation.

Is it suitable for tax-deferred retirement accounts? Yes. Stocks are suitable for IRAs, Keoghs, 401(K) plans, and other tax-deferred plans.

Can I borrow against it? Yes, subject to Federal Reserve margin rules and lender policies concerning marketable securities collateral.

Risk Considerations

How assured can I be of getting my full investment back? There is no concrete assurance. There is always the risk that market prices will decline in value, though some stocks are more volatile than others. When a company goes out of business and liquidates its assets, common shareholders are paid last—after preferred stockholders and creditors.

How assured is my income? Dividends come out of earnings and are declared at the discretion of the board of directors. They can be suspended if profits are off, or if the directors decide reinvestment is preferable. Older, established, blue chip companies are the most dependable dividend payers; young, growth-oriented firms tend to reinvest earnings and thus pay no (or low) dividends.

Are there any other risks unique to this investment? Anything that can affect the fortunes of a company can affect its stock value and dividend payments.

Is it commercially rated? Yes, Moody's, Standard & Poor's, Value Line Investment Survey, and others rate many publicly traded issues.

Tax Considerations

What tax advantages (or disadvantages) does common stock offer? Dividends to individuals are fully taxable in the year they are paid, at 5% or 15% depending on the shareholder's tax rate. Gains on the sale of stock held more than one year receive a preferential long-term capital gains rate. After-tax corporate earnings not paid out as dividends accumulate without being taxed. Corporations can exclude 70% of dividends received from other domestic corporations.

Economic Considerations

What economic factors most affect buy, hold, or sell decisions? Stocks are most attractive as holdings when inflation is moderate, interest rates are low, and business conditions are generally favorable to growth and bigger profits.

CONVERTIBLE SECURITY

Convertible securities—bonds (debentures) or preferred stock convertible into common stock (usually of the issuer but, in rare cases, of the issuer's subsidiary or affiliate)—offer both fixed income and appreciation potential but are not quite the best of both worlds. The yield on the convertible bond or preferred is normally less than that of a "straight" bond or preferred, and the potential for capital gain is less than with a common stock investment.

On the other hand, convertibles (sometimes called CVs and identified that way in the newspaper bond tables, but not the stock tables) do offer less credit risk and market risk than common shares while providing an opportunity to share in the future wealth of the corporation for whose shares the convertible can be exchanged.

In terms of priority of claim on earnings and assets, convertible bonds and convertible preferred stock have the same status as regular bonds and preferred. Bonds, whether convertible or straight, receive payments before preferred stock, whatever its type, and both bonds and preferred have precedence over common stock.

From the investor's standpoint, convertibles must be understood in terms of what is called their *investment value* and their *conversion value*. Investment value is the market value the convertible would have if it were not convertible—its value as a straight bond or straight preferred. Conversion value is the market price of the common stock times the number of shares into which the bond or preferred is convertible (called the conversion rate or ratio).

Since convertible owners hope to capitalize on rises in common shares through conversion and therefore value the conversion privilege, CVs begin trading at a premium over conversion value. As the common rises and the CV is viewed more and more as a common stock investment, the CV tends to sell for its common stock equivalent. Conversion is not advisable until the common dividend has more value than the income on the CV and it is normal for the common price to rise beyond the CV price until that equation is reached.

Of course, common-share prices cannot be guaranteed to rise, and in a down market convertible holders look at their investment in terms of its value as a bond or preferred stock. This investment value represents downside risk protection in the sense that the convertible will never be worth less than this value. Investment value is, however, subject to market risk; it can be pushed down by a general rise in interest rates. But should that happen, investors have downside protection in that the CV will never drop significantly below its conversion value.

Conventional wisdom holds that investors should not buy convertibles unless attracted by the soundness of the underlying common stock. They should be wary also of issues selling at high premiums over the value of the common stock or the prices at which they are callable.

See also the discussion of Zero-Coupon Securities.

* * *

What Is a Convertible Security?

A convertible security is a preferred stock or debenture (unsecured bond) paying a fixed dividend or rate of interest and convertible into common stock, usually of the issuer, at a specified price or conversion ratio.

Buying, Selling, and Holding

How do I buy and sell a convertible security? Through a securities broker-dealer.

Is there a minimum purchase amount and what is the price range? Convertible preferred stock typically trades in 10-share round lots and has par values ranging from $100 down to $10. Bonds sell in $1000 units but exceptions, called baby bonds, can have lower par values, usually $500 down to $25. Brokers often have minimum orders of 10 bonds or, frequently, 100 bonds. Odd lots involve higher commissions or dealer spreads.

What fees and charges are involved? Standard brokerage commissions or dealer spreads. Bonds usually involve a per-bond commission of $2.50 to $20, depending on the broker and the size of the order. However, a minimum of $30 is common.

Does it mature, expire, or otherwise terminate? Bonds mature; preferred stocks do not. Both may be callable, however, and the regular redemption and retirement of both shares and bonds may be provided for by sinking fund agreements. Of course, once converted to common stock, there are no maturities or calls.

Can I sell it quickly? Most can be readily sold, but trading volume is not ordinarily heavy and prices can fluctuate significantly.

How is market value determined and how do I keep track of it? Market value is influenced both by the market price of the underlying common stock and the investment value of the convertible security—that is, its value as a bond or preferred stock exclusive of the conversion feature. When the conversion premium—the amount by which the price of the convertible security exceeds the price of the underlying common stock—is high, the convertible trades like a bond or preferred stock. When trading like a fixed-income investment, its value fluctuates in inverse relation to interest rates, though it will not decline below its investment value. Once parity has been reached—that is, the price of the convertible and its value assuming conversion are the same—the convertible will rise along with the underlying common stock. Prices of convertibles are reported in the stock or bond tables of daily newspapers and in electronic databases.

Investment Objectives

Should I buy a convertible security if my objective is capital appreciation? Yes; convertibles offer the opportunity to capitalize on growth in common share values while enjoying the greater yield and safety of bonds or preferred.

Should I buy this if my objective is income? Yes; but since growth is a feature, the yield is less than on a straight bond or preferred.

To what extent does it protect against inflation? Convertible prices tend to rise with common share prices, which tend to rise with inflation.

Is it suitable for tax-deferred retirement accounts? Yes, CVs qualify for IRAs, Keoghs, 401(k) plans, and other tax-deferred plans.

Can I borrow against it? Yes, subject to margin rules. CVs are acceptable general collateral, with bonds having more loan value than stock.

Risk Considerations

How assured can I be of getting my full investment back? CVs have downside protection in that their value will not sink below the market value the same investment would have as a straight (nonconvertible) bond or preferred. That "investment value" varies inversely with rates, however, so when rates go up the "floor" goes down. The price of a CV is determined, on the other hand, by the value of its conversion feature, so as long as the common holds up, the CV should not decline to its investment value. Of course, once converted, your investment becomes subject to all the risks of common stock. In liquidation, convertible bonds are paid before convertible preferred stock, and both have precedence over the corporation's common stock.

How assured is my income? The interest on convertible bonds, as a legal obligation of the issuer, has a higher claim on earnings than dividends on convertible preferred stock, which can be omitted if the issuer gets tight for cash. Preferred dividends must be paid before common dividends, however. Assuming the issuer is strong financially and has dependable earnings, there is little to worry about.

Are there any other risks unique to this investment? Dilution—a decrease in the value of common shares into which the CV converts—can happen for many reasons. Provision for such obvious corporate actions as stock splits, new issues, or spinoffs of stock or other properties, is normally made in the bond indenture or preferred stock agreement, but subtle developments, such as small quarterly stock dividends or unplanned events, can be a risk.

Is it commercially rated? Yes, by Moody's, Standard & Poor's, Value Line, and other services.

Tax Considerations

What tax advantages (or disadvantages) does it offer? None, except that gains resulting from conversion to the issuer's common stock are not treated as gains for tax purposes, provided the stock you receive is that of the same corporation that issued the convertible. Corporations can exclude from taxes 70% of preferred dividends.

Economic Considerations

What economic factors most affect buy, hold, or sell decisions? Assuming economic conditions are not threatening the issuer's financial health, convertibles offer holders protection from adverse factors affecting both common stock and fixed-income securities. The CV is thus a security for all seasons, though the price of having it both ways is less appreciation potential than common stock and less yield than straight bonds or preferred stock. It follows that CVs are popular in times of economic and market uncertainty. The ideal time to buy is when rates are high and stocks are low and the best time to hold is in a rising stock market. Stagflation is the worst scenario because stocks are hurt by the stagnation and fixed-income securities are hurt by the inflation; both the conversion and investment values of CVs thus suffer.

EXCHANGE-TRADED FUNDS

Passive investing through index funds—mutual funds that replicate or are representative of stock indexes—has been a popular alternative to investing in managed funds that aim, but too often fail, to beat the market. In normal times, a market index can be expected to outperform 75% of actively managed funds. Because they require minimal active management and thus have minimal management fees, index funds can assure investors of doing no worse (or no better) than "the market."

As an alternative to index funds, a wide and expanding variety of exchange-traded funds has become available recently. Although S&P-based SPDRS ("spiders") were pioneered in 1993, the bulk of ETFs are less than 10 years old and have broken records for their acceptability as new products. Also called exchange index securities, exchange shares, listed index securities, and HOLDRs (Merrill Lynch), they are unique investments that trade like stocks, are exchange-listed, and represent ownership of indexes tracking the broad market, industry sectors and sub-sectors, geographical regions, or countries. ETFs based on bond indexes are also available.

Legally, ETFs are structured as portfolio-holding unit investment trusts, closed-end funds, or American Depositary Receipts. But they look, quack, and waddle like common stocks, without the volatility of particular companies. Whereas mutual funds are priced at the net asset value at the end of each day, ETFs can be bought or sold anytime during the trading day at the market price. NTSE Amex Equities (né The American Stock Exchange) generates a number every 15 seconds that translates the index value into the ETFs' share price. Unlike closed-end funds, discounts or premiums to net asset value are eliminated by professional traders specializing in arbitrage and by features that allow investors to exchange the ETF for the underlying stock, thus profiting on any discrepancy between the two.

Like stocks, ETFs can be traded using conditional orders, such as limit orders and stop orders, can be bought on margin, and even sold short (with the additional advantage that they avoid the up-tick rule).

Expense ratios, a big selling point with ETFs, vary, but get lower as ETFs grow in size. The Vanguard 500 (S&P) Index Fund has the lowest expense ratio among straight index funds at 18 bps (basis points). Other index funds range up to 30 bps. The expense ratio of the SPDR, the ETF equivalent, was 18 bps in 2000 and was reduced to 12 bps in 2001. iShares, MSCI Index Fund shares (formerly known as WEBs), a popular category of ETFs, have expense ratios as high as 99 bps, although the iShares S&P 500 Index shares have a ratio of 9 bps.

But expense comparisons aren't that easy. ETFs always involve brokerage commissions and occasionally trade at slight discounts and premiums. Dividend reinvestment, automatic with index funds, is more difficult with ETFs, where share prices are higher, fractional shares don't exist, and odd-lots cost higher commissions. Dividends have to be accumulated and reinvested. Dollar cost averaging is more costly with an ETF.

ETFs are more tax-advantageous than index funds, however. Most trading in ETFs is between shareholders, sparing the fund the need to sell stock to meet redemptions. Redemptions by large investors are paid in kind, again protecting shareholders from taxable events. Generally speaking, the significant capital gains in ETFs are realized only when the investor sells the ETF. This gives the investor control over the timing, whereas straight funds make distributions as events require.

In general, most ETFs have not been around long enough to have a real track record, and while appearing to have a cost advantage over straight funds, their trading costs can quickly add up. Especially if you are looking for a fund that tracks a broad index such as the S&P 500, or if you plan to invest regular sums of money, you are probably better off with a straight index fund. Unless you are interested in narrower industrial sectors or foreign countries, you might consider SPDRS and Diamonds (DJIA) if you tend to buy stocks directly through a discount broker. If you are a mutual fund investor and already belong to a family, you might want to opt for an index fund.

In the event of a market crash, would you be better off in a fund required to be fully invested or in an ETF whose market is ultimately in the hands of a specialist or market-maker? That's anybody's guess.

Exchange-traded Notes (ETNs) entered the scene just before the financial crisis hit in 2008 and not much has been heard about them since the credit crunch put a spotlight on COUNTERPARTY RISK. Like ETFs, they both represent indexes or sectors and trade on exchanges. The difference is that instead of holding a portfolio, an ETN holds a senior unsecured debt instrument, such as a zero-coupon security (discussed later), that guarantees repayment of your investment and entails a credit risk. Accompanying this is an agreement that promises to adjust the investment value of the debt instrument by the performance of a specified index. Whereas ETFs are taxed at the rates applying to the underlying securities, ETNs lump interest and gains or losses on index performance into one total return figure, taxed when the ETN expires. The information below applies to ETFs only.

* * *

What Is an Exchange-Traded Fund (ETF)?

An exchange-traded fund is a mutual fund holding a portfolio of stocks or bonds usually replicating a benchmark index that may be broad or narrow, domestic or foreign, and is traded like a listed share of common stock.

Buying, Selling, and Holding

How do I buy and sell it? Through a securities broker-dealer.

Is there a minimum purchase amount, and what is the price range? Round-lot 100 share purchases save commissions. Prices vary, but the majority are under $100.

What fees and charges are involved? Same as common stock.

Does it mature, expire, or otherwise terminate? No, although securities comprising a portfolio may change periodically.

Can I sell it quickly? Yes.

How is market value determined and how do I keep track of it? Market value is the aggregate of the market value of the common stock or other securities comprising the portfolio. Discrepancies between the market value of the ETF and underlying portfolio, called TRACING RISK, are eliminated by arbitrage and other means. ETFs are listed with other common stocks in the stock tables or, as in *The Wall Street Journal*, listed separately as Exchange-Traded Portfolios.

Investment Objectives

Should I buy it if my objective is capital appreciation? Yes.

Should I buy it if my objective is income? Yes, but you might prefer a straight fund investing only in income-producing securities. Bond ETFs provide interest income.

To what extent does it protect against inflation? ETFs with stock portfolios offer the same inflation protection as stocks. Those with fixed-income portfolios *do not offer protection.*

Is it suitable for tax-deferred accounts? Capital gains in ETF portfolios are not taxable until the ETF itself is sold, so at least part of your investment is tax-deferred. For that reason, it would make sense to use tax-deferred accounts for investments where gains distributions would otherwise be taxable in the year they are received.

Can I borrow against it? Yes, subject to the same Federal Reserve margin rules and lender policies concerning marketable securities collateral.

Risk Considerations

How assured can I be of getting my full investment back? ETFs have the same downside risks as the portfolios they hold.

How assured is my income? Common stock dividends, generated by the underlying stock portfolio, are discretionary but to varying degrees, reliable.

Are there other risks unique to this investment? None other than the risks of common stocks and whatever other risks are associated with their portfolio holdings. The SEC and Depository Trust Clearing Corporation watch ETFs closely and the risk of fraud is negligible.

Is it commercially rated? Yes. Morningstar and Standard & Poor's rate ETFs.

Tax Considerations

What tax advantages (or disadvantages) does it offer? Capital gains are minimized because ETFs are traded between shareholders and redemptions by large investors are paid in kind.

Economic Considerations

What economic factors most affect buy, hold, and sell decisions? ETFs, although traded like common stocks, are subject to the economic factors affecting common stocks only when their portfolios are composed of common stocks. ETFs with fixed-income portfolios are subject to economic factors affecting fixed-income investments.

FOREIGN STOCKS AND BONDS

Foreign stocks and bonds—those of foreign issuers denominated in foreign currencies—offer opportunities (1) to invest where economies or industry sectors may be more attractive than those at home and (2) to augment total returns through profits on currency movements.

Foreign securities have gained popularity as ways to shift money from sluggish U.S. markets into more vibrant overseas economies and as "dollar plays," ways of capitalizing on expected declines in the value of the U.S. dollar vis-à-vis foreign currencies. Generally, foreign investment activity picked up with capital market expansion, deregulation of foreign markets, improved communications, and increased internationalization of business.

The 1990s, however, brought good news and bad news. What had been hailed as the "Asian miracle," an explosive economic boom in the Asian-Pacific region, suddenly and without warning gave way to economic turmoil and currency collapses that caused investment values to sink not only in that region, but also in Latin America and to some extent in Europe. That, in turn, spurred massive capital flows into the U.S. economy, helping to fuel a raging bull market and making the dollar strong.

The second decade of the 2000s finds the U.S. dollar trending weaker against most European and Asian currencies as mounting U.S. national debt is financed by foreign investment from China, Japan, and other foreign countries; as an excess of imports over exports results in widening U.S. trade deficits reflecting the continuing shift of the American economy from manufacturing to services, and as the Federal Reserve's proclivity to stimulate consumer spending by expending the money supply raises concern about the U.S. dollar's declining purchasing power.

On January 1, 2002, the euro officially became the common currency of the now 27 European Union countries comprising Euroland, or the Eurozone, as the EU is alternatively called, an integrated financial and trading marketplace having its own central bank, rivaling the United States in size and potential importance, and making foreign investment in the area a process of company rather than country selection. The aim is an economic community where markets, not governments, steer economies and where the euro will counterbalance the global importance of the dollar. In 2010, however, economic problems are afflicting a number of EU members, notably Greece, Ireland, Italy, Spain, and Portugal (informally grouped as the PIIGs) causing the euro to weaken against the dollar and giving rise to speculation about how the EU, which is not a political union, would deal with a default by one of its members.

Problems with foreign investments, depending on the country, the issue, and the market, include inadequate financial information and regulation; high minimum purchase requirements; additional transaction costs and risks; taxes; possible illiquidity; political risk; and the possibility of currency losses. DEVELOPED COUNTRIES (or ECONOMIES), which lead a hierarchy of categories defined by economic advancement, have liquid markets, generally observe the same accounting and disclosure practices as the United States, and are free of political risk. *Developing countries*, which are one echelon below developed countries, do have all the aforementioned risks to varying degrees but represent greater growth and profit potential. They include the so-called BRIC economies, meaning Brazil, Russia, India, and China, which have huge populations, are rapidly industrializing, and will be the real engines of future international economic progress.

Foreign investment is greatly simplified by the availability of AMERICAN DEPOSITARY RECEIPTS (ADRs). Many foreign stocks can be owned by way of these negotiable receipts, which are issued by U.S. banks and represent actual shares held in their foreign branches. ADRs actively traded on the major stock exchanges are called sponsored ADRs and while currency risks and foreign withholding taxes remain, the depositary pays dividends and capital gains in U.S. dollars and handles rights offerings, splits, stock dividends, and other corporate actions. ADRs eliminate trading inconveniences and custodial problems that otherwise exist with foreign stocks. The main drawback is that only the largest and most actively traded foreign companies sponsor ADRs. Smaller companies that are undervalued and have more exciting growth potential have to be bought directly or through open-end, closed-end, or exchange-traded funds.

Eurobonds—bonds issued by governments and their agencies, banks, international institutions, and corporations (U.S. and foreign) and sold outside their countries through international syndicates for purchase by international investors—also warrant a special word. They may be denominated in foreign currencies, Eurodollars, or composite currency units, such as Special Drawing Rights (SDRs) or European Units of Account (EUAs) whose certificates representing the combined value of two or more currencies are designed to minimize the effects of currency fluctuations. Most are fixed-income obligations, but some Eurodollar issues have floating rates tied to the London Interbank Offered Rate (LIBOR). Eurobonds, which are issued in bearer form, attract upscale personal investors because they are available in a wide range of maturities, are not subject to a withholding tax, and offer good liquidity.

Traditionally, new issues of Eurobonds may not be sold legally to U.S. investors until a 90-day seasoning period has expired. Actually, most U.S. broker-dealers extend this rule to include all new issues in foreign currencies; foreign banks and broker-dealers are generally more solicitous of U.S. investors in selling new issues. Except for Yankee bonds, obligations of foreign borrowers issued in the United States and denominated in dollars, foreign bonds are not subject to Securities and Exchange Commission regulation.

* * *

What Are Foreign Stocks and Bonds?

Foreign stocks and bonds are non-dollar denominated shares of foreign companies listed on foreign exchanges and sometimes also on U.S. exchanges or represented by listed American Depositary Receipts (ADRs); bonds of foreign government entities and corporations, including Eurobonds and non-dollar-denominated bonds issued by local syndicates.

Buying, Selling, and Holding

How do I buy and sell foreign stocks and bonds? Through securities broker-dealers with foreign offices or with expertise in foreign markets, and through foreign banks and their American offices. (ADRs and shares traded on U.S. exchanges can be bought and sold through any broker.) Pink Sheet offerings available through domestic brokers, even the major ones, may conceal excessive mark-ups.

Is there a minimum purchase amount, and what is the price range? ADRs and U.S. exchange-listed foreign stocks trade just like domestic common stock. Minimums on other stocks and bonds vary widely by issue and dealer, but are often high, reflecting low share prices, in some cases literally in pennies. With the extra risks, diversification is important, which raises the cost even higher.

What fees and charges are involved? Transaction costs can be a significant consideration. They vary depending on many factors, but may include custodial fees, local turnover or transfer taxes, and currency conversion fees, in addition to broker commissions or dealer spreads. Transaction and custodial costs are minimized with ADRs.

Do foreign stocks and bonds mature, expire, or otherwise terminate? Bonds mature; stocks do not.

Can I sell them quickly? U.S. exchange-listed foreign stocks and ADRs normally enjoy high liquidity. With other foreign securities, illiquidity is often a problem. Even widely held issues are often kept as permanent investments by governments, banks, and other companies and may not trade actively. Canada, England, and Japan have high average turnover on their stock exchanges.

How is market value determined and how do I keep track of it? Economic, market, and monetary (interest-rate) factors affect foreign stock and bond values the same way they do domestic equity and debt securities, though conditions and growth rates differ among countries. Traditionally, foreign stocks, on average, have been less volatile than domestic issues, because issuers tended to be older firms whose stock was held largely by long-term investors. Today, foreign exchanges list a growing number of young, dynamic companies whose shares are actively traded and often quite volatile. *The Wall Street Journal,* the *Financial Times* (London), and other leading newspapers report on major foreign exchanges, as well as ADRs and foreign stocks and bonds traded in domestic markets.

Investment Objectives

Should I buy foreign stocks and bonds if my objective is capital appreciation? Especially in growing economies, stocks offer potential for both capital and currency appreciation. Unless bought at a discount or in a period of declining interest rates, bonds do not appreciate, although gains due to currency movements are possible.

Should I buy them if my objective is income? Yes, but exchange-rate fluctuations are a factor in the returns of both stocks and bonds.

To what extent do they protect against inflation? Foreign stocks can hedge inflation to the extent local economies and industry sectors offer better growth prospects than exist in the United States. But gains from dividends and appreciation can be eroded by foreign-exchange losses.

Are they suitable for tax-deferred retirement accounts? Yes.

Can I borrow against them? Yes; quality securities are acceptable collateral at most banks, and banks headquartered in the country of the issuer will often lend higher percentages of value. Foreign stocks listed on American exchanges are subject to Federal Reserve margin requirements.

Risk Considerations

How assured can I be of getting my full investment back? Although more young, growing firms appear every day on foreign exchanges, most shares represent solid issuers and volatility has traditionally been low, so foreign equities, on average, may actually be safer than many domestic issues, assuming no adverse currency fluctuations. Bondholders, who lack regulatory protection and full credit information, may have more credit risk than owners of domestic issues, in addition to having political, interest rate, and currency risks. (Foreign exchange risk can be hedged using currency futures and options.)

How assured is my income? Since issuers tend to be established, reputable firms or governments, there have historically been few defaults on payments of interest or instances of omitted dividends. On the other hand, a lack of full financial disclosure and regulatory supervision, a problem in less-developed countries, makes it difficult to anticipate adverse financial developments. Also, many newer companies, whose securities are riskier than those of traditional foreign issuers, are likewise listed on foreign exchanges. Foreign-exchange risk can also affect income.

Are there any other risks unique to this investment? Political or sovereign risk—the risk, for example, that foreign assets might be expropriated or devalued or that local tax policies might adversely affect debt or equity holders; the risk of transactional losses caused by settlement delays or fraud; with stock not registered with the Securities and Exchange Commission, there are legal difficulties for Americans in subscribing to rights offerings, a fact which can also affect the salability of rights (rights problems do not exist with ADRs or U.S. exchange-listed foreign shares).

Are they commercially rated? Some foreign debt issues are rated.

Tax Considerations

What tax advantages (or disadvantages) do they offer? Some countries impose a withholding tax, typically from 15% to 20%, on dividends and interest (except Eurobonds). U.S. tax treaties can result in partial reclamation of withholdings in some countries, and the tax can be offset to some extent against federal income taxes. There is usually no capital gains tax imposed by foreign governments, though such gains are taxed by the U.S. government. Special rules apply to 10% or more ownership of a foreign corporation.

Economic Considerations

What economic factors most affect buy, hold, or sell decisions? Foreign securities are best bought when the U.S. dollar is strong against the currency of denomination and sold when the dollar is declining against the local currency. Foreign equities are attractive relative to American investments when the foreign economy or industrial sector has a better outlook than its domestic counterpart. Foreign bonds rise and fall in inverse relation to market interest rates.

FUTURES CONTRACT ON A COMMODITY

A futures contract is a commitment to buy or sell a specified quantity of a commodity or financial instrument at a specified price during a particular delivery month. Once restricted largely to agricultural commodities and metals, futures contracts have in recent years been extended to include what are broadly termed financial futures—contracts on debt instruments, such as Treasury bonds and Government National Mortgage Association ("Ginnie Mae") certificates and on foreign currencies—and, even more recently, contracts on stock indexes. Contract prices are determined through open outcry—a system of verbal communication between sellers and buyers on the floors of regulated commodities exchanges.

The futures markets are broadly divided into two categories of participants: (1) Hedgers have a position in (i.e., own) the underlying commodity or instrument (such as a farmer in the case of an agricultural commodity or an investor in the case of a financial or index future). Hedgers use futures to create countervailing positions, thus protecting against loss due to price (or rate) changes. (2) Speculators do not own the underlying asset for commercial or investment purposes, but instead aim to capitalize on the ups and downs (the volatility) of the contracts themselves. It is the speculators who provide the liquidity essential to the efficient operation of the futures markets.

As with option contracts, which are also discussed in this section, the great majority of futures contracts are closed out before their expiration—or delivery— date. This is done by buying or selling an offsetting contract. It is vital to note that with futures, in contrast to options (which simply expire), the alternative to an offset is a delivery, though this is done with title documentation or, in the case of index futures, cash, not by the legendary dumping of pork bellies on the front steps of absentminded contract holders. When the future is a contract to buy value, delivery of the future is avoided by buying an offsetting future to sell.

The attraction of futures for speculators, again like options, is the enormous leverage they provide. Although brokers normally require investors to meet substantial net worth and income requirements, it is possible to trade contracts with outlays of cash (or sometimes U.S. Treasury securities) equal to 5% to 10% of contract values. Such "margins" (actually good-faith deposits, more in the nature of performance bonds and required of both buyers and sellers) are set by the exchanges, although brokers normally have their own maintenance requirements. Margin calls are normally made when deposits drop to one half the original percentage value.

The commodity exchanges, with oversight by the Commodities Futures Trading Commission (CFTC), each day set limits, based on the previous day's closing price, to the extent a given contract's trading price may vary. While these trading limits help preclude exaggerated short-term volatility and thus make it possible for margin requirements to be kept low, they can also lock a trader into a losing position, where he must meet a margin call but is prevented from trading out of the position because the contract is either up limit or down limit (as high or as low as the daily limit permits it to be traded).

Speculators in futures contracts fall into three groups: (1) the exchange floor traders (scalpers), who make markets in contracts and turn small profits usually within the trading day; (2) spread traders, who hope to profit from offsetting positions in contracts having different maturities but the same underlying commodity or instrument, similar maturities but different (although usually closely related) underlying commodities, or similar contracts in different markets; and (3) position traders, who have the expertise and financial ability to analyze longer-term factors and ride out shorter-term fluctuations in the expectation of ultimate gains.

While speculation in futures contracts is not recommended for the average investor, individuals with the money and risk tolerance may participate by choosing among the following alternatives: trading for one's own account, which involves time and expertise; trading through a managed account or a discretionary account with a commodities broker, which utilizes a professional's time and expertise for a fee or sometimes involves a participation in profits; or mutual funds, which offer both professional management and diversification and are regulated by both the CFTC and the Securities and Exchange Commission.

* * *

What Is a Commodity Futures Contract?

A commodity futures contract is an agreement to buy or sell a specific amount of a commodity at a particular price in a stipulated future month.

Buying, Selling, and Holding

How do I buy and sell it? Through a full-service broker or firm specializing in commodities transactions.

Is there a minimum purchase amount, and what is the price range? Contract sizes and unit prices vary widely from commodity to commodity, but the exchanges have liberal margin rules making it possible to trade with as little as 5% to 10% down. In some commodities, that can be $100, but brokers often have minimum deposits of $1000 to $2500. (They may also have strict personal income and net worth rules for investors.) One national exchange, the Mid America Commodity Exchange, offers minicontracts in a number of commodities, currencies, and instruments; they range from one fifth to one half the size of regular contracts.

What fees and charges are involved? Broker commissions, which vary by contract but average $25 to $50 for a round-turn (buy and sell) trade with lower rates for intraday and spread (e.g., buy soybeans, sell soybean oil) transactions. Managed accounts involve management fees and, sometimes, participation in profits.

Does a commodity futures contract mature, expire, or otherwise terminate? Yes. All contracts have a stipulated expiration date.

Can I sell it quickly? Most established contracts are liquid, though daily price limits can create illiquidity when a commodity is down limit or up limit (as high or as low as the daily trading limit permits).

How is market value determined and how do I keep track of it? By supply and demand, which is affected by natural causes as well as general economic developments. Futures prices are quoted daily in the financial pages of newspapers and electronic databases.

Investment Objectives

Should I buy a commodity futures contract if my objective is capital appreciation? Only if you are expert, wealthy, and have a high tolerance for risk. Then, with the high leverage possible, capital gains (and losses) can be huge.

Should I buy this if my objective is income? No. Contracts pay no income.

To what extent does it protect against inflation? Forward commodity prices reflect inflation expectations, but since contracts are short-term oriented, inflation protection is a secondary consideration.

Is it suitable for tax-deferred retirement accounts? Although not prohibited by the Internal Revenue Service, most brokerage firms rule out futures contracts as too risky for retirement accounts. They may have a limited role in managed accounts, primarily as a hedging tool. Certain pooled investment vehicles trading in futures may be appropriate in selected situations for people with high risk tolerance.

Can I borrow against it? Futures are not acceptable collateral with most lenders. Of course, they provide leverage inherently because of the relatively small deposits required to control contracts.

Risk Considerations

How assured can I be of getting my full investment back? Commodity futures are inherently speculative and it is actually possible to lose more than your investment (though margin calls would usually limit losses to the amount deposited if the account was sold out—that is, liquidated by the broker to meet the margin call).

How assured is my income? Futures provide no income.

Are there any other risks unique to this investment? The possibility of losses in excess of investment and the risk of illiquidity when a contract is down or up limit (thus making it impossible to trade out of a position) are risks unique to commodity futures trading. Of course, there is the risk (nightmare?) of actual delivery of a commodity if you fail to close out a position prior to expiration of a contract.

Is it commercially rated? No.

Tax Considerations

What tax advantages (or disadvantages) does a commodity futures contract offer? Speculators' open positions are marked to market at year-end and paper profits and losses taxed as though realized. Sixty percent of profits are taxed as long-term capital gains and 40% at short-term (ordinary income) rates. Other tax treatments apply to nonspeculative and hedging uses and tax advice is recommended.

Economic Considerations

What economic factors most affect buy, hold, and sell decisions? Anything that affects supply and demand for a commodity makes contract values move up and down.

FUTURES CONTRACT ON AN INTEREST RATE

For a general discussion of a futures contract, see Futures Contract on a Commodity.

* * *

What Is a Futures Contract on an Interest Rate?

A futures contract on an interest rate is an agreement to buy or sell a given amount of a fixed-income security, such as a Treasury bill, bond, or note or Government National Mortgage Association security at a particular price in a stipulated future month.

Buying, Selling, and Holding

How do I buy and sell it? Through a full-service broker or firm specializing in commodities transactions.

Is there a minimum purchase amount, and what is the price range? Contract sizes vary with the underlying security and the exchange, but range from $20,000 to $1 million; since exchange margin rules allow trading with as little as 5% deposited, the actual cost of investing can be relatively low.

What fees and charges are involved? Broker commissions averaging $25 to $50 per contract transaction.

Does it mature, expire, or otherwise terminate? Yes; futures contracts have specific expiration dates.

Can I sell it quickly? Yes, except that liquidity may become a problem if the contract reaches the maximum price movement allowable in one day, in effect locking you into a position.

How is market value determined and how do I keep track of it? By market interest rate movements, essentially. When rates go up, the prices of fixed-income securities (and futures related to them) go down, and vice versa. Prices are reported daily in newspapers and electronic databases.

Investment Objectives

Should I buy a futures contract on an interest rate if my objective is capital appreciation? Speculators use the leverage available with futures to capitalize on expected interest rate movements, standing to gain (or lose) substantially more than the amount invested.

Should I buy this if my objective is income? No, though you might use futures to hedge the value of securities bought for income or to lock in the yield on a security to be bought at a later date.

To what extent does it protect against inflation? To the extent inflation expectations are a factor in the volatility of fixed-income investments, futures can offer some protection against loss.

Is it suitable for tax-deferred retirement accounts? Although not prohibited by the Internal Revenue Service, most brokerage firms rule out futures contracts as too risky for retirement accounts. They may have a limited role in managed accounts, primarily as a hedging tool. Certain pooled investment vehicles trading in futures may be appropriate in selected situations for people with high risk tolerance.

Can I borrow against it? No; futures contracts are not acceptable collateral at most lenders. Of course, there is considerable leverage inherent in the small deposit required to control contracts.

Risk Considerations

How assured can I be of getting my full investment back? Just as interest rate movements cannot be predicted with certainty, interest rate futures can result in losses as well as gains; it is in fact possible to lose more than your investment (called open-ended risk) but margin calls would normally limit losses to the amount invested, assuming the account was sold out (liquidated) to meet the call.

How assured is my income? Futures do not provide income.

Are there any other risks unique to this investment? Open-ended risk and the risk of illiquidity when a contract is down limit or up limit, making it impossible to trade out of a position, are risks unique to futures contracts.

Is it commercially rated? No.

Tax Considerations

What tax advantages (or disadvantages) does it offer? Speculators' open positions are marked to market at year end and paper profits and losses taxed as though realized. Sixty percent of profits are taxed as long-term capital gains and 40% at short-term (ordinary income) rates. Other tax treatments apply to nonspeculative and hedging uses and tax advice is recommended.

Economic Considerations

What economic factors most affect buy, hold, and sell decisions? Economic and monetary factors affecting interest rates govern choices having to do with interest rate futures.

FUTURES CONTRACT ON A STOCK INDEX

For a general discussion of a futures contract, see Futures Contract on a Commodity.

* * *

What Is a Futures Contract on a Stock Index?

A futures contract on a stock index is an agreement to buy or sell a stock index at a price based on the index value in a stipulated future month with settlement in cash.

Buying, Selling, and Holding

How do I buy and sell it? Through a full-service broker or firm specializing in commodities transactions.

Is there a minimum purchase amount, and what is the price range? Contracts are priced according to formulas based on index values, and vary in terms both of formulas and index values. For example, the contracts on the New York Stock Exchange Composite Index, the Standard & Poor's 500 Stock Index, and The Value Line Stock Index are priced by multiplying $500 times the index value, which ranges roughly between 100 and 300; if one of those indexes had a value of 200, a contract would cost $100,000, which might require a deposit of 10% or $10,000. To play, though, you would probably have to meet an income and liquid net worth test requiring substantial means.

What fees and charges are involved? Broker commissions.

Does it mature, expire, or otherwise terminate? Yes, all contracts have specific expirations.

Can I sell it quickly? Yes, except that liquidity may become a problem if the contract reaches the maximum price movement allowable in one day (i.e., becomes down limit or up limit).

How is market value determined and how do I keep track of it? By the market performance of the stocks comprising the index as they affect the index value. Index futures are reported with other futures prices in the financial pages of daily newspapers and electronic databases.

Investment Objectives

Should I buy a futures contract on a stock index if my objective is capital appreciation? Speculators use the leverage available with futures to capitalize on expected market movements, standing to gain (or lose) substantially more than the amount invested.

Should I buy this if my objective is income? No, but they are used, mainly by professionals, to hedge the value of income-producing stocks.

To what extent does it protect against inflation? This is not an investment you would hold as an inflation hedge.

Is it suitable for tax-deferred retirement accounts? Although not prohibited by the Internal Revenue Service, most brokerage firms rule out futures contracts as too risky for retirement accounts. They may have a limited role in managed accounts, primarily as a hedging tool. Certain pooled investment vehicles trading in futures may be appropriate in selected situations for people with high risk tolerance.

Can I borrow against it? No; futures are not acceptable collateral at most lenders. Of course, there is considerable leverage inherent in the relatively small deposit required to control contracts.

Risk Considerations

How assured can I be of getting my full investment back? Just as market movements cannot be predicted with certainty, index futures can result in losses as well as gains; in fact, it is quite possible to lose more than your investment (called open-ended risk), although margin calls are a safeguard against losses in excess of investment if an account is sold out (liquidated) to meet the call.

How assured is my income? Index futures do not provide income.

Are there any other risks unique to this investment? Index futures and the individual stocks comprising the index may not move exactly together, so it is not a perfect hedging tool.

Is it commercially rated? No.

Tax Considerations

What tax advantages (or disadvantages) does it offer? Speculators' open positions are marked to market at year end and paper profits and losses taxed as though realized. Sixty percent of profits are taxed as long-term capital gains and 40% at short-term (ordinary income) rates. Other tax treatments apply to nonspeculative and hedging uses and tax advice is recommended.

Economic Considerations

What economic factors most affect buy, hold, and sell decisions? The myriad factors affecting the market outlook affect choices having to do with stock index futures, whether they are used to speculate or as a hedging tool.

GOVERNMENT AGENCY SECURITY

Government agency securities, popularly called agencies, are indirect obligations of the United States government, issued by federal agencies and government-sponsored corporations under authority from the United States Congress, but, with a few exceptions, not backed, as U.S. Treasury securities are, by the full faith and credit of the government.

While it is highly unlikely—even unthinkable—that they could ever be allowed to default on principal or interest, these agency securities cannot be considered absolutely risk-free, and therein lies their attraction—because of the slight difference in safety, they generally yield as much as a half percentage point more than direct obligations.

Agencies are also, like Treasuries, exempt from state and local taxes, although there are exceptions—for example, securities guaranteed by the Government National Mortgage Association (GNMA), and issues of the Federal National Mortgage Association (FNMA) and the Federal Home Loan Mortgage Corporation (FHLMC), including both mortgage-backed pass-throughs and bonds and notes issued to finance their operations. Mortgage-backed securities are discussed separately.

Unlike Treasuries, agencies are not sold by auction but rather are marketed at the best yield possible by the Federal Reserve Bank of New York, as fiscal agent, through its network of primary dealers. Information can be obtained from the Federal Reserve Bank of New York, Treasury and Agency Issues Division, from the issuing agencies, or from dealer commercial banks and securities brokers.

Agencies that have issued or guaranteed securities include:

Asian Development Bank

College Construction Loan Insurance Corporation (Connie Lee)

District of Columbia Armory Board (D.C. Stadium)

Export-Import Bank of the United States

Farm Credit Financial Assistance Corporation

Farmers Home Administration

Federal Agricultural Mortgage Corporation (Farmer Mac)

Federal Farm Credit Consolidated System-Wide Securities

Federal Home Loan Bank

Federal Home Loan Mortgage Corporation

Federal Housing Administration (FHA)

Federal National Mortgage Association (FNMA)

Financing Corp. (FICO)

Government National Mortgage Association (GNMA)

Interamerican Development Bank

International Bank for Reconstruction and Development (World Bank)

Maritime Administration

Resolution Funding Corporation (Refcorp.)

Resolution Trust Corporation (RTC)

Small Business Administration (SBA)

Student Loan Marketing Association (SLMA)

Tennessee Valley Authority (TVA)

United States Postal Service

Washington Metropolitan Area Transit Authority

* * *

What Is a Government Agency Security?

A government agency security is a negotiable debt obligation of an agency of the United States government, which may be backed by the full faith and credit of the federal government but is more often guaranteed by the sponsoring agency with the implied backing of Congress.

Buying, Selling, and Holding

How do I buy and sell it? Through a securities broker-dealer or at many commercial banks.

Is there a minimum purchase amount, and what is the price range? Denominations and minimums vary widely from $1000 to $25,000 and up, depending on the issue, the issuing agency, and the dealer.

What fees and charges are involved? None in the case of new issues bought from a member of the underwriting group; otherwise a commission or dealer markup.

Does it mature, expire, or otherwise terminate? Yes, maturities range from 30 days to 30 years.

Can I sell it quickly? Yes, but bid and asked spreads tend to be wider than with direct Treasury obligations, which raises the cost of trading in the secondary market. Inflation-indexed bonds may be less liquid.

How is market value determined and how do I keep track of it? Market values of fixed-income securities vary inversely with market interest rate movements. Daily newspapers, brokers, and large banks provide price information.

Investment Objectives

Should I buy a government agency security if my objective is capital appreciation? No, though appreciation is possible when fixed-rate securities are bought prior to a drop in market interest rates.

Should I buy this if my objective is income? Yes. Yields are a bit higher than those of direct government obligations, but lower than those of corporate obligations.

To what extent does it protect against inflation? As fixed-income securities, agencies offer no protection, though shorter-term issues offer less exposure to inflation risk. Some agencies, such as Tennessee Valley Authority and the

Federal Home Loan Bank, have begun issuing inflation-indexed securities, which protect against inflation but would be a risk in deflation.

Is it suitable for tax-deferred retirement accounts? Yes.

Can I borrow against it? Yes; lenders will often lend 90% of value.

Risk Considerations

How assured can I be of getting my full investment back? Agencies are second only to Treasury securities as good credit risks. Market prices fall as interest rates rise, however, so you may not get a full return of principal if you sell in the secondary market prior to maturity. Some sophisticated investors hedge market risk using options, futures, and futures options that are available on certain Treasury securities and Government National Mortgage Association securities.

How assured is my income? Very assured. It is highly unlikely the U.S. Treasury, Congress, or a regulatory body like the Federal Reserve Board would allow a government agency to default on interest.

Are there any other risks unique to a government agency security? No, but mortgage-backed pass-through securities issued by government-sponsored entities have different characteristics and are covered separately in this section.

Is it commercially rated? Some issues are rated by major services.

Tax Considerations

What tax advantages (or disadvantages) does it offer? Agencies are fully taxable at the federal level but are exempt from state and local taxes with certain exceptions, such as issues of the Federal National Mortgage Association and the Government National Mortgage Association. With inflation-indexed bonds, the annual inflation adjustment is taxable but not paid out until maturity.

Economic Considerations

What economic factors most affect buy, hold, or sell decisions? It is best to buy when interest rates are high and the best yields can be obtained. Holding is most attractive when rates are declining, causing an upward move in the market values of fixed-income securities, and high inflation is not present to erode the value of fixed returns.

LIFE INSURANCE (CASH VALUE)

For young families as yet without sufficient financial security to provide for expenses in the event of the premature death of the breadwinner or homemaker, life insurance provides essential protection. By far the cheapest and simplest way to obtain that protection is *term life insurance,* a no-frills deal whereby premiums buy insurance but do not create cash value. The alternatives—variously called cash value, straight, whole, permanent, or ordinary life insurance—combine protection with an investment program.

The traditional cash value policy requires a fixed premium for the life of the insured and promises a fixed sum of money on the death of the insured. A portion of the premium covers expenses and actual insurance, the rest earns interest in a tax-deferred savings program, gradually building up a cash value.

The latter can be cashed in by canceling the policy (hence the term "cash surrender value"), can be used to buy more protection, or can be borrowed at a below-market or even zero interest rate with the loan balance deducted from the death benefit. On the death of the insured, the beneficiary receives only the death benefit.

Variations called single-premium or limited-payment life policies, have higher up-front premiums so that a policy becomes paid-up—the cash value becomes sufficient to cover the death benefit without further premiums. Later, if the insured is still living, the policy begins paying benefits that can supplement retirement income or be converted to an annuity, thus guaranteeing income for life.

The one serious drawback of cash value policies has been that the interest rate is not competitive with other investments. With soaring interest rates and inflation in the 1970s and in the excitement of new investment products spawned by deregulation in the 1980s, upwardly mobile young investors began questioning the value of insurance policies providing neither competitive investment returns nor the flexibility their dynamic personal financial circumstances required. Faced with cancellations and poor sales, insurers came forth with the following:

> *Universal Life,* which clearly separates the cash value and protection elements of the policy and invests the cash value in a tax-deferred savings program tied to a money market rate. The cost of the insurance is fixed, based on the insured's age and sex, so depending on what the cash value portion earns (it is guaranteed to earn a minimum rate, but can earn more if market rates rise), the premium can vary. The insured may also change the amount of protection at any time. Flexibility is the main feature of this type of policy.

> *Variable Life,* which has a fixed premium like straight life, but the cash value goes into a choice of stock, bond, or money market portfolios, which the investor can alternate. The insurer guarantees a minimum death benefit regardless of portfolio performance, although excess gains buy additional coverage. The attraction here is capital growth opportunity.

> *Universal Variable Life,* a mid-1980s innovation that combines the flexibility of universal life with the growth potential of variable life.

Even with modern policies, however, the question persists: Why sacrifice a portion of income to an insurance company when pure protection can be more cheaply obtained through term insurance and returns as good or better can be obtained by investing directly? The answer depends on an individual's expertise, self-confidence, and willingness to spend time managing investments.

* * *

What Is Cash Value Life Insurance?

Cash value life insurance is a contract combining payment to beneficiaries, in the event of the insured's premature death, with investment programs.

Buying, Selling, and Holding

How do I buy and sell it? Through insurance brokers, insurance company sales agents, savings institutions, full-service brokers, commercial banks, financial planners, and other financial services organizations.

Is there a minimum purchase amount, and what is the price range? Annual premiums vary widely with the type of policy and such factors as the age and sex of the insured.

What fees and charges are involved? Cost of coverage, sales commissions, and insurance company operating costs are built into premiums. Some policies have penalties for cancellation before specified dates.

Does it mature, expire, or otherwise terminate? Policies mature in 10 years to life, depending on the program.

Can I sell it quickly? Yes. Policies can be canceled and cash values claimed anytime (although actual payment may require several weeks of processing time).

How is market value determined and how do I keep track of it? Policies are not traded in a secondary market. Cash values are determined by accumulated premiums plus investment income and performance.

Investment Objectives

Should I buy cash value life insurance if my objective is capital appreciation? Assuming death benefits are your primary objective, you might buy a variable life insurance policy or a universal variable life insurance policy with investments in a stock fund to gain capital appreciation.

Should I buy this if my objective is income? No, although policies combining annuities provide for income payments on annuitization.

To what extent does it protect against inflation? Universal, variable, and universal variable policies can offer some inflation protection through adjustable death benefits and the investment of cash values in inflation-sensitive securities.

Is it suitable for tax deferred retirement accounts? No; life insurance is not an eligible investment.

Can I borrow against it? Yes. Insurance companies will normally loan cash value at lower-than-market rates and reduce the death benefit by the amount of the loan.

Risk Considerations

How assured can I be of getting my full investment back? Insurance companies are highly regulated and there is little risk they will not meet commitments. However, policies that provide for market returns on cash value investments also carry market risk: e.g., a variable life policy invested in a bond fund would lose cash value if interest rates rose, while one invested in stocks would lose in a down market.

How assured is my income? That depends on how cash values are invested. Policies that invest cash value in money market instruments, for example, are subject to fluctuating income.

Are there any other risks unique to cash value life insurance? Although heavily regulated, insurance companies are potentially subject to mismanagement and fraud and are not themselves covered by federal protection in the sense that banks, for example, are covered by the Federal Deposit Insurance Corporation.

Is it commercially rated? Yes. Insurance companies are rated by A.M. Best Co. or Weiss Research.

Tax Considerations

What tax advantages (or disadvantages) does it offer? Income earned on cash value accumulates and compounds tax-deferred. Though subject to federal estate taxes and local inheritance taxes, life insurance proceeds paid to a named beneficiary avoid probate. Proceeds to beneficiaries are normally not subject to federal income taxes. Single-premium life insurance, which offers tax-free cash value accumulation and tax-free access to funds in the form of policy loans, was one of the few tax shelters to survive the Tax Reform Act of 1986. In 1987, however, tax legislation made tax-free borrowings possible only when a test is met requiring substantial insurance coverage relative to premiums over a lengthy time period.

Economic Considerations

What economic factors most affect buy, hold, and sell decisions? Inflation and volatility of interest rates gave rise to life insurance policies whose cash values vary with market conditions. Investors concerned about such factors can choose among such "new breed" alternatives, rather than buying traditional fixed-rate policies, and make their choices based on their expectations. Thus an investor anticipating high inflation and high interest rates would not choose a variable life policy invested in fixed-income bonds but might choose one with a stock fund or one that is money market-oriented. Variable and universal variable life insurance permit switching between bond, stock, and money market funds to afford maximum market flexibility.

MONEY MARKET FUND

This special breed of mutual fund gives personal investors the opportunity to own money market instruments that would otherwise be available only to large institutional investors. The attraction is higher yields than individuals could obtain on their own or from FDIC-insured bank *money market accounts*, plus a high degree of safety and excellent liquidity, complete with checkwriting.

Money market funds are sponsored by mutual fund organizations (investment companies), brokerage firms, and institutions, like insurance companies, which sell and redeem shares without any sales charges or commissions. The company charges only an annual management fee, usually under 1%, although extra services may entail additional charges. Income earned from interest-bearing investments is credited and reinvested (in effect compounded) for shareholders on a daily basis.

The disadvantage of money market funds over other short-term investment alternatives is that income (although normally paid out monthly) fluctuates daily as investments in the fund's portfolio mature and are replaced with new investments bearing current interest rates. In a declining rate market, this can be a disadvantage as compared, say, to a certificate of deposit, which would continue to pay an above-market rate until maturity. As a general rule, fund dividend rates lag behind money market rate changes by a month or so, depending on the average length of their portfolios, which is controlled to an extent by the manager's expectations as to where rates will go. Major sponsors permit switching among different funds in their families.

The market value of a money market fund investment is maintained at a constant $1 a share and while that is not guaranteed, there is only one exception on record. After the bankruptcy of Lehman Brothers in September 2008, The Reserve Primary Fund, a highly respected money market fund that held

Lehman Brothers debt instruments, "broke the buck," causing shock waves that forced several other funds to use their own money to maintain the $1 value. Fearing a run on money market funds, the Treasury Department announced a guarantee program that remained in effect from September 19, 2008 to December 19, 2009. While it would take a near-death financial crisis like 2008 to cause a recurrence, you might feel safer opting for a fund investing exclusively in U.S. government paper, or at least buying a fund run by a substantial manager that could afford to shore up its fund in an emergency. The fixed market value also means capital gains (and the favorable tax treatment they receive) are not a feature of money market funds, though investors may achieve some growth through compounding by opting to reinvest monthly payments.

Funds may differ in terms of the type of securities comprising their portfolios, some specializing only in U.S. Treasury bills or in tax-exempt municipal securities. A general portfolio, however, would typically be comprised of bank and industrial commercial paper, certificates of deposit, acceptances, certain asset-backed securities, repurchase agreements, direct and indirect U.S. government obligations, Eurodollar CDs, and other safe and liquid investments. Bonds and foreign debt securities are sometimes included to lift yields.

Money market funds are not covered by federal insurance the way bank deposits are, although funds sponsored by brokerage firms are insured by the Securities Investor Protection Corporation (SIPC) against losses caused by a failure of the firm. Some funds may also be covered by private insurance.

For longer-term investment purposes, alternative investments offer better yield with comparable safety while also providing growth opportunity, tax advantages, and similar inflation protection. The convenience and income of money market funds, although increasingly challenged by bank deposit products, remain attractive for providing for emergencies and for parking temporarily idle cash.

* * *

What Is a Money Market Fund?

A money market fund is a type of mutual fund in which a pool of money is invested in various money market securities (short-term debt instruments) and which compounds interest daily and pays out (or reinvests) dividends to shareholders monthly.

Buying, Selling, and Holding

How do I buy and sell it? Through sponsoring brokerage firms and mutual fund organizations. Accounts are also offered by insurance companies and other financial institutions as a parking place for temporarily idle funds.

Is there a minimum purchase amount, and what is the price range? The minimum investment usually ranges from $500 to $5000. For funds offered through brokers, $1000 is typical; $2500 is a typical minimum investment for funds offered directly by fund sponsors. Additional investment is usually allowed in increments as small as $100.

What fees and charges are involved? Most are no-load (without sales fee), charging only an annual management fee, which is usually less than 1% of the investment. There may be extra fees for special services, such as money transfers.

Does it mature, expire, or otherwise terminate? No.

Can I sell it quickly? Yes. Shares are redeemable anytime and most funds offer checkwriting privileges, though $500 minimums for checks are common.

How is market value determined and how do I keep track of it? Market values of shares are kept constant. Yields change in response to money market conditions as investments turn over and are calculated on a daily basis. Seven and 30-day average yields are reported weekly in the financial pages of newspapers and current information can be obtained directly by calling the sponsoring organizations.

Investment Objectives

Should I buy this if my objective is capital appreciation? No.

Should I buy this if my objective is income? Yes. The attraction of money market funds is that the individuals can earn the same high yields that would otherwise be available only to institutional investors. Of course, income fluctuates and there is little protection against a decline in market rates.

To what extent does it protect against inflation? Because interest rates on newly offered debt instruments rise with inflation, money market funds, being composed of constantly rotating short-term investments, have performed well in inflation and paid dividends that kept pace with rising price levels.

Is it suitable for tax-deferred retirement accounts? Yes.

Can I borrow against it? Yes, banks and brokers will lend a high percentage (often 90%) of the value of your shares.

Risk Considerations

How assured can I be of getting my full investment back? Your investment in a money market fund is quite safe, since by law portfolios must comprise securities of banks, governments, and top corporations. Investors seeking maximum safety can choose funds investing exclusively in U.S. government direct obligations, though at some sacrifice of yield; while this does not mean the fund is guaranteed by Uncle Sam, the fact that its investments are so guaranteed actually does provide a high degree of security. A financially strong fund manager makes it more likely that backup funds would be available in the unlikely event a crisis such as the Lehman bankruptcy in 2008 were to occur again. Some funds are privately insured against default.

How assured is my income? While the risk of default is very small, there is no way of preventing fluctuations in money market interest rates. Dividend rates could therefore decline, although the reaction to market rate changes may be more or less delayed, depending on the average maturity of a portfolio. Most fund sponsors permit shifting into other investment vehicles within their families when adverse developments can be foreseen or when better opportunities exist.

Are there any other risks unique to this investment? A fund that invested relatively long-term just prior to a drastic rise in rates could be forced to sell investments at a loss to meet redemptions. Well-managed and established funds are aware of this obvious risk and take measures to avoid it. Overall, the industry, which is regulated by the Securities and Exchange Commission, has enjoyed an excellent safety record.

Is it commercially rated? A number of organizations record past performance and a few predict future yields, but money market funds are not rated in the sense that bonds and stocks are.

Tax Considerations

What tax advantages (or disadvantages) does it offer? Where portfolios are comprised of tax-exempt securities, investors are exempt from federal taxes and, depending on state laws, possibly state and local taxes. (States may treat tax-exempt funds differently from tax-exempt direct investments.) Otherwise, dividends are fully taxable. Some states that do not tax interest earned on direct investments will tax dividends from funds, even though the fund's income is from interest earned.

Economic Considerations

What economic factors most affect buy, hold, and sell decisions? Money market funds are most attractive when short-term interest rates are high and alternative investments are beset with uncertainty. As a rule, investors use money market funds to park cash temporarily, choosing other investments for longer-term purposes.

MORTGAGE-BACKED (PASS-THROUGH) SECURITY

Although mortgage-backed securities (MBS) were the weak link in the chain reaction that caused the financial crisis of 2007, those held by individual investors were virtually all backed by U.S. government guarantees or by government-sponsored entities that the government took over. They have traditionally offered one of the best risk/return deals available to investors, plus excellent liquidity. Their most notable drawbacks, though, are that, due to prepayments on mortgages comprising the underlying pools, monthly income payments fluctuate and the term of the investment cannot be predicted with certainty. The trade-off for this is a rate premium.

Pass-through, created through a process called securitization, securities represent shares in pools of home mortgages having approximately the same terms and interest rates. They were introduced in the 1960s to make lenders liquid and stimulate home buying.

The process begins when prospective homeowners apply for mortgages to banks, savings and loan associations, and mortgage bankers. The loan paper is sold to intermediaries, such as Fannie Mae and Freddie Mac who pool and then repackage it as bonds, which are marketed to investors. Interest and principal, including prepayments, pass from the homeowner through the intermediary to the investor. When the mortgages mature or are prepaid, the investment expires.

Pass-throughs have also enjoyed an active secondary market, where securities trade either at discounts or premiums depending on prevailing interest rates. Interestingly, pass-throughs representing pools of low-rate mortgages, when they can be bought favorably to result in attractive yields, are the most desirable holdings because the prepayment risk is low.

The following are principal mortgage-backed securities:

Government National Mortgage Association (GNMA): Ginnie Maes are the most widely held pass-throughs and are backed by Federal Housing Administration (FHA)-insured and Veterans Administration (VA) guaranteed mortgages plus the general guarantee of GNMA, which (by virtue of rulings of the Treasury and Justice departments) brings the full faith and credit of the U.S. government behind these securities. They are as safe as Treasury bonds but typically yield 1% to 2% higher.

Federal Home Loan Mortgage Corporation (FHLMC): Freddie Mac PCs (Participation Certificates) are backed by both FHA and VA mortgages and privately insured conventional mortgages plus the general guarantee of FHLMC, a government-sponsored entity until 2008, when it was taken over by the government.

Federal National Mortgage Association (FNMA): Fannie Mae MBSs (Mortgage-Backed Securities) are issued and guaranteed by FNMA, a government-sponsored, publicly held (NYSE-traded) company that, like Freddie Mac, was taken over by the government in 2008. Its MBSs are backed by both conventional and FHA and VA mortgages. They are essentially similar to Freddie Macs and tend to have similar yields.

Private mortgage participation certificates issued by lending institutions or conduit firms have varying characteristics and different ratings, depending on such factors as private mortgage insurance, cash-fund backing, and over-collateralization (the extent to which the market values of underlying properties exceed the mortgages). These include jumbo pools of mortgages from different lenders.

Collateralized mortgage obligations (CMOs), or collateralized debt obligations (CDOs), are instruments, technically mortgage-backed bonds, that break up mortgage pools into separate maturity or risk classes, called TRANCHES. This is accomplished by applying mortgage income first to the bonds with the shortest maturity (CMOs) or by separating pools into classes based on credit quality (CDOs). Tranches pay different rates of interest and typically mature in 2, 5, 10, and 20 years. Issued by Freddie Mac and private issuers, CMOs are usually backed by government-guaranteed or other top-grade mortgages and most have AAA bond ratings. For a slight sacrifice of yield, CMOs lessen anxiety about the uncertain term of pass-through investments.

CDOs, which were issued by investment banks that bought subprime mortgages not meeting the requirements of Ginnie, Fannie, or Freddie, were sold to hedge funds and institutional investors looking for yield rather than liquidity, many of which found themselves in liquidation after the mortgage meltdown.

Real estate mortgage investment conduits (REMICs), still another variation, were created by the Tax Reform Act of 1986. REMICs offer issuers, who may be government or private entities, more flexibility than CMOs and protection from double taxation, which CMOs have avoided with legal technicalities. They are thus able to separate mortgage pools not only into maturity classes but also into classes of risk. The practical effect of this has been that whereas CMOs have financed top-quality mortgages in order to obtain AAA ratings, REMICs have been used to finance mortgages of lesser quality, even some that are financially distressed. More often than not, a REMIC obligation is a high-yield, junk mortgage bond.

New on the scene since the meltdown are RE-REMICs, standing for resecuritization of real estate mortgage investment conduits. As a practical matter, they are CMOs or CDOs that have been recycled with tranches finagled to have AAA ratings. Unless the real estate market goes up instead of continuing down, they are probably as ill-fated as the original CDOs.

Strips: Mortgage-backed securities are also stripped and sold as zero-coupon securities. See the section Zero-Coupon Security for a discussion of this alternative.

* * *

What Is a Mortgage-Backed (Pass-Through) Security?

A mortgage-backed security is a share in an organized pool of residential mortgages, the principal and interest payments on which are passed through to shareholders, usually monthly. The category includes collateralized mortgage obligations (CMOs), technically mortgage-backed bonds, which provide for different maturities, collateralized debt obligations (CDOs) with different risk calculations, and real estate mortgage investment conduits (REMICs) and RE-REMICs, which provide for both separate maturity and separate risk classes. It does not include mortgage-backed securities that are corporate bonds or government agency securities and are covered in those sections.

Buying, Selling, and Holding

Where do I buy and sell it? At a securities broker-dealer.

Is there a minimum purchase amount, and what is the price range? Most new pass-throughs are sold in minimum amounts of $25,000, although some older issues can be bought with less and some private issues and CMOs and REMICs can be bought for as little as $1000. Shares of funds, limited partnerships, and unit investment trusts that buy such securities range from $1000–$5000.

What fees and charges are involved? This varies among vehicles and brokers, but can be either a flat fee or a dealer spread. Sponsors deduct modest fees from passed-through income.

Does it mature, expire, or otherwise terminate? Yes, the life of a pool, and its related securities, ends when the mortgages mature or are prepaid. CMOs and REMICs offer investors a choice of earlier or later payouts.

Can I sell it quickly? Yes, liquidity has traditionally been very good.

How is market value determined and how do I keep track of it? Market value, to the extent mortgage pools have fixed-rate obligations, goes up when market interest rates go down, and vice versa. On the other hand, prepayments rise when rates decline, shrinking the pool and lowering share values. Daily price and yield information is published in the financial pages of newspapers and in electronic databases.

Investment Objectives

Should I buy this if my objective is capital appreciation? Although most investors plan to hold for the life of the issue, capital appreciation is possible as the result of declining market interest rates.

Should I buy this if my objective is income? Yes; mortgage pass-throughs generally offer good yields. The most conservative, Ginnie Maes, normally yield at least 1% more than U.S. Treasury bonds and have the same safety from default.

To what extent does it protect against inflation? Because they are based largely on fixed-income mortgages, pass-throughs suffer in high inflation.

Is it suitable for tax-deferred retirement accounts? Yes; except for rollovers, however, the minimum investments exceed IRA limits.

Can I borrow against it? Yes.

Risk Considerations

How assured can I be of getting my full investment back? Although some issues are safer than others (Ginnie Maes are U.S. government-guaranteed against default on underlying mortgages, for example), Fannie Mae and Freddie Mac are now government-owned. Others are insured in addition to being over-collateralized (i.e., the market value of the real estate behind the mortgages exceeds the face value of the mortgages), but bond insurers have largely gone out of business and real estate prices are declining as this is written, making any mortgage-related investments questionable unless they are government-guaranteed. REMICs tend to have riskier backing and should be analyzed, the more so with RE-REMICs.

How assured is my income? Income is as safe as the issuer, but can vary from month to month as the result of prepayments and other factors.

Are there any other risks unique to this investment? Prepayments may shorten the life of the investment, although the cash they create is of course passed through to investors.

Is it commercially rated? Yes, Standard & Poor's and other bond-rating services rate mortgage-backed securities, although their ratings have lost credibility since the late 2000s.

Tax Considerations

What tax advantages (or disadvantages) does it offer? None. Interest is taxed as ordinary income and profits or losses from the sale of pass-through securities in the secondary market are taxed as capital gains or losses. But the monthly payment received by an investor in a pass-through is only partly interest. Because payments to the investor are simply pass-throughs of payments by homeowners on their mortgages, and those payments are part interest and part principal, the investor pays taxes only on the portion of his payment representing interest; the rest, as principal, is treated as a nontaxable return of capital. Since home mortgage payments have a higher ratio of interest to principal in the earlier years of the mortgage, it follows that income payments on pass-through securities normally have a higher proportion of taxable interest in the earlier years of the life of the pool.

Economic Considerations

What economic factors most affect buy, hold, and sell decisions? Mortgage-backed pass-throughs are most attractive to hold when general interest rates are low relative to the yield on the mortgage pool. However, this scenario can also cause a high rate of prepayments just when the investment is most attractive. The best holding is a pool of low-rate mortgages whose shares are bought at a good discount; that results in an attractive yield for investors, but since the homeowners are also happy with their low-rate mortgages, the risk of prepayment is much less. Of course, inflation erodes the value of fixed payments, which are the basis of income from pass-throughs.

MUNICIPAL SECURITY

A municipal security, or muni, is a debt obligation of a U.S. state, territory, or political subdivision, such as a county, city, town, village, or authority.

What makes munis special is that those classified as public purpose bonds enjoy exemption from federal income taxes and, frequently, from state and local income taxes as well. Tax-exempt munis pay lower rates of interest than taxable securities, making their after-tax return more attractive as an individual's income moves into higher brackets. Another classification of municipal bonds, called *Private Purpose Bonds* because they involve 10% or more benefit to private parties, are taxable unless specifically exempted.

Whether tax-exempt or not, munis are either (1) general obligations, notes or bonds backed by the full faith and credit (including the taxing power) of the issuing entity and used to finance capital expenditures or improvements; or (2) *revenue obligations,* which are used to finance specific projects and are repaid from the revenues of the facilities they finance.

Although munis vary in the degree of credit strength backing them, their safety record has traditionally been excellent, earning them a place between Treasuries and high-grade corporate bonds in terms of investor confidence. Defaults, even in bad times, have been far fewer than with corporate bonds having the same ratings and their recovery rate has been much higher. The most famous default in recent years was Orange County, California in 1994, where investors eventually got back 100 cents on the dollar.

One important reason munis have a reputation as prudent investments is that municipalities, unlike Uncle Sam, can't print money to reduce deficits. They are legally required to balance their budgets and this has forced fiscal prudence during good times and provided a cushion during periods of economic stress.

Also, many lower-rated muni issues have traditionally been privately insured by bond insurers such as AMBAC FINANCIAL GROUP, MUNICIPAL BOND INVESTORS ASSURANCE CORPORATION (MBIA), Assured Guaranty Ltd (known by its symbol, AGO), and other specialty and general insurers.

All that said, however, how did the late 2000's financial crisis, followed by what is commonly called the worst recession since The Great Depression, affect municipal bonds? The answer, in a word, is hugely. Yet all the news is not bad.

As a direct result of the financial crisis, bond insurers that got involved with bonds backed by subprime mortgage paper, such as COLLATERALIZED BOND OBLIGATIONS, took a devastating hit. AMBAC and MBIA are threatened with bankruptcy and have written no bond insurance at all in 2010. AGO avoided the subprime crisis and is the only major company writing bond insurance as this is written. Institutional buyers of munis and the dealers who serve them have been greatly reduced in number because they were heavily invested in subprime mortgage paper and took big losses. Also, the supply of AAA-rated municipal bonds has shrunk, mainly for two reasons, the first being that they got their high ratings because of bond insurance, the second reason being that the general credit quality of municipals has been declining due to rising spending, collapsing revenues, mounting retiree expenses, and other factors. The result of all this has been a situation where most of the demand is coming from wealthy individuals with less to choose from and a market that, absent institutional traders, is less liquid.

On the other hand, such inventory as is available is attractively priced and higher yielding than would be the case under more normal conditions and while the outlook for municipalities is increasingly gloomy, federal stimulus money aimed at municipal deficits and infrastructure projects and other forms of federal aid designated for education, health, and social services should help municipalities preserve their good default record.

The bottom line is that credit quality has become the prime focus of investors at a time when the rating agencies themselves have lost credibility, so it is incumbent on investors and their advisors to do careful research. Assuming credit can be established, munis offer unique opportunity for high-income investors who benefit from the tax exemption.

The ECONOMIC RECOVERY AND REINVESTMENT ACT introduced BUILD AMERICA BONDS (BAB) in April 2009 to expand the market for municipal bonds by attracting lower income buyers and public pension funds that would not otherwise buy tax-exempt bonds. The aim was to help municipalities raise money during the credit crunch and to create infrastructure-related jobs. BABs are taxable bonds issued by municipalities, but the Federal government provides either an investor tax credit equal to 35% of the coupon or directly subsidizes 35% of the issuer's coupon payments. The program was scheduled to expire one year later, although there is a good chance it will be extended or made permanent. In April 2009, a 30-year, A-rated BAB issued by the Pennsylvania Turnpike Authority sold at 6.10%, 150 points above 30-year Treasuries. After the subsidy, the issuer's borrowing cost was 3.97%. A comparable tax-free bond would have cost 5%–5.10%. The only thing the government guarantees is the 35% subsidy, so there is credit risk.

In addition to taxable bonds, recent innovations in the municipal securities field have included *tax-exempt commercial paper,* short-term discounted notes usually backed by bank lines of credit; *bonds with put options* typically exercisable after one to five years, which carry a somewhat lower yield in exchange for the put privilege; *floating (or variable) rate* issues tied to the Treasury bill or another market rate; and *enhanced security issues,* in which the credit of the municipal entity is supplemented by bank lines of credit or other outside resources.

For smaller investors, open- and closed-end funds, unit investment trusts, and other pooled vehicles with portfolios of municipal obligations offer diversification and professional management with lower minimums.

Munis are also available as zero-coupon securities and are covered in the section dealing with that investment alternative.

* * *

What Is a Municipal Security?

A municipal security is a negotiable bond or note issued by a U.S. state or subdivision. A muni may be a general obligation backed by the full faith and credit (i.e., the borrowing and taxing power) of a government; a revenue obligation paid out of the cash flow from an income-producing project; or a special assessment obligation paid out of taxes specially levied to finance specific public works. Some municipal bonds, such as those to finance low-income housing, may be backed by a federal government agency.

Buying, Selling, and Holding

How do I buy and sell it? Most securities broker-dealers handle municipal securities.

Is there a minimum purchase amount, and what is the price range? Although munis are issued in units of $5000 or $1000 par value as a rule, with exceptions as low as $100, broker-dealers usually require minimum orders of at least

$5000 and often want $10,000, $25,000, or up to $100,000. Odd lots are some-times available from broker-dealers at extra commissions or spreads. Smaller investments can be made through mutual funds, closed-end funds, unit invest-ment trusts and other pooled vehicles with tax-exempt portfolios.

What fees and charges are involved? Sometimes a commission, but usually a spread (rarely exceeding 5%) between the dealer's buying and selling prices.

Does it mature, expire, or otherwise terminate? Yes. Maturities range from one month (notes) to 30 years (bonds). Serial bonds mature in scheduled stages. Munis may also be callable or have put features.

Can I sell it quickly? Some munis have good liquidity, although issues of obscure municipalities and authorities can have inactive markets and be hard to sell.

How is market value determined and how do I keep track of it? Most munis are fixed-income securities and thus rise and fall in opposite relationship to market interest rates. Variable-rate issues, whose rates are periodically ad-justed to reflect changes in U.S. Treasury bill yields or other money market rates, tend to sell at or close to their par values. Muni quotes are not nor-mally published in daily newspapers, but prices published in *The Bond Buyer* (mainly new muni issues) and the *Blue List of Current Municipal Offerings* (a Standard & Poor's publication reporting details of secondary market offerings and their size) are available through brokers or directly by subscription.

Investment Objectives

Should I buy a municipal security if my objective is capital appreciation? No, although appreciation is possible when munis sell at discounts because rates have risen or credit questions arise.

Should I buy this if my objective is income? Yes, but in the case of tax-free bonds, only if the after-tax yield in your tax bracket compares favorably to the yield on a taxable investment of comparable safety.

To what extent does it protect against inflation? Fixed-income munis offer no inflation protection. Variable-rate munis would offer some, if interest rates rose.

Is it suitable for tax-deferred accounts? Tax-exempt issues bearing a lower interest rate than a taxable security are not suitable. Taxable *private purpose* munis and BABs are suitable.

Can I borrow against it? You can, but the interest you pay is not tax-deduct-ible if the proceeds are used to buy municipals. With the lower rate you earn on most munis, it would hardly pay. While munis are acceptable collateral for other loans, care must be taken to avoid the appearance of a violation of the rule against deducting interest.

Risk Considerations

How assured can I be of getting my full investment back? Munis have an excellent default record, but they can and do default, especially in bad econ-omies. In most cases, you can be quite sure of getting your investment back at maturity. Munis generally rank between U.S. government securities and corporate bonds in credit safety. But the risk of default varies with the credit of the issuer and the type of obligation (mainly general obligation or rev-enue obligations). Some munis are covered for default by private insurers, but several leading insurers got into trouble with mortgage-backed bonds in the late 2000s. Of course, prices of all fixed-income securities decline when interest rates go up.

How assured is my income? Munis are relatively safe (see the preceding question) but defaults are possible due to such factors as limited ability to impose taxes, disappointing revenues from the use of facilities, or mismanagement of municipal finances. Issues may also be callable, enabling the issuer to force redemption after specified times.

Are there any other risks unique to this investment? Munis are not subject to Securities and Exchange Commission regulation, so the legality of the issue must be established. Make sure a legal opinion accompanies the issue.

Is it commercially rated? Moody's Investors Service, Standard & Poor's, and others rate credit. White's Tax-Exempt Bond Rating Service rates market risk.

Tax Considerations

What tax advantages (or disadvantages) does it offer? Interest may be exempt from federal income taxes and frequently from state and local income taxes (36 states tax exempt munis of other states but not their own; 5 states tax their own exempt munis and those of other states; 9 states plus the District of Columbia do not tax any exempt munis). Munis issued by Puerto Rico, Guam, and the Virgin Islands (U.S. territories) are tax-exempt in all states. Capital gains are taxable. Permitted private purpose bond interest may be a tax preference item in computing the Alternative Minimum Tax. Up to 85% of Social Security benefits can be taxed if municipal bond interest income plus adjusted gross income plus half the Social Security payments exceeds $32,000 for couples or $25,000 for single taxpayers.

Economic Considerations

What economic factors most affect buy, hold, or sell decisions? Personal tax considerations, of course, then interest rate levels and the inflation rate. Buy when rates are high to get good yields; hold as rates decline to see market values rise. Because tax-exempt munis pay a relatively low interest rate, inflation is especially devastating if the rate is fixed. Prolonged economic downturns can increase the risk of municipal defaults.

MUTUAL FUNDS (OPEN END)

An open-end mutual fund is so named because its sponsoring organization, called an investment company or a management company, stands ready at any time to issue new shares or to redeem existing shares at their daily-computed net asset value. It offers small investors diversification and professional management otherwise available only to large investors.

Mutual funds are designed for a wide variety of investment objectives and risk levels. The HEDGE FUND, a specialized type of fund using ALTERNATIVE INVESTMENTS and restricted to wealthy investors, is not in this category. The following is a partial list of types of funds, with their basic portfolio or mode of operation:

> *Asset Allocation Fund* (management rotates mix of stocks, bonds, and cash to favor best-performing asset class)

Life Cycle (or Strategy) Fund (asset allocation fund that becomes more conservative as your target retirement date approaches)

Income Fund (stocks paying dividends, preferred stocks, corporate bonds)

Growth Fund (growth stocks)

Aggressive Growth Fund (smaller, riskier growth stocks)

Balanced Fund (stocks and bonds)

Performance Fund (high-risk stocks, venture capital investments, etc.)

Conservative Balanced Fund (high-grade income and growth securities)

United States Government Bond Fund (U.S. Treasury or agency bonds)

International Fund (foreign stocks or bonds)

Global Fund (foreign and U.S. stocks or bonds)

Domestic Taxable Bond Fund (corporate bonds with investment-grade ratings)

Corporate High-Yield Bond Fund (corporate bonds with ratings below investment grade)

Municipal Bond Fund (tax-exempt municipal securities)

Special Situations Fund (venture capital, debt/equity securities)

Stock Index Fund (replicating or representative of the major stock indexes)

Market Sector Fund or *Specialized Fund* (securities of high-growth industries or specialized industries like gold-mining)

Tax-managed Fund (utility stocks whose dividends are reinvested for long-term capital gains)

Speculative Fund (engages in selling short and leverage)

Commodities Fund (commodity futures contracts)

Option Fund (sells puts and calls for extra income, sometimes speculating by taking positions without owning underlying securities or instruments)

Socially-conscious Fund (excludes investments offensive on moral or ethical grounds)

Fund of Funds (invests in other funds with top performance)

Money Market Fund (short-term, interest-bearing debt instruments)

Tax-exempt Money Market Fund (trades long-term and short-term municipals for best yields and capital gains)

Ginnie-Mae Fund (mortgage-backed pass-through securities guaranteed by Government National Mortgage Association)

Major sponsors allow switching of investments from shares of one fund to another within their fund families. Other services commonly available to investors include term life insurance; automatic reinvestment plans; regular income checks; open account plans allowing fractional share purchases with Social Security or pension checks or other relatively small amounts of cash; loan programs; and toll-free information services.

A recent development has been the issuance of share classes distinguished by different fee structures and identified by an alphabetical designation following a fund's name in the newspaper listings. Class A shares typically have a FRONT-END LOAD, a sales charge payable when you buy the fund. Class B shares typically have a BACK-END LOAD, payable when you redeem your fund shares, but declining the longer you hold the fund until, finally, after 6 to 8 years, it "converts" to zero. Both A and B shares usually have an additional 12b-1 marketing fee, higher in the case of B shares. Class C shares have no front-end load, a rear-end load ranging from very low (1 percent) to nothing, but have relatively high 12b-1 fees (translating into high EXPENSE RATIOS.) Class A, B, and C shares are by far the most common. Class D shares, where they exist, differ from one mutual fund company to another, in one case signifying front-end loads and no 12b-1 fees, in others high 12b-1 and no front-end loads, in still others, a rear-end load structured differently than that fund company's B shares. Class I and Class Y shares are institutional shares, not available to retail investors; if they are included in your 401(k) plan, they probably have low annual expenses and don't have a sales charge. M and T Class shares are different for each fund company, but are usually a variation on C shares. Z Class shares are either owned by the fund company's employees or by investors who got into a fund when it originally started as a no-load fund and stayed in after it became a load fund.

† † †

What Is an Open-End Mutual Fund?

An open-end mutual fund is an investment company that pools shareholder funds and invests in a diversified securities portfolio having a specified objective. It provides professional management and stands ready to sell new shares and redeem outstanding shares on a continuous (open-end) basis.

Buying, Selling, and Holding

Where do I buy and sell it? Load funds, in which a sales charge is deducted from the amount invested, are bought from securities brokers and financial planners. No-load funds are bought directly from the sponsor. Shares are not sold in the sense that shares of stock are transferred to other owners; rather they are redeemed (by phone, mail, or checkwriting privilege) by the fund at net asset value. We exclude from this definition the specialized category called HEDGE FUNDS. Hedge funds have high-risk portfolios comprising ALTERNATIVE INVESTMENTS and are legally restricted to high-net worth individuals. Although exceptions to net worth requirements have been made by hedge fund managers using the *fund-of-funds* structure as a technicality, hedge funds are not suitable investments for individuals of average means.

Is there a minimum purchase amount, and what is the price range? Some funds have minimum deposits of $1000–$2500. Others have no minimum. Share prices vary, but a majority are under $20. Many funds offer convenient share accumulation plans for investors of modest means.

What fees and charges are involved? Load funds charge a sales commission, typically $8^{1}/2$% of the amount invested, though with larger purchases the load can go as low as $1^{1}/2$%. No-load funds have no sales commissions. Hybrid, low-load funds charge commissions of 3% or less. Both load and no-load funds charge annual management fees of from $^{1}/2$% to 1% of the value of the investment. There is usually no redemption charge (back-end load, or exit fee) with load funds; no-loads may or may not have a 1% to 2% redemption fee to discourage short-term trading. Various share accumulation plans may involve extra service charges. Some funds discourage frequent switching by imposing extra charges. 12b-1 mutual funds, a type of fund that covers all or part of its sales and marketing expenses by charging fees to shareholders, may charge $^{1}/4$% or less of assets in the case of no-load funds, ranging to $8^{1}/2$% for load funds. Share classes having different fee structures are described on page 56.

Does it mature, expire, or otherwise terminate? No.

Can I sell it quickly? Funds stand ready to redeem shares daily, but there may be an "exit fee" (back-end load). Some managing companies allow switching among different funds they sponsor at either no charge (no-load fund families) or a small transaction fee.

How is market value determined and how do I keep track of it? Market value, called net asset value, depends on the way various economic and market forces affect the type of investments composing a particular fund's portfolio; a given economic or interest-rate scenario will have a different effect on bond fund values than stock fund values. Mutual fund quotations are reported daily in newspapers and fund management company reports, usually quarterly, on the composition of portfolios and transactions during the reporting period. Your website or that of Morningstar will give you net asset values.

Investment Objectives

Should I buy an open-end mutual fund if my objective is capital apprecia-tion? Yes, but you would buy a fund with capital gains as a primary objective, such as a growth stock or special situations fund.

Should I buy this if my objective is income? Yes, but you would buy a fund with income as its primary objective, such as a bond or money market fund or a stock fund investing in high-yield stocks.

To what extent does it protect against inflation? That depends on the type of fund. Equity-oriented funds or money market funds offer more protection than fixed income bond portfolios, which provide little or no protection.

Is it suitable for tax-deferred retirement accounts? Yes, except when the fund is invested in tax-exempt securities, such as municipal bonds.

Can I borrow against it? Yes, subject to Federal Reserve margin rules. Collateral value varies with the type of fund. A lender that might loan 90% of the value of money market fund shares might find a high-risk fund unacceptable as collateral.

Risk Considerations

How assured can I be of getting my full investment back? It depends on the type of fund, the quality of the portfolio, and the adroitness of management in avoiding adverse developments. A money market fund has high safety of principal, whereas a bond fund is vulnerable to interest rate movements and a stock fund is subject to market risk, for example.

How assured is my income? Again, it depends on the type of portfolio, its quality, and the skill of the manager. A fund with AAA bonds will be a safer source of income than one comprised of higher-yielding but riskier junk bonds. Other funds stress capital growth at the expense of income. Money market funds offer assured income at a conservative rate, which goes up and down with market conditions.

Are there any other risks unique to this investment? Except for the fact that funds provide automatic diversification, the same risk considerations apply as affect individual investments.

Is it commercially rated? Some funds invest exclusively in securities with given commercial ratings, and a number of organizations, most notably Morningstar, rate mutual funds in terms of historical performance and other factors.

Tax Considerations

What tax advantages (or disadvantages) does it offer? Income is subject to the same federal income taxes as the investments from which it derives. Thus, a shareholder pays taxes just as if he owned the portfolio directly, except that all capital gains distributions are considered long-term, regardless of the time the fund has been held. Funds invested in tax-exempt municipal securities (some are triple— federal, state, and local—tax-exempt) provide tax-free income, at least at the federal level. States vary in their tax treatment of income from municipal securities (see the discussion of tax considerations in the section on Municipal Securities) and the same rules usually apply to fund income. Some states that would not tax interest will tax dividends from funds, however, even though the fund's income is from interest earned. In such states, dividends from a tax-exempt fund would be taxable.

Economic Considerations

What economic factors most affect buy, hold, or sell decisions? The same economic and market forces that affect individual investments affect funds made up of those investments, so choices should be made in the same terms.

OPTION CONTRACT (PUT OR CALL)

Put and call options are contracts that give holders the right, for a price, called a premium, to sell or buy an underlying stock or financial instrument at a specified price, called the exercise or strike price, before a specified expiration date. Option sellers are called writers—covered writers if they own the underlying security or financial instrument, naked writers if they don't—and buyers of options are called option buyers. A put is an option to sell and a call is an option to buy.

Listed options are options traded (since 1973) on national stock and commodity exchanges and thus have both visibility and liquidity, as opposed to conventional over-the-counter options, which are individually negotiated, more expensive, and less liquid. Listed options are available on stocks, stock indexes, debt instruments, foreign currencies, and futures of different types. The issuance and settlement—all the mechanics of options clearing—are handled by the options clearing corporation (OCC), which is owned by the exchanges.

Options make it possible to control a large amount of value with a much smaller amount of money. Because a small percentage change in the value of a financial instrument can result in a much larger percentage change in the value of an option, large gains (and losses) are possible with the leverage that options provide. Although sometimes options are bought with the idea of holding the underlying security as an investment after the exercise of the option, options are usually bought and sold without ever being exercised and settled. They have a life of their own.

The value of options—that is, the amount of their premiums—is mainly determined by the relationship between the exercise price and the market price of the underlying instrument, by the volatility of the underlying instrument, and by the time remaining before expiration.

When the relationship between an option's strike price (exercise price) and the underlying market price is such that the holder would profit (transaction costs aside) by exercising it, an option has intrinsic value and is said to be in the money. In contrast, there is no intrinsic value in an out-of-the-money option— such as a put whose strike price is below the market price or a call whose strike price is above the market price. A premium will normally trade for at least its intrinsic value, if any. An out-of-the-money option, on the other hand, has obviously more risk and a lower premium than an option that is more likely to become profitable. Options on highly volatile securities and instruments command higher premiums because they are more likely to produce profits when and if they move.

Time value influences premiums because the longer the time remaining, the greater the chance of a favorable movement and the higher the present value of the underlying instrument if exercised. This time value, also called net premium, decreases as the option approaches its expiration. (For this reason, options are called wasting assets.) The value of an out-of-the-money option is all time value; that of an in-the-money option is a combination of time value and intrinsic value. In general, the greater the potential for gain, the greater the risk of not achieving it. The farther from expiration and the greater the volatility, the higher the premium an option will have.

Professional traders have multioption strategies, some quite complex, designed to limit risk while capitalizing on premium movements. Called straddles, combinations, and spreads (which have many varieties), they involve close monitoring, expertise, and sometimes onerous commissions. Options trading is not for the average investor.

Options do have a conservative role, however, for personal as well as institutional investors. Options can be used very much like term life insurance policies to protect investors against losses in investments already owned. Option selling (writing) can be a source of added returns.

The use of options as insurance involves the purchase of a put to limit losses or lock in the profit on a position already owned, or the purchase of a call to limit losses or lock in the profit on a short sale. For example, an individual with 100 shares of XYZ at a market value of $60 who expects the price to rise to $70 might buy, at a premium of $125, a put at $55 expiring in three months. If the stock rises, the insurance would have cost $125 and that amount would have to be subtracted from the capital gain. If the stock dropped, however, the put could be exercised and the stock sold for no lower than $55; that would limit the investor's loss to $625—$60 less $55 (times 100 shares) plus the premium of $125. The investor who thought the stock would drop could have sold it short and bought a call to assure the ability to buy the shares to cover at the call price.

Covered option writing—writing calls on stock or other instruments that are owned—is a safe way to increase the income return on an investment, provided the investor is prepared to sell the underlying holding at the exercise price if the price moves that way. Potential gains are limited to the amount of the premium (a significant drawback if the underlying holding rises in value and the option is exercised).

Calls can be written at, in, deep in, out of, or deep out of the money. The farther out of the money it is, the less the chance of exercise and the lower the premium it will command. The main problem with writing covered calls is that to warrant a premium high enough to offset the commissions, the underlying asset has to be volatile, and the option close to the money; the more volatile it is and the closer the option is to the money, the greater the chance it will be exercised. If it's exercised the writer's profit is limited to the premium, when a greater profit could have been made by holding the investment.

Mutual funds that make their income by writing and trading options are an alternative for small investors.

What are LEAPS? LEAPS are among the most notable innovations of the 1990s. An acronym for Long-Term Equity Anticipation Securities, LEAPS were introduced by the Chicago Board Options Exchange (CBOE) in October 1990. LEAPS are long-term put and call options that by the mid-nineties were being traded (on the NYSE, Amex, Philadelphia, and options exchanges) on about 150 stocks and several stock indexes. LEAPS are presently available with expirations of 1 to 3 years. Generally speaking, everything that is said in the following pages about regular puts and calls applies to LEAPS, except, of course, that being longer in term, LEAPS have higher premiums.

* * *

What Is an Option Contract (Put or Call)?

An option contract is a contract that grants the right, in exchange for a price or premium to buy (call) or sell (put) an underlying security at a specified price within a specified period of time.

Buying, Selling, and Holding

Where do I buy and sell it? At a full-service or discount broker.

Is there a minimum purchase amount, and what is the price range? The minimum is one option contract covering 100 shares. Contracts typically cost a few hundred dollars (usually less than $500).

What fees and charges are involved? In addition to the premium, brokerage commissions are charged for buying, selling, and exercising options. The maximum charge is $25 for a transaction covering one option; the average for multiple-contract transactions is about $14.

Does it mature, expire, or otherwise terminate? Yes; options have a specified expiration date, usually within nine months.

Can I sell it quickly? Yes; most options enjoy good liquidity.

How is market value determined and how do I keep track of it? The market value of an option is its premium value, which is determined by a combination of its intrinsic value (the difference between its exercise price and the market value of the underlying stock) and its time value (the value investors place on the amount of time until the expiration of the option). A small change in a stock price can cause a larger percentage change in an option premium; premium changes are reported daily in the financial sections of newspapers.

Investment Objectives

Should I buy an option contract if my objective is capital appreciation? Because a small change in a stock price causes a higher percentage change in a related option premium, speculators gain leverage using options. Of course, if the underlying stock fails to move in the right direction, the speculator is out the cost of the premium. Options are also used as hedging tools to protect the value of shares held for capital gains.

Should I buy this if my objective is income? Although sellers (writers) of options receive income from premiums and thereby augment the income return on the underlying holding, they may be forced to buy or sell the underlying holding if its price moves adversely. Options are not themselves income-producing investments, although speculators and some mutual funds create income through option writing and various spread strategies.

To what extent does it protect against inflation? Puts and calls, as short-term options, are not designed to capitalize on longer-term movements in common stock prices as might be caused by inflationary factors. Of course, LEAPS, subscription warrants, and employee stock options, which are related to put and call options, could be viewed as inflation protection.

Is it suitable for tax-deferred retirement accounts? Although not prohibited by the Internal Revenue Service, most brokerage firms rule out options contracts as too risky for retirement accounts. They may have a limited role in managed accounts, primarily as a hedging tool. Mutual funds or other pooled investments that generate income by writing and speculating in options may be appropriate investments in selected situations for people with high risk tolerance.

Can I borrow against it? No. Although Federal Reserve margin rules allow options transactions in margin accounts, options cannot be used as part of the borrowing base. Of course, options are themselves a source of considerable leverage.

Risk Considerations

How assured can I be of getting my full investment back? Your investment is the premium plus commissions. It is recovered only if the underlying stock or instrument moves favorably to such an extent that the profit gained from selling or exercising the option exceeds the investment; whether it does or not is pure speculation.

How assured is my income? The only income that options provide is from premiums earned in selling them. That is assured income, but it can be more than offset if the underlying stock moves adversely and the option is exercised by its holder.

Are there any other risks unique to this investment? The risk in options ranges from the simple loss of a premium if the option proves valueless to the risk of a magnified loss in the case of uncovered or naked positions—that is, where a put or call is sold without owning the underlying security or instrument. Upon exercise, the security or instrument must be bought or sold at a market price that may be in wide variance from the exercise price.

Is it commercially rated? No.

Tax Considerations

What tax advantages (or disadvantages) does it offer? Options on stocks are subject to the same capital gains taxation as the stocks themselves. Some traditional uses of options to defer income from one year to another have been curtailed by recent tax legislation and advice should be sought. See also the entry for Tax Straddle in Part IV.

Economic Considerations

What economic factors most affect buy, hold, and sell decisions? The same economic factors that affect stock investments in the short term apply essentially to decisions involving put and call options used in speculation and hedging.

OPTION CONTRACT ON A FUTURES CONTRACT (FUTURES OPTION)

For a general discussion of an option, see Option Contract (Put or Call).

* * *

What Is an Option Contract on a Futures Contract?

A futures option is a contract that grants the right, in exchange for a price (premium) to buy (call) or sell (put) a specified futures contract within a specified period of time.

Buying, Selling, and Holding

How do I buy and sell it? At a full service or discount broker.

Is there a minimum purchase amount, and what is the price range? The minimum purchase is one option on one futures contract. It can cost several hundred to several thousand dollars, depending on the underlying future.

What fees and charges are involved? In addition to the premium, brokerage commissions are charged for buying, selling, and exercising an option. Generally, the maximum charge is $25, and the average charge for multiple option transactions is around $14, with lower rates for high-volume transactions.

Does it mature, expire, or otherwise terminate? Yes; options have a specified expiration date, usually within one year.

Can I sell it quickly? Yes; most futures options have good liquidity and they are not subject to daily trading limits that can affect the liquidity of futures themselves.

How is market value determined and how do I keep track of it? The same factors that affect the market value of futures affect the premium values of futures options. (See the sections Futures Contract on a Commodity and Futures Contract on an Interest Rate.) Prices are reported daily in newspapers and electronic databases.

Investment Objectives

Should I buy a futures option if my objective is capital appreciation? Only if you are a speculator attracted to the high degree of leverage offered by options, although options on futures are used by investors to hedge the value of other investments held for capital gains.

Should I buy this if my objective is income? Although selling options is a source of income, options are not themselves an income-producing investment. Some mutual funds trade in options for the purpose of generating income, however.

To what extent does it protect against inflation? Only to the limited extent that futures offer the opportunity to capitalize on inflation expectations and their effects on interest rates and commodity prices.

Is it suitable for tax-deferred retirement accounts? Although not prohibited by the Internal Revenue Service, most brokerage firms rule out options contracts as too risky for retirement accounts. They may have a limited role in managed accounts, primarily as a hedging tool. Mutual funds or other pooled investments that generate income by writing and speculating in options may be appropriate investments in selected situations for people with high risk tolerance.

Can I borrow against it? No. Although Federal Reserve margin rules allow options transactions in margin accounts, options cannot be used as part of the borrowing base. Of course, options are themselves a source of significant leverage.

Risk Considerations

How assured can I be of getting my full investment back? Your investment is the premium plus commissions. It is recovered only if the underlying futures contract moves favorably to such an extent that the proceeds realized from selling or exercising the option exceed the amount expended; whether it does or not is pure speculation.

How assured is my income? The only income that options provide is from premiums earned in selling them. That is assured income, but it can be more than offset if the underlying future moves adversely and the option is exercised by the holder.

Are there any other risks unique to this investment? Essentially the same risks apply as are involved with regular options and futures on the same underlying assets. A special positive feature, however, is that futures options, particularly on debt instruments, have better liquidity than either straight options or straight futures; that is because of less restrictive trading limits on futures options than on futures, and because the open interest on futures options tends to be much higher than on regular interest-rate (debt) options.

Is it commercially rated? No.

Tax Considerations

What tax advantages (or disadvantages) does it offer? Options on futures are subject to the same tax treatment as futures are. See the section on a Futures Contract on a Commodity.

Economic Considerations

What economic factors most affect buy, hold, and sell decisions? The same economic forces that affect interest rate and commodity futures affect the options available on those contracts.

OPTION CONTRACT ON AN INTEREST RATE (DEBT OPTION)

For a general discussion of an option, see Option Contract (Put or Call).

* * *

What Is an Option Contract on an Interest Rate?

An interest-rate option is a contract that grants the right, in exchange for a price (premium), to buy (call option) or sell (put option) a certain debt security at a specified price within a specified period of time, thereby producing a particular yield.

Buying, Selling, and Holding

How do I buy and sell it? Through a full-service or discount broker.

Is there a minimum purchase amount, and what is the price range? The minimum purchase is one contract. Premiums, where the underlying security is interest-bearing, are determined as a percentage (in 32nds for Treasury bonds and notes) of par value. Thus a contract on a $100,000 par value U.S. Treasury bond with a premium of 2.50 would cost $2500, while a $20,000 minicontract with a premium of 1.24 would cost $350. Where the underlying security is discounted rather than interest-bearing, as with the 13-week Treasury bill, premiums are quoted with reference to basis point (100ths of one percent) differences between prices, expressed as complements of annualized discount rates. For example, with a 9% yield, a 13-week Treasury bill (par value $1 million) would have a price basis of 91 and might have an option trading at 92.20. With a premium thus quoted at 1.20 (120 basis points), it would cost $3000, calculated: $.012 \times ^{13}/_{52} \times \$1$ million. (A quick way of approximating dollar premiums is to multiply basis points times $25.)

What fees and charges are involved? Brokerage commissions are charged for buying, selling, or exercising options. The maximum charge is $25 for a transaction covering one contract, with reduced rates for larger trades. Margin accounts may entail interest and other added charges. There may also be income and net worth rules to qualify investors.

Does it mature, expire, or otherwise terminate? Yes. All options have expiration dates, usually within nine months.

Can I sell it quickly? Interest rate options have generally good liquidity. Those with the most contracts outstanding (represented by open interest figures in newspapers) are usually easiest to trade.

How is market value determined and how do I keep track of it? Market value, which is premium value, is determined by a combination of intrinsic value (exercise value less market value of the underlying security) and time value (the diminishing value investors place on the time remaining to expiration). Intrinsic value changes with interest rate movements, which are influenced by Federal Reserve Board monetary policy and other economic factors. Option prices are reported daily in newspapers and electronic databases.

Investment Objectives

Should I buy an interest-rate option if my objective is capital appreciation? Speculators use the high leverage possible with options to capitalize on the price volatility resulting from interest rate movements.

Should I buy this if my objective is income? Option writers earn income in addition to the interest they receive on the underlying security, while taking the risk that the option will be exercised if rates move adversely. Investors also use interest rate options to hedge the value of other income-producing investments.

To what extent does it protect against inflation? As short-term instruments, interest-rate options are not designed for dealing with the longer-term effects of inflation on debt securities. However, inflation expectations are a factor in the term structure of interest rates, and it is possible, using options, to capitalize on short-term movements.

Is it suitable for tax-deferred retirement accounts? Although not prohibited by the Internal Revenue Service, most brokerage firms rule out options contracts as too risky for retirement accounts. They may have a limited role in managed accounts, primarily as a hedging tool. Mutual funds or other pooled investments that generate income by writing and speculating in options may be appropriate investments in selected situations for people with high risk tolerance.

Can I borrow against it? No. Although Federal Reserve margin rules allow options transactions in margin accounts, options cannot be used as part of the borrowing base. Of course, options are themselves a source of considerable leverage.

Risk Considerations

How assured can I be of getting my full investment back? Your investment is recovered only if interest rates move favorably to the extent that the proceeds of the sale of the option exceed the premium plus commissions already expended; that is a matter of pure speculation.

How assured is my income? The only income is from premiums earned in selling options and even that can be negated by losses resulting from exercise by the holder.

Are there any other risks unique to this investment? The marketplace of interest-rate options is dominated on one hand by large institutional investors and their portfolio managers and on the other by dealers who handle the large volumes of high-denomination securities that underlie the options. This puts the smaller investor at a disadvantage in terms both of information and transaction cost. Other special risks have to do with the Option Clearing Corporation's power to remedy shortages of underlying securities by permitting substitutions and adjusting strike prices, and with trading hour differences between options and underlying debt instruments. Sellers of options on discount instruments settled in current instruments take a risk to the extent that they cannot hedge perfectly against exercise.

Is it commercially rated? No.

Tax Considerations

What tax advantages (or disadvantages) does it offer? Unlike regular put and call options, traders in interest-rate options are subject to tax rules covering futures trading; this means open positions are marked to market at year-end with paper gains or losses treated as if realized and taxed as net capital gains (see page 32). Tax advice should be sought.

Economic Considerations

What economic factors most affect buy, hold, and sell decisions? Economic and monetary factors affecting interest rates govern choices having to do with interest-rate options.

OPTION CONTRACT ON A STOCK INDEX

For a general discussion of an option, see Option Contract (Put or Call).

* * *

What Is an Option Contract on a Stock Index?

A stock-index option is a contract that grants the right, in exchange for a price (premium), to buy (call option) or sell (put option) the value of an underlying stock index or subindex at a specified price within a specified period of time with settlement in cash.

Buying, Selling, and Holding

How do I buy and sell it? Through a full-service or discount broker.

Is there a minimum purchase amount, and what is the price range? The minimum purchase is one contract. The premium is the difference in index values times $100. A contract based on a 5-point difference between the current (base) value and the exercise value would thus cost $500. Because contracts are settled in cash, margin security in the form of cash or securities is required by brokers, who may also have suitability requirements calling for substantial net worth and income.

What fees and charges are involved? In addition to the premium, brokerage commissions are charged for buying, selling, and exercising options. The maximum charge is $25 for a transaction covering one contract, with reduced rates for large trades. Margin accounts may entail interest and other additional charges.

Does it mature, expire, or otherwise terminate? Yes; options have a specified expiration date.

Can I sell it quickly? Most stock-index options have good liquidity, though newly introduced contracts may have less active markets than contracts that are better established and more popular. Those with many contracts outstanding (represented by large open interest figures in the newspapers) are generally the easiest to trade.

How is market value determined and how do I keep track of it? Premium value is determined by a combination of intrinsic value (exercise price less the index value) and time value (the value investors place on the amount of time remaining to expiration). The intrinsic value is subject to all the forces that make the stock market go up and down; a small movement in the market, as represented by the index, will result in a much larger percentage change in premium value. Indexes are revalued constantly during the trading day and closing prices are published in daily newspapers and electronic databases along with the option values based on them.

Investment Objectives

Should I buy a stock-index option if my objective is capital appreciation? You might if you were a speculator expecting a move in the stock market and were attracted to the high leverage provided by options. You might also use index options to hedge against possible losses in other securities being held for capital gains.

Should I buy this if my objective is income? Although sellers of options receive premium income and thereby increase the income return on their portfolios, options are not themselves income securities.

To what extent does it protect against inflation? Index options are short-term investments and not designed to capitalize on longer-term market movements as might be caused by inflation.

Is it suitable for tax-deferred retirement accounts? Although not prohibited by the Internal Revenue Service, most brokerage firms rule out options contracts as too risky for retirement accounts. They may have a limited role in managed accounts, primarily as a hedging tool. Mutual funds or other pooled investments that generate income by writing and speculating in options may be appropriate investments in selected situations for people with high risk tolerance.

Can I borrow against it? No. Although Federal Reserve margin rules allow options transactions in margin accounts, options cannot be used as part of the borrowing base. Of course, options are themselves a source of significant leverage.

Risk Considerations

How assured can I be of getting my full investment back? Your investment is recovered only if the underlying index value moves favorably to such an extent that the proceeds gained from selling or exercising the option exceed the cost plus commissions; whether it does is pure speculation.

How assured is my income? The only income that options provide is from premiums earned in selling the options. Even that, however, can be negated if the underlying index moves adversely and the option is exercised by the holder.

Are there any other risks unique to this investment? Index options share the same risks as regular puts and calls, but have a few that are unique. These have basically to do with (1) the limitations of index options as a hedging tool (it is impractical to compose a portfolio that duplicates an index exactly and even then there is rarely dollar-for-dollar variation) and with (2) the fact that settlement is made in cash; the settlement figure is the difference between the strike price and the closing value of the index on the day of exercise, and since the seller is not informed of the assignment until the next business day or even later, his hedge position may have lost value. This timing risk must be considered in all multioption strategies using index options. Other risks have to do with trading halts affecting underlying shares (but not the indexes) and causing index values to be based on noncurrent prices, or trading halts in the index options themselves, with the risk that the index value will move adversely before a position can be closed out.

Is it commercially rated? No.

Tax Considerations

What tax advantages (or disadvantages) does it offer? Unlike regular put and call options, index options are subject to tax rules covering futures trading. This means open positions are marked to market at year-end; paper profits or losses are treated as if realized and taxed as net capital gains (see page 34). Tax advice should be sought.

Economic Considerations

What economic factors most affect buy, hold, and sell decisions? Index options are used to make market bets or to protect other holdings against market risk. Any and all economic factors affecting the market become relevant to decisions involving stock options.

OPTION CONTRACT OR FUTURES CONTRACT ON A CURRENCY

For a general discussion of an option, see Option Contract (Put or Call); for a general discussion of a futures contract, see Futures Contract on a Commodity.

* * *

What Is an Option Contract or a Futures Contract on a Currency?

They are contracts to buy or sell (futures) or that represent rights (options) to buy or sell a foreign currency at a particular price within a specified period of time.

Buying, Selling, and Holding

How do I buy and sell them? Through a full-service broker or commodities dealer.

Is there a minimum purchase amount, and what is the price range? Contract sizes vary with different currencies and different markets. The minimum purchase is one contract, which, for an option, typically costs a few hundred dollars. Futures contracts tend to be sizable (standard-size contracts are 12.5 million yen and 125,000 Swiss francs, for example, which on one day in the mid-1980s both equalled about $62,500) but they can be bought with small (1.5% to 4.2%) margins. Also, minicontracts are traded in several currencies on the Mid-America Commodity Exchange—6.25 million yen and 62,500 Swiss francs, for example.

What fees and charges are involved? Broker's commissions, typically $25 or less per contract for options; $50 to $80 for a round-trip futures contract transaction (purchase and sale). In the event of actual delivery, other fees, charges, or taxes may be required.

Do they mature, expire, or otherwise terminate? Yes; all contracts have specified expiration dates.

Can I sell them quickly? Yes; option and futures contracts enjoy good liquidity, although daily price limits on futures can create illiquidity when contracts are down limit or up limit and it is impossible to trade out of a position, because maximum allowable price movement has occurred during the trading day.

How is market value determined and how do I keep track of it? Premiums and contract values change as the exchange rate between the dollar and the foreign currency changes. The exchange rate is determined by the relative value of two currencies, which can change as events affect either or both of the underlying currencies. Daily prices are published in newspapers and electronic databases.

Investment Objectives

Should I buy them if my objective is capital appreciation? Speculators use the high leverage afforded by options and futures contracts to seek gains on relative currency values.

Should I buy them if my objective is income? Except for premium income earned from selling (writing) options, contracts do not provide income. Contracts are frequently used in hedging strategies to protect other income-producing securities from losses due to currency values.

To what extent do they protect against inflation? Because they are short-term contracts, currency options and futures are not affected directly by inflation.

Are they suitable for tax-deferred retirement accounts? Although not prohibited by the Internal Revenue Service, most brokerage firms rule out options and futures contracts as too risky for retirement accounts. They may have a limited role in managed accounts, primarily as a hedging tool. Mutual funds or other pooled investments that generate income through options and futures may be appropriate investments in selected situations for people with high risk tolerance.

Can I borrow against them? Options can be traded in margin accounts but cannot be used as collateral. Moreover, since foreign currency does not have borrowing value either for margin purposes, purchases as the result of exercise may require extra cash or securities. Futures cannot be used as collateral, but provide leverage because they can be held with small margins, actually good faith deposits.

Risk Considerations

How assured can I be of getting my full investment back? With options, the only investment is the premium plus commissions and it is recovered only when the underlying rate of exchange moves favorably to such an extent that the proceeds gained from sale or exercise exceed the amount expended. Futures are inherently speculative and it is possible to lose more than your investment, although margin calls would normally limit losses to the amount invested, assuming the account was closed out (liquidated) to meet the call.

How assured is my income? Other than premium income from option writing (selling), options and futures provide no income.

Are there any other risks unique to these investments? Since two currencies are involved, developments in either country can affect the values of options and futures. Risks include general economic factors as well as government actions affecting currency valuation and the movements of currencies from one country to another. The quantities of currency underlying option contracts represent odd lots in a market dominated by transactions between banks; this can mean extra transaction costs upon exercise. The fact that options markets may be closed while round-the-clock interbank currency markets are open can create problems due to price and rate discrepancies. With futures, there is always the risk of actual delivery if a position is not closed out prior to expira tion of the contract.

Are they commercially rated? No, neither options nor futures are rated.

Tax Considerations

What tax advantages (or disadvantages) do they offer? Options are subject to the same capital gains rules as the underlying assets. Futures are subject to special rules requiring that open positions be marked to market at year-end and be taxed as realized capital gains (see page 34). Net trading losses can be applied against capital gains on other investments and unused portions carried forward. Other tax treatments may apply where contracts are used for hedging purposes. Tax advice should be sought.

Economic Considerations

What economic factors most affect buy, hold, and sell decisions? All factors that affect either currency affect the values of options and futures contracts.

PRECIOUS METALS

Precious metals—gold, silver, platinum, and palladium—are bought by investors primarily to hedge against inflation, economic uncertainty, and foreign exchange risk, in the belief that these metals, particularly gold, are repositories of absolute value, whereas paper currencies and securities denominated in such currencies have relative value and are vulnerable to loss.

The economics of precious metals have less to do with the production process, industrial demand, or their greatly diminished monetary role than with the psychology of the financial marketplace. There, precious metals—gold especially—are perceived to be the best store of value available when anxiety causes the value of other assets to go into a tailspin. Historically, in such scenarios gold and other precious metals have risen.

An instructive example was in January 1980 when double digit inflation led by rising oil prices amid the American-hostage crisis in Iran, and civil disorder in Saudi Arabia caused a bear market rally in precious metals, which drove gold from $40 an ounce in 1974 to a record price of $887.50 per ounce and led silver and platinum to peak levels as well. When calmer times returned, however, prices soon fell and fluctuated between $250 and $450 an ounce for the next 20 years. It was a memorable lesson in how volatile this store of value can be.

Since 2000, however, gold has been in a bull market reflecting a decline in the value of the U.S. dollar against major foreign currencies as America has run huge trade deficits financed by mounting debt. Gold hit an all-time high of over $1,000 an ounce in March of 2008 as the financial crisis was unfolding, saw a correction to $850 an ounce in November of that year following the bankruptcy of Lehman Brothers, and an irrational flight to the perceived safety of the U.S. dollar, and then resumed its bull trend, rising to a new record over $1,000 an ounce. Silver, which has wider industrial demand than gold, tends to follow similar price trends but has greater upside as well as downside. Platinum and palladium (part of the platinum group, but used in technology, as in catalytic converters) tend to rise and fall with commodities generally. In tough economic times, gold and silver, having once been money, tend to acquire a monetary premium.

Physical ownership is one way of owning precious metals, available in bullion form in units ranging from 400-Troy-ounce gold bars to 1-ounce platinum ingots. These are sold by dealers at markups or premiums that fall as weights and dollar values rise. Gold can also be held in coins, such as the South African Krugerrand, the Canadian Maple Leaf, and the U.S. Eagle series, introduced in 1986. Generally, the more popular the coin, the greater its liquidity and the higher its premium. Silver can be bought in bags containing U.S. coins of $1000 total face value, priced at a discount to the silver value to cover melting and refining costs. The drawbacks of physical ownership are mainly the high premiums, safekeeping and insurance costs, and sales taxes.

Certificates—actually warehouse receipts issued by some banks, dealers, and full-service brokers—represent gold, silver, platinum, or palladium held in safekeeping. Typically, for a fee of 3% or higher, the bank or dealer will buy metals in $1000 units and, for a small annual charge, provide insurance and storage. It will also, for 1% or so, sell the bullion or deliver it without a sales tax. The attraction is the convenience and lower transaction costs compared to physical ownership.

Other alternatives include *securities* of companies engaged in mining or processing, including some exchange-traded South African companies (many represented by American Depositary Receipts) as well as highly speculative penny stocks, traded over-the-counter or on regional or Canadian exchanges. There are also *mutual funds* and *closed-end funds* that specialize in both debt and equity issues of precious metals firms. Exchange-traded funds holding 1 gold (GETFs) and silver bullion certificates are also available.

Finally, *commodity futures, options,* and *options on futures* are traded on precious metals. They provide leverage and hedging opportunities for well-capitalized investors with high expertise and risk tolerance. See separate discussions of these investment vehicles.

* * *

What Are Investments in Precious Metals?

Investments in precious metals involve gold, silver, platinum, and palladium as commodities (i.e., not as money), owned by investors, in physical form or through securities, because of their presumed value as stores of wealth and as hedges against inflation and economic uncertainty. Precious metals are traded by speculators who hope to profit from volatility in the financial marketplace.

Buying, Selling, and Holding

How do I buy and sell them? Through various dealers and brokers, depending on the form of ownership. Coins and certificates are bought and sold through major banks.

Is there a minimum purchase amount and what is the price range? Precious metals can be bought with almost any amount of money, depending on the form of investment. Certificates generally have $1000 minimums.

What fees and charges are involved? Bullion involves a dealer markup, varying with quantity. Certificates cost 3% and up, with storage and insurance another 1% or more and sales fees of 1% or higher. Domestic and foreign securities and other forms of investment, like mutual funds, are subject to standard fees and commissions. Depending on the form of ownership, other costs may include sales or transfer taxes, shipping and handling, assay fees, insurance, storage, and safekeeping. Physical ownership involves an opportunity cost as well, since the money tied up could otherwise be invested in assets producing income. Storage costs vary with the commodity and the amount of space required (e.g., silver is bulkier than gold and may cost more to secure).

Do they mature, expire, or otherwise terminate? Certain investment vehicles, such as options and futures, have specified expirations.

Can I sell them quickly? Usually yes, though platinum and palladium are less liquid than gold and silver. Larger ingots and less popular gold coins can have uncertain liquidity.

How is market value determined and how do I keep track of it? Market value is a complex affair. While investor demand is highest when inflation and economic uncertainty loom largest, industrial demand depends on economic health and certainty. Other factors, such as interest rates and foreign exchange rates, play a key role, and speculators are active. Different forms of investment may be affected in different ways at different times. Dealers are a source of information concerning physical assets; securities and commodities information is reported in the financial pages of daily newspapers. Coins involve production costs and are more expensive than equal weights of bullion.

Investment Objectives

Should I invest in precious metals if my objective is capital appreciation? Yes, but myriad forces affect market value, and a high degree of expertise is required to achieve short-term gains.

Should I buy them if my objective is income? Some forms of ownership, like stocks and mutual funds, may provide income, while others, like physical ownership, provide none and may involve negative returns. In general, precious metals are not purchased for income.

To what extent do they protect against inflation? Although used by investors primarily to hedge political and economic uncertainty, precious metals over the long term have risen in value with inflation. Investors buying precious metals for inflation protection should be mindful, however, that many factors can cause volatility in the shorter term.

Are they suitable for tax-deferred retirement accounts? Except for American gold and silver coins, physical investment is not permitted. Common stocks and mutual fund shares involving precious metals may be suitable for some accounts.

Can I borrow against them? Yes; depending on the form of investment, there are various ways to leverage investments and use them as loan collateral.

Risk Considerations

How assured can I be of getting my full investment back? Precious metals tend to be volatile and offer no assurance that values will be retained.

How assured is my income? Where such investments provide income at all, such as mining stocks paying dividends, the risk is often great.

Are there any other risks unique to these investments? Many investors in precious metals have lost money doing business with unscrupulous dealer-brokers. Political risks in countries where mining is done and related developments, such as the sentiment in the mid-1980s for divestiture of shares of firms doing

business in South Africa, can jeopardize investment values. Inaccurate or misleading estimates of reserves of mining companies is another risk. Confiscation
of gold has precedent in the United States. Gold coins, in periods of high demand, are sold at outrageously high commissions by unscrupulous dealers.

Are they commercially rated? Some common stocks are rated by Standard
& Poor's and other major services.

Tax Considerations

What tax advantages (or disadvantages) do they offer? Assuming you are
not engaged in mining or processing or using gold in a business or profession, dividend income and capital gains and losses are subject to the usual
tax treatment. In addition, you may have to pay state sales taxes on physical
purchases.

Economic Considerations

What economic factors most affect buy, hold, and sell decisions? Investors
favor precious metals to hedge anticipated high inflation; however, many
other economic factors can affect the value of precious metals and related
investment alternatives, often in different ways.

PREFERRED STOCK (NONCONVERTIBLE)

Preferred stock is a hybrid security that combines features of both common
stock and bonds. It is equity, not debt, however, and is thus riskier than bonds.
It rarely carries voting rights.

Preferred dividends, like bond interest, are usually a fixed percentage of
par value, so share prices, like bond prices, go up when interest rates move
down and vice versa. But whereas bond interest is a contractual expense of
the issuer, preferred dividends, although payable before common dividends,
can be skipped if earnings are low. If the issuer goes out of business, preferred
shareholders do not share in assets until bondholders are paid in full, though
preferred shareholders rank ahead of common stockholders. Like bonds,
preferreds may have sinking funds, be callable, or be redeemable by their
holders.

Because preferred issues are designed for insurance companies and other
institutional investors which, as corporations, enjoy a 70% tax exclusion on
dividends earned, fully taxable yields for individuals are not much better than
those on comparable bonds offering more safety. Moreover, trading is often
inactive or in big blocks, meaning less liquidity and higher transaction costs
for small investors.

Still, personal investors do hold preferred stock. A broker can usually find
good buys as investor perceptions of risk in different industrial sectors create
yield differences in stocks that are otherwise comparable. Capital appreciation
can result from shares bought at a discount from the prices at which a sinking
fund will purchase them, or from discounted shares of turnaround firms with
dividend arrearages.

Different types of preferred stock include:

> *Convertible preferred,* convertible into common shares and thus
> offering growth potential plus fixed income; tends to behave dif-
> ferently in the marketplace than straight preferred (see Convert-
> ible Security).

Noncumulative preferred is a hangover from the heyday of the railroads and is rare today. Dividends, if unpaid, do not accumulate.

Cumulative preferred is the most common type. Dividends, if skipped, accrue, and common dividends cannot be paid while arrearages exist.

Participating preferred is unusual and typically issued by firms desperate for capital. Holders share in profits with common holders by way of extra dividends declared after regular dividends are paid. This type may have voting rights.

Adjustable (floating or variable) rate preferred adjusts the dividend rate quarterly (usually based on the 3-month U.S. Treasury bill) to reflect money market rates. It is aimed at corporate investors seeking after-tax yields combined with secondary market price stability. Individuals, looking at modest, fully taxable dividends that can go down as well as up, might prefer the safety of a money market fund.

Prior preferred stock (or preference shares) has priority of claim on assets and earnings over other preferred shares.

PIK Preferred Stock—PIK is an acronym for payment in kind— refers to an oddity spawned in the wave of leveraged buyouts in the 1980s. PIK preferred pays its dividend in the form of additional preferred stock. It is highly speculative almost by definition, since it implies a dearth of cash and raises a question about the adequacy of the issuer's working capital.

⁂

What Is Nonconvertible Preferred Stock?

Nonconvertible preferred is a form of owner's equity, usually nonvoting, paying dividends at a specified rate and having prior claim over common stock on earnings and assets in liquidation. The category does not include INCOME PREFERRED SECURITIES, a hybrid on a hybrid issued by special-purpose entities (SPEs) organized as corporate subsidiaries, limited partnerships, or trusts, which loan the invested funds to the issuer's parent company. The parent company books the proceeds as deeply subordinated debt on which it pays tax-deductible interest to the SPE, which pays preferred dividends to the investor. These securities, which come in varieties known by such names as MIPS, QUIPS, MIDS, QUICS, TOPrS, and QUIDS, offer substantial benefits to the parent companies and account for most of the new preferreds being issued in the 2000s. They are sophisticated products, however, and while they pay attractive returns, are suitable only for investors who understand them and are willing to follow them closely.

Buying, Selling, and Holding

How do I buy and sell it? Through a securities broker-dealer.

Is there a minimum purchase amount, and what is the price range? Buying round lots (usually 10 shares) saves commissions. Shares have par (face) values normally ranging from $100 down to $10, and market prices may be higher or lower than par values to bring yields in line with prevailing interest rate levels.

What fees and charges are involved? Standard commissions, with added transaction charges on inactively traded shares.

Does it mature, expire, or otherwise terminate? Preferred stock may be outstanding indefinitely, but many issues have call features or sinking fund provisions, whereby the issuer, usually for a small premium over par value, can require holders to redeem shares. Preferred issues may also have put features, which allow holders to redeem shares.

Can I sell it quickly? In most cases, yes. As a rule, preferreds are less liquid than common stocks and more liquid than bonds. Because large corporate investors dominate, smaller lots can sometimes be difficult for brokers to transact quickly.

How is market value determined and how do I keep track of it? Assuming good financial condition, fixed-income preferreds vary inversely with market interest rates. Adjustable-rate preferreds tend to be less volatile because dividends are adjusted quarterly to reflect money market conditions. Preferred prices are reported daily in the stock tables of newspapers and in databases, identified by the abbreviation "PF" in newspapers and "PR" in most electronic media.

Investment Objectives

Should I buy nonconvertible preferred stock if my objective is capital appreciation? No, although appreciation is possible in shares bought at a discount from par or redemption value or bought prior to a decline in interest rates. Substantial appreciation is possible in turnaround situations where cumulative preferred issues of troubled companies are selling at big discounts and there is a sizable accumulated dividend obligation.

Should I buy this if my objective is income? Yes, but unless you're a corporation or you buy at a discount, your yield won't be much better than that on a comparable corporate bond, and bonds are less risky in terms of both income and principal.

To what extent does it protect against inflation? Fixed-rate preferred offers no protection against inflation. Adjustable-rate preferred offers some.

Is it suitable for tax-deferred retirement accounts? Yes.

Can I borrow against it? Yes, subject to lender policies and Federal Reserve margin requirements.

Risk Considerations

How assured can I be of getting my full investment back? The market value of fixed-rate preferred stock declines as interest rates rise. (Adjustable-rate preferred has greater price stability.) In liquidation, holders of preferred stock are paid after bondholders but before common stockholders.

How assured is my income? Dividends, unlike interest, are not legal obligations and are paid from earnings, so income is as reliable as the issuer's earnings are stable. Established companies, such as utilities, with predictable cash flows are better bets than young firms or firms in cyclical industries, such as housing. Preferred dividends must be paid before common distributions, however; that means common dividends wait until all unpaid preferred dividends of cumulative issues are satisfied.

Are there any other risks unique to this investment? Call features, when present, allow the issuer to force holders to redeem shares, usually at par value plus a small premium. Firms normally call issues when market rates have declined and they can obtain financing more cheaply. But it is exactly under such circumstances that shares are enjoying higher market values and paying higher than market yields to holders who bought before rates declined. So call features represent a risk to investors; indeed the very presence of a call feature can limit upside price potential. Another risk of preferred stock is that should a dividend be omitted, the market may perceive financial weakness and drive down the share values

Is it commercially rated? Yes. Major issues are rated by Moody's, Standard & Poor's, Value Line Investment Survey, and other services.

Tax Considerations

What tax advantages (or disadvantages) does it offer? Dividends are taxed at a minimum of 15%. Corporations enjoy a 70% exemption from federal income taxes on dividends from other domestic corporations, effectively raising returns.

Economic Considerations

What economic factors most affect buy, hold, or sell decisions? Since most preferred stock pays a fixed dividend, it is best to buy when market rates are high and the issuer is forced to offer a competitive yield. Prices vary inversely with interest rates, so values increase as interest rates decline. Fixed-rate preferred stock loses value in inflation. Poor business conditions may affect profits and threaten dividends.

REAL ESTATE INVESTMENT TRUST (REIT AND FREIT)

REITs were authorized by Congress in the early 1960s to provide small investors with an opportunity to invest in large-scale real estate. The main attraction of REITs is income, and as this is written in 2010, they are doing surprisingly well. Real estate prices show no clear evidence of recovery despite abnormally low interest rates, so it would appear investors are buying REITs for the yield advantage they provide.

Like shares of stock, REITs trade publicly, and like mutual funds their money is invested in a diverse array of real estate assets, from shopping malls and office buildings to health care facilities, apartment complexes, and hotels, usually with geographical diversification as well.

Some REITs, called *equity REITs,* take ownership positions in real estate; shareholders receive income from the rents received from the properties and receive capital gains as properties are sold at a profit. Because both rents and property values rise with inflation, inflation protection is an important benefit of equity-oriented real estate investments. Other REITs specialize in lending money to real estate developers. Called *mortgage REITs,* they pass interest income on to shareholders. *Hybrid* or *balanced REITs* feature a mix of equity and debt investments.

By law, REITs must derive 75% of income from rents, dividends, interest, and gains from the sale of real estate properties, and must pay out 90% to shareholders. Companies meeting those requirements are exempt from federal taxation at the corporate level, although dividends are taxable to shareholders. REITs thus allow investors to share, with limited liability, the financial and tax benefits of real estate while avoiding the double taxation of corporate ownership. REITs also offer liquidity, since you can sell your shares on the market any time you wish.

On the negative side, REIT shares can be just as volatile as shares of stock. When conditions are unfavorable, such as when interest rates are high, materials are short, and the real-estate market is overbuilt, share values suffer.

FREITS: A variation of the REIT is the *finite life real estate investment trust,* or FREIT. FREITs, like limited partnerships, are self-liquidating—that is, they aim to sell or finance their holdings by a given date and distribute the proceeds to investors, thereby enabling them to realize capital gains. Investors thus have the choice of (1) selling their FREIT shares in the market (share values tend to more closely reflect market values of property holding than with REITs) or of (2) waiting to receive the full value of their shares when the portfolio is sold and the cash is distributed. Of course, the disadvantages of REITs apply to FREITs as well—the risk of a soft market at the time of sale or liquidation, and the inability to share in tax-deductible losses.

* * *

What Is a Real Estate Investment Trust (REIT)?

A REIT is a trust that invests in real estate-related assets, such as properties or mortgages, with funds obtained by selling shares, usually publicly traded, to investors. REITs are thus stock, although they offer advantages discussed below. At least one mutual fund group, Vanguard, has an open-end REIT fund and there are exchange-traded funds holding REITs.

Buying, Selling, and Holding

How do I buy and sell it? Through a securities broker-dealer.

Is there a minimum purchase amount, and what is the price range? Like common stocks, shares trade in round lots of 100 shares, with odd-lot transactions involving higher commissions. Prices vary, but most shares trade under $50.

What fees and charges are involved? Standard brokerage commissions.

Does it mature, expire, or otherwise terminate? Not normally. A variation, called the finite life real estate investment trust or FREIT, is self-liquidating— that is, the management has an expressed intention to sell all its properties and distribute the proceeds within a specified time frame.

Can I sell it quickly? Yes, good liquidity is a major attraction.

How is market value determined and how do I keep track of it? Shares of equity REITs reflect property values, rent trends, and market sentiment about real estate. Mortgage REITs fluctuate as market interest rates affect profits. Balanced REITs—part equity, part mortgage—tend to have greater price stability. CMO REITs tend to rise in value as interest rates increase, and vice versa. FREITs, because shareholders will sooner or later realize capital gains income, tend to have share values somewhat more reflective of underlying property values. Share prices are reported in the stock tables of daily newspapers and in electronic databases.

Investment Objectives

Should I buy this if my objective is capital appreciation? Yes, but the potential for share value increases is greater with equity REITs than mortgage

REITs. Also, automatic reinvestment of dividends increases capital gains potential. FREITs aim to pay out realized capital gains within a targeted period.

Should I buy this if my objective is income? Yes, especially since yields are not reduced by taxation at the corporate level. Mortgage REITs are more income-oriented than equity REITs.

To what extent does it protect against inflation? Since income from rents and capital gains increases with inflation, equity REITs provide excellent inflation protection. Mortgage REITs provide less.

Is it suitable for tax-deferred retirement accounts? Yes.

Can I borrow against it? Yes, subject to Federal Reserve margin rules and individual lender policies.

Risk Considerations

How assured can I be of getting my full investment back? REITs shares have the same market risks as common stocks plus the risk of a decline in property values. Mortgage REIT shares suffer when rising interest rates squeeze profits, and unless insured, can involve the risk of default on mortgages. You should not buy REITs if safety of principal is a paramount concern.

How assured is my income? Assuming REITs are well managed, income, which derives from rents or mortgage interest primarily, should be relatively secure. Still, real estate is sensitive to economic adversity, and there are many safer ways to invest for income.

Are there any other risks unique to this investment? Much depends on expert management in terms of selecting, diversifying, and managing portfolios. Valuation of real estate is anything but an exact science. Certain types of REIT portfolios are riskier than others, those whose portfolios comprise short-term construction loan paper being the riskiest.

Is it commercially rated? Yes, by Standard & Poor's, Moody's, and others.

Tax Considerations

What tax advantages (or disadvantages) does it offer? REITs are not taxed at the corporate level, so more of their income is paid out than would be the case with ordinary stocks. But shareholders personally are taxed. Because REITS do not generally pay corporate taxes, the majority of REIT dividends (excluding portions representing capital gains) continue to be taxed as ordinary income. The maximum 15% capital gains rate applies to the sale of REIT stock. Unlike real estate limited partnerships, REITs cannot offer flow-through tax benefits, but some trustees pass on tax-sheltered cash flow (in excess of income) as a nontaxable return of capital. When shares are sold, however, the cost basis must be adjusted by such returns of capital in calculating capital gains taxes. To meet Internal Revenue Service tax-exemption requirements, 75% of a REIT's income must be real estate-related and 90% of it must be paid out to shareholders.

Economic Considerations

What economic factors most affect buy, hold, or sell decisions? REITs are most attractive to buy and hold when interest rates are low and supply and demand factors in the real estate industry favor growth in property values.

Shares tend to be inflation-sensitive as values increase and dividends rise with higher rentals. Real estate is a cyclical industry and the risk-return relationship is maximized when investments are made over the long term.

REAL ESTATE, PHYSICAL

This inflation-sensitive investment in a basic life necessity—shelter—with its high potential for leverage through mortgage financing, its abundant tax benefits, and a history of demographics-driven appreciation of value going back to the end of World War II, was a no-brainer for increasingly affluent baby boomers who viewed their growing home equity as collateral for loans financing lifestyle upgrades, as all or at least part of their retirement nest-eggs, and finally as an asset to leave the kids.

After a market bubble in the 1990s that ended with the collapse of the "dot com" stocks and the start of a recession, the same Federal Reserve Chairman Alan Greenspan, who had described that period with the words "irrational exuberance," made a fateful decision to restart the economy by dropping the base federal funds rate to 1% in 2001. That caused historically low mortgage rates which Greenspan made even more seductive by promoting adjustable rate mortgages (ARMs) and encouraging more relaxed credit policies at the government-sponsored entities (GSEs), such as Fannie Mae and Freddie Mac. The GSEs, together with investment banks that were eager to serve subprime borrowers that the GSEs rejected, bought mortgages from originating banks and other lenders and repackaged them as mortgage-backed securities sporting investment grade ratings from credit rating agencies whose revenues came from the same bond issuers. The MBSs and Collateralized Debt Obligations (CDOs) backed by MBSs were marketed worldwide, thus creating the cash flow to buy and repackage even more mortgages.

Home values tripled and quadrupled as speculators joined the fray and traditionally unqualified homebuyers were seduced by mortgage brokers in cahoots with corrupt appraisers into taking on ARMs with low teaser rates and often requiring no documentation of income, employment, or assets. When the teaser rates reset at higher levels, payments were made by borrowings against home equity or, alternatively, the mortgages allowed "negative amortization," an arrangement whereby the portion of payments representing principal were simply added to the unpaid balance and thus deferred. Everything depended on the prices of houses continuing to appreciate, and "everything," as it turned out when the bubble burst in 2007, meant nothing less than a global financial system.

Since the bubble burst, and despite Federal Reserve policies keeping rates low, the government's bailing out of banks and other lenders, and other government measures to prevent foreclosures and encourage home buying, residential home prices have dropped at least 50% nationwide and are expected to drop further.

So is residential real estate a good investment? First of all, where nothing is invested, as with a mortgage with no down payment, the word becomes a misnomer, although more traditionally strict credit qualifications, including down payments, can be expected in the future. If nothing else was impressed on investors by the real estate meltdown, however, it should be that there is nothing in the holy writ that says real estate necessarily appreciates in value with time. Indeed, logic would tell us that in the absence of monetary or fiscal stimulation aimed at raising real estate values, prices should decline as a function of time as a result of wear and tear, obsolescence, and other factors unless money is invested in maintenance and improvement.

Real estate, on the other hand, is by nature cyclical, and the time-honored truism and industry mantra, "location, location, location," guarantees that opportunities for capital gains (and losses) will always exist regardless of general industry trends.

Commercial real estate correlates with economic growth in essentially the same way as residential real estate, but with different timing and shorter-term financing. Individual investors normally participate through REITs and other investment vehicles.

Even in normal times, real estate has many drawbacks and risks, however, whether owned as an individual; in one of the several forms of joint ownership, which are distinguished mainly in terms of how an interest can be terminated and what happens to it in death or divorce; or through a corporation, which has the advantage of limited liability and the disadvantage of double taxation.

Among the problems of real estate ownership are high carrying costs in the form of property taxes, insurance, maintenance, and repairs; the risk of illiquidity; the risk of loss of value as the result of deflation or of demographic factors, declining neighborhoods, local economic changes, or government policies (such as a rise in property taxes or the imposition of rent controls); competition from professional and institutional investors affecting local supply and demand factors; changes in federal tax provisions; high costs of selling; and a host of special risks associated with specific types of holdings.

Physical real estate can be categorized as (1) residential, where, because the owner lives there, the utility of shelter or recreational use is an important part of the value but depreciation and maintenance are not allowable tax deductions; (2) rental, where income and tax benefits are primary goals, and appreciation secondary; (3) speculative, where income and utilitarian values are traded off for capital gains potential and losses can result from carrying costs (an example is investment in raw land); and (4) multipurpose, such as a multifamily residence used partly to live in and partly to rent, or a vacation property combining recreational use and rental income (tax implications where the status is not clearly established can be serious).

Properties can also be held in forms of shared ownership, which bring tax advantages and other benefits of home ownership to apartments and town houses. Cooperatives, where owners hold shares in total projects, and condominiums, where apartment units are owned along with a share of commonly shared facilities and amenities, often require a tradeoff of certain lifestyle prerogatives (e.g., a ban on pets) and have eligibility criteria advertising restrictions, or even prohibitions against renting that can severely limit liquidity. Condominium time-shares, where each of two or more owners has exclusive right of occupancy for a defined period, make condominium units much more affordable. The occupancy rights of some time-shared property even trade in a secondary market, not unlike securities.

The inflation protection, tax breaks, and total returns of real estate are also available through limited partnerships and real estate investment trusts (REITs). Such syndications offer diversification (by type of holding and geography), professional management, economies of scale, and limited liability for small investments, along with some risks and costs of their own.

* * *

What Is Physical Real Estate?

Physical real estate includes personal residences and investment properties in the form of developed and undeveloped land, established commercial or residential properties, condominiums, and cooperatives.

Buying, Selling, and Holding

How do I buy and sell it? Through a real estate broker or direct negotiation.

Is there a minimum purchase amount, and what is the price range? There is no minimum purchase amount; the price range is limitless. Properties can generally be financed with a down payment of 5% to 50% of value.

What fees and charges are involved? Real estate involves broker commissions and carrying costs in the form of debt interest, real estate taxes, and maintenance costs. Though there are many tax benefits associated with such costs, they can nonetheless be highly burdensome, especially if a property is not producing income.

Does it mature, expire, or otherwise terminate? Not in a financial sense, although related debt instruments have fixed maturities. Physical real estate is, of course, subject to destructive acts of nature, vandalism, and deterioration from use and time.

Can I sell it quickly? Liquidity varies with the type of property and market conditions; as a general rule, real estate is not a liquid investment.

How is market value determined and how do I keep track of it? Although general economic conditions and such factors as money supply and mortgage interest rates have an important effect, real estate is often characterized by independent markets. One segment of the industry (such as residential homes) can be booming, while another (such as office buildings) is depressed, and market conditions can vary widely from one community or geographical area to another. There is no formalized source of information about real estate prices. Trade associations can be a source of (optimistic) national and regional statistics and real estate brokers keep abreast of local values.

Investment Objectives

Should I buy this if my objective is capital appreciation? Yes.

Should I buy this if my objective is income? Yes, but only rental properties provide regular income.

To what extent does it protect against inflation? Real estate is inflation-sensitive, that is, both property values and rental income increase with inflation, although abnormally high inflation can affect values adversely.

Is it suitable for tax-deferred retirement accounts? Personal residences are not legal investments. Real estate securities, such as real estate investment trusts (REITs) or income-oriented limited partnerships, can be appropriate investments, however.

Can I borrow against it? Yes; first, second, even third mortgages are common ways of borrowing against real estate. Home equity loans, a popular product of banks and other financial services institutions, are a convenient form of borrowing for home owners. On a professional scale, substantial fortunes have been made and lost using the financial leverage provided by real estate.

Risk Considerations

How assured can I be of getting my full investment back? Real estate offers no guarantees that values will not decline.

How assured is my income? A lease assures income for its term, to the extent the tenant is dependable and creditworthy.

Are there any other risks unique to this investment? Yes, many—including some not invented yet. Common risks include shifting population centers, changing local economies (including tax policies and rent control legislation), zoning changes, acts of nature, crimes like vandalism and arson, and physical deterioration.

Is it commercially rated? No.

Tax Considerations

What tax advantages (or disadvantages) does it offer? The main tax benefits are deductibility from federal income taxes of mortgage interest and property taxes, and on investment property, depreciation (which reduces taxable income without affecting cash flow), and deductible maintenance costs. All rental income is passive, but a limited amount of passive activity losses can be offset against nonpassive income (phased out for high-income taxpayers). Owners of personal residences classified as primary may be exempt from capital gains taxes every two years, profits up to $500,000 for married couples filing jointly, and up to $250,000 for single taxpayers. Unlike other consumer interest, which became nondeductible at the end of 1991, interest on loans secured by home equity is deductible up to $100,000 and on higher amounts if the proceeds are used to purchase investments or for business purposes. The tax code on this has changed several times, however, and you should get up-to-date advice.

Economic Considerations

What economic factors most affect buy, hold, and sell decisions? Real estate values parallel general economic cycles but are also subject to supply and demand conditions in local markets and in segments of the industry (such as commercial, industrial, residential). The most successful real estate investors have diversified portfolios (in terms of geography and type of holding) and stay in an investment until it becomes profitable. These opportunities, together with professional management and economies of scale, are available to individuals through real estate investment trusts (REITs), exchange-traded funds holding REITs, and limited partnerships.

SAVINGS ALTERNATIVES

For emergencies and for the sake of prudence, every investor should keep a certain amount of money in a form that makes it readily accessible and spendable. Depending on one's need for liquidity, this often means choosing among the deposit accounts and certificates of deposit offered by banks and thrift institutions and U.S. Savings Bonds.

The following are brief descriptions of major savings alternatives:

Deposit accounts Depositors in subscribing banks, savings and loans, and credit unions are insured up to $250,000, respectively, by the Deposit Insurance Fund (DIF), a unit of the Federal Deposit Insurance Corporation (FDIC), and the National Credit Union Administration (NCUA). Different accounts have different features, however.

With full deregulation in March 1986, institutions became legally free to pay any rate of interest. Because banks and thrift institutions must keep costly reserves, however, and because their federal insurance gives them a marketing advantage, their best rates tend generally to be a hair below money market mutual funds. The exceptions are the more aggressive money center banks and institutions with riskier (thus higher-yielding) loan portfolios or skimpier services.

Certificates of Deposit   CDs are issued by banks, savings and loan associations (S&Ls), and credit unions, in various denominations and maturities (some institutions offer designer CDs, with maturities to suit the customer) and are also federally insured at member institutions. CDs, which can have similar maturities and vary a couple of points between issuers, are issued both in discount and interest-bearing form and sometimes with variable rates. Other variations include split-rate CDs, where a higher rate is paid early in the CD's term than in its later life; convertible-term CDs, which convert from fixed-rate to variable-rate instruments; and expandable CDs, which allow adding to the investment at the original rate. CDs can also be bought from some brokers, who make bulk purchases of high-yielding CDs from issuing institutions around the country and then resell them; since the brokers make markets in such CDs, buyers have liquidity they would not enjoy as direct investors.

Savings Bonds   Savings bonds come with deferred federal taxability and exemption from state and local taxes. Series EE bonds have been issued since 1980, when they replaced Series E bonds, which were first issued in 1941. Series H bonds were issued June 1, 1952 and succeeded by Series HH bonds between 1980 and September 1, 2004, when they were discontinued. In 1998, inflation-indexed I-Bonds made their debut.

Series EE bonds are issued in paper form (called Patriot Bonds) at half their face values and in electronic form (through *www.treasurydirect.gov*) at face value. Issue prices range from $25 to $10,000, to the penny, for electronic bonds and in denominations from $50 to $10,000 for paper bonds with an overall limit of $20,000 per person per calendar year or $40,000 for two co-owners. (An individual can invest $5,000 a year in paper EEs, $5,000 in electronic EEs, $5,000 in paper I-Bonds, and $5,000 in electronic I-Bonds, bringing the maximum for a couple to $40,000.) Series EE bonds issued on or after May 1, 2005 earn a fixed rate of interest set each May 1 and November 1 by the Department of the Treasury. The new rate will apply for the 30-year life of each bond, including a 10-year extended maturity period, unless a different rate or rate structure is announced for the extension period. Interest accrues monthly and is compounded semiannually. EE bonds with issue dates prior to May 1, 2005 will continue to earn interest according to the terms in effect when they were issued. (Most recently the rate was 90% of the average yield on five-year Treasury securities based on the previous six months.)

Savings bonds must be held for a minimum of one year and bonds held for less than five years are subject to a penalty equal to three months interest. If a bond does not double in value as the result of applying the fixed rate before the 20-year original maturity, the Treasury will make a one-time adjustment at original maturity to make up the difference, and the original fixed rate will continue unless a new rate or rate structure is announced. Taxpayers meeting income qualifications can buy EE bonds to save for higher education expenses and enjoy total or partial federal tax exemption (see Tax Considerations).

Series HH bonds that were issued after March 1, 1993 are interest-bearing, pay a fixed 4% annual rate in two semiannual payments, and mature in 20 years. Issuance of HH bonds was discontinued September 1, 2004.

Series I, inflation-indexed savings bonds, introduced in September 1998, are issued at face value with a 30-year maturity in eight denominations ranging from $50 to $30,000. The $30,000 limit per person per calendar year applies to the issuance of I-Bonds. I-Bonds, as they are called, protect investors from rising prices because the payments are adjusted semiannually to reflect the going inflation rate. The payout, which is not actually paid out but is instead reinvested and compounded semiannually, is determined by two rates. A fixed rate, that ranged from 3% to 3.5% when the bonds were first introduced, is set by the Treasury Department. A second rate, a rate of inflation, is determined every six months by the Bureau of Labor Statistics to reflect changes in a version of the Consumer Price Index. The second rate is added to (or subtracted from, if there is deflation) the principal at the end of each year, so that the following year, the fixed rate is based on the adjusted principal. Interest is exempt from state and local taxes and federal taxes are deferred until the bonds mature or are cashed in. If the bond is redeemed to pay for college tuition or other college fees, investors may exclude part or all from federal taxes, depending on the holder's income level. In addition, you can't redeem your I-Bonds during the first six months, and you'll lose three months of earnings if you cash them in before the end of the first five years. Some protection against deflation exists in that any decline in the CPI could eat into the fixed rate, but not the principal.

* * *

What Are Savings Alternatives?

Savings alternatives include interest-bearing deposit accounts at banks, savings and loans, and credit unions; bank certificates of deposit (CDs); and Series EE, HH (now discontinued), and inflation-indexed U.S. Savings Bonds (I-Bonds).

Buying, Selling, and Holding

How do I buy and sell them? Deposit accounts, CDs, and savings bonds may be transacted at banks or other savings and financial services institutions. Series EE bonds and I-Bonds may also be available through employer-sponsored payroll savings programs. Electronic Series EE and Series I-Bonds can be purchased through Treasury Direct at *www.treasurydirect.gov.*

Is there a minimum purchase amount, and what is the price range? Deposit accounts are available with no minimum deposits, but interest may vary with balances and some banks impose charges (negative interest) when low balances become an administrative burden. CDs are usually issued for $500 and up, although some $100 CDs are available. Jumbo CDs are issued for $100,000 and up. Series EE and I paper bonds sell for $25 ($50 face value) to $5000 ($10,000 face value). Electronic EE bonds and I-Bonds are issued at face values from $25 to $10,000. Paper bonds you buy as gifts are not subject to your individual limits.

What fees and charges are involved? Fees and charges on deposit accounts vary with the institution and its product. As a general rule, the higher the balance, the longer the commitment, and the less service, the less the cost to the depositor. Such factors usually are reflected both in rates and in fees and charges. Although CDs involve no fees or charges to buy or to redeem at maturity, the Federal Reserve Board voted in March 1986 to impose a penalty of seven days' interest on amounts withdrawn within the first week from personal CDs. (Institutional CDs were made subject to other penalties for early withdrawal.) Savings bonds involve no fees or charges.

Do they mature, expire, or otherwise terminate? CDs have maturities ranging from 32 days to 10 years. Series EE bonds and I-Bonds have 30-year maturities, but may be redeemed after five years without penalties. Series HH bonds mature in 20 years.

Can I sell them quickly? Certain deposit accounts may require notice of withdrawal. CDs may be subject to early withdrawal penalties or the issuer may refuse withdrawal prior to maturity, except in cases of hardship. (Of course, it is usually possible to borrow against such collateral and interest is tax-deductible.) NOW and other savings accounts offer instant liquidity through checkwriting. CDs bought through brokers can be sold in the secondary market. Savings bonds may be redeemed after six months, but there are interest penalties if held for less than five years.

How is market value determined and how do I keep track of it? Large CDs traded by dealers and institutional investors and smaller CDs marketed by brokers have secondary market values that rise and fall in inverse relation to prevailing interest rates. There is no secondary market for consumer-size CDs bought directly from banks and other issuing institutions or for savings bonds and deposit accounts.

Investment Objectives

Should I buy these if my objective is capital appreciation? Other than interest compounding, there is no capital gains opportunity except in CDs traded in the secondary market.

Should I buy these if my objective is income? Deposit accounts provide income, although they vary in terms of how rates are determined, how interest is compounded and credited, and how effective annual yields compare competitively. CDs are used for income, but those due in less than one year and zero-coupon CDs are issued on a discount basis—that is, they are sold at less than face value and redeemed at face value. Series EE bonds and I-Bonds do not pay interest until maturity or redemption, and must be held five years to receive the full rate on redemption. Series HH bonds issued after March 1, 1993 pay a fixed rate of 4%.

To what extent do they protect against inflation? To the extent rates move with inflation, deposit accounts offer some protection. Fixed-rate CDs provide none, but short maturities limit risk. Variable-rate CDs provide some protection. Series EE bonds offer some protection because the rate is adjustable. I-Bonds are designed to protect against inflation and there is deflation protection to the extent declines in the Consumer Price Index cannot reduce underlying principal. Series HH bonds have a fixed rate and offer none.

Are they suitable for tax-deferred retirement accounts? Deposit accounts are legally eligible, but CDs are a better choice due to their higher yields. Because savings bonds already offer tax deferral, there would be no advantage in putting them in such accounts.

Can I borrow against them? Yes.

Risk Considerations

How assured can I be of getting my full investment back? Most deposits and CDs are insured to $100,000 per depositor by the Deposit Insurance Fund, a unit of the Federal Deposit Insurance Corporation (FDIC)—and by the National Credit Union Administration (NCUA). The FDIC and NCUA are federally sponsored agencies. (Nonmembers are insured by state-backed or private insurers, but check the exact conditions.) Savings bonds are direct obligations of the federal government and are risk-free.

How assured is my income? Although rates may in some cases fluctuate, income is very safe because the agencies that insure principal oversee the financial affairs of the institutions.

Are there any other risks unique to these investments? No.

Are they commercially rated? Moody's and other services rate CDs.

Tax Considerations

What tax advantages (or disadvantages) do they offer? Savings bonds are exempt from state and local taxes. Interest on Series EE bonds and I-Bonds is tax-deferred until cashed in or redeemed at maturity; when exchanged for Series HH bonds, interest on EE bonds is tax-deferred until the HH bonds are redeemed (although interest on the HH bonds, paid semiannually, is taxed in the year received). Qualifying taxpayers may enjoy total or partial exemption from federal income taxes on income from EE bonds and I-Bonds that is used to finance a child's higher education (tuition and fees, but not room and board).

Economic Considerations

What economic factors most affect buy, hold, and sell decisions? Safety and growth of principal through interest compounding are the main objectives with savings vehicles, although expectations concerning interest rate movements and inflation may guide decisions.

TREASURY SECURITIES (BILLS, BONDS, AND NOTES)

United States Treasury securities, called Treasuries for short, are backed by the full faith and credit of the U.S. government and are issued to finance activities ranging from daily cash management to the refinancing of long-term bonded debt.

Investors seeking income thus have a wide choice of maturities, yields, and denominations along with the utmost safety. The government would have to become insolvent before default could occur, and as long as it has the power to create money, that is not a real possibility. Of course, creating money can mean creating inflation, a current concern as the government stimulates economic "recovery" with programs financed by printing money. Normal inflation expectations are built into the long-term rate, but unexpected inflation is not and the only protection the investor has in that case is to keep maturities short.

Treasuries also offer excellent liquidity and exemption from taxation at the state and local (but not federal) levels, an advantage that can add significantly to yield in high-tax states and localities.

Being fixed-income securities, however, Treasuries, unless they are inflation-indexed, are not immune, as noted, to the ravages of rising prices, nor are they safe from market risk. When general interest rates move up, the prices of fixed-rate Treasuries move down—unluckily for investors forced to sell prior to maturity in the secondary market. On the other hand, Treasuries, unlike many other fixed-income investments, are not usually callable. With the exception of a recent 20-year issue with a 5-year call provision and some 30-year bonds callable 5 years before maturity, the government cannot force redemption when rates move down.

The major categories of Treasury securities are:

Treasury bills   Called T-bills for short, they are issued weekly with 13-week and 26-week maturities and monthly with a 52-week maturity, on a discount basis and in denominations beginning at $10,000 with multiples of $5000 thereafter. They are issued through the Federal Reserve System, and investors may submit tenders either on a competitive basis, specifying terms and risking rejection, or on a noncompetitive basis, in which case the average rate established in the regular auction applies and purchase is assured. T-bills can also be bought for a fee through banks and other dealers.

Treasury bonds and notes   These are interest-bearing, paying semi-annually in most cases, and, like T-bills, sold through Federal Reserve banks and branches on a competitive or noncompetitive basis. Maturities of bonds range from 10 to 30 years, those of notes from 2 to 10 years. Bonds and notes can be bought in denominations as low as $1000. Except for 2-year notes, which are usually sold monthly, bonds and notes are offered as the need arises. Of course, outstanding issues with almost any maturity can be bought in the secondary market.

Treasury Inflation Protected Securities (TIPS)   United States Treasury securities issued at a fixed rate of interest but with principal adjusted every six months based on changes in the Consumer Price Index. At maturity, TIPS, which are issued in January and July as 5-year and 10-year notes and in October as 30-year bonds, are redeemable either at their inflation-adjusted principal or their face value, whichever is greater. TIPS sacrifice some yield as a tradeoff for inflation protection, and the inflation adjustment is federally taxable annually, although not paid out until maturity.

Other Treasury securities, covered elsewhere, include savings bond Series EE and inflation-indexed I-Bonds and zero-coupon products created by separating the principal and interest coupons from Treasury bonds.

Investors may also buy shares of mutual funds or unit investment trusts that invest in portfolios of Treasury securities.

* * *

What Is a Treasury Security?

A Treasury security is a negotiable debt obligation of the United States government, backed by its full faith and credit, and issued with various maturities.

Buying, Selling, and Holding

How do I buy and sell it? New issues of bills, bonds, and notes may be purchased through competitive or noncompetitive auction at Federal Reserve banks and branches. They can also be bought and sold at commercial banks, securities broker-dealers, and other financial services companies or through Treasury Direct at *www.treasurydirect.com.*

Is there a minimum purchase amount, and what is the price range? Treasury bills are issued in minimum denominations of $10,000 and multiples of $5000 thereafter. Notes and bonds are issued in denominations of $1000, $5000, $10,000, $100,000, and $1 million.

What fees and charges are involved? Treasury securities bought and redeemed through Federal Reserve banks and branches are without fees. Purchases and sales through banks or broker-dealers involve modest fees (about $25) and/or markups.

Does it mature, expire, or otherwise terminate? Yes. Maturities range from 23 days (cash management bills) to 30 years (bonds).

Can I sell it quickly? Yes; bills, bonds, and notes enjoy an active secondary market and are highly liquid. Inflation-indexed notes and bonds, being introduced in the late 1990s when inflation was low, were not as widely sold and were less liquid.

How is market value determined and how do I keep track of it? As wholly or partly fixed income securities, Treasuries rise and fall in price in inverse relation to market interest rates. Because they are risk-free investments, money flows into Treasuries when investors are worried about the credit safety of other debt securities, causing lower yields and higher prices. The financial sections of daily newspapers report new offerings and secondary market yields. The Bureau of Public Debt (Washington, DC 20226) or the Federal Reserve bank or branch in your district will respond to inquiries concerning upcoming offerings. Information on Treasury securities is available at *www.treasurydirect.com.*

Investment Objectives

Should I buy this if my objective is capital appreciation? No, but appreciation is possible if market rates decline.

Should I buy this if my objective is income? Yes, particularly Treasuries with longer maturities, but you are sacrificing yield in return for safety. After-tax yields get a boost in high-tax states and localities because interest is not taxed at the state and local levels.

To what extent does it protect against inflation? Fixed-income issues provide no protection, though short maturities offer less exposure to the risk of inflation. Inflation-indexed securities protect against inflation, but deflation is a risk.

Is it suitable for tax-deferred retirement accounts? Yes.

Can I borrow against it? Yes, to 90% at most banks and brokers.

Risk Considerations

How assured can I be of getting my full investment back? From the credit standpoint, Treasuries offer the highest degree of safety available. You can be assured of getting your money back at maturity. Should you wish to sell earlier in the secondary market, you may find market prices have declined because of rising market interest rates. (Experts sometimes hedge this risk using interest-rate options, futures, and futures options.) Inflation, of course, erodes dollar values and inflation-indexed securities have the risk of deflation.

How assured is my income? There is virtually no risk the government will default on interest. Some bonds may be callable, terminating interest prematurely. Inflation, of course, can erode the value of fixed-interest payments, and low-yielding securities, like Treasuries, are especially vulnerable in hyperinflation, where the inflation rate can exceed the interest rate. Inflation-indexed securities would, of course, be an exception.

Are there any other risks unique to this investment? No.

Is it commercially rated? No, since Treasuries are risk-free, there is no need for commercial credit ratings.

Tax Considerations

What tax advantages (or disadvantages) does it offer? Treasuries are fully taxable at the federal level but are exempt from state and local taxes. With inflation-indexed bonds, the annual inflation adjustment is taxable but not paid out until maturity. Savings bonds, discussed in the section dealing with savings alternatives, are exempt from federal taxes in a specific instance.

Economic Considerations

What economic factors most affect buy, hold, or sell decisions? As with any fixed-income investment, it is best to buy when market rates are high and issues carry a competitive yield. Since prices vary inversely with market interest rates, the holding becomes more attractive as market rates decline. Inflation-indexed bonds and notes, being only partially fixed rate, would be less vulnerable to rate increases accompanied by inflation. As low-yielding, fixed-income securities, treasuries fare poorly in inflation. Because they are virtually default-proof, they are highly desirable holdings when poor business conditions make other investments vulnerable to default, though yields of Treasuries may decline as a result.

UNIT INVESTMENT TRUST

Like a mutual fund, a unit investment trust (UIT) offers to small investors the advantages of a professionally selected and diversified portfolio. Unlike a mutual fund, however, its portfolio is fixed; once structured, it is not actively managed, except for some limited surveillance. It is also self-liquidating, distributing principal as debt securities mature or are redeemed, and paying out the proceeds from equities as they are sold in accordance with predetermined timetables. A onetime sales charge of less than 5% is the only significant cost, and considering this can buy you a share in a "millionaire's portfolio" of municipal bonds, it is one of the attractions.

While sponsors commonly offer instant liquidity as a feature of UITs, liquidity is provided specifically through agreements to make markets in shares or to redeem them; there is not an active secondary market in the public sense, and investors should read the prospectus to determine whether and by what means liquidity provisions exist.

The most time-honored form of UIT is made up of tax-exempt municipal bonds, put together by an investment firm with special expertise in the municipals field. The bonds are deposited with a trustee, usually a bank, which distributes interest and the proceeds from redemptions, calls, and maturities and provides unitholders with audited annual reports. Since unitholders pay taxes as though they were direct investors, portions of income payments representing interest are not taxable, nor are portions representing principal, which are tax-free returns of capital. Capital gains, however, are taxable, technically at the time the trust realizes them, although unit holders commonly recognize them only after their investment in the trust has been recovered from distributions of principal or at the time they sell their shares. It is important to get tax advice on this.

The 1990s saw an explosion in popularity of equity UITs holding as few as 5 or 10 stocks, maturing annually, and following a formula investing approach. The typical equity trust has a total fee of around 2.75%, which is reduced when the trust is renewed.

Unit investment trusts are also available with portfolios of money market securities; corporate bonds of different grades; mortgage-backed securities; U.S. government securities; adjustable and fixed-rate preferred stocks; utility common stocks; foreign bonds; replications of stock indexes; and other investments. New varieties of UITs are being created all the time.

This discussion does not include investments that are legally organized as unit investment trusts, but are exchange listed and traded as common stocks. Examples would be Spiders and Diamonds, which are shares in long-term trusts holding portfolios of stocks that track the S&P 500 Index and the Dow Jones Industrial Average, respectively. For that discussion, see Exchange-Traded Funds (ETFs).

* * *

What Is a Unit Investment Trust?

A unit investment trust (UIT) is a trust that invests in a fixed portfolio of income-producing securities and sells shares to investors.

Buying, Selling, and Holding

How do I buy and sell it? UITs are bought from sponsoring broker-dealers, who usually stand ready to redeem shares.

Is there a minimum purchase amount, and what is the price range? Shares (units) costing $1000 ($250 for IRAs) are typical.

What fees and charges are involved? A sales charge (load) ranging from less than 1% to 5% of your investment (4% is typical, with discounts for volume). An annual fee, usually 0.15%, is factored into the yield. Additional fees (0.30% typically) may apply when the portfolio is insured.

Does it mature, expire, or otherwise terminate? Trusts are self-liquidating. Proceeds are distributed as securities mature or are sold. The life of most municipal UITs is 25 to 30 years, but 10-year trusts are common and some are as short as 6 months.

Can I sell it quickly? Liquidity is not guaranteed, but it usually exists to some extent because of most sponsors' intentions, once shares are sold, to make markets as an accommodation to holders wishing to sell. Trustees may also redeem shares, but such provisions should be investigated before buying shares. Sponsors may also allow switching into their other investment products at little or no cost.

How is market value determined and how do I keep track of it? Since shares represent units in an investment pool, values are determined by the forces affecting the securities in the pool. Thus trusts composed of fixed-income bonds will increase in value as interest rates decline and vice versa. A trust made up of stocks will be affected by market movements and earnings forecasts for individual stocks, among other factors. Details of a particular trust and its portfolio are set forth in the prospectus that, by law, is provided to investors.

Investment Objectives

Should I buy this if my objective is capital appreciation? UITs usually are set up to provide income (but even with a fixed portfolio, capital gains and losses can result from interest rate movements and other factors). Stock index trusts and other equity products have capital gains or total returns as a primary goal.

Should I buy this if my objective is income? Yes.

To what extent does it protect against inflation? Bond trusts offer no protection; equity trusts and floating-rate trusts offer some.

Is it suitable for tax-deferred retirement accounts? Yes, except those with portfolios of securities that are already tax-exempt.

Can I borrow against it? Yes, subject to Federal Reserve margin rules. The lack of an active secondary market raises a question about ready marketability and the attractiveness of shares as collateral.

Risk Considerations

How assured can I be of getting my full investment back? This varies with the safety of the investments in the trust, government bonds and common equities being at opposite ends of the spectrum. Interest rates may decrease the value of bonds, and therefore of shares, unless held for the life of the trust; market risk is always a question with equities. A growing number of trusts purchase insurance against credit risk.

How assured is my income? Portfolios are well diversified, making income relatively secure.

Are there any other risks unique to this investment? The lack of active management, once the portfolio is established and the shares sold, limits responsive corrective action in the face of adverse portfolio developments. Diversification provides some protection, however. Trusts holding foreign securities have political and currency risk.

Is it commercially rated? Yes.

Tax Considerations

What tax advantages (or disadvantages) does it offer? None. UITs are subject to the same taxes (or exemptions) as the investments comprising them. But trusts composed of municipal bonds, some specializing in triple-tax-exempt portfolios for qualified residents, are common, and many taxable UITs are designed for tax-deferred retirement programs. Equity trusts expiring in a year technically create a long-term tax event for all the stocks in the trust, but the IRS has made an exception in the case of stocks that remain in the portfolios when the trusts are renewed.

Economic Considerations

What economic factors most affect buy, hold, or sell decisions? Unit investment trusts are bought with the intention of holding until they self-liquidate. The same considerations that would guide an investor in choosing debt, equity, or money market securities would guide the choice of a particular UIT.

ZERO-COUPON SECURITY

Zero-coupon securities don't pay out their fixed rate of interest like other debt securities; they are issued at deep discounts and accumulate and compound the interest, then pay the full face value at maturity. The attractions for the investor are mainly twofold: (1) They can be bought at very low prices because of the deep discount and (2) Their yield to maturity is locked in, which takes the guesswork out of interest reinvestment.

The mathematical effects of a zero-coupon security, unless one is used to thinking in terms of compound interest over long periods, can seem astonishing: $1000 invested today in a 7%, 30-year zero-coupon bond will bring $7878 at maturity!

The disadvantages of zeros are that income taxes (unless they are tax-exempt) are payable as interest accrues (and out of cash raised from another source); they are highly volatile; and their value at maturity can erode with inflation. (Of course, the opposites are also true: Higher volatility means advantageously higher capital gains when rates are declining, and in a deflationary environment, value at maturity would be greater.) Credit risk, especially with corporate zeros, can be greater than with a regular bond; if the issuer defaults after a certain amount of time has passed, the investor has more to lose, since nothing has been received along the way.

Not surprisingly, a popular use of taxable zeros, with their low purchase prices and automatic compounding, is tax-deferred retirement accounts, where they are sheltered from taxability on imputed interest.

The following are principal types of zeros:

Corporate zero-coupon securities   These are not usually recommended for individual investors because of credit risk and because the yield tends not to be competitive in relation to the risk. One explanation is that these issues are marketed to investors who do not have to pay taxes on imputed interest such as foreign investors.

Strips and STRIPS   Strips are U.S. Treasury or municipal securities that brokerage firms have separated into principal and interest which, represented by certificates (the actual securities are held in escrow), are marketed as zero-coupon securities under proprietary acronyms. Although the obligor is actually the broker, the escrow arrangement assures a high degree of security. Free of risk altogether are STRIPS, Separate Trading of Registered Interest and Principal of Securities, the Treasury's acronym for its own zero-coupon securities. STRIPS are Treasury bonds issued in the traditional way but separated into interest and principal components at the discretion of bondholders using book entry accounts at Federal Reserve banks.

Strips of mortgage-backed securities placed privately or by government agencies are also available. To enter the Federal Reserve's book-entry system, however, federal agency strips must satisfy a technicality requiring a minimum of 1% of the principal of the underlying loans; in other words, they can't be 100% interest.

Municipal zero-coupon securities   These securities are issued by state and local governments and are usually exempt from federal taxes and from state taxes in the state of issue. They provide a convenient way of providing for the future goals of high-bracket investors who get an after-tax benefit from their lower interest rates. One caveat, however: some are issued with call features, which can defeat the purpose of a zero from the investor's standpoint, so avoid those.

Zero-coupon convertibles   Introduced in the mid-1980s, these convertibles come in two varieties: one, issued with a put option, converts into common stock, thus providing growth potential; the other, usually a municipal bond, converts into an interest-paying bond, thus enabling the investor to lock in a rate, then, 15 years later, to begin collecting interest.

* * *

What Is a Zero-Coupon Security?

A zero-coupon security is a debt security or instrument that does not pay periodic interest but is issued at a deep discount and redeemed at face value.

Buying, Selling, and Holding

How do I buy and sell it? Through a securities broker-dealer and many banks. Some products are proprietary, available only at the dealers marketing them.

Is there a minimum purchase amount, and what is the price range? Because of their deep discount, zero-coupon securities can be bought quite cheaply; a $1000 20-year bond yielding 6% would cost about $312, for example. Broker-dealer minimums of 10 bonds or more are common.

What fees and charges are involved? A broker commission or a dealer spread.

Does it mature, expire, or otherwise terminate? Yes; zero-coupon securities have a specified maturity, although some may have put options or be convertible into common stock or interest-bearing bonds. Some zeros have been issued with call features.

Can I sell it quickly? Investors generally buy zeros intending to hold them until maturity. Should you need to sell, the broker-dealer you bought it from can probably make a market, although you would certainly pay a higher transaction cost. Zeros based on treasury securities are somewhat more liquid than corporate or municipal zeros.

How is market value determined and how do I keep track of it? Zeros, being essentially fixed-rate investments, rise and fall in inverse relation to interest rates and are especially volatile. Zeros are listed along with regular bonds in daily newspapers.

Investment Objectives

Should I buy zeros if my objective is capital appreciation? Investing one sum of money and getting back a larger sum is what zeros are all about, so the answer is really yes. Strictly speaking, however, the appreciation is not a capital gain, but is rather compounded interest. Capital gains are possible from secondary market sales after interest rates have declined.

Should I buy this if my objective is income? No. Zeros pay no periodic income.

To what extent does it protect against inflation? As fixed-rate investments, zeros generally offer no inflation protection. Zeros convertible into common stock offer some.

Is it suitable for tax-deferred retirement accounts? Because zeros are taxed as though annual interest were being paid, they are considered ideal candidates for tax-deferred plans. An exception, of course, would be municipal zeros, which are tax-exempt anyway.

Can I borrow against it? Yes, subject to Federal Reserve margin rules and lender policies.

Risk Considerations

How assured can I be of getting my full investment back? Corporate and municipal issues, unless insured, vary with the credit of the issuer, so credit ratings are important. Treasury issues that are stripped (split into two parts principal and interest) by brokerage houses and marketed separately as zero-coupon securities represented by receipts or certificates, are highly safe as long as the broker holds the underlying Treasury security in escrow, as is the practice. Some municipal strips issued by brokers (e.g., M-CATS) have indirect U.S. government backing, since they represent prefundings invested in Treasury securities. Direct Treasury zeros (STRIPS) are risk-free. Zeros sold in the secondary market are susceptible to interest rate risk and a wide dealer spread. Of course, full investment, when talking zeros, means face value, not the small amount originally invested, since money is assumed to have a time value.

How assured is my income? Zeros do not pay income; the income return is built into the redemption value.

Are there any other risks unique to this investment? Other than the small risk of an issuing firm going bankrupt in the case of receipts and certificates issued by brokerages, the unique risk of zeros has to do with the degree of exposure; should a zero default, there is more to lose compared with an interest-bearing security, where some portion of interest would have been paid out and presumably been reinvested. Some municipal issues may be callable, which largely defeats the purpose for which most investors hold zeros. Mortgage-backed strips respond to the prepayment experience of the underlying loans. If rates fall, prepayments increase. This shortens the life of strips and decreases the amount of interest earned.

Is it commercially rated? Municipal and corporate issues are rated.

Tax Considerations

What tax advantages (or disadvantages) does it offer? Interest is taxable as it accrues each year, just as if it were paid out. An exception, of course, is tax-exempt municipal zeros, which may also be exempt from taxes in the state of issue. U.S. government zeros are taxable at the federal level but exempt from state and local taxes.

Economic Considerations

What economic factors most affect buy, hold, and sell decisions? Zeros are purchased based on competitive yield considerations and are normally held until maturity, their appeal being a locked-in interest rate as opposed to a yield that varies with the reinvestment value of periodic interest payments in changing markets. Should it be necessary to sell in the secondary market, lower rates mean higher prices. Considerations governing convertible zeros are complex and vary with the provisions of the issue.

PART II

How to Read an
Annual Report

How to Read a Quarterly Report

HOW TO READ AN
ANNUAL REPORT

Weekend sailors know an axiom that if you can understand a dinghy you can sail a yacht. It's all in grasping the fundamentals. Annual reports are the yachts of corporate communications, and in full regalia they can be as formidable as they are majestic. Fashioned by accountants and lawyers as well as marketers and executives, the reports are aimed at a variety of audiences— stockholders, potential stockholders, securities analysts, lenders, customers, and even employees. Essentially, however, they are financial statements, and if you can understand the basics, you will find that the rest is elaboration, much of which is legally required and very helpful. Of course, there are other parts that are simply embellishment, and those you take with a grain of salt.

The 2000s will be remembered as years when reporting chicanery shook the faith of investors and challenged Congress, the Securities and Exchange Commission, and the accounting profession to adopt reforms to protect investors in the future.

In the most egregious case, Houston-based Enron Corporation, with the complicity of one of the nation's most prominent auditing firms, inflated its profits and hid massive debt through a variety of schemes involving some 3,000 partnerships or "special purpose entities" whose results were excluded from the company's consolidated financial statements. Earlier, Cendant Corporation, primarily by misusing acquisition accounting to create huge reserves that could be released as fake revenue to meet Wall Street earnings expectations, settled shareholder suits for $2.8 billion, then brought suit against its former auditors for allegedly being aware of fraud and covering it up. In the case of Tyco International, top executives were accused of looting the company of some $600 million by making and then forgiving large loans to employees. The loans were allegedly disguised as relocation expenses offset by bonuses charged to other expenses.

The financial crisis following the real estate meltdown later in the decade had more to do with misguided risk management policies and financial product complexity than with financial reporting to shareholders, but there were examples of that as well. In one case, Lehman Brothers, prior to its bankruptcy in 2008, allegedly hid toxic assets using repurchase arrangements. Also, the Financial Accounting Standards Board (FASB) waived mark-to-market rules, which were forcing banks to write down mortgage-related assets to fair market value at a time when virtually no market existed. This impaired their balance sheets and restricted their ability to make loans during an historic credit crunch. The mark-to-market accounting rule was thus frustrating efforts to stimulate economic recovery and the FASB was persuaded to suspend it. Bank balance sheet presentations suddenly reflected an empowering strength that wasn't previously there, thanks to a perfectly legal accounting technicality.

Sarbanes-Oxley, erected in 2002, and other SEC and FASB rulings, which require disclosure of "all material facts" and fuller explanation of transactions related to off-balance sheet and special purpose entities, have tended to result in somewhat greater complexity in annual reports. This is especially true where previously reported results are required to be restated to "reflect all material correcting adjustments."

The added complexity is usually in clearly worded explanations found in the Notes to Financial Statements and Management's Discussion and Analysis. It is a small tradeoff for its value in improving the quality of reported earnings.

By and large, corporate management and the accounting and auditing establishment can be relied upon to act in the interest of shareholders. Annual reports will continue to be a source of useful and accurate information for readers who know what to look for. As with investments themselves, the best rule to follow is to be skeptical of what you don't understand. The legendary investor, Warren Buffett, was recently quoted as saying that if he could not understand an annual report, perhaps the company did not intend for him to understand it. From the Oracle of Omaha!

Essential to understanding annual reports, of course, is knowing the basics. Now let's look at our dinghy.

Basically, a financial statement comprises a *balance sheet* and an *income statement.* Exhibit 1A illustrates a balance sheet reduced to "bare timbers."

EXHIBIT 1A

BALANCE SHEET
December 31, 20XX

Cash/near cash	**5**	Accounts and notes payable	15
Accounts receivable	**20**	Accrued liabilities	5
Inventory	35	Current portion, long-term debt	5
CURRENT ASSETS	**60**	**CURRENT LIABILITIES**	**25**
		Long-term liabilities	25
		TOTAL LIABILITIES	**50**
Net fixed assets	35		
Other assets	5	Capital stock	10
		Retained earnings	40
		NET WORTH	**50**
TOTAL ASSETS	**$100**	**TOTAL LIABILITIES AND NET WORTH**	**$100**

THE BASIC BALANCE SHEET

A balance sheet (also called a statement of financial position or a statement of condition) is simply the status of a company's accounts at one moment in time, usually the last business day of a quarter or year. It is often compared to a snapshot, in contrast to a motion picture. On one side, it lists what the company owns—its assets. On the other side it lists what the company owes—its liabilities—and its net worth, or owners' equity, which is what investors have put into the firm plus earnings that have been retained in the business rather than paid out in dividends. The two sides are always equal. Even if a firm were insolvent—that is, owed more than it had in assets—the sides would be equalized by showing a negative (or deficit) net worth. (A minor technical point: Balance sheets can be presented with opposing sides, as just described, which is known as the account form, or with the assets above the liabilities and owners' equity, which is called the report form.)

Exhibit 1B illustrates a very basic income statement.

EXHIBIT 1B
INCOME STATEMENT
for the year ended December 31, 20XX

SALES		**$110**
Cost of goods sold	80	
Depreciation	5	
Selling, general, and administrative expenses	15	
	100	
NET OPERATING PROFIT		**10**
Other income or expense	1	
Interest expense	2	
Income taxes	2	
NET INCOME	5	**5**

THE BASIC INCOME STATEMENT

The income statement, which goes by such other names as statement of profit and loss, operating statement, and earnings statement, reports the results of operations over a specified period of time—12 months in the case of an annual report. As customers are billed, and as the costs and expenses of producing goods, running the business, and creating sales are incurred and recorded, the information summarized in the income statement is accumulated.

The income statement will be discussed on page 111 in more detail; it is enough for now to understand that its highlights are sales (or revenues), net operating profit (or operating income), and net income. It is this last amount—popularly called the bottom line because it comes after interest expense, unusual income and charges, and income taxes—that is available to pay dividends to shareholders or to be kept in the business as retained earnings.

A word about one expense item, called depreciation, which is important to understand because it is a major factor in cash flow, the net amount of cash taken into the business during a given period and the cash paid out during that period. Depreciation, which is sometimes combined in the figure for cost of goods sold, is merely a bookkeeping entry that reduces income without reducing cash. In other words, depreciation is a noncash expense, and it is added back to net income to determine a company's cash earnings. Net income plus depreciation equals cash flow from operations. More about depreciation and cash flow later.

BASIC RATIO TESTS

With the foregoing information on balance sheets and income statements, it is possible to look at a firm's year-to-year financial statements and make some tentative judgments about the firm's basic financial health and operating trends, particularly if you can compare the figures with those of other firms in a comparable industry. An in-depth look at important financial ratios is at the end of the discussion of the annual report, but much can be learned at a glance by applying the following basic ratio tests.

Current Ratio The current ratio is current assets divided by current liabilities. Current assets are assets expected to be converted to cash within a normal business cycle (usually one year), and current liabilities are obligations that must be paid during the same short-term period. For a manufacturing company (standards vary from industry to industry), a ratio of between 1.5 to 1 and 2 to 1—$1.50 to $2.00 of current assets for each $1.00 of current liabilities—is generally considered an indication that the firm is sufficiently liquid. In other words, there is enough net working capital (the difference between the two figures) to ensure that the firm can meet its current obligations and operate comfortably.

It is important that a company have this cushion because the liquidity of current assets, with the exception of cash and its equivalents, cannot be taken for granted; receivables can become slow or uncollectible (although a reserve for expected write-offs is normally provided) and inventory can lose value or become unsalable. Such things happen in recessions, and can result from poor credit, purchasing, or marketing decisions. Liabilities, unfortunately, remain constant. Of course, a company can have too much liquidity, suggesting inefficient use of cash resources, shrinking operations, or even vulnerability to a takeover attempt by an outside party. Well-run companies are lean, not fat.

Quick Ratio   The quick ratio, which is also known as the acid-test ratio, is the current ratio, with inventory, its least liquid and riskiest component, excluded. It is calculated by adding cash, near-cash (for instance, marketable securities), and accounts receivable (sometimes collectively termed monetary assets), and dividing by current liabilities. Assuming no negative trends are revealed in year-to-year comparisons, a ratio of between .50 to 1 and 1 to 1 generally signifies good health, depending on the quality of the accounts receivable.

Average Collection Period   A quick way of testing accounts receivable quality is to divide annual sales by 360 and divide the result into the accounts receivable. That tells you the average number of days it takes to collect an account. Since terms of sale in most industries are 30 days, a figure of 30 to 60 would indicate normal collections and basically sound receivables—at least up to the date of the statement. It may be helpful to compare a company's figure with that of other firms in the same industry.

Inventory Turnover   Inventory turnover ratio tells the approximate number of times inventory is sold and replaced over a 12-month period and can be a tipoff, when compared with prior years' figures or comparative industry data, to unhealthy accumulations. Inventory should be kept adequate but trim, because it ties up costly working capital and carries market risks. To calculate turnover, divide the balance sheet inventory into sales. (*Note:* Industry comparative data published by Dun & Bradstreet and other firms providing financial data on companies compute this ratio using sales, not cost of goods sold. While cost of goods sold, because it does not include profit, produces a purer result, it is necessary to use sales for the sake of comparability.) As a general rule, high inventory turnover reflects efficient inventory management, but there are exceptions. A firm may be stockpiling raw materials in anticipation of shortages, for instance, or preparing to meet firm orders not yet reflected as sales. If inventory turnover is falling compared to prior years or is out of line with industry data, you should investigate the reasons. Year-to-year comparisons of inventory turnover are of particular significance in high volume–low profit margin industries such as garment manufacturing and retailing.

Debt-to-Equity Ratio   The debt-to-equity ratio can be figured in several ways, but for our purposes it is total liabilities divided by net worth. It measures reliance on creditors to finance operations and is one of several capitalization ratios summarized below. Although financial leverage—using other people's money to increase earnings per share—is desirable to a point, too much debt can be a danger sign. Debt involves contractual payments that must be made regardless of earnings levels; it must usually be refinanced when it matures at prevailing (perhaps much higher) money costs; and it has a prior claim on assets in the event of liquidation. Moreover, debt can limit a company's ability to finance additional growth and can adversely affect a firm's credit rating, with implications for the market value of shares. What is considered a proper debt-to-equity ratio varies with the type of company. Those with highly stable earnings, such as many utilities, are able to afford higher ratios than companies with volatile or cyclical earnings. For a typical industrial company, a debt-to-equity ratio significantly higher than 1 to 1 should be looked at carefully.

Operating Profit Margin   This figure, obtained by dividing a firm's net operating profit by sales, is a measure of operating efficiency. (Analysts sometimes add depreciation back into net operating profit since it is not a cash expense.) Year-to-year comparisons can be a reflection on cost control or on purchasing and pricing policies. Comparisons with other firms in the same industry provide insight into a company's ability to compete.

Return on Equity   This is the bottom line as a percentage of net worth (net worth is divided into net income), and it tells how much the company is earning on shareholder investment. Compared with the figures of prior years and similar companies, it is a measure of overall efficiency—a reflection on financial as well as operational management. But it can also be affected by factors beyond the control of management, such as general economic conditions or higher tax rates. And be suspicious of a firm with abnormally high returns; it could be in for competition from firms willing to sacrifice returns to gain a larger market share. As a rule of thumb, return on equity should be between 10% and 20%.

By applying the foregoing ratio tests to a company's basic balance sheet and income statement, particularly with the help of data on the company's prior years and on other companies in the same industry, you get a sense of whether the company's financial structure and operational trends are essentially sound. There is, however, a great deal you still don't know, such as:

- How reliable are the numbers?
- Are results affected by changes in accounting methods?
- Have there been changes in the company's top management?

- From what product lines did sales and profits largely derive?
- Did any special events affect last year's results?
- What new products are on the horizon?
- Are there any lawsuits or other contingent liabilities that could affect future results or asset values?
- To what extent are the company's operations multinational, and what is its exposure to foreign exchange fluctuations and/or political risk?
- If the company is labor-intensive, what is the status of its union contracts?
- What is the status of the company's debt? Is any financing or refinancing planned that could affect share values?
- How sensitive is the company to changes in interest rates (which, in 2010, are rising and projected to keep rising for the foreseeable future)?
- What were the sources and applications of cash?
- Are any major capital expenditures (for instance, real estate, machinery, equipment) being planned? How are existing fixed assets depreciated?
- How much is allocated to research and development?
- What other operational or financial changes has management planned?
- Does the company have a broad base of customers, or a few major customers?
- To what extent is the company dependent on government contracts?
- What is the company's pension liability, and what are its pension assets? Has it adequately provided for other postretirement employee obligations?
- Does the company have significant financial assets (such as leases or "derivatives") that may represent "off-balance sheet" risk, deferral of losses, or premature recognition of gains?
- If the company has been "downsizing" is it clear what impact discontinued operations have had and what the future of continuing operations is likely to be?

WHAT THE ANNUAL REPORT INCLUDES

The majority of annual reports of major public companies include a table of contents on the inside front cover. The following is typical:

Contents
Highlights
Letter to Shareholders
Review of Operations
Financial Statements
    Report of Independent Accountants
    Consolidated Financial Statements
    Statement of Consolidated Cash Flows
    Notes to Financial Statements
    Supplementary Tables
    Management's Discussion and Analysis
Investor's Information
Directors and Officers

Highlights

The highlights greet you at the start of an annual report. Often including charts and other graphics, they present basic information in a clear, comparative way that requires little explanation. At the very least, you should expect to find the company's total sales for the past two years and its net income, expressed both as a total and on a per-share basis. Needless to say, upward trends (usually, but with exceptions) are positive and downward trends negative. But what is most important to understand is that the company and its public relations advisors can include here whatever other information they feel will create the desired impression on the shareholder. That usually means you can expect to find highlights that add up to a positive impression, although it has become lately a matter both of fashion and good business to include a downward trend or two for the sake of credibility. Basically, though, what you can expect to find highlighted, aside from the unavoidable, are the statistics of which the company is most proud. If dividends were up, they will probably be highlighted; if they were down, the same space might be devoted to an increase in research and development (R&D) expenditures, with the implicit promise of a future payoff for shareholders.

Where earnings are presented on a per-share basis, accounting regulations now require that they be reported two ways. The first, called "basic earnings per share," represents earnings per share of stock presently outstanding. The second, called "diluted earnings per share," shows earnings per share assuming the conversion or exercise of all outstanding securities and rights potentially causing the issuance of additional shares. The second figure is normally lower because more shares are competing for the same amount of earnings. Potentially dilutive items would include convertible bonds, convertible preferred stock, warrants, and executive or employee stock options. Under accounting regulations existing prior to December 1997, the terminology used was "primary" and "fully diluted" earnings per share and companies were required to make the distinction only when the effect was deemed significant.

Should you encounter any other unfamiliar figures in the highlights, consult the Ratio Analysis Summary at the end of this discussion of an annual report.

Letter to Shareholders

In the many spoofs that have been written about corporate annual reports and their reputation for obfuscation, the least mercy has been reserved for the letter to shareholders. This review of the year just passed and look at the year ahead leads off the textual part of the report. It is usually signed by the chairperson and president and is often accompanied by a picture of the two together, suggesting amity not always characteristic of their day-to-day relationship.

While it is certainly true that the letter to shareholders is worded to put the best face on the past year's results and to soothe any anxieties that might be aroused by the financial figures to follow, it is nonetheless a statement of management's intentions and, when compared to prior years' messages, a test of management's credibility. Although it is not an audited, formal part of the report, it purports to be a serious comment on the year's results and their financial impact, a report that puts into perspective the major developments affecting shareholders, a statement of management's position on relevant social issues, and an expression of management's plans for the company's future. An impressive letter is one that compares past predictions with actual results and explains in a candid way the disappointments as well as the successes. Be wary of euphemisms (a "challenging" year was probably a bad one) and wording that is vague or qualified; a product area "positioned for growth" may sound promising, but it's not growing yet. If it were, the letter would say so. Much of the meaning of the letter to shareholders is between the lines.

Review of Operations

This review section consists of pictures and prose and often occupies the bulk of the pages of an annual report. Frequently slick, public relations-oriented, and designed to impress a corporation's various publics, the review can nonetheless be a valuable source of information about the company's products, services, facilities, and future direction. Unfortunately, it is also sometimes designed to divert the reader's attention from unpleasant realities. Be suspicious of reviews that stress the future and give the present short shrift or that are built around themes, such as the loyalty of employees or the company's role in building a stronger America. Also, what is not discussed can be more significant that what is discussed. Lack of reference to an aspect of operations described in the preceding year's annual report as an area of rapid growth and expansion may indicate that the company's expectations were not fulfilled and a write-off may be on the horizon. By and large, though, companies are responding to pressures for greater straightforwardness in the way they present themselves. In addition, companies these days are required to provide detailed financial information about the various segments contributing to their sales and profits. Although that information appears later in the supplementary financial data, it allows you to relate the activities being "promoted" to actual results and thus to evaluate the financial significance of different product areas. The Securities and Exchange Commission (SEC) has imposed stricter disclosure requirements in recent years, and these requirements have had a generally positive effect in terms of making annual reports more credible documents.

Financial Statements

Financial statements are, of course, the basic purpose of annual reports, and as the result both of expanded SEC disclosure regulation and companies' own interest in satisfying the information requirements of securities and credit analysts, financial statements have evolved over the years into presentations that elaborate substantially on the basic balance sheet and income statements. Reporting has also become more complex due to the complexity of the companies themselves, which have become diversified in terms both of product lines and geography, with a trend toward multinational operations involving political and currency risks.

Report of Independent Accountants: This report, also known as the auditor's opinion, is sometimes found at the beginning of the financial statement section and sometimes at the end, but it should be the first thing you read. Numbers are only numbers, and the opinion of an independent accounting firm, which is legally required of public companies, certifies that the financial statements were examined and validated. A "clean" or unqualified opinion—we'll get to what a qualified opinion means in a minute—typically reads as shown in Exhibit 2.

EXHIBIT 2

Report of Independent Accountants

To the Shareholders of XYZ Corporation:

We have audited the accompanying consolidated balance sheets of XYZ Corporation and subsidiaries as of December 31, 2009 and 2008 and the related consolidated statements of earnings, shareholders' equity, and cash flows for each of the three years in the period ended December 31, 2009. These financial statements are the responsibility of the Company's management. Our responsibility is to express an opinion on these financial statements based on our audits.

We conducted our audits in accordance with generally accepted auditing standards. Those standards require that we plan and perform the audit to obtain reasonable assurance about whether the financial statements are free of material misstatement. An audit includes examining, on a test basis, evidence supporting the amounts and disclosures in the financial statements. An audit also includes assessing the accounting principles used and significant estimates made by management, as well as evaluating the overall financial statement presentation. We believe that our audits provide a reasonable basis for our opinion.

In our opinion, the financial statements referred to above present fairly, in all material respects, the consolidated financial position of XYZ Corporation and subsidiaries as of 2009 and 2008, and the consolidated results of their operations and their cash flows for each of the three years in the period ended December 31, 2009, in conformity with generally accepted accounting principles.

The above format would explain any exceptions to "present fairly." It is thus possible to have an opinion that is clean but followed by explanations of potential problems.

Such "modified opinions" challenge the reader to understand the issues raised. Explanations are usually found in footnotes to the financial statements and/or the management's discussion and analysis section.

Qualified opinions include a statement that "except for" specified problems or departures from generally accepted accounting principles, the report would present fairly the company's financial position. Such language is rare, since it means the Securities and Exchange Commission will require the company to resolve the problem or make the accounting treatment acceptable.

Even rarer are two other types of auditor's opinion, the disclaimer of opinion and the adverse opinion. A disclaimer of opinion states that an opinion is not possible because of a material restriction on the scope of the audit (for example, an inability to verify inventory quantities) or a material uncertainty about the accounts (for example, doubt about the company's continued existence as a going concern). An adverse opinion states that the company's financial statements do not present fairly the financial position or results of operations in accordance with generally accepted accounting principles. Either type of opinion is cause for concern, but you are unlikely to run into these types of opinions since the company will normally take the auditor's advice and make the necessary corrections.

You should be wary of a company's figures if the company regularly replaces the independent auditors. Such conduct could indicate that the company is opinion shopping— looking for auditors whose approach would produce the most favorable sales and earnings figures for the company and thereby perhaps hide problem areas or potential problem areas.

Report by Management: Accompanying the Report of Independent Accountants is a similar Report by Management certifying responsibility for the information examined by the accounting firm. This section attests to the objectivity and integrity of the data, estimates, and judgments on which the financial statements were based. It alludes to the company's internal controls and oversight responsibility of the board of directors for the financial statements as carried out through an audit committee composed of directors who are not employees. It is signed by the chief financial officer of the company and the chief executive officer.

Consolidated Financial Statements—Part 1: The Balance Sheet: In the following pages, we will discuss the financial statement of our hypothetical company, XYZ Corporation. As required, the statement presents comparative balance sheets as of the company's two most recent fiscal year ends and income statements for the past three years. Many variations exist on the accounts discussed below, and there are as many unique items as there are companies. But if you grasp the following, you will understand the basis of the vast majority of balance sheets and income statements.

First, an item-by-item explanation of XYZ's balance sheet (see Exhibit 3).

CURRENT ASSETS

Cash and Cash Equivalents   Cash requires little explanation; it is cash in the bank, on its way to the bank, or in the till. Cash equivalents, sometimes listed separately under cash and called marketable securities, represent idle funds invested in highly safe, highly liquid securities with a maturity, when acquired, of less than 3 months. Examples would be U.S. Treasury bills, certificates of deposit, and commercial paper. They are carried at the lower of their cost or market value. If they are shown at cost, their market value is indicated parenthetically or in a footnote.

Accounts and Notes Receivable   These are customer balances owing. When a company makes a sale, a customer is required either to pay in cash (cash sales) or, as in the majority of cases, within credit terms (credit sales), which tend to be standardized within industries but are typically 30 days and rarely more than 90 days.

Accounts receivable—sometimes called just receivables—are credit accounts that are not yet received. Often there is a reference to a footnote containing an aging schedule, a breakdown of accounts in terms of where they stand in relation to their due dates. This reveals delinquency and trends and is a valuable tool for analysts. Of course, a company expects a certain percentage of uncollectible accounts and, based on its historical experience and current policies (it might, for example decide to liberalize credit policy to boost sales), it sets up a reserve (or allowance) for bad debts, which is deducted from gross receivables to arrive at the balance sheet value. This is either noted on the balance sheet or explained in a footnote. Special attention should be paid to accounts receivable if a company does a significant percentage of its business with a few key customers. If any of these key customers were to have financial problems, the worth of the receivables carried on the company's books would quickly be in jeopardy.

Notes receivable normally account for a small portion of the total and usually represent cases in which special terms were granted and obligations were documented with promissory notes. If a short-term note receivable arose out of a loan or the sale of property or some other nontrade transaction, it would, if material, normally be shown separately or footnoted.

Inventories   This figure, when a company is engaged in manufacturing, is a combination of finished goods, work in process, and raw materials. Conservative accounting practice requires that inventories be carried at the

EXHIBIT 3

XYZ CORPORATION
Balance Sheet
As of December 31
(Dollars in Millions)

	2009	2008
ASSETS		
Cash and cash equivalents	**7.6**	7.0
Accounts and notes receivable	**10.2**	9.5
Inventories	**23.0**	20.9
Prepaid expenses	**.3**	.2
Total Current Assets	**41.1**	37.6
Property, plant and equipment	**83.3**	79.4
Less: Accumulated Depreciation	**23.5**	21.3
Net Fixed Assets	**59.8**	58.1
Other assets	**3.8**	3.0
Intangible assets	**.9**	.9
TOTAL ASSETS	**105.6**	99.6
LIABILITIES AND SHAREHOLDERS' EQUITY		
Accounts payable	**4.2**	4.3
Notes payable	**.8**	—
Accrued liabilities	**3.2**	2.7
Federal income taxes payable	**8.2**	7.1
Current portion (maturity) of long-term debt	**.7**	.8
Dividends payable	**1.4**	.9
Total Current Liabilities	**18.5**	15.8
Other liabilities	**2.0**	1.4
Long-term debt	**16.2**	17.0
Deferred federal income taxes	**.9**	.7
TOTAL LIABILITIES	**37.6**	34.9
6% cumulative preferred stock ($100 par value; authorized and outstanding: 50,000 shares)	**5.0**	5.0
Common stock ($10 par value; authorized 2,500,000 shares; outstanding 1,555,000 shares)	**15.6**	15.6
Capital surplus	**8.2**	8.2
Retained earnings	**39.2**	35.9
TOTAL STOCKHOLDERS' EQUITY	**68.0**	64.7
TOTAL LIABILITIES AND STOCKHOLDERS' EQUITY	**105.6**	99.6

lower of cost or market value, but there are different methods of inventory valuation, principally First In, First Out (FIFO) and Last In, First Out (LIFO).

Under the FIFO method, inventory is assumed to be sold in the chronological order in which it was purchased. Under the LIFO method, the reverse is true: The goods sold in a period are assumed to be those most recently bought. When prices are rising or falling, the difference is reflected in the balance sheet value of inventory. A company using the LIFO method during a period of inflation, because its cost of goods sold reflects the most recent—and higher—prices, will show lower profits on its income statement and a lower balance sheet inventory, since its ending inventory remains valued at older (lower) prices. Because LIFO produces lower taxable income in times of inflation, it is the method adopted by a majority of companies in recent years. Thus, the balance sheet inventories of these companies are undervalued—in other words, they have a "LIFO cushion." It is important to remember that *de*flation would produce the opposite result. An explanation of inventory valuation methods (or, significantly, any change in methods) is provided in the footnotes to the statements, which will also explain adjustments required by the tax law changes.

A company's inventory figure cannot be analyzed in a vacuum. To determine if a company is maintaining adequate inventory control, relate the inventory figure to the growth in sales. Inventory growth should keep pace with sales growth, not exceed it. A buildup of inventory relative to sales should be viewed with skepticism.

Prepaid Expenses This account represents expenses paid in advance, such as rent, insurance, subscriptions, or utilities, that are capitalized—that is, recognized as asset values, and gradually written off as expenses, as their benefit is realized during the current accounting period. If the amount is important, this account is usually deducted from current assets in computing the current ratio. However, it usually represents an insignificant percentage of current assets and is thus ignored for analytical purposes.

NET FIXED ASSETS

Property, Plant and Equipment This section of the balance sheet lists the company's fixed assets, sometimes called capital assets or long-term assets. These assets include land, buildings, machinery and equipment, furniture and fixtures, and leasehold improvements—relatively permanent assets that are used in the production of income. The word tangible is sometimes used in describing these assets, to distinguish them from intangible assets (described below), which similarly produce economic benefits for more than a year but which lack physical substance.

Fixed assets are carried—that is, recorded on the books of the company and therefore reported on its balance sheet—at original cost (the cost the company incurred to acquire them) less accumulated depreciation—the cumulative amount of that original cost that the company has written off through annual depreciation expenses charged to income. Land, however, because it is assumed to have unlimited useful life, is not depreciated. (Companies engaged in mining and other extractive industries, whose capital assets represent natural resources, enjoy depletion allowances, a concept similar to depreciation write-offs.) As a result of depreciation writedowns and inflation, it is not unusual for the book value of a company's fixed assets to be considerably lower than their market value. On the other hand, market value is an indication of what it will cost to keep fixed assets up to date and maintain sufficient capacity to support sales growth. The relationship between sales levels and capital expenditures is therefore an important factor in evaluating a firm's viability. However, businesses vary in terms of how capital-intensive they are; manufacturers rely more on fixed assets to produce sales than wholesalers, for example.

The existence of fully depreciated assets on a company's balance sheet may signal that the company is a likely candidate for a takeover attempt or a leveraged buyout. The company's plant, for instance, has most likely appreciated in market value over the years and the depreciated basis on which it is carried on the balance sheet may have no relationship to reality. Thus, new owners could in part finance the purchase of the company by selling some assets at their higher market value.

OTHER ASSETS

This category can include any number of items such as cash surrender value of life insurance policies taken out to insure the lives of key executives; notes receivable after one year; long-term advance payments; small properties not used in daily business operations; and minority stock ownership in other companies or in subsidiaries that for some reason are not consolidated. Additional types of assets, if significant, would be discussed in the footnotes.

Another category of other assets, which is sometimes broken out separately (as in our example), is generally called intangible assets. These are nonphysical rights or resources presumed to represent an advantage to the firm in the marketplace. The most common intangibles are (1) goodwill and (2) a grouping typically labeled patents, trademarks, and copyrights.

Goodwill refers to a company's worth as an operating entity, or going concern—the prestige and visibility of its name, the morale of its employees, the loyalty of its customers, and other going-concern values. These are values beyond the book value of the firm's assets. Thus, when a company is purchased at a price exceeding its book value, the difference—the value of its goodwill—represents a real cost to the acquiring company. Goodwill, though intangible and abstract, can be valued. Because it has no liquidation value, however, it is classified as an intangible asset and must be amortized (written off) over time if certain impairment tests are met. As with fixed assets and depreciation, this is done by annual noncash charges to income.

Patents, trademarks and copyrights, the other most common intangible assets, have economic value in the sense that they translate into profits, but their carrying value is based on their cost. Being intangibles, they are written off over what accounting practice deems to be their useful lives.

Other intangible assets might include capitalized advertising costs, organization costs, licenses, permits of various sorts, brand names, and franchises.

Because intangible assets are assumed not to have value in liquidation, they are excluded from most ratios used in analyzing values. The term tangible net worth is used to mean shareholder equity less intangible assets.

CURRENT LIABILITIES

Accounts Payable   This account represents amounts owed to suppliers for raw materials and other goods, supplies, and services purchased on credit for use in the normal operating cycle of the business. In other words, one company's account payable is another company's account receivable. As with receivables, conventional credit terms vary from industry to industry, but 30 days is standard and anything over 90 days is the exception (except in highly seasonal industries, such as garment manufacturing, where longer-term dating is commonplace and liquidity is provided by cashing accounts receivable with finance companies known as factors). The level of accounts payable should vary with sales levels, or, more specifically, with the amount of annual purchases—a part of the cost of goods sold. Any bulging of accounts payable in relation to purchases could mean a firm is relying to an unhealthy extent on trade suppliers as a source of working capital.

Notes Payable These are usually amounts due banks or financial institutions on short-term loans, often under lines of credit. A line of credit is an arrangement by which a company may borrow working capital up to a limit, and details are usually covered in the footnotes. Notes payable may also be due suppliers under special credit arrangements.

Accrued Liabilities Accrued liabilities arise when an expense is recognized as an obligation but the cash has not yet actually been paid out. Expenses commonly reflected in this account include payroll, commissions, rent, interest, taxes, and other routine expenses.

Federal Income Taxes Payable This account is similar to accrued liabilities, but is usually broken out in recognition of its importance. (It is to be distinguished from the account called deferred federal income taxes, a noncurrent liability discussed below.)

Current Portion (Maturity) of Long-Term Debt When a company has a long-term debt obligation that requires regular payments, the amount due in the next 12 months is recorded here as a current liability.

Dividends Payable These represent dividends that have been declared by the board of directors but have not been paid. Dividends become an obligation when they are declared, and are normally paid quarterly. They include both preferred and common dividends.

LONG-TERM LIABILITIES

These are debt obligations due after one year. Included are term loans from financial institutions, mortgages, and debentures (unsecured bonds), as well as capital lease obligations, pension liabilities, and estimated liabilities under long-term warranties. Details are provided in footnotes.

Depending on a company's accounting practices, long-term liabilities may also include an item called deferred federal income taxes. This is often due to the fact that companies may use different rules for tax purposes and reporting purposes, and this creates timing differences. For example, a company using accelerated depreciation for tax purposes would get large depreciation write-offs in the early years of an asset's life, thus saving taxes, but would have higher taxable income in the later years. For reporting purposes, however, the company might wish to use the straight line method of depreciation, which each year produces equal (and lower) charges, thus resulting in higher reported earnings. The amount of taxes deferred is shown on the statement used for reporting purposes (the annual report) as deferred federal income taxes.

SHAREHOLDERS' EQUITY

This section of the balance sheet represents the owner's interest—the value of assets after creditors, who have a prior legal claim, have all been paid. It includes accounts for preferred stock, common stock, capital surplus, and retained earnings.

Preferred Stock Not all companies issue preferred stock, and it exists in several varieties. Several general characteristics are particularly notable: It usually pays a fixed dividend that must be paid before common dividends can be paid; it has precedence over common stock in the distribution of assets in liquidation; and if it is cumulative, unpaid dividends accumulate and must be paid in full before common dividends can be declared.

In recent years companies have used preferred stock as part of antitakeover programs. Referred to as poison-pill preferreds, these shares are created when a hostile takeover attempt is imminent. The new class of preferred stock is designed to raise the cost of the acquisition to a point where it may be abandoned by the company attempting the takeover. You should check whether a company has issued preferred specifically to fend off a takeover attempt and, if so, try to determine the implications such preferred may have for common shareholders.

Common Stock   Shares of common stock are the basic units of ownership in a corporation. Common shareholders follow behind creditors and preferred shareholders in claims on assets and therefore take all the risks inherent in the business. But, with rare exceptions, they vote in elections of directors and on all important matters, and while they may or may not receive dividends, depending on earnings and whether the directors vote to declare dividends, the book value of their shares stands to grow as net worth (shareholders' equity) expands through earnings retained in the business. Common shareholders in publicly traded companies also stand to profit from increases in market prices of shares, which normally reflect expectations of future earnings. But on the balance sheet, common shares are listed either at a par or stated value, an accounting/legal value signifying nothing other than the lowest price at which shares can be initially sold. Sometimes different classes of stock exist and are listed separately, with the privileges or limitations of each indicated parenthetically or in referenced notes.

Capital Surplus   Sometimes seen as additional paid-in capital (as preferred stock and common stock are sometimes called paid-in capital), this account reflects proceeds from issuances of stock that were in excess of the par or stated value of shares. For example, XYZ common has a par value of $10 per share; when 100,000 shares were issued at $12 a share, $1,000,000 was added to common stock and $200,000 was added to capital surplus.

Retained Earnings   This account is made up of corporate earnings not paid out in dividends and instead retained in the business. Retained earnings are not put in a special bank account or stuffed into a figurative mattress—they are simply absorbed as working capital or to finance fixed assets in order to generate more earnings.

Consolidated Financial Statements—Part 2: The Income Statement: The income statement shows the results of operations over a period of 12 months. Results of the two years prior to the year reported on are included for comparative purposes (see Exhibit 4).

NET SALES

Most income statements (or, more formally, Statements of Income), lead off with Net Sales—the total of cash sales (negligible for most industrial companies) and credit sales for the accounting period (12 months for annual reports). Net simply means after returns of merchandise shipped; freight-out; and allowances for shortages, breakage, and other adjustments having to do with day-to-day commerce. (Note that some service companies, including utilities, and financial organizations use the term revenues instead of sales.) Needless to say, the trend of sales as revealed in the three years'

EXHIBIT 4

XYZ CORPORATION
Income Statement
Fiscal Year Ended December 31
(Dollars in Millions)

	2009	2008	2007
Net Sales	98.4	93.5	88.8
Cost of goods sold	64.9	62.2	59.7
Depreciation and amortization	2.2	3.0	2.0
Selling, general, and administrative expenses	12.1	11.1	10.3
	79.2	76.3	72.0
Net Operating Profit	19.2	17.2	16.8
Other Income or (Expenses)			
Income from dividends and interest	.2		
Interest expense	(1.0)	(.9)	(1.0)
Earnings before income taxes	18.4	16.3	15.8
Provision for income taxes	8.3	7.5	7.3
Net Income	10.1	8.8	8.5

Common shares outstanding: 1,555,000
Net earnings per share (after preferred dividend
requirements in 2009 and 2008: 2008: $6.30; 2007: $5.47;
2006: $5.47)

Statement of Retained Earnings

	2009	2008	2007
Retained Earnings Beginning of Year	35.9	33.6	31.3
Net Income for Year	10.1	8.8	8.5
Less: Dividends Paid on:			
Preferred stock ($6 per share)	.3	.3	
Common stock (per share): 2009: $4.20; 2008: $4.00;	6.5	6.2	6.2
2007: $4.00			
Retained Earnings End of Year	39.2	35.9	33.6

worth of figures is a key indicator of how a company is faring in the market-place. The figures should of course be adjusted for inflation to give an accurate reading of year-to-year changes.

Changes in the components of a company's sales can be more significant than changes in sales figures. If, for example, a chemical company can shift from marketing bulk chemicals (which have a relatively small profit margin) to marketing specialty chemicals (which have a relatively large profit margin) it will ultimately earn more even without an increase in sales. Changes in sales components can be determined by reviewing the business segment information in the annual report (discussed below.)

COST OF GOODS SOLD

This is the cost of producing inventory and includes raw materials, direct labor, and other overhead that can be directly related to production. It is directly affected by the company's choice of the FIFO or LIFO inventory valuation methods (see Inventories, page 106). The reason becomes clear when you look at the formula by which cost of goods sold is determined:

Beginning inventory + Purchases during the period – Ending inventory
= Cost of goods sold

When the ending inventory (the balance sheet inventory) is the oldest stock, which is the case when the LIFO method is used, the cost of goods sold, assuming prices are rising with inflation, becomes a higher number than would be the case using FIFO. Of course, the higher the cost of goods sold, the lower will be taxable income, as we will see.

DEPRECIATION

This noncash expense was alluded to at the start of the discussion of an annual report and again under Deferred Federal Income Taxes Payable in the discussion of balance sheet liabilities. To encourage firms to keep facilities modern and thus spur the economy, the U.S. government provides businesses a way to pay less tax and thereby conserve cash. This is accomplished by allowing firms to take an annual percentage (called a depreciation write-off) of what they spent for certain types of fixed assets, such as buildings, machinery, and equipment, and to treat the amount as though it were an actual expense thus reducing taxable income without requiring an outlay of cash.

Depreciation is a highly complex tax accounting concept, and for purposes of reading annual reports it is not necessary to understand it completely. It is enough to know that tax rules make it possible for companies to recover the cost of certain fixed asset investments on an accelerated basis and thus to get the benefit of tax savings sooner than they would using the straight-line method (now required for newly purchased real property). At the same time, companies are allowed, for purposes of annual reports, to reflect depreciation charges based on the straight line method, whereby the estimated useful life of the asset is divided into its cost to get a uniform annual depreciation charge, which is generally much lower than the figure used for tax purposes. Annual reports thus show higher earnings, while the stockholder has the satisfaction of knowing that the company's tax liability has been minimized. It is all spelled out in the footnotes.

What is more important to know is that depreciation charges have a relationship to the age of the assets and vary with the amount of investment in fixed assets. An increase in depreciation usually reflects increases in depreciable assets—fixed assets like plant and equipment. Decreases usually mean fixed assets have been disposed of or have become fully depreciated. Particularly since straight line depreciation is used by most companies for reporting purposes, lower depreciation charges can signal a need for fixed asset expenditures meaning long-term financing, which has implications for shareholders in the form either of dilution of share values or higher interest costs. Of course, increased or modernized plant capacity should also translate eventually into higher sales, greater operating efficiency and higher earnings per share.

SELLING, GENERAL, AND ADMINISTRATIVE (SG&A) EXPENSES

These are all the expenses associated with the normal operations of the business that were not included in cost of goods sold, which represented direct costs of production. Salaries, rent, utilities, advertising, travel and entertainment, commissions, office payroll, office expenses, and other such items are representative of this category, which varies from industry to industry in terms of its composition and the relative importance of selling expenses versus administrative expenses.

A good test of the quality of a company's management is its ability to control selling, general, and administrative expenses. Many companies have fallen into bankruptcy simply because management was unable or unwilling to control expenses and keep them in line with the growth of sales.

NET OPERATING PROFIT

The net operating profit is what is left over after costs of goods sold, depreciation, and SG&A expenses are deducted from sales, and it tells you the company's profit on a normal operating basis—that is, without taking into account unusual items of income or expense or nonoperating expenses such as interest and taxes. As stated above, it is a measure of operating efficiency, and significant variations from year to year or from industry standards should be investigated by looking more closely at the figures behind the totals, many of which are supplied in footnotes or published in the company's form 10-K (see Investor's Information, page 122). Lower than expected profit due to a rise in SG&A expenses as a percentage of sales might be traceable to a single factor, such as a rise in officers' salaries, for example.

OTHER INCOME OR EXPENSES

This category picks up any unusual or nonoperating income or expense items. Examples might include income, gains, or losses from other investments; gains or losses on the sale of fixed assets; or special payments to employees. Nonrecurring items are usually explained in detail in footnotes. In this category is *interest expense,* which, unlike dividends, is a pretax expense. For companies with bonds or other debt outstanding, however, interest expense is a recurring item. Because interest on funded debt is a contractual, fixed expense that, if unpaid, becomes an event of default, analysts follow closely a company's fixed-charge coverage—how many times such fixed charges are covered by pretax annual earnings.

EARNINGS BEFORE INCOME TAXES

This figure nets out all pretax income and expense items, but it would not be accurate to say it is the figure on which federal income taxes are based. That is because tax returns of corporations, as we have seen, use different methods of depreciation for tax purposes than they use for reporting to shareholders and because other factors, such as tax-loss carrybacks and carryforwards, which are not visible on the current year's statement, may affect the company's tax liability.

PROVISION FOR INCOME TAXES

After taking advantage of all available benefits, this is the company's tax liability for the year in question. Note that it is termed a *provision*. Payments based on estimated taxes have been made during the year, and net payments on this liability are payable according to a timetable determined by the Internal Revenue Service. A portion of the liability will be reflected as an accrued liability, as described above.

A company's effective tax rate should be compared with other companies in the same or similar industries. Although many tax loopholes have been ended by recent tax legislation, it may be a mark of smart and aggressive management if a company has a lower effective rate than other companies similarly engaged.

NET INCOME

This is the bottom line, the "after everything except dividends" figure. Dividends, by law, must be paid out of earnings, though not necessarily out of current earnings. Below the bottom line, figures for common shares outstanding and earnings per common share are given. Securities analysts usually focus on earnings per share in assessing a company's status. As a rule, earnings per share are expected to grow from year to year, and it may be a sign of trouble if they do not grow according to predictions or if they do not grow at all.

Consolidated Financial Statements—Part 3: The Statement of Retained Earnings (Shareholders' Equity): What typically follows the Income Statement is an analysis showing retained earnings at the beginning of the period; how net income increased retained earnings; dividends paid on preferred stock and common stock during the period; and the retained earnings account at the end of the fiscal year being reported (see Exhibit 4). The last figure will, of course, be the same as the retained earnings figure in the stockholders' equity section of the balance sheet.

A Statement of Retained Earnings may reflect stock dividends—new shares issued to existing shareholders. Stock dividends are accounted for by decreasing retained earnings and increasing common stock in equal amounts (using par or stated value if the stock dividend represents more than 20 to 25 percent of outstanding shares, and market value if it represents less). Many investors are attracted to companies that regularly declare stock dividends. It should be borne in mind, however, that stock dividends in no way enhance the actual assets of a company.

Statement of Consolidated Cash Flows: By requiring an analysis of changes affecting cash, the Financial Accounting Standards Board (FASB) was recognizing that the viability of a company hinges ultimately on liquidity and that increases in working capital do not necessarily translate into increased cash. For example, a company that relaxed its credit standards to generate increased sales might show higher profits and working capital from one year to another, but it would not be able to meet its obligations unless and until its accounts receivable were collected in cash. Cash means cash and equivalents, defined by the FASB as all highly liquid securities with a known market value and a maturity, when acquired, of less than 3 months.

The statement of cash flows puts operating results on a cash basis while showing balance sheet changes as they affect the cash account. (In order to provide a complete "bridge" between two balance sheets, the statement of cash flows will also show major balance sheet changes not affecting cash, such as an exchange of bonds for stock or the purchase of a fixed asset that is 100% financed by long-term debt.)

The FASB requires that cash flows be analyzed in three separate categories: cash flows from operating activities, cash flows from investing activities, and cash flows from financing activities. The most commonly used format is XYZ Corporation's, illustrated in Exhibit 5.

The operating analysis begins with the net income figure (from the income statement) and follows with the adjustments necessary to convert that figure to a cash basis.

Depreciation and amortization, as earlier discussed, are bookkeeping transactions that reduced the net income figure without any expenditure of cash; this item (found on the income statement) is thus added back to net income. The increase in the (balance sheet liability) account called deferred federal income taxes represents the portion of income tax expense not actually paid in cash and is similarly added back to net income.

Next are adjustments to assets and liabilities that changed because of operating activities and provided or used cash. The increase in the accounts and notes receivable is subtracted because it represents sales revenue included in net income but not collected in cash. The increase in inventories is also subtracted because it represents cash spent for inventory purchases in excess of the expense recognized through cost of goods sold. The increase in prepaid expenses is deducted because it represents cash spent but not charged against income. The decrease in XYZ's accounts payable between 2009 and 2008 is subtracted because the cash paid to vendors in 2009 was greater than the amount of expense recorded. (Cash was paid for some 2008 accounts.) Increases in accrued liabilities and federal income taxes payable were charged to income but not (yet) paid in cash and are thus added back. Other assets and liabilities were either net users (2009) or providers of cash.

(Note: Adjustments to particular asset and liability accounts will not always equal changes in balance sheet figures as they do in the case of XYZ Corporation. In the case of companies with foreign operations, operating assets and liabilities translated from other currencies have been purified of the effects of currency exchange and a separate line is provided to show the effect of exchange rate changes on cash and cash equivalents. Also, the effects of acquisitions, when accounted for by the PURCHASE ACQUISITION method, and divestitures have been excluded from the operating cash flow adjustments although they are reflected in the balance sheet accounts.)

Cash flows from investing activities include changes in the company's investments in property, plant, and equipment; investments in other companies; and loans made and collected. An increase in investment reduces cash and a decrease (sale) increases cash. It is notable that dividends and interest received are typically treated as operating cash flow, although changes in the same investments are analyzed here. In the case of XYZ, the only changes were those affecting fixed assets. XYZ's only other investments are in the securities comprising cash equivalents; since the whole cash flow statement focuses on cash and cash equivalents, it would be redundant to show those changes here. The small amount of income XYZ received on its cash equivalents is reflected in the net income figure above.

Cash flows from financing activities include all changes in cash resulting from financing, such as short- and long-term borrowings, the issuance or repurchase of common and preferred stock, dividends paid, and changes in dividends payable.

EXHIBIT 5

XYZ CORPORATION
Statement of Consolidated Cash Flow
Fiscal Year Ended December 31
(Dollars in Millions)

	2009	2008	2007
CASH FLOWS FROM OPERATING ACTIVITIES			
Net Income	10.1	8.8	8.5
Adjustments to reconcile net income to net cash provided by operating activities:			
Depreciation and amortization	2.2	3.0	2.0
Deferred income taxes	.2	.3	.2
Accounts receivable	(.7)	(.6)	(.8)
Inventories	(2.1)	(1.9)	(1.2)
Prepaid expenses	(.1)	—	(.1)
Accounts payable	(.1)	1.2	.7
Accrued liabilities	.5	.3	.3
Federal income taxes payable	1.1	.8	.6
Other assets and liabilities, net	(.2)	.5	.5
Net cash from operating activities	**10.9**	**12.4**	**10.7**
CASH FLOWS FROM INVESTING ACTIVITIES			
Additions: property, plant, equipment	(3.9)	(4.2)	(2.8)
Net cash used for investing activities	**(3.9)**	**(4.2)**	**(2.8)**
CASH FLOWS FROM FINANCING ACTIVITIES			
Net change in short-term debt	.7	—	—
Repayments of long-term debt	(.8)	(6.5)	(1.0)
Proceeds from sale of preferred stock		5.0	
Payments of dividends	(6.8)	(6.5)	(6.2)
Increase in dividends payable	.5	.3	—
Net cash used for financing activities	**(6.4)**	**(7.7)**	**(7.2)**
NET INCREASE IN CASH AND EQUIVALENTS	.6	.5	.7
Cash and equivalents, beginning of year	7.0	6.5	5.8
Cash and equivalents at end of year	7.6	7.0	6.5

To interpret the cash flow statement it is helpful to remember a basic rule of thumb: In a conservatively operated company, *permanent* capital requirements—fixed assets and the portion of working capital that is not seasonal—should be financed through a combination of retained earnings and either long-term debt or equity. *Short-term* requirements should be financed with short-term liabilities in a cycle that begins when accounts payable are created to purchase inventory, which in turn is sold to create accounts receivable, which are collected to produce cash, and so on.

Once that is understood, the statement can be a valuable analytical tool that reveals healthy or unhealthy trends; a company's capacity for future investment; its future cash requirements; its cash position compared to similar companies; and its actual cash flows versus those anticipated.

A look at Exhibit 5 tells us XYZ Corporation has been generating operating cash flows that generally support its steadily increasing sales. Cash flow from operations has been sufficient to finance annual additions and improvements to its plant and equipment and still pay dividends without impairing its working capital. The statement reveals that in 2008 the company, despite profitable operations, would have had a negative cash flow (more cash flowing out than in), after meeting $6.5 million of long-term debt repayments, had management not properly planned for the requirement by issuing $5 million of preferred stock.

Discontinued Operations: One final observation: Discontinued operations, although not a factor in XYZ's case, show up frequently as a separate section of the income statements of large companies. Readers are thus able to distinguish between operating results that can be expected to continue in the future and those that have only historical significance. Discontinued operations are those that have been sold, abandoned, or otherwise disposed of. Any gain or loss from the disposal of a segment must be shown along with the operating results of the discontinued segment.

In their statement of cash flows, however, companies are permitted but not required to separately disclose the flows from discontinued operations and extraordinary items. When companies voluntarily make the separation, they indicate clearly that the analysis of net income and adjustments relates to continuing operations and includes a separate line for net cash provided (or used) by discontinued operations. But when discontinued operations that show up in the income statement are not broken out in the statement of cash flows, it is up to the reader to ascertain if a significant portion of the flows relate to operations that are not ongoing.

Notes to Financial Statements: Footnotes to financial statements, sometimes just called notes, are unfortunately named if there's any implication that they represent superfluous detail. Indeed, the balance sheet, the income statement, and the statement of cash flows contain the sentence: "The Notes to Financial Statements are an integral part of this statement." Footnotes set forth the accounting policies of the business—and provide additional disclosure. They contain information having profound significance for the financial values presented elsewhere in the financial statements.

It would be impossible to list here all the types of information one might find in the notes to financial statements. Here is a sampling, though, and if it succeeds in impressing you with the importance of reading this section of a financial report, it will have accomplished its purpose.

Accounting procedure changes   Changes in methods of valuing inventory or depreciating fixed assets significantly affect reported earnings and asset values. Frequent changes in methodology have always been a red flag possibly signaling that a company is hiding operational weaknesses.

Since the passage of Sarbanes-Oxley, accounting rules have been adopted that have caused many companies to change procedures and to reflect the application of such changes to prior years.

For example, in December 2004, the Financial Accounting Standards Board adopted a revised standard requiring companies to record share-based payment transactions as compensation expense at fair market value. Previously, companies had in effect been inflating earnings by rewarding executives with stock options, a form of compensation that would have major impact on future earnings when the options were exercised, but that were not booked as an expense at the time they were awarded. The revised rule, which requires companies to recognize annual expense based on an estimate of option values, results in a more realistic annual earnings figure.

Pension and postretirement benefits In rising securities markets, some companies have used overfunded pension plans to generate cash windfalls, but the reverse also occurs: Some are underfunded, so that the company may be faced with the prospect of cash burdens later on. Pension funding is, at best, an inexact science. Estimates based on a variety of actuarial, personnel, and financial assumptions determine the amount of annual expense required to cover future benefits earned by each year's additional service. Not only are these estimates subject to error, but management has used its discretion over the rate at which pension liabilities are funded to smooth out reported earnings by underfunding in poor years and overfunding in good years. Patterns of underfunding or overfunding can portend future deficiency or surplus, even when estimates are accurate. A liability account termed Unfunded Projected Benefit Obligation is another red flag, in this case meaning that the current return on pension fund investments is inadequate to cover projected future benefit payments.

Closely related are Postemployment Benefits Other than Pensions, consisting mainly of health care benefits payable to employees after retirement and before their eligibility for government benefits such as Medicare and Medicaid. The FASB now requires that if funding is elected, companies fund the present value of estimated future benefits earned by employees. Funding forces an estimate of future liability. It should be noted, however, that whereas with pensions, an additional liability has to be recognized if the accumulated benefit obligation is greater than the fair value of the plan assets, no such additional liability is required for postretirement benefits other than pensions.

Long-term debt Detail on debt maturities makes it possible to anticipate refinancing needs, which have implications for investors in terms of the effect of interest costs on profits or potential dilution of common share values. A company's ability to manage its debt structure so as to obtain money at the lowest rate for the longest maturity is viewed by analysts as demonstrating that the company has a capable management team.

Look here (and also in footnotes concerning preferred stock) for information about antitakeover provisions, or "poison pills." The recent wave of hostile takeovers, usually taking the form of leveraged buyouts, has caused many companies to adopt provisions in their indentures or preferred stock agreements designed to make takeovers prohibitively expensive for acquirers or to protect existing holders from the adverse effects of additional debt or liquidation of assets. A common variety is the "poison put," a provision giving bondholders the right to redeem their bonds at par value in the event of a hostile takeover, thus creating an onerous cash requirement for the acquirer. Although generally designed to protect existing investors from unfavorable events, poison pill provisions can have major implications for a company's finances, and it is important to understand them.

Treasury stock By buying their own shares in the market, companies decrease shares outstanding and thus increase earnings per share for existing stockholders. The existence of an active stock purchase program can be viewed as a two-edged sword. On the one hand, such a program provides in effect a support price for the company's shares as well as a buyer with deep pockets—the company itself. On the other hand, a stock purchase program is frequently used as a defense against a hostile takeover attempt and raises the question whether repurchase of stock is the best way to use assets of the company.

Taxes The prospect of an assessment for a prior year's taxes may be disclosed in the footnotes. Of particular significance is any footnote disclosing that a company's tax returns are being audited or that any of the assumptions utilized by the company in determining the taxable basis of its assets are being questioned by the Internal Revenue Service.

Leases One of the most significant of the off-balance sheet liabilities is the long-term noncapital lease. A footnote dealing with a long-term lease should be reviewed carefully.

Financial assets With computerization and internationalization have come sophisticated derivative instruments—contracts whose value is related to the value of underlying financial assets, including various financial instruments and securities. They come in different forms, including exotica such as interest rate swaps and caps, collateralized mortgage obligations, and financial futures and forward contracts. Some, having the effect of financial guarantees or loan commitments, may be, like the operating leases discussed above, off-balance sheet. Companies use financial assets for a variety of purposes, including financing, hedging, and investment.

The analytical challenge they present is that they are always complex and sometimes speculative, raising questions about unjustifiable deferral of losses, premature recognition of gains, and inadequate disclosure about risks.

SFAS (Statement of Financial Accounting Standard) No. 105 requires that financial statements provide significant information relating to all financial instruments with or without off-balance sheet risk. SFAS No. 107 requires disclosure about fair value of all financial instruments, assets, and liabilities both on and off the balance sheet.

Supplementary Tables: The principal supplementary tables are the following.

SEGMENT REPORTING

The FASB requires companies meeting certain criteria having to do with product and geographical diversification to present certain information in segment form—that is, by product or industry category or markets serviced and by geographical territory. Although this can be done in the body of the financial statement, with supporting footnotes, or in the footnotes section itself, most companies do it in a separate schedule that is an integral part of the financial statements. The information required, which covers the same three-year period as the income statement, includes sales or revenues; operating profit or loss; the book value of identifiable assets; aggregate depreciation, depletion, or amortization; and capital expenditures.

These breakdowns enable shareholders to evaluate a company's exposure to the vagaries of various geographical markets, including political and other risks to a company that has foreign operations. For industry or product-line segments, a stockholder is able to evaluate the company's activities in particular areas in terms of the amount of its investment and the return it is realizing on the investment, as well as the year-to-year trends.

FINANCIAL REPORTING AND CHANGING PRICES

Another ruling of the FASB is aimed at accounting for the effect of inflation or deflation on the inventory, fixed assets, and the income statement values for cost of goods sold and depreciation as they are related to those assets. Thus, companies are encouraged to present the historical figures showing the effects of declines in the purchasing power of the dollar in contrast to the primary values as shown in the financial statements, based on historical cost.

FIVE-YEAR SUMMARY OF OPERATIONS

This required schedule essentially extends the three-year income statement to five years, including preferred and common stock dividend history. It is a useful supplement in terms of permitting analysis of operating trends, and a number of corporations have taken it upon themselves to provide summaries of the last ten years of operations.

TWO-YEAR QUARTERLY DATA

This schedule provides a quarterly breakdown of sales, net income, the high and low stock price, and the common dividend. The operating data is most valuable when a company's operations are subject to seasonal factors, as, for example, a retailer is subject to heavy demand during the Christmas season. The market price and dividend data reveal stock price volatility and the regularity with which the company has made dividend payments.

Management's Discussion and Analysis: *Management's Discussion and Analysis of the Financial Condition and Results of Operations* is a narrative presentation required and monitored by the Securities and Exchange Commission to present management's candid comments on three key areas of a company's business: results of operations, capital resources, and liquidity. Companies are required to address all material developments affecting these three key areas, favorable or unfavorable, including the effects of inflation. In discussing results of operations, companies are required not only to detail operating and unusual events that affected results for the period under discussion, but also any trends or uncertainties that might affect results in the future. The capital resources part involves questions of fixed asset expenditures and considerations of whether it benefits shareholders more to finance such outlays with stock, bonds, or through lease arrangements. Addressing liquidity means discussing anything that affects net working capital, such as the convertibility into cash of accounts receivable or inventory and the availability of bank lines of credit.

When it made this section a requirement, the SEC sought to elicit, in a company's own words, an interpretation of the significance of past and future financial developments.

Investor's Information

This section of the annual report lists the name of the transfer agent, registrar, and trustees; the exchanges on which the company's securities are traded; the date, time, and place of the annual meeting; and a notice as to when proxy materials will be made available to shareholders of record. If the company has an automatic dividend reinvestment plan, the terms and procedures for participating are stated here.

The number of common shareholders (and preferred, if any) as of the fiscal year-end is also usually indicated in this section.

This section may also invite requests for Form 10-K, the annual Securities and Exchange Commission filing corporations are required to make available to shareholders. The 10-K is filed within 90 days of a company's fiscal year-end. It is a thick, drab report containing a mass of detail. Much of what it contains is in the annual report to shareholders or is incorporated by reference to the public annual report, but other information is unique to the 10-K. Such unique information includes historical background; names of principal security holders; security holdings of management; more detailed financial schedules; information about products or services, properties, markets, distribution systems, backlogs, and competitive factors; detail about patents, licenses, or franchises; number of employees; environmental and other regulatory compliances; information concerning amounts paid directors and their share holdings; and background, including employment history, of executives and their relationships to the firm.

Form 10-Q is a shorter, unaudited, update of the 10-K. It must be filed within 45 days of the end of a company's first, second, and third fiscal quarters and be certified by the chief executive officer and chief financial officer. It is mainly useful as a source of information about changes in the status of securities outstanding, compliance with debt agreements, and information on matters to be voted on by shareholders, such as the election of directors.

Major corporations commonly provide a variety of financial information, product and company news through the Internet. A home page address is usually found in the Investor's Information section of the annual report.

Directors and Officers

The names of members of the board of directors and their affiliations are listed here as are the names and titles of senior executives. Also usually indicated is the membership of board members on various committees, such as the executive committee, the finance committee, the compensation committee, the committee on corporate responsibility, the research and development committee, and the audit committee. Corporations vary in terms of the use to which they put the backgrounds of their directors—in some cases the role of directors is ceremonial, in others directors are used to advantage—and this section can sometimes provide meaningful insight. The absence of directors unaffiliated with management may indicate a company dominated by senior officers and not responsive to the concerns of outside shareholders. Senior management can also become more entrenched in companies that stagger the terms of directors to help prevent a hostile takeover.

* * *

RATIO ANALYSIS SUMMARY

Ratios are the principal tools of financial statement analysis. By definition, however, ratios indicate relationships, and by excluding considerations such as dollar amounts and the overall size of a company, their meaning in and of themselves can be limited if not misleading. Ratios have their greatest significance when used to make year-to-year comparisons for the purpose of determining trends or when used in comparison with industry data. Composite ratios for different industries are published by Standard & Poor's Corporation, Dun & Bradstreet, Robert Morris Associates, and the Federal Trade Commission. The following is a summary of key ratios and what they signify. Each ratio is computed for XYZ Corporation, whose hypothetical financial statements are shown in the discussion above of the annual report.

Ratios That Measure Liquidity

Ratio	Calculation	XYZ Computation
Current ratio	$\dfrac{\text{Current assets}}{\text{Current liabilities}}$	$\dfrac{41.1}{18.5} = 2.22$

The current ratio measures the extent to which the claims of a firm's short-term creditors are covered by assets expected to be convened to cash within the same short-term period. In XYZ's industry, the standard is 1.9, so its 2.2 ratio indicates comfortable liquidity, although down slightly from last year's ratio of 2.4. In a recession, extra liquidity protection could make a vital difference; slack consumer demand would mean that XYZ's wholesale customers would have lower sales. That would mean less sales and lower inventory turnover for XYZ. As XYZ's customers became tighter for cash and slower paying, or went out of business, XYZ's accounts receivable would become less collectible. Ultimately that could mean insolvency. Hence the importance of this key measure of short-term solvency. Of course, in other types of companies, the current ratio would have less significance. A company whose sales were largely under United States government contracts would have less receivables and inventory risk, for example, and could thus afford a lower current ratio.

Quick ratio	$\dfrac{\text{Current assets-inventory}}{\text{Current liabilities}}$	$\dfrac{41.1 - 23.0}{18.5} = .97$

A refinement of the current ratio, the quick or acid-test ratio answers the question: If sales stopped, could the company meet its current obligations with the readily convertible assets on hand? XYZ has a quick ratio of .97, almost a dollar of quick assets for each dollar of current liabilities, and virtually in line with the industry standard of 1.0. Last year it was slightly better, 1.04 times, but that small a year-to-year difference is probably not enough to signify a negative trend.

Ratios That Measure Activity

Ratio	Calculation	XYZ Computation
Inventory turnover	$\dfrac{\text{Net Sales}}{\text{Inventory}}$	$\dfrac{98.4}{23.0} = 4.3$ times

This tells us the number of times inventory is sold in the course of the year. As a general rule, high turnover means efficient inventory management and more marketable inventory with a lower risk of illiquidity. But it could also be a reflection on pricing policies or could reflect shortages and an inability to meet new orders. XYZ's turnover ratio is 4.3 times, down slightly from the prior year's 4.5 times, and the industry standard is 6.7 times. This should be looked into.

Average collection period	$\dfrac{\text{Accounts receivable}}{\text{Annual credit sales/360 days}}$	$\dfrac{10.2}{.270} = 37$ days

Assuming a company's terms of sale are standard for its industry, the average collection period—which tells if customers are paying bills on time—can be a reflection on credit policy (a liberal policy, involving relaxed credit standards to generate higher sales volume, will usually result in a longer average collection period); on the diligence of a firm's collection effort; on the attractiveness of discounts offered for prompt payment; or on general economic conditions as they affect the finances of the firm's customers. XYZ's collection period was 38 days this year and 37 days last year compared with an industry average of 37 days. It thus enjoys typical collections, apparently reflecting a sound and competitive credit policy. Of course, there could be potential problems not revealed by this test; for example, a concentration of accounts receivable in one industry or with a few customers, which, if affected by adversity, would have a disproportionate effect on the total receivables portfolio. Footnotes to the financial statements will often contain information concerning the composition of accounts receivable and their age relative to the invoice date.

Fixed assets turnover	$\dfrac{\text{Net sales}}{\text{Net fixed assets}}$	$\dfrac{98.4}{59.8} = 1.6$ times

Measured over time and against competitors, this ratio indicates how efficiently a firm is using its property, plant and equipment—its "plant capacity." Increases in fixed assets should produce increases in sales, although the investment will normally lag the sales effect. If, given time, sales fail to increase in relation to plant capacity, it usually reflects poor marketing strategy. XYZ's ratio is low by industry standards. It has recently added to its capacity and has plans to pursue a more aggressive policy aimed at higher sales and increased market share.

Total assets turnover	$\dfrac{\text{Net sales}}{\text{Total assets}}$	$\dfrac{98.4}{105.6} = .93 \text{ times}$

This ratio measures the amount of sales volume the company is generating on its investment in assets and is thus an indication of the efficiency with which assets are utilized. The relationship between sales and assets is sometimes called operating leverage, since any sales increases that can be generated from the same amount of assets increase profits and return on equity and vice versa. XYZ's turnover of .93, virtually unchanged from the prior year, is considerably under the industry standard of 2.1 meaning XYZ had better increase sales or dispose of some assets. As we observed above, however, it has plans to increase sales and recently added fixed assets in preparation.

Ratios That Measure Profitability

Ratio	Calculation	XYZ Computation
Operating profit margin	$\dfrac{\text{Net operating profit}}{\text{Net sales}}$	$\dfrac{19.2}{98.4} = 19.5\%$

This ratio is the key to measuring a firm's operating efficiency. It is a reflection on management's purchasing and pricing policies and its success in controlling costs and expenses directly associated with the running of the business and the creation of sales, excluding other income and expenses, interest, and taxes. (Some analysts exclude depreciation from this ratio, but we include it here for the sake of comparability.) XYZ's operating profit margin has been quite consistent over the past three years and is somewhat higher than industry averages. That could mean it is in for some competition or that it is exceptionally good at controlling costs. To zero in on the reasons for XYZ's better-than-average performance, relate cost of goods sold to sales and selling, general, and administrative expenses to sales. The explanation may lie in pricing policy or somewhere in the area of selling, general, and administrative expenses.

Net profit margin	$\dfrac{\text{Net income}}{\text{Net sales}}$	$\dfrac{10.1}{98.4} = 10.3\%$

This measures management's overall efficiency—its success not only in managing operations but in terms of borrowing money at a favorable rate, investing idle cash to produce extra income, and taking advantage of tax benefits. XYZ's ratio of 10.3% compares favorably with industry standards. A company in a field where the emphasis was on high volume—a supermarket, for instance—might show a net profit margin of much less—2% for example.

Return on equity	$\dfrac{\text{Net income}}{\text{Total stockholders' equity}}$	$\dfrac{10.1}{68.0} = 15\%$

This ratio measures the overall return on stockholders' equity. It is the bottom line measured against the money shareholders have invested. XYZ's 15% return is above average for the industry, which is good for shareholders as long as it doesn't invite competition.

Ratios That Measure Capitalization (Leverage)

Ratio	Calculation	XYZ Computation
Debt to total assets	$\dfrac{\text{Total liabilities}}{\text{Total assets}}$	$\dfrac{37.6}{105.6} = 36\%$

This measures the proportion of assets financed with debt as opposed to equity. Creditors, such as bankers, prefer that this ratio be low, since it means a greater cushion in the event of liquidation. Owners, on the other hand, may seek higher leverage in order to magnify earnings or may prefer to finance the company's activities through debt rather than yield control. XYZ's ratio is about average for its industry.

Ratio	Calculation	XYZ Computation
Long-term debt to total capitalization	$$\dfrac{\text{Long-term debt}}{\text{Long-term debt} + \text{stockholders' equity}}$$	$$\dfrac{16.2}{68.0} = 24\%$$

This ratio tells us the proportion of permanent financing that is represented by long-term debt versus equity. XYZ's ratio of 24% (24% of its permanent capital is debt) is low by industry standards, suggesting it might consider increasing its leverage—that is, financing its future growth through bonds rather than stock.

Debt to equity (debt ratio)	$$\dfrac{\text{Total liabilities}}{\text{Total stockholders' equity}}$$	$$\dfrac{37.6}{68.0} = 55\%$$

This is the basic ratio. It measures the reliance on creditors—short and long term— to finance total assets and becomes critical in the event of liquidation, when the proceeds from the sale of assets go to creditors before owners. Since assets tend to shrink in liquidation, the lower this ratio the more secure owners can feel. Also, a high debt ratio makes it more difficult to borrow should the need arise. XYZ's debt ratio of 55% is very conservative, and is another indication that its shareholders could safely benefit from greater leverage.

Times interest earned	$$\dfrac{\text{Earnings before taxes and interest charges}}{\text{Interest charges}}$$	$$\dfrac{19.4}{1.0} = 19 \text{ times}$$

This ratio measures the number of times fixed interest charges are covered by earnings. Since failure to meet interest payments would be an event of default under the terms of most debenture agreements, this coverage ratio indicates a margin of safety. Put another way, it indicates the extent to which earnings could shrink—in a recession, for example—before the firm became unable to meet its contractual interest charges. XYZ earns 19 times its annual interest payments, which is substantially more than is normally considered conservative. It is another indication that XYZ should consider increasing its leverage.

Fixed charge coverage	$$\dfrac{\text{Earnings before taxes and interest charges}}{\text{Interest charges} + \text{lease payments}}$$	$$\dfrac{19.4}{1.0} = 19 \text{ times}$$

This is the times interest earned ratio expanded to include other fixed charges, notably annual lease payments. XYZ has no lease obligations, so the ratio is the same. It is important to note, however, that the extent of this coverage should be sufficient to ensure that a company can meet its fixed contractual obligations in bad times as well as good times.

Ratios That Measure Stock Values

Ratio	Calculation	XYZ Computation
Price-earnings ratio	$\dfrac{\text{Market price of common share}}{\text{Earnings per common share}}$	$\dfrac{63.00}{6.30} = 10 \text{ times}$

This ratio reflects the value the marketplace puts on a company's earnings and the prospect of future earnings. It is important to shareholders because it represents the value of their holdings, and it is also important from the corporate standpoint in that it is an indication of the firm's cost of capital—the price it could expect to receive if it were to issue new shares. XYZ's multiple of ten times earnings is about average for an established company.

Ratio	Calculation	XYZ Computation
Market-to-book ratio	$\dfrac{\text{Market price of common share}}{\begin{array}{c}\text{Book value per share (total}\\\text{assets} - \text{intangible assets}\\- \text{total liabilities and preferred}\\\text{stock common shares outstanding)}\end{array}}$	$\dfrac{63.00}{40.00} = 1.58 \text{ times}$

This indicates the value the market places on a firm's expected earnings—its value as a going concern—in relation to the value of its shares if the company were to be liquidated and the proceeds from the sale of assets, after creditor claims were satisfied, were paid to shareholders. XYZ's common shares have a market value that is half again as much as their value in liquidation, assuming its assets could be liquidated at book value.

Ratio	Calculation	XYZ Computation
Dividend payout ratio	$\dfrac{\text{Dividends per common share}}{\text{Earnings per common share}}$	$\dfrac{4.20}{6.30} = 67\%$

This ratio indicates the percentage of common share earnings that are paid out in dividends. As a general rule, young, growing companies tend to reinvest their earnings to finance expansion and thus have low dividend payout ratios or ratios of zero. XYZ's ratio of 67% is higher than most established companies show.

HOW TO READ A QUARTERLY REPORT

In addition to annual reports, publicly held companies issue interim reports usually on a quarterly basis, which update shareholders about sales and earnings and report any material changes in the company's affairs. Companies are also required to file quarterly information, certified by the chief executive and financial officers, with the Securities and Exchange Commission on Form 10-Q within 45 days of the end of the first, second, and third fiscal quarters. These reports, which contain unaudited financial information and news of changes in securities outstanding, compliance with debt agreements, and matters to be voted on by shareholders, may be available from companies directly; at SEC libraries in Atlanta, Boston, Chicago, Denver, Fort Worth, Los Angeles, New York, Seattle, and the District of Columbia; through firms that provide all SEC filings (and that advertise in the financial sections of newspapers), or on the Internet, at EDGAR (*www.freeedgar.com*), the financial database of SEC filings.

Quarterly shareholder reports vary in comprehensiveness. Some reports provide complete, though usually unaudited, financial statements, but most simply contain summarized updates of the operating highlights of the annual report. Accounting regulations require that companies give at least the following information.

- Sales (or revenues)
- Net income (before and after potential dilution, if pertinent)
- Provision for federal income taxes
- Nonrecurring items of income or expense, with tax implications
- Significant acquisitions or disposals of business segments
- Material contingencies, such as pending lawsuits
- Accounting changes
- Significant changes in financial position, including working capital and capital structure

Accounting regulations require that figures be presented either for the quarter in question or cumulatively for the year-to-date, but prior year data must be included on a comparative basis. That requirement is designed to deal with seasonal factors. For example, the quarterly results of a department store, to cite an industry with marked seasonality (sales bulge at Christmastime), would be meaningless unless compared with the same quarter of the prior year.

The main thing to remember about quarterly reports is that they are designed to update existing shareholders, not to provide prospective shareholders with an overall perspective on the company. They should be read in conjunction with the annual report.

PART III

Understanding the Financial News

How to Read Ticker Tapes

UNDERSTANDING THE
FINANCIAL NEWS

Making sense of financial news has been compared to drinking from a fire hose, and that metaphor has never been more apt. As in so many areas of communication, the Internet, now accessible ubiquitously from hand-held smart phones, has been a game changer in the way most people get their financial news.

Unlike print media, online publishers provide free-of-charge real-time (or slightly-delayed, usually 15 minutes) coverage with no space constraints. This enables them to provide a more diverse population of users with greatly expanded quantities of data.

Of course, that means there's a lot more data to sort out, and what doesn't pertain to your own finances can become a bothersome distraction. It would be confusing enough if all the news and numbers weren't changing from minute to minute as they are when the markets are open.

There is also the question of how much knowledge the reader brings to the task. Newspapers and magazines aim at an average level of financial sophistication. Websites just put it all out there, although they make a largely successful effort to clarify and educate with built-in glossaries and tutorials.

In previous editions of the Handbook, we have used the print version of *The Wall Street Journal's Money and Investing* section to show how its top-flight editors distill the previous day's financial news and market data in a few pages. The *Journal* remains the gold standard of financial journalism and as other major newspapers, notably *The New York Times,* have reduced their financial sections to highlights and have referred readers to online editions, the print edition of the *Journal,* which also has an online counterpart for subscribers, is still going strong. If you wouldn't be found dead carrying a newspaper, your state-of-the-art i-Pad has an "app" containing the print edition of *The Wall Street Journal.* A pass or two of your index finger and you have the best of both worlds.

In this edition of the Handbook we will focus mainly on financial websites, the most heavily trafficked of which are *www.bloomberg.com; www.CNBC. com; www.CNNMoney.com; www.MSNMoney.com;* and *www.Yahoo!Finance. com.* The model of a news "package," which we have used in the past to illustrate how print editors prioritize news for consumption, serves us here as well, although electronic media have different opportunities and limitations. Websites offer more detail, but instead of a linear flow from the general to the specific, they have a home screen that provides an overview and displays key words that you click on to bring up other screens containing progressive degrees of elaboration and detail.

The end result is essentially the same, however. Whether the medium is print or electronic, financial publishers have three basic goals: (1) To pack as much news as possible into a given space or, in the case of a website, a human attention span; (2) To attract as many readers/users as possible; and (3) To allow busy people to obtain a quick overview and/or easily find whatever specific information they are seeking. These aims are accomplished by way of a news package, and if we understand how the packaging is done, we can unwrap it to suit ourselves.

THE FINANCIAL NEWS PACKAGE

The home screen of a financial website, like the front page of a newspaper's financial section, is aimed at the broadest audience: the consumer, the investor, the civic minded, the curious—all of us, in one way or another.

As you move deeper inside, the information becomes more detailed. Market indicators relate to a broader range of asset classes, and news reports dig well beneath the headlines. The deepest level of the package focuses on specific data, such as a company's share price or bond yield, earnings information, key ratios, and research reports on issuers of securities. Newspapers present this in tabular form. With websites, you enter a symbol and the company information comes up.

The Home Screen or Front Page

This is the outside of the news package. It contains statistical highlights along with headlines or summaries of the developments comprising the current news background. It sets a tone and provides a context within which statistical highlights relate to each other and the relevance of deeper levels of information becomes clear. The news leads are usually drawn from one or more of the following story categories:

The Economics Story

The fact that a general economics story often appears on the outside of the package is a comment on the inseparability of economics and life in general. It also reflects the fact that government economic data is scheduled for release well in advance, giving editors and reporters time to reserve space, pull out charts for updating, and line up experts to offer commentary. A monthly cycle of major statistics often starts with the release of data on construction spending and the employment situation (the latter generally is released on the first Friday of the month) and continues with statistics on chain-store sales, crop production, consumer installment credit, industrial production, capacity utilization, housing starts and building permits, producer (wholesale) prices, personal income and outlays, consumer prices, average hourly wages, savings flows, and other matters. The month often ends with a report on the indexes of leading, coincident, and lagging economic indicators. Most of the statistics refer to the previous month, some to two months before. Motor vehicle manufacturers report on sales every ten days.

Important statistics are also released on a quarterly basis. These statistics include information on U.S. import and export prices, corporate profits, and of particular significance—the gross domestic product (GDP). The GDP (especially its inflation-adjusted version, constant dollar or real GDP) is a measure of the total value of goods and services produced by the United States economy. Of key interest is how the seasonally adjusted annual growth rate of the GDP in a particular quarter compares to the previous quarter and to the same quarter in the previous year. Trends in the GDP are our primary measures of whether the U.S. economy is strong or weak, growing or in recession.

For investment purposes, watch for basic themes in overall stories on the economy. Favorable economic signals bode well for corporate profits, and therefore usually for stock prices, and unfavorable signals can have the opposite effect. A weakening economy can lift bond prices, however, because economic slackness means weaker demand for credit and thus lower rates for new loans. Because bond prices and interest rates move inversely, this translates into higher prices for existing bonds and notes. But one monthly figure doesn't make a trend, and other factors, including speculation about Federal Reserve

Board monetary policy, also affect securities prices. In any event, between the time economic data is released and its appearance in newspapers, there has been ample opportunity for financial markets to react—to "discount the news," as they say on Wall Street. Most stock markets remained open until 4 P.M. EST the day before (the Pacific Stock Exchange closes 30 minutes later) while the bond market, which is mainly located in brokerage house trading rooms, has no official closing. Thus, the opportunity to react effectively to an economic event may have passed by the time you read of it in the newspaper.

The International Story

Just how global the financial markets have become was demonstrated in the financial crisis of 2008. When the big housing bubble burst in the United States, banks, investment banks, institutional investors, and other players holding highly inflated real estate loans and investments, discovered their mortgage paper or derivatives thereof had suddenly become "toxic." With their capital severely constricted or eliminated, banks couldn't lend, investors facing margin calls were forced to liquidate assets at substantial loss, and a credit freeze resulted that quickly spread internationally. The commercial paper market, a source of life blood in day-to-day American commerce, dried up. One prominent money market mutual fund, holding commercial paper investments in its portfolio, was forced to "break the buck," meaning it couldn't redeem the $1 net asset value per share that is a constant upon which confidence in money market funds depends. In that case, the FDIC came to the rescue, putting the U.S. government's guarantee behind an investment tantamount to a bank account for a large part of the population. Where institutions were deemed to represent systemic risk by being "too big to fail," the U.S. government and Federal Reserve stepped up with taxpayer bailout money. That, along with other emergency measures, precluded a total economic collapse, but the bankruptcy of Lehman Brothers in 2008 certainly created something akin to an international nervous breakdown with signs of recovery still fragile as this is written. The U.S. economy and its trading partners were plunged into deep recession while their debt, already excessive in most cases, mounted, raising concern that future collapses would create greater havoc.

Bearing out a popular cliché, America sneezed and the world got a cold. Foreign securities markets swooned to levels even lower than American markets and in countries having stronger economic fundamentals than America. Dollar-traded commodities like gold and oil became extremely volatile as highly leveraged funds and institutions sold their most liquid assets to meet margin calls and other investors holding foreign stocks liquidated portfolios and rushed into dollars, which they perceived to be a temporary safe haven until the economic storm passed.

That the cold didn't turn into global pneumonia as the cliché implied, however, seemed to assure that foreign investing as a way of diversifying domestic portfolios was a trend that, having been well underway before the crisis, would resume. Foreign markets in developed countries having fundamentally strong economies that were producing and exporting goods actually recovered more quickly than U.S. markets. Markets here at home continued to behave erratically, reflecting an economy that after 20 years of debt-financed consumer spending was brought to its knees, yet was now creating massive new debt to stimulate more consumer spending. The Federal Reserve was printing more and more money to finance bailouts of banks, investment banks, automobile manufacturers, and government-related entities like Fannie Mae and Freddie Mac, in the process laying the groundwork for future high inflation. With the U.S. dollar in a declining long-term trend, investment by Americans in foreign stocks denominated in currencies gaining value relative to the dollar has been growing. Giving impetus has been a proliferation of exchange-traded funds (ETFs), which facilitate investing selectively in prospering sectors and subsectors of both developed and emerging foreign economies.

With the weakness in the American economy and in the Eurozone, and with the BRIC countries (Brazil, Russia, India, and China) in the early stages of industrial revolutions promising unprecedented market opportunity for emerging economies everywhere, globalization is an established reality. It guarantees that the international perspective will be an integral part of the financial news picture.

The Stock Market Story

Although broader-based and more scientifically weighted indexes exist, the Dow Jones Industrial Average, which tracks 30 blue chip stocks, continues to be the most widely watched barometer and almost invariably is featured in the stock market story. A good roundup should give you the widest possible exploration of factors—the effect of other markets (bonds, commodities, currencies, and to an increased extent, stock options and financial futures), corporate earnings, takeover bids and merger rumors, stock repurchase announcements, hedge fund activities, economic developments both domestic and foreign, and changing market forecasts. The article should differentiate between different groups of stocks and different markets. The New York Stock Exchange (NYSE) activity often reflects buying and selling by institutional investors while the NYSE Amex Equities (formerly the American Stock Exchange) has a greater concentration of smaller capitalization and younger companies, foreign stocks, and exchange-traded funds. The NASDAQ is an electronic exchange—as opposed to the brick and mortar (sometimes anachronistically termed "organized") exchanges—and the world's largest exchange company. It lists some 3,500 actively traded companies and exchange-traded funds in what has traditionally been called the over-the-counter market, a term still in use but primarily used these days for less actively traded off-exchange issues. It has traditionally comprised growth stocks of young domestic companies often in high technology and foreign issues, but has exceptions like Microsoft and Intel and encourages trades in NYSE and NYSE Amex issues.

Market volatility has been intensified by program trading, the computer-driven buying and selling by institutional traders and HEDGE FUND arbitrage specialists of all stocks in a "basket" or index. Some forms of program trading, particularly index arbitrage, also involve index options, index futures, and stock options, all of which expire together on the third Fridays of March, June, September, and December. Although measures have been instituted to process this extra activity with minimum disruption, expiration dates still cause a surge of trading, and the market closing on those Fridays is known on Wall Street as "the triple witching hour." A complete stock market story will usually include predictions by analysts who engage either in fundamental analysis, which focuses on business conditions and the financial strength of companies, or technical analysis, which concentrates on the conditions of the stock market, such as the supply and demand for shares and the emotional cycles of investors. Technical analysts, including those called chartists, who analyze historical market patterns, are usually more willing than fundamentalists to predict near-term market movements for financial news stories.

The Interest Rate/Bond Market Story

As market interest rates move up or down, the prices of fixed income securities move in the opposite direction to adjust yields to market levels. Yield determines price, and vice versa. Thus, the daily bond market story is essentially an interest rate story. Major daily newspapers always reserve inside space for this story and move it to the outside of the financial package when warranted by major developments. The event could be a big move in bond values, a new prediction by a widely followed interest-rate forecaster, Congressional testimony or other action by the Federal Reserve Board (especially its chairman), or policy changes by foreign central banks. The bigger the development, the more attention will be focused on its significance to consumers—the prospect of higher or lower mortgage and personal borrowing costs, for instance. A complete story will also explain the significance of such news to investors and include comments by analysts and economists. The Federal Reserve's weekly report on the money supply (usually released on Thursday) provides much of the grist for late-week interest rate stories. If the money supply grows faster than the Federal Reserve had planned, the Fed may be tempted to adopt a restrictive monetary policy. That is, the Federal Reserve may reduce the amount of money in the economy to prevent a rise in inflation. Tighter money means higher interest rates, at least on short-term loans and securities, which usually exerts downward pressure on stock and bond prices. If the Fed thinks the money supply is growing too slowly, especially during an economic slowdown, the Fed could be expected to try to ease monetary policy and stimulate money growth. This often leads to lower interest rates and higher prices for fixed income securities, as well as to optimism and higher prices in the stock markets.

The Commodities Story

The roller coaster action in the prices of oil, gold, and silver in recent years helped make activity in the commodities markets a more frequent front-of-the-package story. When the commodities story gets front-page treatment, the consumer implications—for example, the effects on retail prices of gasoline or orange juice—will usually receive most attention. But there will also be economic and market forecasts and comments by professional analysts and traders, designed to inform investors about commodities futures or futures options contracts. Typical questions answered include: How fast has the price of the commodity futures contract reversed direction in the past? Are there new sources of supply that could affect prices—for example, soybeans from Brazil to replace those from Kansas, or beef from Argentina to replace meat from Texas? Is anything happening that could limit supply? What is the outlook for a political development causing activity in precious metals contracts?

The Takeover or Merger Story

Major takeover bids (called public tender offers) or merger announcements make big news partly because they have important implications for the securities prices of the companies involved. In a takeover or merger story look for (1) the price, total and per share, that's being offered for the target company. Also look at the form of payment cash, securities, or a combination—and how it's being raised. A leveraged buyout, for instance, can sometimes leave the acquired company laden with debt. (2) The reasons for the merger—to combine businesses for greater financial or marketing strength; to avoid an unfriendly takeover; to bail out a troubled corporation, for example. An unfriendly or hostile tender offer could trigger a bidding war which would drive up the price of the target company's stock or prompt legal action. Also, a large-scale takeover or merger runs the risk of antitrust action by the federal government in addition to other impediments. When takeover plans are set back or collapse, the price of the target's stock will most likely drop. (3) Comments by analysts on the acquirer's motives and management skills. A bid substantially above market could mean shares are undervalued or that the acquirer has exciting plans; particularly with reduced float, it might be wiser to hold than tender.

A complete takeover or merger story will also uncover what the risk arbitragers—professional traders who speculate in merger situations—are doing. Heavy buying of the stock of the takeover target combined with short selling of the shares of the acquirer, usually means the professionals think the takeover will succeed.

The Company Story

Sometimes company stories are the result of breaking news—a profit report, a takeover attempt, a new product—and sometimes they are features that have been planned, and even written, well in advance of publication. Newspapers often carry a company stock story as part of their regular stock market coverage or because it is an important company to the newspaper's readership (it has a plant in town, for instance). Because stories on publicly owned companies can influence market values, there are laws to prevent capitalizing on advance knowledge of their content.

Among the things that you, as an investor or potential investor in a company, want to learn are: (1) The nature of the company's business, and whether or not it's diversified or a one-product operation; the size of its customer base; whether it does business mainly with the government or with private firms; whether it relies heavily on exports and is therefore sensitive to fluctuations in the dollar's value; whether its sources of supply are secure; and whether it can easily pass costs on to consumers. (2) The amount of debt of the company relative to its overall capital and whether it plans to borrow funds, issue more shares, or pay back loans. Among other things, this financial information will tell you whether the value of shares you may already own will undergo dilution, which could reduce earnings per share and thus reduce the market value of shares. (3) The nature of the company's ownership. Is a substantial proportion of stock held by the company's founders or by its current management? Closely held companies cannot be taken over by unwelcome acquirers as easily as widely held companies, but that can also deprive shareholders of profits they might otherwise gain through public tender offers at premiums to market value. You should also be told if financial institutions own large blocks of shares; big institutional positions are an indication of how professional investors regard the company. In the case of companies with relatively few shares, however, that can also cause substantial price swings should institutions gobble up or dump large amounts of shares. Trends in insider or institutional ownership can be solid signals as to the prospects of a company—if top management is accumulating or selling shares, they may know before the public about events that might cause the stock to rise or fall. (4) Trends in the company's earnings history. How steady have profits been? Have they been increasing on a per-share basis? Is the company emerging from a period of weakness? Are earnings mainly the result of ongoing operations or of one-time extraordinary items, such as the sale of company property? (5) Trends in dividend payments.

The Industry Story

You'll find many of the same elements of a company story in an industry story, and you will in addition have the opportunity to look at one company in relation to others. These stories are often accompanied by charts comparing companies in an industrial sector (computer chip makers, retailers, or utilities, for instance) according to sales, per-share earnings, stock price range, recent stock price, price-earnings ratio, and other important data.

A Word About Advertisements

The popular websites are free, at least for the time being, because throughout the financial news you will find advertisements for bank deposit instruments, various funds, and other investments. Early in the year many advertisements for individual retirement accounts appear. Some ads encourage you to supply a credit or debit card number right away. Mutual funds and sponsors of other publicly offered securities, however, can't accept an investment from you without first sending you a prospectus. A mutual fund sometimes will print the prospectus as part of the advertisement. Never react impulsively to an attractive rate or yield or special deal. It is difficult to compare rates, yields, and terms because each situation is unique and different institutions use various methods to compute yields. Some have withdrawal penalties and other restrictions that might not be obvious in the ad.

You will also find advertisements for financial publications, advisory newsletters, and computer databases and software, among other products. Often these products can be very helpful, but it is usually best to request a sample or a demonstration to make sure the product suits your needs.

Another form of financial advertising is the tombstone ad. Found only in the print media, it is really a formal announcement, by investment bankers in a public sale of securities, or by other financial institutions announcing major developments. This kind of ad is discussed later.

HOME PAGE HIGHLIGHTS AND WHAT TO MAKE OF THEM

Figure 1 shows what greeted you if you went to the home page of *Yahoo! Finance* on May 20, 2010 at 2:41 PM.

Yahoo! Finance's home page is basically typical of what you'd find on the other websites in that it highlights significant market statistics and summarizes leading financial news headlines. Statistical highlights change constantly while markets are open and top stories also change, although less frequently as the day goes on. Other sites may have a few more or a few less highlights on their home pages, but they all provide a quick overview of how the important markets are doing. At the very top of the page is a line with headings you can click on to get directly to major categories of information. *Yahoo!* headings after *Home* are *Investing, News & Opinion, Personal Finance, My Portfolios* (an interactive feature where you can track your own investments), and *Tech Ticker*, a general news and data section specializing in tech stocks.

But throughout the page, and an integral part of it, are less conspicuous messages inviting you click for information expanding on what you are looking at. For example, the left hand column is headed Market Summary and under it you see the Dow, the Nasdaq, the S&P 500, the 10-year bond yield, and oil and gold prices. The Market Summary heading gives you the options to click on Europe or Asia and bring up comparable highlights for those markets. At the bottom of the Market Summary column, in tiny red type, you are invited to click on "View more indices," and "View more bonds." To the right of that in blue type are the words "Customize summary," an interactive option enabling you to personalize the data selection.

These are all outer package options enabling you to select alternative highlights more suitable for you. If all your investments are in Europe, for example, you'll want your Market Summary to show how stocks did on the major exchanges there. If you live in a foreign country, you can go to the bottom of the page and click on one of the selections under the heading *Yahoo! Finance Worldwide*. That has everything in your own language and from your country's point of view.

FIGURE 1. *Yahoo! Finance* website. Reproduced with permission of Yahoo! Inc. ©2010 Yahoo! Inc. YAHOO! and the YAHOO! logo are trademarks of Yahoo! Inc.

The news lead in Fig. 1 is basically an international story about problems in the European Union and an economics story about disappointing employment news in the United States, both having a major negative effect on stocks. We are looking at a day when stocks took an unusually heavy hit, both here and abroad. The statistical highlights will reflect that news background in significant ways and by taking them one by one we will see how they interrelate.

Stock Prices

Immediately under the heading, Market Summary, U.S. stock prices are represented by the "Dow," the "NASDAQ," and the "S&P 500."

It wouldn't be obvious to the uninitiated, but the Dow refers to the Dow Jones Industrial Average of 30 blue-chip stocks (DJIA), one of a number of Dow Jones stock indices and averages, and the flagship of all stock indicators. Whether it's up, down, or sideways at any given moment, the DJIA's change is the universal answer to the question, "How is the market doing?" If the answer is "up 60" it means the average is up 60 points. As indicated earlier, however, it has its limitations. Strictly speaking, it is not an index, but a simple arithmetic average that has been regularly adjusted over the years to ensure continuity whenever component companies split their stock, merge with other companies, or are replaced by other companies. (Such adjustments are made by changing the "divisor," which explains why the DJIA is expressed in points instead of dollars and has a value of over 10,000 when it is unusual for a component stock to trade at over $100.) Being an average, however, means it is "price-weighted"—the pricier the component stock, the more it weights the average. Conceivably a couple of the highest priced stocks could drop so sharply that the Dow—synonymous to so many people with the "market"— would appear to decline even though the other 28 stocks gained moderately and the market was actually up. Also, its composition of only 30 blue chip corporations, although no longer a concentration of industrial issues, is obviously less representative of the overall market than the S&P with 500 blue chip stocks. Nonetheless, the Dow's very prominence makes it an influential force in market psychology. If the Dow is up, it creates a positive mood, which might inspire more buyers and cause it to rise higher. It is also true, however, that the Dow and the S&P 500 have tended historically to move in parallel lines. The differences in the way they are composed and weighted may on very rare occasions create an anomaly, but they are both reliable indicators of the direction the blue chips are going in. We'll see shortly, though, that their respective percentage movements can be meaningful.

The "Nasdaq," referring to the Nasdaq Composite Index, and the "S&P 500," referring to the Standard & Poor's 500 Stock Index, are similarly the flagships of groups of indices. Both are market-capitalization-weighted, meaning the number of shares outstanding is multiplied by the market price per share, and the larger that figure is, the more it influences the index. (Market-weighted and capitalization-weighted are terms used synonymously, and you'll also see the term free-float capitalization weighted, meaning only shares available for trading are counted. This makes a difference where significant blocks of shares are owned but never traded, as in Japan where company partner shares would otherwise be counted as capitalization.) With market capitalization weighting, the market size of the component company has more influence on the index than the price of a particular stock, as in the case of the DJIA.

The Nasdaq Composite measures the performance of the 3,200 or so stocks listed on the electronic Nasdaq Stock Market, including common stock, American Depositary Receipts (ADRs), limited partnership interests, ordinary shares, real estate investment trusts, shares of beneficial interest (SBIs), and TRACKING STOCKS. Although it includes some very large companies also included in the Dow Jones Industrial Average, the Nasdaq is dominated by younger, smaller, growth-oriented companies that are often engaged in high technology.

The Standard & Poor's 500 Stock Index comprises mostly New York Stock Exchange companies, but also includes some of the larger American Stock Exchange and Nasdaq issues.

As a general rule, lower-priced, smaller capitalization stocks do better in sharply rising markets and conservative blue chips, seen as safer, fare better when the market is sharply off. The Nasdaq Index is the main small stock proxy for *Yahoo!* and the other popular sites, and in Figure 1 it predictably shows the largest percentage decline at –2.48% while the purely blue chip Dow and the broader but still blue chip S&P took lesser hits at –2.21% and –2.16%, respectively.

Other websites sometimes add the Russell 2000, a capitalization-weighted index comprising the 2000 smallest companies in the Russell 3000 Index. The latter includes the 3000 largest American companies based on market capitalization, but the Russell 2000 is nonetheless a reliable indicator of small cap performance. (Put in perspective, the average market capitalization of the Russell 2000 is under $1 billion. The market capitalization of Exxon Mobil, a component in the Dow, the S&P 500, and the Russell 3000, is just under $300 billion.) A sneak peek inside the package reveals that the Russell 2000 is down 3.57%, worse than the Nasdaq.

Had we clicked on the market summary for Europe, we would have seen three indices: The FTSE, the DAX 30, and the CAC 40. All three are market capitalization-weighted indexes. The FTSE is the Financial Times-Stock Exchange 100 Stock Index, popularly called the Footsie, which includes 100 blue chip stocks traded on the London Stock Exchange. The DAX 30 represents 30 blue chip stocks traded on the Frankfurt Stock Exchange (FWB), which accounts for some 85 percent of the stock turnover of Germany, the Eurozone's most powerful economy. The DAX is a total return index, meaning it adds dividends to price changes and reinvests them in shares of the paying company proportionately to its capitalization weighting. It is thus possible for the index to gain while its components do not. The CAC 40 is made up of 40 of the 100 stocks traded on Euronext Paris (formerly the Paris Bourse) that are judged by an Index Steering Committee to be a relevant benchmark for portfolio management and a suitable underlying asset for derivatives products. It is one of the main national indexes of the pan-European stock exchange group. The component companies, all French domiciled, are heavily multinational and about 45 percent owned by foreign investors, especially German, Japanese, American, and British.

Not surprisingly, since France and Germany are expected to bear the brunt of financial support required by weaker Eurozone members, the CAC was off the most at –2.25%, the DAX next at –2.02% and the FTSE, the UK being outside the Eurozone, losing the least at –1.65%.

The Asian indexes featured are the Hang Seng Index, the Nikkei 225 Index, and the Straits Times Index.

The Hang Seng has 42 components traded on the Main Board of the Stock Exchange of Hong Kong and divided into four sub-indexes: Finance (11), Utilities (4), Properties (6), and Commerce and Industry (21). It is a market capitalization weighted index and components are selected based on their market capitalization and turnover, their representation of industry sectors, and their financial performance. Hong Kong has the highest concentration of corporate headquarters in the Asia-Pacific region. The Hong Kong Stock Exchange is the sixth largest in the world and more than half of its nearly $3 trillion (U.S.) represents mainland Chinese companies.

The Nikkei 225 refers to the Nikkei Stock Average of 225 stocks traded on the Tokyo Stock Exchange, which is the world's second largest exchange after the New York Stock Exchange. The Nikkei is the most widely quoted Japanese stock index and was called the Nikkei Dow Jones Stock Average until it changed its name in 1985. Like the Dow, it is composed of blue chip (called first section) stocks and is price-weighted, all companies having a par value of 50 yen. Its components are in 35 industries representative of the Japanese economy. The Bloomberg web site also highlights the Topix, formally the Tokyo Stock Price Index, tracking all 1700-plus companies listed in the First Section of the Tokyo Stock Exchange on a free-float market capitalization weighted basis.

The benchmark Straits Times Index, calculated and put out by FTSE, is a market value-weighted index of 30 stocks listed on the Singapore Stock Exchange. Singapore is a sovereign city-state and the smallest country in Southeast Asia. It is also a highly developed, free market economy with stable prices, very low unemployment, and a per capita GDP equal to that of the four largest West European countries. Its manufacturing base is heavy in consumer electronics and information technology products, and diversified in petroleum refining, chemicals, mechanical engineering, and biomedical sciences. The stock exchange has the third largest listing of Chinese companies after Hong Kong and the United States.

The Asian companies are big exporters to Europe and the U.S. and the stock indices were all negative there as well.

The 10-year Bond

As was observed earlier, bond prices move in the opposite direction from interest rates, the market's way of bringing yields in line with prevailing rates. When yields rise, prices of existing fixed-rate bonds decline, and vice versa. Of course, bond prices and yields are strongly influenced by risk factors, by inflation expectations, by Federal Reserve monetary policy, and by supply and demand. Different types of bonds reflect these characteristics to different degrees.

The 10-year Treasury bond (or note, as many professionals prefer to call bonds with a maturity of 10 years or less) is issued at auctions held four times a year, roughly in the middle of each quarter. Treasury obligations have the "full faith and credit" of the U.S. Government behind them and are free of risks other than those associated with fluctuating interest rates and inflation. Because the 10-year note is relatively long-term and not, like short-term Treasury bills, a direct instrument of Federal Reserve monetary policy, its price and yield normally reflect more purely than other investments the market's expectations with respect to interest rates and inflation. With the country in a recession led by falling home prices, the Fed has been buying heavily both at the short and long ends of the government's maturity spectrum to stimulate economic activity and keep mortgage rates low. This has kept interest rates abnormally low across the maturity spectrum, setting the stage for a collapse in bond prices when the Federal Reserve ends its stimulus programs and raises rates to attract capital and fight inflation.

With stocks being clobbered as this is written, money is flowing to the safety of bonds, another factor driving their prices higher and yields lower. It is not surprising that the 10-year Treasury yield is off nearly a full point amid a stock market rout.

Oil

Oil and other commodities are traded world-wide in United States dollars and the price shown is for one barrel of crude. Recessions diminish demand. Inflation, which reduces the purchasing power of the dollar, forces oil prices higher although the producers, mainly the OPEC countries, can control production and regulate prices so that demand doesn't suffer significantly. Events like the British Petroleum disaster off the Gulf Coast in 2010 would tend to stir fears of shortages, but with the U.S. in recession and pursuing policies that will lead to future inflation, with Europe in crisis and doing the same thing to finance the bailout of Greece, Iran threatening the world with its nuclear ambitions, constant threats of terrorism, and other factors creating uncertainty, the price of oil, always a major cost of living factor, can go either way from day to day. But most economists believe it will head higher primarily as a function of potential inflation and growing demand from the BRIC countries (Brazil, Russia, India, and China). In any event, it is a price everybody follows, especially after crude reached $145 in the summer of 2008 and forced gasoline prices at the pump to $4 a gallon.

That the oil price dropped along with stocks probably owes to the generally pessimistic view of the global economy and the belief that lower growth means lower prices and less inflation, not more.

Gold

Gold is a store of value and tends to rise as currencies lose value to inflation. It continues to hit historical highs (the chart plots the nearest month future price in U.S. dollars of one Troy ounce on the Comex) as the U.S. and now Europe spend trillions to bail out over-indebted economies with printed money that can only produce high rates of inflation in the not-distant future. Before the U.S. dollar abandoned its international gold backing in 1971, the Federal Reserve couldn't create additional money supply without increasing its gold reserves proportionately. Today all the world's economies have fiat currency, meaning currency having no intrinsic value and worth only what it will buy. Rampant inflation is a problem existing and getting worse in every developed country and many people believe a return to the gold standard, by governments or private companies accepting deposits in gold and charging debt cards, is the only way purchasing power in money form can be preserved. Central banks in China and elsewhere are adding to their gold reserves as world currencies lose value and this demand is driving the gold price higher. Of course, where prices are significantly rising, speculation increases and volatility becomes a factor.

The same psychology affecting oil prices may also explain the drop in gold, which had been breaking records with new highs as economic uncertainly spread and massive expenditures to revive growth threatened to create a wave of high inflation. The pullback in this time-honored inflation hedge may simply reflect a view that less growth means less price escalation. Also, gold is a highly liquid asset and often the first to be sold when investors need cash quickly. That need arises when sudden, large declines in stock prices cause margin calls.

Currencies

For the same reasons that gold has been rising, fiat currencies, led by the U.S. dollar and now by the euro, have been losing value everywhere. Despite a bailout agreement that precluded imminent default in Greece, that country's continuing problems and financial weakness in Portugal, Ireland, Italy, and Spain (known as the PIIGS) raise questions about the longer-term viability of the European Union and, in the shorter term, threaten to add a debt burden on economically stronger Germany and France. While it is true that a weak currency benefits exporters to countries with stronger currencies because the exports are effectively cheaper and more attractive, a country with chronically weak economic fundamentals and trade imbalances will become poorer and its currency will lose value. Investors who buy stocks and other assets with dollars that are weak relative to the currencies of the countries they invest in, make a currency profit when they convert the foreign currency back to dollars, assuming the foreign currency gains strength or the dollar gets weaker. Travelers from countries with strong currencies relative to the local currencies where they are traveling benefit from the foreign exchange (forex) rate and vice versa.

Explanation of currency terms and abbreviations:

The currencies table shows three currency pairs and their change from the previous day's close. A currency pair is a base currency and a quote currency separated by a slash. The price of the pair is the value of the quote currency when the base currency is exchanged for it. Which currency of the pair is the base and which is the quote is a matter of accepted convention. One group of currencies, called the *Majors,* comprises the U.S. dollar (USD), euro (EUR), Japanese yen (JPY), British pound (GBP), Australian dollar (AUD), New Zealand dollar (NZD), Canadian dollar (CAD), and the Swiss franc (CHF). Of that group, the USD is the base only in a pair with JPY, the CAD, and the CHF. Currency pairs not including the USD are *cross currency pairs,* but if the EUR is included in a pair and the USD isn't, it's called a *euro cross.* All other currencies are called *Minors* and when they are paired with Majors they become the quotes.

Getting back to *Yahoo!,* then, one euro exchanged for 1.2570 U.S. dollars and the euro increased slightly relative to the dollar, meaning the euro got slightly stronger or the dollar got slightly weaker, or both. If the price were lower, the opposite would be true. The yen exchanged for 90.1550 dollars and the yen decreased relative to the dollar, meaning the yen got weaker or the dollar got stronger, or both. The GBP/USD pair would be read the same way as the EUR/USD. In this case, the exchange rate was virtually unchanged with the pound gaining on the dollar by a negligible amount.

The second table, the Currency Converter, shows how much of the base currency a U.S. dollar would be worth in exchange.

Other Highlights

The *Yahoo!* home page has a few more self-explanatory data, such as surveys of nationwide and local area rates for mortgages, home equity and auto loans, savings, credit cards; newsworthy ETF quotes, and stocks notable because of unusual activity, percentage price changes, trading volume or industry affiliation.

DEEPER INTO THE PACKAGE

Here we leave the home screen and move to the inner news package. The headings differ from site to site, but look for categories generically designating (1) *News,* meaning the full stories behind the headlines shown on the home screen along with news of lesser importance as well as commentary and opinion; (2) *Markets*, meaning more specifics backing up the statistical highlights; and (3) *Investing*, which is sometimes combined with (2), but turns a spotlight respectively on stocks, rates and bonds, currencies, mutual funds, exchange-traded funds, and commodities. Headings like *Yahoo! Personal Finance*, which gets into college planning, careers, auto financing, and retirement issues, and *My Portfolios*, where you enter personal portfolio data that the site will track for you, are beyond the scope of this discussion but are self-explanatory and well worth exploring. All the major financial websites have interactive features providing customized displays.

News

Here you'll find the complete form of news stories that were summarized or headlined on the home page along with editorial opinion, expert commentary, related articles, other background, and generally a wealth of information greatly exceeding what you'd get in a single print publication. It is drawn from a variety of sources that are specified. The websites provide links directly to the world wide web if something you want isn't covered. Since news speaks for itself and unfamiliar terms and concepts are explained elsewhere within the framework in which it is communicated, there is no elaboration needed here.

Markets
Stocks

At this level, information about stocks focuses on what various market averages and indices measure and what predictive value they have. Market movements upward, downward, or sideways don't necessarily signal trends, however, which is why we need additional statistical information.

	NYSE	AMEX	NASDAQ	BB
Advancing Issues	395 (10%)	63 (11%)	259 (9%)	314 (22%)
Declining Issues	3,515 (89%)	504 (86%)	2,494 (89%)	751 (53%)
Unchanged Issues	39 (1%)	19 (3%)	57 (2%)	340 (24%)
New Highs	65	6	10	141
New Lows	154	16	145	332
Up Volume	747,081,141 (30%)	4,527,815 (2%)	162,078,772 (7%)	160,333,272 (17%)
Down Volume	1,729,816,426 (69%)	240,883,602 (98%)	2,162,093,971 (93%)	617,365,606 (65%)
Unchanged	19,100,889 (1%)	193,555 (0%)	11,589,238 (0%)	165,753,924 (18%)

The table above compares advance, decline, and volume figures for four markets, the large-company-dominated NYSE (New York Stock Exchange), the emerging, small-company-dominated AMEX, the technology-dominated NASDAQ and, abbreviated BB, the high-risk, young company issues traded on the over-the-counter Bulletin Board (OTCBB). Figures represent stocks except in the case of volume, where they represent shares. The figures represent approximately the same intraday point on May 20, 2010 as Figure 1.

The advance and decline numbers are called breadth indicators and show the market's direction at the time reported. In a severe market drop such as was in progress on the day in question, the numbers confirm that the declines were across the board and not reflective of any industry or significant capitalization bias. (One is tempted to pay less attention to the OTCBB figures, given that the overall market, reacting today to negative economic news both in

Europe and at home, was in a volatile phase caused by mixed economic signals and general uncertainty. The OTCBB group would probably not attract active investors in any major way as the large unchanged volume number would seem to bear out.)

Volume, the amount of buying and selling, is an important market datum that can help you determine in which direction the stock market will continue to move. If stock prices rise amid heavy volume, the indication is that many investors chose to invest heavily in stocks, and they intend to hold out for further price rises. Similarly, a market drop on heavy volume is considered a more serious setback than a drop on light volume. A market rise on light volume will cause the market rise to be questioned. On the exchanges shown here, volume was on an intraday track to end at levels well above average.

Under the heading *Major US Indices*, the *Yahoo! Finance* website displays a total of 35 indices in five groupings labeled Dow Jones, New York Stock Exchange, Nasdaq, S&P, and Other U.S. Each grouping is displayed in a boxed table under the headings: *Symbol, Name, Last Trade, Change and Related Information*. For example, one boxed table lists four major Dow Jones averages: the Composite, the Industrial, the Transportation, and the Utility averages.

The Dow Jones Industrial Average (DJIA), of course, is the mother of U.S. market indicators and has already been explained in some detail. The Dow Jones Composite Average Index is a 65 stock average combining the components of the Dow's industrial, transportation, and utilities averages. The Dow Jones Transportation Average comprises 20 stocks, representing airlines, railroads, and trucking companies. Transportation stocks have traditionally been watched because the amount of shipping activity, meaning either raw materials going to factories or finished goods to distributors, provides a confirming indication of manufacturing and business activity and thus of the direction of the stock market. One time-honored if not consistently reliable market predictor, the Dow Theory, holds that when both the DJIA and the Dow Jones Transportation average both reach new highs or new lows, a market trend is afoot. The Dow Jones Utilities Average is made up of 15 large electricity and natural gas utilities. Because utilities are big borrowers, and because lower rates mean higher profits, a rise in the utilities index normally augurs well for the market in general and vice versa.

A click on the symbol at the left of the box brings up additional market data for the particular average, including the value at the previous day's close and at the opening at the current session, plus the value range for the day and for the previous 52 weeks. This information, which is illustrated by an accompanying chart that plots the minute to minute movement of the average, gives you an idea of the market's volatility and also puts the current value in the perspective of the past year.

In addition to that current market information, you can go back to the box and, under the *Related Information* heading, access the components of each average along with charts that plot the index value. If you click on charts, the basic chart appears and gives you your choice of seven time frames, ranging from one day to five years and your choice of bar, line, or candle graphs. You then get two graphs, one plotting index value, the other plotting volume. Naturally you would want an idea of what normal volume is for any given index during any particular session. These charts show the relationship between price and volume clearly.

An interesting feature of the basic chart screen is a place in which you can enter the symbol of another index or a particular stock, click "compare," and get another basic chart with two lines comparing relative performance over the period you select. A stock investor might want to compare, for example, how small capitalization stocks as represented by the Russell 2000 performed relative to the blue chip S&P 500 over a period during which there were significant highs and lows and how the differences correlated with volume at various points.

Another option is "Historical Prices," where you enter a symbol, a start and end date, and a choice of daily, weekly, monthly, or dividends only, then click on "Get Prices." Up comes a seven-column list headed: Date, Open, High, Low, Close, Volume, and Adjusted (for dividends and splits) Close. This kind of historical detail, useful for back-testing hypothetical portfolios or reconstructing history for tax and other purposes, was very hard to come by before financial websites.

Technical Analysis Tools

The Charts menu has a heading Basic Technical Analysis that brings up the basic chart along with a selection of overlay options that will take you further into the realm of technical analysis than most people are prepared to go, although the website's educational page will show you to appropriate tutorials on the subject. For example, you might want to see a 1-year line graph of the Dow Jones Industrial Average with an overlay of a 50-day moving average. The moving average—"moving" because each new each day it drops the oldest day—is an indicator of trend. There are two things to look for here. One is a "crossover," where the daily plottings of the DJIA cross over the 50-day moving average line, indicating a short-term countertrend, which may or may not have longer-term significance. Crossovers that are indicative of longer-term trends (it is by no means to be assumed that they are) eventually show up in what are called "reversals" of the moving average line. Technical analysis, which gets highly complicated, is used mainly by short-term, "swing traders," and is better left to professionals. But if you're into exponential moving averages, MACDs, slow and fast stochastics, Bollinger Bands, and other such arcana, look no further than the financial websites.

Other Indexes

Of the other indexes reported in the *Yahoo! Finance* groupings, the following are particularly noteworthy:

New York Stock Exchange Indices

The NYSE Composite Index (New Method) (NYSE:NYA) was reintroduced in January 2003 with a value of 5000 points to exclude all closed-end funds, ETFs, limited partnerships, and derivatives. It now includes all NYSE common stocks, including REITs, ADRs, and TRACKING STOCKS. It lists over 2000 domestic and foreign issues, and is adjusted to eliminate the effects of capitalization changes, new listings, and delistings. It is weighted using free-float market capitalization and calculated on a continuously computed total return basis. Of the 100 companies having the largest market capitalization (and thus weighted most heavily), more than 50 percent are non-U.S. issues. It is the basis of the exchange-traded fund iShares NYSE Composite Index Fund (NYC).

NASDAQ Indices

The *NASDAQ 100* (NDX) is notable for two reasons primarily, its frequent confusion with the NASDAQ Composite (IXIC), the main NASDAQ index discussed earlier, and being the basis for the exchange-traded fund (ETF) known as the "Cubes" because of its NASDAQ symbol QQQQ. Cubes was the most actively traded security in the United States at the peak of the "Dot Com" bubble in 2000 when it was traded on the American Stock Exchange with the symbol QQQ. It is still among the five most actively traded stocks and ETFs. Its components are the 100 largest non-financial companies listed on the NASDAQ, namely Industrial, Technology, Retail, Telecommunications, Biotechnology, Health Care, Transportation, Media and Service companies. The NASDAQ Financial Index lists financial services companies and there are other specialized NASDAQ indexes. The NASDAQ 100 is "modified capital weighted," meaning that the largest components are subject to certain rules limiting their influence on the index. It includes 15 companies not incorporated in the United States.

Standard & Poor's Indexes

The S&P 100 stock index is a subset of the widely published S&P 500 Index and is notable because the 100 sector-balanced components tend to be the largest and most established stocks of the 500 and all have exchange-listed options. Index options on it are highly popular and recognizable by their ticker symbol, OEX. S&P's other subset indices include the *S&P 400 MidCap Index* and the *S&P 600 SmallCap Index,* the latter composed of a sector-balanced sampling of the same capitalization range as the more widely quoted Russell 2000, which has an almost identical historical graph line. The S&P Composite 1500 Index is simply a combination of the 500, 400, and 600 stock indices.

Other Stock Indices

The Amex Composite Index was renamed the *NYSE Amex Composite Index* after the American Stock Exchange was acquired in 2008 by NYSE Euronext. Its symbol is XAX. It is a market-capitalization-weighted index and its 494 components are all the equities listed on the NYSE Amex Equities exchange, which is primarily a market for emerging growth companies. Its trading, the volume of which makes it the third largest U.S. exchange, is almost entirely in small-cap stocks, exchange-traded funds, and derivatives.

In 2005, Wilshire Associates, most famous for the Wilshire 5000 Index, which measures the performance of all U.S. equity securities with readily available price data and has grown to include more than 7000 stocks, teamed up with Dow Jones to launch a series of capitalization-weighted indexes. Hence the *Dow Jones Wilshire 5000*, which is the broadest of all stock indexes, and the *Dow Jones Wilshire 2500*, which comprises the largest 2500 of the issues included in the broader index. Other Dow Jones Wilshire indexes listed were designed as benchmarks to evaluate active managers. They separate the 5000 index into four capitalization groups (Large, Small, Mid, and Micro) and then divide the Large, Small, and Mid-cap issues by float-adjusted capitalization equally into growth and value indexes.

The Value Line Composite Average is unique in that its components, 1700 companies from the New York, NYSE Amex, NASDAQ, and over-the-counter markets, are equally weighted and represent more than 90 industries.

Two other Dow Jones indexes, although not included in the *Yahoo!* groupings cited above, are the *Global Titans 50, the Asian Titans 50,* and the *DJ Stoxx 50.* These are float-adjusted, market-capitalization-weighted indexes representing blue-chip companies worldwide, in Asia, and in Europe, respectively.

Commodities

Following the stock indices, the *Yahoo! Finance* website has another boxed table displaying three major commodities indices.

The Goldman Sachs Commodity Index was bought by Standard & Poor's in 2007 and is now properly called the *S&P GSCI*. Traded on the Chicago Mercantile Exchange, it is a benchmark for investment in commodities and comprises 24 commodities representing the standard commodity sectors, namely energy products, industrial metals, agricultural products, livestock products, and precious metals. Its diversity of subsectors is considered to minimize its vulnerability to events that would impact individual commodity markets. It is a world-production-weighted index based on the average quantity produced of each component commodity, which makes it a measure of investment performance as well as an economic indicator. Commodities are traded internationally in U.S. dollars, giving the asset class value as an inflation hedge. Historically, stocks and commodities have trended in countercyclical patterns, a bull market in commodities accompanied by a bear market in stocks and vice versa.

The PHLX Gold/Silver Sector refers to the *Philadelphia Gold and Silver Index,* which comprises sixteen precious metal mining companies and is traded on the Philadelphia Stock Exchange. Gold, of course, is a time-honored "store of value" and inflation hedge and gave international backing to the U.S. dollar until the gold standard was abandoned in 1971. Silver also has a monetary history and is considered a store of value. There is much more of it, however, although that factor is offset by its wider industrial demand compared to gold. Both metals, and to a lesser extent platinum and palladium, can be owned in physical form although there are associated safety and storage costs, the more so with bulkier silver. Mining stocks can be a bad hold when demand is slack and production, which is costly, is curtailed. When demand takes off, however, as is happening as this is written in 2010, high prices get the benefit of leverage and mining stocks can be a source of huge capital gains and rich dividends. In the Great Depression of the 1930s, stocks generally collapsed, but gold mining shares quadrupled. And non-gold precious metals, particularly silver, have even more upside than gold. Investors in precious metals keep their eye on the gold to silver ratio. Silver rises faster than gold in a bull market for precious metals, but the ratio narrows the higher both metals go.

Rogers International Commodities Index (RICI) is a composite, U.S. dollar based, total return index calculated from 36 commodities traded on 11 international exchanges and possibly the most diversified of all the commodity indexes. It has three segments that provide the basis for three sub-indices, namely RICI Agriculture, RICI Energy, and RICI Metals. Each commodity is rebalanced to its initial weight at the start of each month and components are reviewed annually, although it changes very rarely and counts stability, consistency, and transparency as attributes. The initial value was set at 1000 July 31, 1998 and eleven years later its value was 2908.59. Its compound annual return has outperformed every other commodity index.

Interest Rates and Bonds

The *Interest Rates & Bonds* section of *The Wall Street Journal's Market's Lineup*, Figure 2, presents an excellent summary. The Consumer Rates Graph selects day-to-day from the various consumer rates listed in the table below it and shows how these rates are affected by the Federal Reserve target rate that is raised, lowered, or left unchanged at meetings of the Federal Open-Market Committee. The Federal Reserve's open market operations involve the buying or selling of government securities to expand or contract the money supply and the reserves banks are required to maintain. By influencing the target Fed Funds rate, the rate banks with excess reserves charge other banks needing to borrow funds to meet reserve requirements, the Fed is able to effect upward or downward movement in rates generally. On the day illustrated, the Fed Funds rate is compared with the average annual rate paid by money market deposit accounts, the most competitive of which are listed to the right of the graph.

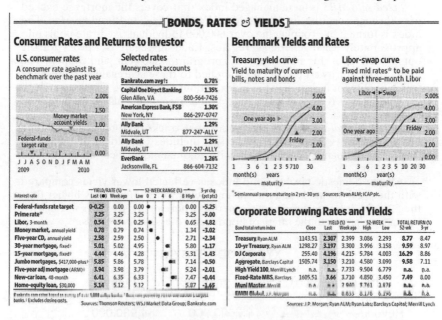

FIGURE 2. WSJ Bond Rates and Yields

The Treasury Yield Curve, compared in the middle graph to the previous year, plots the yields on one-, three-, and six-month bills, one-year, two-year, 3-year, 5-year, and 7-year notes, and 10-year and 30-year bonds. The yield curve is a benchmark for mortgage and other bank lending rates, but it is also an economic indicator. A normal curve rises as the months and years go out and protection against inflation and other uncertainties is reflected in higher rates. An inverted yield curve—where short-term rates are higher than long-term rates—is often a signal of an oncoming recession.

The Libor/Swap Curve, illustrated on the right, is not something most people are concerned with. It compares the London Interbank Offering Rate, a benchmark rate charged by international banks on large Eurodollar loans to the most creditworthy customers, to the rate being commanded by credit-equivalent interest rate swaps at various future points in time. Swaps are used by sophisticated, professional traders, although the Libor/Swap Curve, like the yield curve, has some value as an economic indicator.

The Corporate Borrowing Rates and Yields table provides benchmark total return indexes in various categories of fixed-income securities.

Treasury shows the 5-10 year Treasury index, and the *10-year Treasury* index comprises maturities from 10 to 30 years.

The *DJ Corporate* is an equally weighted basket of 96 recently issued investment grade corporate bonds with laddered maturities.

Aggregate tracks the total U.S. bond market, including Treasuries, government agency securities, and investment-grade corporate debt, and the U.S. Government/Credit Index, which includes a blend of U.S. Treasury, U.S. agency, and supranational, mortgage, and corporate securities of varying maturities.

The *High Yield 100* Index tracks the high-yield ("junk bond") sector of the U.S. corporate bond market, defined as bonds with credit ratings below investment grade, which are bonds rated BBB or below by Standard & Poor's or BAA or below by Moody's Investor Services.

Fixed-rate MBS is an unmanaged index that covers the mortgage-backed pass-through securities of Ginnie Mae, Fannie Mae, and Freddie Mac. The index is formed by grouping the over 600,000 individual fixed-rate pools into approximately 3,500 generic aggregates. Each aggregate is a proxy for the outstanding pools for a given agency, program, issue year, and coupon. The index and maturity criteria are then applied to these aggregates to determine which qualify for inclusion in the index. About 600 qualify.

Muni Master is a broad gauge index of tax-free municipal bonds published by Merrill Lynch.

EMBI Global is a J.P. Morgan index that tracks total returns for traded debt instruments in emerging markets. It includes U.S. dollar denominated Brady Bonds, loans, and Eurobonds with an outstanding face value of at least $500 million.

All the domestic taxable bond indexes reflected lower yields compared with the previous week, and the current yields were only slightly higher than the 52-week lows, unsurprising in a period where many investors were gravitating from stocks to the safety of bonds regardless of poor yields.

XYZ PRODUCTS (N)

Qtr to March 31	2010	2009
Revenue	$5,600,000	$4,980,000
Net income	463,000	452,000
Share earns—basic	.22	.22
Share earns—diluted	.20	.20
Shares outstanding	2,100,000	2,050,000

Earnings Reports

Quarterly profit reports for corporations are carried in major newspapers like *The Wall Street Journal* and *Investor's Business Daily,* as well as in financial web sites. In most cases, the abbreviated reports appear in one place, and include the latest sales, net income, net income per share, and shares outstanding, compared with the year-earlier figures. Using year-earlier comparisons rather than comparisons with the previous quarter excludes purely seasonal fluctuations. Department stores, for example, as a rule report the most sales in the fourth quarter, owing to the Christmas season. Comparing the fourth and third quarters, therefore, might give an inaccurate impression of the health of a department-store chain. It is very important also to look at earnings on a per-share basis. Per-share earnings, more than total earnings, are a major determinant of stock prices.

Starting in 1998, companies were required to report earnings per share on two bases: Basic earnings per share is simply the number of shares outstanding divided by a company's net profit. Diluted earnings per share, normally a lower figure, assumes that all potentially dilutive securities, such as convertible bonds and preferred stock, warrants, and options were actually converted or exercised, thus increasing shares outstanding.

XYZ PRODUCTS (N)

Qtr to March 31	2010	2009
Revenue	$5,600,000	$4,980,000
Net income	463,000	452,000
Share earns—basic	.22	.22
Share earns—diluted	.20	.20
Shares outstanding	2,100,000	2,050,000

Dividend Reports

Lists of quarterly dividends, organized alphabetically by corporation, appear in greater number during the third through fifth weeks of each calendar quarter when earnings reports are most numerous. The dividend reports are generally divided into categories: Irregular, Increased, Reduced, and Regular. The organization of columns looks like this:

DIVIDEND REPORTS

	Regular			
	Period	Rate	Stk of Record	Pay-able
XYZ Corp.	Q	.30	4–10	4–30

The table tells you that the regular dividend for the hypothetical XYZ Corporation is paid quarterly, that the dividend is 30 cents per share (which would result in $1.20 per share annually if the rate held steady), that the dividend will be paid to shareowners of record April 10, and that the actual payment will be made on April 30. It's important to remember that stocks go ex-dividend during the interval between the dividend announcement and the actual payment. This means that the dividend isn't payable to investors who buy the stock during that interval. (On the other hand, if you sell the stock during the ex-dividend period, you still collect the dividend.) Shares listed on the NYSE generally go ex-dividend four days before the stockholder of record date. Stocks normally decline by the amount of the dividend when they enter an ex-dividend trading period.

Securities Offerings

Announcements of newly issued or about-to-be issued stocks and bonds come in two forms. Large newspapers include calendars and digests of expected and newly announced securities issues to be distributed by underwriting groups or syndicates. These groups of investment banking houses also place paid advertisements, known as tombstones in the language of Wall Street, which give a very basic summary of the offerings. (Tombstone ads are also used for other purposes, such as announcing major personnel changes or a firm's important role in an acquisition or merger.)

The newspaper listings come under such headings as Finance Briefs (*The New York Times*) or New Securities Issues (*The Wall Street Journal*). Because a high proportion of the offerings are bonds, these listings can usually be found near the bond tables and the interest rate/bond market news story.

One advantage of buying new issues (which are often reserved for favored customers) over buying existing securities, is that the buyer pays no commission. The broker-dealer is paid out of the underwriting spread, the difference between the price at which the securities are sold to the public and the lower price paid to the issuer by the underwriters. Even if you're not interested in purchasing securities, these notices give you an idea of the prevailing interest rates (in the case of bonds) and the types of companies that are able to attract capital by issuing shares.

In the accompanying illustration of a typical tombstone ad, the boilerplate (standard legal language) advises you to read the prospectus before you buy. Many investors, of course, simply rely on the word of their brokers anyway, but the prospectus is a legally required summary of the facts and risks concerning the issue, and investors are well-advised to read it. The tombstone lists the names of the firms comprising the underwriting group and, by alphabetically organized groups, the relative importance of their participation. The par value of the stock, if any, is usually listed, but has no meaning in terms of market value. The offering price, of course, is included; however, this announcement doesn't tell you anything more, for example, how the proceeds of the sale are to be used.

Tender Offer Announcements

In both friendly and unfriendly takeover situations, the advertisements placed by corporations soliciting your shares may offer the greatest source of practical information regarding what you should or could do with your shares. Among other things, these comprehensive tombstone type notices identify the company seeking to acquire another company; state the price being offered for your shares and whether payment will be in cash or securities or a combination of the two; inform you of various deadlines to send in your shares or to withdraw your offer; and announce various other conditions, such as the minimum number of shares the acquiring company requires for the deal to be completed. These notices also include the names of companies that act as soliciting and information agents, such as D.F. King & Co., or Georgeson Shareholder Communication, Inc., along with their addresses and phone numbers. Such companies have been paid to provide you with information and prospectuses. Of course, these ads can also be biased and are often followed in a few days with ads placed by the target company, citing reasons to reject the bid.

Redemption Notices

Callable bonds and preferred stock can be redeemed by the issuer prior to maturity, and the likelihood of this happening is greatest when the issuer can replace them with new securities providing lower interest rate or dividends. When redemption takes place, issuers often place paid notices in a local newspaper and/or a major publication, such as *The Wall Street Journal.* These notices provide the serial numbers and denominations of the securities being redeemed and the call price of the securities.

This announcement is neither an offer to sell nor a solicitation of an offer to buy these Securities
The offer is made only by the Prospectus

New Issue   October 2, 20--

750,000 Shares

ABXY Corporation

Common Stock
($.10 par value)

Price $30 per Share

Copies of the Prospectus may be obtained in any State in which this announcement is circulated only from such of the undersigned as may legally offer these securities in such state.

First XYZ Inc.

          MNO Inc.   TUV Securities

  ABC Inc.   CDE & Co.   Monopoly Inc.

  Ajax Inc.   Dustby Inc.   ZXZ Inc.

          HIJ Securities

Short Interest

Around the twentieth of each month, the New York and American stock exchanges and Nasdaq release data on short interest—shares sold when they are not actually owned by the seller (usually they are borrowed). The exchanges break down the statistics by individual stocks and also give a total number of shorted shares of their listed companies compared to the total the month before.

Short interest figures generally signify that professional investors anticipate a decline in share prices. However, the figures are somewhat inflated by the inclusion of the short positions of exchange floor specialists; they sell short as part of their stabilizing function as well as for investment purposes. Market analysts also view large short interest positions as potential buying pressure since short positions must ultimately be covered by purchasing shares.

Other Economic and Financial Indicators

Among the more common weekly graphic and tabular features relating to business activity, securities prices, and returns on your savings are the following:

Treasury Bill Bar Chart: This appears usually on Tuesday, following the Treasury bill auction of the preceding day. This table of 3-month Treasury bill yields shows how discount rates have changed on a weekly basis over the past three months, and gives the year-earlier yield as well. This chart gives you an idea of the direction in which rates on adjustable rate mortgages are heading, and whether you'll earn more or less income from a money market fund or an adjustable rate CD.

Federal Reserve Data: This table appears on Friday, following the weekly report on the nation's money supply released by the Federal Reserve Board on Thursday and covering the period ended Wednesday. The money supply— the amount of money people have to spend, whether it is in cash or liquid investments like money market funds—is a measure of whether the economy is expanding or contracting. When the economy is strong, the money supply tends to increase by itself and vice versa. When the economy is growing too fast or not fast enough, the Federal Reserve has traditionally used its powers to expand or contract the money supply. The money supply is expressed as four classifications: The first three, called M1, M2, and M3 comprise a category called Monetary Aggregates, and the classifications represent degrees of liquidity. M1, for example, is immediately spendable cash and money in checking accounts; M2 includes M1 plus savings accounts and time deposits; M3 includes M1, M2 plus long-term deposits, and the assets and liabilities of financial institutions. The fourth category, designated "L" adds to M3 other highly liquid assets, such as short-term bonds and commercial paper.

Since the early 1990s, the Fed, believing it could no longer accurately measure a key variable in the money supply—velocity, or the number of times money changed hands—has periodically changed the Fed Funds rate, rather than attempting to target the money supply directly. At each of the eight meetings per year of the Federal Open Market Committee (FOMC), the Fed announces its decision to raise, lower, or keep unchanged the Fed Funds target rate and issues a "balance of risks statement," from which can be inferred the Fed's bias with respect to future rate actions.

Although the Monetary Aggregates, Member Bank Reserve Changes, and Reserve Aggregates data shown in the table are used by economists and securities professionals as factors in projecting the direction of interest rates, this table has less predictive value for the non-professional, who is better guided by the periodic announcements of the Federal Open Markets Committee.

THE INNER PACKAGE
Stocks

Here we get down to basics—the specific data about particular stocks. Websites provide this information when you enter the stock symbol and click on "quotes." Newspapers like *The Wall Street Journal* provide the prior day's closing results in tabular form.

The *Journal* recently revised its format to present one table headed *Biggest 1,000 Stocks*, which it describes as applying to NYSE, NYSE Arca, NYSE Amex, and Nasdaq Stock Market listed securities with prices representing composite quotations that include primary market trades as well as trades reported by Nasdaq OMX BXSM (formerly Boston), Chicago Stock Exchange, CBOE, National Stock Exchange, ISE, and BATS (BATS Exchange Inc., a recently formed and rapidly growing electronic exchange).

The *Journal* presentation begins with a note explaining the table and what various indications mean. For example, underlining indicates that the volume of trading in a stock was greater than average for that stock. Boldface type indicates a 5 percent or greater price change.

1,000 LARGEST STOCKS

①	②		③	④ ⑤		⑥	⑦	⑧
Ytd	52-Week			Yld				Net
% Chg.	High	Low	Stock	SYM	%	PE	Last	Chg.
–3.90	55.64	40	XYZ Cp	XYZ	2.7	6	48.44	–1.65

1. YTD % CHG This shows the percentage change in the stock price since the close of the last trading day of the previous year.

2. 52-week High-Low The high-low column gives you the annual trading range, the highest and lowest prices of the previous 52 weeks plus the current trading week, up to, but not through, the last session. A broad range indicates that a stock has demonstrated the potential to make—and lose—money for shareholders. Sometimes, a stock that has traded up and down within a range will meet resistance when it approaches its previous high point, because some investors will use this high point as a benchmark to sell. Similarly, the low point could serve as a buffer against further price drops. At the low point, buyers, hoping history will repeat itself and the stock rise, may purchase shares and thus provide support for the stock's price.

3. Name It's not always easy to locate a particular stock, because the names are usually radically abbreviated. The abbreviation systems used by the Associated Press and United Press International, which supply most of the tables you see, are different (and not to be confused with stock ticker symbols used on the exchanges); thus, the alphabetical order will differ from one system to the other. Stocks like IBM and AT&T are easy to find; few investors, however, would know immediately that J.P. Morgan Chase is listed under J. Unless otherwise identified, these are names of common stock. A "v" indicates that trading was suspended in the primary market. Stock tables are usually accompanied by explanatory notes defining any letters that may appear. An "A," "B," or other capital letter differentiates between one class of stock and another. A "wt" identifies the security as a warrant. A "vj" indicates that the company is in bankruptcy proceedings, and "wi" means when issued, signifying that the shares have not yet been issued. If the issuance is canceled, the trades will also be canceled. Also included are exchange-listed American Depositary Receipts (ADRs), which are negotiable receipts representing shares of foreign issuers. They are usually identified by the letters ADS (American Depositary Shares) and are sometimes broken out separately. Closed-end and Exchange-Traded Funds (ETFs), mutual funds, and other portfolios that are traded like stocks are usually listed in similar but separate tables. Preferred stocks are listed in separate tables in *The Wall Street Journal*, but included with common stocks in some newspapers, identified as "pr."

2. Annual dividend Dividends are listed by dollars and cents per share. Don't confuse this figure with the amount you'll receive in the mail each quarter. The annual dividend is an estimate, based on the most recent quarterly dividend multiplied by four. If a company has a history of steadily rising dividends, consider this a conservative estimate. An "e" in this column indicates that dividends have been irregular, and that the figure represents the amount paid over the past year, rather than an estimate of future dividends. A "g" means dividends are paid in Canadian currency, although the other stock market data is given in terms of U.S. dollars.

4. *SYM* is the stock symbol. It is how you identify the stock on the consolidated tape (which is why it is still sometimes anachronistically called the "ticker symbol)" and is the symbol you would put in the "quote" box at a financial website to bring up the real-time version of the information in newspaper stock tables.

5. *Yield* This is the current dividend divided by the latest closing price, rounded off to the nearest tenth of a percent. A low- or no-yield stock may be a growth stock, which means that profits are reinvested rather than paid out in dividends. Investors purchase growth stocks for capital gains, not for dividends; they hope that stock prices will increase as profits do. Some investors, however, purchase stocks for dividends, or income. This yield figure allows you to compare the dividend income with the income from other types of investments. Careful, though. A high dividend yield can be a sign of trouble. For example, when the Gulf of Mexico oil spill occurred in April of 2010 and the shares of BP Corporation plunged, the stock was suddenly yielding 8 percent, not because it was rewarding shareholders but rather because it was looking at liability that threatened its very existence.

6. *PE ratio* The price earnings ratio is the latest price divided by the last 12 months' earnings per share, rounded to the nearest whole number. Be sure not to confuse PEs with dividends. PEs are used to compare the perceived value of stocks in the marketplace. PEs indicate how investors view the value of a company's profits. Stocks representing solid, uninflated profits that are expected to grow usually have higher PEs than stocks with questionable profits and profit-growth potential. Growth companies may have PEs of 20 or more. On the other hand, a high PE could be the result of a recent drop in earnings, and the prelude to a drop in the stock's price that will drop the PE to its former, lower level. A start-up or turnaround could be attractive, but could have no earnings— and therefore no PE. PEs give you a way to calculate per share earnings roughly: divide the stock price by the PE. PE ratios are meaningful only when the earnings component is a normal and representative number.

7. *Last.* The last sale is the closing price at the end of the trading day. After-hours trading is shown elsewhere.

8. *NET CHG* This figure represents the change in closing price from the previous day.

Other Over-the-Counter Stocks Tables

The quantity of information available for over-the-counter stocks has grown dramatically over the years. It's still often necessary, however, to call your broker for a price because many of the lesser-known, less expensive stocks aren't included in the daily tables. Your broker will use the pink sheets published by the Pink Sheets LLC, which list bid and asked prices, to give you a price. *Barron's* provides extensive over-the-counter tables on a weekly basis. The *OTC Journal,* another weekly, carries information about penny stocks, which usually sell for less than $1.00. The daily tables included in large newspapers have expanded, in part because of the efforts of the Financial Industry Regulatory Authority (FINRA), the umbrella group for over-the-counter dealers. Since the early 1970s, the NASD Automated Quotations, or Nasdaq Stock Market, has allowed dealers using desktop terminals to view each other's bid quotations (the highest prices they're willing to pay), and asked quotations (the lowest prices they'd accept). Nasdaq also passes this and other information on to wire services for use in daily stock tables. Since the early 1980s, the system has been upgraded to allow dealers to enter transaction prices and sizes of trades. As a result, the tables for the more expensive or more heavily traded Nasdaq stocks are identical to the NYSE and AMEX tables. Stocks that are subject to this full-line reporting system are included in tables headed Nasdaq National Market Issues.

However, not all the companies meeting NASD criteria to have their shares listed as part of the National Market System are included there. Instead, more limited market information for the shares of these and other Nasdaq-listed companies is included under the heading Nasdaq Small Cap Market.

International Foreign Stock Market Tables

Of increasing importance are stocks traded on foreign markets. Information about the more important stocks are carried in *Investor's Business Daily, The Wall Street Journal,* and on web sites. The stocks are organized by the exchange on which they're traded. The data carried for foreign stocks is limited, to often only the name and the closing price and daily change, given in local currency, such as Japanese yen, British pence, euro, and so on. It's up to the reader to make use of the foreign exchange tables to translate the price into U.S. dollars and cents.

STOCK OPTIONS TABLES

Stock options give you both a conservative way to increase the income on your holdings or insure your portfolio against losses, as well as relatively inexpensive if highly speculative ways to invest in stocks. In any case, don't assume you understand these investment vehicles until you at least understand the stock option tables. Although unheard of a generation ago, these tables now comprise a major portion of the inside of financial news packages. The longest tables are generated by the principal options exchanges, the Chicago Board Options Exchange, NYSE-Amex, and the Philadelphia Stock Exchange. Shorter tables are included for small options trading operations found on other exchanges.

A 1990s innovation that has rapidly been gaining popularity is LEAPS, a term now used generically but that started as a proprietary acronym of the Chicago Board Options Exchange, meaning Long-Term Equity AnticiPation Securities. LEAPS are long-term options expiring in 2 to 5 years. Currently being traded on some 150 stocks and several stock indexes, LEAPS are listed separately in some financial pages. Although the following explanations apply to traditional conventional options expiring typically in 9 months or less, LEAPS are essentially no different except that in having longer terms, they logically trade at higher premiums.

Daily Stock Options Tables

Options tables give you the prices of wasting assets. These contracts, which as a rule last no longer than nine months, give the holder the right, but not the obligation, to buy (call) or sell (put) shares of stock at a specified strike price by a specified expiration date. The daily table format, and what it includes, by columns, is as follows.

LISTED OPTIONS QUOTATIONS

①	②	③	④		⑤	
			Call		**Put**	
Option/Strike		**Exp.**	**Vol.**	**Last**	**Vol.**	**Last**
XYZ	42.50	Jan	—	—	670	0.85
57.98	50	Oct	4	8	2763	0.15
57.98	55	Oct	350	3.60	743	0.65
57.98	55	Jan	132	5.60	1249	2.95
57.98	60	Oct	824	0.60	440	2.65

1. Name of the underlying stock and, under it, the closing price of the underlying stock, repeated for each row of stock prices. (Since the New York Stock Exchange tables include sales of NYSE stocks on other exchanges, the NY Close may differ from the NYSE table, which reports later sales on the Pacific Exchange and elsewhere.) In this example, XYZ Corporation stock closed at $57.98 on the principal stock exchange on which it is traded, most likely the NYSE. Because the stock is worth $57.98 per share, each 100-share option contract has an exercise value of $5,798.

2. The strike price is given in this column. This is the price per share at which the option holder is entitled to buy or sell the stock. The accompanying table includes options series for five strike prices—$42.50, $50, $55, $55, and $60 per share. Therefore, values of the 100-share contracts are $4250, $5000, $5500, $5500, and $6000, respectively.

3. This column shows the month each option expires. Expiration is on the third Friday of the month. For example, an XYZ January 55 means that any time up to the third Friday in January, that option holder could buy or sell 100 shares of XYZ for $55 a share. Other January expirations are listed at their strike prices.

4/5. These columns tell us, for calls and puts, respectively, the number of contracts transacted the previous day (volume) and the closing price paid for a contract. For example, 350 of the October 55 calls were traded the previous day and the last price paid was $360 for an option on 100 shares at $55. Whether you gain or lose in options trading usually depends on movements in the premium price. That is because options positions are generally closed out with an offsetting purchase or sale or are allowed to expire. Having to exercise the option, that is, actually buying the stock in the case of calls or coming up with the shares to sell in the case of puts, involves more cash than many options holders want to commit.

Notice how the strike prices of the options series straddle the current market value of the stock. This gives investors a choice of intrinsically worthless—but cheap—options as well as options that have considerable value, but which are expensive to buy. Options exchanges constantly create series with new strike prices to maintain this situation as the price of the underlying stock changes. For stocks selling at $25 to $50 per share, the strike prices are usually set in increments of $5; the increments are $10 on contracts for stocks priced $50 to $200 per share. For options on stocks worth $200 or more per share, strike prices are set $20 apart, and for options on stocks worth less than $25 per share, the increments are $2.50.

The cheapest options are those on which you would lose money (even before considering commission costs) if you exercised them. These are referred to as out-of-the-money options.

Options with intrinsic value are naturally more expensive than those with no intrinsic value. The percentage gains or losses on such options are less than the volatile out-of-the-money options, but there is also less chance that these options will have to be allowed to expire worthless.

These tables also indicate how much money you can make by selling options and thus increase the income from your stock portfolio. For example, if you own 100 shares of XYZ, you may decide to sell calls; that is, you may give another person the right to buy your shares. In return, you receive the premium. Assuming the price of options held steady from the previous day's closing levels, you could expect to receive $560 for selling an XYZ Jan55 call. Of course, if the stock price should rise, the call holder could exercise the option, and you would lose the capital gain. Ideally, you would hope that XYZ stock would hold at around 45 until the option you sold expired. In that case, after brokerage commissions were factored into the equation, it would not be worthwhile for another investor to exercise the option you sold.

If you are worried that your XYZ stock might drop, you can lock in a value of $55 a share through most of October by buying an October55 put (which gives you the right to get $55 a share) for $65 a contract.

In addition to options on individual stocks, options are traded on debt instruments (interest rate options), foreign currencies, stock indexes, and certain futures contracts. What applies to puts and calls on stocks also applies to options on other instruments, with one major exception—index options. Because they are settled in cash and have other distinct features, they deserve special attention.

Daily Index Options Tables

Index options give you the right to buy and sell the dollar value of an index (rather than 100 shares of stock, as with stock options). They often dominate the most-active lists that appear at the head of daily option tables. Index options tables in *The Wall Street Journal* run under their exchange headings: Chicago Board Options Exchange (often referred to in the tables as Chicago Board or just Chicago), the American, Philadelphia, Pacific, and International Stock Exchanges.

Index options are popular because they allow investors to play the whole market, in the case of broad-based indexes, or segments of the market, in the case of indexes that track technology stocks or gold stocks, among others. An index is assigned a value of a certain number of dollars per point—$100, for example. Standard & Poor's and, more recently, Dow Jones, have allowed their indexes to be used for such purposes, as have the New York Stock Exchange and Value Line. Sometimes indexes are created specifically for trading options on them. Using *The Wall Street Journal* format, a hypothetical XYZ index option, which for example, tracks hundreds of stocks, would appear like the accompanying example.

INDEX OPTIONS

			①		②	③	④	⑤
	XYZ Index							
			Strike		**Vol**	**Last**	**Net Chg**	**Open Int**
Ⓐ	Nov	395p	10	15	4.00	42
Ⓑ	Oct	400c	86	20.50	−7.90	1159
Ⓒ	Oct	400p	3647	8.30	1.00	10053
Ⓓ	Nov	400c	2	31	−1.50	132
Ⓔ	Nov	400p	61	15	−0.70	1374
Ⓕ	Dec	420c	33	24.50	−1.50	1865
Ⓖ	Dec	420p	35	29.50	−0.50	2823

Explanation of columns

1. Shows the expiration month, the strike price (the price you would pay for the index if you exercised a call or that you would receive if you exercised a put) and the lower-case "p" or "c" indicating whether the contract is a put or call. To compute the dollar value, multiply by $100 per point, which is the assigned value of the XYZ index. The 400 strike price, for example, would require the payment of $40,000.

2. Indicates the number of contracts traded the previous day.

3. Shows the closing price, or premium, of the last contract traded. For example, the November 395 put traded at 15, meaning $1500 was paid for a contract exercisable for $39,500.

4. Net change is the dollars and cents difference between the previous day's closing price and the closing price the day before that.

5. Open interest is the total number of contracts held but not exercised.

At the bottom of the table relating to each index is a summary of the call and put volume for all the contracts listed and the total open interest for each type of option respectively. These figures give some indication of investor sentiment, since calls are bets that the market will rise and puts are a bet that the market will fall.

The Wall Street Journal tables are accompanied by a box listing each of the underlying indexes with their highs, lows, closes, and net changes from the previous day and for the year to date. By relating the closing price shown in the box to the exercise price shown in the table, we are able to see which contracts are in the money and which are out of the money, and how the option premiums, which move in opposite directions for puts and calls, get more expensive as the contract approaches intrinsic value. XYZ, for example, closed at $412.27 on October 3, down 3.66 (information not illustrated but that would be shown in the underlying indexes box). The November 400 call (D), which is in the money (because you could buy for $400 an index already selling at $412.27), closed at $31, down $1.50 from the prior day, logical since there was a 3.66 decline in the index putting the contract further out of the money. The November 400 put (E), out of the money by the same amount but moving closer into the money as the index value declines, should probably be expected to close fractionally higher, although the fact that it closed marginally lower could be explained by a number of factors, including volume, and is not significant. The December 420 calls and puts (F&G), out of the money and in the money respectively, are appropriately priced lower and higher relative to the November 400s and the closing prices reflect the movement of the index.

Weekly Options Tables

Weekly options tables, such as those found in *Barron's* follow a format different from the daily tables. Calls and puts are stacked rather than placed next to each other. More information is included in these tables. Index options are still run separately.

In the accompanying example of a typical stock-option table, the columns include the following information:

1. Name of the option, as identified by the underlying stock, the expiration month, and the strike price. The closest expiration months and lowest strike prices appear first. A "p" identifies puts; the other options are calls.

2. Sales for the week, in terms of the number of contracts that changed hands.

WEEKLY OPTIONS TABLE

①	②	③	④	⑤		⑥	⑦
Option	Sales	Open Int.	High	Low	Last	Net Chg.	Stock close
ABZ Mar35	1437	10921	6.1	3.75	4.00	–1.15	39
ABZ Mar35 p	99	5089	.15	.15	.15	–.15	39
ABZ Mar40	5981	7332	1.95	.5	.60	–.15	39
ABZ Mar40 p	237	402	2.00	1.00	1.75	+.25	39

3. Open interest—the number of contracts in investor and dealer hands that haven't been exercised or closed out yet. Comparing the number of outstanding calls to puts helps you assess the direction speculators expect the price of the stock to take.

4. The highest and lowest premiums, per share, paid for a particular contract during the past week.

5. The closing premium, or price, per share, at the end of the week.

6. Net Change—how much premiums per share rose or fell from the previous weekly close. The $1.15 per share loss for ABZ Mar35 calls indicates that the contracts lost $115 each.

FUTURES TABLES

Futures tables are grouped by broad categories—agricultural (grains, edible oils, livestock, coffee, sugar, cocoa, orange juice), metals (gold, silver, platinum, palladium, copper), industrials (lumber, cotton, crude oil, heating oil, gasoline), and financial (U.S. Treasury bonds, notes, and bills, foreign currencies, certificates of deposit, stock index futures). About 50 contracts are listed in various futures markets and included in newspaper tables. Commodity contracts are agreements to deliver or take delivery of a commodity in the future. Hence, the "Futures Prices" label for these tables. Most investors in commodities futures contracts are speculators who hope to make big profits by predicting correctly the change in commodity prices. The contracts are identified by their delivery months. A typical table, in this case for cattle, is presented here. The type of contract and the exchange (CME, or Chicago Mercantile Exchange) as well as the size (44,000 pounds) and the units of trade (pennies per pound) are shown in lines B and C.

Other information is presented as follows:

1. The highest and lowest prices paid for a particular delivery month contract since the contract was listed. This indicates the price swings of the contract. The April futures (*Line D*) ranged between 67.07 cents and 55.30 cents per pound, or $29,510 and $24,332 per 44,000-pound contract—a difference of $5178. An investor smart enough or lucky enough to invest $2433 (10% margin when the contract reached its $24,332 low point) and sell when prices peaked would have more than doubled his or her money. On the other hand, someone who invested at the high point could easily have lost all of his or her money. When the loss of a contract's value equals the amount of money that's been invested, brokers will usually demand more margin. If they don't get it, they will sell the contract.

CATTLE FUTURES

	①	②	③	④	⑤	⑥
	...Season...					Open
Ⓐ	High	Low	High	Low	Close	Chg.	Int.
Ⓑ	CATTLE, LIVE BEEF (CME)						
Ⓒ	44,000 lb.; ¢ per lb.						
Ⓓ	67.07	55.30 Apr	61.75	60.32	60.40	−.30	29,042
Ⓔ	66.60	56.25 Jun	60.52	59.35	59.47	−.28	17.547
Ⓕ	61.75	55.20 Aug	58.40	57.45	57.47	−.25	5,939
Ⓖ	60.60	55.70 Oct	57.20	56.37	56.50	−.15	2,705
Ⓗ	61.75	57.55 Dec	58.80	58.10	58.35	−.02	612
Ⓘ	60.20	58.00 Feb	58.90	58.77	58.77	+.07	56
Ⓙ	Est. sales 21,859. Wed's sales 21.607.						
Ⓚ	Wed.'s open Int 55,901, up 63.						

2. The delivery months differentiate one contract from another. The spacing between delivery months and the length of the longest contract varies from one commodity to the next. Most contracts last no longer than one year.

3. The daily high and low prices.

4. The closing price. At 60.40 cents, the close in the April future made that contract worth $26,576.

5. The change in price—the difference from one close to the next. The .3 cent loss for April cattle signifies a $132 loss for the contract.

6. The open interest—the number of contracts that have not been closed through delivery or offsetting transactions. This indicates which contracts will experience the heaviest trading in the future, as most contracts will be closed out through either a sale or a purchase of an offsetting contract, rather than by the delivery of the commodity.

J. This line estimates the number of contracts that changed hands during the last session, as well as the volume of the previous session.

K. This line presents the total open interest of the two previous days, and the change in the number of open contracts.

A great deal of information is omitted from these tables, including delivery days, delivery specifications (the locations to which the commodities would be sent and how they would arrive), and the daily limits in price changes that exchanges impose on most futures contracts. The contract specifications are available from the exchange on which the commodity is traded. Commodities don't possess the uniform qualities of options contracts; the sequence of delivery months and the maximum length of contracts varies from one commodity to another.

Comprehensive commodities tables also include a listing of cash prices, gathered from various sources each day—exchanges, warehouses, fabricators—which give you the immediate value of many of the commodities for which futures contracts are traded as well as other materials, such as wool and cloth and mercury, which have no formal futures market. In the case of futures-related commodities, remember that the current cash price, while often determining the direction of futures contract prices, is usually different. A glut in grain during the harvest could cause an immediate plunge in prices, while prices in the futures market, which anticipate conditions further down the road, could rise.

CORPORATE BOND TABLES

Although corporate bond tables give you valuable insight into a key financial market, they present only part of the picture. While several thousand corporate bonds are traded on the New York and American stock exchanges, many more that are traded through broker/dealers do not appear in the tables of exchange-listed bonds. In addition, exchange-listed bonds traded in lots of 10 or more are also handled off the exchange. According to the Nine Bond Rule, only lots of nine or fewer must be sent to the exchange floor.

Nevertheless, these tables are important because they (1) give you specific information about bonds you may own or are considering buying and (2) indicate the prevailing yields, which can help you estimate the value of similar bonds that you may have in your portfolio or are considering buying.

The table listings look like this:

CORPORATE BONDS

①	②	③	④	⑤	⑥	⑦	⑧
Company (Ticker)	Coupon	Maturity	Last Price	Last Yield	Est. Spread	UST	Est. $ Vol.
BellSouth Corp(BLS)	6.00	Nov 15,2034	92.618	6.576	142	30	40,216
Alcoa (AA)	6.50	Jun 1, 2011	104.348	5.508	63	5	26,982

The accompanying bond table, in this case using *The Wall Street Journal's* format, presents information as follows:

1. The company abbreviations may vary from the abbreviations used in the stock tables, although the ticker symbol is the same.

2. The coupon is the annual interest rate of the bond. A $1000 bond with a coupon of 5% will pay $50 annually until it matures or unless it defaults. A noninterest bearing or "zero coupon" bond would be identified as 0 or, sometimes, as "zr."

3. The maturity is the date the bonds become due for repayment and expire.

4. The last price is the last sale in terms of $100 units. Multiply by 10 to get the price per $1,000 bond. Prices are quoted as a percentage of par value, as though the face value was $100, not $1,000.

5. The last yield is what the bond, based on its coupon and last price, would yield to the new holder. The higher the last price, the lower the last yield, and vice versa.

6. The spread, expressed in basis points (a basis point is 1/100 of 1%), is the difference between the corporate yield and the yield on a comparable Treasury note or bond. The wider the spread, the riskier the corporate bond.

7. This is the maturity of the comparable Treasury security.

8. The estimated dollar volume in thousands.

The *WSJ* corporate bond table lists the forty most active fixed-coupon bonds. It is footnoted with the information on price/yield data for trades of $1 million and greater, and gives the maturities and yields of the Treasury securities used in calculating estimated spreads.

You should also be familiar with the following information, which is not included in the corporate bond tables:

Ratings These indicate the risk of default by the issuer on payments of interest or principal. The major bond rating agencies are Fitch Investor's Service, Moody's Investors Service, and Standard & Poor's Corporation.

Denominations Not all bonds are available in denominations of $1000. Some, called baby bonds, are denominated in amounts of $500 or less.

Yield to maturity   This represents the return, including both the annual interest payments and the gain or loss realized when the bonds are redeemed, taking into account the timing of payments and the time value of money. Yield to maturity will vary depending on whether you bought the bonds at a discount or a premium in relation to their face value, and with the time remaining to maturity. This type of yield calculation allows you to more easily compare bonds with other types of fixed income investments.

Payment dates   Interest payments on corporate bonds are usually, but not always, made semiannually. In any case, the payment cycles vary.

Callability   If a bond can be redeemed prior to maturity by the issuer, it will most likely be called when rates decline and conditions are favorable to the issuer. For this reason, another yield calculation, yield to call, can have more significance than yield to maturity.

GOVERNMENT SECURITIES TABLES

There's no uniform method of quoting the prices of government securities. In addition, the methods of presenting the values of these bills, notes, and bonds are sometimes as obscure as these markets once were to general investors. Because of the numbers of investors who are now familiar with these markets, however, it's worthwhile for you to know how to extract information from these tables.

Treasury Bills

These obligations—or IOUs—of the U.S. Treasury, are backed by the full faith and credit of the U.S. government. They always mature within one year (3 months, 6 months, 9 months, and one year), and are included in many major daily newspapers in the form used in the accompanying table. Information is provided as follows.

TREASURY BILLS

①	②	③	④	⑤
Date	Bid	Asked	Chg	Ask Yield
Aug 20, 2015	5.02	4.98	+0.01	5.05

1.   This is the date on which the bills mature. The maturity date distinguishes one bill from another.

2.   The bid is the price dealers were willing to pay late (there is never an official end) in the last trading session. A bid is presented in a way you may find confusing. It's the discount from the face value demanded by dealers, expressed as an annual percentage. The reason for this is that Treasury bills do not pay interest in the usual sense. Instead, you pay less than the face value of the bills, but you receive the full value when the bills mature. The difference equals the interest you would receive. Thus, if you pay $9000 for a one-year $10,000 bill ($10,000 is the minimum size for a Treasury bill), you're paying 10% less than par, or buying the bill at a 10% discount. A bid of 10 would appear in the table. The higher the discount, the lower the price.

3.   The asked price is the price the dealer is willing to accept, again expressed as an annualized percentage discount rate. In these tables, the percentages are carried out to the nearest hundredth, or basis point. Note that the dealer demands a smaller discount—a higher price—when he resells the bonds.

4.   The change indicates how much the bid discount rate rose or fell during the session. A plus change actually represents a drop in prices, because it indicates an increased discount from par. Just as a larger discount on merchandise in a store window signifies lower prices, so the +0.01, or one basis point, indicates an increase in the discount. A minus change means that Treasury bill prices have risen and that the discount rate—and often other types of yields and rates—has dropped.

5.   The yield represents a yield to maturity, based on the price you would actually pay for the Treasury bill, rather than its face value. The 10% discount rate tells you that you would pay 10% less than $10,000—or $9000 for a one year Treasury bill, for a difference—representing interest—of $1000. The actual yield, however, is better expressed in terms of the amount you would really pay for this investment—$9000. In addition, a return of $1000 on a $9000 investment is greater than the 10% discount rate; it's an 11.11% yield. Note that the yield shown in the sample table, 5.05, is higher than the 5.02 discount rate bid shown in column 2.

Treasury Notes and Bonds

Treasury note and bond prices are included in the same tables. The only difference is that the notes, designated by an "n" or a "p," mature in from one to ten years after they are issued, while bonds mature in ten years or longer. These tables present the securities in the order of their maturity dates, with the closest maturity date at the top and the furthest (always the much-quoted government long bond) at the bottom. Notice the increase in yields as the period of maturity increases; this reflects the fact that lenders demand a greater return for locking up their money for longer time periods. As with other government bonds, prices are given as dealer bid and asked quotes, not in terms of last sales. The reason for this is that there is no way for the extensive network of government bond dealers to report transaction prices and amounts in order to register them onto a last-sale "tape." Extra care must be taken in reading the bid and asked quotes because the two digits following the decimal points are 32nds rather than hundredths, reflecting the traditional language of the government bond market.

The information on a typical daily table is as follows:

TREASURY BONDS

① Rate	② Maturity Mo/Yr	③ Bid	④ Asked	⑤ Chg.	⑥ Ask Yield
6.000	Aug 09n	103.13	103.14	2	4.86
12.500	Aug 14	123.03	123.04	1	4.84
7.875	Feb 21	127.13	127.14	11	5.20
6.500	Nov 26	116.01	116.02	14	5.22

1. The rate is the coupon rate, or the annual interest rate, expressed as a percentage of the face value ($1000 minimum denominations for bonds and $1000 or $5000 for notes).

2. The date identifies the note or bond by its month and year of maturity; thus an "09" means 2009, a "26" means 2026. In addition, an "n" signifies a note.

3. The bid is the price dealers were offering to pay late in the session. It's presented as a percentage of face value. Note, however, that the two digits following the colon are 32nds, not tenths or hundredths. The 103:13 bid for the Aug 09 notes equals $103^{13}\!/\!32$. Because $1/32\%$ of $1000 is $31^{1}\!/\!4$ cents, $^{13}\!/\!32$ equals $4.06; the total bid, per $1000 of notes, equals $1034.06.

4. The asked, the price at which dealers are offering to sell the securities, is calculated similarly to the bid.

5. The daily change from two previous sessions to yesterday's session is based on the rise or fall of the bid price.

6. This figure represents yield to maturity, which combines your current yield (the percentage return in interest based on the price you actually pay) and the difference between the price you paid and the face value at redemption.

Government Agency Bonds

Securities of U.S. agencies such as the Federal Home Loan Bank and Government National Mortgage Association that appear in *The Wall Street Journal* use the same type of bid and asked quotes, expressed in 32nds of a percent, as appear in the Treasury note and bond tables.

Municipal Bonds

You probably won't find individual municipal bond prices in the financial pages, although *The Wall Street Journal* on Wednesdays publishes Merrill Lynch's Muni Master Index along with the latest yields on a variety of municipal bond categories. Even major financial publications include only a sampling of revenue bonds—those repaid from the income of a particular project rather than from general tax dollars. Such tables, typically headed Tax-exempt Authority Bonds, include the issuer's name, maturity date, the bid, the asked, and the daily change in the bid. Information on general obligation bonds is even harder to find. One way of approximating the value of your holdings, though, is to look at yields on newly issued bonds as revealed in tombstone ads placed by underwriters or in the short lists of new issues some papers provide. If the yields on new issues are lower than those your municipals are earning, your bonds are probably selling above face value and vice versa, assuming the bonds are comparable in terms of quality and type of issuer.

MUTUAL FUNDS TABLES

Mutual fund prices are listed several ways in newspapers and at financial websites. Prices of a fund offered by an open-end management company that invests in long-term securities, either stocks or bonds, change with changes in market segments or the market as a whole. These funds sell and redeem their own shares. These prices are generally listed under the heading Mutual Funds.

MUTUAL FUNDS

①	②	③	④
	NAV	Buy	Chg.
ABZ Grp:			
Genrl Fd	14.38	NL	+ .03
AB Growth	10.50	11.03	+ .01
ABZ Incm	5.22	NL	+ .02
Tax Ex	8.21	NL	− .01

These tables contain the following information, by column:

1. The names of mutual funds are clustered by family of funds—funds sponsored by a particular management company. The names often reflect the type of investments that comprise each fund; for example, a general stock fund, growth stock fund, income fund, or tax-exempt bond fund.

Some fund names are followed by lowercase letters such as "a" (meaning a stock dividend was paid in the past 12 months), "d" (new 52-week low), "f" (quotation refers to previous day), "r" (redemption charge may apply), "u" (new 52-week high), and "x" (fund is trading ex-dividend).

2. NAV stands for net asset value, the per-share value of the fund's assets, minus management costs. This is the amount you would receive, per share, if you redeemed your shares. The numbers indicate dollars and cents per share. Sometimes the column carries the heading Sell, meaning that you would receive this amount per share if you were the seller.

3. The Buy column may also be headed Offer Price. It tells you, in dollars and cents per share, the price per share, the price you would pay to buy the shares. Funds that carry a sales charge, or front end load, cost more per share than their net asset value. Funds with back end loads discourage withdrawals by charging a fee to redeem your shares. Many funds, however, carry no sales charge; these are no-load funds whose buy-in costs are the same as their net asset values. These funds carry an "NL" or just "n" in the Buy column.

4. Change refers to the daily change in net asset value, determined at the close of each trading day.

Share prices of a fund offered by a closed-end management company, which issues a fixed number of shares that are then traded among investors, are often included in the daily stock tables. Some newspapers also provide weekly tables listing the prices and values of the shares as of the previous day's close-of-the-market.

CLOSED-END FUNDS

①	②	③	④
	N.A. Value	Stk Price	% Diff
Diversified funds			
ABZ Fund	17.55	21.5	+ 3.1
WXY Fund	10.81	11.3	− 1.8
ZBF Fund	24.74	20.5	− 5.0
Specialized Equity and Convertible Funds			
ABZ Gold	33.10	33.5	+ 2.2
XYZ Conv	15.77	16	+ 1.6
XYZ Tech	9.97	10.3	− 4.4

1. Fund names are grouped alphabetically by fund type.

2. Net Asset Values, as of the last close (unless otherwise indicated) are listed in terms of dollars and cents per share.

3. Stock prices are the last close.

4. Percent difference represents the weekly rise or fall of the net asset value of the shares.

Listings of shares of dual purpose funds can be found in stock exchange tables. These closed-end funds have two classes of shares. One class entitles shareholders to capital gains based on the market value of the assets. The other class entitles holders to dividend and interest income from the fund. Some major newspapers also carry weekly tables of the per share prices of the capital shares, the net asset value of the capital shares, and the weekly percentage or loss of price of those shares. These tables are useful because the daily stock tables don't include net asset values.

Tables for money market funds appear weekly, usually Thursday, after the release of data by iMoneyNet Money Fund Report Average or the National Association of Securities Dealers. Some newspapers print the tables again on Sunday. If you need information on a money market fund before Thursday, you can call the fund organizations. Many fund groups have toll-free 800 phone numbers for shareholders. Most investors need no more than weekly updates because per share values should remain constant at $1.00. These funds, which invest in short-term debt instruments, often are bought because they are liquid (most allow check-writing) and the yield fluctuates with short-term interest rates. Market movements and the accompanying capital gains and losses don't play a major role in the decision to buy or sell shares. The yield is the main information included in such tables.

EXCHANGE-TRADED FUNDS

Exchange-traded funds (ETFs), which are also called exchange-traded port-folios reflecting the recent trend toward broadening an asset class dominated by geographical or industrial sector index funds to include managed designer portfolios, are reported like stocks, but separately. Financial websites offer a wealth of information not found in print publications, including breakdowns of price and performance data by sector.

MONEY MARKET FUNDS

①	②	③	④	⑤
Fund	Assets ($ million)	Average maturity (days)	7-day average yield (%)	Effective 7-day average yield (%)
ABzz Safety Fst	344.7	20	5.61	5.90
Blxx Liquid Secs	1,343.9	26	5.57	5.73
Xymo Govt. Fund	299.0	22	4.11	4.46

The accompanying table includes the following information, by column:

1. Name of the money-market fund.

2. Assets are stated in millions of dollars, to the nearest $100,000. These figures indicate the size of the fund. Investors constantly debate the advantages and disadvantages of size.

3. The average maturity figure represents how long, on average, it takes for the securities in a money fund's portfolio to mature. Shorter average maturities mean that the fund's yield will react more quickly to general interest-rate changes in the fixed-income securities market. This is beneficial when rates are rising, but disad-vantageous when rates are dropping. In the latter case, you would want your fund to hold onto higher-yielding securities as long as possible. The move in the average maturity figure is considered by some to be a good predictor of short-term interest rate direc-tion. If a fund's average maturity increases by several days for several weeks, this is an indication that portfolio managers expect short-term rates to drop. If the average maturity decreases, the managers probably expect short-term rates to rise.

4. The 7-day average yield indicates the average daily total return for that period, and is determined largely by subtract-ing the fund's costs from the investment income. The result is expressed as a percentage of the average share price:

5. The effective 7-day average yield is the 7-day average yield computed after assuming that the rate continues for a year and that dividends are reinvested. This permits comparison with other instruments whose yields are expressed on the same basis, such as bank certificates of deposit.

OTHER TABLES

Interest and Currency Rates

The key rates highlighted earlier are followed up with more detailed summaries throughout the inside of the major print and website news packages.

A complete rate and yield table. for example, would additionally list, with comparisons to the previous day and year ago, the (Federal Reserve) discount rate and the prime rate, whose significance we have already discussed. It might also list yields on 7-year Treasury notes, an important benchmark for intermediate-term corporate and other non-Treasury fixed-income obligations; yields on 30-year Treasury bonds, the ultimate indicator of the entire bond market and often of the stock market, where prices normally move inversely to "long bond" yields; and top-rated obligations of public utilities whose yield is a direct benchmark for other corporate bonds that are riskier to varying degrees. Major newspapers also carry additional lists of rates that are mainly of interest to professional traders. Some, like Eurodollar time deposits, the London Interbank Offered Rate (LIBOR), and commercial paper, were discussed above. Others include banker's acceptances, which are time drafts created in commerce, accepted (guaranteed, in effect) by major banks, and traded as money market instruments; and the broker loan rate (or call loan rate), which is the rate banks charge brokers for overnight loans to cover securities positions of customers. This rate, which usually hovers just above the rate on (also overnight) federal funds, has meaning to individual investors because it determines what brokers charge on margin loans.

Many financial newspapers and other media now carry weekly listings of the banks currently offering the highest interest rates on deposit accounts and certificates of deposit.

The meaning and importance of currency exchange rates was discussed earlier. In addition to highlighting major currency changes, most major financial papers carry full exchange tables, listed alphabetically by country, which provide the exchange rates from the previous two days in four columns—two in terms of dollars per unit of foreign currency, two in terms of units of foreign currency per dollar. Major currencies also list 30-, 90-, and 180-day forward rates. These represent guaranteed future delivery rates offered by banks for customers who must plan ahead and are willing to pay a premium to eliminate the risk of exchange rates moving adversely in the interim.

Some publications, including *The Wall Street Journal* and financial website, contain a table showing key currency cross rates. This table lists currencies in terms of each other's value. Complete currency sections also cover futures, options, and futures options on leading currencies.

HOW TO READ TICKER TAPES

With the growth of cable television, an increasing number of investors pick up financial news from cablecasters that cover the securities and commodities markets continuously throughout the business day. Like daily newspapers, the purveyors of electronic financial news aim for a broad audience. Through the creative use of graphics and commentary, they manage generally to communicate complex information in a way nonprofessionals can understand.

But unless you work for an investment firm or spend your leisure time sitting around a board room of a brokerage, the figures and symbols that pass constantly—sometimes with maddening rapidity—across the lower portion of the TV screen may require explanation. What you see there is the stock ticker tape, the same report of trading activity displayed on the floors of the major stock exchanges. The only difference is that to give stock exchange members an advantage, it is transmitted with a 15-minute delay.

The most frequently seen display is the consolidated tape, a combination of two networks (not to be confused with television networks): Network A reports all New York Stock Exchange issues traded on the NYSE or other identified markets, which include five regional exchanges, the over-the-counter market, and other electronic communication networks are traded. Network B reports all American Stock Exchange issues traded on the Amex or other identified markets. National Association of Securities Dealers (NASDAQ) over-the-counter quotes are presented separately in the lower band.

Elements of the consolidated tape; which reports actual transactions (the term quotes is loosely used to mean trades in ticker tape jargon, although its proper financial meaning refers to bid and asked quotations) are explained as follows:

Stock Symbol The first letters are the stock ticker symbol—XOM for ExxonMobil, C for Citicorp. IBM for IBM, for example. (There is one exception to this, which is that the prefix Q is used when a company is in receivership or bankruptcy.) The ticker symbol may be followed by an abbreviation designating a type of issue, such as Pr to signify preferred stock, which may, in turn, be followed by a letter indicating a class of preferred. Thus XYZ-PrE means XYZ Corporation's preferred stock series E. If XYZ's preferred stock series E was convertible, the abbreviation .CV would be added to read XYZPrE.CV. Common stock classes, if any, are indicated by a period plus a letter following the ticker symbol. Thus XYZ's class B common would be designated XYZ.B. (A list of ticker symbols is included at the end of Part V of this book.)

Other abbreviations placed after the ticker symbol as necessary are rt for rights; wi for when issued; .WD for when distributed; .WS for warrants (the abbreviation may be preceded by another period and letter to identify the particular issue of warrant); and .XD for ex-dividend.

Market Identifiers When the information about the stock is followed by an ampersand (&) and a letter, the transaction took place in a market other than the New York Stock Exchange, if you are looking at Network A, or the American Stock Exchange, if you are looking at Network B. The letter identifies the market as follows:

A	American Stock Exchange
B	Boston Stock Exchange
C	The National Stock Exchange
M	Chicago Stock Exchange
N	New York Stock Exchange
O	Other Markets (electronic communication networks)
P	Pacific Stock Exchange
T	Third market (mainly Nasdaq)
X	Philadelphia Stock Exchange

Volume The next portion of the transaction information provided on a ticker tape may appear below or to the right of the above stock symbol and market designation. It reports the number of shares traded. However, if the trade is in a round lot of 100 shares, which it usually is, no volume is indicated and the tape simply shows the issue and the price. Thus XYZ 26.5 simply means that 100 shares of XYZ were traded at 26.50 a share. Where larger round lot transactions take place, the number of round lots is indicated followed by the letter "s" followed by the price. Thus, XYZ 4 s 26.5 means 400 shares were traded at $26.50 a share. Similarly, 1700 shares would be XYZ 17 s 26.5 and so on, except that when the volume is 10,000 shares or more the full number is given—XYZ 16,400 s 26.5, for example.

Odd lots quantities other than multiples of 100 or whatever other unit represents the round lot—are not printed on the ticker tape unless approved by an exchange official. If approval is given, odd lots of 50 shares and 150 shares of XYZ would be displayed respectively: XYZ 50 SHRS 26.5 and XYZ 150 SHRS 26.5.

A limited number of issues—mainly inactive stocks or higher priced preferred issues—trade in round lots of less than 100 shares. On the New York Stock Exchange such round lots are always 10 shares, but on the Amex these round lots can be 10, 25, or 50 shares. Transactions in these special round lots are designated by a number indicating how many lots were traded followed by the symbols. Thus, on the New York Stock Exchange, XYZ Pr 3 55 means 3 10-share lots (30 shares) of XYZ preferred stock were traded at $55 a share. If XYZ were listed on the AMEX, you would not know by looking at the tape whether the lot involved was 10, 25, or 50 shares. For that information, you would have to consult a stock guide.

Active Market Procedures When trading becomes sufficiently heavy to cause the tape to run more than a minute behind, shortcuts are implemented. The most frequently taken measure to keep up with heavy trading is signified by the tape printout DIGITS AND VOLUME DELETED. This means only the unit price digit and fraction will be printed (for example, 9.5 instead of 19.5) except when the price ends in zero or is an opening transaction. In addition, volume information will be deleted except when trades are 5000 shares or more (the threshold can be raised if required). Another common procedure is to announce REPEAT PRICES OMITTED, meaning that successive transactions at the same price will not be repeated. When activity slackens to a more normal level, the tape will read DIGITS AND VOLUME RESUMED with similar indications for the other measures.

Other Abbreviations When a transaction is being reported out of its proper order, the letters .SLD will follow the symbol as in XYZ .SLD 3s 26.5. SLR followed by a number signifies seller's option and number of days until settlement. This indication is found after the price. CORR indicates that a correction of information follows. ERR or CXL indicates a print is to be ignored. OPD signifies an opening transaction that was delayed or one whose price is significantly changed from the previous day's close.

PART IV

Dictionary of Finance and Investment

HOW TO USE THIS DICTIONARY EFFECTIVELY

Alphabetization: All entries are alphabetized by letter rather than by word so that multiple-word terms are treated as single words. For example, **NET ASSET VALUE** follows **NET ASSETS** as though it were spelled **NETASSETVALUE,** without spacing. Similarly, **ACCOUNT EXECUTIVE** follows **ACCOUNTANT'S OPINION.** In unusual cases, abbreviations or acronyms appear as entries in the main text, in addition to appearing in the back of the book in the separate listing of Abbreviations and Acronyms. This is when the short form, rather than the formal name, predominates in common business usage. For example, NASDAQ is more commonly used in speaking of the National Association of Securities Dealers Automated Quotations system than the name itself, so the entry is at **NASDAQ.** Numbers in entry titles are alphabetized as if they were spelled out.

Abbreviations and Acronyms: A separate list of abbreviations and acronyms follows the Dictionary. It contains shortened versions of terms defined in the book, plus several hundred related business terms.

Cross-references: In order to gain a fuller understanding of a term, it will sometimes help to refer to the definition of another term. In these cases the additional term is printed in SMALL CAPITALS. Such cross-references appear in the body of the definition or at the end of the entry (or sub-entry). Cross-references at the end of an entry (or sub-entry) may refer to related or contrasting concepts rather than give more information about the concept under discussion. As a rule, a term is printed in small capitals only the first time it appears in an entry. Where an entry is fully defined at another entry, a reference rather than a definition is provided; for example, **EITHER-OR ORDER** *see* ALTERNATIVE ORDER.

Italics: Italic type is generally used to indicate that another term has a meaning identical or very closely related to that of the entry. Occasionally, italic type is also used to highlight the fact that a word used is a business term and not just a descriptive phrase. Italics are also used for the titles of publications.

Parentheses: Parentheses are used in entry titles for two reasons. The first is to indicate that an entry's opposite is such an integral part of the concept that only one discussion is necessary; for example, **REALIZED PROFIT (OR LOSS).** The second and more common reason is to indicate that an abbreviation is used with about the same frequency as the term itself; for example, **OVER THE COUNTER (OTC).**

Examples, Illustrations, and Tables: The numerous examples in this Dictionary are designed to help readers gain understanding and to help them relate abstract concepts to the real world of finance and investment. Line drawings are provided in addition to text to clarify concepts best understood visually; for example, technical chart patterns used by securities analysts and graphic concepts used in financial analysis.

A

ABANDONMENT voluntarily giving up all rights, title, or claims to property that rightfully belongs to the owner. An example of abandoned property would be stocks, bonds, or mutual funds held in a brokerage account for which the firm is unable to locate the listed owner over a specified period of time, usually a few years. If ruled to be abandoned, the property may revert to the state under the laws of ESCHEAT. In addition to financial assets, other kinds of property that are subject to abandonment include patents, inventions, leases, trademarks, contracts, and copyrights.

ABEYANCE indefinite legal status of real estate title when lawful ownership is in question and being determined.

ABILITY TO PAY

Finance: borrower's ability to meet principal and interest payments on long-term obligations out of earnings. Also called *ability to service. See also* FIXED CHARGE COVERAGE.

Industrial relations: ability of an employer, especially a financial organization to meet a union's financial demands from operating income.

Municipal bonds: issuer's present and future ability to generate enough tax revenue to meet its contractual obligations, taking into account all factors concerned with municipal income and property values.

Taxation: the concept that tax rates should vary with levels of wealth or income; for example, the progressive income tax.

ABNORMAL RETURN *see* EXCESS RETURN.

ABOVE PAR *see* PAR VALUE.

ABROGATE nullify a contract or law.

ABS *see* AUTOMATED BOND SYSTEM.

ABSOLUTE PRIORITY RULE rule that creditor claims have precedence over shareholder claims in BANKRUPTCY or LIQUIDATION.

ABSORBED

Business: a cost that is treated as an expense rather than passed on to a customer.

Also, a firm merged into an acquiring company.

Cost accounting: indirect manufacturing costs (such as property taxes and insurance) are called absorbed costs. They are differentiated from variable costs (such as direct labor and materials). *See also* DIRECT OVERHEAD.

Finance: an account that has been combined with related accounts in preparing a financial statement and has lost its separate identity. Also called *absorption account* or *adjunct account.*

Securities: issue that an underwriter has completely sold to the public.

Also, in market trading, securities are absorbed as long as there are corresponding orders to buy and sell. The market has reached the *absorption point* when further assimilation is impossible without an adjustment in price. *See also* UNDIGESTED SECURITIES.

ABSORPTION RATE estimated rate at which real estate properties can be sold or leased in a particular area.

ABUSIVE TAX SHELTER any investment used to avoid taxes that is not in compliance with the law, such as a LIMITED PARTNERSHIP the Internal Revenue Service deems to be claiming illegal tax deductions—typically, one that inflates the value of acquired property beyond its fair market value. If these writeoffs are denied by the IRS, investors must pay severe penalties and interest charges, on top of back taxes.

ACCELERATED COST RECOVERY SYSTEM (ACRS) provision instituted by the ECONOMIC RECOVERY TAX ACT OF 1981 (ERTA) and modified by the TAX REFORM ACT OF 1986, which established rules for the DEPRECIATION (the recovery of cost through tax deductions) of qualifying assets within a shorter period than the asset's expected useful (economic) life. With certain exceptions, ACRS rules provided for greater acceleration over longer periods of time than ERTA rules, and were effective for property placed in service between 1980 and 1987. The ACRS was superseded by the Modified Accelerated Cost Recovery System (MACRS) for assets placed in service after 1986. *See also* MODIFIED ACCELERATED COST RECOVERY SYSTEM.

ACCELERATED DEPRECIATION depreciation methods that allow faster write-offs than straight-line rates in earlier periods of the useful life of an asset. For example, in the first few years of recovery, MACRS allows a 200% DOUBLE-DECLINING BALANCE write-off, which is twice the rate of STRAIGHT-LINE DEPRECIATION. Depreciable assets other than buildings fall into 3-, 5-, 7-, 10-, 15-, or 20-year recovery periods under the general depreciation system.

ACCELERATION CLAUSE provision, normally present in an INDENTURE agreement, mortgage, or other contract, that the unpaid balance is to become due and payable if specified events of default should occur. Such events include failure to meet interest, principal, or sinking fund payments; insolvency; and nonpayment of taxes on mortgaged property.

ACCELERATED DEATH BENEFIT provision in a life insurance policy that allows greater benefits to be paid to a terminally ill patient by reducing death benefits.

ACCEPTANCE

In general: agreement created when the drawee of a TIME DRAFT (bill of exchange) writes the word "accepted" above the signature and designates a date of payment. The drawee becomes the acceptor, responsible for payment at maturity.

Also, paper issued and sold by sales finance companies, such as General Motors Acceptance Corporation.

Banker's acceptance: time draft drawn on and accepted by a bank, the customary means of effecting payment for merchandise sold in import-export transactions and a source of financing used extensively in international trade. With the credit strength of a bank behind it, the banker's acceptance usually qualifies as a MONEY MARKET instrument. The liability assumed by the bank is called its acceptance liability. *See also* LETTER OF CREDIT.

Trade acceptance: time draft drawn by the seller of goods on the buyer, who becomes the acceptor, and which is therefore only as good as the buyer's credit.

ACCIDENTAL DEATH BENEFIT value paid to the benficiary of an accidental death insurance policy or a life insurance policy having an accidental death clause or rider, in the event the insured dies because of an accident. Such policies or clauses often provide also for bodily injury causing various forms of dismemberment, in which case the benefit is paid to the insured. Double or triple idemnity policies pay twice or three times the face value of the policy. Exclusions typically apply to death or injury caused by war, illegal activities, or noncommercial aviation. Time (meaning death or dismemberment must occur within a specified period following an accident) and age limits usually apply.

ACCOMMODATION ENDORSEMENT third-party guarantee of an obligation without compensation.

ACCOMMODATIVE MONETARY POLICY Federal Reserve policy to increase the amount of money available for lending by banks. When the Fed implements an accommodative policy, it is known as easing the money supply. During a period of easing, interest rates fall, making it more attractive for borrowers to borrow, thereby stimulating the economy. The Fed will initiate an accommodative policy when interest rates are high, the economy is weak, and there is little fear of an outbreak of inflation. Once interest rates have been lowered enough to stimulate the economy, the Fed may become concerned about inflation again and switch to a TIGHT MONEY policy. *See also* MONETARY POLICY.

ACCOUNT

In general: contractual relationship between a buyer and seller under which payment is made at a later time. The term *open account* or *charge account* is used, depending on whether the relationship is commercial or personal.

Also, the historical record of transactions under the contract, as periodically shown on the *statement of account.*

Banking: relationship under a particular name, usually evidenced by a deposit against which withdrawals can be made. Among them are demand, time, custodial, joint, trustee, corporate, special, and regular accounts. Administrative responsibility is handled by an *account officer.*

Bookkeeping: assets, liabilities, income, and expenses as represented by individual ledger pages to which debit and credit entries are chronologically posted to record changes in value. Examples are cash, accounts receivable, accrued interest, sales, and officers' salaries. The system of recording, verifying, and reporting such information is called accounting. Practitioners of accounting are called *accountants.*

Investment banking: financial and contractual relationship between parties to an underwriting syndicate, or the status of securities owned and sold.

Securities: relationship between a broker-dealer firm and its client wherein the firm, through its registered representatives, acts as agent in buying and selling securities and sees to related administrative matters. *See also* ACCOUNT EXECUTIVE; ACCOUNT STATEMENT.

ACCOUNT AGGREGATION *see* AGGREGATION.

ACCOUNTANT'S OPINION statement signed by an independent public accountant describing the scope of the examination of an organization's books and records. Because financial reporting involves considerable discretion, the accountant's opinion is an important assurance to a lender or investor. Depending on the scope of an audit and the auditor's confidence in the veracity of the information, the opinion can be unqualified or, to some degree, qualified. Qualified opinions, though not necessarily negative, warrant investigation. Also called *auditor's certificate.*

ACCOUNT BALANCE net of debits and credits at the end of a reporting period. Term applies to a variety of account relationships, such as with banks, credit card companies, brokerage firms, and stores, and to classifications of transactions in a bookkeeping system. The same account may be an asset account balance or a liability account balance, depending on which side of the transaction you are on. For example, your bank balance is an asset account to you and a liability account to the bank. Your credit card (debit) balance is a liability account to you and an asset account (account receivable) to the credit card company.

ACCOUNT EXECUTIVE *see* REGISTERED REPRESENTATIVE.

ACCOUNT RECONCILIATION the process of adjusting the balance in your checkbook to match your bank statement. Your checkbook balance, plus outstanding checks, less bank charges, plus interest (if any), should equal the balance shown on your bank statement.

ACCOUNTS PAYABLE amounts owing on open account to creditors for goods and services. Analysts look at the relationship of accounts payable to purchases for indications of sound day-to-day financial management. *See also* TRADE CREDIT.

ACCOUNTS RECEIVABLE money owed to a business for merchandise or services sold on open account, a key factor in analyzing a company's LIQUIDITY—its ability to meet current obligations without additional revenues. *See also* ACCOUNTS RECEIVABLE TURNOVER; AGING SCHEDULE; COLLECTION RATIO.

ACCOUNTS RECEIVABLE FINANCING short-term financing whereby accounts receivable serve as collateral for working capital advances. *See also* FACTORING.

ACCOUNTS RECEIVABLE TURNOVER ratio obtained by dividing total credit sales by accounts receivable. The ratio indicates how many times the receivables portfolio has been collected during the accounting period. *See also* ACCOUNTS RECEIVABLE; AGING SCHEDULE; COLLECTION RATIO.

ACCOUNT STATEMENT
In general: any record of transactions and their effect on charge or open-account balances during a specified period.
Banking: summary of all checks paid, deposits recorded, and resulting balances during a defined period. Also called a *bank statement.*
Securities: statement summarizing all transactions and showing the status of an account with a broker-dealer firm, including long and short positions. Such statements must be issued quarterly, but are generally provided monthly when accounts are active. Also, the OPTION AGREEMENT required when an option account is opened.

ACCREDITED INVESTOR under the SECURITIES ACT OF 1933, a company may be exempt from registration requirements when selling its securities to accredited investors. Among those considered accredited investors under Rule 501 of Securities and Exchange Commission Regulation D are banks, insurance companies, employee benefit plans, and charitable organizations, corporations, or partnerships with assets exceeding $5 million. Also in this category are individuals or married couples with a net worth of at least $1 million at the time of purchase and individuals with income exceeding $200,000 in each of the two most recent years ($300,000 for married couples).

ACCREDITED PERSONAL FINANCIAL PLANNING SPECIALIST
see FINANCIAL PLANNER.

ACCRETION
1. asset growth through internal expansion, acquisition, or such causes as aging of whisky or growth of timber.
2. adjustment of the difference between the price of a bond bought at an original discount and the par value of the bond.

ACCRUAL BASIS accounting method whereby income and expense items are recognized as they are earned or incurred, even though they may not have been received or actually paid in cash. The alternative is CASH BASIS accounting.

ACCRUAL BONDS bonds that do not make periodic interest payments, but instead accrue interest until the bond matures. Also known as *zero-coupon bonds*. *See also* ZERO-COUPON SECURITIES.

ACCRUED BENEFITS pension benefits that an employee has earned based on his or her years of service at a company. *See also* VESTING.

ACCRUED INTEREST interest that has accumulated between the most recent payment and the sale of a bond or other fixed-income security. At the time of sale, the buyer pays the seller the bond's price plus accrued interest, calculated by multiplying the coupon rate by the number of days that have elapsed since the last payment.

Accrued interest is also used in a real estate LIMITED PARTNERSHIP when the seller of a building takes a lump sum in cash at the time of sale and gives a second mortgage for the remainder. If the rental income from the building does not cover the mortgage payments, the seller agrees to let the interest accrue until the building is sold to someone else. Accrued interest deals were curtailed by the 1984 tax act.

ACCRUED MARKET DISCOUNT increase in market value of a DISCOUNT BOND that occurs because of its approaching MATURITY DATE (when it is redeemable at PAR) and not because of declining market interest rates.

ACCUMULATE *see* BROKER RECOMMENDATIONS (or OPINIONS or RATINGS).

ACCUMULATED BENEFIT OBLIGATION (ABO) estimated liabilty of a pension plan assuming immediate termination. Differs from *projected benefit obligation (PBO)*, which makes a similar calculation assuming plan is ongoing.

ACCUMULATED DEPRECIATION *see* BOOK VALUE (meaning number 1).

ACCUMULATED DIVIDEND dividend due, usually to holders of cumulative preferred stock, but not paid. It is carried on the books as a liability until paid. *See also* CUMULATIVE PREFERRED.

ACCUMULATED PROFITS TAX surtax on earnings retained in a business to avoid the higher personal income taxes they would be subject to if paid out as dividends to the owners.

Accumulations above the specified limit, which is set fairly high to benefit small firms, must be justified by the reasonable needs of the business or be subject to the surtax. Because determining the reasonable needs of a business involves considerable judgment, companies have been known to pay excessive dividends or even to make merger decisions out of fear of the accumulated profits tax. Also called *accumulated earnings tax*.

ACCUMULATION

Corporate finance: profits that are not paid out as dividends but are instead added to the company's capital base. *See also* ACCUMULATED PROFITS TAX.

Investments: purchase of a large number of shares in a controlled way so as to avoid driving the price up. An institution's accumulation program, for instance, may take weeks or months to complete.

Mutual funds: investment of a fixed dollar amount regularly and reinvestment of dividends and capital gains.

ACCUMULATION AREA price range within which buyers accumulate shares of a stock. Technical analysts spot accumulation areas when a stock does not drop below a particular price. Technicians who use the ON-BALANCE VOLUME method of analysis advise buying stocks that have hit their accumulation area, because the stocks can be expected to attract more buying interest. *See also* DISTRIBUTION AREA.

ACCUMULATION AREA

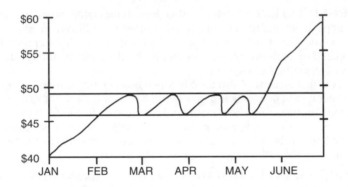

ACCUMULATION BOND term used occasionally to describe a bond issued at an ORIGINAL ISSUE DISCOUNT (OID) with interest that accumulates but is not paid out until maturity. Also called ACCRUAL BONDS and DISCOUNTED BONDS, but not to be confused with DISCOUNT BONDS, which trade below face value but are interest-bearing, that is, pay out interest on a regular basis. *See also* IMPUTED INTEREST; ZERO COUPON SECURITY.

ACCUMULATION PERIOD years during which a working person is making contributions to a DEFERRED ACCOUNT.

ACES PASS-THRU run by the FINANCIAL INDUSTRY REGULATORY AUTHORITY (FINRA), ACES Pass-Thru automates trades between order-entry and market-maker firms that have established trading relationships with each other, designating securities at specified quantities for automatic execution. Once trading parameters are set, ACES Pass-Thru facilitates order entry, best-price order execution, and limited-order maintenance, as well as a variety of inventory control capabilities. Trades are then automatically reported for public dissemination and sent for comparison and clearing.

ACID-TEST RATIO *see* QUICK RATIO.

ACKNOWLEDGMENT verification that a signature on a banking or brokerage document is legitimate and has been certified by an authorized person. Acknowledgment is needed when transferring an account from one broker to another, for instance. In banking, an acknowledgment verifies that an item has been received by the paying bank and is or is not available for immediate payment.

ACQUIRED SURPLUS uncapitalized portion of the net worth of a successor company in a POOLING OF INTERESTS combination. In other words, the part of the combined net worth not classified as CAPITAL STOCK.

In a more general sense, the surplus acquired when a company is purchased.

ACQUISITION one company taking over controlling interest in another company. Investors are always looking out for companies that are likely to be acquired, because those who want to acquire such companies are often willing to pay more than the market price for the shares they need to complete the acquisition. *See also* MERGER; POOLING OF INTERESTS; TAKEOVER.

ACQUISITION COST
Finance: price plus CLOSING COSTS to buy a company, real estate or other property.
Investments: SALES CHARGE incurred to buy a LOAD FUND or the original price, plus brokerage commissions, of a security. *See also* TAX BASIS.

ACROSS THE BOARD movement in the stock market that affects almost all stocks in the same direction. When the market moves up across the board, almost every stock gains in price.

An across-the-board pay increase in a company is a raise of a fixed percent or amount for all employees.

ACTING IN CONCERT two or more investors working together to achieve the same investment goal—for example, all buying stock in a company they want to take over. Such investors must inform the Securities and Exchange Commission if they intend to oust the company's top management or acquire control. It is illegal for those acting in concert to manipulate a stock's price for their own gain.

ACTIVE ACCOUNT account at a bank or brokerage firm in which there are many transactions. An active banking account may generate more fees for each check written or ATM transaction completed. An active brokerage account will generate more commission revenue for the brokerage firm than an inactive account. Banks usually impose minimum charges for maintaining a checking and savings account. Many brokerage firms levy a fee if an account does not generate a high enough level of activity. If there is no activity in an account for five years or more, the account may be subject to ESCHEAT procedures in which the account's assets revert to the state.

ACTIVE BOX collateral available for securing brokers' loans or customers' margin positions in the place—or *box*—where securities are held in safekeeping for clients of a broker-dealer or for the broker-dealer itself. Securities used as collateral must be owned by the firm or hypothecated—that is, pledged or assigned—by the customer to the firm, then by the broker to the lending bank. For margin loans, securities must be hypothecated by the customer to the broker.

ACTIVE MANAGEMENT
1. INVESTMENT MANAGEMENT where the PORTFOLIO MANAGER actively makes investment decisions and initiates buying and selling of securities in an

effort to maximize RETURN. It is the opposite of PASSIVE MANAGEMENT, where the money manager oversees a fixed portfolio structured to match the performance of the overall market or a preselected part of it, a strategy called INDEXING.

The terms active and passive management apply at the level of portfolio management; the operative concept is management, implying professional management. PASSIVE INVESTING is something else. An individual who buys an INDEX FUND is engaging in passive investing as is an investor in a LIMITED PARTNERSHIP deemed *passive* by the Internal Revenue Service. But should the same individual hire an INVESTMENT COUNSEL, who chose to place his or her client's funds in passive investments, the investment counsel would be making investment choices and thus be engaged in active management. The passive investments themselves might or might not be under active management; an index fund would be under passive management, while the passive limited partnership, having business activities, would be under active management.

2. bond terminology meaning a strategy of buying and selling rather than holding to maturity.

ACTIVE MARKET heavy volume of trading in a particular stock, bond, or commodity. The spread between bid and asked prices is usually narrower in an active market than when trading is quiet.

Also, a heavy volume of trading on the exchange as a whole. Institutional money managers prefer such a market because their trades of large blocks of stock tend to have less impact on the movement of prices when trading is generally active.

ACTIVE MONEY same as CURRENCY IN CIRCULATION.

ACT OF GOD unavoidable destructive event caused by natural forces and that may excuse parties to a contract from responsibility.

ACT OF STATE DOCTRINE principle followed by federal courts in the United States that domestic actions of a sovereign nation cannot be adjudicated in the courts of another nation. Its purpose is to prevent U.S. courts from interfering with actions of the executive branch of the U.S. government with respect to claims by U.S. nationals against foreign governments, such as cases where property is expropriated through nationalization.

ACTUALS any physical commodity, such as gold, soybeans, or pork bellies. Trading in actuals ultimately results in delivery of the commodity to the buyer when the contract expires. This contrasts with trading in commodities of, for example, index options, where the contract is settled in cash, and no physical commodity is delivered upon expiration. However, even when trading is in actuals most futures and options contracts are closed out before the contract expires, and so these transactions do not end in delivery.

ACTUARY mathematician employed by an insurance company to calculate premiums, reserves, dividends, and insurance, pension, and annuity rates, using risk factors obtained from experience tables. These tables are based on both the company's history of insurance claims and other industry and general statistical data.

ADDITIONAL BONDS TEST test limiting the amount of new bonds that can be issued. Since bonds are secured by assets or revenues of a corporate or governmental entity, the underwriters of the bond must insure that the bond issuer can meet the debt service requirements of any additional bonds. The test usually sets specific financial benchmarks, such as what portion of an issuer's revenues or cash flow can be devoted to paying interest.

ADDITIONAL PAID-IN CAPITAL *see* PAID-IN CAPITAL.

ADDITIONAL VOLUNTARY CONTRIBUTIONS contributions made by an employee into a tax-deferred savings account, such as a 401(k) or 403(b), beyond the level at which an employer will match the investment. Depending on the level of contributions, these may be made on a pretax or aftertax basis. Tax law limits the total amount of money that can be contributed to such a tax-deferred account. In any case, all funds so contributed accumulate without taxation until withdrawn at retirement. The employee chooses the investment vehicles in which the money is invested.

ADD-ON privilege offered by some issuers of CERTIFICATES OF DEPOSIT (CDs) whereby funds can be added prior to maturity and earn the original interest rate, a benefit in periods of declining rates.

ADEQUACY OF COVERAGE test of the extent to which the value of an asset, such as real property, securities, or a contract subject to currency exchange rates, is protected from potential loss either through INSURANCE or HEDGING.

ADJUSTABLE LIFE INSURANCE LIFE INSURANCE that gives a policyholder power to change the face amount, premium, coverage period, or other features of the policy.

ADJUSTABLE RATE MORTGAGE (ARM) mortgage agreement between a financial institution and a real estate buyer stipulating predetermined adjustments of the interest rate at specified intervals. Mortgage payments are tied to some index outside the control of the bank or savings and loan institution, such as the interest rates on U.S. Treasury bills or the average national mortgage rate. Adjustments are made regularly, usually at intervals of one, three, or five years. In return for taking some of the risk of a rise in interest rates, borrowers get lower rates at the beginning of the ARM than they would if they took out a fixed rate mortgage covering the same term. A homeowner who is worried about sharply rising interest rates should probably choose a fixed rate mortgage, whereas one who thinks rates will rise modestly, stay stable, or fall should choose an adjustable rate mortgage. Critics of ARMs charge that these mortgages entice young homeowners to undertake potentially onerous commitments.

Also called a Variable Rate Mortgage (VRM), the ARM should not be confused with the GRADUATED PAYMENT MORTGAGE, which is issued at a fixed rate with monthly payments designed to increase as the borrower's income grows. *See also* CAP; COST OF FUNDS; GROWING EQUITY MORTGAGE; MORTGAGE INTEREST DEDUCTION; OPTION ARM; SELF-AMORTIZING MORTGAGE; SHARED APPRECIATION MORTGAGE; TEASER RATE.

ADJUSTABLE RATE PREFERRED STOCK (ARPS) PREFERRED STOCK, whose dividend instead of being fixed is adjusted, usually quarterly, based on changes in the Treasury bill rate or other money market rate. The prices of adjustable rate preferreds are less volatile than fixed rate preferreds. Also called *floating rate* or *variable rate* preferred. *See also* CAPS; DUTCH AUCTION PREFERRED STOCK; MANDATORY CONVERTIBLES.

ADJUSTED BALANCE METHOD formula for calculating finance charges based on ACCOUNT BALANCE remaining after adjusting for payments and credits posted during the billing period. Interest charges under this method are lower than those under the AVERAGE DAILY BALANCE and PREVIOUS BALANCE METHOD.

ADJUSTED BASIS base price from which to judge capital gains or losses upon sale of an asset like a stock or bond. The cost of commissions in effect is deducted at the time of sale when net proceeds are used for tax purposes. The price must be adjusted to account for any stock splits that have occurred since the initial purchase before arriving at the adjusted basis.

ADJUSTED (OR MODIFIED) BOOK VALUE BOOK VALUE adjusted for MARKET VALUE on a BALANCE SHEET.

ADJUSTED DEBIT BALANCE (ADB) formula for determining the position of a margin account, as required under Regulation T of the Federal Reserve Board. The ADB is calculated by netting the balance owing the broker with any balance in the SPECIAL MISCELLANEOUS ACCOUNT (SMA), and any paper profits on short accounts. Although changes made in Regulation T in 1982 diminished the significance of ADBs, the formula is still useful in determining whether withdrawals of cash or securities are permissible based on SMA entries.

ADJUSTED EXERCISE PRICE term used in put and call options on Government National Mortgage Association (Ginnie Mae) contracts. To make sure that all contracts trade fairly, the final exercise price of the option is adjusted to take into account the coupon rates carried on all GNMA mortgages. If the standard GNMA mortgage carries an 8% yield, for instance, the price of GNMA pools with 12% mortgages in them are adjusted so that both instruments have the same yield to the investor.

ADJUSTED GROSS INCOME (AGI) income on which an individual or couple computes federal income tax. AGI is determined by subtracting from gross income any unreimbursed business expenses and other allowable adjustments—for example, INDIVIDUAL RETIREMENT ACCOUNTS, SEP and Keogh payments, and alimony payments. Other adjustments include forfeiture of interest penalties because of premature withdrawals from a certificate of deposit; capital loss deductions up to $3,000; rent and royalty expenses; 50% of self-employed tax liability; health insurance deductions for the self-employed; and net operating losses. Other adjustments include student loan interest; jury duty pay turned over to your employer; moving expenses; health savings account contributions; tuition and fees deductions; and hybrid vehicle deductions. AGI is the individual's or couple's income before itemized deductions such as medical expenses, state and local income taxes, and real estate taxes. Once AGI exceeds certain income thresholds detailed in the tax code, some itemized deductions are disallowed. For example, for those married couples filing jointly in 2009 with adjusted gross incomes of more than $159,950, itemized deductions are reduced by 3% of the amount by which the AGI exceeds $159,950. These thresholds are adjusted upward annually and the phaseout of exemptions will be gradually eliminated by 2010.

ADJUSTMENT BOND bond issued in exchange for outstanding bonds when recapitalizing a corporation that faces bankruptcy. Authorization for the exchange comes from the bondholders, who consider adjustment bonds a lesser evil. These bonds promise to pay interest only to the extent earned by the corporation. This gives them one of the characteristics of income bonds, which trade flat—that is, without accrued interest.

ADJUSTMENT DATE effective date of rate change on an ADJUSTABLE RATE MORTGAGE (ARM).

ADMINISTRATOR court-appointed individual or bank charged with carrying out the court's decisions with respect to a decedent's estate until it is fully distributed to all claimants. Administrators are appointed when a person dies without having made a will or without having named an executor, or when the named executor cannot or will not serve. The term *administratrix* is sometimes used if the individual appointed is a woman.

In a general sense, an administrator is a person who carries out an organization's policies.

ADR *see* AMERICAN DEPOSITARY RECEIPT (ADR); ASSET DEPRECIATION RANGE SYSTEM (ADR).

AD VALOREM Latin term meaning "according to value" and refer-ring to a way of assessing duties or taxes on goods or property. As one example, ad valorem DUTY assessment is based on the value of the imported item rather than on its weight or quantity. As another example, the city of Englewood, New Jersey, levies an ad valorem property tax based on the assessed value of property rather than its size.

ADVANCE

Employee benefits: cash given to an employee before it is needed or earned. A travel advance is supplied so that an employee has cash to use on an upcoming business trip. A salary advance is provided to help the employee cover emergency expenses.

Securities: increase in the price of stocks, bonds, commodities, or other assets. Often heard when referring to the movement of broad indexes, e.g., "The Dow Jones Industrials advanced 15 points today."

Trade: advance payment for goods or services that will be delivered in the near future. For example, home contractors require an advance from homeowners to pay for building materials.

ADVANCED DETECTION SYSTEM (ADS) FINANCIAL INDUSTRY REGULATORY AUTHORITY (FINRA) automated surveillance system, used to monitor member firms' trading and reporting in order to uncover operational irregularities that could negatively impact the quality of market information and order processing.

ADVANCE-DECLINE (A-D) measurement of the number of stocks that have advanced and the number that have declined over a particular period. It is the ratio of one to the other and shows the general direction of the market. It is considered bullish if more stocks advance than decline on any trading day. It is bearish if declines outnumber advances. The steepness of the A-D line graphically shows whether a strong bull or bear market is underway.

ADVANCE-DECLINE LINE

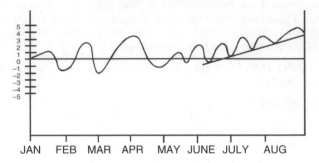

ADVANCED FUNDED PENSION PLAN pension plan under which assets are set aside in amounts and at times approximately coincident with the accruing of benefit rights. In this way, funds are set aside in advance of the date of retirement.

ADVANCE REFUNDING

Government securities: exchange of maturing government securities prior to their due date for issues with a later maturity. It is through advance refunding that the national debt is extended as an alternative to the economic disruptions that would result from eliminating the debt all at once.

Municipal bonds: sale of new bonds (the refunding issue) in advance, usually by some years, of the first call date of the old bonds (the issue to be refunded). The refunding issue would normally have a lower rate than the issue to be refunded, and the proceeds would be invested, usually in government securities, until the higher-rate bonds become callable. This practice, also called *prerefunding*, has been curtailed by several tax acts. *See also* REFUNDING ESCROW DEPOSITS (REDs).

ADVERSE OPINION opinion expressed by a company's independent auditors that the firm's financial statements do not accurately reflect the company's current financial position or operating results. An adverse opinion is a far more serious finding than a QUALIFIED OPINION, in which only some issues are of concern to the auditor. Investors should be extremely cautious about investing in any company with an adverse opinion from its auditors.

ADVERSE SELECTION tendency of people with significant potential to file claims wanting to obtain insurance coverage. For example, those with severe health problems want to buy health insurance, and people going to a dangerous place such as a war zone want to buy more life insurance. Companies employing workers in dangerous occupations want to buy more worker's compensation coverage. In order to combat the problem of adverse selection, insurance companies try to reduce their exposure to large claims by either raising premiums or limiting the availability of coverage to such applicants.

ADVISORY ACCOUNT brokerage account in which broker's discretion in making investment decisions is limited to goals defined by the customer. *Compare* DISCRETIONARY ACCOUNT.

ADVISORY LETTER newsletter aiming to offer financial advice to subscribers. The letter may offer a broad economic and market outlook, or it may focus on a particular sector of the stock, bond, or commodity markets. Some advisory letters specialize in recommending only mutual funds. Some letters also advise their subscribers of new recommendations through a toll-free hotline, which can be updated much more quickly than a printed letter. If the advisory letter recommends specific securities, the author usually is registered with the Securities and Exchange Commission as a REGISTERED INVESTMENT ADVISOR. *See also* HULBERT RATING.

AFFIDAVIT written statement made under oath before an authorized person, such as a notary public.

AFFIDAVIT OF DOMICILE AFFIDAVIT made by the executor of an estate that certifies the decedent's place of residence at the time of death. Before securities can be transferred from an estate, it must be verified that no liens exist against them in the home state of the decedent.

AFFILIATE
In general: two companies are affiliated when one owns less than a majority of the voting stock of the other, or when both are subsidiaries of a third company. A SUBSIDIARY is a company of which more than 50% of the voting shares are owned by another corporation, termed the PARENT COMPANY. A subsidiary is always, by definition, an affiliate, but subsidiary is the preferred term when majority control exists. In everyday use, affiliate is the correct word for intercompany relationships, however indirect, where the parent-subsidiary relationship does not apply.
Banking Act of 1933: any organization that a bank owns or controls by stock holdings, or which the bank's shareholders own, or whose officers are also directors of the bank.
Internal Revenue Service: for purposes of consolidated tax returns an affiliated group is composed of companies whose parent or other inclusive corporation owns at least 80% of voting stock
Interstate Commerce Commission, Account 706: 1. Controlled by the accounting company alone or with others under a joint agreement. **2.** Controlling the accounting company alone or with others under a joint agreement.
Investment Company Act: company in which there is any direct or indirect ownership of 5% or more of the outstanding voting securities.

AFFILIATED CORPORATION corporation that is an AFFILIATE.

AFFILIATED PERSON individual in a position to exert direct influence on the actions of a corporation. Among such persons are owners of 10% or more of the voting shares, directors, and senior elected officers and any persons in a position to exert influence through them—such as members of their immediate family and other close associates. Sometimes called a *control person.*

AFFINITY CARD credit card co-issued by a bank and a sponsoring organization that gets a percentage of the revenue generated by use of the card. Cardholder may also get discounts or other advantages when the card is used to buy sponsor's products or services.

AFFIRMATIVE OBLIGATIONS FINANCIAL INDUSTRY REGULATORY AUTHORITY (FINRA) requirement that MARKET MAKERS quote firm prices, make continuous TWO-SIDED MARKETS, participate in the Small Order Entry (or Execution) System (SOES), and report price and volume data for each transaction in a NASDAQ security within 90 seconds of execution.

AFFORDABILITY INDEX standard established by the National Association of Realtors (NAR) to gauge the financial ability of consumers to buy a home. A reading of 100 means a family earning the national median family income (reported by the Census Bureau) can qualify for a mortgage on a typical median-priced existing single-family home. An index above 100 signifies that a family earning the median income more than qualifies for a mortgage loan on a median-priced home, assuming a 20% down payment. Therefore, an increase in the Affordability Index shows that a family is more able to afford the median-priced home. The prevailing mortgage interest rate is the effective rate on loans closed on existing homes from the Federal Housing Finance Agency (for the United States) and HSH Associates Financial Publishers (for various regions). The mortgage is based on an 80% loan (20% down payment) and a qualifying ratio of 25%, meaning that 25% of the borrower's gross monthly income will be needed to cover housing costs, including the mortgage. The 25% qualifying ratio covers expected principal and interest payments but does not cover taxes and insurance.

There are three different types of indices calculated by NAR. The Fixed Rate Index is based on the current effective interest rate on 30-year fixed rate mortgages. The Adjustable Rate Index is calculated using the prevailing effective interest rate on adjustable rate mortgages. The Composite Index uses a weighted average of the interest rates on fixed and adjustable rate mortgages, weighted by the relative proportion of fixed and adjustable rate loans closed on existing homes.

NAR also calculates a first-time home buyer Affordability Index, which recognizes the special characteristics of first-time home buyers and the homes they purchase. The group most likely to purchase a first home consists of a young renter family with a head of household aged 25 to 44 and a lower median income than the overall population. This index assumes a 10% DOWN PAYMENT, and adds one quarter of a percentage point to the mortgage rate for the required private mortgage insurance. The first-time home is calculated at 85% of the median price of all existing homes purchased. Some economists maintain that every one-point increase in the home mortgage interest rate results in 300,000 fewer home sales.

AFTER ACQUIRED CLAUSE clause in a mortgage agreement providing that any additional mortgageable property acquired by the borrower after the mortgage is signed will be additional security for the obligation.

While such provisions can help give mortgage bonds a good rating and enable issuing corporations to borrow at favorable rates, by precluding additional first mortgages, they make it difficult to finance growth through new borrowings. This gives rise to various maneuvers to remove after acquired clauses, such as redemption or exchange of bonds or changes in indenture agreements.

AFTER-HOURS DEALING OR TRADING trading of stocks and bonds after regular trading hours on organized exchanges. This may occur when there is a major announcement about positive or negative earnings or a takeover at a particular company. The stock price may therefore soar or plummet from the level at which it closed during regular trading hours. Some brokerage firms specialize in making over-the-counter markets around the clock to accommodate after-hours dealing. *See also* MAKE A MARKET.

AFTERMARKET trading activity immediately following an INITIAL PUBLIC OFFERING (IPO). *See also* SECONDARY MARKET.

AFTERTAX BASIS basis for comparing the returns on a corporate taxable bond and a municipal tax-free bond. For example, a corporate bond paying 10% would have an aftertax return of 6.5% for someone in the 35% tax bracket. So any municipal bond paying higher than 6.5% would yield a higher aftertax return.

AFTERTAX REAL RATE OF RETURN amount of money, adjusted for inflation, that an investor can keep, out of the income and capital gains earned from investments. Every dollar loses value to inflation, so investors have to keep an eye on the aftertax real rate of return whenever they commit their capital. By and large, investors seek a rate of return that will match if not exceed the rate of inflation.

AGAINST THE BOX SHORT SALE by the holder of a LONG POSITION in the same stock. BOX refers to the physical location of securities held in safekeeping. When a stock is sold against the box, it is sold short, but only in effect. A short sale is usually defined as one where the seller does not own the shares. Here the seller *does* own the shares (holds a long position) but does not wish to disclose ownership; or perhaps the long shares are too inaccessible to deliver in the time required; or, prior to the TAXPAYER RELIEF ACT OF 1997, he may have been holding his existing position to get the benefit of long-term capital gains tax treatment. In any event, when the sale is made against the box, the shares needed to cover are borrowed, probably from a broker. This technique was eliminated as a way to reduce tax liabilities in the TAXPAYER RELIEF ACT OF 1997. *See also* SELLING SHORT AGAINST THE BOX.

AGED FAIL contract between two broker-dealers that is still not settled 30 days after the settlement date. At that point the open balance no longer counts as an asset, and the receiving firm must adjust its capital accordingly.

AGENCY
In general: relationship between two parties, one a principal and the other an AGENT who represents the principal in transactions with a third party.
Finance: certain types of accounts in trust institutions where individuals, usually trust officers, act on behalf of customers. Agency services to corporations are related to stock purchases and sales. Banks also act as agents for individuals.
Government: securities issued by government-sponsored entities and federally related institutions. Agency securities are exempt from Securities and Exchange Commission (SEC) registration requirements. *See also* AGENCY SECURITIES.
Investment: act of buying or selling for the account and risk of a client. Generally, an agent, or broker, acts as intermediary between buyer and seller, taking no financial risk personally or as a firm, and charging a commission for the service.

AGENCY SECURITIES securities issued by U.S. government-sponsored entities (GSEs) and federally related institutions. GSEs currently issuing securities comprise eight privately owned, publicly chartered entities created to reduce borrowing costs for certain sectors of the economy, such as farmers, home owners, and students. They include the Federal Farm Credit Bank System, Farm Credit Financial Assistance Corporation, Federal Home Loan Bank, FEDERAL HOME LOAN MORTGAGE CORPORATION, FEDERAL NATIONAL MORTGAGE ASSOCIATION (FANNIE MAE), FINANCING CORPORATION (FICO). GSEs issue discount notes (with maturities ranging from overnight to 360 days) and bonds. With the exception of the Farm Credit Financial Assistance Corporation, GSE securities are not backed by the full faith and credit of the U.S. government. Other GSEs that formerly issued directly now borrow from the FEDERAL FINANCING BANK (FFB).

Federally related institutions are arms of the U.S. government and generally have not issued securities directly into the marketplace since the Federal Financing Bank was established to meet their consolidated borrowing needs in 1973. They include the EXPORT-IMPORT BANK (Eximbank) of the United States, the Commodity Credit Corporation, the Farmers Housing Administration, the General Services Administration, the GOVERNMENT NATIONAL MORTGAGE ASSOCIATION (GNMA), the Maritime Administration, the Private Export Funding Corporation, the Rural Electrification Administration, the Rural Telephone Bank, the SMALL BUSINESS ADMINISTRATION (SBA), the Tennessee Valley Authority (TVA), and the Washington Metropolitan Area Transit Authority. Except for the Private Export Funding Corporation and the TVA, federally related institution obligations are backed by the full faith and credit of the U.S. government.

Agency securities are exempt from SEC registration and from state and local income taxes. *See also* FEDERAL FARM CREDIT SYSTEM; FEDERAL HOME LOAN BANK SYSTEM.

AGENT individual authorized by another person, called the principal, to act in the latter's behalf in transactions involving a third party. Banks are frequently appointed by individuals to be their agents, and so authorize their employees to act on behalf of principals. Agents have three basic characteristics:

1. They act on behalf of and are subject to the control of the principal.
2. They do not have title to the principal's property.
3. They owe the duty of obedience to the principal's orders.

  See also ACCOUNT EXECUTIVE; BROKER; TRANSFER AGENT.

AGGREGATE EXERCISE PRICE in stock options trading, the number of shares in a put or call CONTRACT (normally 100) multiplied by the EXERCISE PRICE. The price of the option, called the PREMIUM, is a separate figure not included in the aggregate exercise price. A July call option on 100 XYZ at 70 would, for example, have an aggregate exercise price of 100 (number of shares) times $70 (price per share), or $7,000, if exercised on or before the July expiration date.

In options traded on debt instruments, which include GOVERNMENT NATIONAL MORTGAGE ASSOCIATION (GNMA) pass-throughs, Treasury bills, Treasury notes, Treasury bonds, and certain municipal bonds, the aggregate exercise price is determined by multiplying the FACE VALUE of the underlying security by the exercise price. For example, the aggregate exercise price of put option Treasury bond December 90 would be $90,000 if exercised on or before its December expiration date, the calculation being 90% times the $100,000 face value of the underlying bond.

AGGREGATE SUPPLY in MACROECONOMICS, the total amount of goods and services supplied to the market at alternative price levels in a given period of time; also called *total output.* The central concept in SUPPLY SIDE ECONOMICS, it corresponds with aggregate demand, defined as the total amount of goods and services demanded in the economy at alternative income levels in a given period, including both consumer and producers' goods; aggregate demand is also called *total spending.* The aggregate supply curve describes the relationship between price levels and the quantity of output that firms are willing to provide.

AGGREGATION

In general: any bringing together of parts or units to form a collective whole; in the case of data, to consolidate and thus reduce it.

Personal finance: Internet-related service, usually called *account aggregation,* that provides all-in-one convenience by consolidating on one web page information and service from various sources, such as your bank account, your brokerage account, and your credit cards. Confidential access is gained by entering a user name and password. Some banks offer account aggregation as a convenience to customers, usually free of charge.

Corporate finance: collecting and treating as one the investment proposals of different operating units.

Futures: combining of all the positions owned or controlled by a trader for reporting and compliance purposes.

AGGRESSIVE GROWTH MUTUAL FUND mutual fund holding stocks of rapidly growing companies. While these companies may be large or small, they all share histories of and prospects for above-average profit growth. Aggressive growth funds are designed solely for capital appreciation, since they produce little or no income from dividends. This type of mutual fund is typically more volatile than the overall stock market, meaning its shares will rise far more than the average stock during bull markets and will fall much farther than the typical stock in a bear market. Investors in aggressive growth funds must realize that the value of their shares will fluctuate sharply over time. Aggressive growth funds are also called *maximum capital gains funds* or *capital appreciation funds.*

AGING SCHEDULE classification of trade ACCOUNTS RECEIVABLE by date of sale. Usually prepared by a company's auditor, the *aging,* as the schedule is called, is a vital tool in analyzing the quality of a company's receivables investment. It is frequently required by grantors of credit.

The schedule is most often seen as: (1) a list of the amount of receivables by the month in which they were created; (2) a list of receivables by maturity, classified as current or as being in various stages of delinquency. The following is a typical aging schedule.

	dollars (in thousands)	
Current (under 30 days)	$14,065	61%
1–30 days past due	3,725	16
31–60 days past due	2,900	12
61–90 days past due	1,800	8
Over 90 days past due	750	3
	$23,240	100%

The aging schedule reveals patterns of delinquency and shows where collection efforts should be concentrated. It helps in evaluating the adequacy of the reserve for BAD DEBTS, because the longer accounts stretch out the more likely they are to become uncollectible. Using the schedule can help prevent the loss of future sales, since old customers who fall too far behind tend to seek out new sources of supply.

AGREEMENT AMONG UNDERWRITERS contract between participating members of an investment banking SYNDICATE; sometimes called *syndicate contract* or *purchase group agreement.* It is distinguished from the *underwriting agreement,* which is signed by the company issuing the securities and the SYNDICATE MANAGER, acting as agent for the underwriting group.

The agreement among underwriters, (1) appoints the originating investment banker as syndicate manager and agent; (2) appoints additional managers, if considered advisable; (3) defines the members' proportionate liability (usually limited to the amount of their participation) and agrees to pay each member's share on settlement date; (4) authorizes the manager to form and allocate units to a SELLING GROUP, and agrees to abide by the rules of the selling group agreement; (5) states the life of the syndicate, usually running until 30 days after termination of the selling group, or ending earlier by mutual consent.

AICPA *see* AMERICAN INSTITUTE OF CERTIFIED PUBLIC ACCOUNTANTS (AICPA).

AIR POCKET STOCK stock that falls sharply, usually in the wake of such negative news as unexpected poor earnings. As shareholders rush to sell, and few buyers can be found, the price plunges dramatically, like an airplane hitting an air pocket.

AIRPORT REVENUE BOND tax-exempt bond issued by a city, county, state, or airport authority to support the expansion and operations of an airport. The repayment of principal and interest is backed by either the general revenues of airport authority or lease payments generated by one or more airlines using the facilities. In some cases, airport revenue bonds are backed directly by the financial strength of the major airline using the airport, which makes the bonds more risky, because airlines are particularly sensitive to economic cycles and could go out of business in a down cycle.

ALGORITHMIC TRADING *see* HIGH-FREQUENCY TRADING.

ALIEN CORPORATION company incorporated under the laws of a foreign country regardless of where it operates. "Alien corporation" can be used as a synonym for the term *foreign corporation.* However, "foreign corporation" also is used in U.S. state law to mean a corporation formed in a state other than that in which it does business.

ALIMONY PAYMENT money paid to a separated or divorced spouse as required by a divorce decree or a legal separation agreement. The IRS allows qualifying payments as DEDUCTIONS by the payor and they are taxable income to the payee.

ALLIED MEMBER a person who is not a member of the New York Stock Exchange, but who is either a general partner of a member organization, an employee who controls a member organization, or a principal executive officer of such an organization.

ALLIGATOR SPREAD spread in the options market that "eats the investor alive" with high commission costs. The term is used when a broker arranges a combination of puts and calls that generates so much commission the client is unlikely to turn a profit even if the markets move as anticipated.

ALL IN underwriting shorthand for *all included,* referring to an issuer's interest rate after giving effect to commissions and miscellaneous related expenses.

ALL OR NONE (AON)
Investment banking: an offering giving the issuer the right to cancel the whole issue if the underwriting is not fully subscribed.
Securities: buy or sell order marked to signify that no partial transaction is to be executed. The order will not automatically be canceled, however, if a complete transaction is not executed; to accomplish that, the order entry must be marked FOK, meaning FILL OR KILL.

ALL-OR-NOTHING OPTION *see* EXOTIC OPTIONS.

ALL ORDINARIES INDEX a MARKET CAPITALIZATION weighted index. The index represents 500 of the largest companies listed on the Australian Securities Exchange (ASX), which was established in 2006 by a merger of the Australian Stock Exchange and the Sydney Futures Exchange. Market capitalization is the only eligibility requirement of constituents, as liquidity is not considered for this index, with the exception of foreign domiciled companies. The index was established by the ASX in 1980 and supplanted as the market's leading indicator by the S&P/ASX 200 in 2000.

ALLOTMENT amount of securities assigned to each of the participants in an investment banking SYNDICATE formed to underwrite and distribute a new issue, called *subscribers* or *allottees.* The financial responsibilities of the subscribers are set forth in an allotment notice, which is prepared by the SYNDICATE MANAGER.

ALLOWANCE deduction from the value of an invoice, permitted by a seller of goods to cover damages or shortages. *See also* RESERVE.

ALL-RISKS COVERAGE *see* NAMED PERILS INSURANCE.

ALPHA
1. coefficient measuring the portion of an investment's RETURN arising from specific (nonmarket) risk. In other words, alpha is a mathematical estimate of the amount of return expected from an investment's inherent values, such as the rate of growth in earnings per share. It is distinct from the amount of return caused by VOLATILITY, which is measured by the BETA coefficient. For example, an alpha of 1.25 indicates that a stock is projected to rise 25% in price in a year when the return on the market and the stock's beta are both zero. An investment whose price is low relative to its alpha is undervalued and considered a good selection.
     In the case of a MUTUAL FUND, or other portfolio, alpha measures the relationship between the portfolio's performance and its beta over a three-year period, and can be viewed as a measure of the value added by the manager.
2. on the London Stock Exchange, *alpha stocks* were the largest and most actively traded companies in a classification system that was adopted after the BIG BANG in October 1986 and was replaced in January 1991 with the NORMAL MARKET SIZE (NMS) classification system.

ALPHABET STOCK categories of common stock associated with particular subsidiaries created by acquisitions and restructuring. Alphabet stock differs from classified stock, which is typically designated Class A and Class B, in that classified stock implies a hierarchy of powers and privileges, whereas an alphabet stock simply separates differences. Also called TRACKING STOCK.

ALT-A LOAN mortgage loan to an applicant that has a good credit score but is classified between PRIME and SUBPRIME because of some deficiency, such as inability to make a down payment or to document steady income because of recent divorce, self-employment, commission-based income, or other factors not necessarily negative. *Alternative documentation loans,* as they are also called, command a higher rate.

ALTERNATIVE INVESTMENTS investments other than stocks and bonds, such as HEDGE FUNDS, LEVERAGED BUY-OUTS (LBOs), DERIVATIVES, private equity, ARBITRAGE, event driven, and other hedging strategies. Term sometimes refers to real estate and venture capital investments.

ALTERNATIVE MINIMUM TAX (AMT) federal tax aimed at ensuring that wealthy individuals, trusts, estates, and corporations pay at least some income tax. For individuals, the AMT is computed by adding TAX PREFERENCE ITEMS to taxable income and making various adjustments to a taxpayer's regular taxable income. Taxpayers must calculate their tax obligations through the regular tax system and through the AMT system, and pay the greater of the two amounts. The most common adjustments and tax preference items include
• addition of personal exemptions
• addition of the standard deduction, if claimed by the taxpayer
• addition of itemized deductions claimed for state and local taxes, certain interest, most miscellaneous deductions, and part of medical expenses
• subtraction of any refund of state and local taxes included in gross income
• changes to accelerated depreciation of certain property
• difference between gain and loss on the sale of property
• addition of certain income from incentive stock options
• change in certain passive activity loss deductions
• addition of certain depletion that is more than the adjusted basis of the property
• addition of part of the deduction for certain intangible drilling costs
• addition of tax-exempt interest on certain private activity bonds
Taxpayers may have to pay the alternative minimum tax if their taxable income for regular tax purposes, combined with these adjustments and tax preference items, is more than $69,950 for married couples filing jointly, $46,200 for those filing as single or head of household, or $34,975 if married filing a separate return. The AMT tax rate on income up to $175,000 ($87,500 for a married couple filing separately) is 26% and 28% for income over $175,000.

Calculating the AMT can be extremely complex and is best left to a professional accountant. *See also* AMT PATCH.

ALTERNATIVE ORDER order giving a broker a choice between two courses of action; also called an *either-or order* or a *one cancels the other order.* Such orders are either to buy or to sell, never both. Execution of one course automatically makes the other course inoperative. An example is a combination buy limit/buy stop order, wherein the buy limit is below the current market and the buy stop is above.

ALTERNATIVE TRADING SYSTEMS *see* ELECTRONIC COMMUNICATIONS NETWORKS (ECN).

AMBAC FINANCIAL GROUP, INC. *see* MUNICIPAL BOND INSURANCE.

AMENDED TAX RETURN Internal Revenue Service tax return filed on Form 1040X to correct mistakes made on the original return. Amended returns must be filed within three years of the original filing.

AMENDMENT addition to, or change, in a legal document. When properly signed, it has the full legal effect of the original document.

AMERICAN ASSOCIATION OF INDIVIDUAL INVESTORS (AAII) nonprofit organization, based in Chicago, designed to educate individual investors about stocks, bonds, mutual funds, and other financial alternatives through seminars, conferences, and publications. The AAII also evaluates investment-oriented software in a publication called *Computerized Investing*. The AAII web site (*www.aaii.org*) provides extensive information on the basics of investing, as well as a reference section on a wide variety of topics such as annuities, mutual funds, dividend reinvestment plans and discount brokers. The AAII regularly polls its members for their outlook on the stock market, and the AAII Index of Bullish, Bearish and Neutral Outlook is published weekly in *Barron's* under Investor Sentiment Readings.

AMERICAN BUSINESS CONFERENCE (ABC) organization representing the combination (in 2002) of the former American Business Conference (ABC), the nation's leading association of midsize businesses, and the Association of Publicly Traded Companies (APTC), the leading lobby for MID CAP and SMALL CAP public companies. Both organizations were formed in the early 1980s and function as bipartisan advocates of policies to promote economic growth, tax reform, open international trade and investment, regulatory and securities litigation reform, and better corporate governance, proxy process, and accounting and capital markets standards.

AMERICAN DEPOSITARY RECEIPT (ADR) receipt for the shares of a foreign-based corporation held in the vault of a U.S. bank and entitling the shareholder to all dividends and capital gains. Instead of buying shares of foreign-based companies in overseas markets, Americans can buy shares in the United States in the form of an ADR. ADRs are available for hundreds of stocks from numerous countries. Those, called *Sponsored ADRs*, which are issued in cooperation with the foreign company whose equity shares will underlie the related AMERICAN DEPOSITARY SHARES (ADS), are eligible for listing on a major U.S. exchange and afford the shareholder rights and benefits associated with direct ownership, such as voting rights, and the right to receive reports. *Unsponsored ADRs*, issued without the involvement of the underlying foreign company, may not have such rights attached and the shares generally trade over-the-counter. *See also* DEPOSITARY RECEIPT; PORTFOLIO DEPOSITARY RECEIPT.

AMERICAN DEPOSITARY RECEIPT RATIO number of ORDINARY SHARES into which an AMERICAN DEPOSITARY RECEIPT (ADR) is convertible. In other words, the number of AMERICAN DEPOSITARY SHARES underlying an ADR.

AMERICAN DEPOSITARY SHARE (ADS) share issued under a deposit agreement representing the underlying ordinary share which trades in the issuer's home market. The terms ADS and ADR tend to be used interchangeably. Technically, the ADS is the instrument that actually is traded, while the ADR is the certificate that represents a number of ADSs.

AMERICAN INSTITUTE OF CERTIFIED PUBLIC ACCOUNTANTS (AICPA) premier professional association for CERTIFIED PUBLIC ACCOUNTANTS (CPAs) in the United States, with more than 330,000 members. Its origins go back to 1887 when the American Association of Public Accountants was formed. After several name changes, and after absorbing in 1936 the American Society of Certified Public Accountants (a federation of state societies founded in 1921), the present name was adopted in 1957. The AICPA is extensively involved in various member services, education and publishing, professional ethical practices, enforcement of professional standards, research, and peer review. It also creates and grades the uniform CPA examination. Until the Financial Accounting Standards Board (FASB) was created in 1973, financial accounting and reporting standards were established by AICPA, first through its Committee on Accounting Procedure and then by its Accounting Principles Board, many of whose pronouncements remain in effect. Through its Rule 203, Rules of Professional Conduct, as amended in May 1973 and May 1979, the AICPA recognizes the FASB as the designated organization for establishing standards of financial accounting and reporting. *See also* GENERALLY ACCEPTED ACCOUNTING PRINCIPLES (GAAP).

AMERICAN RECOVERY AND REINVESTMENT ACT OF 2009 federal law enacted to stimulate economic recovery from the recession and financial crisis of the previous year by spending $790 billion on infrastructure, providing tax incentives, and giving money to states and localities. The Act had three components:

Spending: billions of dollars were appropriated for projects including modernization of the electrical grid, computerization of medical records in hospitals and other medical facilities, energy-efficient upgrades to public facilities, road and bridge construction, public transit, high-speed rail, and water infrastructure.

Aid to states and localities: billions of dollars were sent to states and localities to supplement their budgets and pay for schools, Medicaid, foreclosure prevention, extension of jobless benefits, and increases in college grants.

Tax cuts: many changes were made in the tax code to allow Americans to keep more of their earnings. Some of the most important tax changes include:

- Extension of alternative minimum tax relief in 2009 by increasing the AMT exemption amount by $70,950 for joint filers and $46,700 for individuals.
- Excluded interest from tax-exempt private activity bonds from the Alternative Minimum Tax.
- Sales and excise tax deduction for new vehicle purchases of $49,500 or less including cars, light trucks, recreational vehicles, and motorcycles through 2009. The deduction is subject to phase out for individuals with adjusted gross income over $125,000 and couples filing jointly with AGIs of over $250,000.
- Institution of plug-in electric vehicle credit of $2,500.
- Computers as a qualifying expense under Section 529 Education Plans.
- American Opportunity Education tax credit up to $2,500 of the cost of college tuition and related expenses in 2009 and 2010. The tax credit is

phased out for individual taxpayers with adjustable gross incomes of $80,000 ($160,000 for couples filing jointly).

- Refundable first-time home buyer credit. Tax credit of up to $8,000 for those who have not owned a home for the past three years if they buy a home between January 1, 2009 and December 1, 2009. The tax credit is phased out for individual taxpayers with adjustable gross incomes of $75,000 ($150,000 for couples filing jointly).
- Making Work Pay tax credit. Provision cuts taxes for 95% of working families by offering a refundable tax credit of up to $400 for working individuals and $800 for working families. Taxpayers can receive this benefit through a reduction in the amount of income tax withheld from their paychecks or through claiming the credit on their tax returns. The tax credit is phased out for individual taxpayers with adjustable gross incomes of $75,000 ($150,000 for couples filing jointly).
- Increase in Earned Income Tax Credit. For working families with three or more children, the earned income credit would increase from 40% to 45% of the family's first $12,570 of earned income.
- Increased eligibility for refundable portion of child credit. The child tax credit is refundable to the extent of 15% of the taxpayer's earned income over $3,000, down from $8,500 previously.
- Tax credits for energy-efficiency improvements in homes. A tax credit of 10% of the amount paid for qualified energy efficiency improvements including natural gas, propane, oil furnace, or hot water boilers, up to $1,500 per property.
- Premium subsidies for COBRA continuation coverage for unemployed workers. 65% of a worker's COBRA premiums would be subsidized for up to 9 months if they had been involuntarily terminated.
- Small business capital gains. Allow small businesses to exclude 75% of a capital gain from the sale of a business held for more than 5 years.
- Enhanced small business expensing. Small business taxpayers are allowed to write off up to $125,000 in capital expenditures once those expenditures exceed $500,000 through the end of 2010.
- Extension of net operating losses from 2 years to 5 years back for small businesses with gross sales of $15 million or less.
- Extension of bonus depreciation. Businesses can recover the costs of capital expenditures to 50% of those costs for depreciable property such as equipment, tractors, wind turbines, solar panels, and computers purchased in 2009.

AMERICAN STOCK EXCHANGE (AMEX) the third largest options exchange in the United States. Located at 86 Trinity Place in lower Manhattan, the AMEX was known as the New York Curb Exchange until 1953. The exchange pioneered index options and trades options on 25 broad-based and sector indices. It is a leader in the development of EXCHANGE TRADED FUNDS (ETFs), and it calculates and publishes a wide variety of indices to support index-based products such as ETFs, index options, and structured products. The Amex is home to about 600 small to mid-size companies and trades 20 corporate bonds. The AMEX was one of the pioneers in index options and trades put-and-call options on broad market, industry sector, and international indexes. Index options make it possible for investors to "trade" an entire market to seek either profit or protection from price movements in a stock market as a whole or in broad segments of a particular market. The exchange trades more than 160 ETFs; 17 Holding Company Depositary Receipts (HOLDRs); and more than 350 structured products such as notes linked to currencies, equities, and indexes. The two main indices tracking AMEX stocks are the AMEX Composite Index and the AMEX Major Market Index. AMEX derivatives include Diamonds, which tracks the Dow Jones Industrial Average, and Standard & Poor's Depositary Receipts (SPDRs), which track the S&P 500 index and are called Spiders. In 1998, the National Association of Securities Dealers, which then operated NASDAQ, merged with the AMEX, but in 2004 the AMEX became independent again. In 2008, the AMEX was acquired by NYSE Euronext. The AMEX's trading environment is largely automated, but still retains its human-based OPEN OUTCRY system of trading for those investors who desire it. Trading hours: 9:30 A.M.–4 P.M., Monday through Friday. *See also* SECURITIES AND COMMODITIES EXCHANGES; SPDRS; STOCK INDICES AND AVERAGES.

AMERICAN-STYLE OPTION put or call OPTION exercisable anytime between the purchase date and the expiration date. *See also* EUROPEAN-STYLE EXERCISE. Most exchange-traded options in the United States are American-style options.

AMORTIZATION accounting procedure that gradually reduces the cost value of a limited life or intangible asset through periodic charges to income. For fixed assets the term used is DEPRECIATION, and for wasting assets (natural resources) it is depletion, both terms meaning essentially the same thing as amortization. Most companies follow the conservative practice of writing off, through amortization, INTANGIBLE ASSETS such as GOODWILL. It is also common practice to amortize any premium over par value paid in the purchase of preferred stock or bond investments. The purpose of amortization is to reflect resale or redemption value.

Amortization also refers to the reduction of debt by regular payments of interest and principal sufficient to pay off a loan by maturity.

Discount and expense on funded debt are amortized by making applicable charges to income in accordance with a predetermined schedule. While this is normally done systematically, charges to profit and loss are permissible at any time in any amount of the remaining discount and expense. Such accounting is detailed in a company's annual report.

AMT PATCH provision in the AMERICAN RECOVERY AND REINVESTMENT ACT OF 2009 that raises the level of income exempted from the ALTERNATIVE MINIMUM TAX (AMT) for the year 2009 ostensibly to add economic stimulus.

ANALYSIS *see* FUNDAMENTAL ANALYSIS; TECHNICAL ANALYSIS.

ANALYST person in a brokerage house, bank trust department, or mutual fund group who studies a number of companies and makes buy or sell recommendations on the securities of particular companies and industry groups. Most analysts specialize in a particular industry, but some investigate any company that interests them, regardless of its line of business. Some analysts have considerable influence, and can therefore affect the price of a company's stock when they issue a buy or sell recommendation. *See also* CREDIT ANALYST.

AND INTEREST phrase used in quoting bond prices to indicate that, in addition to the price quoted, the seller will receive ACCRUED INTEREST.

ANGEL
1. INVESTMENT GRADE bond, as distinguished from FALLEN ANGEL.
2. an original VENTURE CAPITAL INVESTOR.

ANKLE BITER stock issue having a MARKET CAPITALIZATION of less than $500 million. Generally speaking, such small-capitalization stocks are more speculative than "high-cap" issues, but their greater growth potential gives them more RELATIVE STRENGTH in recessions. *See also* SMALL FIRM EFFECT.

ANNUAL BASIS statistical technique whereby figures covering a period of less than a year are extended to cover a 12-month period. The procedure, called *annualizing,* must take seasonal variations (if any) into account to be accurate.

ANNUAL EXCLUSION tax rule allowing a taxpayer to exclude certain kinds of income from taxation on a tax return. For example, interest earned from municipal bonds must be reported, even though it is not taxed by the federal government. Proceeds from life insurance policies paid by reason of the death of the insured are not taxable. Gifts received of $13,000 or less are also not taxable, and are therefore subject to the annual exclusion rule. This $13,000 gift tax exclusion limit is subject to upward revision in $1,000 increments tied to the rate of inflation based on the TAXPAYER RELIEF ACT OF 1997.

ANNUAL MORGATOR STATEMENT statement provided to the morgator (borrower) by the mortgagee (lender) showing taxes and interest paid during the year and the outstanding mortgage loan balance.

ANNUALIZE to convert to an annual basis. For example, if a mutual fund earns 1% in a month, it would earn 12% on an annualized basis, by multiplying the monthly return by 12. Many economists annualize a monthly number such as auto sales or housing starts to make it easier to compare to prior years.

ANNUAL MEETING once-a-year meeting when the managers of a company report to stockholders on the year's results, and the board of directors stands for election for the next year. The chief executive officer usually comments on the outlook for the coming year and, with other senior officers, answers questions from shareholders. Stockholders can also request that resolutions on corporate policy be voted on by all those owning stock in the company. Stockholders unable to attend the annual meeting may vote for directors and pass on resolutions through the use of PROXY material, which must legally be mailed to all shareholders of record.

ANNUAL PERCENTAGE RATE (APR) cost of credit that consumers pay, expressed as a simple annual percentage. According to the federal Truth in Lending Act, every consumer loan agreement must disclose the APR in large bold type. *See also* CONSUMER CREDIT PROTECTION ACT OF 1968.

ANNUAL RENEWABLE TERM INSURANCE *see* TERM INSURANCE.

ANNUAL REPORT yearly record of a corporation's financial condition that must be distributed to shareholders under SECURITIES AND EXCHANGE COMMISSION regulations. Included in the report is a description of the company's operations as well as its balance sheet and income statement. The long version of the annual report with more detailed financial information— called the 10-K—is available upon request from the corporate secretary.

ANNUAL RETURN TOTAL RETURN per year from an investment, including dividends or interest and capital gains or losses but excluding commissions and other transactions costs and taxes. A *compound annual return* represents the annual rate at which money would have to compound to reach the cumulative figure resulting from annual total returns. It is a discount rate and different from *average annual return,* which is simply an arithmetic mean of annual returns.

ANNUITANT individual receiving benefits from an annuity. The annuity owner can choose to annuitize the policy, meaning that he or she begins to receive regular payments from the annuity.

ANNUITIZE to begin a series of payments from the capital that has built up in an ANNUITY. The payments may be a fixed amount, or for a fixed period of time, or for the lifetimes of one or two *annuitants,* thus guaranteeing income payments that cannot be outlived. *See also* DEFERRED PAYMENT ANNUITY; FIXED ANNUITY; IMMEDIATE PAYMENT ANNUITY; VARIABLE ANNUITY.

ANNUITY form of contract sold by life insurance companies that guarantees a fixed or variable payment to the annuitant at some future time, usually retirement. In a FIXED ANNUITY the amount will ultimately be paid out in regular installments varying only with the payout method elected. In a VARIABLE ANNUITY, the payout is based on a guaranteed number of units; unit values and payments depend on the value of the underlying investments. All capital in the annuity grows TAX-DEFERRED. Key considerations when buying an annuity are the financial soundness of the insurance company (*see* BEST'S RATING), the returns it has paid in the past, and the level of fees and commissions paid to salesmen. *See also* REFUND ANNUITY.

ANNUITY CERTAIN annuity that pays a specified monthly level of income for a predetermined time period, frequently ten years. The annuitant is guaranteed by the insurance company to receive those payments for the agreed upon time period without exception or contingency. If the annuitant dies before the time period expires, the annuity payments are then made to the annuitant's designated beneficiaries. The level of payment in an annuity certain will be higher than for a LIFE ANNUITY because the insurance company knows exactly what its liability will be, whereas with a life annuity, payments depend on how long the annuitant lives.

ANNUITY STARTING DATE date on which an ANNUITANT begins receiving payments from an annuity. Generally, any distributions before age 59½ are subject to a 10% penalty from the IRS, so most annuities start paying after the annuitant has attained that age. The later an annuitant waits to start receiving payments, the higher his or her monthly payments will be under a life annuity, because the insurance company has had more time to invest the money, and the annuitant's remaining life expectancy is shorter.

ANTICIPATED HOLDING PERIOD time during which a limited partnership expects to hold onto an asset. In the prospectus for a real estate limited partnership, for instance, a sponsor will typically say that the anticipated holding period for a particular property is five to seven years. At the end of that time the property is sold, and, usually, the capital received is returned to the limited partners in one distribution.

ANTICIPATION
In general: paying an obligation before it falls due.

Finance: repayment of debt obligations before maturity, usually to save interest. If a formalized discount or rebate is involved, the term used is *anticipation rate*.

Mortgage instrument: when a provision allows prepayment without penalty, the mortgagee is said to have the *right of anticipation*.

Trade payments: bill that is paid before it is due, not discounted.

ANTIDILUTIVE effect on EARNINGS PER SHARE assuming conversion of COMMON STOCK EQUIVALENTS, when the effect is to increase, rather than decrease, earnings per share. For example, if a convertible bond was converted into common stock, net earnings would increase by the amount of bond interest saved, and the number of shares outstanding would increase by the conversion ratio. If the former (the numerator) divided by the latter (the denominator) resulted in increased earnings per share, the effect of the conversion would be antidilutive. Conservative accounting principles require that EARNINGS PER SHARE (EPS) not be inflated by antidilutive effects.

ANTITRUST LAWS federal legislation designed to prevent monopolies and restraint of trade. Landmark statutes include
1. the Sherman Anti-Trust Act of 1890, which prohibited acts or contracts tending to create monopoly and initiated an era of trustbusting.
2. the Clayton Anti-Trust Act of 1914, which was passed as an amendment to the Sherman Act and dealt with local price discrimination as well as with the INTERLOCKING DIRECTORATES. It went further in the areas of the HOLDING COMPANY and restraint of trade.
3. the Federal Trade Commission Act of 1914, which created the Federal Trade Commission or FTC, with power to conduct investigations and issue orders preventing unfair practices in interstate commerce.

ANY-AND-ALL BID offer to pay an equal price for all shares tendered by a deadline; contrasts with TWO-TIER BID. *See also* TAKEOVER.

ANY-INTEREST-DATE CALL provision found in some municipal bond indentures that gives the issuer the right to redeem on any interest payment due date, with or without a premium (depending on the indenture).

APPRAISAL FEE fee charged by an expert to estimate, but not determine, the market value of property. An appraisal is an opinion of value, and is usually required when real property is sold, financed, condemned, taxed, insured, or partitioned. For example, the appraisal of a work of art done to establish value for the IRS when the art is to be donated to a charity may differ from the appraisal if the piece of art is about to be sold at auction. Similarly, the appraisal of a piece of real estate for insurance purposes may differ from an appraisal for determining property taxes. The appraisal fee is usually a set dollar amount, though in some cases may be calculated as a percentage of the value of the property appraised.

APPRECIATION increase in the value of an asset such as a stock, bond, commodity, or real estate.

APPROVED LIST list of investments that a mutual fund or other financial institution is authorized to make. The approved list may be statutory where a fiduciary responsibility exists. *See also* LEGAL LIST.

APS acronym for *Auction Preferred Stock*, Goldman Sach's DUTCH AUCTION PREFERRED STOCK product.

ARBITRAGE profiting from differences in price when the same security, currency, or commodity is traded on two or more markets. For example, an *arbitrageur* simultaneously buys one contract of gold in the New York market and sells one contract of gold in the Chicago market, locking in a profit because at that moment the price on the two markets is different. (The arbitrageur's selling price is higher than the buying price.) *Index arbitrage* exploits price differences between STOCK INDEX FUTURES and underlying stocks. By taking advantage of momentary disparities in prices between markets, arbitrageurs perform the economic function of making those markets trade more efficiently. *See also* RISK ARBITRAGE.

ARBITRAGE BONDS bonds issued by a municipality in order to gain an interest rate advantage by refunding higher-rate bonds in advance of their call date. Proceeds from the lower-rate refunding issue are invested in treasuries until the first call date of the higher-rate issue being refunded. Arbitrage bonds, which always raised a question of tax exemption, were further curtailed by the TAX REFORM ACT OF 1986.

ARBITRAGE PRICING THEORY (APT) alternative to the CAPITAL MARKET PRICING MODEL (CAPM) based on arbitrage arguments and assuming multiple risk factors in the calculation of ALPHA.

ARBITRAGEUR person or firm engaged in ARBITRAGE. Arbitrageurs attempt to profit when the same security or commodity is trading at different prices in two or more markets. Those engaged in RISK ARBITRAGE attempt to profit from buying stocks of announced or potential TAKEOVER targets. Also called Arb.

ARBITRATION dispute resolution mechanism designed to help aggrieved parties recover damages. In arbitration, an impartial person or panel hears all sides of the issues as presented by the parties, evaluates the evidence, and decides how the matter should be resolved. Arbitration is final and binding, and is subject to review by a court only on a very limited basis. *See also* ARBITRATION PANEL.

ARBITRATION PANEL each sponsoring organization maintains a roster of individuals whose professional experience qualifies them for service as arbitrators. The arbitrators are not employees of the sponsoring organization and they, not the sponsoring organization, determine the outcome of the dispute. The arbitrators receive an honorarium from the SELF-REGULATORY ORGANIZATIONS.

ARCHIPELAGO an ELECTRONIC COMMUNICATIONS NETWORK (ECN) formed in 1996 that was merged with the NEW YORK STOCK EXCHANGE (NYSE) in 2006 to form the NYSE Group.

ARITHMETIC MEAN simple average obtained by dividing the sum of two or more items by the number of items.

ARMS' INDEX better known as TRIN; technical indicator named for *Barron's* writer Richard Arms.

ARM'S LENGTH TRANSACTION transaction that is conducted as though the parties were unrelated, thus avoiding any semblance of conflict of interest. For example, under current law parents may rent real estate to their children and still claim business deductions such as depreciation as long as the parents charge their children what they would charge if someone who is not a relative were to rent the same property.

ARREARAGE
In general: amount of any past-due obligation.
Investments: amount by which interest on bonds or dividends on CUMULATIVE PREFERRED stock is due and unpaid. In the case of cumulative preferred stock, common dividends cannot be paid by a company as long as preferred dividends are in arrears.

ARTICLES OF INCORPORATION document filed with a U.S. state by
the founders of a corporation. After approving the articles, the state issues a certificate of incorporation; the two documents together become the CHARTER that gives the corporation its legal existence. The charter embodies such information as the corporation's name, purpose, amount of authorized shares, and number and identity of directors. The corporation's powers thus derive from the laws of the state and from the provisions of the charter. Rules governing its internal management are set forth in the corporation's BYLAWS, which are drawn up by the founders.

ARTIFICIAL CURRENCY *currency substitute,* such as SPECIAL DRAWING
RIGHTS (SDRs) and EUROPEAN CURRENCY UNITS (ECUs).

ASCENDING TOPS chart pattern tracing a security's price over a period of
time and showing that each peak in a security's price is higher than the preceding peak. This upward movement is considered bullish, meaning that the upward trend is likely to continue. *See also* DESCENDING TOPS.

ASCENDING TOPS

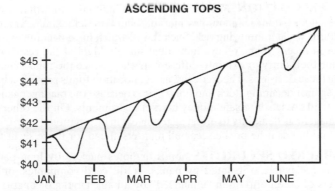

ASIAN OPTION OPTION contract in which settlement is based on the average
value of the underlying asset over the contract period. Also called *average rate option.*

ASKED PRICE
1. price at which a security or commodity is offered for sale on an exchange or in the over-the-counter market. Generally, it is the lowest round lot price at which a dealer will sell. Also called the *ask price, asking price, ask,* or OFFERING PRICE.
2. per-share price at which mutual fund shares are offered to the public, usually the NET ASSET VALUE per share plus a sales charge, if any.

ASPIRIN acronym for *Australian Stock Price Riskless Indexed Notes.* Zero-coupon, four-year bonds guaranteed by the Treasury of New South Wales repayable at face value plus the percentage increase by which the Australian Stock Index of All Ordinaries (common stocks) rises above 1372 points during the period. *See also* ALL ORDINARIES INDEX.

ASSAY test of a metal's purity to verify that it meets the standards for trading on a commodities exchange. For instance, a 100 troy-ounce bar of refined gold must be assayed at a fineness of not less than 995 before the Comex will allow it to be used in settlement of a gold contract.

ASSESSED VALUATION dollar value assigned to property by a municipality for purposes of assessing taxes, which are based on the number of mills per dollar of assessed valuation. If a house is assessed at $100,000 and the tax rate is 50 mills, the tax is $5000. Assessed valuation is important not only to homeowners but also to investors in municipal bonds that are backed by property taxes.

ASSET anything having commercial or exchange value that is owned by a business, institution, or individual. *See also* CAPITAL ASSET; CURRENT ASSETS; DEFERRED CHARGE; FIXED ASSET; INTANGIBLE ASSET; NONCURRENT ASSET.

ASSET ALLOCATION apportioning of investment funds among categories of assets, such as CASH EQUIVALENTS, STOCK, FIXED-INCOME INVESTMENTS, and such tangible assets as real estate, precious metals, and collectibles. Also applies to subcategories such as government, municipal, and corporate bonds, and industry groupings of common stocks. Asset allocation affects both risk and return and is a central concept in personal financial planning and investment management.

ASSET ALLOCATION MUTUAL FUND mutual fund that switches between stocks, bonds, and money market securities to maximize shareholders' returns while minimizing risk. Such funds, which have become extremely popular in recent years, relieve individual shareholders of the responsibility of timing their entry or exit into different markets, since the fund manager is making those decisions. Theoretically, asset allocation funds provide a built-in buffer against declining stock and bond prices because the manager can move all the fund's assets into safe money market instruments. On the other hand, the manager has flexibility to invest aggressively in international and domestic stocks and bonds if he or she sees bull markets ahead for those securities.

ASSET-BACKED SECURITIES bonds or notes backed by loan paper or accounts receivable originated by banks, credit card companies, or other providers of credit and often "enhanced" by a bank LETTER OF CREDIT or by insurance coverage provided by an institution other than the issuer. Typically, the originator of the loan or accounts receivable paper sells it to a specially created trust, which repackages it as securities with a minimum denomination of $1,000 and a term of five years or less. The securities are then underwritten by brokerage firms who reoffer them to the public. Examples are CERTIFICATES FOR AUTOMOBILE RECEIVABLES (CARs) and so-called *plastic bonds,* backed by credit card receivables. Because the institution that originated the underlying loans or receivables is neither the obligor nor the guarantor, investors should evaluate the quality of the original paper, the worth of the guarantor or insurer, and the extent of the protection. *See also* PASS-THROUGH SECURITY.

ASSET CLASS category of ASSETS, such as cash equivalents, stocks, bonds, and their subcategories, as well as tangible assets, such as real estate, precious metals, and collectibles. Asset class is a central concept in ASSET ALLOCATION.

ASSET COVERAGE extent to which a company's net assets cover a particular debt obligation, class of preferred stock, or equity position.

Asset coverage is calculated as follows: from assets at their total book value or liquidation value, subtract intangible assets, current liabilities, and all obligations prior in claim to the issue in question. Divide the result by the dollar amount of the subject issue (or loan) to arrive at the asset coverage ratio. The same information can be expressed as a percentage or, by using units as the divisor, as a dollar figure of coverage per unit. The variation to determine preferred stock coverage treats all liabilities as paid; the variation to arrive at common stock coverage considers both preferred stock and liabilities paid. The term most often used for the common stock calculation is *net book value per share of common stock.*

These calculations reveal *direct* asset coverage. *Overall* asset coverage is obtained by including the subject issue with the total of prior obligations and dividing the aggregate into total tangible assets at liquidating value.

Asset coverage is important as a cushion against losses in the event of liquidation.

ASSET DEPRECIATION RANGE SYSTEM (ADR) range of depreciable lives allowed by the Internal Revenue Service for particular classes of depreciable assets. The ADR system was replaced when the ECONOMIC RECOVERY TAX ACT OF 1981 (ERTA) introduced the ACCELERATED COST RECOVERY SYSTEM (ACRS) but was revived with modifications of ACRS under the TAX REFORM ACT OF 1986. The ADR system assigns an upper and lower limit to the estimated useful lives of asset classes. ACRS classes are based on the mid-points of these ranges. Under the alternative depreciation system, taxpayers may elect STRAIGHT LINE DEPRECIATION over the applicable ADR-class life.

ASSET FINANCING financing that seeks to convert particular assets, such as accounts receivable or inventory, into working cash in exchange for a security interest in those assets. The term is replacing *commercial financing* as major banks join commercial finance companies in addressing the financing needs of companies that do not fit the traditional seasonal borrower profile.

ASSET INFLATION INFLATION primarily affecting a particular asset class, such as stocks, or, in the 2000s, residential real estate.

ASSET-LIABILITY MANAGEMENT matching an individual's level of debt and amount of assets. Someone who is planning to buy a new car, for instance, would have to decide whether to pay cash, thus lowering assets, or to take out a loan, thereby increasing debts (or liabilities). Such decisions should be based on interest rates, on earning power, and on the comfort level with debt. Financial institutions carry out asset-liability management when they match the maturity of their deposits with the length of their loan commitments to keep from being adversely affected by rapid changes in interest rates.

ASSET MANAGEMENT ACCOUNT account at a brokerage house, bank, or savings institution that combines banking services like check writing, credit cards, and debit cards; brokerage features like buying securities and making loans on margin; automatic investment of overnight funds; and the convenience of having all financial transactions listed on one monthly statement. Such accounts are also termed *central asset accounts* and are known by such proprietary names as the Cash Management Account (Merrill Lynch), Active Assets Account (Morgan Stanley Dean Witter), or Schwab One Account (Charles Schwab). *See also* AGGREGATION; SWEEP ACCOUNT.

ASSET PLAY stock market term for a stock that is attractive because the current price does not reflect the value of the company's assets. For example, an analyst could recommend a hotel chain, not because its hotels are run well but because its real estate is worth far more than is recognized in the stock's current price. Asset play stocks are tempting targets for takeovers because they provide an inexpensive way to buy assets.

ASSET STRIPPER corporate raider who takes over a company planning to sell large assets in order to repay debt. The raider calculates that after selling the assets and paying off the debt, he or she will be left with valuable assets that are worth more than his or her purchase price.

ASSETS UNDER MANAGEMENT total value of ASSETS under management by a PORTFOLIO MANAGER. Management fees are based on a percentage of assets under management.

ASSET VALUE net market value of a company's assets on a per-share basis as opposed to the market value of the shares. A company is undervalued by the stock market when asset value exceeds share value.

ASSIGN sign a document transferring ownership from one party to another. Ownership can be in a number of forms, including tangible property, rights (usually arising out of contracts), or the right to transfer ownership at some later time. The party who assigns is called the *assignor* and the party who receives the transfer of title—the assignment—is the *assignee.*

Stocks and registered bonds can be assigned by completing and signing a form printed on the back of the certificate—or, as is sometimes preferred for safety reasons, by executing a separate form, called an *assignment separate from certificate* or *stock/bond power.*

When the OPTIONS CLEARING CORPORATION learns of the exercise of an option, it prepares an assignment form notifying a broker-dealer that an option written by one of its clients has been exercised. The firm in turn assigns the exercise in accordance with its internal procedures.

An assignment for the benefit of creditors, sometimes called simply an *assignment,* is an alternative to bankruptcy, whereby the assets of a company are assigned to the creditors and liquidated for their benefit by a trustee.

ASSIGNED RISK PLANS facilities available in all 50 states in which drivers can obtain auto insurance if they are unable to buy it in the regular or "voluntary" market. Every insurer licensed in the state must participate in these facilities, which are also known as *joint underwriting facilities.* When premiums are too low to cover losses, insurers are usually assessed to make up the difference, and these costs are passed on to all of their customers.

ASSIMILATION absorption of a new issue of stock by the investing public after all shares have been sold by the issue's underwriters. *See also* ABSORBED.

ASSOCIATED PERSON
1. any person in the securities business who is affiliated with a NASDAQ member firm, whether or not the person is registered or exempt from registration with the FINANCIAL INDUSTRY REGULATORY AUTHORITY (FINRA).
2. anyone associated with a member organization of the NEW YORK STOCK EXCHANGE, such as a partner, employee, officer, or member.
3. a person registered with the COMMODITY FUTURES TRADING COMMISSION (CFTC) or the NATIONAL FUTURES ASSOCIATION (NFA) who solicits orders, customers, or customer funds on behalf of a futures commission merchant, an introducing broker, a commodity trading advisor, or a commodity pool operator.

ASSOCIATION FOR INVESTMENT MANAGEMENT AND RESEARCH (AIMR) *see* CHARTERED FINANCIAL ANALYST (CFA) INSTITUTE.

ASSUMED BOND corporate bond issued by one company but payable by another because the liability has been assumed.

ASSUMED INTEREST RATE rate of interest that an insurance company uses to determine the payout on an ANNUITY contract. The higher the assumed interest rate, the higher the monthly payout will be.

ASSUMPTION act of taking on responsibility for the liabilities of another party, usually documented by an *assumption agreement*. In the case of a MORTGAGE assumption, the seller remains secondarily liable unless released from the obligations by the lender.

ASYMMETRY any absence of balance or equivalence between two things that are otherwise comparable. Examples are *asymmetric information*, meaning some people have more information than others; *asymmetric taxes,* where parties to a transaction have different tax rates; *asymmetric volatility*, where there is more volatility in down markets than in up markets. *See also* FED BIAS.

ATM (AUTOMATIC TELLER MACHINE) unmanned location where the insertion of a precoded credit or debit card and the entry of a PIN NUMBER in a machine provides access to bank teller services, including cash. A small transaction fee is typically charged, especially when the customer is not a client of the bank providing the service.

ATP acronym for *arbitrage trading program,* better known as PROGRAM TRADING. Program traders simultaneously place orders for stock index futures and the underlying stocks in an attempt to exploit price variations. Their activity is often blamed for excessive VOLATILITY.

AT PAR at a price equal to the face, or nominal, value of a security. *See also* PAR VALUE.

AT RISK exposed to the danger of loss. Investors in a limited partnership can claim tax deductions only if they can prove that there's a chance of never realizing any profit and of losing their investment as well. Deductions will be disallowed if the limited partners are not exposed to economic risk—if, for example, the general partner guarantees to return all capital to limited partners even if the business venture should lose money.

ATHENS EXCHANGE (ATHEX) formed in 2002 by a merger of the Athens Stock Exchange and the Athens Derivatives Exchange. The ATHEX is the principal stock exchange in Greece, trading stocks and bonds through the fully computerized OASIS system. Screen-based futures, and options trading is conducted on indices, stock futures, and options. The ATHEX offers more than 20 indices, including the three international indices: FTSE/ASE 20 Index, FTSE/ASE Mid 40 Index, and FTSE/ASE 80 Small Cap Index. The exchange introduced the FTSE Med 100 Index in 2003, a joint index involving the ATHEX, the TEL AVIV STOCK EXCHANGE, and the Cyprus Exchange. The ATHEX trades a general index and a total return general index on the main share market and one on the parallel market, as well as a total return parallel market index, in addition to 19 sector indices. The FTSE/ASE indices are reevaluated quarterly. Settlement of equity transactions is T + 3. Trading hours are 10 A.M. to 5:20 P.M., Monday through Friday. *www.ase.gr.*

ATTAINED AGE age at which a person is eligible to receive certain benefits. For example, someone may be eligible to receive the proceeds from a trust when they reach age 21. Or someone who has attained the age of 65 may be eligible for certain pension or other retirement benefits. In some cases, the person may have to take some action when they reach the attained age, such as retire from a company.

AT THE CLOSE ORDER
Securities: market order that is to be executed in its entirety at the closing price on the exchange of the stock named in the order. If it is not so executed, the order is to be treated as canceled.
Futures/Options: in futures and options, a MARKET ON CLOSE ORDER, which is a contract to be executed on some exchanges during the closing period, during which there is a range of prices.

AT THE MARKET *see* MARKET ORDER.

AT THE MONEY at the current price, as an option with an exercise price equal to or near the current price of the stock or underlying futures contract. *See also* DEEP IN/OUT OF THE MONEY; IN THE MONEY; OUT OF THE MONEY.

AT THE OPENING ORDER
Securities: market or limited price order to be executed on the opening trade of the stock on the exchange. If the order, or any portion of it, is not executed in this manner, it is to be treated as canceled.
Futures/Options: in futures and options, a MARKET ON OPEN ORDER, during which there is a range of prices at the opening.

AUCTION MARKET system by which securities are bought and sold through brokers on the securities exchanges, as distinguished from the over-the-counter market, where trades are negotiated. Best exemplified by the NEW YORK STOCK EXCHANGE, it is a double auction system or TWO-SIDED MARKET. That is because, unlike the conventional auction with one auctioneer and many buyers, here we have many sellers and many buyers. As in any auction, a price is established by competitive bidding between brokers acting as agents for buyers and sellers. That the system functions in an orderly way is the result of several trading rules: (1) The first bid or offer at a given price has priority over any other bid or offer at the same price. (2) The high bid and low offer "have the floor." (3) A new auction begins whenever all the offers or bids at a given price are exhausted. (4) Secret transactions are prohibited. (5) Bids and offers must be made in an audible voice.

Also, the competitive bidding by which Treasury bills are sold. *See also* BILL; DUTCH AUCTION.

AUCTION-RATE PREFERRED STOCK *see* DUTCH AUCTION PREFERRED STOCK.

AUDIT professional examination and verification of a company's accounting documents and supporting data for the purpose of rendering an opinion as to their fairness, consistency, and conformity with GENERALLY ACCEPTED ACCOUNTING PRINCIPLES. *See also* ACCOUNTANT'S OPINION.

AUDITOR'S CERTIFICATE *see* ACCOUNTANT'S OPINION.

AUDITOR'S REPORT public accountant's declaration following the completion of an examination of corporate financial statements. Also called *accountant's opinion.*

AUDIT TRAIL step-by-step record by which accounting data can be traced to their source. Questions as to the validity or accuracy of an accounting figure can be resolved by reviewing the sequence of events from which the figure resulted.

AUNT MILLIE derogatory term for an unsophisticated investor. Wall Street professionals may say that "This investment will interest Aunt Millie," meaning that it is simple to understand. It may also imply that such small investors will not be able to appreciate the amount of risk posed by the investment relative to the opportunity for profit. Brokers and financial advisors, using the KNOW YOUR CUSTOMER rule, should not recommend complex and risky investments to Aunt Millie investors.

AUSTRALIAN SECURITIES EXCHANGE (ASX) formed in 2006 from the merger of the Australian Stock Exchange and the Sydney Futures Exchange. The fully automated exchange is Australia's primary national market for equities, derivatives, and fixed-interest securities. The ASX demutualized in 1998; its shares trade on its own market. The Australian market, formerly dominated by mining, resources, and manufacturing companies, now registers significant growth for financial services and service sectors such as telecommunications. Retail investors have grown substantially, with 55% of the adult Australian population owning shares. The majority of trading takes place during normal trading hours of 10 A.M. to 4 P.M. SEATS (Stock Exchange Automated Trading System) is an all-electronic trading system and is used to trade shares, warrants, and other securities. The market's leading indicator is the S&P/ASX 200 Index.

AUSTRIAN SCHOOL OF ECONOMICS school of economic thought founded in 1871 with the publication of Carl Menger's *Principles of Economics.* Considered a heterodox school from the mid-20th century forward, it has gotten renewed attention since 2007 when adherents predicted the financial crisis. The Austrian School supports the Libertarian philosophy without espousing a political position, although its rejection of the inflationary approach of Keynesian economics attracts the conservative element. It holds that efficiency is achieved through free market forces, which maximize value as sought by individuals acting consistent with MARGINAL UTILITY. Inefficiency and ineffectualness, by the same token, result from government intervention, extending even to defense, police, court systems, electricity, infrastructure, and such externalities as polluters and free riders. Inflation means expansion, and expansion of the money supply without an offsetting expansion of goods and services creates inflation. The Austrian view of recent events holds that Federal Reserve actions to keep long-term rates low to avoid the bust that should have been allowed to correct the excesses of the "dot com" boom that preceded it, created the "malinvestments" that caused the housing bubble, and that the bailouts and stimulus the government is using to prevent the consequences of the housing bust will inevitably cause hyperinflation and economic collapse if allowed to proceed.

AUTARKY an economic policy of self-sufficiency, wherein trade and financial transactions with external parties are forbidden despite adverse effects on the standard of living. Also called *closed economy*. Examples were commonplace in the 17th and 18th centuries under mercantilism, where transactions were prohibited outside sovereign boundaries. Afghanistan under the Taliban between 1996 and 2001 is a rare recent example.

AUTEX SYSTEM electronic system for alerting brokers that other brokers want to buy or sell large blocks of stock. Once a match is made, the actual transaction takes place over the counter or on the floor of an exchange.

AUTHENTICATION identification of a bond certificate as having been issued under a specific indenture, thus validating the bond. Also, legal verification of the genuineness of a document, as by the certification and seal of an authorized public official.

AUTHORITY BOND bond issued by and payable from the revenue of a government agency or a corporation formed to administer a revenue producing public enterprise. One such corporation is the Port Authority of New York and New Jersey, which operates bridges and tunnels in the New York City area. Because an authority usually has no source of revenue other than charges for the facilities it operates, its bonds have the characteristics of revenue bonds. The difference is that bondholder protections may be incorporated in the authority bond contract as well as in the legislation that created the authority.

AUTHORIZED SHARES maximum number of shares of any class a company may legally create under the terms of its ARTICLES OF INCORPORATION. Normally, a corporation provides for future increases in authorized stock by vote of the stockholders. The corporation is not required to issue all the shares authorized and may initially keep issued shares at a minimum to hold down taxes and expenses. Also called *authorized stock*.

AUTOMATED BOND SYSTEM (ABS) New York Stock Exchange computerized system that records bids and offers for inactively traded bonds until they are cancelled or executed. Before the ABS, such limit orders were kept in steel cabinets, giving rise to the terms CABINET SECURITY and CABINET CROWD (traders in inactive bonds).

AUTOMATED CLEARING HOUSE (ACH) nationwide electronic network that processes debit and credit transactions between participating banks and reduces FLOAT to one day.

AUTOMATED CONFIRMATION TRANSACTION (ACT) SERVICE
postexecution service of NASDAQ that speeds price and volume reporting,
comparison, and clearing of prenegotiated trades in NASDAQ and OTC BUL-
LETIN BOARD securities.

AUTOMATED ORDER ENTRY SYSTEM electronic system that expedites
the execution of smaller orders by channeling them directly to the specialist
on the exchange floor, bypassing the FLOOR BROKER. The New York Stock
Exchange calls its system DOT (Designated Order Turnaround). Other
systems include Auto Ex, OSS, PACE, SOES, and SOREX.

AUTOMATIC EXTENSION granting of more time for a taxpayer to file a
tax return. By filing an IRS Form 4868 by the original due date of the tax
return, a taxpayer can automatically extend his or her filing date by four
months, though the tax payment (based on the taxpayer's best estimate) is
still due on the original filing date.

AUTOMATIC FUNDS TRANSFER fast and accurate transfer of funds,
often internationally, from one account or investment vehicle to another
without direct management, using modern electronic and telecommunications technology. A broker's instant transfer of stock sale proceeds to a
money market fund is one example.

AUTOMATIC INVESTMENT PROGRAM any program in which an
investor can accumulate or withdraw funds automatically. Some of the most
popular automatic investment programs include:
- mutual fund debit programs, in which a mutual fund will automatically debit
  a preset amount from a bank savings or checking account to buy fund shares
  on a weekly, monthly, quarterly, or annual basis.
- mutual fund reinvestment programs, in which all dividends and capital
  gains are automatically reinvested in more shares of the fund.
- stock dividend reinvestment plans, in which companies offer their shareholders the opportunity to reinvest their dividends in more shares of the
  company, and in some cases, buy additional shares at a discount with little
  or no brokerage commissions.
- defined contribution plans, offered by employers to their employees, which
  allow automatic investment in several funds through payroll deduction. Corporate plans are called 401(k), nonprofit and educational plans are called
  403(b), and federal and municipal government plans are called 457s. To
  entice employees to participate in these plans, many employers match
  employee contributions.
- savings bond payroll savings plans, which allow employees to purchase
  savings bonds through payroll deduction.

   In addition to allowing automatic purchases of shares, automatic investment programs also permit participants to withdraw a set amount of money
on a regular basis. These are known as AUTOMATIC WITHDRAWAL plans. For
example, a retiree may request that a mutual fund automatically sell a fixed
dollar amount of shares every month and send him or her a check.

AUTOMATIC REINVESTMENT *see* CONSTANT DOLLAR PLAN; DIVIDEND
REINVESTMENT PLAN.

AUTOMATIC STABILIZERS expenditures or receipts of the federal government that have stabilizing economic effects but increase and decrease

automatically and without action by Congress or the president. Examples are income taxes and unemployment compensation.

AUTOMATIC WITHDRAWAL mutual fund program that entitles shareholders to a fixed payment each month or each quarter. The payment comes from dividends, including realized capital gains and income on securities held by the fund.

AVAILABILITY FLOAT *see* UNCOLLECTED FUNDS.

AVERAGE appropriately weighted and adjusted ARITHMETIC MEAN of selected securities designed to represent market behavior generally or important segments of the market. Among the most familiar averages are the Dow Jones industrial and transportation averages.

Because the evaluation of individual securities involves measuring price trends of securities in general or within an industry group, the various averages are important analytical tools.

See also STOCK INDEXES AND AVERAGES.

AVERAGE COST
Investing: average cost of shares of stock or in a fund bought at different prices. *See also* AVERAGE DOWN; AVERAGE UP; CONSTANT DOLLAR PLAN.
Manufacturing: total of fixed and variable costs divided by units of production. Companies with relatively low average costs are better able to withstand price-cutting pressures from competition. Term also describes INVENTORY valuation method whereby the cost of goods available for sale is divided by the number of units available for sale.

AVERAGE DAILY BALANCE method for computing interest or finance charges on bank deposit accounts, credit cards, and charge accounts. Deposit accounts use the daily closing balance divided by the number of days in the period and apply the interest rate to that. Credit and charge cards divide the balances owed each day by the number of days and apply the finance charge. The average daily balance method, widely used by department stores, is less favorable to the consumer than the ADJUSTED BALANCE METHOD used for interest earned on bank deposit accounts but more favorable than the PREVIOUS BALANCE METHOD used by most credit cards.

AVERAGE DIRECTIONAL INDEX (ADX) indicator used in TECHNICAL ANALYSIS to show the strength of a trend. On a scale of 100, it nets the weight of positive and negative directional indicators (+ DIs and − DIs) and assigns a value. An ADX value above 40 indicates a trend strong enough to base a strategy on, for example, whereas a value of 20 indicates a trend probably too weak to be reliable.

AVERAGE DOWN strategy to lower the average price paid for a company's shares. An investor who wants to buy 1,000 shares, for example, could buy 400 at the current market price and three blocks of 200 each as the price fell. The average cost would then be lower than it would have been if all 1,000 shares had been bought at once. Investors also average down in order to realize tax losses. Say someone buys shares at $20, then watches them fall to $10. Instead of doing nothing, the investor can buy at $10, then sell the $20 shares at a capital loss, which can be used at tax time to offset other gains. However, the WASH SALE rule says that in order to claim the capital loss, the investor must not sell the $20 stock until at least 30 days after buying the stock at $10. *See also* CONSTANT DOLLAR PLAN.

AVERAGE EQUITY average daily balance in a trading account. Brokerage firms calculate customer equity daily as part of their procedure for keeping track of gains and losses on uncompleted transactions, called MARK TO THE MARKET. When transactions are completed, profits and losses are booked to each customer's account together with brokerage commissions. Even though daily fluctuations in equity are routine, average equity is a useful guide in making trading decisions and ensuring sufficient equity to meet MARGIN REQUIREMENTS.

AVERAGE LIFE average length of time before the principal of a debt issue is scheduled to be repaid through AMORTIZATION or SINKING FUND payments. *See also* HALF-LIFE.

AVERAGE MATURITY average time to maturity of bonds, instruments, and other fixed-term investments in a MUTUAL FUND portfolio. The shorter the average maturity, the more sensitive the portfolio is to market interest rate changes.

AVERAGE RATE OF RETURN
1. **Investments:** arithmetic average of the ANNUAL RETURNS of two or more investments.
2. **Corporate finance:** abbreviated ARR, ratio of the average cash inflow to the amount invested.
    See also RATE OF RETURN.

AVERAGE RATE OPTION *see* ASIAN OPTION.

AVERAGE SHARES OUTSTANDING average number of shares of common stock OUTSTANDING during a specified period of time, such as a quarter or a year.

AVERAGE UP buy on a rising market so as to lower the overall cost. Buying an equal number of shares at $50, $52, $54, and $58, for instance, will make the average cost $53.50. This is a mathematical reality, but it does not determine whether the stock is worth buying at any or all of these prices.

AVERAGING *see* CONSTANT DOLLAR PLAN.

AWAY FROM THE MARKET expression used when the bid on a LIMIT ORDER is lower or the offer price is higher than the current market price for the security. Away from the market limit orders are held by the specialist for later execution unless FILL OR KILL (FOK) is stipulated on the order entry.

B

B2B widely used abbreviation for *business-to-business,* meaning Internet marketing between businesses as opposed to marketing by businesses directly to consumers.

B2C Internet marketing between businesses and consumers. Example: Amazon. com.

BABY BELLS the seven regional telephone companies created when AT&T was broken up in 1984. The original consent decree creating the Baby Bells gave them a monopoly over local phone service but banned them from participating in the long-distance or equipment manufacturing business. AT&T was excluded from the local phone business in return. Over time, these distinctions eroded. According to the Telecommunications Act of 1996, the Baby Bells can offer long-distance service; AT&T and other long-distance providers can offer local service. The original seven Baby Bells were NYNEX in the Northeast; Bell Atlantic in the Mid-Atlantic states; BELLSOUTH in the South; SBC (Southwestern Bell Corp.) in the Southwest; Ameritech in the Midwest; U.S. West in the Rocky Mountain States; and Pacific Telesis in the West. After numerous mergers and name changes, including the 2004 acquisition by SBC Corp. of AT&T itself and the 2006 acquisition of BELL-SOUTH by AT&T, there were two Baby Bells left—Qwest and Verizon.

BABY BOND convertible or straight debt bond having a par value of less than $1000, usually $500 to $25. Baby bonds bring the bond market within reach of small investors and, by the same token, open a source of funds to corporations that lack entree to the large institutional market. On the negative side, they entail higher administrative costs (relative to the total money raised) for distribution and processing and lack the large and active market that ensures the liquidity of conventional bonds. *See also* PREFERRED EQUITY TRADED BONDS (PETS).

BACKDATING
In general: dating any statement, document, check or other instrument earlier than the date drawn.
Mutual funds: feature permitting fundholders to use an earlier date on a promise to invest a specified sum over a specified period in exchange for a reduced sales charge. Backdating, which usually accompanies a large transaction, gives retroactive value to purchases from the earlier date in order to meet the requirements of the promise, or LETTER OF INTENT. *See also* OPTIONS BACKDATING.

BACK-END LOAD redemption charge an investor pays when withdrawing money from an investment. Most common in mutual funds and annuities, the back-end load is designed to discourage withdrawals. Back-end loads typically decline for each year that a shareholder remains in a fund. For example, if the shareholder sells shares in the first year, a 5% sales charge is levied. The charge is 4% in the second year, 3% in the third year, 2% in the fourth year, 1% in the fifth year, and no fee is charged if shares are sold after the fifth year. Also called *contingent deferred sales load, deferred sales charge, exit fee, redemption charge. See also* MUTUAL FUND SHARE CLASSES.

BACKING AWAY broker-dealer's failure, as market maker in a given security, to make good on a bid for the minimum quantity. This practice is considered unethical under the RULES OF FAIR PRACTICE of the FINANCIAL INDUSTRY REGULATORY AUTHORITY (FINRA).

BACKLOG value of unfilled orders placed with a manufacturing company. Whether the firm's backlog is rising or falling is a clue to its future sales and earnings.

BACK MONTHS in futures and options trading, the months with the expiration dates furthest out in time. *See also* FURTHEST MONTH.

BACK OFFICE bank or brokerage house departments not directly involved in selling or trading. The back office sees to accounting records, compliance with government regulations, and communication between branches. When stock-market trading is particularly heavy, order processing can be slowed by massive volume; this is called a back office crunch.

BACK TAXES taxes that have not been paid when due. Taxpayers may owe back taxes if they underreported income or overstated deductions, either accidentally, or by design. The Internal Revenue Service and state and local taxing authorities have the right to audit past tax returns and demand payment of back taxes, plus interest and penalties.

BACK-TESTING applying current stock selection criteria to prior periods to create hypothetical PORTFOLIO performance history. A major limitation of back-testing is that it ignores the effect of an investment strategy's popularity on portfolio total returns.

BACK UP turn around; reverse a stock market trend. When prices are moving in one direction, traders would say of a sudden reversal that the market backed up.

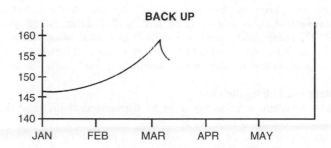

BACKUP LINE BANK LINE of credit in the name of an issuer of commercial paper, covering maturing notes in the event that new notes cannot be marketed to replace them. Ideally, the unused line should always equal the commercial paper outstanding. In practice, something less than total coverage is commonplace, particularly because the compensating balances normally required in support of the line are also available to meet maturing paper.

BACKUP WITHHOLDING system used by the Internal Revenue Service to ensure that taxpayers without Social Security numbers have taxes withheld on earnings. In an instance where a Form 1099 can not be filed by a payor, such as a bank or brokerage, 28% of the interest or dividends is withheld and remitted to the IRS. To avoid backup withholding, you must fill out a federal

W-9 form for the financial institution, verifying that your Social Security number is correct.

BACKWARDATION
1. pricing structure in commodities or foreign-exchange trading in which deliveries in the near future have a higher price than those made later on. Backwardation occurs when demand is greater in the near future. *See also* CONTANGO.

2. London Stock Exchange term for the fees and interest due on short sales of stock with delayed delivery.

BACKWARD INTEGRATION acquisition by a business of its own suppliers.

BAD DEBT
Banks and Corporations: open account balance or loan receivable that has proven uncollectible and is written off. Traditionally, companies and financial institutions have maintained a RESERVE for uncollectible accounts, charging the reserve for actual bad debts and making annual, tax deductible charges to income to replenish or increase the reserve. Companies and large banks ($500 million or more in assets) must generally use the direct charge-off method for tax purposes, although bad debt reserves continue to appear on balance sheets for reporting purposes. Small banks and thrift institutions continue using the reserve method for tax purposes, although with strict limitations. The relationship of bad debt WRITE-OFFS and recoveries to accounts receivable can reveal how liberal or conservative a firm's credit and charge-off policies are.

Individuals: Individuals lending money may deduct bad debts on their tax return when the debtor does not repay the loan. Bad business debts are fully deductible from gross income on Schedule C for self-employed individuals. Nonbusiness bad debts can be deducted as short-term capital losses on Schedule D. These short-term losses can offset capital gains plus $3,000 of other income. Any excess bad debt losses can be carried forward into future tax years. In order to determine whether a bad debt deduction is legitimate:

1. the debt must be legally valid

2. A debtor-creditor relationship must be formalized at the time the debt arose

3. the funds providing the loan must have previously been reported as income or part of the individual's capital and

4. the individual must prove that the debt became worthless in that tax year.

BAD DELIVERY opposite of GOOD DELIVERY.

BAD TITLE title to property that does not clearly confer ownership. Most frequently applied to real estate, a bad title may prevent a homeowner from selling the property. Title may be clouded by unpaid taxes or other unsatisfied liens, a faulty or incomplete certificate of occupancy, an incorrect survey, or uncorrected building violations, among other causes. Steps must be taken to rectify these problems before title to a property can be legally transferred. Also called *cloud on title.*

BAILOUT BOND bond issued by RESOLUTION FUNDING CORPORATION (REFCORP) to finance the rescue or disposition of SAVINGS AND LOAN ASSO-

CIATIONS that were failing in the 1980s and 1990s. The principal of REFCORP securities is backed by zero-coupon Treasury bonds and the U.S. Treasury guarantees interest payments. Because this is stronger backing than that enjoyed by other GOVERNMENT SECURITIES issued by agencies, bailout bonds yield only slightly more than TREASURIES of comparable maturity. Once the savings and loan crisis ended in the mid-1990s, no more bailout bonds were issued, though existing issues continued to trade in the bond market. *See also* OFFICE OF THRIFT SUPERVISION (OTS).

BAKED IN THE CAKE already reflected in a stock's market price. Said of projected earnings or an unconfirmed news development. *See also* DISCOUNTING THE NEWS.

BALANCED BUDGET *see* BUDGET.

BALANCED MUTUAL FUND fund that buys common stock, preferred stock, and bonds in an effort to obtain the highest return consistent with a low-risk strategy. A balanced fund typically offers a higher yield than a pure stock fund and performs better than such a fund when stocks are falling. In a rising market, however, a balanced mutual fund usually will not keep pace with all-equity funds.

BALANCE OF PAYMENTS system of recording all of a country's economic transactions with the rest of the world during a particular time period. Double-entry bookkeeping is used, and there can be no surplus or deficit on the overall balance of payments. The balance of payments is typically divided into three accounts—current, capital, and gold—and these can show a surplus or deficit. The current account covers imports and exports of goods and services; the capital account covers movements of investments; and the gold account covers gold movements. The balance of payments helps a country evaluate its competitive strengths and weaknesses and forecast the strength of its currency. From the standpoint of a national economy, a surplus on a part of the balance of payments is not necessarily good, nor is a deficit necessarily bad; the state of the national economy and the manner of financing the deficit are important considerations. *See also* BALANCE OF TRADE.

BALANCE OF RISKS STATEMENT *see* FED BIAS.

BALANCE OF TRADE net difference over a period of time between the value of a country's imports and exports of merchandise. Movable goods such as automobiles, foodstuffs, and apparel are included in the balance of trade; payments abroad for services and for tourism are not. When a country exports more than it imports, it is said to have a favorable balance of trade; when imports predominate the balance is called unfavorable. The balance of trade should be viewed in the context of the country's entire international economic position, however. For example, a country may consistently have an unfavorable balance of trade that is offset by considerable exports of services; this country would have a balanced current account and a good international economic position. *See also* BALANCE OF PAYMENTS.

BALANCE SHEET financial report, also called *statement of condition* or *statement of financial position,* showing the status of a company's assets, liabilities, and owners' equity on a given date, usually the close of a month. One way of looking at a business enterprise is as a mass of capital (ASSETS) arrayed against the sources of that capital (LIABILITIES and EQUITY). Assets are equal to liabilities and equity, and the balance sheet is a listing of the items making up the two sides of the equation. Unlike a PROFIT AND LOSS STATEMENT, which shows the results of operations over a period of time, a balance sheet shows the state of affairs at one point in time. It is a snapshot, not a motion picture, and must be analyzed with reference to comparative prior balance sheets and other operating statements.

BALLOON final payment on a debt that is substantially larger than the preceding payments. Loans or mortgages are structured with balloon payments when some projected event is expected to provide extra cash flow or when refinancing is anticipated. Balloon loans are sometimes called *partially amortized loans.*

BALLOON INTEREST in serial bond issues, the higher COUPON rate on bonds with later maturities.

BALLOON MATURITY bond issue or long-term loan with larger dollar amounts of bonds or payments falling due in the later years of the obligation.

BAN *see* BOND ANTICIPATION NOTE.

BANKER'S ACCEPTANCE *see* ACCEPTANCE.

BANK DISCOUNT BASIS *see* DISCOUNT YIELD.

BANKER'S YEAR twelve months of 30 days for a total of 360 days.

BANK HOLDING COMPANY company that owns or controls two or more banks or other bank holding companies. As defined in the Bank Holding Company Act of 1956, such companies must register with the BOARD OF GOVERNORS of the FEDERAL RESERVE SYSTEM and hence are called registered bank holding companies. Amendments to the 1956 act set standards for acquisitions (1966) and ended the exemption enjoyed by one-bank holding companies (1970), thus restricting bank holding companies to activities related to banking. The FINANCIAL SERVICES MODERNIZATION ACT OF 1999 liberated Bank Holding Companies that qualify as FINANCIAL HOLDING COMPANIES to acquire or create as subsidiaries securities firms and insurance companies.

BANK INSURANCE FUND (BIF) unit of FEDERAL DEPOSIT INSURANCE CORPORATION (FDIC) providing deposit insurance for banks other than thrifts. BIF was formed as part of the 1989 savings and loan association bailout bill to keep separate the administration of the bank and thrift insurance programs. There were thus two distinct insurance entities under the FDIC: BIF and SAVINGS ASSOCIATION INSURANCE FUND (SAIF). In 2005, Congress passed legislation merging the SAIF and BIF into one insurance fund called the Deposit Insurance Fund (DIF). The same law also raised the federal deposit insurance level from $100,000 to $250,000 on retirement accounts. In 2008, the insurance ceiling on regular bank accounts was also raised from $100,000 to $250,000. *See also* OFFICE OF THRIFT SUPERVISION (OTS).

BANK INVESTMENT CONTRACT (BIC) bank-guaranteed interest in a portfolio providing a specified yield over a specified period. For insurance company equivalent, *see* GUARANTEED INVESTMENT CONTRACT (GIC).

BANK LINE bank's moral commitment, as opposed to its contractual commitment, to make loans to a particular borrower up to a specified maximum during a specified period, usually one year. Because a bank line—also called a *line of credit*—is not a legal commitment, it is not customary to charge a commitment fee. It is common, however, to require that compensating balances be kept on deposit—typically 10% of the line, with an additional 10% of any borrowings under the line. A line about which a customer is officially notified is called an *advised line* or *confirmed line*. A line that is an internal policy guide about which the customer is not informed is termed a *guidance line.*

BANKMAIL bank's agreement with a company involved in a TAKEOVER not to finance another acquirer's bid.

BANK QUALITY *see* INVESTMENT GRADE.

BANKRUPTCY state of insolvency of an individual or an organization—in other words, an inability to pay debts. There are two kinds of legal bankruptcy under U.S. law: involuntary, when one or more creditors petition to have a debtor judged insolvent by a court; and voluntary, when the debtor brings the petition. In both cases, the objective is an orderly and equitable settlement of obligations.

The 1978 Bankruptcy Reform Act removed some of the rigidities of the old law and permitted more flexibility in procedures. The Bankruptcy Reform Act of 1984 curtailed some of the more liberal provisions (mainly affecting consumer bankruptcy) of the 1978 act.

Chapter 7 of the 1978 act, dealing with LIQUIDATION, provides for a court-appointed interim trustee with broad powers and discretion to make management changes, arrange unsecured financing, and generally operate the debtor business in such a way as to prevent loss. Only by filing an appropriate bond is the debtor able to regain possession from the trustee.

Chapter 11, which deals with REORGANIZATION of businesses, provides that, unless the court rules otherwise, the debtor remains in possession of the business and in control of its operation. Debtor and creditors are allowed considerable flexibility in working together.

Chapter 13, which deals with debt adjustment or reorganization for individuals, allows people to put forward a plan to repay creditors over time, usually from future income. Most consumer reorganizations take place under Chapter 13 of the bankruptcy law. A Chapter 13 bankruptcy normally requires monthly payments to the bankruptcy trustee for a period of three to five years. Once payments have been completed under the plan, the debtors are entitled to a discharge. Chapter 13 reorganizations also allow debtors to keep more property than in a Chapter 7 liquidation. *See also* PREPACKAGED BANKRUPTCY.

BANKRUPTCY ABUSE PREVENTION AND CONSUMER PROTECTION ACT OF 2005 legislation reforming the bankruptcy code designed to make filing for bankruptcy more difficult for debtors. Among the major provisions of the law:

1. **Means test for Chapter 7 eligibility**: A test of the debtor's income determining whether he or she can file under Chapter 7 or 13. If the debtor's income is greater than the state's median income, the debtor would most likely have to file a Chapter 13 repayment plan and not be able to file a Chapter 7 liquidation plan.

2. **Mandatory credit counseling**: Debtors must receive credit counseling from an approved nonprofit budget and credit counseling agency before they can file for bankruptcy.

3. **Limit on auto lien-stripping**: A secured creditor such as an auto lender can retain its lien until the payment of the entire debt, not just the secured portion, where the creditor holds a security interest in a motor vehicle purchased within 910 days of the filing.

4. **Mandatory debtor education**: A Chapter 13 bankruptcy filing will not be approved unless the debtor has completed an education course in personal financial management approved by the U.S. Bankruptcy Trustee.

5. **Scope of discharge**: Debts owed to a single creditor of more than $500 for luxury goods incurred within 90 days of the filing or cash advances up to $750 within 70 days cannot be discharged.

6. **Serial filings**: A Chapter 13 filing will not be granted if the debtor has obtained a Chapter 7, 11, or 12 discharge within the previous 4 years. A Chapter 7 debtor cannot receive a discharge if the previous discharge was received within the previous 8 years.

7. **Homestead exemption**: Debtors can elect the state exemption for the value of their home up to $125,000 if it was acquired within 1,215 days before the filing. This federal law overrides certain states such as Florida and Texas that formerly had unlimited homestead exemptions.

8. **Reaffirmations**: New disclosures are required detailing the rights of the debtor and specifying the amount of debt reaffirmed, rates of interest, when payments begin, court filing requirements; the right to rescind and certification that the agreement does not impose an undue hardship on the debtor.

9. **Limit on automatic stay**: Limits the application of the stay and provides that it does not go into effect where there have been serial filings or under other circumstances that would indicate bad faith or abusive filings.

10. **Duration of Chapter 13 plans**: If the debtor's income is greater than the state median income, a Chapter 13 plan must be for five years.

11. **Dismissal for failure to file documents**: Failure to file proper documents within 45 days of filing the petition will result in automatic dismissal of the case.

12. **Attorney verification**: Attorneys who sign the bankruptcy petition with the debtor must make reasonable inquiry to verify that the information in the petition is well grounded in fact. If the information later turns out to be false, the attorney can be held responsible.

13. **Debtor statement of intent**: Debtors must provide a statement of intent about their secured property within 30 days after the date set for the first creditor's meeting.

14. **Eviction proceedings**: The bankruptcy filing will not prevent an eviction if the debtor does not pay his or her rent after the filing.

15. **Nondischargeable student loans**: Student loans are not dischargeable through bankruptcy, and this is extended to loans from for-profit and nongovernmental institutions.

BANK TRUST DEPARTMENT part of a bank engaged in settling estates, administering trusts and guardianships, and performing AGENCY services. As part of its personal trust and ESTATE PLANNING services, it manages investments for large accounts. People who cannot or do not want to make investment decisions are commonly bank trust department clients. Known for their conservative investment philosophy, such departments have custody over billions of dollars, making them a major factor in the movement of stock and bond prices.

Among other things, the departments also act as trustee for corporate bonds, administer pension and profit-sharing plans, and function as TRANSFER AGENTS.

BANK WIRE computerized message system owned and administered by participating banks. It provides information about loan participations, securities transactions, Federal Reserve System funds borrowings, credit history, the payment or nonpayment of "wire fate" items, and other essential matters requiring prompt communication. *See also* ELECTRONIC FUNDS TRANSFER (EFT).

BAR
1. slang for one million dollars.
2. sanction of the FINANCIAL INDUSTRY REGULATORY AUTHORITY (FINRA) that expels an individual guilty of a disciplinary violation from FINRA membership and prohibits associating with a FINRA member. *See also* GOLD BARS.

BARBELL PORTFOLIO portfolio of bonds distributed like the shape of a barbell, with most of the portfolio in short-term and long-term bonds, but few bonds in intermediate maturities. This portfolio can be adjusted to emphasize short- or long-term bonds, depending on whether the investor thinks interest rates are rising or falling. A portfolio with a higher concentration in medium term bonds than short- or long-term bonds is called a *bell-shaped curve portfolio.*

BAREFOOT PILGRIM unsophisticated investor who has lost his or her shirt and shoes in securities trading.

BARGAINING UNIT group of labor union members organized to negotiate with management.

BAROMETER selective compilation of economic and market data designed to represent larger trends. Consumer spending, housing starts, and interest rates are barometers used in economic forecasting. The Dow Jones Industrial Average and the Standard & Poor's 500 Stock Index are prominent stock market barometers. The Dow Jones Utility Average is a barometer of market trends in the utility industry.

A *barometer stock* has a price movement pattern that reflects the market as a whole, thus serving as a market indicator. General Motors, for example, is considered a barometer stock.

BARRA'S PERFORMANCE ANALYSIS (PERFAN) devised by BARRA, Inc., a California consulting firm, a method of PERFORMANCE ATTRIBUTION ANALYSIS used by institutional investors to measure the performance of PORTFOLIO MANAGERS.

BARRIER OPTIONS *see* EXOTIC OPTIONS.

BARRIERS TO ENTRY anything that makes it difficult for new competitors to enter a particular industry or type of business. Examples would include excessive capital investment, inability to achieve required economies of scale, prohibitive government policies, and inadequate labor supply.

BARRON'S CONFIDENCE INDEX weekly index of corporate bond yields published by *Barron's,* a Dow Jones financial newspaper. The index shows the ratio of the average yield on 10 top-grade bonds to the average yield on 10 intermediate-grade bonds. People who are worried about the economic outlook tend to seek safety in a FLIGHT TO QUALITY, whereas investors who feel secure about the economy are more likely to buy lower-rated bonds. The spread between high- and low-grade bonds thus reflects investor confidence about the economy. *Barron's* also publishes other confidence indicators, such as the TED SPREAD (the difference between Treasury Bill Futures and Euro-dollar Futures contract prices); the Lehman Brothers Treasury Bond Index; the Lehman Brothers Corporate Bond Index; the Ryan Labs Treasury Index; the Bond Buyer 20 Bond Index; the Bond Buyer Municipal Bond Index, and the Stock/Bond Yield Gap, which is the difference between the yield on the highest-grade corporate bonds and the yield on the stocks in the Dow Jones Industrial Average.

BARTER trade of goods or services without use of money. When money is involved, whether in such forms as wampum, checks, or bills or coins, a transaction is called a SALE. Although barter is usually associated with unde-veloped economies, it occurs in modern complex societies. In conditions of extreme inflation, it can be a preferred mode of commerce. Where a popula-tion lacks confidence in its currency or banking system, barter becomes commonplace. In international trade, barter can provide a way of doing business with countries whose soft currencies would otherwise make them unattractive trading partners.

BASE in TECHNICAL ANALYSIS, a chart pattern in which the SUPPORT LEVEL and the RESISTANCE LEVEL come together. During a *basing* period, supply and demand are in relative equilibrium and the stock trades in a narrow range. A positive or negative BREAKOUT from a basing period can be a powerful buy or sell signal.

BASE CURRENCY currency used as a basis for measuring profits or losses in an international portfolio, usually of equities.

BASE MARKET VALUE average market price of a group of securities at a given time. It is used as a basis of comparison in plotting dollar or percent-age changes for purposes of market INDEXING.

BASE PERIOD particular time in the past used as a yardstick when measur-ing economic data. A base period is usually a year or an average of years; it can also be a month or other time period. The U.S. rate of INFLATION is determined by measuring current prices against those of a base period; for instance, the CONSUMER PRICE INDEX is determined by comparing current prices with prices in the base reference years of 1982–1984 and the PRODUCER PRICE INDEX is determined by comparing current prices with prices in the base reference year of 1987.

BASE RATE
1. interest rate charged by banks to their best corporate customers in Great Britain. It is the British equivalent of the PRIME RATE in the United States.
2. interest rate used as the basis for setting and adjusting rates described as

adjustable, floating, or variable, usually the base or prime rate as defined above; a BENCHMARK, such as an index or the 10-year Treasury note; or a MONEY MARKET rate, such as the rate on Treasury bills. *See also* COST-OF-FUNDS INDEX (COFI).

BASIC EARNINGS PER SHARE *see* EARNINGS PER SHARE.

BASIC MATERIALS *see* SECTOR ROTATION.

BASIS

In general: short for TAX BASIS, the original cost plus out-of-pocket expenses that must be reported to the Internal Revenue Service when an investment is sold and must be used in calculating capital gains or losses. If a stock was bought for $1,000 two years ago and is sold today for $2,000, the basis is $1,000 plus expenses and the profit is a capital gain.

Bonds: an investor's YIELD TO MATURITY at a given bond price. A 10% bond selling at 100 has a 10% basis.

Commodities: the difference between the cash price of a hedged money market instrument and a FUTURES CONTRACT.

BASIS POINT smallest measure used in quoting yields on bills, notes, and bonds. One basis point is .01%, or one one-hundredth of a percent of yield. Thus, 100 basis points equal 1%. A bond's yield that increased from 8.00% to 8.50% would be said to have risen 50 basis points.

BASIS PRICE

In general: price an investor uses to calculate capital gains when selling a stock or bond. *See also* BASIS; STEPPED-UP BASIS.

Odd-lot trading: the price arbitrarily established by an exchange floor official at the end of a trading session for a buyer or seller of an odd lot when the market bid and asked prices are more than $2 apart, or if no round-lot trans-actions have occurred that day. The customer gets the basis price plus or minus the odd-lot differential, if any. This procedure for determining prices is rare, since most odd lots are transacted at the market bid (if a sale) or asked (if a buy) or at prices based on the next round-lot trade.

BASKET

1. unit of 15 or more stocks used in PROGRAM TRADING.
2. program trading vehicles offered by the NEW YORK STOCK EXCHANGE (NYSE) (called Exchange Stock Portfolio or ESP) and the CHICAGO BOARD OPTIONS EXCHANGE (CBOE) (called Market Basket) to institutional investors and index arbitrageurs. Both baskets permit the purchase in one trade of all the stocks making up the Standard & Poor's 500 Composite Index. ESP's design requires a minimum trade of approximately $5 million, and Market Basket's, around $1.7 million. The baskets were introduced in late 1989 to solve problems revealed when institutions tried to negotiate large block trades on BLACK MONDAY and to head off an exodus of program trading business to overseas exchanges. Subsequently, trading in these instruments ceased due to lack of trading volume. *See also* DIAMONDS; EXCHANGE-TRADED FUNDS (ETF); SPDR.

BASKET OPTIONS *see* EXOTIC OPTIONS; FOREIGN CURRENCY FUTURES AND OPTIONS.

BD FORM document that brokerage house must file and keep current with the Securities and Exchange Commission, detailing the firm's finances and officers.

BEACON acronym for the *Boston Exchange Automated Communication Order-routing Network.* This electronic system allows the automatic execution of trades based on the prevailing stock prices on the consolidated market, any of the seven U.S. securities exchanges.

BEAR person with a pessimistic market outlook. Contrast with BULL.

BEAR CD *see* CERTIFICATE OF DEPOSIT (CD).

BEARER BOND *see* COUPON BOND.

BEARER FORM security not registered on the books of the issuing corporation and thus payable to the one possessing it. A bearer bond has coupons attached, which the bondholder sends in or presents on the interest date for payment, hence the alternative name COUPON BONDS. Bearer stock certificates are negotiable without endorsement and are transferred by delivery. Dividends are payable by presentation of dividend coupons, which are dated or numbered. Most securities issued today, with the exception of foreign stocks, are in registered form, including municipal bonds issued since 1983.

BEAR ETF *see* INVERSE EXCHANGE-TRADED FUNDS (ETFs).

BEAR FUNDS specialized MUTUAL FUNDS or HEDGE FUNDS that use SELLING SHORT to make money in declining markets. Such funds are either actively managed funds that short individual stocks or inverse-index funds that short entire indexes, some positioned to double the inverse of a particular index. With the advent of EXCHANGE TRADED FUNDS (ETFs), individual investors can short indexes.

BEAR HUG TAKEOVER bid so attractive in terms of price and other features that TARGET COMPANY directors, who might be opposed for other reasons, must approve it or risk shareholder protest.

BEAR MARKET prolonged period of falling prices. A bear market in stocks is usually brought on by the anticipation of declining economic activity, and a bear market in bonds is caused by rising interest rates.

BEAR RAID attempt by investors to manipulate the price of a stock by selling large numbers of shares short. The manipulators pocket the difference between the initial price and the new, lower price after this maneuver. Bear raids are illegal under Securities and Exchange Commission rules, which stipulate that every SHORT SALE be executed on an UPTICK (the last price was higher than the price before it) or a ZERO PLUS TICK (the last price was unchanged but higher than the last preceding different price).

BEARS acronym for *Bonds Enabling Annual Retirement Savings* and the flip side of *CUBS*, acronym for *Calls Underwritten By Swanbrook*. Holders of BEARS receive the face value of bonds underlying call options but exercised by CUBS holders. If the calls are exercised, BEARS holders receive the aggregate of the exercise prices.

BEAR SPREAD strategy in the options market designed to take advantage of a fall in the price of a security or commodity. Someone executing a bear spread could buy a combination of calls and puts on the same security at different *strike prices* in order to profit as the security's price fell. Or the investor could buy a put of short maturity and a put of long maturity in order to profit from the difference between the two puts as prices fell. *See also* BULL SPREAD.

BEAR TRAP situation confronting short sellers when a bear market reverses itself and turns bullish. Anticipating further declines, the bears continue to sell, and then are forced to buy at higher prices to cover. *See also* SELLING SHORT.

BEGGAR-THY-NEIGHBOR competitive international trade policies whereby one trading partner gains an advantage at the expense of another by devaluing its currency or erecting trade barriers.

BEHAVIORAL FINANCE (OR INVESTING) new area of financial research that recognizes a psychological element in financial decision making, thus challenging traditional models that assume investors will always weigh risk/return factors rationally and act without bias. For example, the human tendency to avoid admitting error, called *fear of regret* by psychologists, can cause an investor to hold a losing stock too long or sell a winner too soon. Similarly, investment choices are influenced positively or negatively by attitudes toward wealth. The success of contrarian and momentum strategies owes largely to psychological factors. The premise of behavioral finance is that taking psychological factors into account can enhance the effectiveness of investment strategies.

BEIGE BOOK FEDERAL RESERVE BOARD report published eight times a year and summarizing current economic conditions.

BELL signal that opens and closes trading on major exchanges—sometimes actually a bell but sometimes a buzzer sound.

BELLWETHER security seen as an indicator of a market's direction. In stocks, 3M Company (MMM) is considered both an economic and a market bellwether because it sells to a diverse range of other producers and because so much of its stock is owned by institutional investors who have much control over supply and demand on the stock market. Institutional trading actions tend to influence smaller investors and therefore the market generally. There are bellwethers in specific industries; for example, Microsoft and Intel act as bellwethers for the technology stocks. In bonds, the 10-year U.S. Treasury note is considered the bellwether, denoting the direction in which all other bonds are likely to move.

BELLY UP slang for bankrupt.

BELOW PAR *see* PAR VALUE.

BENCHMARK any basis of measurement, such as an interest rate, an index or peer grouping of stock or bond prices or other values, used as a reference point. For example, the STANDARD & POOR'S 500 COMPOSITE INDEX is the most commonly used benchmark for comparing the performance of stock PORTFOLIO MANAGERS. The 10-year Treasury note yield is a benchmark that might be used to adjust a FLOATING RATE NOTE. Benchmark indexes are also called REFERENCE indexes. *See also* BASE RATE.

BENEFICIAL OWNER person who enjoys the benefits of ownership even though title is in another name. When shares of a mutual fund are held by a custodian bank or when securities are held by a broker in STREET NAME, the real owner is the beneficial owner, even though, for safety or convenience, the bank or broker holds title.

BENEFICIARY
1. person to whom an inheritance passes as the result of being named in a will.
2. recipient of the proceeds of a life insurance policy.
3. party in whose favor a LETTER OF CREDIT is issued.
4. one to whom the amount of an ANNUITY is payable.
5. party for whose benefit a TRUST exists.

BEQUEST giving of assets, such as stocks, bonds, mutual funds, real estate, and personal property, to beneficiaries through the provisions of a will.

BERMUDA OPTION *see* EXOTIC OPTIONS.

BEST EFFORT arrangement whereby investment bankers, acting as agents, agree to do their best to sell an issue to the public. Instead of buying the securities outright, these agents have an option to buy and an authority to sell the securities. Depending on the contract, the agents exercise their option and buy enough shares to cover their sales to clients, or they cancel the incompletely sold issue altogether and forgo the fee. Best efforts deals, which were common prior to 1900, entailed risks and delays from the issuer's standpoint. What is more, the broadening of the securities markets has made marketing new issues easier, and the practice of outright purchase by investment bankers, called FIRM COMMITMENT underwriting, has become commonplace. For the most part, the best efforts deals we occasionally see today are handled by firms specializing in the more speculative securities of new and unseasoned companies. *See also* BOUGHT DEAL.

BEST EXECUTION REQUIREMENT regulation specified in FINRA Rule 2320 and elsewhere that broker-dealers, MARKET MAKERS, and others acting on behalf of investors execute orders at the best available price.

BEST-OF-TWO OPTION *see* EXOTIC OPTIONS.

BEST'S RATING rating assigned to insurance companies by A.M. Best Co. A Best's Rating is important to buyers of insurance or annuities because it provides an opinion of a company's ability to meet its obligations to policyholders. Best's Ratings are also important to investors in insurance stocks. The top rating is A++. Other companies providing ratings of insurance companies include FITCH RATINGS in New York and London, MOODY'S INVESTORS SERVICES in New York, STANDARD & POOR'S in New York, and Weiss Research in Palm Beach Gardens, Florida.

BETA coefficient is the covariance of a stock or portfolio in relation to the rest of the stock market. The Standard & Poor's 500 Stock Index has a beta coefficient of 1. Any stock or portfolio with a higher beta is more volatile than the market, and any with a lower beta can be expected to rise and fall more slowly than the market. A conservative investor whose main concern is preservation of capital should focus on stocks with low betas, whereas one willing to take high risks in an effort to earn high rewards should look for high-beta stocks. *See also* ALPHA; VOLATILE.

BETTER-OF-TWO OPTIONS *see* EXOTIC OPTIONS.

BID
1. price a prospective buyer is ready to pay. Term is used by traders who MAKE A MARKET (maintain firm bid and OFFER prices) in a given security by standing ready to buy or sell round lots at publicly quoted prices and by the SPECIALIST in a stock, who performs a similar function on an exchange.
2. TENDER OFFER in a TAKEOVER attempt.
3. any offer to buy at a specified price.

    See also ANY-AND-ALL BID; COMPETITIVE BID; TREASURIES.

BID AND ASKED bid is the highest price a prospective buyer is prepared to pay at a particular time for a trading unit of a given security; asked is the lowest price acceptable to a prospective seller of the same security. Together, the two prices constitute a QUOTATION; the difference between the two prices is the SPREAD. Although the bid and asked dynamic is common to all securities trading, "bid and asked" usually refers to UNLISTED SECURITIES traded OVER THE COUNTER.

BID-ASKED SPREAD difference between BID and offer prices. The term *asked* is usually used in OVER-THE COUNTER trading; *offered* is used in exchange trading. The bid and asked (or offered) prices together comprise a QUOTATION (or *quote*).

BIDDER party that is ready to buy at a specified price in a TWO-SIDED MARKET or DUTCH AUCTION.

BIDDING UP practice whereby the price bid for a security is successively moved higher lest an upswing in prices leaves orders unexecuted. An example would be an investor wanting to purchase a sizable quantity of shares in a rising market, using buy limit orders (orders to buy at a specified price or lower) to ensure the most favorable price. Since offer prices are moving up with the market, the investor must move his limit buy price upward to continue accumulating shares. To some extent the buyer is contributing to the upward price pressure on the stock, but most of the price rise is out of his control.

BID-TO-COVER RATIO number of bids received in a Treasury security auction compared to the number of bids accepted. A high ratio (over 2.0) is an indication that bidding was aggressive and the auction successful. A low ratio, indicating the government had difficulty selling its securities, is usually accompanied by a long TAIL, a wide spread between the average and high yield (the average and lowest accepted bid).

BID WANTED (BW) announcement that a holder of securities wants to sell and will entertain bids. Because the final price is subject to negotiation, the bid submitted in response to a BW need not be specific. A BW is frequently seen on published market quotation sheets.

BIG BANG deregulation on October 27, 1986, of London-based securities markets, an event comparable to MAY DAY in the United States and marking a major step toward a single world financial market.

BIG BLUE popular name for International Business Machines Corporation (IBM), taken from the color of its logotype.

BIG BOARD popular term for the NEW YORK STOCK EXCHANGE.

BIG BOX RETAILER physically large store, typically part of a chain, and occupying between 50,000 and 200,000 square feet of single floor space that sells general merchandise (e.g., Wal-Mart and Target) or specialty products (e.g., Home Depot, Best Buy, Barnes & Noble). Chains operate nationally and, increasingly, internationally.

BIG FOUR largest U.S. accounting firms as measured by revenue. They do the accounting and auditing for most major corporations, signing the AUDI-TOR'S REPORT that appears in every annual report. They also offer various consulting services. Over time, there have been several mergers among the top accounting firms, which formerly were called the Big Eight. In alphabetical order they are PricewaterhouseCoopers; Deloitte & Touche; Ernst & Young; and KPMG International.

BIG PRODUCER broker who is very successful, and thereby produces a large volume of commission dollars for the brokerage firm he or she represents. Big producers typically will bring in $1 million or more per year in commissions for their firms. In order to retain big producers, many brokerage firms try to tie them to the firm with GOLDEN HANDCUFFS.

BIG THREE the three large automobile companies in America, which are, alphabetically, Chrysler, Ford, and General Motors. Since the automobile business has such a major influence on the direction of the economy, the Big Three's fortunes are closely followed by investors, analysts, and economists. Because auto company profits rise and fall with the economy, they are considered to be CYCLICAL STOCKS. In 1998, Chrysler merged with Daimler-Benz to create DaimlerChrysler AG. In 2007, Chrysler was sold to Cerberus Capital Management. On April 30, 2009, Chrysler LLC filed for Chapter 11 bankruptcy protection, and in June the formation of a "New Chrysler" called Chrysler Group LLC was announced that would buy most of the former company's assets with the U.S. government providing $6.6 billion financing. The Italian automaker Fiat would hold a 20% stake with an option to increase this eventually to 51%. General Motors emerged from a Chapter 11 bankruptcy reorganization on July 10, 2009, and is now majority owned by the U.S. Treasury and Canadian governments. No GM shares are currently available to the public, but the company plans an initial public offering (IPO) in 2010.

BIG UGLIES stocks that are out of favor with the investing public. These usually are large industrial companies such as steel or chemical firms that are not in glamorous businesses. Because they are unpopular, Big Uglies typically sell at low price/earnings and price/book value ratios.

BILL
In general: (1) short for *bill of exchange,* an order by one person directing a second to pay a third. (2) document evidencing a debtor's obligation to a creditor, the kind of bill we are all familiar with. (3) paper currency, like the $5 bill. (4) *bill of sale,* a document used to transfer the title to certain goods from seller to buyer in the same way a deed to real property passes.
Investments: short for *due bill,* a statement of money owed. Commonly used to adjust a securities transaction when dividends, interest, and other distributions are reflected in a price but have not yet been disbursed. For example, when a stock is sold ex-dividend, but the dividend has not yet been paid, the buyer would sign a due bill stating that the amount of the dividend is payable to the seller.

A due bill may accompany delivered securities to give title to the buyer's broker in exchange for shares or money.

U.S. Treasury bill: commonly called bill or T-bill by money market people, a Treasury bill is a short-term (maturities up to a year), discounted government security sold through competitive bidding at weekly and monthly auctions in denominations from $10,000 to $1 million.

The auction at which bills are sold differs from the two-sided auction used by exchanges. Here, in what is sometimes termed a *Dutch auction,* the Treasury invites anyone interested to submit a bid, called a TENDER, then awards units to the highest bidders going down a list. Three- and six-month bills are auctioned weekly, nine-month and one-year bills monthly. Although the yield on bills may barely top the inflation rate, the high degree of safety together with the liquidity provided by an active SECONDARY MARKET make bills popular with corporate money managers as well as with banks and other government entities.

Individuals may also purchase bills directly, in amounts under $500,000, at no transaction charge, from a Federal Reserve bank, the Bureau of Federal Debt, or certain commercial banks. Bills bought on this basis are priced by noncompetitive bidding, with subscribers paying an average of the accepted bids.

Treasury bills are the most widely used of all government debt securities and are a primary instrument of Federal Reserve monetary policy. *See also* TAX ANTICIPATION BILL; TREASURY DIRECT.

BILLING CYCLE interval between periodic billings for goods sold or services rendered, normally one month, or a system whereby bills or statements are mailed at periodic intervals in the course of a month in order to distribute the clerical workload.

BILL OF EXCHANGE *see* DRAFT.

BILL PASS Federal Reserve purchases of Treasury bills from dealers. *See also* FED PASS.

BINDER sum of money paid to evidence good faith until a transaction is finalized. In insurance, the binder is an agreement executed by an insurer (or sometimes an agent) that puts insurance coverage into force before the contract is signed and the premium paid. In real estate, the binder holds the sale until the closing and is refundable.

BI-WEEKLY MORTGAGE LOAN mortgage loan on which the borrower makes 26 half-month payments a year, resulting in earlier loan retirement and lower total interest costs than with a fully amortized loan with regular monthly payments. For example, a 30-year mortgage may be retired in 20 years if paid bi-weekly. Many bi-weekly plans offer automatic electronic debiting of the borrower's bank account.

BLACK BOX designation sometimes applied to breakthrough systems that, while not necessarily black or even boxed, use advanced technology to provide data or perform functions of unique value. Their methodologies are arcane and usually not understood by the people who use them. Airliner flight recorders are the most familiar examples. Financial uses of the term included early electronic trading systems and, currently, HIGH-FREQUENCY TRADING technology.

BLACK-BOX ACCOUNTING financial statements based on accounting methodologies so complex that numbers, although accurate and legal, obfuscate rather than clarify. Restatements of revenues, inventory, and earnings, and the use of derivatives and off-the-books partnerships are examples.

BLACK FRIDAY sharp drop in a financial market. The original Black Friday was September 24, 1869, when a group of financiers tried to corner the gold market and precipitated a business panic followed by a depression. The panic of 1873 also began on Friday, and Black Friday now applies to any Friday when there is a debacle affecting the financial markets.

BLACK MARKET illegal commercial market in which goods or services are in short supply and buyers seek out sellers willing to sell at prices exceeding the EQUILIBRIUM PRICE or the price set by government price controls.

BLACK MONDAY October 19, 1987, when the Dow Jones Industrial Average plunged 508 points, or a record 22.6%, following sharp drops the previous week, reflecting investor anxiety about inflated stock price levels, federal budget and trade deficits, and foreign market activity. Many blamed PROGRAM TRADING for the extreme VOLATILITY. The greatest point loss of the Dow Jones Industrial Average was 777.68 points on September 29, 2008.

BLACK-SCHOLES OPTION PRICING MODEL see DERIVATIVE PRICING MODELS.

BLACK TUESDAY October 29, 1929, the day of the great CRASH on the NEW YORK STOCK EXCHANGE. That event, a 30-point, 11.7% drop to 230.07 from the previous day's close, triggered bank failures and eventually led to the Great Depression of the 1930s.

BLANK CHECK check drawn on a bank account and signed by the maker, but with the amount of the check to be supplied by the drawee. Term is used as a metaphor for any situation where inordinate trust is placed in another person.

BLANK CHECK OFFERING INITIAL PUBLIC OFFERING (IPO) by a company whose business activities have yet to be determined and which is therefore speculative. Similar to the BLIND POOL concept of limited partnerships.

BLANKET CERTIFICATION FORM see NASD FORM FR-1.

BLANKET FIDELITY BOND insurance coverage against losses due to employee dishonesty. Brokerage firms are required to carry such protection in proportion to their net capital as defined by the Securities and Exchange Commission. Contingencies covered include securities loss, forgery, and fraudulent trading. Also called *blanket bond.*

BLANKET RECOMMENDATION communication sent to all customers of a brokerage firm recommending that they buy or sell a particular stock or stocks in a particular industry regardless of investment objectives or portfolio size.

BLENDED RATE mortgage financing term used when a lender, to avoid assuming an old mortgage at an obsoletely low rate, offers the incentive to refinance at a rate somewhere between the old rate and the rate on a new loan.

BLEND FUND MUTUAL FUND holding stocks, bonds, and MONEY MARKET instruments to provide diversification; differs from an ASSET ALLOCATION MUTUAL FUND, which may choose among classes of assets rather than be constantly diversified by asset classes.

BLIND BID large investor's BID on a BASKET of unidentified stocks in hopes of adding to a position without upsetting the market in the stocks desired.

BLIND POOL limited partnership that does not specify the properties the general partner plans to acquire. If, for example, a real estate partnership is offered in the form of a blind pool, investors can evaluate the project only by looking at the general partner's track record. In a *specified pool,* on the other hand, investors can look at the prices paid for property and the amount of rental income the buildings generate, then evaluate the partnership's potential. In general, blind pool partnerships do not perform better or worse than specified pool partnerships.

BLIND TRUST trust in which a fiduciary third party, such as a bank or money management firm, is given complete discretion to make investments on behalf of the trust beneficiaries. The trust is called blind because the beneficiary is not informed about the holdings of the trust. Blind trusts often are set up when there is a potential conflict of interest involving the beneficiary and the investments held in the trust. For example, a politician may be required to place his assets in a blind trust so that his votes are not influenced by his trust's portfolio holdings.

BLITZKREIG TENDER OFFER TAKEOVER jargon for a tender offer that is completed quickly, usually because it was priced attractively. *Blitzkreig* translates from the German as "lightning-like war" and was used to describe World War II bombing raids. Legislation passed in the 1960s was aimed at curtailing surprise takeovers, so the term is relative. *See also* SATURDAY NIGHT SPECIAL.

BLOCK large quantity of stock or large dollar amount of bonds held or traded. As a general guide, 10,000 shares or more of stock and $200,000 or more worth of bonds would be described as a block.

BLOCK POSITIONER dealer who, to accommodate the seller of a block of securities, will take a position in the securities, hoping to gain from a rise in the market price. Block positioners must register with the Securities and Exchange Commission and the New York Stock Exchange (if member firms). Typically they engage in ARBITRAGE, HEDGING, and SELLING SHORT to protect their risk and liquidate their position.

BLOCK TRADE *see* BLOCK.

BLOODY MONDAY *see* BLACK MONDAY.

BLOOMBERG, LP New York City-based financial software, news, and data company founded in 1981 and 92 percent-owned by Michael Bloomberg, Mayor of New York since 2002 and beginning an unprecedented third four-year term in 2010. The core business, Bloomberg Terminal, provides analytics, equity trading platforms, and other financial software tools along with data and news services to financial companies and organizations around the world, including radio and television broadcasting and Internet, and print publications. It commands one-third of a market that includes SNL Financial, Thompson Reuters, Capital IQ, Dow Jones Newswires, FactSet Research Systems, and numerous smaller competitors. Revenues in 2007 were $5.4 billion.

BLOW OFF TOP in TECHNICAL ANALYSIS, a chart pattern showing a sharp rise and a sharp fall in both price and volume within a short (four days to six weeks) time period. Also called a *parabolic blow off,* the pattern signifies panic buying followed by a SELL-OFF, called a *blow off move* or an *exhaustion move.*

BLOWOUT quick sale of all shares in a new offering of securities. Corporations like to sell securities in such environments, because they get a high price for their stock. Investors are likely to have a hard time getting the number of shares they want during a blowout. Also called *going away* or *hot issue.*

BLUE CHIP common stock of a nationally known company that has a long record of profit growth and/or dividend payment and a reputation for quality management, products, and services. Some examples of blue chip stocks: International Business Machines, General Electric, and Du Pont. Blue chip stocks typically are relatively high priced and have moderate dividend yields.

BM&F BOVESPA a securities, commodities, and futures exchange based in Sao Paulo and created in 2008 by the merger of the Brazilian Mercantile and Futures Exchange (BM&F) and the Sao Paulo Stock Exchange (Bovespa). The third largest exchange in the world in terms of market value, it is the second largest in the Americas and the largest in Latin America. Its trading products include equities, securities, financial assets, indices, interest rates, agricultural commodities, and foreign exchange futures and spot contracts. The exchange dates back to 1890. In 1990, trading began through the Computer Assisted Trading System (CATS), which operates simultaneously with the OPEN OUTCRY trading floor. The Home Broker and After-Market systems allow small and medium-sized investors to participate in the market. In 2007, the exchange was demutualized. *www.bmfbovespa.com.br.*

BLUE LIST daily financial publication listing bonds offered for sale by several hundred dealers and banks and representing billions of dollars in par value. The *Blue List,* published by a Standard & Poor's subsidiary, mainly contains data on municipal bonds. With its pertinent price, yield, and other data, the *Blue List* is the most comprehensive source of information on activity and volume in the secondary market for tax-exempt securities. Some corporate bonds offered by the same dealers are also included. Full name, *Blue List of Current Municipal Offerings.* The *Blue List* is also available through an online database on the Internet at *www.bluelist.com.*

BLUE-SKY LAW law of a kind passed by various states to protect investors against securities fraud. These laws require sellers of new stock issues or mutual funds to register their offerings and provide financial details on each issue so that investors can base their judgments on relevant data. The term is said to have originated with a judge who asserted that a particular stock offering had as much value as a patch of blue sky.

BOARD BROKER employee of the CHICAGO BOARD OPTIONS EXCHANGE who handles AWAY FROM THE MARKET orders, which cannot immediately be executed. If board brokers act as agents in executing such orders, they notify the exchange members who entered the orders.

BOARD OF DIRECTORS group of individuals elected, usually at an annual meeting, by the shareholders of a corporation and empowered to carry out certain tasks as spelled out in the corporation's charter. Among such powers are appointing senior management, naming members of executive and finance committees (if any), issuing additional shares, and declaring dividends. Boards normally include the top corporate executives, termed *inside directors,* as well as OUTSIDE DIRECTORS chosen from business and from the community at large to advise on matters of broad policy. Directors meet several times a year and are paid for their services. They are considered control persons under the securities laws, meaning that their shares are restricted. As insiders, they cannot (1) buy and sell the company's stock within a 6-month period; (2) sell short in the company's stock, and if they sell owned shares must deliver in 20 days and/or place certificates in mail within 5 days; (3) effect any foreign or arbitrage transaction in the company's stock; (4) trade on material information not available to the public.

BOARD OF GOVERNORS OF THE FEDERAL RESERVE SYSTEM seven-member managing body of the FEDERAL RESERVE SYSTEM, commonly called the Federal Reserve Board. The board sets policy on issues relating to banking regulations as well as to the MONEY SUPPLY.

BOARD ROOM
Brokerage house: room where customers can watch an electronic board that displays stock prices and transactions.
Corporation: room where the board of directors holds its meetings.

BOARD LOT the standard unit of trading on a stock exchange. In the United States, where the synonym ROUND LOT is more commonly used, it is 100 shares on all the stock exchanges (10 shares if a stock is thinly traded). In countries where exchanges list a high proportion of low-priced shares, board lots are often higher or set at levels proportionate to price ranges. In Canada, for example, the board lot for shares priced under 10 cents (Canadian) is 1,000 shares; 10 cents to a dollar, 500 shares, and a dollar or more, 100 shares. Board lots in Hong Kong vary by security in a range of 500 to 100,000 shares. Exceptions to board or round lots are called ODD LOTS. The additional work and expense traditionally associated with processing odd lots has been largely eliminated by computers, although most trades are still made in round (board) lots, one reason being that put and call OPTIONS trade in 100 share units.

BOGEY target for purchasing or selling a security or achieving some other objective. An investor's bogey may be a 10% rate of return from a particular stock. Or it may be locking in an 8% yield on a bond. A money manager's bogey may be to beat the Standard & Poor's 500 index.

BOILERPLATE standard legal language, often in fine print, used in most contracts, wills, indentures, prospectuses, and other legal documents. Although what the boilerplate says is important, it rarely is subject to change by the parties to the agreement, since it is the product of years of legal experience.

BOILER ROOM place where high-pressure salespeople use banks of telephones to call lists of potential investors (known in the trade as sucker lists) in order to peddle speculative, even fraudulent, securities. They are called boiler rooms because of the high-pressure selling. Boiler room methods, if not illegal, clearly violate the FINANCIAL INDUSTRY REGULATORY AUTHORITY (FINRA) RULES OF FAIR PRACTICE, particularly those requiring that recommendations be suitable to a customer's account. *See also* BUCKET SHOP; PUMP AND DUMP.

BOLLINGER BANDS TECHNICAL ANALYSIS technique invented by John Bollinger that plots STANDARD DEVIATION levels above and below a moving average. This differs from a typical MOMENTUM OSCILLATOR, which plots fixed percentages above and below the moving average, creating *"envelopes"* that represent the normal trading range of the security.

Since standard deviation measures VOLATILITY, the Bollinger bands, typically based on a 20-day time span, expand and contract as the volatility of the price series changes. In volatile markets the bands widen and in calm markets they narrow. Both envelopes and Bollinger lines take their significance from the fact that prices normally stay within them and that when overzealous buyers and sellers push prices to the extremes they represent, reversals are likely to follow.

Steven B. Achelis, in his book *Technical Analysis from A to Z,* reports Mr. Bollinger's own interpretation of Bollinger bands: (1) sharp price changes tend to occur after the bands tighten, signifying less volatility; (2) when prices move outside the bands, a continuation of the current trend is implied; (3) bottoms and tops made outside the bands followed by bottoms and tops made inside the bands call for reversals in the trend; and (4) a move that originates at one band tends to go all the way to the other band, a useful observation when projecting price targets.

BOLSA Spanish term for *stock exchange.* There are bolsas in Spain, Latin America, Central America, and other Spanish-speaking countries. In French, the term is *bourse;* in Italian, *borsa.*

BOLSA DE COMMERCIO DE SANTIAGO (SSE) founded in 1893, Chile's dominant stock exchange trades stocks, bonds, investment funds, stock options, futures, gold and silver coins minted by the Banco Central de Chile, and U.S. dollars on Telepregon, its electronic platform; the only floor trading conducted is in the share market, concurrent with screen trading. Three stock indices are published. The General Stock Price Index (IGPA) is a market capitalization weighted index that measures price variations of the majority of the exchange's listed stocks, classified by sectors according to their activity and revised annually. The Selective Stock Price Index (IPSA) is composed of the 40 most heavily traded stocks and revised annually. The Inter-10 Index is a volume-weighted index of the 10 main Chilean stocks listed in foreign markets through ADRs; its stocks are selected from the IPSA, which trades ADRS, and is revised quarterly. Futures are traded on the IPSA, U.S. dollar, and on bonds of the Banco Central de Chile. Settlement for shares is T + 2. Trading hours: 9:30 A.M. to 5:30 P.M. for all products but futures and options, which trade from 9:30 A.M. to 1:20 P.M., Monday to Friday. *www.bolsadesantiago.com.*

BOLSA DE MADRID largest and most international of Spain's four regional stock exchanges in Barcelona, Bilbao, and Valencia that trade shares and convertible bonds and fixed-income securities, both government and private-sector debt. The reorganization of Spain's financial market under the national umbrella of the Spanish Stock Market includes the bolsas, the derivatives markets, and fixed-income markets. Trading is linked through the electronic Spanish Stock Market Interconnection System (SIBE), which handles more than 90% of transactions; all fixed-income assets are traded through SIBE. The Madrid Stock Exchange General Index (IGBM) is the exchange's principal index and represents the construction, financial services, communications, consumer, capital/intermediate goods, energy, and market services sectors. The Ibex-35 Index is a capitalization-weighted index comprising the 35 most liquid Spanish stocks traded in the continuous market, and is Bolsa de Madrid's BENCHMARK. Bolsa de Madrid also offers the FTSE–Latibex Index, a European market for Latin American stocks; and the Ibex New Market Index for emerging companies. Settlement is T + 3. Trading on SIBE is conducted from 9 A.M. to 5:30 P.M.; open outcry, from 10 A.M. to 11:30 A.M., both Monday through Friday. *See also* BOLSAS Y MERCADOS ESPANOLES. *www. bolsamadrid.es.*

BOLSA MEXICANA DE VALORES (BMV) based in Mexico City, BMV is Mexico's only stock exchange and the second largest stock exchange in Latin America. Founded in 1859 and a public company since 2008, the exchange trades debt instruments including federal Treasury certificates (CETES), federal government development bonds (BONDES), investment unit bonds, banker's acceptances, promissory notes with yield payable at maturity, commercial paper and development bank bonds. It also trades stocks, debentures, mutual fund shares, and warrants. The BMV calculates 13 indices of stock prices. Each index can be used as an underlying value for derivative products listed on specialized markets. The Price and Quotation Index, or IPC (Indice de Precios y Cotizaciones), is the broadest indicator of the BMV's overall performance. It is made up of a balanced weighted selection of shares that are representative of all the shares listed on the exchange from various sectors across the economy, and is revised twice a year. Weight is determined by market capitalization. The IPC's value is related to the previous day's value, rather than the base date of October 30, 1978. Indice México (INMEX) is a market capitalization-weighted index of 20 to 25 of the BMV's most highly marketable issuers, using their most representative series. The sample is limited to issuers with a minimum market value of $100 million and is revised every six months. The weighting cannot be greater than 10% at the start of each calculation period. The Mid-Capitalization Index (IMC30) includes 30 stocks' series representative of the market's middle level of capitalization, and is aimed at mutual funds and derivatives markets as a reference for indexed instruments. Seven sector indices are calculated for mining, manufacturing, construction, retail, communications and transportation, services, and others. Three mutual fund indices are calculated. Trading is conducted electronically through the BMV-SENTRA Equities System. Settlement is T + 3. Trading hours: 8:30 A.M. to 3 P.M. for the capital markets; 8 A.M. to 2:30 P.M. for debt instruments, both Monday through Friday. *www. bmv.com.mx.*

BOLSAS Y MERCADOS ESPANOLES (BME) based in Madrid, BME integrates the securities markets and financial systems in Spain. It includes the Madrid, Barcelona, Bilbao, and Valencia stock exchanges, MF Mercados Financieros, Iberclear and BME Consulting. BME provides trading facilities for equities, derivatives, warrants, and fixed-income securities. It also provides clearing and settlement services, distribution of information, and consulting and technology services. *www.bolsasymercados.es*. *See also* BOLSA DE MADRID.

BOMBAY STOCK EXCHANGE (BSE) founded in 1875 and the oldest stock exchange in Asia. Formerly called The Stock Exchange, Mumbai, the BSE, with 4,700 listed companies, has the greatest number of listed companies in the world. The exchange is a market for trading equity, debt instruments, and derivatives. In 1995, it migrated from an OPEN OUTCRY system to a fully automated computerized mode of trading called BOLT (BSE Online Trading). The BSE benchmark index, SENSEX (Sensitive Index), contains 30 stocks representing 12 major sectors. Trading Hours: 9:55 A.M. to 3:30 P.M., Monday through Friday. *www.bseindia.com*.

BOND any interest-bearing or discounted government or corporate security that obligates the issuer to pay the bondholder a specified sum of money, usually at specific intervals, and to repay the principal amount of the loan at maturity. Bondholders have an IOU from the issuer, but no corporate ownership privileges, as stockholders do.

An owner of *bearer bonds* presents the bond coupons and is paid interest, whereas the owner of *registered bonds* appears on the records of the bond issuer.

See also CONVERTIBLE; DEBENTURE; INDENTURE; PERFORMANCE BOND; SECURED BOND; SURETY; ZERO-COUPON SECURITY.

BOND ANTICIPATION NOTE (BAN) short-term debt instrument issued by a state or municipality that will be paid off with the proceeds of an upcoming bond issue. To the investor, BANs offer a safe, tax-free yield that may be higher than other tax-exempt debt instruments of the same maturity.

BOND BROKER broker who executes bond trades on the floor of an exchange. Also, one who trades corporate, U.S. government, or municipal debt issues over the counter, mostly for large institutional accounts.

BOND BUYER, **THE** daily publication containing most of the key statistics and indexes used in the fixed-income markets. *See also* BOND BUYER'S INDEX; THIRTY-DAY VISIBLE SUPPLY.

BOND BUYER'S MUNICIPAL BOND INDEX index published daily by the *BOND BUYER,* a newspaper covering the municipal bond market. The index tracks municipal bond prices and is composed of 40 actively traded general obligation and revenue issues rated A or better with a term portion of at least $50 million ($75 million for housing issues); at least 19 years remaining to maturity; a first call date between 7 and 16 years; and at least one call at par before redemption. Starting in July 1, 1995, noncallable bonds became eligible for inclusion in the index. The publication also tracks the Bond Buyer 20 Bond Index, which is an index of yields of 20 general obligation municipal bonds. Investors use the publication's Bond Buyer indices to plot interest rate patterns in the muni market. Traders use the daily Bond Buyer Index to trade municipal bond index futures and futures options at the CHICAGO BOARD OF TRADE.

BOND COUNSEL attorney or law firm that prepares the LEGAL OPINION for a municipal bond issue.

BOND CROWD exchange members who transact bond orders on the floor of the exchange. The work area in which they congregate is separate from the stock traders, hence the term bond crowd.

BOND DISCOUNT amount by which the MARKET PRICE of a bond is lower than its FACE VALUE. Outstanding bonds with fixed COUPONS go to discounts when market interest rates rise. Discounts are also caused when supply exceeds demand and when a bond's CREDIT RATING is reduced. When opposite conditions exist and market price is higher than face value, the difference is termed a *bond premium.* Premiums also occur when a bond issue with a CALL FEATURE is redeemed prior to maturity and the bondholder is compensated for lost interest. *See also* ORIGINAL ISSUE DISCOUNT.

BOND EQUIVALENT YIELD restatement of a DISCOUNT YIELD as its interest-bearing equivalent.

BONDHOLDER owner of a bond. Bondholders may be individuals or institutions such as corporations, banks, insurance companies, or mutual funds. Bondholders are entitled to regular interest payments as due and return of principal when the bond matures. Bondholders may own corporate, government, or municipal issues. For corporate bonds, bondholders' claims on the assets of the issuing corporation take precedence over claims of stockholders in the event of liquidation. Unlike stockholders, however, straight bondholders do not own an equity interest in the issuing company. Some bonds, such as convertible bonds, do have some claim on the equity of the issuing corporation.

BOND MUTUAL FUND mutual fund holding bonds. Such funds may specialize in a particular kind of bond, such as government, corporate, convertible, high-yield, mortgage-backed, municipal, foreign, or zero-coupon bonds. Other bond mutual funds will buy some or all of these kinds of bonds. Most bond mutual funds are designed to produce current income for shareholders. Bond funds also produce capital gains when interest rates fall and capital losses when interest rates rise. Unlike the bonds in these funds, the funds themselves never mature. There are two types of bond mutual funds: open- and closed-end. *Open-end funds* continually create new shares to accommodate new money as it flows into the funds and they always trade at NET ASSET VALUE. *Closed-end funds* issue a limited number of shares and trade on stock exchanges. Closed-end funds trade at either higher than their net asset value (a premium) or lower than their net asset value (a discount), depending on investor demand for the fund.

BOND PREMIUM *see* BOND DISCOUNT.

BOND POWER form used in the transfer of registered bonds from one owner to another. Sometimes called *assignment separate from certificate,* it accomplishes the same thing as the assignment form on the back of the bond certificate, but has a safety advantage in being separate. Technically, the bond power appoints an attorney-in-fact with the power to make a transfer of ownership on the corporation's books.

BOND RATING method of evaluating the possibility of default by a bond issuer. Fitch Ratings, Standard & Poor's, and Moody's Investors Service analyze the financial strength of each bond's issuer, whether a corporation or a government body. Their ratings range from AAA (highly unlikely to default) to D (in default). Bonds rated BB or below are not INVESTMENT GRADE—in other words, institutions that invest other people's money may not under most state laws buy them. *See also* RATING.

BOND RATIO *leverage* ratio measuring the percentage of a company's capitalization represented by bonds. It is calculated by dividing the total bonds due after one year by the same figure plus all equity. A bond ratio over 33% indicates high leverage—except in utilities, where higher bond ratios are normal. *See also* DEBT-TO-EQUITY RATIO.

BOND SWAP simultaneous sale of one bond issue and purchase of another. The motives for bond swaps vary: *maturity swaps* aim to stretch out maturities but can also produce a profit because of the lower prices on longer bonds; *yield swaps* seek to improve return and *quality swaps* seek to upgrade safety; *tax swaps* create tax-deductible losses through the sale, while the purchase of a substitute bond effectively preserves the investment. *See also* SWAP, SWAP ORDER.

BON VOYAGE BONUS *see* GREENMAIL.

BOOK
1. in an underwriting of securities, (1) preliminary indications of interest rate on the part of prospective buyers of the issue ("What is the book on XYZ Company?") or (2) record of activity in the syndicate account ("Who is managing the book on XYZ?").
2. record maintained by a specialist of buy and sell orders in a given security. The term derives from the notebook that specialists traditionally used for this purpose. Also, the aggregate of sell orders left with the specialist, as in BUY THE BOOK.
3. as a verb, to book is to give accounting recognition to something. ("They booked a profit on the transaction.")
4. collectively, books are the journals, ledgers, and other accounting records of a business.
   See also BOOK VALUE.

BOOK-ENTRY SECURITIES securities that are not represented by a certificate. Purchases and sales of some municipal bonds, for instance, are merely recorded on customers' accounts; no certificates change hands. This is increasingly popular because it cuts down on paperwork for brokers and leaves investors free from worry about their certificates. *See also* CERTIFICATE-LESS MUNICIPALS.

BOOK PROFIT OR LOSS *see* UNREALIZED PROFIT OR LOSS.

BOOKRUNNER *see* MANAGING UNDERWRITER.

BOOK-TO-BILL RATIO The ratio of orders booked for future delivery to orders being shipped immediately, and therefore billed. The book-to-bill ratio is released on a monthly basis for the semiconductor industry because it provides a very sensitive indicator of whether orders for chips are rising or falling and at what pace. The release of the chip book-to-bill ratio can have a major impact on the stock prices of semiconductor stocks in particular and technology stocks in general. Also called CARRYING VALUE.

BOOK VALUE
1. value at which an asset is carried on a balance sheet. For example, a piece

of manufacturing equipment is put on the books at its cost when purchased. Its value is then reduced each year as depreciation is charged to income. Thus, its book value at any time is its cost minus accumulated depreciation. However, the primary purpose of accounting for depreciation is to enable a company to recover its cost, not replace the asset or reflect its declining usefulness. Book value may therefore vary significantly from other objectively determined values, most notably MARKET VALUE.

2. net asset value of a company's securities, calculated by using the following formula:

Total assets *minus* intangible assets (goodwill, patents, etc.) *minus* current liabilities *minus* any long-term liabilities and equity issues that have a prior claim (subtracting them here has the effect of treating them as paid) *equals* total net assets available for payment of the issue under consideration.

The total net asset figure, divided by the number of bonds, shares of preferred stock, or shares of common stock, gives the *net asset value*—or book value—per bond or per share of preferred or common stock.

Book value can be a guide in selecting underpriced stocks and is an indication of the ultimate value of securities in liquidation. *See also* ASSET COVERAGE.

BOOT STRAP to help a company start from scratch. Entrepreneurs founding a company with little capital are said to be boot strapping it in order to become established.

BORROWED RESERVES funds borrowed by member banks from a FEDERAL RESERVE BANK for the purpose of maintaining the required reserve ratios. Actually, the proper term is *net borrowed reserves*, since it refers to the difference between borrowed reserves and excess or free reserves. Such borrowings, usually in the form of advances secured by government securities or eligible paper, are kept on deposit at the Federal Reserve bank in the borrower's region. Net borrowed reserves are an indicator of heavy loan demand and potentially TIGHT MONEY.

BORROWING POWER OF SECURITIES amount of money that customers can invest in securities on MARGIN, as listed every month on their brokerage account statements. This margin limit usually equals 50% of the value of their stocks, 30% of the value of their bonds, and the full value of their CASH EQUIVALENT assets, such as MONEY MARKET account funds. The term also refers to securities pledged (hypothecated) to a bank or other lender as loan COLLATERAL. The loan value in this case depends on lender policy and type of security.

BORSA ITALIANA organizes and runs the Italian regulated markets for equities, bonds, and derivatives. The company was founded in 1808, privatized in 1997, and acquired by the London Stock Exchange Group in 2007. It offers a full and diversified set of products and services covering the entire business system: listing, trading, the various post-trading components, and guarantee and custody operations. The Borsa Italiana subsidiaries are BIT Systems, the ICT company that provides investment banks, brokerage houses, institutional investors, Internet brokers, and companies that operate marketplaces with high-quality IT consulting services; Cassa di Compensazione & Garanzia (CC&G), the Italian clearing house that operates as central counter party for equities, derivatives, and government bonds securities; Monte Titoli, the Central Securities Depository, also with settlement functions; and Piazza Affari Gestione e Servizi, which is responsible for the management of the Congress and Training Center located in Palazzo Mezzanotte, the building in Milan where Borsa Italiana is based. All the markets managed by Borsa Italiana are electronic and order-driven (the computerized order-driven trading system was introduced in 1991, and since 1994, all listed securities have been traded electronically). Markets can be grouped, based on the type of instruments traded, as follows: Equities Markets, MTA for companies operating in traditional segments, MTAX for high-tech companies, and Mercato Expandi for Italian micro caps. MTA and MTAX are organized into three equal segments: Blue-Chips for large companies; STAR for mid-size and small companies that adopt more stringent requirements in terms of liquidity, transparency, and corporate governance; Standard for mid-size and small companies complying with the general rules defined for the overall market. Normal trading sessions are held from 9:05 A.M. to 5:35 P.M. Borsa Italiana's main indices are S&P/MIB, MIDEX, STAR, techSTAR, ALL STAR, MIBTEL, and MIB. Shares included in S&P/MIB, MIB30, and MIDEX indices are also traded in the after-hours market lasting from 6 P.M. to 8:30 P.M. STAR shares may be traded in the after-hours market if supported by a specialist. *www.borsaitaliana.com.*

BOSTON STOCK EXCHANGE (BSE) established in 1834, the BSE is the first American exchange to open its membership to foreign brokers. It is the first U.S. exchange with a foreign linkage to the Montreal Exchange (1984), and the first with an off-site, backup trading floor. The BSE trades listed equities and, through its facility, the Boston Options Exchange (BOX), began trading equity options in an all-electronic format in February 2004. The BSE competes with other national stock exchanges, with more than 200 members and approximately 50 of its own primary listed companies. In 1994 the exchange introduced the Competing Specialists Initiative (CSI) in an auction market environment. The BSE operates the BEACON automated trading system. In 2001 BEACON Remote was launched, the first all-inclusive remote access trading system offered by a U.S. stock exchange; it allows primary and competing specialists with the exchange to trade from remote sites across the United States. In 1998, the exchange introduced EXCHANGE TRADED FUNDS (ETFs), a hybrid version of MUTUAL FUNDS. In 1999 the exchange moved to a state-of-the-art facility in downtown Boston. In 2002 the exchange began trading NASDAQ-listed stocks, and launched derivatives trading on its facility BOX in 2004. BOX currently trades the top 400 OCC listed options and is averaging more than 7% of the market in which it trades. In 2008 the BSE was acquired by the NASDAQ OMX Group. Trading hours are Monday through Friday, 9:30 A.M. to 4 P.M., with a limited crossing network at 5 P.M. *www.bostonstock.com* and *www.bostonoptions.com.*

BOT
1. stockbroker shorthand for bought, the opposite of SL for sold.
2. in finance, abbreviation for balance of trade.
3. in the mutual savings bank industry, abbreviation for board of trustees.

BOTTOM
In general: support level for market prices of any type. When prices fall below that level and appear to be continuing downward without check, we say that the *bottom dropped out.* When prices begin to trend upward again,

we say they have *bottomed out.*
Economics: lowest point in an economic cycle.
Securities: lowest market price of a security or commodity during a day, a season, a year, a cycle. Also, lowest level of prices for the market as a whole, as measured by any of the several indexes.

BOTTOM FISHER investor who is on the lookout for stocks that have fallen to their bottom prices before turning up. In extreme cases, bottom fishers buy stocks and bonds of bankrupt or near-bankrupt firms.

BOTTOM-UP APPROACH TO INVESTING search for outstanding performance of individual stocks before considering the impact of economic trends. The companies may be identified from research reports, stock screens, or personal knowledge of the products and services. This approach assumes that individual companies can do well, even in an industry that is not performing well. *See also* TOP-DOWN APPROACH TO INVESTING.

BOUGHT DEAL in securities underwriting, a FIRM COMMITMENT to purchase an entire issue outright from the issuing company. Differs from a STAND-BY COMMITMENT, wherein, with conditions, a SYNDICATE of investment bankers agrees to purchase part of an issue if it is not fully subscribed. Also differs from a BEST EFFORTS commitment, wherein the syndicate agrees to use its best efforts to sell the issue. Most issues in recent years have been bought deals. Typically, the syndicate puts up a portion of its own capital and borrows the rest from commercial banks. Then, perhaps through a selling group, the syndicate resells the issue to the public at slightly more than the purchase price.

BOUNCE return of a check by a bank because it is not payable, usually due to insufficient funds. In securities, the rejection and subsequent RECLAMATION of a security because of *bad delivery.* Term also refers to stock price's sudden decline and recovery.

BOURSE French term for *stock exchange. See also* PARIS BOURSE.

BOUTIQUE small, specialized brokerage firm that deals with a limited clientele and offers a limited product line. A highly regarded securities analyst may form a research boutique, which clients use as a resource for buying and selling certain stocks. A boutique is the opposite of a FINANCIAL SUPERMARKET, which offers a wide variety of services to a wide variety of clients.

BOWIE BONDS bonds representing the SECURITIZATION of INTELLECTUAL PROPERTY. Name derives from the issuance in 1997 of bonds by rock star David Bowie that raised $55 million repayable from future royalties earned from Bowie's 25-album catalog. Other Bowie bonds, also called *celebrity bonds,* have been issued subsequently by other artists.

BOX physical location of securities or other documents held in safekeeping. The term derives from the large metal tin, or tray, in which brokerage firms and banks actually place such valuables. Depending on rules and regulations concerned with the safety and segregation of clients' securities, certificates held in safekeeping may qualify for stock loans or as bank loan collateral.

BRACKET CREEP edging into higher tax brackets as income rises to compensate for inflation.

BRADY BONDS public-issue, U.S. dollar-denominated bonds of developing countries, mainly in Latin America, that were exchanged in a restructuring for commercial bank loans in default. The securities, named for former Bush administration Treasury Secretary Nicholas Brady, are collateralized by U.S. Treasury zero-coupon bonds to ensure principal.

BRANCH OFFICE MANAGER person in charge of a branch of a securities brokerage firm or bank. Branch office managers who oversee the activities of three or more brokers must pass tests administered by various stock exchanges. A customer who is not able to resolve a conflict with a REGISTERED REPRESENTATIVE should bring it to the attention of the branch office manager, who is responsible for resolving such differences.

BREADTH OF THE MARKET percentage of stocks participating in a particular market move. Analysts say there was good breadth if two thirds of the stocks listed on an exchange rose during a trading session. A market trend with good breadth is more significant and probably more long-lasting than one with limited breadth, since more investors are participating. Breadth-of-the-market indexes are alternatively called ADVANCE/DECLINE indexes. *See also* DEPTH OF THE MARKET.

BREAK
Finance: in a pricing structure providing purchasing discounts at different levels of volume, a point at which the price changes—for example, a 10% discount for ten cases.
Investments: (1) sudden, marked drop in the price of a security or in market prices generally; (2) discrepancy in the accounts of brokerage firms; (3) stroke of good luck.

BREAKEVEN
Finance: the point at which sales equal costs. The point is located by breakeven analysis, which determines the volume of sales at which fixed and variable costs will be covered. All sales over the breakeven point produce profits; any drop in sales below that point will produce losses.
    Because costs and sales are so complex, breakeven analysis has limitations as a planning tool and is being supplanted by computer based financial planning systems. *See also* LEVERAGE (operating).
Securities:
1. dollar price at which a transaction produces neither a gain nor a loss.
2. The time required to recoup the dollar amount of the CONVERSION PREMIUM from the interest income on a convertible instrument.
    In options strategy the term has the following definitions:
1. long calls and short uncovered calls: strike price plus premium.
2. long puts and short uncovered puts: strike price minus premium.
3. short covered call: purchase price minus premium.
4. short put covered by short stock: short sale price of underlying stock plus premium.

BREAKING THE BUCK decline in the normally constant $1 net asset value (NAV) of a MONEY MARKET FUND. This could happen if the fund suffered severe losses or if investment income fell below operating expenses.

BREAKING THE SYNDICATE terminating the investment banking group formed to underwrite a securities issue. More specifically, terminating the AGREEMENT AMONG UNDERWRITERS, thus leaving the members free to sell remaining holdings without price restrictions. The agreement among underwriters usually terminates the syndicate 30 days after the selling group, but the syndicate can be broken earlier by agreement of the participants.

BREAKOUT rise in a security's price above a resistance level (commonly its previous high price) or drop below a level of support (commonly the former lowest price). A breakout is taken to signify a continuing move in the same direction.

BREAKOUT

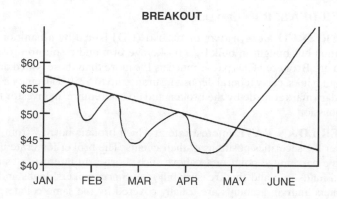

BREAKPOINT SALE in mutual funds, the dollar investment required to make the fundholder eligible for a lower sales charge. *See also* LETTER OF INTENT; RIGHT OF ACCUMULATION.

BREAKUP VALUE *see* PRIVATE MARKET VALUE.

BRETTON WOODS AGREEMENT OF 1944 *see* FIXED EXCHANGE RATE; INTERNATIONAL BANK FOR RECONSTRUCTION AND DEVELOPMENT (IBRD); INTERNATIONAL MONETARY FUND (IMF).

BRIC acronym for the world's four largest DEVELOPING ECONOMIES, namely Brazil, Russia, India, and China.

BRICKS AND MORTAR a physical business location as distinguished from a Web site.

BRIDGE LOAN short-term loan, also called a *swing loan,* made in anticipation of intermediate-term or long-term financing.

BRITISH CLEARERS the large banks, comparable to MONEY CENTER BANKS in the United States, that accept deposits, clear checks, and engage in short-term lending in the domestic sterling market.

BROAD TAPE enlargement of the Dow Jones news ticker tape, projected on a screen in the board room of a brokerage firm. It continually reports major news developments and financial information. The term can also refer to similar information provided by Associated Press, United Press International, Reuters, or Munifacts. The broad tape is not allowed on the exchange floor because it would give floor traders an unfair edge.

BROKER
Insurance: person who finds the best insurance deal for a client and then sells the policy to the client.

Real estate: person who represents the seller and gets a commission when the property is sold.

Securities: person who acts as an intermediary between a buyer and seller, usually charging a commission. A broker who specializes in stocks, bonds, commodities, or options acts as AGENT and must be registered with the exchange where the securities are traded. Hence the term *registered representative. See also* ACCOUNT EXECUTIVE; DEALER; DISCOUNT BROKER.

BROKER-DEALER *see* DEALER.

BROKERED CD a CERTIFICATE OF DEPOSIT (CD) issued by a bank or thrift institution but bought in bulk by a brokerage firm and resold to brokerage customers. Brokered CDs pay as much as 1% more than those issued directly by major banks, carry federal deposit insurance up to $250,000, enjoy a liquid secondary market made by the broker, and do not require an investor to pay a commission.

BROKER LOAN RATE interest rate at which brokers borrow from banks to cover the securities positions of their clients. The broker loan rate usually hovers a percentage point or so above such short-term interest rates as the federal funds rate and the Treasury bill rate. Since brokers' loans and their customers' margin accounts are usually covered by the same collateral, the term REHYPOTHECATION is used synonymously with *broker loan borrowing.* Because broker loans are callable on 24-hour notice, the term *call loan rate* is also used, particularly in money rate tables published in newspapers.

BROKER RECOMMENDATIONS (OR OPINIONS OR RATINGS) buy, sell, or hold recommendations and variations thereof, sometimes called *opinions* or ratings and expressed in numbers or alphanumerically, assigned by securities analysts working in broker research departments to stocks they cover. Different brokers use different variations, and research reports usually indicate what they mean. Commonly used variations include: strong buy, buy, accumulate, hold, outperform, market perform, underperform, and sell. Strong buy, buy, hold, and sell are self-explanatory. "Accumulate" is the weakest form of buy recommendation, generally implying that if you are following a CONSTANT DOLLAR PLAN, you would not exclude these shares at this time. It may have a more negative implication, however, if "accumulate" represents a DOWNGRADE from a previous buy recommendation; that says, in effect, "Buy it, but not with the degree of confidence previously warranted." Outperform, market perform, and underperform project 12-month price behavior relative to the overall market as measured by the STANDARD & POOR'S 500 COMPOSITE INDEX. *See also* TARGET PRICE.

BROUGHT OVER THE WALL when somebody in the research department of an investment bank is pressed into the service of the underwriting department in reference to a particular corporate client, the individual has been "brought over the ("Chinese") wall" that legally divides the two functions and, being thus privy to INSIDE INFORMATION, is precluded from providing opinions about the company involved. *See also* CHINESE WALL.

BUBBLE THEORY belief that stock or real estate prices will sometimes inflate to levels well beyond reasonable VALUATION before "the bubble bursts" and prices return to normal. The real estate bubble in the mid-2000s is a recent example. One explanation of the phenomenon is the GREATER FOOL THEORY.

BUCK in common usage, slang for one dollar. In professional stock trader's vernacular, slang for one million dollars.

BUCKETING illegal practice in which a broker, hoping to profit from an offsetting transaction at a later time, executes a customer's order for the broker's own account instead of releasing the order to the market or OPEN OUTCRY system. *See also* BUCKET SHOP.

BUCKET SHOP illegal brokerage firm, of a kind now almost extinct, which accepts customer orders but does not execute them right away as Securities and Exchange Commission regulations require. Bucket-shop brokers confirm the price the customer asked for, but in fact make the trade at a time advantageous to the broker, whose profit is the difference between the two prices. Sometimes bucket shops neglect to fill the customer's order and just pocket the money. *See also* BOILER ROOM; PUMP AND DUMP.

BUDGET estimate of revenue and expenditure for a specified period. Of the many kinds of budgets, a CASH BUDGET shows cash flow, an expense budget shows projected expenditures, and a CAPITAL BUDGET shows anticipated capital outlays. The term refers to a preliminary financial plan. In a *balanced budget*, revenues cover expenditures.

BUDGET DEFICIT excess of spending over income for a government, corporation, or individual over a particular period of time. A budget deficit accumulated by the federal government of the United States must be financed by the issuance of Treasury bonds. Corporate budget deficits must be reduced or eliminated by increasing sales and reducing expenditures, or the company will not survive in the long run. Similarly, individuals who consistently spend more than they earn will accumulate huge debts, which may ultimately force them to declare bankruptcy if the debt cannot be serviced.

BUDGET SURPLUS excess of income over spending for a government, corporation, or individual over a particular period of time. A government with a budget surplus may choose to start new programs or cut taxes. A corporation with a surplus may expand the business through investment or acquisition, or may choose to buy back its own stock. An individual with a budget surplus may choose to pay down debt or increase spending or investment.

BUILD AMERICA BONDS (BABs) taxable bonds issued by municipalities designed to encourage spending on infrastructure and create jobs. The issuance of these bonds was authorized by the AMERICAN RECOVERY AND REINVESTMENT ACT OF 2009. Municipalities can issue BABs only for new capital spending projects such as schools, hospitals, and roads and cannot be issued to refinance old debt. The federal government provides a tax credit of 35% of the interest expense, which can be given to either the bondholder or the municipality. This provision allows municipal issuers to recognize significantly lower borrowing costs than if they issued traditional tax-free bonds. The program was scheduled to end on December 31, 2010.

BULGE quick, temporary price rise that applies to an entire commodities or stock market, or to an individual commodity or stock.

BULGE BRACKET the group of firms in an underwriting syndicate that share the largest participation. TOMBSTONE ads list the participants alphabetically within groupings organized by size of participation and presented in tiers. The first and lead grouping is the "bulge bracket." *See also* MEZZANINE BRACKET.

BULK SEGREGATION separation of securities owned by a firm from securities held by the same firm in STREET NAME for customers.

BULL person who thinks prices will rise. One can be bullish on the prospects for an individual stock, bond, or commodity, an industry segment, or the market as a whole. In a more general sense, bullish means optimistic, so a person can be bullish on the economy as a whole.

BULL AND BEAR BONDS securities representing bonds issued with two TRANCHES respectively designed to benefit from upward and downward movements in a designated index or other security.

BULL CD *see* CERTIFICATE OF DEPOSIT (CD).

BULLDOG SECURITIES in London market, foreign (non-British) securities, generally INVESTMENT GRADE long-term bonds, denominated in sterling. Analagous to securities traded in YANKEE BOND MARKET.

BULLET BOND a bond that is not CALLABLE and whose FACE VALUE is repayable at maturity.

BULLET CONTRACT single-premium GUARANTEED INVESTMENT CONTRACT.

BULLET LOAN term loan repayable in one BALLOON payment. Also called BALLOON MATURITY LOAN, although the concept of no AMORTIZATION is essential.

BULLION COINS coins composed of metal such as gold, silver, platinum, or palladium. Bullion coins provide the purest play on the "up or down" price moves of the underlying metal, and are the most actively traded. These coins trade at a slight premium over their metal content, unlike NUMISMATIC COINS, which trade on their rarity and artistic value. Some of the most popular bullion coins minted by major governments around the world include the American Eagle, the Canadian Maple Leaf, the South African Kruggerand, and the Australian Kangaroo. In addition to trading bullion in coin form, nearly pure precious metals also are available in bar form.

BULL MARKET prolonged rise in the prices of stocks, bonds, or commodities. Bull markets usually last at least a few months and are characterized by high trading volume.

BULL SPREAD option strategy, executed with puts or calls, that will be profitable if the underlying stock rises in value. The following are three varieties of bull spread:
Vertical spread: simultaneous purchase and sale of options of the same class at different strike prices, but with the same expiration date.
Calendar spread: simultaneous purchase and sale of options of the same class and the same price but at different expiration dates.
Diagonal spread: combination of vertical and calendar spreads wherein the investor buys and sells options of the same class at different strike prices and different expiration dates.

An investor who believes, for example, that XYZ stock will rise, perhaps only moderately, buys an XYZ 30 call for 1½ and sells an XYZ 35 call for ½; both options are OUT OF THE MONEY. The 30 and 35 are strike prices and the 1½ and ½ are premiums. The net cost of this spread, or the difference between the premiums, is $1. If the stock rises to 35 just prior to expiration, the 35 call becomes worthless and the 30 call is worth $5. Thus the spread provides a profit of $4 on an investment of $1. If on the other hand the price of the stock goes down, both options expire worthless and the investor loses the entire premium.

BUMP-UP CD certificate of deposit that gives its owner a one-time right to increase its yield for the remaining term of the CD if interest rates have risen from the date of issuance. The CD's yield will not be adjusted downward if rates fall, however. If rates remain stable or decline, the CD will pay its stated rate of interest until maturity.

BUNCHING

1. combining many round-lot orders for execution at the same time on the floor of an exchange. This technique can also be used with odd lot orders, when combining many small orders can save the odd-lot differential for each customer.

2. pattern on the ticker tape when a series of trades in the same security appear consecutively.

3. aggregating income items or deductions in a single year to minimize taxes in that year.

BUNDLING *see* UNBUNDLING.

BUREAU OF ECONOMIC ANALYSIS agency of the U.S. Department of Commerce that provides GROSS DOMESTIC PRODUCT statistics and other economic data.

BURNOUT exhaustion of a tax shelter's benefits, when an investor starts to receive income from the investment. This income must be reported to the Internal Revenue Service, and taxes must be paid on it.

BURN RATE in venture capital financing, the rate at which a start-up company spends capital to finance overhead before generating a positive cash flow from operations.

BURSA MALAYSIA dates back to 1930 when it was set up as a formal organization dealing in securities in Malaya. Bursa Malaysia was known as the Kuala Lumpur Stock Exchange until 2004, when it was demutualized and renamed. A fully integrated exchange, its holdings include the stock exchange, a derivatives exchange, an off-shore international financial exchange, equity and derivatives clearing houses, a central depository, an information services provider, and an information technology services provider. *www.bursamalaysia.com.*

BUSINESS COMBINATION *see* MERGER.

BUSINESS CYCLE recurrence of periods of expansion (RECOVERY) and contraction (RECESSION) in economic activity with effects on inflation, growth, and employment. One cycle extends from a GROSS DOMESTIC PRODUCT (GDP) base line through one rise and one decline and back to the base line, a period typically averaging about 2½ years. The 1990s, however, saw an extended period of expansion. A business cycle affects profitability and CASH FLOW, making it a key consideration in corporate dividend policy, and a factor in the rise and fall of the inflation rate, which in turn affects return on investments. *See also* SOFT LANDING.

BUSINESS DAY
In general: hours when most businesses are in operation. Although individual working hours may differ, and particular firms may choose staggered schedules, the conventional business day is 9 A.M. to 5 P.M.
Finance and investments: day when financial marketplaces are open for trading. In figuring the settlement date on a *regular way* securities transaction—which is the fifth business day after the trade date—Saturday, Sunday, and a legal holiday would not be counted, for example.

BUSINESS LIFE INSURANCE also called KEY MAN (OR WOMAN) INSURANCE. Life insurance bought by a company, usually a small business, on the life of a key executive, with the company as beneficiary.

BUSINESS PLAN a comprehensive analysis of all aspects of a business enterprise relevant to its viability, including its history, management, competitive position, market, activities, products, policies, finances, and projected finances. Its purpose is usually to attract financing or investment capital.

BUSINESS SEGMENT REPORTING reporting the results of the divisions, subsidiaries, or other segments of a business separately so that income, sales, and assets can be compared. When not a separate part of the business structure, a segment is generally defined as any grouping of products and services comprising a significant industry, which is one representing 10% or more of total revenues, assets, or income. Allocation of central corporate expenses is not required by the Financial Accounting Standards Board. Also called *line of business reporting*.

BUSTED CONVERTIBLES CONVERTIBLES that trade like fixed-income investments because the market price of the common stock they convert to has fallen so low as to render the conversion feature valueless. Also called *fixed income equivalent*.

BUST-UP TAKEOVER LEVERAGED BUYOUT in which TARGET COMPANY assets or activities are sold off to repay the debt that financed the TAKEOVER.

BUTTERFLY SPREAD complex option strategy that involves selling two calls and buying two calls on the same or different markets, with several maturity dates. One of the options has a higher exercise price and the other has a lower exercise price than the other two options. An investor in a butterfly spread will profit if the underlying security makes no dramatic movements because the premium income will be collected when the options are sold.

BUY acquire property in return for money. Buy can be used as a synonym for bargain.

BUY AND HOLD STRATEGY strategy that calls for accumulating shares in a company over the years. This allows the investor to pay favorable long-term capital gains tax on profits and requires far less attention than a more active trading strategy.

BUY AND WRITE STRATEGY conservative options strategy that entails buying stocks and then writing covered call options on them. Investors receive both the dividends from the stock and the premium income from the call options. However, the investor may have to sell the stock below the current market price if the call is exercised.

BUYBACK purchase of a long contract to cover a short position, usually arising out of the short sale of a commodity. Also, purchase of identical securities to cover a short sale. Synonym: *short covering. See also* STOCK BUYBACK; STOCK REPURCHASE PLAN (OR PROGRAM).
Bond buyback: corporation's purchase of its own bonds at a discount in the open market. This is done in markets characterized by rapidly rising interest rates and commensurately declining bond prices.

BUY DOWN cash payment by a mortgage lender allowing the borrower to receive a lower rate of interest on a mortgage loan. For example, a home builder having trouble selling homes may offer a buy down with a local lender which will enable home buyers to qualify for mortgages that they would otherwise not qualify for. The buy down may lower the mortgage rate for the life of the loan, or sometimes just for the first few years of the loan.

BUYER'S MARKET market situation that is the opposite of a SELLER'S MARKET. Since there is more supply of a security or product than there is current demand, the prices tend to fall allowing buyers to set both the price and terms of the sale. It contrasts with a seller's market, characterized by excess demand, high prices, and terms suited to seller's desires.

BUY HEDGE *see* LONG HEDGE.

BUY IN
Options trading: procedure whereby the responsibility to deliver or accept stock can be terminated. In a transaction called *buying-in* or CLOSING PURCHASE, the writer buys an identical option (only the premium or price is different). The second of these options offsets the first, and the profit or loss is the difference in premiums.
Securities: transaction between brokers wherein securities are not delivered on time by the broker on the sell side, forcing the buy side broker to obtain shares from other sources.

BUYING CLIMAX rapid rise in the price of a stock or commodity, setting the stage for a quick fall. Such a surge attracts most of the potential buyers of the stock, leaving them with no one to sell their stock to at higher prices. This is what causes the ensuing fall. Technical chartists see a buying climax as a dramatic runup, accompanied by increased trading volume in the stock.

BUYING ON MARGIN buying securities with credit available through a relationship with a broker, called a MARGIN ACCOUNT. Arrangements of this kind are closely regulated by the Federal Reserve Board. *See also* MARGIN.

BUYING OUTRIGHT in securities terminology, opposite of buying on MARGIN.

BUYING POWER amount of money available to buy securities, determined by tabulating the cash held in brokerage accounts, and adding the amount that could be spent if securities were margined to the limit. The market cannot rise beyond the available buying power. *See also* PURCHASING POWER.

BUY MINUS order to buy a stock at a price lower than the current market price. Traders try to execute a buy minus order on a temporary dip in the stock's price.

BUY ON THE BAD NEWS strategy based on the belief that, soon after a company announces bad news, the price of its stock will plummet. Those who buy at this stage assume that the price is about as low as it can go, leaving plenty of room for a rise when the news improves. If the adverse development is indeed temporary, this technique can be quite profitable. *See also* BOTTOM FISHER.

BUY ORDER in securities trading, an order to a broker to purchase a specified quality of a security at the MARKET PRICE or at another stipulated price.

BUYOUT purchase of at least a controlling percentage of a company's stock to take over its assets and operations. A buyout can be accomplished through negotiation or through a tender offer. A LEVERAGED BUYOUT occurs when a small group borrows the money to finance the purchase of the shares. The loan is ultimately repaid out of cash generated from the acquired company's operations or from the sale of its assets. *See also* GOLDEN PARACHUTE.

BUY-SIDE ANALYST SECURITIES ANALYST who works in the RESEARCH DEPARTMENT of an institutional investor, such as a MUTUAL FUND, and whose research is used internally by money managers. In contrast, *sell-side analysts* are typically employed by brokerage firms, where their research is used as a selling tool and made available to indi-vidual investing clients. *See also* BROKER RECOMMENDATIONS (or OPINIONS or RATINGS).

BUY SIGNAL in TECHNICAL ANALYSIS, a chart configuration, such as a DOUBLE BOTTOM, indicating there is price support and that it is time to buy a security or position. In general, any combination of factors indicating conditions favorable for buying. Opposite of *sell signal.*

BUY STOP ORDER BUY ORDER marked to be held until the market price rises to the STOP PRICE, then to be entered as a MARKET ORDER to buy at the best available price. Sometimes called a *suspended market order,* because it remains suspended until a market transaction elects, activates, or triggers the stop. Such an order is not permitted in the over-the-counter market. *See also* STOP ORDER.

BUY THE BOOK order to a broker to buy all the shares available from the specialist in a security and from other brokers and dealers at the current offer price. The book is the notebook in which specialists kept track of buy and sell orders before computers. The most likely source of such an order is a professional trader or a large institutional buyer.

BYLAWS rules governing the internal management of an organization which, in the case of business corporations, are drawn up at the time of incorporation. The charter is concerned with such broad matters as the number of directors and the number of authorized shares; the bylaws, which can usually be amended by the directors themselves, cover such points as the election of directors, the appointment of executive and finance committees, the duties of officers, and how share transfers may be made. Bylaws, which are also prevalent in not-for-profit organizations, cannot countermand laws of the government.

BYPASS TRUST agreement allowing parents to pass assets on to their children to reduce estate taxes. The trust must be made irrevocable, meaning that the terms can never be changed. Assets put in such a trust usually exceed the amount that the children and other heirs can receive tax-free at a parent's death. The estate tax exclusion amount was $3.5 million in 2009, according to the ECONOMIC GROWTH AND TAX RELIEF RECONCILIATION ACT OF 2001. Parents can arrange to receive income from the assets during their lifetimes and may even be able to touch the principal in case of dire need. One variation of a bypass trust is the qualified terminable interest property trust, or Q-TIP TRUST.

C

C2C *see* ELECTRONIC COMMERCE.

CABINET SECURITY stock or bond listed on a major exchange but not actively traded. There are a considerable number of such bonds and a limited number of such stocks, mainly those trading in ten-share units. Cabinets are the metal storage racks that LIMIT ORDERS for such securities are filed in pending execution or cancellation. *See also* AUTOMATED BOND SYSTEM (ABS).

CABLE as a verb, to send money abroad by transoceanic cable lines or by wireless. Noun is slang for the (U.S.) dollar/sterling spot exchange rate.

CAC 40 INDEX broad-based index of common stocks on the Paris Bourse, based on 40 of the 100 largest companies listed on the forward segment of the official list (reglement menseul); it has a base of 100. It is comparable to the Dow Jones Industrial Average. There are index futures and index options contracts based on the CAC 40 index.

CAFETERIA EMPLOYEE BENEFIT PLAN plan offering employees numerous options among their employee benefits. Each employee is able to pick the benefits that are most valuable in his or her particular situation. For example, a young employee with children may want to receive more life and health insurance than a mid-career employee who is more concerned with building up retirement plan assets.

CAGE section of a brokerage firm's back office where funds are received and disbursed.

Also, the installation where a bank teller works.

CALENDAR list of securities about to be offered for sale. Separate calendars are kept for municipal bonds, corporate bonds, government bonds, and new stock offerings.

CALENDAR EFFECT historical tendency of stocks to perform better or worse on certain days of the week, weeks of the month, or months of the year. Examples would be the JANUARY BAROMETER and the HALLOWEEN STRATEGY.

CALENDAR SPREAD options strategy that entails buying two options on the same security with different maturities. If the EXERCISE PRICE is the same (a June 50 call and a September 50 call) it is a HORIZONTAL SPREAD. If the exercise prices are different (a June 50 call and a September 45 call), it is a DIAGONAL SPREAD. Investors gain or lose as the difference in price narrows or widens.

CALL

Banking: demand to repay a secured loan usually made when the borrower has failed to meet such contractual obligations as timely payment of interest. When a banker calls a loan, the entire principal amount is due immediately. *See also* BROKER LOAN RATE.

Bonds: right to redeem outstanding bonds before their scheduled maturity. The first dates when an issuer may call bonds are specified in the prospectus of every issue that has a call provision in its indenture. *See also* CALLABLE; CALL PRICE.

Options: right to buy a specific number of shares at a specified price by a fixed date. *See also* CALL OPTION.

CALLABLE redeemable by the issuer before the scheduled maturity. The issuer must pay the holders a premium price if such a security is retired early. Bonds are usually called when interest rates fall so significantly that the issuer can save money by floating new bonds at lower rates. *See also* CALL PRICE; DEMAND LOAN.

CALL DATE date on which a bond may be redeemed before maturity. If called, the bond may be redeemed at PAR or at a slight premium to par. For example, a bond may be scheduled to mature in 20 years but may have a provision that it can be called in 10 years if it is advantageous for the issuer to refinance the issue. The date 10 years from the issue date is the call date. When buying a bond, it is important to know the bond's call date, because you cannot be assured that you will receive interest from that bond beyond the call date.

CALLED AWAY term for a bond redeemed before maturity, or a call or put option exercised against the stockholder, or a delivery required on a short sale.

CALL FEATURE part of the agreement a bond issuer makes with a buyer, called the indenture, describing the schedule and price of redemptions before maturity. Most corporate and municipal bonds have 10-year call features (termed CALL PROTECTION by holders); government securities usually have none. *See also* CALL PRICE.

CALL LOAN any loan repayable on demand, but used in newspaper money rate tables as a synonym for *broker loan* or *broker overnight loan*. *See also* BROKER LOAN RATE.

CALL LOAN RATE *see* BROKER LOAN RATE.

CALL MARKET *see* WALRASIAN MARKET.

CALL OPTION right to buy 100 shares of a particular stock or stock index at a predetermined price before a preset deadline, in exchange for a premium. For buyers who think a stock will go up dramatically, call options permit a profit from a smaller investment than it would take to buy the stock. These options can also produce extra income for the seller, who gives up ownership of the stock if the option is exercised. *See also* EXOTIC OPTIONS; OPTIONS; PUT OPTIONS.

CALL PREMIUM amount that the buyer of a call option has to pay to the seller for the right to purchase a stock or stock index at a specified price by a specified date.

In bonds, preferreds, and convertibles, the amount over par that an issuer has to pay to an investor for redeeming the security early.

CALL PRICE price at which a bond or preferred stock with a *call provision* or CALL FEATURE can be redeemed by the issuer; also known as *redemption price*. To compensate the holder for loss of income and ownership, the call price is usually higher than the par value of the security, the difference being the CALL PREMIUM. *See also* CALL PROTECTION.

CALL PROTECTION length of time during which a security cannot be redeemed by the issuer. U.S. government securities are generally not callable, although there is an exception in certain 30-year Treasury bonds, which become callable after 25 years. Corporate and municipal issuers generally provide 10 years of call protection. Investors who plan to live off the income from a bond should be sure they have call protection, because without it the bond could be CALLED AWAY at any time specified in the indenture. *See also* PROVISIONAL CALL FEATURE.

CALL PROVISION clause in a bond's INDENTURE that allows the issuer to redeem the bond before maturity. The call provision will spell out the first CALL DATE and whether the bond will be called at PAR or at a slight premium to par. Some preferred stock issues also have call provisions spelling out the conditions of a redemption. *See also* PROVISIONAL CALL FEATURE.

CALL RISK risk to a bondholder that a bond may be redeemed before scheduled maturity. Bondholders should read the CALL PROVISIONS in a bond's INDENTURE to understand the earliest potential CALL DATE for their bond. The main risk of having a bond called before maturity is that the investor will be unable to replace the bond's yield with another similar-quality bond paying the same yield. The reason the bond issuer will call the bond is that interest rates will have fallen from the time of issuance, and the bond can be refinanced at lower rates.

CALL SWAPTION *see* SWAPTION.

CAMBRIST a foreign currency expert, usually a trader.

CAMPS acronym for *Cumulative Auction Market Preferred Stocks,* Oppenheimer & Company's DUTCH AUCTION PREFERRED STOCK product.

CANCEL
In general: void a negotiable instrument by annulling or paying it; also, prematurely terminate a bond or other contract.
Securities trading: void an order to buy or sell. *See also* GOOD TILL CANCELED ORDER.

CAP
Bonds: highest level interest rate that can be paid on a floating-rate debt instrument. For example, a variable-rate note might have a cap of 8%, meaning that the yield cannot exceed 8% even if the general level of interest rates goes much higher than 8%.
Mortgages: highest interest rate level that an adjustable-rate mortgage (ARM) can rise to over a particular period of time. For example, an ARM contract may specify that the rate cannot jump more than two points in any year, or a total of six points during the life of the mortgage.
Stocks: short for CAPITALIZATION, or the total current value of a company's outstanding shares in dollars. A stock's capitalization is determined by multiplying the total number of shares outstanding by the stock's price. Analysts also refer to small-, medium-, and large-cap stocks as a way of distinguishing the capitalizations of companies they are interested in. Many mutual funds restrict themselves to the small-, medium-, or large-cap universes. *See also* COLLAR.

CAPACITY
Debt: ability to repay loans, as measured by credit grantors. Creditors judge an applicant's ability to repay a loan based on assets and income, and assign a certain capacity to service debt. If someone has many credit cards and credit lines outstanding, even if there are no outstanding balances, that is using up that person's debt capacity.
Economics: the amount of productive capacity in the economy is known as *industrial capacity.* This figure is released on a monthly basis by the Federal Reserve to show how much of the nation's factories, mines, and utilities are in

use. If more than 85% of industrial capacity is in use, economists worry that production bottlenecks may form and create inflationary pressure. On the other hand, if less than 80% of capacity is in use, industrial production may be slack and inflationary pressures low.

CAPACITY UTILIZATION RATE percentage of production capacity in use by a particular company, an industry, or the entire economy. While in theory a business can operate at 100% of its productive capacity, in practice the maximum output is less than that, because machines need to be repaired, employees take vacations, etc. The operating rate is expressed as a percentage of the potential 100% production output. For example, a company may be producing at an 85% operating rate, meaning its output is 85% of the maximum that could be produced with its existing resources. *See also* CAPACITY.

CAP AND TRADE informal phrase for *emissions trading,* an environmental policy approach whereby the government sets a limit (cap) on the overall amount of pollutants emitted and individual companies trade assigned permits, called credits, among themselves. The overall aim is to reduce emissions. This goal is further advanced as the authorities periodically lower the overall caps and as market prices of credits are forced higher by reductions in the available supply. The United States has one national cap and trade program (Acid Rain Program) and three regional programs.

A hot button political issue currently is the U.S. Carbon Cap and Trade Program proposed by President Obama and passed by the U.S. House of Representatives by a narrow vote as *H.R. 2452: American Clean Energy and Security Act of 2009.* Its expressed aim is to create clean energy jobs, achieve energy independence, reduce global warming pollution, and transition to a clean energy economy. President Obama proposes reducing U.S. emissions 14% below 2005 levels by 2020 and 83% below by 2050. His 2009 budget proposal has the government raising $646 billion from 2012 to 2019 by taxing energy usage via carbon permit auctions. Opponents of the "Cap and Trade" bill say it amounts to an unacceptable tax because it will hike the price of electricity and gas and thus add to the cost of living and cause higher unemployment.

CAPITAL ASSET long-term asset that is not bought or sold in the normal course of business. Generally speaking, the term includes FIXED ASSETS—land, buildings, equipment, furniture and fixtures, and so on. The Internal Revenue Service definition of capital assets includes security investments.

CAPITAL ASSET PRICING MODEL (CAPM) sophisticated model of the relationship between *expected risk* and *expected return.* The model is grounded in the theory that investors demand higher returns for higher risks. It says that the return on an asset or a security is equal to the risk-free return—such as the return on a short-term Treasury security—plus a risk premium.

CAPITAL BUDGET program for financing long-term outlays such as plant expansion, research and development, and advertising. Among methods used in arriving at a capital budget are NET PRESENT VALUE (NPV), INTERNAL RATE OF RETURN (IRR), and PAYBACK PERIOD.

CAPITAL BUILDER ACCOUNT (CBA) brokerage account offered by Merrill Lynch that allows investors to buy and sell securities. It may be a cash or credit account that allows an investor to access the loan value of his or her eligible securities. Unlike a regular brokerage account, with a CBA one can choose from a money market fund or an insured money market deposit account to have one's idle cash invested or deposited on a regular basis, without losing access to the money.

CAPITAL CONSUMPTION ALLOWANCE amount of depreciation included in the GROSS DOMESTIC PRODUCT (GDP), normally around 11%. This amount is subtracted from GDP, on the theory that it is needed to maintain the productive capacity of the economy, to get net national product (NNP). When adjusted further for indirect taxes, NNP equals national income. Economists use GDP rather than NNP in the analyses we read every day largely because capital consumption allowance figures are not always available or reliable. *See also* DEPRECIATION.

CAPITAL DIVIDEND Same as RETURN OF CAPITAL.

CAPITAL EXPENDITURE outlay of money to acquire or improve CAPITAL ASSETS such as buildings and machinery.

CAPITAL FLIGHT movement of large sums of money from one country to another to escape political or economic turmoil or to seek higher rates of return. For example, periods of high inflation or political revolution have brought about an exodus of capital from many Latin American countries to the United States, which is seen as a safe haven.

CAPITAL FORMATION creation or expansion, through savings, of capital or of *producer's goods*—buildings, machinery, equipment that produce other goods and services, the result being economic expansion.

CAPITAL GAIN difference between an asset's adjusted purchase price and selling price when the difference is positive. A long-term capital gain is achieved once an asset such as a stock, bond, or mutual fund has been held for more than 12 months. Such long-term gains are taxed at a maximum rate of 15%. Those in the 15% tax bracket pay a 5% tax on long-term capital gains. Selling assets for a profit after holding them for 12 months or less generates short-term capital gains, which are subject to regular income tax rates. Assets purchased starting January 1, 2000 and held for more than five years qualify for a maximum capital gains tax rate of 8%. Capital gains are reported on Schedule D of a tax return.

CAPITAL GAINS DISTRIBUTION mutual fund's distribution to shareholders of the profits derived from the sale of stocks or bonds. Shareholders must pay long-term capital gains tax rates of as much as 15% if the fund held the securities for at least 12 months, no matter how long the shareholder owned shares in the mutual fund. Shareholders must pay short-term capital gains taxes at regular income tax rates on securities sold by the mutual fund that have been held for less than 12 months, no matter how long the shareholder owned shares in the mutual fund. Distributions that are reinvested by shareholders are taxed in the same way as distributions paid to shareholders in cash. If a capital gain distribution is declared in October, November, or December, but paid in January, the fund will still report the distribution as taxable in the year it was declared. Mutual funds report capital gains distributions to shareholders annually on Form 1099-DIV.

CAPITAL GAINS TAX tax on profits from the sale of CAPITAL ASSETS. Traditionally, the tax law specified a minimum holding period after which a capital gain is taxed at a more favorable rate (recently, a maximum of 15%

for individuals) than ordinary income. A long-term capital gain is achieved once an asset such as a stock, bond, or mutual fund is held for more than 12 months. Such long-term gains are taxed at a maximum rate of 15% for taxpayers. Those in the 15% tax bracket pay a 5% tax on long-term capital gains. Assets sold for a profit after having been held for 12 months or less generate short-term capital gains, which are subject to ordinary income tax rates. Assets purchased starting January 1, 2000 and held for more than five years qualify for a maximum capital gains tax rate of 8%.

CAPITAL GOODS goods used in the production of other goods—industrial buildings, machinery, equipment—as well as highways, office buildings, government installations. In the aggregate such goods form a country's productive capacity.

CAPITAL-INTENSIVE requiring large investments in CAPITAL ASSETS. Motorvehicle and steel production are capital-intensive industries. To provide an acceptable return on investment, such industries must have a high margin of profit or a low cost of borrowing. Sometimes used to mean a high proportion of fixed assets to labor.

CAPITAL INVESTMENT *see* CAPITAL EXPENDITURE.

CAPITALISM economic system in which (1) private ownership of property exists; (2) aggregates of property or capital provide income for the individuals or firms that accumulated it and own it; (3) individuals and firms are relatively free to compete with others for their own economic gain; (4) the profit motive is basic to economic life.

Among the synonyms for capitalism are LAISSEZ-FAIRE economy, private enterprise system, and free-price system. In this context *economy* is interchangeable with *system*.

CAPITALIZATION *see* CAPITALIZE; CAPITAL STRUCTURE; MARKET CAPITALIZATION.

CAPITALIZATION RATE rate of interest used to convert a series of future payments into a single PRESENT VALUE.

CAPITALIZATION RATIO analysis of a company's capital structure showing what percentage of the total is debt, preferred stock, common stock, and other equity. The ratio is useful in evaluating the relative RISK and leverage that holders of the respective levels of security have. *See also* BOND RATIO.

CAPITALIZE
1. convert a schedule of income into a principal amount, called *capitalized value,* by dividing by a rate of interest.
2. issue securities to finance *capital outlays* (rare).
3. record capital outlays as additions to asset accounts, not as expenses. *See also* CAPITAL EXPENDITURE.
4. convert a lease obligation to an asset/liability form of expression called a *capital lease,* that is, to record a leased asset as an owned asset and the lease obligation as borrowed funds.
5. turn something to one's advantage economically—for example, sell umbrellas on a rainy day.

CAPITALIZED COST REDUCTION in automotive leasing, a down payment designed to lower monthly lease payments. It does not reduce the residual value (purchase price) of the vehicle when the lease expires.

CAPITAL LEASE lease that under Statement 13 of the Financial Accounting Standards Board must be reflected on a company's balance sheet as an asset and corresponding liability. Generally, this applies to leases where the lessee acquires essentially all of the economic benefits and risks of the leased property. Also called FINANCIAL LEASE.

CAPITAL LOSS amount by which the proceeds from the sale of a CAPITAL ASSET are less than the adjusted cost of acquiring it. Capital losses are deducted first against capital gains, and then against up to $3,000 of other income for married couples filing jointly, and up to $1,500 for married couples filing separately. Any capital losses in excess of $3,000 may be carried over into future tax years. Short-term losses realized on assets sold 12 months or less after purchase are offset against short-term capital gains. Long-term capital losses on assets sold more than 12 months after purchase are offset against long-term capital gains. Capital losses are reported on Schedule D of a tax return. *See also* TAX LOSS CARRYBACK, CARRYFORWARD.

CAPITAL MARKET EFFICIENCY extent to which available information is reflected in the market price of an ASSET, in accordance with the EFFICIENT MARKET theory.

CAPITAL MARKET IMPERFECTIONS VIEW approach to FINANCIAL LEVERAGE decisions that recognizes that a CAPITAL STRUCTURE optimal in terms of debt versus equity mathematics may not benefit shareholders equally unless it takes account of such factors as ASYMMETRY in personal tax brackets.

CAPITAL MARKET LINE *see* CAPITAL ASSET PRICING MODEL.

CAPITAL MARKETS markets where capital funds—debt and equity—are traded. Included are private placement sources of debt and equity as well as organized markets and exchanges. *See also* PRIMARY MARKET.

CAPITAL OUTFLOW exodus of capital from a country. A combination of political and economic factors may encourage domestic and foreign owners of assets to sell their holdings and move their money to other countries that offer more political stability and economic growth potential. If a capital outflow becomes large enough, some countries may try to restrict investors' ability to remove money from the country with currency controls or other measures.

CAPITAL OUTLAY *see* CAPITAL EXPENDITURE.

CAPITAL PURCHASE PROGRAM (CPP) program run by the Treasury Department under its TARP authority to reinforce the solvency of major banks. The Treasury purchased billions of dollars in nonvoting preferred stock and equity warrants in many major banks, which gave the government an ownership stake in these banks, though not a controlling position. Banks taking CPP funds were subject to government policies, such as caps on executive bonuses and pay and restrictions on dividend payments. Many large banks eventually repaid their CPP investments, thereby freeing themselves from these government policies.

CAPITAL RATIONING a situation in capital budgeting in which acceptable investments (capital investment opportunities whose projected rate of return exceeds the firm's risk-adjusted cost of capital) compete for a limited amount of funds available for capital spending. The implication is that the costs of raising new capital are prohibitively high relative to expected returns. The ranking of projects competing for limited funds is called the PROFITABILITY INDEX.

CAPITAL REQUIREMENTS

1. permanent financing needed for the normal operation of a business; that is, the long-term and working capital.
2. appraised investment in fixed assets and normal working capital. Whether patents, rights, and contracts should be included is moot.

CAPITAL SHARES one of the two classes of shares in a dual-purpose investment company. The capital shares entitle the owner to all appreciation (or depreciation) in value in the underlying portfolio in addition to all gains realized by trading in the portfolio. The other class of shares in a dual-purpose investment company are INCOME SHARES, which receive all income generated by the portfolio. If the fund guarantees a minimum level of income payable to the income shareholders, it may be necessary to sell some securities in the portfolio if the existing securities do not provide a high enough level of dividends and interest. In this case, the value of the capital shares will fall.

CAPITAL STOCK stock authorized by a company's charter and having PAR VALUE, STATED VALUE, or NO PAR VALUE. The number and value of issued shares are normally shown, together with the number of shares authorized, in the capital accounts section of the balance sheet.

Informally, a synonym for COMMON STOCK, though capital stock technically also encompasses PREFERRED STOCK.

CAPITAL STRUCTURE corporation's financial framework, including LONG-TERM DEBT, PREFERRED STOCK, and NET WORTH. It is distinguished from FINANCIAL STRUCTURE, which includes additional sources of capital such as short-term debt, accounts payable, and other liabilities. It is synonymous with *capitalization,* although there is some disagreement as to whether capitalization should include long-term loans and mortgages. Analysts look at capital structure in terms of its overall adequacy and its composition as well as in terms of the DEBT-TO-EQUITY RATIO, called *leverage. See also* CAPITALIZATION RATIO; PAR VALUE.

CAPITAL SURPLUS

1. EQUITY—or NET WORTH—not otherwise classifiable as CAPITAL STOCK or RETAINED EARNINGS. Here are five ways of creating surplus:
   a. from stock issued at a premium over par or stated value.
   b. from the proceeds of stock bought back and then sold again.
   c. from a reduction of par or stated value or a reclassification of capital stock.
   d. from donated stock.
   e. from the acquisition of companies that have capital surplus.
2. common umbrella term for more specific classifications such as ACQUIRED SURPLUS, ADDITIONAL PAID-IN CAPITAL, DONATED SURPLUS, and REEVALUATION SURPLUS (arising from appraisals). Most common synonyms: *paid-in surplus; surplus.*

CAPITAL TURNOVER annual sales divided by average stockholder equity (net worth). When compared over a period, it reveals the extent to which a company is able to grow without additional capital investment. Generally, companies with high profit margins have a low capital turnover and vice versa. Also called *equity turnover.*

CAPITULATION the terminal stage of a market collapse, when investors give up hope and take losses, and prices bottom out. Capitulations stir bullish sentiment since they create opportunities for VALUE INVESTING and are a TECHNICAL SIGN that DOWNSIDE RISK is being replaced by UPSIDE POTENTIAL. Market bottoms are confirmable only in hindsight, however, so there is always an element of speculation.

CAPS acronym for *convertible adjustable preferred stock,* whose adjustable interest rate is pegged to Treasury security rates and which can be exchanged, during the period after the announcement of each dividend rate for the next period, for common stock (or, usually, cash) with a market value equal to the par value of the CAPS. CAPS solved a problem inherent with DUTCH AUCTION PREFERRED STOCK, which was that the investor could not be certain of the principal value of the preferred. *See also* MANDATORY CONVERTIBLES.

CAPTIVE AGENT insurance agent working exclusively for one company. Such an agent will tend to have more in-depth knowledge of that company's policies than an INDEPENDENT AGENT, who can sell policies from many companies. Captive agents are usually paid on a combination of salary and commissions earned from selling policies, in the first few years they sell policies. Later, they are usually paid exclusively on a commission basis.

CAPTIVE FINANCE COMPANY company, usually a wholly owned subsidiary, that exists primarily to finance consumer purchases from the parent company. Example: Ford Motor Credit Company. Although these subsidiaries stand on their own financially, parent companies frequently make SUBORDINATED LOANS to add to their equity positions. This supports the high leverage on which the subsidiaries operate and assures their active participation in the COMMERCIAL PAPER and bond markets.

CARROT EQUITY British slang for an equity investment with a KICKER in the form of an opportunity to buy more equity if the company meets specified financial goals.

CARRYBACK,   CARRYFORWARD   *see*   TAX   LOSS   CARRYBACK, CARRYFORWARD.

CARRYING CHARGE
Commodities: charge for carrying the actual commodity, including interest, storage, and insurance costs.
Margin accounts: fee that a broker charges for carrying securities on credit.
Real estate: carrying cost, primarily interest and taxes, of owning land prior to its development and resale.
Retailing: seller's charge for installment credit, which is either added to the purchase price or to unpaid installments.

CARRYOVER *see* TAX LOSS CARRYBACK, CARRYFORWARD.

CARRYING VALUE Also called BOOK VALUE.

CARRY TRADE practice of borrowing money in a market where interest rates are low and investing that money at a profit where the return is higher. A popular strategy between 2000 and 2008, for example, was to borrow yen when the Japanese interest rate was near zero and invest the converted dollar proceeds in U.S. Treasury bonds paying over 3%. Investors enjoyed a *positive carry* exceeding 3%, while additionally benefiting from the dollar's rise against the yen when the dollars were converted back at the end of the loan. The risk: that relative interest rates and/or currency exchange rates will change adversely, resulting in a *negative carry*.

CARS *see* CERTIFICATE FOR AUTOMOBILE RECEIVABLES.

CARTEL group of businesses or nations that agree to influence prices by regulating production and marketing of a product. The most famous contemporary cartel is the ORGANIZATION OF PETROLEUM EXPORTING COUNTRIES (OPEC), which, notably in the 1970s, restricted oil production and sales and raised prices. A cartel has less control over an industry than a MONOPOLY. A number of nations, including the United States, have laws prohibiting cartels. TRUST is sometimes used as a synonym for cartel.

CARVE OUT *see* EQUITY CARVE OUT.

CASH asset account on a balance sheet representing paper currency and coins, negotiable money orders and checks, and bank balances. Also, transactions handled in cash. In the financial statements of annual reports, cash is usually grouped with CASH EQUIVALENTS, defined as all highly liquid securities with a known market value and a maturity, when acquirerest rate charged on the cash advance is usually different from the rate charged on purchases made with the same card. Frequently, the cash advance rate is higher. In many cases advance rates are variable, and are usually tied to a certain number of percentage points over the prime rate.

CASH ASSET RATIO balance sheet LIQUIDITY RATIO representing cash (and equivalents) and marketable securities divided by current liabilities. Stricter than the *quick ratio*.

CASH BASIS
Accounting: method that recognizes revenues when cash is received and recognizes expenses when cash is paid out. In contrast, the *accrual method* recognizes revenues when goods or services are sold and recognizes expenses when obligations are incurred. A third method, called *modified cash basis,* uses accrual accounting for long-term assets and is the basis usually referred to when the term cash basis is used.
Series EE Savings Bonds: paying the entire tax on these bonds when they mature. The alternative is to prorate the tax each year until the bonds mature.

CASHBOOK accounting book that combines cash receipts and disbursements. Its balance ties to the cash account in the general ledger on which the balance sheet is based.

CASH BUDGET estimated cash receipts and disbursements for a future period. A comprehensive cash budget schedules daily, weekly, or monthly expenditures together with the anticipated CASH FLOW from collections and other operating sources. Cash flow budgets are essential in establishing credit and purchasing policies, as well as in planning credit line usage and short-term investments in COMMERCIAL PAPER and other securities.

CASH COMMODITY commodity that is owned as the result of a completed contract and must be accepted upon delivery. Contrasts with futures contracts, which are not completed until a specified future date. The cash commodity contract specifications are set by the commodity exchanges.

CASH CONVERSION CYCLE elapsed time, usually expressed in days, from the outlay of cash for raw materials to the receipt of cash after the finished goods have been sold. Because a profit is built into the sales, the term *earnings cycle* is also used. The shorter the cycle, the more WORKING CAPITAL a business generates and the less it has to borrow. This cycle is directly affected by production efficiency, credit policy, and other controllable factors.

CASH COW business that generates a continuing flow of cash. Such a business usually has well-established brand names whose familiarity stimulates repeated buying of the products. For example, a magazine company that has a high rate of subscription renewals would be considered a cash cow. Stocks that are cash cows have dependable dividends.

CASH DISCOUNT TRADE CREDIT feature providing for a deduction if payment is made early. For example: trade terms of "2% 10 days net 30 days" allow a 2% cash discount for payment in 10 days. Term also refers to the lower price some merchants charge customers who pay in cash rather than with credit cards, in which case the merchant is passing on all or part of the merchant fee it would otherwise pay to the credit card company.

CASH DIVIDEND cash payment to a corporation's shareholders, distributed from current earnings or accumulated profits and taxable as income. Cash dividends are distinguished from STOCK DIVIDENDS, which are payments in the form of stock. *See also* YIELD.

INVESTMENT COMPANY cash dividends are usually made up of dividends, interest income, and capital gains received on its investment portfolio.

CASH EARNINGS cash revenues less cash expenses—specifically excluding noncash expenses such as DEPRECIATION.

CASH EQUIVALENTS instruments or investments of such high liquidity and safety that they are virtually as good as cash. Examples are a MONEY MARKET FUND and a TREASURY BILL. The FINANCIAL ACCOUNTING STANDARDS BOARD (FASB) defines cash equivalents for financial reporting purposes as any highly liquid security with a known market value and a maturity, when acquired, of less than three months.

CASH FLOW
1. in a larger financial sense, an analysis of all the changes that affect the cash account during an accounting period. The STATEMENT OF CASH FLOWS included in annual reports analyzes all changes affecting cash in the categories of operations, investments, and financing. For example: net operating income is an increase; the purchase of a new building is a decrease; and the issuance of stock or bonds is an increase. When more cash comes in than goes out, we speak of a *positive cash flow;* the opposite is a *negative cash flow.* Companies with assets well in excess of liabilities may nevertheless go bankrupt because they cannot generate enough cash to meet current obligations.
2. in investments, NET INCOME plus DEPRECIATION and other noncash charges. In this sense, it is synonymous with CASH EARNINGS. Investors focus on cash flow from operations because of their concern with a firm's ability to pay dividends. *See also* CASH BUDGET.

CASH FLOW MATCHING *see* PORTFOLIO DEDICATION.

CASH FOR CLUNKERS federal bill passed in June 2009 to boost slumping auto sales and effect energy savings by allowing consumers to turn in gas-guzzling cars and trucks for vouchers worth up to $4,500 toward more fuel efficient vehicles. The $1 billion originally allocated to the subsidy had been used up by late July, and an additional $2 billion of vouchers was gone by late August when the program was terminated.

CASHIERING DEPARTMENT *see* CAGE.

CASHIER'S CHECK check that draws directly on a customer's account; the bank becomes the primary obligor. Consumers requiring a cashier's check must pay the amount of the check to the bank. The bank will then issue a check to a third party named by the consumer. Many businesses require that bills be paid by cashier's check instead of personal check, because they are assured that the funds are available with a cashier's check.

CASH INDEX PARTICIPATIONS (CIPS) *see* BASKET.

CASH MANAGEMENT
Corporate finance: efficient mobilization of cash into income-producing applications, using computers, telecommunications technology, innovative investment vehicles, and LOCK BOX arrangements.
Investing: broker's efficient movement of cash to keep it working. Merrill Lynch pioneered its proprietary Cash Management Account to combine securities trading, checking account services, money market investment services, and a debit (Visa) card. *See also* AGGREGATION; SWEEP ACCOUNT.

CASH MARKET transactions in the cash or spot markets that are completed; that is, ownership of the commodity is transferred from seller to buyer and payment is given on delivery of the commodity. The cash market contrasts with the futures market, in which contracts are completed at a specified time in the future.

CASH-ON-CASH RETURN method of yield computation used for investments lacking an active secondary market, such as LIMITED PARTNERSHIPS. It simply divides the annual dollar income by the total dollars invested; a $10,000 investment that pays $1,000 annually thus has a 10% cash-on-cash return. Investments having a market value and a predictable income stream to a designated maturity or call date, such as bonds, are better measured by CURRENT YIELD or YIELD-TO-MATURITY (or to call).

CASH ON DELIVERY (COD)
Commerce: transaction requiring that goods be paid for in full by cash or certified check or the equivalent at the point of delivery. The term *collect on delivery* has the same abbreviation and same meaning. If the customer refuses delivery, the seller has round-trip shipping costs to absorb or other, perhaps riskier, arrangements to make.
Securities: a requirement that delivery of securities to institutional investors be in exchange for assets of equal value—which, as a practical matter, means cash. Alternatively called *delivery against cost* (DAC) or *delivery versus payment* (DVP). On the other side of the trade, the term is *receive versus payment*.

CASH OR DEFERRED ARRANGEMENT (CODA) *see* 401(k) PLAN.

CASH OUT REFINANCING mortgage refinancing where the new loan exceeds the unpaid balance of the original loan because of amortization and/ or appreciation, and the difference is withdrawn in cash.

CASH RATIO ratio of cash and marketable securities to current liabilities; a refinement of the QUICK RATIO. The cash ratio tells the extent to which liabilities could be liquidated immediately. Sometimes called *liquidity ratio*.

CASH SETTLEMENT in the United States, settlement in cash on the TRADE DATE rather than the SETTLEMENT DATE of a securities transaction. In Great Britain, delivery and settlement on the first business day after the trade date.

CASH SURRENDER VALUE in insurance, the amount the insurer will return to a policyholder on cancellation of the policy. Sometimes abbreviated *CSVLI* (cash surrender value of life insurance), it shows up as an asset on the balance sheet of a company that has life insurance on its principals, called *key man insurance.* Insurance companies make loans against the cash value of policies, often at a better-than-market rate.

CASH VALUE INSURANCE life insurance that combines a death benefit with a potential tax-deferred buildup of money (called cash value) in the policy. The three main kinds of cash value insurance are WHOLE LIFE INSURANCE, VARIABLE LIFE INSURANCE, and UNIVERSAL LIFE INSURANCE. In whole life, cash value is accumulated based on the return on the company's investments in stocks, bonds, real estate, and other ventures. In variable life, the policyholder chooses how to allocate the money among stock, bond, and money market options. In universal life, a policyholder's cash value is invested in investments such as money market securities and medium-term Treasury bonds to build cash value. All cash values inside an insurance policy remain untaxed until they are withdrawn from the policy. Unlike cash value insurance, TERM LIFE INSURANCE offers only a death benefit, and no cash value buildup.

CASUALTY-INSURANCE insurance that protects a business or homeowner against property loss, damage, and related liability.

CASUALTY LOSS financial loss caused by damage, destruction, or loss of property as the result of an identifiable event that is sudden, unexpected, or unusual. Casualty and theft losses are considered together for tax purposes; are covered by most *casualty insurance* policies; and are tax deductible provided the loss is (1) not covered by insurance or (2) if covered, a claim has been made and denied.

CATASTROPHE CALL premature redemption of a municipal revenue bond because a catastrophe destroyed the source of the revenue backing the bond. For example, a bond backed by toll revenues from a bridge might be called, meaning bondholders will receive their principal back, if a storm destroyed the bridge. Usually, the proceeds for the payment will come from a commercial insurance policy covering the revenue-producing asset such as the bridge. A bond's INDENTURE will spell out the conditions under which a catastrophe call can be implemented.

CATASTROPHIC COVERAGE
1. insurance coverage for a catastrophe hazard (such as a hurricane or flood) that cannot or will not be provided by commercial insurers and may be covered through government agency programs.

2. medical coverage made afforable by a high DEDUCTIBLE and that covers everything above a certain amount. Also called *catastrophe insurance*.

CATCH-UP CONTRIBUTIONS supplemental tax-deferred contributions to IRAs and qualified plans permitted for individuals and employees 50 years old or older. Congress added the new catch-up contribution limits out of concern that baby boomers had not been saving enough for retirement. The provisions apply in 401(k), 403(b), and 457 plans and IRAs, but the rules differ among plans. Permitted IRA catch-up contributions are $1,000 a year; thus the maximum contribution to a traditional IRA for 2008 is $5,000, plus $1,000 more if 50 or older. Contributions are made on top of current limits.

CATS *see* CERTIFICATE OF ACCRUAL ON TREASURY SECURITIES.

CATS AND DOGS speculative stocks that have short histories of sales, earnings, and dividend payments. In bull markets, analysts say disparagingly that even the cats and dogs are going up.

CAVEAT EMPTOR, CAVEAT SUBSCRIPTOR *buyer beware, seller beware*. A variation on the latter is *caveat venditor*. Good advice when markets are not adequately protected, which was true of the stock market before the watchdog SECURITIES AND EXCHANGE COMMISSION was established in the 1930s.

CBO *see* COLLATERALIZED BOND (OR DEBT) OBLIGATION (CBO OR CDO).

CDO *see* COLLATERALIZED BOND (OR DEBT) OBLIGATION (CBO OR CDO).

CEILING highest level allowable in a financial transaction. For example, someone buying a stock may place a ceiling on the stock's price, meaning they are not willing to pay more than that amount for the shares. The issuer of a bond may place a ceiling on the interest rate it is willing to pay. If market interest rates rise beyond that ceiling, the underwriter must cancel the issue. *See also* CAP.

CENTRAL BANK country's bank that (1) issues currency; (2) administers monetary policy, including OPEN MARKET OPERATIONS; (3) holds deposits representing the reserves of other banks; and (4) engages in transactions designed to facilitate the conduct of business and protect the public interest. In the United States, central banking is a function of the FEDERAL RESERVE SYSTEM.

CENTRAL LIMIT ORDER BOOK (CLOB) proposed system to consolidate securities *limit orders* received from specialists and market makers and electronic trading systems. The idea has been opposed by securities exchanges fearing lost volume, but advocated by the SEC and others worried about the fragmentation of markets caused by electronic trading systems. A CLOB would be "hard" or "soft," depending on whether orders were executed or merely facilitated by consolidated information.

CENTRAL REGISTRATION DEPOSITORY (CRD) also known as WebCRD, on-line registration, and licensing data bank, developed by the FINANCIAL INDUSTRY REGULATORY AUTHORITY (FINRA) and the North American Securities Administrators Association (NASAA), containing information on some 500,000 registered securities employees of FINRA member, broker/dealer firms.

CERTIFICATE formal declaration that can be used to document a fact, such as a birth certificate.

The following are certificates with particular relevance to finance and investments.

1. auditor's certificate, sometimes called certificate of accounts, or ACCOUNTANT'S OPINION.
2. bond certificate, certificate of indebtedness issued by a corporation containing the terms of the issuer's promise to repay principal and pay interest, and describing collateral, if any. Traditionally, bond certificates had coupons attached, which were exchanged for payment of interest. Now that most bonds are issued in registered form, coupons are less common. The amount of a certificate is the par value of the bond.
3. CERTIFICATE OF DEPOSIT.
4. certificate of INCORPORATION.
5. certificate of indebtedness, government debt obligation having a maturity shorter than a bond and longer than a treasury bill (such as a Treasury Note).
6. PARTNERSHIP certificate, showing the interest of all participants in a business partnership.
7. PROPRIETORSHIP certificate, showing who is legally responsible in an individually owned business.
8. STOCK CERTIFICATE, evidence of ownership of a corporation showing number of shares, name of issuer, amount of par or stated value represented or a declaration of no-par value, and rights of the shareholder. Preferred stock certificates also list the issuer's responsibilities with respect to dividends and voting rights, if any.

CERTIFICATE FOR AMORTIZED REVOLVING DEBT *see* CARDS.

CERTIFICATE FOR AUTOMOBILE RECEIVABLES (CARS) PASS-THROUGH SECURITY backed by automobile loan paper of banks and other lenders. *See also* ASSET-BACKED SECURITIES.

CERTIFICATELESS MUNICIPALS MUNICIPAL BONDS that have no certificate of ownership for each bondholder. Instead, one certificate is valid for the entire issue. Certificateless municipals save paperwork for brokers and municipalities and allow investors to trade their bonds without having to transfer certificates. *See also* BOOK ENTRY SECURITIES.

CERTIFICATE OF ACCRUAL ON TREASURY SECURITIES (CATS) U.S. Treasury issues, sold at a deep discount from face value. A ZERO-COUPON security, they pay no interest during their lifetime, but return the full face value at maturity. They are appropriate for retirement or education planning. AS TREASURY SECURITIES, CATS cannot be CALLED AWAY.

CERTIFICATE OF DEPOSIT (CD) debt instrument issued by a bank that usually pays interest. Institutional CDs are issued in denominations of $100,000 or more, and individual CDs start as low as $100. Maturities range from a few weeks to several years. Interest rates are set by competitive forces in the marketplace. *See also* BROKERED CD; MARKET-INDEXED CD.

CERTIFICATE OF INDEBTEDNESS *see* TREASURIES.

CERTIFIED CHECK check for which a bank guarantees payment. It legally becomes an obligation of the bank, and the funds to cover it are immediately withdrawn from the depositor's account.

CERTIFIED FINANCIAL PLANNER (CFP) person who has passed examinations accredited by the Denver-based Certified Financial Planner Board of Standards, testing the ability to coordinate a client's banking, estate, insurance, investment, and tax affairs. Financial planners usually specialize in one or more of these areas and consult outside experts as needed. Some planners charge only fees and make no money on the implementation of their plans. Others charge a commission on each product or service they sell. *See also* FINANCIAL PLANNER.

CERTIFIED FINANCIAL STATEMENTS financial statements accompanied by an ACCOUNTANT'S OPINION.

CERTIFIED PUBLIC ACCOUNTANT (CPA) accountant who has passed certain exams, achieved a certain amount of experience, reached a certain age, and met all other statutory and licensing requirements of the U.S. state where he or she works. In addition to accounting and auditing, CPAs prepare tax returns for corporations and individuals.

CFA INSTITUTE A global, nonprofit professional organization of more than 83,000 investment practitioners in 129 countries, formerly known as the Association for Investment Management and Research. Its membership includes the world's 64,000 CFA charter holders, as well as 135 affiliated professional societies in 56 countries and territories. The group was created in 1999 from the merger of the Financial Analysts Federation (FAF) and the Institute of Chartered Financial Analysis (ICFA). The CFA Institute administers the Chartered Financial Analyst (CFA) curriculum and examination program worldwide and sets voluntary, ethics-based professional and performance-reporting standards for the investment industry, such as its Code of Ethics and Standards of Professional Conduct, the Asset Manager Code of Professional Conduct, Trade Management Guidelines, and the Global Investment Performance Standards (GIPS). CFA Institute members are employed as securities analysts, portfolio managers, strategists, consultants, educators, and other investment specialists, who practice in a variety of fields, including investment counseling and management, banking, insurance, and investment banking and brokerage. *See also* SECURITIES ANALYST; PORTFOLIO MANAGER.

CHAEBOLS major Korean business conglomerates.

CHAIRMAN OF THE BOARD member of a corporation's board of directors who presides over its meetings and who is the highest ranking officer in the corporation. The chairman of the board may or may not have the most actual executive authority in a firm. The additional title of CHIEF EXECUTIVE OFFICER (CEO) is reserved for the principal executive, and depending on the particular firm, that title may be held by the chairman, the president, or even an executive vice president. In some corporations, the position of chairman is either a prestigious reward for a past president or an honorary position for a prominent person, a large stockholder, or a family member; it may carry little or no real power in terms of policy or operating decision making.

CHANNEL in TECHNICAL ANALYSIS charting, the space, representing a TRADING RANGE, between two parallel trend lines, one connecting the highs, the other connecting the lows in a price series. Channels can be ascending, descending, or horizontal, but the lines should be near parallel and, respectively, represent RESISTANCE LEVELS (top) and SUPPORT LEVELS (bottom). A BREAKOUT in the opposite direction of either line may signify a trend reversal. Channels are used to guide short- and medium-term trading decisions. *See* illustration.

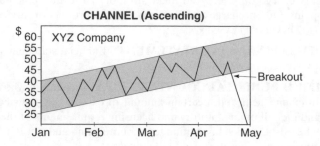

CHANNEL (Ascending)

CHAPTER 7 *see* BANKRUPTCY.

CHAPTER 10 federal BANKRUPTCY law section providing for reorganization under a court-appointed independent manager (trustee in bankruptcy) rather than under existing management as in the case with Chapter 11.

CHAPTER 11 *see* BANKRUPTCY.

CHAPTER 13 *see* BANKRUPTCY.

CHARGE OFF *see* BAD DEBT.

CHARITABLE LEAD TRUST *see* CHARITABLE REMAINDER TRUST.

CHARITABLE REMAINDER TRUST IRREVOCABLE TRUST that pays income to one or more individuals until the GRANTOR's death, at which time the balance, which is tax free, passes to a designated charity. It is a popular tax-saving alternative for individuals who have no children or who are wealthy enough to benefit both children and charity.

The charitable remainder trust is the reverse of a *charitable lead trust,* whereby a charity receives income during the grantor's life and the remainder passes to designated family members upon the grantor's death. The latter trust reduces estate taxes while enabling the family to retain control of the assets.

CHARTER *see* ARTICLES OF INCORPORATION.

CHARTERED FINANCIAL ANALYST (CFA) designation awarded by the Institute of Chartered Financial Analysts (ICFA), a unit of Charlottesville, Virginia-based CFA INSTITUTE, to experienced financial analysts who pass examinations in economics, financial accounting, portfolio management, security analysis, and standards of conduct.

CHARTERED FINANCIAL CONSULTANT (ChFC) designation awarded by American College, Bryn Mawr, PA, to a professional FINANCIAL PLANNER who completes a four-year program covering economics, insurance, taxation, real estate, and other areas related to finance and investing.

CHARTERED INVESTMENT COUNSEL (CIC) designation awarded by the Investment Counsel Association of America (ICAA), Washington, D.C., a national association of REGISTERED INVESTMENT ADVISERS founded in 1937, to CHARTERED FINANCIAL ANALYSTS (CFA), who have had significant experience in investment counseling or portfolio management, are employed by an ICAA member firm, have provided work and character references, endorse the ICAA's Standards of Practice, and provide professional ethical information.

CHARTERED LIFE UNDERWRITER (CLU) designation granted by American College, Bryn Mawr, PA, the insurance and financial service industry's oldest and largest fully accredited institution of higher learning in the United States. Designation requires completion of ten college-level courses, three years of qualifying experience, and adherence to a strict code of ethics. All CLUs may join the American Society of CLU and ChFC, a professional association also headquartered in Bryn Mawr, for continuing education opportunities and other member services. The American Society has chapters in all 50 states.

CHARTIST technical analyst who charts the patterns of stocks, bonds, and commodities to make buy and sell recommendations to clients. Chartists believe recurring patterns of trading can help them forecast future price movements. *See also* TECHNICAL ANALYSIS.

CHASING THE MARKET purchasing a security at a higher price than intended because prices have risen sharply, or selling it at a lower level when prices fall. For example, an investor may want to buy shares of a stock at $20 and place a limit order to do so. But when the shares rise above $25, and then $28, the customer decides to enter a market order and buy the stock before it goes even higher. Investors can also chase the market when selling a stock. For example, if an investor wants to sell a stock at $20 and it declines to $15 and then $12, he may decide to sell it at the market price before it declines even further.

CHASTITY BONDS bonds that become redeemable at par value in the event of a TAKEOVER.

CHATTEL MORTGAGE a mortgage loan collateralized by personal property other than physical real estate, such as automobiles, inventories, furniture, or real estate leases.

CHATTER *see* WHIPSAWED.

CHEAPEST TO DELIVER futures contract seller's term for a Treasury security with the highest implied repurchase rate, which is the most profitable issue for the seller to buy and then deliver on the settlement date.

CHECK bill of exchange, or draft on a bank drawn against deposited funds to pay a specified sum of money to a specified person on demand. A check is considered as cash and is NEGOTIABLE when endorsed.

CHECKING THE MARKET canvassing securities market-makers by telephone or other means in search of the best bid or offer price.

CHICAGO BOARD OF TRADE (CBOT) the CBOT is the world's oldest futures and options exchange. CBOT volume in 2004 totaled nearly 600 million contracts, representing about 15% of the total global listed futures and options on futures trades executed during that year. With its diverse mix of more than 50 financial, equity, and commodity futures and options on futures products, the CBOT advances into the future on the strength of its market integrity and the deep, liquid, and transparent trading environment that it provides. Formed in 1848 as a centralized marketplace for the grain trade, the CBOT's product line has grown to include contracts on agricultural commodities (such as corn, soybeans, wheat, and rough rice) and financial instruments (such as U.S. Treasury bonds and notes, 30-Day Federal Funds, Dow Jones stock indexes and swaps). In 2004 the CBOT launched 100 oz. Gold and 5,000 oz. silver futures contracts traded exclusively through its on-line platform. The CBOT became a public company in 2005 and merged with the Chicago Mercantile Exchange in 2007 to form the CME Group, the nation's largest derivatives market. Approximately 3,000 members trade the CBOT's products through its open auction and electronic trading platforms. The CBOT has also deployed new technology to its open auction platform, creating greater efficiencies in the trading environment through the use of electronic terminals and hand-held devices. The CBOT's open-outcry trading platform is available Monday through Friday, 7:20 A.M. to 2 P.M. (financial); 9:30 A.M. to 1:15 P.M. (agricultural); and 7:20 A.M. to 3:15 P.M. (equities). The CBOT's electronic trading platform is available from 6 P.M. to 4 P.M. (financial); 6:30 P.M. to 6 A.M. (agricultural); 6:15 P.M. to 4 P.M. (equities); and 6:16 P.M. to 4 P.M. (metals). *www.cbot.com.*

CHICAGO BOARD OPTIONS EXCHANGE (CBOE) the world's largest options marketplace and the creator of listed options. Options traded at CBOE include options on equity, index, ETFs, structured products, and interest rates. The CBOE traded 911 contracts when it opened on April 26, 1973, listing call options on 16 stocks. Today it lists equity options on some 1,700 stocks and American Depositary Receipts (ADRs). The exchange launched index options in 1983 with the STANDARD & POOR'S 100 INDEX (OEX). The contract is the most actively traded index option in the world. ·The CBOE holds over 90% of the index options market, trading cash-settled index options on more than 40 indices. It also trades LEAPS, FLEX options, exchange-traded funds, structured products, and interest rate options. Among the most heavily traded index options are contracts on the Dow Jones, S&P, Russell, and NASDAQ indices. CBOE also trades a family of options on international indices as well as industry sector indices. The CBOE trades European-style cash-settled options on the yield of U.S. Treasury securities. The CBOE Volatility Index, known as the VIX, is a measure of the volatility of the U.S. equity market, using real-time S&P 500 Index option bid/ask quotes. In 2004, CBOE founded the CBOE Futures Exchange, LLC. CFE is a wholly-owned subsidiary of CBOE that operates as an all-electronic exchange, using CBOEdirect as its trading platform, with trades cleared through the Options Clearing Corporation. Trading hours: Monday through Friday, from 8:30 A.M. to 3:15 P.M. *www.cboe.com. See also* SECURITIES AND COMMODITIES EXCHANGES.

CHICAGO MERCANTILE EXCHANGE U.S. derivatives exchange founded in 1898 as the Chicago Butter and Egg Board, evolving into Chicago Mercantile Exchange in 1919. The exchange is a major global marketplace for trading futures and options on interest rates, equities, foreign exchange, commodities, and alternative investment products nearly 24 hours a day via the CME Globex electronic trading platform and on its OPEN OUTCRY trading floors. CME became a for-profit, shareholder-owned corporation in November 2000, the first U.S. financial exchange to demutualize by converting its membership interests into shares of common stock that can be traded separately from exchange trading privileges. In December 2002, CME became the first publicly traded U.S. financial exchange when shares of the parent company, Chicago Mercantile Exchange Holdings, Inc. began trading on the New York Stock Exchange. CME has greatly expanded its international presence through strategic alliances with exchanges and clearing organizations. As a result of its transaction processing agreement with the CHICAGO BOARD OF TRADE, CME's Clearing House now clears approximately 90% of all U.S. futures trading. CME has an agreement with REUTERS to bring direct foreign exchange futures trading to the interbank foreign exchange market. The CME has a mutual offset system with Singapore Exchange Derivatives Trading Ltd. (SGX). The exchange has entered into memoranda of understanding with the Shanghai Stock Exchange, the Shanghai Futures Exchange, and the China Foreign Exchange Trading System. CME is a partner in ONE CHICAGO LLC, a joint venture created to trade single-stock futures and narrow-based stock indices. *See also* SECURITIES AND COMMODITIES EXCHANGE.

CHICAGO STOCK EXCHANGE (CHX) founded in 1882, CHX is a regional exchange complementing in and adding diversity to the National Market System. CHX merged with the stock exchanges in St. Louis, Minneapolis-St. Paul, and Cleveland in 1949 to form the Midwest Stock Exchange. Ten years later, the exchange in New Orleans also joined the Midwest Stock Exchange. The Midwest Stock Exchange changed its name to the Chicago Stock Exchange in 1993. In 2005, CHX members voted to demutualize, resulting in a new corporation named CHX Holdings, Inc. that owns and operates the Chicago Stock Exchange. The majority of trades executed on the Exchange are automated and its customer base includes a wide spectrum of participants bringing together on-line, full-service, professional, and institutional customers. CHX trades stocks and exchange-traded funds that are listed on the New York Stock Exchange, American Stock Exchange, NASDAQ Stock Market, and exclusively on CHX. *www.chx.com.*

CHIEF EXECUTIVE OFFICER (CEO) officer of a firm principally responsible for the activities of a company. CEO is usually an additional title held by the CHAIRMAN OF THE BOARD, the president, or another senior officer such as a vice chairman or an executive vice president.

CHIEF FINANCIAL OFFICER (CFO) executive officer who is responsible for handling funds, signing checks, keeping financial records, and financial planning for a corporation. He or she typically has the title of vice president-finance or financial vice president in large corporations, that of treasurer or controller (also spelled comptroller) in smaller companies. Since many state laws require that a corporation have a treasurer, that title is often combined with one or more of the other financial titles.

The controllership function requires an experienced accountant to direct

internal accounting programs, including cost accounting, systems and procedures, data processing, acquisitions analysis, and financial planning. The
controller may also have internal audit responsibilities.

   The treasury function is concerned with the receipt, custody, investment,
and disbursement of corporate funds and for borrowings and the maintenance of a market for the company's securities.

CHIEF OPERATING OFFICER (COO) officer of a firm, usually the president or an executive vice president, responsible for day-to-day management.
The chief operating officer reports to the CHIEF EXECUTIVE OFFICER and may
or may not be on the board of directors (presidents typically serve as board
members). *See also* CHAIRMAN OF THE BOARD.

CHINESE HEDGE *see* REVERSE HEDGE.

CHINESE WALL imaginary barrier between the investment banking, corporate finance, and research departments of a brokerage house and the sales
and trading departments. Since the investment banking side has sensitive
knowledge of impending deals such as takeovers, new stock and bond issues,
divestitures, spinoffs and the like, it would be unfair to the general investing
public if the sales and trading side of the firm had advance knowledge of
such transactions. So several SEC and stock exchange rules mandate that a
Chinese Wall be erected to prevent premature leakage of this market-moving
information. It became law with the passage of SEC Rule 10b-5 of the Securities Exchange Act of 1934. The investment banking department uses code
names and logs of the people who have access to key information in an
attempt to keep the identities of the parties secret until the deal is publicly
announced.

CHUNNEL tunnel crossing the English Channel between Great Britain and
France. The Chunnel project took years to build and cost billions of dollars,
but was finally opened for passenger and freight traffic in 1994. The Chunnel
was built and is operated by Euro-Tunnel PLC.

CHURNING excessive trading of a client's account. Churning increases the
broker's commissions, but usually leaves the client worse off or no better off
than before. Churning is illegal under SEC and exchange rules, but is difficult
to prove.

CIRCLE underwriter's way of designating potential purchasers and amounts
of a securities issue during the REGISTRATION period, before selling is permitted. Registered representatives canvass prospective buyers and report any
interest to the underwriters, who then circle the names on their list.

CIRCUIT BREAKERS measures instituted by the major stock and commodities exchanges to halt trading temporarily in stocks and stock index futures
when the market has fallen by an amount based on specified percentage
declines in a specified period. For example, circuit breakers instituted at the
NEW YORK STOCK EXCHANGE in spring 1998 halt stock trading when the Dow
Jones Industrial Average falls 10%, 20%, and 30%, with the point settings
revised quarterly on the first day of January, April, July, and October. Circuit
breakers were originally instituted after BLACK MONDAY in 1987 and modified
following another sharp market drop in October 1989. They are subject to
change from time to time, but may include trading halts, curtailment of automated trading systems, and/or price movement limits on index futures. Their

purpose is to prevent a market free-fall by permitting a rebalancing of buy and sell orders. *See also* CURBS IN; PROGRAM TRADING.

CIRCUS SWAP currency SWAP where one side is a fixed-rate currency and the other a floating U.S. dollar LIBOR payment.

CITIZEN BONDS form of CERTIFICATELESS MUNICIPALS. Citizen bonds may be registered on stock exchanges, in which case their prices are listed in daily newspapers, unlike other municipal bonds. *See also* BOOK-ENTRY SECURITIES.

CITY CODE ON TAKEOVERS AND MERGERS *see* DAWN RAID.

CIVILIAN LABOR FORCE all members of the population aged 16 or over in the United States who are not in the military or institutions such as prisons or mental hospitals and who are either employed or are unemployed and actively seeking and available for work. Every month, the U.S. Department of Labor releases the unemployment rate, which is the percentage of the civilian labor force who are unemployed. The Labor Department also releases the percentage of the civilian non-institutional population who are employed.

CLASS
1. securities having similar features. Stocks and bonds are the two main classes; they are subdivided into various classes—for example, mortgage bonds and debentures, issues with different rates of interest, common and preferred stock, or Class A and Class B common. The different classes in a company's capitalization are itemized on its balance sheet.
2. options of the same type—put or call—with the same underlying security. A class of option having the same expiration date and EXERCISE PRICE is termed a SERIES.

CLASS A/CLASS B SHARES *see* CLASSIFIED STOCK; MUTUAL FUND SHARE CLASSES.

CLASS ACTION legal complaint filed on behalf of a group of shareholders having an identical grievance. Shareholders in a class action are typically represented by one lawyer or group of attorneys, who like this kind of business because the awards tend to be proportionate to the number of parties in the class. *See also* DERIVATIVE SUIT.

CLASSES OF MUTUAL FUND SHARES *see* MUTUAL FUND SHARE CLASSES.

CLASS OF OPTIONS *see* CLASS (2).

CLASSIFIED STOCK separation of equity into more than one CLASS of common, usually designated Class A and Class B. The distinguishing features, set forth in the corporation charter and bylaws, usually give an advantage to the Class A shares in terms of voting power, though dividend and liquidation privileges can also be involved. Classified stock is less prevalent today than in the 1920s, when it was used as a means of preserving minority control.

CLAWBACK a provision in a law or contract that limits or reverses a payment or distribution for specified reasons. For example, a limited partnership agreement might have a clawback provision requiring that when cumulative profits are tallied at expiration, distributions received by the general partner in excess of a certain percentage will be deemed excessive and returned to limited partners. Another example: In the PRIVATIZATION of an enterprise owned by a national government, the anticipated demand for shares may be so great that the underwriting agreement will contain a clawback provision that restricts foreign subscriptions until domestic demand is satisfied. A dividend clawback requires the sponsors of a project to contribute dividend payouts as equity to cover future cash deficiencies. It is also a legal measure to force individuals to give up bonuses received from a company.

CLAYTON ANTI-TRUST ACT *see* ANTITRUST LAWS.

CLEAN
Finance: free of debt, as in a clean balance sheet. In banking, corporate borrowers have traditionally been required to *clean up* for at least 30 days each year to prove their borrowings were seasonal and not required as permanent working capital.
International trade: without documents, as in clean vs. documentary drafts.
Securities: block trade that matches buy or sell orders, sparing the block positioner any inventory risk. If the transaction appears on the exchange tape, it is said to be *clean on the tape.* Sometimes such a trade is called a *natural:* "We did a natural for 80,000 XYZ common."

CLEAR
Banking: COLLECTION of funds on which a check is drawn, and payment of those funds to the holder of the check. *See also* CLEARING HOUSE FUNDS.
Finance: asset not securing a loan and not otherwise encumbered. As a verb, to clear means to make a profit: "After all expenses, we *cleared* $1 million."
Securities: COMPARISON of the details of a transaction between brokers prior to settlement; final exchange of securities for cash on delivery.

CLEARING CORPORATIONS organizations, such as the NATIONAL SECURITIES CLEARING CORPORATION (NSCC), that are exchange-affiliated and facilitate the validation, delivery, and settlement of securities transactions.

CLEARING FIRM *see* CLEARING CORPORATION.

CLEARING HOUSE FUNDS funds represented by checks or drafts that pass between banks through the FEDERAL RESERVE SYSTEM. Unlike FEDERAL FUNDS, which are drawn on reserve balances and are good the same day, clearing house funds require three days to clear. Also, funds used to settle transactions on which there is one day's FLOAT.

CLEAR TITLE title that is clear of all claims or disputed interests. It is necessary to have clear title to a piece of real estate before it can be sold by one party to another. In order to obtain a clear title, it is usually necessary to have a title search performed by a title company, which may find various clouds on the title such as an incomplete certificate of occupancy, outstanding building violations, claims by neighbors for pieces of the property, or an inaccurate survey. Once these objections have been resolved, the owner will have a clear and marketable title. *See also* BAD TITLE; CLOUD ON TITLE.

CLOB *see* CENTRAL LIMIT ORDER BOOK (CLOB).

CLONE FUND in a FAMILY OF FUNDS, new fund set up to emulate a successful existing fund.

CLOSE
1. the price of the final trade of a security at the end of a trading day.
2. the last half hour of a trading session on the exchanges.

3. in commodities trading, the period just before the end of the session when trades marked for execution AT THE CLOSE are completed.

4. to consummate a sale or agreement. In a REAL ESTATE closing, for example, rights of ownership are transferred in exchange for monetary and other considerations. At a *loan* closing, notes are signed and checks are exchanged. At the close of an *underwriting* deal, checks and securities are exchanged.

5. in accounting, the transfer of revenue and expense accounts at the end of the period—called *closing the books.*

CLOSE A POSITION to eliminate an investment from one's portfolio. The simplest example is the outright sale of a security and its delivery to the purchaser in exchange for payment. In commodities futures and options trading, traders commonly close out positions through offsetting transactions. Closing a position terminates involvement with the investment; HEDGING, though similar, requires further actions. *See also* REVERSING TRADE.

CLOSE CORPORATION PLAN plan in which the surviving holders of a CLOSED CORPORATION buy the shares of a deceased holder.

CLOSE MARKET market in which there is a narrow spread between BID and OFFER prices. Such a market is characterized by active trading and multiple competing market makers. In general, it is easier for investors to buy and sell securities and get good prices in a close market than in a wide market characterized by wide differences between bid and offer prices.

CLOSED CORPORATION corporation owned by a few people, usually management or family members. Shares have no public market. Also known as *private corporation* or *privately held corporation.*

CLOSED-END FUND type of fund that has a fixed number of shares usually listed on a major stock exchange. Unlike open-end mutual funds, closed end funds do not stand ready to issue and redeem shares on a continuous basis. They tend to have specialized portfolios of stocks, bonds, CONVERTIBLES, or combinations thereof, and may be oriented toward income, capital gains, or a combination of these objectives. Examples are the Korea Fund, which specializes in the stocks of Korean firms, and ASA Ltd., which specializes in South African gold mining stocks. Both are listed on the New York Stock Exchange. Because the managers of closed-end funds are perceived to be less responsive to profit opportunities than open-end fund managers, who must attract and retain shareholders, closed-end fund shares often sell at a discount from net asset value. *See also* DUAL-PURPOSE FUND; EXCHANGE-TRADED FUNDS (ETFs).

CLOSED-END MANAGEMENT COMPANY INVESTMENT COMPANY that operates a mutual fund with a limited number of shares outstanding. Unlike an OPEN-END MANAGEMENT COMPANY, which creates new shares to meet investor demand, a closed-end fund has a set number of shares. These are often listed on an exchange. *See also* CLOSED-END FUND.

CLOSED-END MORTGAGE mortgage-bond issue with an indenture that prohibits repayment before maturity and the repledging of the same collateral without the permission of the bondholders; also called closed mortgage. It is distinguished from an OPEN-END MORTGAGE, which is reduced by amortization and can be increased to its original amount and secured by the original mortgage.

CLOSED FUND MUTUAL FUND that has become too large and is no longer issuing shares.

CLOSED OUT liquidated the position of a client unable to meet a margin call or cover a short sale. *See also* CLOSE A POSITION.

CLOSELY HELD corporation most of whose voting stock is held by a few shareholders; differs from a CLOSED CORPORATION because enough stock is publicly held to provide a basis for trading. Also, the shares held by the controlling group are not considered likely to be available for purchase.

CLOSET INDEXING structuring a mutual fund or other managed portfolio to replicate an index and avoid the risk of underperforming it, which would reflect negatively on the manager. Closet indexers charge the regular fees for active management but deliver the same results as index funds, which are unmanaged and have much lower fees.

CLOSING BELL *see* BELL.

CLOSING COSTS expenses involved in transferring real estate from a seller to a buyer, among them lawyer's fees, survey charges, title searches and insurance, and fees to file deeds and mortgages.

CLOSING PRICE price of the last transaction completed during a day's trading session on an organized securities exchange. *See also* CLOSING RANGE.

CLOSING PURCHASE option seller's purchase of another option having the same features as an earlier one. The two options cancel each other out and thus liquidate the seller's position.

CLOSING QUOTE last bid and offer prices recorded by a specialist or market maker at the close of a trading day.

CLOSING RANGE range of prices (in commodities trading) within which an order to buy or sell a commodity can be executed during one trading day.

CLOSING SALE sale of an option having the same features (i.e., of the same series) as an option previously purchased. The two have the effect of canceling each other out. Such a transaction demonstrates the intention to liquidate the holder's position in the underlying securities upon exercise of the buy.

CLOSING TICK gauge of stock market strength that nets the number of stocks whose New York Stock Exchange closing prices were higher than their previous trades, called an UPTICK or plus tick, against the number that closed on a DOWNTICK or minus tick. When the closing tick is positive, that is, when more stocks advanced than declined in the last trade, traders say the market closed on an uptick or was "buying at the close," a bullish sign. "Selling at the close," resulting in a minus closing tick or downtick, is bearish. *See also* TRIN.

CLOSING TRIN *see* TRIN.

CLOUD ON TITLE any document, claim, unreleased lien, or encumbrance that may superficially impair or injure the title to a property or make the title doubtful because of its apparent or possible validity. Clouds on title are usually uncovered in a TITLE SEARCH. These clouds range from a recorded mortgage paid in full, but with no satisfaction of mortgage recorded, to a property sold without a spouse's release of interest, to an heir of a prior owner with a questionable claim to the property. The property owner may initiate a quitclaim deed or a quiet title proceeding to remove the cloud on title from the record. Also called *bad title.*

CMO *see* COLLATERALIZED MORTGAGE OBLIGATION (CMO).

CMO REIT specialized type of REAL ESTATE INVESTMENT TRUST (REIT) that invests in the residual cash flows of COLLATERALIZED MORTGAGE OBLIGATIONS (CMOs). CMO cash flows represent the spread (difference) between the rates paid by holders of the underlying mortgage loans and the lower, shorter term rates paid to investors in the CMOs. Spreads are subject to risks associated with interest rate levels and are considered risky investments. Also called *equity CMOs.*

COATTAIL INVESTING following on the coattails of other successful investors, usually institutions, by trading the same stocks when their actions are made public. This risky strategy assumes the research that guided the investor wearing the coat is still relevant by the time the coattail investor reads about it.

COBRA *see* CONSOLIDATED OMNIBUS BUDGET RECONCILIATION ACT (COBRA).

CODE OF PROCEDURE rules provided by FINANCIAL INDUSTRY REGULATORY AUTHORITY (FINRA) to guide its District Business Conduct Committees in hearing and adjudicating complaints filed between or against FINRA members under its Rules of Fair Practice.

CODICIL legal document that amends a will.

C.O.D. TRANSACTION *see* DELIVERY VERSUS PAYMENT.

COEFFICIENT OF DETERMINATION *see* R-SQUARE.

COINCIDENT INDICATORS economic indicators that coincide with the current pace of economic activity. The Index of Coincident Indicators is published monthly by the CONFERENCE BOARD along with the Index of LEADING INDICATORS and the Index of LAGGING INDICATORS to give the public a reading on whether the economy is expanding or contracting and at what pace. The components of the Index of Coincident Indicators are: non-farm payroll workers, personal income less transfer payments, industrial production, manufacturing, and trade sales.

COINSURANCE sharing of an insurance risk, common when claims could be of such size that it would not be prudent for one company to underwrite the whole risk. Typically, the underwriter is liable up to a stated limit, and the coinsurer's liability is for amounts above that limit.

Policies on hazards such as fire or water damage often require coverage of at least a specified coinsurance percentage of the replacement cost. Such clauses induce the owners of property to carry full coverage or close to it.

COLA acronym for *cost-of-living adjustment,* which is an annual addition to wages or benefits to compensate employees or beneficiaries for the loss of purchasing power due to inflation. Many union contracts contain a COLA providing for salary increases at or above the change in the previous year's

CONSUMER PRICE INDEX (CPI). Social Security recipients also have their monthly payments adjusted annually based on a COLA tied to the CPI.

COLD CALLING practice of making unsolicited calls to potential customers by brokers. Brokers hope to interest customers in stocks, bonds, mutual funds, financial planning, or other financial products and services in their cold calls. In some countries, such as Great Britain and parts of Canada, cold calling is severely restricted or even prohibited.

COLLAR
1. in new issue underwriting, the lowest rate acceptable to a buyer of bonds or the lowest price acceptable to the issuer. In an adjustable rate issue, refers to the maximum and minimum rates payable based on par value.
2. in ACQUISITION terminology, feature of an agreement that protects the acquirer from having to put up additional stock or cash in the event the market value of the acquirer falls between the agreement and closing.
3. in options trading, selling an OUT-OF-THE MONEY call and buying an IN-THE-MONEY put, thus limiting both upside and downside.
4. index level at which a CIRCUIT BREAKER is triggered.

COLLATERALIZE *see* ASSIGN; COLLATERAL; HYPOTHECATION.

COLLATERALIZED BOND (OR DEBT) OBLIGATION (CBO OR CDO) INVESTMENT-GRADE bond backed by a pool of variously rated bonds, including JUNK BONDS. CBOs are similar in concept to COLLATERALIZED MORTGAGE OBLIGATIONS (CMOs), but differ in that CBOs represent different degrees of credit quality rather than different maturities. Underwriters of CBOs package a large and diversified pool of bonds, including high-risk, high-yield JUNK BONDS, which is then separated into tiers, called TRANCHES. Typically, a top tier represents the higher quality collateral and pays the lowest interest rate; a middle tier is backed by riskier bonds and pays a higher rate; the bottom tier represents the lowest credit quality and, instead of receiving a fixed interest rate, receives the residual interest payments—money that is left over after the higher tiers have been paid. CBOs, like CMOs, are substantially overcollateralized and this, plus the diversification of the pool backing them, earns them investment-grade bond ratings. Holders of third-tier CBOs stand to earn high yields or less money depending on the rate of defaults in the collateral pool. CBOs provide a way for big holders of junk bonds to reduce their portfolios and for securities firms to tap a new source of buyers in the disenchanted junk bond market of the early 1990s.

COLLATERALIZED MORTGAGE OBLIGATION (CMO) mortgage-backed bond that separates mortgage pools into different *tranches* based on maturity and risk. This is accomplished by applying income (payments and prepayments of principal and interest) from mortgages in the pool in the order that the CMOs pay out. Tranches pay different rates of interest and can mature in a few months, or as long as 20 years. Issued by the Federal Home Loan Mortgage Corporation (Freddie Mac) and private issuers, CMOs are usually backed by government-guaranteed or other top-grade mortgages and have AAA ratings. In return for a lower yield, CMOs provide investors with increased security about the life of their investment compared to purchasing a whole mortgage-backed security. Even so, if mortgage rates drop sharply, causing a flood of refinancings, prepayment rates will soar and CMO tranches will be repaid before their expected maturity. CMOs are broken into different classes, called COMPANION BONDS or PLANNED AMORTIZATION CLASS (PAC) BONDS.

COLLATERAL TRUST BOND corporate debt security backed by other securities, usually held by a bank or other trustee. Such bonds are backed by collateral trust certificates and are usually issued by parent corporations that are borrowing against the securities of wholly owned subsidiaries.

COLLECTIBLE rare object collected by investors. Examples: stamps, coins, oriental rugs, antiques, baseball cards, photographs. Collectibles typically rise sharply in value during inflationary periods, when people are trying to move their assets from paper currency as an inflation hedge, then drop in value during low inflation. Collectible trading for profit can be difficult, because of limited buyers and sellers, but the Internet, notably eBay, is helping.

COLLECTION
1. presentation of a negotiable instrument such as a draft or check to the place at which it is payable. The term refers not only to check clearing and payment, but to such special banking services as foreign collections, coupon collection, and collection of returned items (bad checks).
2. referral of a past due account to specialists in collecting loans or accounts receivable, either an internal department or a private collection agency.
3. in a general financial sense, conversion of accounts receivable into cash.

COLLECTION PERIOD *see* COLLECTION RATIO.

COLLECTION RATIO ratio of a company's accounts receivable to its average daily sales. Average daily sales are obtained by dividing sales for an accounting period by the number of days in the accounting period— annual sales divided by 365, if the accounting period is a year. That result, divided into accounts receivable (an average of beginning and ending accounts receivable is more accurate), is the collection ratio—the average number of days it takes the company to convert receivables into cash. It is also called *average collection period*. *See* ACCOUNTS RECEIVABLE TURNOVER for a discussion of its significance.

COLLECTIVE BARGAINING process by which members of the labor force, operating through authorized union representatives, negotiate with their employers concerning wages, hours, working conditions, and benefits.

COLLEGE CONSTRUCTION LOAN INSURANCE ASSOCIATION federal agency established in 1987 to guarantee loans for college building programs. Informally called *Connie Lee*.

COLLEGE SAVINGS PLAN *see* QUALIFIED TUITION PROGRAM (529 PLAN).

COLTS acronym for *Continuously Offered Longer-term Securities,* 3-year to 30-year fixed rate, variable rate, or zero-coupon bonds offered on an ongoing basis by the INTERNATIONAL BANK FOR RECONSTRUCTION AND DEVELOPMENT (World Bank). Bonds finance general operations of the bank and the terms are determined by bank management at the time of each new offering.

CO-MAKER *see* MAKER.

COMBINATION
1. arrangement of options involving two long or two short positions with

different expiration dates or strike (exercise) prices. A trader could order a combination with a long call and a long put or a short call and a short put.
2. joining of competing companies in an industry to alter the competitive balance in their favor is called a combination in restraint of trade.
3. joining two or more separate businesses into a single accounting entity; also called *business combination. See also* MERGER.

COMBINATION ANNUITY *see* HYBRID ANNUITY.

COMBINATION BOND bond backed by the full faith and credit of the governmental unit issuing it as well as by revenue from the toll road, bridge, or other project financed by the bond.

COMBINATION ORDER *see* ALTERNATIVE ORDER.

COMBINATION PLAN (OR POLICY)
1. a life insurance policy with elements of both term and whole life coverage.
2. a pension plan that combines an insurance policy with some type of auxiliary fund.
3. an automobile policy with two or more insurers.

COMBINED FINANCIAL STATEMENT financial statement that brings together the assets, liabilities, net worth, and operating figures of two or more affiliated companies. In its most comprehensive form, called a combining statement, it includes columns showing each affiliate on an "alone" basis; a column "eliminating" offsetting intercompany transactions; and the resultant combined financial statement. A combined statement is distinguished from a CONSOLIDATED FINANCIAL STATEMENT of a company and subsidiaries, which must reconcile investment and capital accounts. Combined financial statements do not necessarily represent combined credit responsibility or investment strength.

COMFORT LETTER
1. independent auditor's letter, required in securities underwriting agreements, to assure that information in the registration statement and prospectus is correctly prepared and that no material changes have occurred since its preparation. It is sometimes called *cold comfort letter*—cold because the accountants do not state positively that the information is correct, only that nothing has come to their attention to indicate it is not correct.
2. letter from one to another of the parties to a legal agreement stating that certain actions not clearly covered in the agreement will—or will not—be taken. Such declarations of intent usually deal with matters that are of importance only to the two parties and do not concern other signers of the agreement.

COMMENT LETTER
1. an INDEPENDENT AUDITOR's letter to a securities UNDERWRITER satisfying a due diligence requirement.
2. SECURITIES AND EXCHANGE COMMISSION (SEC) letter requesting changes or amendments to a REGISTRATION STATEMENT.

COMMERCIAL HEDGERS companies that take positions in commodities markets in order to lock in prices at which they buy raw materials or sell their products. For instance, Alcoa might hedge its holdings of aluminum with contracts in aluminum futures, or Eastman Kodak, which must buy great quantities of silver for making film, might hedge its holdings in the silver futures market.

COMMERCIAL LOAN short-term (typically 90-day) renewable loan to finance the seasonal WORKING CAPITAL needs of a business, such as purchase of inventory or production and distribution of goods. Commercial loans—shown on the balance sheet as notes payable—rank second only to TRADE CREDIT in importance as a source of short-term financing. Interest is based on the prime rate. *See also* CLEAN.

COMMERCIAL PAPER short-term obligations with maturities ranging from 2 to 270 days issued by banks, corporations, and other borrowers to investors with temporarily idle cash. Such instruments are unsecured and usually discounted, although some are interest-bearing. They can be issued directly— *direct issuers* do it that way—or through brokers equipped to handle the enormous clerical volume involved. Issuers like commercial paper because the maturities are flexible and because the rates are usually marginally lower than bank rates. Investors—actually lenders, since commercial paper is a form of debt—like the flexibility and safety of an instrument that is issued only by top-rated concerns and is nearly always backed by bank lines of credit. Both Moody's and Standard & Poor's assign ratings to commercial paper.

COMMERCIAL PROPERTY real estate that includes income-producing property, such as office buildings, restaurants, shopping centers, hotels, industrial parks, warehouses, and factories. Commercial property usually must be zoned for business purposes. It is possible to invest in commercial property directly, or through REAL ESTATE INVESTMENT TRUSTS or REAL ESTATE LIMITED PARTNERSHIPS. Investors receive income from rents and capital appreciation if the property is sold at a profit. Investing in commercial property also entails large risks, such as nonpayment of rent by tenants or a decline in property values because of overbuilding or low demand.

COMMERCIAL WELLS oil and gas drilling sites that are productive enough to be commercially viable. A limited partnership usually syndicates a share in a commercial well.

COMMERCIAL YEAR 12 months times 30 days.

COMMINGLING
Securities: mixing customer-owned securities with those owned by a firm in its proprietary accounts. REHYPOTHECATION—the use of customers' collateral to secure brokers' loans—is permissible with customer consent, but certain securities and collateral must by law be kept separate.
Trust banking: pooling the investment funds of individual accounts, with each customer owning a share of the total fund. Similar to a MUTUAL FUND.

COMMISSION
Real estate: percentage of the selling price of the property, paid by the seller.
Securities: fee paid to a broker for executing a trade based on the number of shares traded or the dollar amount of the trade. Since 1975, when regulation ended, brokers have been free to charge whatever they like.

COMMISSION BROKER broker, usually a floor broker, who executes trades of stocks, bonds, or commodities for a commission.

COMMITMENT FEE lender's charge for contracting to hold credit available. Fee may be replaced by interest when money is borrowed or both fees and interest may be charged, as with a REVOLVING CREDIT.

COMMITTEE ON FOREIGN INVESTMENT IN THE UNITED STATES (CFIUS) committee comprising representatives from nine U.S. government agencies and chaired by the secretary of the Treasury that reviews the national security implications of foreign investment in the United States. CFIUS, pronounced "sifius," was instrumental in thwarting the attempted acquisition of UNOCAL by the state-owned China National Offshore Oil Corporation in 2005 and the Dubai Ports World's planned acquisition of P&O, the U.S. ports operator, in 2006. *See also* SOVEREIGN WEALTH FUND.

COMMITTEE ON UNIFORM SECURITIES IDENTIFICATION PROCEDURES (CUSIP) committee that assigns identifying numbers and codes for all securities. These CUSIP numbers and symbols are used when recording all buy or sell orders. For International Business Machines the CUSIP symbol is IBM and the CUSIP number is 45920010.

COMMODITIES bulk goods such as grains, metals, and foods traded on a commodities exchange or on the SPOT MARKET. *See also* SECURITIES AND COMMODITIES EXCHANGES.

COMMODITIES EXCHANGE CENTER former home of New York commodity exchanges at the former World Trade Center.

COMMODITY-BACKED BOND bond tied to the price of an underlying commodity. An investor whose bond is tied to the price of silver or gold receives interest pegged to the metal's current price, rather than a fixed dollar amount. Such a bond is meant to be a hedge against inflation, which drives up the prices of most commodities.

COMMODITY FUTURES CONTRACT FUTURES CONTRACT tied to the movement of a particular commodity. This enables contract buyers to buy a specific amount of a commodity at a specified price on a particular date in the future. The price of the contract is determined using the OPEN OUTCRY system on the floor of a commodity exchange such as the Chicago Board of Trade or the Commodity Exchange in New York. There are commodity futures contracts based on meats such as cattle and pork bellies; grains such as corn, oats, soybeans and wheat; metals such as gold, silver, and platinum; and energy products such as heating oil, natural gas, and crude oil. For a complete listing of commodity futures contracts, *see* SECURITIES AND COMMODITIES EXCHANGES.

COMMODITY FUTURES TRADING COMMISSION (CFTC) independent agency created by Congress in 1974 responsible for regulating the U.S. commodity futures and options markets. The CFTC is responsible for insuring market integrity and protecting market participants against manipulation, abusive trade practices, and fraud.

COMMODITY INDICES indices that measure either the price or performance of physical commodities, or the price of commodities as represented by the price of futures contracts that are listed on commodity exchanges. Due to the complexities of holding physical commodities, investors tend to focus on futures indices that are liquid baskets of commodities. Institutional investors prohibited from investing directly in the futures market can include commodities in their portfolios through these indices. The leading indices include the **Continuous Commodity Index (CCI),** the commodities index algorithm that, until June 17, 2005, had been known as the Reuters CRB Index. On June 20, 2005, the Reuters CRB Index was renamed the Reuters Jefferies CRB Index and given a new algorithm. The old algorithm is now published as the CCI. The CCI is made up of 17 commodities whose futures trade on U.S. exchanges. The index is a broad measure of overall commodity price trends. There are six component groups: Energy (17.6%)—crude oil, heating oil, natural gas; Grains (17.6%)—corn, wheat, soybeans; Industrials (11.8%)—copper, cotton; Precious Metals (17.6%)—gold, silver, platinum; Livestock (11.8%)—live cattle, lean hogs; Softs (23.5%)—coffee, cocoa, sugar, orange juice. Equal weighting is used for both arithmetic averaging of individual commodity months and for geometric averaging of the 17 commodity averages. As a result, no single month or commodity has undue impact on the index. Futures and options on the CCI trade on the INTERCONTINENTAL EXCHANGE (ICE). Futures are settled at contract maturity by cash payment. *www.theice.com.*

Dow Jones-AIG Commodity Index (DJ–AIGCI): This is an index composed of commodities traded on U.S. exchanges, with the exception of aluminum, nickel, and zinc, which are traded on the LONDON METAL EXCHANGE (LME). Weighting is based on liquidity, the relative amount of trading activity of a particular commodity, and the dollar-adjusted production data. All data used are averaged over a five-year period. Indexes are calculated on both an excess return and total return basis. The excess return indexes reflect the return of underlying commodity futures price movements only, whereas the total return indexes reflect the theoretical return on fully collateralized futures positions. The DJ–AIGCI is also available in EURO, YEN, Swiss franc, pound sterling, and Australian dollar denominated versions, as well as a spot price and currency hedged versions. There are nine subindexes representing the index's major sectors: Precious Metals, Industrial Metals, Energy, Grains, Livestock, Petroleum, Softs, Agriculture, and ExEnergy. To ensure that commodity exposure is diversified, no single commodity (e.g., natural gas or silver) may constitute more than 15% of the index or less than 2% of the index. Annual rebalancing and reweighting ensure that diversity is maintained over time. The indexes underlie several exchange-traded products, including futures contracts at the CBOT and EUREX. *djindexes.com.*

S&P GSCI: a composite index of commodity sector returns, representing an unleveraged, long-only investment in commodity futures that is broadly diversified. The index was purchased by Standard & Poor's from Goldman Sachs in 2007. Inclusion is based on liquidity and world production weight. Each component is weighted by its respective world production quantities in the last five years, enabling the S&P GSCI to respond to world economic growth. The total number of constituent commodities, as well as the number in each sector, is adjusted for liquidity in the underlying futures markets, just as the dollar weights and index values are adjusted daily, based on real-time prices. As of April 9, 2009, the index consisted of 25 commodities from all commodity sectors: Energy; Industrial Metals; Precious Metals; Agricultural;

and Livestock. Following are the weightings for these groups and their components: Energy (66.77%)—crude oil (35.90%), Brent crude (12.94%), unleaded gasoline (4.65%), heating oil (4.20%), gas oil (4.48%), natural gas (4.60%); Industrial Metals (7.13%)—aluminum (2.39%), copper (3.12%), lead (0.43%), nickel (0.59%), zinc (0.60%); Precious Metals (3.43%)—gold (3.09%), silver (0.33%); Agriculture (16.77%)—wheat (4.19%), Kansas wheat (0.91%), corn (4.47%), soybeans (3.11%), cotton (0.98%), sugar (1.85%), coffee (0.86%), cocoa (0.40%); Livestock (5.03%)—feeder cattle (0.64%), live cattle (3.22%), lean hogs (2.05%), biofuel (0.05%). The index has a rolling yield, reflecting expiration and rolling forward of underlying futures contracts. Three S&P GSCI indices are published. The S&P GSCI Excess Return Index measures the returns accrued from investing in uncollateralized nearby commodity futures. The S&P GSCI Total Return Index measures the return from investing in fully collateralized nearby commodity futures. The S&P GSCI Spot Index measures the level of nearby commodity prices. Futures and options on the S&P GSCI are traded on the CHICAGO MERCANTILE EXCHANGE. *www.spgsci.com.*

COMMODITY PAPER inventory loans or advances secured by commodities. If the commodities are in transit, a bill of lading is executed by a common carrier. If they are in storage, a trust receipt acknowledges that they are held and that proceeds from their sale will be transmitted to the lender; a warehouse receipt lists the goods.

COMMODITY POOL *see* POOL (INVESTMENTS).

COMMODITY RESEARCH BUREAU (CRB) world's leading commodities and futures research, data, and analysis firm, founded in 1934 and based in Chicago, Illinois. Its flagship index, reformulated and renamed (from CRB Commodity Index) in 2005, is the *Continuous Commodity Index (CCI),* an equally weighted index of the following 17 commodities: corn, wheat, soybeans, live cattle, lean hogs, gold, silver, copper, cocoa, coffee, sugar #11, cotton, orange juice, platinum, crude oil, heating oil, and natural gas. The CCI should not be confused with the Reuters/Jeffries-CRB Futures Price Index, which is less representative and 33% oil weighted.

COMMODITY TRADING ADVISOR (CTA) individual or organization that directly or indirectly advises others as to the value or advisability of buying or selling FUTURES CONTACTS or OPTIONS. Indirect advice includes exercising trading authority over a customer's account. Registered CTAs are registered with the COMMODITIES FUTURES TRADING COMMISSION (CFTA) and are generally required to be members of the NATIONAL FUTURES ASSOCIATION (NFA).

COMMON MARKET *see* EUROPEAN ECONOMIC COMMUNITY.

COMMON SIZE STATEMENT presentation showing BALANCE SHEET and PROFIT AND LOSS STATEMENT as percentages of total ASSETS and sales, respectively, rather than (or in addition to) dollars. Common size analysis, which is also called *vertical analysis,* facilitates the comparison of one period to another and helps identify trends. Also called *one hundred percent statement.*

COMMON STOCK units of ownership of a public corporation. Owners typically are entitled to vote on the selection of directors and other important matters as well as to receive dividends on their holdings. In the event that a corporation is liquidated, the claims of secured and unsecured creditors and owners of bonds and preferred stock take precedence over the claims of those who own common stock. For the most part, however, common stock has more potential for appreciation. *See also* CAPITAL STOCK.

COMMON STOCK EQUIVALENT preferred stock or bond convertible into common stock, or warrant to purchase common stock at a specified price or discount from market price. Common stock equivalents represent potential dilution of existing common shareholder's equity, and their conversion or exercise is assumed in calculating fully diluted earnings per share. *See also* ANTIDILUTIVE; FULLY DILUTED EARNINGS PER SHARE.

COMMON STOCK FUND MUTUAL FUND that invests only in common stocks.

COMMON STOCK RATIO percentage of total capitalization represented by common stock. From a creditor's standpoint a high ratio represents a margin of safety in the event of LIQUIDATION. From an investor's standpoint, however, a high ratio can mean a lack of *leverage*. What the ratio should be depends largely on the stability of earnings. Electric utilities can operate with low ratios because their earnings are stable. As a general rule, when an industrial company's stock ratio is below 30%, analysts check on earnings stability and fixed charge coverage in bad times as well as good.

COMMUNITY PROPERTY property and income accumulated by a married couple and belonging to them jointly. The two have equal rights to the income from stocks, bonds, and real estate, as well as to the appreciated value of those assets.

COMMUNITY REINVESTMENT ACT OF 1977 law passed in 1977 and implemented by Federal Reserve Board Regulation BB, revised in 1995, encouraging depository institutions to help meet the credit needs of communities in which they operate, including low- and moderate-income neighborhoods. The Act requires federal agencies responsible for supervising such institutions to evaluate their compliance periodically and to take their records into account in considering applications for deposit facilities. *See also* FINANCIAL HOLDING COMPANY.

COMPANION BONDS one class of a COLLATERALIZED MORTGAGE OBLIGATION (CMO) which is paid off first when the underlying mortgages are prepaid as interest rates fall. When interest rates rise and there are fewer prepayments, the principal on companion bonds will be prepaid more slowly. Companion bonds therefore absorb most of the prepayment risk inherent in a CMO, and are therefore more volatile. In return, they pay higher yields than the other class within a CMO, called PLANNED AMORTIZATION CLASS (PAC) bonds.

COMPANY organization engaged in business as a proprietorship, partnership, corporation, or other form of enterprise. Originally, a firm made up of a group of people as distinguished from a sole proprietorship. However, since few proprietorships owe their existence exclusively to one person, the term now applies to proprietorships as well.

COMPANY DOCTOR executive, usually recruited from the outside, specialized in corporate turnarounds.

COMPARATIVE STATEMENTS financial statements covering different dates but prepared consistently and therefore lending themselves to comparative analysis, as accounting convention requires. Comparative figures reveal trends in a company's financial development and permit insight into the dynamics behind static balance sheet figures.

COMPARISON
1. short for *comparison ticket*, a memorandum exchanged prior to settlement by two brokers in order to confirm the details of a transaction to which they were parties. Also called comparison sheet.
2. verification of collateral held against a loan, by exchange of information between two brokers or between a broker and a bank.

COMPENSATING BALANCE or COMPENSATORY BALANCE average balance required by a bank for holding credit available. The more or less standard requirement for a bank line of credit, for example, is 10% of the line plus an additional 10% of the borrowings. Compensating balances increase the effective rate of interest on borrowings.

COMPETITIVE BID sealed bid, containing price and terms, submitted by a prospective underwriter to an issuer, who awards the contract to the bidder with the best price and terms. Many municipalities and virtually all railroads and public utilities use this bid system. Industrial corporations generally prefer NEGOTIATED UNDERWRITING on stock issues but do sometimes resort to competitive bidding in selecting underwriters for bond issues.

COMPETITIVE TRADER *see* REGISTERED COMPETITIVE TRADER.

COMPLETE AUDIT usually the same as an unqualified audit, because it is so thoroughly executed that the auditor's only reservations have to do with unobtainable facts. A complete audit examines the system of internal control and the details of the books of account, including subsidiary records and supporting documents. This is done with an eye to locality, mathematical accuracy, accountability, and the application of accepted accounting principles.

COMPLETED CONTRACT METHOD accounting method whereby revenues and expenses (and therefore taxes) on long-term contracts, such as government defense contracts, are recognized in the year the contract is concluded, except that losses are recognized in the year they are forecast. This method differs from the *percentage-of-completion method,* where sales and costs are recognized each year based on the value of the work performed. Under the TAX REFORM ACT OF 1986, manufacturers with long-term contracts must elect either the latter method or the *percentage-of-completion capitalized cost method,* requiring that 40% of the contract be included under the percentage-of-completion method and 60% under the taxpayer's normal accounting method.

COMPLETION PROGRAM oil and gas limited partnership that takes over drilling when oil is known to exist in commercial quantities. A completion program is a conservative way to profit from oil and gas drilling, but without the capital gains potential of exploratory wildcat drilling programs.

COMPLIANCE DEPARTMENT department set up by brokers and all organized stock exchanges to oversee market activity and make sure that trading and other activities comply with Securities and Exchange Commission and exchange regulations. A company that does not adhere to the rules can be delisted, and a trader or brokerage firm that violates the rules can be barred from trading.

COMPOSITE
1. in financial analysis, a BALANCE SHEET and/or PROFIT AND LOSS STATEMENT representing averages of the accounts of a number of companies in the same industry. The accounts of a particular company can thus be compared with a composite to identify abnormalities.
2. an INDEX or AVERAGE combining other indexes or averages. For example, the NEW YORK STOCK EXCHANGE Composite Index combines the NYSE Finance, Industrials, Transportation, and Utilities indexes.

COMPOSITE TAPE *see* TAPE.

COMPOSITE QUOTATION SYSTEM (CQS) *see* CONSOLIDATED QUOTATION SYSTEM (CQS).

COMPOUND ANNUAL RETURN investment return, discounted retroactively from a cumulative figure, at which money, compounded annually, would reach the cumulative total. Also called INTERNAL RATE OF RETURN.

COMPOUND ANNUAL GROWTH RATE (CAGR) Same as COMPOUND GROWTH RATE.

COMPOUND ARBITRAGE ARBITRAGE involving four or more markets.

COMPOUND GROWTH RATE rate of growth of a number, compounded over several years. Securities analysts check a company's compound growth rate of profits for five years to see the long-term trend.

COMPOUND INTEREST interest earned on principal plus interest that was earned earlier. If $100 is deposited in a bank account at 10%, the depositor will be credited with $110 at the end of the first year and $121 at the end of the second year. That extra $1, which was earned on the $10 interest from the first year, is the compound interest. This example involves interest compounded annually: interest can also be compounded on a daily, quarterly, half-yearly, or other basis. *See also* COMPOUND ANNUAL RETURN.

COMPOUND OPTION an OPTION on an option.

COMPREHENSIVE INSURANCE automobile insurance covering losses due to damage or theft, but not covering collision.

COMPTROLLER OF THE CURRENCY federal official, appointed by the President and confirmed by the Senate, who is responsible for chartering, examining, supervising, and liquidating all national banks. In response to the *comptroller's call,* national banks are required to submit *call reports* of their financial activities at least four times a year and to publish them in local newspapers. National banks can be declared insolvent only by the Comptroller of the Currency.

COMPUTERIZED MARKET TIMING SYSTEM system of picking buy and sell signals that puts together voluminous trading data in search of patterns and trends. Often, changes in the direction of moving average lines form the basis for buy and sell recommendations. These systems, commonly used by commodity funds and by services that switch between mutual funds, tend to work well when markets are moving steadily up or down, but not in trendless markets.

CONCENTRATED FUND *see* NONDIVERSIFIED MANAGEMENT COMPANY.

CONCERT PARTY person ACTING IN CONCERT.

CONCESSION
1. SELLING GROUP's per-share or per-bond compensation.
2. right, usually granted by a government entity, to use property for a specified purpose, such as a service station on a highway.

CONDEMNATION legal seizure of private property by a public authority for public use. Using the powers and legal procedures of EMINENT DOMAIN, a state, city, or town may condemn a property owner's home to make way for a highway, school, park, hospital, public housing project, parking facility, or other public project. The homeowners must give up the property even if they do not want to, and in return they must be compensated at fair market value by the public authority.

CONDITIONAL CALL OPTIONS form of CALL PROTECTION available to holders of some HIGH-YIELD BONDS. In the event the bond is called, the issuing corporation is obligated to substitute a non-callable bond having the same life and terms as the bond that is called.

CONDITIONAL ORDER order to buy or sell stock that, unlike a MARKET ORDER, has specified conditions. Examples are LIMIT ORDERS and STOP ORDERS, which have different variations.

CONDITIONAL RATING bond RATING conditional on the completion of a specified circumstance.

CONDITIONAL SALES CONTRACT (OR AGREEMENT) sales (as opposed to LEASE) contract where the buyer takes possession but ownership is not transferred until the terms of payment have been met.

CONDOMINIUM form of real estate ownership in which individual residents hold a deed and title to their houses or apartments and pay a maintenance fee to a management company for the upkeep of common property such as grounds, lobbies, and elevators as well as for other amenities. Condominium owners pay real estate taxes on their units and can sublet or sell as they wish. Some real estate limited partnerships specialize in converting rental property into condominiums. *See also* COOPERATIVE.

CONDOR options spread using four contracts, either puts or calls, with the same underlying security and the same expiration dates, two of which are LONG LEGS and have consecutive exercise prices, the other two being short legs priced immediately higher and lower respectively than the first two. The image of a long position surrounded by two shorts suggests a condor's body and wings.

CONDUIT IRA *see* CONDUIT THEORY.

CONDUIT THEORY theory regulating investment companies such as REAL ESTATE INVESTMENT TRUSTS and MUTUAL FUNDS holding that since such companies are pure conduits for all capital gains, dividends, and interest to be passed through to shareholders, the investment company should not be taxed at the corporate level. As long as the investment company adheres to certain regulations, shareholders are therefore taxed only once—at the individual level—on income and capital gains. In contrast, shareholders of corporations are taxed twice: once at the corporate level in the form of corporate income taxes and once at the individual level in the form of individual income taxes on all dividends paid by the corporation. The same concept defines a *conduit IRA,* where funds in a qualified retirement plan with one employer can be held without tax consequences pending their ROLLOVER into a new employer's QUALIFIED PLAN OR TRUST.

CONFERENCE BOARD, THE New York City-based, not-for-profit, membership and research organization that sponsors economic surveys and publishes such useful statistical information as the monthly CONSUMER CONFIDENCE INDEX and the *Help-Wanted Index,* which is based on the number of help-wanted ads in 51 newspapers in major employment areas nationwide. *See also* LEADING INDICATORS.

CONFIDENCE INDEX (OR INDICATOR) any of several indicators that measure consumers' or investors' optimism or pessimism with respect to the economy or the stock market. High consumer/investor confidence is generally bullish for the economy and the market, although TECHNICAL ANALYSIS practitioners may see it differently, pointing out that contractions follow expansions and vice versa. *See also* BARRON'S CONFIDENCE INDEX; CONSUMER CONFIDENCE INDEX; MISERY INDEX; SENTIMENT INDICATORS.

CONFIDENCE LEVEL in risk analysis, a statistical calculation measuring the validity of a correlation or the certainty of a forecast. For investors in a START-UP, for example, the confidence level is a measure of the likelihood that goals described in the BUSINESS PLAN will be met.

CONFIRMATION
1. formal memorandum from a broker to a client giving details of a securities transaction. When a broker acts as a dealer, the confirmation must disclose that fact to the customer.
2. document sent by a company's auditor to its customers and suppliers requesting verification of the book amounts of receivables and payables. *Positive confirmations* request that every balance be confirmed, whereas *negative confirmations* request a reply only if an error exists.

CONFORMED COPY copy of an original document with the essential legal features, such as the signature and seal, being typed or indicated in writing.

CONFORMING LOANS mortgage loans that meet the qualifications of FREDDIE MAC or FANNIE MAE, which buy them from lenders and then issue PASS-THROUGH SECURITIES.

CONGLOMERATE corporation composed of companies in a variety of businesses. Conglomerates were popular in the 1960s, when they were thought to provide better management and sounder financial backing, and therefore to generate more profit, than small independent companies. However, some conglomerates became so complex that they were difficult to manage. In the 1980s and 1990s, many conglomerates sold off divisions and concentrated on a few core businesses. Analysts generally consider stocks of conglomerates difficult to evaluate because they are involved in so many unrelated businesses.

CONNIE LEE nickname for COLLEGE CONSTRUCTION LOAN INSURANCE ASSOCIATION.

CONSENSUS FORECAST EARNINGS PER SHARE prediction representing the collective judgment of SECURITIES ANALYSTS following a stock, who are canvassed by research services such as FIRST CALL and ZACKS ESTIMATE SYSTEM.

CONSERVATOR individual appointed by a court to manage the property of a person who lacks the capacity to manage his own property. A conservator may be charged with liquidating the assets of a business in bankruptcy, or may have to take control of the personal finances of an incompetent individual who needs to be protected by the court.

CONSIDERATION something of value that one party gives to another in exchange for a promise or act. In law, a requirement of valid contracts. A consideration can be in the form of money, commodities, or personal services; in many industries the forms have become standardized.

CONSOL British term for a PERPETUAL BOND.

CONSOLIDATED FINANCIAL STATEMENT financial statement that brings together all assets, liabilities, and operating accounts of a parent company and its subsidiaries. *See also* COMBINED FINANCIAL STATEMENT.

CONSOLIDATED MORTGAGE BOND bond issue that covers several units of property and may refinance separate mortgages on these properties. The consolidated mortgage with a single coupon rate is a traditional form of financing for railroads because it is economical to combine many properties in one agreement.

CONSOLIDATED OMNIBUS BUDGET RECONCILIATION ACT (COBRA) federal legislation under which group health plans sponsored by employers with 20 or more employees must offer continuation of coverage to employees who leave their jobs, voluntarily or otherwise, and their dependents. The employee must pay the entire premium up to 102% of the cost of coverage extended by COBRA. Depending on circumstances, COBRA permits employees to extend their coverage for up to 18 months and that of surviving dependents for up to 36 months. COBRA was designed to help former employees maintain health insurance coverage at group rates which may otherwise be unobtainable or unaffordable.

CONSOLIDATED QUOTATION SYSTEM (CQS) electronic service providing quotations on issues traded on the NEW YORK STOCK EXCHANGE, the AMERICAN STOCK EXCHANGE, regional stock exchanges, and the NASDAQ STOCK MARKET. NASDAQ reprocesses the information and provides it to subscribers to its Composite Quotation System, also known by the initials CQS.

CONSOLIDATED TAPE combined tapes of the New York Stock Exchange and the American Stock Exchange. It became operative in June 1975. Network A covers NYSE-listed securities and identifies the originating market. Network B does the same for Amex-listed securities and also reports on securities listed on regional exchanges.

CONSOLIDATED TAX RETURN return combining the reports of the companies in what the tax law defines as an affiliated group. A firm is part of an affiliated group if it is at least 80% owned by a parent or other inclusive corporation. "Owned" refers to voting stock. (Before the TAX REFORM ACT OF 1986 it also included nonvoting stock.)

CONSOLIDATION LOAN loan that combines and refinances other loans or debt. It is normally an installment loan designed to reduce the dollar amount of an individual's monthly payments.

CONSORTIUM group of companies formed to promote a common objective or engage in a project of benefit to all the members. The relationship normally entails cooperation and a sharing of resources, sometimes even common ownership.

CONSTANT DOLLAR PLAN method of accumulating assets by investing a fixed amount of dollars in securities at set intervals. The investor buys more shares when the price is low and fewer shares when the price is high; the overall cost is lower than it would be if a constant number of shares were bought at set intervals. Also called *dollar cost averaging.*

CONSTANT DOLLARS dollars of a base year, used as a gauge in adjusting the dollars of other years in order to ascertain actual purchasing power. Denoted as C$ by the FINANCIAL ACCOUNTING STANDARDS BOARD (FASB), which defines constant dollars as hypothetical units of general purchasing power.

CONSTANT RATIO PLAN type of FORMULA INVESTING whereby a predetermined ratio is maintained between stock and FIXED INCOME INVESTMENTS through periodic adjustments. For example, an investor with $200,000 and a 50-50 formula might start out with $100,000 in stock and $100,000 in bonds. If the stock increased in value to $150,000 and the bonds remained unchanged over a given adjustment period, the investor would restore the ratio at $125,000–$125,000 by selling $25,000 of stock and buying $25,000 of bonds.

CONSTANT YIELD METHOD method of allocating annual interest on a ZERO-COUPON SECURITY for income tax purposes. IRS Publication 1212 explains how to figure taxable interest on such ORIGINAL ISSUE DISCOUNT securities.

CONSTRUCTION LOAN short-term real estate loan to finance building costs. The funds are disbursed as needed or in accordance with a prearranged plan, and the money is repaid on completion of the project, usually from the proceeds of a mortgage loan. The rate is normally higher than prime, and there is usually an origination fee. The effective yield on these loans tends to be high, and the lender has a security interest in the real property.

CONSTRUCTION LOAN NOTE (CLN) note issued by a municipality to finance the construction of multi-family housing projects. The notes, which typically mature in three years or less, are normally repaid out of the proceeds of a long-term bond issue.

CONSTRUCTIVE RECEIPT term used by Internal Revenue Service for the date when a taxpayer received dividends or other income. IRS rules say that constructive receipt of income is established if the taxpayer has the right to claim it, whether or not the choice is exercised. For instance, if a bond pays interest on December 29, the taxpayer must report the income in that tax year and not in the following year.

CONSUMER CONFIDENCE INDEX indicator, published monthly by the CONFERENCE BOARD, of consumers' attitudes and buying intentions. It surveys

5,000 U.S. households, using 1985 as a base year with an index of 100. Subsequent periods are recorded as a percentage change. *See also* CONFIDENCE INDEX.

CONSUMER CREDIT debt assumed by consumers for purposes other than home mortgages. Interest on consumer loans had been 100% deductible until the TAX REFORM ACT OF 1986 mandated that the deduction be phased out by 1991. Consumers can borrow through credit cards, lines of credit, loans against insurance policies, and many other methods. The Federal Reserve Board releases the amount of outstanding consumer credit on a monthly basis.

CONSUMER CREDIT PROTECTION ACT OF 1968 landmark federal legislation establishing rules of disclosure that lenders must observe in dealings with borrowers. The act stipulates that consumers be told annual percentage rates, potential total cost, and any special loan terms. The act, enforced by the Federal Reserve Bank, is also known as the *Truth in Lending Act.*

CONSUMER DEBENTURE investment note issued by a financial institution and marketed directly to the public. Consumer debentures were a popular means of raising lendable funds for banks during tight money periods prior to deregulation, since these instruments, unlike certificates of deposit, could compete freely with other money-market investments in a high-rate market.

CONSUMER DURABLES products bought by consumers that are expected to last three years or more. These include automobiles, appliances, boats, and furniture. Economists look at the trend in consumer expenditure on durables as an important indicator of the strength of the economy, since consumers need confidence to make such large and expensive purchases. Stock market analysts also classify companies that produce appliances, furniture, cars, and similar items as consumer durables manufacturers, contrasting them with consumer non-durables manufacturers, which make consumable items such as food or drugs.

CONSUMER FINANCE COMPANY *see* FINANCE COMPANY.

CONSUMER GOODS goods bought for personal or household use, as distinguished from CAPITAL GOODS or *producer's goods,* which are used to produce other goods. The general economic meaning of consumer goods encompasses consumer services. Thus the *market basket* on which the CONSUMER PRICE INDEX is based includes clothing, food, and other goods as well as utilities, entertainment, and other services.

CONSUMER INTEREST interest paid on consumer loans. Consumer interest is paid on credit cards, bank lines of credit, retail purchases, car and boat loans, and educational loans. Since the end of 1991, such interest is no longer deductible for tax purposes, based on provisions of the TAX REFORM ACT OF 1986. That tax law distinguished nondeductible consumer interest from other forms of interest which can be deductible, including business interest, investment interest, and mortgage-related interest.

CONSUMER PRICE INDEX (CPI) measures the average monthly change for a market basket of goods and services bought by a typical consumer, including food, transportation, shelter, utilities, clothing, medical care, and entertainment. The CPI, published by the Bureau of Labor Statistics in the Department of Labor, uses the years 1982–1984 as a reference base. It is widely used as a cost-of-living benchmark to adjust Social Security payments and other payment schedules, union contracts, and tax brackets. Also known as the cost-of-living index, it is a common indicator of price inflation.

CONSUMER STOCK *see* SECTOR ROTATION.

CONSUMPTION TAX a tax on what people spend instead of what they earn, such as a SALES TAX, a VALUE-ADDED TAX (VAT), or a consumption tax system that, similar to an INDIVIDUAL RETIREMENT ACCOUNT (IRA), excludes from taxation all income that is saved, then taxes withdrawals from savings. Advocates of a consumption tax as a replacement for the income tax favor the consumption tax system approach, arguing that the gains from additional saving and investment would offset the higher tax rate necessitated by the removal of saved income from the tax base.

CONTAGION the spreading of an economic crisis from one geographical area to another. For example, the "Asian contagion" in the late 1990s spread from the Pacific Rim to parts of South America. Contagion can also refer to a higher than normal correlation among returns from different market investments in the areas affected by economic crisis. *See also* DECOUPLING.

CONTANGO
1. pricing situation in which futures prices get progressively higher as maturities get progressively longer, creating negative spreads as contracts go farther out. The increases reflect carrying costs, including storage, financing, and insurance. The reverse condition, an inverted market, is termed BACKWARDATION.
2. in finance, the costs that must be taken into account in analyses involving forecasts.

CONTINGENT BENEFICIARY person named in an insurance policy to receive the policy benefits if the primary beneficiary dies before the benefits become payable.

CONTINGENT CONVERTIBLE BONDS *see* COCO BONDS.

CONTINGENT DEFERRED SALES LOAD sales charge levied by a mutual fund if a customer sells fund shares within a specified number of years. Instead of charging a traditional FRONT END LOAD of 5%, for example, a brokerage firm may offer the same fund with a contingent deferred sales load. Customers who sell the fund within the first year pay a 5% load. In the second year, the charge would be 4%. Each year the charge declines by one percentage point until there is no fee for selling fund shares after the fifth year. Also called *back-end load. See also* MUTUAL FUND SHARE CLASSES.

CONTINGENT IMMUNIZATION PORTFOLIO management policy requiring that active management be replaced by an immunization strategy when returns decline to a specified level. Immunization occurs when the DURATIONS of the assets and liabilities of a portfolio are the same.

CONTINGENT LIABILITIES
Banking: potential obligation of a guarantor or accommodation endorser; or the position of a customer who opens a letter of credit and whose account

will be charged if a draft is presented. The bank's own ultimate responsibility for letters of credit and other commitments, individually and collectively, is its contingent liability.

Corporate reports: pending lawsuits, judgments under appeal, disputed claims, and the like, representing potential financial liability.

CONTINGENT ORDER securities order whose execution depends on the execution of another order; for example, a sell order and a buy order with prices stipulated. Where the purpose is to effect a swap, a price difference might be stipulated as a condition of the order's execution. Generally, brokers discourage these orders, favoring firm instructions.

CONTINGENT PENSION LIABILITY the liability of a firm to its PENSION PLAN participants. The EMPLOYEE RETIREMENT INCOME SECURITY ACT (ERISA) limits this liability to 39% of the firm's NET WORTH.

CONTINUING EDUCATION PROGRAM any formal educational program designed to keep professionals abreast of new developments and that, in some cases, may be required to maintain certifications. The FINANCIAL INDUSTRY REGULATORY AUTHORITY (FINRA) has a continuing education program for securities professionals that has two elements: the regulatory element requires ongoing periodic training in applicable rules and laws; the firm element, in job- and product-related areas.

CONTINUOUS COMMODITY INDEX (CCI) *see* COMMODITY RESEARCH BUREAU (CRB).

CONTINUOUS INVENTORY *see* PERPETUAL INVENTORY.

CONTINUOUS NET SETTLEMENT (CNS) method of securities clearing and settlement that eliminates multiple fails in the same securities. This is accomplished by using a clearing house, such as the National Securities Clearing Corporation, and a depository, such as DEPOSITORY TRUST COMPANY, to match transactions to securities available in the firm's position, resulting in one net receive or deliver position at the end of the day. By including the previous day's fail position in the next day's selling trades, the firm's position is always up-to-date and money settlement or withdrawals can be made at any time with the clearing house. The alternative to CNS is window settlement, where the seller delivers securities to the buyer's cashier and receives payment.

CONTRA BROKER broker on the opposite side—the buy side of a sell order or the sell side of a buy order.

CONTRACT in general, agreement by which rights or acts are exchanged for lawful consideration. To be valid, it must be entered into by competent parties, must cover a legal and moral transaction, must possess mutuality, and must represent a meeting of minds. Countless transactions in finance and investments are covered by contracts.

CONTRACT MARKET market in which OPTIONS and FUTURES CONTRACTS are traded. *See also* FUTURES MARKET.

CONTRACTUAL PLAN plan by which fixed dollar amounts of mutual fund shares are accumulated through periodic investments for 10 or 15 years. The legal vehicle for such investments is the *plan company* or *participating unit investment trust,* a selling organization operating on behalf of the fund's underwriter. The plan company must be registered with the Securities and Exchange Commission, as the underlying fund must be, so the investor receives two prospectuses. Investors in these plans commonly receive other benefits in exchange for their fixed periodic payments, such as decreasing term life insurance. *See also* FRONT-END LOAD.

CONTRARIAN investor who does the opposite of what most investors are doing at any particular time. According to contrarian opinion, if everyone is certain that something is about to happen, it won't. This is because most people who say the market is going up are fully invested and have no additional purchasing power, which means the market is at its peak. When people predict decline they have already sold out, so the market can only go up. Some mutual funds follow a contrarian investment strategy, and some investment advisers suggest only out-of-favor securities, whose price/earnings ratio is lower than the rest of the market or industry.

CONTRIBUTED CAPITAL payments made in cash or property to a corporation by its stockholders either to buy capital stock, to pay an assessment on the capital stock, or as a gift. Also called *paid-in capital.* The contributed or paid-in capital of a corporation is made up of capital stock and capital (or contributed) surplus, which is contributed (or paid-in) capital in excess of PAR value or STATED VALUE. Donated capital and DONATED SURPLUS are freely given forms of contributed (paid-in) capital, but DONATED STOCK refers to fully paid (previously issued) capital stock that is given as a gift to the issuing corporation.

CONTROLLED AND RESTRICTED STOCK *see* LETTER SECURITY.

CONTROLLED COMMODITIES commodities regulated by the Commodities Exchange Act of 1936, which set up trading rules for futures in commodities markets in order to prevent fraud and manipulation.

CONTROLLED FOREIGN CORPORATION an ALIEN CORPORATION whose voting stock is more than 50% owned by U.S. shareholders, each of which owns at least 10% of the voting power.

CONTROLLED WILDCAT DRILLING drilling for oil and gas in an area adjacent to but outside the limits of a proven field. Also known as a *field extension.* Limited partnerships drilling in this area take greater risks than those drilling in areas of proven energy reserves, but the rewards can be considerable if oil is found.

CONTROLLER or COMPTROLLER chief accountant of a company. In small companies the controller may also serve as treasurer. In a brokerage firm, the controller prepares financial reports, supervises internal audits, and is responsible for compliance with Securities and Exchange Commission regulations.

CONTROLLING INTEREST ownership of more than 50% of a corporation's voting shares. A much smaller interest, owned individually or by a group in combination, can be controlling if the other shares are widely dispersed and not actively voted.

CONTROL STOCK shares owned by holders who have a CONTROLLING INTEREST.

CONVENTIONAL MORTGAGE residential mortgage loan, usually from a bank or savings and loan association, with a fixed rate and term. It is repayable in fixed monthly payments over a period usually 30 years or less, secured by real property, and not insured by the FEDERAL HOUSING ADMINISTRATION or guaranteed by the Veterans Administration.

CONVENTIONAL OPTION put or call contract arranged off the trading floor of a listed exchange and not traded regularly. It was commonplace when options were banned on certain exchanges, but is now rare.

CONVENTIONAL PASS-THROUGH a PASS-THROUGH SECURITY that, unlike an *agency pass-through,* is backed by mortgages not guaranteed by U.S. government agencies. Also called *private label pass-through.*

CONVERGENCE movement of the price of a futures contract toward the price of the underlying CASH COMMODITY. At the start of the contract price is higher because of the time value. But as the contract nears expiration the futures price and the cash price converge.

CONVERSION
1. exchange of a convertible security such as a bond into a fixed number of shares of the issuing corporation's common stock.
2. transfer of mutual-fund shares without charge from one fund to another fund in a single family; also known as fund switching.
3. in insurance, switch from short-term to permanent life insurance.

CONVERSION FEATURE right to convert a particular holding to another form of holding, such as the SWITCHING within a mutual fund family, the right to convert certain preferred stock or bonds to common stock, or the right to switch from one type of insurance policy to another. *See also* CONVERTIBLES.

CONVERSION PARITY common-stock price at which a convertible security can become exchangeable for common shares of equal value.

CONVERSION PREMIUM amount by which the price of a convertible tops the market price of the underlying stock. If a stock is trading at $50 and the bond convertible at $45 is trading at $50, the premium is $5. If the premium is high the bond trades like any fixed income bond. If the premium is low the bond trades like a stock.

CONVERSION PRICE the dollar value at which convertible bonds, debentures, or preferred stock can be converted into common stock, as announced when the convertible is issued.

CONVERSION RATIO relationship that determines how many shares of common stock will be received in exchange for each convertible bond or preferred share when the conversion takes place. It is determined at the time of issue and is expressed either as a ratio or as a conversion price from which the ratio can be figured by dividing the par value of the convertible by the conversion price. The indentures of most convertible securities contain an antidilution clause whereby the conversion ratio may be raised (or the conversion price lowered) by the percentage amount of any stock dividend or split, to protect the convertible holder against dilution.

CONVERSION VALUE
In general: value created by changing from one form to another. For example, converting rental property to condominiums adds to the value of the property.

Convertibles: the price at which the exchange can be made for common stock.

CONVERTIBLE ADJUSTABLE PREFERRED STOCK *see* CAPS.

CONVERTIBLE CURRENCY currency that can be readily exchanged for other currencies.

CONVERTIBLE EUROBOND EUROBOND convertible into COMMON STOCK or another corporate asset, usually by exercising an attached SUBSCRIPTION WARRANT.

CONVERTIBLE 100 index compiled by Goldman Sachs comprising the 100 CONVERTIBLE SECURITIES most popular with INSTITUTIONAL INVESTORS.

CONVERTIBILITY in foreign exchange, ability to exchange money for other currencies or for gold without government restriction. Also said of a currency that foreign residents will accept as payment for goods or services. *See also* HARD MONEY (HARD CURRENCY).

CONVERTIBLES corporate securities (usually preferred shares or bonds) that are exchangeable for a set number of another form (usually common shares) at a prestated price. Convertibles are appropriate for investors who want higher income than is available from common stock, together with greater appreciation potential than regular bonds offer. From the issuer's standpoint, the convertible feature is usually designed as a sweetener, to enhance the marketability of the stock or preferred. Also called DEFERRED EQUITY.

CONVERTIBLE TERM LIFE INSURANCE TERM LIFE INSURANCE that can be converted into WHOLE LIFE INSURANCE without a physical examination and regardless of health. *See also* GUARANTEED INSURABILITY.

CONVEXITY mathematical concept that measures sensitivity of the market price of an interest-bearing bond to changes in interest rate levels. *See also* DURATION.

COOK THE BOOKS to falsify the financial statements of a company intentionally. A firm in financial trouble may want to cook the books to prevent investors from pushing down the company's stock price. Companies may also falsify their records to lower their tax liabilities. Whatever the reason, the practice is illegal under SEC, IRS, and stock exchange rules as well as the ethical code of the accounting profession. *See also* SARBANES-OXLEY ACT OF 2002.

COOKIE JAR RESERVES *see* MANAGED EARNINGS.

COOLING-OFF PERIOD
1. interval (usually 20 days) between the filing of a preliminary prospectus with the Securities and Exchange Commission and the offer of the securities to the public. *See also* REGISTRATION.
2. period during which a union is prohibited from striking, or an employer from locking out employees. The period, typically 30 to 90 days, may be required by law or provided for in a labor agreement.

COOPERATIVE organization owned by its members.
     In real estate, a property whose residents own shares in a cooperative giving them exclusive use of their apartments. Decisions about common

areas—hallways, elevators, grounds—are made by a vote of members' shares. Members also approve sales of apartments.

Agriculture cooperatives help farmers sell their products more efficiently. Food cooperatives buy food for their members at wholesale prices, but usually require members to help run the organization.

COPYRIGHT legal protection given to authors of literary, musical, and artistic works and similar INTELLECTUAL PROPERTY. A copyright conveys the exclusive right to print, reprint, and copy the work; to sell, assign, and distribute copies; and to perform the work. The legal life of a copyright is the life of the author plus 70 years.

CORE CAPITAL thrift institution's bedrock capital, which must be at least 2% of assets to meet proposed rules of the Federal Home Loan Bank. It comprises capital stock and surplus accounts, including perpetual preferred stock, plus minority interests in consolidated subsidiaries.

CORE COMPETENCY a company's basic business and area of greatest expertise. A core competency can take many forms, including subject matter know-how, a reliable process, or close relationships with customers and suppliers.

CORE HOLDING a security owned as part of a portfolio's primary, permanent holdings.

CORE INFLATION increases in the PRODUCER PRICE INDEX (PPI) likely to spill over into consumer prices and become the basis of a long-term inflationary trend. Food and energy prices, which tend to be volatile and to cause temporary price shocks, are usually excluded from core inflation calculations. Other measures of core inflation use the CONSUMER PRICE INDEX (CPI), excluding food, energy, and other products where price changes reflect volatility rather than trends.

CORNERING THE MARKET purchasing a security or commodity in such volume that control over its price is achieved. A cornered market in a security would be unhappy news for a short seller, who would have to pay an inflated price to cover. Cornering has been illegal for some years.

CORPORATE BOND debt instrument issued by a private corporation, as distinct from one issued by a government agency or a municipality. Corporates typically have four distinguishing features: (1) they are taxable; (2) they usually have a par value of $1,000; (3) they have a term maturity—which means they come due all at once—and are paid for out of a sinking fund accumulated for that purpose; (4) they are traded on major exchanges, with prices published in newspapers. *See also* BOND; MUNICIPAL BOND.

CORPORATE CHARTER *see* ARTICLES OF INCORPORATION.

CORPORATE EQUIVALENT YIELD comparison that dealers in government bonds include in their offering sheets to show the after-tax yield of government bonds selling at a discount and corporate bonds selling at par.

CORPORATE FINANCE also called corporation finance, one of the three main divisions of finance, the others being personal finance and public finance. Corporate finance deals with the promotion, organization, capitalization, financing, investing, and financial administration of the corporation from the firm's point of view. CAPITAL BUDGETING is an important function of corporate finance.

CORPORATE FINANCING COMMITTEE NATIONAL ASSOCIATION OF SECURITIES DEALERS standing committee that reviews documentation submitted by underwriters in compliance with Securities and Exchange Commission requirements to ensure that proposed markups are fair and in the public interest.

CORPORATE GOVERNANCE
1. In general: management of a corporation for the benefit of its shareholders in compliance with laws and ethical standards.
2. NASDAQ: term for non-quantitative standards companies must meet before their securities qualify for trading.

CORPORATE INCOME FUND (CIF) UNIT INVESTMENT TRUST with a fixed portfolio made up of high-grade securities and instruments, similar to a MONEY MARKET FUND. Most CIFs pay out investment income monthly.

CORPORATE RESPONSIBILITY ACT OF 2002 *see* SARBANES-OXLEY ACT OF 2002.

CORPORATE SECURITIES (LIMITED) REPRESENTATIVE (CS) a person who has passed the Corporate Securities Limited Representative (Series 62) examination administered by the FINANCIAL INDUSTRY REGULATORY AUTHORITY (FINRA) and is licensed to trade corporate securities, including common and preferred stocks, corporate bonds, rights, warrants, closed-end investment companies, money market mutual funds, privately issued mortgage-backed securities, other asset-backed securities, and real estate investment trusts, but not municipal securities, direct participation programs, other securities registered under the Investment Company Act of 1940, variable contracts, or options. Other limited representatives are licensed by FINRA (*see* SERIES 6 REGISTERED). To trade all securities (except commodities futures), brokers must pass the General Securities Representative Examination (SERIES 7) and, in some cases, Series 63 state examinations.

CORPORATION legal entity, chartered by a U.S. state or by the federal government, and separate and distinct from the persons who own it, giving rise to a jurist's remark that it has "neither a soul to damn nor a body to kick." Nonetheless, it is regarded by the courts as an artificial person; it may own property, incur debts, sue, or be sued. It has three chief distinguishing features:
1. limited liability; owners can lose only what they invest.
2. easy transfer of ownership through the sale of shares of stock.
3. continuity of existence.
   Other factors helping to explain the popularity of the corporate form of organization are its ability to obtain capital through expanded ownership, and the shareholders' ability to profit from the growth of the business.

CORPUS Latin for *body*.
1. in trust banking, the property in a trust—real estate, securities and other personal property, cash in bank accounts, and any other items included by the donor.
2. body of an investment or note, representing the principal or capital as distinct from the interest or income.

CORRECTION reverse movement, usually downward and exceeding 10%, in the price of an individual stock, bond, commodity, or index. If prices have been rising on the market as a whole, then fall dramatically, this is known as a *correction within an upward trend.* Technical analysts note that markets do not move straight up or down and that corrections are to be expected during any long-term move.

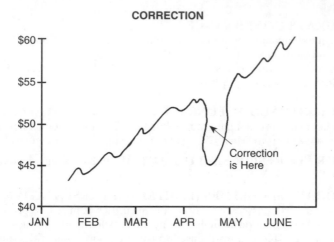

CORRECTION

CORRELATION COEFFICIENT statistical measure of the degree to which the movements of two variables are related.

CORRESPONDENT financial organization that regularly performs services for another in a market inaccessible to the other. In banking there is usually a depository relationship that compensates for expenses and facilitates transactions.

COSIGNER party, also called co-maker, who accepts joint responsibility for a debt obligation.

COST ACCOUNTING branch of accounting concerned with providing the information that enables the management of a firm to evaluate production costs.

COST BASIS original price of an asset, used in determining capital gains. It usually is the purchase price, but in the case of an inheritance it is the appraised value of the asset at the time of the donor's death.

COST-BENEFIT ANALYSIS method of measuring the benefits expected from a decision, calculating the cost of the decision, then determining whether the benefits outweigh the costs. Corporations use this method in deciding whether to buy a piece of equipment, and the government uses it in determining whether federal programs are achieving their goals.

COST-BENEFIT RATIO the relationship considered in a COST-BENEFIT ANAL- YSIS. In capital budgeting, it is the NET PRESENT VALUE (NPV) of an investment divided by its initial cost. *See also* CAPITAL RATIONING.

COST OF CAPITAL rate of return that a business could earn if it chose another investment with equivalent risk—in other words, the OPPORTUNITY COST of the funds employed as the result of an investment decision. Cost of capital is also calculated using a weighted average of a firm's costs of debt and classes of equity. This is also called the *composite cost of capital.*

COST OF CARRY out-of-pocket costs incurred while an investor has an investment position, among them interest on long positions in margin accounts, dividends lost on short margin positions, and incidental expenses.

COST OF FUNDS interest cost paid by a financial institution for the use of money. Brokerage firms' cost of funds are comprised of the total interest expense to carry an inventory of stocks and bonds. In the banking and savings and loan industry, the cost of funds is the amount of interest the bank must pay on money market accounts, passbooks, CDs, and other liabilities. Many adjustable rate mortgage loans are tied to a cost-of-funds index, which rises and falls in line with the banks' interest expenses.

COST-OF-FUNDS INDEX (COFI) index used by mortgage lenders on adjustable rate mortgage loans. Borrower's mortgage payments rise or fall based on the widely published COFI, which is based on what financial institutions are paying on money market accounts, passbooks, CDs, and other liabilities. The COFI tends to move far more slowly, both up and down, than other indexes for adjustable rate mortgages, such as one-year Treasuries or the prime rate. *See also* BASE RATE.

COST OF GOODS SOLD figure representing the cost of buying raw materials and producing finished goods. Depreciation is considered a part of this cost but is usually listed separately. Included in the direct costs are clear-cut factors such as direct factory labor as well as others that are less clear-cut, such as overhead. *Cost of sales* may be used as a synonym or may mean selling expenses. *See also* DIRECT OVERHEAD; FIRST IN, FIRST OUT; LAST IN, FIRST OUT.

COST-OF-LIVING ADJUSTMENT (COLA) adjustment of wages designed to offset changes in the cost of living, usually as measured by the CONSUMER PRICE INDEX. COLAs are key bargaining issues in labor contracts and are politically sensitive elements of Social Security payments and federal pensions because they affect millions of people.

COST-OF-LIVING INDEX *see* CONSUMER PRICE INDEX.

COST OF LIVING RIDER feature of a life insurance policy that adjusts the FACE VALUE, typically with term insurance, to keep up with changes in the CONSUMER PRICE INDEX (CPI). Also found in some DISABILITY INCOME INSURANCE.

COST OF SALES *see* COST OF GOODS SOLD.

COST-PLUS CONTRACT contract basing the selling price of a product on the total cost incurred in making it plus a stated percentage or a fixed fee— called a *cost-plus-fixed-fee contract.* Cost-plus contracts are common when there is no historical basis for estimating costs and the producer would run a risk of loss—defense contracts involving sophisticated technology, for example. The alternative is a FIXED PRICE contract.

COST-PUSH INFLATION inflation caused by rising prices, which follow on the heels of rising costs. This is the sequence: When the demand for raw materials exceeds the supply, prices go up. As manufacturers pay more for these raw materials they raise the prices they charge merchants for the finished products, and the merchants in turn raise the prices they charge consumers. *See also* DEMAND-PULL INFLATION; INFLATION.

COST RECORDS
1. investor records of the prices at which securities were purchased, which provide the basis for computing capital gains.
2. in finance, anything that can substantiate the costs incurred in producing goods, providing services, or supporting an activity designed to be productive. Ledgers, schedules, vouchers, and invoices are cost records.

COTTAGE INDUSTRY home-based, rather than factory-based, industry. Often implies a new industry serendipitously created as an offspring of a larger activity.

COUNCIL OF ECONOMIC ADVISERS group of economists appointed by the President of the United States to provide counsel on economic policy. The council helps to prepare the President's budget message to Congress, and its chairman frequently speaks for the administration's economic policy.

COUNCIL OF INSTITUTIONAL INVESTORS Washington, D.C.-based organization founded in 1985 and comprising more than 140 public, union, and corporate pension funds with more than $3 trillion of total assets. The Council advocates regulatory issues affecting its members and provides research, educational, and legal services.

COUNTERCYCLICAL STOCKS stocks that tend to rise in value when the economy is turning down or is in recession. Traditionally, companies in industries with stable demand, such as drugs and food, are considered countercyclical. Some firms actually do better when the economy or stock market is in turmoil. For example, firms offering money market mutual funds may enjoy an inflow of cash when stock prices fall. Temporary-help firms may benefit if companies are cutting costs by laying off full-time employees and replacing them with temps. Companies that can perform various functions for other companies more efficiently and at lower cost (called *outsourcing firms*) will tend to benefit during economic downturns. *See also* CYCLICAL STOCKS.

COUNTERPARTY RISK the mutual risk that one of the parties to a contract will default or fail to perform as agreed. The term applies generally to any credit transaction where one party agrees to lend and the other agrees to repay, but there are many more complicated examples. A FUTURES CONTRACT, for example, obligates the buyer and a seller of a commodity, but the counterparty risk may be the potential bankruptcy of the futures exchange on which the trade is executed. In the now famous case of AIG, the insurer was the counterparty to banks holding CREDIT DEFAULT SWAPS to hedge their exposure to MORTGAGE CREDIT DERIVATIVES. AIG, whose risk analysis took into account historical foreclosure experience but did not factor in the possibility of a market-wide housing collapse, was unable to meet its obligations and had to be bailed out by the government. Evaluations of counterparty risk should also confirm that the risk factors of the respective counterparties do not correlate adversely, causing *wrong way risk*.

COUNTRY BASKET general term for exchange-traded funds, such as iSHARES, that enable investors to own portfolios of stocks in specific countries with a single security at regular transaction costs.

COUPON interest rate on a debt security the issuer promises to pay to the holder until maturity, expressed as an annual percentage of face value. For example, a bond with a 10% coupon will pay $10 per $100 of the face amount per year, usually in installments paid every six months. The term derives from the small detachable segment of a bond certificate which, when presented to the bond's issuer, entitles the holder to the interest due on that date. As the REGISTERED BOND becomes more widespread, coupons are gradually disappearing.

COUPON BOND bond issued with detachable coupons that must be presented to a paying agent or the issuer for semiannual interest payment. These are bearer bonds, so whoever presents the coupon is entitled to the interest. Once universal, the coupon bond has been gradually giving way to the REGISTERED BOND, some of which pay interest through electronic transfers. *See also* BOOK-ENTRY SECURITIES; CERTIFICATELESS MUNICIPALS; COUPON.

COUPON COLLECTION *see* COLLECTION.

COUPON-EQUIVALENT RATE same as EQUIVALENT BOND YIELD.

COUPON PASS canvassing by the DESK of the Federal Reserve's Open-Market Committee of PRIMARY DEALERS to determine the inventory and maturities of their Treasury securities. Desk then decides whether to buy or sell specific issues (coupons) to add or withdraw reserves. *See also* BILL PASS; FED PASS.

COUPON YIELD (OR RATE) *see* COUPON.

COVARIANCE statistical term for the correlation between two variables multiplied by the standard deviation for each of the variables.

COVENANT promise in a trust indenture or other formal debt agreement that certain acts will be performed and others refrained from. Designed to protect the lender's interest, covenants cover such matters as working capital, debt-equity ratios, and dividend payments. Also called *restrictive covenant* or *protective covenant.*

COVER
1. to buy back contracts previously sold; said of an investor who has sold stock or commodities short.
2. in corporate finance, to meet fixed annual charges on bonds, leases, and other obligations, out of earnings.
3. amount of net-asset value underlying a bond or equity security. Coverage is an important aspect of a bond's safety rating.

COVERAGE *see* FIXED-CHARGE COVERAGE.

COVERAGE INITIATED indication by a RESEARCH DEPARTMENT that its analysts have just begun to follow a particular stock, usually a favorable development for holders of that company's shares. *See also* NEGLECTED FIRM EFFECT.

COVERDELL EDUCATION SAVINGS ACCOUNT account created by the ECONOMIC GROWTH AND TAX RELIEF RECONCILIATION ACT OF 2001 to encourage parents to save for their children's education. The ESA, formerly called the Education IRA, was named after Georgia Senator Paul Coverdell, who championed the idea. Parents can contribute up to $2,000 annually per child into an account held at a bank, mutual fund, insurance company, or brokerage firm, which can be invested in stocks, bonds, mutual funds, CDs, money market accounts, and other securities. When the money is withdrawn for use by a designated beneficiary for a qualified education expense at a public, private, or religious school, it is distributed tax-free. Only married couples filing jointly with modified adjusted gross income (MAGI) of up to $190,000 may contribute the full $2,000 to a Coverdell. The contribution limit is phased down for MAGI up to $220,000, after which no contributions are allowed. Singles with MAGI up to $95,000 may make the full contribution, and those with MAGI between $95,000 and $110,000 may make limited contributions. Contributions are not deductible and can be made up to the due date of the tax return—usually April 15. Funds in the Coverdell account can be used for a wide array of educational expenses, including elementary school, secondary school, and college tuition and fees, room and board, tutoring, uniforms, transportation, and books, supplies, and equipment.

COVERED BOND a corporate bond, typically issued by a bank, that is backed by cash flows from a pool of assets, typically mortgages, but that differs from ASSET-BACKED SECURITIES in the important respect that the bond remains on the issuer's books. The investor, in the event of default, has recourse both to the pool and to the issuer. In 2008, then Treasury Secretary Paulson announced that along with four large U.S. banks, the Treasury would attempt to create a market for bonds covered by pools of eligible mortgages. At the same time, the Federal Reserve said it would consider accepting highly rated covered bonds as collateral for emergency fund requests.

COVERED INTEREST ARBITRAGE ARBITRAGE that exploits and thereby eliminates differences between spot exchange rates, forward exchange rates, and interest rates on deposits, thus creating *interest rate parity*.

COVERED OPTION option contract backed by the shares underlying the option. For instance, someone who owns 300 shares of XYZ and sells three XYZ call options is in a covered option position. If the XYZ stock price goes up and the option is exercised, the investor has the stock to deliver to the buyer. Selling a call brings a premium from the buyer. *See also* NAKED OPTION.

COVERED WRITER seller of covered options—in other words, an owner of stock who sells options against it to collect premium income. For example, when writing a CALL OPTION, if a stock price stays stable or drops, the seller will be able to hold onto the stock. If the price rises sharply enough, it will have to be given up to the option buyer.

COVERING SHORT *see* COVER.

CPI *see* CONSUMER PRICE INDEX (CPI).

CRAM-DOWN feature of the bankruptcy law that allows a debtor to force confirmation of a plan over the objections of dissenting classes if certain tests are met. When junior classes impose a cram-down on a senior class, the term "cram-up" is used. More recently cram-down is used to describe a measure that would allow bankruptcy judges to modify mortgage loans and reduce payments for homeowners facing foreclosure.

CRAM-DOWN DEAL merger or leveraged buyout slang for situation in which stockholders are forced, for lack of attractive alternatives, to accept undesirable terms, such as JUNK BONDS instead of cash or equity.

CRAM-UP *see* CRAM-DOWN.

CRASH precipitate drop in stock prices and economic activity, as in the crash of 1929 or BLACK MONDAY in 1987. Crashes are usually brought on by a loss in investor confidence following periods of highly inflated stock prices.

CREATIVE DESTRUCTION free market concept popularized by economist Joseph Schumpeter holding that economic progress results from entrepreneurial innovation, a necessary consequence of which is the destruction of established businesses that then become obsolete. Example: The invention of the automobile destroyed the buggy whip industry but created a vital new industry contributing to growth and progress.

CREDIT
In general: loans, bonds, charge-account obligations, and open-account balances with commercial firms. Also, available but unused bank letters of credit and other standby commitments as well as a variety of consumer credit facilities.
    On another level, discipline in which lending officers and industrial credit people are professionals. At its loftiest it is defined in Dun & Bradstreet's motto: "Credit—Man's Confidence in Man."
Accounting: entry—or the act of making an entry—that increases liabilities, owners' equity, revenue, and gains, and decreases assets and expenses. *See also* CREDIT BALANCE.
Customer's statement of account: adjustment in the customer's favor, or increase in equity.

CREDIT ANALYST person who (1) analyzes the record and financial affairs of an individual or a corporation to ascertain creditworthiness or (2) determines the credit ratings of corporate and municipal bonds by studying the financial condition and trends of the issuers.

CREDIT BALANCE
In general: account balance in the customer's favor. *See also* CREDIT.
Securities: in cash accounts with brokers, money deposited and remaining after purchases have been paid for, plus the uninvested proceeds from securities sold. In margin accounts, (1) proceeds from short sales, held in escrow for the securities borrowed for these sales; (2) free credit balances, or net balances, which can be withdrawn at will. SPECIAL MISCELLANEOUS ACCOUNT balances are not counted as free credit balances.

CREDIT BUREAU agency that gathers information about the credit history of consumers and relays it to credit grantors for a fee. Credit bureaus maintain files on millions of consumers detailing which lines of credit they have applied for and received, and whether they pay their bills in a timely fashion. Bureaus receive this information from credit grantors such as credit card issuers, retail stores, gasoline companies, and others. Credit grantors look at this information, which is constantly being updated, in making their decision as to whether or not to grant credit to a particular consumer, and if so, how much credit is appropriate. Consumers have rights under the FAIR CREDIT REPORTING ACT to see a copy of their credit report and to dispute any item they think is inaccurate. Credit data are maintained by 500 credit bureaus which operate off of three automated systems: Equifax, based in Georgia, Experian, based in California, and Trans-Union, based in Illinois. *See also* CREDIT SCORING.

CREDIT CARD plastic card issued by a bank, savings and loan, retail store, oil company, or other credit grantor giving consumers the right to charge purchases and pay for them later. Most credit cards offer a grace period of about 25 days, during which interest charges do not accrue. After that, consumers pay nondeductible CONSUMER INTEREST on the remaining balance until it is paid off. Some credit cards start charging interest from the day the purchase is registered. Most credit cards also permit consumers to obtain cash on their card in the form of a CASH ADVANCE. *See also* CONSUMER CREDIT PROTECTION ACT OF 1968.

CREDIT CARD ACCOUNTABILITY, RESPONSIBILITY, AND DIS-CLOSURE ACT OF 2009 legislation designed to curb fees and interest rate increases and other abusive practices by credit card companies. The legislation went into effect fully in February 2010 and provided:
- Change in existing balance rates: Credit card issuers may no longer retroactively change rates on existing balances unless a card is 60 days delinquent or increase rates under universal default rules, which hold that if a consumer pays any bill late, the credit card company can increase the consumer's rate even though the consumer has not paid the credit card bill late.
- Cardholder rights: Gives cardholders the right to cancel their card and pay off an existing balance at the existing interest rate if they get hit with an interest rate hike.
- Application of payments: Consumer payments above the minimum due must be applied first to balances with higher rates before being applied to those with lower rates.
- Teaser rates: Promotional rates must last at least 6 months, and issuers cannot raise rates for the first year after an account is opened.
- Due dates: Bills must be sent at least 21 days before the date the payment is due. Requires that payments made before 5 P.M. on the due date be considered timely. Prohibits card companies from charging late fees when a cardholder provides proof of mailing the bill within 7 days of the due date.
- Overlimit fees: Issuers cannot charge overlimit fees unless consumers have signed up to allow such fees. Requires companies to offer consumers the option of having a fixed credit limit that cannot be exceeded.
- Minors getting credit cards: Issuers must either get proof of income or other ability to repay a debt for any applicant under age 21 or the applicant must get a co-signer for the application, such as the applicant's parents.
- Double-cycle billing: Prohibits practice of assessing interest on a prior month's balance that had been paid in full for a late-paying customer.
- Increased warning time: Cardholders must receive at least 45 days notice in writing before any significant change is made in the terms of the card account.
- More disclosure: Cardholders must be informed about how long it will take to pay off a balance if they make only the minimum payment, and the language and print in credit card statements must be made easier to read and understand.
- Subprime cards: Requires that all fees for subprime cards be paid up front

before the card is issued. Subprime cards are defined as having total fixed fees over a year exceed 25% of the credit limit.

CREDIT DEFAULT SWAP (CDS) in its most basic form, a contract whereby one party, called a *protection buyer,* periodically makes fixed payments to another party, the *protection seller,* in exchange for an agreement to pay an amount of money in the event of default by a third party, called the *reference entity.* The reference entity is typically a loan or bond but can also be a company in some sort of duress. What makes the CDS different from an insurance contract is that the buyer need not have any interest whatsoever in the reference entity or its debt and doesn't even need to have a loss if the entity defaults. Like other financial DERIVATIVES, CDSs are traded OVER-THE-COUNTER, although with varying degrees of liquidity. Their market value is the *credit default swap spread,* which is the annual amount the buyer must pay the seller over the length of the contract as a percentage of NOTIONAL VALUE and that fluctuates with the likelihood that the seller will have to pay. CDSs are used by investors for hedging (to protect an investment); speculation (on changes in spreads); and arbitrage (to exploit changes in the correlation between a company's CDS spread and its stock price). CDSs became a major issue in 2008 by causing the collapse of Bear Stearns, the bankruptcy of Lehman Brothers, and the bailout of American International Group (AIG) and by 2009 the NOTIONAL VALUE of the CDS market had dropped to $30 trillion from a 2007 high of $45 trillion. In March 2009 the International Swaps and Derivatives Association (ISDA) introduced a central U.S. clearing house operated by InterContinental Exchange (ICE) to act as the counterparty for both sides of a CDS, thus reducing risks of buyers and sellers.

CREDIT DEFAULT SWAP SPREAD *see* CREDIT DEFAULT SWAP (CDS).

CREDIT DERIVATIVE *see* COLLATERALIZED BOND (OR DEBT) OBLIGATION (CBO or CDO).

CREDIT ENHANCEMENT techniques used by debt issuers to raise the credit rating of their offering, and thereby lower their interest costs. A municipality may have their bond insured by one of the large insurance companies such as Municipal Bond Investor's Assurance (MBIA) or American Municipal Bond Assurance Corporation (AMBAC), thereby raising the bond's credit rating to AAA. A corporate bond issuer may arrange for a bank letter of credit to back its issue, raising its rating to AAA. While investors in such credit-enhanced issuers feel safer because an insurance company or bank stands ready to step in if there is a default by the underlying issuer, the yield received by the investor is lower than if the bond were uninsured. *See also* CREDIT DEFAULT SWAP.

CREDIT INSURANCE protection against *abnormal* losses from unpaid accounts receivable, often a requirement of banks lending against accounts receivable.

In consumer credit, life or accident coverage protecting the creditor against loss in the event of death or disability, usually stated as a percentage of the loan balance.

CREDIT (OR CREDITOR) LIFE INSURANCE individual or group life insurance payable to a lender upon the death of a borrower in the amount of the outstanding balance of the loan.

CREDIT LIMIT credit card term, meaning the maximum balance allowed for a particular customer.

CREDITOR party that extends credit, such as a trade supplier, a bank lender, or a bondholder.

CREDITOR'S COMMITTEE group representing firms that have claims on a company in financial difficulty or bankruptcy; sometimes used as an alternative to legal bankruptcy, especially by smaller firms.

CREDIT RATING formal evaluation of an individual's or company's credit history and capability of repaying obligations. Any number of firms investigate, analyze, and maintain records on the credit responsibility of individuals and businesses—Experian (individuals) and Dun & Bradstreet (commercial firms), for example. The bond ratings assigned by Standard & Poor's, Fitch Ratings, and Moody's are also a form of credit rating. Bond ratings agencies have come under scrutiny regarding their ability to remain objective, since the majority of their income comes from fees paid by the issuing organizations. In addition, because ratings agencies work so closely with their customers, there is the possibility that analysts could assign a more or less favorable rating based on their relationships with executives in companies or governments issuing debt.

CREDIT RATING AGENCY REFORM ACT OF 2006 federal law enacted September 29, 2006, to encourage competition among firms engaged in CREDIT RATING of government and business obligations. It defined "nationally recognized statistical rating organization" (NRSRO) and required they register with the SECURITIES AND EXCHANGE COMMISSION (SEC) and comply with oversight rules. The financial crisis that broke soon after the act was passed revealed glaring deficiencies in the ways credit rating agencies performed and has spurred ongoing discussion of new proposals that would improve transparency, tighten oversight, and reduce reliance on credit agencies. A central issue is the conflict of interest inherent in the way agencies are compensated. Currently they earn their revenues from the issuers they rate, not from their subscribers as was once the case.

CREDIT RISK financial and moral risk that an obligation will not be paid and a loss will result.

CREDIT SCORING objective methodology used by credit grantors to determine how much, if any, credit to grant to an applicant. Credit scoring is devised by three different methods: by a third-party firm, by the credit grantor, or by the credit bureau in cooperation with the credit grantor. Some of the most common factors in scoring are income, assets, length of employment, length of living in one place, and past record of using credit. Any negative events in the past, such as bankruptcies or tax delinquencies, will sharply reduce an applicant's credit score. CREDIT BUREAU scores are commonly called "*FICO scores*" because the three main credit reporting agencies (Equifax, Experian, and TransUnion) use scores produced from software developed by Fair Isaac and Company.

CREDIT SPREAD difference in the value of two options, when the value of the one sold exceeds the value of the one bought. The opposite of a DEBIT SPREAD.

CREDIT UNION not-for-profit financial institution typically formed by employees of a company, a labor union, or a religious group and operated as a cooperative. Credit unions may offer a full range of financial services and pay higher rates on deposits and charge lower rates on loans than commercial banks. Federally chartered credit unions are regulated and insured by the National Credit Union Administration.

CREDIT WATCH used by bond RATING agencies to indicate that a company's credit is under review and its rating subject to change. The implication is that if the rating is changed, it will be lowered, usually because of some event that affects the income statement or balance sheet adversely.

CREDITWORTHINESS general eligibility of a person or company to borrow money. *See also* CREDIT RATING; CREDIT SCORING.

CREEPING TENDER OFFER strategy whereby individuals ACTING IN CONCERT circumvent WILLIAMS ACT provisions by gradually acquiring TARGET COMPANY shares from arbitrageurs and other sellers in the open market. *See also* TENDER OFFER.

CRITICAL MASS the size or scale at which a business activity acquires self-sustaining viability.

CRONY CAPITALISM favoritism that develops in free market economics because of close personal relationships between government officials and industry leaders or other powers, such as labor unions or, in some societies, ethnic, religious, or racial interests. Theories vary as to where the blame belongs. Capitalists blame latent socialism, arguing that socialist governments reward business operators for their cooperation. Socialists blame capitalists for cultivating government officials that might otherwise threaten their power. Others argue that since capitalism is all about benefiting friends and associates anyway, the word "crony" is superfluous. The concept, previously associated with Third World despots and their like, took on fresh life in the latter 2000s when the American financial crisis raised questions, fairly or not, about Goldman Sachs getting bailed out by a U.S. Treasury led by its former CEO; about Fannie Mae and Freddie Mac being taken over by the government to avoid insolvency caused by government policies; and about BERNARD MADOFF's ability to run a $65 billion PONZI SCHEME for a number of years without being stopped by an SEC staffed with members of the same Wall Street community.

CROSS securities transaction in which the same broker acts as agent in both sides of the trade. The practice—called crossing—is legal only if the broker first offers the securities publicly at a price higher than the bid.

CROSS BORDER country to country.

CROSSED MARKET situation in which one broker's bid is higher than another broker's lowest offer, or vice versa. FINANCIAL INDUSTRY REGULATORY AUTHORITY (FINRA) rules prohibit brokers from crossing the market deliberately.

CROSSED TRADE manipulative practice prohibited on major exchanges whereby buy and sell orders are offset without recording the trade on the exchange, thus perhaps depriving the investor of the chance to trade at a more favorable price. Also called *crossed sale*.

CROSS-HEDGING hedging a cash (spot) commodity or security with a FUTURES CONTRACT where the underlying commodity is similar but not identical to the commodity or security being hedged. Cross-hedging is used when no future is available on the commodity being hedged and a future with a high degree of price correlation can be substituted.

CROSS-HOLDINGS one corporation's holdings of another corporation's stock. Cross-holdings must be eliminated to avoid double-counting when consolidating or combining capital accounts.

CROSSOVER FUND a MUTUAL FUND that invests in equity shares of both publicly held and privately held companies.

CROSS RATES in foreign exchange, determining the EXCHANGE RATE between a domestic currency and a foreign currency by comparing the exchange rates of each with another foreign currency.

CROWD group of exchange members with a defined area of function tending to congregate around a trading post pending execution of orders. These are specialists, floor traders, odd-lot dealers, and other brokers as well as smaller groups with specialized functions—the INACTIVE BOND CROWD, for example.

CROWDING OUT heavy federal borrowing at a time when businesses and consumers also want to borrow money. Because the government can pay any interest rate it has to and individuals and businesses can't, the latter are crowded out of credit markets by high interest rates. Crowding out can thus cause economic activity to slow.

CROWN CORPORATION a corporation that is organized and owned by a soverign government, that serves a public purpose, and is administered by a government-appointed board of directors allowed to operate in a business-like way with minimal government supervision.

CROWN JEWELS the most desirable entities within a diversified corporation as measured by asset value, earning power and business prospects. The crown jewels usually figure prominently in takeover attempts; they typically are the main objective of the acquirer and may be sold by a takeover target to make the rest of the company less attractive.

CUBES *see* QUBES.

CUM DIVIDEND with dividend; said of a stock whose buyer is eligible to receive a declared dividend. Stocks are usually cum dividend for trades made on or before the fifth day preceding the RECORD DATE, when the register of eligible holders is closed for that dividend period. Trades after the fifth day go EX-DIVIDEND.

CUM RIGHTS with rights; said of stocks that entitle the purchaser to buy a specified amount of stock that is yet to be issued. The cut-off date when the stocks go from cum rights to EX-RIGHTS (without rights) is stipulated in the prospectus accompanying the rights distribution.

CUMULATIVE ANNUAL RETURN *see* COMPOUND ANNUAL RETURN.

CUMULATIVE PREFERRED preferred stock whose dividends if omitted because of insufficient earnings or any other reason accumulate until paid out. They have precedence over common dividends, which cannot be paid as long as a cumulative preferred obligation exists. Most preferred stock issued today is cumulative.

CUMULATIVE VOTING voting method that improves minority shareholders' chances of naming representatives on the board of directors. In regular or statutory voting, stockholders must apportion their votes equally among candidates for director. Cumulative voting allows shareholders to cast all their votes for one candidate. Assuming one vote per share, 100 shares owned, and six directors to be elected, the regular method lets the shareholder cast 100 votes for each of six candidates for director, a total of 600 votes. The cumulative method lets the same 600 votes be cast for one candidate or split as the shareholder wishes. Cumulative voting is a popular cause among advocates of corporate democracy, but it remains the exception rather than the rule.

CURB *see* AMERICAN STOCK EXCHANGE.

CURBS IN indication that CIRCUIT BREAKERS have been activated because of abnormal price movements on exchanges. "Curbs in" is perhaps most familiar as a bug on the TV screen during financial news broadcasts, such as on CNBC. When trading in a single stock has been halted, the term TRADING CURB is used. *See also* TICK TEST.

CURRENCY CONVERTIBILITY *see* CONVERTIBILITY.

CURRENCY FUTURES contracts in the futures markets that are for delivery in a major currency such as U.S. dollars, British pounds, Euros, German marks, Swiss francs, or Japanese yen. Corporations that sell products around the world can hedge their currency risk with these futures. *See also* FUTURES CONTRACT.

CURRENCY IN CIRCULATION paper money and coins circulating in the economy, counted as part of the total money in circulation, which includes DEMAND DEPOSITS in banks.

CURRENCY OPTION *see* OPTION.

CURRENCY RISK *see* TRANSACTION RISK.

CURRENCY SWAP *see* SWAP.

CURRENEX independent multibank on-line global currency exchange used by corporate and institutional foreign exchange traders.

CURRENT ACCOUNT (1) an active TRADE CREDIT account; (2) an account with an extender of credit that is up to date; (3) *See also* BALANCE OF PAYMENTS.

CURRENT ASSETS cash, accounts receivable, inventory, and other assets that are likely to be converted into cash, sold, exchanged, or expensed in the normal course of business, usually within a year.

CURRENT COUPON BOND corporate, federal, or municipal bond with a coupon within half a percentage point of current market rates. These bonds are less volatile than similarly rated bonds with lower coupons because the interest they pay is competitive with current market instruments.

CURRENT INCOME money that is received on an ongoing basis from investments in the form of dividends, interest, rents, or other income sources.

CURRENT LIABILITY debt or other obligation coming due within a year.

CURRENT MARKET VALUE present worth of a client's portfolio at today's market price, as listed in a brokerage statement every month— or more often if stocks are bought on margin or sold short. For listed stocks and bonds the current market value is determined by closing prices; for over-the-counter securities the bid price is used.

CURRENT MATURITY interval between the present time and the maturity date of a bond issue, as distinguished from original maturity, which is the time difference between the issue date and the maturity date. For example, in 2009 a bond issued in 2007 to mature in 2027 would have an original maturity of 20 years and a current maturity of 18 years.

CURRENT PRODUCTION RATE top interest rate allowed on current GOVERNMENT NATIONAL MORTGAGE ASSOCIATION mortgage-backed securities, usually half a percentage point below the current mortgage rate to defray administrative costs of the mortgage servicing company. For instance, when homeowners are paying 6½% on mortgages, an investor in a GNMA pool including those mortgages will get a current production rate of 6%.

CURRENT RATIO current assets divided by current liabilities. The ratio shows a company's ability to pay its current obligations from current assets. For the most part, a company that has a small inventory and readily collectible accounts receivable can operate safely with a lower current ratio than a company whose cash flow is less dependable. *See also* QUICK RATIO.

CURRENT YIELD annual interest on a bond divided by the market price. It is the actual income rate of return as opposed to the coupon rate (the two would be equal if the bond were bought at par) or the yield to maturity. For example, a 10% (coupon rate) bond with a face (or par) value of $1,000 is bought at a market price of $800. The annual income from the bond is $100. But since only $800 was paid for the bond, the current yield is $100 divided by $800, or 12½%.

CUSHION
1. interval between the time a bond is issued and the time it can be called. Also termed CALL PROTECTION.
2. margin of safety for a corporation's financial ratios. For instance, if its DEBT-TO-EQUITY RATIO has a cushion of up to 40% debt, anything over that level might be cause for concern.
3. *see* LAST IN, FIRST OUT.

CUSHION BOND callable bond with a coupon above current market interest rates that is selling for a premium. Cushion bonds lose less of their value as rates rise and gain less in value as rates fall, making them suitable for conservative investors interested in high income.

CUSHION THEORY theory that a stock's price must rise if many investors are taking short positions in it, because those positions must be covered by purchases of the stock. Technical analysts consider it particularly bullish if the short positions in a stock are twice as high as the number of shares traded daily. This is because price rises force short sellers to cover their positions, making the stock rise even more.

CUSIP NUMBER number identifying all stocks and registered bonds, using the COMMITTEE ON UNIFORM SECURITIES IDENTIFICATION PROCEDURES (CUSIP). Brokers will use a security's CUSIP number to look it up on a computer terminal to get further information. The CUSIP number will also be listed on any trading confirmation tickets. The CUSIP system makes it easier to settle and clear trades. Foreign securities use a similar identification system called the CUSIP International Numbering System (CINS).

CUSTODIAL ACCOUNT account that is created for a minor, usually at a bank, brokerage firm, or mutual fund. Minors cannot make securities transactions without the approval of the custodian, who manages cash and other property gifted to minors under the UNIFORM GIFTS TO MINORS ACT (UGMA) or the UNIFORM TRANSFER TO MINORS ACT (UTMA). Any earnings or interest from the account up to $900 are tax-free if the child is under age 14. Earnings from $900 to $1,800 are taxed at the child's tax rate. Any earnings over $1,800 are taxed at the parents' rate. Once the child turns 14, the earnings are taxed at the child's tax rate. When the child reaches the age of majority, usually 18, the child has full discretion over the account, unless the account is set up in a trust controlled by the parent. *See also* KIDDIE TAX; UNIFORM GIFTS TO MINORS ACT.

CUSTODIAN bank or other financial institution that keeps custody of stock certificates and other assets of a mutual fund, individual, or corporate client. *See also* CUSTODIAL ACCOUNT.

CUSTODY legal responsibility for someone else's assets or for a child. Term implies management as well as safekeeping. The IRS does not require custodial parents or guardians to declare child support as income, nor is child support deductible by the noncustodial parent.

CUSTOMER'S LOAN CONSENT agreement signed by a margin customer permitting a broker to borrow margined securities to the limit of the customer's debit balance for the purpose of covering other customers' short positions and certain failures to complete delivery.

CUSTOMERS' NET DEBIT BALANCE total credit extended by New York Stock Exchange member firms to finance customer purchases of securities.

CUTOFF POINT in capital budgeting, the minimum rate of return acceptable on investments.

CYBER-INVESTING using the computer as a tool to acquire, analyze, and screen information relevant to an investment decision, and to execute trades and keep records. *See also* INTERNET INVESTING; STOCK SCREENING.

CYCLE *see* BUSINESS CYCLE.

CYCLICAL STOCK stock that tends to rise quickly when the economy turns up and to fall quickly when the economy turns down. Examples are housing, automobiles, and paper. Stocks of noncyclical industries—such as foods, insurance, drugs—are not as directly affected by economic changes. *See also* COUNTERCYCLICAL STOCKS; INDUSTRIAL SECTORS.

D

DAILY LIST NASDAQ STOCK MARKET list providing daily update of all market participants on securities additions, anticipated securities additions, issue deletions, name/symbol changes, or newspaper changes. *See also* BLUE LIST; YELLOW SHEETS.

DAILY TRADING LIMIT maximum that many commodities and options markets are allowed to rise or fall in one day. When a market reaches its limit early and stays there all day, it is said to be having an up-limit or down-limit day. Exchanges usually impose a daily trading limit on each contract. For example, the Chicago Board of Trade limit is two points ($2,000 per contract) up or down on its treasury bond futures options contract.

DAISY CHAIN trading between market manipulators to create the appearance of active volume as a lure for legitimate investors. When these traders drive the price up, the manipulators unload their holdings, leaving the unwary investors without buyers to trade with in turn.

DATABASE store of information that is sorted, indexed, and summarized and accessible to people with computers. Databases containing market and stock histories are available from a number of commercial sources.

DATA MINING sifting historical data for evidence that appears to support a premise. Implication is that only favorable data are selected, making the conclusion dubious.

DATED DATE date from which accrued interest is calculated on new bonds and other debt instruments. The buyer pays the issuer an amount equal to the interest accrued from the dated date to the issue's settlement date. With the first interest payment on the bond, the buyer is reimbursed.

DATE OF ISSUE
Bonds: date on which a bond is issued and effective. Interest accrues to bondholders from this date.
Insurance: date on which a policy is issued. Normally, the policy is also declared effective on that date, though not in every case.
Stocks: date on which a new stock is publicly issued and begins trading.

DATE OF RECORD date on which a shareholder must officially own shares in order to be entitled to a dividend. For example, the board of directors of a corporation might declare a dividend on November 1 payable on December 1 to stockholders of record on November 15. After the date of record the stock is said to be EX-DIVIDEND. Also called *record date.*

DATING in commercial transactions, extension of credit beyond the supplier's customary terms—for example, 90 days instead of 30 days. In industries marked by high seasonality and long lead time, dating, combined with ACCOUNTS RECEIVABLE FINANCING, makes it possible for manufacturers with lean capital to continue producing goods. Also called *seasonal dating, special dating.*

DATS *see* DIRECT ACCESS.

DAWN RAID British term for a practice whereby a RAIDER instructs brokers to buy all the available shares of another company at the opening of the market, thus giving the acquirer a significant holding before the TARGET COMPANY gets wise to the undertaking. In London based markets, the practice is restricted by the *City Code on Takeovers and Mergers. See also* SATURDAY NIGHT SPECIAL.

DAX 100 price-weighted index of the 100 most widely traded stocks on the DAX Index, the German market index.

DAY LOAN loan from a bank to a broker for the purchase of securities pending delivery through the afternoon clearing. Once delivered the securities are pledged as collateral and the loan becomes a regular broker's CALL LOAN. Also called *morning loan.*

DAY OF DEPOSIT TO DAY OF WITHDRAWAL ACCOUNT bank account that pays interest based on the actual number of days that money is on deposit. Also called *actual balance method.*

DAY ORDER order to buy or sell securities that expires unless executed or canceled the day it is placed. All orders are day orders unless otherwise specified. The main exception is a GOOD-TILL-CANCELED ORDER, though even it can be executed the same day if conditions are right.

DAY TRADE purchase and sale of a position during the same day.

DAY TRADER person who makes DAY TRADES on a regular basis. *See also* IN-AND-OUT TRADER.

DEAD CAT BOUNCE sharp rise in stock prices after a severe decline. The saying refers to the fact that a dead cat dropped from a high place will bounce. Often, the bounce is the result of short-sellers covering their positions at a profit

DEALER
1. individual or firm acting as a PRINCIPAL in a securities transaction. Principals trade for their own account and risk. When buying from a broker acting as a dealer, a customer receives securities from the firm's inventory; the confirmation must disclose this. When specialists trade for their own account, as they must as part of their responsibility for maintaining an orderly market, they act as dealers. Since most brokerage firms operate both as brokers and as principals, the term *broker-dealer* is commonly used.
2. one who purchases goods or services for resale to consumers. The element of inventory risk is what distinguishes a dealer from an agent or sales representative.

DEALER MARKET securities market in which transactions are between principals acting as DEALERS for their own accounts rather than between brokers acting as agents for buyers and sellers. Municipal and U.S. government securities are largely traded in dealer markets. *See also* AUCTION MARKET.

DEALER'S SPREAD *see* MARKDOWN; UNDERWRITING SPREAD.

DEAL FLOW rate of new deals being referred to the investment banking division of a brokerage firm. This might refer to proposals for new stock and bond issues, as well as mergers, acquisitions, and takeovers.

DEAL STOCK stock that may be rumored to be a TAKEOVER target or the party to some other major transaction such as a merger or leveraged buyout. The stock may be subject to a rumor of a prospective deal, or a deal may have been announced that attracts additional bidders and the company is said to be *in play*. Arbitrageurs and other speculators will attempt to buy deal stocks before the deal is finalized or profit when the stock price rises. Of course, if there is no deal, these speculators may lose money if the stock falls back to its pre-rumor price.

DEAR MONEY British equivalent of TIGHT MONEY.

DEATH-BACKED BONDS bonds backed by policyholder loans against life insurance policies. The loans will be repaid either by the policyholder while he or she is alive or from the proceeds of the insurance policy if the policyholder dies. Also called *policyholder loan bonds*.

DEATH BENEFIT amount of money to be paid to beneficiaries when a policyholder dies. The death benefit is the face value of the policy less any unpaid policy loans or other insurance company claims against the policy. Beneficiaries are not taxed on the death benefit when they receive it.

DEATH PLAY stock bought or sold short on the expectation that a key executive will die and a profit on the shares will be made as a result. For example, there might be reason to believe that upon the imminent death of a CEO, a company will be broken up and that the shares will be worth more at their PRIVATE MARKET VALUE.

DEATH SPIRAL type of convertible (to common stock) bond or preferred stock issued by a distressed company where the conversion ratio increases as the market price of the common stock drops. As the common drops because of potential and actual dilution, deteriorating finances, and short selling, original common holders progressively lose control.

DEATH TAX synonym for ESTATE TAX favored by those who would reduce or eliminate it.

DEATH VALLEY CURVE venture capital term that describes a start-up company's rapid use of capital. When a company begins operations, it uses a great deal of its equity capital to set up its offices, hire personnel, and do research and development. It may be several months or even years before the company has products or services to sell, creating a stream of revenues. The Death Valley Curve is the time period before revenues begin, when it is difficult for the company to raise more equity or issue debt to help it through its cash-flow difficulties.

DEBENTURE general debt obligation backed only by the integrity of the borrower and documented by an agreement called an INDENTURE. An *unsecured bond* is a debenture.

DEBENTURE STOCK stock issued under a contract providing for fixed payments at scheduled intervals and more like preferred stock than a DEBENTURE, since their status in liquidation is equity and not debt.

Also, a type of bond issued by Canadian and British corporations, which refer to debt issues as stock.

DEBIT BALANCE
1. account balance representing money owed to the lender or seller.
2. money a margin customer owes a broker for loans to purchase securities.

DEBIT CARD card issued by a bank to allow customers access to their funds electronically. Debit cards could replace checks as a method of payment for goods and services, and are more convenient because they are more widely accepted than checks. Debit cards can also be used to withdraw cash from automatic teller machines. Many debit cards combine the features of CREDIT CARDS such as Visa.

DEBIT SPREAD difference in the value of two options, when the value of the one bought exceeds the value of the one sold. The opposite of a CREDIT SPREAD.

DEBT
1. money, goods, or services that one party is obligated to pay to another in accordance with an expressed or implied agreement. Debt may or may not be secured.
2. general name for bonds, notes, mortgages, and other forms of paper evidencing amounts owed and payable on specified dates or on demand.

DEBT BOMB situation in which a major financial institution defaults on its obligations, causing major disruption to the financial system of the institution's home country. If a major multinational bank were to run into such trouble, it could have a major negative impact on the global financial system.

DEBT CEILING maximum amount of money that the federal government is allowed to borrow. When the federal government approaches the ceiling, Congress has to raise it in order to authorize additional borrowing and issuance of new debt by the Treasury. *See also* DEBT LIMIT.

DEBT DISCHARGE INCOME outstanding debt that is forgiven and therefore legally becomes income taxable to the borrower unless exempted. Following the real estate meltdown in 2008, debt discharge income resulting from mortgages renegotiated to avoid foreclosures, was ruled to be nontaxable.

DEBT INSTRUMENT written promise to repay a debt; for instance, a BILL, NOTE, BOND, banker's ACCEPTANCE, CERTIFICATE OF DEPOSIT, or COMMERCIAL PAPER.

DEBT LIMIT maximum amount of debt that a municipality can incur. If a municipality wants to issue bonds for an amount greater than its debt limit, it usually requires approval from the voters.

DEBTOR any individual or company that owes money. If debt is in the form of a loan from a financial institution, you might use *borrower*. If indebtedness is in the form of securities, such as bonds, you would refer to the *issuer*. *See also* OBLIGOR.

DEBTOR IN POSSESSION debtor in a Chapter 11 BANKRUPTCY reorganization, who keeps control of the business and performs the duties of a trustee.

DEBT RATIO *see* DEBT-TO-EQUITY RATIO.

DEBT RETIREMENT repayment of debt. The most common method of retiring corporate debt is to set aside money each year in a SINKING FUND.

Most municipal bonds and some corporates are issued in serial form, meaning different portions of an issue—called series—are retired at different times, usually on an annual or semiannual schedule.

Sinking fund bonds and serial bonds are not classes of bonds, just methods of retiring them that are adaptable to debentures, convertibles, and so on. *See also* REFUNDING.

DEBT SECURITY security representing money borrowed that must be repaid and having a fixed amount, a specific maturity or maturities, and usually a specific rate of interest or an original purchase discount. For instance, a BILL, BOND, COMMERCIAL PAPER, or a NOTE.

DEBT SERVICE cash required in a given period, usually one year, for payments of interest and current maturities of principal on outstanding debt. In corporate bond issues, the annual interest plus annual sinking fund payments; in government bonds, the annual payments into the debt service fund. *See also* ABILITY TO PAY.

DEBT SERVICE COVERAGE
Corporate finance: amount, usually expressed as a ratio, of CASH FLOW available to meet annual interest and principal payments on debt, including SINKING FUND payments.
Government finance: export earnings required to cover annual principal and interest payments on a country's external debts.
Personal finance: ratio of monthly installment debt payments, excluding mortgage loans and rent, to monthly take-home pay.
 See also FIXED-CHARGE COVERAGE.

DEBT SWAP exchange, between banks, of a loan, usually to a third-world country in local currency. *See also* SWAP.

DEBT-TO-EQUITY RATIO
1. total liabilities divided by total shareholders' equity. This shows to what extent owner's equity can cushion creditors' claims in the event of liquidation. Usually called DEBT RATIO.
2. total long-term debt divided by total shareholders' equity. This is a measure of LEVERAGE—the use of borrowed money to enhance the return on owners' equity.
3. long-term debt and preferred stock divided by common stock equity. This relates securities with fixed charges to those without fixed charges.

DECIMAL TRADING quotation of stock prices in decimals. American markets changed from traditional dollars and fractions to dollars and cents (from 50½ to 50.50, for example) in 2001, having already changed the minimum increment in stock prices from ⅛ to 1/16 in 1999. Decimal trading saves investors money by narrowing the spread between BID AND ASKED prices, and by making stock prices easier to understand.

DECLARATION DATE date on which a company announces the amount and date of its next dividend payment. There is normally an interim period of a few days between the declaration date and the EX-STOCK DIVIDEND date which allows people to buy shares and still qualify to receive the upcoming dividend.

DECLARE authorize the payment of a dividend on a specified date, an act of the board of directors of a corporation. Once declared, a dividend becomes an obligation of the issuing corporation.

DECLINING BALANCE METHOD *see* DOUBLE DECLINING BALANCE DEPRECIATION METHOD (DDB).

DECOUPLING concept, analogous to a railroad car decoupling from a train, that a DEVELOPED COUNTRY can keep its financial markets (*financial decoupling*) and its economy (*economic decoupling*) viable when one or more countries in the global economy, with which it has trade and other commercial and financial interrelationships, are economically distressed. The cliché, "When America sneezes, the world gets a cold," assuming the germs in a worst case scenario are life-threatening, is what the concept of decoupling refutes. As events of 2008 demonstrated, foreign markets and economies, especially those with large holdings of American debt and those with large exports to the United States, were severely impacted by America's credit problems and deep recession. (*See* CONTAGION.) Adherents to the decoupling concept maintain, however, that the basic strength of the developed foreign economies, the ultimate resilience of their financial markets, and their potential ability to replace American consumers with consumers in their own populations, was never in serious question. In other words, healthy developed countries, despite all the interdependence implied by globalization, have economies and financial markets that are basically self-sufficient and able to remain viable thanks to their ability to decouple from sick economies that might otherwise drag them down.

DECREASING TERM LIFE INSURANCE form of life insurance coverage in which premiums remain constant for the life of the policy while the death benefit declines. Term insurance premiums usually increase every year as the policyholder ages, and the policy is renewed. If there is less need for coverage because, for example, children have become self-sufficient, it may be prudent to decrease the amount of outstanding coverage.

DECREMENTAL decline in corporate profitability; opposite of incremental. It measures the degree to which earnings decline with each dollar of sales lost. For example, if a company sells $100 less products and profit falls by $30, the margin on decremental sales is 30%. Decremental margins are most significant early in an economic downturn because sales tend to fall faster than companies can cut back their costs.

DEDICATED CAPITAL (OR VALUE) the par (assigned) value of a company's shares multiplied by the number of shares issued (shares outstanding plus shares held in treasury).

DEDICATION STRATEGY *see* PORTFOLIO DEDICATION.

DEDUCTIBLE
Insurance: amount of money that the policyholders must pay out of their pockets before reimbursements from the insurance company begin. The deductible is usually set as a fixed dollar amount, though in some cases it can also be a percentage of the premium paid or some other formula. Some group health insurance plans set the deductible at a set percentage of the employee's salary, for example. In general, the higher a deductible a policyholder will accept, the lower insurance premiums will be. The insurance company is willing to lower its premiums because the company is no longer liable for small claims.
Taxes: *see* TAX DEDUCTIBLE.

DEDUCTION

1. expense allowed by the Internal Revenue Service as a subtraction from adjusted gross income in arriving at a person's taxable income. Such deductions include some interest paid, state and local taxes, charitable contributions.
2. adjustment to an invoice allowed by a seller for a discrepancy, shortage, and so on.

DEED written instrument containing some transfer, bargain, or contract relating to property—most commonly, conveying the legal title to real estate from one party to another.

DEED OF TRUST *see* INDENTURE.

DEEP DISCOUNT BOND bond selling for a discount of more than about 20% from its face value. Unlike a CURRENT COUPON BOND, which has a higher interest rate, a deep discount bond will appreciate faster as interest rates fall and drop faster as rates rise. Unlike ORIGINAL ISSUE DISCOUNT bonds, deep discounts were issued at a par value of $1,000.

DEEP IN/OUT OF THE MONEY CALL OPTION whose exercise price is well below the market price of the underlying stock (deep *in* the money) or well above the market price (deep *out of* the money). The situation would be exactly the opposite for a PUT OPTION. The premium for buying a deep-in-the-money option is high, since the holder has the right to purchase the stock at a striking price considerably below the current price of the stock. The premium for buying a deep-out-of-the-money option is very small, on the other hand, since the option may never be profitable.

DEEP MARKET *see* DEPTH OF THE MARKET.

DEFAULT failure of a debtor to make timely payments of interest and principal as they come due or to meet some other provision of a bond indenture. In the event of default, bondholders may make claims against the assets of the issuer in order to recoup their principal.

DEFAULT RISK risk that a debtholder will not receive interest and principal when due. One way to gauge default risk is the RATINGS issued by credit rating agencies such as Fitch Investors Service, Moody's, and Standard & Poor's. The higher the rating (AAA or Aaa is highest), the less risk of default. Some issues, such as Treasury bonds backed by the full faith and credit of the U.S. government, are considered free of default risk. Other bonds, such as JUNK BONDS, carry a much higher default risk. One investor defense against default for municipal bonds is MUNICIPAL BOND INSURANCE. *See also* PURCHASING POWER RISK.

DEFEASANCE

In general: provision found in some debt agreements whereby the contract is nullified if specified acts are performed.
Corporate finance: short for in-substance defeasance, a technique whereby a corporation discharges old, low-rate debt without repaying it prior to maturity. The corporation uses newly purchased securities with a lower face value but paying higher interest or having a higher market value. The objective is a cleaner (more debt free) balance sheet and increased earnings in the amount by which the face amount of the old debt exceeds the cost of the new securi-

ties. The use of defeasance in modern corporate finance began in 1982 when Exxon bought and put in an irrevocable trust $312 million of U.S. government securities yielding 14% to provide for the repayment of principal and interest on $515 million of old debt paying 5.8% to 6.7% and maturing in 2009. Exxon removed the defeased debt from its balance sheet and added $132 million— the after-tax difference between $515 million and $312 million—to its earnings that quarter.

In another type of defeasance, a company instructs a broker to buy, for a fee, the outstanding portion of an old bond issue of the company. The broker then exchanges the bond issue for a new issue of the company's stock with an equal market value. The broker subsequently sells the stock at a profit.

DEFENSIVE INTERVAL RATIO ratio showing how long a company can operate on its current liquid assets without having to rely on additional revenues. The ratio divides cash and equivalents, marketable securities, and accounts receivable (DEFENSIVE ASSETS) by projected daily operating expenses less NONCASH CHARGES. The denominator is determined by dividing COST OF GOODS SOLD plus operating expenses and other ordinary cash expenses by 360.

DEFENSIVE SECURITIES stocks and bonds that are more stable than average and provide a safe return on an investor's money. When the stock market is weak, defensive securities tend to decline less than the overall market.

DEFERRAL OF TAXES postponement of tax payments from this year to a later year. For instance, an INDIVIDUAL RETIREMENT ACCOUNT (IRA) defers taxes until the money is withdrawn.

DEFERRED ACCOUNT account that postpones taxes until a later date. Some examples: ANNUITY, INDIVIDUAL RETIREMENT ACCOUNT, KEOGH PLAN accounts, PROFIT-SHARING PLAN, SALARY REDUCTION PLAN, SIMPLIFIED EMPLOYEE PENSION (SEP) PLAN.

DEFERRED ANNUITY *see* DEFERRED PAYMENT ANNUITY.

DEFERRED CHARGE expenditure carried forward as an asset until it becomes relevant, such as an advance rent payment or insurance premium. The opposite is *deferred income,* such as advance rent received.

DEFERRED COMPENSATION currently earned compensation that, under the terms of a profit-sharing, pension, or stock option plan, is not actually paid until a later date and is therefore not taxable until that date.

DEFERRED EQUITY securities convertible into COMMON STOCK. *See* CONVERTIBLES.

DEFERRED INTEREST BOND bond that pays interest at a later date. A ZERO COUPON BOND, which pays interest and repays principal in one lump sum at maturity, is in this category. In effect, such bonds automatically reinvest the interest at a fixed rate. Prices are more volatile for a deferred interest bond than for a CURRENT COUPON BOND.

DEFERRED ORDINARY SHARES *see* ORDINARY SHARES.

DEFERRED PAYMENT ANNUITY ANNUITY whose contract provides that payments to the annuitant be postponed until a number of periods have elapsed—for example, when the annuitant attains a certain age. Also called a *deferred annuity.*

DEFERRED SALES CHARGE *see* BACK-END LOAD.

DEFICIENCY LETTER written notice from the Securities and Exchange Commission to a prospective issuer of securities that the preliminary prospectus needs revision or expansion. Deficiency letters require prompt action; otherwise, the registration period may be prolonged.

DEFICIT
1. excess of liabilities and debts over income and assets. Deficits usually are corrected by borrowing or by selling assets.
2. in finance, an excess of expenditures over budget.

DEFICIT FINANCING borrowing by a government agency to make up for a revenue shortfall. Deficit financing stimulates the economy for a time but eventually can become a drag on the economy by pushing up interest rates. *See also* CROWDING OUT; KEYNESIAN ECONOMICS.

DEFICIT SPENDING excess of government expenditures over government revenue, creating a shortfall that must be financed through borrowing. *See also* DEFICIT FINANCING.

DEFINED BENEFIT PENSION PLAN plan that promises to pay a specified amount to each person who retires after a set number of years of service. Such plans pay no taxes on their investments. Employees contribute to them in some cases; in others, all contributions are made by the employer.

DEFINED CONTRIBUTION PENSION PLAN pension plan in which the level of contributions is fixed at a certain level, while benefits vary depending on the return from the investments. In some cases, such as 401(k), 403(b), and 457 plans, employees make voluntary contributions into a tax-deferred account, which may or may not be matched by employers. The level of contribution may be selected by the employee within a range set by the employer, such as between 2% and 10% of annual salary. In other cases, contributions are made by an employer into a profit-sharing account based on each employee's salary level, years of service, age, and other factors. Defined contribution pension plans, unlike DEFINED BENEFIT PENSION PLANS, give the employee options of where to invest the account, usually among stock, bond and money market accounts. Defined contribution plans have become increasingly popular in recent years because they limit a company's pension outlay and shift the liability for investment performance from the company's pension plan to employees.

DEFLATION decline in the prices of goods and services. Deflation is the reverse of INFLATION; it should not be confused with DISINFLATION, which is a slowing down in the rate of price increases. Generally, the economic effects of deflation are the opposite of those produced by inflation, with two notable exceptions: (1) prices that increase with inflation do not necessarily decrease with deflation—union wage rates, for example; (2) while inflation may or may not stimulate output and employment, marked deflation has always affected both negatively.

DEFLATIONARY GAP the amount by which a recession causes the GROSS DOMESTIC PRODUCT (GDP) to shrink from its full employment level.

DEFLATOR statistical factor used to convert current dollar activity into inflation-adjusted activity—in effect, a measure of prices. The change in the gross domestic product (GDP) deflator, for example, is a measure of economy-wide inflation.

DEFLECTION OF TAX LIABILITY legal shift of one person's tax burden to someone else through such methods as the CLIFFORD TRUST, CUSTODIAL ACCOUNTS, and SPOUSAL REMAINDER TRUSTS. Such devices were curtailed but not eliminated by the TAX REFORM ACT OF 1986.

DE JURE CORPORATION corporation lawfully chartered by a state government. Generally, the term *de jure* connotes "as a matter of law," as distinguished from *de facto,* which connotes "as a matter of practice not founded on law."

DELAYED DELIVERY the delivery of securities later than the scheduled date, which is ordinarily three business days after the trade date. A contract calling for delayed delivery, known as a SELLER'S OPTION, is usually agreed to by both parties to a trade. *See also* DELIVERY DATE.

DELAYED OPENING postponement of the start of trading in a stock until a gross imbalance in buy and sell orders is overcome. Such an imbalance is likely to follow on the heels of a significant event such as a takeover offer.

DELEVERAGE to become less reliant on debt. Traditionally, the term usually referred to financial LEVERAGE in corporations. Since the 2007 credit crisis, usage has broadened to include any entity that suffers from too much debt, including the American government, economic sectors such as real estate, and individuals.

DELINQUENCY failure to make a payment on an obligation when due. In finance company parlance, the amount of past due balances, determined either on a contractual or recency-of-payment basis.

DELISTING removal of a company's security from an exchange because the firm did not abide by some regulation or the stock does not meet certain financial ratios or sales levels.

DELIVERABLE BILLS financial futures and options trading term meaning Treasury bills that meet all the criteria of the exchange on which they are traded. One such criterion is that the deliverable T-bill is the current bill for the week in which settlement takes place.

DELIVERY *see* DELIVERY DATE; GOOD DELIVERY.

DELIVERY DATE
1. first day of the month in which delivery is to be made under a futures contract. Since sales are on a SELLER'S OPTION basis, delivery can be on any day of the month, as long as proper notice is given.
2. third business day following a REGULAR WAY transaction of stocks or bonds. Seller's option delivery can be anywhere from 3 to 60 days, though there may be a purchase-price adjustment to compensate for DELAYED DELIVERY. The SETTLEMENT DATE was changed from 5 days to 3 days effective June 1, 1995, after approval by the SEC. New deadline is known as *T* (for trade)-*plus-three.*

DELIVERY NOTICE
1. notification from the seller to the buyer of a futures contract indicating the date when the actual commodity is to be delivered.

2. in general business transactions, a formal notice documenting that goods have been delivered or will be delivered on a certain date.

DELIVERY VERSUS PAYMENT securities industry procedure, common with institutional accounts, whereby delivery of securities sold is made to the buying customer's bank in exchange for payment, usually in the form of cash. (Institutions are required by law to require "assets of equal value" in exchange for delivery.) Also called CASH ON DELIVERY, delivery against payment, delivery against cash, or, from the sell side, RECEIVE VERSUS PAYMENT.

DELTA
1. measure of the relationship between an option price and the underlying futures contract or stock price. For a call option, a delta of 0.50 means a half-point rise in premium for every dollar that the stock goes up. For a put option contract, the premium rises as stock prices fall. As options near expiration, IN-THE-MONEY contracts approach a delta of 1.
2. on the London Stock Exchange, *delta stocks* were the smallest capitalization issues before the system was replaced with today's NORMAL MARKET SIZE.

DELTA HEDGING HEDGING method used in OPTION trading and based on the change in premium (option price) caused by a change in the price of the underlying instrument. The change in the premium for each one-point change in the underlying security is called DELTA and the relationship between the two price movements is called the *hedge ratio*. For example, if a call option has a hedge ratio of 40, the call should rise 40% of the change in the security move if the stock goes down. The delta of a put option, conversely, has a negative value. The value of the delta is usually good the first one-point move in the underlying security over a short time period. When an option has a high hedge ratio, it is usually more profitable to buy the option than to be a WRITER because the greater percentage movement vis-à-vis the underlying security's price and the relatively little time value erosion allow the purchaser greater leverage. The opposite is true for options with a low hedge ratio.

DEMAND DEPOSIT account balance which, without prior notice to the bank, can be drawn on by check, cash withdrawal from an automatic teller machine, or by transfer to other accounts using the telephone or home computers. Demand deposits are the largest component of the U.S. MONEY SUPPLY, and the principal medium through which the Federal Reserve implements monetary policy. *See also* COMPENSATING BALANCE.

DEMAND DESTRUCTION in economics, a permanent reduction of demand caused by a prolonged period of high prices or constrained supply. A recent example is the effect of high gasoline prices on the demand for gas-guzzling sports utility vehicles. Since the 2008 financial crisis, usage of the term has broadened to include demand destruction caused by lower personal incomes, unavailable credit, and extended economic contraction. Housing, retailing, and education are among many sectors of the economy where demand driven by consumer debt is now being destroyed by DELEVERAGING.

DEMAND LOAN loan with no set maturity date that can be called for repayment when the lender chooses. Banks usually bill interest on these loans at fixed intervals.

DEMAND-PULL INFLATION price increases occurring when supply is not adequate to meet demand. *See also* COST-PUSH INFLATION.

DEMONETIZATION withdrawal from circulation of a specified form of currency. For example, the Jamaica Agreement between major INTERNATIONAL MONETARY FUND countries officially demonetized gold starting in 1978, ending its role as the major medium of international settlement.

DEMUTUALIZATION conversion of a member-owned institution or mutually owned company to another form of organization, usually a shareholder-owned company. Demutualization, which is usually done to make access to capital easier, has been a trend in the insurance industry and has been done in the case of several stock exchanges, such as the Chicago Mercantile Exchange and the Philadelphia Stock Exchange.

DENATIONALIZATION opposite of NATIONALIZATION. *See also* PRIVATIZATION.

DENOMINATION face value of currency units, coins, and securities. *See also* PAR VALUE.

DEPARTMENT OF VETERANS AFFAIRS (VA) Cabinet-level department that succeeded the Veterans Administration in 1989. The VA is responsible for providing federal benefits to veterans and their families and operates nationwide programs for health care, financial assistance, and burial benefits. It also guarantees home mortgage loans to veterans.

DEPLETION accounting treatment available to companies that extract oil and gas, coal, or other minerals, usually in the form of an allowance that reduces taxable income. Oil and gas limited partnerships pass the allowance on to their limited partners, who can use it to reduce other tax liabilities.

DEPOSIT
1. cash, checks, or drafts placed with a financial institution for credit to a customer's account. Banks broadly differentiate between demand deposits (checking accounts on which the customer may draw at any time) and time deposits, which usually pay interest and have a specified maturity or require 30 days' notice before withdrawal.
2. securities placed with a bank or other institution or with a person for a particular purpose.
3. sums lodged with utilities, landlords, and service companies as security.
4. money put down as evidence of an intention to complete a contract and to protect the other party in the event that the contract is not completed.

DEPOSITARY RECEIPT alternatively spelled depositary or depository, a negotiable certificate issued by a trust company or security depository (such as DEPOSITORY TRUST AND CLEARING CORPORATION) evidencing the deposit of publicly traded securities and facilitating the trading of such securities on stock exchanges. AMERICAN DEPOSITARY RECEIPTS represent shares of foreign companies and trade on American exchanges. *Global Depositary Receipts (GDR)*, which are sometimes called *European Depositary Receipts (EDR)*, represent shares of foreign stock that can be traded on the exchanges of the depository's country. As a legal vehicle, depositary receipts can be EXCHANGE-TRADED FUNDS (ETFs) representing indexes or other portfolios (such as HOLDRs) traded like stocks. *See also* PORTFOLIO DEPOSITARY RECEIPTS.

DEPOSIT INSURANCE FUND (DIF) *see* CREDIT UNION; FEDERAL DEPOSIT INSURANCE CORPORATION.

DEPOSITORY INSTITUTIONS DEREGULATION AND MONETARY CONTROL ACT federal legislation of 1980 providing for deregulation of the banking system. The act established the Depository Institutions Deregulation Committee, composed of five voting members, the Secretary of the Treasury and the chair of the Federal Reserve Board, the Federal Home Loan Bank Board, the Federal Deposit Insurance Corporation, and the National Credit Union Administration, and one nonvoting member, the Comptroller of the Currency. The committee was charged with phasing out regulation of interest rates of banks and savings institutions over a six-year period (passbook accounts were de-regulated effective April 1986, under a different federal law). The act authorized interest-bearing NEGOTIABLE ORDER OF WITHDRAWAL (NOW) accounts to be offered anywhere in the country. The act also overruled state usury laws on home mortgages over $25,000 and otherwise modernized mortgages by eliminating dollar limits, permitting second mortgages, and ending territorial restrictions in mortgage lending. Another part of the law permitted stock brokerages to offer checking accounts. *See also* DEREGULATION.

DEPOSITORY TRUST AND CLEARING CORPORATION (DTCC) a holding company that, through subsidiaries, provides clearance, settlement, and information services for equities, corporate and municipal bonds, mutual funds, annuities and insurance, government and mortgage-backed securities, over-the-counter credit derivatives, and emerging market debt trades. Its Depository Trust Company (DTC) subsidiary is a central securities repository where stock and bond certificates are held and exchanged, mostly electronically. Another subsidiary is National Securities Clearing Corporation (NSCC), which provides connectivity to thousands of brokers, dealers, banks, mutual funds, insurance carriers, and other financial intermediaries. Fixed-Income Clearing Corporation (FICC), which began operations on January 1, 2003, is DTCC's newest clearing corporation, formed by the merger of the Government Securities Clearing Corporation (GSCC) and the MBS Clearing Corporation (MBSCC). FICC clears and settles U.S. government securities and mortgage-backed securities trades. In 2004, DTCC handled an average of more than $4 trillion in trades daily. Other subsidiaries include DTCC Deriv/SERV LLC, which provides matching, confirmation, and payment services for the global over-the-counter derivatives market, and Global Asset Solutions LLC, which provides a global information service on corporate actions worldwide.

DEPRECIATED COST original cost of a fixed asset less accumulated DEPRECIATION; this is the *net book value* of the asset.

DEPRECIATION

Economics: consumption of capital during production—in other words, wearing out of plant and capital goods, such as machines and equipment.

Finance: amortization of fixed assets, such as plant and equipment, so as to allocate the cost over their depreciable life. Depreciation reduces taxable income but does not reduce cash.

Among the most commonly used methods are STRAIGHT-LINE DEPRECIATION; ACCELERATED DEPRECIATION; the ACCELERATED COST RECOVERY SYSTEM, and the MODIFIED ACCELERATED COST RECOVERY SYSTEM. Others include the annuity, appraisal, compound interest, production, replacement, retirement, and sinking fund methods. *See also* JOB CREATION AND WORKER ASSISTANCE ACT OF 2002; RECAPTURE.

Foreign exchange: decline in the price of one currency relative to another.

DEPRESSED MARKET market characterized by more supply than demand and therefore weak (depressed) prices. *See also* SYSTEMATIC RISK.

DEPRESSED PRICE price of a product, service, or security that is weak because of a DEPRESSED MARKET. Also refers to the market price of a stock that is low relative to comparable stocks or to its own ASSET VALUE because of perceived or actual risk. Such stocks are identified by high dividend yield, abnormally low PRICE/EARNINGS RATIOS and other such yardsticks. *See also* FUNDAMENTAL ANALYSIS.

DEPRESSION economic condition characterized by falling prices, reduced purchasing power, an excess of supply over demand, rising unemployment, accumulating inventories, deflation, plant contraction, public fear and caution, and a general decrease in business activity. The Great Depression of the 1930s, centered in the United States and Europe, had worldwide repercussions.

DEPTH OF THE MARKET measure of how many units of a security, usually shares of stock, can be bought or sold without causing a significant change in the MARKET PRICE. A DEEP MARKET in a stock means that numerous and sizeable bids and offers exist and that the stock thus has high LIQUIDITY.

DEREGULATION greatly reducing government regulation in order to allow freer markets to create a more efficient marketplace. After the stock-brokerage industry was deregulated in the mid-1970s, commissions were no longer fixed. After the banking industry was deregulated in the early 1980s, banks were given greater freedom in setting interest rates on deposits and loans. Industries such as communications and transportation have also been deregulated, with similar results: increased competition, heightened innovation, and mergers among weaker competitors. Some government oversight usually remains after deregulation.

DERIVATIVE short for *derivative instrument,* a contract whose value is based on the performance of an underlying financial asset, index, or other investment. For example, an ordinary *option* is a derivative because its value changes in relation to the performance of an underlying stock. A more complex example would be an option on a FUTURES CONTRACT, where the option value varies with the value of the futures contract which, in turn, varies with the value of an underlying commodity or security. Derivatives are available based on the performance of assets, interest rates, currency exchange rates, and various domestic and foreign indexes. Derivatives afford leverage and, when used properly by knowledgeable investors, can enhance returns and be useful in HEDGING portfolios. They gained notoriety in the late '80s because of problems involved in PROGRAM TRADING; in the '90s, when a number of mutual funds, municipalities, corporations, and leading banks suffered large losses because of unexpected movements in interest rates; and in the mid-2000s when defaults stemming from COUNTER-PARTY RISK caused the economy to collapse. *See also* BEARS, CERTIFICATES OF ACCRUAL ON TREASURY

SECURITIES (CATS), COLLATERALIZED BOND OR DEBT OBLIGATION (CBO OR CDO); COLLATERALIZED MORTGAGE OBLIGATION (CMO); CREDIT DEFAULT SWAPS; CUBS; DIAMONDS; INDEX OPTIONS; OEX; SPDR; STRIP; SUBSCRIPTION RIGHT; SUBSCRIPTION WARRANT; SWAP; TIGER.

DERIVATIVE INSTRUMENT *see* DERIVATIVE.

DERIVATIVE PRICING MODELS models that relate a number of variables and yield a theoretical price that is useful in judging whether an option or other derivative is fairly priced by the market or is overvalued or undervalued. The best-known and most widely adapted model is the basic BLACK-SCHOLES OPTION PRICING MODEL, developed by Fischer Black and Myron Scholes in the 1960s for options on stocks and modified in the 1970s for options on futures. Others are the *Cox-Ross Pricing Model* and the *Bi Nomal Option Pricing Model.* Black-Scholes uses the following five variables: 1. time remaining to expiration; 2. market price of the underlying stock or futures contract; 3. the exercise or strike price of the option; 4. carrying charges (interest rate, dividends for stocks); and 5. the volatility of the underlying stock or contract. Among other benefits, the Black-Scholes formula calculates the hedge ratio or DELTA, the theoretical percentage change in an option price caused by each one-point change in the price of the underlying stock or future. The delta thus provides a comparative valuation between the options price movement and the underlying asset over a one point move in the asset, assuming no change in time to expiration. A move of more than one point or a change in time, however, causes a change in the delta. A change in the delta, called a gamma, is measured by another model called the *Gamma Pricing Model.* The *Vega Pricing Model* measures the change in the option price caused by a change in volatility. The *Theta Pricing Model* measures the change in the option price caused by a change in the time value.

Derivative pricing is highly complex and has been made easier by available computer programs and Internet services.

DERIVATIVE SUIT a suit brought by shareholders on behalf of a corporation to enforce corporate rights against directors or other insiders, or to assert rights of the corporation in the absence of corporate action to protect such rights. Differs from a CLASS ACTION, where shareholders or other plaintiffs bring suit on their own behalf.

DESCENDING TOPS chart pattern wherein each new high price for a security is lower than the preceding high. The trend is considered bearish.

DESIGNATED ORDER TURNAROUND (DOT) electronic system used by the New York Stock Exchange to expedite execution of small MARKET ORDERS by routing them directly from the member firm to the SPECIALIST, thus bypassing the FLOOR BROKER. A related system called *Super DOT* routes LIMIT ORDERS.

DESK trading desk, or Securities Department, at the New York FEDERAL RESERVE BANK, which is the operating arm of the FEDERAL OPEN MARKET COMMITTEE. The Desk executes all transactions undertaken by the FEDERAL RESERVE SYSTEM in the money market or the government securities market, serves as the Treasury Department's eyes and ears in these and related markets, and encompasses a foreign desk which conducts transactions in the FOREIGN EXCHANGE market.

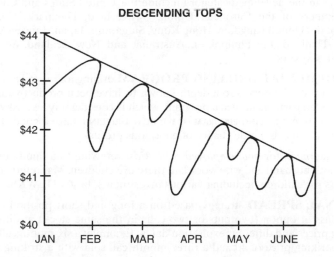

DESCENDING TOPS

DESKTOP TICKER computer screen display of REAL-TIME or delayed QUOTA-TIONS available through various services.

DEUTSCHE BÖRSE AG principal unit of Deutsche Börse Group, Germany's umbrella group for financial markets trading, trading services, and systems applications. The group operates the Xetra trading platform, which has made Deutsche Börse the world's second-largest fully electronic cash market; EUREX, the world's largest derivatives market; and Clearstream, the European clearing house for stocks and bonds. Deutsche Börse operates the Frankfurt Stock Exchange, and six other securities markets in Germany. *www.deutsche-borse.com. See also* EUREX, FRANKFURT STOCK EXCHANGE.

DEUTSCHE TERMINBORSE (DTB) *see* EUREX.

DEVALUATION lowering of the value of a country's currency relative to gold and/or the currencies of other nations. Devaluation can also result from a rise in value of other currencies relative to the currency of a particular country.

DEVELOPED COUNTRY (OR ECONOMY) countries at the top of a hierarchy that also includes, in descending order of development, *developing (also called less-developed or emerging)* and *underdeveloped (or non-industrialized or Third World) countries.* UNDERDEVELOPED COUNTRIES are agricultural economies, but there is no universal agreement on what precisely distinguishes developed from developing. DEVELOPING COUNTRIES, which include those in the BRIC group, have, among other things, a stock market accessible by foreigners and providing a reasonable degree of liquidity, an absence of prohibitive regulation and taxation, a unified currency, a growing industrial base, and economic potential even though the standard of living may be low. Developed countries have accelerated rates of economic growth, pro-business regulatory systems, high savings rates, comfortable standards of living, an educated populace, a potential for consumption, and a functional combination of free market forces and government intervention. In 2009, countries in the developed category include the United States and Canada, the members of the European Union, Switzerland, Denmark, Norway, Sweden, the United Kingdom, Hong Kong, Singapore, Japan, Taiwan, South Korea, Thailand, the Philippines, Australia, and New Zealand. *See also* FRONTIER MARKETS.

DEVELOPMENTAL DRILLING PROGRAM drilling for oil and gas in an area with proven reserves to a depth known to have been productive in the past. Limited partners in such a program, which is considerably less risky than an EXPLORATORY DRILLING PROGRAM or WILDCAT DRILLING, have a good chance of steady income, but little chance of enormous profits.

DEWKS acronym for *dual-employed, with kids,* referring to a family unit in which both husband and wife work and there are children. Marketers selling products for children, including various investments, target DEWKS.

DIAGONAL SPREAD strategy based on a long and short position in the same class of option (two puts or two calls in the same stock) at different striking prices and different expiration dates. Example: a six-month call sold with a striking price of 40 and a three-month call sold with a striking price of 35. *See also* CALENDAR SPREAD; VERTICAL SPREAD.

DIALING AND SMILING expression for COLD CALLING by securities brokers and other salespeople. Brokers must not only make unsolicited telephone calls to potential customers, but also gain the customer's confidence with their upbeat tone of voice and sense of concern for the customer's financial well-being.

DIALING FOR DOLLARS expression for COLD CALLING in which brokers make unsolicited telephone calls to potential customers, hoping to find people with investable funds. The term has a derogatory implication, and is typically applied to salespeople working in BOILER ROOMS, selling speculative or fraudulent investments such as PENNY STOCKS.

DIAMOND INVESTMENT TRUST unit trust that invests in high-quality diamonds. Begun in the early 1980s by Thomson McKinnon, these trusts let shareholders invest in diamonds without buying and holding a particular stone. Shares in these trusts do not trade actively and are therefore difficult to sell if diamond prices fall, as they did soon after the first trust was set up.

DIAMONDS units of beneficial interest in the Diamonds Trust, a UNIT INVESTMENT TRUST that holds the 30 component stocks of the Dow Jones Industrial Average. First introduced in January, 1998, Diamonds trade under the ticker symbol "DIA" like any other stock on the American Stock Exchange. They are designed to offer investors a low-cost means of tracking the Dow Jones Industrial Average, the most widely recognized indicator of the American stock market. Diamonds pay monthly DIVIDENDS (which can be reinvested into more shares of the trust) that correspond to the dividend yields of the component stocks of the Dow and pay capital gains distributions once a year. Diamonds are designed to trade at about 1/100 the level of the Dow Jones Industrial Average, so if the parent group comprises the Madrid, Barcelona, Bilbao, and Valencia stock exchanges, MF Mercados Financieros, Iberclear, and BME Consulting, low is at 10000, Diamonds will trade at about $100 per unit. Unlike open-end mutual funds, Diamonds trade like stocks, allowing investors to buy or sell at any time during the trading day, whereas index mutual funds are priced only once at the end of each trading day Like open-end index funds, Diamonds charge low-management fees because there is little research or trading conducted by the trust's management. There are also no LOADS to buy Diamonds, though normal brokerage commissions do apply to trades. Whereas closed-end funds often trade at discounts to their NET ASSET VALUES, investors can create an unlimited number of Diamonds trading units, which helps insure they will correlate closely with the performance of the Dow stocks in the portfolio. *See also* INDEX FUND; SPDR; EXCHANGE-TRADED FUNDS (ETFs). *www.amex.com/dia.*

DIFFERENTIAL small extra charge sometimes called the *odd-lot-differential*—usually ⅛ of a point—that dealers add to purchases and subtract from sales in quantities less than the standard trading unit or ROUND LOT. Also, the extent to which a dealer widens his round lot quote to compensate for lack of volume.

DIGITAL MONEY electronic payment systems used in lieu of coin and currency. Although the terms *electronic money* and, the short version, *e-money*, are commonly used interchangeably with digital money (or digital cash), digital, strictly defined, refers to e-cash that is off-line, meaning you can conduct a transaction without interacting with a bank and anonymous, meaning the identity of the person who originally withdrew the money from a bank is protected through the use of blind signatures. The technology underlying digital money is complex and problematic; a number of companies providing digital money services have come and gone, and the technology is still evolving. E-money that is "on-line" and "identified" is more common, an example being the ELECTRONIC WALLET.

DIGITS DELETED designation on securities exchange tape meaning that because the tape has been delayed, some digits have been dropped.

DILUTION effect on earnings per share and book value per share if all convertible securities were converted or all warrants or stock options were exercised. *See also* FULLY DILUTED EARNINGS PER (COMMON) SHARE.

DILUTION PROTECTION any right or provision designed to protect existing investors from DILUTION. Examples would include provisions that adjust the CONVERSION RATIO of CONVERTIBLES in the event of a stock dividend or other unusual COMMON STOCK distribution, PREEMPTIVE RIGHT statutes, and VENTURE CAPITAL *full ratchet* provisions, specifying that options and conversion privileges be exercisable at the lowest stock price at which stock was issued following issuance of the option or convertible.

DINKS acronym for *dual-income, no kids,* referring to a family unit in which there are two incomes and no children. The two incomes may result from both husband and wife working, or one spouse holding down two jobs. Since the couple do not have children, they typically have more disposable income than those with children, and therefore are the prime targets of marketers selling luxury products and services, including various investments. *See also* DENKS; DEWKS.

DIP slight drop in securities prices after a sustained uptrend. Analysts often advise investors to buy on dips, meaning buy when a price is momentarily weak.

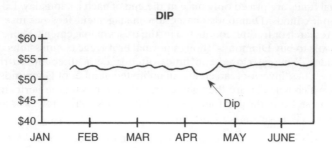

DIP

DIRECT ACCESS service offered by *direct access brokers*, that uses complicated computer software to enable clients to trade directly with exchanges
or other buyers and sellers through electronic communications networks
(ECN) at reduced commission rates. Using *direct access trading systems
(DATS),* active traders, such as DAY TRADERS, enjoy speedy order execution
by eliminating the third party, and receive other services, such as Level II
Nasdaq quotes, interactive charts, and other real-time information. Direct
access is provided by Charles Schwab, Ameritrade, and others.

DIRECT FINANCING any financing transaction where there is no intermediary between the lender and the borrower. Where securities are sold directly
to institutional lenders or investors and the cost of UNDERWRITING is being
avoided, the terms DIRECT PLACEMENT and PRIVATE PLACEMENT are interchangeably used. *See also* LETTER SECURITY.

DIRECT INVESTMENT (1) purchase of a controlling interest in a foreign
(international) business or subsidiary. (2) in domestic finance, the purchase
of a controlling interest or a minority interest of such size and influence that
active control is a feasible objective.

DIRECT ISSUER a company that sells COMMERCIAL PAPER directly to investors rather than through a broker.

DIRECT OBLIGATIONS debt securities backed by FULL FAITH AND CREDIT.

DIRECTOR *see* BOARD OF DIRECTORS.

DIRECTORS' AND OFFICERS' LIABILITY INSURANCE *see* DIREC-
TORS' IDEMNITIES.

DIRECTORS' INDEMNITIES corporate agreements to pay liabilities
board members may incur while acting as directors. DIRECTORS' AND OFFICERS'
LIABILITY INSURANCE, usually with a large deductible, covers the exposure of
directors and officers to personal suits for making misleading or false statements or commiting negligent acts or omissions, along with related legal fees
and court costs.

DIRECT OVERHEAD portion of overhead costs—rent, lights, insurance—
allocated to manufacturing, by the application of a standard factor termed a
burden rate. This amount is absorbed as an INVENTORY cost and ultimately
reflected as a COST OF GOODS SOLD.

DIRECT PARTICIPATION PROGRAM program letting investors participate directly in the cash flow and tax benefits of the underlying investments. Such programs are usually organized as LIMITED PARTNERSHIPS, although their uses as tax shelters have been severely curtailed by tax legislation affecting PASSIVE investments.

DIRECT PLACEMENT direct sale of securities to one or more professional investors. Such securities may or may not be registered with the SECURITIES AND EXCHANGE COMMISSION. They may be bonds, private issues of stock, limited partnership interests, mortgage-backed securities, venture capital investments, or other sophisticated instruments. These investments typically require large minimum purchases, often in the millions of dollars. Direct placements offer higher potential returns than many publicly offered securities, but also present more risk. Buyers of direct placements are large, sophisticated financial institutions including insurance companies, banks, mutual funds, foundations, and pension funds that are able to evaluate such offerings. Also called *private placement.*

DIRECT PURCHASE purchasing shares in a no-load or low-load OPEN-END MUTUAL FUND directly from the fund company. Investors making direct purchases deal directly with the fund company over the phone, in person at investor centers, or by mail. This contrasts with the method of purchasing shares in a LOAD FUND through a financial intermediary such as a broker or financial planner, who collects a commission for offering advice on which fund is appropriate for the client. Many companies also now allow shareholders to purchase "no-load" stock directly from the company, thereby avoiding brokers and sales commissions. *See also* TREASURY DIRECT.

DIRECT ROLLOVER distribution from a QUALIFIED PLAN OR TRUST that is remitted directly to the trustee, custodian, or issuer of a receiving INDIVIDUAL RETIREMENT ACCOUNT (IRA) ROLLOVER account. Tax-and penalty-free rollovers are allowed once a year. The years begin on the date of the first distribution.

DIRECT TRANSFER direct movement of assets from one QUALIFIED PLAN OR TRUST to another. Such transfers are not considered withdrawals and involve no taxes or penalties. Differs from a DIRECT ROLLOVER, in which assets go to a tax-deferred personal retirement account. Here they go from one corporate pension plan, 401(k), or 403(b), to another, as in a job change, for example.

DIRTY FLOAT occasional exception to a country's floating exchange rate system whereby a central bank intervenes to prevent large-scale speculation or some other external force from destabilizing its currency and threatening its economy.

DIRTY STOCK stock that fails to meet the requirements for GOOD DELIVERY.

DISABILITY INCOME INSURANCE insurance policy that pays benefits to a policyholder when that person becomes incapable of performing one or more occupational duties, either temporarily or on a long-term basis, or totally. The policy is designed to replace a portion of the income lost because of the insured's disability. Payments begin after a specified period, called the *elimination period,* of several weeks or months.

Some policies remain in force until the person is able to return to work, or to return to a similar occupation, or is eligible to receive benefits from another program such as Social Security disability. Disability insurance payments are normally tax-free to beneficiaries as long as they paid the policy premiums. Many employers offer disability income insurance to their employees, though people are able to buy coverage on an individual basis as well.

DISBURSEMENT paying out of money in the discharge of a debt or an expense, as distinguished from a distribution.

DISCHARGE OF BANKRUPTCY order terminating bankruptcy proceedings, ordinarily freeing the debtor of all legal responsibility for specified obligations.

DISCHARGE OF LIEN order removing a lien on property after the originating legal claim has been paid or otherwise satisfied.

DISCLAIMER OF OPINION auditor's statement, sometimes called an *adverse opinion,* that an ACCOUNTANT'S OPINION cannot be provided because of limitations on the examination or because some condition or situation exists, such as pending litigation, that could impair the financial strength or profitability of the client.

DISCLOSURE release by companies of all information, positive or negative, that might bear on an investment decision, as required by the Securities and Exchange Commission and the stock exchanges. *See also* FINANCIAL PUBLIC RELATIONS; INSIDE INFORMATION; INSIDER; TRANSPARENCY.

DISCONTINUED OPERATIONS operations of a business that have been sold, abandoned, or otherwise disposed of. Accounting regulations require that continuing operations be reported separately in the income statement from discontinued operations, and that any gain or loss from the disposal of a segment (an entity whose activities represent a separate major line of business or class of customer) be reported along with the operating results of the discontinued segment.

DISCOUNT
1. difference between a bond's current market price and its face or redemption value.
2. manner of selling securities such as treasury bills, which are issued at less than face value and are redeemed at face value.
3. relationship between two currencies. The English pound may sell at a discount to the Euro, for example.
4. to apply all available news about a company in evaluating its current stock price (e.g., taking into account the introduction of an exciting new product).
5. method whereby interest on a bank loan or note is deducted in advance.
6. reduction in the selling price of merchandise or a percentage off the invoice price in exchange for quick payment.

DISCOUNT BOND bond selling below its redemption value. *See also* DEEP DISCOUNT BOND.

DISCOUNT BROKER brokerage house that executes orders to buy and sell securities at commission rates sharply lower than those charged by a FULL SERVICE BROKER.

DISCOUNT DIVIDEND REINVESTMENT PLAN *see* DIVIDEND REINVESTMENT PLAN.

DISCOUNTED CASH FLOW value of future expected cash receipts and expenditures at a common date, which is calculated using NET PRESENT VALUE or INTERNAL RATE OF RETURN and is a factor in analyses of both capital investments and securities investments. The net present value (NPV) method applies a rate of discount (interest rate) based on the marginal cost of capital to future cash flows to bring them back to the present. The internal rate of return (IRR) method finds the average return on investment earned through the life of the investment. It determines the discount rate that equates the present value of future cash flows to the cost of the investment.

DISCOUNTING THE NEWS bidding a firm's stock price up or down in anticipation of good or bad news about the company's prospects.

DISCOUNT POINTS *see* POINT.

DISCOUNT RATE
  1. interest rate that the Federal Reserve charges member banks for loans, using government securities or ELIGIBLE PAPER as collateral. This provides a floor on interest rates, since banks set their loan rates a notch above the discount rate. *See also* DISCOUNT WINDOW.
  2. interest rate used in determining the PRESENT VALUE of future CASH FLOWS. *See also* CAPITALIZATION RATE.

DISCOUNT WINDOW place in the Federal Reserve where banks go to borrow money at the DISCOUNT RATE. Borrowing from the Fed has been a last resort for banks short of reserves, but in 2002, the Fed began encouraging direct loans to reduce volatility in the FEDERAL FUNDS RATE. During the late 2000s credit crunch, the Fed encouraged banks to use the window to increase liquidity.

DISCOUNT YIELD yield on a security sold at a discount—U.S. treasury bills sold at $9,750 and maturing at $10,000 in 90 days, for instance. Also called *bank discount basis*. To figure the annual yield, divide the discount ($250) by the face amount ($10,000) and multiply that number by the approximate number of days in the year (360) divided by the number of days to maturity (90). The calculation looks like this:

$$\frac{\$250}{\$10,000} \times \frac{360}{90} = .025 \times 4 = .10 = 10\%.$$

DISCRETIONARY ACCOUNT account empowering a broker or adviser to buy and sell without the client's prior knowledge or consent. Some clients set broad guidelines, such as limiting investments to blue chip stocks.

DISCRETIONARY INCOME amount of a consumer's income spent after essentials like food, housing, and utilities and prior commitments have been covered. The total amount of discretionary income can be a key economic indicator because spending this money can spur the economy.

DISCRETIONARY ORDER order to buy a particular stock, bond, or commodity that lets the broker decide when to execute the trade and at what price.

DISCRETIONARY SPENDING in general, any spending that is nonessential. In U.S. government financing, it is the portion of the budget subject to annual review and appropriation. It is distinguished from MANDATORY SPENDING, which refers to expenditures authorized by existing laws, such as Social Security, Medicare, and other entitlement programs and including spending from the Troubled Asset Relief Program (TARP) and other voted stabilization programs.

DISCRETIONARY TRUST
1. mutual fund or unit trust whose investments are not limited to a certain kind of security. The management decides on the best way to use the assets.
2. personal trust that lets the trustee decide how much income or principal to provide to the beneficiary. This can be used to prevent the beneficiary from dissipating funds.

DISHONOR to refuse to pay, as in the case of a check that is returned by a bank because of insufficient funds.

DISINFLATION slowing down of the rate at which prices increase— usually during a recession, when sales drop and retailers are not always able to pass on higher prices to consumers. Not to be confused with DEFLATION, when prices actually drop.

DISINTERMEDIATION movement of funds from low-yielding accounts at traditional banking institutions to higher-yielding investments in the general market—for example, withdrawal of funds from a short-term certificate of deposit paying 1½% to buy a Treasury bond paying 3%. As a countermove, banks may pay higher rates to depositors, then charge higher rates to borrowers, which leads to tight money and reduced economic activity. Since banking DEREGULATION, disintermediation is not the economic problem it once was.

DISINVESTMENT reduction in capital investment either by disposing of capital goods (such as plant and equipment) or by failing to maintain or replace capital assets that are being used up.

DISPOSABLE INCOME personal income remaining after personal taxes and noncommercial government fees have been paid. This money can be spent on essentials or nonessentials or it can be saved. *See also* DISCRETIONARY INCOME.

DISSOLUTION ending (dissolving) of the legal existence of a corporation after the sale of its assets and the satisfaction of its preferred, secured, and unsecured creditors (in that order), and, finally, its owners.

DISTRESS SALE sale of property under distress conditions. For example, stock, bond, mutual fund or futures positions may have to be sold in a portfolio if there is a MARGIN CALL. Real estate may have to be sold because a bank is in the process of FORECLOSURE on the property. A brokerage firm may be forced to sell securities from its inventory if it has fallen below various capital requirements imposed by stock exchanges and regulators. Because distress sellers are being forced to sell, they usually do not receive as favorable a price as if they were able to wait for ideal selling conditions.

DISTRIBUTING SYNDICATE group of brokerage firms or investment bankers that join forces in order to facilitate the DISTRIBUTION of a large block of securities. A distribution is usually handled over a period of time to avoid upsetting the market price. The term distributing syndicate can refer to a primary distribution or a secondary distribution, but the former is more commonly called simply a syndicate or an underwriting syndicate.

DISTRIBUTION
Corporate finance: allocation of income and expenses to the appropriate subsidiary accounts.

Economics: (1) movement of goods from manufacturers; (2) way in which wealth is shared in any particular economic system.

Estate law: parceling out of assets to the beneficiaries named in a will, as carried out by the executor under the guidance of a court.

Mutual funds and closed-end investment companies: payout of realized capital gains on securities in the portfolio of the fund or closed-end investment company.

Securities: sale of a large block of stock in such manner that the price is not adversely affected. Technical analysts look on a pattern of distribution as a tipoff that the stock will soon fall in price. The opposite of distribution, known as ACCUMULATION, may signal a rise in price.

DISTRIBUTION AREA price range in which a stock trades for a long time. Sellers who want to avoid pushing the price down will be careful not to sell below this range. ACCUMULATION of shares in the same range helps to account for the stock's price stability. Technical analysts consider distribution areas in predicting when stocks may break up or down from that price range. *See also* ACCUMULATION AREA.

DISTRIBUTION PERIOD period of time, usually a few days, between the date a company's board of directors declares a stock dividend, known as the DECLARATION DATE, and the DATE OF RECORD, by which the shareholder must officially own shares to be entitled to the dividend.

DISTRIBUTION PLAN plan adopted by a mutual fund to charge certain distribution costs, such as advertising, promotion and sales incentives, to shareholders. The plan will specify a certain per-centage, usually .75% or less, which will be deducted from fund assets annually. *See also* 12b-1 MUTUAL FUND.

DISTRIBUTION STOCK stock part of a block sold over a period of time in order to avoid upsetting the market price. May be part of a primary (underwriting) distribution or a secondary distribution following SHELF REGISTRATION.

DISTRIBUTOR wholesaler of goods to dealers that sell to consumers.

DIVERGENCE in TECHNICAL ANALYSIS, graphic plottings of prices or indicators that are moving in directions that fail to confirm a trend. *See also* MOVING AVERAGE CONVERGENCE/DIVERGENCE (MACD).

DIVERSIFICATION
1. spreading of risk by putting assets in several categories of investments— stocks, bonds, money market instruments, and precious metals, for instance, or several industries, or a mutual fund, with its broad range of stocks in one portfolio.

2. at the corporate level, entering into different business areas, as a CON-
GLOMERATE does.

DIVERSIFIED INVESTMENT OR MANAGEMENT mutual fund or
unit trust that invests in a wide range of securities. Under the Investment
Company Act of 1940, such a company may not have more than 5% of its
assets in any one stock, bond, or commodity and may not own more than
10% of the voting shares of any one company.

DIVESTITURE disposition of an asset or investment by outright sale,
employee purchase, liquidation, and so on.
    Also, one corporation's orderly distribution of large blocks of another
corporation's stock, which were held as an investment. Du Pont was ordered
by the courts to divest itself of General Motors stock, for example.

DIVIDEND distribution of earnings to shareholders, prorated by class of
security and paid in the form of money, stock, scrip, or, rarely, company
products or property. The amount is decided by the board of directors and is
usually paid quarterly. Dividends must be declared as income in the year they
are received. According to the JOBS AND GROWTH TAX RELIEF RECONCILIATION
ACT OF 2003, dividends are taxed at either the 5% or 15% tax rate, depending
on the taxpayer's tax bracket.
    Mutual fund dividends are paid out of income, usually on a quarterly
basis from the fund's investments. The tax on such dividends depends on
whether the distributions resulted from capital gains, interest income, or
dividends received by the fund. *See also* EQUALIZING DIVIDEND; EXTRA
DIVIDEND.

DIVIDEND CAPTURE *see* DIVIDEND ROLLOVER PLAN.

DIVIDEND CLAWBACK *see* CLAWBACK.

DIVIDEND COVER British equivalent of the dividend PAYOUT RATIO.

DIVIDEND DISCOUNT MODEL mathematical model used to determine
the price at which a stock should be selling based on the discounted value
of projected future dividend payments. It is used to identify undervalued
stocks representing capital gains potential.

DIVIDEND EXCLUSION domestic corporations may exclude from taxable
income 70% of dividends received from other domestic corporations.

DIVIDEND IN ARREARS ACCUMULATED DIVIDEND on CUMULATIVE PRE-
FERRED stock, which is payable to the current holder. Preferred stock in a
TURNAROUND situation can be an attractive buy when it is selling at a discount
and has dividends in arrears.

DIVIDEND NOTIFICATION requirement of FINANCIAL INDUSTRY REGULA-
TORY AUTHORITY (FINRA) that its Uniform Practice Department be notified
of a dividend 10 days prior to the RECORD DATE so that FINRA can set the
EX-DIVIDEND DATE.

DIVIDEND PAYOUT RATIO percentage of earnings paid to shareholders
in cash. In general, the higher the payout ratio, the more mature the company.
Electric and telephone utilities tend to have the highest payout ratios,
whereas fast-growing companies usually reinvest all earnings and pay no
dividends.

DIVIDENDS RECEIVED DEDUCTION *see* DIVIDEND EXCLUSION.

DIVIDEND RECORD publication of Standard & Poor's Corporation that provides information on corporate policies and payment histories.

DIVIDEND REINVESTMENT PLAN (DRP) automatic reinvestment of shareholder dividends in more shares of the company's stock. Some companies absorb most or all of the applicable brokerage fees, and some also discount the stock price. Dividend reinvestment plans allow shareholders to accumulate capital over the long term using DOLLAR COST AVERAGING. For corporations, dividend reinvestment plans are a means of raising capital funds without the FLOTATION COSTS of a NEW ISSUE. *See also* NO-LOAD STOCK.

DIVIDEND REQUIREMENT amount of annual earnings necessary to pay contracted dividends on preferred stock.

DIVIDEND ROLLOVER PLAN method of buying and selling stocks around their EX-DIVIDEND dates so as to collect the dividend and make a small profit on the trade. This entails buying shares about two weeks before a stock goes ex-dividend. After the ex-dividend date the price will drop by the amount of the dividend, then work its way back up to the earlier price. By selling slightly above the purchase price, the investor can cover brokerage costs, collect the dividend, and realize a small capital gain in three or four weeks. Also called *dividend capture*. *See also* TRADING DIVIDENDS.

DIVIDENDS PAYABLE dollar amount of dividends that are to be paid, as reported in financial statements. These dividends become an obligation once declared by the board of directors and are listed as liabilities in annual and quarterly reports.

DIVIDENDS-RECEIVED DEDUCTION tax deduction allowed to a corporation owning shares in another corporation for the dividends it receives. In most cases, the deduction is 70%, but in some cases it may be as high as 100% depending on the level of ownership the dividend receiving company has in the dividend-paying entity.

DIVIDEND YIELD annual percentage of return earned by an investor on a common or preferred stock. The yield is determined by dividing the amount of the annual dividends per share, called the INDICATED DIVIDEND, by the current market price per share of the stock. For example, a stock paying a $1 dividend per year that sells for $10 a share has a 10% dividend yield.

DIVISOR flexible numerical value (a denominator) that is adjusted to reflect stock splits and other events that would distort the comparability of a stock average. When divided into the unadjusted overall value of the average (the numerator), the divisor normalizes that value and gives it period-to-period comparability and historical continuity. For example, since 1928, the Dow Jones Industrial Average, which, because of multitudinous adjustments, is expressed in points, has been based on an unweighted, or price-weighted, arithmetic average of the dollar prices of 30 component stocks. Every time an event, such as a split, stock dividend, merger, or substitution, would cause a distortion of 10 points or more, the divisor has been adjusted. A one-point move in any component stock pushed the average up or down almost eight points at the end of 2008. To understand how the formula works, assume the average originally comprised four stocks priced as follows: $10, $30, $60, $80.

Those four amounts total $180, which, divided by four gives us an average of $45. But now assume the $80 stock split two for one, giving the holder two shares priced at $40 each. The list would now comprise four stocks priced at $10, $30, $60, and $40, which totals $140 and divided by four equals $35. Shareholder value has remained constant, but the average is now distorted. One way to adjust the distortion would be to count the split stock twice at $40. But Dow Jones & Company decided instead to use the following formula:

$$\frac{140}{X} = 45; \ 45X = 140; \ X = \frac{140}{45} = 3.11$$

So the divisor in this example is 3.11, which restores the post-split average to 45. The Dow Jones Industrial Average divisor on April 3, 2009, was 0.1255527093. It is reported daily in the Markets Lineup section of *The Wall Street Journal*.

DOCUMENTARY DRAFT *see* DRAFT.

DOGS OF THE DOW strategy of buying the 10 high-yielding stocks in the DOW JONES INDUSTRIAL AVERAGE. Over one-year periods, these 10 stocks tend to outperform all 30 Dow stocks because investors are buying them at depressed prices and earning the highest yields, and the stocks tend to bounce back. The Dogs of the Dow strategy was popularized by Michael B. O'Higgins and John Downes in their book and newsletter *Beating the Dow*. (Downes is the co-author of this *Handbook*.)

DOING BUSINESS AS (DBA) name used for business purposes that is not the legal name of the individual or organization actually conducting the business. DBAs are usually on file as a certificate in the courthouse of the business's jurisdiction. A PROPRIETORSHIP commonly operates under a DBA, as in John Smith DBA John's Auto Body.

DOLLAR BEARS traders who think the dollar will fall in value against other foreign currencies. Dollar bears may implement a number of investment strategies to capitalize on a falling dollar, such as buying Japanese yen, Deutsche marks, British pounds or other foreign currencies directly, or buying futures or options contracts on those currencies.

DOLLAR BOND
1. municipal revenue bond quoted and traded on a dollar price basis instead of yield to maturity.
2. bond denominated in U.S. dollars but issued outside the United States, principally in Europe.
3. bond denominated in U.S. dollars and issued in the United States by foreign companies.
   See also EUROBOND; EURODOLLAR BOND.

DOLLAR COST AVERAGING *see* CONSTANT DOLLAR PLAN.

DOLLAR DRAIN amount by which a foreign country's imports from the United States exceed its exports to the United States. As the country spends more dollars to finance the imports than it receives in payment for the exports, its dollar reserves drain away.

DOLLAR INDEX *see* UNITED STATES DOLLAR INDEX (USDX).

DOLLAR PRICE bond price expressed as a percentage of face value (normally $1000) rather than as a yield. Thus a bond quoted at $97\frac{1}{2}$ has a dollar price of $975, which is $97\frac{1}{2}$% of $1,000.

DOLLAR SHORTAGE situation in which a country that imports from the United States can no longer pay for its purchases without U.S. gifts or loans to provide the necessary dollars. After World War II a world-wide dollar shortage was alleviated by massive infusions of American money through the European Recovery Program (Marshall Plan) and other grant and loan programs.

DOLLAR VOLUME
1. VOLUME, which is normally expressed as the number of shares traded in a period, multiplied by the dollar value of shares.
2. in finance, synonymous with sales and used to distinguish dollar volume from UNIT volume.

DOLLAR-WEIGHTING OF RETURNS investment performance measurement method that equates changes in the dollar value of a portfolio to TOTAL RETURN. While dollar-weighting enables investors to compare absolute dollars with financial goals, manager-to-manager comparisons are not possible unless performance is isolated from external cash flows; this is accomplished with the TIME-WEIGHTING OF RETURNS.

DOMESTIC ACCEPTANCE *see* ACCEPTANCE.

DOMESTIC CORPORATION corporation doing business in the U.S. state in which it was incorporated. In all other U.S. states its legal status is that of a FOREIGN CORPORATION.

DOMICILE place where a person has established permanent residence. It is important to establish a domicile for the purpose of filing state and local income taxes, and for filing estate taxes upon death. The domicile is created based on obtaining a driver's license, registering to vote, and having a permanent home to which one returns. Usually, one must be a resident in a state for at least six months of the year to establish a domicile.

DONATED STOCK fully paid capital stock of a corporation contributed without CONSIDERATION to the same issuing corporation. The gift is credited to the DONATED SURPLUS account at PAR VALUE.

DONATED SURPLUS shareholder's equity account that is credited when contributions of cash, property, or the firm's own stock are freely given to the company. Also termed *donated capital*. Not to be confused with contributed surplus or contributed capital, which is the balances in CAPITAL STOCK accounts plus capital contributed in excess of par or STATED VALUE accounts.

DO NOT INCREASE abbreviated *DNI*. Instruction on good-till-cancelled buy limit and sell stop orders that prevent the quantity from changing in the event of a stock SPLIT or stock dividend.

DO NOT REDUCE (DNR) instruction on a LIMIT ORDER to buy, or on a STOP ORDER to sell, or on a STOP-LIMIT ORDER to sell, not to reduce the order when the stock goes EX-DIVIDEND and its price is reduced by the amount of the dividend as usually happens. DNRs do not apply to rights or stock dividends.

DONOR individual who donates property to another through a TRUST. Also called a *grantor*. Donors also make tax-deductible charitable contributions of securities or physical property to nonprofit institutions such as schools, philanthropic groups, and religious organizations.

DON'T FIGHT THE TAPE don't trade against the market trend. If stocks are falling, as reported on the BROAD TAPE, some analysts say it would be foolish to buy aggressively. Similarly, it would be fighting the tape to sell short during a market rally.

DON'T KNOW Wall Street slang for a *questioned trade*. Brokers exchange comparison sheets to verify the details of transactions between them. Any discrepancy that turns up is called a don't know or a *QT*.

DOT-COM an Internet-related stock, such as Amazon.com.

DOUBLE AUCTION SYSTEM *see* AUCTION MARKET.

DOUBLE-BARRELED municipal revenue bond whose principal and interest are guaranteed by a larger municipal entity. For example, a bridge authority might issue revenue bonds payable out of revenue from bridge tolls. If the city or state were to guarantee the bonds, they would be double-barreled, and the investor would be protected against default in the event that bridge usage is disappointing and revenue proves inadequate.

DOUBLE BOTTOM technical chart pattern showing a drop in price, then a rebound, then another drop to the same level. The pattern is usually interpreted to mean the security has much support at that price and should not drop further. However, if the price does fall through that level, it is considered likely to reach a new low. *See also* DOUBLE TOP.

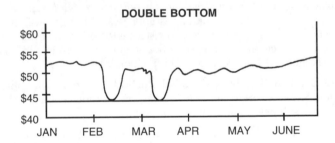

DOUBLE BOTTOM

DOUBLE-DECLINING-BALANCE   DEPRECIATION   METHOD (DDB) method of accelerated depreciation, approved by the Internal Revenue Service, permitting twice the rate of annual depreciation as the straight-line method. It is also called the 200 percent declining-balance method. The two methods are compared below, assuming an asset with a total cost of $1,000, a useful life of four years, and no SALVAGE VALUE.

With STRAIGHT-LINE DEPRECIATION the useful life of the asset is divided into the total cost to arrive at the uniform annual charge of $250, or 25% a year. DDB permits twice the straight-line annual percentage rate—50% in this case—to be applied each year to the undepreciated value of the asset. Hence: 50% × $1,000 = $500 the first year, 50% × $500 = $250 the second year, and so on.

YEAR	STRAIGHT LINE		DOUBLE DECLINING BALANCE	
	Expense	Cumulative	Expense	Cumulative
1	$250	$250	$500	$500
2	250	500	250	750
3	250	750	125	875
4	250	1,000	63	938
	$1,000		$938	

A variation of DDB, called *150 percent declining balance method,* uses 150% of the straight-line annual percentage rate.

A switch to straight-line from declining balance depreciation is permitted once in the asset's life—logically, at the third year in our example. When the switch is made, however, salvage value must be considered. *See also* MODIFIED ACCELERATED COST RECOVERY SYSTEM; DEPRECIATION.

DOUBLE (TAX) EXEMPT descriptive of a MUNICIPAL BOND or other security exempt from federal and state income taxes. *See also* TRIPLE TAX EXEMPT.

DOUBLE HEDGING HEDGING of a SPOT PRICE by using both a FUTURES CONTRACT and an OPTION.

DOUBLE TAXATION taxation of earnings at the corporate level, then again as stockholder dividends. *See also* CONDUIT THEORY.

DOUBLE TOP technical chart pattern showing a rise to a high price, then a drop, then another rise to the same high price. This means the security is encountering resistance to a move higher. However, if the price does move through that level, the security is expected to go on to a new high. *See also* DOUBLE BOTTOM.

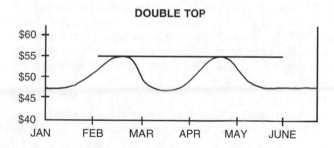

DOUBLE TOP

DOUBLE UP sophisticated stock buying (or selling short) strategy that reaffirms the original rationale by doubling the risk when the price goes (temporarily it is hoped) the wrong way. For example, an investor with confidence in XYZ buys 10,000 shares at $40. When the price drops to $35, the investor buys 10,000 additional shares, thus doubling up on a stock he feels will ultimately rise.

DOUBLE WITCHING DAY day when two related classes of options and futures expire. For example, index options and index futures on the same underlying index may expire on the same day, leading to various strategies by ARBITRAGEURS to close out positions. *See also* TRIPLE WITCHING HOUR.

DOW DIVIDEND THEORY *see* DOGS OF THE DOW.

DOW JONES AVERAGES *see* STOCK INDICES AND AVERAGES.

DOW JONES & COMPANY major financial publisher since 1882 that was acquired by News Corporation in 2007. The company is comprised of four essential segments: Consumer Media includes *The Wall Street Journal* and seven related special and foreign editions, *Barron's*, *MarketWatch*, and the *Far Eastern Economic Review*; Enterprise Media includes Dow Jones Newswires, Factiva, Dow Jones Indexes and other service entities; Local Media includes 8 daily and 14 weekly newspapers with Internet sites; and Strategic Alliances includes 50% of SmartMoney, Vendomosti, and 33% of STOXX Ltd.

DOW JONES INDUSTRIAL AVERAGE *see* STOCK INDEXES AND AVERAGES.

DOWNGRADE lowering of the RATING of a bond or other rated security or of the recommendation of a stock by a research department or rating service. *See also* BROKER RECOMMENDATIONS (OR RATINGS).

DOWN PAYMENT up-front payment of a portion of a purchase price, thereby reducing the balance. *See also* CAPITAL REDUCTION.

DOWNSIDE RISK estimate that a security will decline in value and the extent of the decline, taking into account the total range of factors affecting market price.

DOWNSIZING term for a corporate strategy popular in the 1990s whereby a company reduces its size and complexity, thereby presumably increasing its efficiency and profitability. Downsizing is typically accomplished through RESTRUCTURING, which means reducing the number of employees and, often, the SPIN-OFF of activities unrelated to the company's core business.

DOWNSTREAM flow of corporate activity from parent to subsidiary. Financially, it usually refers to loans, since dividends and interest generally flow upstream. Term is also used by securities analysts, particularly oil analysts, meaning earnings or operations at or near the end-product stage. In an integrated oil company, for example, downstream would refer to the retail gas pump, *upstream* to exploration.

DOWNTICK sale of a security at a price below that of the preceding sale. If a stock has been trading at $15 a share, for instance, the next trade is a downtick if it is down $1/16$ at 14.94. Also known as MINUS TICK. *See also* SHORT-SALE RULE.

DOWNTURN shift of an economic or stock market cycle from rising to falling.

DOW THEORY theory that a major trend in the stock market must be confirmed by a similar movement in the Dow Jones Industrial Average and the Dow Jones Transportation Average. According to Dow Theory, a significant trend is not confirmed until both Dow Jones indexes reach the new highs or lows; if they don't, the market will fall back to its former trading range. Dow Theory proponents often disagree on when a true breakout has occurred and, in any case, miss a major portion of the up or down move while waiting for their signals.

DRAFT signed, written order by which one party (drawer) instructs another party (drawee) to pay a specified sum to a third party (payee). Payee and drawer are usually the same person. In foreign transactions, a draft is usually called a *bill of exchange.* When prepared without supporting papers, it is a *clean draft.* With papers or documents attached, it is a *documentary draft.* A *sight draft* is payable on demand. *A time draft* is payable either on a definite date or at a fixed time after sight or demand.

DRAG ALONG RIGHTS right of majority shareholders to force minority shareholders to consent to an agreement to sell or liquidate a company. Right prevents smaller shareholders from blocking a deal in order to raise share.

DRAGON BOND United States dollar-denominated bond issued in Asia.

DRAINING RESERVES actions by the Federal Reserve System to decrease the money supply by curtailing the funds banks have available to lend. The Fed does this in three ways: (1) by raising reserve requirements, forcing banks to keep more funds on deposit with Federal Reserve banks; (2) by increasing the rate at which banks borrow to maintain reserves, thereby making it unattractive to deplete reserves by making loans; and (3) by selling bonds in the open market at such attractive rates that dealers reduce their bank balances to buy them. *See also* MULTIPLIER.

DRAWBACK rebate of taxes or duties paid on imported goods that have been reexported. It is in effect a government subsidy designed to encourage domestic manufacturers to compete overseas.

DRAWER *see* DRAFT.

DRAWN BONDS (SECURITIES) bonds or other securities that have been subjected to a CALL and have been redeemed.

DRESSING UP A PORTFOLIO practice of money managers to make their portfolio look good at the end of a reporting period. For example, a mutual fund or pension fund manager may sell certain stocks that performed badly during the quarter shortly before the end of that quarter to avoid having to report that holding to shareholders. Or they may buy stocks that have risen during the quarter to show shareholders that they owned winning stocks. Because these portfolio changes are largely cosmetic, they have little effect on portfolio performance except they increase transaction costs. In the final few days of a quarter, market analysts frequently comment that certain stocks rose or fell because of end-of-quarter WINDOW DRESSING.

DRILLING PROGRAM *see* BALANCED DRILLING PROGRAM; COMPLETION PROGRAM; DEVELOPMENTAL DRILLING PROGRAM; EXPLORATORY DRILLING PROGRAM; OIL AND GAS LIMITED PARTNERSHIP.

DRIP *see* DIVIDEND REINVESTMENT PLAN.

DRIP FEED supplying capital to a new company as its growth requires it, rather than in a lump sum at the beginning. *See also* EVERGREEN FUNDING.

DRIVER the aspect of a business mainly responsible for its growth and viability.

DROP-DEAD DAY day on which a deadline, such as the expiration of the national debt limit, becomes absolutely final.

DROP-DEAD FEE British term meaning a fee paid to a lender only if a deal requiring financing from that lender falls through.

DROPLOCK SECURITY FLOATING RATE NOTE or bond that becomes a FIXED INCOME INVESTMENT when the rate to which it is pegged drops to a specified level.

DUAL BANKING U.S. system whereby banks are chartered by the state or federal government. This makes for differences in banking regulations, in lending limits, and in services available to customers.

DUAL LISTING listing of a security on more than one exchange, thus increasing the competition for bid and offer prices as well as the liquidity of the securities. Furthermore, being listed on an exchange in the East and another in the West would extend the number of hours when the stock can be traded. Securities may not be listed on both the New York and American stock exchanges.

DUAL PURPOSE FUND exchange-listed CLOSED-END FUND that has two classes of shares. Preferred shareholders receive all the income (dividends and interest) from the portfolio, while common shareholders receive all the capital gains. Such funds are set up with a specific expiration date when preferred shares are redeemed at a predetermined price and common shareholders claim the remaining assets, voting either to liquidate or to continue the fund on an open-end basis. Dual purpose funds are not closely followed on Wall Street, and there is little trading in them.

DUAL TRADING commodities traders' practice of dealing for their own and their clients' accounts at the same time. Reformers favor restricting dual trading to prevent FRONT RUNNING; advocates claim the practice is harmless in itself and economically vital to the industry.

DUE BILL *see* BILL.

DUE DATE date on which a debt-related obligation is required to be paid.

DUE DILIGENCE MEETING meeting conducted by the underwriter of a new offering at which brokers can ask representatives of the issuer questions about the issuer's background and financial reliability and the intended use of the proceeds. Brokers who recommend investment in new offerings without very careful due diligence work may face lawsuits if the investment should go sour later. Although, in itself, the legally required due diligence meeting typically is a perfunctory affair, most companies, recognizing the importance of due diligence, hold informational meetings, often in different regions of the country, at which top management representatives are available to answer questions of securities analysts and institutional investors.

DUE-ON-SALE CLAUSE clause in a mortgage contract requiring the borrower to pay off the full remaining principal outstanding on a mortgage when the mortgaged property is sold, transferred, or in any way encumbered. Due-on-sale clauses prevent the buyer of the property from assuming the mortgage loan.

DUMPING

International finance: selling goods abroad below cost in order to eliminate a surplus or to gain an edge on foreign competition. The U.S. Antidumping Act of 1974 was designed to prevent the sale of imported goods below cost in the United States.

Securities: offering large amounts of stock with little or no concern for price or market effect.

DUN & BRADSTREET (D & B) company that combines credit information obtained directly from commercial firms with data solicited from their creditors, then makes this available to subscribers in reports and a ratings directory. D & B also offers an accounts receivable collection service and publishes financial composite ratios and other financial information.

DUN'S NUMBER short for Dun's Market Identifier. It is published as part of a list of firms giving information such as an identification number, address code, number of employees, corporate affiliations, and trade styles. Full name: Data Universal Numbering System.

DUPONT SYSTEM system devised in 1919 by E. I. Du Pont de Nemours & Company to appraise financial performance. The Du Pont method or formula determines return on assets (ROA) by multiplying asset turnover (sales divided by assets) by return on sales (net income divided by net sales).

DURABLE GOODS goods that have a useful life of more than three years. Orders for durable goods, which are tracked by the Commerce Department on a monthly basis, indicate the extent to which businesses and manufacturers are willing to invest capital for future needs Several months of increases in durable goods orders are a sign of a strong economy, and vice versa. The term *hard goods* is sometimes used synonymously, but more properly refers to durable consumer goods, such as appliances, as opposed to *soft goods,* which are consumer nondurables, such as textiles. The official economic opposite of durable goods is *nondurable goods,* which includes food, fuel, cosmetics, drugs, clothing, and services.

DURABLE POWER OF ATTORNEY legal document by which a person with assets (the principal) appoints another person (the agent) to act on the principal's behalf, even if the principal becomes incompetent. If the power of attorney is not "durable," the agent's authority to act ends if the principal becomes incompetent. The agent's power to act for the principal may be broadly stated, allowing the agent to buy and sell securities, or narrowly stated to limit activity to selling a car.

DURATION concept first developed by Frederick Macaulay in 1938 that measures bond price VOLATILITY by measuring the "length" of a bond. It is a weighted-average term-to-maturity of the bond's cash flows, the weights being the present value of each cash flow as a percentage of the bond's full price. A Salomon Smith Barney study compared it to a series of tin cans equally spaced on a seesaw. The size of each can represents the cash flow due, the contents of each can represent the present values of those cash flows, and the intervals between them represent the payment periods. Duration is the distance to the fulcrum that would balance the seesaw. The duration of a zero-coupon security would thus equal its maturity because all the cash flows—all the weights—are at the other end of the seesaw. The greater the duration of a bond, the greater its percentage volatility. In general, duration rises with maturity, falls with the frequency of coupon payments, and falls as the yield rises (the higher yield reduces the present values of the cash flows.) Duration (the term *modified duration* is used in the strict sense because of modifications to Macaulay's formulation) as a measure of percentage of volatility is valid only for small changes in yield. For working purposes, duration can be defined as the approximate percentage change in price for a 100-basis-point change in yield. A duration of 5, for example, means the price of the bond will change by approximately 5% for a 100-basis point change in yield.

For larger yield changes, volatility is measured by a concept called *convexity*. That term derives from the price-yield curve for a normal bond, which is convex. In other words, the price is always falling at a slower rate as the yield increases. The more convexity a bond has, the merrier, because it means the bond's price will fall more slowly and rise more quickly on a given movement in general interest rate levels. As with duration, convexity on straight bonds increases with lower coupon, lower yield, and longer maturity. Convexity measures the rate of change of duration, and for an option-free bond it is always positive because changes in yield do not affect cash flows. When a bond has a call option, however, cash flows are affected. In that case, duration gets smaller as yield decreases, resulting in *negative convexity*.

When the durations of the assets and the liabilities of a portfolio, say that of a pension fund, are the same, the portfolio is inherently protected against interest-rate changes and you have what is called *immunization*. The high volatility and interest rates in the early 1980s caused institutional investors to use duration and convexity as tools in immunizing their portfolios.

DUTCH AUCTION auction system in which the price of an item is gradually lowered until it meets a responsive bid and is sold. U.S. Treasury bills are sold under this system. Contrasting is the two-sided or DOUBLE AUCTION SYSTEM exemplified by the major stock exchanges. *See also* BILL.

DUTCH AUCTION PREFERRED STOCK type of adjustable-rate PREFERRED STOCK whose dividend is determined every seven weeks in a DUTCH AUCTION process by corporate bidders. Shares are bought and sold at FACE VALUES ranging from $100,000 to $500,000 per share. Also known as *auction rate preferred stock. See also* APS.

DUTY tax imposed on the importation, exportation, or consumption of goods. *See also* TARIFF.

DWARFS pools of mortgage-backed securities, with original maturity of 15 years, issued by the Federal National Mortgage Association (FANNIE MAE).

DYNAMIC ASSET ALLOCATION ASSET ALLOCATION strategy involving frequent changes in asset proportion or composition in response to changing economic or market conditions.

E

EACH WAY commission made by a broker involved on both the purchase and the sale side of a trade. *See also* CROSSED TRADE.

EAFE acronym for the *Europe and Australasia, Far East Equity* index, calculated by the Morgan Stanley Capital International (MSCI) group. EAFE is composed of stocks screened for liquidity, cross-ownership, and industry representation. Stocks are selected by MSCI's analysts in Geneva. The index acts as a benchmark for managers of international stock portfolios. There are financial futures and options contracts based on EAFE.

EARLY WITHDRAWAL PENALTY charge assessed against holders of fixed-term investments if they withdraw their money before maturity. Such a penalty would be assessed, for instance, if someone who has a six-month certificate of deposit withdrew the money after four months.

EARNED INCOME income (especially wages and salaries) generated by providing goods or services. Also, pension or annuity income.

EARNED INCOME CREDIT TAX CREDIT for qualifying taxpayers with at least one child in residence for more than half the year and incomes below a specified dollar level.

EARNED SURPLUS *see* RETAINED EARNINGS.

EARNEST MONEY good faith deposit given by a buyer to a seller prior to consummation of a transaction. Earnest money is usually forfeited in the event the buyer is unwilling or unable to complete the sale. In real estate, earnest money is the down payment, which is usually put in an escrow account until the closing.

EARNING ASSET income-producing asset. For example, a company's building would not be an earning asset normally, but a financial investment in other property would be if it provided rental income.

EARNINGS BEFORE TAXES corporate profits after interest has been paid to bondholders, but before taxes have been paid.

EARNINGS MANAGEMENT *see* MANAGED EARNINGS.

EARNINGS MOMENTUM pattern of increasing rate of growth in EARNINGS PER SHARE from one period to another, which usually causes a stock price to go up. For example, a company whose earnings per share are up 15% one year and 35% the next has earnings momentum and should see a gain in its stock price.

EARNINGS MULTIPLE Same as PRICE/EARNINGS RATIO (P/E).

EARNINGS PER SHARE portion of a company's profit allocated to each outstanding share of common stock. For instance, a corporation that earned $10 million last year and has 10 million shares outstanding would report earnings of $1 per share. The figure is calculated after paying taxes and after paying preferred shareholders and bondholders, as required by FINANCIAL ACCOUNTING STANDARDS BOARD (FASB) Rule 128. Companies must report earnings per share on two bases: BASIC EARNINGS PER SHARE which doesn't count stock options, warrants, and convertible securities, and (fully) *diluted* *earnings per share,* which includes those securities. *See also* FULLY DILUTED EARNINGS PER (COMMON) SHARE.

EARNINGS-PRICE RATIO relationship of earnings per share to current stock price. Also known as *earnings yield,* it is used in comparing the relative attractiveness of stocks, bonds, and money market instruments. Inverse of PRICE-EARNINGS RATIO.

EARNINGS REPORT statement issued by a company to its shareholders and the public at large reporting its earnings for the latest period, which is either on a quarterly or annual basis. The report will show revenues, expenses, and net profit for the period. Earnings reports are released to the press and reported in newspapers and electronic media, and are also mailed to shareholders of record. Also called *profit and loss statement* (P&L) or *income statement.*

EARNINGS SURPRISE EARNINGS REPORT that reports a higher or lower profit than analysts have projected. If earnings are higher than expected, a company's stock price will usually rise sharply. If profits are below expectations, the company's stock will often plunge. Many analysts on Wall Street study earnings surprises very carefully on the theory that when a company reports a positive or negative surprise, it is typically followed by another surprise in the same direction. Two firms that follow general trends in earnings surprises are FIRST CALL and ZACKS ESTIMATE SYSTEM.

EARNINGS YIELD *see* EARNINGS-PRICE RATIO.

EARN-OUT in mergers and acquisitions, supplementary payments, not part of the original ACQUISITION COST, based on future earnings of the acquired company above a predetermined level.

EASY MONEY *see* TIGHT MONEY.

EATING SOMEONE'S LUNCH expression that an aggressive competitor is beating their rivals. For example, an analyst might say that one retailer is "eating the lunch" of a competitive retailer in the same town if it is gaining market share through an aggressive pricing strategy. The implication of the expression is that the winning competitor is taking food away from the losing company or individual.

EATING STOCK a block positioner or underwriter who can't find buyers may find himself eating stock, that is, buying it for his own account.

E-BANK *see* ONLINE BANKING.

EBIDTA acronym meaning earnings before interest, taxes, depreciation, and amortization; pronounced *ee' bitda.*

ECHO BOOMERS generation representing the children of *baby boomers* who were born immediately following World War II.

ECI *see* EMPLOYMENT COST INDEX (ECI).

ECM *see* EMERGING COMPANY MARKETPLACE (ECM).

ECONOMETRICS use of computer analysis and modeling techniques to describe in mathematical terms the relationship between key economic forces such as labor, capital, interest rates, and government policies, then test the effects of changes in economic scenarios. For instance, an econometric model might show the relationship of housing starts and interest rates.

ECONOMIC GROWTH AND TAX RELIEF RECONCILIATION ACT OF 2001 (EGTRRA) landmark legislation designed to cut taxes by $1.35 trillion over ten years. It was signed into law by President Bush on June 7, 2001. Following are the highlights of the law:

Lowers Tax Rates: The tax rate on the first $6,000 of taxable income is lowered from 15% to 10% for singles and married couples filing separately. For heads of household, the first $10,000 of income is taxed at 10% and for married couples filing jointly, the first $12,000 in income is taxed at 10%.

Marginal tax rates are reduced in phases over five years according to this schedule:

Year	15% rate	28% rate	31% rate	36% rate	39.8% rate
2001	refund credit	27.5%	30.5%	35.5%	39.1%
2002–03	partial 10%	27%	30%	35%	38.6%
2004–05	partial 10%	26%	29%	34%	37.6%
2006 on	partial 10%	25%	28%	33%	35%

Repeal of deduction and personal exemption limitations The limit on itemized deductions is phased out in stages starting in 2006 and is completely repealed in 2010. In addition, the phase-out of personal exemptions for high-income taxpayers is repealed starting in 2006 and in 2010 there will no longer be any phase-out of the personal exemption.

Provided 2001 Tax Refund Because the new 10% rate reduction on the first $6,000 of income was retroactive to January 1, 2001, taxpayers who paid income taxes for 2000 received tax refund checks of $300 for a single, $500 for a head of household, and $600 for a married couple filing jointly.

Alternative Minimum Tax exemptions increased the AMT exemption amounts for individuals increased in 2001 through 2004 to $49,000 for married couples filing jointly and surviving spouses, to $35,750 for singles, and to $24,500 for married couples filing separately.

Marriage Penalty Relief the penalty imposed on couples who pay more tax when filing a joint return than they would if filing as singles is gradually phased out through 2009. This is accomplished by increasing the standard deduction from 2005 through 2009 so that when fully phased in the deduction for a married couple is twice the deduction for a single. This phase-in of the deduction is shown in this table:

Year	% of standard deduction for single taxpayers
2005	174%
2006	184%
2007	187%
2008	190%
2009	200%

In addition, the size of the 15% income tax bracket for a married couple filing jointly expands to twice the size of the corresponding bracket for a single from 2005 through 2009 according to this table:

Year	Phase-in amount of increase
2005	180%
2006	187%
2007	193%
2008	200%

The earned income credit is also equalized so that married and single taxpayers receive the same benefit by 2008 according to this schedule:

Year	Increase in EIC phase-out amount
2002–2004	$1000
2005–2007	$2000
2008 and later	$3000

Child, Adoption, and Dependent Care Credits Expanded the child tax credit was doubled from $500 to $1,000 per child over 10 years through 2010 using this table:

Year	Maximum child credit
2001–2004	$600
2005–2008	$700
2009	$800
2010	$1000

In addition, this child tax credit can be applied against a taxpayer's Alternative Minimum Tax (AMT) liability on a permanent basis. The credit is also refundable to the extent that 10% of the taxpayer's earned income exceeds $10,000 for 2001 through 2004. The refundable amount of the credit increases to 15% of the income over $10,000 after 2004.

The adoption credit for the adoption of a child was raised from $5,000 to $10,000 for both a non-special needs and a special needs child. This credit is phased out for couples with adjusted gross incomes of $150,000 (up from $75,000 under previous law).

The dependent care credit rate was increased from 30% to 35% and the amount of eligible employment-related expenses to which the credit rate can be applied rose from $2,400 to $3,000. The beginning point of the income phase-out range for the credit was raised from $10,000 to $15,000.

Education Tax Breaks Expanded several provisions of the law were designed to help save and pay for educational expenses including:

Deductions for college tuition for qualified higher education expenses were introduced. For the years 2002–2003, for singles with adjusted gross incomes below $65,000 and married couples filing jointly with AGI below $130,000, an above-the-line deduction of $3,000 is allowed each year. In 2004 and 2005, the deduction rises to $4,000. Singles with incomes up to $80,000 and joint filers with incomes up to $160,000 can take a maximum tuition deduction of $2,000 in 2004 and 2005. This deduction sunsets after 2005. In the past, deductions for student loan interest were only allowed for five years after payments began—this limitation was repealed by the new law.

Education IRAs were renamed Coverdell Education Savings Accounts and were expanded greatly. The contribution limit was raised from $500 to $2,000 per year per child from birth to age 18. The Adjusted Gross Income limitation was raised to $95,000 for singles and $190,000 for married couples.

Contributions can now be made up until April 15 after the close of the applicable tax year instead of December 31 under previous law. Distributions from Coverdell ESAs can be used for a much wider array of education expenses including higher education, elementary or secondary school tuition, or expenses at either a public or private school. Some of the eligible expenses include tutoring, computer equipment, room and board, uniforms, and extended day programs.

In addition, the law allowed taxpayers to claim a Hope and Lifetime Learning Credit in the same year that they took a distribution from a Coverdell ESA as long as the distribution is not used to pay for the same expense for which the education credits are claimed. Contributions to Coverdell ESAs and qualified state tuition 529 plans were allowed in the same year without penalty.

Qualified tuition plans were improved and expanded. Plans were allowed to be sponsored by both state and private institutions. Distributions from state-sponsored plans were made completely tax-free after December 31, 2001 and distributions from school-sponsored plans were made tax-free after December 31, 2003.

The law extended and made permanent the income-tax exclusion up to $5,250 for employer-provided educational assistance to pay for undergraduate and graduate courses.

Retirement Savings Plans Expanded a variety of new features of the law allows people to contribute more to their retirement savings plans including:

Maximum annual contributions to Individual Retirement Arrangements (IRAs) were expanded from $2,000 a year to $5,000 in 2008 under the following phase-in schedule:

Year	Maximum IRA contribution
2002	$3000
2003	$3000
2004	$3000
2005	$4000
2006	$4000
2007	$4000
2008	$5000

After 2008, the $5,000 maximum will be adjusted for inflation.

For those at least 50 years old in 2002, an additional "catch-up" contribution is allowed. The catch-up amount is phased in according to this schedule:

Year	IRA catch-up amount
2002	$500
2003	$500
2004	$500
2005	$500
2006	$1000
2007	$1000
2008	$1000

Retirement account rollover rules were simplified and pension plan portability increased, so that IRA holders are allowed to roll over balances from their IRA into any eligible retirement plan, whether it is another IRA or a plan sponsored by an employer. Taxpayers who had received after-tax contributions to their pension plans from their employers are also able to roll over those contributions to an IRA or other employer's defined contribution plan.

A new retirement savings tax credit was introduced. For married couples filing jointly with an adjusted gross income of $50,000 or less, a credit of as much as $2,000 is available. The same credit can apply to heads of households earning $37,500 or less or singles with $25,000 or less in income. This credit is in addition to any other deduction or exclusion that applies to retirement savings contributions.

The limit on contributions to defined contribution plans such as 401(k) salary reduction plans was raised from $10,500 to $15,000 by the year 2006. In addition, those over age 50 can make additional "catch-up" contributions rising from $1,000 to $5,000 by 2006 under the following schedule:

Year	Maximum 401 (k) contribution	Catch-up contribution
2001	$10,500	$0
2002	$11,000	$1000
2003	$12,000	$2000
2004	$13,000	$3000
2005	$14,000	$4000
2006	$15,000	$5000

After 2006 the limit will be adjusted for inflation.

Limits on contributions for SIMPLE plans were also raised, and will be phased in from $6,500 in 2001 to $10,000 in 2006, with an additional catch-up amount allowed for those over age 50, according to this schedule:

Year	Maximum SIMPLE contribution	Catch-up contribution
2001	$6500	$0
2002	$7000	$500
2003	$8000	$1000
2004	$9000	$1500
2005	$10,000	$2000
2006	$10,000	$2500

After 2006 the limit will be adjusted for inflation.

The limit on annual additions to a small business defined contribution plan jumped from $35,000 to $40,000 in 2002 with future adjustments for inflation in $1,000 increments. In addition, the total amount of compensation that employers may consider when calculating an employee's contribution rose from $170,000 to $200,000.

To stimulate the savings capability of newer businesses and those without an existing pension plan, the law granted a special tax credit of up to 50% of the first $1,000 in start-up expenses for three years after establishing the plan for businesses with less than 100 employees. The law also raised the tax-deductibility limits for profit-sharing and stock-bonus plans from 15% to 25%.

Vesting rules for qualified retirement plan employer matches were accelerated. Two vesting schedules were introduced: Under one, participants would have the right to 100% of their employer match after three years. Under the other, vesting of the match would be 20% each year starting in the second year, reaching 100% after six years.

The limit on current liability pension funding is repealed over time. In an effort to strengthen pension security, the current liability full funding limit is first increased and then repealed based on this schedule:

Year	Funding limit
2001	160%
2002	165%
2003	170%
2004 and later	No limit

The law created Roth 401(k) and Roth 403(b) plans, starting in 2006. Employers will allow employees to contribute after-tax dollars to these plans and eventually take the money out of the Roths in retirement tax-free.

Estate Tax Changes the law phases out much of the estate tax over nine years until the tax is repealed in 2010. However, the entire estate tax law was scheduled to be automatically reinstated in 2011 unless Congress changed the law again.

The estate tax rate was scheduled to drop in phases from 55% in 2001 to 45% in 2009 and the amount of property that can be exempted from estate tax was scheduled to rise in phases from $675,000 in 2001 to $3.5 million in 2009 according to this schedule:

Year	Exemption	Highest tax rate
2001	$675,000	55%
2002	$1 million	50%
2003	$1 million	49%
2004	$1.5 million	48%
2005	$1.5 million	47%
2006	$2 million	46%
2007	$2 million	45%
2008	$2 million	45%
2009	$3.5 million	45%
2010	repealed	0%
2011	$1 million	55%

The generation-skipping tax (GST) is a tax on the transfer of property to a person more than one generation below, such as a grandchild. The tax rate for the GST is usually the highest estate tax rate. The federal estate tax allows a credit for state death taxes. The new law mandated that the GST and state death tax credit be coordinated under the phase-out schedule. The amount of the state death tax credit will be reduced according to this schedule:

Year	Reduction in credit
2002	25%
2003	50%
2004	75%
2005	No-credit-deduction only

The maximum tax rate on gifts made during a lifetime was reduced in phases from 50% in 2002 to 35% in 2010. The amount that a person can exempt from gift tax during his or her lifetime remains at $1 million. The annual amount that can be excluded on a gift to any individual remains at

$11,000, though that amount is adjusted for inflation. Transfers between spouses remain free of gift taxes.

The carryover basis system for those inheriting property was changed. Under the current system, heirs receive property with a higher stepped-up basis based on the value of the property on the day of the death of the grantor. Under the new law in 2010, when there will be no estate tax, property received by heirs will not automatically receive a step-up in value. Instead, it will have the same basis as it did before the death. This new arrangement is called a modified carryover basis. Some relief will be available in that an estate will be allowed a basis step-up of $1.3 million and there will be an extra $3 million step-up in basis on property left to a spouse.

ECONOMIC GROWTH RATE rate of change in the GROSS NATIONAL PRODUCT, as expressed in an annual percentage. If adjusted for inflation, it is called the *real economic growth rate.* Two consecutive quarterly drops in the growth rate mean recession, and two consecutive advances in the growth rate reflect an expanding economy.

ECONOMIC INDICATORS key statistics showing the direction of the economy. Among them are the unemployment rate, inflation rate, factory utilization rate, and balance of trade. *See also* LEADING INDICATORS.

ECONOMIC ORDER QUANTITY (EOQ) amount of orders necessary to minimize costs related to the ordering and carrying of inventory.

ECONOMIC RECOVERY TAX ACT OF 1981 (ERTA) tax-cutting legislation. Among the key provisions:
1. across-the-board tax cut, which took effect in three stages ending in 1983.
2. indexing of tax brackets to the inflation rate.
3. lowering of top tax rates on long-term capital gains from 28% to 20%. The top rate on dividends, interest, rents, and royalties income dropped from 70% to 50%.
4. lowering of MARRIAGE PENALTY tax, as families with two working spouses could deduct 10% from the salary of the lower-paid spouse, up to $3,000.
5. expansion of INDIVIDUAL RETIREMENT ARRANGEMENTS to all working people, who can contribute up to $2,000 a year, and $250 annually for nonworking spouses. Also, expansion of the amount self-employed people can contribute to KEOGH PLAN account contributions.
6. creation of the *all-savers certificate,* which allowed investors to exempt up to $1,000 a year in earned interest. The authority to issue these certificates expired at the end of 1982.
7. deductions for reinvesting public utility dividends.
8. reductions in estate and gift taxes, phased in so that the first $600,000 of property can be given free of estate tax starting in 1987. Annual gifts that can be given free of gift tax were raised from $3,000 to $10,000. Unlimited deduction for transfer of property to a spouse at death.
9. lowering of rates on the exercise of stock options.
10. change in rules on DEPRECIATION and INVESTMENT CREDIT.
  See also TAX REFORM ACT OF 1986.

ECONOMICS study of the economy. Classic economics concentrates on how the forces of supply and demand allocate scarce product and service resources. MACROECONOMICS studies a nation or the world's economy as a whole, using data about inflation, unemployment and industrial production to understand the past and predict the future. MICROECONOMICS studies the behavior of specific sectors of the economy, such as companies, industries, or households. Various schools of economic thought have gained prominence, including AUSTRIAN ECONOMICS, KEYNESIAN ECONOMICS, MONETARISM, and SUPPLY-SIDE ECONOMICS.

ECONOMIES OF SCALE economic principle that as the volume of production increases, the cost of producing each unit decreases. Therefore, building a large factory will be more efficient than a small factory because the large factory will be able to produce more units at a lower cost per unit than the smaller factory. The introduction of mass production techniques in the early twentieth century, such as the assembly line production of Ford Motor Company's Model T, put the theory of economies of scale into action.

ECU *see* EUROPEAN CURRENCY UNIT (ECU).

EDGAR *see* SEC EDGAR.

EDGE ACT banking legislation, passed in 1919, which allows national banks to conduct foreign lending operations through federal or state chartered subsidiaries, called Edge Act corporations. Such corporations can be chartered by other states and are allowed, unlike domestic banks, to own banks in foreign countries and to invest in foreign commercial and industrial firms. The act also permitted the FEDERAL RESERVE SYSTEM to set reserve requirements on foreign banks that do business in America. Edge Act corporations benefited further from the 1978 International Banking Act, which instructs the Fed to strike any regulations putting American banks at a disadvantage compared with U.S. operations of foreign banks.

EDUCATION IRA form of INDIVIDUAL RETIREMENT ARRANGEMENT allowing parents to save money for their children's educational expenses. Originally created in the TAXPAYER RELIEF ACT OF 1997, the Education IRA became the COVERDELL EDUCATION SAVINGS ACCOUNT in the ECONOMIC GROWTH AND TAX RELIEF RECONCILIATION ACT OF 2001.

EEC *see* EUROPEAN ECONOMIC COMMUNITY.

EFFECTIVE DATE
In general: date on which an agreement takes effect.
Securities: date when an offering registered with the Securities and Exchange Commission may commence, usually 20 days after filing the registration statement. *See also* SHELF REGISTRATION.
Banking and insurance: time when an insurance policy goes into effect. From that day forward, the insured party is covered by the contract.

EFFECTIVE DEBT total debt owed by a firm, including the capitalized value of lease payments.

EFFECTIVE NET WORTH net worth plus subordinated debt, as viewed by senior creditors. In small business banking, loans payable to principals are commonly subordinated to bank loans. The loans for principals thus can be regarded as effective net worth as long as a bank loan is outstanding and the subordination agreement is in effect.

EFFECTIVE RATE yield on a debt instrument as calculated from the purchase price. The effective rate on a bond is determined by the price, the coupon rate, the time between interest payments, and the time until maturity. Every bond's effective rate thus depends on when it was bought. The effective rate is a more meaningful yield figure than the coupon rate. *See also* RATE OF RETURN.

EFFECTIVE SALE price of a ROUND LOT that determines the price at which the next ODD LOT will be sold. If the last round-lot price was 15, for instance, the odd-lot price might be 15⅛. The added fraction expressed in decimals is the *odd-lot differential.*

EFFECTIVE TAX RATE tax rate paid by a taxpayer. It is determined by dividing the tax paid by the taxable income in a particular year. For example, if a taxpayer with a taxable income of $100,000 owes $30,000 in a year, he has an effective tax rate of 30%. The effective tax rate is useful in tax planning, because it gives a taxpayer a realistic understanding of the amount of taxes he is paying after allowing for all deductions, credits, and other factors affecting tax liability.

EFFICIENT MARKET theory that market prices reflect the knowledge and expectations of all investors. Those who adhere to this theory consider it futile to seek undervalued stocks or to forecast market movements. Any new development is reflected in a firm's stock price, they say, making it impossible to beat the market. This vociferously disputed hypothesis also holds that an investor who throws darts at a newspaper's stock listings has as good a chance to outperform the market as any professional investor. The theory, also known as the RANDOM WALK theory, was first set forth in 1900 by the French mathematician Louis Bachelier, and received modern treatment in Burton Malkiel's book *A Random Walk Down Wall Street. See also* ACTIVE MANAGEMENT; BEHAVIORAL FINANCE (OR INVESTING).

EFFICIENT PORTFOLIO portfolio that has a maximum EXPECTED RETURN for any level of risk or a minimum level of risk for any expected return. It is arrived at mathematically, taking into account the expected return and standard deviation of returns for each security, as well as the covariance of returns between different securities in the portfolio.

EITF *see* EMERGING ISSUES TASK FORCE.

EITHER-OR ORDER *see* ALTERNATIVE ORDER.

ELASTICITY OF DEMAND AND SUPPLY
Elasticity of demand: responsiveness of buyers to changes in price. Demand for luxury items may slow dramatically if prices are raised, because these purchases are not essential, and can be postponed. On the other hand, demand for necessities such as food, telephone service, and emergency surgery is said to be inelastic. It remains about the same despite price changes because buyers cannot postpone their purchases without severe adverse consequences.
Elasticity of supply: responsiveness of output to changes in price. As prices move up, the supply normally increases. If it does not, it is said to be inelastic. Supply is said to be elastic if the rise in price means a rise in production.

ELECT
In general: choose a course of action. Someone who decides to incorporate a certain provision in a will elects to do so.
Securities trading: make a conditional order into a market order. If a customer has received a guaranteed buy or sell price from a specialist on the

floor of an exchange, the transaction is considered elected when that price is reached. If the guarantee is that a stock will be sold when it reaches 20, and a stop order is put at that price, the sale will be elected at 20.

ELECTRONIC BANKING *see* ONLINE BANKING.

ELECTRONIC BLUE SHEET (EBS) format used by clearing firms to provide the SEC with detailed information about trading activity, including the security traded, the trade date, price, transaction size, and a list of the parties involved. Preelectronics, information was communicated on blue paper.

ELECTRONIC CASH (E-CASH) *see* DIGITAL MONEY; ELECTRONIC WALLET.

ELECTRONIC COMMERCE buying and selling on the Internet. Also called *e-commerce*, it has three subcategories: business-to-business (B2B), business-to-consumer (B2C), and consumer-to-consumer (C2C).

ELECTRONIC COMMUNICATIONS NETWORK (ECN) any one of a number of electronic systems that displays and matches orders placed on exchanges and over-the-counter by market makers and traders. A prominent example is Inet, a business of Instinet Group. Inet represents the consolidation of the order flow of the former Instinet ECN and former Island ECN. In 2005, Instinet was acquired by NASDAQ and is now part of NASDAQ OMX. *See also* NATIONAL MARKET SYSTEM; SUPER MONTAGE.

ELECTRONIC DATA GATHERING ANALYSIS AND RETRIEVAL (EDGAR) *see* SEC EDGAR.

ELECTRONIC FUNDS TRANSFER (EFT) as defined in the Electronic Fund Transfer Act (Title XX of the Financial Institutions Regulatory and Interest Rate Control Act of 1978), any transfer of funds, other than a transaction originated by a paper instrument, that is initiated through an electronic terminal, telephone, or computer or magnetic tape and that orders or authorizes a financial institution to debit or credit an account. An example would be an ATM (AUTOMATIC TELLER MACHINE) transaction. Also called *wire transfer*.

ELECTRONIC QUOTATION SERVICE Internet service providing information of PINK SHEETS LLC.

ELECTRONIC WALLET computer technology that stores a coded credit card number in the hard drive and permits purchases at web sites without reentering card information. *See also* DIGITAL MONEY.

ELEPHANTS expression describing large institutional investors. The term implies that such investors, including mutual funds, pension funds, banks, and insurance companies, tend to move their billions of dollars in assets in a herd-like manner, driving stock and bond prices up and down in concert. CONTRARIAN investors specialize in doing the opposite of the elephants—buying when institutions are selling and selling when the elephants are buying. The opposite of elephants are SMALL INVESTORS, who buy and sell far smaller quantities of stocks and bonds.

ELEVEN BOND INDEX average yield on a particular day of 11 selected general obligation municipal bonds with an average AA rating, maturing in 20 years. It is comprised of 11 of the 20 bonds in the Twenty Bond Index, also referred to as the BOND BUYER'S MUNICIPAL BOND INDEX, published by the *BOND BUYER* and used as a benchmark in tracking municipal bond yields.

ELIGIBLE PAPER commercial and agricultural paper, drafts, bills of exchange, banker's acceptances, and other negotiable instruments that were acquired by a bank at a discount and that the Federal Reserve Bank will accept for rediscount.

ELIGIBILITY REQUIREMENTS
Insurance: requirements by an insurance company to qualify for coverage. For example, a life insurance company may require that because of a person's health condition, a potential policyholder would need to pay a higher premium to obtain coverage. In this circumstance, the policyholder's ability to pay becomes a primary issue.

For employer group health insurance coverage, an employer may require a person be a full-time employee for coverage of the employee and the employee's dependents.

Pensions: conditions an employee must satisfy to become a participant in a pension plan, such as completing one year of service and reaching the age of 21. Federal pension laws allow plan participants to become VESTED after five years of service. Alternatively, some companies implement a graduated vesting schedule. Public pension plans sponsored by federal, state, and local governments have their own eligibility requirements.

ELLIOTT WAVE THEORY TECHNICAL ANALYSIS concept first put forth by Ralph Nelson Elliott in 1939, then discussed in a 1978 book by Robert Prechter and A. J. Frost, *The Elliott Wave Principle*. Mr. Prechter also has a newsletter, "The Elliott Wave Theorist." The theory holds that all human activities, including stock market movements, can be predicted by identifying a repetitive pattern of building up and tearing down, represented graphically as eight waves, five in the direction of the main trend, followed by three corrective waves. A 5–3 move completes a cycle, although cycles and the underlying waves vary in duration. Some practitioners believe the most recent "supercycle" began in 1932 and ended with BLACK MONDAY in 1987, but there is not unanimous agreement and the predictive value of the theory has been in question since then. The *skyscraper indicator,* which correlates the construction of the world's tallest buildings with stock market tops, was popularized by "The Elliott Wave Theorist."

EMANCIPATION freedom to assume certain legal responsibilities normally associated only with adults, said of a minor who is granted this freedom by a court. If both parents die in an accident, for instance, the 16-year-old eldest son may be emancipated by a judge to act as guardian for his younger brothers and sisters.

EMBARGO government prohibition against the shipment of certain goods to another country. An embargo is most common during wartime, but is sometimes applied for economic reasons as well. For instance, the Organization of Petroleum Exporting Countries placed an embargo on the shipment of oil to the West in the early 1970s to protest Israeli policies and to raise the price of petroleum.

EMERGENCY ECONOMIC STABILIZATION ACT (EESA) OF 2008 legislation designed to assist large financial institutions to prevent failure and to signal to worldwide financial markets that the U.S. government would stand behind major American banks and other important financial entities to prevent disruptive collapses. The EESA set up and funded the TROUBLED ASSET RELIEF PROGRAM (TARP) with $700 billion, which was spent to bolster banks, automakers, and insurance companies such as American International Group; reduce home foreclosures; and buy mortgages and commercial and consumer loans through the TALF.

EMERGENCY FUND cash reserve that is available to meet financial emergencies, such as large medical bills or unexpected auto or home repairs. Most financial planners advocate maintaining an emergency reserve of two to three months' salary in a liquid interest-bearing account such as a money market mutual fund or bank money market deposit account.

EMERGENCY HOME FINANCE ACT OF 1970 act creating the quasi-governmental Federal Home Loan Mortgage Corporation, also known as Freddie Mac, to stimulate the development of a secondary mortgage market. The act authorized Freddie Mac to package and sell Federal Housing Administration- and Veterans Administration-guaranteed mortgage loans. More than half the home mortgages were subsequently packaged and sold to investors in the secondary market in the form of pass-through securities.

EMERGING GROWTH STOCK a young company in a fast-growing industry. DOT-COM companies in the 1990s were a good example of this asset class, which is typically characterized by high risk, high return, and high failure rates.

EMERGING ISSUES TASK FORCE group founded in 1984 by the FINANCIAL ACCOUNTING STANDARDS BOARD (FASB) to hold public meetings and identify accounting issues so they can be resolved with standard practices before divergent practices become widespread.

EMERGING MARKET a foreign economy that is developing in response to the spread of capitalism and has created its own stock market. Analagous to small growth companies, emerging markets have high potential as well as high risk. PACIFIC RIM Markets, which grew rapidly and then collapsed in 1997 and 1998, are a good example.

EMERGING MARKETS FREE (EMF) INDEX index developed by Morgan Stanley Capital International to follow stock markets in Mexico, Malaysia, Chile, Jordan, Thailand, the Philippines, and Argentina, countries selected because of their accessibility to foreign investors.

EMINENT DOMAIN right of a government entity to seize private property for the purpose of constructing a public facility. Federal, state, and local governments can seize people's homes under eminent domain laws as long as the homeowner is compensated at fair market value. Some public projects that may necessitate such CONDEMNATION include highways, hospitals, schools, parks, or government office buildings.

EMPLOYEE RETIREMENT INCOME SECURITY ACT (ERISA) 1974 law governing the operation of most private pension and benefit plans. The law eased pension eligibility rules, set up the PENSION BENEFIT GUARANTY CORPORATION, and established guidelines for the management of pension funds.

EMPLOYEE STOCK OWNERSHIP PLAN (ESOP) program encouraging employees to purchase stock in their company. Employees may participate in the management of the company and even take control to rescue the company or a particular plant that would otherwise go out of business. Employees may offer wage and work rule concessions in return for ownership privileges in an attempt to keep a marginal facility operating.

EMPLOYEE STOCK PURCHASE PLAN (ESPP) program offered by employers that enables employees to purchase company stock at a discount to fair market value. Sometimes called *employee stock fund,* although it differs from an EMPLOYEE STOCK OWNERSHIP PLAN (ESOP), which is a trust fund qualified as a retirement plan. Also differs from an *employee stock repurchase agreement*, in which the employer reserves the right to repurchase.

EMPLOYEE STOCK REPURCHASE AGREEMENT *see* EMPLOYEE STOCK PURCHASE PLAN (ESSP).

EMPLOYMENT COST INDEX (ECI) report issued quarterly by the U.S. Department of Labor tracking changes in employer payroll costs, including salaries, wages, benefits, and bonuses. Marked increases or upward trends signal INFLATION.

EMPTY HEAD AND PURE HEART TEST SEC Rule 14e-3, subparagraph (b), which, with strict exceptions, prohibits any party other than the bidder in a TENDER OFFER to trade in the stock while having INSIDE INFORMATION.

EMTA new name adopted in 2000 by Emerging Markets Traders Association, which was formed in 1990 by the financial community in response to the trading opportunities created by debt restructurings using BRADY BONDS. EMTA's projects now involve market practices, standard documentation and infrastructure for emerging markets bonds, derivatives, foreign exchange, equities and local currency instruments, as well as advocacy of positions that promote emerging markets as an asset class.

ENCUMBERED owned by one party but subject to another party's valid claim. A homeowner owns his mortgaged property, for example, but the bank has a security interest in it as long as the mortgage loan is outstanding.

ENDORSE transfer ownership of an asset by signing the back of a negotiable instrument. One can endorse a check to receive payment or endorse a stock or bond certificate to transfer ownership.

    See also QUALIFIED ENDORSEMENT.

ENDOWMENT permanent gift of money or property to a specified institution for a specified purpose. Endowments may finance physical assets or be invested to provide ongoing income to finance operations.

ENDOWMENT INSURANCE form of LIFE INSURANCE where the face value is paid out to the insured or a beneficiary after a specified contract period. For example, an endowment policy that provides benefits for 20 years until the insured is 65, pays its face value after 20 years whether the insured lives or dies.

ENERGY MUTUAL FUND mutual fund that invests solely in energy stocks such as oil, oil service, gas, solar energy, and coal companies and makers of energy-saving devices.

ENERGY TAX INCENTIVES ACT OF 2005 legislation designed to improve energy production, transportation, and efficiency, signed into law on August 10, 2005. Some of the bill's most important provisions include

1. **Deduction for energy-efficient buildings**. A new deduction was instituted for expenses incurred to improve the energy efficiency of existing or new buildings. This applies to improvements in lighting, heating, cooling, ventilation, and hot water systems.
2. **Tax credit for building energy-efficient homes.** Taxpayers may claim a lifetime nonrefundable credit of up to $500 for making qualifying energy-saving improvements to an existing home. This includes solar water heaters, solar panels to produce electricity, fuel cell property, and energy-efficient air conditioners, heat pumps, and other equipment.
3. **Tax credits for alternative power vehicles.** Credits were introduced for fuel cell, lean burn technology, hybrid, and other alternative fuel motor vehicles.
4. **Energy-related cost recovery provisions.** These include the ability of oil and gas producers to use percentage depletion under the independent producer exception, expensing for investments that increase capacity of oil refineries, two-year amortization of geological costs from domestic oil and gas exploration and seven-year write-off rules for new natural gas gathering lines.
5. **Business tax credits.** Several new business tax credits were created for manufacturing energy-efficient appliances, for fuel cell power plants, for microturbine power plants, for small agribiodiesel producers, and for ethanol producers. Other new credits created were for hydropower, geothermal and solar power, advanced coal and gasification projects.

ENGLE'S LAW economic precept that as income rises the percentage of income spent on food (the Engle coefficient) declines. Generally, the lower the Engle coefficient, the higher the standard of living.

ENHANCED INCOME SECURITY (EIS) *see* INCOME DEPOSIT SECURITY (IDS).

ENHANCED INDEXING managing an index fund with the aim of outperforming the underlying index, by weighting undervalued components, for example. Contrast with PURE INDEX FUND.

ENRONITIS said of a stock that has declined because of suspected accounting irregularities. Reference is to investor anxieties caused by the bankruptcy of Enron Corporation in late 2001 after alleged misrepresentations by the accounting firm of Arthur Andersen. *See also* SARBANES-OXLEY ACT OF 2002.

ENTERPRISE a business firm. The term often is applied to a newly formed venture.

ENTERPRISE ZONE geographical area targeted by the federal, state, or municipal government where small businesses are given incentives to create employment opportunities. Incentives may include tax credits, favorable financing terms, contract set-asides, zoning regulation relief, and other types of help.

ENTREPRENEUR person who takes on the risks of starting a new business. Many entrepreneurs have technical knowledge with which to produce a saleable product or to design a needed new service. Often, VENTURE CAPITAL is used to finance the startup in return for a piece of the equity. Once an entrepreneur's business is established, shares may be sold to the public as an INITIAL PUBLIC OFFERING, assuming favorable market conditions.

ENVIRONMENTAL FUND MUTUAL FUND specializing in stocks of companies having a role in the bettering of the environment. Not to be confused with a SOCIALLY CONSCIOUS MUTUAL FUND, which aims in part to satisfy social values, an environmental fund is designed to capitalize on financial opportunities related to the environmental movement.

EOM DATING arrangement—common in the wholesale drug industry, for example—whereby all purchases made through the 25th of one month are payable within 30 days of the end of the following month; EOM means *end of month.* Assuming no prompt payment discount, purchases through the 25th of April, for example, will be payable by the end of June. If a discount exists for payment in ten days, payment would have to be made by June 10th to take advantage of it. End of month dating with a 2% discount for prompt payment (10 days) would be expressed in the trade either as: *2%-10 days, EOM, 30,* or *2/10 prox. net 30,* where prox., or proximo, means "the next."

EOQ *see* ECONOMIC ORDER QUANTITY.

EPS *see* EARNINGS PER SHARE.

EQUAL CREDIT OPPORTUNITY ACT federal legislation passed in the mid-1970s prohibiting discrimination in granting credit, based on race, religion, sex, ethnic background, or whether a person is receiving public assistance or alimony. The Federal Trade Commission enforces the act.

EQUALIZING DIVIDEND special dividend paid to compensate investors for income lost because a change was made in the quarterly dividend payment schedule.

EQUILIBRIUM PRICE
1. price when the supply of goods in a particular market matches demand.
2. for a manufacturer, the price that maximizes a product's profitability.

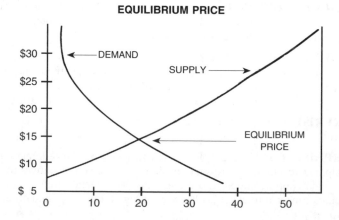

EQUILIBRIUM PRICE

EQUIPMENT LEASING PARTNERSHIP limited partnership that buys equipment such as computers, railroad cars, and airplanes, then leases it to businesses. Limited partners receive income from the lease payments as well as tax benefits such as depreciation. Whether a partnership of this kind works out well depends on the GENERAL PARTNER's expertise. Failure to lease the equipment can be disastrous, as happened with railroad hopper cars in the mid-1970s.

EQUIPMENT TRUST CERTIFICATE bond, usually issued by a transportation company such as a railroad or shipping line, used to pay for new equipment. The certificate gives the bondholder the first right to the equipment in the event that interest and principal are not paid when due. Title to the equipment is held in the name of the trustee, usually a bank, until the bond is paid off.

EQUITABLE OWNER beneficiary of property held in trust.

EQUITY
In general: fairness. Law courts, for example, try to be equitable in their judgments when splitting up estates or settling divorce cases.
Banking: difference between the amount a property could be sold for and the claims held against it.
Brokerage account: excess of securities over debit balance in a margin account. For instance, equity would be $28,000 in a margin account with stocks and bonds worth $50,000 and a debit balance of $22,000.
Investments: ownership interest possessed by shareholders in a corporation—stock as opposed to bonds.

EQUITY CARVE OUT initial public sale of a minority position (20% or less, typically) in the stock of a subsidiary or division by a larger corporation. The parent company will often SPIN OFF the remaining shares to its existing stockholders at a future date. Also called CARVE OUT; SPLIT-OFF IPO.

EQUITY CMO *see* CMO REIT.

EQUITY COMMITMENT NOTES *see* MANDATORY CONVERTIBLES.

EQUITY CONTRACT NOTES *see* MANDATORY CONVERTIBLES.

EQUITY FINANCING raising money by issuing shares of common or preferred stock. Usually done when prices are high and the most capital can be raised for the smallest number of shares.

EQUITY FUNDING type of investment combining a life insurance policy and a mutual fund. The fund shares are used as collateral for a loan to pay the insurance premiums, giving the investor the advantages of insurance protection and investment appreciation potential.

EQUITY-INDEXED ANNUITY an ANNUITY whose interest earnings during the ACCUMULATION PERIOD are linked to rises in a stock index. Such contracts have a minimum annual return that guarantees principal, so they can offer upside potential and downside protection. They sometimes come with a CAP and usually have early withdrawal penalties.

EQUITY KICKER offer of an ownership position in a deal that involves loans. For instance, a mortgage real estate limited partnership that lends to real estate developers might receive as an equity kicker a small ownership position in a building that can appreciate over time. When the building is sold, limited partners receive the appreciation payout. In return for that equity kicker, the lender is likely to charge a lower interest rate on the loan. Convertible features and warrants are offered as equity kickers to make securities attractive to investors.

EQUITY REIT REAL ESTATE INVESTMENT TRUST that takes an ownership position in the real estate it invests in. Stockholders in equity REITs earn dividends on rental income from the buildings and earn appreciation if properties are sold for a profit. The opposite is a MORTGAGE REIT.

EQUIVALENT BOND YIELD comparison of discount yields and yields on bonds with coupons. Also called *coupon-equivalent rate.* For instance, if a 10%, 90-day Treasury bill with a face value of $10,000 cost $9,750, the equivalent bond yield would be:

$$\frac{\$250}{\$9750} \times \frac{365}{90} = 10.40\%$$

EQUIVALENT TAXABLE YIELD comparison of the taxable yield on a corporate or government bond and the tax-free yield on a municipal bond. Depending on the tax bracket, an investor's aftertax return may be greater with a municipal bond than with a corporate or government bond offering a highest interest rate. For someone in a 31% federal tax bracket, for instance, a 7% municipal bond would have an equivalent taxable yield of 10.4%. An investor living in a state that levies state income tax should add in the state tax bracket to get a true measure of the equivalent taxable yield. *See* YIELD EQUIVALENCE for method of calculation.

ERISA *see* EMPLOYEE RETIREMENT INCOME SECURITY ACT.

ERM acronym for *exchange rate mechanism,* by which participating member countries agree to maintain the value of their own currencies through intervention.

ERTA *see* ECONOMIC RECOVERY TAX ACT OF 1981.

ESCALATOR CLAUSE provision in a contract allowing cost increases to be passed on. In an employment contract, an escalator clause might call for wage increases to keep employee earnings in line with inflation. In a lease, an escalator clause could obligate the tenant to pay for increases in fuel or other costs.

ESCHEAT return of property (for example, land, bank balances, insurance policies) to the state if abandoned or left by a person who died without making a will. If rightful owners or heirs later appear, they can claim the property.

ESCROW money, securities, or other property or instruments held by a third party until the conditions of a contract are met.

ESCROWED TO MATURITY (ETM) holding proceeds from a new bond issue in a separate escrow account to pay off an existing bond issue when it matures. Bond issuers will implement an ADVANCE REFUNDING when interest rates have fallen significantly, making it advantageous to pay off the existing issue before scheduled maturity at the first CALL DATE. The funds raised by the refunding are invested in government securities in the escrow account until the principal is used to prepay the original bond issue at the first call date. The escrowed funds may also pay some of the interest on the original issue up until the bonds are redeemed.

ESCROW RECEIPT in options trading, a document provided by a bank to guarantee that the UNDERLYING SECURITY is on deposit and available for potential delivery.

ESSENTIAL PURPOSE (or FUNCTION) BOND *see* PUBLIC PURPOSE BOND.

ESTATE all the assets a person possesses at the time of death—such as securities, real estate, interests in business, physical possessions, and cash. The estate is distributed to heirs according to the dictates of the person's will or, if there is no will, a court ruling.

ESTATE PLANNING planning for the orderly handling, disposition, and administration of an estate when the owner dies. Estate planning includes drawing up a will, setting up trusts, and minimizing estate taxes, perhaps by passing property to heirs before death or by setting up a BYPASS TRUST or a TESTAMENTARY TRUST.

ESTATE TAX tax imposed by a state or federal government on assets left to heirs. Under the ECONOMIC RECOVERY TAX ACT OF 1981, there is no estate tax on transfers of property between spouses, an action known as the MARITAL DEDUCTION. According to the ECONOMIC GROWTH AND TAX RELIEF RECONCILIATION ACT OF 2001, the amount of assets that each person can exclude from federal taxes is $3.5 million in 2009. Unless extended in 2010, the estate tax is completely repealed, and in 2011 the estate tax law returns using 2001 rules, except that the exemption goes to $1 million. Any assets passed to beneficiaries over these limits that are not protected by TRUSTS are assessed estate taxes of 45% in 2009. Many states impose their own estate taxes on top of federal levies. Careful ESTATE PLANNING, involving the writing of a will and the establishment of trusts, is essential for those wishing to minimize estate taxes. *Also called* DEATH TAX; INHERITANCE TAX.

ESTIMATED TAX amount of estimated tax for the coming year, minus tax credits, based on the higher of regular or ALTERNATIVE MINIMUM TAX (AMT). Corporations, estates and trusts, self-employed persons, and persons for whom less than a fixed percentage of income is withheld by employers must compute estimated tax and make quarterly tax payments to the IRS and state tax authorities, if required. Generally, a taxpayer must pay at least 90% of his or her total tax liability for the year in withholding and/or quarterly estimated tax payments. Alternatively, taxpayers may base their current year's estimated tax on the prior year's income tax. For taxpayers with adjusted gross income (AGI) in the prior tax year of $150,000 or less, estimated taxes must equal 100% of the prior year's tax. For those reporting AGI of more than $150,000, the current year's estimated taxes must be based on 110% of the prior year's tax liability. Thus, for someone reporting an AGI of more than $150,000 who paid $50,000 in taxes in the prior year, estimated taxes of at least $55,000 will be due in the current tax year. Severe penalties are imposed by the IRS and state tax authorities for underpayment of estimated taxes.

ETHICAL FUND *see* SOCIAL CONSCIOUSNESS MUTUAL FUND.

E-TRADE any securities purchase or sale made electronically by computer. May or may not be by DIRECT ACCESS.

EUREX one of the world's largest derivatives exchanges and the leading clearing house in Europe. The fully electronic exchange has more than 400 participants in about 20 countries, creating decentralized and standardized access to its markets. Members are linked to the Eurex system through a dedicated wide-area communications network (WAN). Access points have been installed in Amsterdam, Chicago, New York, Helsinki, London, Madrid, Paris, Hong Kong, Tokyo, and Sydney. Eurex is the successor to DEUTSCHE TERMINBORSE (DTB), Germany's first fully computerized exchange and the first German exchange for trading financial futures. DTB merged with DEUTSCHE BÖRSE AG and in 1998 merged with the SWISS OPTIONS AND FINANCIAL FUTURES EXCHANGE (SOFFEX) to form Eurex. In 2007, Eurex acquired the International Securities Exchange. Eurex lists some 20 product groups, including Dutch, Scandinavian, French, German, Italian, Russian, Spanish, Swiss, and U.S. equities; Finnish, German, and Swiss index products; and Finnish, German, and Swiss fixed-income products. In the derivatives markets, Eurex lists futures and options on the Euro-SCHATZ, Euro-BOBL, Euro-BUND, Euro-BUXL, and CONF futures; futures and options on the three-month EURIBOR and futures on the one-month EURIBOR; futures and options on the VDAX, NEMAX 50, VSMI, and HEX 25 indices; Dow Jones Global Titans 50 Index futures and options; and futures and options on a family of Dow Jones STOXX products. Eurex operates in three trading phases: pretrading, from 7:30 A.M. to 9 A.M.; trading, 9 A.M. to 8 P.M.; and post-trading, 8 P.M. to 8:30 P.M. *www. eurexchange.com. See also* DEUTSCHE BÖRSE AG; STOXX.

EUREX ZURICH The 50% joint venture holding company between Deutsche Borse AG and SWX Swiss Exchange, under which the Eurex companies operate. *See also* EUREX.

EURIBOR Eurozone interbank offering rate denominated Euros.

EURO single currency adopted originally by 11 European nations starting January 1, 1999. The first to adopt the Euro were Austria, Belgium, Finland, France, Germany, Ireland, Italy, Luxembourg, the Netherlands, Portugal, and Spain. On that date, the conversion rates of the participating currencies were irrevocably fixed, both among themselves and against the Euro. In January 2001, Greece became the 12th country to adopt the Euro, followed by Slovenia in 2007, Cyprus and Malta in 2008, and Slovakia in 2009. It is also used as the official currency in five other European countries and territories. At first, the Euro was used in financial markets by companies and governments issuing bonds and by banks issuing credit cards. Starting January 1, 2002, the Euro went into circulation and replaced all national currencies of the participating countries. Dual circulation ended on February 28, 2002. Euro banknotes are issued in denominations of 5, 10, 20, 50, 100, 200, and 500 Euro. There are eight different coins ranging from one cent (one hundredth of a Euro) to 2 Euro. The Euro replaced the ECU (European Currency Unit) on January 1, 1999, and is now the currency of 329 million people in the 16 Euro-area countries, known collectively as the Eurozone.

EUROBOND bond denominated in U.S. dollars or other currencies and sold to investors outside the country whose currency is used. The bonds are usually issued by large underwriting groups composed of banks and issuing houses from many countries. An example of a Eurobond transaction might be a dollar-denominated debenture issued by a Belgian corporation through an underwriting group comprised of the overseas affiliate of a New York investment banking house, a bank in Holland, and a consortium of British merchant banks; a portion of the issue is sold to French investors through Swiss investment accounts. The Eurobond market is an important source of capital for multinational companies and foreign governments, including Third World governments.

EUROCLEAR Brussels-based settlement house established in 1968 by a group of banks for the clearance of EUROBONDS.

EUROCURRENCY money deposited by corporations and national governments in banks away from their home countries, called *Eurobanks*. The terms Eurocurrency and Eurobanks do not necessarily mean the currencies or the banks are European, though more often than not, that is the case. For instance, dollars deposited in a British bank or Japanese Yen deposited in a bank in South Africa are considered to be Eurocurrency. The Eurodollar is only one of the Eurocurrencies, though it is the most prevalent. Also known as *Euromoney*.

EURODOLLAR U.S. currency held in banks outside the United States, mainly in Europe, and commonly used for settling international transactions. Some securities are issued in Eurodollars—that is, with a promise to pay interest in dollars deposited in foreign bank accounts.

EURODOLLAR BOND bond that pays interest and principal in Eurodollars, U.S. dollars held in banks outside the United States, primarily in Europe. Such a bond is not registered with the Securities and Exchange Commission, and because there are fewer regulatory delays and costs in the Euromarket, Eurodollar bonds generally can be sold at lower than U.S. interest rates. *See also* EUROBOND.

EURODOLLAR CERTIFICATE OF DEPOSIT CDs issued by banks outside the United States, primarily in Europe, with interest and principal paid in dollars. Such CDs usually have minimum denominations of $100,000 and short-term maturities of less than two years.

EURONEXT NV Europe's first cross-border grouping of stock exchanges and their derivatives markets, formed in 2000 by the merger of the stock exchanges of Amsterdam, Brussels, and Paris. The Euronext group expanded in early 2002 with the acquisition of LIFFE (London International Financial Futures and Options Exchange) and the merger with the Portuguese exchange BVLP (Bolsa de Valores de Lisboa e Porto), renamed Euronext Lisbon. In 2007, Euronext merged with the NYSE Group to create NYSE Euronext. Local regulators continue to have jurisdiction over the respective exchanges. The markets are regulated and unregulated. Euronext uses a single platform for cash trading, derivatives, and clearing. For cash trading NSC is used: For derivatives trading the platform is LIFE CONNECT. Clearing is outsourced to LCH.Clearnet: Euronext has cross-membership and cross-access agreements with the WARSAW STOCK EXCHANGE for their cash and derivatives products, and with the HELSINKI EXCHANGES on cash trading; ownership agreements are excluded. The Euronext List encompasses all quoted companies. It has two segments: NextEconomy, consisting of companies whose equities are traded continuously and active in sectors such as information technology and biotechnology, and NextPrime, consisting of companies in more traditional sectors that are traded continuously. Inclusion in the segments is voluntary. Euronext manages two broad-based indices.

The EURONEXT 100 INDEX is the blue-chip index. The Next 150 Index is a market capitalization index of the 150 next largest stocks, representing the large to mid-capitalization segment of listed stocks at Euronext. The Next-Economy and NextPrime segments each have a price index and a total return index, weighted by market capitalization and excluding the shares listed in the Euronext 100 Index. The indices have a base date of December 31, 2001, with a starting level of 1,000 points. Six NextWeather weather indices for France, launched in January 2002, are among the indices calculated by Euronext. EXCHANGE-TRADED FUNDS, called trackers, comprise Euronext's NextTrack product segment, and have been introduced on the AEX INDEX, CAC40 INDEX, DJ EURO STOXX 50 INDEX, and various pan-European regional and sector indices. Euronext has introduced several commodity futures contracts, available to all constituents. *www.euronext.com.*

EURONEXT 100 INDEX the blue chip index of the pan-European exchange, comprised of the largest and most liquid traded stocks traded on Euronext. Each stock must trade more than 20% of its issued shares over the course of the rolling one-year analysis period. The index is reviewed quarterly through a size and liquidity analysis of the investment universe. Stocks in the index represent 80% of the total market capitalization of the investment universe as of December 31, 2002. Each stock in the index is given a sector classification. Analysis indicates a high correlation with the CAC 40 INDEX.

EUROPEAN CENTRAL BANK (ECB) bank founded to oversee monetary policy for the countries that converted their local currencies into the EURO. The bank's primary mission is to maintain price stability and issue Euro currency. It replaces the Frankfurt-based European Monetary Institute (EMI), which was established in 1994 to prepare the way for a single currency. The bank is run by a Governing Council, which is composed of members of the Executive Board and the governors of National Central Banks. The Executive Board consists of a president, vice president, and four other members.

EUROPEAN CURRENCY QUOTATION the value of a U.S. dollar in terms of a foreign currency. For example, if the British pound is $1.60, there are 0.625 pounds to the dollar. An *American Currency Quotation,* using the same exchange rate, would be 1.60, indicating there are 1.60 dollars to the pound.

EUROPEAN DEPOSITARY RECEIPTS *see* DEPOSITARY RECEIPTS.

EUROPEAN-STYLE EXERCISE system of exercising options contracts in which the option buyer can exercise the contract only on the last business day prior to expiration (normally Friday). This system is widely used with index options traded on various U.S. exchanges. *See also* AMERICAN-STYLE OPTION; ASIAN OPTION.

EUROPEAN UNION (EU) group established in 1992 by the European Union Treaty (also known as the Maastricht Treaty) and amended by various treaties thereafter. Initially, the EU consisted of six countries: Belgium, Germany, France, Italy, Luxembourg, and the Netherlands. Denmark, Ireland, and the United Kingdom joined in 1973, Greece in 1981, Spain and Portugal in 1986, Austria, Finland, and Sweden in 1995. The largest expansion occurred in 2004 with 10 new countries joining. They are

Cyprus, the Czech Republic, Estonia, Hungary, Latvia, Lithuania, Malta, Poland, Slovakia, and Slovenia. In 2007, two more countries from Eastern Europe, Bulgaria and Romania, joined, bringing the total number to 27. Others are expected to join as well. At its core, the EU is a group of democratic countries working together on economic, judicial, and security issues. It has taken several steps toward a more unified Europe. For example, in 1992, the EU made the decision to move toward a single European currency, known as the EURO. The EU is governed by a five-part institutional system, including the European Commission, the EU Council of Ministers, the European Parliament, the European Court of Justice, and the Court of Auditors, which monitors EU budget spending. *europa.eu.int/index_en.htm.*

EUROYEN BOND EUROCURRENCY deposits in Japanese yen.

EVALUATOR independent expert who appraises the value of property for which there is limited trading—antiques in an estate, perhaps, or rarely traded stocks or bonds. The fee for this service is sometimes a flat amount, sometimes a percentage of the appraised value.

EVENT RISK risk that a bond will suddenly decline in credit quality and warrant a lower RATING because of a TAKEOVER-related development, such as additional debt or a RECAPITALIZATION. Corporations whose INDENTURES include protective COVENANTS, such as POISON PUT provisions, are assigned *Event Risk Covenant Rankings* by Standard & Poor's Corporation. Ratings range from E-1, the highest, to E-5 and supplement basic bond ratings.

EVERGREEN FUNDING similar to DRIP FEED, British term for the gradual infusion of capital into a new or recapitalized enterprise. In the United States, banks use the term *evergreen* to describe short-term loans that are continuously renewed rather than repaid.

EXACT INTEREST interest paid by a bank or other financial institution and calculated on a 365-days-per-year basis, as opposed to a 360-day basis, called ordinary interest. The difference—the ratio is 1.0139—can be material when calculating daily interest on large sums of money.

EX-ALL sale of a security without dividends, rights, warrants, or any other privileges associated with that security.

EXCESS MARGIN equity in a brokerage firm's customer account, expressed in dollars, above the legal minimum for a margin account or the maintenance requirement. For instance, with a margin requirement of $25,000, as set by REGULATION T and a maintenance requirement of $12,500 set by the stock exchange, the client whose equity is $100,000 would have excess margin of $75,000 and $87,500 in terms of the initial and maintenance requirements, respectively.

EXCESS PROFITS TAX extra federal taxes placed on the earnings of a business. Such taxes may be levied during a time of national emergency, such as in wartime, and are designed to increase national revenue. The excess profits tax differs from the WINDFALL PROFITS TAX, designed to prevent excessive corporate profits in special circumstances.

EXCESS RESERVES money a bank holds over and above the RESERVE REQUIREMENT. The money may be on deposit with the Federal Reserve System or with an approved depository bank, or it may be in the bank's possession.

For instance, a bank with a reserve requirement of $5 million might have $4 million on deposit with the Fed and $1.5 million in its vaults and as till cash. The $500,000 in excess reserves is available for loans to other banks or customers or for other corporate uses.

EXCESS RETURN TOTAL RETURN of an asset or security portfolio less the risk-free return (usually defined as the return on the 90-day Treasury bill) for the period being measured. In modern portfolio theory, excess return represents the RISK PREMIUM—the reward for taking risk—and is correlated with BETA—the measure of market risk—to produce a *risk-adjusted return*. Excess return is sometimes used to mean *abnormal return*, the difference between the expected return, given beta, and the actual return.

EXCHANGE
Barter: to trade goods and services with another individual or company for other goods and services of equal value.
Corporate finance: offer by a corporation to exchange one security for another. For example, a company may want holders of its convertible bonds to exchange their holdings for common stock. Or a company in financial distress may want its bondholders to exchange their bonds for stock in order to reduce or eliminate its debt load. *See also* SWAP.
Currency: trading of one currency for another. Also known as *foreign exchange*.
Mutual funds: process of switching from one mutual fund to another, either within one fund family or between fund families, if executed through a brokerage firm offering funds from several companies. In many cases, fund companies will not charge an additional LOAD if the assets are kept within the same family. If one fund is sold to buy another, a taxable event has occurred, meaning that capital gains or losses have been realized, unless the trade was executed within a tax-deferred account, such as an IRA or Keogh account.
Trading: central location where securities or futures trading takes place. The New York and American Stock Exchanges are the largest centralized place to trade stocks in the United States, for example. Futures exchanges in Chicago, Kansas City, New York, and elsewhere facilitate the trading of futures contracts. *See also* OVER THE COUNTER (OTC); SECURITIES AND COMMODITIES EXCHANGES.

EXCHANGEABLE DEBENTURE like CONVERTIBLES, with the exception that this type of debenture can be converted to the common stock of a SUBSIDIARY or AFFILIATE of the issuer.

EXCHANGE CONTROLS government regulation of foreign exchange (currency trading).

EXCHANGE DISTRIBUTION (OR ACQUISITION) block trade carried out on the floor of an exchange between customers of a member firm. Someone who wants to sell a large block of stock in a single transaction can get a broker to solicit and bunch a large number of orders. The seller transmits the securities to the buyers all at once, and the trade is announced on the BROAD TAPE as an exchange distribution. The seller, not the buyers, pays a special commission to the broker who executes the trade.

EXCHANGE INDEX SECURITIES *see* EXCHANGE-TRADED FUNDS (ETFs).

EXCHANGE-LISTED PORTFOLIOS *see* EXCHANGE-TRADED FUNDS (ETFs).

EXCHANGE MEMBERS see MEMBER FIRM; SEAT.

EXCHANGE NOTES see INCOME PREFERRED SECURITIES.

EXCHANGE PRIVILEGE right of a shareholder to switch from one mutual fund to another within one fund family—often, at no additional charge. This enables investors to put their money in an aggressive growth-stock fund when they expect the market to turn up strongly, then switch to a money-market fund when they anticipate a downturn. Some discount brokers allow shareholders to switch between fund families in pursuit of the best performance.

EXCHANGE RATE price at which one country's currency can be converted into another's. The exchange rate between the U.S. dollar and the British pound is different from the rate between the dollar and the Euro, for example. A wide range of factors influences exchange rates, which generally change slightly each trading day. Some rates are fixed by agreement; see FIXED EXCHANGE RATE.

EXCHANGE SHARES see EXCHANGE-TRADED FUNDS (ETFs).

EXCHANGE STOCK PORTFOLIO (ESP) see BASKET.

EXCHANGE-TRADED FUNDS (ETFs) SECURITIES representing MUTUAL FUNDS that are traded like stocks on the exchanges. Also called exchange-listed portfolios, exchange index securities, exchange shares, and listed index securities, they are organized as index shares (UNIT INVESTMENT TRUSTS (UITs)) or OPEN-END MANAGEMENT COMPANIES holding baskets of stocks, or as PORTFOLIO DEPOSITARY SHARES (DEPOSITARY RECEIPTS). They differ from CLOSED-END FUNDS, which typically trade at substantial premiums or discounts to their net asset values; in the case of ETFs, arbitrage traders exploit and thus largely eliminate pricing discrepancies between the fund shares and the underlying portfolio values. Arbitrageurs and other large investors, such as market makers and institutions, trade in creation units, typically 50,000 share blocks, that are bought and sold "in kind" and are the only way shares can be bought at net asset value (unless, of course, the market price and NAV happen to be equal). ETFs start as creation units and subsequently issue retail shares.

Compared with open-end index funds, ETFs have a number of advantages. Unlike mutual fund shares, which are priced at their net asset values at the end of each day, ETFs can be bought or sold anytime during the trading day at the market price. The stock exchanges generate a number every 15 seconds that translates the index value into the ETF share value. Like stocks, ETF shares can be traded using CONDITIONAL ORDERS, can be bought on MARGIN, and can be sold short. Expense ratios are low relative to regular index funds but vary and tend to get lower as ETFs grow in size. Expense savings in any event have to be weighed against commissions and the fact that they occasionally trade at slight discounts or premiums. Dividend reinvestment, easy if not automatic with straight index funds, is more difficult with ETFs, where relatively high share prices, unavailability of fractional shares, and higher brokerage costs for odd lots mean dividends have to be accumulated and then reinvested at what might be a higher price. Dollar cost averaging is less practical with ETFs than straight index funds. Even more than straight index funds, ETFs minimize capital gains taxes. Most trading in ETFs is between shareholders, sparing the fund the need to sell stocks to meet redemptions. Redemptions by large investors are paid in kind, protecting shareholders from taxable events. Capital gains generated when ETFs adjust for changes in their underlying indexes are relatively infrequent. The significant capital gains are realized when the investor sells the ETF, giving the investor control over the timing of taxability. Some popular ETFs being currently traded include SPDRS, DIAMONDS, ISHARES, and QUBES (QQQ). ETFs, the majority of which are listed on the American Stock Exchange, are reported in a separate table in the *Wall Street Journal* under Exchange-Traded Portfolios. *See also* HOLDRS.

EXCHANGE TRADED NOTES (ETNs) security similar to an EXCHANGE TRADED FUND (ETF) but that holds, instead of a portfolio of stocks, a senior unsecured debt instrument that promises to repay the principal amount adjusted by applicable fees and by the performance of a specified index. No period coupons are distributed. As with ETFs, they can be exchange-traded like stocks, bought and sold using conditional orders, sold short, and owned on margin. Unlike ETFs, there is no TRACKING RISK, but the investor is a creditor and thus has COUNTERPARTY RISK. Like bonds, ETNs may be held to maturity or sold prior to maturity at market value. Unlike ETFs, which are taxed at the rates applying to the underlying securities as if they were sold at year-end, ETNs lump interest and gains or losses on index performance as one total return figure, taxable when the ETN is closed out or matures. Some types of ETNs may be taxable as ordinary income.

EXCISE TAX federal or state tax on the sale or manufacture of a commodity, usually a luxury item. Examples: federal and state taxes on alcohol and tobacco.

EXCLUSION
Contracts: item not covered by a contract. For example, an insurance policy may list certain hazards, such as acts of war, that are excluded from coverage.
Taxes: on a tax return, items that must be reported, but not taxed. For example, corporations are allowed to exclude 70% of dividends received from other domestic corporations. Gift tax rules allow DONORS to exclude up to $12,000 worth of gifts to donees annually.

EXCLUSIVE LISTING written listing agreement giving an agent the right to sell a specific property for a period of time with a definite termination date, frequently three months. There are two types of exclusive listings. With the exclusive agency, the owner reserves the right to sell the property himself without owing a commission; the exclusive agent is entitled to a commission if he or she personally sells the property, or if it is sold by anyone other than the seller. Under the exclusive right to sell, a broker is appointed as exclusive agent, entitled to a commission if the property is sold by the owner, the broker, or anyone else. "Right to sell" means the right to find a buyer. Sellers opt for exclusive listings because they think an agent will give their property more attention. An agent with an exclusive listing will not have to share the commission with any other agent as they would under a multiple-listing arrangement. If the property is not sold within the specified time, the seller may expand the selling group through an open, multiple listing.

EX-DIVIDEND interval between the announcement and the payment of the next dividend. An investor who buys shares during that interval is not entitled to the dividend. Typically, a stock's price moves up by the dollar amount of the dividend as the ex-dividend date approaches, then falls by the amount of the dividend after that date. A stock that has gone ex-dividend is marked with an *x* in newspaper listings.

EX-DIVIDEND DATE date on which a stock goes EX-DIVIDEND, typically about three weeks before the dividend is paid to shareholders of record. Shares listed on the New York Stock Exchange go ex-dividend four business days before the RECORD DATE. This NYSE rule is generally followed by the other exchanges.

EXECUTION
Law: the signing, sealing, and delivering of a contract or agreement making it valid.
Securities: carrying out a trade. A broker who buys or sells shares is said to have executed an order.

EXECUTOR/EXECUTRIX administrator of the estate who gathers the estate assets; files the estate tax returns and final personal income tax returns, and administers the estate; pays the debts of and charges against the estate; and distributes the balance in accordance with the terms of the will. The executor's responsibility is relatively short term, one to three years, ending when estate administration is completed. An executor (executrix if a female) may be a bank trust officer, a lawyer, or a family member or trusted friend.

EXEMPTION IRS-allowed direct reductions from gross income. Personal and dependency exemptions are allowed for: individual taxpayers; elderly and disabled taxpayers; dependent children and other dependents more than half of whose support is provided; total or partial blindness; and a taxpayer's spouse.

EXEMPT SECURITIES stocks and bonds exempt from certain Securities and Exchange Commission and Federal Reserve Board rules. For instance, government and municipal bonds are exempt from SEC registration requirements and from Federal Reserve Board margin rules.

EXERCISE make use of a right available in a contract. In options trading a buyer of a call contract may exercise the right to buy underlying shares at a particular price by informing the option seller. A put buyer's right is exercised when the underlying shares are sold at the agreed-upon price.

EXERCISE LIMIT limit on the number of option contracts of any one class that can be exercised in a span of five business days. For options on stocks, the exercise limit is usually 2,000 contracts.

EXERCISE NOTICE notification by a broker that a client wants to exercise a right to buy the underlying stock in an option contract. Such notice is transmitted to the option seller through the Options Clearing Corporation, which ensures that stock is delivered as agreed upon.

EXERCISE PRICE price at which the stock or commodity underlying a call or put option can be purchased (call) or sold (put) over the specified period. For instance, a call contract may allow the buyer to purchase 100 shares of XYZ at any time in the next three months at an exercise or STRIKE PRICE of $63.

EXHAUST PRICE price at which broker must liquidate a client's holding in a stock that was bought on margin and has declined, but has not had additional funds put up to meet the MARGIN CALL.

EXIMBANK *see* EXPORT-IMPORT BANK.

EXIT FEE *see* BACK-END LOAD.

EXIT STRATEGY an investor's advance plan to get out of an investment at an opportune time. The most common example is a VENTURE CAPITAL investment, which is illiquid at the outset, but where the investor plans on an INITIAL PUBLIC OFFERING (IPO) as an opportunity to cash out. A stock trader's use of a STOP ORDER would be another example.

EX-LEGAL municipal bond that does not have the legal opinion of a bond law firm printed on it, as most municipal bonds do. When such bonds are traded, buyers must be warned that legal opinion is lacking.

EXOTIC OPTIONS OPTION contracts that are variations on simple puts and calls or are different products with optionality built into them. Exotic options are available in various asset classes on which options are available, but are mostly found in the foreign exchange market. A common example is the BARRIER OPTION, which itself comes in various forms such as *knock-in options* and *knock-out options* (and reversed versions of both) that can be either *single-barrier options* or *double-barrier options*. What those terms refer to and what barrier options have in common are one or two trigger prices that, if touched, will cause an option with predetermined characteristics to be created (knock-in option) or will cause an existing option to cease to exist (knock-out option). A double-barrier option has barriers on either side of the exercise price (i.e., one trigger price is higher than the strike price and the other is lower), whereas a single-barrier option has one trigger price that may be higher or lower than the strike price. Barrier options, because they risk either not being knocked in, or being knocked out, are cheaper than ordinary puts and calls, and a double knockout option is cheaper than a single knockout option.

Other examples of exotic options: *basket options,* which give the owner the right to receive two or more designated foreign currencies in exchange for a base currency, either at a prearranged rate of exchange or at the prevailing spot market rate; *compound options*, which are options on options, whereby the holder has the right to purchase another option at a pre-set date, at a pre-set option premium (a put on a call or a call on a put or a put on a put or a call on a call), and are used by corporations to hedge the foreign exchange risk of an uncertain acquisition or by speculators to bet on the volatility of volatility; *Bermuda options*, which combine the attributes of an AMERICAN-STYLE OPTION and a EUROPEAN-STYLE EXERCISE; *all-or-nothing options* that pay out a set amount if the underlying asset price is above or below the exercise price at the time of expiration; *best-of- two options* that pay off based on the independent performances of two different securities or indexes, or *better-of-two options* that pay off on the better performing of two underlying assets or indexes; and others. *See also* ASIAN OPTIONS; LADDER OPTIONS; LOOKBACK OPTIONS.

EXPECTED RETURN the return a portfolio would earn based on its BETA. *See also* MEAN RETURN.

EXPENSE RATIO amount, expressed as a percentage of total investment, that shareholders pay annually for mutual fund operating expenses and management fees. These expenses include shareholder service, salaries for money managers and administrative staff, and investor centers, among many others.

The expense ratio, which may be as low as 0.2% or as high as 2% of shareholder assets, is taken out of the fund's current income and is disclosed in the prospectus to shareholders.

EXPERIENCE RATING insurance company technique to determine the correct price of a policy premium. The company analyzes past loss experience for others in the insured group to project future claims. The premium is then set at a rate high enough to cover those potential claims and still earn a profit for the insurance company. For example, life insurance companies charge higher premiums to smokers than to non-smokers because smokers' experience rating is higher, meaning their chance of dying is much higher.

EXPIRATION
Banking: date on which a contract or agreement ceases to be effective.
Options trading: last day on which an option can be exercised. If it is not, traders say that the option *expired worthless.*

EXPIRATION CYCLE *see* OPTION CYCLES.

EX-PIT TRANSACTION purchase of commodities off the floor of the exchange where they are regularly traded and at specified terms.

EXPLORATORY DRILLING PROGRAM search for an undiscovered reservoir of oil or gas—a very risky undertaking. Exploratory wells are called *wildcat* (in an unproven area); *controlled wildcat* (in an area outside the proven limits of an existing field); or *deep test* (within a proven field but to unproven depths). Exploratory drilling programs are usually syndicated, and units are sold to limited partners.

EXPORT-IMPORT BANK (EXIMBANK) bank set up by Congress in 1934 to encourage U.S. trade with foreign countries. Eximbank is an independent entity that borrows from the U.S. Treasury to (1) finance exports and imports; (2) grant direct credit to non-U.S. borrowers; (3) provide export guarantees, insurance against commercial and political risk, and discount loans.

EXPOSURE extent of RISK.

EX-RIGHTS without the RIGHT to buy a company's stock at a discount from the prevailing market price, which was distributed until a particular date. Typically, after that date the rights trade separately from the stock itself. *See also* EX-WARRANTS.

EX-STOCK DIVIDENDS interval between the announcement and payment of a stock dividend. An investor who buys shares during that interval is not entitled to the announced stock dividend; instead, it goes to the seller of the shares, who was the owner on the last recorded date before the books were closed and the stock went EX-DIVIDEND. Stocks cease to be ex-dividend after the payment date.

EXTENDED COVERAGE insurance protection that is extended beyond the original term of the contract. For example, consumers can buy extended warranties when they purchase cars or appliances, which will cover repairs beyond the original warranty period.

EXTENSION OF TIME FOR FILING TAXES time period beyond the original tax filing date. For example, taxpayers who file Form 4868 may get an automatic extension of six months to file their tax returns with the IRS.

Though the return will then be due on October 15, the estimated tax is still due on the original filing date of April 15.

EXTERNAL FUNDS funds brought in from outside the corporation, perhaps in the form of a bank loan, or the proceeds from a bond offering, or an infusion of cash from venture capitalists. External funds supplement internally generated CASH FLOW and are used for expansion, as well as for seasonal WORKING CAPITAL needs.

EXTRA DIVIDEND dividend paid to shareholders in addition to the regular dividend. Such a payment is made after a particularly profitable year in order to reward shareholders and engender loyalty.

EXTRAORDINARY CALL early redemption of a revenue bond by the issuer due to elimination of the source of revenue to pay the stipulated interest. For example, a mortgage revenue municipal bond may be subject to an extraordinary call if the issuer is unable to originate mortgages to homeowners because mortgage rates have dropped sharply, making the issuer's normally below-market mortgage interest rate suddenly higher than market rates. In this case, the bond issuer is required to return the money raised from the bond issue to bondholders because the issuer will not be able to realize the expected interest payments from mortgages. Extraordinary calls may also be necessary if another revenue-producing project such as a road or bridge is not able to be built for some reason. Calls are usually made at PAR. Also called a *special call.*

EXTRAORDINARY ITEM unusual and infrequent occurrence that must be explained to shareholders in an annual or quarterly report. Some examples: fire loss, writeoff of a division, acquisition of another company, sale of a large amount of real estate, or uncovering of employee fraud that negatively affects the company's financial condition. Earnings are usually reported before and after taking into account the effects of extraordinary items.

EX-WARRANTS stock sold with the buyer no longer entitled to the WARRANT attached to the stock. Warrants allow the holder to buy stock at some future date at a specified price. Someone buying a stock on June 3 that had gone ex-warrants on June 1 would not receive those warrants. They would be the property of the stockholder of record on June 1.

F

FACE-AMOUNT CERTIFICATE debt security issued by face-amount certificate companies, one of three categories of mutual funds defined by the INVESTMENT COMPANY ACT OF 1940. The holder makes periodic payments to the issuer, and the issuer promises to pay the purchaser the face value at maturity or a surrender value if the certificate is presented prior to maturity.

FACE VALUE value of a bond, note, mortgage, or other security as given on the certificate or instrument. Corporate bonds are usually issued with $1,000 face values, municipal bonds with $5,000 face values, and federal government bonds with $10,000 face values. Although the bonds fluctuate in price from the time they are issued until redemption, they are redeemed at maturity at their face value, unless the issuer defaults. If the bonds are retired before maturity, bondholders normally receive a slight premium over face value. The face value is the amount on which interest payments are calculated. Thus, a 10% bond with a face value of $1,000 pays bondholders $100 per year. Face value is also referred to as PAR VALUE or *nominal value.*

FACTORING type of financial service whereby a firm sells or transfers title to its accounts receivable to a factoring company, which then acts as principal, not as agent. The receivables are sold without recourse, meaning that the factor cannot turn to the seller in the event accounts prove uncollectible. Factoring can be done either on a *notification basis,* where the seller's customers remit directly to the factor, or on a *non-notification basis,* where the seller handles the collections and remits to the factor. There are two basic types of factoring:
1. **Discount factoring** arrangement whereby seller receives funds from the factor prior to the average maturity date, based on the invoice amount of the receivable, less cash discounts, less an allowance for estimated claims, returns, etc. Here the factor is compensated by an interest rate based on daily balances and typically 2% to 3% above the bank prime rate.
2. **Maturity factoring** arrangement whereby the factor, who performs the entire credit and collection function, remits to the seller for the receivables sold each month on the average due date of the factored receivables. The factor's commission on this kind of arrangement ranges from 0.75% to 2%, depending on the bad debt risk and the handling costs.

Factors also accommodate clients with "overadvances," loans in anticipation of sales, which permit inventory building prior to peak selling periods. Factoring has traditionally been most closely associated with the garment industry, but is used by companies in other industries as well.

FAIL POSITION securities undelivered due to the failure of selling clients to deliver the securities to their brokers so the latter can deliver them to the buying brokers. Since brokers are constantly buying and selling, receiving and delivering, the term usually refers to a net delivery position—that is, a given broker owes more securities to other brokers on sell transactions than other brokers owe to it on buy transactions. *See also* FAIL TO DELIVER; FAIL TO RECEIVE.

FAIL TO DELIVER situation where the broker-dealer on the sell side of a contract has not delivered securities to the broker-dealer on the buy side. A fail to deliver is usually the result of a broker not receiving delivery from its selling customer. As long as a fail to deliver exists, the seller will not receive payment. *See also* FAIL TO RECEIVE.

FAIL TO RECEIVE situation where the broker-dealer on the buy side of a contract has not received delivery of securities from the broker-dealer on the sell side. As long as a fail to receive exists, the buyer will not make payment for the securities. *See also* FAIL TO DELIVER.

FAIR AND ACCURATE CREDIT TRANSACTIONS ACT OF 2003 (FACTA) legislation designed to help consumers protect their credit identities and recover from identity theft. Among the key provisions of the law:

1. **Free credit report.** Consumers are entitled to one free copy of their credit report annually from each of the three credit bureaus (Equifax, Experian, and Trans Union) by calling 877-322-8228 or logging on to *www.annual creditreport.com.*

2. **Fraud alerts.** Consumers were given the right to contact a credit reporting agency to order a fraud alert if they become victims of identity theft. The fraud alert is effective for 90 days and may be extended for as long as seven years. If a consumer has instituted a fraud alert, any creditor that is asked to extend credit must contact the consumer by phone to make sure that the credit application was not made by an identity thief. The National Fraud Alert System is to be set up to track fraudulent activity.

3. **Blocking inaccurate information.** Victims of identity theft are given the right to block inaccurate items that appear on a credit report because of the identity theft.

4. **Account number truncation.** Receipts for credit and debit card transactions may no longer include more than the last five digits of the card number or the expiration date. Consumers who request a copy of their credit file from a credit bureau may also request that the first five numbers of their Social Security number not be included in the file.

5. **Imposter information.** Victims of identity theft must be given the imposter's account application and transactions in order to be able to find and prosecute them.

6. **Collection agencies.** If an identity theft victim is contacted by a collection agency about a debt that resulted from the theft, the collection agency must inform the creditor of the fraud. The victim is also entitled to receive all information about the debt, such as the application, account statements, and late notices. Creditors cannot place this debt into collection or sell the debt once they are notified of the theft.

7. **Red flags.** Creditors must adopt procedures to spot identity theft before it occurs. Events such as change of address, request for replacement cards, and efforts to reactivate dormant card accounts must be considered potential signs of fraud.

8. **Consumer rights notice.** Credit reporting agencies are required to give identity theft victims notice of their rights. These include the right to file a fraud alert, to block fraudulent information from getting on the credit report, and the right to obtain copies of documents used to commit the fraud.

9. **Credit scores.** Consumers may request their credit SCORE from credit reporting agencies including an explanation of the factors that went into computing the score, for a reasonable fee.

10. **Disputing inaccurate information.** Consumers may dispute inaccurate information on their credit reports directly with the furnisher of the information, rather than with the credit reporting agency. Once notified, the furnisher of the information must investigate and cannot report negative information while the investigation is pending. Furnishers who have been notified that the information is the result of identity theft must not report it to a credit reporting agency.

11. **Notice of negative information.** Consumers must be given "early warning" notice before negative information is reported to a credit reporting agency. Financial institutions must send consumers notice before or no later than 30 days after negative information is furnished to a credit bureau. Negative information includes late, partial, or missed payments, or any other form of default on the account.

12. **Medical information and credit reports.** Consumer reporting agencies may not report the name, address, or telephone number of any medical creditor unless the information is provided in codes that do not identify the provider of medical care or the individual's medical condition. Creditors may also not obtain or use medical information to make credit decisions.

13. **Opt-out marketing.** Consumers are given the right to opt out to stop a corporation's affiliates from sharing consumer data for marketing purposes.

14. **Risk-based pricing.** Consumers who are offered credit on terms that are materially less favorable than others must receive a notice of this fact. Therefore, consumers who might be approved for a loan, but at a much higher interest rate than a standard applicant, must be notified and get a free copy of their credit report.

FAIR CREDIT BILLING ACT (FCBA) federal law designed to facilitate the handling of credit complaints and eliminate abusive credit billing practices. It applies to OPEN END CREDIT accounts, such as credit cards and revolving charge accounts. For example, the law requires that complaints about credit bills be acknowledged within 30 days.

FAIR CREDIT REPORTING ACT (FCRA) federal law enacted in 1971 giving persons the right to see their credit records at credit reporting bureaus. Designed to improve the confidentiality and accuracy of credit reports, the law is enforced by the FEDERAL TRADE COMMISSION (FTC) and state consumer protection agencies. Individuals may challenge and correct negative aspects of their record if they can prove there is a mistake. Consumers may also submit statements explaining why they received certain negative credit marks. Congress passed amendments to the FCRA that went into effect on October 1, 1997 which augmented consumers' privacy rights and further protected the accuracy of credit report information. For example, the amendments made it a civil law violation for someone to obtain a consumer report without a permissible purpose. Cpnsumers must now give written permission before their credit reports are obtained for employment purposes. Consumers also have the right not to be included in direct mail or telemarketing solicitations based on prescreened lists obtained from credit bureaus. The amendments also state that when a consumer disputes information, the consumer reporting agency and the original furnisher of the information must investiate the claim. Agencies must finish their investigations within 30 days and report their results back to consumers. The law also stipulates that there be a "date certain" for the calculation of the length of time that information can remain in consumer report files in situations involving collections or charge-offs. The FCRA was further strengthened by the passage of the FAIR AND ACCURATE CREDIT TRANSACTIONS ACT OF 2003, which, among many other provisions, gave consumers the right to receive one free copy of their credit report annually. *See also* CREDIT RATING.

FAIR MARKET VALUE price at which an asset or service passes from a willing seller to a willing buyer. It is assumed that both buyer and seller are rational and have a reasonable knowledge of relevant facts. *See also* MARKET; MARK TO MARKET.

FAIRNESS OPINION professional judgment offered for a fee by an investment banker on the fairness of the price being offered in a merger, takeover, or leveraged buyout. For example, if management is trying to take over a company in a leveraged buyout, it will need a fairness opinion from an independent source to verify that the price being offered is adequate and in the best interests of shareholders. If shareholders sue on the grounds that the offer is not adequate, management will rely on the fairness opinion in court to prove its case. Fairness opinions are also obtained when a majority shareholder is trying to buy out the minority shareholders of a company.

FAIR PRICE *see* FAIR VALUE.

FAIR RATE OF RETURN level of profit that a utility is allowed to earn as determined by federal and/or state regulators. Public utility commissions set the fair rate of return based on the utility's needs to maintain service to its customers, pay adequate dividends to shareholders and interest to bondholders, and maintain and expand plant and equipment.

FAIR TRADE ACTS state laws protecting manufacturers from price-cutting by permitting them to establish minimum retail prices for their goods. Fair trade pricing was effectively eliminated in 1975 when Congress repealed the federal laws upholding resale price maintenance.

FAIR VALUE
In general: *see* FAIR MARKET VALUE.
Stocks: price of a stock assuming appropriate VALUATION. *See also* FULLY VALUED.
Futures contracts: the *theoretical futures price* obtained by continuously compounding the SPOT PRICE at the COST OF CARRY rate for some time interval. It is an equilibrium price and any discrepancy would be closed by arbitrage. Also called *fair price.*

FALLEN ANGELS bonds that were INVESTMENT GRADE at the time they were issued but have since declined in quality to below investment grade (BB or lower). Fallen angels are a type of JUNK BOND, but the latter term is usually reserved for bonds that are originally issued with ratings of BB or lower.

FALL OUT OF BED sharp drop in a stock's price, usually in response to negative corporate developments. For example, a stock may fall out of bed if a takeover deal falls apart or if profits in the latest period fall far short of expectations.

FAMILY OF FUNDS *see* FUND FAMILY.

FAMILY TRUST trust that bypasses surviving spouse and distributes assets to children or other heirs. *See also* SPRINKLING TRUST.

FANNIE MAE (FEDERAL NATIONAL MORTGAGE ASSOCIATION) publicly owned, government-sponsored corporation established in 1938 to purchase both government-backed and conventional mortgages from lenders and securitize them. Its objective is to increase the affordability of home mortgage funds for low-, moderate-, and middle-income home buyers. Fannie Mae is a congressionally chartered company and the largest source of home mortgage funds in the United States. Fannie Mae is a large issuer of debt securities, which are used to finance its activities. The federal government seized control of Fannie Mae in September 2008 by placing it into conservatorship as the foreclosure crisis mushroomed.

FARMER MAC *see* FEDERAL AGRICULTURAL MORTGAGE CORPORATION.

FARMER'S HOME ADMINISTRATION (FHA) federal agency under the Department of Agriculture that makes loans in low-income, rural areas of the United States for farms, homes, and community facilities.

FAR MONTH trading month that is farthest in the future in an options or futures contract. This may be a few months or up to a year or more. Under normal conditions, there is far less trading activity in the far month contracts than in the NEAREST MONTH or SPOT DELIVERY MONTH contracts. Also called *furthest month.*

FARTHER OUT; FARTHER IN relative length of option-contract maturities with reference to the present. For example, an options investor in January would call an option expiring in October farther out than an option expiring in July. The July option is farther in than the October option. *See also* DIAGONAL SPREAD.

FASB *see* FINANCIAL ACCOUNTING STANDARDS BOARD.

FAT CAT wealthy person who has become lazy living off the dividends and interest from investments. Fat cats also tend to be offered special treatment by brokers and other financial professionals because they have so much money and their accounts can therefore generate large fees and commissions.

FAVORABLE TRADE BALANCE situation that exists when the value of a nation's exports is in excess of the value of its imports. *See* BALANCE OF PAYMENTS; BALANCE OF TRADE.

FAVORITE FIFTY *see* NIFTY FIFTY.

FEAR INDEX *see* VIX INDEX.

FED BIAS expressed inclination of the FEDERAL OPEN MARKET COMMITTEE (FOMC), to raise, lower, or keep unchanged, the target FEDERAL FUNDS RATE, based on current economic conditions. Although it no longer adopts a formal policy bias toward raising or lowering rates, the FOMC communicates its intentions by issuing a *"balance of risks" statement* when it announces rate actions at its regularly scheduled meetings eight times a year or about every six weeks. The committee may also vote to authorize the chairman, with or without consulation, to take actions between meetings. Such authorizations are called *asymmetric directives.*

FEDERAL AGENCY SECURITY debt instrument issued by an agency of the federal government such as the Federal National Mortgage Association, Federal Farm Credit Bank, and the Tennessee Valley Authority (TVA). Though not general obligations of the U.S. Treasury, such securities are sponsored by the government and therefore have high safety ratings.

FEDERAL AGRICULTURAL MORTGAGE CORPORATION federal agency established in 1988 to provide a secondary market for farm mortgage loans. Informally called *Farmer Mac*.

FEDERAL DEFICIT (SURPLUS) federal shortfall that results when the government spends more in a fiscal year than it receives in revenue. To cover the shortfall, the government usually borrows from the public by floating long- and short-term debt. Federal deficits, which started to rise in the 1970s, exploded to enormous proportions of hundreds of billions of dollars per year in the 80s and 90s. By the late 90s, revenues from an extended period of strong economic growth and soaring stock prices were applied to eliminate the deficit in accordance with budget balancing legislation which resulted in a *federal surplus*. Though this scenario did not come to pass in the 80s and 90s, some economists think that massive federal deficits can lead to high interest rates and inflation, since they compete with private borrowing by consumers and businesses. Deficits also add to the demand for money from the FEDERAL RESERVE BANK. *See also* CROWDING OUT; NATIONAL DEBT.

FEDERAL DEPOSIT INSURANCE CORPORATION (FDIC) federal agency established in 1933 that guarantees (within limits) funds on deposit in member banks and thrift institutions and performs other functions, such as making loans to or buying assets from member institutions to facilitate mergers or prevent failures. In 1989, Congress passed savings and loan association bailout legislation that reorganized FDIC into two insurance units: the BANK INSURANCE FUND (BIF) continued the traditional FDIC functions with respect to banking institutions and the SAVINGS ASSOCIATION INSURANCE FUND (SAIF) insured thrift institution deposits, replacing the FEDERAL SAVINGS AND LOAN INSURANCE CORPORATION (FSLIC), which ceased to exist. In 2005, Congress passed the FDI Reform Act merging the SAIF and BIF into one insurance fund called the DEPOSIT INSURANCE FUND (DIF). The same law also raised the federal deposit insurance level from $100,000 to $250,000 on retirement accounts and gave the FDIC the option to increase insurance ceilings on regular bank accounts from $100,000 by $10,000 a year, based on inflation, every five years thereafter starting April 1, 2010. In 2008, Congress passed the Emergency Economic Stabilization Act that temporarily increased the basic limit on deposit insurance for all ownership categories from $100,000 to $250,000. *See also* OFFICE OF THRIFT SUPERVISION (OTS).

FEDERAL FARM CREDIT BANK government-sponsored institution that consolidates the financing activities of the Federal Land Banks, the Federal Intermediate Credit Banks, and the Banks for Cooperatives. *See also* FEDERAL FARM CREDIT SYSTEM.

FEDERAL FARM CREDIT SYSTEM system established by the Farm Credit Act of 1971 to provide credit services to farmers and farm-related enterprises through a network of 12 Farm Credit districts. Each district has a Federal Land Bank, a Federal Intermediate Credit Bank, and a Bank for Cooperatives to carry out policies of the system. The system sells short-term

(5- to 270-day) notes in increments of $50,000 on a discounted basis through a national syndicate of securities dealers. Rates are set by the FEDERAL FARM CREDIT BANK, a unit established to consolidate the financing activities of the various banks. An active secondary market is maintained by several dealers. The system also issues Federal Farm Credit System Consolidated Systemwide Bonds on a monthly basis with six- and nine-month maturities. The bonds are sold in increments of $5,000 with rates set by the system. The bonds enjoy a secondary market even more active than that for the discounted notes. *See also* SECONDARY MARKET.

FEDERAL FINANCING BANK (FFB) U.S. government-owned bank that consolidates financing activities of government AGENCIES in order to reduce borrowing costs.

FEDERAL FUNDS
1. funds deposited by commercial banks at Federal Reserve Banks, including funds in excess of bank reserve requirements. Banks may lend federal funds to each other on an overnight basis at the federal funds rate. Member banks may also transfer funds among themselves or on behalf of customers on a same-day basis by debiting and crediting balances in the various reserve banks. *See also* FED WIRE.
2. money used by the Federal Reserve to pay for its purchases of government securities.
3. funds used to settle transactions where there is no FLOAT.

FEDERAL FUNDS RATE interest rate charged by banks with excess reserves at a Federal Reserve district bank to banks needing overnight loans to meet reserve requirements. The rate is determined by the balance of supply and demand for funds, which is influenced by OPEN MARKET OPERATIONS pursuant to decisions made by the FEDERAL OPEN MARKET COMMITTEE (FOMC). The FOMC establishes a *target rate* and expands or contracts the money supply with the aim that the federal funds rate, a market rate, will approximate the target rate. *See also* FED BIAS; DISCOUNT WINDOW.

FEDERAL GIFT TAX federal tax imposed on the transfer of securities, property, or other assets. The donor must pay the tax based on the fair market value of the transferred assets. However, federal law allows donors to give up to $13,000 per year to any individual without incurring gift tax liability. So, a husband and wife may give $26,000 to their child in one year without tax if each parent gives $13,000. This practice is known as GIFT SPLITTING. According to the TAXPAYER RELIEF ACT OF 1997, this gift tax limit is indexed to inflation in $1,000 increments. Gifts between spouses are not subject to the gift tax. For those making gifts over the limit, a gift tax return using IRS form 709 must be filed by April 15th of the year following the year of the gift. Many states match the $13,000 gift tax exemption, but some allow a smaller amount to be gifted tax-free.

FEDERAL HOME LOAN BANK SYSTEM system supplying credit reserves for SAVINGS AND LOANS, cooperative banks, and other mortgage lenders in a manner similar to the Federal Reserve's role with commercial banks. The Federal Home Loan Bank System is made up of 12 regional Federal Home Loan Banks. It raises money by issuing notes and bonds and lends money to savings and loans and other mortgage lenders based on the amount of collateral the institution can provide. The system was established in 1932 after a massive wave of bank failures. In 1989, Congress passed savings and loan bailout legislation revamping the regulatory structure of the industry. The Federal Home Loan Bank Board was dismantled and replaced with the Federal Housing Finance Board, which has since been replaced by the FEDERAL HOUSING FINANCE AGENCY. The FINANCIAL SERVICES MODERNIZA-TION ACT OF 1999 expanded the collateral that member banks could use to obtain an advance. In addition to traditional mortgage loans, banks can now put up rural, agricultural, and small business loans. *See also* OFFICE OF THRIFT SUPERVISION (OTS).

FEDERAL HOUSING ADMINISTRATION (FHA) federally sponsored agency that insures lenders against loss on residential mortgages. It was founded in 1934 in response to the Great Depression to execute the provi-sions of the National Housing Act. The FHA was the forerunner of a group of government agencies responsible for the growing secondary market for mortgages, such as the Government National Mortgage Association (Ginnie Mae) and the Federal National Mortgage Association (Fannie Mae).

FEDERAL HOUSING FINANCE AGENCY (FHFA) U.S. government agency created in 2008 under the Housing and Economic Recovery Act to replace the Federal Housing Finance Board and assume oversight of the FEDERAL HOME LOAN BANK SYSTEM that includes the housing related GSEs, Fannie Mae, Freddie Mac, and the Federal Home Loan Banks. It was granted enhanced powers to establish standards, restrict asset growth, increase enforcement, and put entities into receivership.

FEDERAL ID NUMBER (FIN) *see* TAXPAYER IDENTIFICATION NUMBER (TIN).

FEDERAL INCOME TAXES *see* INCOME TAXES.

FEDERAL INSURANCE CONTRIBUTIONS ACT (FICA) commonly known as Social Security, the federal law requiring employers to withhold wages and make payments to a government trust fund providing retirement and other benefits. *See also* SOCIAL SECURITY.

FEDERAL INTERMEDIATE CREDIT BANK one of 12 banks that make funds available to production credit associations, commercial banks, agricul-tural credit corporations, livestock loan companies, and other institutions extending credit to crop farmers and cattle raisers. Their stock is owned by farmers and ranchers, and the banks raise funds largely from the public sale of short-term debentures. *See also* FEDERAL FARM CREDIT BANK; FEDERAL FARM CREDIT SYSTEM.

FEDERAL LAND BANK one of 12 banks under the U.S. Farm Credit Admin-istration that extends long-term mortgage credit to crop farmers and cattle raisers for buying land, refinancing debts, or other agricultural purposes. To obtain a loan, a farmer or rancher must purchase stock equal to 5% of the loan in any one of approximately 500 local land bank associations; these, in turn, purchase an equal amount of stock in the Federal Land Bank. The stock is retired when the loan is repaid. The banks raise funds by issuing Consolidated Systemwide Bonds to the public. *See also* FEDERAL FARM CREDIT BANK; FEDERAL FARM CREDIT SYSTEM.

FEDERAL OPEN-MARKET COMMITTEE (FOMC) committee that sets interest rate and credit policies for the Federal Reserve System, the

United States' central bank. The FOMC has 12 members. Seven are the members of the Federal Reserve Board, appointed by the president of the United States. The other five are presidents of the 12 regional Federal Reserve banks. Of the five, four are picked on a rotating basis; the other is the president of the Federal Reserve Bank of New York, who is a permanent member. The Committee decides whether to increase or decrease interest rates through open-market operations of buying or selling government securities. The Committee's decisions are closely watched and interpreted by economists and stock and bond market analysts, who try to predict whether the Fed is seeking to tighten credit to reduce inflation or to loosen credit to stimulate the economy.

FEDERAL RESERVE BANK one of the 12 banks that, with their branches, make up the FEDERAL RESERVE SYSTEM. These banks are located in Boston, New York, Philadelphia, Cleveland, Richmond, Atlanta, Chicago, St. Louis, Minneapolis, Kansas City, Dallas, and San Francisco. The role of each Federal Reserve Bank is to monitor the commercial and savings banks in its region to ensure that they follow Federal Reserve Board regulations and to provide those banks with access to emergency funds from the DISCOUNT WINDOW. The reserve banks act as depositories for member banks in their regions, providing money transfer and other services. Each of the banks is owned by the member banks in its district.

FEDERAL RESERVE BOARD (FRB) governing board of the FEDERAL RESERVE SYSTEM. Its seven members are appointed by the president of the United States, subject to Senate confirmation, and serve 14-year terms. The Board establishes Federal Reserve System policies on such key matters as reserve requirements and other bank regulations, sets the discount rate, tightens or loosens the availability of credit in the economy, and regulates the purchase of securities on margin.

FEDERAL RESERVE OPEN MARKET COMMITTEE *see* FEDERAL OPEN-MARKET COMMITTEE.

FEDERAL RESERVE SYSTEM system established by the Federal Reserve Act of 1913 to regulate the U.S. monetary and banking system. The Federal Reserve System (the Fed) is comprised of 12 regional Federal Reserve Banks, their 24 branches, and all national and state banks that are part of the system. National banks are stockholders of the FEDERAL RESERVE BANK in their region.

The Federal Reserve System's main functions are to regulate the national money supply, set reserve requirements for member banks, supervise the printing of currency at the mint, act as clearinghouse for the transfer of funds throughout the banking system, and examine member banks to make sure they meet various Federal Reserve regulations. Although the members of the system's governing board are appointed by the President of the United States and confirmed by the Senate, the Federal Reserve System is considered an independent entity, which is supposed to make its decisions free of political influence. Governors are appointed for terms of 14 years, which further assures their independence. *See also* FEDERAL OPEN-MARKET COMMITTEE; FEDERAL RESERVE BOARD; OPEN-MARKET OPERATIONS.

FEDERAL SAVINGS AND LOAN ASSOCIATION federally chartered institution with a primary responsibility to collect people's savings deposits and to provide mortgage loans for residential housing. Federal Savings and

Loans may be owned either by stockholders, who can trade their shares on stock exchanges, or by depositors, in which case the associations are considered mutual organizations. Federal Savings and Loans are members of the Federal Home Loan Bank System. After deregulation, S&Ls expanded into nonhousing-related financial services such as discount stock brokerage, financial planning, credit cards, and consumer loans. *See also* FINANCIAL SUPERMARKET; MUTUAL ASSOCIATION; OFFICE OF THRIFT SUPERVISION (OTS); SAVINGS AND LOAN ASSOCIATION.

FEDERAL SAVINGS AND LOAN INSURANCE CORPORATION (FSLIC) federal agency established in 1934 to insure deposits in member savings institutions. In 1989, Congress passed savings and loan bailout legislation revamping the regulatory structure of the industry. FSLIC was disbanded and its insurance activities were assumed by a new agency, SAVINGS ASSOCIATION INSURANCE FUND (SAIF), a unit of the FEDERAL DEPOSIT INSURANCE CORPORATION (FDIC). Responsibility for insolvent institutions previously under FSLIC's jurisdiction was assumed by another newly created agency, RESOLUTION FUNDING CORPORATION (REFCORP). *See also* OFFICE OF THRIFT SUPERVISION (OTS).

FEDERAL SURPLUS *see* FEDERAL DEFICIT (SURPLUS).

FEDERAL TRADE COMMISSION (FTC) federal agency established in 1914 to foster free and fair business competition and prevent monopolies and activities in restraint of trade. It administers both antitrust and consumer protection legislation.

FEDERAL UNEMPLOYMENT TAX ACT (FUTA) legislation under which federal and state governments require employers (and in some states, such as New Jersey, employees) to contribute to a fund that pays unemployment insurance benefits.

FED PASS move by the Federal Reserve to add reserves to the banking system, thereby making credit more available. The Fed will initiate an open-market operation when it wants to add or subtract reserves in the banking system. It transacts these operations through a group of dealers called PRIMARY DEALERS, banks or security houses with which the Fed has agreed to do business. For example, the buying of securities by the Federal Reserve can be done in such a way that will make reserves more available, thus encouraging banks to lend and making credit easier to obtain by consumer and business borrowers. *See also* BILL PASS; COUPON PASS.

FED WIRE high-speed, computerized communications network that connects all 12 Federal Reserve Banks, their 24 branches, the Federal Reserve Board office in Washington, D.C., U.S. Treasury offices in Washington, D.C., and Chicago, and the Washington, D.C. office of the Commodity Credit Corporation; also spelled FedWire and Fedwire. The Fed wire has been called the central nervous system of money transfer in the United States. It enables banks to transfer reserve balances from one to another for immediate available credit and to transfer balances for business customers. Using the Fed wire, Federal Reserve Banks can settle interdistrict transfers resulting from check collections, and the Treasury can shift balances from its accounts in different reserve banks quickly and without cost. It is also possible to transfer bearer short-term government securities within an hour at no cost. This is done through a procedure called CPD (Commissioner of Public Debt of the Treasury) transfers, whereby one Federal Reserve Bank "retires" a seller's security, while another reserve bank makes delivery of a like amount of the same security from its unissued stock to the buyer.

FEEDER FUND a fund that is similar to a FUND OF FUNDS except that virtually all the underlying investments are held by a *master fund*, which is responsible for managing them. A typical HEDGE FUND arrangement, called a *master feeder structure,* has three entities: a master fund and two feeder funds, the sole investment of the feeder funds being an ownership interest in the master fund. One feeder fund is for U.S. investors and the other for non-U.S. investors. The master fund, usually an offshore entity organized as a limited liability company to preserve the tax treatment of both the U.S. and non-U.S. investors, consolidates all the trading activities into a single portfolio, providing operational efficiencies and ensuring that the performance of each feeder fund mirrors the other.

FIAT MONEY currency that has no intrinsic metallic or redemption value. Its nominal value is what the issuing sovereign government engraves on paper, and its real value is what it will buy in the marketplace, in other words, its purchasing power. Internationally, its value is what it is worth in exchange for another country's currency. The U.S. dollar has been a fiat currency since the abandonment of the international gold standard in 1971, and all the world's currencies are now fiat money. The purchasing power of fiat money depends on the issuer's economic strength and how its money supply is managed. Lacking intrinsic value, fiat money becomes vulnerable to loss of purchasing power when central banks allow INFLATION to get out of control. Gold, although not officially money, is a universally accepted store of value and a popular inflation hedge that tends to rise in value as fiat currency loses purchasing power.

FICA *see* FEDERAL INSURANCE CONTRIBUTIONS ACT.

FICO *see* FINANCING CORPORATION.

FICO SCORE *see* CREDIT SCORING.

FICTITIOUS CREDIT the credit balance in a securities MARGIN ACCOUNT representing the proceeds from a short sale and the margin requirement under Federal Reserve Board REGULATION T (which regulates margin credit). Because the proceeds, which are held as security for the loan of securities made by the broker to effect the short sale, and the margin requirement are both there to protect the broker's position, the money is not available for withdrawal by the customer; hence the term "fictitious" credit. It is in contrast to a free credit balance, which can be withdrawn anytime.

FIDELITY BOND *see* BLANKET FIDELITY BOND.

FIDUCIARY person, company, or association holding assets in trust for a beneficiary. The fiduciary is charged with the responsibility of investing the money wisely for the beneficiary's benefit. Some examples of fiduciaries are executors of wills and estates, receivers in bankruptcy, trustees, and those who administer the assets of underage or incompetent beneficiaries. Most U.S. states have laws about what a fiduciary may or may not do with a beneficiary's assets. For instance, it is illegal for fiduciaries to invest or misappropriate the money for their personal gain. *See also* LEGAL LIST; PRUDENT MAN RULE.

FIDUCIARY LIABILITY INSURANCE policy that covers legal-defense costs and any payouts in lawsuits against corporate pension plan trustees and other fiduciaries who oversee retirement savings plans.

FIFO *see* FIRST IN, FIRST OUT.

FILING STATUS category a taxpayer chooses in filing a tax return. It determines the filing requirements, standard deduction, eligibility to claim certain deductions and credits, and tax rates. Filing status is determined on the last day of the tax year. The four filing status categories are single, married filing jointly, married filing separately, and head of household. Depending upon the taxpayer's family situation and income, it is more advantageous to file using one category over others. Many accountants figure out a taxpayer's liability using two filing statuses—filing jointly or filing separately—to calculate which one results in the lower tax.

FILL execute a customer's order to buy or sell a stock, bond, or commodity. An order is filled when the amount of the security requested is supplied. When less than the full amount of the order is supplied, it is known as a *partial fill.*

FILL OR KILL (FOK) order to buy or sell a particular security which, if not executed immediately, is canceled. Often, fill or kill orders are placed when a client wants to buy a large quantity of shares of a particular stock at a particular price. If the order is not executed because it will significantly upset the market price for that stock, the order is withdrawn.

FINANCE CHARGE cost of credit, including interest, paid by a customer for a consumer loan. Under the Truth in Lending Act, the finance charge must be disclosed to the customer in advance. *See also* CONSUMER CREDIT PROTECTION ACT OF 1968; REGULATION Z.

FINANCE COMPANY company engaged in making loans to individuals or businesses. Unlike a bank, it does not receive deposits but rather obtains its financing from banks, institutions, and other money market sources. Generally, finance companies fall into three categories: (1) consumer finance companies, also known as *small loan* or *direct loan companies,* lend money to individuals under the small loan laws of the individual U.S. states; (2) sales finance companies, also called *acceptance companies,* purchase retail and wholesale paper from automobile and other consumer and capital goods dealers; (3) commercial finance companies, also called *commercial credit companies,* make loans to manufacturers and wholesalers; these loans are secured by accounts receivable, inventories, and equipment. Finance companies typically enjoy high credit ratings and are thus able to borrow at the lowest market rates, enabling them to make loans at rates not much higher than banks. Even though their customers usually do not qualify for bank credit, these companies have experienced a low rate of default. Finance companies in general tend to be interest rate-sensitive—increases and decreases in market interest rates affect their profits directly. For this reason, publicly held finance companies are sometimes referred to as money stocks. *See also* CAPTIVE FINANCE COMPANY.

FINANCIAL ACCOUNTING STANDARDS BOARD (FASB) group establishes standards of financial accounting and reporting for private-sector entities, including businesses and not-for-profit organizations. It was formed in 1973, and its standards are officially recognized as authoritive by the Securities and Exchange Commission (SEC). The mission of the FASB is to establish and improve standards of financial accounting and reporting for the guidance and education of the public, including issuers, auditors, and users of financial information. FASB decision making follows an extensive due process that is open to public observation and participation. In addition, the FASB's Financial Accounting Standards Advisory Council, Investors Technical Advisory Committee, Investors Task Force, Small Business Advisory Committee, and Private Company Financial Reporting Committee also serve as resources to the board, both in formulating the technical agenda and advising on specific agenda projects. The Emerging Issues Task Force assists the FASB in improving financial reporting through the timely identification, discussion, and resolution of financial accounting issues within the framework of existing authoritarian literature. The FASB standards have been represented by statements numbered 1 through 163 and summaries are available on-line at *www.fasb.org/st*. In July 2009 the FASB Accounting Standards Codification became the single official source of authoritative U.S. GENERALLY ACCEPTED ACCOUNTING PRINCIPLES (GAAP). New statements are issued as Codification Updates, rather than numerical statements. An example of a statement summary is FASB Statement No. 157, Fair Value Measurements, defines fair value and establishes a framework for measuring fair value in generally accepted accounting principles and expands disclosures about fair value measurements. *See also* GENERALLY ACCEPTED ACCOUNTING PRINCIPLES. *www.fasb.org.*

FINANCIAL ADVISER professional adviser offering financial counsel. Some financial advisers charge a fee and earn commissions on the products they recommend to implement their advice. Other advisers only charge fees, and do not sell any products or accept commissions. Some financial advisers are generalists, while others specialize in specific areas such as investing, insurance, estate planning, taxes, or other areas.

FINANCIAL ANALYSIS analysis of the FINANCIAL STATEMENT of a company. *See also* FUNDAMENTAL ANALYSIS.

FINANCIAL ASSETS assets in the form of stocks, bonds, rights, certificates, bank balances, etc., as distinguished from tangible, physical assets. For example, real property is a physical asset, but shares in a REAL ESTATE INVESTMENT TRUST (REIT) or the stock or bonds of a company that held property as an investment would be financial assets.

FINANCIAL FUTURE FUTURES CONTRACT based on a financial instrument. Such contracts usually move under the influence of interest rates. As rates rise, contracts fall in value; as rates fall, contracts gain in value. Examples of instruments underlying financial futures contracts: Treasury bills, Treasury notes, Government National Mortgage Association (Ginnie Mae) pass-throughs, foreign currencies, and certificates of deposit. Trading in these contracts is governed by the federal Commodities Futures Trading Commission. Traders use these futures to speculate on the direction of interest rates. Financial institutions (banks, insurance companies, brokerage firms) use them to hedge financial portfolios against adverse fluctuations in interest rates.

FINANCIAL GUARANTEE INSURANCE covers losses from specific financial transactions. The coverage guarantees investors in debt instruments that they will receive timely payment of principal and interest if there is a default on underlying debts. For example, this insurance backs loan portfolios composed of credit card and auto loans.

FINANCIAL HOLDING COMPANY BANK HOLDING COMPANY or securities firm affiliate that meets qualifications specified in the FINANCIAL SERVICES MODERNIZATION ACT OF 1999 and is therefore permitted to engage in activities previously prohibited by the GLASS-STEAGALL ACT OF 1933 and the Bank Holding Company Act of 1956. Glass-Steagall had prevented banks from engaging in most securities activities and securities firms from engaging in banking activities. The Bank Holding Company Act of 1956 had prohibited affiliations between banks and insurance companies. These "firewall" restrictions are eliminated under the powers given to financinal holding companies by the 1999 Act. A Bank Holding Company qualifies as a Financial Holding Company if its banking subsidiaries are "well capitalized" and "well managed," and it files with the Federal Reserve Board a certification to such effect and a declaration that it elects to become a Financial Holding Company. For such a declaration to be effective, at the date of the election, all the subsidiary insured depository institutions of the Bank Holding Company must have received a satisfactory or better *Community Reinvestment Act (CRA)* rating. (The 1977 CRA requires that banks lend in the communities from which they obtain deposits.) Securities firms and insurance companies, in a two-step process, must first qualify Bank Holding Companies under the 1956 law and then qualify Financial Holding Companies.

FINANCIAL INDUSTRY REGULATORY AUTHORITY (FINRA) a SELF-REGULATORY ORGANIZATION (SRO) and the largest non-governmental regulator of securities firms in the United States. Created in July 2007 by the consolidation of the National Association of Securities Dealers (NASD) and the member regulation, enforcement, and arbitration functions of the NEW YORK STOCK EXCHANGE (NYSE). FINRA oversees 5,100 brokerage firms, about 173,000 branch offices, and more than 676,000 registered securities representatives. It touches virtually every aspect of the securities business, including registering and providing qualification examinations to industry professionals, writing rules for securities trading, educating the investing public, providing trade reporting, and administering an arbitration forum to resolve disputes between customers and member firms. FINRA levied fines totaling $40 million against financial firms in 2008.

FINANCIAL INSTITUTION institution that collects funds from the public to place in financial assets such as stocks, bonds, money market instruments, bank deposits, or loans. Depository institutions (banks, savings and loans, savings banks, credit unions) pay interest on deposits and invest the deposit money mostly in loans. Nondepository institutions (insurance companies, pension plans) collect money by selling insurance policies or receiving employer contributions and pay it out for legitimate claims or for retirement benefits. Increasingly, many institutions are performing both depository and nondepository functions. For instance, brokerage firms now place customers' money in certificates of deposit and money market funds and sell insurance. *See also* FINANCIAL SUPERMARKET.

FINANCIAL INSTITUTIONS REFORM, RECOVERY AND ENFORCEMENT ACT OF 1989 (FIRREA) legislation enacted into law on August 9, 1989, to resolve the crisis affecting U.S. savings and loan associations. Known as the *bailout bill,* it revamped the regulatory, insurance, and financing structures and established the OFFICE OF THRIFT SUPERVISION. The act created (1) the RESOLUTION TRUST CORPORATION (RTC), which, operating under the management of the FEDERAL DEPOSIT INSURANCE CORPORATION (FDIC), was charged with closing or merging institutions that had become insolvent beginning in 1989; (2) the RESOLUTION FUNDING CORPORATION (REFCORP), charged with borrowing from private capital markets to fund RTC activities and to manage the remaining assets and liabilities taken over by the FEDERAL SAVINGS AND LOAN INSURANCE CORPORATION (FSLIC) prior to 1989; (3) the SAVINGS ASSOCIATION INSURANCE FUND (SAIF) (pronounced "safe"), to replace FSLIC as insurer of thrift deposits and to be administered by the FDIC separately from its bank deposit insurance program, which became the BANK INSURANCE FUND (BIF); and (4) the FEDERAL HOUSING FINANCE BOARD (FHFB), charged with overseeing the FEDERAL HOME LOAN BANKS.

The RTC was authorized to accept additional insolvent institutions through June 1995; after that date, responsibilities for newly failed institutions shifted to the SAIF.

See also BAILOUT BOND.

FINANCIAL INTERMEDIARY commercial bank, savings and loan, mutual savings bank, credit union, or other "middleman" that smooths the flow of funds between "savings surplus units" and "savings deficit units." In an economy viewed as three sectors—households, businesses, and government— a *savings surplus unit* is one where income exceeds consumption; a *savings deficit unit* is one where current expenditures exceed current income and external sources must be called upon to make up the difference. As a whole, households are savings surplus units, whereas businesses and governments are savings deficit units. Financial intermediaries redistribute savings into productive uses and, in the process, serve two other important functions: By making savers infinitesimally small "shareholders" in huge pools of capital, which in turn are loaned out to a wide number and variety of borrowers, the intermediaries provide both diversification of risk and liquidity to the individual saver. *See also* DISINTERMEDIATION; FINDER'S FEE.

FINANCIALIZATION concept associated with developments leading up to the 2008–2009 crisis and defined differently by various people, but referring generally to the dominance of financial services over industry as the primary creator of wealth. Whereas, traditionally, the capital markets made bank-based savings available to producers who created wealth, capital market systems became themselves the generator of profit making and wealth. DERIVATIVES, such as futures contracts, swaps, and options, originally designed as tools for use in hedging and risk management, became widely traded financial assets. For one startling example: The Comptroller of the Currency reported the total U.S. credit derivatives positions (CREDIT DEFAULT SWAPS) increased from $492 billion at the beginning of 2003 to $11.8 trillion as of June 2007. Financialization is increasingly seen as a root cause of systemic economic challenges because it can misrepresent reality and lead to dangerous errors. According to one theory, the recent mortgage meltdown and ensuing financial crisis was rooted in the fact that so many mortgages ceased to accurately represent the risk to the lender or the future value to the borrower, ultimately resulting in the misuse of credit default swaps as collateralized debt obligations became widely traded.

FINANCIAL LEASE *see* CAPITAL LEASE.

FINANCIAL LEVERAGE *see* LEVERAGE.

FINANCIAL MARKET market for the exchange of capital and credit in the economy. Money markets concentrate on short-term debt instruments; capital markets trade in long-term debt and equity instruments. Examples of financial markets: stock market, bond market, commodities market, and foreign exchange market.

FINANCIAL NEEDS APPROACH technique to assess the proper amount of life insurance for an individual. The person, either on his or her own or with the help of an insurance adviser, must estimate the financial needs of survivors in case the person dies unexpectedly. Projections for expenses, income, taxes, funeral costs, and other financial factors lead to an understanding of the amount of insurance proceeds that would be needed to allow the survivors to continue in their present lifestyle. Once the optimal amount of insurance protection is determined, various kinds of TERM and CASH VALUE INSURANCE programs can be designed to meet these needs.

FINANCIAL PLANNER professional who analyzes personal financial circumstances and prepares a program to meet financial needs and objectives. Financial planners, who may be accountants, bankers, lawyers, insurance agents, real estate or securities brokers, or independent practitioners, should have knowledge in the areas of wills and estate planning, retirement planning, taxes, insurance, family budgeting, debt management, and investments.

Fee-only planners charge on the basis of service and time and have nothing to sell. *Commission-only planners* offer their services for free but sell commission-producing products such as MUTUAL FUNDS, LIMITED PARTNERSHIPS, insurance products, stocks, and bonds. *Fee-plus-commission planners* charge an upfront fee for consultation and their written plan, then charge commissions on the financial products they sell. *Fee-offset planners* charge fees against which they apply credits when they sell commission-producing products.

The Certified Financial Planner Board of Standards, Inc., in Denver, Colorado, issues the CERTIFIED FINANCIAL PLANNER (CFP) license, and the Financial Planning Association, also in Denver, maintains a referral list. The American Institute of Certified Public Accountants in New York City provides a list of CPAs who offer financial planning services. The National Association of Personal Financial Advisors (NAPFA) in Arlington Heights, Illinois, lists fee-only planners. The International Association of Registered Financial Consultants (IARFC) in Middletown, Ohio, lists financial consultants and planners. The National Endowment for Financial Education, in Denver, offers a financial planning starter kit to consumers, on request. *See also* ACCREDITED PERSONAL FINANCIAL PLANNING SPECIALIST.

FINANCIAL POSITION status of a firm's assets, liabilities, and equity accounts as of a certain time, as shown on its FINANCIAL STATEMENT. Also called *financial condition*.

FINANCIAL PUBLIC RELATIONS branch of public relations specializing in corporate disclosure responsibilities, stockholder relations, and relations with the professional investor community. Financial public relations is concerned not only with matters of corporate image and the cultivation of a favorable financial and investment environment but also with legal interpretation and adherence to Securities and Exchange Commission and other government regulations, as well as with the DISCLOSURE requirements of the securities exchanges. Its practitioners, therefore, include lawyers with expertise in such areas as tender offers and takeovers, public offerings, proxy solicitation, and insider trading. *See also* INVESTOR RELATIONS DEPARTMENT.

FINANCIAL PYRAMID
1. risk structure many investors aim for in spreading their investments between low-, medium-, and high-risk vehicles. In a financial pyramid, the largest part of the investor's assets is in safe, liquid investments that provide a decent return. Next, some money is invested in stocks and bonds that provide good income and the possibility for long-term growth of capital. Third, a smaller portion of one's capital is committed to speculative investments which may offer higher returns if they work out well. At the top of the financial pyramid, where only a small amount of money is committed, are high-risk ventures that have a slight chance of success, but which will provide substantial rewards if they succeed.
2. acquisition of holding company assets through financial leverage. *See also* PYRAMIDING.

 Financial pyramid is not to be confused with fraudulent selling schemes, also sometimes called *pyramiding*.

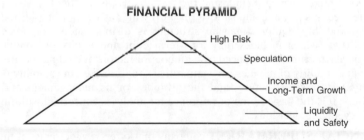

FINANCIAL PYRAMID

High Risk

Speculation

Income and Long-Term Growth

Liquidity and Safety

FINANCIAL SERVICES MODERNIZATION ACT OF 1999 law enacted November 12, 1999, also known as the *Gramm-Leach-Bliley Act*, that repealed parts of the GLASS-STEAGALL ACT OF 1933 and the BANK HOLDING COMPANY Act of 1956, eliminating remaining FIREWALLs between banks, securities firms, and insurance companies. The Act permits commercial banks, merchant banks, securities firms and insurers to affiliate through a structure called the FINANCIAL HOLDING COMPANY. Nationally chartered banks are permitted to engage in most financial activities through direct subsidiaries. The principle of functional regulation is maintained, meaning banking activities are regulated by bank regulators, securities activities by securities regulators, and insurance activities by (state) insurance regulators (who are prohibited from interfering with non-insurance financial activities). Activities permitted Financial Holding Companies and the financial subsidiaries of national banks include lending, exchanging, transferring, investing for others, or safeguarding money or securities; engaging in insurance activities, including insuring and acting as principal, agent, or broker for all types of insurance, including health; financial advice, including advising an investment company; issuing or selling instruments representing interests in pools of assets permissible for a bank to hold indirectly; underwriting, dealing in, or making a market in securities with no limitation as to revenue; directly or indirectly acquiring a company or other entity engaged in any activity that is not financial in nature as a bona fide underwriting or merchant banking activity; engaging in any activity that a Bank Holding Company may engage in outside the United States and that the Federal Reserve Board has determined to be usual in connection with the transaction of banking or other financial operations abroad; insurance company portfolio investments; and activities previously permissible as closely related to banking.

Other provisions of the Act continue to exclude commercial enterprises from controlling banking institutions, including Financial Holding Companies, and limit the commercial activities in which such a Financial Holding Company can engage. Still others relate to disclosure of ATM fees, fair treatment of women by financial advisers, privacy of personal information, and FEDERAL HOME LOAN BANK SYSTEM modernization.

FINANCIAL STATEMENT written record of the financial status of an individual, association, or business organization. The financial statement includes a BALANCE SHEET and an INCOME STATEMENT (or operating statement or profit and loss statement) and may also include a STATEMENT OF CASH FLOWS, a statement of changes in retained earnings, and other analyses.

FINANCIAL STRUCTURE makeup of the right-hand side of a company's BALANCE SHEET, which includes all the ways its assets are financed, such as trade accounts payable and short-term borrowings as well as long-term debt and ownership equity. Financial structure is distinguished from CAPITAL STRUCTURE, which includes only long-term debt and equity. A company's financial structure is influenced by a number of factors, including the growth rate and stability of its sales, its competitive situation (i.e., the stability of its profits), its asset structure, and the attitudes of its management and its lenders. It is the basic frame of reference for analyses concerned with financial leveraging decisions.

FINANCIAL SUPERMARKET company that offers a wide range of financial services under one roof. For example, some large retail organizations offer stock, insurance, and real estate brokerage, as well as banking services. For customers, having all their assets with one institution can make financial transactions and planning more convenient and efficient, since money does not constantly have to be shifted from one institution to another. For institutions, such all-inclusive relationships are more profitable than dealing with just one aspect of a customer's financial needs. Institutions often become financial supermarkets in order to capture all the business of their customers. The financial crisis of the late 2000s raised the question that some institutions had become "too big to fail." As regulatory reform is considered a major question is how to prevent institutions from becoming so big and powerful they present SYSTEMIC RISK.

FINANCIAL TABLES tables found in newspapers listing prices, dividends, yields, price/earnings ratios, trading volume, and other important data on stocks, bonds, mutual funds, and futures contracts. While local newspapers may carry limited tables, more extensive listings are available in *Barron's, Investor's Business Daily,* the *Wall Street Journal,* and other publications.

FINANCING CORPORATION (FICO) agency set up by Congress in 1987 to issue bonds and bail out the FEDERAL SAVINGS AND LOAN INSURANCE CORPORATION (FSLIC). *See also* BAILOUT BOND.

FINDER'S FEE fee charged by a person or company acting as a finder (intermediary) in a transaction.

FINITE LIFE REAL ESTATE INVESTMENT TRUST (FREIT) REAL ESTATE INVESTMENT TRUST (REIT) that promises to try to sell its holdings within a specified period to realize CAPITAL GAINS.

FINITE RISK INSURANCE a non-life insurance arrangement in which the limit of coverage, the time period involved, and the premium paid are based on the time value of money. Finite risk contracts, although they must involve some transfer of risk, are multiyear contracts that spread risk over time. Premiums are invested in an experience fund, often based offshore to avoid taxation, that accrues interest and pays losses. The experience fund reverts to the insured at the end of the transaction period. For example, an insurance company might use a finite insurer to reinsure a medical malpractice claim where the harm caused may not be evident for some time and the final claim not determined for years. The key risk in this instance would be the time element, since with enough time, the experience fund would pay the claim and leave a profit. In the mid-2000s, finite risk (or "loss-mitigation") insurance was abused by some primary insurers to disguise under-reserving for losses stemming from the World Trade Center disaster.

FINRA *see* FINANCIAL INDUSTRY REGULATORY AUTHORITY.

FINRA FORM FR-1 form required of foreign dealers in securities subscribing to new securities issues in the process of distribution, whereby they agree to abide by FINANCIAL INDUSTRY REGULATORY AUTHORITY rules concerning a HOT ISSUE. Under FINRA Rules of Fair Practice, firms participating in the distribution must make a bona fide public offering at the public offering price. Any sale designed to capitalize on a hot issue—one that on the first day of trading sells at a substantial premium over the public offering price—would be in violation of FINRA rules. Violations include a sale to a member of the dealer's family or to an employee, assuming such sales could not be defended as "normal investment practice." Also called *blanket certification form.*

FIREWALL metaphor for any strictly enforced legal separation of activities. For example, in a securities firm, underwriting and investment banking activities are separated from the firm's research and brokerage functions by a firewall, to avoid conflicts of interest. The GLASS-STEAGALL ACT created a firewall between commercial banking and investment banking until it was eliminated by the FINANCIAL SERVICES MODERNIZATION ACT OF 1999.

FIRM

1. general term for a business, corporation, partnership, or proprietorship. Legally, a firm is not considered a corporation since it may not be incorporated and since the firm's principals are not recognized as separate from the identity of the firm itself. This might be true of a law or accounting firm, for instance.
2. solidity with which an agreement is made. For example, a firm order with a manufacturer or a firm bid for a stock at a particular price means that the order or bid is assured.

FIRM COMMITMENT

Lending: term used by lenders to refer to an agreement to make a loan to a specific borrower within a specific period of time and, if applicable, on a specific property. *See also* COMMITMENT FEE.

Securities underwriting: arrangement whereby investment bankers make outright purchases from the issuer of securities to be offered to the public; also called *firm commitment underwriting.* The underwriters, as the investment bankers are called in such an arrangement, make their profit on the difference between the purchase price—determined through either competitive bidding or negotiation—and the public offering price. Firm commitment underwriting is to be distinguished from conditional arrangements for distributing new securities, such as standby commitments and best efforts commitments. The word *underwriting* is frequently misused with respect to such conditional arrangements. It is used correctly only with respect to firm commitment underwritings or, as they are sometimes called, BOUGHT DEALS. *See also* BEST EFFORT; STANDBY COMMITMENT.

FIRM ORDER

Commercial transaction: written or verbal order that has been confirmed and is not subject to cancellation.

Securities: (1) order to buy or sell for the proprietary account of the broker-dealer firm; (2) buy or sell order not conditional upon the customer's confirmation.

FIRM QUOTE securities industry term referring to any round lot bid or offer price of a security stated by a market maker and not identified as a nominal (or subject) quote. Under FINANCIAL INDUSTRY REGULATORY AUTHORITY (FINRA) rules and practice, quotes requiring further negotiation or review must be identified as nominal quotes. *See also* NOMINAL QUOTATION.

FIRREA *see* FINANCIAL INSTITUTIONS REFORM AND RECOVERY ACT.

FIRST BOARD delivery dates for futures as established by the Chicago Board of Trade and other exchanges trading in futures.

FIRST CALL *see* THOMSON FINANCIAL.

FIRST CALL DATE first date specified in the indenture of a corporate or municipal bond contract on which part or all of the bond may be redeemed at a set price. An XYZ bond due in 2030, for instance, may have a first call date of May 1, 2013. This means that, if XYZ wishes, bondholders may be paid off starting on that date in 2013. Bond brokers typically quote yields on such bonds with both yield to maturity (in this case, 2030) and yield to call (in this case, 2013). *See also* DURATION; YIELD TO CALL; YIELD TO MATURITY; YIELD TO WORST.

FIRST IN, FIRST OUT (FIFO) method of accounting for inventory whereby, quite literally, the inventory is assumed to be sold in the chronological order in which it was purchased. For example, the following formula is used in computing the cost of goods sold:

Under the FIFO method, inventory costs flow from the oldest purchases forward, with beginning inventory as the starting point and ending inventory representing the most recent purchases. The FIFO method contrasts with the LIFO or LAST IN, FIRST OUT method, which is FIFO in reverse. The significance of the difference becomes apparent when inflation or deflation affects inventory prices. In an inflationary period, the FIFO method produces a higher ending inventory, a lower cost of goods sold figure, and a higher gross profit. LIFO, on the other hand, produces a lower ending inventory, a higher cost of goods sold figure, and a lower reported profit.

In accounting for the purchase and sale of securities for tax purposes, FIFO is assumed by the IRS unless it is advised of the use of an alternative method.

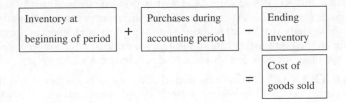

FIRST MORTGAGE real estate loan that gives the mortgagee (lender) a primary lien against a specified piece of property. A primary lien has precedence over all other mortgages in case of default. *See also* JUNIOR MORTGAGE; SECOND MORTGAGE.

FIRST PREFERRED STOCK preferred stock that has preferential claim on dividends and assets over other preferred issues and common stock.

FIRST TIME HOMEBUYER TAX CREDIT program enacted in 2009 to encourage first time home buyers to buy homes and qualify for a tax credit of 10% of a home's purchase price up to $8,000. Participants in the program could not have owned a principal residence in the previous three years and had to use the money to purchase their primary home.

FISCAL AGENT
1. usually a bank or a trust company acting for a corporation under a corporate trust agreement. The fiscal agent handles such matters as disbursing funds for dividend payments, redeeming bonds and coupons, handling taxes related to the issue of bonds, and paying rents.
2. agent of the national government or its agencies or of a state or municipal government that performs functions relating to the issue and payment of bonds. For example, the Federal Reserve is the U.S. government's fiscal agent.

FISCAL DRAG the negative effect on demand for goods and services caused by progressive taxation during periods of economic expansion. Tax revenues tend to expand as a percentage of GDP as personal incomes rise, indicating that spending is being diverted to taxes causing reduced demand.

FISCAL POLICY federal taxation and spending policies designed to level out the business cycle and achieve full employment, price stability, and sustained growth in the economy. Fiscal policy basically follows the economic theory of the 20th-century English economist John Maynard Keynes that insufficient demand causes unemployment and excessive demand leads to inflation. It aims to stimulate demand and output in periods of business decline by increasing government purchases and cutting taxes, thereby releasing more disposable income into the spending stream, and to correct overexpansion by reversing the process. Working to balance these deliberate fiscal measures are the so-called built-in stabilizers, such as the progressive income tax and unemployment benefits, which automatically respond countercyclically. Fiscal policy is administered independently of MONETARY POLICY, by which the Federal Reserve Board attempts to regulate economic activity by controlling the money supply. The goals of fiscal and monetary policy are the same, but Keynesians and Monetarists disagree as to which of the two approaches works best. At the basis of their differences are questions dealing with the velocity (turnover) of money and the effect of changes in the money supply on the equilibrium rate of interest (the rate at which money demand equals money supply). *See also* KEYNESIAN ECONOMICS.

FISCAL YEAR (FY) accounting period covering 12 consecutive months, 52 consecutive weeks, 13 four-week periods, or 365 consecutive days, at the end of which the books are closed and profit or loss is determined. A company's fiscal year is often, but not necessarily, the same as the calendar year. A seasonal business will frequently select a fiscal rather than a calendar year, so that its year-end figures will show it in its most liquid condition, which also means having less inventory to verify physically. The FY of the U.S. government ends September 30.

FISCHER EFFECT hypothesis of Irving Fischer that the real interest rate is constant and independent of monetary measures and that it is equal to the nominal interest rate minus the expected rate of inflation. The *international Fischer effect* holds that, assuming capital is free to flow across borders, a change in the difference in nominal interest rates between two countries determines the change in the exchange rates between their currencies, the currency of the country with the lower nominal interest rate being the one that moves.

FIT a situation where the features of a particular investment perfectly match the portfolio requirements of an investor.

FITCH RATINGS New York and London-based subsidiary of Fimmalac, Paris and one of the three nationally recognized statistical ratings organizations designated by the SECURITIES AND EXCHANGE COMMISSION (SEC). Fitch Ratings has 50 offices worldwide that provide ratings and research covering 1,600 financial institutions, 1,000 corporations, and maintain surveillance on 3,300 structured financings and 17,000 municipal bond ratings in the U.S. tax-exempt market. Fitch Ratings also covers over 800 insurance companies, plus over 100 sovereigns.

FITCH SHEETS sheets indicating the successive trade prices of securities listed on the major exchanges. They are published by Francis Emory Fitch, Inc. in New York City.

FIVE HUNDRED DOLLAR RULE REGULATION T provision of the Federal Reserve that exempts deficiencies in margin requirements amounting to $500 or less from mandatory remedial action. Brokers are thus not forced to resort to the liquidation of an account to correct a trivial deficiency in a situation where, for example, a customer is temporarily out of town and cannot be reached. *See also* MARGIN CALL.

FIVE PERCENT RULE one of the Rules of Fair Practice of the FINANCIAL INDUSTRY REGULATORY AUTHORITY (FINRA). It proposes an ethical guideline for spreads in dealer transactions and commissions in brokerage transactions, including PROCEEDS SALES and RISKLESS TRANSACTIONS.

501-(c)(3) BOND debt instrument issued by a tax-exempt nonprofit organization and paying interest not subject to the ALTERNATIVE MINIMUM TAX (AMT).

FIVE PERCENT RULE one of the Rules of Fair Practice of the National Association of Securities Dealers (NASD). It proposes an ethical guideline for spreads in dealer transactions and commissions in brokerage transactions, including PROCEEDS SALES and RISKLESS TRANSACTIONS.

FIXATION setting of a present or future price of a commodity, such as the twice-daily London GOLD FIXING. In other commodities, prices are fixed further into the future for the benefit of both buyers and sellers of that commodity.

FIXED ANNUITY investment contract sold by an insurance company that guarantees fixed payments, either for life or for a specified period, to an annuitant. In fixed annuities, the insurer takes both the investment and the mortality risks. A fixed annuity contrasts with a VARIABLE ANNUITY, where payments depend on an uncertain outcome, such as prices in the securities markets. *See also* ANNUITY.

FIXED ASSET tangible property used in the operations of a business, but not expected to be consumed or converted into cash in the ordinary course of events. Plant, machinery and equipment, furniture and fixtures, and leasehold improvements comprise the fixed assets of most companies. They are normally represented on the balance sheet at their net depreciated value.

FIXED BENEFITS payments to a BENEFICIARY that are fixed rather than variable.

FIXED-CHARGE COVERAGE ratio of profits before payment of interest and income taxes to interest on bonds and other contractual long-term debt. It indicates how many times interest charges have been earned by the corporation on a pretax basis. Since failure to meet interest payments would be a default under the terms of indenture agreements, the coverage ratio measures a margin of safety. The amount of safety desirable depends on the stability of a company's earnings. (Too much safety can be an indication of an undesirable lack of leverage.) In cyclical companies, the fixed-charge coverage in periods of recession is a telling ratio. Analysts also find it useful to calculate the number of times that a company's *cash flow*—i.e., *after*-tax earnings plus noncash expenses (for example, depreciation)—covers fixed charges. Also known as *times fixed charges*.

FIXED COST cost that remains constant regardless of sales volume. Fixed costs include salaries of executives, interest expense, rent, depreciation, and insurance expenses. They contrast with *variable costs* (direct labor, materials costs), which are distinguished from *semivariable costs.* Semivariable costs vary, but not necessarily in direct relation to sales. They may also remain fixed up to a level of sales, then increase when sales enter a higher range. For example, expenses associated with a delivery truck would be fixed up to the level of sales where a second truck was required. Obviously, no costs are purely fixed; the assumption, however, serves the purposes of cost accounting for limited planning periods. Cost accounting is also concerned with the allocation of portions of fixed costs to inventory costs, also called indirect costs, overhead, factory overhead, and supplemental overhead. *See also* DIRECT OVERHEAD; VARIABLE COST.

FIXED EXCHANGE RATE set rate of exchange between the currencies of countries. At the Bretton Woods international monetary conference in 1944, a system of fixed exchange rates was set up, which existed until the early 1970s, when a FLOATING EXCHANGE RATE system was adopted and international gold backing was abandoned.

FIXED EXPENSES *see* FIXED COSTS.

FIXED-INCOME EQUIVALENT *see* BUSTED CONVERTIBLES.

FIXED-INCOME INVESTMENT security that pays a fixed rate of return. This usually refers to government, corporate, or municipal bonds, which pay a fixed rate of interest until the bonds mature, and to preferred stock, paying a fixed dividend. Such investments are advantageous in a time of low inflation, but do not protect holders against erosion of buying power in a time of rising inflation, since the bondholder or preferred shareholder gets the same amount of interest or dividends, even though consumer goods cost more.

FIXED PREMIUM equal installments payable to an insurance company for INSURANCE or an ANNUITY. *See also* SINGLE-PREMIUM DEFERRED ANNUITY (SPDA) and SINGLE-PREMIUM LIFE INSURANCE.

FIXED PRICE
Contracts: type of contract where the price is preset and invariable, regardless of the actual costs of production. *See also* COST-PLUS CONTRACT.
Investment: in a public offering of new securities, price at which investment bankers in the underwriting SYNDICATE agree to sell the issue to the public. The price remains fixed as long as the syndicate remains in effect. The proper term for this kind of system is *fixed price offering system.* In contrast, Eurobonds, which are also sold through underwriting syndicates, are offered on a basis that permits discrimination among customers; i.e., the underwriting spread may be adjusted to suit the particular buyer. *See also* EUROBOND.

FIXED RATE (LOAN) type of loan in which the interest rate does not fluctuate with general market conditions. There are fixed rate mortgage (also known as conventional mortgage) and consumer installment loans, as well as fixed rate business loans. Fixed rate loans tend to have higher original interest rates than flexible rate loans such as an ADJUSTABLE RATE MORTGAGE (ARM), because lenders are not protected against a rise in the cost of money when they make a fixed rate loan.
　　The term fixed rate may also refer to fixed currency exchange rates. *See also* FIXED EXCHANGE RATE.

FIXED TERM REVERSE MORTGAGE mortgage granted by a bank or other lending institution providing payments to a homeowner for a fixed number of years. A retired couple who have paid off their traditional mortgage might be interested in such a plan if they do not want to move out of their house, but want to be able to tap the equity in their house for current cash income.

FIXED TRUST UNIT INVESTMENT TRUST that has a fixed portfolio of previously agreed upon securities; also called *fixed investment trust.* The securities are usually of one type, such as corporate, government, or municipal bonds, in order to afford a regular income to holders of units. A fixed trust is distinguished from a PARTICIPATING TRUST.

FIXTURE attachment to real property that is not intended to be moved and would create damage to the property if it were moved—for example, a plumbing fixture. Fixtures are classified as part of real estate when they share the same useful life. Otherwise, they are considered equipment.

FLAG technical chart pattern resembling a flag shaped like a parallelogram with masts on either side, showing a consolidation within a trend. It results from price fluctuations within a narrow range, both preceded and followed by sharp rises or declines. If the flag—the consolidation period—is preceded by a rise, it will usually be followed by a rise; a fall will follow a fall.

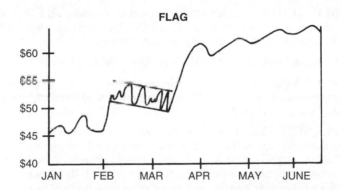

FLAG

FLASH tape display designation used when volume on an exchange is so heavy that the tape runs more than five minutes behind. The flash interrupts the display to report the current price—called the *flash price*—of a heavily traded security. Current prices of two groups of 50 stocks are flashed at five-minute intervals as long as the tape is seriously behind.

FLASH TRADING *see* HIGH-FREQUENCY TRADING.

FLAT
1. in bond trading, without accrued interest. This means that accrued interest will be received by the buyer if and when paid but that no accrued interest is payable to the seller. Issues in default and INCOME BONDS are normally quoted and traded flat. The opposite of a flat bond is an AND INTEREST bond. *See also* LOANED FLAT.
2. inventory of a market maker with a net zero position—i.e., neither long nor short.
3. position of an underwriter whose account is completely sold.

FLAT MARKET market characterized by HORIZONTAL PRICE MOVEMENT. It is usually the result of low activity. However, STABILIZATION, consolidation, and DISTRIBUTION are situations marked by both horizontal price movement and active trading.

FLAT SCALE
Industry: labor term denoting a uniform rate of pay that makes no allowance for volume, frequency, or other factors.
Municipal bonds: bond trader's term describing a situation where shorter and longer term yields show little difference over the maturity range of a new serial bond issue.

FLAT TAX tax applied at the same rate to all levels of income. It is often discussed as an alternative to the PROGRESSIVE TAX. Proponents of a flat tax argue that people able to retain larger portions of higher income would have an added incentive to earn, thus stimulating the economy. Advocates also note its simplicity. Opponents argue it is a REGRESSIVE TAX in effect, comparing it to the sales tax, a uniform tax that puts a greater burden on households with lower incomes. The TAX REFORM ACT OF 1986 instituted a modified flat tax system—a progressive tax with fewer tax brackets and lower rates. However, the trend towards a flat tax was reversed with the REVENUE RECONCILIATION ACT OF 1993, which added another tax bracket and a tax surcharge to the income tax system. *See also* CONSUMPTION TAX.

FLEXIBLE BUDGET statement of projected revenue and expenditure based on various levels of production. It shows how costs vary with different rates of output or at different levels of sales volume.

FLEXIBLE EXCHANGE RATE *see* FLOATING EXCHANGE RATE.

FLEXIBLE EXPENSES in personal finance, expenses that can be adjusted or eliminated, such as those for luxuries, as opposed to fixed expenses, such as rent or car payments.

FLEXIBLE MUTUAL FUND fund that can invest in stocks, bonds, and cash in whatever proportion the fund manager thinks will maximize returns to shareholders at the lowest level of risk. Flexible funds, also called ASSET ALLOCATION funds, can provide high returns if they are fully invested in stocks when stock prices soar, and they can also protect shareholders' assets by going largely to cash during a stock bear market. Flexible mutual funds are popular because the fund manager, not the shareholder, must make the difficult decisions on asset allocation and market timing. Some flexible funds allow managers to buy securities anywhere in the world in their quest to maximize shareholder returns.

FLEXIBLE SPENDING ACCOUNTS (FSAs) CAFETERIA EMPLOYEE BENEFIT PLANS established by Section 125 of the Internal Revenue Code that allow unlimited (except for limits that may be set by employers) pretax contributions for certain health-care, dependent-care, insurance, and adoption costs, any or all of which categories may be elected. Accounts can be opened as either *premium-only plans*, where contributions are remitted to an insurer, or *reimbursement plan*s, where contributions are based on estimated expenses for the plan year and unspent contributions are forfeited. Contributions by employers, which include nonprofit organizations, are permitted on either basis. Medical-expense FSAs allow for reimbursement of nonprescription drug services.

FLIGHT OF CAPITAL *see* CAPITAL FLIGHT.

FLIGHT TO QUALITY moving capital to the safest possible investment to protect oneself from loss during an unsettling period in the market. For example, when a major bank fails, cautious money market investors may buy only government-backed money market securities instead of those issued by major banks. A flight to quality can be measured by the differing yields resulting from such a movement of capital. In the example just given, the yields on bank-issued money market paper will rise since there will be less demand for it, and the rates on government securities will fall, because there will be more demand for them.

FLIP-IN POISON PILL *see* POISON PILL.

FLIP-OVER POISON PILL *see* POISON PILL.

FLIPPING buying and selling immediately for a profit. Brokerage firms underwriting new stock issues tend to discourage flipping, and will often try to allocate shares to investors who say they plan to hold on to the shares for some time. Still, the temptation to flip a new issue once it has risen in price sharply is too irresistible for many investors lucky enough to be allocated shares in a HOT ISSUE. An investor who flips assets is called a *flipper*. Flipping of real estate was commonplace during the recent housing bubble but ended abruptly in 2007.

FLOAT
Banking: time between the deposit of a check in a bank and payment. Long floats are to the advantage of checkwriters, whose money may earn interest until a check clears. They are to the disadvantage of depositors, who must wait for a check to clear before they have access to the funds. As a rule, the further away the paying bank is from the deposit bank, the longer it will take for a check to clear. Some U.S. states limit the amount of float a bank can impose on the checks of its depositors. *See also* UNCOLLECTED FUNDS.
Investments: number of shares of a corporation that are outstanding and available for trading by the public. A small float means the stock will be more volatile, since a large order to buy or sell shares can influence the stock's price dramatically. A larger float means the stock will be less volatile.

FLOATER
Bonds: debt instrument with a variable interest rate tied to another interest rate, e.g., the rate paid by Treasury bills. A FLOATING RATE NOTE, for instance, provides a holder with additional interest if the applicable interest rate rises and less interest if the rate falls. It is generally best to buy floaters if it appears that interest rates will rise. If the outlook is for falling rates, investors typically favor fixed rate instruments. Floaters spread risk between issuers and debtholders.
Insurance: endorsement to a homeowner's or renter's insurance policy, a form of property insurance for items that are moved from location to location. Typically, a floater is bought to cover jewelry, furs, and other items whose full value is not covered in standard homeowner's or renter's policies. A standard homeowner's policy typically covers $1,000 to $2,000 for jewelry, furs, and watches. Also called a *rider*.

FLOATING AN ISSUE *see* NEW ISSUE; UNDERWRITE.

FLOATING DEBT continuously renewed or refinanced short-term debt of companies or governments used to finance ongoing operating needs.

FLOATING EXCHANGE RATE movement of a foreign currency exchange rate in response to changes in the market forces of supply and demand; also known as *flexible exchange rate.* Currencies strengthen or weaken based on a nation's reserves of hard currency and gold, its international trade balance, its rate of inflation and interest rates, and the general strength of its economy. Nations generally do not want their currency to be too strong, because this makes the country's goods too expensive for foreigners to buy. A weak currency, on the other hand, may signify economic instability if it has been caused by high inflation or a weak economy. The opposite of the floating exchange rate is the FIXED EXCHANGE RATE system. *See also* PAR VALUE OF CURRENCY.

FLOATING LIEN LIEN attached to a company's ASSETS or class of assets.

FLOATING RATE NOTE debt instrument with a variable interest rate. Interest adjustments are made periodically, often every six months, and are tied to a money-market index such as Treasury bill rates. Floating rate notes usually have a maturity of about five years. They provide holders with protection against rises in interest rates, but pay lower yields than fixed rate notes of the same maturity. Also known as a FLOATER.

FLOATING SECURITIES
1. securities bought for the purpose of making a quick profit on resale and held in a broker's name.
2. outstanding stock of a corporation that is traded on an exchange.
3. unsold units of a newly issued security.

FLOATING SUPPLY
Bonds: total dollar amount of municipal bonds in the hands of speculators and dealers that is for sale at any particular time as offered in the BLUE LIST. Someone might say, for instance, "There is $10 billion in floating supply available now in the municipal bond market."
Stocks: number of shares of a stock available for purchase. A dealer might say, "The floating supply in this stock is about 200,000 shares." Sometimes called simply the *float.*

FLOOR in general, the lower limit of something. In securities, the part of a stock exchange where active trading takes place or the price at which a STOP LOSS order is activated. *See also* FLOOR BROKER.

FLOOR BROKER member of an exchange who is an employee of a member firm and executes orders, as agent, on the floor of the exchange for clients. The floor broker receives an order via teletype machine from his firm's trading department, then proceeds to the appropriate trading post on the exchange floor. There he joins other brokers and the specialist in the security being bought or sold, and executes the trade at the best competitive price available. On completion of the transaction, the customer is notified through his registered representative back at the firm, and the trade is printed on the consolidated ticker tape, which is displayed electronically around the country. A floor broker should not be confused with a FLOOR TRADER, who trades as a principal for his or her own account, rather than as a broker.

FLOOR OFFICIAL securities exchange employee, who is present on the floor of the exchange to settle disputes in the auction procedure, such as questions about priority or precedence in the settling of an auction. The floor official makes rulings on the spot and his or her judgment is usually accepted.

FLOOR TICKET summary of the information entered on the ORDER TICKET by the registered representative on receipt of a buy or sell order from a client. The floor ticket gives the floor broker the information needed to execute a securities transaction. The information required on floor tickets is specified by securities industry rules.

FLOOR TRADER member of a stock or commodities exchange who trades on the floor of that exchange for his or her own account. The floor trader must abide by trading rules similar to those of the exchange specialists who trade on behalf of others. The term should not be confused with FLOOR BROKER. *See also* REGISTERED COMPETITIVE TRADER.

FLOTATION (FLOATATION) COST cost of issuing new stocks or bonds. It varies with the amount of underwriting risk and the job of physical distribution. It comprises two elements: (1) the compensation earned by the investment bankers (the underwriters) in the form of the spread between the price paid to the issuer (the corporation or government agency) and the offering price to the public, and (2) the expenses of the issuer (legal, accounting, printing, and other out-of-pocket expenses). Securities and Exchange Commission studies reveal that flotation costs are higher for stocks than for bonds, reflecting the generally wider distribution and greater volatility of common stock as opposed to bonds, which are usually sold in large blocks to relatively few investors. The SEC also found that flotation costs as a percentage of gross proceeds are greater for smaller issues than for larger ones. This occurs because the issuer's legal and other expenses tend to be relatively large and fixed, also, smaller issues tend to originate with less established issuers, requiring more information development and marketing expense. An issue involving a RIGHTS OFFERING can involve negligible underwriting risk and selling effort and therefore minimal flotation cost, especially if the underpricing is substantial.

The UNDERWRITING SPREAD is the key variable in flotation cost, historically ranging from 23.7% of the size of a small issue of common stock to as low as 1.25% of the par value of high-grade bonds. Spreads are determined by both negotiation and competitive bidding.

FLOW OF FUNDS
Economics: in referring to the national economy, the way funds are transferred from savings surplus units to savings deficit units through financial intermediaries. *See also* FINANCIAL INTERMEDIARY.
Municipal bonds: statement found in the bond resolutions of municipal revenue issues showing the priorities by which municipal revenue will be applied. Typically, the flow of funds in decreasing order of priority is operation and maintenance, bond debt service, expansion of the facility, and sinking fund for retirement of debt prior to maturity. The flow of funds statement varies in detail from issue to issue.
Mutual funds: movement of money into or out of mutual funds or between various fund sectors. Heavy inflows and outflows are viewed respectively as bullish or bearish indicators for the stock market in general or for stock prices of the underlying companies in different sectors.

FLUCTUATION

1. change in prices or interest rates, either up or down. Fluctuation may refer to either slight or dramatic changes in the prices of stocks, bonds, or commodities. *See also* FLUCTUATION LIMIT.
2. the ups and downs in the economy.

FLUCTUATION LIMIT limits placed on the daily ups and downs of futures prices by the commodity exchanges. The limit protects traders from losing too much on a particular contract in one day. If a commodity reaches its limit, it may not trade any further that day. *See also* LIMIT UP, LIMIT DOWN.

FLURRY sudden increase in trading activity in a particular security. For example, there will be a flurry of trading in the stock of a company that was just the target of a surprise takeover bid. There are often trading flurries right after a company releases its quarterly earnings.

FNMA *see* FEDERAL NATIONAL MORTGAGE ASSOCIATION.

FOB *see* FREE ON BOARD.

FOCUS REPORT FOCUS is an acronym for the Financial and Operational Combined Uniform Single report, which broker-dealers are required to file monthly and quarterly with self-regulatory organizations (SROs). The SROs include exchanges, securities associations, and clearing organizations registered with the Securities and Exchange Commission and required by federal securities laws to be self-policing. The FOCUS report contains figures on capital, earnings, trade flow, and other required details.

FOLIO *see* SELF-DIRECTED PORTFOLIO.

FOOTSIE popular name for the *Financial Times'* FT-SE 100 Index (Financial Times-Stock Exchange 100 stock index), a market-value (capitalization)-weighted index of 100 BLUE CHIP stocks traded on the London Stock Exchange.

FORBES 500 annual listing by *Forbes* magazine of the largest U.S. publicly-owned corporations ranked four ways: by sales, assets, profits, and market value. *See also* FORTUNE 500.

FORCED CONVERSION when a CONVERTIBLE security is called in by its issuer. Convertible owners may find it to their financial advantage either to sell or to convert their holdings into common shares of the underlying company or to accept the call price. Such a conversion usually takes place when the convertible is selling above its CALL PRICE because the market value of the shares of the underlying stock has risen sharply. *See also* CONVERTIBLE.

FORCE MAJEURE event that absolves parties to a contract from responsibility by making it impossible for one or the other to perform. Examples might be a war, a strike, or an ACT OF GOD.

FORECASTING projecting current trends using existing data.

Stock market forecasters predict the direction of the stock market by relying on technical data of trading activity and fundamental statistics on the direction of the economy.

Economic forecasters foretell the strength of the economy, often by utilizing complex econometric models as a tool to make specific predictions of future levels of inflation, interest rates, and employment. *See also* ECONOMETRICS.

Forecasting can also refer to various PROJECTIONS used in business and financial planning.

FORECLOSURE process by which a homeowner who has not made timely payments of principal and interest on a mortgage loses title to the home. The holder of the mortgage, whether it be a bank, a savings and loan, or an individual, must go to court to seize the property, which may then be sold to satisfy the claims of the mortgage.

FOREIGN BOND a debt security issued by a foreign entity in a domestic market in the domestic market's currency. Attraction to domestic investors is international diversification without currency exchange risk *See also* EURO-BONDS, BULLDOG SECURITIES, MATILDA BONDS, SAMURAI BONDS, YANKEE BONDS.

FOREIGN CORPORATION corporation chartered under the laws of a state other than the one in which it conducts business. Because of inevitable confusion with the term ALIEN CORPORATION, out-of-state corporation is preferred.

FOREIGN CORRUPT PRACTICES SECURITIES EXCHANGE ACT OF 1934 amendment passed in 1977 providing internal controls and penalties aimed at curtailing bribery by publicly held companies of foreign government officials and personnel.

FOREIGN CROWD New York Stock Exchange members who trade on the floor in foreign bonds.

FOREIGN CURRENCY FUTURES AND OPTIONS futures and options contracts based on foreign currencies, such as the Euro, Japanese yen, and British pound. The buyer of a foreign currency futures contract acquires the right to buy a particular amount of that currency by a specific date at a fixed rate of exchange, and the seller agrees to sell that currency at the same fixed price. *Call options* give call buyers the right, but not the obligation, to buy the underlying currency at a particular price by a particular date. Call options on foreign currency futures give call buyers the right to a long underlying futures contracts. Those buying *put options* have the right to sell the underlying currencies at a specific price by a specific date. Most buyers and sellers of foreign currency futures and options do not exercise their rights to buy or sell, but trade out of their contracts at a profit or loss before they expire. SPECULATORS hope to profit by buying or selling a foreign currency futures or options contract before a currency rises or falls in value. HEDGERS buy or sell such contracts to protect their cash market position from fluctuations in currency values. These contracts are traded on SECURITIES AND COMMODITIES EXCHANGES throughout the world, including the CHICAGO MERCANTILE EXCHANGE (CME), FINEX, the Mid-America Commodity Exchange, and the PHILADELPHIA STOCK EXCHANGE (PHLX). *See also* EXOTIC OPTIONS.

FOREIGN DIRECT INVESTMENT
1. investment in U.S. businesses by foreign citizens; usually involves majority stock ownership of the enterprise.
2. joint ventures between foreign and U.S. companies.

FOREIGN EXCHANGE instruments employed in making payments between countries—paper currency, notes, checks, bills of exchange, and electronic notifications of international debits and credits.

FOREIGN EXCHANGE CONTROLS restrictions a government puts on the purchase or sale of foreign currencies by its residents or on the purchase or sale of its own currency by nonresidents. Such controls have been instituted by countries with weak currencies to prevent its citizens from holding and using currencies of other nations or to inhibit foreign investors from extricating their funds.

FOREIGN EXCHANGE RATE *see* EXCHANGE RATE; FOREIGN EXCHANGE.

FOREIGN SALES CORPORATION (FSC) *see* TAX REFORM ACT OF 1984 (number 22).

FORFEITURE loss of rights or assets due to failure to fulfill a legal obligation or condition and as compensation for resulting losses or damages.

FORENSIC ACCOUNTING the integration of accounting and investigative techniques to produce analysis suitable for use in courts of law.

FOREX MARKET the exchanges and electronic trading systems comprising the market for FOREIGN EXCHANGE, including the SPOT MARKET for currencies, FOREIGN CURRENCY FUTURES AND OPTIONS, and FORWARD EXCHANGE TRANSACTIONS. Participants include central banks, commercial and investment banks, hedge funds, international corporations, and individual traders. The Forex operates 24 hours a day, five days a week. *See also* NONDELIVERABLE FORWARD (NDF) MARKET.

FORM 8-K Securities and Exchange Commission required form that a publicly held company must file, reporting on any material event that might affect its financial situation or the value of its shares, ranging from merger activity to amendment of the corporate charter or bylaws. The SEC considers as material all matters about which an average, prudent investor ought reasonably to be informed before deciding whether to buy, sell, or hold a registered security. Form 8-K must be filed within a month of the occurrence of the material event. Timely disclosure rules may require a corporation to issue a press release immediately concerning an event subsequently reported on Form 8-K.

FORM 4 document, filed with the Securities and Exchange Commission and the pertinent stock exchange, which is used to report changes in the holdings of (1) those who own at least 10% of a corporation's outstanding stock and (2) directors and officers, even if they own no stock. When there has been a major change in ownership, Form 4 must be filed within ten days of the end of the month in which the change took place. Form 4 filings must be constantly updated during a takeover attempt of a company when the acquirer buys more than 10% of the outstanding shares.

FORM T National Association of Securities Dealers (NASD) form for reporting equity transaction executed after the market's normal hours.

FORM 10-K annual report required by the Securities and Exchange Commission of every issuer of a registered security, every exchange-listed company, and any company with 500 or more shareholders or $1 million or more in gross assets. The form provides for disclosure of total sales, revenue, and pretax operating income, as well as sales by separate classes of products for each of a company's separate lines of business for each of the past five years. A source and application of funds statement presented on a comparative basis for the last two fiscal years is also required. Form 10-K becomes public information when filed with the SEC.

FORM 10-Q quarterly report required by the Securities and Exchange Commission of companies with listed securities. Form 10-Q is less comprehensive than the FORM 10-K annual report and does not require that figures be audited. It may cover the specific quarter or it may be cumulative. It should include comparative figures for the same period of the previous year.

FORM 13D form used to comply with SCHEDULE 13D.

FORM 13G short form of SCHEDULE 13D for positions acquired in the ordinary course of business and not to assume control or influence.

FORM 3 form filed with the Securities and Exchange Commission and the pertinent stock exchange by all holders of 10% or more of the stock of a company registered with the SEC and by all directors and officers, even if no shares are owned. Form 3 details the number of shares owned as well as the number of warrants, rights, convertible bonds, and options to purchase common stock. Individuals required to file Form 3 are considered insiders, and they are required to update their information whenever changes occur. Such changes are reported on FORM 4.

FORMULA INVESTING investment technique based on a predetermined timing or asset allocation model that eliminates emotional decisions. One type of formula investing, called dollar cost averaging, involves putting the same amount of money into a stock or mutual fund at regular intervals, so that more shares will be bought when the price is low and less when the price is high. Another formula investing method calls for shifting funds from stocks to bonds or vice versa as the stock market reaches particular price levels. If stocks rise to a particular point, a certain amount of the stock portfolio is sold and put in bonds. On the other hand, if stocks fall to a particular low price, money is brought out of bonds into stocks. *See also* CONSTANT DOLLAR PLAN; CONSTANT RATIO PLAN.

FORTUNE 500 listings of the top 500 U.S. corporations compiled by *Fortune* magazine. The companies are ranked by 12 indices, among them revenues, profits; assets; stockholders' equity; market value; profits as a percentage of revenues, assets, and stockholders' equity; earnings per share growth over a 10-year span; total return to investors in the year; and the 10-year annual rate of total return to investors. In separate listings, companies also are ranked by performance and within states. Headquarters city, phone number, and the name of the chief executive officer are included. In another listing 1,000 companies are ranked within 61 different industry groups.

FORWARD CONTRACT purchase or sale of a specific quantity of a commodity, government security, foreign currency, or other financial instrument at the current or SPOT PRICE, with delivery and settlement at a specified future date. Because it is a completed contract—as opposed to an options contract, where the owner has the choice of completing or not completing—a forward contract can be a COVER for the sale of a FUTURES CONTRACT. *See also* HEDGE.

FORWARD EXCHANGE TRANSACTION purchase or sale of foreign currency at an exchange rate established now but with payment and delivery at a specified future time. Most forward exchange contracts have one-, three-, or six-month maturities, though contracts in major currencies can normally be arranged for delivery at any specified date up to a year, and sometimes up to three years.

FORWARD-LOOKING STATEMENTS statements in annual reports and other financial communications that are based on management's expectations, estimates, projections, and assumptions and are made pursuant to the SAFE HARBOR provisions of the PRIVATE SECURITIES LITIGATION REFORM ACT OF 1995, as amended. Such statements are accompanied by caveats saying actual future results and trends may differ materially from what is forecast.

FORWARD P/E *see* PRICE/EARNINGS RATIO (P/E).

FORWARD PRICING Securities and Exchange Commission requirement that open-end investment companies, whose share price is always determined by the NET ASSET VALUE of the outstanding shares, base all incoming buy and sell orders on the next net asset valuation of fund shares. *See also* INVESTMENT COMPANY.

FOR YOUR INFORMATION (FYI) prefix to a security price quote by a market maker that indicates the quote is "for your information" and is not a firm offer to trade at that price. FYI quotes are given as a courtesy for purposes of valuation. FVO (for valuation only) is sometimes used instead.

401(k) PLAN plan whereby employees may elect, as an alternative to receiving taxable cash in the form of compensation or a bonus, to contribute pretax dollars to a qualified tax-deferred retirement plan. Starting in 2006, some employees had the option of ROTH-IRA-type 401(k) plans as well, into which after-tax dollars are contributed, but in which all earnings grow tax-free. Elective deferrals are limited to $15,000 a year (the amount is revised each year by the IRS based on inflation). Many companies, to encourage employee participation in the plan, match employee contributions anywhere from 10% to 100% annually. All employee contributions and employer matching funds can be invested in several options, usually including several stock mutual funds, bond mutual funds, a GUARANTEED INVESTMENT CONTRACT, a money market fund, and company stock. Employees control how the assets are allocated among the various choices, and can usually move the money at least once a year, and sometimes even daily. Withdrawals from 401(k) plans prior to age $59\frac{1}{2}$ are subject to a 10% penalty tax except for death, disability, termination of employment, or qualifying hardship. Withdrawals after the age of $59\frac{1}{2}$ are subject to taxation in the year the money is withdrawn. "Highly compensated" employees are subject to special limitations. 401(k) plans have become increasingly popular in recent years, in many cases supplanting traditional DEFINED BENEFIT PENSION PLANS. Companies favor these plans because they are less costly than traditional pension plans. Also called *cash or deferred arrangement* (CODA) or *salary reduction plan.*

403(b) PLAN type of INDIVIDUAL RETIREMENT ACCOUNT (IRA) covered in Section 403(b) of the Internal Revenue Code that permits employees of qualifying nonprofit organizations to set aside tax-deferred funds.

408(k) PLAN *see* SALARY REDUCTION SIMPLIFIED EMPLOYEE PENSION PLAN (SARSEP).

FOURTH MARKET direct trading of large blocks of securities between institutional investors to save brokerage commissions. The fourth market is aided by computers, notably by a computerized subscriber service called *INSTINET.*

FRACTIONAL DISCRETION ORDER buy or sell order for securities that allows the broker discretion within a specified fraction of a point. For example, "Buy 1,000 XYZ at 28, discretion $\frac{1}{2}$ point" means that the broker may execute the trade at a maximum price of 28.50.

FRACTIONAL SHARE unit of stock less than one full share. For instance, if a shareholder is in a dividend reinvestment program, and the dividends being reinvested are not adequate to buy a full share at the stock's current price, the shareholder will be credited with a fractional share until enough dividends accumulate to purchase a full share.

FRAGMENTATION dispersion of securities markets as a result of proliferating electronic communications networks. Fragmentation entails the risk of executions at less than optimum prices. *See also* CENTRAL LIMIT ORDER BOOK (CLOB).

FRANCHISE
In general: (1) privilege given a dealer by a manufacturer or franchise service organization to sell the franchisor's products or services in a given area, with or without exclusivity. Such arrangements are sometimes formalized in *a franchise agreement,* which is a contract between the franchisor and franchisee wherein the former may offer consultation, promotional assistance, financing, and other benefits in exchange for a percentage of sales or profits. (2) The business owned by the franchisee, who usually must meet an initial cash investment requirement.
Government: legal right given to a company or individual by a government authority to perform some economic function. For example, an electrical utility might have the right, under the terms of a franchise, to use city property to provide electrical service to city residents.

FRANCHISED MONOPOLY monopoly granted by the government to a company. The firm will be protected from competition by government exclusive license, permit, patent, or other device. For example, an electric utility will be granted the exclusive right to generate and sell electricity in a particular locality in return for agreeing to be subject to governmental rate regulation.

FRANCHISE TAX state tax, usually regressive (that is, the rate decreases as the tax base increases), imposed on a state-chartered corporation for the right to do business under its corporate name. Franchise taxes are usually levied on a number of value bases, such as capital stock, capital stock plus surplus, capital, profits, or property in the state.

FRANKFURT STOCK EXCHANGE (FWB) the largest of seven German securities exchanges operated by DEUTSCHE BÖRSE AG. The exchange has about 330 market participants, and it is the world's third-largest securities exchange in terms of turnover and dealings. It accounts for more than 90% of Germany's securities turnover. The exchange uses the Xetra computerized trading system, originally for German and cross-border trading in Frankfurt. It features other electronic systems and traditional floor trading. The DAX Share Index is its benchmark index of securities. Settlement is T + 2. Trading hours are 9 A.M. to 5:30 P.M., Monday through Friday. *www.deutsche-borse. com.*

FRAUD intentional misrepresentation, concealment, or omission of the truth for the purpose of deception or manipulation to the detriment of a person or an organization. Fraud is a legal concept and the application of the term in a specific instance should be determined by a legal expert.

FREDDIE MAC

1. nickname for FEDERAL HOME LOAN MORTGAGE CORPORATION (FHLMC), a publicly owned, government-sponsored corporation. The federal government seized control of Freddie Mac in September 2008 by placing it into conservatorship as the foreclosure crisis mushroomed.
2. mortgage-backed securities, issued in minimum denominations of $25,000, that are packaged, guaranteed, and sold by the FHLMC. Mortgage-backed securities are issues in which residential mortgages are packaged and sold to investors.

FREE AND OPEN MARKET market in which price is determined by the free, unregulated interchange of supply and demand. The opposite is a *controlled market,* where supply, demand, and price are artificially set, resulting in an *inefficient market.*

FREE BOX securities industry jargon for a secure storage place ("box") for fully paid ("free") customers' securities, such as a bank vault or the DEPOSITORY TRUST COMPANY.

FREE CASH FLOW the amount of cash a company has after expenses, debt service, capital expenditures, and dividends. Free cash flow measures the financial comfort level of the company as a going concern. The higher the free cash flow, the stronger the company's BALANCE SHEET.

FREED UP securities industry jargon meaning that the members of an underwriting syndicate are no longer bound by the price agreed upon and fixed in the AGREEMENT AMONG UNDERWRITERS. They are thus free to trade in the security on a market basis.

FREE ON BOARD (FOB) transportation term meaning that the invoice price includes delivery at the seller's expense to a specified point and no further. For example, "FOB our Newark warehouse" means that the buyer must pay all shipping and other charges associated with transporting the merchandise from the seller's warehouse in Newark to the buyer's receiving point. Title normally passes from seller to buyer at the FOB point by way of a bill of lading.

FREERIDING

1. practice, prohibited by the Securities and Exchange Commission and the National Association of Securities Dealers, whereby an underwriting SYNDICATE member withholds a portion of a new securities issue and later resells it at a price higher than the initial offering price.
2. practice whereby a brokerage client buys and sells a security in rapid order without putting up money for the purchase. The practice violates REGULATION T of the Federal Reserve Board concerning broker-dealer credit to customers. The penalty requires that the customer's account be frozen for 90 days. *See also* FROZEN ACCOUNT.

FREE RIGHT OF EXCHANGE ability to transfer securities from one name to another without paying the charge associated with a sales transaction. The free right applies, for example, where stock in STREET NAME (that is, registered in the name of a broker-dealer) is transferred to the customer's name in order to be eligible for a dividend reinvestment plan. *See also* REGISTERED SECURITY.

FREE STOCK (1) stock that is fully paid for and is not assigned as collateral. (2) stock held by an issuer following a PRIVATE PLACEMENT but that can be traded free of the restrictions bearing on a LETTER SECURITY.

FREEZE OUT put pressure on minority shareholders after a takeover to sell their shares to the acquirer.

FREIT *see* FINITE LIFE REAL ESTATE INVESTMENT TRUST.

FRICTIONAL COST in an INDEX FUND, the amount by which the fund's return, excluding investment performance, is less than that of the index it replicates. The difference, assuming it is not otherwise adjusted, represents the fund's management fees and transaction costs.

FRIENDLY TAKEOVER merger supported by the management and board of directors of the target company. The board will recommend to shareholders that they approve the takeover offer, because it represents fair value for the company's shares. In many cases, the acquiring company will retain many of the existing managers of the acquired company to continue to run the business. A friendly takeover is in contrast to a HOSTILE TAKEOVER, in which management actively resists the acquisition attempt by another company or RAIDER.

FRINGE BENEFITS compensation to employees in addition to salary. Some examples of fringe benefits are paid holidays, retirement plans, life and health insurance plans, subsidized cafeterias, company cars, stock options, and expense accounts. In many cases, fringe benefits can add significantly to an employee's total compensation, and are a key ingredient in attracting and retaining employees. For the most part, fringe benefits are not taxable to the employee, though they are generally tax-deductible for the employer.

FRONT-END LOAD sales charge applied to an investment at the time of initial purchase. There may be a front-end load on a mutual fund, for instance, which is sold by a broker. Annuities, life insurance policies, and limited partnerships can also have front-end loads. From the investor's point of view, the earnings from the investment should make up for this up-front fee within a relatively short period of time. *See also* INVESTMENT COMPANY; MUTUAL FUND SHARE CLASSES.

FRONTIER MARKETS markets a tier below EMERGING MARKETS in terms of their stage of development, meaning market capitalizations or rates of annual turnover are smaller or market restrictions are greater but they are nonetheless accessible to foreign investors and meet acceptable standards of economic and political stability.

FRONT OFFICE sales personnel in a brokerage, insurance, or other financial services operation. Front office workers produce revenue, in contrast to BACK OFFICE workers, who perform administrative and other support functions for the front office.

FRONT RUNNING practice whereby a securities or commodities trader takes a POSITION to capitalize on advance knowledge of a large upcoming transaction expected to influence the market price. In the stock market, this might be done by buying an OPTION on stock expected to benefit from a large BLOCK transaction. In commodities, DUAL TRADING is common practice and provides opportunities to profit from front running. *See also* RUNNING AHEAD.

FROZEN ACCOUNT
Banking: bank account from which funds may not be withdrawn until a lien is satisfied and a court order is received freeing the balance.

A bank account may also be frozen by court order in a dispute over the ownership of property.
Investments: brokerage account under disciplinary action by the Federal Reserve Board for violation of REGULATION T. During the period an account is frozen (90 days), the customer may not sell securities until their purchase price has been fully paid and the certificates have been delivered. The penalty is invoked commonly in cases of FREERIDING.

FULL COUPON BOND bond with a coupon rate that is near or above current market interest rates. If interest rates are generally about 8%, for instance, a $7\frac{1}{2}$% or 9% bond is considered a full coupon bond.

FULL DISCLOSURE
In general: requirement to disclose all material facts relevant to a transaction.
Securities industry: public information requirements established by the Securities Act of 1933, the Securities Exchange Act of 1934, and the major stock exchanges.

See also DISCLOSURE; TRANSPARENCY.

FULL FAITH AND CREDIT phrase meaning that the full taxing and borrowing power, *plus* revenue other than taxes, is pledged in payment of interest and repayment of principal of a bond issued by a government entity. U.S. government securities and general obligation bonds of states and local governments are backed by this pledge.

FULL RATCHET PROVISION *see* DILUTION PROTECTION.

FULL REPLACEMENT COVERAGE *see* GUARANTEED REPLACEMENT COST COVERAGE INSURANCE.

FULL-SERVICE BROKER broker who provides a wide range of services to clients. Unlike a DISCOUNT BROKER, who just executes trades, a full-service broker offers advice on which stocks, bonds, commodities, and mutual funds to buy or sell. A full-service broker may also offer an ASSET MANAGEMENT ACCOUNT; advice on financial planning, tax shelters, and INCOME LIMITED PARTNERSHIPS; and new issues of stock. A full-service broker's commissions will be higher than those of a discount broker. The term *brokerage* is gradually being replaced by variations of the term *financial services* as the range of services offered by brokers expands.

FULL TRADING AUTHORIZATION freedom, even from broad guidelines, allowed a broker or adviser under a DISCRETIONARY ACCOUNT.

FULLY DEPRECIATED said of a fixed asset to which all the DEPRECIATION the tax law allows has been charged. Asset is carried on the books at its RESIDUAL VALUE, although its LIQUIDATING VALUE may be higher or lower.

FULLY DILUTED EARNINGS PER (COMMON) SHARE figure showing earnings per common share after assuming the exercise of warrants and stock options, and the conversion of convertible bonds and preferred stock (all potentially *dilutive* securities). Actually, it is more analytically correct to define the term as the smallest earnings per common share that can be obtained by computing EARNINGS PER SHARE (EPS) for all possible combinations of assumed exercise or conversion (because antidilutive securities—securities whose conversion would add to EPS—may not be assumed to be exercised or converted). Under accounting rules adopted in 1998, companies must report EPS on two bases: Basic EPS, which does not count stock options, warrants, and convertible securities, and (fully) Diluted EPS, which includes those securities. *See also* ANTIDILUTIVE; DILUTION; EARNINGS PER SHARE; PRIMARY EARNINGS PER (COMMON) SHARE.

FULLY DISCLOSED *see* FUTURES COMMISSION MERCHANT (FCM).

FULLY DISTRIBUTED term describing a new securities issue that has been completely resold to the investing public (that is, to institutions and individuals and other investors rather than to dealers).

FULLY INVESTED said of an investor or a portfolio when funds in cash or CASH EQUIVALENTS are minimal and assets are totally committed to other investments, usually stock. To be fully invested is to have an optimistic view of the market.

FULLY VALUED said of a stock that has reached a price at which analysts think the underlying company's fundamental earnings power has been recognized by the market. If the stock goes up from that price, it is called OVERVALUED. If the stock goes down, it is termed UNDERVALUED.

FUND *see* FUND FAMILY; FUNDING; MUTUAL FUND.

FUNDAMENTAL ANALYSIS
Economics: research of such factors as interest rates, gross domestic product, inflation, unemployment, and inventories as tools to predict the direction of the economy.
Investment: analysis of the balance sheet and income statements of companies in order to forecast their future stock price movements. Fundamental analysts consider past records of assets, earnings, sales, products, management, and markets in predicting future trends in these indicators of a company's success or failure. By appraising a firm's prospects, these analysts assess whether a particular stock or group of stocks is UNDERVALUED or OVERVALUED at the current market price. The other major school of stock market analysis is TECHNICAL ANALYSIS, which relies on price and volume movements of stocks and does not concern itself with financial statistics.

FUNDED DEBT
1. debt that is due after one year and is formalized by the issuing of bonds or long-term notes.
2. bond issue whose retirement is provided for by a SINKING FUND.
   See also FLOATING DEBT.

FUNDED PENSION PLAN pension plan in which all liabilities are fully funded. A pension plan's administrator knows the potential payments necessary to make to pensioners over the coming years. In order to be funded, the plan must have enough capital contributions from the plan sponsor, plus returns from investments, to pay those claims. Employees are notified annually of the financial strength of their pension plans, and whether or not the plans are fully funded. If the plans are not funded, the PENSION BENEFIT GUARANTY CORPORATION (PBGC), which guarantees pension plans, will act to try to get the plan sponsor to contribute more money to the plan. If a company fails with an underfunded pension plan, the PBGC will step in to make the promised payments to pensioners.

FUND FAMILY mutual fund company offering funds with many investment objectives. A fund family may offer several types of stock, bond, and money market funds and allow free switching among their funds. Large no-load fund families include American Century, Fidelity, Dreyfus, T. Rowe Price, USAA, and Vanguard. Most major brokerage houses such as Merrill Lynch, Smith Barney, Goldman Sachs, and UBS also sponsor fund families of their own. Many independent firms such as American Funds, Federated, Loomis–Sayles, Putnam, and Pioneer distribute their funds with a sales charge through brokerage firms and financial planners. Many investors find it convenient to place most of their assets with one or two fund families because of the convenience offered by such switching privileges. In recent years, several discount brokerage firms have offered the ability to shift assets from one fund family to another, making it less important than it had been to consolidate assets in one fund family. *See also* INVESTMENT COMPANY.

FUNDING
1. refinancing a debt on or before its maturity; also called REFUNDING and, in certain instances, PREREFUNDING.
2. putting money into investments or another type of reserve fund, to provide for future pension or welfare plans.
3. in corporate finance, the word *funding* is preferred to *financing* when referring to bonds in contrast to stock. A company is said to be funding its operations if it floats bonds.
4. to provide funds to finance a project, such as a research study.
   See also SINKING FUND.

FUND MANAGER manager of a pool of money such as a mutual fund, pension fund, insurance fund, or bank-pooled fund. Their job is to maximize the fund's returns at the least risk possible. Each fund manager tries his or her best to realize the fund's objectives, whether it be growth, income, or some combination of the two. Different fund managers use different styles to accomplish their objectives. For example, some stock fund managers use the value style of investing, while others concentrate on growth stocks. In picking a fund, it is important to know the fund manager's style, and how long he or she has been managing the fund. This information is generally available for publicly offered mutual funds from fund company literature or fund representatives.

FUND OF FUNDS mutual fund that invests in other mutual funds. The concept behind such funds is that they are able to move money between the best funds in the industry, and thereby increase shareholders' returns with more diversification than is offered by a single fund. The fund of funds has been criticized as adding another layer of management expenses on shareholders, however, because fees are paid to the fund's management company as well as to all the underlying fund management companies. The SEC limits the total amount of fees that shareholders can pay in such a fund. Funds of funds are usually organized in a fund family of their own, offering funds that will specialize in international stocks, aggressive growth, income, and other objectives. Funds of funds were extremely popular in the 1960s, but then faded in popularity in the 1970s because of a scandal involving Equity Funding, which was a fund of funds. In the mid-2000s, they were being used to circumvent laws requiring that HEDGE FUNDS be restricted to investors meeting high net worth requirements, since the fund holding the hedge funds was not itself a hedge fund. *See also* FEEDER FUND.

FUND SWITCHING moving money from one mutual fund to another, within the same FUND FAMILY or among fund families. Purchases and sales of funds may be done to time the ups and downs of the stock and bond markets, or because investors' financial needs have changed. Several newsletters and fund managers specialize in advising clients on which funds to switch into and out of, based on market conditions. Switching among funds within a fund family is usually allowed without sales charges. Unless practiced inside a tax-deferred account such as an IRA or Keogh account, a fund switch creates a taxable event, since CAPITAL GAINS OR LOSSES are realized.

FUNGIBLES bearer instruments, securities, or goods that are equivalent, substitutable, and interchangeable. Commodities such as soybeans or wheat, common shares of the same company, and dollar bills are all familiar examples of fungibles.

Fungibility (interchangeability) of listed options, by virtue of their common expiration dates and strike prices, makes it possible for buyers and sellers to close out their positions by putting offsetting transactions through the OPTIONS CLEARING CORPORATION. *See also* OFFSET; STRIKE PRICE.

FUN MONEY money that is not necessary for everyday living expenses, and can therefore be risked in volatile, but potentially highly profitable, investments. If the investment pans out, the investor has had some fun speculating. If the investment turns sour, the investor's lifestyle has not been put at risk because he or she could afford to lose the money.

FURTHEST MONTH in commodities or options trading, the month that is furthest away from settlement of the contract. For example, Treasury bill futures may have outstanding contracts for three, six, or nine months. The six- and nine-month contracts would be the furthest months, and the three-month contract would be the NEAREST MONTH.

FUTA *see* FEDERAL UNEMPLOYMENT TAX ACT (FUTA).

FUTOP screen-traded, Danish derivatives market that merged with the COPEN-HAGEN STOCK EXCHANGE in 1997. *See also* COPENHAGEN STOCK EXCHANGE.

FUTURES COMMISSION MERCHANT (FCM) an individual, firm, or trust that acts as a broker in FUTURES MARKET transactions, which include FUTURES CONTRACTS and futures OPTIONS, and that accepts money or other assets from customers in connection with such orders. FCMs, sometimes called commission firms, futures commission firms, or commodity brokerage firms must be registered with the Commodity Futures Trading Commission (CFTC). They have two basic account types: *fully disclosed* accounts are carried in the names of individual customers, while *omnibus accounts* are opened in the name of one FCM at another FCM and comprise multiple individual accounts whose names are not disclosed.

FUTURES CONTRACT agreement to buy or sell a specific amount of a commodity, a currency, or a financial instrument at a particular price on a stipulated future date. The price is established between buyer and seller on the floor of a commodity exchange, using the OPEN OUTCRY system. A futures contract obligates the buyer to purchase the underlying commodity and the seller to sell it, unless the contract is sold to another before settlement date, which may happen if a trader waits to take a profit or cut a loss. This contrasts with options trading, in which the option buyer may choose whether or not to exercise the option by the exercise date. *See also* FORWARD CONTRACT; FUTURES MARKET.

FUTURES MARKET exchange where futures contracts and options on futures contracts are traded. Exchanges may trade commodities, financial derivatives, or a combination of the two, as well as futures and options on indices and equity products. The major exchanges in the U.S. are the NEW YORK BOARD OF TRADE and its subsidiaries, the COFFEE, SUGAR, AND COCOA EXCHANGE, FINEX, NEW YORK COTTON EXCHANGE and NEW YORK FUTURES EXCHANGE; NEW YORK MERCANTILE EXCHANGE; CHICAGO BOARD OF TRADE; CHICAGO MERCANTILE EXCHANGE; KANSAS CITY BOARD OF TRADE; and MINNEAPOLIS GRAIN EXCHANGE.

International futures markets from around the world are also described elsewhere in this *Dictionary,* including: EUREX; HONG KONG FUTURES EXCHANGE; INTERNATIONAL PETROLEUM EXCHANGE; LONDON INTERNATIONAL FINANCIAL FUTURES AND OPTIONS EXCHANGE (LIFFE); LONDON METAL EXCHANGE; MATIF; MONTREAL EXCHANGE; SYDNEY FUTURES EXCHANGE (SFE). *See also* SECURITIES AND COMMODITIES EXCHANGES; SPOT MARKET.

FUTURES OPTION OPTION on a FUTURES CONTRACT.

FUTURE VALUE reverse of PRESENT VALUE.

FVO (FOR VALUATION ONLY) *see* FOR YOUR INFORMATION.

G

GAAP *see* GENERALLY ACCEPTED ACCOUNTING PRINCIPLES (GAAP).

GAIJIN non-Japanese investor in Japan. The Japanese refer to foreign competitors, on both the individual and institutional levels, as gaijin. In particular, the large, prestigious American and European brokerage firms that compete with the major Japanese brokerage firms, such as Nomura and Nikko, are called gaijin.

GAIN profit on the sale of an asset. A gain is realized when a stock, bond, mutual fund, futures contract, or other financial instrument is sold for more than its purchase price. If the instrument was held for more than a year, the gain is taxable at more favorable capital gains tax rates of 5% or 15%, depending on the investor's tax bracket. If held for 12 months or less, the gain is taxed at regular income tax rates.

GAMMA PRICING MODEL *see* DERIVATIVE PRICING MODELS.

GAP

Finance: amount of a financing need for which provision has yet to be made. For example, ABC company might need $1.5 million to purchase and equip a new plant facility. It arranges a mortgage loan of $700,000, secures equipment financing of $400,000, and obtains new equity of $150,000. That leaves a gap of $250,000 for which it seeks gap financing. Such financing may be available from state and local governments concerned with promoting economic development.

Securities: securities industry term used to describe the price movement of a stock or commodity when one day's trading range for the stock or commodity does not overlap the next day's, causing a range, or gap, in which no trade has occurred. This usually takes place because of some extraordinary positive or negative news about the company or commodity. See chart on next page. *See also* PRICE GAP.

GAP

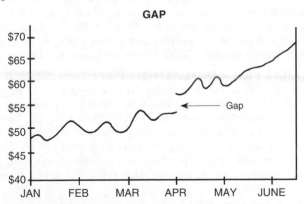

GAP OPENING opening price for a stock that is significantly higher or lower than the previous day's closing price. For example, if XYZ Company was the subject of a $50 takeover bid after the market closed with its shares trading at $30, its share price might open the next morning at $45 a share. There would therefore be a gap between the closing price of $30 and the opening price of $45. The same phenomenon can occur on the downside if a company reports disappointing earnings or a takeover bid falls through, for example. Stocks trading on the New York or American Stock Exchange may experience a delayed opening when such an event occurs as the specialist deals with the rush of buy or sell orders to find the stock's appropriate price level.

GARAGE annex floor on the north side of the main trading floor of the New York Stock Exchange.

GARMAN-KOHLGAGEN OPTION PRICING MODEL *see* DERIVATIVE PRICING MODELS.

GARNISHMENT court order to an employer to withhold all or part of an employee's wages and send the money to the court or to a person who has won a lawsuit against the employee. An employee's wages will be *garnished* until the court-ordered debt is paid. Garnishing may be used in a divorce settlement or for repayment of creditors.

GARP *see* GROWTH AT A REASONABLE PRICE (GARP).

GATE clause, also called a *gating clause,* in the agreements many HEDGE FUNDS have with their investors, which limits the percentage of the fund's assets that can be redeemed in a given period. The rationale is that funds would be restricted from profitable long-term bets if they had to fear sudden redemptions requiring liquidity. Some analysts speculate that gating clauses may explain why more hedge funds didn't fail during the period of heavy DELEVERAGING in 2008 and that gating clauses may be hiding losses. There has been a more recent trend where funds have traded shorter *lock-up periods* for higher fees and vice versa.

GATHER IN THE STOPS stock-trading tactic that involves selling a sufficient amount of stock to drive down the price to a point where stop orders (orders to buy or sell at a given price) are known to exist. The stop orders are then activated to become market orders (orders to buy or sell at the best available price), in turn creating movement which touches off other stop orders in a process called SNOWBALLING. Because this can cause sharp trading swings, floor officials on the exchanges have the authority to suspend stop orders in individual securities if that seems advisable. *See also* STOP ORDER.

GDP IMPLICIT PRICE DEFLATOR ratio of current-dollar GROSS DOMESTIC PRODUCT (GDP) to constant-dollar GDP. Changes in the implicit price deflator reflect both changes in prices of all goods and services that make up GDP and changes in the composite of GDP. Over time, the implicit price deflator understates inflation because people tend to shift consumption from goods that have high prices or rapidly increasing prices to goods that have less rapidly increasing prices. Therefore, theoretically, prices of all goods and service could increase and the implicit price deflator could decrease. *See also* PERSONAL INFLATION RATE.

G-8 FINANCE MINISTERS the finance ministers of the eight largest industrial countries: Canada, France, Germany, Great Britain, Italy, Japan, Russia, and the United States. Meetings of the G-8 take place at least once a year and are important in coordinating economic policy among the major industrial countries. The political leaders of the G-8 countries also meet once a year, usually in July, at the Economic Summit, which is held in one of the eight countries. Before the admission of Russia in 1998, the group was called G-7 Finance Ministers. *See also* GROUP OF 20 (G-20).

G-20 *see* GROUP OF 20 (G-20).

GEM *see* GROWING EQUITY MORTGAGE.

GENERAL ACCOUNT Federal Reserve Board term for brokerage customer margin accounts subject to REGULATION T, which covers extensions of credit by brokers for the purchase and short sale of securities. The Fed requires that all transactions in which the broker advances credit to the customer be made in this account. *See also* MARGIN ACCOUNT.

GENERAL AGREEMENT ON TARIFFS AND TRADE (GATT) United Nations-associated international treaty organization headquartered in Geneva that works to eliminate barriers to trade between nations. In 1995 if was replaced by the WORLD TRADE ORGANIZATION (WTO).

GENERAL LEDGER formal ledger containing all the financial statement accounts of a business. It contains offsetting debit and credit accounts, the totals of which are proved by a trial balance. Certain accounts in the general ledger, termed *control accounts,* summarize the detail booked on separate subsidiary ledgers.

GENERAL LIEN LIEN against an individual that excludes real property. The lien carries the right to seize personal property to satisfy a debt. The property seized need not be the property that gave rise to the debt.

GENERAL LOAN AND COLLATERAL AGREEMENT continuous agreement under which a securities broker-dealer borrows from a bank against listed securities to buy or carry inventory, finance the underwriting of new issues, or carry the margin accounts of clients. Synonymous with *broker's loan. See also* BROKER LOAN RATE; MARGIN ACCOUNT; UNDERWRITE.

GENERALLY ACCEPTED ACCOUNTING PRINCIPLES (GAAP) conventions, rules, and procedures that define accepted accounting practice, including broad guidelines as well as detailed procedures. The basic doctrine was set forth by the Accounting Principles Board of the American Institute of Certified Public Accountants, which was superseded in 1973 by the FINANCIAL ACCOUNTING STANDARDS BOARD (FASB), an independent self-regulatory organization.

GENERAL MORTGAGE mortgage covering all the mortgageable properties of a borrower and not restricted to any particular piece of property. Such a blanket mortgage can be lower in priority of claim in liquidation than one or more other mortgages on specific parcels.

GENERAL OBLIGATION BOND municipal bond backed by the FULL FAITH AND CREDIT (which includes the taxing and further borrowing power) of a municipality. A *GO bond,* as it is known, is repaid with general revenue and borrowings, in contrast to the revenue from a specific facility built with the borrowed funds, such as a tunnel or a sewer system. *See also* REVENUE BOND.

GENERAL PARTNER
1. one of two or more partners who are jointly and severally responsible for the debts of a partnership.

2. managing partner of a LIMITED PARTNERSHIP, who is responsible for the operations of the partnership and, ultimately, any debts taken on by the partnership. The general partner's liability is unlimited. In a real estate partnership, the general partner will pick the properties to be bought and will manage them. In an oil and gas partnership, the general partner will select drilling sites and oversee drilling activity. In return for these services, the general partner collects certain fees and often retains a percentage of ownership in the partnership.

GENERAL REVENUE when used in reference to state and local governments taken separately, the term refers to total revenue less revenue from utilities, sales of alcoholic beverages, and insurance trusts. When speaking of combined state and local total revenue, the term refers only to taxes, charges, and miscellaneous revenue, which avoids the distortion of overlapping intergovernmental revenue.

GENERAL REVENUE SHARING unrestricted funds (which can be used for any purpose) provided by the federal government until 1987 to the 50 states and to more than 38,000 cities, towns, counties, townships, Indian tribes, and Alaskan native villages under the State and Local Fiscal Assistance Act of 1972.

GENERAL SECURITIES REPRESENTATIVE EXAMINATION *see* SERIES 7.

GENERATION-SKIPPING TRANSFER OR TRUST arrangement whereby your principal goes into a TRUST when you die, and transfers to your grandchildren when your children die, but which provides income to your children while they live. Once a major tax loophole for the wealthy because taxes were payable only at your death and your grandchildren's death, now $2 million can be transferred tax-free to the grandchildren. Otherwise, a special generation-skipping tax—with rates equal to the maximum ESTATE TAX rate of 46% in 2006, falling to 45% in 2007 and thereafter—applies to transfers to grandchildren, whether the gifts are direct or from a trust.

GESTATION REPO REVERSE REPURCHASE AGREEMENT whereby a MORTGAGE BANKER sells federal agency-guaranteed mortgage-backed securities to a securities dealer and agrees to repurchase them at a fixed price on a future date.

GHOSTING illegal manipulation of a company's stock price by two or more market makers. One firm will push a stock's price higher or lower, and the other firms will follow their lead in collusion to drive the stock's price up or down. The practice is called ghosting because the investing public is unaware of this coordinated activity among market makers who are supposed to be competing with each other.

GIC *see* GUARANTEED INVESTMENT CONTRACT.

GIFT INTER VIVOS gift of property from one living person to another, without consideration.

GIFT SPLITTING dividing a gift into $12,000 pieces to avoid GIFT TAX. For example, a husband and wife wanting to give $24,000 to their child will give $12,000 each instead of $24,000 from one parent, so that no gift tax is due.

GILT-EDGED SECURITY stock or bond of a company that has demonstrated over a number of years that it is capable of earning sufficient profits to cover dividends on stocks and interest on bonds with great dependability. The term is used with corporate bonds more often than with stocks, where the term BLUE CHIP is more common.

GILTS bonds issued by the British government. Gilts are the equivalent of Treasury securities in the United States in that they are perceived to have no risk of default. Income earned from investing in gilts is therefore guaranteed. Gilt yields act as the benchmark against which all other British bond yields are measured. Gilt futures are traded on the LONDON INTERNATIONAL FINANCIAL FUTURES AND OPTIONS EXCHANGE (LIFFE). The name gilt is derived from the original British government certificates, which had gilded edges.

GINNIE MAE nickname for the GOVERNMENT NATIONAL MORTGAGE ASSOCIATION and the securities guaranteed by that agency. *See also* GINNIE MAE PASS-THROUGH.

GINNIE MAE PASS-THROUGH security, backed by a pool of mortgages and guaranteed by the GOVERNMENT NATIONAL MORTGAGE ASSOCIATION (Ginnie Mae), which passes through to investors the interest and principal payments of homeowners. Homeowners make their mortgage payments to the bank or savings and loan that originated their mortgage. After deducting a service charge (usually $\frac{1}{2}\%$), the bank forwards the mortgage payments to the pass-through buyers, who may be institutional investors or individuals. Ginnie Mae guarantees that investors will receive timely principal and interest payments even if homeowners do not make mortgage payments on time.

Ginnie Maes are available in three types:
1. *GNMA 1* securities are single issuer pools whose certificates pay principal and interest separately.
2. *GNMA 2* securities represent multiple-issuer pools (called *jumbos*) that are longer and more geographically diverse than single issuer pools, with certificate holders receiving aggregate principal and interest payments from a central paying agent.
3. *GNMA Midgets,* a term dealers use that is not an official GNMA designation, are certificates backed by fifteen-year fixed rate mortgages.

The introduction of Ginnie Mae pass-throughs has benefited the home mortgage market, since more capital has become available for lending. Investors, who are able to receive high, government-guaranteed interest payments, have also benefited. For investors, however, the rate of principal repayment on a Ginnie Mae pass-through is uncertain. If interest rates fall, principal will be repaid faster, since homeowners will refinance their mortgages. If rates rise, principal will be repaid more slowly, since homeowners will hold onto the underlying mortgages. *See also* HALF-LIFE.

GIPS *see* GLOBAL INVESTMENT PERFORMANCE STANDARDS (GIPS).

GIVE BACK a relinquishment of benefits by employees to the corporation providing them, typically to make the employer more competitive in foreign markets. Bad news for employees; good news for investors.

GIVE UP
1. term used in a securities transaction involving three brokers, as illustrated by the following scenario: Broker A, a FLOOR BROKER, executes a buy order

for Broker B, another member firm broker who has too much business at
the time to execute the order. The broker with whom Broker A completes
the transaction (the sell side broker) is Broker C. Broker A "gives up"
the name of Broker B, so that the record shows a transaction between
Broker B and Broker C even though the trade was actually executed
between Broker A and Broker C.

2. another application of the term: A customer of brokerage firm ABC Co.
travels out of town and, finding no branch office of ABC, places an order
with DEF Co., saying he is an account of ABC. After confirming the
account relationship, DEF completes a trade with GHI Co., advising GHI
that DEF is acting for ABC ("giving up" ABC's name). ABC will then
handle the clearing details of the transaction with GHI. Alternatively,
DEF may simply send the customer's order directly to ABC for execution.
Whichever method is used, the customer pays only one commission.

GLAMOR STOCK stock with a wide public and institutional following.
Glamor stocks achieve this following by producing steadily rising sales and
earnings over a long period of time. In bull (rising) markets, glamor stocks
tend to rise faster than market averages. Although a glamor stock is often
in the category of a BLUE CHIP stock, the glamor is characterized by a higher
earnings growth rate.

GLASS-STEAGALL ACT OF 1933 legislation passed by Congress authorizing deposit insurance and prohibiting commercial banks from owning full-
service brokerage firms. Under Glass-Steagall, these banks were prohibited
from investment banking activities, such as underwriting corporate securities
or municipal revenue bonds. The law was designed to insulate bank depositors from the risk involved when a bank deals in securities and to prevent a
bank collapse like the one that occurred during the Great Depression. The
original separation of commercial and investment banking had already significantly eroded when, on November 12, 1999 the FINANCIAL SERVICES MOD-
ERNIZA-TION ACT OF 1999 was signed into law, repealing parts of the 1933
GLASS-STEAGALL ACT and the 1956 BANK HOLDING COMPANY ACT and effectively
allowing banks, brokers, and insurers into each other's businesses. Basically,
the 1999 Act allows banks to affiliate with securities firms and insurers
through a holding company structure and permits nationally chartered banks
to engage in most financial activities through direct subsidiaries. While provisions of Glass-Steagall continue to restrict banks from most underwriting
activities and securities firms from taking deposits, these restrictions apply
only to the banks and securities firms, not to their Financial Holding Company
affiliates and are, therefore, technical.

GLOBAL BONDS bonds simultaneously issued in all the major domestic and
foreign capital markets.

GLOBAL DEPOSITARY RECEIPT (GDR) receipt for shares in a foreign-
based corporation traded in capital markets around the world. While AMERI-
CAN DEPOSITARY RECEIPTS permit foreign corporations to offer shares to
American citizens, Global Depositary Receipts (GDRs) allow companies in
Europe, Asia, the United States and Latin America to offer shares in many
markets around the world. The advantage to the issuing company is that they
can raise capital in many markets, as opposed to just their home market. The
advantage of GDRs to local investors is that they do not have to buy shares

through the issuing company's home exchange, which may be difficult and expensive. In addition, the share price and all dividends are converted into the shareholder's home currency. Many GDRs are issued by companies in emerging markets such as China, India, Brazil, and South Korea and are traded on major stock exchanges, particularly the London SEAQ International Trading system. Because the companies issuing GDRs are not as well established and do not use the same accounting systems as traditional Western corporations, their stocks tend to be more volatile and less liquid. *See also* DEPOSITARY RECEIPTS.

GLOBAL INVESTMENT PERFORMANCE STANDARDS (GIPS) standardized rules relating to the reporting of investment performance by money managers worldwide, adopted in February 2005 by the CFA INSTITUTE after revision of previous rules by its Investment Performance Council. The full report is available at the CFA Institute Web site.

GLOBAL MUTUAL FUND mutual fund that can invest in stocks and bonds throughout the world. Such funds typically have a portion of their assets in American markets as well as Europe, Asia, and developing countries. Global funds differ from INTERNATIONAL MUTUAL FUNDS, which invest only in non-U.S. securities. The advantage of global funds is that the fund managers can buy stocks or bonds anywhere they think has the best opportunities for high returns. Thus if one market is underperforming, they can shift assets to markets with better potential. Though some global funds invest in both stocks and bonds, most funds specialize in either stocks or bonds.

GLOBAL SHARES shares of the same class issued in the United States, registered in different countries, traded in different currencies, providing equal corporate rights to all shareholders. Also called *global registered shares*, they are foreign securities and not to be confused with AMERICAN DEPOSITARY RECEIPTS (ADRs) or GLOBAL DEPOSITARY RECEIPTS (GDRs), which are domestic securities representing foreign interests.

GNMA 1; GNMA 2; GNMA MIDGET *see* GINNIE MAE PASS-THROUGH.

GNOMES OF ZÜRICH term coined by Labour ministers of Great Britain, during the sterling crisis of 1964, to describe the financiers and bankers in Zürich, Switzerland, who were engaged in foreign exchange speculation.

GNP *see* GROSS NATIONAL PRODUCT.

GOAL financial objective set by an individual or institution. For example, an individual investor might set a goal to accumulate enough capital to finance a child's college education. A pension fund's goal is to build up enough money to pay pensioners their promised benefits. Investors may also set specific price objectives when buying a security. For example, an investor buying a stock at $30 may set a price goal of $50, at which point he or she will sell shares, or at least reevaluate whether or not to continue holding the stock. Also called *target price*.

GO AROUND term used to describe the process whereby the trading desk at the New York Federal Reserve Bank ("the DESK"), acting on behalf of the FEDERAL OPEN MARKET COMMITTEE, contacts primary dealers for bid and offer prices. Primary dealers are those banks and investment houses approved for direct purchase and sale transactions with the Federal Reserve System in its OPEN MARKET OPERATIONS.

GODFATHER OFFER takeover offer that is so generous that management of the target company is unable to refuse it out of fear of shareholder lawsuits.

GO-GO FUND MUTUAL FUND that invests in highly risky but potentially rewarding stocks. During the 1960s many go-go funds shot up in value, only to fall dramatically later and, in some cases, to go out of business as their speculative investments fizzled.

GOING AHEAD unethical securities brokerage act whereby the broker trades first for his own account before filling his customers' orders. Brokers who go ahead violate the RULES OF FAIR PRACTICE of the FINANCIAL INDUSTRY REGULATORY AUTHORITY (FINRA).

GOING AWAY bonds purchased by dealers for immediate resale to investors, as opposed to bonds purchased *for stock*—that is, to be held in inventory for resale at some future time. The significance of the difference is that bonds bought going away will not overhang the market and cause adverse pressure on prices.

   The term is also used in new offerings of serial bonds to describe large purchases, usually by institutional investors, of the bonds in a particular maturity grouping (or series).

GOING-CONCERN VALUE value of a company as an operating business to another company or individual. The excess of going-concern value over asset value, or LIQUIDATING VALUE, is the value of the operating organization as distinct from the value of its assets. In acquisition accounting, going-concern value in excess of asset value is treated as an intangible asset, termed *goodwill.* Goodwill is generally understood to represent the value of a well-respected business name, good customer relations, high employee morale, and other such factors expected to translate into greater than normal earning power. *See also* GOODWILL.

GOING LONG purchasing a stock, bond, or commodity for investment or speculation. Such a security purchase is known as a LONG POSITION. The opposite of going long is GOING SHORT, when an investor sells a security he does not own and thereby creates a SHORT POSITION.

GOING PRIVATE movement from public ownership to private ownership of a company's shares either by the company's repurchase of shares or through purchases by an outside private investor. A company usually goes private when the market price of its shares is substantially below their BOOK VALUE and the opportunity thus exists to buy the assets cheaply. Another motive for going private is to ensure the tenure of existing management by removing the company as a takeover prospect.

GOING PUBLIC securities industry phrase used when a private company first offers its shares to the public. The firm's ownership thus shifts from the hands of a few private stockowners to a base that includes public shareholders. At the moment of going public, the stock is called an INITIAL PUBLIC OFFERING. From that point on, or until the company goes private again, its shares have a MARKET VALUE. *See also* NEW ISSUE; GOING PRIVATE.

GOING SHORT selling a stock or commodity that the seller does not have. An investor who goes short borrows stock from his or her broker, hoping to purchase other shares of it at a lower price. The investor will then replace the borrowed stock with the lower priced stock and keep the difference as profit. *See also* SELLING SHORT; GOING LONG.

GOLD BARS bars made out of 99.5% to 99.99% pure gold which can be traded for investment purposes or held by central banks. Gold bars range in size from 400 troy ounces to as little as 1 ounce of gold; an individual can either hold on to these bars or store them in a safe deposit box. Central banks store gold bars weighing 400 troy ounces in vaults. In the United States, gold is stored at a few Federal Reserve banks and Fort Knox, for example. In the past, this gold directly backed the American currency, but now it serves more as a symbolic backing for dollars issued by the Federal Reserve.

GOLD BOND bond backed by gold. Such debt obligations are issued by gold-mining companies, who peg interest payments to the level of gold prices. Investors who buy these bonds therefore anticipate a rising gold price. Silver mining firms similarly issue silver-backed bonds.

GOLDBUG analyst enamored of gold as an investment. Goldbugs usually are worried about possible disasters in the world economy, such as a depression or hyperinflation, and recommend gold as a HEDGE.

GOLD BULLION gold in its purest form. The metal may be smelted into GOLD COINS or GOLD BARS of different sizes. The price of gold bullion is set by market forces of supply and demand. Twice a day, the latest gold price is fixed at the London GOLD FIXING. Gold bullion is traded in physical form, and also through futures and options contracts. Certain gold-oriented mutual funds also hold small amounts of gold bullion.

GOLD CERTIFICATE paper certificate providing evidence of ownership of gold bullion. An investor not wanting to hold the actual gold in his or her home because of lack of security, for example, may prefer to hold gold in certificate form; the physical gold backing the certificate is held in a secure bank vault. Certificate owners pay a small custodial charge each year to the custodian bank.

GOLD COIN coin minted in gold. Bullion coins are minted by governments and are traded mostly on the value of their gold content. Major gold bullion coins include the American Eagle, the Canadian Maple Leaf, the Mexican Peso, the Australian Kangaroo, and the South African Kruggerand. Other gold coins, called NUMISMATIC COINS, are minted in limited quantity and trade more on the basis of their aesthetic value and rarity, rather than on their gold content. Numismatic coins are sold at a hefty markup to their gold content, and are therefore not as pure a play on gold prices as bullion coins.

GOLDEN BOOT inducement, using maximum incentives and financial benefits, for an older worker to take "voluntary" early retirement, thus circumventing age discrimination laws.

GOLDEN HANDCUFFS contract that ties a broker to a brokerage firm. If the broker stays at the firm, he or she will earn lucrative commissions, bonuses, and other compensation. But if the broker leaves and tries to lure clients to another firm, the broker must promise to give back to the firm much of the compensation received while working there. Golden handcuffs are a response by the brokerage industry to the frequent movement of brokers from one firm to another.

GOLDEN HANDSHAKE generous payment by a company to a director, senior executive, or consultant who is let go before his or her contract expires because of a takeover or other development. *See also* GOLDEN PARACHUTE.

GOLDEN HELLO bonus paid by a securities firm, usually in England, to get a key employee away from a competing firm.

GOLDEN PARACHUTE lucrative contract given to a top executive to provide lavish benefits in case the company is taken over by another firm, resulting in the loss of the job. A golden parachute might include generous severance pay, stock options, or a bonus. The TAX REFORM ACT OF 1984 eliminated the deductibility of "excess compensation" and imposed an excise tax. The TAX REFORM ACT OF 1986 covered matters of clarification.

GOLD FIXING daily determination of the price of gold by selected gold specialists and bank officials in London, Paris, and Zürich. The price is fixed at 10:30 A.M. and 3:30 P.M. London time every business day, according to the prevailing market forces of supply and demand.

GOLDILOCKS ECONOMY term coined in the mid-90s to describe an economy that was "not too hot, not too cold, just right," as was the porridge in the children's story of "Goldilocks and the Three Bears." Adroit MONETARY POLICY was credited for an economy that enjoyed steady growth with a nominal rate of inflation. *See also* SOFT LANDING.

GOLD MUTUAL FUND mutual fund investing in gold mining shares. Some funds limit themselves to shares in North American mining companies, while others can buy shares anywhere in the world, including predominantly South Africa and Australia. Such mutual funds offer investors diversification among many gold mining companies, somewhat reducing risks. Still, such funds tend to be volatile, since the prices of gold mining shares tend to move up or down far more than the price of gold itself. Gold funds also tend to pay dividends, since many gold mining companies pay dividends based on gold sales.

GOLD STANDARD monetary system under which units of currency are convertible into fixed amounts of gold. Such a system is said to be anti-inflationary. The United States has been on the gold standard in the past but was taken off in 1971. *See also* HARD MONEY.

GOODBYE KISS *see* GREENMAIL.

GOOD DELIVERY securities industry designation meaning that a certificate has the necessary endorsements and meets all other requirements (signature guarantee, proper denomination, and other qualifications), so that title can be transferred by delivery to the buying broker, who is then obligated to accept it. Exceptions constitute *bad delivery*. *See also* DELIVERY DATE.

GOOD FAITH DEPOSIT
In general: token amount of money advanced to indicate intent to pursue a contract to completion.
Commodities: initial margin deposit required when buying or selling a futures contract. Such deposits generally range from 2% to 10% of the contract value.

Securities:
1. deposit, usually 25% of a transaction, required by securities firms of individuals who are not known to them but wish to enter orders with them.
2. deposit left with a municipal bond issuer by a firm competing for the underwriting business. The deposit typically equals 1% to 5% of the principal amount of the issue and is refundable to the unsuccessful bidders.

GOOD MONEY
Banking: federal funds, which are good the same day, in contrast to CLEARING HOUSE FUNDS. Clearing house funds are understood in two ways: (1) funds requiring three days to clear and (2) funds used to settle transactions on which there is a one-day FLOAT.

Gresham's Law: theory that money of superior intrinsic value, "good money," will eventually be driven out of circulation by money of lesser intrinsic value. *See also* GRESHAM'S LAW.

GOOD-THIS-MONTH ORDER (GTM)
order to buy or sell securities (usually at a LIMIT PRICE or STOP PRICE set by the customer) that remains in effect until the end of the month. In the case of a limit price, the customer instructs the broker either to buy at the stipulated limit price or anything lower, or to sell at the limit price or anything higher. In the case of a stop price, the customer instructs the broker to enter a market order once a transaction in the security occurs at the stop price specified.

A variation on the GTM order is the *good-this-week-order* (GTW), which expires at the end of the week if it is not executed.

See also DAY ORDER; GOOD-TILL-CANCELED ORDER; LIMIT ORDER; OPEN ORDER; STOP ORDER.

GOOD THROUGH
order to buy or sell securities or commodities at a stated price for a stated period of time, unless canceled, executed, or changed. It is a type of LIMIT ORDER and may be specified GTW (good this week), GTM (GOOD-THIS-MONTH ORDER), or for shorter or longer periods.

GOOD-TILL-CANCELED ORDER (GTC)
brokerage customer's order to buy or sell a security, usually at a particular price, that remains in effect until executed or canceled. If the GTC order remains unfilled after a long period of time, a broker will usually periodically confirm that the customer still wants the transaction to occur if the stock reaches the target price. *See also* DAY ORDER; GOOD-THIS-MONTH ORDER; OPEN ORDER; TARGET PRICE.

GOODWILL
intangible asset representing GOING CONCERN VALUE in excess of asset value paid by a company for another company in a PURCHASE ACQUISITION. Under FINANCIAL ACCOUNTING STANDARDS BOARD (FASB) rule 142 issued June 2001, goodwill cannot be amortized unless an impairment test is satisfied. Before that ruling, goodwill and related intangible assets were amortized and deducted on a straight-line basis over a 15-year period.

GOVERNMENT NATIONAL MORTGAGE ASSOCIATION (GNMA)
government-owned corporation, nicknamed Ginnie Mae, which is an agency of the U.S. Department of Housing and Urban Development. GNMA guarantees, with the full faith and credit of the U.S. Government, full and timely payment of all monthly principal and interest payments on the mortgage-backed PASS-THROUGH SECURITIES of registered holders. The securities, which are issued by private firms, such as MORTGAGE BANKERS and savings institutions, and typically marketed through security broker-dealers, represent pools of residential mort-

gages insured or guaranteed by the Federal Housing Administration (FHA), the Farmer's Home Administration (FmHA), or the Veterans Administration (VA). *See also* FEDERAL HOME LOAN MORTGAGE CORPORATION; FEDERAL NATIONAL MORTGAGE ASSOCIATION; GINNIE MAE PASS-THROUGH.

GOVERNMENT OBLIGATIONS U.S. government debt instruments (Treasury bonds, bills, notes, savings bonds) the government has pledged to repay. *See* GOVERNMENTS.

GOVERNMENTS
1. securities issued by the U.S. government, such as Treasury bills, bonds, notes, and savings bonds. Governments are the most creditworthy of all debt instruments since they are backed by the FULL FAITH AND CREDIT of the U.S. government, which if necessary can print money to make payments. Also called TREASURIES.
2. debt issues of federal agencies, which are not directly backed by the U.S. government. *See also* GOVERNMENT SECURITIES.

GOVERNMENT SECURITIES securities issued by U.S. government agencies, such as the RESOLUTION FUNDING CORPORATION (REFCORP) or the Federal Land Bank; also called *agency securities.* Although these securities have high credit ratings, they are not considered to be GOVERNMENT OBLIGATIONS and therefore are not directly backed by the FULL FAITH AND CREDIT of the government as TREASURIES are. *See also* AGENCY SECURITIES.

GOVERNMENT SECURITIES CLEARING CORPORATION (GSCC) nonprofit subsidiary of the NATIONAL SECURITIES CLEARING CORPORATION (NSCC) that provides clearing and settlement of United States government securities.

GRACE PERIOD period of time provided in most loan contracts and insurance policies during which default or cancellation will not occur even though payment is due.
Credit cards: number of days between when a credit card bill is sent and when the payment is due without incurring interest charges. Most banks offer credit card holders a 25-day grace period, though some offer more and others fewer days.
Insurance: number of days, typically 30, during which insurance coverage is in force and premiums have not been paid.
Loans: provision in some long-term loans, particularly EUROCURRENCY syndication loans to foreign governments and multinational firms by groups of banks, whereby repayment of principal does not begin until some point well into the lifetime of the loan. The grace period, which can be as long as five years for international transactions for corporations, is an important point of negotiation between a borrower and a lender; borrowers sometimes will accept a higher interest rate to obtain a longer grace period.

GRADUATED CALL WRITING strategy of writing (selling) covered CALL OPTIONS at gradually higher EXERCISE PRICES so that as the price of the underlying stock rises and the options are exercised, the seller winds up with a higher average price than the original exercise price. The premiums naturally rise as the underlying stock rises, representing income to the seller that helps offset the loss if the stock should decline.

GRADUATED FLAT TAX a compromise between a FLAT TAX and a progressive tax, such as the modified flat tax system instituted by the Tax Reform Act of 1986, with its fewer tax brackets and lower rates.

GRADUATED LEASE longer-term lease in which payments, instead of being fixed, are adjusted periodically based on appraisals or a benchmark rate, such as increases in the CONSUMER PRICE INDEX.

GRADUATED-PAYMENT MORTGAGE (GPM) mortgage featuring lower monthly payments at first, which steadily rise until they level off after a few years. GPMs, also known as "jeeps," are designed for young couples whose income is expected to grow as their careers advance. A graduated-payment mortgage allows such a family to buy a house that would be unaffordable if mortgage payments started out at a high level. Persons planning to take on such a mortgage must be confident that their income will be able to keep pace with the rising payments. *See also* ADJUSTABLE-RATE MORTGAGE; CONVENTIONAL MORTGAGE; REVERSE-ANNUITY MORTGAGE; VARIABLE-RATE MORTGAGE.

GRADUATED SECURITY security whose listing has been upgraded by moving from one exchange to another—for example, from the American Stock Exchange to the more prestigious New York Stock Exchange, or from a regional exchange to a national exchange. An advantage of such a transfer is to widen trading in the security.

GRAHAM AND DODD METHOD OF INVESTING fundamental investment approach outlined in Benjamin Graham and David Dodd's landmark book *Security Analysis,* published in the 1930s. Graham and Dodd founded the modern discipline of security analysis with their work. They believed that investors should buy stocks with undervalued assets and that eventually those assets would appreciate to their true value in the marketplace. Graham and Dodd advocated buying stocks in companies where current assets exceed current liabilities and all long-term debt, and where the stock is selling at a low PRICE/EARNINGS RATIO. They suggested that the stocks be sold after a profit objective of between 50% and 100% was reached, which they assumed would be three years or less from the time of purchase. Analysts today who call themselves Graham and Dodd investors hunt for stocks selling below their LIQUIDATING VALUE and do not necessarily concern themselves with the potential for earnings growth.

GRAMM-LEACH-BLILEY ACT *see* FINANCIAL SERVICES MODERNIZATION ACT OF 1999.

GRANDFATHER CLAUSE provision included in a new rule that exempts from the rule a person or business already engaged in the activity coming under regulation. For example, the Financial Accounting Standards Board might adopt a rule effective in 1998 relating, say, to depreciation that, under a grandfather clause, would exempt assets put in service before 1998.

GRANTOR
Investments: options trader who sells a CALL OPTION or a PUT OPTION and collects PREMIUM INCOME for doing so. The grantor sells the right to buy a security at a certain price in the case of a call, and the right to sell at a certain price in the case of a put.
Law: one who executes a deed conveying title to property or who creates a trust. The grantor of an irrevocable *grantor trust* is taxed on the income.

Where title to property is irrevocably transferred, as with a *qualified personal residence trust (QPRT)*, the grantor is responsible for property taxes and normal expenses of repair. Also called a *settlor*. *See also* GRANTOR RETAINED INCOME TRUST (GRIT).

GRANTOR RETAINED INCOME TRUST (GRIT) type of TRUST designed to save estate taxes in the event the GRANTOR outlives the trust termination date. Under such a trust, which must be irrevocable and have a life of at least 15 years, the grantor transfers property immediately to the beneficiary but receives income until termination, at which time the beneficiary begins receiving it. At that point the grantor pays a GIFT TAX based on the original value of the gift. When the grantor dies, the gift is added back to the grantor's estate at the value as of the day of the gift, not its (presumably) higher current value.

GRAVEYARD MARKET bear market wherein investors who sell are faced with substantial losses, while potential investors prefer to stay liquid, that is, to keep their money in cash or cash equivalents until market conditions improve. Like a graveyard, those who are in can't get out and those who are out have no desire to get in.

GRAY KNIGHT acquiring company that, acting to advance its own interests, outbids a WHITE KNIGHT but that, not being unfriendly, is preferable to a hostile bidder.

GRAY LIST a list of stocks that an investment banking firm can transact as regular and block trades in its capacity as agent (broker) but not as principal (dealer) because the firm, in its other capacity as an investment banker, is involved with the issuing company in nonpublic activities, such as merger and acquisition defense, affiliate ownership, or underwriting. Since a company's presense on the gray list would indicate that market-conditioning developments are in progress, the list is kept highly confidential within the trading area of the firm to avoid conflicts of interest. Term is often used interchangeably with *restricted list*, although the latter also refers to lists of securities that employees of banks and other organizations having fiduciary relationships with issuers are not permitted to own.

GRAY MARKET
Consumer goods: sale of products by unauthorized dealers, frequently at discounted prices. Consumers who buy gray market goods may find that the manufacturer refuses to honor the product warranty. In some cases, gray market goods may be sold in a country they were not intended for, so, for example, instructions may be in another language than the home market language.
Securities: sale of securities that have not officially been issued yet by a firm that is not a member of the underwriting syndicate. Such trading in the when-issued, or gray, market can provide a good indication of the amount of demand for an upcoming new stock or bond issue.

GREATER FOOL THEORY theory that even though a stock or the market as a whole is FULLY VALUED, speculation is justified because there are enough fools to push prices further upward.

GREEN COLLAR JOBS jobs in industries that foster environmental sustainability or energy conservation such as solar and wind energy, biomass, recycling, and smart electrical grids.

GREENMAIL payment of a premium to a raider trying to take over a company through a proxy contest or other means. Also known as BON VOYAGE BONUS, it is designed to thwart the takeover. By accepting the payment, the raider agrees not to buy any more shares or pursue the takeover any further for a specified number of years. *See also* GOODBYE KISS.

GREEN INVESTING owning the stock of environmentally friendly companies.

GREEN SHOE clause in an underwriting agreement saying that, in the event of exceptional public demand, the issuer will authorize additional shares for distribution by the syndicate.

GREEN SHOOTS botanical metaphor for early indications that an economy in recession may be recovering. For example, in mid-2009 a jobs report showing that fewer jobs were lost in the most recent reporting period than in the previous one and that housing starts were up by several percentage points were optimistically cited as green shoots, although their significance was by no means certain.

GRESHAM'S LAW theory in economics that bad money drives out good money. Specifically, people faced with a choice of two currencies of the same nominal value, one of which is preferable to the other because of metal content or because it resists mutilation, will hoard the good money and spend the bad money, thereby driving the good money out of circulation. The observation is named for Sir Thomas Gresham, master of the mint in the reign of Queen Elizabeth I.

GRIT *see* GRANTOR RETAINED INCOME TRUST (GRIT).

GROSS DOMESTIC PRODUCT (GDP) market value of the goods and services produced within the borders of the United States. GDP is made up of consumer and government purchases, private domestic investments, and net exports of goods and services. Figures for GDP are released by the Commerce Department on a quarterly basis. Growth of the U.S. economy is measured by the change in inflation-adjusted GDP, or real GDP. In 1991, GDP replaced *Gross National Product* (GNP), which includes American producers outside the U.S. and excludes foreign producers in the U.S.

GROSS EARNINGS personal taxable income before adjustments made to arrive at ADJUSTED GROSS INCOME.

GROSS ESTATE total value of a person's assets before liabilities such as debts and taxes are deducted. After someone dies, the executor of the will makes an assessment of the stocks, bonds, real estate, and personal possessions that comprise the gross estate. Debts and taxes are paid, as are funeral expenses and estate administration costs. Beneficiaries of the will then receive their portion of the remainder, which is called the *net estate.*

GROSS INCOME total personal income before exclusions and deductions.

GROSS LEASE property lease under which the lessor (landlord) agrees to pay all the expenses normally associated with ownership (insurance, taxes, utilities, repairs). An exception might be that the lessee (tenant) would be required to pay real estate taxes above a stipulated amount or to pay for certain special operating expenses (snow removal, grounds care in the case of a shopping center, or institutional advertising, for example). Gross leases are the most common type of lease contract and are typical arrangements for short-term tenancy. They normally contain no provision for periodic rent adjustments, nor are there preestablished renewal arrangements. *See also* NET LEASE.

GROSS NATIONAL PRODUCT (GNP) *see* GROSS DOMESTIC PRODUCT.

GROSS PER BROKER gross amount of commission revenues attributable to a particular REGISTERED REPRESENTATIVE during a given period. Brokers, who typically keep one third of the commissions they generate, are often expected by their firms to meet productivity quotas based on their gross.

GROSS PROFIT net sales less the COST OF GOODS SOLD. Also called *gross margin*. *See also* NET PROFIT.

GROSS SALES total sales at invoice values, not reduced by customer discounts, returns or allowances, or other adjustments. *See also* NET SALES.

GROSS SPREAD difference (spread) between the public offering price of a security and the price paid by an underwriter to the issuer. The spread breaks down into the manager's fee, the dealer's (or underwriter's) discount, and the selling concession (i.e., the discount offered to a selling group). *See also* CONCESSION; FLOTATION (FLOATATION) COST.

GROUND LEASE lease on the land. Typically, the land will be under a building, which will have its own leases with tenants.

GROUP INSURANCE insurance coverage bought for and provided to a group instead of an individual. For example, an employer may buy disability, health, and term life insurance for its employees at a far better rate than the employees could obtain on their own. Credit unions, trade associations, and other groups may also offer their members preferential group insurance rates. Group insurance is not only advantageous to employees or group members because it is cheaper than they could obtain on their own, but some people may be able to get coverage under the group umbrella when they would be denied coverage individually because of preexisting conditions or other factors.

GROUP OF EIGHT (G-8) *see* G-8 FINANCE MINISTERS.

GROUP OF 20 (G-20) group of finance ministers and central bank governors established in 1999, representing 19 globally important industrial and emerging-market countries plus the European Union. It normally meets once a year to promote understanding and cooperation on key issues related to global economic stability and to give greater recognition to key emerging-market countries. Members represent 90% of global GDP, 80% of world trade, and two-thirds of the world's population. The chair, which will be South Korea in 2010, is part of a revolving three-member Troika of past, present, and future chairs.

GROUP ROTATION tendency of stocks in one industry to outperform and then underperform other industries. This may be due to the economic cycle or what industry is popular or unpopular with investors at any particular time. For example, CYCLICAL stocks in the auto, paper, or steel industry may be group leaders when the economy is showing robust growth, while stocks of stable-demand firms such as drug or food companies may be market leaders in a recession. Alternatively, investor demand for stocks in certain industries, such as biotechnology, computer software, or real estate investment trusts may rise and fall because of enthusiasm or disappointment with the group, creating rotation into or out of such stocks. Market analysts watch which industry group is coming into and going out of vogue in recommending stocks that might lead or lag in coming months. Also called *sector rotation*. *See also* INDUSTRIAL SECTORS.

GROUP SALES term used in securities underwriting that refers to block sales made to institutional investors. The securities come out of a syndicate "pot" with credit for the sale prorated among the syndicate members in proportion to their original allotments.

GROUP UNIVERSAL LIFE POLICY (GULP) UNIVERSAL LIFE INSURANCE offered on a group basis, and therefore more cheaply than one could obtain it personally, to employees and, sometimes, their family members.

GROWING EQUITY MORTGAGE (GEM) mortgage with a fixed interest rate and growing payments. This technique allows the homeowner to build equity in the underlying home faster than if they made the same mortgage payment for the life of the loan. Borrowers who take on GEM loans should be confident in their ability to make higher payments over time based on their prospects for rising income.

GROWTH AND INCOME FUND MUTUAL FUND that seeks earnings growth as well as income. These funds invest mainly in the common stock of companies with a history of capital gains but that also have a record of consistent dividend payments.

GROWTH AT A REASONABLE PRICE (GARP) investment approach combining VALUE INVESTING and GROWTH STOCK investing.

GROWTH FUND mutual fund that invests in growth stocks. The goal is to provide capital appreciation for the fund's shareholders over the long term. Growth funds are more volatile than more conservative income or money market funds. They tend to rise faster than conservative funds in bull (advancing) markets and to drop more sharply in bear (falling) markets. *See also* GROWTH STOCK.

GROWTH RATE percentage rate at which the economy, stocks, or earnings are growing. The economic growth rate is normally determined by the growth of the GROSS DOMESTIC PRODUCT. Individual companies try to establish a rate at which their earnings grow over time. Firms with long-term earnings growth rates of more than 15% are considered fast-growing companies. Analysts also apply the term *growth rate* to specific financial aspects of a company's operations, such as dividends, sales, assets, and market share. Analysts use growth rates to compare one company to another within the same industry.

GROWTH RECESSION economy in which gross domestic product and unemployment both rise. Also called *jobless recovery.*

GROWTH STOCK stock of a corporation that has exhibited faster-than-average gains in earnings over the last few years and is expected to continue to show high levels of profit growth. Over the long run, growth stocks tend to outperform slower-growing or stagnant stocks. Growth stocks are riskier investments than average stocks, however, since they usually sport higher price/earnings ratios and make little or no dividend payments to shareholders. *See also* PRICE/EARNINGS RATIO.

GUARANTEE to take responsibility for payment of a debt or performance of some obligation if the person primarily liable fails to perform. A guarantee is a CONTINGENT LIABILITY of the guarantor—that is, it is a potential liability not recognized in accounts until the outcome becomes probable in the opinion of the company's accountant.

GUARANTEED BOND bond on which the principal and interest are guaranteed by a firm other than the issuer. Such bonds are nearly always railroad bonds, arising out of situations where one road has leased the road of another and the security holders of the leased road require assurance of income in exchange for giving up control of the property. Guaranteed securities involved in such situations may also include preferred or common stocks when dividends are guaranteed. Both guaranteed stock and guaranteed bonds become, in effect, DEBENTURE (unsecured) bonds of the guarantor, although the status of the stock may be questionable in the event of LIQUIDATION. In any event, if the guarantor enjoys stronger credit than the railroad whose securities are being guaranteed, the securities have greater value.

Guaranteed bonds may also arise out of parent-subsidiary relationships where bonds are issued by the subsidiary with the parent's guarantee.

GUARANTEED INSURABILITY feature offered as an option in life and health insurance policies that enables the insured to add coverage at specified future times and at standard rates without evidence of insurability.

GUARANTEED INVESTMENT CONTRACT contract between an insurance company and a corporate profit-sharing or pension plan that guarantees a specific rate of return on the invested capital over the life of the contract. Many defined contribution plans, such as 401(k) and 403(b) plans, offer guaranteed investment contracts as investment options to employees. Although the insurance company takes all market, credit, and interest rate risks on the investment portfolio, it can profit if its return exceeds the guaranteed amount. Only the insurance company backs the guarantee, not any governmental agency, so if the insurer fails, it is possible that there could be a default on the contract. For pension and profit-sharing plans, guaranteed investment contracts, also known as GICs, are a conservative way of assuring beneficiaries that their money will achieve a certain rate of return. *See also* BANK INVESTMENT CONTRACT.

GUARANTEED RENEWABLE POLICY INSURANCE policy that requires the insurer to renew the policy for a period specified in the contract provided premiums are paid in a timely fashion. The insurer cannot make any changes in the provisions of the policy other than a change in the premium rate for all insureds in the same class.

GUARANTEED REPLACEMENT COST COVERAGE INSURANCE policy that pays for the full cost of replacing damaged property without a deduction for depreciation and without a dollar limit. This policy is different from an actual cash value policy, which takes into account depreciation for lost and damaged items, if the damage resulted from an insured peril.

GUARANTEED STOCK *see* GUARANTEED BOND.

GUARANTEE LETTER letter by a commercial bank that guarantees payment of the EXERCISE PRICE of a client's PUT OPTION (the right to sell a given security at a particular price within a specified period) if or when a notice indicating its exercise, called an assignment notice, is presented to the option seller (writer).

GUARANTEE OF SIGNATURE certificate issued by a bank or brokerage firm vouching for the authenticity of a person's signature. Such a document may be necessary when stocks, bonds, or other registered securities are transferred from a seller to a buyer. Banks also require guarantees of signature before they will process certain transactions.

GUARANTY PROGRAM FOR MONEY MARKET FUNDS program instituted in 2008 to guarantee the safety of money market mutual funds after the Reserve Fund "broke the buck" by being forced to redeem shares at less than the $1 per share net asset value typically maintained by money funds because of the fund's large holdings in Lehman Bros. securities, which became worthless after Lehman's bankruptcy filing. Reserve's action caused a run on all money funds by panicky investors, causing the Treasury to intervene with this program, which reassured investors. The program expired in 2009 when calm returned to the money market fund industry.

GUARDIAN individual who has the legal right to care for another person as a parent or to act as an administrator of the assets of a person declared incompetent for mental or physical reasons. Guardians can be *testamentary*, meaning appointed in a parent's will; *general,* meaning having the general responsibility to care for another person and that person's estate; or *special,* meaning the guardian has limited authority, such as half the responsibility of a general guardian but not the other.

GULP *see* GROUP UNIVERSAL LIFE POLICY (GULP).

GUN JUMPING
1. trading securities on information before it becomes publicly disclosed.
2. illegally soliciting buy orders in an underwriting, before a Securities and Exchange Commission REGISTRATION is complete.

GUNSLINGER aggressive portfolio manager who buys speculative stocks, often on margin. In the great bull market of the 1960s, several hot fund managers gained reputations and had huge followings as gunslingers by producing enormous returns while taking great risks. However, the bear market of the early 1970s caused many of these gunslingers to lose huge amounts of money, and in most cases, their followings. The term is still used when referring to popular managers who take big risks in search of high returns.

H

HAIRCUT securities industry term referring to the formulas used in the valuation of securities for the purpose of calculating a broker-dealer's net capital. The haircut varies according to the class of a security, its market risk, and the time to maturity. For example, cash equivalent GOVERNMENTS could have a 0% haircut, equities could have an average 30% haircut, and fail positions (securities with past due delivery) with little prospect of settlement could have a 100% haircut. *See also* CASH EQUIVALENTS; FAIL POSITION.

HALF-LIFE point in time in which half the principal has been repaid in a mortgage-backed security guaranteed or issued by the GOVERNMENT NATIONAL MORTGAGE ASSOCIATION, the FEDERAL NATIONAL MORTGAGE ASSOCIATION, or the FEDERAL HOME LOAN MORTGAGE CORPORATION. Normally, it is assumed that such a security has a half-life of 12 years. But specific mortgage pools can have vastly longer or shorter half-lives, depending on interest rate trends. If interest rates fall, more homeowners will refinance their mortgages, meaning that principal will be paid off more quickly, and half-lives will drop. If interest rates rise, homeowners will hold onto their mortgages longer than anticipated, and half-lives will rise.

HALF-STOCK common or preferred stock with a $50 PAR value instead of the more conventional $100 par value.

HALF-YEAR CONVENTION in tax law, the assumption that an asset acquired at any point in the taxable year was placed in service halfway during the year.

HALLOWEEN STRATEGY stock investment strategy based on the historical fact that most capital gains (80 percent by some estimates) occur between October 31 and May 1. An investor using the *Halloween indicator,* as it is also called, would be FULLY INVESTED for that six-month period and out of the stock market for the other six months of the year, theoretically enjoying the major part of an annual return with half the EXPOSURE.

HAMMERING THE MARKET intense selling of stocks by those who think prices are inflated. Speculators who think the market is about to drop, and therefore sell short, are said to be hammering the market. *See also* SELLING SHORT.

HANDS-OFF INVESTOR investor willing to take a passive role in the management of a corporation. An individual or corporation with a large stake in another company may decide to adopt a "hands-off" policy if it is satisfied with the current performance of management. However, if management falters, it may become more actively involved in corporate strategy.

HANDS-ON INVESTOR investor who takes an active role in the management of the company whose stock he or she has bought.

HANG SENG INDEX the major indicator of stock market performance in Hong Kong. The index is comprised of 33 companies with aggregate capitalization that represents 70% of total market capitalization of all eligible stocks listed on the Main Board of the Stock Exchange of Hong Kong. There are four sector indices: commerce and industry, finance, properties, and utilities.

HARD DOLLARS actual payments made by a customer for services, including research, provided by a brokerage firm. For instance, if a broker puts together a financial plan for a client, the fee might be $1,000 in hard dollars. This contrasts with SOFT DOLLARS, which refers to compensation by way of the commissions a broker would receive if he were to carry out any trades called for in that financial plan. Brokerage house research is sold for either hard or soft dollars.

HARD GOODS consumer DURABLE GOODS.

HARD MONEY (HARD CURRENCY)
1. currency in which there is widespread confidence. It is the currency of an economically and politically stable country, such as the U.S. or Switzerland. Countries that have taken out loans in hard money generally must repay them in hard money.
2. gold or coins, as contrasted with paper currency, which is considered *soft money*. Some hard-money enthusiasts advocate a return to the GOLD STANDARD as a method of reducing inflation and promoting economic growth.

HART-SCOTT-RODINO ACT OF 1976 United States Department of Justice regulation enforced by the FEDERAL TRADE COMMISSION that requires notification by an investor seeking to acquire an interest in the lesser amount of 15% or $15 million of a firm's capitalization. The filing prompts a 30-day review of antitrust considerations.

HEAD AND SHOULDERS patterns resembling the head and shoulders outline of a person, which is used to chart stock price trends. The pattern signals the reversal of a trend. As prices move down to the right shoulder, a head and shoulders top is formed, meaning that prices should be falling. A reverse head and shoulders pattern has the head at the bottom of the chart, meaning that prices should be rising.

HEAD AND SHOULDERS

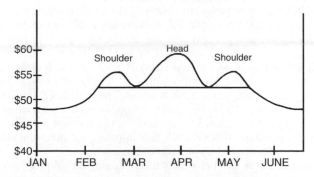

HEADLINE INFLATION an increase in inflation as measured by the CONSUMER PRICE INDEX (CPI) or, when specified, the PRODUCER PRICE INDEX (PPI) including all prices making up the index, which means that the most volatile prices excluded to arrive at CORE INFLATION, namely food and energy, are added back.

HEADLINE RISK the risk that a major news story about a company, whether true or not, will adversely affect the value of its stock.

HEAD OF HOUSEHOLD tax filing status available in the tax code to individuals who provide more than half of the financial support to their household during the tax year. Heads of household can be married or single, as long as they support dependent children or grandchildren, parents, or other close relatives living at home. Those qualifying for head-of-household status pay the same tax rates as singles and married couples filing jointly, but the rates apply at different income levels. For example, a head of household in 2005 paid a 28% tax rate on taxable income between $102,800 and $166,450, while a single paid the same tax rate on income between $71,950 and $150,150 and a married couple filing jointly paid 28% on $119,950 to $182,800.

HEALTH INSURANCE in popular usage, any insurance plan that covers medical expenses or health care services, including HMOs, insured plans, preferred provider organizations, etc. In insurance, protection against loss by sickness or bodily injury, in which sense it is synonymous with accident and health, accident and sickness, accident, or disability income insurance.

HEALTH SAVING ACCOUNT (HSA) created by the Medicare bill in 2003 that allows tax-free contributions, earnings, and withdrawals from an HSA if used for medical care. HSAs must be used in conjunction with a high-deductible health plan. Allowable contributions depend on the deductible but were limited to $3,000 in 2009 for an individual and $5,950 for family, plus an additional $1,000 for people 55 or over. Within limits, accounts can be drawn down without penalty at any time for medical bills.

HEAVY MARKET stock, bond, or commodity market with falling prices resulting from a larger supply of offers to sell than bids to buy.

HEDGE/HEDGING strategy used to offset investment risk. A perfect hedge is one eliminating the possibility of future gain or loss.

A stockholder worried about declining stock prices, for instance, can hedge his or her holdings by buying a PUT OPTION on the stock or selling a CALL OPTION. Someone owning 100 shares of XYZ stock, selling at $70 per share, can hedge his position by buying a put option giving him the right to sell 100 shares at $70 at any time over the next few months. This investor must pay a certain amount of money, called a PREMIUM, for these rights. If XYZ stock falls during that time, the investor can exercise his option—that is, sell the stock at $70—thereby preserving the $70 value of the XYZ holdings. The same XYZ stockholder can also hedge his position by selling a call option. In such a transaction, he sells the right to buy XYZ stock at $70 per share for the next few months. In return, he receives a premium. If XYZ stock falls in price, that premium income will offset to some extent the drop in value of the stock.

SELLING SHORT is another widely used hedging technique.

Investors often try to hedge against inflation by purchasing assets that will rise in value faster than inflation, such as gold, real estate, or other tangible assets.

Large commercial firms that want to be assured of the price they will receive or pay for a commodity will hedge their position by buying and selling simultaneously in the FUTURES MARKET. For example, Hershey's, the chocolate company, will hedge its supplies of cocoa in the futures market to limit the risk of a rise in cocoa prices.

Managers of large pools of money such as pension and mutual funds frequently hedge their exposure to currency or interest rate risk by buying or selling futures or options contracts. For example, a GLOBAL MUTUAL FUND manager with a large position in Japanese stocks who thinks the Japanese yen is about to fall in value against the U.S. dollar may buy futures or options on the Japanese yen to offset the projected loss on the currency.

HEDGE CLAUSE disclaimer seen in market letters, security research reports, or other printed matter having to do with evaluating investments, which purports to absolve the writer from responsibility for the accuracy of information obtained from usually reliable sources. Despite such clauses, which may mitigate liability, writers may still be charged with negligence in their use of information. Typical language of a hedge clause: "The information furnished herein has been obtained from sources believed to be reliable, but its accuracy is not guaranteed."

HEDGED TENDER SELLING SHORT a portion of the shares being tendered to protect against a price drop in the event all shares tendered are not accepted. For example, ABC Company or another company wishing to acquire ABC Company announces a TENDER OFFER at $52 a share when ABC shares are selling at a market price of $40. The market price of ABC will now rise to near the tender price of $52. An investor wishing to sell all his or her 2,000 shares at $52 will tender 2,000 shares, but cannot be assured all shares will be accepted. To lock in the $52 price on the tendered shares the investor thinks might not be accepted—say half of them or 1,000 shares—he or she will sell short that many shares. Assuming the investor has guessed correctly and only 1,000 shares are accepted, when the tender offer expires and the market price of ABC begins to drop, the investor will still have sold all 2,000 shares for $52 or close to it—half to the tenderer and the other half when the short sale is consummated.

HEDGE FUND private investment partnership (for U.S. investors) or an off-shore investment corporation (for non-U.S. or tax-exempt investors) in which the general partner has made a substantial personal investment, and whose offering memorandum allows for the fund to take both long and SHORT POSITIONS, use leverage and derivatives, and invest in many markets. Hedge funds often take large risks on speculative strategies, including PROGRAM TRADING, SWAPS, ARBITRAGE, and other MARKET-NEUTRAL INVESTING. A fund need not employ all of these tools all of the time; it must merely have them at its disposal. Since hedge funds are not limited to buying securities, they can potentially profit in any market environment, including one with sharply declining prices. Because they move billions of dollars in and out of markets quickly, hedge funds can have a significant impact on the day-to-day trading developments in the stock, bond, and futures markets.

Hedge funds entitle the general partner to an additional incentive management fee based upon positive returns—the higher the returns, the higher their fee. Traditional hedge funds require that 65% of all investors be of the *accredited* type, defined as an individual or couple who have a net worth of at least $1 million, or an individual who had income in the previous year of at least $200,000, or a couple with at least $300,000 of income in the previous year. In reality, though, an investor needs much more than that.

The funds also require substantial minimum investments that can make it hard even for accredited investors to ante up. Minimums typically range from about $250,000 to $10 million. An investor gives up liquidity in hedge funds. They typically have a one-year lock-up for first-time investors. Since 2000, some mutual fund families and mainstream financial services firms have begun offering hedge funds aimed at the semi-affluent retail market, some with minimum investment requirements as low as $25,000. These are offered as open-end mutual funds or FUNDS-OF-FUNDS and as such innovative products as CLOSED-END FUNDS that do not trade on exchanges, and usually offer investors the opportunity to sell shares only quarterly or annually. New rules adopted December 2, 2004, amending the Investment Advisers Act of 1940 require hedge fund managers to register as advisers with the Securities and Exchange Commission (SEC). *See also* GATE; TWO AND TWENTY.

HEDGE RATIO *see* DELTA HEDGING.

HEDGE WRAPPER options strategy where the holder of a long position in an underlying stock buys an OUT OF THE MONEY put and sells an out of the money call. It defines a range where the stock will be sold at expiration of the option, whatever way the stock moves. The maximum profit is made if the call is exercised at expiration, since the holder gets the strike price plus any dividends. The maximum loss occurs if the put option is exercised, and represents the cost of the hedge wrapper less the strike price plus dividends received. The cost of the hedge wrapper less dividends received is the breakeven point. The strategy produces a loss whenever the breakeven price is higher than the strike price of the call.

HEIR one who inherits some or all of the estate of a deceased person by virtue of being in the direct line (*heir of the body*), or being designated in a will or by a legal authority (*heir at law*).

HELP-WANTED INDEX *see* CONFERENCE BOARD, THE.

HEMLINE THEORY whimsical idea that stock prices move in the same general direction as the hemlines of women's dresses. Short skirts in the 1920s and 1960s were considered bullish signs that stock prices would rise, whereas longer dresses in the 1930s and 1940s were considered bearish (falling) indicators. Despite its sometimes uncanny way of being prophetic, the hemline theory has remained more in the area of wishful thinking than serious market analysis.

HERSTATT RISK *see* SETTLEMENT RISK.

HIBOR acronym for *Hong Kong Interbank Offer Rate,* the annualized offer rate paid by banks for Hong Kong dollar-denominated three-month deposits. It acts as a benchmark for many interest rates throughout the Far East.

HIDDEN INFLATION INFLATION that is not reflected in a price but rather in the quantity or quality of a product sold at price that remains constant. The classic example is a candy bar that sells at the same price even though the amount inside the package is smaller. *See also* QUANTITY THEORY OF MONEY.

HIDDEN LOAD sales charge which may not be immediately apparent to an investor. For example, a 12b-1 MUTUAL FUND assesses an annual asset base charge of up to 0.75% to cover marketing, distribution, and promotion expenses incurred by the fund. Even though it has been disclosed in the prospectus, many investors do not realize that they are paying this load. The sales charges levied on insurance policies are also hidden, because they are not explicitly disclosed to customers, and are instead subtracted from premiums paid by policyholders. *See also* MUTUAL FUND SHARE CLASSES.

HIDDEN VALUES assets owned by a company but not yet reflected in its stock price. For example, a manufacturing firm may own valuable real estate that could be sold at a much higher price than it appears on the company's books, which is usually the price at which the real estate was purchased. Other undervalued assets that could have significant value include patents, trademarks, or exclusive contracts. Value-oriented money managers search for stocks with hidden values on their balance sheet in the hope that some day, those values will be realized through a higher stock price either by actions of the current management or by a takeover. Also called HIDDEN RESERVES.

HIGH CREDIT
Banking: maximum amount of loans outstanding recorded for a particular customer.
Finance: the highest amount of TRADE CREDIT a particular company has received from a supplier at one time.

HIGH CURRENT INCOME MUTUAL FUND mutual fund with the objective of paying high income to shareholders. Such funds usually take higher risks than more conservative, but lower-yielding funds in order to provide an above-market rate of current yield. For example, JUNK BOND funds buy corporate bonds with below investment grade credit ratings in order to pay higher levels of income to shareholders than would be available from Treasury or high-quality corporate bonds. Another example of a high current income mutual fund is an international bond fund.

HIGH FLYER high-priced and highly speculative stock that moves up sharply over a short period. The stock of unproven high-technology companies might be high flyers, for instance.

HIGH-FREQUENCY TRADING trading, also called "flash" trading, done in microseconds (one-millionth of a second) using supercomputers and making it possible for traders to exploit subtle and obscure market signals and inefficiencies and to earn rebates paid by exchanges for quickly providing shares when needed. The practice attracted attention when it produced huge profits for firms using it in the highly volatile markets of 2007 and 2008. Regulators are concerned that unscrupulous operators could trade ahead of orders and affect prices. Flash-order advocates fear banning high-frequency trading would cause a drop in trading volume of the exchanges.

HIGH-GRADE BOND bond rated triple-A or double-A by Standard & Poor's, Moody's, and other RATING services.

HIGHJACKING Japanese term for a TAKEOVER.

HIGHLY CONFIDENT LETTER letter from an investment banking firm that it is "highly confident" that it will be able to arrange financing for a securities deal. This letter might be used to finance a leveraged buyout or multibillion-dollar takeover offer, for example. The board of directors of the target firm might request a highly confident letter in evaluating whether a proposed takeover can be financed. After the letter has been issued and the deal approved, the investment bankers will attempt to line up financing from banks, private investors, stock and bond offerings, and other sources. Though the investment banker professes to be highly confident he can arrange financing, the letter is not an ironclad guarantee of his ability to do so.

HIGHLY LEVERAGED TRANSACTION (HLT) loan, usually by a bank, to an already highly LEVERAGED COMPANY.

HIGH-PREMIUM CONVERTIBLE DEBENTURE bond with a long-term, high-premium, common stock conversion feature and also offering a fairly competitive interest rate. Premium refers in this case to the difference between the market value of the CONVERTIBLE security and the value at which it is convertible into common stock. Such bonds are designed for bond-oriented portfolios, with the "KICKER," the added feature of convertibility to stock, intended as an inflation hedge.

HIGH RATIO MORTGAGE mortgage loan exceeding 80% of property value.

HIGH WATER MARK POLICY rule followed by most HEDGE FUNDS that managers must earn back account losses before collecting further performance fees. The high water mark is the amount of losses in an account. The underlying rationale is that hedge funds, by definition, should be profitable in any kind of market.

HIGHS stocks that have hit new high prices in daily trading for the current 52-week period. (They are listed as "highs" in daily newspapers.) Technical analysts consider the ratio between new highs and new LOWS in the stock market to be significant for pointing out stock market trends.

HIGH-TECH STOCK stock of companies involved in high-technology fields (computers, Internet related businesses, semiconductors, biotechnology, robotics, electronics). Successful high-tech stocks have above-average earnings growth and therefore typically very volatile stock prices.

HIGH-TICKET ITEMS items with a significant amount of value, such as jewelry and furs. Most standard homeowner's/renter's policies have limits on specific types of high-ticket items. Most policies have a limit of $1,000–$2,000 for all jewelry and furs. To provide appropriate coverage for these items, they should be scheduled separately in the form of a FLOATER or endorsement. Also called *valuables.*

HIGH-YIELD BOND bond that has RATING of BB or lower and that pays a higher yield to compensate for its greater risk. *See also* JUNK BOND.

HISTORICAL COST accounting principle requiring that all financial statement items be based on original cost or acquisition cost. The dollar is assumed to be stable for the period involved.

HISTORICAL EXCHANGE RATE the EXCHANGE RATE in effect at the time an ASSET or LIABILITY was acquired.

HISTORICAL TRADING RANGE price range within which a stock, bond, or commodity has traded since going public. A VOLATILE stock will have a wider trading range than a more conservative stock. Technical analysts see the top of a historical range as the RESISTANCE LEVEL and the bottom as the SUPPORT LEVEL. They consider it highly significant if a security breaks above the resistance level or below the support level. Usually such a move is interpreted to mean that the security will go onto new highs or new lows, thus expanding its historical trading range.

HISTORICAL YIELD yield provided by a mutual fund, typically a money market fund, over a particular period of time. For instance, a money market fund may advertise that its historical yield averaged 5% over the last year.

HISTORIC REHABILITATION LIMITED PARTNERSHIP partnership designed to take advantage of the historic rehabilitation tax credit available in the Internal Revenue Code. These partnerships rehabilitate structures to their original condition, and limited partners receive credits that reduce partners' taxes dollar for dollar. For example, $5,000 in tax credits reduces the amount of taxes due by $5,000. Tax credits of 20% are available if the partnership rehabilitates a historic structure built before 1936. Tax credits of 10% are available for the restoration of buildings built before 1936 that are not certified as historic by the Department of the Interior. Historic rehabilitation limited partnerships can be assembled by local builders and investors, or by professional general partners specializing in such projects.

HIT informally, a significant securities loss or a development having a major impact on corporate profits, such as a large WRITE-OFF. Term is also used in the opposite sense to describe an investing success, similar to a "hit" in show business.

HIT THE BID to accept the highest price offered for a stock. For instance, if a stock's ask price is $50.25 and the current bid price is $50, a seller will hit the bid if he or she accepts $50 a share.

HOCKEY STICK projection showing rapidly rising trend following a flat period and appearing on a graph to have the shape of a hockey stick.

HOLD
Banking: retaining an asset in an account until the item has been collected. For example, a hold can be put on a certain amount of funds in a checking account if a certified check has been issued for that amount.
Securities: maintaining ownership of a stock, bond, mutual fund, or other security for a long period of time. Proponents of the BUY AND HOLD STRATEGY try to buy high-quality securities which they hope will grow in value over many years. By holding for a long time, the investor can delay capital gains taxes until the position is sold many years in the future.

Securities analysts also issue a HOLD recommendation if they are not enthusiastic enough about a security to recommend purchasing it, yet are not pessimistic enough to recommend selling it. However, many analysts who downgrade a stock from a buy to a hold rating are in fact saying that investors should sell the stock, since there are better opportunities to invest elsewhere.

HOLDER OF RECORD owner of a company's securities as recorded on the books of the issuing company or its TRANSFER AGENT as of a particular date. Dividend declarations, for example, always specify payability to holders of record as of a specific date.

HOLDING COMPANY corporation that owns enough voting stock in another corporation to influence its board of directors and therefore to control its policies and management. A holding company need not own a majority of the shares of its subsidiaries or be engaged in similar activities. However, to gain the benefits of tax consolidation, which include tax-free dividends to the parent and the ability to share operating losses, the holding company must own 80% or more of the subsidiary's voting stock.

Among the advantages of a holding company over a MERGER as an approach to expansion are the ability to control sizeable operations with fractional ownership and commensurately small investment; the somewhat theoretical ability to take risks through subsidiaries with liability limited to the subsidiary corporation; and the ability to expand through unobtrusive purchases of stock, in contrast to having to obtain the approval of another company's shareholders.

Among the disadvantages of a holding company are partial multiple taxation when less than 80% of a subsidiary is owned, plus other special state and local taxes; the risk of forced DIVESTITURE (it is easier to force dissolution of a holding company than to separate merged operations); and the risks of negative leverage effects in excessive PYRAMIDING.

The following types of holding companies are defined in special ways and subject to particular legislation: public utility holding company (*see* PUBLIC UTILITY HOLDING COMPANY ACT), BANK HOLDING COMPANY, FINANCIAL HOLDING COMPANY, railroad holding company, and air transport holding company.

HOLDING PERIOD length of time an asset is held by its owner. Capital assets held for more than 12 months qualify for preferential capital gains tax treatment. Assets sold after being held for more than 12 months are subject to a maximum capital gains tax rate of 15%, while assets sold after being held for 12 months or less are taxed at regular income tax rates up to 35%. *See also* ANTICIPATED HOLDING PERIOD; CAPITAL GAIN; INVESTMENT LETTER.

HOLDING THE MARKET entering the market with sufficient buy orders to create price support for a security or commodity, for the purpose of stabilizing a downward trend. The Securities and Exchange Commission views "holding" as a form of illegal manipulation except in the case of stabilization of a new issue cleared with the SEC beforehand.

HOLDRs acronym for holding company depositary receipts, HOLDRs are a proprietary product of Merrill Lynch representing an EXCHANGE-TRADED FUND (ETF) bought and sold in 100-share increments and exchangeable for the underlying stocks at any time. The exchange feature keeps the price of HOLDRs in line with the value of the underlying portfolios (which start with 20 stocks but, being unmanaged, can change through mergers and other developments), since investors can profit on any difference between the two. HOLDRs offer diversification, liquidity, and flexibility.

HOME BANKING service offered by banks allowing consumers and small businesses to perform many banking functions at home through computers, telephones, and cable television links to the bank, thereby providing them with a number of convenience services. Bank customers are able to shift money between accounts, apply for loans and make loan payments, pay bills, check balances, and buy and sell securities, among other services. As home banking becomes easier and more convenient to use, more and more consumers sign up for it. It offers the advantages of privacy, speed, accuracy and the ability to perform transactions at any time. Most banks charge an extra fee for access to home banking services. Home banking does not currently offer the ability to obtain cash, for which customers must still visit a bank teller or automatic teller machine. *See also* ON-LINE BANKING.

HOME EQUITY CONVERSION MORTGAGE (HECM) *see* REVERSE MORTGAGE.

HOME MORTGAGE DISCLOSURE ACT (HMDA) act passed by Congress in 1975 and implemented by the FEDERAL RESERVE BOARD's Regulation C, requiring lending institutions to report data that is used to determine if financial institutions are serving the housing needs of their communities, if discriminatory lending policies are in effect, and if public sector or private sector investments are needed in particular areas. *See also* COMMUNITY REINVESTMENT ACT OF 1977.

HOMEOWNER'S EQUITY ACCOUNT credit line offered by banks, savings and loans, brokerage firms, credit unions and other mortgage lenders allowing a homeowner to tap the built-up equity in his or her home. Such an account is, in effect, a REVOLVING CREDIT second mortgage, which owners can access with the convenience of a check. Most lenders will provide a line of credit up to 70% or 80% of the appraised value of a home, minus any outstanding first mortgage debt. Some home equity lenders will lend as much as 125% of the home's value, although this is risky for both the lender and the borrower; if the borrower defaults, he must come up with 25% more equity than his home is worth to satisfy the loan. When a homeowner receives the loan, a LIEN is automatically placed against the house and removed when the loan is repaid. A homeowner's equity account often carries a lower interest rate than a second mortgage; typically, the rate is tied to the PRIME RATE. Often, a lender will offer a below-market rate at or below the prime rate for some introductory period of six months to a year to entice the borrower. After that, many banks charge between the prime rate and two percentage points over prime for the long term. Most programs require an initial sign-up fee, an annual maintenance fee and additional fees called POINTS when the credit line is tapped. Interest is tax deductible up to $100,000 married filing jointly, no matter how loan proceeds are used. Interest on loans exceeding $100,000 may be deductible if the proceeds are used to purchase investments or for business purposes. Consult a tax specialist for the latest information on what qualifies as a deduction. *See also* SECOND MORTGAGE LENDING.

HOMEOWNER'S INSURANCE POLICY policy protecting a homeowner against property and casualty perils. A basic HO-3 policy (HO stands for homeowner's) is a standard policy and the most comprehensive. It will cover damage to the home from natural causes such as fire, lightning, windstorms, hail, rain, or volcanic eruption. In addition, man-made disasters such as riots, vandalism, damage from cars or airplanes, explosions, and theft will also be reimbursed. Damage caused by falling objects, the weight of ice, snow or sleet, freezing of plumbing, heating or air conditioning systems, electrical discharges, or the rupture of water heating or protective sprinkler systems also fall under the HO-3 policy. Flood, earthquake, war, and nuclear accident are not covered; flood and earthquake insurance can be purchased separately. Other types of homeowner's policies include HO-4 for renters (which also could include co-ops), HO-6 for condominium owners, and HO-8 for older homes. In general, homeowners should try to purchase coverage that will pay for the replacement of damaged or stolen items at current market prices, not at the prices for which those items may have been acquired years ago. There are dollar limits for high-ticket items such as jewelry. A FLOATER or an endorsement, purchased separately, can provide the additional coverage needed.

The average homeowner's or renter's policy provides approximately $100,000 of liability protection. A special policy is required for homeowner's business risk coverage. Home business owners need both property and liability insurance, since the homeowner's policy provides only limited coverage for business equipment, in most cases up to $2,500 for business equipment in the home and $250 away from the home.

Most mortgage lenders require homeowners to obtain adequate insurance coverage before they agree to provide a mortgage.

HOME RUN large gain by an investor in a short period of time. Someone who aims to hit an investment home run may be looking for a potential TAKEOVER target, for example, since takeover bids result in sudden price spurts. Such investing is inherently more risky than the strategy of holding for the long term.

HONG KONG EXCHANGES AND CLEARING LIMITED (HKEx) company formed in 2000 after The Stock Exchange of Hong Kong Limited and the Hong Kong Futures Exchange Limited demutualized and merged with Hong Kong Securities Clearing Company Limited. The HKEx ranks fifth in the world by market capitalization of listed companies. Trading is conducted Monday through Friday. The morning session is from 10 A.M. to 12:30 P.M. and the afternoon session is from 2:30 P.M. to 4 P.M. *www.hkex.com.hk/index.htm.*

HORIZON ANALYSIS method of measuring the discounted cash flow (time-adjusted return) from an investment, using time periods or series *(horizons)* that differ from the investment's contractual maturity. The horizon date might be the end of a BUSINESS CYCLE or some other date determined in the perspective of the investor's overall portfolio requirements. Horizon analysis calculations, which include reinvestment assumptions, permit comparison with alternative investments that is more realistic in terms of individual portfolio requirements than traditional YIELD-TO-MATURITY calculations.

HORIZONTAL MERGER *see* MERGER.

HORIZONTAL PRICE MOVEMENT movement within a narrow price range over an extended period of time. A stock would have a horizontal price movement if it traded between $47 and $51 for more than six months, for instance. Also known as *sideways price movement. See also* FLAT MARKET.

HORIZONTAL PRICE MOVEMENT

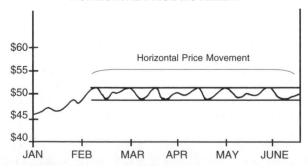

HORIZONTAL SPREAD options strategy that involves buying and selling the same number of options contracts with the same exercise price, but with different maturity dates; also called a CALENDAR SPREAD. For instance, an investor might buy ten XYZ call options with a striking price of $70 and a maturity date of October. At the same time, he would sell ten XYZ call options with the same striking price of $70 but a maturity date of July. The investor hopes to profit by moves in XYZ stock by this means.

HOSPITAL REVENUE BOND bond issued by a municipal or state agency to finance construction of a hospital or nursing home. The latter is then operated under lease by a not-for-profit organization or a for-profit corporation such as Columbia/ HCA. A hospital revenue bond, which is a variation on the INDUSTRIAL DEVELOPMENT BOND, is tax exempt, but there may be limits to the exemption. *See also* REVENUE BOND.

HOSTILE TAKEOVER takeover of a company against the wishes of current management and the board of directors. This takeover may be attempted by another company or by a well-financed RAIDER. If the price offered is high enough, shareholders may vote to accept the offer even if management resists and claims that the company is actually worth even more. If the acquirer raises the price high enough, management may change its attitude, converting the hostile takeover into a friendly one. Management has many weapons at its disposal to fend off a hostile takeover, such as GREENMAIL, POISON PILLS, the SCORCHED EARTH POLICY, and SUICIDE PILLS, among others. Also called *unfriendly takeover. See also* TAKEOVER.

HOT ISSUE newly issued stock that is in great public demand. Hot issue stocks usually shoot up in price at their initial offering, since there is more demand than there are shares available. Special National Association of Securities Dealers rules apply to the distribution of hot issues by the selling investment banking syndicate. *See also* UNDERWRITE.

HOT MONEY investment funds capriciously seeking high, short-term yields. Borrowers attracting hot money, such as banks issuing high-yielding CERTIFICATES OF DEPOSIT, should be prepared to lose it as soon as another borrower offers a higher rate.

HOT STOCK
1. stock that has been stolen.
2. newly issued stock that rises quickly in price. *See also* HOT ISSUE.
3. any stock rising quickly and consistently because it is attracting buyers.

HOUSE
1. firm or individual engaged in business as a broker-dealer in securities and/ or investment banking and related services.
2. nickname for the London Stock Exchange.

HOUSE ACCOUNT account handled at the main office of a brokerage firm or managed by an executive of the firm; in other words, an account distinguished from one that is normally handled by a salesperson in the territory. Ordinarily, a salesperson does not receive a commission on a house account, even though the account may actually be in his or her territory.

HOUSE CALL brokerage house notification that the customer's EQUITY in a MARGIN ACCOUNT is below the maintenance level. If the equity declines below that point, a broker must call the client, asking for more cash or securities.

If the client fails to deliver the required margin, his or her position will be liquidated. House call limits are usually higher than limits mandated by the FINANCIAL INDUSTRY REGULATORY AUTHORITY (FINRA), a self-regulatory group, and the major exchanges with jurisdiction over these rules. Such a margin MAINTENANCE REQUIREMENT is in addition to the initial margin requirements set by REGULATION T of the Federal Reserve Board. *See also* HOUSE MAINTENANCE REQUIREMENT; MARGIN CALL.

HOUSE MAINTENANCE REQUIREMENT internally set and enforced rules of individual broker-dealers in securities with respect to a customer's MARGIN ACCOUNT. House maintenance requirements set levels of EQUITY that must be maintained to avoid putting up additional equity or having collateral sold out. These levels are normally higher than maintenance levels required by the FINANCIAL INDUSTRY REGULATORY AUTHORITY (FINRA) and the stock exchange. *See also* HOUSE CALL; MINIMUM MAINTENANCE.

HOUSE OF ISSUE investment banking firm that underwrites a stock or bond issue and offers the securities to the public. *See also* UNDERWRITE.

HOUSE POOR short of cash because the bulk of your money is tied up in your house. Implication is that without the real estate investment and associated mortgage, you would be financially comfortable.

HOUSE RULES securities industry term for internal rules and policies of individual broker-dealer firms concerning the opening and handling of customers' accounts and the activities of the customers in such accounts. House rules are designed to assure that firms are in comfortable compliance with the requirements of outside regulatory authorities and in most cases are more stringent than the outside regulations. *See also* HOUSE CALL; HOUSE MAINTENANCE REQUIREMENT.

HOUSING AFFORDABILITY INDEX *see* AFFORDABILITY INDEX.

HOUSING AND ECONOMIC RECOVERY ACT OF 2008 legislation passed to address the subprime housing crisis. The Act created a new regulator for the housing-related GSEs: Fannie Mae, Freddie Mac, and the Federal Home Loan Banks. The Federal Housing Finance Agency (FHFA) was granted enhanced powers to establish standards, restrict asset growth, increase enforcement, and put entities into receivership. This agency takes over from the Federal Housing Finance Board and the Office of Federal Housing Enterprise Oversight. The Act also created the Hope For Homeowners program allowing the Federal Housing Authority (FHA) to insure up to $300 billion of distressed homeowners' FHA-insured mortgages. It requires mortgage holders to accept the proceeds of the insured loan as payment in full for all pre-existing indebtedness. The bill includes the FHA Modernization ACT, which increased the FHA loan limit from 95% to 110% of area median home prices up to 150% of the GSE conforming loan limit of $625,000. It required a down payment of at least 3.5% for any FHA loan and prohibited seller-financed down payments and allows down payment assistance from family members. The Act also includes the Secure and Fair Enforcement (SAFE) for Mortgage Licensing Act, which requires states to have a loan originator licensing and registration system in place by August 1, 2009, which provides uniform licensing standards nationwide.

HOUSING AND URBAN DEVELOPMENT, DEPARTMENT OF (HUD) cabinet-level federal agency, founded in 1965, which is responsible for stimulating housing development in the United States. HUD has several programs to subsidize low- and moderate-income housing and urban renewal projects, often through loan guarantees. The GOVERNMENT NATIONAL MORT-GAGE ASSOCIATION (Ginnie Mae), which fosters the growth of the secondary mortgage market, is within HUD.

HOUSING BOND short- or long-term bond issued by a local housing authority to finance short-term construction of (typically) low- or middle-income housing or long-term commitments for housing, plants, pollution control facilities, or similar projects. Such bonds are free from federal income taxes and from state and local taxes where applicable.

Shorter-term bonds sell in $5,000 denominations and have maturities from 18 months to 4 years. They cannot be called (redeemed prior to maturity) and are paid at maturity with the proceeds from Federal Housing Administration-insured loans. Longer-term bonds are typically issued by local authorities under federal agency contracts, thus providing complete safety. Yields are competitive.

Term is also used to describe *mortgage-backed revenue bonds,* municipal bonds that provide financial institutions with the funds to make low-rate mortgage loans, which collateralize and eventually repay the bonds.

HOUSING MARKET INDEX (HMI) a weighted, seasonally-adjusted statistic derived from ratings for present single family sales, single family sales in the next six months, and buyers traffic. The HMI is published by the National Association of Home Builders (NAHB) and is based on a monthly survey sent to NAHB members, who are asked to rate general economic and housing market conditions. The first two components are measured on a scale of "good," "fair," and "poor," and the last one on a scale of "high," "average," and "low." A rating of 50 indicates that the number of positive, or good, responses received from the builders is about the same as the number of negative, or poor, responses. Ratings higher than 50 indicate more positive, or good, responses.

HOUSING STARTS category of residential construction monitored by the Department of Commerce. Housing starts represent the start of construction of a house or apartment building, which means the digging of the foundation. Other categories are housing permits, housing completions, and new home sales. In normal times, residential construction accounts for roughly 3% of GROSS DOMESTIC PRODUCT.

HULBERT RATING rating by Hulbert Financial Digest, a service of Dow Jones Marketwatch (*www.marketwatch.com*) of how well the recommendations of various investment advisory newsletters have performed. The ratings cover performance as far back as 1980, if data are available. The Digest ranks over 180 investment advisory newsletters covering stocks, bonds, mutual funds, futures, and options by tabulating the profits and losses subscribers would have received had they followed the newsletter's advice exactly.

HUMAN CAPITAL skills acquired by a worker through formal education and experience that improve the worker's productivity and increase his or her income.

HUNG UP term used to describe the position of an investor whose stocks or bonds have dropped in value below their purchase price, presenting the problem of a substantial loss if the securities were sold.

HUNKERING DOWN trader's term for working to sell off a big position in a stock.

HURDLE RATE term used in the budgeting of capital expenditures, meaning the REQUIRED RATE OF RETURN in a DISCOUNTED CASH FLOW analysis. If the EXPECTED RATE OF RETURN on an investment is below the hurdle rate, the project is not undertaken. The hurdle rate should be equal to the INCREMENTAL COST OF CAPITAL.

HYBRID ANNUITY contract offered by an insurance company that allows an investor to mix the benefits of both fixed and variable annuities. Also called *combination annuity.* For instance, an annuity buyer may put a portion of his assets in a FIXED ANNUITY, which promises a certain rate of return, and the remainder in a stock or bond fund VARIABLE ANNUITY, which offers a chance for higher return but takes more risk.

HYBRID INVESTMENT OR SECURITY investment vehicle that combines two different kinds of underlying investments. For example, a structured note, which is a form of a bond, may have the interest rate it pays tied to the rise and fall of a commodity's price. Hybrid investments are also called *derivatives.*

HYPERINFLATION *see* INFLATION.

HYPOTHECATION
Banking: pledging property to secure a loan. Hypothecation does not transfer title, but it does transfer the right to sell the hypothecated property in the event of default.
Securities: pledging of securities to brokers as collateral for loans made to purchase securities or to cover short sales, called margin loans. When the same collateral is pledged by the broker to a bank to collateralize a broker's loan, the process is called *rehypothecation.*

I

IBC'S MONEY FUND REPORT AVERAGE *see* IMONEYNET MONEY FUND REPORT AVERAGE.

I/B/E/S INTERNATIONAL INC. provides the I/B/E/S data base, which comprises analysts' estimates of future earnings for thousands of publicly traded companies. I/B/E/S was combined with First Call, a division of THOMSON FINANCIAL.

I-BONDS inflation-indexed SAVINGS BONDS issued by the United States Treasury in eight denominations ranging from $50 to $10,000 with a 30-year maturity. Unlike other inflation-adjusted bonds, but like other savings bonds, the securities, which were introduced in 1998, offer special tax benefits. As long as investors hold their bonds, they may defer paying taxes on their earnings, which are automatically reinvested and added to the principal. Like other Treasury bonds, I-Bonds are exempt from state and local income taxes. If the bond is redeemed to pay for college tuition or other college fees, investors may exclude part or all of the income in calculating their taxes. The payout on the bonds is determined by two rates. A fixed rate, ranging from 3% to 3.5% when the bonds were first introduced, is set by the Treasury Department. The second rate, a rate of inflation, is determined every six months by the Bureau of Labor Statistics to reflect changes in a version of the Consumer Price Index. Some protection against deflation exists in that any decline in the CONSUMER PRICE INDEX (CPI) could eat into the fixed rate, but not affect the underlying principal. *See also* INFLATION INDEXED SECURITIES; TREASURY INFLATION PROTECTED SECURITIES (TIPS).

ICELAND STOCK EXCHANGE (ICEX) established in 1985 as a joint venture of several banks and brokerage firms at the initiative of the Central Bank. In 1999 the exchange became a private company and in 2002 it adopted the Icelandic name Kauphöll Islandshf. In 2006 ICEX was acquired by the OMX Nordic Exchange, which is now part of the NASDAQ OMX Group. Trading has always used electronic systems. The exchange has been a member of the NOREX alliance since 2000, which allows for the cross-listing of stocks on Nordic stock exchanges. In 2003 the exchange listed Faroese bonds, which was a major step toward expanding the market, and in 2007 it listed Faroese equities. The exchange opened an ETF market in 2004. *www.icex.is. See also* NOREX.

IDEM the Italian derivatives market, managed by BORSA ITALIANA. Futures and options are traded on the MIB 30 Index, a capitalization-weighted index based on the 30 most liquid and capitalized stocks listed on the Italian stock market. Futures are traded on all major shares listed on the Italian stock market and several shares listed on Nuovo Mercato, and on the MIDEX Index and the miniFIB, a new contract based on the MIB Index. Trading is electronic, Monday to Friday, from 9 A.M. to 5:30 P.M. *www.borsaitaliana.it. See also* BORSA ITALIANA.

IDENTIFIED SHARES shares of stock or a mutual fund identified as having been bought at a particular price on a particular date. If a shareholder wishes to minimize his tax liability when selling shares, he must identify which shares were bought at what price in order to determine his cost basis. If he has acquired shares over a long period of time, through a CONSTANT DOLLAR PLAN or a DIVIDEND REINVESTMENT PLAN, for example, he will have many shares at many different prices. By identifying the shares with the highest cost basis, he will generally pay lower capital gains taxes than if he identified shares bought at a lower cost. If shares are sold at a loss, the shareholder can pick how large or small a loss he wants to take based on which shares he identifies. In addition, if the identified shares were held for 12 months or more, the investor qualifies for long-term capital gains tax rates. If the identified shares were held for less than 12 months, he will have to pay regular income tax rates on the gain.

ILLEGAL DIVIDEND dividend declared by a corporation's board of directors in violation of its charter or of state laws. Most states, for example, stipulate that dividends be paid out of current income or RETAINED EARNINGS; they prohibit dividend payments that come out of CAPITAL SURPLUS or that would make the corporation insolvent. Directors who authorize illegal dividends may be sued by stockholders and creditors and may also face civil and criminal penalties. Stockholders who receive such dividends may be required to return them in order to meet the claims of creditors.

ILLIQUID
Finance: firm that lacks sufficient CASH FLOW to meet current and maturing obligations.
Investments: not readily convertible into cash, such as a stock, bond, or commodity that is not traded actively and would be difficult to sell at once without taking a large loss. Other assets for which there is not a ready market, and which therefore may take some time to sell, include real estate and collectibles such as rare stamps, coins, or antique furniture.

IMBALANCE OF ORDERS too many orders of one kind—to buy or to sell—without matching orders of the opposite kind. An imbalance usually follows a dramatic event such as a takeover, the death of a key executive, or a government ruling that will significantly affect the company's business. If it occurs before the stock exchange opens, trading in the stock is delayed. If it occurs during the trading day, the specialist suspends trading until enough matching orders can be found to make for an orderly market.

IMF *see* INTERNATIONAL MONETARY FUND.

IMMEDIATE FAMILY parents, brothers, sisters, children, relatives supported financially, father-in-law, mother-in-law, sister-in-law, and brother-in-law. This definition is incorporated in the NATIONAL ASSOCIATION OF SECURITIES DEALERS RULES OF FAIR PRACTICE on abuses of *hot issues* through such practices as FREERIDING and WITHHOLDING. The ruling prohibits the sale of such securities to members of a broker-dealer's own family or to persons buying and selling for institutional accounts and their families.

IMMEDIATE OR CANCEL ORDER order requiring that all or part of the order be executed as soon as the broker enters a bid or offer; the portion not executed is automatically canceled. Such stipulations usually accompany large orders.

IMMEDIATE PAYMENT ANNUITY annuity contract bought with a single payment and with a specified payout plan that starts right away. Payments may be for a specified period or for the life of the annuitant and are usually on a monthly basis. *See also* ANNUITIZE.

IMMUNIZATION *see* DURATION.

IMMUNIZATION STRATEGY bond portfolio management strategy that uses DURATION to eliminate INTEREST RATE RISK. *See also* CONTINGENT IMMUNIZATION.

iMoneyNet MONEY FUND REPORT AVERAGE average for all major taxable and tax-free money market mutual fund yields published weekly for 7- and 30-day simple and compound (assumes reinvested dividends) yields. iMoneyNet also tracks the average maturity of securities in money fund portfolios. A short maturity of about 30 days or less reflects the conviction of funds managers that interest rates will rise, and a long maturity of 60 days or more reflects a sentiment that rates will fall. Investors can compare the yield and average maturity against the industry average to ascertain if their money fund's return is competitive, and how their fund manager's views on the direction of interest rates compares to industry peers. iMoneyNet's Money Fund Report Average is published in major newspapers, including *The Wall Street Journal, The New York Times,* and *Barron's. Barron's* also publishes a list of the 7- and 30-day yields of most major money market mutual funds, along with each fund's net assets and average maturity as compiled by iMoneyNet of Westborough, Massachusetts. Web site: (*www. imoneynet.com*).

IMPAIRED CAPITAL total capital that is less than the stated or par value of the company's CAPITAL STOCK. *See also* DEFICIT NET WORTH.

IMPAIRED CREDIT deterioration in the credit rating of a borrower, which may result in a reduction in the amount of credit made available by lenders. For example, a company may launch a product line that is a failure, and the resulting losses will seriously weaken the company's finances. Concerned lenders may reduce the firm's credit lines as a result. The same process can apply to an individual who has been late paying bills, or in an extreme case, has filed for bankruptcy protection. Also called *adverse credit.*

IMPORT DUTY *see* TARIFF.

IMPUTED INTEREST interest considered to have been paid in effect even though no interest was actually paid. For example, the Internal Revenue Service requires that annual interest be recognized on a ZERO-COUPON SECURITY.

IMPUTED VALUE logical or implicit value that is not recorded in any accounts. Examples: in projecting annual figures, values are imputed for months about which actual figures are not yet available; cash invested unproductively has an imputed value consisting of what it would have earned in a productive investment (OPPORTUNITY COST); in calculating national income, the U.S. Department of Commerce imputes a dollar value for wages and salaries paid in kind, such as food and lodging provided on ships at sea.

INACTIVE ASSET asset not continually used in a productive way, such as an auxiliary generator.

INACTIVE BOND CROWD *see* CABINET CROWD.

INACTIVE POST trading post on the New York Stock Exchange at which inactive stocks are traded in 10-share units rather than the regular 100-share lots. Known to traders as *Post 30. See also* ROUND LOT.

INACTIVE STOCK/BOND security traded relatively infrequently, either on an exchange or over the counter. The low volume makes the security ILLIQUID, and small investors tend to shy away from it.

IN-AND-OUT TRADER one who buys and sells the same security in one day, aiming to profit from sharp price moves. *See also* DAY TRADE.

INCENTIVE FEE compensation for producing above-average results. Incentive fees are common for commodities trading advisers who achieve or top a preset return, as well as for a GENERAL PARTNER in a real estate or oil and gas LIMITED PARTNERSHIP.

INCENTIVE STOCK OPTION (ISO) plan created by the ECONOMIC RECOVERY TAX ACT OF 1981 (ERTA) under which qualifying options are free of tax at the date of grant and the date of exercise. Profits on shares sold after being held at least two years from the date of grant or one year from the date of transfer to the employee are subject to favorable CAPITAL GAINS TAX rates. *See also* QUALIFYING STOCK OPTION.

INCESTUOUS SHARE DEALING buying and selling of shares in each other's companies to create a tax or other financial advantage.

INCOME AVAILABLE FOR FIXED CHARGES *see* FIXED-CHARGE COVERAGE.

INCOME AVERAGING method of computing personal income tax whereby tax is figured on the average of the total of current year's income and that of the three preceding years. According to 1984 U.S. tax legislation, income averaging was used when a person's income for the current year exceeded 140% of the average taxable income in the preceding three years. The TAX REFORM ACT OF 1986 repealed income averaging.

INCOME BOND obligation on which the payment of interest is contingent on sufficient earnings from year to year. Such bonds are traded FLAT—that is, with no accrued interest—and are often an alternative to bankruptcy. *See also* ADJUSTMENT BOND.

INCOME DEPOSIT SECURITY (IDS) first introduced in 2004 and also called an *income participating security (IPS)* and an *enhanced income security (EIS),* an IDS consists of two securities "clipped" together. One is common stock, the other a fixed-rate debt instrument, and the two together produce a blended yield. IDSs are exchange-listed, but the underlying securities cannot be unclipped and traded until a period of time has expired, typically 45 to 90 days after the closing of the offering. Such offerings are priced to reflect a yield based on expected cash flow, which is distributed similarly to a REAL ESTATE INVESTMENT TRUST or other income trust. To ensure that equity and debt are kept separate and interest remains tax-deductible, at least 10% of the equity and 10% of the debt are placed with holders who do not own any IDSs. Companies with predictable cash flows, limited capital expenditure needs, and moderate growth potential are likely issuers.

INCOME DIVIDEND payout to shareholders of interest, dividends, or other income received by a mutual fund. By law, all such income must be distributed to shareholders, who may choose to take the money in cash or reinvest it in more shares of the fund. All income dividends are taxable to shareholders in the year they are received, unless the fund is held in a tax-deferred account such as an IRA or Keogh plan.

INCOME EXCLUSION RULE INCOME TAX rule excluding certain items from taxable income. Personal exclusions include interest on tax-exempt securities, returns of capital, life insurance death benefits, dividends on veterans' life insurance, child support, welfare payments, disability benefits paid by the Veterans Administration, and amounts received from an insurer because of the loss of use of a home. *See also* EXCLUSION.

INCOME INVESTMENT COMPANY management company that operates an income-oriented MUTUAL FUND for investors who value income over growth. These funds may invest in bonds or high-dividend stocks or may write covered call options on stocks. *See also* INVESTMENT COMPANY.

INCOME LIMITED PARTNERSHIP real estate, oil and gas, or equipment leasing LIMITED PARTNERSHIP whose aim is high income, much of which may be taxable. Such a partnership may be designed for tax-sheltered accounts like Individual Retirement Accounts, Keogh plan accounts, or pension plans.

INCOME MUTUAL FUND mutual fund designed to produce current income for shareholders. Some examples of income funds are government, mortgage-backed security, municipal, international, and junk bond funds. Several kinds of equity-oriented funds also can have income as their primary investment objective, such as utilities income funds and equity income funds. All distributions from income funds are taxable in the year received by the shareholder unless the fund is held in a tax-deferred account such as an IRA or Keogh or the distributions come from tax-exempt bonds, such as with a municipal bond fund.

INCOME PARTICIPATING SECURITY (IPS) *see* INCOME DEPOSIT SECURITY (IDS).

INCOME PREFERRED SECURITIES hybrid PREFERRED STOCK issued by special-purpose entities (SPE) organized as corporate subsidiaries, limited partnerships, or trusts, with the proceeds loaned to the parent company. The parent company books the proceeds as deeply SUBORDINATED debt on which it pays tax-deductible interest to the SPE, which pays preferred dividends to the buyers of the securities. Because the parent company, with debt repackaged as equity, gets the best of both worlds, some 70% of all new preferred issues are now income preferred securities, whose yield to investors is normally higher than the prevailing yield on conventional preferred issues. (Corporate investors are not allowed the 70% dividend exclusion, so the investors are largely individuals.) Since the issuer has the option of temporarily deferring dividend payments, the investor may have a tax liability on income allocated but not yet received.

The first hybrid securities of this type to be issued were *Monthly Income Preferred Securities (MIPS)*, which typically have a $25 par value, are NYSE-listed, and make cumulative monthly payments. *Quarterly Income Preferred Securities (QUIPS)* are similarly structured but pay dividends quarterly.

Hybrids of hybrids now include *Monthly Income Debt Securities (MIDS),* which are subordinated debentures with 30–50-year maturities, issued directly by the parent company, which guarantees monthly payments; the quarterly version of MIDS, called *QUIDS*; *Trust Originated Preferred Securities (TOPrS)*, which make quarterly payments guaranteed by the parent company, although they are direct obligations of the trust; and *Quarterly Income Capital Securities (QUICS)*, which are similar to QUIDS. Related, are *Exchangeable Notes,* which, after an initial period and at the company's option, can be exchanged or converted into the issuer's preferred stock.

INCOME PROPERTY real estate bought for the income it produces. The property may be placed in an INCOME LIMITED PARTNERSHIP, or it may be owned by individuals or corporations. Buyers also hope to achieve capital gains when they sell the property.

INCOME SHARES one of two kinds or classes of capital stock issued by a DUAL-PURPOSE FUND or split investment company, the other kind being *capital shares.* Holders of income shares receive dividends from both classes of shares, generated from income (dividends and interest) produced by the portfolio, whereas holders of capital shares receive capital gains payouts on both classes. Income shares normally have a minimum income guarantee, which is cumulative.

INCOMES POLICY controversial anti-inflation approach whereby a government attempts, either through voluntary guidelines or mandatory controls to regulate wage and price levels. The policy was used to control wartime inflation during World War II and the Korean War and was tried in the early 1970s but abandoned when it produced shortages, inferior quality, and burdensome bureaucracy.

INCOME STATEMENT *see* PROFIT AND LOSS STATEMENT.

INCOME STOCK stock paying high and regular dividends to shareholders. Some industries known for income stocks include gas, electric, and telephone utilities; real estate investment trusts; banks; and insurance companies. High-quality income stocks have established a long history of paying dividends, and in many cases have a track record of regularly increasing dividends. All dividends paid to shareholders of income stocks are taxable in the year received unless the stock is held in a tax-deferred account such as an IRA or Keogh plan.

INCOME TAX annual tax on income levied by the federal government and by certain state and local governments. There are two basic types: the personal income tax, levied on incomes of households and unincorporated businesses, and the corporate (or corporation) income tax, levied on net earnings of corporations.

Under present tax law, there are six tax brackets for individual taxpayers: 10%, 15%, 25%, 28%, 33%, and 35%. The level of TAXABLE INCOME for each bracket differs according to filing status (such as married filing jointly, singles, or heads of household) and is revised slightly every year. Long-term CAPITAL GAINS receive preferential tax treatment both for individuals and corporations. Assets held for more than 12 months are taxed at a top rate of 15%, versus a top rate of 35% for short-term gains on assets held for 12 months or less. Because capital gains rates reward taxpayers in a position to take risks, and because LOOPHOLES and TAX SHELTERS enable the wealthiest corporations and individuals to escape the higher tax brackets, the progressiveness of the tax system has often been more theoretical than real. There have been many sweeping changes in the tax code, creating an enormous amount of complexity. In 1998, the INTERNAL REVENUE SERVICE RESTRUCTURING AND REFORM ACT OF 1998 instituted numerous changes in the way the Internal Revenue Service conducts business, including shifting the burden of proof from taxpayers to the IRS in court disputes over the amount of taxes owed by a taxpayer. The progression of changes in the tax code is described in great detail in other *Dictionary* entries, including: ECONOMIC GROWTH AND TAX RELIEF RECONCILIATION ACT OF 2001; ECONOMIC RECOVERY TAX ACT OF 1981 (ERTA); ENERGY TAX INCENTIVES ACT OF 2005; INTERNAL REVENUE SERVICE RESTRUCTURING AND REFORM ACT OF 1998; JOBS AND GROWTH TAX RELIEF RECONCILIATION ACT OF 2003; REVENUE RECONCILIATION ACT OF 1993; MILITARY FAMILY TAX RELIEF ACT OF 2003; TAX EQUITY AND FISCAL RESPONSIBILITY ACT OF 1982 (TEFRA); TAX REFORM ACT OF 1976; TAX REFORM ACT OF 1984; TAX REFORM ACT OF 1986; TAXPAYER RELIEF ACT OF 1997; and the WORKING FAMILIES TAX RELIEF ACT OF 2004.

INCOME TAX REBATE PLAN part of a $168 billion economic stimulus bill proposed by President George W. Bush and enacted February 2008 that eliminated taxes on the first $6,000 of taxable income ($12,000 for couples) and paid out in rebate checks up to $300 for individuals, $1,200 to married couples, and $300 per dependent child. Rebate amounts were reduced for individuals with incomes over $75,000 (couples over $150,000). The bill also raised load limits for Fannie Mae, Freddie Mac, and the FHA. Businesses got an extra 50% deduction for new equipment purchases, and small business got liberalized expensing benefits.

INCOME TRUST investment company holding assets that generate cash flow, which is passed on to unit holders, usually with tax advantages. Real estate and natural resources are asset categories favored by income trusts. *See also* INCOME DEPOSIT SECURITY (IDS); REAL ESTATE INVESTMENT TRUST (REIT).

INCONTESTABILITY CLAUSE provision in a life insurance contract stating that the insurer cannot revoke the policy after it has been in force for one or two years if the policyholder concealed important facts from the company during the application process. For example, a policyholder who stated that he had never had a heart attack, but in fact had experienced one, would still be covered by the policy if the insurance company had not discovered this discrepancy within one or two years. However, if a policyholder lies about his age on the application, the policy's death benefit can be adjusted higher retroactively to account for the insured's true age.

INCORPORATION process by which a company receives a state charter allowing it to operate as a corporation. The fact of incorporation must be acknowledged in the company's legal name, using the word *incorporated,* the abbreviation *inc.,* or other acceptable variations. *See also* ARTICLES OF INCORPORATION.

INCREMENTAL CASH FLOW net of cash outflows and inflows attributable to a corporate investment project.

INCREMENTAL COST OF CAPITAL weighted cost of the additional capital raised in a given period. Weighted cost of capital, also called *composite cost of capital,* is the weighted average of costs applicable to the issues of debt and classes of equity that compose the firm's capital structure. Also called *marginal cost of capital.*

INDEMNIFY agree to compensate for damage or loss. The word is used in insurance policies promising that, in the event of a loss, the insured will be restored to the financial position that existed prior to the loss.

INDENTURE formal agreement, also called a deed of trust, between an issuer of bonds and the bondholder covering such considerations as: (1) form of the bond; (2) amount of the issue; (3) property pledged (if not a debenture issue); (4) protective COVENANTS including any provision for a sinking fund; (5) WORKING CAPITAL and CURRENT RATIO; and (6) redemption rights or call privileges. The indenture also provides for the appointment of a trustee to act on behalf of the bondholders, in accordance with the TRUST INDENTURE ACT OF 1939.

INDEPENDENT AGENT agent representing several insurance companies. The agent is independent from all the companies he or she sells for, and can therefore in theory evaluate different insurance policies objectively. Independent agents pay all their own expenses and keep their own records and earn their income from commissions on the policies they sell. The opposite of an independent agent is a CAPTIVE AGENT, who works exclusively for one company.

INDEPENDENT AUDITOR certified public accountant (CPA) who provides the ACCOUNTANT'S OPINION.

INDEPENDENT BROKER New York Stock Exchange member who executes orders for other floor brokers who have more volume than they can handle, or for firms whose exchange members are not on the floor. Formerly called $2 brokers because of their commission for a round lot trade, independent brokers are compensated by commission brokers with fees that once were fixed but are now negotiable. *See also* GIVE UP.

INDEPENDENT DIRECTOR same as OUTSIDE DIRECTOR.

INDEX statistical composite that measures changes in the economy or in financial markets, often expressed in percentage changes from a base period or from the previous month. For instance, the CONSUMER PRICE INDEX uses 1982–84 as the base period. That index, made up of the prices for key consumer goods and services, moves up and down as the rate of inflation changes. By March 2009 the seasonally adjusted index climbed to over 212, meaning that the basket of goods and services that the index is based on has more than doubled since the base period.

Indices also measure the ups and downs of stock, bond, and commodities markets, reflecting market prices and the number of shares outstanding for the companies in the index. Some well-known indices are the Dow Jones Averages, the New York Stock Exchange Composite Index, the American Stock Exchange Composite Index, the Standard & Poor's 500 Index, the NASDAQ Composite Index, the Russell 2000 Index, and the Value Line Composite Index. Subindices for industry groups such as drugs, railroads, or computers are also tracked. Stock market indices form the basis for trading in INDEX OPTIONS. *See also* INDEXING; STOCK INDICES AND AVERAGES.

INDEX ARBITRAGE *see* ARBITRAGE.

INDEXATION *see* INDEXING, at meaning (2).

INDEX BOND bond whose cash flow is linked to the purchasing power of the dollar or a foreign currency. For example, a bond indexed to the CON-SUMER PRICE INDEX (CPI) would ensure that the bondholder receives real value by making an upward adjustment in the interest rate to reflect higher prices.

INDEX FUND mutual fund that has a portfolio matching that of a broad-based portfolio. This may include the Dow Jones Industrial Average, Standard & Poor's 500 Index, indices of mid- and small-capitalization stocks, foreign stock indices, and bond indices, to name a few. Many institutional and individual investors, especially believers in the EFFICIENT MARKET theory, put money in index funds on the assumption that trying to beat the market averages over the long run is futile, and their investments in these funds will at least keep pace with the index being tracked. In addition, since the cost of managing an index fund is far cheaper than the cost of running an actively managed portfolio, index funds have a built-in cost advantage.

INDEX FUND SHARES a subcategory of EXCHANGE-TRADED FUNDS, representing ownership in equity funds. *See also* INDEX SHARES.

INDEXING
1. weighting one's portfolio to match a broad-based index such as Standard & Poor's so as to match its performance—or buying shares in an INDEX FUND.
2. tying wages, taxes, or other rates to an index. For example, a labor contract may call for indexing wages to the consumer price index to protect against loss of purchasing power in a time of rising inflation.

INDEXING PLUS *see* ENHANCED INDEXING.

INDEX OF LEADING INDICATORS *see* LEADING INDICATORS.

INDEX OPTIONS calls and puts on indexes of stocks. These options are traded on the New York, American, and Chicago Board Options Exchanges, among others. Broad-based indexes cover a wide range of companies and industries, whereas narrow-based indexes consist of stocks in one industry or sector of the economy. Index options allow investors to trade in a particular market or industry group without having to buy all the stocks individually. For instance, someone who thought oil stocks were about to fall could buy a put on the oil index instead of selling short shares in half a dozen oil companies.

INDEX PARTICIPATION *see* BASKET.

INDEX SHARES one of two categories of EXCHANGE-TRADED FUNDS. There are two forms of index shares: PORTFOLIO DEPOSITARY RECEIPTS and INDEX FUND SHARES. Index shares represent ownership in either funds or UNIT INVESTMENT TRUSTS that hold portfolios of common stock that closely track the performance and dividend yield of specific indices—broad market, sector, or international. Investors can buy or sell an entire portfolio of stocks embedded in a single security in the same manner they would buy any shares of common stock. *See also* PORTFOLIO DEPOSITARY RECEIPTS; INDEX FUND SHARES.

INDEX TRACKING STOCK same as INDEX SHARES.

INDICATED DIVIDEND the most recent quarterly dividend multiplied by four (annualized). The indicated dividend is used in the calculation of DIVIDEND YIELD, shown in the column headed YLD in newspaper stock tables.

INDICATED YIELD coupon or dividend rate as a percentage of the current market price. For fixed-rate bonds it is the same as CURRENT YIELD. For common stocks, it is the market price divided into the annual indicated dividend. For preferred stocks, it is the market price divided into the contractual dividend.

INDICATION approximation of what a security's TRADING RANGE (bid and offer prices) will be when trading resumes after a delayed opening or after being halted because of an IMBALANCE OF ORDERS or another reason. Also called *indicated market.*

INDICATION OF INTEREST securities underwriting term meaning a dealer's or investor's interest in purchasing securities that are still *in registration* (awaiting clearance by) the Securities and Exchange Commission. A broker who receives an indication of interest should send the client a preliminary prospectus on the securities. An indication of interest is not a commitment to buy, an important point because selling a security while it is in registration is illegal. *See also* CIRCLE; RESTRICTED.

INDICATOR technical measurement securities market analysts use to forecast the market's direction, such as investment advisory sentiment, volume of stock trading, direction of interest rates, and buying or selling by corporate insiders.

INDIRECT COST AND EXPENSE *see* DIRECT OVERHEAD; FIXED COST.

INDIRECT LABOR COSTS wages and related costs of factory employees, such as inspectors and maintenance crews, whose time is not charged to specific finished products.

INDIVIDUAL RETIREMENT ARRANGEMENT (OR ACCOUNT) (IRA) personal, tax-deferred, retirement account that an employed person can set up, with a deposit limited to $5,000 per year ($10,000 for a married couple filing jointly, whether or not both spouses work). For those 50 or older, additional catch-up contributions of $1,000 are allowed, meaning an annual contribution limit of $6,000. IRAs can be invested in almost every kind of instrument, including stocks, bonds, mutual funds, certificates of deposit, annuities, real estate, and precious metals.

    IRA contributions are deductible regardless of income if neither the taxpayer nor the taxpayer's spouse is covered by a QUALIFIED PLAN OR TRUST. In 2008 a taxpayer covered by a qualified plan could make a full IRA deduction if Modified Adjusted Gross Income (MAGI) was up to $85,000 on a joint return or $53,000 on a single return. Couples with incomes between $85,000 and $105,000, and single taxpayers with incomes between $53,000 and $63,000 were allowed partial deductions. Taxpayers with incomes of $105,000 or more (joint) and $63,000 or more (single) were not allowed deductions, but could make the same contributions (treated as a nontaxable

RETURN OF CAPITAL upon withdrawal) and thus gain the benefit of tax-deferral. Taxpayers who cannot make deductible contributions because of participation in qualified retirement plans may make nondeductible contributions. Withdrawals from IRAs prior to age 59½ are generally subject to a 10% (of principal) penalty tax. Withdrawals after age 59½ are fully taxable if the original contributions generated deductions. If the original contributions were nondeductible, taxes need not be paid on the amount of those contributions. No IRA withdrawals are required until age 70½, when minimum required distributions must be made according to an IRS schedule based on life expectancy.

The 1997 tax act created the ROTH IRA, named after Delaware Republican Senator William V. Roth, Jr., who championed the idea. Individuals can invest up to $5,000 a year ($6,000 if 50 or older) in a Roth IRA, even after reaching the age of 70½. As long as the assets have remained inside the account for five years, all earnings and principal can be withdrawn totally tax-free after age 59½. Participants do not have to take distributions from a Roth IRA starting at age 70½. In fact, they don't have to take distributions at all in their lifetimes, allowing them to pass the assets in the Roth IRA to beneficiaries income-tax-free. Contributors to Roth IRAs do not receive a tax deduction for making the contribution, but the value of tax-free withdrawals often exceeds the tax break from upfront deductions. Roth IRA rules also permit participants to withdraw assets prior to age 59½ without the usual 10% early withdrawal penalty, if they use the money for the purchase of a first home (withdrawals are limited to up to $10,000), or if they become disabled. In 2008 only married couples with MAGIs of less than $159,000 and singles with MAGIs of less than $101,000 could contribute the full amount to Roth IRAs. The amount that could be contributed was phased out for MAGIs between $159,000 and $169,000 for married couples and between $101,000 and $116,000 for singles. No contributions are allowed over these income limits. The tax law allows ROLLOVERS of existing deductible and nondeductible IRA balances into a Roth IRA. Taxpayers who roll over, however, must pay income tax on all previously untaxed contributions and earnings in the year the rollover occurs.

The 1997 tax act also created another form of IRA called the EDUCATION IRA. It allows parents to contribute up to $2,000 per year for each child up to the age of 18. The Education IRA became the COVERDELL EDUCATION SAVINGS ACCOUNT as a result of the ECONOMIC GROWTH AND TAX RELIEF RECONCILIATION ACT OF 2001. *See also* COVERDELL EDUCATION SAVINGS ACCOUNT; EDUCATION IRA; ROTH IRA; SELF-DIRECTED IRA; SIMPLE IRA; SIMPLIFIED EMPLOYEE PENSION (SEP) PLAN.

INDIVIDUAL RETIREMENT ARRANGEMENT (IRA) ROLLOVER provision of the IRA law that enables persons receiving LUMP-SUM payments from their company's pension, profit-sharing, or SALARY REDUCTION PLAN— due to retirement or other termination of employment—to roll over the amount into an IRA investment plan within 60 days. Also, current IRAs may be transferred to other investment options or financial institutions within a 60-day period. Through an IRA rollover, the capital continues to accumulate tax-deferred until time of withdrawal. In order to avoid a 20% withholding by the IRA trustee, assets should be rolled over from one place to another as a *direct transfer*, made by instructing the IRA trustee to transfer the assets directly to another IRA trustee. Tax-free rollovers may only occur once in a one-year period starting on the date of the first distribution. Otherwise, the distribution amount would be subject to regular income tax and a 10% premature distribution penalty. IRA account holders can also take advantage of the rollover rules to borrow funds from their IRAs for a 60-day loan. As long as the money is redeposited within 60 days, there is no tax on the withdrawal, which is considered a tax-free rollover. *See also* ROLLOVER.

INDIVIDUAL TAX RETURN tax return filed by an individual instead of a corporation. The 1040 tax form used by individuals comes in three basic varieties: the 1040EZ basic form, the 1040A short form, and the 1040 long form. Attached to the 1040 are several schedules, including Schedule A for itemized deductions, Schedule B for interest and dividend income, Schedule C for profits and losses from a business, Schedule D for reporting capital gains and losses, Schedule E for supplemental income and losses, Schedule F for profit or loss from farming, Schedule H for household employment taxes, Schedule K-1 for a limited partner's share of gains, losses, and credits, Schedule R for the credit for the elderly or the disabled and Schedule SE for self-employment tax. The 1040PC allows taxpayers to file their tax returns electronically through what is known as an *IRS e-file*. Form 1040X allows taxpayers to amend their return if they discover mistakes in their original filing. Form 1040 ES is designed for taxpayers making quarterly estimated tax payments.

INDONESIA STOCK EXCHANGE traces its roots back to 1912 during the Dutch colonial era. Established under its present name in 2007 by the merger of the Jakarta Stock Exchange and the Surabaya Stock Exchange. An order-driven market and open-auction system, the exchange trades shares, rights, warrants, bonds, and convertible bonds. Trading is Monday through Friday. *www.idx.co.id*.

INDUSTRIAL in stock market vernacular, general, catch-all category including firms producing or distributing goods and services that are not classified as utility, transportation, or financial companies. *See also* STOCK INDICES AND AVERAGES; FORBES 500; FORTUNE 500.

INDUSTRIAL BANK bank owned by an industrial corporation such as General Electric, Pitney Bowes, BMW, and Target that primarily make loans to businesses. They were originally set up to offer loans to factory workers who could not normally qualify for credit. More recently, they make loans to a wide variety of businesses. The banks, most of which are based in Utah, Nevada, and California, are regulated by the states, not supervised by the Federal Reserve. They are barred from offering checking accounts and have no retail branches. Industrial bank's parents are not required to set aside capital reserves like banks supervised by the Fed. Companies that own industrial banks can typically fund their lending operations more cheaply than federally chartered banks relying on insured deposits.

INDUSTRIAL DEVELOPMENT BOND (IDB) type of MUNICIPAL REVENUE BOND issued to finance FIXED ASSETS that are then leased to private firms, whose payments AMORTIZE the debt. IDBs were traditionally tax-exempt to buyers, but under the TAX REFORM ACT OF 1986, large IDB issues ($1 million plus) became taxable effective August 15, 1986, while tax-exempt small issues for commercial and manufacturing purposes were prohibited after 1986 and 1989 respectively. Also, effective August 7, 1986, banks lost their 80% interest deductibility on borrowings to buy IDBs.

INDUSTRIAL PRODUCTION monthly statistic released by the FEDERAL RESERVE BOARD on the total output of all U.S. factories and mines. These numbers are a key ECONOMIC INDICATOR.

INDUSTRIAL REVENUE BOND *see* INDUSTRIAL DEVELOPMENT BOND.

INDUSTRIAL SECTORS groupings of companies that react similarly to given economic conditions. SECTORS can be as broadly defined as producer stocks and *consumer stocks* or specifically defined as sub-sectors. Twelve sectors that have the size, individuality, and representational value to be useful for investment purposes are cyclicals, noncyclicals, basic materials, energy, financial, technology, media and entertainment, utilities, health care, real estate, transportation, and retailers/wholesalers. These have been broken down into one hundred or more sub-sectors representing types of business, such as airlines and chemicals. *See also* SECTOR ROTATION; SPECIAL-IZED MUTUAL FUND.

INEFFICIENCY IN THE MARKET failure of investors to recognize that a particular stock or bond has good prospects or may be headed for trouble. According to the EFFICIENT MARKET theory, current prices reflect all knowledge about securities. But some say that those who find out about securities first can profit by exploiting that information; stocks of small, little-known firms with a large growth potential most clearly reflect the market's inefficiency, they say.

INELASTIC DEMAND OR SUPPLY *see* ELASTICITY OF DEMAND OR SUPPLY.

IN ESCROW *see* ESCROW.

INFANT INDUSTRY ARGUMENT case made by developing sectors of the economy that their industries need protection against international competition while they establish themselves. In response to such pleas, the government may enact a TARIFF or import duty to stifle foreign competition. The infant industry argument is frequently made in developing nations that are trying to lessen their dependence on the industrialized world. In Brazil, for example, such infant industries as automobile production argue that they need protection until their technological capability and marketing prowess are sufficient to enable competition with well-established foreigners.

INFLATION rise in the prices of goods and services, as happens when spending increases relative to the supply of goods on the market—in other words, too much money chasing too few goods. Moderate inflation is a common result of economic growth. Hyperinflation, with prices rising at 100% a year or more, causes people to lose confidence in the currency and put their assets in hard assets like real estate or gold, which usually retain their value in inflationary times. *See also* COST-PUSH INFLATION; DEMAND-PULL INFLATION.

INFLATION ACCOUNTING showing the effects of inflation in financial statements. The Financial Accounting Standards Board (FASB) requires major companies to supplement their traditional financial reporting with information showing the effects of inflation. The ruling applies to public companies having inventories and fixed assets of more than $125 million or total assets of more than $1 billion.

INFLATION HEDGE investment designed to protect against the loss of purchasing power from inflation. Traditionally, gold and real estate have a reputation as good inflation hedges, though growth in stocks also can offset inflation in the long run. Money market funds, which pay higher yields as interest rates rise during inflationary times, can also be a good inflation hedge. In the case of hyperinflation, hard assets such as precious metals and real estate are normally viewed as inflation hedges, while the value of paper-based assets such as stocks, bonds, and currency erodes rapidly.

INFLATION-INDEXED SECURITIES bonds or notes that guarantee a return that beats INFLATION if held to maturity. Also applied to shares in mutual funds that hold such securities. Inflation-indexed Treasury securities were introduced in 1997 in 10-year maturities and were subsequently issued as 5-year notes. Similar offerings followed by issuers such as the Tennessee Valley Authority and the Federal Home Loan Bank. In April 1998, the first 30-year inflation-indexed Treasury bonds were issued. Inflation-indexed Treasuries offer a fixed rate of return, as well as a fluctuating rate of return that matches inflation. The fixed portion is paid out as INTEREST, while the indexed portion is represented by an annual adjustment of PRINCIPAL. For example, a $1,000 inflation-indexed Treasury is issued at auction with a 3.5% INTEREST RATE and inflation that year turns out to be 3%. The 3.5% interest on $1,000 would be paid out and, at the end of the year, the inflation rate would adjust the principal, bringing it to $1,030. The following year, the fixed 3.5% interest rate would be applied to the new principal of $1,030 and the principal would again be adjusted according to that year's inflation rate. With low inflation prevailing in the late 90s, anti-inflation securities met a lackluster reception, although longer-term bonds were in somewhat greater demand. Chief drawbacks are the prospect of DEFLATION, a lack of LIQUIDITY, and the fact that the inflation adjustment is taxable annually but not paid out until maturity. *See also* I-BONDS; TREASURY INFLATION PROTECTED SECURITIES (TIPS).

INFLATION RATE rate of change in prices. Two primary U.S. indicators of the inflation rate are the CONSUMER PRICE INDEX and the PRODUCER PRICE INDEX, which track changes in prices paid by consumers and by producers. The rate can be calculated on an annual, monthly, or other basis.

INFLATION RISK *see* PURCHASING POWER RISK; RISK.

INFLEXIBLE EXPENSES *see* FLEXIBLE EXPENSES.

INFORMATION RATIO variation of the SHARPE RATIO that measures the consistency of a portfolio manager's performance. It is calculated by taking the average EXCESS RETURN and dividing by the STANDARD DEVIATION of the excess return.

INFRASTRUCTURE a nation's basic system of transportation, communication, and other aspects of its physical plant. Building and maintaining road, bridge, sewage, and electrical systems provides millions of jobs nationwide. For developing countries, building an infrastructure is a first step in economic development.

INGOT bar of metal. The Federal Reserve System's gold reserves are stored in ingot form. Individual investors may take delivery of an ingot of a precious metal such as gold or silver or may buy a certificate entitling them to a share in an ingot.

INHERITANCE part of an estate acquired by an HEIR.

INHERITANCE TAX *see* ESTATE TAX.

INHERITANCE TAX RETURN state counterpart to the federal ESTATE TAX return, required of the executor or administrator to determine the amount of state tax due on the inheritance.

INITIAL MARGIN amount of cash or eligible securities required to be deposited with a broker before engaging in margin transactions. A margin transaction is one in which the broker extends credit to the customer in a margin account. Under REGULATION T of the Federal Reserve Board, the initial margin is currently 50% of the purchase price when buying eligible stock or convertible bonds or 50% of the proceeds of a short sale. *See also* MAINTENANCE REQUIREMENT; MARGIN CALL; MARGIN REQUIREMENT; MARGIN SECURITY.

INITIAL PUBLIC OFFERING (IPO) corporation's first offering of stock to the public. IPO's are almost invariably an opportunity for the existing investors and participating venture capitalists to make big profits, since for the first time their shares will be given a market value reflecting expectations for the company's future growth. *See also* HOT ISSUE.

INITIATE COVERAGE *see* COVERAGE INITIATED.

INJUNCTION court order instructing a defendant to refrain from doing something that would be injurious to the plaintiff, or face a penalty. The usual procedure is to issue a temporary restraining order, then hold hearings to determine whether a permanent injunction is warranted.

IN PLAY stock affected by TAKEOVER rumors or activities.

INSIDE INFORMATION corporate affairs that have not yet been made public. The officers of a firm would know in advance, for instance, if the company was about to be taken over, or if the latest earnings report was going to differ significantly from information released earlier. Under Securities and Exchange Commission rules, an INSIDER is not allowed to trade on the basis of such information.

INSIDE MARKET bid or asked quotes between dealers trading for their own inventories. Distinguished from the retail market, where quotes reflect the prices that customers pay to dealers. Also known as *inter-dealer market; wholesale market.*

INSIDER person with access to key information before it is announced to the public. Usually the term refers to directors, officers, and key employees, but the definition has been extended legally to include relatives and others in a position to capitalize on INSIDE INFORMATION. Insiders are prohibited from trading on their knowledge.

INSIDER TRADING practice of buying and selling shares in a company's stock by that company's management or board of directors, or by a holder of more than 10% of the company's shares. Managers may trade their company's stock as long as they disclose their activity within ten days of the close of the month within the time the transactions took place. However, it is illegal for insiders to trade based on their knowledge of material corporate developments that have not been announced publicly. Developments that would be considered *material* include news of an impending takeover, introduction of a new product line, a divestiture, a key executive appointment, or other news that could affect the company's stock positively or negatively. Insider trading laws have been extended to other people who have knowledge of these developments but who are not members of management, including investment bankers, lawyers, printers of financial disclosure documents, or relatives of managers and executives who learn of these material developments.

INSIDER TRADING AND SECURITIES FRAUD ENFORCEMENT ACT OF 1988 expanded the coverage of the ITSA to include the punishment of employees who fail to fulfill their obligation as "controlling persons" to prevent their employees from becoming involved in INSIDER TRADING.

INSIDER TRADING SANCTIONS ACT OF 1984 (ITSA) amendment to the SECURITIES EXCHANGE ACT OF 1934 that gave the SEC the authority to ask the courts to impose penalties on illegal traders and on those who pass on private information to third parties.

INSOLVENCY inability to pay debts when due. *See also* BANKRUPTCY; CASH FLOW; SOLVENCY.

INSTALLMENT SALE
In general: sale made with the agreement that the purchased goods or services will be paid for in fractional amounts over a specified period of time.
Securities: transaction with a set contract price, paid in installments over a period of time. Gains or losses are generally taxable on a prorated basis.

INSTINET GROUP through affiliates, this is the largest global electronic agency securities broker and has been providing investors with electronic trading solutions and execution services for 40 years. It operates two major businesses through Instinet, LLC, The Institutional Broker, and Inet ATS, Inc., the electronic marketplace. Inet represents the consolidation of the order flow of the former Instinet ECN and former Island ECN, providing its U.S. broker-dealer customers one of the largest liquidity pools in NASDAQ-listed securities. In 2005 Instinet Group was acquired by NASDAQ and is now part of NASDAQ OMX. *See also* ELECTRONIC COMMUNICATIONS NETWORK.

INSTITUTE FOR SUPPLY MANAGEMENT (ISM) Tempe, Arizona-based not-for-profit association founded in 1916 and formerly known as the National Association of Purchasing Management (NAPM). Through various resources and 180 affiliated organizations, ISM offers a wide range of educational products and programs to more than 48,000 purchasing and supply management professionals. Its monthly publication, "Inside Supply Management" forecasts economic trends for the nonmanufacturing sector.

INSTITUTIONAL BROKER broker who buys and sells securities for banks, mutual funds, insurance companies, pension funds, or other institutional clients. Institutional brokers deal in large volumes of securities and generally charge their customers lower per-unit commission rates than individuals pay.

INSTITUTIONAL INVESTOR organization that trades large volumes of securities. Some examples are mutual funds, banks, insurance companies, pension funds, labor union funds, corporate profit-sharing plans, and college endowment funds. Typically, upwards of 70% of the daily trading on the New

York Stock Exchange is on behalf of institutional investors. *See also* QUALIFIED INSTITUTIONAL INVESTOR.

INSTITUTIONAL SHAREHOLDER SERVICES (ISS) leading provider of PROXY voting and CORPORATE GOVERNANCE services. ISS serves more than 1,500 institutional and corporate clients worldwide with its core businesses— analyzing proxies and issuing informed research and objective vote recommendations for more than 33,000 companies across 115 markets worldwide.

INSTRUMENT legal document in which some contractual relationship is given formal expression or by which some right is granted—for example, notes, contracts, agreements. *See also* NEGOTIABLE INSTRUMENT.

INSTRUMENTALITY federal agency whose obligations, while not direct obligations of the U.S. Government, are sponsored or guaranteed by the government and backed by the FULL FAITH AND CREDIT of the government. Well over 100 series of notes, certificates, and bonds have been issued by such instrumentalities as Federal Home Loan Bank, and Student Loan Marketing Association.

INSURABILITY conditions under which an insurance company is willing to insure a risk. Each insurance company applies its own standards based on its own underwriting criteria. For example, some life insurance companies do not insure people with high-risk occupations such as stuntmen or firefighters, while other companies consider these people insurable, though the premiums they must pay are higher than for those in low-risk professions.

INSURABLE INTEREST relationship between an insured person or property and the potential beneficiary of the policy. For example, a wife has an insurable interest in her husband's life, because she would be financially harmed if he were to die. Therefore, she could receive the proceeds of the insurance policy if he were to die while the policy was in force. If there is no insurable interest, an insurance company will not issue a policy.

INSURANCE system whereby individuals and companies that are concerned about potential hazards pay premiums to an insurance company, which reimburses them in the event of loss. The insurer profits by investing the premiums it receives. Some common forms of insurance cover business risks, automobiles, homes, boats, workers' compensation, and health. Life insurance guarantees payment to the beneficiaries when the insured person dies. In a broad economic sense, insurance transfers risk from individuals to a larger group, which is better able to pay for losses.

INSURANCE AGENT representative of an insurance company who sells the firm's policies. CAPTIVE AGENTS sell the policies of only one company, while INDEPENDENT AGENTS sell the policies of many companies. Agents must be licensed to sell insurance in the states where they solicit customers.

INSURANCE BROKER independent broker who searches for the best insurance coverage at the lowest cost for the client. Insurance brokers do not work for insurance companies, but for the buyers of insurance products. They constantly are comparing the merits of competing insurance companies to find the best deal for their customers.

INSURANCE CLAIM request for payment from the insurance company by the insured. For example, a homeowner files a claim if he or she suffered damage because of a fire, theft, or other loss. In life insurance, survivors submit a claim when the insured dies. The insurance company investigates the claim and pays the appropriate amount if the claim is found to be legitimate, or denies the claim if it determines the loss was fraudulent or not covered by the policy.

INSURANCE DIVIDEND money paid to cash value life insurance policyholders with participating policies, usually once a year. Dividend rates are based on the insurance company's mortality experience, administrative expenses, and investment returns. Lower mortality experience (the number of policyholders dying) and expenses, combined with high investment returns, will increase dividends. Technically, dividends are considered a return of the policyholder's premiums, and are thus not considered taxable income by the IRS. Policyholders may choose to take these dividends in cash or may purchase additional life insurance.

INSURANCE POLICY insurance contract specifying what risks are insured and what premiums must be paid to keep the policy in force. Policies also spell out DEDUCTIBLES and other terms. Policies for life insurance specify whose life is insured and which beneficiaries will receive the insurance proceeds. HOMEOWNER'S INSURANCE POLICIES specify which property and casualty perils are covered. *Health insurance policies* detail which medical procedures, drugs, and devices are reimbursed. *Auto insurance policies* describe the conditions under which car owners will be covered in case of accidents, theft, or other damage to their cars. *Disability policies* specify the qualifying conditions of disability and how long payments will continue. *Business insurance policies* describe which liabilities are reimbursable. The policy is the written document that both insured and insurance company refer to when determining whether or not a claim is covered.

INSURANCE PREMIUM payment made by the insured in return for insurance protection. Premiums are set based on the probability of risk of loss and competitive pressures with other insurers. An insurance company's actuary will figure out the expected loss ratio on a particular class of customers, and then individual applicants will be evaluated based on whether they present higher or lower risks than the class as a whole. If a policyholder does not pay the premium, the insurance or policy may lapse. If the policy is a cash value policy, the policyowner can choose to take a paid-up insurance policy with a lower face value amount or an extended term policy.

INSURANCE SETTLEMENT payment of proceeds from an insurance policy to the insured under the terms of an insurance contract. Insurance settlements may be either in the form of one lump-sum payment or a series of payments.

INSURED individual, group, or property that is covered by an INSURANCE POLICY. The policy specifies exactly which perils the insured is indemnified against. The insured may be a particular individual, such as someone covered by a life insurance policy. It may be a group of people, such as those covered by a group life insurance policy purchased by a company on behalf of its employees. The insured may also refer to property, such as a house and its possessions which are covered by a HOMEOWNER'S INSURANCE POLICY.

INSURED ACCOUNT account at a bank, savings and loan association, credit union, or brokerage firm that belongs to a federal or private insurance organization. Bank accounts are insured by the DEPOSIT INSURANCE FUND (DIF) administered by the FEDERAL DEPOSIT INSURANCE CORPORATION (FDIC). In 2005 Congress raised the federal deposit insurance level from $100,000 to $250,000 on retirement accounts and gave the FDIC the option to increase insurance ceilings on regular bank accounts from $100,000 by $10,000 a year, based on inflation, every five years thereafter starting April 1, 2010. Credit union accounts are insured by the National Credit Union Administration. In 2008 Congress passed the Emergency Economic Stabilization Act that temporarily increased the basic limit on deposit insurance for all ownership categories from $100,000 to $250,000. Brokerage accounts are insured by the SECURITIES INVESTOR PROTECTION CORPORATION. Such insurance protects depositors against loss in the event that the institution becomes insolvent. Federal insurance systems were set up in the 1930s, after bank failures threatened the banking system with collapse.

INSURED BONDS municipal bonds that are insured against default by a MUNICIPAL BOND INSURANCE company. The company pledges to make all interest and principal payments when due if the issuer of the bonds defaults on its obligations. In return, the bond's issuer pays a premium to the insurance company. Insured bonds usually trade based on the credit rating of the insurer rather than the rating of the underlying issuer, since the insurance company is ultimately at risk for the repayment of principal and interest. Insured bonds will pay slightly lower yields, because of the cost of the insurance protection, than comparable noninsured bonds. Some of the major municipal bond insurance firms include MBIA and AMBAC Indemnity Corporation.

INTANGIBLE ASSET right or nonphysical resource that is presumed to represent an advantage to the firm's position in the marketplace. Such assets include copyrights, patents, TRADEMARKS, goodwill, computer programs, capitalized advertising costs, organization costs, licenses, LEASES, FRANCHISES, exploration permits, and import and export permits.

INTANGIBLE COST tax-deductible cost. Such costs are incurred in drilling, testing, completing, and reworking oil and gas wells—labor, core analysis, fracturing, drill stem testing, engineering, fuel, geologists' expenses; also abandonment losses, management fees, delay rentals, and similar expenses.

INTELLECTUAL PROPERTY INTANGIBLE ASSETS representing ideas and knowledge that can be protected by copyright, patent, or trademark.

INTERBANK RATE *see* LONDON INTERBANK OFFERED RATE (LIBOR).

INTERCOMMODITY SPREAD spread consisting of a long position and a short position in different but related commodities—for example, a long position in gold futures and a short position in silver futures. The investor hopes to profit from the changing price relationship between the commodities.

INTERCONTINENTAL EXCHANGE (ICE) established in 2000 by leading energy companies and global banks as an electronic marketplace for energy commodities. It operates regulated global futures exchanges, as well as markets for agricultural, energy, equity index, and currency contracts. In

2001 ICE acquired the International Petroleum Exchange, now called ICE Futures Europe. In 2007 ICE acquired the New York Board of Trade, now called ICE Futures U.S.

INTERDELIVERY SPREAD futures or options trading technique that entails buying one month of a contract and selling another month in the same contract—for instance, buying a June wheat contract and simultaneously selling a September wheat contract. The investor hopes to profit as the price difference between the two contracts widens or narrows.

INTEREST
  1. cost of using money, expressed as a rate per period of time, usually one year, in which case it is called an annual rate of interest.
  2. share, right, or title in property.

INTEREST COVERAGE *see* FIXED-CHARGE COVERAGE.

INTEREST DEDUCTION DEDUCTION allowable for certain types of interest expense, such as for interest on a home mortgage or interest on a MARGIN ACCOUNT.

INTEREST-ONLY LOAN form of loan where the only current obligation is interest and where repayment of principal is deferred.

INTEREST OPTION insurance policyholder's choice to reinvest dividends with the insurer to earn a guaranteed rate of interest. A beneficiary may also reinvest proceeds to earn interest.

INTEREST RATE rate of interest charged for the use of money, usually expressed at an annual rate. The rate is derived by dividing the amount of interest by the amount of principal borrowed. For example, if a bank charged $10 per year in interest to borrow $100, they would be charging a 10% interest rate. Interest rates are quoted on bills, notes, bonds, credit cards, and many kinds of consumer and business loans.

INTEREST-RATE FUTURES CONTRACT futures contract based on a debt security or inter-bank deposit. In theory, the buyer of a bond futures contract agrees to take delivery of the underlying bonds when the contract expires, and the contract seller agrees to deliver the debt instrument. However, most contracts are not settled by delivery, but instead are traded out before expiration. The value of the contract rises and falls inversely to changes in interest rates. For example, if Treasury bond yields rise, futures contracts on Treasury bonds will fall in price. Conversely, when yields fall, Treasury bond futures prices rise. There are many kinds of interest rate futures contracts, including those on Treasury bills, notes, and bonds; Government National Mortgage Association (GNMA) mortgage-backed securities; municipal bonds; and inter-bank deposits such as Eurodollars. Speculators believing that interest rates are about to rise or fall trade these futures. Also, companies with exposure to fluctuations in interest rates, such as brokerage firms, banks, and insurance companies, may use these contracts to HEDGE their holdings of Treasury bonds and other debt instruments or their costs of future borrowings. For a list of interest rate futures contracts, *see* SECURITIES AND COMMODITIES EXCHANGES.

INTEREST-RATE OPTIONS CONTRACT options contract based on an underlying debt security. Options, unlike futures, give their buyers the right, but not the obligation, to buy the underlying bond at a fixed price before a specific date in the future. Option sellers promise to sell the bonds at a set price anytime until the contract expires. In return for granting this right, the option buyer pays a premium to the option seller. Yield-based calls become more valuable as yields rise, and puts become more valuable as yields decline. There are interest rate options on Treasury bills, notes, and bonds; GNMA mortgage-backed securities; certificates of deposit; municipal bonds; and other interest-sensitive instruments. For a complete list of these contracts, *see* SECURITIES AND COMMODITIES EXCHANGES.

INTEREST RATE PARITY *see* COVERED INTEREST ARBITRAGE.

INTEREST-RATE RISK RISK that changes in interest rates will adversely affect the value of an investor's securities portfolio. For example, an investor with large holdings in long-term bonds and utilities has assumed a significant interest-rate risk, because the value of those bonds and utility stocks will fall if interest rates rise. Investors can take various precautionary measures to HEDGE their interest-rate risk, such as buying INTEREST-RATE FUTURES or INTEREST-RATE OPTIONS CONTRACTS.

INTEREST-SENSITIVE INSURANCE POLICY cash value life insurance with dividend rates tied to the fluctuations in interest rates. For example, holders of UNIVERSAL LIFE INSURANCE policies will be credited with a greater increase in cash values when interest rates rise and a slower rate of increase in cash values when interest rates fall.

INTEREST-SENSITIVE STOCK stock of a firm whose earnings change when interest rates change, such as a bank or utility, and which therefore tends to go up or down on news of rate movements.

INTERIM DIVIDEND DIVIDEND declared and paid before annual earnings have been determined, generally quarterly. Most companies strive for consistency and plan quarterly dividends they are sure they can afford, reserving changes until fiscal year results are known.

INTERIM FINANCING temporary, short-term loan made conditional on a TAKEOUT by intermediate or long-term financing. Also called *bridge loan* financing.

INTERIM LOAN *see* CONSTRUCTION LOAN.

INTERIM STATEMENT financial report covering only a portion of a fiscal year. Public corporations supplement the annual report with quarterly statements informing shareholders of changes in the balance sheet and income statement, as well as other newsworthy developments.

INTERLOCKING DIRECTORATE membership on more than one company's board of directors. This is legal so long as the companies are not competitors. Consumer activists often point to interlocking directorates as an element in corporate conspiracies. The most flagrant abuses were outlawed by the Clayton Anti-Trust Act of 1914.

INTERMARKET SPREAD *see* INTERDELIVERY SPREAD.

INTERMARKET SURVEILLANCE INFORMATION SYSTEM (ISIS) DATABASE sharing information provided by the major stock exchanges in the United States. It permits the identification of CONTRA BROKERS and aids in preventing violations.

INTERMARKET TRADING SYSTEM (ITS) computer system that links the New York, American, Boston, Chicago, National, Pacific, and Philadelphia stock exchanges, the Chicago Board Options Exchange, and the NASDAQ. A specialist (or MARKET MAKER) at one exchange may direct an order to another exchange where the quote is better by sending the order through the electronic workstation. A transaction that is accepted at the other exchange is analogous to an electronic handshake and constitutes a contract. In recent times, ITS has come under criticism for being out of date and no longer needed in the wake of regulatory changes.

INTERMEDIARY person or institution empowered to make investment decisions for others. Some examples are banks, savings and loan institutions, insurance companies, brokerage firms, mutual funds, and credit unions. These specialists are knowledgeable about investment alternatives and can achieve a higher return than the average investor can. Furthermore, they deal in large dollar volumes, have lower transaction costs, and can diversify their assets easily. Also called *financial intermediary*.

INTERMEDIATE TERM period between the short and long term, the length of time depending on the context. Stock analysts, for instance, mean 6 to 12 months, whereas bond analysts most often mean 3 to 10 years.

INTERMEDIATION placement of money with a financial INTERMEDIARY like a broker or bank, which invests it in bonds, stocks, mortgages, or other loans, money-market securities, or government obligations so as to achieve a targeted return. More formally called *financial intermediation*. The opposite is DISINTERMEDIATION, the withdrawal of money from an intermediary.

INTERNAL AUDITOR employee of a company who examines records and procedures to ensure against fraud and to make certain board directives and management policies are being properly executed.

INTERNAL CONTROL method, procedure, or system designed to promote efficiency, assure the implementation of policy, and safeguard assets.

INTERNAL EXPANSION asset growth financed out of internally generated cash—usually termed INTERNAL FINANCING—or through ACCRETION or APPRECIATION. *See also* CASH EARNINGS.

INTERNAL FINANCING funds produced by the normal operations of a firm, as distinguished from external financing, which includes borrowings and new equity. *See also* INTERNAL EXPANSION.

INTERNAL RATE OF RETURN (IRR) discount rate at which the present value of the future cash flows of an investment equal the cost of the investment. When the net present values of cash outflows (the cost of the investment) and cash inflows (returns on the investment) equal zero, the rate of discount being used is the IRR. When IRR is greater than the required return—called the hurdle rate in capital budgeting—the investment is acceptable.

INTERNAL REVENUE CODE blanket term for complexity of statutes comprising the federal TAX law.

INTERNAL REVENUE SERVICE (IRS) U.S. agency charged with collecting nearly all federal taxes, including personal and corporate income taxes, social security taxes, and excise and gift taxes. Major exceptions include taxes having to do with alcohol, tobacco, firearms, and explosives, and customs duties and tariffs. The IRS administers the rules and regulations that are the responsibility of the U.S. Department of the Treasury and investigates and prosecutes (through the U.S. Tax Court) tax illegalities.

INTERNAL REVENUE SERVICE RESTRUCTURING AND REFORM ACT OF 1998 legislation designed to reform the Internal Revenue Service, lower the holding period for CAPITAL GAINS, and make various technical corrections in the TAXPAYER RELIEF ACT OF 1997. Some of the major provisions of law, which was enacted in the summer of 1998, include:

1. **Reduction in the capital gains holding period:** Under the Taxpayer Relief Act of 1997, the holding period to qualify for preferential long-term 20% (10% for those in the 15% tax bracket) capital gains tax rates had been raised from 12 to 18 months. This law lowered the holding period back to 12 months, effective retroactively to January 1, 1998.

2. **Restructuring the Internal Revenue Service:** The IRS Commissioner was instructed to modify the organization and governance of the agency by replacing the National-Regional-District structure with operating units to serve particular groups of taxpayers such as individuals, small businesses, big businesses, and tax-exempt organizations. In addition, the Act created an independent Oversight Board to supervise strategic IRS plans and modernization. The National Taxpayer Advocate was made independent of IRS control, now reporting directly to the Treasury Secretary. Local Taxpayer Advocates will help taxpayers resolve disputes separate from IRS examination, collection, and appeals functions.

3. **Taxpayer protections and rights:** Several sections of the law were designed to help taxpayers in disputes with the IRS during the audit and collection process:

   Shift in burden of proof: The burden of proof shifts from the taxpayer to the IRS in any court proceeding on income, gift, estate, or generation-skipping tax liability on factual issues. This applies only if the taxpayer introduces credible evidence on factual issues, maintains records and substantiates claims, and cooperates with reasonable IRS requests for meetings, interviews, witnesses, information, and documents. These rules apply to all court proceedings arising from audits after the Act was signed into law in July 1998. It does not apply to court proceedings started before that date. The burden of proof remains on corporations, trusts, and partnerships with a net worth over $7 million.

   Confidentiality privilege: The Act extends the existing attorney-client privilege of confidentiality to non-lawyers who are authorized to practice before the IRS, such as accountants or enrolled agents. This privilege may be asserted in any noncriminal tax proceeding before the IRS or federal courts.

   Innocent spouse relief: Spouses who become divorced, legally separated, or live apart for at least 12 months are entitled to relief from tax liabilities if their former mates made tax mistakes without their knowledge. Spouses may elect to make a separate-liability claim if the taxes paid were understated as late as two years after the IRS has initiated collection activities. The IRS also must inform taxpayers of their joint and several liability and innocent spouse rights.

   Liberalizes installment agreements and offers-in-compromise: The Act makes offers-in-compromise and installment agreements more flexible and accessible to taxpayers. The IRS is directed to try to negotiate deals with taxpayers instead of battling them in drawn-out court proceedings. If the taxpayer owes $10,000 or less, the IRS is required to allow the tax liability to be paid in installments.

Increases safeguards against IRS collection abuses: The Act imposes a list of "due-process" procedures the IRS must follow as it attempts to collect taxes. For example, taxpayers can request a hearing before Tax Court before property is seized and they can appeal IRS liens more easily. Higher dollar amounts were instituted for property that is exempt from liens and levies. The IRS must follow fair debt collection practices imposed on private-sector collection agencies, such as the prohibition against late-night calls to taxpayers.

Interest and penalty relief: The Act suspends interest and time-related penalties if the IRS does not provide appropriate notice of tax liability to a taxpayer within 18 months after a timely return is filed. In addition, taxpayers are entitled to a 0% interest rate when outstanding overpayments and underpayments of income and self-employment taxes are equal. The interest rate paid on refunds was raised to the same rate as the underpayment interest rate.

4. **Electronic filing incentives:** The Act encourages more filing of returns electronically, with the goal of limiting paper returns to 20% of all returns by the year 2007. By 2002, taxpayers who prepare their returns electronically but send a printout to the IRS will be required to file electronically. Those who file information returns electronically after 1999 get an extra month to file, from February 28 under the old law to March 31 under the new rules.

5. **Limit the tax benefits of "paired-share" REITs:** A small number of Real Estate Investment Trusts, called "paired-share" REITs, had been taking advantage of a tax loophole allowing them to put the revenues from operating businesses through their tax-sheltered REIT structures. This practice was curtailed.

6. **Changes to Roth IRA rules:** Several changes were made to clarify regulations related to the Roth IRA, which was created in the TAXPAYER RELIEF ACT OF 1997. For example, those who convert to Roth IRAs from regular IRAs may elect to recognize all income in the year of conversion rather than over four years. In addition, taxpayers have until the due date of their return to change their minds about any Roth IRA conversion that took place at any time in the past tax year. This rule was designed to help taxpayers who incorrectly projected the size of their adjusted gross income as less than $100,000 when converting assets from a regular IRA to a Roth IRA.

7. **Pre-rata gains from sales of principal residences:** The Act settled the question of how to apply the capital gain exclusion to the sale of a residence that had been owned and occupied for less than two years. Such homeowners can now exclude the amount of the capital gain ($500,000 for couples and $250,000 for singles) that is equal to the fraction of the two years that the property was owned and occupied.

INTERNATIONAL ACCOUNTING STANDARDS BOARD (IASB)
London-based, privately funded organization formed in 1973 as the International Accounting Standards Committee. Its mission is to develop, in the public interest, a single set of high-quality, understandable, and international

financial reporting standards (IFFRSs) for general-purpose financial statements.

INTERNATIONAL BANK FOR RECONSTRUCTION AND DEVELOPMENT (IBRD) organization set up by the Bretton Woods Agreement of 1944 to help finance the reconstruction of Europe and Asia after World War II. That task accomplished, the *World Bank,* as IBRD is known, turned to financing commercial and infrastructure projects, mostly in developing nations. It does not compete with commercial banks, but it may participate in a loan set up by a commercial bank. World Bank loans must be backed by the government in the borrowing country.

INTERNATIONAL FISCHER EFFECT *see* FISCHER EFFECT.

INTERNATIONAL ORGANIZATION OF SECURITIES COMMISSIONS (IOSCO) based in Madrid, Spain and with membership agencies comprising securities commissions and regulators in their home countries, IOSCO provides standards, surveillance, and enforcement of regulations having to do with international securities transactions.

INTERNATIONAL MARKET INDEX market-value weighted proprietary index of the American Stock Exchange which tracks the performance of 50 American Depositary Receipts traded on the American Stock Exchange, New York Stock Exchange and NASDAQ Market. Options are no longer traded on the index.

INTERNATIONAL MONETARY FUND (IMF) organization set up by the Bretton Woods Agreement in 1944. Unlike the World Bank, whose focus is on foreign exchange reserves and the balance of trade, the IMF focus is on lowering trade barriers and stabilizing currencies. While helping developing nations pay their debts, the IMF usually imposes tough guidelines aimed at lowering inflation, cutting imports, and raising exports. IMF funds come mostly from the treasuries of industrialized nations. *See also* INTERNATIONAL BANK FOR RECONSTRUCTION AND DEVELOPMENT.

INTERNATIONAL MONETARY MARKET (IMM) division of the Chicago Mercantile Exchange that trades futures in U.S. Treasury bills, foreign currency, certificates of deposit, and Eurodollar deposits.

INTERNATIONAL MUTUAL FUND mutual fund that invests in securities markets throughout the world so that if one market is in a slump, profits can still be earned in others. Fund managers must be alert to trends in foreign currencies as well as in world stock and bond markets. Otherwise, seemingly profitable investments in a rising market could lose money if the national currency is falling against the dollar. While international mutual funds tend to concentrate only on non-American securities, GLOBAL MUTUAL FUNDS buy both foreign and domestic stocks and bonds.

INTERNATIONAL CAPITAL MARKET ASSOCIATION Zurich, Switzerland-based self-regulatory organization for the international securities market formed through the July 2005 merger of its predecessors the International Securities Market Association and the International Primary Market Association. The group has more than 400 members in about 50 countries. It plays an active role in the shaping of the financial regulatory framework in Europe.

INTERNATIONAL PETROLEUM EXCHANGE (IPE) the leading European marketplace for regulated trading of energy contracts, the IPE is a London-based energy futures and options exchange. The IPE lists the benchmark Brent crude oil futures contract, which is relied upon for pricing an estimated two-thirds of the world's traded oil products. The IPE offers fully electronic trading in futures and options on Brent crude oil and gas oil, and futures on emissions, natural gas, and electricity. In June 2001, the IPE became a wholly owned subsidiary of INTERCONTINENTAL EXCHANGE (ICE), an electronic marketplace for trading both futures and over-the-counter (OTC) contracts in natural gas, power, and oil. Trading hours: 2 A.M. to 10 P.M. *See also* INTERCONTINENTAL EXCHANGE. *www.theipe.com.*

INTERNATIONAL SECURITIES EXCHANGE (ISE) New York City-based, SEC-registered, securities exchange started in 2000 for electronic trading of options. ISE is funded by a consortium of broker-dealers.

INTERNATIONAL SECURITIES REGULATORY ORGANIZATION (ISRO) *see* INTERNATIONAL STOCK EXCHANGE OF THE UNITED KINGDOM AND THE REPUBLIC OF IRELAND (ISE).

INTERNET INVESTING general term for using the Internet to obtain investment information and execute trades. Tools available on the Internet include sources of quotes, financial news, company information, Wall Street research, message boards, stock screening, and on-line brokerage sites. *See also* ON-LINE TRADING.

INTERPOLATION estimation of an unknown number intermediate between known numbers. Interpolation is a way of approximating price or yield using bond tables that do not give the net yield on every amount invested at every rate of interest and for every maturity. Interpolation is based on the assumption that a certain percentage change in yield will result in the same percentage change in price. The assumption is not altogether correct, but the variance is small enough to ignore.

INTERPOSITIONING placement of a second broker in a securities transaction between two principals or between a customer and a marketmaker. The practice is regulated by the Securities and Exchange Commission, and abuses such as interpositioning to create additional commission income are illegal.

INTERSTATE COMMERCE COMMISSION (ICC) federal agency created by the Interstate Commerce Act of 1887 to insure that the public receives fair and reasonable rates and services from carriers and transportation service firms involved in interstate commerce. Legislation enacted in the 1970s and 80s substantially curtailed the regulatory activities of the ICC, particularly in the rail, truck, and bus industries.

INTER VIVOS TRUST trust established between living persons—for instance, between father and child. In contrast, a TESTAMENTARY TRUST goes into effect when the person who establishes the trust dies. Also called *living trust.*

INTESTACY; INTESTATE a person who dies without a valid will is said to die *intestate* or *in intestacy.* State law determines who is entitled to inherit and who is entitled to manage the decedent's estate.

INTESTATE DISTRIBUTION distribution of assets to beneficiaries from the estate of a person who dies without a written will of instructions. This distribution is overseen by a PROBATE court and the appointed EXECUTOR of the estate. Each state has specific laws outlining how intestate distributions are to be made.

IN THE MONEY option contract on a stock whose current market price is above the striking price of a call option or below the striking price of a put option. A call option on XYZ at a striking price of 100 would be in the money if XYZ were selling for 102, for instance, and a put option with the same striking price would be in the money if XYZ were selling for 98. *See also* AT THE MONEY; OUT OF THE MONEY.

IN THE TANK slang expression meaning market prices are dropping rapidly. Stock market observers may say, "The market is in the tank" after a day in which stock prices fell.

INTRACOMMODITY SPREAD futures position in which a trader buys and sells contracts in the same commodity on the same exchange, but for different months. For instance, a trader would place an intracommodity spread if he bought a pork bellies contract expiring in December and at the same time sold a pork bellies contract expiring in April. His profit or loss would be determined by the price difference between the December and April contracts.

INTRADAY within the day; often used in connection with high and low prices of a stock, bond, or commodity. For instance, "The stock hit a new intraday high today" means that the stock reached an all-time high price during the day but fell back to a lower price by the end of the day. The listing of the high and low prices at which a stock is traded during a day is called the *intraday price range*.

INTRASTATE OFFERING securities offering limited to one state in the United States. *See also* BLUE-SKY LAW.

INTRINSIC VALUE
Financial analysis: valuation determined by applying data inputs to a valuation theory or model. The resulting value is comparable to the prevailing market price.
Options trading: difference between the EXERCISE PRICE or strike price of an option and the market value of the underlying security. For example, if the strike price is $53 on a call option to purchase a stock with a market price of $55, the option has an intrinsic value of $2. Or, in the case of a put option, if the strike price was $55 and the market price of the underlying stock was $53, the intrinsic value of the option would also be $2. Options AT THE MONEY or OUT OF THE MONEY have no intrinsic value.

INVENTORY
Corporate finance: value of a firm's raw materials, work in process, supplies used in operations, and finished goods. Since inventory value changes with price fluctuations, it is important to know the method of valuation. There are a number of inventory valuation methods; the most widely used are FIRST IN, FIRST OUT (FIFO) and LAST IN, FIRST OUT (LIFO). Financial statements normally indicate the basis of inventory valuation, generally the lower figure of either cost price or current market price, which precludes potentially

overstated earnings and assets as the result of sharp increases in the price of raw materials.

Personal finance: list of all assets owned by an individual and the value of each, based on cost, market value, or both. Such inventories are usually required for property insurance purposes and are sometimes required with applications for credit.

Securities: net long or short position of a dealer or specialist. Also, securities bought and held by a dealer for later resale.

INVENTORY FINANCING

Factoring: sometimes used as a synonym for overadvances in FACTORING, where loans in excess of accounts receivable are made against inventory in anticipation of future sales.

Finance companies: financing by a bank or sales finance company of the inventory of a dealer in consumer or capital goods. Such loans, also called wholesale financing or *floorplanning*, are secured by the inventory and are usually made as part of a relationship in which retail installment paper generated by sales to the public is also financed by the lender. *See also* FINANCE COMPANY.

INVENTORY TURNOVER ratio of annual sales to inventory, which shows how many times the inventory of a firm is sold and replaced during an accounting period; sometimes called *inventory utilization ratio*. Compared with industry averages, a low turnover might indicate a company is carrying excess stocks of inventory, an unhealthy sign because excess inventory represents an investment with a low or zero rate of return and because it makes the company more vulnerable to falling prices. A steady drop in inventory turnover, in comparison with prior periods, can reveal lack of a sufficiently aggressive sales policy or ineffective buying.

Two points about the way inventory turnover may be calculated: (1) Because sales are recorded at market value and inventories are normally carried at cost, it is more realistic to obtain the turnover ratio by dividing inventory into cost of goods sold rather than into sales. However, it is conventional to use sales as the numerator because that is the practice of Dun & Bradstreet and other compilers of published financial ratios, and comparability is of overriding importance. (2) To minimize the seasonal factor affecting inventory levels, it is better to use an average inventory figure, obtained by adding yearly beginning and ending inventory figures and dividing by 2.

INVERSE EXCHANGE-TRADED FUNDS (ETFs) EXCHANGE-TRADED FUNDS (ETFs) that track the reverse, or opposite, direction of their benchmark indexes. Also called *short ETFs* or *bear ETFs*. For example, an inverse ETF tracking the S&P 500 INDEX will rise 4% if the index falls 4%, assuming no TRACKING error. Their principal advantage is that by buying an inverse ETF an investor can effectively be SELLING SHORT in a down market without having a MARGIN ACCOUNT. In mid-2009 the SEC said investors should be wary of such products, particularly when they use SWAPS or DERIVATIVES to amplify returns.

INVERSE FLOATER derivative instrument whose coupon rate is inversely related to some multiple of a specified market rate of interest. Typically a cap and floor are placed on the coupon. As interest rates go down, the amount of interest the inverse floater pays goes up. For example, if the inverse floater rate is 32% and the multiple is four times the London Interbank Offered Rate (LIBOR) of 7%, the coupon is valued at 4%. If the LIBOR goes to 6%, the new coupon is 8%. Many inverse floaters are based on pieces of mortgage-backed securities such as COLLATERALIZED MORTGAGE OBLIGATIONS which react inversely to movements in interest rates.

INVERTED SCALE serial bond offering where earlier maturities have higher yields than later maturities. *See also* SERIAL BOND.

INVERTED YIELD CURVE unusual situation where short-term interest rates are higher than long-term rates. Normally, lenders receive a higher yield when committing their money for a longer period of time; this situation is called a POSITIVE YIELD CURVE. An inverted YIELD CURVE occurs when a surge in demand for short-term credit drives up short-term rates on instruments like Treasury bills and money-market funds, while long-term rates move up more slowly, since borrowers are not willing to commit themselves to paying high interest rates for many years. This situation happened in the early 1980s, when short-term interest rates were around 20%, while long-term rates went up to only 16% or 17%. The existence of an inverted yield curve can be a sign of an unhealthy economy, marked by high inflation and low levels of confidence. Also called *negative yield curve.*

INVERTED YIELD CURVE

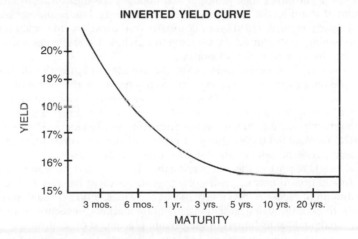

INVESTMENT use of capital to create more money, either through income-producing vehicles or through more risk-oriented ventures designed to result in capital gains. *Investment* can refer to a financial investment (where an investor puts money into a vehicle) or to an investment of effort and time on the part of an individual who wants to reap profits from the success of his labor. Investment connotes the idea that safety of principal is important. SPECULATION, on the other hand, is far riskier.

INVESTMENT ADVISERS ACT legislation passed by Congress in 1940 that requires all investment advisers to register with the Securities and Exchange Commission. The Act is designed to protect the public from fraud or misrepresentation by investment advisers. One requirement, for example, is that advisers must disclose all potential *conflicts of interest* with any recommendations they make to those they advise. A potential conflict of interest might exist where the adviser had a position in a security he was recommending. *See also* INVESTMENT ADVISORY SERVICE.

INVESTMENT ADVISORY SERVICE service providing investment advice for a fee. Investment advisers must register with the Securities and Exchange Commission and abide by the rules of the INVESTMENT ADVISERS ACT. Investment advisory services usually specialize in a particular kind of investment—for example, emerging growth stocks, international stocks, mutual funds, or commodities. Some services only offer advice through a newsletter; others will manage a client's money. The performance of many investment advisory services is ranked by the *Hulbert Financial Digest. See also* HULBERT RATING.

INVESTMENT BANKER firm, acting as underwriter or agent, that serves as intermediary between an issuer of securities and the investing public. In what is termed FIRM COMMITMENT underwriting, the investment banker, either as manager or participating member of an investment banking syndicate, makes outright purchases of new securities from the issuer and distributes them to dealers and investors, profiting on the spread between the purchase price and the selling (public offering) price. Under a conditional arrangement called BEST EFFORT, the investment banker markets a new issue without underwriting it, acting as agent rather than principal and taking a commission for whatever amount of securities the banker succeeds in marketing. Under another conditional arrangement, called STANDBY COMMITMENT, the investment banker serves clients issuing new securities by agreeing to purchase for resale any securities not taken by existing holders of RIGHTS.

Where a client relationship exists, the investment banker's role begins with pre-underwriting counseling and continues after the distribution of securities is completed, in the form of ongoing expert advice and guidance, often including a seat on the board of directors. The direct underwriting responsibilities include preparing the Securities and Exchange Commission registration statement; consulting on pricing of the securities; forming and managing the syndicate; establishing a selling group if desired; and PEGGING (stabilizing) the price of the issue during the offering and distribution period.

In addition to new securities offerings, investment bankers handle the distribution of blocks of previously issued securities, either through secondary offerings or through negotiations; maintain markets for securities already distributed; and act as finders in the private placement of securities.

Along with their investment banking functions, the majority of investment bankers also maintain broker-dealer operations, serving both wholesale and retail clients in brokerage and advisory capacities and offering a growing number of related financial services. *See also* FLOTATION COST; SECONDARY DISTRIBUTION; UNDERWRITE.

INVESTMENT CERTIFICATE certificate evidencing investment in a savings and loan association and showing the amount of money invested. Investment certificates do not have voting rights and do not involve stockholder responsibility. Also called *mutual capital certificate. See also* MUTUAL ASSOCIATION.

INVESTMENT CLIMATE economic, monetary, and other conditions affecting the performance of investments.

INVESTMENT CLUB group of people who pool their assets in order to make joint investment decisions. Each member of the club contributes a certain amount of capital, with additional money to be invested every month or quarter. Decisions on which stocks or bonds to buy are made by a vote of members. Besides helping each member become more knowledgeable about investing, these clubs allow people with small amounts of money to participate in larger investments, own part of a more diversified portfolio, and pay lower commission rates than would be possible for individual members on their own. The trade group for investment clubs is the National Association of Investors Corporation (NAIC) in Madison Heights, Michigan. The NAIC helps clubs get started and offers several programs, such as the Low-Cost Investment Plan allowing clubs to purchase an initial share of individual stocks at low commissions and reinvest dividends automatically at no charge.

INVESTMENT COMPANY firm that, for a management fee, invests the pooled funds of small investors in securities appropriate for its stated investment objectives. It offers participants more diversification, liquidity, and professional management service than would normally be available to them as individuals.

There are two basic types of traditional investment companies: (1) *open-end,* better known as a MUTUAL FUND, which has a floating number of outstanding shares (hence the name *open-end*) and stands prepared to sell or redeem shares at their current NET ASSET VALUE; and (2) *closed-end,* also known as an *investment trust,* which, like a corporation, has a fixed number of outstanding shares that are traded like a stock, often on the New York and American Stock Exchanges. Two other varieties of investment companies, EXCHANGE-TRADED FUNDS (ETFs) and UNIT INVESTMENT TRUSTS (UITs), have more recently become commonplace and are covered separately.

Open-end management companies are basically divided into two categories, based on the way they distribute their funds to customers. The first category is *load funds,* which are sold in the over-the-counter market by broker-dealers, who do not receive a sales commission; instead a "loading charge" is added to the net asset value at time of purchase. For many years the charge was 8½%, but more recently it has been reduced to 4.5%–5%. Many load funds do not charge an upfront load, but instead impose a BACK-END LOAD which customers must pay if they sell fund shares within a certain number of years, usually five. Funds are available as classes of shares, each having a different fee structure. The second category is *no-load funds,* which are bought directly from sponsoring fund companies. Such companies do not charge a loading fee, although some funds levy a redemption fee if shares are sold within a specified number of years.

Some funds, both load and no-load, are called 12b-1 MUTUAL FUNDS because they levy an annual 12b-1 charge of up to 0.75% of assets to pay for promotional and marketing expenses.

Dealers in closed-end investment companies obtain their revenue from regular brokerage commissions, just as they do in selling any individual stock.

Both open-end and closed-end investment companies charge annual management fees, typically ranging from 0.25% to 2% of the value of the assets in the fund.

Under the INVESTMENT COMPANY ACT OF 1940, the registration statement and prospectus of every investment company must state its specific investment objectives. Investment companies fall into many categories, including: diversified common stock funds (with growth of capital as the principal objective); balanced funds (mixing common and preferred stocks, bonds, and cash); bond and preferred stock funds (emphasizing current income); specialized funds (by industry, groups of industries, geography, or size of company); income funds buying high-yield stocks and bonds; dual-purpose funds (a form of closed-end investment company offering a choice of income shares or capital gains shares); and money market funds which invest in money market instruments.

INVESTMENT COMPANY ACT OF 1940 legislation passed by Congress requiring registration and regulation of investment companies by the Securities and Exchange Commission. The Act sets the standards by which mutual funds and other investment vehicles of investment companies operate, in such areas as promotion, reporting requirements, pricing of securities for sale to the public, and allocation of investments within a fund portfolio. *See also* INVESTMENT COMPANY.

INVESTMENT COMPANY AMENDMENTS ACT OF 1970 amendments to the Investment Company Act of 1940 that established regulations concerning sales charges, fees, and withdrawal penalties.

INVESTMENT COMPANY INSTITUTE (ICI) Washington, D.C.-based trade association for U.S. investment companies. Founded in 1940, membership in 2008 consisted of 9,114 MUTUAL FUNDS, 675 CLOSED-END FUNDS, 649 EXCHANGE-TRADED FUNDS, and 3,421 UNIT INVESTMENT TRUSTS. ICI's mission is to encourage high ethical standards; to advance the interests of funds, their shareholders, directors, and investment advisors; and to promote public understanding of mutual funds and other investment companies.

INVESTMENT COUNSEL person with the responsibility for providing investment advice to clients and executing investment decisions. *See also* PORTFOLIO MANAGER.

INVESTMENT COUNSEL ASSOCIATION OF AMERICA (ICAA) a not-for-profit organization that represents the interests of SEC-registered investment advisory firms. It was founded in 1937 and lists some 300 registered advisory firms that manage in excess of $3 trillion for individual and institutional clients. *www.icaa.org*.

INVESTMENT CREDIT reduction in income tax liability granted by the federal government over the years to firms making new investments in certain asset categories, primarily equipment; also called *investment tax credit.* The investment credit, designed to stimulate the economy by encouraging capital expenditure, has been a feature of tax legislation on and off, and in varying percentage amounts, since 1962; in 1985 it was 6% or 10% of the purchase price, depending on the life of the asset. As a credit, it has been deducted from the tax bill, not from pretax income, and it has been independent of DEPRECIATION. The TAX REFORM ACT OF 1986 generally repealed the investment credit retroactively for any property placed in service after January 1, 1986. The 1986 Act also provided for a 35% reduction of the value of credits carried over from previous years, which was later changed to 50%.

INVESTMENT GRADE bond with a RATING of AAA to BBB. *See also* JUNK BOND.

INVESTMENT HISTORY body of prior experience establishing "normal investment practice" with respect to the account relationship between a member firm and its customer. For example, the Rules of Fair Practice of the FINANCIAL INDUSTRY REGULATORY AUTHORITY (FINRA) prohibit the sale of a new issue to members of a distributing dealer's immediate family, but it there was sufficient precedent in the investment history of this particular dealer-customer relationship, the sale would not be a violation.

INVESTMENT INCOME income from securities and other nonbusiness investments; such as DIVIDENDS, INTEREST, OPTION PREMIUMS, and income from a ROYALTY or ANNUITY. Interest on MARGIN ACCOUNTS may be used to offset investment income without limitation. Investment income earned by passive activities must be treated separately from other PASSIVE income. Expenses incurred to generate investment income can reduce investment income to the extent they exceed 2% of adjusted gross income. By excluding capital gains from the calculation, tax law, in effect, prevents a taxpayer from claiming an ordinary deduction for margin interest incurred to carry an investment that is taxable at the favorable capital gains rate. Also called UNEARNED INCOME and *portfolio income.*

INVESTMENT LETTER in the private placement of new securities, a letter of intent between the issuer of securities and the buyer establishing that the securities are being bought as an investment and are not for resale. This is necessary to avoid having to register the securities with the Securities and Exchange Commission. (Under provisions of SEC Rule 144, a purchaser of such securities may eventually resell them to the public if certain specific conditions are met, including a minimum holding period of at least two years.) Use of the investment letter gave rise to the terms *letter stock* and *letter bond* in referring to unregistered issues. *See also* LETTER SECURITY.

INVESTMENT MANAGEMENT in general, the activities of a portfolio manager. More specifically, it distinguishes between managed and unmanaged portfolios, examples of the latter being UNIT INVESTMENT TRUSTS and INDEX FUNDS, which are fixed portfolios not requiring ongoing decisions.

INVESTMENT OBJECTIVE financial objective that an investor uses to determine which kind of investment is appropriate. For example, if the investor's objective is growth of capital, he may opt for growth-oriented mutual funds or individual stocks. If he is more interested in income, he might purchase income-oriented mutual funds or individual bonds instead. Consideration of investment objectives, combined with the risk tolerance of investors, helps an investor narrow his search to an investment vehicle designed for his needs at a particular time.

INVESTMENT PHILOSOPHY style of investment practiced by an individual investor or money manager. For example, some investors follow the growth philosophy, concentrating on stocks with steadily rising earnings. Others are value investors, searching for stocks that have fallen out of favor, and are therefore cheap relative to the true value of their assets. Some managers favor small-capitalization stocks, while others stick with large BLUE CHIP companies. Some managers have a philosophy of remaining fully invested at all times, while others believe in market timing, so that their portfolios can accumulate cash if the managers think stock or bond prices are about to fall. Styles encompass international and fixed-income investing and combinations of all the foregoing. Styles are cyclical, but since cycles cannot be predicted with any certainty, patience and discipline are the time-honored elements of successful investing. Managers who have not consistently stayed with their styles have historically been unsuccessful and *style drift* is viewed as a negative in the analysis of a manager's record. Example: The phenomenal performance of dot-com stocks in the late 1990s tempted some managers to depart from their styles, and the subsequent decline in tech stocks caught them unprepared.

INVESTMENT SOFTWARE software designed to aid investors' decision-making. Some software packages allow investors to perform TECHNICAL ANALYSIS, charting stock prices, volume, and other indicators. Other programs allow FUNDAMENTAL ANALYSIS, permitting investors to SCREEN STOCKS based on financial criteria such as earnings, price/earnings ratios, book value, and dividend yields. Some software offers recordkeeping, so that an investor can keep track of the value of his portfolio and the prices at which he bought or sold securities. Many software packages allow investors to tap into databases to update securities prices, scan news items, and execute trades. Specialty programs allow investors to value options, calculate yield analysis on bonds, and screen mutual funds.

INVESTMENT STRATEGY plan to allocate assets among such choices as stocks, bonds, CASH EQUIVALENTS, commodities, and real estate. An investment strategy should be formulated based on an investor's outlook on interest rates, inflation, and economic growth, among other factors, and also taking into account the investor's age, tolerance for risk, amount of capital available to invest, and future needs for capital, such as for financing children's college educations or buying a house. An investment adviser will help to devise such a strategy. *See also* INVESTMENT ADVISORY SERVICE.

INVESTMENT STRATEGY COMMITTEE committee in the research department of a brokerage firm that sets the overall investment strategy the firm recommends to clients. The director of research, the chief economist, and several top analysts typically sit on this committee. The group advises clients on the amount of money that should be placed into stocks, bonds, or CASH EQUIVALENTS, as well as the industry groups or individual stocks or bonds that look particularly attractive.

INVESTMENT STYLE *see* INVESTMENT PHILOSOPHY.

INVESTMENT TAX CREDIT *see* INVESTMENT CREDIT.

INVESTMENT TRUST *see* INVESTMENT COMPANY.

INVESTMENT VALUE OF A CONVERTIBLE SECURITY estimated price at which a CONVERTIBLE security (CV) would be valued by the marketplace if it had no stock conversion feature. The investment value for CVs of major companies is determined by investment advisory services and, theoretically, should never fall lower than the price of the related stock. It is arrived at by estimating the price at which a nonconvertible ("straight") bond or preferred share of the same issuing company would sell. The investment value reflects the interest rate; therefore, the market price of the security will go up when rates are down and vice versa. *See also* PREMIUM OVER BOND VALUE.

INVESTOR party who puts money at risk; may be an individual or an institutional investor.

INVESTOR RELATIONS DEPARTMENT in major listed companies, a staff position responsible for investor relations, reporting either to the chief financial officer or to the director of public relations. The actual duties will vary, depending on whether the company retains an outside financial public relations firm, but the general responsibilities are as follows:

- to see that the company is understood, in terms of its activities and objectives, and is favorably regarded in the financial and capital markets and the investment community; this means having input into the annual report and other published materials, coordinating senior management speeches and public statements with the FINANCIAL PUBLIC RELATIONS effort, and generally fostering a consistent and positive corporate image.
- to ensure full and timely public DISCLOSURE of material information, and to work with the legal staff in complying with the rules of the SEC, the securities exchanges, and other regulatory authorities.
- to respond to requests for reports and information from shareholders, professional investors, brokers, and the financial media.
- to maintain productive relations with the firm's investment bankers, the specialists in its stock, major broker-dealers, and institutional investors who follow the company or hold sizeable positions in its securities.
- to take direct measures, where necessary, to see that the company's shares are properly valued. This involves identifying the firm's particular investment audience and the professionals controlling its stock float, arranging analysts' meetings and other presentations, and generating appropriate publicity.

The most successful investor relations professionals have been those who follow a policy of full and open dissemination of relevant information, favorable and unfavorable, on a consistent basis. The least successful, over the long run, have been the "touts"—those who emphasize promotion at the expense of credibility.

INVESTORS SERVICE BUREAU New York Stock Exchange public service that responds to written inquiries of all types concerning securities investments.

INVOICE bill prepared by a seller of goods or services and submitted to the purchaser. The invoice lists all the items bought, together with amounts.

INVOLUNTARY BANKRUPTCY *see* BANKRUPTCY.

IRA *see* INDIVIDUAL RETIREMENT ARRANGEMENT (OR ACCOUNT).

IRA ROLLOVER *see* INDIVIDUAL RETIREMENT ACCOUNT ROLLOVER.

IRA TRANSFER a change of trustees with no tax consequences to the holder, but possibly a loss of income while funds are in transit.

IRISH STOCK EXCHANGE (ISE) founded in 1793 in Dublin, the exchange is a limited company trading equities, government and corporate bonds, investment funds, and specialist securities such as asset-backed debt, securitized bonds, and warrants. Most company securities trade on ISE Xetra, the exchange's electronic trading system, and are settled in CREST. Irish government bonds are traded on EuroMTS, the electronic trading system for market makers in Irish government bonds, and are settled through Euroclear. CRESTCo merged with the Euroclear group in September 2002. Continuous trading runs from 8 A.M. to 4:28 P.M., with an 80-minute pre-market session starting at 6:30 A.M. and 10-minute auctions before the opening and two minutes after the close. A post-trading session runs from 4:30 P.M. to 5:15 P.M. *www.ise.ie.*

IRRATIONAL EXUBERANCE characterization of market mood in a 1996 speech by then Federal Reserve Chairman Alan Greenspan. In context, the typically cautious Greenspan posed the question, "How do we know when irrational exuberance has unduly escalated asset values, which then become subject to unexpected and prolonged contraction . . . ?" *Irrational Exuberance* was used as the title of a 2000 book by Yale economics professor Robert Shiller, who argued that the stock market had indeed become dangerously overvalued.

IRREDEEMABLE BOND
1. bond without a CALL FEATURE (issuer's right to redeem the bond before maturity) or a REDEMPTION privilege (holder's right to sell the bond back to the issuer before maturity).
2. PERPETUAL BOND.

IRREVOCABLE something done that cannot legally be undone, such as an IRREVOCABLE TRUST.

IRREVOCABLE LIVING TRUST trust usually created to achieve some tax benefit, or to provide a vehicle for managing assets of a person the creator believes cannot or should not be managing his or her own property. This trust cannot be changed or reversed by the creator of the trust.

IRREVOCABLE TRUST trust that cannot be changed or terminated by the one who created it without the agreement of the BENEFICIARY.

IRS *see* INTERNAL REVENUE SERVICE.

IRS PRIVATE LETTER RULING *see* PRIVATE LETTER RULING.

iSHARES EXCHANGE-TRADED FUNDS of Barclays Global Investors that replaced and expanded a product line formerly known as WEBS (World Equity Benchmark Shares). Some 75 iSHARE portfolios are currently traded on the American Stock Exchange with two more trading on the New York Stock Exchange and the Chicago Board Options Exchange. Represented are 20 Standard & Poor's domestic and international stock indexes, 23 MSCI (MORGAN STANLEY CAPITAL INTERNATIONAL) INDEXES representing foreign country and regional markets, 15 Dow Jones INDUSTRIAL SECTOR indexes, 12 RUSSELL INDICES, 5 Goldman Sachs specialized indexes, a NASDAQ biotechnology index, a Cohen & Steers real estate index, and a Lehman Aggregate ETF (AGG) fixed-income fund.

ISIS *see* INTERMARKET SURVEILLANCE INFORMATION SYSTEM (ISIS).

ISMA *see* INTERNATIONAL SECURITIES MARKET ASSOCIATION (ISMA).

ISSUE
1. stock or bonds sold by a corporation or a government entity at a particular time.
2. selling new securities by a corporation or government entity, either through an underwriter or by a private placement.
3. descendants, such as children and grandchildren. For instance, "This man's estate will be passed, at his death, to his issue."

ISSUED AND OUTSTANDING shares of a corporation, authorized in the corporate charter, which have been issued and are outstanding. These shares represent capital invested by the firm's shareholders and owners, and may be all or only a portion of the number of shares authorized. Shares that have been issued and subsequently repurchased by the company are called *treasury stock,* because they are held in the corporate treasury pending reissue or retirement. Treasury shares are legally issued but are not considered outstanding for purposes of voting, dividends, or earnings per share calculations. Shares authorized but not yet issued are called *unissued shares.* Most companies show the amount of authorized, issued and outstanding, and treasury shares in the capital section of their annual reports. *See also* TREASURY STOCK.

ISSUER legal entity that has the power to issue and distribute a security. Issuers include corporations, municipalities, foreign and domestic governments and their agencies, and investment trusts. Issuers of stock are responsible for reporting on corporate developments to shareholders and paying dividends once declared. Issuers of bonds are committed to making timely payments of interest and principal to bondholders.

ISSUER-PAID RESEARCH equities research paid for by the companies who stand to gain or lose depending on whether a report is positive or negative. Actions taken to eliminate conflicts of interest between underwriters and their research departments after the corporate scandals of the early 2000s resulted in investment banking firms downsizing their research units and covering fewer companies. At the same time, the bull market of the 1990s increased the number of public companies desiring coverage. The ironic result was an issuer-paid research industry with its own obvious conflict of interest issues. CFA INSTITUTE and NIRI established a joint task force to recommend preventive guidelines.

ITALIAN STOCK EXCHANGE (ISE) *see* BORSA ITALIANA.

ITEMIZED DEDUCTION item that allows a taxpayer to reduce adjusted gross income on his or her tax return. For example, mortgage interest, charitable contributions, state and local income and property taxes, unreimbursed business expenses, IRA contributions, and other miscellaneous items are considered deductible under certain conditions and are listed as itemized deductions on Schedule A of an individual's tax return. However, at certain income levels, deductions are phased out. For example, in the 2008 tax year, itemized deductions for married couples filing jointly were phased out by 3% of the excess of adjusted gross income over $159,950 (over $79,975 if married and filing separately). Some deductions are not subject to the 3% reduction, including medical and dental expenses, investment interest, casualty and theft losses, and gambling losses.

ITS/CAES *see* NATIONAL MARKET SYSTEM.

J

JANUARY BAROMETER market forecasting tool popularized by *The Stock Traders Almanac,* whose statistics show that with 90% consistency since 1950, the market has risen in years when the STANDARD & POOR'S INDEX of 500 stocks was up in January and dropped when the index for that month was down.

JANUARY EFFECT phenomenon that stocks (especially small stocks) have historically tended to rise markedly during the period starting on the last day of December and ending on the fourth trading day of January. The January Effect is owed to year-end selling to create tax losses, recognize capital gains, effect portfolio WINDOW DRESSING, or raise holiday cash; since such selling depresses the stocks but has nothing to do with their fundamental worth, bargain hunters quickly buy in, causing the January rally.

J-CURVE graph pattern showing the effect of depreciation of a currency on a country's trade DEFICIT. Higher prices on imports will offset the reduced volume of imports, thus increasing the deficit in the short run, although in the long run the deficit will decrease.

JEEP *see* GRADUATED PAYMENT MORTGAGE.

JENSEN INDEX index that uses the CAPITAL ASSET PRICING MODEL to determine the ALPHA of an investment or a portfolio, that is, the portion of the return arising from company-specific (nonmarket) risk.

JINGLE MAIL expression born of the real estate meltdown meaning envelopes containing house keys mailed to mortgage lenders by home owners walking away from UPSIDE-DOWN MORTGAGES in massive numbers.

JOBBER
1. wholesaler, especially one who buys in small lots from manufacturers, importers, and/or other wholesalers and sells to retailers.
2. London Stock Exchange term for MARKET MAKER.

JOB CREATION AND WORKER ASSISTANCE ACT OF 2002 legislation passed by Congress and signed into law on March 9, 2002 to stimulate the economy out of the recession and economic contraction caused by the terrorist attacks of September 11, 2001. Here are some of the main provisions of the law:
Provisions Affecting Individuals
1. Extended unemployment benefits for 13 weeks for workers who filed an initial claim for unemployment benefits on or after March 15, 2001.
2. Extends the use of personal credits such as the child tax and adoption credits through December 31, 2003 for use in calculating the alternative minimum tax.
3. Creates above-the-line deduction for classroom expenses for elementary and secondary school teachers up to $250 annually for supplies, books and computer equipment.
4. Archer Medical Savings Accounts extends through December 31, 2003.
5. Allows taxpayers to claim the education IRA exclusion and HOPE scholarship credit in the same year.

Provisions Affecting Business
1. Business taxpayers become entitled to take an additional first-year depreciation deduction equal to 30% of the adjusted basis of qualified property. This 30% bonus depreciation is allowable for regular and AMT purposes for the tax year in which the property is placed into service after September 10, 2001. Property eligible for this treatment includes property with a recovery period of 20 years or less; water utility property; and certain kinds of computer software and qualified leasehold improvements.
2. Net operating losses (NOLs) can now be carried forward for five years instead of two years if the losses arise in tax years 2001 or 2002.
3. Taxpayers using the accrual method of accounting can now exclude from income money earned from the performance of qualified services that they think will not be collected. Qualified services include health, law and consulting services, and other services, provided to small businesses.
4. Allows Subchapter S corporations to discharge certain indebtedness for tax purposes when they become insolvent.
5. Extended many expiring business tax credits until December 31, 2003 including: Work Opportunity Tax Credit; Welfare-to-Work Credit; credit for producing electricity from wind, biomass, and poultry litter; clean-fuel vehicle deduction; qualified zone academy bonds; tax incentives for investment in Native American reservations; and other energy incentives.

Creation of New York City Liberty Zone
   Created special tax breaks for taxpayers in the Liberty Zone of southern Manhattan to encourage them to rebuild after the events of September 11:
1. The maximum deduction amount for qualifying property used in the Liberty Zone is increased to the cost of the property or $35,000, whichever is less.
2. An additional first-year 30% depreciation deduction is created for qualifying property, on top of normal first-year depreciation deductions.
3. The Work Opportunity Tax Credit is added for Liberty Zone taxpayers who work in a business in the Zone or for a business that relocated from the Zone to another location in New York City due to the terrorist attacks.
4. A five-year replacement period (instead of the usual two-year period) is created for involuntarily converted property due to the terrorist attacks, if the property is replaced with other property used in New York City.
5. Qualified leasehold improvement depreciation is allowed for five-year property put into service from September 10, 2001 through January 1, 2007.

JOBS AND GROWTH TAX RELIEF RECONCILIATION ACT OF 2003 legistlation providing significant tax relief for individuals, investors, and businesses that was signed into law on May 28, 2003. The major provisions of the law are:

1. **Accelerated expansion of the 10% tax bracket.** The 10% tax bracket applies to the first $7,000 of taxable income for singles and $14,000 for married couples filing jointly. Beginning in 2004, the taxable income levels for the 10% bracket will be adjusted for inflation.
2. **Accelerated reduction of individual income tax brackets above 15%.** The new tax brackets above 15% are 25%, 28%, 33%, and 35%.
3. **Accelerated increase in the child credit.** Starting in 2003, the child tax credit is increased to $1,000.
4. **Elimination of the marriage penalty.** The standard deduction for married

couples filing jointly becoms twice the deduction for single taxpayers. The size of the 15% tax bracket is widened so that the married level of income is double the size of the single level of income.

5. **Increase in AMT exemption amount for individuals.** The exemption amount is increased to $58,000 for married couples filing jointly, $29,000 for married couples filing singly, and $40,250 for singles.

6. **Adjustments in withholding tables.** The IRS changed its withholding tables so that less tax is withheld from workers' paychecks because of the reductions in tax rates.

7. **Long-term capital gains tax rates reduced to 5% and 15%.** Capital gains tax rates were reduced from 10% to 5% and from 20% to 15% for asset sales after May 5, 2003 for assest held a year or longer. Gains from property purchased after 2000 and held more than five years are taxed at an 8% capital gains rate.

8. **Tax rate on noncorporate taxpayers' dividend income cut to 5% and 15%.** Dividends are taxed at 5% for those in the two lowest tax brackets, and 15% for those in the higher tax brackets. Previously, dividends had been taxed at regular income tax rates.

9. **Expanded expensing election for businesses.** The amount of expense that a business can deduct in the year it buys equipment rises from $25,000 to $100,000, as an incentive to increase capital expenditures.

10. **Bonus first-year depreciation allowance liberalized.** The bonus for first-year depreciation for property bought after May 5, 2003 is boosted from 30% to 50%. This bonus applies to equipment, property, and autos.

11. **Accumulated earnings tax and personal holding company tax rates reduced to 15%.** Formerly, accumulated earnings and profits that were taxed at regular income tax rates as high as 38.6% were reduced to a 15% tax rate.

12. **Collapsible corporation rules repealed.** A collapsible corporation is one that had assets that had appreciated in value and before the corporation realized the increased value from the property, was liquidated, or made a distribution to shareholders. Such gains were formerly taxed at ordinary income rates. After the repeal of these rules, distributions are taxed at capital gains rates.

JOINT ACCOUNT bank or brokerage account owned jointly by two or more people. Joint accounts may be set up in two ways: (1) either all parties to the account must sign checks and approve all withdrawals or brokerage transactions or (2) any one party can take such actions on his or her own. *See also* JOINT TENANTS WITH RIGHT OF SURVIVORSHIP.

JOINT ACCOUNT AGREEMENT form needed to open a JOINT ACCOUNT at a bank or brokerage. It must be signed by all parties to the account regardless of the provisions it may contain concerning signatures required to authorize transactions.

JOINT AND SURVIVOR ANNUITY annuity that makes payments for the lifetime of two or more beneficiaries, often a husband and wife. When one of the annuitants dies, payments continue to the survivor annuitant in the same amount or in a reduced amount as specified in the contract. Also called JOINT LIFE ANNUITY.

JOINT BOND bond that has more than one obligator or that is guaranteed by a party other than the issuer; also called *joint and several bond.* Joint bonds are common where a parent corporation wishes to guarantee the bonds of a subsidiary. *See also* GUARANTEED BOND.

JOINT ECONOMIC COMMITTEE the ten U.S. House members and ten U.S. Senate members who review and recommend national economic policy.

JOINT LIFE ANNUITY *see* JOINT AND SURVIVOR ANNUITY.

JOINT LIABILITY mutual legal responsibility by two or more parties for claims on the assets of a company or individual. *See also* LIABILITY.

JOINTLY AND SEVERALLY
In general: legal phrase used in definitions of liability meaning that an obligation may be enforced against all obligators jointly or against any one of them separately.
Securities: term used to refer to municipal bond underwritings where the account is undivided and syndicate members are responsible for unsold bonds in proportion to their participations. In other words, a participant with 5% of the account would still be responsible for 5% of the unsold bonds, even though that member might already have sold 10%. *See also* SEVERALLY BUT NOT JOINTLY.

JOINT OWNERSHIP equal ownership by two or more people, who have right of survivorship.

JOINT STOCK COMPANY form of business organization that combines features of a corporation and a partnership. Under U.S. law, joint stock companies are recognized as corporations with unlimited liability for their stockholders. As in a conventional corporation, investors in joint stock companies receive shares of stock they are free to sell at will without ending the corporation; they also elect directors. Unlike in a limited liability corporation, however, each shareholder in a joint stock company is legally liable for all debts of the company.
    There are some advantages to this form of organization compared with limited-liability corporations: fewer taxes, greater ease of formation under the common law, more security for creditors, mobility, and freedom from regulation, for example. However, the disadvantages—such as the fact that the joint stock company usually cannot hold title to real estate and, particularly, the company's unlimited liability—tend to outweigh the advantages, with the result that it is not a popular form of organization.

JOINT TAX RETURN tax return filed by two people, usually a married couple. Both parties must sign the return, and they are equally responsible for paying the taxes due. Thus if one party does not pay the taxes, the IRS can come after the other party to make the required payment. Because of the way the tax tables are designed, it is frequently more advantageous for a married couple to file a joint return than for them to file separate returns. *See also* FILING STATUS; HEAD OF HOUSEHOLD; MARRIAGE PENALTY.

JOINT TENANCY *see* TENANCY IN COMMON; JOINT TENANTS WITH RIGHT OF SURVIVORSHIP.

JOINT TENANTS WITH RIGHT OF SURVIVORSHIP when two or more people maintain a JOINT ACCOUNT with a brokerage firm or a bank, it is normally agreed that, upon the death of one account holder, ownership of the account assets passes to the remaining account holders. This transfer of assets escapes probate, but estate taxes may be due, depending on the amount of assets transferred.

JOINT VENTURE agreement by two or more parties to work on a project together. Frequently, a joint venture will be formed when companies with complementary technology wish to create a product or service that takes advantage of the strengths of the participants. A joint venture, which is usually limited to one project, differs from a partnership, which forms the basis for cooperation on many projects.

JOINT WILL single document setting forth the testamentary instructions of a husband and wife. The use of joint wills is not common in the United States, and it may create tax and other problems.

JONESTOWN DEFENSE tactics taken by management to ward off a hostile TAKEOVER that are so extreme that they appear suicidal for the company. For example, the company may try to sell its CROWN JEWELS or take on a huge amount of debt to make the company undesirable to the potential acquirer. The term refers to the mass suicide led by Jim Jones in Jonestown, Guyana, in the early 1980s. *See also* SCORCHED EARTH POLICY.

JSE LIMITED located in Sandton, South Africa, JSE is the largest stock exchange in Africa. It was established in 1887 as the Johannesburg Exchange and Chambers Company and later became the Johannesburg Stock Exchange to raise financing for the mining industry. In 1995 the JSE opened its doors to foreign and corporate members. The following year, the JSE Equities Trading (JET) electronic system was introduced, discontinuing trading on the floor. This trading platform was subsequently replaced with SETS. In 2000 the exchange changed its name to JSE Securities Exchange South Africa. The present name was adopted in 2005. The JSE bought out SAFEX, the South Africa Futures Exchange, in 2001, under a mutual agreement whereby the JSE retained the Safex branding and created two divisions— Safex Financial Derivatives and Safex Agricultural Derivatives. The mining sector dominates market capitalization of quoted companies, but financial services is a growing area. In 2002 the FTSE/JSE Africa Index series was launched, providing free-float adjusted, total return indices for the African and international markets that can serve as BENCHMARKS and are tradable. These are the FTSE/JSE Africa Top 40, Africa Resource 20, Africa Industrial 25, Africa Financial 15, and Africa Financial and Industrial 30. Electronic clearing and settlement is conducted through the STRATE system. Settlement is T + 3. Trading hours: 9 A.M. to 5 P.M., Monday through Friday. *www.jse.co.za.*

JUDGMENT decision by a court of law ordering someone to pay a certain amount of money. For instance, a court may order someone who illegally profited by trading on INSIDE INFORMATION to pay a judgment amounting to all the profits from the trade, plus damages. The term also refers to condemnation awards by government entities in payment for private property taken for public use.

JUMBO CERTIFICATE OF DEPOSIT certificate with a minimum denomination of $100,000. Jumbo CDs are usually bought and sold by large institutions such as banks, pension funds, money market funds, and insurance companies.

JUMBO LOANS loans in amounts exceeding the national guidelines of FREDDIE MAC and FANNIE MAE.

JUNIOR ISSUE issue of debt or equity that is subordinate in claim to another issue in terms of dividends, interest, principal, or security in the event of liquidation. *See also* JUNIOR SECURITY; PREFERRED STOCK; PRIORITY; PRIOR LIEN BOND: PRIOR PREFERRED STOCK.

JUNIOR MORTGAGE mortgage that is subordinate to other mortgages—for example, a second or a third mortgage. If a debtor defaults, the first mortgage will have to be satisfied before the junior mortgage.

JUNIOR REFUNDING refinancing government debt that matures in one to five years by issuing new securities that mature in five years or more.

JUNIOR SECURITY security with lower priority claim on assets and income than a SENIOR SECURITY. For example, a PREFERRED STOCK is junior to a DEBENTURE, but a debenture, being an unsecured bond, is junior to a MORTGAGE BOND. COMMON STOCK is junior to all corporate securities. Some companies—finance companies, for example—have senior SUBORDINATED and junior subordinated issues, the former having priority over the latter, but both ranking lower than senior (unsubordinated) debt.

JUNK BOND bond with a credit rating of BB or lower by RATING agencies. Although commonly used, the term has a pejorative connotation, and issuers and holders prefer the securities be called *high-yield bonds*. Junk bonds are issued by companies without long track records of sales and earnings, or by those with questionable credit strength. In the 1980s, they were a popular means of financing TAKEOVERS. Since they are more volatile and pay higher yields than INVESTMENT GRADE bonds, many risk-oriented investors specialize in trading them. Institutions with FIDUCIARY responsibilities are regulated (*see* PRUDENT-MAN RULE). *See also* FALLEN ANGELS

JURISDICTION defined by the American Bankers Association as "the legal right, power or authority to hear and determine a cause; as in the jurisdiction of a court." The term frequently comes up in finance and investment discussions in connection with the jurisdictions of the various regulatory authorities bearing on the field. For example, the Federal Reserve Board, not the Securities and Exchange Commission (as might be supposed), has jurisdiction in a case involving a brokerage MARGIN ACCOUNT (*see also* REGULATION T).

The term also is important with respect to EUROCURRENCY loan agreements, where it is possible for a loan to be funded in one country but made in another by a group of international banks each from different countries, to a borrower in still another country. The determination of jurisdiction, not to mention the willingness of courts in different countries to accept that jurisdiction, is a matter of obvious urgency in such cases.

JURY OF EXECUTIVE OPINION forecasting method whereby a panel of experts—perhaps senior corporate financial executives—prepare individual forecasts based on information made available to all of them. Each expert then reviews the others' work and modifies his or her own forecasts accordingly. The resulting composite forecast is supposed to be more realistic than any individual effort could be. Also known as *Delphi forecast*.

JUSTIFIED PRICE fair market price an informed buyer will pay for an asset, whether it be a stock, a bond, a commodity, or real estate. *See also* FAIR MARKET VALUE.

JUST-IN-TIME INVENTORY SYSTEM computer-age inventory management system that coordinates delivery of raw materials or components from suppliers with production schedule, thereby minimizing inventory carrying costs.

JUST TITLE title to property that is supportable against all legal claims. Also called *clear title, good title, proper title.*

K

K abbreviation for $1,000.

KAFFIRS informal term for South African gold mining shares traded on the LONDON STOCK EXCHANGE. These shares are traded over the counter in the U.S. in the form of American Depositary Receipts, which are claims to share certificates deposited in a foreign bank. Under South African law, Kaffirs must pay out almost all their earnings to shareholders as dividends. These shares thus not only provide stockholders with a gold investment to hedge against inflation, but also afford substantial income in the form of high dividend payments. However, investors in Kaffirs must also consider the political risks of investing in South Africa, as well as the risk of fluctuations in the price of gold. *See also* AMERICAN DEPOSITARY RECEIPT.

KANGAROOS nickname for Australian stocks. The term normally refers to stocks in the ALL ORDINARIES INDEX, and refers to the animal most closely associated with Australia.

KANSAS CITY BOARD OF TRADE (KCBT) formed in 1856 as a chamber of commerce, it reorganized after the Civil War as an exchange. The KCBT is the principal market for hard, red winter wheat futures and options. It was the first exchange to trade stock index futures contracts when it launched Value Line Stock Index futures; options on the index also are traded. Trading hours for index products are 7:15 P.M. to 3:15 P.M. by electronic trading and wheat from 9:30 A.M to 1:15 P.M. for open outcry and 7:32 P.M. to 6 A.M. for electronic trading, all Monday through Friday. *www.kcbt. com.*

KAPPA DERIVATIVE PRICING MODEL that measures the effect of volatility. Used interchangeably with *vega* and also with OMEGA, SIGMA PRIME, and ZETA.

KEOGH PLAN tax-deferred pension account designated for employees of unincorporated businesses or for persons who are self-employed (either full-time or part-time). Like the INDIVIDUAL RETIREMENT ARRANGEMENT (IRA), the Keogh plan (also known as HR 10) allows all investment earnings to grow tax-deferred until capital is withdrawn, as early as age $59\frac{1}{2}$ and starting no later than age $70\frac{1}{2}$. Almost any investment, except physical real estate and collectibles, can be used for a Keogh account. Typically, people place Keogh assets in stocks, bonds, money-market funds, certificates of deposit, mutual funds, or limited partnerships. The Keogh plan, named after U.S. Representative Eugene James Keogh, was established by Congress in 1962 and was expanded in the ECONOMIC RECOVERY TAX ACT OF 1981 (ERTA). Employers can deduct, up to certain limits, the contributions they make to Keogh plans, including those made for their own retirement.

KEY INDUSTRY industry of primary importance to a nation's economy. For instance, the defense industry is called a key industry since it is crucial to maintaining a country's safety. The automobile industry is also considered key since so many jobs are directly or indirectly dependent on it.

KEYNESIAN ECONOMICS body of economic thought originated by the British economist and government adviser, John Maynard Keynes (1883–1946), whose landmark work, *The General Theory of Employment, Interest* *and Money,* was published in 1935. Writing during the Great Depression, Keynes took issue with the classical economists, like Adam Smith, who believed that the economy worked best when left alone. Keynes believed that active government intervention in the marketplace was the only method of ensuring economic growth and stability. He held essentially that insufficient demand causes unemployment and that excessive demand results in inflation; government should therefore manipulate the level of aggregate demand by adjusting levels of government expenditure and taxation. For example, to avoid depression Keynes advocated increased government spending and EASY MONEY, resulting in more investment, higher employment, and increased consumer spending.

Keynesian economics has had great influence on the public economic policies of industrial nations, including the United States. In the 1980s, however, after repeated recessions, slow growth, and high rates of inflation in the U.S., a contrasting outlook, uniting monetarists and "supply siders," blamed excessive government intervention for troubles in the economy.

See also AGGREGATE SUPPLY; AUSTRIAN ECONOMICS; LAISSEZ-FAIRE; MACRO-ECONOMICS; MONETARIST; SUPPLY-SIDE ECONOMICS.

KEY PERSON INSURANCE *see* BUSINESS LIFE INSURANCE.

KICKBACK
Finance: practice whereby sales finance companies reward dealers who discount installment purchase paper through them with cash payments.
Government and private contracts: payment made secretly by a seller to someone instrumental in awarding a contract or making a sale—an illegal payoff.
Labor relations: illegal practice whereby employers require the return of a portion of wages established by law or union contract, in exchange for employment.

KICKER added feature of a debt obligation, usually designed to enhance marketability by offering the prospect of equity participation. For instance, a bond may be convertible to stock if the shares reach a certain price. This makes the bond more attractive to investors, since the bondholder potentially gets the benefit of an equity security in addition to interest payments. Other examples of equity kickers are RIGHTS and WARRANTS. Some mortgage loans also include kickers in the form of ownership participation or in the form of a percentage of gross rental receipts. Kickers are also called *sweeteners.*

KIDDIE TAX tax filed by parents on Form 8615 for the investment income of children under age 14 exceeding $1,800. Tax is at parent's top tax rate. In some cases, however, parents may elect to report such children's income on their own returns.

KILLER BEES those who aid a company in fending off a takeover bid. "Killer bees" are usually investment bankers who devise strategies to make the target less attractive or more difficult to acquire.

KITCHEN SINK BOND bond representing a bundling of miscellaneous, usually hard-to-sell, TRANCHES of COLLATERALIZED MORTGAGE OBLIGATIONS (CMOs) and REMICS. With different underlying mortgage pools and different expected cash flows—"everything but the kitchen sink"—such bonds defy analysis from a risk standpoint, and their future price behavior is impossible to model and predict.

KITING
Commercial banking: (1) depositing and drawing checks between accounts at two or more banks and thereby taking advantage of the FLOAT—that is, the time it takes the bank of deposit to collect from the paying bank. (2) fraudently altering the figures on a check to increase its face value.
Securities: driving stock prices to high levels through manipulative trading methods, such as the creation of artificial trading activity by the buyer and the seller working together and using the same funds.

KNOCK-OUT OPTION form of derivative that gives the buyer the right, but not the obligation, to buy an underlying commodity, currency, or other position at a preset price. Unlike regular options, however, knock-out options expire worthless, or are "knocked out" if the underlying commodity or currency goes through a particular price level. For example, a knock-out option based on the value of the U.S. dollar against the German mark gets knocked out if the dollar falls below a specified exchange rate against the mark. Regular options can have unlimited moves up or down. Knock-out options are much cheaper to buy than regular options, allowing buyers to take larger positions with less money than regular options. Knock-out options are frequently used by hedge funds and other speculators. Knock-in options are the same concept with the trigger on the other side of the price. *See also* EXOTIC OPTIONS.

KNOW YOUR CUSTOMER ethical concept in the securities industry either stated or implied by the rules of the exchanges and the other authorities regulating broker-dealer practices. Its meaning is expressed in the following paragraph from Article 3 of the FINRA Rules of Fair Practice: "In recommending to a customer the purchase, sale or exchange of any security, a member shall have reasonable grounds for believing that the recommendation is suitable for such customer upon the basis of the facts, if any, disclosed by such customer as to his other security holdings and as to his financial situation and needs." Customers opening accounts at brokerage firms must supply financial information that satisfies the know-your-customer requirement for routine purposes.

KONDRATIEFF WAVE theory of the Soviet economist Nikolai Kondratieff in the 1920s that the economies of the Western capitalist world were prone to major up-and-down "supercycles" lasting 50 to 60 years. He claimed to have predicted the economic crash of 1929–30 based on the crash of 1870, 60 years earlier. The Kondratieff wave theory has adherents, but is controversial among economists. Also called *Kondratieff cycle.*

KRUGGERAND gold bullion coin minted by the Republic of South Africa which comes in one-ounce, half-ounce, quarter-ounce and one-tenth-ounce sizes. Kruggerands usually sell for slightly more than the current value of their gold content. Kruggerands, which had been the dominant gold coin in the world, were banned from being imported into the United States in 1985 because of the South African government's policy of apartheid. The ban was lifted on July 10, 1991. Other GOLD COINS traded in addition to the Kruggerand include the United States Eagle, Canadian Maple Leaf, Mexican Peso, Austrian Philharmonic, and Australian Kangaroo.

L

LABOR-INTENSIVE requiring large pools of workers. Said of an industry in which labor costs are more important than capital costs. Deep-shaft coal mining, for instance, is labor-intensive.

LADDERING Same as STAGGERING MATURITIES.

LADDER OPTION EXOTIC OPTION that allows the holder to lock-in gains on the underlying security during the life of the option. Also called *step-lock option.*

LADY MACBETH STRATEGY TAKEOVER tactic whereby a third party poses as a white knight then turns coat and joins an unfriendly bidder.

LAFFER CURVE curve named for U.S. economics professor Arthur Laffer, postulating that economic output will grow if marginal tax rates are cut. The curve is used in explaining SUPPLY-SIDE ECONOMICS, a theory that noninflationary growth is spurred when tax policies encourage productivity and investment.

LAGGING INDICATORS economic indicators that lag behind the overall pace of economic activity. The Conference Board publishes the Index of Lagging Indicators monthly along with the index of LEADING INDICATORS and the index of COINCIDENT INDICATORS. The six components of the lagging indicators are the unemployment rate, business spending, unit labor costs, bank loans outstanding, bank interest rates, and the book value of manufacturing and trade inventories.

LAISSEZ-FAIRE doctrine that interference of government in business and economic affairs should be minimal. Adam Smith's *The Wealth of Nations* (1776) described laissez-faire economics in terms of an "invisible hand" that would provide for the maximum good for all, if businessmen were free to pursue profitable opportunities as they saw them. The growth of industry in England in the early 19th century and American industrial growth in the late 19th century both occurred in a laissez-faire capitalist environment. The laissez-faire period ended by the beginning of the 20th century, when large monopolies were broken up and government regulation of business became the norm. The Great Depression of the 1930s saw the birth of KEYNESIAN ECONOMICS, an influential approach advocating government intervention in economic affairs. The movement toward deregulation of business in the United States that began in the 1970s and 80s is to some extent a return to the laissez-faire philosophy. *Laissez-faire* is French for "allow to do." *See also* AUSTRIAN ECONOMICS.

LAND CONTRACT creative real estate financing method whereby a seller with a mortgage finances a buyer by taking a down payment and being paid installments but not yielding title until the mortgage is repaid. Also called *contract for deed* and *installment sales contract.*

LANDLORD owner of property who rents it to a TENANT.

LAPSE expiration of a right or privilege because one party did not live up to its obligations during the time allowed. For example, a life insurance policy will lapse if the policyholder does not make the required premium payments on time. This means that the policyholder is no longer protected by the policy.

LAPSED OPTION OPTION that reached its expiration date without being exercised and is thus without value.

LARGE CAP stock with a large capitalization (numbers of shares outstanding times the price of the shares). Large Cap stocks typically have at least $5 billion in outstanding MARKET VALUE. Numerous mutual funds specialize in Large Cap stocks, and many have the words Large Cap in their names.

LAST IN FIRST OUT (LIFO) method of accounting for INVENTORY that ties the cost of goods sold to the cost of the most recent purchases. The formula for cost of goods sold is:

> beginning inventory + purchases – ending inventory = cost of goods sold

In contrast to the FIRST IN, FIRST OUT (FIFO) method, in a period of rising prices LIFO produces a higher cost of goods sold and a lower gross profit and taxable income. The artificially low balance sheet inventories resulting from the use of LIFO in periods of inflation give rise to the term *LIFO cushion.*

LAST SALE most recent trade in a particular security. Not to be confused with the final transaction in a trading session, called the CLOSING SALE. The last sale is the point of reference for two Securities and Exchange Commission rules: (1) On a national exchange, no SHORT SALE may be made below the price of the last regular sale. (2) No short sale may be made at the same price as the last sale unless the last sale was at a price higher than the preceding different price. PLUS TICK, MINUS TICK, ZERO MINUS TICK, and ZERO PLUS TICK, used in this connection, refer to the last sale.

LAST TRADING DAY final day during which a futures contract may be settled. If the contract is not OFFSET, either an agreement between the buying and selling parties must be arranged or the physical commodity must be delivered from the seller to the buyer.

LATE CHARGE fee charged by a grantor of credit when the borrower fails to make timely payment.

LATE TAPE delay in displaying price changes because trading on a stock exchange is particularly heavy. If the tape is more than five minutes late, the first digit of a price is deleted. For instance, a trade at 62.75 is reported as 2.75. *See also* DIGITS DELETED.

LATE TRADING *see* MARKET TIMING.

LAUNDER to make illegally acquired cash look as if it were acquired legally. The usual practice is to transfer the money through foreign banks, thereby concealing its purpose. SEC Rule 17a-8 prohibits using broker-dealers for this purpose.

LAW OF LARGE NUMBERS statistical concept holding that the greater the number of units in a projection, the less important each unit becomes. Group insurance, which gets cheaper as the group gets larger, is an example of the principle in application; actuarial abnormalities have less influence on total claims.

LAY OFF

Investment banking: reduce the risk in a standby commitment, under which the bankers agree to purchase and resell to the public any portion of a stock issue not subscribed to by shareowners who hold rights. The risk is that the market value will fall during the two to four weeks when shareholders are deciding whether to exercise or sell their rights. To minimize the risk, investment bankers (1) buy up the rights as they are offered and, at the same time, sell the shares represented by these rights; and (2) sell short an amount of shares proportionate to the rights that can be expected to go unexercised—to $\frac{1}{2}$% of the issue, typically. Also called *laying off.*

Labor: temporarily or permanently remove an employee from a payroll because of an economic slowdown or a production cutback, not because of poor performance or an infraction of company rules.

LEADER

1. stock or group of stocks at the forefront of an upsurge or a downturn in a market. Typically, leaders are heavily bought and sold by institutions that want to demonstrate their own market leadership.
2. product that has a large market share.

LEADING INDICATORS components of indicators released monthly by the CONFERENCE BOARD, along with the Index of LAGGING INDICATORS and the Index of COINCIDENT INDICATORS. The 11 components are: the average work-week of production workers; average weekly claims for state unemployment insurance; manufacturers' new orders for consumer goods and materials; vendor performance (companies receiving slower deliveries from suppliers); contracts and orders for plant and equipment; building permits; change in manufacturers' unfilled orders for durable goods; changes in sensitive materials prices; stock prices; MONEY SUPPLY (M-2); and index of consumer expectations. The index of leading indicators, the components of which are adjusted for inflation, accurately forecasts the ups and downs of the business cycle.

LEAD REGULATOR leading self-regulatory organization (SRO) taking responsibility for investigation of a particular section of the law and all the cases that pertain to it. In the securities business, for example, the New York Stock Exchange may take the lead in investigating certain kinds of fraud or suspicious market activity, while the American Stock Exchange or NASDAQ may be the lead regulator in other areas. The lead regulator will report its findings to the other self-regulatory organizations, and ultimately to a government oversight agency, such as the Securities and Exchange Commission.

LEAPS acronym for Long-Term Equity AnticiPation Securities, LEAPS are long-term equity options traded on U.S. exchanges and over the counter. Instead of expiring in two near-term and two farther out months as most equity OPTIONS do, LEAPS expire in two to five years, giving the buyer a longer time for his strategy to come to fruition. LEAPS are traded on many individual stocks listed on the New York Stock Exchange, the American Stock Exchange, and NASDAQ.

LEARNING CURVE predictable improvements following the early part of the life of a production contract, when costly mistakes are made.

LEASE contract granting use of real estate, equipment, or other fixed assets for a specified time in exchange for payment, usually in the form of rent. The owner of the leased property is called the lessor, the user the lessee. *See also* CAPITAL LEASE; FINANCIAL LEASE; OPERATING LEASE; SALE AND LEASEBACK.

LEASE ACQUISITION COST price paid by a real estate LIMITED PARTNERSHIP, when acquiring a lease, including legal fees and related expenses. The charges are prorated to the limited partners.

LEASEBACK transaction in which one party sells property to another and agrees to lease the property back from the buyer for a fixed period of time. For example, a building owner wanting to get cash out of the building may decide to sell the building to a real estate or leasing company and sign a long-term lease to occupy the space. The original owner is thereby able to receive cash for the value of his property, which he can reinvest in his business, as well as remain in the property. The new owner is assured of the stability of a long-term tenant and a steady income. Leaseback deals (also called sale and leaseback deals) also are executed for business equipment such as computers, cars, trucks, and airplanes. Partial ownership interests in leasing deals are sold to investors in LIMITED PARTNERSHIP form, and are designed to produce a fixed level of income to limited partners for the lease term.

LEASEHOLD asset representing the right to use property under a LEASE.

LEASEHOLD IMPROVEMENT modification of leased property. The cost is added to fixed assets and then amortized.

LEASE-PURCHASE AGREEMENT agreement providing that portions of LEASE payments may be applied toward the purchase of the property under lease.

LEG
1. sustained trend in stock market prices. A prolonged bull or bear market may have first, second, and third legs.
2. one side of a spread transaction. For instance, a trader might buy a CALL OPTION that has a particular STRIKE PRICE and expiration date, then combine it with a PUT OPTION that has the same striking price and a different expiration date. The two options are called legs of the spread. Selling one of the options is termed LIFTING A LEG.

LEGACY gift under a WILL of cash or some other specific item of personal property, such as a stock certificate, a car, or a piece of jewelry. The legacy usually is conditioned, meaning the legatee is required to be employed by the TESTATOR—the person who makes the will—or related to the testator by marriage. In other cases, a legacy to a legatee who has not attained a particular age at the testator's death will be held in trust for the legatee, instead of being distributed outright.

LEGACY ASSETS TOXIC ASSETS, in the form of mortgage loans held directly by banks (*legacy loans*) or mortgage-related ASSET-BACKED SECURITIES (ABSs) and COLLATERALIZED DEBT OBLIGATIONS (CDOs) held by banks as investments (*legacy securities*), following the real estate meltdown in 2007. *See also* PUBLIC-PRIVATE INVESTMENT PROGRAM FOR LEGACY ASSETS.

LEGACY COST the cost of retiree pension, health, insurance, and other benefits to an employer.

LEGAL computerized data base maintained by the New York Stock Exchange to track enforcement actions against member firms, audits of member firms, and customer complaints. LEGAL is not an acronym, but is written in all capitals.

LEGAL AGE age at which a person can enter into binding contracts or agree to other legal acts without the consent of another adult. In most states, the legal age, also called the *age of majority,* is 18 years old.

LEGAL ENTITY person or organization that has the legal standing to enter into a contract and may be sued for failure to perform as agreed in the contract. A child under legal age is not a legal entity; a corporation is a legal entity since it is a person in the eyes of the law.

LEGAL INVESTMENT investment permissible for investors with FIDUCIARY responsibilities. INVESTMENT GRADE bonds, as rated by Standard & Poor's or Moody's, usually qualify as legal investments. Guidelines designed to protect investors are set by the state in which the fiduciary operates. *See also* LEGAL LIST.

LEGAL LIABILITY (1) monies owed, shown on a balance sheet. (2) individual's or company's obligation to act responsibly or face compensatory penalties. *See also* LIABILITY.

LEGAL LIST securities selected by a state agency, usually a banking department, as permissible holdings of mutual savings banks, pension funds, insurance companies, and other FIDUCIARY institutions. To protect the money that individuals place in such institutions, only high quality debt and equity securities are generally included. As an alternative to the legal list, some states apply the PRUDENT MAN RULE.

LEGAL MONOPOLY exclusive right to offer a particular service within a particular territory. In exchange, the company agrees to have its policies and rates regulated. Some electric and water utilities are legal monopolies.

LEGAL OPINION
1. statement as to legality, written by an authorized official such as a city attorney or an attorney general.
2. statement as to the legality of a MUNICIPAL BOND issue, usually written by a law firm specializing in public borrowings. It is part of the *official statement,* the municipal equivalent of a PROSPECTUS. Unless the legality of an issue is established, an investor's contract is invalid at the time of issue and he cannot sue under it. The legal opinion is therefore required by a SYNDICATE MANAGER and customarily accompanies the transfer of municipal securities as long as they are outstanding.

LEGAL TRANSFER transaction that requires documentation other than the standard stock or bond power to validate the transfer of a stock certificate from a seller to a buyer—for example, securities registered to a corporation or to a deceased person. It is the selling broker's responsibility to supply proper documentation to the buying broker in a legal transfer.

LEGISLATIVE RISK risk that a change in legislation could have a major positive or negative effect on an investment. For instance, a company that is a large exporter may be a beneficiary of a trade agreement that lowers tariff barriers, and therefore may see its stock price rise. On the other hand, a company that is a major polluter may be harmed by laws that stiffen fines for polluting the air or water, thereby making its share price fall.

LEMON product or investment producing poor performance. A car that continually needs repairs is a lemon, and consumers are guaranteed a full refund in several states under so-called lemon laws. A promising stock that fails to live up to expectations is also called a lemon.

LENDER individual or firm that extends money to a borrower with the expectation of being repaid, usually with interest. Lenders create debt in the form of loans, and in the event of LIQUIDATION they are paid off before stockholders receive distributions. But the investor deals in both debt (bonds) and equity (stocks). It is useful to remember that investors in commercial paper, bonds, and other debt instruments are in fact lenders with the same rights and powers enjoyed by banks.

LENDER OF LAST RESORT
1. characterization of a central bank's role in bolstering a bank that faces large withdrawals of funds. The U.S. lender of last resort is the FEDERAL RESERVE BANK. Member banks may borrow from the DISCOUNT WINDOW to maintain reserve requirements or to meet large withdrawals. The Fed thereby maintains the stability of the banking system, which would be threatened if major banks were to fail.
2. government small business financing programs and municipal economic development organizations whose precondition to making loans to private enterprises is an inability to obtain financing elsewhere.

LENDING AGREEMENT contract between a lender and a borrower. *See also* INDENTURE; REVOLVING CREDIT; TERM LOAN.

LENDING AT A PREMIUM term used when one broker lends securities to another broker to cover customer's short position and imposes a charge for the loan. Such charges, which are passed on to the customer, are the exception rather than the rule, since securities are normally LOANED FLAT between brokers, that is, without interest. Lending at a premium might occur when the securities needed are in very heavy demand and are therefore difficult to borrow. The premium is in addition to any payments the customer might have to make to the lending broker to MARK TO THE MARKET or to cover dividends or interest payable on the borrowed securities.

LENDING AT A RATE paying interest to a customer on the credit balance created from the proceeds of a SHORT SALE. Such proceeds are held in ESCROW to secure the loan of securities, usually made by another broker, to cover the customer's short position. Lending at a rate is the exception rather than the rule.

LENDING SECURITIES securities borrowed from a broker's inventory, other MARGIN ACCOUNTS, or from other brokers, when a customer makes a SHORT SALE and the securities must be delivered to the buying customer's broker. As collateral, the borrowing broker deposits with the lending broker an amount of money equal to the market value of the securities. No interest or premium is ordinarily involved in the transaction. The Securities and Exchange Commission requires that brokerage customers give permission to have their securities used in loan transactions, and the point is routinely covered in the standard agreement signed by customers when they open general accounts.

LESS DEVELOPED COUNTRIES (LDC) countries that are not fully industrialized or do not have sophisticated financial or legal systems. These countries, also called members of the *Third World,* typically have low levels of per-capita income, high inflation and debt, and large trade deficits. The World Bank may be helping them by providing loan assistance. Loans to such countries are commonly called *LDC debt.*

LESSEE *see* LEASE.

LESSOR *see* LEASE.

LETTER BOND *see* LETTER SECURITY.

LETTER OF CREDIT (L/C) instrument or document issued by a bank guaranteeing the payment of a customer's drafts up to a stated amount for a specified period. It substitutes the bank's credit for the buyer's and eliminates the seller's risk. It is used extensively in international trade. A *commercial letter of credit* is normally drawn in favor of a third party, called the beneficiary. A *confirmed letter of credit* is provided by a correspondent bank and guaranteed by the issuing bank. A *revolving letter of credit* is issued for a specified amount and automatically renewed for the same amount for a specified period, permitting any number of drafts to be drawn so long as they do not exceed its overall limit. A *traveler's letter of credit* is issued for the convenience of a traveling customer and typically lists correspondent banks at which drafts will be honored. A *performance letter of credit* is issued to guarantee performance under a contract.

LETTER OF INTENT
1. any letter expressing an intention to take (or not take) an action, sometimes subject to other action being taken. For example, a bank might issue a letter of intent stating it will make a loan to a customer, subject to another lender's agreement to participate. The letter of intent, in this case, makes it possible for the customer to negotiate the participation loan.
2. preliminary agreement between two companies that intend to merge. Such a letter is issued after negotiations have been satisfactorily completed.
3. promise by a MUTUAL FUND shareholder to invest a specified sum of money monthly for about a year. In return, the shareholder is entitled to lower sales charges.
4. INVESTMENT LETTER for a LETTER SECURITY.

LETTER OF LAST INSTRUCTIONS letter placed with a WILL containing instructions on carrying out the provisions of the will. These letters generally are not binding on the executors, but many executors feel morally bound to follow the wishes of the TESTATORS who appointed them. Florida is one of several states where the law allows these letters to be incorporated by reference if the language of the will shows this intent and identifies the letter's purpose clearly.

LETTER SECURITY stock or bond that is not registered with the Securities and Exchange Commission and therefore cannot be sold in the public market. When an issue is sold directly by the issuer to the investor, registration with the SEC can be avoided if a LETTER OF INTENT, called an INVESTMENT LETTER, is signed by the purchaser establishing that the securities are being bought for investment and not for resale. The letter's integral association with the security gives rise to the terms *letter security, letter stock,* and *letter bond.* Also called *144 stock and controlled and restricted stock. See also* SECURITIES AND EXCHANGE COMMISSION RULES; RESTRICTED SECURITIES.

LETTER STOCK *see* LETTER SECURITY.

LEVEL DEBT SERVICE provision in a municipal charter stipulating that payments on municipal debt be approximately equal every year. This makes it easier to project the amount of tax revenue needed to meet obligations.

LEVEL I, II, III levels of service available to firms trading NASDAQ stocks. Level I provides a single median quote and is intended for firms not engaged in trading over-the-counter stocks, such as the OTC BULLETIN BOARD service and other market news vendors. Level II is a component of NASDAQ Workstation II, a network of workstations providing quotations, executions, trade reporting, and trade negotiations and clearing. Level II provides current bid and offer quotes by all market makers for firms trading for themselves and for customers. Level III, designed for market makers, provides Level II services plus the ability to enter quotations, direct/execute orders, and send information.

LEVEL LOAD sales charge that does not change over time. In mutual funds, level load shares are called *C class shares,* compared to *A class* for upfront loads and *B class* for back-end loads. A level load will typically be 1% to 2% of assets each year, which is lower than an upfront load of 4% to 5% or the back-end load, which starts at 5% and declines each year until it disappears if the fund shares are held for five years. Though the level load may be lower than an upfront or back-end load, an investor ends up paying a higher commission if he holds the fund for many years.

LEVEL PLAYING FIELD condition in which competitors operate under the same rules. For example, all banks must follow the same regulations set down by the Federal Reserve. In some situations, competitors complain to regulators or Congress that they are not playing on a level playing field. For example, banks contend that brokerage firms can offer certain banking services without the same rules imposed on banks. Companies wanting to export to a particular country may complain that domestic companies are protected by various trade barriers, creating an uneven playing field. Various sections of the tax code may favor some companies more than others, prompting cries from the disadvantaged firms to "level the playing field."

LEVEL TERM INSURANCE life insurance policy with a fixed face value and rising insurance premiums.

LEVERAGE

Operating leverage: extent to which a company's costs of operating are fixed (rent, insurance, executive salaries) as opposed to variable (materials, direct labor). In a totally automated company, whose costs are virtually all fixed, every dollar of increase in sales is a dollar of increase in operating income once the BREAKEVEN POINT has been reached, because costs remain the same at every level of production. In contrast, a company whose costs are largely variable would show relatively little increase in operating income when production and sales increased because costs and production would rise together. The leverage comes in because a small change in sales has a magnified percentage effect on operating income and losses. The *degree of operating leverage*—the ratio of the percentage change in operating income to the percentage change in sales or units sold—measures the sensitivity of a firm's profits to changes in sales volume. A firm using a high degree of operating leverage has a breakeven point at a relatively high sales level.

Financial leverage: debt in relation to equity in a firm's capital structure—its LONG-TERM DEBT (usually bonds), PREFERRED STOCK, and SHAREHOLDERS' EQUITY—measured by the DEBT-TO-EQUITY RATIO. The more long-term debt there is, the greater the financial leverage. Shareholders benefit from financial leverage to the extent that return on the borrowed money exceeds the interest costs and the market value of their shares rises. For this reason, financial leverage is popularly called *trading on the equity.* Because leverage also means required interest and principal payments and thus ultimately the risk of default, how much leverage is desirable is largely a question of stability of earnings. As a rule of thumb, an industrial company with a debt to equity ratio of more than 30% is highly leveraged, exceptions being firms with dependable earnings and cash flow, such as electric utilities.

Since long-term debt interest is a fixed cost, financial leverage tends to take over where operating leverage leaves off, further magnifying the effects on earnings per share of changes in sales levels. In general, high operating leverage should accompany low financial leverage, and vice versa.

Investments: means of enhancing return or value without increasing investment. Buying securities on margin is an example of leverage with borrowed money, and extra leverage may be possible if the leveraged security is convertible into common stock. RIGHTS, WARRANTS, and OPTION contracts provide leverage, not involving borrowings but offering the prospect of high return for little or no investment. *See also* DELEVERAGE.

LEVERAGED BUYOUT (LBO) takeover of a company, using borrowed funds. Most often, the target company's assets serve as security for the loans taken out by the acquiring firm, which repays the loan out of cash flow of the acquired company. Management may use this technique to retain control by converting a company from public to private. A group of investors may also borrow funds from banks, using their own assets as collateral, to take over another firm. In almost all leveraged buyouts, public shareholders receive a premium over the current market value for their shares. When a company that has gone private in a leveraged buyout offers shares to the public again, it is called a REVERSE LEVERAGED BUYOUT.

LEVERAGED COMPANY company with debt in addition to equity in its capital structure. In its popular connotation, the term is applied to companies that are highly leveraged. Although the judgment is relative, industrial companies with more than one third of their capitalization in the form of debt are considered highly leveraged. *See also* LEVERAGE.

LEVERAGED EMPLOYEE STOCK OWNERSHIP PLAN (LESOP) EMPLOYEE STOCK OWNERSHIP PLAN (ESOP) in which employee pension plans and profit-sharing plans borrow money to purchase stock in the company or issue CONVERTIBLES exchangeable for common stock. In addition to the usual advantages of employee ownership, the LESOP is a way to ensure that majority ownership remains in friendly hands.

LEVERAGED INVESTMENT COMPANY

1. open-end INVESTMENT COMPANY, or MUTUAL FUND, that is permitted by its charter to borrow capital from a bank or other lender.
2. dual-purpose INVESTMENT COMPANY, which issues both income and capital shares. Holders of income shares receive dividends and interest on investments, whereas holders of capital shares receive all capital gains on investments. In effect each class of shareholder leverages the other.

LEVERAGED LEASE LEASE that involves a lender in addition to the lessor and lessee. The lender, usually a bank or insurance company, puts up a percentage of the cash required to purchase the asset, usually more than half. The balance is put up by the lessor, who is both the equity participant and the borrower. With the cash the lessor acquires the asset, giving the lender (1) a mortgage on the asset and (2) an assignment of the lease and lease payments. The lessee then makes periodic payments to the lessor, who in turn pays the lender. As owner of the asset, the lessor is entitled to tax deductions for DEPRECIATION on the asset and INTEREST on the loan.

LEVERAGED RECAPITALIZATION corporate strategy to fend off potential acquirers by taking on a large amount of debt and making a large cash distribution to shareholders. For example, XYZ Company, selling at $50 a share, may borrow $3 billion to make a one-time distribution of $20 a share to stockholders. After the distribution, the stock price will drop to $30. By replacing equity with $3 billion in debt, XYZ is a far less attractive takeover target for a raider or other company than it was before. Also called *leveraged recap* for short.

LEVERAGED STOCK stock financed with credit, as in a MARGIN ACCOUNT. Although not, strictly speaking, leveraged stock, securities that are convertible into common stock provide an extra degree of leverage when bought on margin. Assuming the purchase price is reasonably close to the INVESTMENT VALUE and CONVERSION VALUE, the downside risk is no greater than it would be with the same company's common stock, whereas the appreciation value is much greater.

LIABILITY claim on the assets of a company or individual—excluding ownership EQUITY. Characteristics: (1) It represents a transfer of assets or services at a specified or determinable date. (2) The firm or individual has little or no discretion to avoid the transfer. (3) The event causing the obligation has already occurred. *See also* BALANCE SHEET.

LIABILITY INSURANCE insurance for money the policyholder is legally obligated to pay because of bodily injury or property damage caused to another person and covered in the policy. Liabilities may result from property damage, bodily injury, libel, or any other damages caused by the insured. The insurance company agrees to pay for such damages if they are awarded by a court, up to the limitations specified in the insurance contract. The insurer may also cover legal expenses incurred in defending the suit.

LIAR LOAN *see* NO DOCUMENTATION LOAN.

LIBOR *see* LONDON INTERBANK OFFERED RATE.

LICENSE legal document issued by a regulatory agency permitting an individual to conduct a certain activity, usually because the person has passed a training course qualifying him. For example, a securities license is required for a broker to sell stocks, bonds, and mutual funds. An insurance license is required before someone can sell insurance products. Before a driver's license is granted, a driver must pass an examination proving that he knows how to drive safely. If the licensed individual violates the regulations, the license can be revoked.

LIEN creditor's claim against property. For example, a mortgage is a lien against a house; if the mortgage is not paid on time, the house can be seized to satisfy the lien. Similarly, a bond is a lien against a company's assets; if interest and principal are not paid when due, the assets may be seized to pay the bondholders. As soon as a debt is paid, the lien is removed. Liens may be granted by courts to satisfy judgments. *See also* MECHANIC'S LIEN.

LIFE ANNUITY ANNUITY that makes a guaranteed fixed payment for the rest of the life of the annuitant. After the annuitant dies, beneficiaries receive no further payments.

LIFE CYCLE most common usage refers to an individual's progression from cradle to grave and the assumption that the choice of appropriate investments changes. Term also applies to the life of a product or of a business, consisting of inception, development, growth, expansion, maturity, and decline (or change). Recently, the term has entered into the vocabulary of the family-owned business, referring to generations of management. The post-World War II baby boom produced entrepreneurs who built businesses that now approach a juncture where a second generation either takes over management or sells out.

LIFE-CYCLE FUND a special breed of BALANCED MUTUAL FUND structured as a FUND OF FUNDS that automatically adjusts asset allocation between equity and fixed income to become more conservative as one's target retirement date approaches. Also called *age-based fund* and *target-date fund.*

LIFE-CYCLE PLANNING planning contemplated by the concept of LIFE CYCLE.

LIFE EXPECTANCY age to which an average person can be expected to live, as calculated by an ACTUARY. Insurance companies base their projections of benefit payouts on actuarial studies of such factors as sex, heredity, and health habits and base their rates on actuarial analysis. Life expectancy can be calculated at birth or at some other age and generally varies according to age. Thus, all persons at birth might have an average life expectancy of 80 years and all persons aged 40 years might have an average life expectancy of 85 years.

Life expectancy projections determine such matters as the ages when an INDIVIDUAL RETIREMENT ACCOUNT may start and finish withdrawing funds. Annuities payable for lifetimes are usually based on separate male or female tables, except that a QUALIFIED PLAN OR TRUST must use unisex tables.

LIFE INSURANCE insurance policy that pays a death benefit to beneficiaries if the insured dies. In return for this protection, the insured pays a premium, usually on an annual basis. *Term insurance* pays off upon the insured's death but provides no buildup of cash value in the policy. Term premiums are cheaper than premiums for *cash value policies* such as whole life, variable life, and universal life, which pay death benefits and also provide for the buildup of cash values in the policy. The cash builds up tax-deferred in the policy and is invested in stocks, bonds, real estate, and other investments. Policyholders can take out loans against their policies, which reduce the death benefit if they are not repaid. Some life insurance provides benefits to policyholders while they are still living, including income payments. *See also* SINGLE PREMIUM LIFE INSURANCE.

LIFE INSURANCE IN FORCE amount of life insurance that a company has issued, including the face amount of all outstanding policies together with all dividends that have been paid to policyholders. Thus a life insurance policy for $500,000 on which dividends of $10,000 have been paid would count as life insurance in force of $510,000.

LIFE INSURANCE POLICY contract between an insurance com-pany and the insured setting out the provisions of the life insurance coverage. These provisions include premiums, loan procedures, face amounts, and the designation of beneficiaries, among many other clauses. Policies may be for term or permanent cash value types of coverage.

LIFETIME REVERSE MORTGAGE type of reverse mortgage agreement whereby a homeowner borrows against the value of the home, retains title, and makes no payments while living in the home. When the home ceases to be the primary residence of the borrower, as when the borrower dies, the lender sells the property, repays the loan, and remits any surplus to the borrower's estate. Such arrangements may be appropriate for older people who need cash and are HOUSE POOR. *See also* REVERSE ANNUITY MORTGAGE (RAM).

LIFO *see* LAST IN, FIRST OUT.

LIFT rise in securities prices as measured by the Dow Jones Industrial Average or other market averages, usually caused by good business or economic news.

LIFTING A LEG closing one side of a HEDGE, leaving the other side as a long or short position. A leg, in Wall Street parlance, is one side of a hedged transaction. A trader might have a STRADDLE—that is, a call and a put on the same stock, at the same price, with the same expiration date. Making a closing sale of the put, thereby lifting a leg—or *taking off a leg,* as it is sometimes called—would leave the trader with the call, or the LONG LEG.

LIGHTEN UP to sell a portion of a stock or bond position in a portfolio. A money manager with a large profit in a stock may decide to realize some of the gains because he is unsure that the stock will continue to rise, or because he is concerned too much of the fund's assets are tied up in the stock. As a result, he will say that he is "lightening up" his position in the stock. However, some of the stock remains in the portfolio.

LIMIT *see* LIMIT ORDER; LIMIT UP, LIMIT DOWN.

LIMITED COMPANY form of business most common in Britain, where registration under the Companies Act is comparable to incorporation under state law in the United States. It is abbreviated Ltd. or PLC.

LIMITED DISCRETION agreement between broker and client allowing the broker to make certain trades without consulting the client—for instance, sell an option position that is near expiration or sell a stock on which there has just been adverse news.

LIMITED LIABILITY underlying principle of the CORPORATION and the LIMITED PARTNERSHIP in the United States and the LIMITED COMPANY in the United Kingdom that LIABILITY is limited to an investor's original investment. In contrast, a general partner or the owner of a PROPRIETORSHIP has unlimited liability.

LIMITED PARTNERSHIP organization made up of a GENERAL PARTNER, who manages a project, and limited partners, who invest money but have limited liability, are not involved in day-to-day management, and usually cannot lose more than their capital contribution. Usually limited partners receive income, capital gains, and tax benefits; the general partner collects fees and a percentage of capital gains and income. Typical limited partnerships are in real estate, oil and gas, and equipment leasing, but they also finance movies, research and development, and other projects. Typically, public limited partnerships are sold through brokerage firms, for minimum investments of $5,000, whereas private limited partnerships are put together with fewer than 35 limited partners who invest more than $20,000 each. *See also* INCOME LIMITED PARTNERSHIP; MASTER LIMITED PARTNERSHIP; OIL AND GAS LIMITED PARTNERSHIP; PASSIVE; RESEARCH AND DEVELOPMENT LIMITED PARTNERSHIP; UNLEVERAGED PROGRAM.

LIMITED PAYMENT POLICY LIFE INSURANCE contract that provides protection for one's whole life but requires premiums for a lesser number of years.

LIMITED RISK risk in buying an options contract. For example, someone who pays a PREMIUM to buy a CALL OPTION on a stock will lose nothing more than the premium if the underlying stock does not rise during the life of the option. In contrast, a FUTURES CONTRACT entails *unlimited risk,* since the buyer may have to put up more money in the event of an adverse move. Thus options trading offers limited risk unavailable in futures trading.

   Also, stock analysts may say of a stock that has recently fallen in price, that it now has limited risk, reasoning that the stock is unlikely to fall much further.

LIMITED TAX BOND MUNICIPAL BOND backed by the full faith of the issuing government but not by its full taxing power; rather it is secured by the pledge of a special tax or group of taxes, or a limited portion of the real estate tax.

LIMITED TRADING AUTHORIZATION *see* LIMITED DISCRETION.

LIMITED VOTING STOCK class of stock that cedes the right to elect directors to another class of stock. Contrast with CONTROL STOCK.

LIMITED WARRANTY warranty that imposes certain limitations, and is therefore not a full warranty. For example, an automaker may issue a warranty that covers parts, but not labor, for a particular period of time.

LIMIT ON CLOSE ORDER order to buy or sell a stated amount of a stock at the closing price, to be executed only if the closing price is a specified price or better, e.g., an order to sell XYZ at the close, if the closing price is $30 or higher.

LIMIT ORDER order to buy or sell a security or commodity at a specific price or better. The broker will execute the trade only within the price restriction. For example, a customer puts in a limit order to buy XYZ Corp. at 30 when the stock is selling for 32. Even if the stock reached 30.01 the broker will not execute the trade. Similarly, if the client put in a limit order to sell XYZ Corp. at 33 when the price is 31, the trade will not be executed until the stock price hits 33.

LIMIT ORDER INFORMATION SYSTEM electronic system that informs subscribers about securities traded on participating exchanges, showing the specialist, the exchange, the order quantities, and the bid and offer prices. This allows subscribers to shop for the most favorable prices.

LIMIT PRICE price set in a LIMIT ORDER. For example, a customer might put in a limit order to sell shares at 45 or to buy at 40. The broker executes the order at the limit price or better.

LIMIT UP, LIMIT DOWN maximum price movement allowed for a commodity FUTURES CONTRACT during one trading day. In the face of a particularly dramatic development, a future's price may move limit up or limit down for several consecutive days.

LINE category of insurance, such as the *liability line,* or the amount of insurance on a given property, such as a $500,000 line on the buildings of the XYZ Company. Term is also used generally, to refer to a product line. *See also* BANK LINE.

LINE CHART in TECHNICAL ANALYSIS, a chart showing a line connecting the closing prices of a stock or index. *See also* MOVING AVERAGE.

LINE OF CREDIT *see* BANK LINE.

LIONS variation of LYONS, or liquid yield option notes. *See also* ZERO-COUPON CONVERTIBLE SECURITY.

LIPPER MUTUAL FUND INDUSTRY AVERAGE average performance level of all mutual funds, as reported by Lipper Analytical Services of New York. The performance of all mutual funds is ranked quarterly and annually, by type of fund—such as aggressive growth fund or income fund. Mutual fund managers try to beat the industry average as well as the other funds in their category. *See also* MUTUAL FUND.

LIQUID ASSET cash or easily convertible into cash. Some examples: money-market fund shares, U.S. Treasury bills, bank deposits. An investor in an ILLIQUID investment such as a real estate or oil and gas LIMITED PARTNERSHIP is required to have substantial liquid assets, which would serve as a cushion if the illiquid deal did not work out favorably.

In a corporation's financial statements, liquid assets are cash, marketable securities, and accounts receivable.

LIQUIDATING DIVIDEND distribution of assets in the form of a DIVIDEND from a corporation that is going out of business. Such a payment may come when a firm goes bankrupt or when management decides to sell off a company's assets and pass the proceeds on to shareholders.

LIQUIDATING VALUE projected price for an asset of a company that is going out of business—for instance, a real estate holding or office equipment.

Liquidating value, also called *auction value*, assumes that assets are sold separately from the rest of the organization; it is distinguished from GOING CONCERN VALUE, which may be higher because of what accountants term *organization value* or GOODWILL.

LIQUIDATION

1. dismantling of a business, paying off debts in order of priority, and distributing the remaining assets in cash to the owners. Involuntary liquidation is covered under Chapter 7 of the federal BANKRUPTCY law. *See also* JUNIOR SECURITY; PREFERRED STOCK.
2. forced sale of a brokerage client's securities or commodities after failure to meet a MARGIN CALL. *See also* SELL OUT.

LIQUIDITY ability to buy or sell an asset quickly and in large volume without substantially affecting the asset's price. Shares in large blue-chip stocks like General Motors or General Electric are liquid, because they are actively traded and therefore the stock price will not be dramatically moved by a few buy or sell orders. However, shares in small companies with few shares outstanding, or commodity markets with limited activity, generally are not considered liquid, because one or two big orders can move the price up or down sharply. A high level of liquidity is a key characteristic of a good market for a security or a commodity.

Liquidity also refers to the ability to convert to cash quickly. For example, a money market mutual fund provides instant liquidity since shareholders can write checks on the fund. Other examples of liquid accounts include checking accounts, bank money market deposit accounts, passbook accounts, and Treasury bills.

LIQUIDITY DIVERSIFICATION purchase of bonds whose maturities range from short to medium to long term, thus helping to protect against sharp fluctuations in interest rates. Also called *laddering* and STAGGERING MATURITIES.

LIQUIDITY RATIO measure of a firm's ability to meet maturing short-term obligations. *See also* CASH ASSET RATIO; CURRENT RATIO; NET QUICK ASSETS; QUICK RATIO.

LIQUIDITY RISK the risk of being unable to sell an ASSET quickly at its FAIR MARKET VALUE. Assets with active markets, such as listed stocks, have lower liquidity risk than assets with fewer potential buyers, such as paintings.

LIQUIDITY TRAP economic situation where adding liquidity by increasing the money supply and lowering target interest rates fail to stimulate borrowing and lending, consumption, and fixed investment. Liquidity traps can sometimes be escaped by resorting to FISCAL POLICY or by using *helicopter money,* meaning distributing money directly to people as though dropping it from a helicopter and thus bypassing a banking system that tends under strained circumstances to hoard cash rather than lend it. The *Lost Decade* in Japan, where recession lasted throughout the 1990s, is an example of how intractable such liquidity problems can be. *See also* PARADOX OF SAVINGS (OR THRIFT).

LIQUID POSITION situation in which an investor's holdings are in cash or NEAR-MONEY rather than in securities or assets vulnerable to DOWNSIDE RISK.

LISBON STOCK EXCHANGE (LSE) founded in January 1769, the exchange and the PORTO DERIVATIVES EXCHANGE were united in a restructuring to form BOLSA DE VALORES DE LISBOA E PORTO (BVLP) the Portuguese Exchange. In 2002, BVLP was acquired by EURONEXT NV, and renamed EURONEXT LISBON. *See also* EURONEXT NV; EURONEXT LISBON.

LISTED FIRM company whose stock trades on the New York Stock Exchange or American Stock Exchange. The company has to meet certain LISTING REQUIREMENTS or it will be delisted. Listed firms are distinguished from unlisted companies, whose stock trades over-the-counter on the NASDAQ market.

LISTED INDEX SECURITIES *see* EXCHANGE TRADED FUNDS (ETFs).

LISTED OPTION put or call OPTION that an exchange has authorized for trading, properly called an *exchange-traded option.*

LISTED SECURITY stock or bond that has been accepted for trading by one of the organized and registered securities exchanges in the United States, which list more than 6,000 issues of securities of some 3,500 corporations. Generally, the advantages of being listed are that the exchanges provide (1) an orderly marketplace; (2) liquidity; (3) fair price determination; (4) accurate and continuous reporting on sales and quotations; (5) information on listed companies; and (6) strict regulations for the protection of security holders. Each exchange has its own listing requirements, those of the New York Stock Exchange being most stringent. Listed securities include stocks, bonds, convertible bonds, preferred stocks, warrants, rights, and options, although not all forms of securities are accepted on all exchanges. Unlisted securities are traded in the OVER-THE-COUNTER market. *See also* LISTING REQUIREMENTS; STOCK EXCHANGE.

LISTING written employment agreement between a property owner and a real estate broker authorizing the broker to find a buyer or tenant for certain property. Oral listings, while not specifically illegal, are unenforceable under many state fraud statutes, and generally are not recommended. The most common form of listing is the exclusive-right-to-sell listing. Others include open listings, net listings and exclusive-agency listings. Listings are personal service contracts and cannot be assigned to another broker, but brokers can delegate the work to other members of the sales office. The listing usually states the amount of commission the seller will pay the broker and the time limit. In a buyer's listing, the buyer hires the broker to locate a property.

LISTING BROKER licensed real estate broker (agent) who secures a listing of a property for sale. A *listing* involves a contract authorizing the broker to perform services for the selling property owner. The listing broker may sell the property, but it may also be sold by the *selling broker,* a different agent, with the two sharing commissions, usually equally.

LISTING REQUIREMENTS rules that must be met before a stock is listed for trading on an exchange. Among the requirements of the New York Stock Exchange: a corporation must have a minimum of one million publicly held shares with a minimum aggregate market value of $16 million as well as an annual net income topping $2.5 million before federal income tax.

LIST PRICE suggested retail price for a product according to the manufacturer. The list price is designed to guide retailers, though they remain free to sell products above or below list price.

LITTLE DRAGONS nickname for developing Asian nations such as Singapore, Hong Kong, South Korea, and Taiwan that pose a threat to Japan (the Big Dragon) because of their lower labor costs, high productivity, and probusiness attitudes. Also known as the *tigers*. Called an "economic miracle" for most of the 1990s, the so-called Pacific Rim region lost its economic underpinnings in 1997, causing currencies and securities markets to plunge.

LIVING BENEFITS life insurance benefits upon which the insured can draw cash while still alive. Some policies allow benefits to be paid to the insured in cases of terminal illness or illness involving certain long-term care costs. Beneficiaries receive any balance upon the insured's death. Also known as *accelerated benefits*.

LIVING DEAD *see* ZOMBIES.

LIVING TRUST *see* INTER VIVOS TRUST.

LIVING WILL document instructing doctors and family members regarding the continuation of life by artificial means or heroic measures, if incapacitated.

LLOYD'S OF LONDON a gathering place in London, England for insurance UNDERWRITERS. Lloyd's is a marketplace made up of hundreds of underwriting syndicates, each of them in effect a mini-insurer. Lloyd's sets standards for its members, but does not issue policies itself. Each syndicate is managed by an underwriter who decides which risks to accept. Typically, a risk underwritten at Lloyd's will be shared by many syndicates. The number of individual investors, known as "names," in a particular syndicate may vary from a few to hundreds. The Lloyd's market is also a major international reinsurer, allowing other insurance companies to limit their risks.

LOAD sales charge paid by an investor who buys shares in a load MUTUAL FUND or ANNUITY. Loads are usually charged when shares or units are purchased; a charge for withdrawing is called a BACK-END LOAD (or *rear-end load*). A fund that does not charge this fee is called a NO-LOAD FUND. *See also* INVESTMENT COMPANY.

LOAD FUND MUTUAL FUND that is sold for a sales charge by a brokerage firm or other sales representative. Such funds may be stock, bond, or commodity funds, with conservative or aggressive objectives. The stated advantage of a load fund is that the salesperson will explain the fund to the customer, and advise him or her when it is appropriate to sell the fund, as well as when to buy more shares. A NO-LOAD FUND, which is sold without a sales charge directly to investors by a fund company, does not give advice on when to buy or sell. Increasingly, traditional no-load funds are becoming *low-load funds,* imposing up-front charges of 3% or less with no change in services. *See also* INVESTMENT COMPANY; MUTUAL FUND SHARE CLASSES.

LOAD SPREAD OPTION method of allocating the annual sales charge on some contractual mutual funds. In a CONTRACTUAL PLAN, the investor accumulates shares in the fund through periodic fixed payments. During the first four years of the contract, up to 20% of any single year's contributions to the fund may be credited against the sales charge, provided that the total charges for these four years do not exceed 64% of one year's contributions. The sales charge is limited to 9% of the entire contract.

LOAN transaction wherein an owner of property, called the LENDER, allows another party, the *borrower*, to use the property. The borrower customarily promises to return the property after a specified period with payment for its use, called INTEREST. The documentation of the promise is called a PROMISSORY NOTE when the property is cash.

LOAN AMORTIZATION reduction of debt by scheduled, regular payments of principal and interest sufficient to repay the loan at maturity.

LOAN COMMITMENT lender's agreement to make money available to a borrower in a specified amount, at a specified rate, and within a specified time. *See also* COMMITMENT FEE.

LOAN CROWD stock exchange members who lend or borrow securities required to cover the positions of brokerage customers who sell short—called a crowd because they congregate at a designated place on the floor of the exchange. *See also* LENDING SECURITIES.

LOANED FLAT loaned without interest, said of the arrangement whereby brokers lend securities to one another to cover customer SHORT SALE positions. *See also* LENDING AT A PREMIUM; LENDING AT A RATE; LENDING SECURITIES.

LOAN ORIGINATION FEE *see* POINT.

LOAN STOCK *see* LENDING SECURITIES.

LOAN-TO-VALUE RATIO (LTV) ratio of money borrowed to fair market value, usually in reference to real property. Residential mortgage loans conventionally have a maximum LTV of 80% (an $80,000 loan on a $100,0000 house).

LOAN VALUE
1. amount a lender is willing to lend against collateral. For example, at 50% of appraised value, a piece of property worth $800,000 has a loan value of $400,000.
2. with respect to REGULATION T of the FEDERAL RESERVE BOARD, the maximum percentage of the current market value of eligible securities that a broker can lend a margin account customer. Regulation T applies only to securities formally registered or having an unlisted trading privilege on a national securities exchange. For securities exempt from Regulation T, which comprise U.S. government securities, municipal bonds, and bonds of the International Bank for Reconstruction and Development, loan value is a matter of the individual firm's policy.

LOCAL member of a futures exchange who trades for his or her own account. The traders in a futures pit are composed of locals and employees of various brokerage firms. Locals initiate their own transactions on the floor of the exchange. Some, termed *dual traders,* also execute orders on behalf of customers.

LOCAL TAXES taxes paid by an individual to his or her locality. This includes city income, property, sewer, water, school, and other taxes. These taxes are usually deductible on the taxpayer's federal income tax return.

LOCK BOX
1. cash management system whereby a company's customers mail payments to a post office box near the company's bank. The bank collects checks from the lock box—sometimes several times a day—deposits them to the account of the firm, and informs the company's cash manager by telephone of the deposit. This reduces processing FLOAT and puts cash to work more quickly. The bank's fee for its services must be weighed against the savings from reduced float to determine whether this arrangement is cost-effective.
2. bank service that entails holding a customer's securities and, as agent, receiving and depositing income such as dividends on stock and interest on bonds.
3. box rented in a post office where mail is stored until collected.

LOCKDOWN freezing of assets in a retirement plan, such as a 401(k) PLAN during a preannounced, temporary period, called *blackout period*, while the sponsoring company is making administrative changes, such as in a corporate merger or a change of money managers. In 2000–2001, lockdowns were misused to prevent employees of Enron and Global Crossing from selling their company stock as questionable accounting practices were revealed.

LOCKED IN
1. unable to take advantage of preferential tax treatment on the sale of an asset because the required HOLDING PERIOD has not elapsed. *See also* CAPITAL GAIN.
2. commodities position in which the market has an up or down limit day, and investors cannot get in or out of the market.
3. said of a rate of return that has been assured for a length of time through an investment such as a certificate of deposit or a fixed rate bond; also said of profits or yields on securities or commodities that have been protected through HEDGING techniques.

LOCKED MARKET highly competitive market environment with identical bid and ask prices for a stock. The appearance of more buyers and sellers unlocks the market.

LOCKUP PERIOD period, usually six months following an IPO, when insiders agree not to sell shares. *See also* GATE.

LOCK-UP CD certificate of deposit issued with the understanding that the buyer will hold it until maturity. Sometimes the issuer will literally lock up the CD in safekeeping.

LOCK-UP OPTION privilege offered a WHITE KNIGHT (friendly acquirer) by a TARGET COMPANY of buying CROWN JEWELS or additional equity. The aim is to discourage a hostile TAKEOVER.

LONDON INTERBANK OFFERED RATE (LIBOR) rate that the most creditworthy international banks dealing in EURODOLLARS charge each other for large loans. The LIBOR rate is usually the base for other large Eurodollar loans to less creditworthy corporate and government borrowers. For instance, a Third World country may have to pay one point over LIBOR when it borrows money.

LONDON METAL EXCHANGE (LME) principal-to-principal market for base metals trading established in 1877. LME prices are used as reference prices in many world markets by metals producers and fabricators of metal products, and are the basis for most major commodity indices. LME contracts assume an eventual delivery of physical metal on the prompt date, but this generally does not occur, since the majority of LME business is for trade hedging LME trades cash and three-month contracts on aluminum, copper, nickel, lead, tin, zinc, aluminum alloy, and North American special aluminum alloy. Traded average price option (TAPOs) contracts are available for these metals. The London Metal Exchange Index (LMEX) is a base metals index comprised of the six nonferrous metals traded on the exchange designed for investors. In 2005, the LME launched the world's first futures contracts for plastics—polypropylene and linear low-density polyethylene, tradable across all platforms. The LME supports three trading platforms; OPEN OUTCRY on the "ring" (11:45 A.M.–5 P.M.), LME Select, the Exchange's electronic trading system (7 A.M.–7 P.M.), and 24 hours via telephone. In open outcry trading, contracts are traded in "rings"—a period of five minutes for each contract beginning at 11.45 A.M. After a break, the process is repeated. The second part of this session results in settlement and official prices, at or near 1:15 P.M. After official prices are announced, a period of trading called "the kerb" begins, with all contracts trading simultaneously. The second ring, or the afternoon session, begins at 3:20 P.M., following the structure of the first ring and ending with a 25-minute kerb period from 4:35 P.M. to 5 P.M. LME Select is the exchange's electronic trading platform, connecting 33 LME member firms.

Accredited traders can execute trades on the screen in addition to open outcry ring trading and the telephone market. All trades are covered by a matching system run by the LCH. Clearnet, which acts as a central counterpart to trades executed between clearing members of the exchange. *www. lme.com.*

LONDON STOCK EXCHANGE (LSE) formed in 1761 as a club at Jonathan's Coffee House by 150 brokers who were kicked out of the Royal Exchange for rowdiness. The Stock Exchange name was adopted in 1773, and it became a regulated exchange in 1801. Following deregulation in 1986—the BIG BANG—the LSE introduced computerized trading via the SEAQ (Stock Exchange Automatic Quotation) and SEAQ International systems that display share price information in brokers' offices throughout the United Kingdom. The LSE became a public limited company in 2000 and transferred its role as the U.K. Listing Authority to the Financial Services Authority. The LSE acquired Borsa Italiana in 2007; also in 2007, Borse Dubai acquired 28% of the LSE. In 2001 the London Stock Exchange's shares were listed on its Main Market. The exchange has two equity markets, the Main Market and AIM, the exchange's international market for growing companies, which was launched in 1995. In 1997 the exchange introduced SETS (Stock Exchange Electronic Trading Service) to bring greater speed and efficiency to the market. CREST, its electronic share settlement system, was also launched that year. The London Stock Exchange is the most international equities exchange by trading in the world and Europe's largest pool of liquidity. In 2008 the total market capitalization of the over 3,500 companies on the London Stock Exchange's markets amounted to £4.4 trillion. Trading hours: Monday through Friday, 8 A.M. to 4:30 P.M. *www.londonstockexchange.com.*

LONG BOND in general, bond that matures in 10 years or more. Since these bonds commit investors' money for a long time, they normally pay investors a higher yield. In Wall Street parlance, the "long bond" is the 30-year Treasury, although none has been issued since 2001.

LONG COUPON
1. bond issue's first interest payment covering a longer period than the remaining payments, or the bond issue itself. Conventional schedules call for interest payments at six-month intervals. A long COUPON results when a bond is issued more than six months before the date of the first scheduled payment. *See also* SHORT COUPON.
2. interest-bearing bond maturing in more than 10 years.

LONG HEDGE
1. FUTURES CONTRACT bought to protect against a rise in the cost of honoring a future commitment. Also called a *buy hedge.* The hedger benefits from a narrowing of the BASIS (difference between cash price and future price) if the future is bought below the cash price, and from a widening of the basis if the future is bought above the cash price.
2. FUTURES CONTRACT or CALL OPTION bought in anticipation of a drop in interest rates, so as to lock in the present yield on a fixed-income security.

LONG LEG part of an OPTION SPREAD representing a commitment to buy the underlying security. For instance, if a spread consists of a long CALL OPTION and a short PUT OPTION, the long call is the long LEG.

LONG POSITION
1. ownership of a security, giving the investor the right to transfer ownership to someone else by sale or by gift; the right to receive any income paid by the security; and the right to any profits or losses as the security's value changes.
2. investor's ownership of securities held by a brokerage firm.

LONG TERM
1. holding period of more than 12 months and applicable in calculating the CAPITAL GAINS TAX.
2. investment approach to the stock market in which an investor seeks appreciation by holding a stock for more than 12 months.
3. bond with a maturity of 10 years or longer.
   See also CAPITAL GAIN; LONG BOND; LONG-TERM DEBT; LONG-TERM FINANCING; LONG-TERM GAIN; LONG-TERM INVESTOR; LONG-TERM LOSS; SHORT TERM.

LONG-TERM DEBT liability due in a year or more. Normally, interest is paid periodically over the term of the loan, and the principal amount is payable as notes or bonds mature. Also, a LONG BOND with a maturity of 10 years or more.

LONG-TERM DEBT RATIO *see* DEBT-TO-EQUITY RATIO (2). *See also* RATIO ANALYSIS.

LONG-TERM CARE INSURANCE insurance policy that pays some or all costs of nursing home care for qualified insureds. Premiums are based on the age of the applicant and are projected to remain stable for the life of the policy. Premium payments stop when the insured meets the qualifications for long-term care, which include medical necessity, cognitive impairment, and inability to carry out certain activities of daily living. Group policies are available.

LONG-TERM FINANCING liabilities not repayable in one year and all equity. *See also* LONG-TERM DEBT.

LONG-TERM GAIN gain on the sale of a CAPITAL ASSET where the HOLDING PERIOD was more than 12 months and the profit was subject to the long-term CAPITAL GAINS TAX.

LONG-TERM GOALS financial goals that an individual sets for five years or longer. Some examples of long-term goals include assembling a retirement fund, saving for a down payment on a house or for college tuition, buying a second home, or starting a business.

LONG-TERM INVESTOR someone who invests in stocks, bonds, mutual funds, or other investment vehicles for a long time, typically at least five years, in order to fund long-term goals. A long-term investor looks for solid investments with a good long-term track record, such as a BLUE CHIP stock or a mutual fund with exemplary performance. As long as the investor holds his investments for more than 12 months, he will pay preferential CAPITAL GAINS TAXES at a maximum 15% tax rate instead of paying higher regular income tax rates, which are due when assets are sold after having been held for 12 months or less.

LONG-TERM LIABILITIES any monies owed that are not payable on demand or within one year. The *current portion of long-term debt* is a current liability, as distinguished from a long-term liability.

LONG-TERM LOSS negative counterpart to LONG-TERM GAIN as defined by the same legislation. A long-term loss is realized when an asset held for more than 12 months is sold at a lower price than its adjusted purchase price. A CAPITAL LOSS can be used to offset a CAPITAL GAIN plus $3,000 of ORDINARY INCOME except that short-term losses exceeding short-term gains must first be applied to long-term gains, if any.

LONG-TERM PLANNING financial planning to accomplish LONG-TERM GOALS. A long-term plan will project how much money will be needed to fund retirement, pay college tuition, or buy a house in five years or more by designing an investment strategy to meet that goal.

LOOKBACK OPTION EXOTIC OPTION whose payout is based on the highest intrinsic value of the underlying security during the life of the option. A lookback call thus uses the highest market price of the underlying, while a lookback put pays off at the lowest market price.

LOONIE popular name for the Canadian dollar, which is engraved with the common loon on one side and Queen Elizabeth on the other.

LOOPHOLE technicality making it possible to circumvent a law's intent without violating its letter. For instance, a TAX SHELTER may exploit a loophole in the tax law, or a bank may take advantage of a loophole in the GLASS-STEAGALL ACT to acquire a DISCOUNT BROKER.

LOOSE CREDIT policy by the Federal Reserve Board to make loans less expensive and thus widely available in the economy. The Fed implements a loose credit policy by reducing interest rates through OPEN MARKET OPERATIONS by buying Treasury securities, which gives banks more funds they need to satisfy loan demand. The Fed initiates a loose credit policy when the economy is weak and inflation is low, in order to stimulate a faster pace of economic activity. Also called *easy money*. The opposite policy is called TIGHT MONEY, in which the Fed sells securities and makes it more difficult and expensive to borrow, and thereby hopes to slow down economic activity. Tight money policy is used to dampen inflation in an overheated economy.

LOSS opposite of PROFIT.

LOSS-CONTROL ACTIVITIES actions initiated by a company or individual at the urging of its insurance company to prevent accidents, losses or other insurance claims. For example, a home insurer may require smoke alarms. A commercial insurer may require certain safety procedures in a manufacturing plant.

LOSS LEADER concept, primarily in retailing, where an item is priced at a loss and widely advertised in order to draw trade into the store. The loss is considered a cost of promotion and is offset by the profits on other items sold. Concept is sometimes used by DISCOUNT BROKERS, who will advertise a particular transaction at a loss price to attract customers, who will enter into other transactions at a profit to the broker.

LOSS-OF-INCOME INSURANCE insurance coverage replacing income lost by a policyholder. For example, *business interruption insurance* will pay employee wages if a business is temporarily out of operation because of a fire, flood, or other disaster. *Disability insurance* will replace a portion of an insured disabled person's income while he or she is disabled due to injury or illness. *Worker's compensation insurance* will reimburse a worker who was injured on the job for lost wages during the disability period.

LOSS PREVENTION programs instituted by individuals or companies to prevent losses. Businesses implement safety programs to prevent workplace injuries. Individuals install fire detectors, burglar alarms, and other protective devices to prevent losses caused by fire and theft. Car owners install special locks to prevent auto theft. Insurance companies usually offer discounts to businesses or individuals taking loss prevention measures.

LOSS RATIO ratio of losses paid or accrued by an insurer to premiums earned, usually for a one-year period. *See also* BAD DEBT.

LOSS RESERVE *see* BAD DEBT.

LOST DECADE *see* LIQUIDITY TRAP.

LOT in a general business sense, a lot is any group of goods or services making up a transaction. *See also* BOARD LOT; ODD LOT; ROUND LOT.

LOW bottom price paid for a security over the past year or since trading in the security began; in the latter sense also called *historic low.*

LOW BALANCE METHOD interest computation method on savings accounts where interest is based on the lowest balance during the period.

LOW GRADE bond RATING of B or lower.

LOWER OF COST OR MARKET generally accepted accounting principle that inventory should be valued at the lower of the cost to produce it, the cost to repurchase it, or its market value.

LOW-INCOME HOUSING LIMITED PARTNERSHIP limited partnership investment in housing complexes occupied by low- and moderate-income tenants paying rent that cannot exceed statutory limits. Such partnerships offer investors annual tax credits over a 10-year period that total approximately 130% to 150% of the amount invested. Due to the restricted rents as required under the tax law, anticipated cash flow during the holding period is minimal. Properties can be sold after a 15-year holding period, which may return some or all of the original investment. The primary investment motivation for limited partners is a predictable stream of annual tax benefits. Limited partners use IRS Form 8586 to claim the credit.

LOW-LOAD FUND *see* LOAD FUND.

LUMP SUM large payment of money received at one time instead of in periodic payments. People retiring from or leaving a company may receive a lump-sum distribution of the value of their pension, salary reduction or profit-sharing plan. (Special tax rules apply to such lump-sum distributions unless the money is rolled into an IRA rollover account.) Some annuities, called *single premium deferred annuities* (SPDAs) require one upfront lump sum which is invested. Beneficiaries of life insurance policies may receive a death benefit in a lump sum. A consumer making a large purchase such as a car or boat may decide to pay in one lump sum instead of financing the purchase over time.

LUXURY TAX tax on goods considered nonessential. For example, in the early 90s a 10% luxury tax was imposed on purchases of cars selling for $30,000 or more, airplanes, boats, furs and expensive jewelry. The result of the tax, however, was that purchases of these items dropped sharply, harming the producers and retailers of these goods severely. That luxury tax was repealed in the REVENUE RECONCILIATION ACT OF 1993.

LYONS *see* ZERO-COUPON CONVERTIBLE SECURITY.

M

MA BELL nickname for AT&T. Before the Bell System was broken up in 1984, AT&T controlled both local and long distance telephone service in the United States. After the breakup, local phone service was performed by the seven regional phone companies and AT&T concentrated on long distance, telecommunications research, equipment, and computer manufacturing. Even though it no longer enjoyed the monopoly it once had, people still refer to AT&T as Ma Bell. In 2004 AT&T Corporation was purchased by SBC Corporation, and SBC took AT&T's name to become AT&T Incorporated. SBC, formerly Southwestern Bell Company, was one of the original seven regional phone companies spun off from AT&T in 1984. In 2006 AT&T acquired BELLSOUTH, another of the seven regional phone companies. AT&T Inc. stock is a component of the Dow Jones Industrial Average and is one of the most widely held and actively traded stocks on the New York Stock Exchange.

MACD *see* MOVING AVERAGE CONVERGENCE/DIVERGENCE.

MACROECONOMICS analysis of a nation's economy as a whole, using such aggregate data as price levels, unemployment, inflation, and industrial production. *See also* MICROECONOMICS.

MADRID STOCK EXCHANGE *see* BOLSA DE MADRID.

MACRS *see* MODIFIED ACCELERATED COST RECOVERY SYSTEM (MACRS).

MADOFF SCANDAL the largest PONZI SCHEME in history, operated by Bernard Madoff, chairman of Bernard L. Madoff Investment Securities LLC, one of the top market makers on Wall Street until his arrest December 11, 2008. Federal prosecutors estimated client losses, including fabricated gains, at nearly $65 billion, including many prominent investors and nonprofit organizations. On June 29, 2009, Madoff was sentenced to 150 years in prison. The fraud dated to the early 1990s and, according to federal investigators, may have begun in the early 1980s. *See also* PYRAMIDING.

MAINTENANCE BOND a bond that guarantees against defects in workmanship or materials for a specified period following completion of a contract.

MAINTENANCE CALL call for additional money or securities when a brokerage customer's margin account equity falls below the requirements of the FINANCIAL INDUSTRY REGULATORY AUTHORITY (FINRA), of the exchanges, or of the brokerage firm. Unless the account is brought up to the levels complying with equity maintenance rules, some of the client's securities may be sold to remedy the deficiency. *See also* MAINTENANCE REQUIREMENT; MINIMUM MAINTENANCE; SELL OUT.

MAINTENANCE FEE annual charge to maintain certain types of brokerage accounts. Such a fee may be attached to an ASSET MANAGEMENT ACCOUNT, which combines securities and money market accounts. Banks and brokers may also charge a maintenance fee for an INDIVIDUAL RETIREMENT ACCOUNT (IRA).

MAINTENANCE REQUIREMENT *see* MINIMUM MAINTENANCE.

MAJORITY SHAREHOLDER one of the shareholders who together control more than half the outstanding shares of a corporation. If the ownership is widely scattered and there are no majority shareholders, effective control may be gained with far less than 51% of the outstanding shares. *See also* WORKING CONTROL.

MAJOR MEDICAL INSURANCE coverage exceeding that of a basic hospital medical insurance plan and typically paying medical expenses relating to room and board, physician fees, X-rays, fluoroscopy, and miscellaneous expenses, such as bandages, operating room expenses, and drugs.

MAKE A MARKET maintain firm bid and offer prices in a given security by standing ready to buy or sell ROUND LOTS at publicly quoted prices. The dealer is called a *market maker* in the over-the-counter market and a SPECIAL-IST on the exchanges. A dealer who makes a market over a long period is said to *maintain* a market. *See also* MARKET MAKER; REGISTERED COMPETITIVE MARKET MAKER.

MAKE A PRICE *see* MAKE A MARKET.

MALONEY ACT legislation, also called the Maloney Amendment, enacted in 1938 to amend the SECURITIES EXCHANGE ACT OF 1934 by adding Section 15A, which provides for the regulation of the OVER-THE-COUNTER (OTC) market through national securities associations registered with the Securities and Exchange Commission. *See also* FINANCIAL INDUSTRY REGULATORY AUTHOR-ITY (FINRA).

MANAGED ACCOUNT investment account consisting of money that one or more clients entrust to a manager, who decides when and where to invest it. Such an account may be handled by a bank trust department or by an investment advisory firm. Clients are charged a MANAGEMENT FEE and share in proportion to their participation in any losses and gains.

MANAGED EARNINGS corporate profits made to appear higher than they actually were by accounting devices, usually with the aim of meeting analysts' projected earnings per share. COOKIE JAR RESERVES, sometimes called *rainy day reserves* or *contingency reserves*, can be overstated in good years, then reversed in bad years to reduce expenses and increase earnings. Other examples are overstated, one-time *"big bath"* charges for restructurings, taken in good years and used in weak years to bolster earnings, and creative acquisition accounting. Earnings management issues became a focus after the 2001 Enron debacle and were a factor prompting the SAR-BANES-OXLEY ACT OF 2002.

MANAGEMENT combined fields of policy and administration and the people who provide the decisions and supervision necessary to implement the owners' business objectives and achieve stability and growth. The formulation of policy requires analysis of all factors having an effect on short- and long-term profits. The administration of policies is carried out by the CHIEF EXECUTIVE OFFICER, his or her immediate staff, and everybody else who possesses authority delegated by people with supervisory responsibility. Thus the size of management can range from one person in a small organization to multilayered management hierarchies in large, complex organizations. The top members of management, called senior management, report to the owners of a firm; in large corporations, the CHAIRMAN OF THE BOARD, the PRESIDENT, and sometimes other key senior officers report to the BOARD OF DIRECTORS, comprising elected representatives of the owning stockholders. The application of scientific principles to decision-making is called management science. *See also* ORGANIZATION CHART.

MANAGEMENT BUYIN purchase of a large, and often controlling, interest in a company by an outside investor group that chooses to retain existing management. In many cases, the outside investors are venture capitalists who believe the company's products, services, and management have bright prospects. The investor group will usually place its representatives on the company's board of directors to monitor the progress of the company.

MANAGEMENT BUYOUT purchase of all of a company's publicly held shares by the existing management, which takes the company private. Usually, management will have to pay a premium over the current market price to entice public shareholders to go along with the deal. If management has to borrow heavily to finance the transaction, it is called a LEVERAGED BUYOUT (LBO). Managers may want to buy their company for several reasons: They want to avoid being taken over by a raider who would bring in new management; they no longer want the scrutiny that comes with running a public company; or they believe they can make more money for themselves in the long run by owning a larger share of the company, and eventually reap substantial profits by going public again with a REVERSE LEVERAGED BUYOUT.

MANAGEMENT COMPANY same as INVESTMENT COMPANY.

MANAGEMENT FEE charge against investor assets for managing the portfolio of an open- or closed-end MUTUAL FUND as well as for such services as shareholder relations or administration. The fee, as disclosed in the PROSPECTUS, is a fixed percentage of the fund's net asset value, typically between 0.5% and 2% per year. The fee also applies to a MANAGED ACCOUNT. The management fee is deducted automatically from a shareholder's assets once a year. *See also* MUTUAL FUND SHARE CLASSES.

MANAGING UNDERWRITER leading—and originating—investment banking firm of an UNDERWRITING GROUP organized for the purchase and distribution of a new issue of securities. The AGREEMENT AMONG UNDERWRITERS authorizes the managing underwriter, or syndicate manager, to act as agent for the group in purchasing, carrying, and distributing the issue as well as complying with all federal and state requirements; to form the selling group; to determine the allocation of securities to each member; to make sales to the selling group at a specified discount—or CONCESSION—from the public offering price; to engage in open market transactions during the underwriting period to stabilize the market price of the security; and to borrow for the syndicate account to cover costs. *See also* FLOTATION COST; INVESTMENT BANKER; UNDERWRITE.

MANDATORY CONVERTIBLES debt-equity hybrids that became popular in the 1980s to meet the strong demand by banks for the raising of capital. One type, *equity contract notes,* is exchangeable at maturity for common stock having a market value equal to the principal amount of the notes. If the holder of the notes does not choose to receive equities at maturity, the issuer will sell the equity on behalf of the holder. Another type, *equity commitment notes,* does not require the holder to purchase equity with the notes but rather commits the issuer to redeem the notes with the proceeds of an equity issue at some future date. The Federal Reserve requires issuers to fund a third of the equity in the first four years, another third in the second four years, and the balance by maturity in the third four years. CAPS are still another form of mandatory convertible.

MANDATORY SPENDING *see* DISCRETIONARY SPENDING.

MANIPULATION buying or selling a security to create a false appearance of active trading and thus influence other investors to buy or sell shares. This may be done by one person or by a group acting in concert. Those found guilty of manipulation are subject to criminal and civil penalties. *See also* MINI-MANIPULATION.

MAPLE LEAF bullion coin minted by the government of Canada in gold (99.99% pure), silver (99.99% pure) and platinum (99.95% pure). The gold and platinum coins are available in one ounce, one-half ounce, one-quarter ounce, one-tenth ounce, one-fifteenth ounce and one-twentieth ounce sizes. The silver coin is available only in the one-ounce size. The Maple Leaf is actively traded throughout the world along with the American Eagle, South African Kruggerand, and other coins. The Maple Leaf usually sells at a slight premium to the bullion value of the coin. *See also* GOLD COIN.

MARGIN in general, amount a customer deposits with a broker when borrowing from the broker to buy securities. Under Federal Reserve Board regulation, the initial margin required since 1945 has ranged from 50% to 100% of the security's purchase price. In 2009 the minimum was 50% of the purchase or short sale price, in cash or eligible securities, with a minimum of $2,000. Thereafter, MINIMUM MAINTENANCE requirements are imposed by the FINANCIAL INDUSTRY REGULATORY AUTHORITY (FINRA) and by the individual brokerage firm, whose requirement is typically higher. Banking: difference between the current market value of collateral backing a loan and the face value of the loan. For instance, if a $100,000 loan is backed by $50,000 in collateral, the margin is $50,000. Corporate finance: difference between the price received by a company for its products and services and the cost of producing them. Also known as gross profit margin. Futures trading: good-faith deposit put up when buying or selling a contract. If the futures price moves adversely, the investor must put up more money to meet margin requirements.

MARGINABLE SECURITIES *see* MARGIN SECURITY.

MARGIN ACCOUNT brokerage account allowing customers to buy securities with money borrowed from the broker. Margin accounts are governed by REGULATION T, by the FINANCIAL INDUSTRY REGULATORY AUTHORITY (FINRA), and by individual brokerage house rules. Margin requirements can be met with cash or with eligible securities. In the case of securities sold short, an equal amount of the same securities is normally borrowed without interest from another broker to cover the sale, while the proceeds are kept in escrow as collateral for the lending broker. *See also* MINIMUM MAINTENANCE.

MARGIN AGREEMENT document that spells out the rules governing a MARGIN ACCOUNT, including the HYPOTHECATION of securities, how much equity the customer must keep in the account, and the interest rate on margin loans. Also known as a *hypothecation agreement.*

MARGINAL COST increase or decrease in the total costs of a business firm as the result of one more or one less unit of output. Also called *incremental cost* or *differential cost.* Determining marginal cost is important in deciding whether or not to vary a rate of production. In most manufacturing firms, marginal costs decrease as the volume of output increases due to economies of scale, which include factors such as bulk discounts on raw materials, specialization of labor, and more efficient use of machinery. At some point, however, diseconomies of scale enter in and marginal costs begin to rise; diseconomies include factors like more intense managerial supervision to control a larger work force, higher raw materials costs because local supplies have been exhausted, and generally less efficient input. The marginal cost curve is typically U-shaped on a graph.

A firm is operating at optimum output when marginal cost coincides with average total unit cost. Thus, at less than optimum output, an increase in the rate of production will result in a marginal unit cost lower than average total unit cost; production in excess of the optimum point will result in marginal cost higher than average total unit cost. In other words, a sale at a price higher than marginal unit cost will increase the net profit of the manufacturer even though the sales price does not cover average total unit cost; marginal cost is thus the lowest amount at which a sale can be made without adding to the producer's loss or subtracting from his profits.

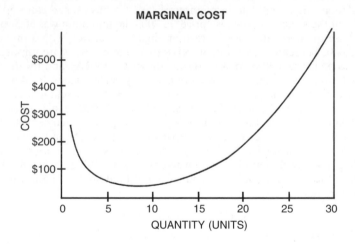

MARGINAL EFFICIENCY OF CAPITAL annual percentage yield earned by the last additional unit of capital. It is also known as *marginal productivity of capital, natural interest rate, net capital productivity,* and *rate of return over cost.* The significance of the concept to a business firm is that it represents the market rate of interest at which it begins to pay to undertake a capital investment. If the market rate is 10%, for example, it would not pay to undertake a project that has a return of $9\frac{1}{2}$%, but any return over 10% would be acceptable. In a larger economic sense, marginal efficiency of capital influences long-term interest rates. This occurs because of the law of diminishing returns as it applies to the yield on capital. As the highest yielding projects are exhausted, available capital moves into lower yielding projects and interest rates decline. As market rates fall, investors are able to justify projects that were previously uneconomical. This process is called *diminishing marginal productivity* or *declining marginal efficiency of capital.*

MARGINAL REVENUE change in total revenue caused by one additional unit of output. It is calculated by determining the difference between the total revenues produced before and after a one-unit increase in the rate of production. As long as the price of a product is constant, price and marginal revenue are the same; for example, if baseball bats are being sold at a constant price of $10 apiece, a one-unit increase in sales (one baseball bat) translates into an increase in total revenue of $10. But it is often the case that additional output can be sold only if the price is reduced, and that leads to a consideration of MARGINAL COST—the added cost of producing one more unit. Further production is not advisable when marginal cost exceeds marginal revenue since to do so would result in a loss. Conversely, whenever marginal revenue exceeds marginal cost, it is advisable to produce an additional unit. Profits are maximized at the rate of output where marginal revenue equals marginal cost.

MARGINAL TAX RATE amount of tax imposed on an additional dollar of income. In the U.S. progressive income tax system, the marginal tax rate increases as income rises. Economists believing in SUPPLY-SIDE ECONOMICS hold that this reduces the incentive to be productive and discourages business investment. In urging that marginal tax rates be cut for individuals and businesses, they argue that the resulting increased work effort and business investment would reduce STAGFLATION. *See also* FLAT TAX.

MARGINAL UTILITY in economics, the addition to total satisfaction from goods or services (called *utility*) that is derived from consuming one more unit of that good or service.

MARGIN CALL demand that a customer deposit enough money or securities to bring a margin account up to the INITIAL MARGIN or MINIMUM MAINTENANCE requirements. If a customer fails to respond, securities in the account may be liquidated. *See also* FIVE HUNDRED DOLLAR RULE; SELL OUT.

MARGIN DEPARTMENT section within a brokerage firm that monitors customer compliance with margin regulations, keeping track of debits and credits, short sales, and purchases of stock on margin, and all other extensions of credit by the broker. Also known as the *credit department. See also* MARK TO THE MARKET.

MARGIN OF PROFIT relationship of gross profits to net sales. Returns and allowances are subtracted from gross sales to arrive at net sales. Cost of goods sold (sometimes including depreciation) is subtracted from net sales to arrive at gross profit. Gross profit is divided by net sales to get the profit margin, which is sometimes called the *gross margin.* The result is a ratio, and the term is also written as *margin of profit ratio.*

The term profit margin is less frequently used to mean the *net margin,* obtained by deducting operating expenses in addition to cost of goods sold and dividing the result by net sales. Operating expenses are usually shown on profit and loss statements as "selling, general and administrative (SG&A) expenses."

Both gross and net profit margins, when compared with prior periods and with industry statistics, can be revealing in terms of a firm's operating efficiency and pricing policies and its ability to compete successfully with other companies in its field.

MARGIN REQUIREMENT minimum amount that a client must deposit in the form of cash or eligible securities in a margin account as spelled out in REGULATION T of the Federal Reserve Board. Reg T requires a minimum of $2,000 or 50% of the purchase price of eligible securities bought on margin or 50% of the proceeds of short sales. Also called INITIAL MARGIN. *See also* MARGIN; MARGIN SECURITY; MINIMUM MAINTENANCE; SELLING SHORT.

MARGIN SECURITY security that may be bought or sold in a margin account. REGULATION T defines margin securities as (1) any *registered security* (a LISTED SECURITY or a security having UNLISTED TRADING privileges); (2) any *OTC margin stock* or *OTC margin bond*, which are defined as any UNLISTED SECURITY that the Federal Reserve Board (FRB) periodically identifies as having the investor interest, marketability, disclosure, and solid financial position of a listed security; (3) any OTC security designated as qualified for trading in the NATIONAL MARKET SYSTEM under a plan approved by the Securities and Exchange Commission; (4) any mutual fund or unit investment trust registered under the Investment Company Act of 1940. Other securities that are not EXEMPT SECURITIES must be transacted in cash.

MARITAL DEDUCTION provision in the federal estate and gift tax law allowing spouses to transfer unlimited amounts of property to each other free of tax. Such transfers may be made during the life or at the death of the transferor, and are intended to treat a couple as an economic unit for transfer tax purposes. Although the deduction is unlimited, passing all assets to a spouse may create transfer tax problems in the surviving spouse's estate; planners should try to fully use each spouse's UNIFIED CREDIT, which offsets up to $3.5 million in transfers in 2009, and equalize the rate of transfer taxes for both spouses to reduce taxes for the couple. According to the ECONOMIC GROWTH AND TAX RELIEF RECONCILIATION ACT OF 2001, the amount of assets that each person can exclude from federal taxes was $3.5 million in 2009. In 2010, the estate tax is completely repealed, and in 2011 the estate tax law returns using 2001 rules, except that the exemption goes to $1 million.

MARKDOWN
1. amount subtracted from the selling price, when a customer sells securities to a dealer in the OVER-THE-COUNTER market. Had the securities been purchased from the dealer, the customer would have paid a markup, or an amount added to the purchase price. The FINANCIAL INDUSTRY REGULATORY AUTHORITY (FINRA) RULES OF FAIR PRACTICE established 5% as a reasonable guideline in markups and markdowns, though many factors enter into the question of fairness, and exceptions are common.
2. reduction in the price at which the underwriters offer municipal bonds after the market has shown a lack of interest at the original price.
3. downward adjustment of the value of securities by banks and investment firms, based on a decline in market quotations.
4. reduction in the original retail selling price, which was determined by adding a percentage factor, called a markon, to the cost of the merchandise. Anything added to the markon is called a markup, and the term markdown does not apply unless the price is dropped below the original selling price.

MARKET

1. public place where products or services are bought and sold, directly or through intermediaries. Also called *marketplace.*
2. aggregate of people with the present or potential ability and desire to purchase a product or service; equivalent to demand.
3. securities markets in the aggregate, or the New York Stock Exchange in particular.
4. short for *market value,* the value of an asset based on the price it would command on the open market, usually as determined by the MARKET PRICE at which similar assets have recently been bought and sold.
5. as a verb, to sell. *See also* MARKETING.

MARKETABILITY speed and ease with which a particular security may be bought and sold. A stock that has a large amount of shares outstanding and is actively traded is highly marketable and also liquid. In common use, marketability is interchangeable with LIQUIDITY, but liquidity implies the preservation of value when a security is bought or sold.

MARKETABLE SECURITIES securities that are easily sold. On a corporation's balance sheet, they are assets that can be readily converted into cash— for example, government securities, banker's acceptances, and commercial paper. In keeping with conservative accounting practice, these are carried at cost or market value, whichever is lower.

MARKETABLE TITLE title to a piece of real estate that is reasonably free from risk of litigation over possible defects, and while it may not be perfect, it is free from plausible or reasonable objections, and is one that a court of law would order the buyer to accept. A seller under a contract of sale is required to deliver marketable title at final closing; this requirement is implicit in law and does not need to be stated in the contract. Usually the property buyer will engage a title insurance company to ensure that the seller has CLEAR TITLE to the real estate before entering into a purchase contract. This search generally is not ordered until financing has been secured. Once the title company has researched the history of ownership of the property and feels sure that the seller owns it, it will issue a title insurance policy. The seller is thus assured that he has a marketable title, which allows him to transfer ownership to the buyer. *See also* BAD TITLE; CLOUD ON TITLE.

MARKET ANALYSIS

1. research aimed at predicting or anticipating the direction of stock, bond, or commodity markets, based on technical data about the movement of market prices or on fundamental data such as corporate earnings prospects or supply and demand.
2. study designed to define a company's markets, forecast their directions, and decide how to expand the company's share and exploit any new trends.

MARKET BASKET *see* BASKET.

MARKET BREAK any sudden drop (BREAK) in the stock market as measured by STOCK INDEXES AND AVERAGES. In SEC parlance, BLACK MONDAY, when the Dow Jones Industrial Average dropped 508 points.

MARKET BREADTH *see* BREADTH OF THE MARKET.

MARKET CAPITALIZATION value of a corporation as determined by the market price of its issued and outstanding common stock. It is calculated by multiplying the number of outstanding shares by the current market price of a share. Institutional investors often use market capitalization as one investment criterion, requiring, for example, that a company have a market capitalization of $100 million or more to qualify as an investment. Analysts look at market capitalization in relation to book, or accounting, value for an indication of how investors value a company's future prospects.

MARKET ECONOMY system wherein resources are allocated and prices are set by the forces of supply and demand and the interference of government is absent or minimal. Also called *free market system. See also* AUSTRIAN ECONOMICS; CAPITALISM.

MARKET EYE financial information service that emanates from the British Broadcasting Company under the sponsorship of the INTERNATIONAL STOCK EXCHANGE OF THE UK AND THE REPUBLIC OF IRELAND (ISE). Market Eye supplies current market information plus statistical information on particular equity and debt issues and is a supplement to the Stock Exchange Automated Quotations System (SEAQ), which records trades.

MARKET IF TOUCHED ORDER (MIT) order to buy or sell a security or commodity as soon as a preset market price is reached, at which point it becomes a MARKET ORDER. When corn is selling for $4.75 a bushel, someone might enter a market if touched order to buy at $4.50. As soon as the price is dropped to $4.50, the contract would be bought on the customer's behalf at whatever market price prevails when the order is executed.

MARKET INDEX numbers representing weighted values of the components that make up the index. A stock market index, for example, is weighted according to the prices and number of outstanding shares of the various stocks. The Standard & Poor's 500 Stock Index is one of the most widely followed, but myriad other indexes track stocks in various industry groups.

MARKET-INDEXED CD CERTIFICATE OF DEPOSIT (CD) with a return tied to a market index, such as the S&P 500 stock index. Principal is typically guaranteed against DOWNSIDE RISK. Product is issued by banks and marketed by brokers.

MARKET INDEX TARGET TERM SECURITIES (MITTS) intermediate-term, senior debt securities issued by Merrill Lynch, which guarantee the original investment plus a percentage of the appreciation of a stock index at maturity. MITTS pay no annual income but are subject to annual taxes.

MARKETING moving goods and services from the provider to consumer. This involves product origination and design, development, distribution, advertising, promotion, and publicity as well as market analysis to define the appropriate market.

MARKET JITTERS state of widespread fear among investors, which may cause them to sell stocks and bonds, pushing prices downward. Investors may fear lower corporate earnings, negative economic news, tightening of credit by the Federal Reserve, foreign currency fluctuations, or many other factors. In some cases, news may be good, but is interpreted as bad because investors are so fearful. For example, investors may think that positive economic or corporate earnings news is putting more pressure on the Federal Reserve to raise interest rates, which would hurt stock and bond prices.

MARKET LETTER newsletter provided to brokerage firm customers or written by an independent market analyst, registered as an investment adviser with the Securities and Exchange Commission, who sells the letter to subscribers. These letters assess the trends in interest rates, the economy, and the market in general. Brokerage letters typically reiterate the recommendations of their own research departments. Independent letters take on the personality of their writers—concentrating on growth stocks, for example, or basing their recommendations on technical analysis. A HULBERT RATING is an evaluation of such a letter's performance.

MARKET MAKER dealer firm that maintains a firm bid and offer price in a given security by standing ready to buy or sell at publicly quoted prices. The NASDAQ Stock Market is a decentralized network of competitive market makers, who process orders for their own customers and for other broker-dealers. All NASDAQ securities are traded through market makers, who will also buy securities from issuers for sale to customers and other broker-dealers. Market makers are broker-dealers who have met the capitalization standards of the FINANCIAL INDUSTRY REGULATORY AUTHORITY (FINRA). *See also* MAKE A MARKET; PINK SHEETS; REGISTERED COMPETITIVE MARKET MAKER.

MARKET NEUTRAL INVESTING investing, such as that done by HEDGE FUNDS, where the direction of the overall market does not affect profit or loss but gains are attempted as the result of market inefficiencies. An example of market neutral investing is PAIRS TRADING, where two highly correlated trading vehicles are bought long and sold short at a moment when the pair's price ratio has diverged. When the pair reverts to its normal price relationship, a profit is made on one or both sides.

MARKET-ON-CLOSE (MOC) ORDER order to buy or sell stocks or futures and options contracts as near as possible to when the market closes for the day. Such an order may be a LIMIT ORDER which had not yet been executed during the trading day.

MARKET OPENING the start of formal trading on an exchange, usually referring to the New York Stock Exchange (NYSE) and marked by an opening bell. All stocks do not necessarily open trading at the bell, since there may be order imbalances causing a DELAYED OPENING. *See also* OPD; OPENING.

MARKET ORDER order to buy or sell a security at the best available price. Most orders executed on the exchanges are market orders.

MARKET OUT CLAUSE escape clause sometimes written into FIRM COMMITMENT underwriting agreements which essentially allows the underwriters to be released from their purchase commitment if material adverse developments affect the securities markets generally. It is not common practice for the larger investment banking houses to write "outs" into their agreements, since the value of their commitment is a matter of paramount concern. *See also* UNDERWRITE.

MARKET PERFORM *See* BROKER RECOMMENDATIONS (AND RATINGS).

MARKET PERFORMANCE COMMITTEE (MPC) New York Stock Exchange (NYSE) SPECIALIST oversight group consisting of members and ALLIED MEMBERS. MOC monitors specialists' effectiveness in maintaining fair prices and orderly markets and is authorized to assign or reassign new or existing issues to specialist units based on their capability.

MARKETPLACE *see* MARKET.

MARKET PRICE last reported price at which a security was sold on an exchange. For stocks or bonds sold OVER THE COUNTER, the combined bid and offer prices available at any particular time from those making a market in the stock. For an inactively traded security, evaluators or other analysts may determine a market price if needed—to settle an estate, for example.

In the general business world, market price refers to the price agreed upon by buyers and sellers of a product or service, as determined by supply and demand.

MARKET RESEARCH exploration of the size, characteristics, and potential of a market to find out, before developing any new product or service, what people want and need. Market research is an early step in marketing—which stretches from the original conception of a product to its ultimate delivery to the consumer.

In the stock market, market research refers to TECHNICAL ANALYSIS of factors such as volume, price advances and declines, and market breadth, which analysts use to predict the direction of prices.

MARKET RISK *see* SYSTEMATIC RISK.

MARKET SHARE percentage of industry sales of a particular company or product.

MARKET SWEEP second offer to institutional investors, made following a public TENDER OFFER, aimed at increasing the buyer's position from a significant interest to a controlling interest. The second offering is usually at a slightly higher price than the original tender offer.

MARKET TIMING
1. strategy of trading or SWITCHING in anticipation of changes in overall market outlook.
2. questionable, sometimes illegal, short-term transactions by MUTUAL FUND MANAGERS or by favored large shareholders. *Rapid in and out trading* can adversely affect long-term investment returns of ordinary holders. *Late trading*, buying after the 4 P.M. (NY) official cutoff when each day's fund share prices are determined and then selling at the following day's official share price, is unfair when done with knowledge of news affecting fund valuations.

MARKET TONE general health and vigor of a securities market. The market tone is good when dealers and market makers are trading actively on narrow bid and offer spreads; it is bad when trading is inactive and bid and offer spreads are wide.

MARKET VALUE
In general: market price—the price at which buyers and sellers trade similar items in an open marketplace. In the absence of a market price, it is the estimated highest price a buyer would be warranted in paying and a seller

justified in accepting, provided both parties were fully informed and acted intelligently and voluntarily.

Investments: current market price of a security—as indicated by the latest trade recorded.

Accounting: technical definition used in valuing inventory or marketable securities in accordance with the conservative accounting principle of "lower of cost or market." While cost is simply acquisition cost, market value is estimated net selling price less estimated costs of carrying, selling, and delivery, and, in the case of an unfinished product, the costs to complete production. The market value arrived at this way cannot, however, be lower than the cost at which a normal profit can be made.

MARKET VALUE-WEIGHTED INDEX index whose components are weighted according to the total market value of their outstanding shares. Also called *capitalization-weighted index.* The impact of a component's price change is proportional to the issue's overall market value, which is the share price times the number of shares outstanding. For example, the AMEX Composite Index (XAX) has more than 800 component stocks. The weighting of each stock constantly shifts with changes in the stock's price and the number of shares outstanding. The index fluctuates in line with the price moves of the stocks.

MARKING UP OR DOWN increasing or decreasing the price of a security based on supply and demand forces. A securities dealer may mark up the price of a stock or bond if prices are rising, and may be forced to mark it down if demand is declining. The markup is the difference, or spread, between the price the dealer paid for the security and the price at which he sells it to the retail customer. *See also* MARKDOWN.

MARK-TO-MODEL practice whereby STRUCTURED PRODUCTS, in the absence of actual markets where real buyers trade with real sellers, are assigned accounting values based on theoretical mathematical models. *See also* MARK TO THE MARKET.

MARK TO THE MARKET adjust the valuation of a security or portfolio to reflect current market values. For example, MARGIN ACCOUNTS are marked to the market to ensure compliance with maintenance requirements. OPTION and FUTURES CONTRACTS are marked to the market at year end with PAPER PROFIT OR LOSS recognized for tax purposes. In a MUTUAL FUND, the daily net asset value reported to shareholders is the result of marking the fund's current portfolio to current market prices. When TOXIC ASSETS were causing bank failures in 2009, the FASB suspended mark-to-market rules, allowing banks to carry mortgage-related assets at the higher values they would presumably have under less distressed market conditions.

MARKUP *see* MARKDOWN.

MARRIAGE PENALTY effect of a tax code that makes a married couple pay more than the same two people would pay if unmarried and filing singly. The ECONOMIC GROWTH AND TAX RELIEF RECONCILIATION ACT OF 2001 gradually phased out the marriage penalty through 2009. This phaseout of the marriage penalty was accelerated in the JOBS AND GROWTH RELIEF RECONCILIATION ACT OF 2003. This act increased the standard deduction for married joint filers to twice the standard deduction for single taxpayers and widened the size of the 15% tax bracket to double the size of the bracket for single taxpayers.

MARRIED PUT option to sell a certain number of securities at a particular price by a specified time, bought simultaneously with securities of the underlying company so as to hedge the price paid for the securities. *See also* OPTION; PUT OPTION.

MASTER LIMITED PARTNERSHIP (MLP) public LIMITED PARTNERSHIP composed of corporate assets spun off *(roll out)* or private limited partnerships *(roll up)* with income, capital gains, and/or TAX SHELTER orientations. Interests are represented by depositary receipts traded in the SECONDARY MARKET. Investors thus enjoy LIQUIDITY. Flow-through tax benefits, previously possible within PASSIVE income restrictions, were limited by tax legislation passed in 1987 that would treat most MLPs as corporations after a GRANDFATHER CLAUSE expired in 1998.

MATCHED AND LOST report of the results of flipping a coin by two securities brokers locked in competition to execute equal trades.

MATCHED BOOK term used for the accounts of securities dealers when their borrowing costs are equal to the interest earned on loans to customers and other brokers.

MATCHED MATURITIES coordination of the maturities of a financial institution's assets (such as loans) and liabilities (such as certificates of deposit and money-market accounts). For instance, a savings and loan might issue 10-year mortgages at 10%, funded with money received for 10-year CDs at 7% yields. The bank is thus positioned to make a three-percentage-point profit for 10 years. If a bank granted 20-year mortgages at a fixed 10%, on the other hand, using short-term funds from money-market accounts paying 7%, the bank would be vulnerable to a rapid rise in interest rates. If yields on the money-market accounts surged to 14%, the bank could lose a large amount of money, since it was earning only 10% from its assets. Such a situation, called a *maturity mismatch,* can cause tremendous problems for financial institutions if it persists, as it did in the early 1980s.

MATCHED ORDERS
1. illegal manipulative technique of offsetting buy and sell orders to create the impression of activity in a security, thereby causing upward price movement that benefits the participants in the scheme.
2. action by a SPECIALIST to create an opening price reasonably close to the previous close. When an accumulation of one kind of order—either buy or sell—causes a delay in the opening of trading on an exchange, the specialist tries to find counterbalancing orders or trades long or short from his own inventory in order to narrow the spread.

MATCHED SALE PURCHASE TRANSACTION FEDERAL OPEN MARKET COMMITTEE procedure whereby the Federal Reserve Bank of New York sells government securities to a nonbank dealer against payment in FEDERAL FUNDS. The agreement requires the dealer to sell the securities back by a specified date, which ranges from one to 15 days. The Fed pays the dealer a rate of interest equal to the discount rate. These transactions, also called reverse repurchase agreements, decrease the money supply for temporary periods by reducing dealer's bank balances and thus excess reserves. The Fed is thus able to adjust an abnormal monetary expansion due to seasonal or other factors. *See also* REPURCHASE AGREEMENT.

MATERIALITY characteristic of an event or information that is sufficiently important (or *material*) to have a large impact on a company's stock price. For example, if a company was about to report its earnings, or make a take-over bid for another company, that would be considered material information. Material information is information the reasonable investor needs to make an informed decision about an investment.

MATILDA BOND FOREIGN BOND denominated in Australian dollars and sold in Australia.

MATRIX TRADING bond swapping whereby traders seek to take advantage of temporary aberrations in YIELD SPREAD differentials between bonds of the same class but with different ratings or between bonds of different classes.

MATURE ECONOMY economy of a nation whose population has stabilized or is declining, and whose economic growth is no longer robust. Such an economy is characterized by a decrease in spending on roads or factories and a relative increase in consumer spending. Many of Western Europe's economies are considerably more mature than that of the United States and in marked contrast to the faster-growing economies of the Far East.

MATURITY
1. reaching the date at which a debt instrument is due and payable. A bond due to mature on January 1, 2010, will return the bondholder's principal and final interest payment when it reaches maturity on that date. Bond yields are frequently calculated on a YIELD-TO-MATURITY basis.
2. when referring to a company or economy, *maturity* means that it is well-established, and has little room for dynamic growth. For example, econo-mists will say that an aging industrial economy has reached maturity. Or stock analysts will refer to a company's market as mature, meaning that demand for the company's products is stagnant.

MATURITY DATE
1. date on which the principal amount of a note, draft, acceptance bond, or other debt instrument becomes due and payable. Also termination or due date on which an installment loan must be paid in full.
2. in FACTORING, average due date of factored receivables, when the factor remits to the seller for receivables sold each month.

MATURITY MATCHING *see* DURATION (*immunization*).

MAXIMUM CAPITAL GAINS MUTUAL FUND fund whose objective is to produce large capital gains for its shareholders. During a bull market it is likely to rise much faster than the general market or conservative mutual funds. But in a falling market, it is likely to drop much farther than the market averages. This increased volatility results from a policy of investing in small, fast-growing companies whose stocks characteristically are more volatile than those of large, well-established companies.

MAY DAY May 1, 1975, when fixed minimum brokerage commissions ended in the United States. Instead of a mandated rate to execute exchange trades, brokers were allowed to charge whatever they chose. The May Day changes ushered in the era of discount brokerage firms that execute buy and sell orders for low commissions, but give no investment advice. The end of fixed commissions also marked the beginning of diversification by the brokerage industry into a wide range of financial services utilizing computer technology and advanced communications systems.

MBS CLEARING CORPORATION (MBSCC) SEC-registered clearing corporation that provides services to the mortgage-backed securities market.

M-CAMP a proprietary product of Morgan Stanley, M-CAMPS are professionally recommended portfolios of six different tax-exempt MUNICIPAL BOND issues, structured with alternating coupon dates that generate twelve consecutive monthly checks. The bonds in the portfolio are marketed together for a total of $30,000, but each $5,000 bond can be sold individually by the investor at any time. They are not mutual funds and, being unmanaged, do not charge ongoing management or maintenance fees.

McCARRAN-FERGUSON ACT OF 1945 federal law in which Congress declared that the states will continue to regulate the insurance business. As a result, insurers are granted a limited exemption to federal antitrust legislation.

MEALS AND ENTERTAINMENT EXPENSE expense for meals and entertainment that qualifies for a tax deduction. Under current tax law, employers may deduct 50% of meals and entertainment expenses that have a bona fide business purpose. For example, a business meal must include a discussion producing a direct business benefit.

MEAN RETURN in security analysis, expected value, or mean, of all the likely returns of investments comprising a portfolio; in capital budgeting, mean value of the probability distribution of possible returns. The portfolio approach to the analysis of investments aims at quantifying the relationship between risk and return. It assumes that while investors have different risk-value preferences, rational investors will always seek the maximum rate of return for every level of acceptable risk. It is the mean, or expected, return that an investor attempts to maximize at each level of risk. Also called *expected return. See also* CAPITAL ASSET PRICING MODEL, EFFICIENT PORTFOLIO, PORTFOLIO THEORY.

MECHANIC'S LIEN LIEN against buildings or other structures, allowed by some states to contractors, laborers, and suppliers of materials used in their construction or repair. The lien remains in effect until these people have been paid in full and may, in the event of a liquidation before they have been paid, give them priority over other creditors.

MEDIAN midway value between two points. There are an equal number of points above and below the median. For example, the number 5 is the median between the numbers 1 and 9, since there are 4 numbers above and below 5 in this sequence. Several important economic numbers use medians, including median household income and median home price.

MEDIATION less time-consuming and less expensive alternative to ARBITRATION for settling disputes between an investor and a broker. Each side agrees to be bound by the third party's resolution, but may walk away any time. *See also* NASD DISPUTE RESOLUTION, INC.

MEDICAID a joint federal-state medical assistance program for financially needy people, including the aged, blind, and disabled, and families with dependent children. Benefits vary from state to state. Officially known as

Title XIX of the Social Security Act, Medicaid was enacted in 1965 at the same time as MEDICARE.

MEDICARE program under Title XVIII of the Social Security Amendments of 1965 that provides hospital insurance, voluntary supplementary medical insurance, and prescription drug benefits to people over 65 or people under 65 who are disabled and have received Social Security disability benefits for 24 consecutive months.

MEDIUM-TERM BOND bond with a maturity of 2 to 10 years. *See also* INTERMEDIATE TERM; LONG TERM; SHORT TERM.

MELLO ROOS FINANCING financing of real estate developments in California authorized by legislation in 1982 sponsored by Henry Mello and Mike Roos of the California legislature. The bill allowed municipalities to float bonds to be repaid from the proceeds of tax revenues generated by real estate sales. The bonds financed construction of a community's infrastructure, such as sewers, roads, and electricity, which developers then finished with homes and businesses.

MEMBER BANK bank that is a member of the FEDERAL RESERVE SYSTEM, including all nationally chartered banks and any state-chartered banks that apply for membership and are accepted. Member banks are required to purchase stock in the FEDERAL RESERVE BANK in their districts. Half of that investment is carried as an asset of the member bank. The other half is callable by the Fed at any time. Member banks are also required to maintain a percentage of their deposits as reserves in the form of currency in their vaults and balances on deposit at their Fed district banks. These reserve balances make possible a range of money transfer and other services using the FED WIRE system to connect banks in different parts of the country.

MEMBER FIRM brokerage firm that has at least one membership on a major stock exchange, even though, by exchange rules, the membership is in the name of an employee and not of the firm itself. Such a firm enjoys the rights and privileges of membership, such as voting on exchange policy, together with the obligations of membership, such as the commitment to settle disputes with customers through exchange arbitration procedures.

MEMBER SHORT SALE RATIO ratio of the total shares sold short for the accounts of New York Stock Exchange members in one week divided by the total short sales for the same week. Because the specialists, floor traders, and off-the-floor traders who trade for members' accounts are generally considered the best minds in the business, the ratio is a valuable indicator of market trends. A ratio of 82% or higher is considered bearish; a ratio of 68% or lower is positive and bullish. The member short sale ratio appears with other NYSE round lot statistics in the Monday edition of *The Wall Street Journal* and in *Barron's,* a weekly financial newspaper.

MERC nickname for the Chicago Mercantile Exchange. The exchange trades many types of futures, futures options, and foreign currency futures contracts. *See also* SECURITIES AND COMMODITIES EXCHANGES.

MERCANTILE AGENCY organization that supplies businesses with credit ratings and reports on other firms that are or might become customers. Such agencies may also collect past due accounts or trade collection statistics, and they tend to industry and geographical specialization. The largest of the agencies, DUN & BRADSTREET, was founded in 1841 under the name Mercantile Agency. It provides credit information on companies of all descriptions along with a wide range of other credit and financial reporting services.

MERCHANT BANK

1. European financial institution that engages in investment banking, counseling, and negotiating in mergers and acquisitions, and a variety of other services including securities portfolio management for customers, insurance, the acceptance of foreign bills of exchange, dealing in bullion, and participating in commercial ventures. Deposits in merchant banks are negligible, and the prominence of such names as Rothschild, Baring, Lazard, and Hambro attests to their role as counselors and negotiators in large-scale acquisitions, mergers, and the like.

2. part of an American bank that engages in investment banking functions, such as advising clients in mergers and acquisitions, underwriting securities, and taking debt or equity positions. The Federal Reserve permits commercial banks to underwrite corporate debt and common stock deals.

3. American bank that has entered into an agreement with a merchant to accept deposits generated by bank credit/charge card transactions.

MERGENT, INC. part of Xinhua Finance, which acquired Moody's publications group in 1998, Mergent provides global business and financial information on publicly traded companies and fixed-income securities. Products include Mergent Online, Mergent BondSource, the Dividend Achiever Index series, Mergent Manuals and Handbooks, and other products. Four exchange-traded funds are based on Dividend Achiever Index methodologies.

MERGER combination of two or more companies, where the amount paid over and above the acquired company's book value is carried on the books of the purchaser as goodwill; or a consolidation, where a new company is formed to acquire the net assets of the combining companies. Strictly speaking, only combinations in which one of the companies survives as a legal entity are called mergers or, more formally, statutory mergers; thus consolidations, or statutory consolidations, are technically not mergers, though the term merger is commonly applied to them. Where an acquisition takes place by the purchase of assets or stock using cash or a debt instrument for payment, the merger is a taxable capital gain to the selling company or its stockholders.

Mergers can also be classified in terms of their economic function. Thus a *horizontal merger* is one combining direct competitors in the same product lines and markets; a *vertical merger* combines customer and company or supplier and company; a *market extension merger* combines companies selling the same products in different markets; a *product extension merger* combines companies selling different but related products in the same market; a *conglomerate merger* combines companies with none of the above relationships or similarities. *See also* ACQUISITION.

MEXICAN STOCK EXCHANGE *see* BOLSA MEXICANA DE VALORES.

MEZZANINE BRACKET members of a securities underwriting group whose participations are of such a size as to place them in the tier second to the largest participants. In the newspaper TOMBSTONE advertisements that announce new securities offerings, the underwriters are listed in alphabetical groups, first the lead underwriters, then the mezzanine bracket, then the remaining participants.

MEZZANINE LEVEL stage of a company's development just prior to its going public, in VENTURE CAPITAL language. Venture capitalists entering at that point have a lower risk of loss than at previous stages and can look forward to early capital appreciation as a result of the MARKET VALUE gained by an INITIAL PUBLIC OFFERING.

MICROCAP stocks in very small companies with market capitalizations of $250 million or less. PINK SHEETS LLC. offers quotes on many microcaps. *See also* PENNY STOCK.

MICROECONOMICS study of the behavior of basic economic units such as companies, industries, or households. Research on the companies in the airline industry would be a microeconomic concern, for instance. *See also* MACROECONOMICS.

MID CAP stock with a middle-level capitalization (numbers of shares outstanding times the price of the shares). Mid Cap stocks typically have between $1 billion and $5 billion in outstanding market value. Many mutual funds specializing in mid cap stocks will use the words mid cap in their names.

MIDS *see* INCOME PREFERRED SECURITIES.

MILITARY FAMILY TAX RELIEF ACT OF 2003 legislation creating new tax breaks for members of the Armed Forces and their families and others serving the United States such as Foreign Service officers. The major provisions of the law include

1. **Ten-year suspension of the five-year homesale exclusion for qualifying military and Foreign Service personnel.** Ordinary taxpayers can exclude up to $250,000 ($500,000 for a married couple) in realized gains on the sale of their primary residence if they have lived in the house for two of the past five years of owning it. This five year rule is suspended for military personnel.

2. **Money received under the Defense Department's Homeowners Assistance Program are excluded from taxable income and Social Security taxes.** If a home's value falls sharply because of a military base realignment or closure, military personnel receive payments to compensate them for these losses. These payments are no longer taxable as they were previously.

3. **Amount of death gratuity payment excluded from gross income increased to $12,000.** For deaths occurring after September 10, 2001, the amount of the death benefit gratuity increases to $12,000 from $6,000. The entire $12,000 can be excluded from gross income for income tax purposes.

4. **Military reservists can deduct away from home expenses.** National Guard or Reservists may claim itemized deductions for nonreimbursable expenses for transportation, meals, and lodging when they have to travel away from home on Reserve duty. These expenses can be taken as an "above-the-line" deduction.

5. **IRS can suspend the tax-exempt status of organizations designated as terrorist organizations.** If an organization is designated as terrorist or supporting terrorists under the Immigration and Nationality Act, the IRS can

suspend its tax-exempt status. Therefore, any contributions to that organization would no longer be tax-deductible to the donor.

MILL one-tenth of a cent, the unit most often used in expressing property tax rates. For example, if a town's tax rate is 5 mills per dollar of assessed valuation, and the assessed valuation of a piece of property is $100,000, the tax is $500, or 0.005 times $100,000.

MINI-MANIPULATION trading in a security underlying an option contract so as to manipulate the stock's price, thus causing an increase in the value of the options. In this way the manipulator's profit can be multiplied many times, since a large position in options can be purchased with a relatively small amount of money.

MINIMUM FLUCTUATION smallest possible price movement of a security or options or futures contract. For example, most stocks on the New York Stock Exchange trade with a minimum fluctuation of one cent. Minimum fluctuations are set by the securities, futures, or options exchanges regulating each security or contract. Also called MINIMUM TICK.

MINIMUM MAINTENANCE equity level that must be maintained in brokerage customers' margin accounts, as required by the New York Stock Exchange (NYSE), Financial Industry Regulatory Authority (FINRA), and individual brokerage firms. Under REGULATION T, $2000 in cash or securities must be deposited with a broker before *any* credit can be extended; then an INITIAL MARGIN requirement must be met, currently 50% of the market value of eligible securities long or short in customers' accounts. The NYSE and FINRA, going a step further, both require that a margin be *maintained* equal to 25% of the market value of securities in margin accounts. Brokerage firm requirements are typically a more conservative 30%. When the market value of margined securities falls below these minimums a MARGIN CALL goes out requesting additional equity. If the customer fails to comply, the broker may sell the margined stock and close the customer out. *See also* MARGIN REQUIREMENT; MARGIN SECURITY; MARK TO THE MARKET; SELL OUT.

MINIMUM PAYMENT minimum amount that a consumer is required to pay on a revolving charge account in order to keep the account in good standing. If the minimum payment is not made, late payment penalties are due. If the minimum is still not paid within a few months, credit privileges may be revoked. If a consumer pays just the minimum due, interest charges continue to accrue on all outstanding balances. In some cases, a credit card issuer will waive the minimum payment for a month or two, as long as the cardholder has demonstrated a good payment history. If the cardholder does not make any minimum payment in such a case, interest charges accrue on the entire outstanding balance.

MINIMUM TICK *see* MINIMUM FLUCTUATION.

MINI-TENDER OFFER offer to buy a company's stock in a quantity of 5% or less, thus being exempt from protective regulations applicable to a regular TENDER OFFER.

MINI-WAREHOUSE LIMITED PARTNERSHIP partnership that invests in small warehouses where people can rent space to store belongings. Such partnerships offer tax benefits such as depreciation allowances, but mostly they provide income derived from rents. When the partnership is liquidated, the general partner may sell the warehouse for a profit, providing capital gains to limited partners.

MINNEAPOLIS GRAIN EXCHANGE (MGEX) formed in 1881 as a centralized cash market for grains grown in the upper Midwest and still the world's largest cash grain market, trading approximately 1 million bushels per day. The exchange was founded as a nonprofit membership organization and maintains that structure today with a membership base of 390 outstanding seats, or memberships. In 1883 MGEX launched its first futures contract, hard red spring wheat, which is the exchange's most heavily traded product today. In addition to futures and options on hard red spring wheat, MGEX is the exclusive market for futures and options on Hard Red Winter Wheat Index (HRWI), Hard Red Spring Wheat Index (HRSI), Soft Red Winter Wheat Index (SRWI), National Corn Index (NCI), and National Soybean Index (NSI). MGEX has exclusive rights to develop index-based futures and options contracts that financially settle to agricultural and weather data collected and disseminated by Data Transmission Network (DTN), a business-to-business electronic commerce and information services company in Omaha, Nebraska. MGEX index contracts trade exclusively on the exchange's electronic trading platform from 7:30 P.M. to 1:45 P.M. (CT). Hard red spring wheat futures trade electronically from 7:32 P.M. to 6 A.M. Sunday–Friday (CT), and options trade electronically from 7:34 P.M. to 6 A.M. Sunday–Friday (CT). *www.mgex.com.*

MINORITY INTEREST interest of shareholders who, in the aggregate, own less than half the shares in a corporation. On the consolidated balance sheets of companies whose subsidiaries are not wholly owned, the minority interest is shown as a separate equity account or as a liability of indefinite term. On the income statement, the minority's share of income is subtracted to arrive at consolidated net income.

MINOR'S ACCOUNT bank savings account in the name of a minor, in which the minor has the power to deposit and withdraw. The minor must be able to sign for the account, but minimum deposit requirements and charges are waived until the child reaches majority (age 18 in most states).

MINUS symbol (–) preceding a fraction or number in the change column at the far right of newspaper stock tables designating a closing sale lower than that of the previous day.

MINUS TICK *see* DOWNTICK.

MIPS *see* INCOME PREFERRED SECURITIES.

MISERY INDEX index that combines the unemployment and inflation rates. The index was devised in the 1970s when both inflation and unemployment rose sharply. The misery index is often credited with political significance, since it may be difficult for a president to be re-elected if there is a high misery index. The misery index is also linked to consumer confidence—the lower the index, in general, the more confident consumers tend to be.

MISSING THE MARKET failing to execute a transaction on terms favorable to a customer and thus being negligent as a broker. If the order is subsequently executed at a price demonstrably less favorable, the broker, as the customer's agent, may have to make up the loss.

MITTS *see* MARKET INDEX TARGET TERM SECURITIES.

MIXED ACCOUNT brokerage account in which some securities are owned (in long positions) and some borrowed (in short positions).

MLP *see* MASTER LIMITED PARTNERSHIP (MLP).

MOB SPREAD difference in yield between a tax-free MUNICIPAL BOND and a Treasury bond with the same maturity. Term is an acronym for *municipals-over-bonds* SPREAD, which will always exist because municipals involve different degrees of risk while Treasuries are risk-free as to principal. The spread between a "muni" of a given rating and a Treasury with the same maturity has significance in tax decisions and in transactions involving financial futures contracts.

MOBILE HOME CERTIFICATE mortgage-backed security guaranteed by the GOVERNMENT NATIONAL MORTGAGE ASSOCIATION consisting of mortgages on mobile homes. Although the maturity tends to be shorter on these securities than on single-family homes, they have all the other characteristics of regular Ginnie Maes, and the timely payment of interest and the repayment of principal are backed by the FULL FAITH AND CREDIT of the U.S. government.

MOCK TRADING simulated trading of stocks, bonds, commodities and mutual funds. Real money is not used. Students learning about investing in schools or brokerage training classes may go through exercises in mock trading, in which securities prices are tracked on a daily basis and fictional trades are made. With commodity futures and options, this may take the form of going through a simulated trading session on the trading floor or using computer programs to illustrate the futures and options strategies.

MODELING designing and manipulating a mathematical representation of an economic system or corporate financial application so that the effect of changes can be studied and forecast. For example, in ECONOMETRICS, a complex economic model can be drawn up, entered into a computer, and used to predict the effect of a rise in inflation or a cut in taxes on economic output.

MODERN PORTFOLIO THEORY *see* PORTFOLIO THEORY.

MODIFIED ACCELERATED COST RECOVERY SYSTEM (MACRS) provision, originally called the Accelerated Cost Recovery System (ACRS), instituted by the Economic Recovery Tax Act of 1981 (ERTA) and modified by the Tax Reform Act of 1986, which establishes rules for the DEPRECIATION (the recovery of cost through tax deductions) of qualifying assets. With certain exceptions, the 1986 Act modifications, which generally provide for greater acceleration over longer periods of time than ERTA rules, are effective for property placed in service after 1986.

Under the modified rules, depreciable assets other than buildings fall within a 3-, 5-, 7-, 10-, 15-, or 20-year class life. The 3-, 5-, 7-, and 10-year classes use the DOUBLE DECLINING BALANCE DEPRECIATION METHOD, with a switch to STRAIGHT LINE DEPRECIATION. Instead of the 200% rate, you may elect a 150% rate. For 15- and 20-year property, the 150% declining balance method is used with a switch to straight line. The conversion to straight line occurs when larger annual deductions may be claimed over the remaining life. Real estate uses the straight line basis. Residential rental property placed in service after December 31, 1986, is depreciated over 27.5 years, while nonresidential property placed in service between December 1, 1986, and May 13, 1993, is depreciated over 31.5 years. A 39-year period applies to nonresidential property placed in service after May 12, 1993, although certain transition rules apply.

MOMENTUM rate of acceleration of an economic, price, or volume movement. An economy with strong growth that is likely to continue is said to have a lot of momentum. In the stock market, technical analysts study stock momentum by charting price and volume trends. *See also* EARNINGS MOMENTUM.

MOMENTUM INDICATORS indicators, called oscillators, used in technical analysis to measure the velocity of price movements (momentum), both up and down. In his book, *Introduction to Technical Analysis,* Martin Pring says, "All momentum series have the characteristics of an oscillator as they move from one extreme to the other. These extremes are known as OVERBOUGHT and OVERSOLD levels. An unruly dog taking a walk strains at the leash, moving from one side of the walk to the other. One moment the dog roams to the curb on his extreme left and the next he scampers back toward the lawns on his right, as far as the leash will allow him. Momentum works in a similar manner, so that when an oscillator is at an overextended reading on the upside, it is said to be overbought. When it reaches the opposite end of the spectrum on the downside, the condition is known as oversold. The horizontal line in between these extremes is called the equilibrium line."

Some of the most widely used momentum indicators are the RELATIVE STRENGTH INDICATOR (RSI), the MOVING AVERAGE CONVERGENCE/DIVERGENCE (MACD) and the STOCHASTICS INDEX. The basic characteristics of any momentum oscillator are illustrated on the previous page.

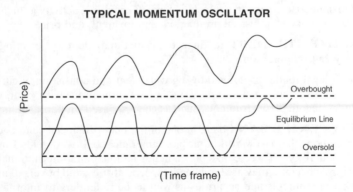

TYPICAL MOMENTUM OSCILLATOR

(Price)

Overbought

Equilibrium Line

Oversold

(Time frame)

M-1, M-2, and M-3 three measures of the money supply as defined by the Federal Reserve Board:

M1 is the narrowest measure of money supply. It includes currency in circulation, checking account balances, NOW accounts and share draft accounts at credit unions, and travelers' checks. M1 represents all money that can be spent or readily converted to cash for immediate spending.

M2 includes everything in M1 plus savings accounts and time deposits such as CDs, money market deposit accounts, and repurchase agreements.

M3 includes everything in M2 plus large CDs and money market fund balances held by institutions. M3 is the broadest measure of money supply tracked by the Fed.

Federal Reserve policymakers carefully watch the growth rate of all three money supply measures, but especially M2, as key indicators of economic growth and the potential for inflation. Most economists maintain that most economic growth and inflation is determined by the rate of growth in the money supply.

MONETARIST economist who believes that the MONEY SUPPLY is the key to the ups and downs in the economy. Monetarists such as Milton Friedman think that the money supply has far more impact on the economy's future course than, say, the level of federal spending—a factor on which KEYNESIAN ECONOMICS puts great stress. Monetarists advocate slow but steady growth in the money supply.

MONETARY INDICATORS economic gauges of the effects of MONETARY POLICY, such as various measures of credit market conditions, U.S. Treasury BILL rates, and the Dow Jones Industrial Average (of common stocks).

MONETARY POLICY FEDERAL RESERVE BOARD decisions on the MONEY SUPPLY. To make the economy grow faster, the Fed can supply more credit to the banking system through its OPEN MARKET OPERATIONS, or it can lower the member bank reserve requirement or lower the DISCOUNT RATE—which is what banks pay to borrow additional reserves from the Fed. If, on the other hand, the economy is growing too fast and inflation is an increasing problem, the Fed might withdraw money from the banking system, raise the reserve requirement, or raise the discount rate, thereby putting a brake on economic growth. Other instruments of monetary policy range from selective credit controls to simple but often highly effective MORAL SUASION. Monetary policy differs from FISCAL POLICY, which is carried out through government spending and taxation. Both seek to control the level of economic activity as measured by such factors as industrial production, employment, and prices.

MONETIZE THE DEBT to finance the national debt by printing new money, causing inflation.

MONEY legal tender as defined by a government and consisting of currency and coin. In a more general sense, money is synonymous with CASH, which includes negotiable instruments, such as checks, based on bank balances.

MONEY CENTER BANK bank in one of the major financial centers of the world, among them New York, Chicago, San Francisco, Los Angeles, London, Paris, and Tokyo. These banks play a major national and international economic role because they are large lenders, depositories, and buyers of money market instruments and securities as well as large lenders to international governments and corporations. In the stock market, bank analysts usually categorize the money center banks as separate from regional banks—those that focus on one area of the country. Also known as *money market bank*.

MONEY FUND REPORT AVERAGE™ average taxable and tax-free money market fund yields published weekly for 7- and 30-day simple and compound (assumed reinvested dividends) yields. Money Fund Report also tracks the average maturity of securities in money market fund portfolios, a short maturity (30 days or less) signifying a manager's conviction that rates will rise, and a longer (60 days or more) maturity that rates will fall. Money Fund Report was formerly known as IBC's Money Fund Report and before that Donoghue's Money Fund Report. The owning company is iMoneyNet, Inc. in Westborough, Massachusetts. iMoneyNet is a subsidiary of London-based Informa Group Plc. The Money Fund Report Average is published in major newspapers, including *The Wall Street Journal, The New York Times,* and *Barron's. Barron's* also publishes a list of the 7- and 30-day yields of most money market mutual funds, along with each fund's net assets and average maturity. The web site, *www.imoneynet.com*, features rate research and analysis on money market funds, banks, thrifts, credit unions, mortgage companies, credit card issuers, and other lenders.

MONEY MANAGEMENT financial planner's responsibility for the general management of monetary matters, including banking, credit management, budgeting, taxation, and borrowing. Term is also a synonym for PORTFOLIO MANAGEMENT.

MONEY MANAGER *see* PORTFOLIO MANAGER.

MONEY MARKET market for SHORT-TERM DEBT INSTRUMENTS—negotiable certificates of deposit, Eurodollar certificates of deposit, commercial paper, banker's acceptances, Treasury bills, and discount notes of the Federal Home Loan Bank, Federal National Mortgage Association, and Federal Farm Credit System, among others. Federal funds borrowings between banks, bank borrowings from the Federal Reserve Bank WINDOW, and various forms of repurchase agreements are also elements of the money market. What these instruments have in common are safety and LIQUIDITY. The money market operates through dealers, MONEY CENTER BANKS, and the Open Market Trading DESK at the New York Federal Reserve Bank. New York City is the leading money market, followed by London and Tokyo. The dealers in the important money markets are in constant communication with each other and with major borrowers and investors to take advantage of ARBITRAGE opportunities, a practice which helps keep prices uniform worldwide. *See also* MONEY MARKET FUND.

MONEY MARKET DEPOSIT ACCOUNT market-sensitive bank account that has been offered since December 1982. Under Depository Institutions Deregulatory Committee rules, such accounts had a minimum of $1,000 (eliminated in 1986) and only three checks may be drawn per month, although unlimited transfers may be carried out at an automated teller machine. The funds are therefore liquid—that is, they are available to depositors at any time without penalty. The interest rate is generally comparable to rates on money market mutual funds, though any individual bank's rate may be higher or lower. These accounts are insured by the FEDERAL DEPOSIT INSURANCE CORPORATION.

MONEY MARKET FUND open-ended MUTUAL FUND that invests in commercial paper, banker's acceptances, repurchase agreements, government securities, certificates of deposit, and other highly liquid and safe securities, and pays money market rates of interest. Launched in the middle 1970s, these funds were especially popular in the early 1980s when interest rates and inflation soared. Management's fee is less than 1% of an investor's assets; interest over and above that amount is credited to shareholders monthly. The fund's net asset value normally remains a constant $1 a share—only the interest rate goes up or down. Such funds usually offer check-writing privileges. In 2008 the government created a temporary money-fund insurance program, guaranteeing share prices if the fund's net asset value falls below $1 a share. In addition, some funds are covered by private insurance. Some funds invest only in government-backed securities, which give shareholders an extra degree of safety. Many money market funds are part of fund families. This means that investors can switch their money from one fund to another and back again without charge. Money in an ASSET MANAGEMENT ACCOUNT usually is automatically swept into a money market fund until the account holder decides where to invest it next. *See also* BREAKING THE BUCK; FAMILY OF FUNDS; IBC'S MONEY FUND REPORT AVERAGE; MONEY MARKET DEPOSIT ACCOUNT; TAX-EXEMPT MONEY MARKET FUND.

MONEY ORDER financial instrument that can be easily converted into cash by the payee named on the money order. The money order lists both the payee and the person who bought the instrument, known as the payor. Money orders are issued by banks, telephone companies, post offices, and traveler's check issuers to people presenting cash or other forms of acceptable payment. A personal money order from a bank can be considered a one-stop checking account, because the purchaser has the ability to stop payment on it; this does not hold true for money orders from other sources. Money orders often are used by people who do not have checking accounts. They can be used to pay bills or any outstanding debts.

MONEY PURCHASE PLAN program for buying a pension annuity that provides for specified, regular payments, usually based on salary.

MONEY SPREAD *see* VERTICAL SPREAD.

MONEY SUPPLY total stock of money in the economy, consisting primarily of (1) currency in circulation and (2) deposits in savings and checking accounts. Too much money in relation to the output of goods tends to push interest rates down and push prices and inflation up; too little money tends to push interest rates up, lower prices and output, and cause unemployment and idle plant capacity. The bulk of money is in demand deposits with commercial banks, which are regulated by the Federal Reserve Board. It manages the money supply by raising or lowering the reserves that banks are required to maintain and the DISCOUNT RATE at which they can borrow from the Fed, as well as by its OPEN MARKET OPERATIONS—trading government securities to take money out of the system or put it in.

Changes in the financial system, particularly since banking deregulation in the 1980s, have caused controversy among economists as to what really constitutes the money supply at a given time. In response to this, a more comprehensive analysis and breakdown of money was developed. Essentially, the various forms of money are now grouped into two broad divisions: M-1, M-2, and M-3, representing money and NEAR MONEY; and L, representing longer-term liquid funds. The table on the next page shows a detailed breakdown of all four categories. *See also* MONETARY POLICY.

MONEY SUPPLY

Classification	Components
M-1	currency in circulation commercial bank demand deposits NOW and ATS (automatic transfer from savings) accounts credit union share drafts mutual savings bank demand deposits nonbank travelers checks
M-2	M-1 overnight repurchase agreements issued by commercial banks overnight Eurodollars savings accounts time deposits under $100,000 money market mutual fund shares
M-3	M-2 time deposits over $100,000 term repurchase agreements
L	M-3 and other liquid assets such as: Treasury bills savings bonds commercial paper bankers' acceptances Eurodollar holdings of United States residents (nonbank)

MONOPOLY control of the production and distribution of a product or service by one firm or a group of firms acting in concert. In its pure form, monopoly, which is characterized by an absence of competition, leads to high prices and a general lack of responsiveness to the needs and desires of consumers. Although the most flagrant monopolistic practices in the United States were outlawed by ANTITRUST LAWS enacted in the late 19th century and early 20th century, monopolies persist in some degree as the result of such factors as patents, scarce essential materials, and high startup and production costs that discourage competition in certain industries. *Public monopolies—* those operated by the government, such as the post office, or closely regulated by the government, such as utilities—ensure the delivery of essential products and services at acceptable prices and generally avoid the disadvantages produced by private monopolies. MONOPSONY, the dominance of a market by one buyer or group of buyers acting together, is less prevalent than monopoly. *See also* CARTEL; OLIGOPOLY; PERFECT COMPETITION.

MONOPSONY situation in which one buyer dominates, forcing sellers to agree to the buyer's terms. For example, a tobacco grower may have no choice but to sell his tobacco to one cigarette company that is the only buyer for his product. The cigarette company therefore virtually controls the price at which it buys tobacco. The opposite of a monopsony is a MONOPOLY.

MONTHLY INCOME DEBT SECURITIES (MIDS) *see* INCOME PREFERRED SECURITIES.

MONTHLY COMPOUNDING OF INTEREST *see* COMPOUND INTEREST.

MONTHLY INCOME PREFERRED SECURITIES (MIPS) *see* INCOME PRE-FERRED SECURITIES.

MONTHLY INVESTMENT PLAN plan whereby an investor puts a fixed dollar amount into a particular investment every month, thus building a position at advantageous prices by means of *dollar cost averaging (see* CONSTANT DOLLAR PLAN).

MONTREAL EXCHANGE (MX) Canada's oldest exchange and the only financial derivatives exchange in the country acquired by the TSX Group in 2008. MX offers individual and institutional investors, both in Canada and abroad, a wide range of risk management products for protecting their investments and ensuring growth. MX is fully electronic, and its services include trading, clearing, training, market information, market operations, and regulations. MX operates a stock options market as well as a futures market. There are more than 88 options classes (regular and long-term expiry cycles) listed on MX. The Montreal Exchange is also a significant shareholder of the Boston Options Exchange (BOX), a U.S. automated equity options exchange whose technical operations are ensured by the Montreal Exchange. With MX interest rates products, investors have access to a wide range of strategies on the yield curve. The BAX is the BENCHMARK for Canadian short-term interest rates. The CGB and CGZ offer investment opportunities for investors in the fields of portfolio enhancement and ARBI-TRAGE and can be used as a risk management tool. The ONX futures contract can be used as an indicator of Canadian interest rate movements. Options on BAX (OBX) are also available. The SXF, an index future, and the SXO, an index option—both based on the S&P/TSX 60 Index—offer investors a wide variety of strategies and approaches to managing equity portfolios while maintaining portfolio integrity. Index futures based upon select sectors of the Canadian economy are also available. The exchange also offers options based on Barclays iUnits Sector Funds. Trading hours for options are 9:30 A.M. to 4:15 P.M. Trading for futures is from 6 A.M. to 4:15 P.M. *www.m-x.ca.*

MOODY'S INVESTORS SERVICE a widely utilized source for credit ratings, research, and risk analysis. The firm publishes market-leading credit opinions, deal research, and commentary that reach more than 2,600 institutions and 16,500 users globally. Moody's ratings and analysis track more than $35 trillion of debt covering nearly 170,000 corporate, government, and structured finance securities, more than 100,000 public finance obligations, 10,000 corporate relationships, and 100 sovereign nations.

In recent years, Moody's has moved significantly beyond its traditional bond rating activities, assigning ratings to issuers of securities, insurance company obligations, bank loans, bank deposits and other bank debt, managed funds, and derivatives. The firm also has expanded into developing markets through affiliations with local rating agencies in Korea, India, Chile, the Czech Republic, Russia, Israel, and Egypt. Moody's maintains offices in most of the world's major financial centers and employs more than 2,000 people worldwide, including more than 1,000 analysts. Clients include investors, depositors, creditors, investment banks, commercial banks, other financial intermediaries, and a wide range of corporate and governmental issuers of securities. Moody's Investors Service is a subsidiary of Moody's Corporation, a publicly traded company. *www.moodys.com. See also* MERGENT, INC.

MORAL OBLIGATION BOND tax-exempt bond issued by a municipality or a state financial intermediary and backed by the moral obligation pledge of a state government. (State financial intermediaries are organized by states to pool local debt issues into single bond issues, which can be used to tap larger investment markets.) Under a moral obligation pledge, a state government indicates its intent to appropriate funds in the future if the primary OBLIGOR, the municipality or intermediary, defaults. The state's obligation to honor the pledge is moral rather than legal because future legislatures cannot be legally obligated to appropriate the funds required.

MORAL SUASION persuasion through influence rather than coercion, said of the efforts of the FEDERAL RESERVE BOARD to achieve member bank compliance with its general policy. From time to time, the Fed uses moral suasion to restrain credit or to expand it.

MORGAN STANLEY CAPITAL INTERNATIONAL (MSCI) develops and maintains equity, REIT, fixed-income, multi-asset class and HEDGE FUND indices that serve as a BENCHMARK for an estimated U.S. $3 trillion on a worldwide basis. The MSCI indices are market capitalization-weighted and cover both developed and emerging markets. In addition to the country indices, MSCI also calculates aggregate indices for the world—Europe, North America, Asia, and Latin America. Most international mutual funds and other international institutional investors measure their performance against MSCI indices.

MORNINGSTAR RATING SYSTEM system for rating open- and closed-end mutual funds, exchange-traded funds (ETFS), separately managed accounts (SMAs), and annuities by Morningstar Inc. of Chicago. The system rates funds from one to five stars, using a risk-adjusted performance rating in which performance equals total return of the fund. The system rates funds assessing down-side risk, which is linked to the three-month U.S. Treasury bill. If a fund underperforms the Treasury bill, it will lower the fund's rating. The score is plotted on a bell curve, and is applied to four distinct categories: all equities, fixed income, hybrids, municipals. The top 10% receive five stars; the top 22.5%, four stars; the top 35%, three stars; the bottom 22.5%, two stars; and the bottom 10%, one star. Morningstar is a subscription-based company, offering its ratings in binders, software, and CD-ROM form. It sells its data to America Online and Realities Telescan Analyzer and other databases, as well as metropolitan newspapers. Morningstar also sells information on U.S. equities and American Depositary Receipts (ADRs), but star ratings are not calculated for them.

MORTGAGE debt instrument by which the borrower (mortgagor) gives the lender (mortgagee) a lien on property as security for the repayment of a loan. The borrower has use of the property, and the lien is removed when the obligation is fully paid. A mortgage normally involves real estate. For personal property, such as machines, equipment, or tools, the lien is called a *chattel mortgage.*

See also ADLUSTABLE RATE MORTGAGE; CLOSED-END MORTGAGE; CONSOLIDATED MORTGAGE BOND; MORTGAGE BOND; OPEN-END MORTGAGE; VARIABLE RATE MORTGAGE.

MORTGAGE ACCELERATION PROGRAM plan offered by financial institutions to homeowners whereby, for a sign-up fee and a monthly charge, 50% of the mortgage payment is made every two weeks instead of 100% each month. This saves about $60,000 in interest on a $200,000, 30-year mortgage and shortens the loan. The problem typically with such programs is that the saving is achieved because 26 payments of 50% add up to 13 payments a year instead of 12 payments. Since most lenders continue to credit the monthly minimum and apply the overpayment at the end of the year, borrowers are paying fees for something they could do by themselves.

MORTGAGE-BACKED CERTIFICATE security backed by mortgages. Such certificates are issued by the FEDERAL HOME LOAN MORTGAGE CORPORATION, and the FEDERAL NATIONAL MORTGAGE ASSOCIATION. Others are guaranteed by the GOVERNMENT NATIONAL MORTGAGE ASSOCIATION. Investors receive payments out of the interest and principal on the underlying mortgages. Sometimes banks issue certificates backed by CONVENTIONAL MORTGAGES, selling them to large institutional investors. The growth of mortgage-backed certificates and the secondary mortgage market in which they are traded has helped keep mortgage money available for home financing. *See also* PASS-THROUGH SECURITY.

MORTGAGE-BACKED REVENUE BONDS *see* HOUSING BONDS.

MORTGAGE-BACKED SECURITY *see* MORTGAGE-BACKED CERTIFICATE.

MORTGAGE BANKER company, or individual, that originates mortgage loans, sells them to other investors, services the monthly payments, keeps related records, and acts as escrow agent to disperse funds for taxes and insurance. A mortgage banker's income derives from origination and servicing fees, profits on the resale of loans, and the spread between mortgage yields and the interest paid on borrowings while a particular mortgage is held before resale. To protect against negative spreads or mortgages that can't be resold, such companies seek commitments from institutional lenders or buy them from the FEDERAL NATIONAL MORTGAGE ASSOCIATION or the GOVERNMENT NATIONAL MORTGAGE ASSOCIATION. Mortgage bankers thus play an important role in the flow of mortgage funds even though they are not significant mortgage holders.

MORTGAGE BOND bond issue secured by a mortgage on the issuer's property, the lien on which is conveyed to the bondholders by a deed of trust. A mortgage bond may be designated senior, underlying, first, prior, overlying, junior, second, third, and so forth, depending on the priority of the lien. Most of those issued by corporations are first mortgage bonds secured by specific real property and also representing unsecured claims on the general assets of the firm. As such, these bonds enjoy a preferred position relative to unsecured bonds of the issuing corporation. *See also* CONSOLIDATED MORTGAGE BOND; MORTGAGE.

MORTGAGE BROKER one who places mortgage loans with lenders for a fee, but does not originate or service loans.

MORTGAGE INTEREST DEDUCTION federal tax deduction for mortgage interest paid in a taxable year. Interest on a mortgage to acquire, construct, or substantially improve a residence is deductible for indebtedness of up to $1 million. In addition, interest on a home equity loan of up to $100,000 is deductible. These amounts are halved for married taxpayers filing separately.

MORTGAGE LIFE INSURANCE policy that pays off the balance of a mortgage on the death of the insured.

MORTGAGE MODIFICATION legislation and Treasury department actions aimed at providing lenders with incentives to work with borrowers to avoid foreclosure by modifying mortgages or refinancing their loans. Flagship $75 billion Obama administration program, called the Home Affordable Modification Program, results in a permanent adjustment of rate, balance, or term. A variation, called *forbearance*, is a time-limited modification designed to forestall foreclosure while temporary financial problems are resolved.

MORTGAGE POOL group of mortgages sharing similar characteristics in terms of class of property, interest rate, and maturity. Investors buy participations and receive income derived from payments on the underlying mortgages. The principal attractions to the investor are DIVERSIFICATION and LIQUIDITY, along with a relatively attractive yield. Those backed by government-sponsored agencies such as the FEDERAL HOME LOAN MORTGAGE CORPORATION, FEDERAL NATIONAL MORTGAGE ASSOCIATION, and GOVERNMENT NATIONAL MORTGAGE ASSOCIATION became popular not only with individual investors but with life insurance companies, pension funds, and even foreign investors.

MORTGAGE REIT invests in loans secured by real estate. These mortgages either may be originated and underwritten by the REAL ESTATE INVESTMENT TRUST or the REIT may purchase preexisting secondary mortgages. The funds the REIT invests may come from either shareholder equity capital or debt borrowed from other lenders. Mortgage REITs earn income from the interest they are paid and fees generated. This net income is generated from the excess of their interest and fee income and their interest expense and administrative fees. The other kind of real estate investment trust—called an EQUITY REIT—takes an ownership position in real estate, as opposed to acting as a lender. Some REITs, called *hybrid REITs,* take equity positions and make mortgage loans.

MORTGAGE SERVICING administration of a mortgage loan, including collecting monthly payments and penalties on late payments, keeping track of the amount of principal and interest that has been paid at any particular time, acting as escrow agent for funds to cover taxes and insurance, and, if necessary, curing defaults and foreclosing when a homeowner is seriously delinquent. For mortgage loans that are sold in the secondary market and packaged into a MORTGAGE-BACKED CERTIFICATE the local bank or savings and loan that originated the mortgage typically continues servicing the mortgages for a fee.

MOSCOW INTERBANK CURRENCY EXCHANGE (MICEX) established in 1992 to handle currency transactions from the former Gosbank of the USSR, MICEX is the largest, most liquid, and best-organized financial exchange in Russia. It is the model for the nationwide system of currency, equity, and derivatives trading spanning Russia's eight main financial centers. The MICEX Group includes the MICEX Stock Exchange, the MICEX Settlement House, the National Depositary Center, and regional exchanges.

Since 1997, the MICEX has calculated the MICEX Index, which is the leading Russian stock market indicator. MICEX's electronic trading and depository system links more than 1,500 remote workstations installed in banks and other financial institutions in 50 cities in Russia and abroad to the exchange. More than 270 broker systems are connected to the MICEX trading system, which serves clients via the Internet; about 50% of securities transactions are conducted through the Internet. The year 2004 marked the completion of the formation of a unified national currency market in Russia, with the unification of the Russia Unified Trading Session (UTS) and the System of Electronic Lot Trades (SELT). Trading hours for listed and unlisted securities are 10:30 A.M. to 6:45 P.M., Monday through Friday. Trading for eurobonds is from 10:30 A.M. to 3 P.M. *www.micex.com.*

MOST ACTIVE LIST stocks with the most shares traded on a given day. Unusual VOLUME can be caused by TAKEOVER activity, earnings releases, institutional trading in a widely held issue, and other factors.

MOVING AVERAGE average of security or commodity prices constructed on a period as short as a few days or as long as several years and showing trends for the latest interval. For example, a thirty-day moving average includes yesterday's figures; tomorrow the same average will include today's figures and will no longer show those for the earliest date included in yesterday's average. Thus every day it picks up figures for the latest day and drops those for the earliest day. *See also* MOMENTUM INDICATORS; 200-DAY MOVING AVERAGE.

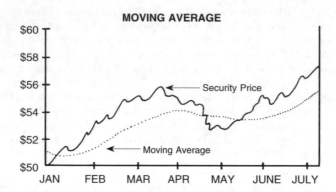

MOVING AVERAGE

MOVING AVERAGE CONVERGENCE/DIVERGENCE (MACD) TECHNICAL ANALYSIS oscillator developed by Gerald Appel that measures OVERBOUGHT and OVERSOLD conditions. MACD, informally called "MacD," uses three exponential MOVING AVERAGES: a short one, a long one, and a third that plots the moving average of the difference between the other two and forms a signal line on an MACD graph. (MACD is usually shown as a histogram, which plots the difference between the signal line and the MACD line). Trend reversals are signaled by the convergence and divergence of these moving averages. A positive BREAKOUT occurs when the histogram crosses the zero line upward (a buy signal) and a negative breakout occurs when the histogram crosses the zero (equilibrium) line downward (a sell signal). One of the most popular MACDs is the 8/17/9 MACD. On a daily MACD, the short moving average would be 8 days, the long one 17 days, and the signal line 9 days. On a weekly MACD, the same numbers would refer to weeks instead of days. The weekly MACD overrides chatter (*see* WHIPSAWED) and is a better indicator of how strongly the market feels about a stock and how likely it is the current trend will continue. *See also* MOMENTUM INDICATORS.

MTN initials standing for *medium-term (5–10–year) notes* that are issued by corporations and distributed by investment banks acting as agents, similar to shorter-term COMMERCIAL PAPER.

MUD acronym for *municipal utility district,* a political subdivision that provides utility-related services and may issue SPECIAL ASSESSMENT BONDS.

MULTINATIONAL CORPORATION corporation that has production facilities or other fixed assets in at least one foreign country and makes its major management decisions in a global context. In marketing, production, research and development, and labor relations, its decisions must be made in terms of host-country customs and traditions. In finance, many of its problems have no domestic counterpart—the payment of dividends in another currency, for example, or the need to shelter working capital from the risk of devaluation, or the choices between owning and licensing. Economic and legal questions must be dealt with in drastically different ways. In addition to foreign exchange risks and the special business risks of operating in unfamiliar environments, there is the specter of political risk—the risk that sovereign governments may interfere with operations or terminate them altogether.

MULTIPLE *see* PRICE-EARNINGS RATIO.

MULTIPLE LISTING listing agreement used by a broker who is a member of a multiple-listing organization that is an exclusive right to sell with an additional authority and obligation on the part of the listing broker to distribute the listing to other brokers in the organization. These listings then are distributed in a multiple-listing service publication. Generally, the listing broker and the selling broker will split the commission, but terms for division can vary. A multiple-listing agreement benefits the seller by exposing his property to a wider group of potential buyers than would be available from one exclusive broker, which should allow the sale to be completed more quickly, and for a higher price. The multiple-listing service, however, has come under close scrutiny by consumer groups and justice departments for alleged antitrust practices.

MULTIPLE PERIL INSURANCE policy that incorporates several different types of property insurance coverage, such as flood, fire, wind, etc. In its broadest application, the term is synonymous with *all-risks insurance,* which covers loss or damage to property from fortuitous circumstances not specifically excluded from coverage. Do not confuse multiple peril insurance with *multiple protection insurance,* which is a form of life insurance policy combining features of term and whole life insurance.

MULTIPLIER the multiplier has two major applications in finance and investments.
   1. *investment multiplier* or *Keynesian multiplier:* multiplies the effects of investment spending in terms of total income. An investment in a small plant facility, for example, increases the incomes of the workers who built it, the merchants who provide supplies, the distributors who supply the merchants, the manufacturers who supply the distributors, and so on. Each

recipient spends a portion of the income and saves the rest. By making an assumption as to the percentage each recipient saves, it is possible to calculate the total income produced by the investment.

2. *deposit multiplier* or *credit multiplier:* magnifies small changes in bank deposits into changes in the amount of outstanding credit and the money supply. For example, a bank receives a deposit of $100,000, and the RESERVE REQUIREMENT is 20%. The bank is thus required to keep $20,000 in the form of reserves. The remaining $80,000 becomes a loan, which is deposited in the borrower's bank. When the borrower's bank sets aside the $16,000 required reserve out of the $80,000, $64,000 is available for another loan and another deposit, and so on. Carried out to its theoretical limit, the original deposit of $100,000 could expand into a total of $500,000 in deposits and $400,000 in credit.

MUNI popular designation for a municipal security, especially a MUNICIPAL BOND.

MUNICIPAL BOND debt obligation of a state or local government entity. The funds may support general governmental needs or special projects. Prior to the TAX REFORM ACT OF 1986, the terms *municipal* and *tax-exempt* were synonymous, since virtually all municipal obligations were exempt from federal income taxes and most from state and local income taxes, at least in the state of issue. The 1986 Act, however, divided municipals into two broad groups: (1) PUBLIC PURPOSE BONDS, which remain tax-exempt and can be issued without limitation, and (2) PRIVATE PURPOSE BONDS, which are taxable unless specifically exempted. The tax distinction between public and private purpose is based on the percentage extent to which the bonds benefit private parties; if a tax-exempt public purpose bond involves more than a 10% benefit to private parties, it is taxable. Permitted private purpose bonds (those specified as tax-exempt) are generally TAX PREFERENCE ITEMS in computing the ALTERNATIVE MINIMUM TAX, and effective August 15, 1986, are subject to volume caps. *See also* ADVANCE REFUNDING; GENERAL OBLIGATION BOND; HOSPITAL REVENUE BOND; INDUSTRIAL DEVELOPMENT BOND; LIMITED TAX BOND; MUNICIPAL INVESTMENT TRUST; MUNICIPAL REVENUE BOND; SINGLE STATE MUNICIPAL BOND FUND; SPECIAL ASSESSMENT BOND; TAXABLE MUNICIPAL BOND; TAX-EXEMPT SECURITY; UNDERLYING DEBT; YIELD BURNING.

MUNICIPAL BOND INSURANCE policies underwritten by private insurers guaranteeing municipal bonds in the event of default. The insurance can be purchased either by the issuing government entity or the investor; it provides that bonds will be purchased from investors at par should default occur. Such insurance is available from a number of large insurance companies, but a major portion is written by the following "monoline" companies, so-called because their primary business is insuring municipal bonds: AMBAC Assurance Corporation (AMBAC); Assured Guaranty Corporation (AGC); CIFG Assurance North America (CIFG); Financial Guaranty Insurance Company (FGIC); Financial Security Assurance (FSA); National Public Finance Guaranty Corporation; and Syncora Guarantee. Insured municipal bonds generally enjoy the highest rating resulting in greater marketability and lower cost to their issuers. From the investor's standpoint, however, their yield is typically lower than similarly rated uninsured bonds because the cost of the insurance is passed on by the issuer to the investor. Some unit investment trusts and mutual funds feature insured municipal bonds for investors willing to trade marginally lower yield for the extra degree of safety.

MUNICIPAL CONVERTIBLE a ZERO-COUPON BOND with the deep discount and VOLATILITY, but without the taxability, and that can be convertible into an interest-bearing security under certain conditions. *See also* ZERO COUPON CONVERTIBLE SECURITY (meaning 2).

MUNICIPAL IMPROVEMENT CERTIFICATE certificate issued by a local government in lieu of bonds to finance improvements or services, such as widening a sidewalk, or installing a sewer, or repairing a street. Such an obligation is payable from a special tax assessment against those who benefit from the improvement, and the payments may be collected by the contractor performing the work. Interest on the certificate is usually free of federal, state, and local taxes. *See also* GENERAL OBLIGATION BOND.

MUNICIPAL INVESTMENT TRUST (MIT) UNIT INVESTMENT TRUST that buys municipal bonds and passes the tax-free income on to shareholders. Bonds in the trust's portfolio are normally held until maturity, unlike the constant trading of bonds in an open-ended municipal bond fund's portfolio. MITs are sold through brokers, typically for a sales charge of about 3% of the principal paid, with a minimum investment of $1000. The trust offers diversification, professional management of the portfolio, and monthly interest, compared with the semiannual payments made by individual municipal bonds.

　　Many MITs invest in the securities of just one state. For California residents who buy a California-only MIT, for example, all the interest is free of federal, state, and local taxes. In contrast, a Californian who buys a national MIT might have to pay state and local taxes on interest derived from out-of-state bonds in the trust's portfolio. Also called MUNICIPAL BOND UNIT TRUST.

MUNICIPAL NOTE in common usage, a municipal debt obligation with an original maturity of two years or less.

MUNICIPAL REVENUE BOND bond issued to finance public works such as bridges or tunnels or sewer systems and supported directly by the revenues of the project. For instance, if a municipal revenue bond is issued to build a bridge, the tolls collected from motorists using the bridge are committed for paying off the bond. Unless otherwise specified in the indenture, holders of these bonds have no claims on the issuer's other resources.

MUNICIPAL SECURITIES RULEMAKING BOARD *see* SELF-REGULATORY ORGANIZATION.

MURPHY'S LAW aphorism that anything that can go wrong will go wrong.

MUTILATED SECURITY certificate that cannot be read for the name of the issue or the issuer, or for the detail necessary for identification and transfer, or for the exercise of the holder's rights. It is then the seller's obligation to take corrective action, which usually means having the transfer agent guarantee the rights of ownership to the buyer.

MUTUAL ASSOCIATION SAVINGS AND LOAN ASSOCIATION organized as a cooperative owned by its members. Members' deposits represent shares; shareholders vote on association affairs and receive income in the form of dividends. Unlike state-chartered corporate S&Ls, which account for a minority of the industry, mutual associations are not permitted to issue stock, and they are usually chartered by the OFFICE OF THRIFT SUPERVISION (OTS) and belong to the Deposit Insurance Fund (DIF). Deposits are technically subject to a waiting period before withdrawal, although in practice withdrawals are usually allowed on demand. *See also* DEMUTUALIZATION.

MUTUAL COMPANY corporation whose ownership and profits are distributed among members in proportion to the amount of business they do with the company. The most familiar examples are (1) mutual insurance companies, whose members are policy holders entitled to name the directors or trustees and to receive dividends or rebates on future premiums; (2) state-chartered MUTUAL SAVINGS BANKS, whose members are depositors sharing in net earnings but having nothing to do with management; and (3) federal savings and loan associations, MUTUAL ASSOCIATIONS whose members are depositors entitled to vote and receive dividends.

MUTUAL EXCLUSION DOCTRINE doctrine which established that interest from municipal bonds is exempt from federal taxation. In return for this federal tax exemption, states and localities are not allowed to tax interest generated by federal government securities, such as Treasury bills, notes, and bonds.

MUTUAL FUND fund operated by an INVESTMENT COMPANY that raises money from shareholders and invests it in stocks, bonds, options, futures, currencies, or money market securities. These funds offer investors the advantages of diversification and professional management. A management fee is charged for these services, typically between 0.5% and 2% of assets per year. Funds also levy other fees such as 12B-1 FEES, EXCHANGE FEES and other administrative charges. Funds that are sold through brokers are called LOAD FUNDS, and those sold to investors directly from the fund companies are called NO-LOAD FUNDS. Mutual fund shares are redeemable on demand at NET ASSET VALUE by shareholders. All shareholders share equally in the gains and losses generated by the fund.

Mutual funds come in many varieties. Some invest aggressively for capital appreciation, while others are conservative and are designed to generate income for shareholders. Investors need to assess their tolerance for risk before they decide which fund would be appropriate for them. In addition, the timing of buying or selling depends on the outlook for the economy, the state of the stock and bond markets, interest rates, and other factors. *See also* CLOSED-END FUNDS; EXCHANGE-TRADED FUNDS (ETFs); MUTUAL FUND SHARE CLASSES.

MUTUAL FUND CASH-TO-ASSETS RATIO amount of mutual fund assets held in cash instruments. A fund manager may choose to keep a large cash position if he is bearish on the stock or bond market, or if he cannot find securities he thinks are attractive to buy. A large cash position (10% or more of the fund's assets in liquid instruments) may also accumulate if many investors buy fund shares and the fund manager cannot put all the money to work at once. On the other hand, a low cash-to-assets ratio is an indication that the fund manager is bullish, because he is fully invested and expects stock or bond prices to rise. Some analysts consider this ratio to be an important indicator of bullish or bearish sentiment among sophisticated investment managers. If many fund managers are increasing their cash positions, the fund managers are becoming more bearish—though some analysts consider it bullish for the market because the managers will have more cash to buy securities. The ratio for the entire mutual fund industry is released on a monthly basis by the Investment Company Institute, the largest mutual fund trade group.

MUTUAL FUND CUSTODIAN commercial bank or trust company that provides safekeeping for the securities owned by a mutual fund and may also act as TRANSFER AGENT, making payments to and collecting investments from shareholders. Mutual fund custodians must comply with the rules set forth in the INVESTMENT COMPANY ACT OF 1940.

MUTUAL FUND SHARE CLASSES alphabetical class designations that follow a mutual fund's name in most newspaper listings and usually, but not always, identify a fee structure as follows: Class A shares typically have a FRONT-END LOAD, a sales charge payable when you buy the fund. Class B shares typically have a BACK-END LOAD, payable when you redeem your fund shares, but declining the longer you hold the fund until finally, after six to eight years, it "converts" to zero. Both A and B shares usually have an additional 12b-1 marketing fee, higher in the case of B shares. Class C shares have no front-end load, a rear-end load ranging from very low (1 percent) to nothing, but have relatively high 12b-1 fees (translating into high EXPENSE RATIOS.) Class A, B, and C shares are by far the most common. Class D shares, where they exist, differ from one mutual fund company to another, in one case signifying front-end loads and no 12b-1 fees, in others high 12b-1 and no front-end loads, in still others, a rear-end load structured differently than that fund company's B shares. Class I and Class Y shares are institutional shares, not available to retail investors; if they are included in your 401k plan, they probably have low annual expenses and don't have a sales charge. M and T Class shares are different for each fund company, but are usually a variation on C shares. Z Class shares are either owned by the fund company's employees or by investors who got into a fund when it originally started as a no-load fund and stayed in after it became a load fund.

MUTUAL FUND SYMBOL five letter symbol ending with an X that identifies a mutual fund. Exchange-traded funds have STOCK SYMBOLS.

MUTUAL IMPROVEMENT CERTIFICATE certificate issued by a local government in lieu of bonds to finance improvements or services, such as widening a sidewalk, or installing a sewer, or repairing a street. Such an obligation is payable from a special tax assessment against those who benefit from the improvement, and the payments may be collected by the contractor performing the work. Interest on the certificate is free of federal, state, and local taxes. *See also* GENERAL OBLIGATION BOND.

MUTUAL SAVINGS BANK SAVINGS BANK organized under state charter for the ownership and benefit of its depositors. A local board of trustees makes major decisions as fiduciaries, independently of the legal owners. Traditionally, income is distributed to depositors after expenses are deducted and reserve funds are set aside as required. In recent times, many mutual savings banks have begun to issue stock and offer consumer services such as credit cards and checking accounts, as well as commercial services such as corporate checking accounts and commercial real estate loans.

N

NAKED OPTION OPTION for which the buyer or seller has no underlying security position. A writer of a naked CALL OPTION, therefore, does not own a LONG POSITION in the stock on which the call has been written. Similarly, the writer of a naked PUT OPTION does not have a SHORT POSITION in the stock on which the put has been written. Naked options are very risky—although potentially very rewarding. If the underlying stock or stock index moves in the direction sought by the investor, profits can be enormous, because the investor would only have had to put down a small amount of money to reap a large return. On the other hand, if the stock moved in the opposite direction, the writer of the naked option could be subject to huge losses.

For instance, if someone wrote a naked call option at $60 a share on XYZ stock without owning the shares, and if the stock rose to $70 a share, the writer of the option would have to deliver XYZ shares to the call buyer at $60 a share. In order to acquire those shares, he or she would have to go into the market and buy them for $70 a share, sustaining a $10-a-share loss on his or her position. If, on the other hand, the option writer already owned XYZ shares when writing the option, he or she could just turn those shares over to the option buyer. This latter strategy is known as writing a COVERED CALL.

NAKED POSITION securities position that is not hedged from market risk—for example, the position of someone who writes a CALL or PUT option without having the corresponding LONG POSITION or SHORT POSITION on the underlying security. The potential risk or reward of naked positions is greater than that of covered positions. *See* COVERED CALL; HEDGE; NAKED OPTION.

NAKED SHORT position of an underwriter who sells more shares than are issued so he or she can become a buyer after the offering and support the market price. *See also* SELLING SHORT. Naked short selling occurs when sellers don't borrow the shares before selling them, and then look to cover their positions sometime after the sale. The Securities and Exchange Commission considers naked short-selling abusive, because it allows short-sellers to push down a stock's price dramatically without even owning the shares. The SEC banned the practice in 2009 by requiring that brokers must promptly buy or borrow securities to deliver on any short sales.

NAKED WRITER seller of a NAKED OPTION.

NAMED PERILS INSURANCE property insurance that covers risks specified in the policy. Contrasts with *all-risks insurance,* which specifies exclusions.

NAREIT *see* NATIONAL ASSOCIATION OF REAL ESTATE INVESTMENT TRUSTS (NAREIT).

NARROW-BASED INDEX (NBI) a futures contract on a small group of stocks, typically under ten, in a specific industry sector, such as airlines, pharmaceuticals, semiconductors, or energy. *See also* SINGLE STOCK FUTURE (SSF).

NARROWING THE SPREAD closing the SPREAD between the bid and asked prices of a security as a result of bidding and offering by market makers and specialists in a security. For example, a stock's bid price—the most anyone is willing to pay—may be $10 a share, and the asked price—the lowest price at which anyone will sell—may be $10\frac{3}{4}$. If a broker or market maker offers to buy shares at $10\frac{1}{4}$, while the asked price remains at $10\frac{3}{4}$, the spread has effectively been narrowed.

NARROW MARKET securities or commodities market characterized by light trading and greater fluctuations in prices relative to volume than would be the case if trading were active. The market in a particular stock is said to be narrow if the price falls more than a point between ROUND LOT trades without any apparent explanation, suggesting lack of interest and too few orders. The terms THIN MARKET and *inactive market* are used as synonyms for narrow market.

NASAA *see* NORTH AMERICAN SECURITIES ADMINISTRATORS ASSOCIATION (NASAA).

NASDAQ OMX GROUP the world's largest exchange company, with more than 3,900 companies representing $5.5 trillion in total market value. Formed on February 27, 2008, when NASDAQ acquired OMX, an integrated securities market in Northern Europe. Later that year, NASDAQ OMX acquired both the Philadelphia Stock Exchange and the Boston Stock Exchange. NASDAQ is the principal home of top U.S. growth companies, as well as international companies trading shares in the United States. It offers trading across multiple asset classes, including equities, derivatives, debt, commodities, structured products, and exchange-traded funds. NASDAQ added an options market in 2008. NASDAQ real-time quotes are transmitted through an international computer and telecommunications network to more than 1.3 million users in 83 countries. The NASDAQ OMX Global Index Group offers full-scale, premium index services, including the NASDAQ-100 Index, launched in 1985, and the NASDAQ Composite Index, launched in 1971. About 300 market makers use their own capital to buy and sell NASDAQ securities, then redistribute the stock as needed. Its U.S. trading platform is a fully integrated order display, execution, and trade reporting system for all NASDAQ-, NEW YORK STOCK EXCHANGE-, and AMERICAN STOCK EXCHANGE-listed securities. The trading platform is the fastest in the industry, with peak trading speeds of 250 microseconds. NASDAQ launched SuperMontage, a new generation system, in 2002. In 2004, NASDAQ bought BRUT LLC, operator of BRUT ECN, an ELECTRONIC COMMUNICATIONS NETWORK. In 2005, it acquired Instinet Group and integrated Instinet's Inet ECN into its operations. The NASDAQ Stock Market is composed of two separate markets. The NASDAQ National Market is the market for NASDAQ's largest and most actively traded securities, among them Microsoft and Intel. The NASDAQ SmallCap Market lists emerging growth companies that move up to the NASDAQ National Market as they become established. Trading hours: 9:30 A.M. to 4 P.M. and 4 P.M. to 6:30 P.M. (NASDAQ Stock Market); 3:30 A.M. to 9 A.M. (NASDAQ International Market); 8 A.M. to 9:30 A.M. and 4 P.M. to 6:30 P.M. (SelectNet). *www.nasdaqomx.com.*

NATIONAL ASSOCIATION OF INVESTORS CORPORATION (NAIC) not-for-profit educational association that helps investment clubs become established. Investment clubs are formed by people who pool their money and make common decisions about how to invest those assets. The NAIC is located in Madison Heights, Michigan. *See also* INVESTMENT CLUB.

NATIONAL ASSOCIATION OF REAL ESTATE INVESTMENT TRUSTS (NAREIT) Washington, D.C.-based national trade association for REAL ESTATE INVESTMENT TRUSTS (REITs) and other businesses that own, operate, and finance income-producing real estate, as well as firms and individuals who advise, study, and service these businesses. NAREIT serves as an advocacy group and as a source of research, news, and other industry information. Its web address is *www.nareit.com.*

NATIONAL BANK internationally, synonymous with CENTRAL BANK. In the United States, a nationally chartered bank. *See also* MEMBER BANK.

NATIONAL BUREAU OF ECONOMIC RESEARCH (NBER) Cambridge, Massachusetts-based private, nonprofit organization "committed to undertaking and disseminating unbiased economic research among public policymakers, business professionals, and the academic community."

NATIONAL CREDIT UNION ADMINISTRATION (NCUA) independent federal agency based in Washington, D.C., established by Congress to oversee the federal credit union system. The NCUA is funded by credit unions and does not receive any tax dollars. The agency supervises nearly 6,600 federal credit unions and insures member accounts in approximately 4,000 state-chartered credit unions. The National Credit Union Share Insurance Fund is the agency's arm that insures member accounts up to $100,000, although that limit was temporarily increased to $250,000. This temporary increase in coverage was originally set to expire in 2010, but was later extended to 2013. The fund is backed by the full faith and credit of the U.S. government and is managed by the NCUA Board, which is comprised of three members appointed by the president.

NATIONAL DEBT debt owed by the federal government. The national debt is made up of such debt obligations as Treasury bills, Treasury notes, and Treasury bonds. Congress imposes a ceiling on the national debt, which has been increased on occasion when accumulated deficits near the ceiling. By the late-2000s, the national debt stood at $12 trillion. The interest due on the national debt is one of the major expenses of the federal government. The national debt, which is the total debt accumulated by the government over many decades, should not be confused with the federal budget deficit, which is the excess of spending over income by the federal government in one fiscal year.

NATIONAL FOUNDATION FOR CREDIT (NFCC) a nonprofit national organization based in Silver Spring, Maryland, created in 1951 to help the increasing number of consumers who have taken on too much debt. The NFCC has more than 150 members operating 1300 locations providing consumers with money management, budget, and wise-credit-use education workshops and counseling sessions. While counselors work with creditors to work out a payment plan, the NFCC does not provide credit or financial assistance. Most members do not charge for counseling; however some members charge a low fee for services such as debt repayment or counseling. No one is turned away due to the inability to pay.

NATIONAL FUTURES ASSOCIATION (NFA) self-regulatory organization of the futures industry. It was authorized by Congress in 1974 and designated by the Commodity Futures Trading Commisssion (CFTC) as a "registered futures association" in 1982. Its mission is to protect the public investor by maintaining the integrity of the marketplace, and it is a source of education, training aids, publications, and information about futures professionals. *www.nfa.futures.org*.

NATIONAL INVESTOR RELATIONS INSTITUTE (NIRI) founded in 1969, NIRI is a professional association of corporate officers and investor relations consultants responsible for communication among corporate management, the investing public, and the financial community. It has more than 4,300 members in 35 chapters around the country. *www.niri.org*. *See also* INVESTOR RELATIONS DEPARTMENT.

NATIONALIZATION takeover of a private company's assets or operations by a government. The company may or may not be compensated for the loss of assets. In developing nations, an operation is typically nationalized if the government feels the company is exploiting the host country and exporting too high a proportion of the profits. By nationalizing the firm, the government hopes to keep profits at home. In developed countries, industries are often nationalized when they need government subsidies to survive as is the case in the United States in 2009. The French government nationalized steel and chemical companies in the mid-1980s in order to preserve jobs that would have disappeared if free market forces had prevailed. In some developed countries, however, nationalization is carried out as a form of national policy, often by Socialist governments, and is not designed to rescue ailing industries.

NATIONAL MARKET SYSTEM (NMS) a concept embodied in the Securities Acts Amendments of 1975 with the goal of fostering greater competition among the stock exchanges and other participants in the U.S. markets. In furtherance of this concept, the AMERICAN STOCK EXCHANGE, BOSTON STOCK EXCHANGE, CHICAGO STOCK EXCHANGE, Cincinnati Stock Exchange (now called the NATIONAL STOCK EXCHANGE), NEW YORK STOCK EXCHANGE, PACIFIC EXCHANGE, and the PHILADELPHIA STOCK EXCHANGE developed the Intermarket Trading System (ITS). NASDAQ subsequently joined ITS. ITS is an electronic linkage among all of the registered national securities exchanges and associations that permits participants to route orders to the participant displaying the best price nationwide. The ITS Plan was filed with the Securities and Exchange Commission as a national market system plan under Section 11A of the Securities Exchange Act of 1934. The commission approved the plan. A second industry group, the Consolidated Tape Association (CTA), has two plans: the Consolidated Tape Plan (CT Plan) and the Consolidated Quotation Plan (CQ Plan), which provide, respectively, trade reports for listed securities and the current bid and offer from each participating market, as well as the national best bid and offer. The CT Plan is a national market system plan, as well as a transaction-reporting plan. The CQ Plan is a national market system plan. In light of the many changes in the securities markets over the years, the ITS plan was amended in 2000 to expand NASDAQ's ITS/CAES (Computer Assisted Execution System) linkage to all listed securities. In 1998, the SEC adopted Regulation ATS (alternative trading systems) to provide a streamlined regulatory structure for ECNs that choose to be regulated as alternative trading systems rather than national securities exchanges, with the aim of integrating them into the NMS. In 2005 the SEC approved a sweeping plan, known as Regulation NMS, to modernize the regulatory structure of the U.S. equity markets. Regulation NMS covers the following areas: order protection, intermarket access, sub-penny pricing, and market data. It also updates the existing Exchange Act rules governing the national market system and consolidates them into a single regulation. Two amendments were also made to the joint industry plans for disseminating market information. *See also* INTERMARKET TRADING SYSTEM.

NATIONAL QUOTATION BUREAU *see* PINK SHEETS, LLC.

NATIONAL SECURITIES TRADING SYSTEM (NSTS) *see* NATIONAL STOCK EXCHANGE (NSX).

NATIONAL STOCK EXCHANGE (NSX) founded in 1885, it was the first all-electronic stock exchange in the United States, having replaced its physical trading floor with a completely automated market in 1980. Exchange membership consists of registered broker-dealers. NSX created the National Securities Trading System (NSTS), which automatically performs all functions of an auction market. NSTS, an electronic securities communication and execution facility, consolidates bids and offers of competing dealers, as well as public orders, for review and execution by users. NSTS contains features envisioned for a national exchange market system. Founded in Cincinnati and formerly called The Cincinnati Stock Exchange, the exchange moved to Chicago in 1995 and changed its name to National Stock Exchange in 2003. NSX was demutualized in 2006. Trading is Monday through Friday. *www.nsx.com.*

NATIONAL STOCK EXCHANGE OF AUSTRALIA (NSX) until 2006, called the Stock Exchange of Newcastle Limited. Founded in 1937, incorporated in 1972 and reactivated in 2000, NSX is the leading market for small to medium regional companies and sub-exchanges in Australia. Trading is all-electronic and settlement is on a T-PLUS-THREE basis. Trading Hours: 9 A.M. to 2:30 P.M., Monday through Friday. *www.newsx.com.au.*

NATIONAL STOCK EXCHANGE OF INDIA (NSE) established in India in 1994 to provide a more transparent alternative to The Bombay Stock Exchange. It is the largest stock exchange in India in both turnover and number of trades. The NSE is a national exchange integrating the country's stock markets through nationwide automated on-line screen operations and electronic clearing and settlement. The exchange's products include equities, exchange-traded funds, stock futures, index futures, interest rate futures, and options. The S&P CNX Nifty, a diversified 50-stock index representing 23 sectors of the Indian economy, is among the exchange's major indices. *www. nseindia.com.*

NEAREST MONTH in commodity futures or OPTION trading, the expiration dates, expressed as months, closest to the present. For a commodity or an option that had delivery or expiration dates available in September, December, March, and June, for instance, the nearest month would be September if a trade were being made in August. Nearest month contracts, called nearbys, are always more heavily traded than FURTHEST MONTH contracts.

NEAR MONEY CASH EQUIVALENTS and other assets that are easily convertible into cash. Some examples are government securities, bank TIME DEPOSITS, and MONEY MARKET FUND shares. Bonds close to REDEMPTION date are also called near money.

NEGATIVE AMORTIZATION LOAN type of OPTION ARM where the current payment is lowered and the difference is added to the balance of the loan.

NEGATIVE CARRY situation in which the cost of money borrowed to finance securities or financial futures positions is higher than the return on those positions. For example, if an investor borrowed at 10% to finance, or "carry," a bond yielding 8%, the bond position would have a negative carry. Negative carry does not necessarily mean a loss to the investor, however, and a positive yield can result on an aftertax basis. In this case, the yield from the 8% bond may be tax-exempt, whereas interest on the 10% loan is tax-deductible. In commodities, this would occur in any month in a BACKWARD-ATION where the price is higher than the spot month. With the negative carry, if the investor holds the physical position in copper, for example, it will continue to lose value.

NEGATIVE CASH FLOW situation in which a business spends more cash than it receives through earnings or other transactions in an accounting period. *See also* CASH FLOW.

NEGATIVE INCOME TAX proposed system of providing financial aid to poverty-level individuals and families, using the mechanisms already in place to collect income taxes. After filing a tax return showing income below sub-sistence levels, instead of paying an income tax, low-income people would receive a direct subsidy, called a negative income tax, sufficient to bring them up to the subsistence level.

NEGATIVE INTEREST RATE a rate below zero, whereby the lender, actually or technically, pays interest to the borrower. In 2002, for example, the FEDERAL FUNDS RATE was lower than the rate of inflation, resulting in a REAL INTEREST RATE that was, technically, negative. An example of a negative inter-est rate in the literal sense is a PRIVATE PLACEMENT with institutional investors of debt-plus-warrants, a security called *Squarz* (pronounced "squares") of Berkshire Hathaway Corporation, controlled by the Wall Street legend Warren Buffett. Goldman Sachs, which designed the structure in mid-2002, called it the "first ever negative-coupon security." Taking advantage of low market interest rates and high stock market volatility, Berkshire would pay about 3% a year on the bonds being issued. But the investor would also receive a warrant allowing the purchase of Berkshire stock and to keep the warrant alive, investors would have to pay a higher rate, perhaps 3.75%, at the same time Berkshire made the interest payments. The net effect was a negative interest rate.

NEGATIVE OBLIGATION NEW YORK STOCK EXCHANGE requirement that a SPECIALIST must "stand out of the way" when a natural match can occur between a buyer and a seller. Any violation of this rule is called *trading ahead*. Decimalization has resulted in a practice called PENNY JUMPING (or PENNYING), whereby a specialist offers the seller a penny over the bid and makes the difference between that price and the offer price, which may be several pennies higher. Penny jumping is controversial because it is similar to the illegal practice of FRONT RUNNING.

NEGATIVE PLEDGE CLAUSE negative covenant or promise in an INDEN-TURE agreement that states the corporation will not pledge any of its assets if doing so would result in less security to the debtholders covered under the indenture agreement. Also called *covenant of equal coverage.*

NEGATIVE WORKING CAPITAL situation in which the current liabilities of a firm exceed its current assets. For example, if the total of cash, MARKET-ABLE SECURITIES, ACCOUNTS RECEIVABLE and notes receivable, inventory, and other current assets is less than the total of ACCOUNTS PAYABLE, short-term notes payable, long-term debt due in one year, and other current liabilities, the firm has a negative working capital. Unless the condition is corrected, the firm will not be able to pay debts when due, threatening its ability to keep operating and possibly resulting in bankruptcy.

To remedy a negative working capital position, a firm has these alternatives: (1) it can convert a long-term asset into a current asset—for example, by selling a piece of equipment or a building, by liquidating a long-term investment, or by renegotiating a long-term loan receivable; (2) it can convert short-term liabilities into long-term liabilities—for example, by negotiating the substitution of a current account payable with a long-term note payable; (3) it can borrow long term; (4) it can obtain additional equity through a stock issue or other sources of paid-in capital; (5) it can retain or "plow back" profits. *See also* WORKING CAPITAL.

NEGATIVE YIELD CURVE *see* INVERTED YIELD CURVE.

NEGLECTED FIRM EFFECT tendency of stocks undiscovered by analysts and institutional investors to outperform the overall market because of the SMALL FIRM EFFECT and to register dramatic gains once discovered.

NEGOTIABLE
In general:
1. something that can be sold or transferred to another party in exchange for money or as settlement of an obligation.
2. matter of mutual concern to one or more parties that involves conditions to be worked out to the satisfaction of the parties. As examples: In a lender-borrower arrangement, the interest rate may be negotiable; in securities sales, brokerage commissions are now negotiable, having historically been fixed; and in divorce cases involving children, the terms of visiting rights are usually negotiable.

Finance: instrument meeting the qualifications of the Uniform Commercial Code dealing with negotiable instruments. *See also* NEGOTIABLE INSTRUMENT.

Investments: type of security the title to which is transferable by delivery. A stock certificate with the stock power properly signed is negotiable, for example.

NEGOTIABLE CERTIFICATE OF DEPOSIT large-dollar-amount, short-term certificate of deposit. Such certificates are issued by large banks and bought mainly by corporations and institutional investors. They are payable either to the bearer or to the order of the depositor, and, being NEGOTIABLE, they enjoy an active SECONDARY MARKET, where they trade in round lots of $5 million. Although they can be issued in any denomination from $100,000 up, the typical amount is $1 million. They have a minimum original maturity of 14 days; most original maturities are under six months. Also called a JUMBO CERTIFICATE OF DEPOSIT.

NEGOTIABLE INSTRUMENT unconditional order or promise to pay an amount of money, easily transferable from one person to another. Examples:

check, promissory note, draft (bill of exchange). The Uniform Commercial Code requires that for an instrument to be negotiable it must be signed by the maker or drawer, must contain an unconditional promise or order to pay a specific amount of money, must be payable on demand or at a specified future time, and must be payable to order or to the bearer.

NEGOTIABLE ORDER OF WITHDRAWAL a bank or savings and loan withdrawal ticket that is a NEGOTIABLE INSTRUMENT. The accounts from which such withdrawals can be made, called NOW accounts, are thus, in effect, interest-bearing checking accounts. They were first introduced in the late 1970s and became available nationally in January 1980. In the early and mid-1980s the interest rate on NOW accounts was capped at $5\frac{1}{2}\%$; the cap was phased out in the late 1980s. *See also* SUPER NEGOTIABLE ORDER OF WITHDRAWAL (NOW) ACCOUNT.

NEGOTIATED COMMISSION brokerage COMMISSION that is determined through negotiation. Prior to 1975, commissions were fixed. Since then, brokerage firms have been free to charge what they want and, although they have minimums and commission schedules, will negotiate commissions on large transactions.

NEGOTIATED UNDERWRITING underwriting of new securities issue in which the SPREAD between the purchase price paid to the issuer and the public offering price is determined through negotiation rather than multiple competitive bidding. The spread, which represents the compensation to the investment bankers participating in the underwriting (collectively called the *syndicate),* is negotiated between the issuing company and the MANAGING UNDERWRITER, with the consent of the group. Most corporate stock and bond issues and municipal revenue bond issues are priced through negotiation, whereas municipal general obligation bonds and new issues of public utilities are generally priced through competitive bidding. Competitive bidding is mandatory for new issues of public utilities holding companies. *See also* COMPETITIVE BID.

NELLIE MAE CORPORATION division of SALLIE MAE providing education financing for undergraduate and graduate students and families.

NEO abbreviation for *nonequity options.* This refers to options contracts on foreign currencies, bonds and other debt issues, commodities, metals, and stock indexes. In contrast, equity options have individual stocks as underlying values.

NEST EGG assets put aside for a person's retirement. Such assets are usually invested conservatively to provide the retiree with a secure standard of living for the rest of his or her life. Investment in an INDIVIDUAL RETIREMENT ACCOUNT would be considered part of a nest egg.

NET

In general: figure remaining after all relevant deductions have been made from the gross amount. For example: net sales are equal to gross sales minus discounts, returns, and allowances; net profit is gross profit less operating (sales, general, and administrative) expenses; net worth is assets (worth) less liabilities.

Investments: dollar difference between the proceeds from the sale of a security and the seller's adjusted cost of acquisition—that is, the gain or loss.

As a verb:
1. to arrive at the difference between additions and subtractions or plus amounts and minus amounts. For example, in filing tax returns, capital losses are netted against capital gains.
2. to realize a net profit, as in "last year we netted a million dollars after taxes."

NET AFTERTAX GAIN capital gain after income taxes.

NET ASSETS difference between a company's total assets and liabilities; another way of saying *owner's equity* or NET WORTH. *See* ASSET COVERAGE for a discussion of net asset value per unit of bonds, preferred stock, or common stock.

NET ASSET VALUE (NAV)
1. in mutual funds, the market value of a fund share, synonymous with *bid price.* In the case of no-load funds, the NAV, market price, and offering price are all the same figure, which the public pays to buy shares; load fund market or offer prices are quoted after adding the sales charge to the net asset value. NAV is calculated by most funds after the close of the exchanges each day by taking the closing market value of all securities owned plus all other assets such as cash, subtracting all liabilities, then dividing the result (total net assets) by the total number of shares outstanding. The number of shares outstanding can vary each day depending on the number of purchases and redemptions.
2. book value of a company's different classes of securities, usually stated as net asset value per bond, net asset value per share of preferred stock, and net book value per common share of common stock. The formula for computing net asset value is total assets less any INTANGIBLE ASSET less all liabilities and securities having a prior claim, divided by the number of units outstanding (i.e., bonds, preferred shares, or common shares). *See* BOOK VALUE for a discussion of how these values are calculated and what they mean. *See also* DEFINED ASSET FUNDS; EXCHANGE TRADED FUNDS.

NET CAPITAL REQUIREMENT Securities and Exchange Commission requirement that member firms as well as nonmember broker-dealers in securities maintain a maximum ratio of indebtedness to liquid capital of 15 to 1; also called *net capital rule* and *net capital ratio.* Indebtedness covers all money owed to a firm, including MARGIN loans and commitments to purchase securities, one reason new public issues are spread among members of underwriting syndicates. Liquid capital includes cash and assets easily converted into cash.

NET CHANGE difference between the last trading price on a stock, bond, commodity, or mutual fund from one day to the next. The net change in individual stock prices is listed in newspaper financial pages. The designation $+2\frac{1}{2}$, for example, means that a stock's final price on that day was $2.50 higher than the final price on the previous trading day. The net changes in prices of NASDAQ STOCK MARKET stocks is usually the difference between bid prices from one day to the next.

NET CURRENT ASSETS difference between current assets and current liabilities; another name for WORKING CAPITAL. Some security analysts divide this figure (after subtracting preferred stock, if any) by the number of ·

common shares outstanding to arrive at working capital per share. Believing working capital per share to be a conservative measure of LIQUIDATING VALUE (on the theory that fixed and other noncurrent assets would more than compensate for any shrinkage in current assets if assets were to be sold), they compare it with the MARKET VALUE of the company's shares. If the net current assets per share figure, or "minimum liquidating value," is higher than the market price, these analysts view the common shares as a bargain (assuming, of course, that the company is not losing money and that its assets are conservatively valued). Other analysts believe this theory ignores the efficiency of capital markets generally and, specifically, obligations such as pension plans, which are not reported as balance sheet liabilities under present accounting rules.

NET DOMESTIC PRODUCT the GROSS DOMESTIC PRODUCT (GDP) less the depreciation of the country's capital goods. A shortfall between GDP and net domestic product is an indication of obsolescence and enables users of the country's national accounts to estimate the amount of capital spending necessary to maintain the current GDP.

NET EARNINGS *see* NET INCOME.

NET ESTATE *see* GROSS ESTATE.

NET INCOME
In general: sum remaining after all expenses have been met or deducted; synonymous with *net earnings* and with *net profit* or *net loss* (depending on whether the figure is positive or negative).
For a business: difference between total sales and total costs and expenses. Total costs comprise cost of goods sold including depreciation; total expenses comprise selling, general, and administrative expenses, plus INCOME DEDUCTIONS. Net income is usually specified as to whether it is before income taxes or after income taxes. Net income after taxes is the *bottom line* referred to in popular vernacular. It is out of this figure that dividends are normally paid. *See also* OPERATING PROFIT (OR LOSS).
For an individual: gross income less expenses incurred to produce gross income. Those expenses are mostly deductible for tax purposes.

NET INCOME PER SHARE OF COMMON STOCK amount of profit or earnings allocated to each share of common stock after all costs, taxes, allowances for depreciation, and possible losses have been deducted. Net income per share is stated in dollars and cents and is usually compared with the corresponding period a year earlier. For example, XYZ might report that second-quarter net income per share was $1.20, up from 90 cents in the previous year's second quarter. Also known as EARNINGS PER SHARE (EPS).

NET INCOME TO NET WORTH RATIO *see* RETURN ON EQUITY.

NET INTEREST COST (NIC) total amount of interest that a corporate or municipal bond entity will end up paying when issuing a debt obligation. The net interest cost factors in the coupon rate, any premiums or discounts, and reduces this to an average annual rate for the number of years until the bond matures or is callable. Underwriters compete to offer issuers the lowest NIC when they bid for the deal. The underwriting syndicate with the lowest NIC is normally awarded the contract.

NET INVESTMENT INCOME PER SHARE income received by an investment company from dividends and interest on securities investments during an accounting period, less management fees and administrative expenses and divided by the number of outstanding shares. Short-term trading profits (net profits from securities held for less than six months) are considered dividend income. The dividend and interest income is received by the investment company, which in turn pays shareholders the net investment income in the form of dividends prorated according to each holder's share in the total PORTFOLIO.

NET LEASE financial lease stipulating that the user (rather than the owner) of the leased property shall pay all maintenance costs, taxes, insurance, and other expenses. Many real estate and oil and gas limited partnerships are structured as net leases with ESCALATOR CLAUSES, to provide limited partners with both depreciation tax benefits and appreciation of investment, minus cash expenses. *See also* GROSS LEASE.

NET OPERATING LOSS (NOL) tax term for the excess of business expenses over income in a tax year. Under TAX LOSS CARRYBACK, CARRYFORWARD provisions, NOLs can (if desired) be carried back two years and forward 20 years. The carryback period for net operating losses caused by casualty and theft losses is three years.

NET PRESENT VALUE (NPV) method used in evaluating investments whereby the net present value of all cash outflows (such as the cost of the investment) and cash inflows (returns) is calculated using a given discount rate, usually a REQUIRED RATE OF RETURN. An investment is acceptable if the NPV is positive. In capital budgeting, the discount rate used is called the HURDLE RATE and is usually equal to the INCREMENTAL COST OF CAPITAL.

NET PROCEEDS amount (usually cash) received from the sale or disposition of property, from a loan, or from the sale or issuance of securities after deduction of all costs incurred in the transaction. In computing the gain or loss on a securities transaction for tax purposes, the amount of the sale is the amount of the net proceeds.

NET PROFIT *see* NET INCOME.

NET PROFIT MARGIN NET INCOME as a percentage of NET SALES. A measure of operating efficiency and pricing strategy, the ratio is usually computed using net profit before extraordinary items and taxes—that is, net sales less COST OF GOODS SOLD and SELLING, GENERAL, AND ADMINISTRATIVE (SG&A) EXPENSES.

NET QUICK ASSETS cash, MARKETABLE SECURITIES, and ACCOUNTS RECEIVABLE, minus current liabilities. *See also* QUICK RATIO.

NET REALIZED CAPITAL GAINS PER SHARE amount of CAPITAL GAINS that an investment company realized on the sale of securities, net of CAPITAL LOSSES, and divided by the number of outstanding shares. Such net gains are distributed annually to shareholders in proportion to their shares in the total portfolio. The distributions are eligible for favorable CAPITAL GAINS TAX rates if the positions were held for more than 12 months. If held for 12 months or less, the gains would be subject to regular income taxes at the shareholder's tax bracket. *See also* REGULATED INVESTMENT COMPANY.

NET SALES gross sales less returns and allowances, freight out, and cash discounts allowed. Cash discounts allowed is seen less frequently than in past years, since it has become conventional to report as net sales the amount finally received from the customer. Returns are merchandise returned for credit; allowances are deductions allowed by the seller for merchandise not received or received in damaged condition; freight out is shipping expense passed on to the customer.

NET TANGIBLE ASSETS PER SHARE total assets of a company, less any INTANGIBLE ASSET such as goodwill, patents, and trademarks, less all liabilities and the par value of preferred stock, divided by the number of common shares outstanding. *See* BOOK VALUE for a discussion of what this calculation means and how it can be varied to apply to bonds or preferred stock shares. *See also* NET ASSET VALUE.

NET TRANSACTION securities transaction in which the buyer and seller do not pay fees or commissions. For instance, when an investor buys a new issue, no commission is due. If the stock is initially offered at $15 a share, the buyer's total cost is $15 per share.

NETWORK A *see* CONSOLIDATED TAPE.

NETWORK B *see* CONSOLIDATED TAPE.

NET WORKING CAPITAL CURRENT ASSETS minus CURRENT LIABILITIES. Usually simply called WORKING CAPITAL.

NET WORTH amount by which assets exceed liabilities. For a corporation, net worth is also known as *stockholders' equity* or NET ASSETS. For an individual, net worth is the total value of all possessions, such as a house, stocks, bonds, and other securities, minus all outstanding debts, such as mortgage and revolving-credit loans. In order to qualify for certain high-risk investments, brokerage houses require that an individual's net worth must be at or above a certain dollar level.

NET YIELD RATE OF RETURN on a security net of out-of-pocket costs associated with its purchase, such as commissions or markups. *See also* MARKDOWN.

NEW ACCOUNT REPORT document filled out by a broker that details vital facts about a new client's financial circumstances and investment objectives. The report may be updated if there are material changes in a client's financial position. Based on the report, a client may or may not be deemed eligible for certain types of risky investments, such as commodity trading or highly leveraged LIMITED PARTNERSHIP deals. *See also* KNOW YOUR CUSTOMER.

NEW HIGH/NEW LOW stock prices that have hit the highest or lowest prices in the last year. Next to each stock's listing in a newspaper will be an indication of a new high with a letter "u" or a new low with the letter "d." Newspapers publish the total number of new highs and new lows each day on the New York and American Stock Exchanges and on the Nasdaq Stock Market. Technical analysts pay great attention to the trend of new highs and new lows. If the number of new highs is expanding, that is considered a bullish indicator. If the number of new lows is rising, that is considered bearish. Many analysts also track the ratio of new highs to new lows as a reflection of the general direction of the stock market.

NEW ISSUE stock or bond being offered to the public for the first time, the distribution of which is covered by Securities and Exchange Commission (SEC) rules. New issues may be initial public offerings by previously private companies or additional stock or bond issues by companies already public and often listed on the exchanges. New PUBLIC OFFERINGS must be registered with the SEC. PRIVATE PLACEMENTS avoid SEC registration if a LETTER OF INTENT establishes that the securities are purchased for investment and not for resale to the public. *See also* HOT ISSUE; LETTER SECURITY; UNDERWRITE.

NEW LISTING security that has just begun to trade on a stock or bond exchange. A new listing on the New York or American Stock Exchange must meet all LISTING REQUIREMENTS, and may either be an INITIAL PUBLIC OFFERING or a company whose shares have previously traded on the NASDAQ STOCK MARKET. New listings on the New York and American Stock Exchanges or a non-U.S. market carry the letter "n" next to their listing in newspaper tables for one year from the date they started trading on the exchange.

NEW MONEY amount of additional long-term financing provided by a new issue or issues in excess of the amount of a maturing issue or by issues that are being refunded.

NEW MONEY PREFERRED PREFERRED STOCK issued after October 1, 1942, when the tax exclusion for corporate investors receiving preferred stock dividends was raised from 60% to 85%, to equal the exclusion on common stock dividends. The change benefited financial institutions, such as insurance companies, which are limited in the amount of common stocks they can hold, typically 5% of assets. New money preferreds offer an opportunity to gain tax advantages over bond investments, which have fully taxable interest. The corporate tax exclusion on dividends is currently 70%.

NEW YORK CURB EXCHANGE *see* AMERICAN STOCK EXCHANGE.

NEW YORK MERCANTILE EXCHANGE (NYMEX) the largest physical commodity exchange in the world, offering futures and options trading in energy and metals contracts and clearing services for off-exchange energy transactions. NYMEX was acquired by the CME Group, parent company of the CHICAGO MERCANTILE EXCHANGE, in 2008. Through a combination of open outcry floor trading and the NYMEX ACCESS and NYMEX ClearPort electronic trading platforms, a wide range of crude oil, petroleum products, natural gas, coal, electricity, gold, silver, copper, aluminum, and platinum group metals markets are available virtually 24 hours a day. *www.nymex.com*. *See also* SECURITIES AND COMMODITIES EXCHANGES.

NEW YORK STOCK EXCHANGE (NYSE) founded in 1792 with the signing of the Buttonwood Agreement, it is the largest equities marketplace and most liquid exchange group in the world. The NYSE is located at 11 Wall Street in New York City and is composed of four rooms used for the facilitation of trading; also known as the Big Board and The Exchange. Approximately 2,700 companies worth $12 trillion in global market capitalization are listed on the exchange, a cross-section of leading blue chip, mid-size, and small capitalization companies that meet the NYSE's stringent listing requirements. It merged with Archipelago, an ELECTRONIC COMMUNICATIONS NETWORK (ECN), in 2006 and became a for-profit, public company. The New York Stock Exchange is a unit of NYSE Euronext, the world's most diverse exchange group, formed when the NYSE Group and Euronext, the European combined stock market, merged in 2007. NYSE Euronext acquired the AMERICAN STOCK EXCHANGE in 2008. The exchange offers an array of financial products and services, including equities, futures, options, interest-rate derivatives, exchange-traded products, bonds, market data, and commercial technology solutions. In 2001 trading in decimals was instituted, replacing trading in fractions. The NYSE also operates an automated bond market offering investors corporate, agency, and government bonds. NYSE-listed equity issuers can list their bonds without charge on the exchange. Corporate debt represents the largest share of NYSE bond volume, with some 85% in nonconvertible bonds and 15% in convertible debt issues. The NYSE is expanding its position in the trading of EXCHANGE-TRADED FUNDS (ETFs), structured products, and other derivative securities and is the largest market for listing iShares ETFs.

Additionally, Dow Jones Indexes developed and maintains a family of NYSE-branded indices that track the performance of NYSE-listed companies in key market sectors and regions. NYSE Euronext is part of the S&P 500 index and is the only exchange operator in the S&P 100 index. Certain operational functions are handled by affiliated corporations, such as Depository Trust Company, National Securities Clearing Corporation (NSCC), and SECURITIES INDUSTRY AUTOMATION CORPORATION (SIAC). Trading on the NYSE is in a continuous auction format, with specialist brokers acting as auctioneers in an OPEN OUTCRY market environment bringing buyers and sellers together—and, on occasion, committing their own capital to a trade. Trading is also conducted electronically. The NYSE sells one-year licenses to trade directly on the exchange. Trading hours: 9:30 A.M. to 4 P.M., followed by after-hours automated Crossing Sessions, Monday through Friday. *www.nyseeuronext.com. See also* SECURITIES AND COMMODITIES EXCHANGES.

NEW YORK STOCK EXCHANGE INDEX *see* STOCK INDEXES AND AVERAGES.

NEW ZEALAND EXCHANGE LIMITED (NZX) operator of New Zealand's sole registered securities exchange. Utilizing its proprietary FASTER technology, NZX facilitates fully electronic trading, clearing, and settlements across its three principal markets: NZSX-Stock Market, the premier equities market; NZDX-Debt Market, for corporate and government bonds and fixed-income securities; and NZAX-Alternative Market, for smaller and growing companies. In addition, NZX offers various data products, indices, and funds and is responsible for the ongoing monitoring, surveillance, and regulation of New Zealand's securities markets. NZX demutualized in 2002 and became a publicly listed company. Trading hours: 10 A.M. to 4:45 P.M. *www.nzx.com.*

NICHE particular specialty in which a firm has garnered a large market share. Often, the market will be small enough so that the firm will not attract very much competition. For example, a company that makes a line of specialty chemicals for use by only the petroleum industry is said to have a niche in the chemical industry. Stock analysts frequently favor such companies, since their profit margins can often be wider than those of firms facing more competition.

NICS acronym for *newly industrialized countries,* which are countries that have rapidly developing industrial economies. Some examples of NICS are Hong Kong, Singapore, Malaysia, South Korea, Mexico, Argentina, and Chile. NICS typically have instituted free-market policies which encourage exports to traditional Western industrialized countries and seek investment from Western corporations. Most NICS have increasingly been reducing trade barriers to imports from Western firms.

NIFTY FIFTY 50 stocks most favored by institutions. The membership of this group is constantly changing, although companies that continue to produce consistent earnings growth over a long time tend to remain institutional favorites. Nifty Fifty stocks also tend to have higher than market average price/earnings ratios, since their growth prospects are well recognized by institutional investors. The Nifty Fifty stocks were particularly famous in the bull markets of the 1960s and early 1970s, when many of the price/earnings ratios soared to 50 or more. *See also* PRICE/EARNINGS RATIO.

NIKKEI INDEX *see* NIKKEI STOCK AVERAGE.

NIKKEI STOCK AVERAGE index of 225 leading stocks traded on the Tokyo Stock Exchange. Called the Nikkei Dow Jones Stock Average until it was renamed in May 1985, it is similar to the Dow Jones Industrial Average because it is composed of representative BLUE CHIP companies (termed *first-section* companies in Japan) and is a PRICE-WEIGHTED INDEX. That means that the movement of each stock, in yen or dollars respectively, is weighed equally regardless of its market capitalization. The Nikkei Stock Average, informally called the Nikkei Index and often still referred to as the Nikkei Dow, is published by the *Nihon Keizai Shimbun (Japan Economic Journal)* and is the most widely quoted Japanese stock index.

   Also widely quoted is the Tokyo Stock Price Index (Topix) of all issues listed in the First Section.

NINA LOANS *see* NO DOCUMENTATION LOAN.

NINE-BOND RULE New York Stock Exchange (NYSE) requirement that orders for nine bonds or less be sent to the floor for one hour to seek a market. Since bond trading tends to be inactive on the NYSE (because of large institutional holdings and because many of the listed bond trades are handled OVER THE COUNTER), Rule 396 is designed to obtain the most favorable price for small investors. Customers may request that the rule be waived, but the broker-dealer in such cases must then act only as a BROKER and not as a PRINCIPAL (dealer for his own account).

9/15 Wall Street shorthand for September 15, 2008, the date Lehman Brothers filed bankruptcy and the full force of the financial crisis was unleashed.

19c3 STOCK stock listed on a national securities exchange, such as the New York Stock Exchange or the American Stock Exchange, after April 26, 1979, and thus exempt from Securities and Exchange Commission rule 19c3 prohibiting exchange members from engaging in OFF-BOARD trading.

NIRI *see* NATIONAL INVESTOR RELATIONS INSTITUTE.

NO-ACTION LETTER letter requested from the Securities and Exchange Commission wherein the Commission agrees to take neither civil nor criminal action with respect to the specific activity and circumstances. LIMITED PARTNER-SHIPS designed as TAX SHELTERS, which are frequently venturing in uncharted legal territory, often seek no-action letters to clear novel marketing or financing techniques.

NO-BRAINER term used to describe a market the direction of which has become obvious, and therefore requires little or no analysis. This means that most of the stocks will go up in a strong bull market and fall in a bear market, so that it does not matter very much which stock investors buy or sell.

NOB SPREAD acronym for *notes over bonds* spread. Traders buying or selling a NOB spread are trying to profit from changes in the relationship between yields in Treasury notes, which are intermediate-term instruments maturing in 2 to 10 years, and Treasury bonds, which are long-term instruments maturing in 15 or more years. Most people trade the NOB Spread by buying or selling futures contracts on Treasury notes and Treasury bonds. *See also* MOB SPREAD.

NO DOCUMENTATION LOAN a mortgage loan, sometimes called a "no doc," where the borrower is not required to provide proof of income, employment, or assets. Such loans evolved from *low documentation loans*, which were originally designed for applicants in the ALT-A LOAN category, who could satisfy credit standards with high credit scores or low loan to value ratios. As the real estate boom of the 2000s gained momentum, Wall Street firms entered an un-served market by securitizing SUBPRIME mortgages. Appraisers, who formerly worked for banks or other originators of qualifying mortgages sold to Fannie Mae or Freddie Mac, were joined by a new breed of appraisers working for mortgage brokers operating on an *originate to distribute* basis. Those brokers paid appraisers to give properties whatever values satisfied firms securitizing subprime mortgages. These developments defeated the original purpose of no documentation loans, and as abuses proliferated after 2006 they not only got a bad name but added new names having negative connotations, such as *liar loans* (usually a reference to reported income), *NINA (no income, no assets) loans, stated income loans*, among others.

NO-FAULT concept used in divorce law and automobile insurance whereby the parties involved are not required to prove blame in an action. The concept recognizes irreconcilable differences as a basis for divorce. In automobile insurance, the accident victim collects directly from his or her own insurance company for medical and hospital expenses, regardless of who was at fault. No-fault statutes vary widely among states that have them. No-fault automobile insurance typically contains provisions aimed at discouraging frivolous lawsuits.

NOISE stock-market activity caused by PROGRAM TRADES and news and comment affecting prices that is unsubstantiated.

NO-LOAD FUND MUTUAL FUND offered by an open-end investment company that imposes no sales charge (load) on its shareholders. Investors buy shares in no-load funds directly from the fund companies, rather than through a BROKER, as is done in load funds. Many no-load fund families (*see* FAMILY OF FUNDS) allow switching of assets between stock, bond, and money market funds. The listing of the price of a no-load fund in a newspaper is accompanied with the designation NL. The net asset value, market price, and offer prices of this type of fund are exactly the same, since there is no sales charge. *See also* LOAD FUND; MUTUAL FUND SHARE CLASSES.

NO-LOAD STOCK shares available for DIRECT PURCHASE from the issuing companies, thus avoiding brokers and sales commissions. Such shares are typically offered as a part of a company's DIVIDEND REINVESTMENT PLAN to encourage long-term investment. Prices are based on an average of recent market prices and may not be as low as the current market price. Broker commissions are payable if and when the shares are sold.

NOMINAL DOLLARS dollars unadjusted for inflation. For example, economists will refer to a product that cost 100 nominal dollars several years ago, and now costs $150. However, adjusted for inflation, the product's current price may be much higher or lower. Most financial statements are reported in nominal dollars.

NOMINAL EXERCISE PRICE EXERCISE PRICE (strike price) of a GOVERNMENT NATIONAL MORTGAGE ASSOCIATION (GNMA or Ginnie Mae) option contract, obtained by multiplying the unpaid principal balance on a Ginnie Mae certificate by the ADJUSTED EXERCISE PRICE. For example, if the unpaid principal balance is $96,000 and the adjusted exercise price is 58, the nominal exercise price is $55,680.

NOMINAL INCOME income unadjusted for changes in the PURCHASING POWER OF THE DOLLAR. GENERALLY ACCEPTED ACCOUNTING PRINCIPLES (GAAP) require certain large, publicly held companies to provide supplementary information adjusting income from continuing operations for changing prices. FINANCIAL ACCOUNTING STANDARDS BOARD (FASB) Statement Number 89 removed the requirement to present general purchasing power and current cost/constant dollar supplement statements, however.

NOMINAL INTEREST RATE *see* NOMINAL YIELD.

NOMINAL QUOTATION bid and offer prices given by a market maker for the purpose of valuation, not as an invitation to trade. Securities industry rules require that nominal quotations be specifically identified as such; usually this is done by prefixing the quote with the letters FYI (FOR YOUR INFORMATION) or FVO (for valuation only).

NOMINAL RATE OF INTEREST rate of interest unadjusted for inflation. The actual interest rate charged by a bank on a loan is in nominal dollars. This is in contrast to interest rates that have been adjusted for either past or projected inflation, called REAL INTEREST RATES.

NOMINAL YIELD annual dollar amount of income received from a fixed-income security divided by the PAR VALUE of the security and stated as a percentage. Thus a bond that pays $90 a year and has a par value of $1,000 has a nominal yield of 9%, called its *coupon rate*. Similarly, a preferred stock that pays a $9 annual dividend and has a par value of $100 has a nominal yield of 9%. Only when a stock or bond is bought exactly at par value is the nominal yield equal to the actual yield. Since market prices of fixed-income securities go down when market interest rates go up and vice versa, the actual yield, which is determined by the market price and coupon rate (nominal yield), will be higher when the purchase price is below par value and lower when the purchase price is above par value. *See also* RATE OF RETURN.

NOMINEE person or firm, such as a bank official or brokerage house, into whose name securities or other properties are transferred by agreement. Securities held in STREET NAME, for example, are registered in the name of a BROKER (nominee) to facilitate transactions, although the customer remains the true owner.

NONACCREDITED INVESTOR investor who does not meet the net worth requirements of SEC Regulation D. Under Rules 505 and 506 of Regulation D, an investment can be offered to a maximum of 35 nonaccredited investors. Such investors tend to be wealthy and sophisticated, and therefore the SEC feels they need less investor protection than smaller, less sophisticated investors. Also called QUALIFIED INVESTORS.

NONCALLABLE preferred stock or bond that cannot be redeemed at the option of the issuer. A bond may offer CALL PROTECTION for a particular length of time, such as ten years. After that, the issuer may redeem the bond if it chooses and can justify doing so. U.S. government bond obligations are not callable until close to maturity. Provisions for noncallability are spelled out in detail in a bond's INDENTURE agreement or in the prospectus issued at the time a new preferred stock is floated. Bond yields are often quoted to the first date at which the bonds could be called. *See also* YIELD TO CALL.

NONCASH CHARGE an accounting charge that reduces taxable income, but does not require an outlay of cash. Examples are DEPRECIATION and DEPLETION.

NONCLEARING MEMBER member firm of the New York Stock Exchange or another organized exchange that does not have the operational facilities for clearing transactions and thus pays a fee to have the services performed by another member firm, called a *clearing member.* The clearing process involves comparison and verification of information between the buying and selling brokers and then the physical delivery of certificates in exchange for payment, called the *settlement.*

NONCOMPETITIVE BID method of buying Treasury bills without having to meet the high minimum purchase requirements of the regular DUTCH AUCTION; also called *noncompetitive tender.* The process of bidding for Treasury bills is split into two parts: competitive and noncompetitive bids.

COMPETITIVE BIDS are entered by large government securities dealers and brokers, who buy millions of dollars worth of bills. They offer the best price they can for the securities, and the highest bids are accepted by the Treasury in what is called the Dutch auction.

Noncompetitive bids are submitted by smaller investors through a Federal Reserve Bank, the Bureau of Federal Debt, or certain commercial banks. These bids will be executed at the average of the prices paid in all the competitive bids accepted by the Treasury. The minimum noncompetitive bid for a Treasury bill is $10,000. *See also* TREASURY DIRECT.

NONCONTESTABILITY CLAUSE provision found in insurance contracts stipulating that policyholders cannot be denied coverage after a specific period of time, usually two years, even if the policyholder provided inaccurate or even fraudulent information in his or her insurance application. In order to contest the policy, the insurer must find out about the incorrect information before the clause goes into effect. *See* INCONTESTABILITY CLAUSE.

NONCONTRIBUTORY PENSION PLAN pension plan that is totally funded by the employer, and to which employees are not expected to contribute. Most DEFINED BENEFIT PENSION PLANS are noncontributory. In contrast, DEFINED CONTRIBUTION PENSION PLANS offer employees the choice to contribute to a plan such as a 401(k) or 403(b).

NONCUMULATIVE term describing a preferred stock issue in which unpaid dividends do not accrue. Such issues contrast with CUMULATIVE PREFERRED issues, where unpaid dividends accumulate and must be paid before dividends on common shares. Most preferred issues are cumulative. On a noncumulative preferred, omitted dividends will, as a rule, never be paid. Some older railroad preferred stocks are of this type.

NONCURRENT ASSET asset not expected to be converted into cash, sold, or exchanged within the normal operating cycle of the firm, usually one year. Examples of noncurrent assets include FIXED ASSETS, such as real estate, machinery, and other equipment; LEASEHOLD IMPROVEMENTS; INTANGIBLE ASSETS, such as goodwill, patents, and trademarks; notes receivable after one year; other investments; miscellaneous assets not meeting the definition of a CURRENT ASSET. Prepaid expenses (also called DEFERRED CHARGES or *deferred expenses),* which include such items as rent paid in advance, prepaid insurance premiums, and subscriptions, are usually considered current assets by accountants. Credit analysts, however, prefer to classify these expenses as noncurrent assets, since prepayments do not represent asset strength and protection in the way that other current assets do, with their convertibility into cash during the normal operating cycle and their liquidation value should operations be terminated.

NONCURRENT LIABILITY LIABILITY due after one year.

NONDELIVERABLE FORWARD (NDF) a short-term forward contract on a thinly traded or nonconvertible foreign currency not otherwise internationally traded. Contracts in the NDF market are settled in cash and the profit or loss is the difference between an exchange rate agreed upon on a *fixing date* and the spot rate at the time on the *settlement date.* NDFs are typically quoted for time periods of one month to one year and are quoted and settled in U.S. dollars. *See also* FOREX MARKET.

NONDISCRETIONARY TRUST TRUST where the trustee has no power to determine the amount of distributions to the beneficiary. Contrast with DISCRETIONARY TRUST.

NONDIVERSIFIED MANAGEMENT COMPANY according to the Investment Company Act of 1940 (Section 5 b.2), any management company that does not meet the requirements of a DIVERSIFIED INVESTMENT [MANAGEMENT] COMPANY. These are mutual funds or closed-end funds, often venture capital funds, operating under policies that permit investment of a relatively large portion of the fund's assets in particular companies or other concentrations. Sometimes also called *concentrated funds, focused funds,* or *undiversified funds.*

NONDURABLE GOODS *see* DURABLE GOODS.

NONFINANCIAL ASSETS assets that are physical, such as REAL ESTATE and PERSONAL PROPERTY.

NON-INTEREST-BEARING NOTE note that makes no periodic interest payments. Instead, the note is sold at a discount and matures at face value. Also called a ZERO-COUPON BOND.

NONMEMBER FIRM brokerage firm that is not a member of an organized exchange. Such firms execute their trades either through member firms, on regional exchanges, or in the THIRD MARKET. *See also* MEMBER FIRM; REGIONAL STOCK EXCHANGES.

NONPARTICIPATING LIFE INSURANCE POLICY life insurance policy that does not pay dividends. Policyholders thus do not participate in the interest, dividends, and capital gains earned by the insurer on premiums paid. In contrast, PARTICIPATING INSURANCE POLICIES pay dividends to policyholders from earnings on investments.

NONPARTICIPATING PREFERRED STOCK *see* PARTICIPATING PREFERRED STOCK.

NONPERFORMING ASSET ASSET not effectual in the production of income. In banking, commercial loans 90 days past due and consumer loans 180 days past due are classified as nonperforming.

NONPRODUCTIVE LOAN type of commercial bank loan that increases the amount of spending power in the economy but does not lead directly to increased output; for example, a loan to finance a LEVERAGED BUYOUT. The Federal Reserve has on occasion acted to curtail such lending as one of its early steps in implementing monetary restraint.

NONPUBLIC INFORMATION information about a company, either positive or negative, that will have a material effect on the stock price when it is released to the public. Insiders, such as corporate officers and members of the board of directors, are not allowed to trade on material nonpublic information until it has been released to the public, since they would have an unfair advantage over unsuspecting investors. Some examples of important nonpublic information are an imminent takeover announcement, a soon-to-be-released earnings report that is more favorable than most analysts expect, or the sudden resignation of a key corporate official. *See also* DISCLOSURE; INSIDER.

NONPURPOSE LOAN loan for which securities are pledged as collateral but which is not used to purchase or carry securities. Under Federal Reserve Board REGULATION U, a borrower using securities as collateral must sign an affidavit called a PURPOSE STATEMENT, indicating the use to which the loan is to be put. Regulation U limits the amount of credit a bank may extend for purchasing and carrying margin securities, where the credit is secured directly or indirectly by stock.

NONQUALIFYING ANNUITY annuity purchased outside of an IRS-approved pension plan. The contributions to such an annuity are made with after-tax dollars. Just as with a QUALIFYING ANNUITY, however, the earnings from the nonqualifying annuity can accumulate tax deferred until withdrawn. Assets may be placed in either a FIXED ANNUITY, a VARIABLE ANNUITY, or a HYBRID ANNUITY.

NONQUALIFYING STOCK OPTION employee stock option not meeting the Internal Revenue Service criteria for QUALIFYING STOCK OPTIONS (INCENTIVE STOCK OPTIONS) and therefore triggering a tax upon EXERCISE. (The issuing employer, however, can deduct the nonqualifying option during the period when it is exercised, whereas it would not have a deduction when a qualifying option is exercised. A STOCK OPTION is a right issued by a corporation to an individual, normally an executive employee, to buy a given amount of shares at a stated price within a specified period of time. Gains realized on the exercise of nonqualifying options are treated as ordinary income in the tax year in which the options are exercised. Qualifying stock options, in contrast, are taxed neither at the time of granting or the time of exercise; only when the underlying stock is sold and a CAPITAL GAIN realized, does a tax event occur.

NONRATED bonds that have not been rated by one or more of the major rating agencies such as STANDARD & POOR'S, MOODY'S INVESTORS SERVICE or FITCH RATINGS. Issues are usually nonrated because they are too small to justify the expense of getting a rating. Nonrated bonds are not necessarily better or worse than rated bonds, though many institutions cannot buy them because they need to hold bonds with an investment-grade rating.

NONRECOURSE LOAN type of financial arrangement used by limited partners in a DIRECT PARTICIPATION PROGRAM, whereby the limited partners finance a portion of their participation with a loan secured by their ownership in the underlying venture. They benefit from the LEVERAGE provided by the loan. In case of default, the lender has no recourse to the assets of the partnership beyond those held by the limited partners who borrowed the money.

NONRECURRING CHARGE one-time expense or WRITE-OFF appearing in a company's financial statement; also called *extraordinary charge.* Nonrecurring charges would include, for example, a major fire or theft, the write-off of a division, and the effect of a change in accounting procedure.

NONREFUNDABLE provision in a bond INDENTURE that either prohibits or sets limits on the issuer's retiring the bonds with the proceeds of a subsequent issue, called REFUNDING. Such a provision often does not rule out refunding altogether but protects bondholders from REDEMPTION until a specified date. Other such provisions may preclude refunding unless new bonds can be issued at a specified lower rate. *See also* CALL PROTECTION.

NONSYSTEMATIC RISK opposite of SYSTEMATIC RISK. Also called company-specific risk, nonmarket risk, security-related risk, and residual risk, this risk classification can be eliminated by DIVERSIFICATION. *See also* ALPHA.

NONVOTING STOCK corporate securities that do not empower a holder to vote on corporate resolutions or the election of directors. Such stock is sometimes issued in connection with a takeover attempt, when management creates nonvoting shares to dilute the target firm's equity and thereby discourage the merger attempt. Except in very special circumstances, the New York Stock Exchange does not list nonvoting stock. Preferred stock is normally nonvoting stock. *See also* VOTING STOCK; VOTING TRUST CERTIFICATE.

NO-PAR-VALUE STOCK stock with no set (par) value specified in the corporate charter or on the stock certificate; also called *no-par stock.* Companies issuing no-par value shares may carry whatever they receive for them either as part of the CAPITAL STOCK account or as part of the CAPITAL SURPLUS (paid-in capital) account, or both. Whatever amount is carried as capital stock has an implicit value, represented by the number of outstanding shares divided into the dollar amount of capital stock.

The main attraction of no-par stock to issuing corporations, historically, had to do with the fact that many states imposed taxes based on PAR VALUE, while other states, like Delaware, encouraged incorporations with no-par-value stock.

For the investor, there are two reservations: (1) that unwise or inept directors may reduce the value of outstanding shares by accepting bargain basement prices on new issues (shareholders are protected, to some extent, from this by PREEMPTIVE RIGHT—the right to purchase enough of a new issue to protect their power and equity) and (2) that too great an amount of shareholder contributions may be channeled into the capital surplus account, which is restricted by the law of many states from being a source of dividend payments. See ILLEGAL DIVIDEND.

Still, no-par stock, along with low-par stock, remains an appealing alternative, from the issuer's standpoint, to par-value shares because of investor confusion of par value and real value.

Most stock issued today is either no-par or low-par value.

NOREX an alliance of Nordic exchanges acting as a single securities market, using the SAXESS electronic trading system. The alliance was formed in 1998 by the Copenhagen Stock Exchange and the Stockholm Stock Exchange, both of which are now owned by NASDAQ OMX. Today, NASDAQ OMX Nordic and NASDAQ OMX Baltic includes the exchanges in Helsinki, Copenhagen, Stockholm, Iceland, Tallinn, Riga, and Vilnius. See also NASDAQ OMX.

NORMAL INVESTMENT PRACTICE history of investment in a customer account with a member of the FINANCIAL INDUSTRY REGULATORY AUTHORITY (FINRA) as defined in its Rules of Fair Practice. It is used to test the bona fide PUBLIC OFFERINGS requirement that applies to the allocation of a HOT ISSUE. If the buying customer has a history of purchasing similar amounts in normal circumstances, the sale qualifies as a bona fide public offering and is not in violation of the Rules of Fair Practice. A record of buying only hot issues is not acceptable as normal investment practice. See also FINRA FORM FR-1.

NORMALIZED EARNINGS earnings, either in the past or the future, that are adjusted for cyclical ups and downs in the economy. Earnings are normalized by analysts by generating a moving average over several years including up and down cycles. Analysts refer to normalized earnings when explaining whether a company's current profits are above or below its long-term trend.

NORMAL RETIREMENT point at which a pension plan participant can retire and immediately receive unreduced benefits. Pension plans can specify age and length-of-service requirements that employees must meet to be eligible for retirement.

NORMAL TRADING UNIT standard minimum size of a trading unit for a particular security; also called a ROUND LOT. For instance, stocks have a normal trading unit of 100 shares, although inactive stocks trade in 10-share round lots. Any securities trade for less than a round lot is called an ODD LOT trade.

NORTH AMERICAN INDUSTRIAL CLASSIFICATION SYSTEM (NAICS) *see* STANDARD INDUSTRIAL CLASSIFICATION (SIC) SYSTEM.

NORTH AMERICAN SECURITIES ADMINISTRATORS ASSOCIA-TION (NASAA) organized in 1919, NASAA is a voluntary association whose membership consists of 67 state, provincial, and territorial securities administrators in the 50 states, the District of Columbia, Puerto Rico, the U.S. Virgin Islands, Canada, and Mexico. Members license firms and their agents, investigate violations of state and provincial law, file enforcement actions, and educate the public about investment fraud.

NOTE *see* MUNICIPAL NOTE; PROMISSORY NOTE; TREASURIES.

NOT-FOR-PROFIT type of incorporated organization in which no stockholder or trustee shares in profits or losses and which usually exists to accomplish some charitable, humanitarian, or educational purpose; also called *nonprofit.* Such groups are exempt from corporate income taxes but are subject to other taxes on income-producing property or enterprises. Donations to these groups are usually tax deductible for the donor. Some examples are hospitals, colleges and universities, foundations, and such familiar groups as the Red Cross and Girl Scouts.

NOT HELD instruction (abbreviated NH) on a market order to buy or sell securities, indicating that the customer has given the FLOOR BROKER time and price discretion in executing the best possible trade but will not hold the broker responsible if the best deal is not obtained. Such orders, which are usually for large blocks of securities, were originally designed for placement with specialists, who could hold an order back if they felt prices were going to rise. The Securities and Exchange Commission no longer allows specialists to handle NH orders, leaving floor brokers without any clear alternative except to persuade the customer to change the order to a LIMIT ORDER. The broker can then turn the order over to a SPECIALIST, who could sell pieces of the block to floor traders or buy it for his own account. *See also* SPECIALIST BLOCK PURCHASE AND SALE. An older variation of NH is DRT, meaning disregard tape.

NOTICE OF SALE advertisement placed by an issuer of municipal securities announcing its intentions to sell a new issue and inviting underwriters to submit COMPETITIVE BIDS.

NOTIONAL VALUE the unrealized value of a derivative or, in other words, the total face value of the underlying security that is controlled by the derivative net of the derivative's cost. For example, an interest-rate SWAP is a derivative arrangement whereby two counterparties agree to exchange periodic interest rate payments based on a predetermined principal amount, which is called the notional value or, in the particular case of an interest-rate swap, the *notational principal amount.* The fact that the notional amount does not change hands gives it the name.

NOT RATED indication used by securities rating services (such as STANDARD & POOR'S, MOODY'S INVESTORS SERVICE, or FITCH RATINGS) and mercantile agencies (such as Dun & Bradstreet) to show that a security or a company has not been rated. It has neither negative nor positive implications. The abbreviation NR is used.

NOT-SUFFICIENT-FUNDS CHECK a bank check written against an inadequate balance. Also called *insufficient-funds check* and, informally, a *bounced check*.

NOUVEAU MARCHE equity market unit of the PARIS BOURSE dedicated to innovative, high-growth companies. Nouveau Marche, in turn, is linked to other European markets in EURO.NM, which is modeled on the NASDAQ market in the United States.

NOVATION
1. agreement to replace one party to a contract with a new party. The novation transfers both rights and duties and requires the consent of both the original and the new party.
2. replacement of an older debt or obligation with a newer one.

NOW ACCOUNT *see* NEGOTIABLE ORDER OF WITHDRAWAL.

NSROS *see* CREDIT RATING AGENCY REFORM ACT OF 2006.

NUMISMATIC COIN coin that is valued based on its rarity, age, quantity originally produced, and condition. These coins are bought and sold as individual items within the coin collecting community. Most numismatic coins are legal tender coins that were produced in limited quantities to give them scarcity value. They are historic coins which also can be rare. The current price of gold is a minor factor when dealing with numismatic coins. Premiums are traditionally far higher than those of BULLION COINS, and values fluctuate to a much wider extent. For example, a $5 gold piece may contain $60 worth of gold and may sell for as much as $700. The minimum amount recovered from numismatic coin investments is always either its face value or its metal content. Most coins, however, sell substantially above these amounts. Since the markup over bullion value can vary widely from one dealer to another, investors need to shop around diligently to avoid paying exhorbitant markups.

O

OBAMANOMICS economic recovery and reform policies championed by President Barack Obama that call for increased involvement by the government in the private sector in areas such as health care, banking, autos, college education finance, consumer protection, and environmental protection where the private sector is not able to function efficiently and effectively on its own. These policies also call for higher tax rates on higher income earners. These policies stand in sharp contrast to politically conservative policies promoted by President Ronald Reagan. *See also* REAGANOMICS.

OBLIGATION legal responsibility, as for a DEBT.

OBLIGATION BOND type of mortgage bond in which the face value is greater than the value of the underlying property. The difference compensates the lender for costs exceeding the mortgage value.

OBLIGOR one who has an obligation, such as an issuer of bonds, a borrower of money from a bank or another source, or a credit customer of a business supplier or retailer. The obligor *(obligator, debtor)* is legally bound to pay a debt, including interest, when due.

ODD LOT securities trade made for less than the NORMAL TRADING UNIT (termed a ROUND LOT). In stock trading, any purchase or sale of less than 100 shares is considered an odd lot, although inactive stocks generally trade in round lots of 10 shares. An investor buying or selling an odd lot pays a higher commission rate than someone making a round-lot trade. This odd-lot differential varies among brokers but for stocks is often 0.125 per share. For instance, someone buying 100 shares of XYZ at $70 would pay $70 a share plus commission. At the same time, someone buying only 50 shares of XYZ would pay $70.125 a share plus commission. *See also* BOARD LOT; ODD-LOT DEALER; ODD-LOT SHORT-SALE RATIO; ODD-LOT THEORY.

ODD-LOT DEALER originally a dealer who bought round lots of stock and resold it in odd lots to retail brokers who, in turn, accommodated their smaller customers at the regular commission rate plus an extra charge, called the odd-lot differential. The assembling of round lots from odd lots is now a service provided free by New York Stock Exchange specialists to member brokers, and odd-lot transactions can be executed through most brokers serving the retail public. Brokers handling odd lots do, however, receive extra compensation; it varies with the broker, but 0.125 per share in addition to a regular commission is typical. *See also* ODD-LOT.

ODD-LOT SHORT-SALE RATIO ratio obtained by dividing ODD LOT short sales by total odd-lot sales, using New York Stock Exchange (NYSE) statistics; also called the *odd-lot selling indicator.* Historically, odd-lot investors—those who buy and sell in less than 100-share round lots—react to market highs and lows; when the market reaches a low point, odd-lot short sales reach a high point, and vice versa. The odd-lot ratio has followed the opposite pattern of the NYSE MEMBER SHORT SALE RATIO. *See also* ODD-LOT THEORY.

ODD-LOT THEORY historical theory that the ODD LOT investor—the small personal investor who trades in less than 100-share quantities—is usually guilty of bad timing and that profits can be made by acting contrary to odd-lot trading patterns. Heavy odd-lot buying in a rising market is interpreted by proponents of this theory as a sign of technical weakness and the signal of a market reversal. Conversely, an increase of odd-lot selling in a declining market is seen as a sign of technical strength and a signal to buy. In fact, analyses of odd-lot trading over the years fail to bear out the theory with any real degree of consistency, and it has fallen into disfavor in recent years. It is also a fact that odd-lot customers generally, who tend to buy market leaders, have fared rather well in the upward market that has prevailed over the last fifty years or so. *See also* ODD-LOT SHORT-SALE RATIO.

OEX pronounced as three letters, Wall Street shorthand for the Standard & Poor's 100 stock index, which comprises stocks for which options are traded on the CHICAGO BOARD OPTIONS EXCHANGE (CBOE). OEX index options are traded on the CHICAGO BOARD OF TRADE (CBOT), and futures are traded on the CHICAGO MERCANTILE EXCHANGE (CME). *See also* STOCK INDICES AND AVERAGES.

OFF-BALANCE-SHEET FINANCING financing that does not add debt on a balance sheet and thus does not affect borrowing capacity as it would be determined by financial ratios. The most common example would be a lease structured as an OPERATING LEASE rather than a CAPITAL LEASE and where management's intent is, in fact, to acquire an asset and corresponding liability without reflecting either on its balance sheet. Other examples include the sale of receivables with recourse, TAKE-OR-PAY CONTRACTS, and bank financial instruments such as guarantees, letters of credit, and loan commitments. GENERALLY ACCEPTED ACCOUNTING PRINCIPLES (GAAP) require that information be provided in financial statements about off-balance-sheet financing involving credit, market, and liquidity risk.

OFF-BOARD off the exchange (the New York Stock Exchange is known as the Big Board, hence the term). The term is used either for a trade that is executed OVER THE COUNTER or for a transaction entailing listed securities that is not completed on a national exchange. Over-the-counter trading is handled by telephone, with competitive bidding carried on constantly by market makers in a particular stock. The other kind of off-board trade occurs when a block of stock is exchanged between customers of a brokerage firm, or between a customer and the firm itself if the brokerage house wants to buy or sell securities from its own inventory. *See also* THIRD MARKET.

OFF-BUDGET federal programs not counted toward budget limits due to provisions in current law. For example, Social Security and the postal service are off-budget based on their intended self-funding. Also, supplemental appropriations, meaning funds needed to meet emergencies, such as disaster relief, are off-budget. Iraq War-related expenses, following similar logic, have been treated as off-budget to the consternation of people who view the Iraq War as a "war of choice."

OFFER price at which someone who owns a security offers to sell it; also known as the ASKED PRICE. This price is listed in newspapers for stocks traded OVER THE COUNTER. The bid price—the price at which someone is prepared to buy— is also shown. The bid price is always lower than the offer price. *See also* OFFERING PRICE.

OFFERING *see* PUBLIC OFFERING.

OFFERING CIRCULAR *see* PROSPECTUS.

OFFERING DATE date on which a distribution of stocks or bonds will first be available for sale to the public. *See also* DATED DATE; PUBLIC OFFERING.

OFFERING PRICE price per share at which a new or secondary distribution of securities is offered for sale to the public; also called PUBLIC OFFERING PRICE. For instance, if a new issue of XYZ stock is priced at $40 a share, the offering price is $40.

When mutual fund shares are made available to the public, they are sold at NET ASSET VALUE, also called the *offering price* or the ASKED PRICE, plus a sales charge, if any. In a NO-LOAD FUND, the offering price is the same as the net asset value. In a LOAD FUND, the sales charge is added to the net asset value, to arrive at the offering price. *See also* OFFER.

OFFERING SCALE prices at which different maturities of a SERIAL BOND issue are offered to the public by an underwriter. The offering scale may also be expressed in terms of YIELD TO MATURITY.

OFFER WANTED (OW) notice by a potential buyer of a security that he or she is looking for an offer by a potential seller of the security. The abbreviation OW is frequently seen in the PINK SHEETS (listing of stocks) and YELLOW SHEETS (listing of corporate bonds) published by the NATIONAL QUOTATION BUREAU for securities traded by OVER THE COUNTER dealers. *See also* BID WANTED.

OFF-FLOOR ORDER order to buy or sell a security that originates off the floor of an exchange. These are customer orders originating with brokers, as distinguished from orders of floor members trading for their own accounts (ON-FLOOR ORDERS). Exchange rules require that off-floor orders be executed before orders initiated on the floor.

OFFICE OF MANAGEMENT AND BUDGET (OMB) at the federal level, an agency within the Office of the President responsible for (1) preparing and presenting to Congress the president's budget; (2) working with the Council of Economic Advisers and the Treasury Department in developing a fiscal program; (3) reviewing the administrative policies and performance of government agencies; and (4) advising the president on legislative matters.

OFFICE OF THRIFT SUPERVISION (OTS) agency of the U.S. Treasury Department created by the FINANCIAL INSTITUTIONS REFORM, RECOVERY AND ENFORCEMENT ACT OF 1989 (FIRREA), the bailout bill enacted to assist depositors that became law on August 9, 1989. The OTS replaced the disbanded FEDERAL HOME LOAN BANK BOARD and assumed responsibility for the nation's savings and loan industry. The legislation empowered OTS to institute new regulations, charter new federal savings and loan associations and federal savings banks, and supervise all savings institutions and their holding companies insured by the SAVINGS ASSOCIATION INSURANCE FUND (SAIF). *See also* BAILOUT BOND.

OFFICIAL NOTICE OF SALE notice published by a municipality inviting investment bankers to submit competitive bids for an upcoming bond issue. The notice provides the name of a municipal official from whom further details can be obtained and states certain basic information about the issue, such as its par value and important conditions. The *Bond Buyer* regularly carries such notices.

OFFICIAL STATEMENT *see* LEGAL OPINION.

OFFSET
Accounting: (1) amount equaling or counterbalancing another amount on the opposite side of the same ledger or the ledger of another account. *See also* ABSORBED. (2) amount that cancels or reduces a claim.
Banking: (1) bank's legal right to seize deposit funds to cover a loan in default—called *right of offset.* (2) number stored on a bank card that, when related to the code number remembered by the cardholder, represents the depositor's identification number, called *PAN-PIN pair.*
Securities, commodities, options: (1) closing transaction involving the purchase or sale of an OPTION having the same features as one already held. (2) HEDGE, such as the SHORT SALE of a stock to protect a capital gain or the purchase of a future to protect a commodity price, or a STRADDLE representing the purchase of offsetting put and call options on a security.

OFFSHORE term used in the United States for any financial organization with a headquarters outside the country. A MUTUAL FUND with a legal domicile in the Bahamas or the Cayman Islands, for instance, is called an *offshore fund.* To be sold in the United States, such funds must adhere to all pertinent federal and state regulations. Many banks have offshore subsidiaries that engage in activities that are either heavily regulated or taxed or not allowed under U.S. law.

OIL AND GAS LIMITED PARTNERSHIP partnership consisting of one or more limited partners and one or more general partners that is structured to find, extract, and market commercial quantities of oil and natural gas. The limited partners, who assume no liability beyond the funds they contribute, buy units in the partnership, typically for at least $5,000 a unit, from a broker registered to sell that partnership. All the limited partners' money then goes to the GENERAL PARTNER, the partner with unlimited liability, who either searches for oil and gas (an exploratory or wildcat well), drills for oil and gas in a proven oil field (a DEVELOPMENTAL DRILLING PROGRAM), or pumps petroleum and gas from an existing well (a COMPLETION PROGRAM). The riskier the chance of finding oil and gas, the higher the potential reward or loss to the limited partner. Conservative investors who mainly want to collect income from the sale of proven oil and gas reserves are safest with a developmental or completion program.

Subject to PASSIVE income rules, limited partners also receive tax breaks, such as depreciation deductions for equipment used for drilling and oil depletion allowances for the value of oil extracted from the fields. If the partnership borrows money for increased drilling, limited partners also can get deductions for the interest cost of the loans. *See also* EXPLORATORY DRILLING PROGRAM; INCOME LIMITED PARTNERSHIP; INTANGIBLE COSTS; LIMITED PARTNERSHIP; WILDCAT DRILLING.

OIL PATCH states in America that produce and refine oil and gas. This includes Texas, Oklahoma, Louisiana, California, and Alaska. Economists refer to oil patch states when assessing the strength or weakness of a region of the country tied to movements in oil prices.

OLIGOPOLY market situation in which a small number of selling firms control the market supply of a particular good or service and are therefore able to control the market price. An oligopoly can be *perfect*—where all firms produce an identical good or service (cement)—or *imperfect*—where each firm's product has a different identity but is essentially similar to the others (cigarettes). Because each firm in an oligopoly knows its share of the total market for the product or service it produces, and because any change in price or change in market share by one firm is reflected in the sales of the others, there tends to be a high degree of interdependence among firms; each firm must make its price and output decisions with regard to the responses of the other firms in the oligopoly, so that oligopoly prices, once established, are rigid. This encourages nonprice competition, through advertising, packaging, and service—a generally nonproductive form of resource allocation. Two examples of oligopoly in the United States are airlines serving the same routes and tobacco companies. *See also* OLIGOPSONY.

OLIGOPSONY market situation in which a few large buyers control the purchasing power and therefore the output and market price of a good or service; the buy-side counterpart of OLIGOPOLY. Oligopsony prices tend to be lower than the prices in a freely competitive market, just as oligopoly prices tend to be higher. For example, the large tobacco companies purchase all the output of a large number of small tobacco growers and therefore are able to control tobacco prices.

OMEGA DERIVATIVE PRICING MODEL that measures the effect of volatility. Used interchangeably with *vega* and also with KAPPA, SIGMA PRIME, and ZETA.

OMITTED DIVIDEND dividend that was scheduled to be declared by a corporation, but instead was not voted for the time being by the board of directors. Dividends are sometimes omitted when a company has run into financial difficulty and its board decides it is more important to conserve cash than to pay a dividend to shareholders. The announcement of an omitted dividend will typically cause the company's stock price to drop, particularly if the announcement is a surprise.

OMNIBUS ACCOUNT *see* FUTURES COMMISSION MERCHANT (FCM).

OMX owns and operates the largest integrated securities market in Northern Europe and is a leading provider of marketplace services and solutions to financial and energy markets around the world. OMX was acquired by NASDAQ in 2008 to form the NASDAQ OMX Group. Among its units are NASDAQ OMX Nordic and NASDAQ OMX Baltic, which offer customers access to about 80% of the Nordic and Baltic securities markets. Included are the stock exchanges in Helsinki, Copenhagen, Stockholm, Iceland, Tallinn, Riga, and Vilnius. Through the OMX Technology division, the company provides transaction technology, processing, and outsourcing services. OMX was established in Stockholm in 1984 and merged with the Stockholm Stock Exchange in 1998. In 2003 it merged with HEX, the owner of the exchanges in Finland, Estonia, and Latvia. In 2004 OMX became the strategic owner of the Vilnius Stock Exchange. And in 2005 OMX merged with the Copenhagen Stock Exchange. Trading in the Nordic markets (Copenhagen, Stockholm, Helsinki, Iceland) takes place between 9 P.M. and 5:30 P.M., except for Copenhagen, where trading ends at 5 P.M. Trading in the Baltic markets (Tallinn, Riga, and Vilnius) takes place between 9 A.M. and 1 P.M. CET. *www.nasdaqomx.com. See also* NOREX.

ON ACCOUNT
In general: in partial payment of an obligation.
Finance: on credit terms. The term applies to a relationship between a seller and a buyer wherein payment is expected sometime after delivery and the obligation is not documented by a NOTE. Synonymous with *open account*.

ON A SCALE *see* SCALE ORDER.

ON-BALANCE VOLUME TECHNICAL ANALYSIS method that attempts to pinpoint when a stock, bond, or commodity is being accumulated by many buyers or is being distributed by many sellers. The on-balance volume line is superimposed on the stock price line on a chart, and it is considered significant when the two lines cross. The chart indicates a buy signal when accumulation is detected and a sell signal when distribution is spotted. The on-balance method can be used to diagnose an entire market or an individual stock, bond, or commodity.

ONECHICAGO LLC a joint venture of IB Exchange Corporation, CHICAGO BOARD OPTIONS EXCHANGE, and CME Group CHICAGO BOARD OF TRADE to trade single-stock futures—futures contracts on individual stocks, EXCHANGE-TRADED FUNDS (ETFs), and narrow-based indices. It was founded in 2001 and is headquartered in Chicago. The more than 185 stocks are all included in the S&P 500. OneChicago operates exclusively as an electronic exchange. Products trade on the CBOEdirect system and are accessible through GLOBEX. Physical settlement of single stock and ETF futures will be done at expiration. Narrow-based indices are cash settled at expiration. OneChicago uses a Lead Market Maker system, where LMMs are responsible for providing continuous two-sided markets for the products to which they are assigned. Security futures can be traded in either a securities or futures brokerage account. *www.onechicago.com.*

ONE-CANCELS-THE-OTHER ORDER *see* ALTERNATIVE ORDER.

ONE DECISION STOCK stock with sufficient quality and growth potential to be suitable for a BUY AND HOLD STRATEGY.

ONE HUNDRED PERCENT STATEMENT *see* COMMON SIZE STATEMENT.

ONE-SHARE-ONE-VOTE RULE the principle that public companies should not reduce shareholder voting rights. Originally, the New York Stock Exchange had a one-share, one-vote requirement for its listed companies. In 1988, the SEC adopted Rule 19c-4, which prohibited companies listed on a national securities exchange or quoted on the National Association of Securities Dealers Automated Quotation System (NASDAQ) from disenfranchising existing shareholders through, for example, issuances of super voting stock. The rule, however, was struck down by the Court of Appeals in *Business Roundtable v. SEC* in 1990. In December 1994, the SEC approved rules proposed by the New York Stock Exchange, American Stock Exchange, and National Association of Securities Dealers that establish a uniform voting standard. This new standard prohibits companies listed on the NYSE, the AMEX, or the NASDAQ system from taking any corporate action or issuing any stock that has the effect of disparately reducing or restricting the voting rights of existing common stock shareholders.

ON-FLOOR ORDER security order originating with a member on the floor of an exchange when dealing for his or her own account. The designation separates such orders from those for customers' accounts (OFF-FLOOR ORDERS), which are generally given precedence by exchange rules.

ONLINE BANKING HOME BANKING systems available through the Internet, provided at their own web sites by traditional banks that also have BRICK AND MORTAR locations (and related overhead), or by banks that exist exclusively on the Internet, called E-BANKS, or VIRTUAL BANKS. Online banking services, which are accessible through passwords, typically include up-to-date account information; transfers of funds between savings, checking, and credit card accounts; electronic bill paying; the purchase and tracking of CERTIFICATES OF DEPOSIT (CDs), and other investment services. Some banks charge fees, but all offer the cost savings afforded by instant transfers of funds; once deposits clear, funds can be held in interest-paying accounts until the last minute and miscellaneous fees, such as overdraft charges, are more easily avoided. Proprietary software is provided by some banks to augment on-line services, and generally marketed systems such as Quicken and Microsoft Money can be used to initiate online banking transactions, while providing a range of budget-and tax-related record-keeping services. Also called *electronic banking*. *See also* DIGITAL MONEY; ELECTRONIC WALLET; AGGREGATION.

ONLINE BROKER in general, any broker that provides trading services to its customers over the Internet, which includes established full-service brokers such as Merrill Lynch as well as a range of discount- and deep discount brokers. The connotation of the term on-line broker, which is used interchangeably with *electronic broker* and *cyberbroker*, is a deep discount broker whose principal, if not only, existence, is on-line. These on-line brokers typically charge flat rates, usually for transactions up to 1,000 shares, with additional fees for larger or more complicated orders, a fraction of the amounts charged by full-service brokers. The downside is minimal service, the risk of technical interruptions, and the possibility that low publicized transaction costs may hide extra costs associated with THIRD MARKET executions. *See also* DIRECT ACCESS.

ONLINE TRADING buying and selling securities using the Internet or broker-provided proprietary software that works through the Internet. Online trading is distinguished from WIRELESS TRADING, a nascent area of service where brokerage customers can trade via cell phones, pagers, and hand-held organizers.

ON MARGIN *see* MARGIN.

ON THE CLOSE ORDER order to buy or sell a specified number of shares in a particular stock as close as possible to the closing price of the day. Brokers accepting on the close orders do not guarantee that the trade will be executed at the final closing price, or even that the trade can be completed at all. On an order ticket, on the close orders are abbreviated as "OTC" orders. *See also* AT THE CLOSE ORDER; MARKET-ON-CLOSE ORDER.

ON THE OPENING ORDER order to buy or sell a specified number of shares in a particular stock at the price of the first trade of the day. If the trader cannot buy or sell shares at that price, the order is immediately cancelled.

ON THE SIDELINES investors who refrain from investing because of market uncertainty are said to be on the sidelines. The analogy is to a football game, in which spectators on the sidelines do not actively participate in the game. Investors on the sidelines normally keep their money in short-term instruments such as money market mutual funds, which can be tapped instantly if the investor sees a good opportunity to reenter the stock or bond markets. Market commentators frequently say that trading activity was light "because investors stayed on the sidelines."

OPD ticker tape symbol designating (1) the first transaction of the day in a security after a DELAYED OPENING or (2) the opening transaction in a security whose price has changed significantly from the previous day's close—usually 2 or more points on stocks selling at $20 or higher, 1 or more points on stocks selling at less than $20.

OPEC *see* ORGANIZATION OF PETROLEUM EXPORTING COUNTRIES (OPEC).

OPEN
Securities:
1. status of an order to buy or sell securities that has still not been executed. A GOOD-TILL-CANCELED ORDER that remains pending is an example of an open order.
2. to establish an account with a broker.
Banking: to establish an account or a LETTER OF CREDIT.
Finance: unpaid balance.
   See also OPEN-END LEASE; OPEN-END MANAGEMENT COMPANY; OPEN-END MORTGAGE; OPEN INTEREST; OPEN ORDER; OPEN REPO.

OPEN-END CREDIT revolving line of credit offered by banks, savings and loans, and other lenders to consumers. The line of credit is set with a particular limit, after which consumers can borrow using a credit card, check, or cash advance. Every time a purchase or cash advance is made, credit is extended on behalf of the consumer. Consumers may pay off the entire balance each month, thereby avoiding interest charges. Or they may pay a minimum amount, with interest accruing on the outstanding balance.

OPEN-END LEASE lease agreement providing for an additional payment after the property is returned to the lessor, to adjust for any change in the value of the property.

OPEN-END MANAGEMENT COMPANY INVESTMENT COMPANY that sells MUTUAL FUNDS to the public. The term arises from the fact that the firm continually creates new shares on demand, although an open-end fund may close itself to new investors when its management decides that it is too large. Mutual fund shareholders buy the shares at NET ASSET VALUE and can redeem them at any time at the prevailing market price, which may be higher or lower than the price at which the investor bought. The shareholder's funds are invested in stocks, bonds, or money market instruments, depending on the type of mutual fund company. The opposite of an open-end management company is a CLOSED-END MANAGEMENT COMPANY, which issues a limited number of shares, which are then traded on a stock exchange. *See also* EXCHANGE-TRADED FUNDS.

OPEN-END MORTGAGE
Real estate finance: MORTGAGE that allows the issuance of additional bonds having equal status with the original issue, but that protects the original

bondholders with specific restrictions governing subsequent borrowing under the original mortgage. For example, the terms of the original INDEN-TURE might permit additional mortgage-bond financing up to 75% of the value of the property acquired, but only if total fixed charges on all debt, including the proposed new bonds, have been earned a stated number of times over the previous 5 years. The open-end mortgage is a more practical and acceptable (to the mortgage holder) version of the *open mortgage,* which allows a corporation to issue unlimited amounts of bonds under the original first mortgage, with no protection to the original bondholders. An even more conservative version is the *limited open-end mortgage,* which usually contains the same restrictions as the open-end, but places a limit on the amount of first mortgage bonds that can be issued, and typically provides that proceeds from new bond issues be used to retire outstanding bonds with the same or prior security.

Trust banking: corporate trust indenture that permits the trustee to authenticate and deliver bonds from time to time in addition to the original issue. *See also* AUTHENTICATION.

OPEN-END (MUTUAL) FUND *see* OPEN-END MANAGEMENT COMPANY.

OPENING
1. price at which a security or commodity starts a trading day. Investors who want to buy or sell as soon as the market opens will put in an order at the opening price.
2. short time frame of market opportunity. For instance, if interest rates have been rising for months, and for a few days or weeks they fall, a corporation that has wanted to FLOAT bonds at lower interest rates might seize the moment to issue the bonds. This short time frame would be called an *opening in the market* or a *window of opportunity. See also* WINDOW.

OPEN INTEREST total number of contracts in a commodity or options market that are still open; that is, they have not been exercised, closed out, or allowed to expire. The term also applies to a particular commodity or, in the case of options, to the number of contracts outstanding on a particular underlying security. The level of open interest is reported daily in newspaper commodity and options pages.

OPEN-MARKET COMMITTEE *see* FEDERAL OPEN MARKET COMMITTEE (FOMC).

OPEN-MARKET OPERATIONS activities by which the Securities Department of the Federal Reserve Bank of New York—popularly called the DESK—carries out instructions of the FEDERAL OPEN MARKET COMMITTEE designed to regulate the money supply. Such operations involve the purchase and sale of government securities, which effectively expands or contracts funds in the banking system. This, in turn, alters bank reserves, causing a MULTIPLIER effect on the supply of credit and, therefore, on economic activity generally. Open-market operations represent one of three basic ways the Federal Reserve implements MONETARY POLICY, the others being changes in the member bank RESERVE REQUIREMENTS and raising or lowering the DIS-COUNT RATE charged to banks borrowing from the Fed to maintain reserves.

OPEN-MARKET RATES interest rates on various debt instruments bought and sold in the open market that are directly responsive to supply and demand. Such open, market rates are distinguished from the DISCOUNT RATE, set by the FEDERAL RESERVE BOARD as a deliberate measure to influence other rates, and from bank commercial loan rates, which are directly influenced by Federal Reserve policy. The rates on short-term instruments like COMMERCIAL PAPER and BANKER'S ACCEPTANCES are examples of open-market rates, as are yields on interest-bearing securities of all types traded in the SECONDARY MARKET.

OPEN ON THE PRINT BLOCK POSITIONER'S term for a BLOCK trade that has been completed with an institutional client and "printed" on the consolidated tape, but that leaves the block positioner open—that is, with a risk position to be covered. This usually happens when the block positioner is on the sell side of the transaction and sells SHORT what he lacks in inventory to complete the order.

OPEN ORDER buy or sell order for securities that has not yet been executed or canceled; a GOOD-TILL-CANCELED ORDER.

OPEN OUTCRY method of trading on a commodity exchange. The term derives from the fact that traders must shout out their buy or sell offers. When a trader shouts he wants to sell at a particular price and someone else shouts he wants to buy at that price, the two traders have made a contract that will be recorded.

OPEN REPO REPURCHASE AGREEMENT in which the repurchase date is unspecified and the agreement can be terminated by either party at any time. The agreement continues on a day-to-day basis with interest rate adjustments as the market changes.

OPERATING INCOME see OPERATING PROFIT (OR LOSS).

OPERATING IN THE RED operating at a loss. See also OPERATING PROFIT (OR LOSS).

OPERATING LEASE type of LEASE, normally involving equipment, whereby the contract is written for considerably less than the life of the equipment and the lessor handles all maintenance and servicing; also called *service lease*. Operating leases are the opposite of capital leases, where the lessee acquires essentially all the economic benefits and risks of ownership. Common examples of equipment financed with operating leases are office copiers, computers, automobiles, and trucks. Most operating leases are cancelable, meaning the lessee can return the equipment if it becomes obsolete or is no longer needed.

OPERATING LEVERAGE see LEVERAGE.

OPERATING PROFIT MARGIN see NET PROFIT MARGIN.

OPERATING PROFIT (OR LOSS) the difference between the revenues of a business and the related costs and expenses, excluding income derived from sources other than its regular activities and before income deductions; synonymous with *net operating profit (or loss), operating income (or loss),* and *net operating income (or loss)*. Income deductions are a class of items comprising the final section of a company's income statement, which, although necessarily incurred in the course of business and customarily charged before arriving at net income, are more in the nature of costs imposed from without than costs subject to the control of everyday operations. They include interest; amortized discount and expense on bonds; income taxes; losses from sales of plants, divisions, major items of property; prior-year adjustments; charges to contingency reserves; bonuses and other periodic profit distributions to officers and employees: write-offs of intangibles: adjustments arising from major changes in accounting methods, such as inventory valuation and other material and nonrecurrent items. In the wake of the Enron debacle in 2002, Standard & Poor's announced a new definition of operating earnings, whereby restructuring and certain other expenses that are not generally included by many companies in their operating earnings figure will be included, and certain gains will be excluded. Two controversial examples: Pension gains are excluded from core earnings by the S&P definition while employee stock-option costs are included. In several highly publicized cases, earnings have been inflated by exaggerated returns on pension fund investments and executive compensation not reflected as an expense.

OPERATING RATE percentage of production capacity in use by a particular company, an industry, or the entire economy. While in theory a business can operate at 100% of its productive capacity, in practice the maximum output is less than that because machines need to be repaired, employees take vacations, etc. The operating rate is expressed as a percentage of the ideal 100% production output. For example, a company may be producing at an 85% operating rate, meaning its output is 85% of the maximum that could be produced with its existing resources. If a company has a low operating rate of under 50%, it usually is suffering meager profits or losses, though it has large potential for profit growth. A company operating at 80% of capacity or more is usually highly profitable, though it has less opportunity for improvement.

The Federal Reserve calculates the operating rate of U.S. industry on a monthly basis when its releases figures for industrial production. An operating rate of 85% or higher is generally considered to be full capacity by economists, who become concerned about inflationary pressures caused by production bottlenecks. An operating rate of less than 80% shows considerable slack in the economy, with few inflationary pressures.

OPERATING RATIO any of a group of ratios that measure a firm's operating efficiency and effectiveness by relating various income and expense figures from the profit and loss statement to each other and to balance sheet figures. Among the ratios used are sales to cost of goods sold, operating expenses to operating income, net profits to gross income, net income to net worth. Such ratios are most revealing when compared with those of prior periods and with industry averages.

OPERATIONS DEPARTMENT BACK OFFICE of a brokerage firm where all clerical functions having to do with clearance, settlement, and execution of trades are handled. This department keeps customer records and handles the day-to-day monitoring of margin positions.

OPINION *see* ACCOUNTANT'S OPINION.

OPINION SHOPPING dubious practice of changing outside auditors until one is found that will give an unqualified ACCOUNTANT'S OPINION.

OPM
1. other people's money; Wall Street slang for the use of borrowed funds by individuals or companies to increase the return on invested capital. *See also* FINANCIAL LEVERAGE.
2. options pricing model. *See also* BLACK-SCHOLES OPTION PRICING MODEL.

OPPORTUNITY COST
In general: highest price or rate of return an alternative course of action would provide.

Corporate finance: concept widely used in business planning; for example, in evaluating a CAPITAL INVESTMENT project, a company must measure the projected return against the return it would earn on the highest yielding alternative investment involving similar risk. *See also* COST OF CAPITAL.

Securities investments: cost of forgoing a safe return on an investment in hopes of making a larger profit. For instance, an investor might buy a stock that shows great promise but yields only 2%, even though a higher safe return is available in a money market fund yielding 5%. The 3% yield difference is called the opportunity cost.

OPTIMUM CAPACITY level of output of manufacturing operations that produces the lowest cost per unit. For example, a tire factory may produce tires at $30 apiece if it turns out 10,000 tires a month, but the tires can be made for $20 apiece if the plant operates at its optimum capacity of 100,000 tires a month. *See also* MARGINAL COST.

OPTION
In general: right to buy or sell property that is granted in exchange for an agreed upon sum. If the right is not exercised after a specified period, the option expires and the option buyer forfeits the money. *See also* EXERCISE.

Securities: securities transaction agreement tied to stocks, commodities, currencies, or stock indexes. Options are traded on many exchanges.

1. a CALL OPTION gives its buyer the right to buy 100 shares of the underlying security at a fixed price before a specified date in the future—usually three, six, or nine months. For this right, the call option buyer pays the call option seller, called the writer, a fee called a PREMIUM, which is forfeited if the buyer does not exercise the option before the agreed-upon date. A call buyer therefore speculates that the price of the underlying shares will rise within the specified time period. For example, a call option on 100 shares of XYZ stock may grant its buyer the right to buy those shares at $100 apiece anytime in the next three months. To buy that option, the buyer may have to pay a premium of $2 a share, or $200. If at the time of the option contract XYZ is selling for $95 a share, the option buyer will profit if XYZ's stock price rises. If XYZ shoots up to $120 a share in two months, for example, the option buyer can EXERCISE his or her option to buy 100 shares of the stock at $100 and then sell the shares for $120 each, keeping the difference as profit (minus the $2 premium per share). On the other hand, if XYZ drops below $95 and stays there for three months, at the end of that time the call option will expire and the call buyer will receive no return on the $2 a share investment premium of $200.

2. the opposite of a call option is a PUT OPTION, which gives its buyer the right to sell a specified number of shares of a stock at a particular price within a specified time period. Put buyers expect the price of the underlying stock to fall. Someone who thinks XYZ's stock price will fall might buy a three-month XYZ put for 100 shares at $100 apiece and pay a premium of $2. If XYZ falls to $80 a share, the put buyer can then exercise his or her right to sell 100 XYZ shares at $100. The buyer will first purchase 100 shares at $80 each and then sell them to the put option seller (writer) at $100 each, thereby making a profit of $18 a share (the $20 a share profit minus the $2

a share cost of the option premium).

In practice, most call and put options are rarely exercised. Instead, investors buy and sell options before expiration, trading on the rise and fall of premium prices. Because an option buyer must put up only a small amount of money (the premium) to control a large amount of stock, options trading provides a great deal of LEVERAGE and can prove immensely profitable. Options traders can write either covered options, in which they own the underlying security, or far riskier naked options, for which they do not own the underlying security. Often, options traders lose many premiums on unsuccessful trades before they make a very profitable trade. More sophisticated traders combine various call and put options in SPREAD and STRADDLE positions. Their profits or losses result from the narrowing or widening of spreads between option prices.

An *incentive stock option* is granted to corporate executives if the company achieves certain financial goals, such as a level of sales or profits. The executive is granted the option of buying company stock at a below-market price and selling the stock in the market for a profit. *See also* CALL; COVERED OPTION; DEEP IN (OUT OF) THE MONEY; EXOTIC OPTIONS; IN THE MONEY; LEAPS; NAKED OPTION; OPTION WRITER; OUT OF THE MONEY.

OPTION ACCOUNT account at a brokerage firm that is approved to contain option positions or trades. Since certain option strategies require margin, an option account may be a margin account or a cash account. There are several prerequisites. The client must be given a copy of "Characteristics and Risks of Standardized Options Contracts," known as the Options Disclosure Documents, before the account can be approved. The client must complete an OPTION AGREEMENT in order to open the account. The client must show that he is suitable for options transactions, both in financial resources and investing experience, before the brokerage firm will approve the account for options trading.

OPTION AGREEMENT form filled out by a brokerage firm's customer when opening an option account. It details financial information about the customer, who agrees to follow the rules and regulations of options trading. This agreement, also called the *option information form,* assures the broker that the customer's financial resources are adequate to withstand any losses that may occur from options trading. The customer must receive a prospectus from the OPTIONS CLEARING CORPORATION before he or she can begin trading.

OPTION ARM ADJUSTABLE RATE MORTGAGES (ARM) where the interest adjusts monthly and the payment adjusts annually. Borrowers have several options affecting the size of their payments, including interest only, and a "minimum" payment that may be even lower than the interest only payment, because it is added to the principal of the loan, a gimmick called *negative amortization.*

OPTION CYCLE cycle of months in which options contracts expire. These cycles are used for options on stocks and indices, as well as options on commodities, currencies, and debt instruments. The three most common cycles are: January, April, July, October (JAJO); February, May, August, November (FMAN); and March, June, September, December (MJSD). In addition to these expiration months, options on individual stocks and indices generally also expire in the current month and subsequent month. As an example, an option in the February cycle trading during May would have May, June and August expiration months listed at a minimum. Because of option cycles, there are four days a year—in March, June, September, and December, when TRIPLE WITCHING DAY takes place, as several options contracts expire on the same day. Also called EXPIRATION CYCLE.

OPTIONAL DIVIDEND dividend that can be paid either in cash or in stock. The shareholder entitled to the dividend makes the choice.

OPTIONAL PAYMENT BOND bond whose principal and/or interest are payable, at the option of the holder, in one or more foreign currencies as well as in domestic currency.

OPTION HOLDER someone who has bought a call or put OPTION but has not yet exercised or sold it. A call option holder wants the price of the underlying security to rise; a put option holder wants the price of the underlying security to fall.

OPTION MARGIN MARGIN REQUIREMENT applicable to OPTIONS, as set forth in REGULATION T and in the internal policies of individual brokers. Requirements vary with the type of option and the extent to which it is IN-THE-MONEY, but are strictest in the case of NAKED OPTIONS and narrow-based INDEX OPTIONS. There, Regulation T requires the option premium plus 20% of the underlying value as the maximum and the premium plus 10% of the underlying value as the minimum. Merrill Lynch, for example, would also require a minimum of $10,000 per account and $1,000 per position.

OPTION MUTUAL FUND MUTUAL FUND that either buys or sells options in order to increase the value of fund shares. OPTION mutual funds may be either conservative or aggressive. For instance, a conservative fund may buy stocks and increase shareholders' income through the PREMIUM earned by selling put and call options on the stocks in the fund's portfolio. This kind of fund would be called an *option income fund*. At the opposite extreme, an aggressive *option growth fund* may buy puts and calls in stocks that the fund manager thinks are about to fall or rise sharply; if the fund manager is right, large profits can be earned through EXERCISE of the options. The LEVERAGE that options provide makes it possible to multiply the return on invested funds many times over.

OPTION PREMIUM amount per share paid by an OPTION buyer to an option seller for the right to buy (call) or sell (put) the underlying security at a particular price within a specified period. Option premium prices are quoted in increments of eighths or sixteenths of 1% and are printed in the options tables of daily newspapers. A PREMIUM of $5 per share means an option buyer would pay $500 for an option on 100 shares. *See also* CALL OPTION; PUT OPTION.

OPTION PRICE market price at which an option contract is trading at any particular time. The price of an option on a stock reflects the fact that it covers 100 shares of a stock. So, for example, an option that is quoted at $7 would cost $700, because it would be an option for 100 shares of stock at a $7 cost per share covered. The option price is determined by many factors, including its INTRINSIC VALUE, time to expiration, volatility of the underlying stock, interest rates, dividends, and marketplace adjustments for supply and demand. Options on indices, debt instruments, currencies, and commodities also have prices determined by many of the same forces. Options prices are published daily in the business pages of many newspapers.

OPTIONS CLEARING CORPORATION (OCC) the largest clearing organization in the world for financial derivative instruments. OCC issues, guarantees, and clears options on underlying financial assets including common stocks, foreign exchange, stock indices, U.S. Treasury securities, and interest rate composites. As the issuer and guarantor of every options contract executed on every securities options exchange in the United States, OCC serves as the counter party for all transactions. OCC's ability to meet its obligations arising from its options contracts earned it an AAA rating by STANDARD & POOR'S CORPORATION. OCC is the only securities clearinghouse in the world to receive this accreditation. Its options disclosure document, "Characteristics and Risks of Standardized Options," is required reading for all investors prior to trading options. OCC is owned by all but one of the U.S. exchanges that trade options. *www.optionsclearing.com. See also* OPTION.

OPTION SERIES options of the same class (puts or calls with the same underlying security) that also have the same EXERCISE PRICE and maturity month. For instance, all XYZ October 80 calls are a series, as are all ABC July 100 puts. *See also* OPTION.

OPTION SPREAD buying and selling of options within the same CLASS at the same time. The investor who uses the OPTION spread strategy hopes to profit from the widening or narrowing of the SPREAD between the various options. Option spreads can be designed to be profitable in either up or down markets.

Some examples:

(1) entering into two options at the same EXERCISE PRICE, but with different maturity dates. For instance, an investor could buy an XYZ April 60 call and sell an XYZ July 60 call.

(2) entering into two options at different STRIKE PRICES with the same expiration month. For example, an investor could buy an XYZ April 60 call and sell an XYZ April 70 call.

(3) entering into two options at different strike prices with different expiration months. For instance, an investor could buy an XYZ April 60 call and sell an XYZ July 70 call.

OPTION WRITER person or financial institution that sells put and call options. A writer of a PUT OPTION contracts to buy 100 shares of stock from the put option buyer by a certain date for a fixed price. For example, an option writer who sells XYZ April 50 put agrees to buy XYZ stock from the put buyer at $50 a share any time until the contract expires in April.

A writer of a CALL OPTION, on the other hand, guarantees to sell the call option buyer the underlying stock at a particular price before a certain date. For instance, a writer of an XYZ April 50 call agrees to sell stock at $50 a share to the call buyer any time before April.

In exchange for granting this right, the option writer receives a payment called an OPTION PREMIUM. For holders of large portfolios of the premiums from stocks, option writing therefore is a source of additional income.

ORAL CONTRACT contract between two parties that has been spoken, but not agreed to in writing or signed by both parties. Oral contracts are usually legally enforceable, though not in the case of real estate.

OR BETTER indication, abbreviated OB on the ORDER TICKET of a LIMIT ORDER to buy or sell securities, that the broker should transact the order at a price better than the specified LIMIT PRICE if a better price can be obtained.

ORDER
Investments: instruction to a broker or dealer to buy or sell securities or commodities. Securities orders fall into four basic categories: MARKET ORDER, LIMIT ORDER, time order, and STOP ORDER.
Law: direction from a court of jurisdiction, or a regulation.
Negotiable instruments: payee's request to the maker, as on a check stating, "Pay to the order of (when presented by) John Doe."
Trade: request to buy, sell, deliver, or receive goods or services which commits the issuer of the order to the terms specified.

ORDER IMBALANCE large number of buy or sell orders for a stock, causing an unusually wide spread between bid and offer prices. Stock exchanges frequently halt trading of a stock with a significant order imbalance until more buyers or sellers appear and an orderly market can be reestablished. A significant order imbalance on the buying side can occur when there is an announcement of an impending takeover of the company, better-than-expected earnings, or other unexpected positive news. A significant order imbalance on the selling side can occur when a takeover offer has fallen through, a key executive has left the company, earnings came in far worse than expected, or there is other unexpected negative news.

ORDER ROOM department in a brokerage firm that receives all orders to buy or sell securities. ORDER TICKETS are processed through the order room.

ORDER SPLITTING practice prohibited by rules of the FINANCIAL INDUSTRY REGULATORY AUTHORITY (FINRA) whereby brokers might split orders in order to qualify them as small orders for purposes of automatic execution by the SMALL ORDER EXECUTION SYSTEM (SOES).

ORDER TICKET form completed by a registered representative (ACCOUNT EXECUTIVE) of a brokerage firm, upon receiving order instructions from a customer. It shows whether the order is to buy or to sell, the number of units, the name of the security, the kind of order (ORDER MARKET, LIMIT ORDER or STOP ORDER) and the customer's name or code number. After execution of the order on the exchange floor or in the firm's trading department (if over the counter), the price is written and circled on the order ticket, and the completing broker is indicated by number. The order ticket must be retained for a certain period in compliance with federal law.

ORDINARY INCOME any income from the normal activities of an individual or business, as distinguished from the sale or exchange of a capital asset held for more than 12 months. Ordinary income is taxed at regular income tax rates, not preferential capital gains rates.

ORDINARY INTEREST simple interest based on a 360-day year rather than on a 365-day year (the latter is called *exact interest*). The difference between the two bases when calculating daily interest on large sums of money can be substantial. The ratio of ordinary interest to exact interest is 1.0139.

ORDINARY LIFE INSURANCE *see* WHOLE LIFE INSURANCE.

ORDINARY SHARES the equivalent of common stock in England, Australia, and certain other English-speaking countries other than the United States. Ordinary shares may be voting or nonvoting. Preferred ordinary shares rank between a preference share (the British equivalent of PREFERRED STOCK) and ordinary shares in the payment of dividends. Deferred ordinary shares fall into two categories: ordinary shares, typically issued to founders, that pay dividends only after ordinary and preferred ordinary dividends are paid, and ordinary shares that pay little or no dividend for a fixed period of years, then rank with other ordinary shares. Also called *ordinaries*.

ORGANIZATION CHART chart showing the interrelationships of positions within an organization in terms of authority and responsibility. There are basically three patterns of organization: *line organization,* in which a single manager has final authority over a group of foremen or middle management supervisors; *functional organization,* in which a general manager supervises a number of managers identified by function; and *line and staff organization,* which is a combination of line and functional organization, with specialists in particular functions holding staff positions where they advise line officers concerned with actual production.

ORGANIZATION OF PETROLEUM EXPORTING COUNTRIES (OPEC) international organization of eleven developing countries dependent on oil exports as a source of revenues. Members are Algeria, Indonesia, Iran, Iraq, Kuwait, Libya, Nigeria, Qatar, Saudi Arabia, the United Arab Emirates, and Venezuela. OPEC members supply about 40% of the world's oil output and claim to possess over three quarters of known oil reserves. Twice a year, or more often if required, the Oil and Energy Ministers of the OPEC Members meet to determine production quotas aimed at optimizing world oil prices given supply and demand conditions.

ORGANIZED SECURITIES EXCHANGE STOCK EXCHANGE as distinguished from an OVER-THE-COUNTER MARKET. *See also* SECURITIES AND COMMODITIES EXCHANGES.

ORIGINAL COST
1. in accounting, all costs associated with the acquisition of an asset.
2. in public utilities accounting, the acquisition cost incurred by the entity that first devotes a property to public use; normally, the utility company's cost for the property. It is used to establish the rate to be charged customers in order to provide the utility company with a FAIR RATE OF RETURN on capital.

ORIGINAL ISSUE DISCOUNT (OID) discount from PAR VALUE at the time a bond or other debt instrument, such as a STRIP, is issued. (Although the par value of bonds is normally $1,000, $100 is used when traders quote prices.) A bond may be issued at $50 ($500) per bond instead of $100 ($1000), for example. The bond will mature at $100 (1,000), however, so that an investor has a built-in gain if the bond is held until maturity. The most extreme version of an original issue discount is a ZERO-COUPON BOND, which is originally sold at far below par value and pays no interest until it matures. The REVENUE RECONCILIATION ACT OF 1993 extended OID rules to include stripped preferred stock.

The tax treatment of original issue discount bonds is complex. The Internal Revenue Service assumes a certain rate of appreciation of the bond every year until maturity. No capital gain or loss will be incurred if the bond is sold for that estimated amount. But if the bond is sold for more than the assumed amount, a CAPITAL GAINS TAX or a tax at the ORDINARY INCOME rate is due.

SAVINGS BONDS are exempt from OID rules.

ORIGINAL MATURITY interval between the issue date and the maturity date of a bond, as distinguished from CURRENT MATURITY, which is the time difference between the present time and the maturity date. For example, in 2001 a bond issued in 1999 to mature in 2014 would have an original maturity of 15 years and a current maturity of 13 years.

ORIGINATOR
1. bank, savings and loan, or mortgage banker that initially made the mortgage loan comprising part of a pool of mortgages.
2. investment banking firm that worked with the issuer of a new securities offering from the early planning stages and that usually is appointed manager of the underwriting SYNDICATE; more formally called the *originating investment banker.*
3. in banking terminology, the initiator of money transfer instructions.

ORPHAN STOCK stock that has been neglected by research analysts. Since the company's story is rarely followed and the stock infrequently recommended, it is considered an orphan by investors. Orphan stocks may not attract much attention because they are too small, or because they have disappointed investors in the past. Because they are followed by so few investors, orphan stocks tend to trade at low price/earnings ratios. However, if the company assembles a solid record of rising profitability, it can be discovered again by research analysts, boosting the stock price and price/earnings ratio significantly. Investors who buy the stock when it is still a neglected orphan can thereby earn high returns. Also called a *wallflower.*

OSCILLATOR *see* MOMENTUM INDICATORS.

OTC *see* OVER THE COUNTER.

OTC BULLETIN BOARD (OTCBB) electronic listing of bid and asked quotations of over-the-counter stocks not meeting the minimum net worth and other requirements of the NASDAQ stock-listing system. The new system, which was approved by the Securities and Exchange Commission in 1990, provides continuously updated data on domestic stocks and twice-daily updates on foreign stocks. It was designed to facilitate trading and provide greater surveillance of stocks traditionally reported on once daily in the *PINK SHEETS* published by PINK SHEETS LLC.

OTC MARGIN STOCK shares of certain large firms traded OVER THE COUNTER that qualify as margin securities under REGULATION T of the Federal Reserve Board. Such stock must meet rigid criteria, and the list of eligible OTC shares is under constant review by the Fed. *See also* MARGIN SECURITY.

OTHER CAPITAL residual category in BALANCE OF PAYMENTS capital account that groups capital transactions not included in direct investment, portfolio investment, and reserves. Other long-term capital includes bank loans, mortgages, and nonnegotiable instruments with a life of a year or more; other short-term capital includes financial assets converting to cash in under one year.

OTHER INCOME heading on a profit and loss statement for income from activities not in the normal course of business: sometimes called *other revenue*. Examples: interest on customers' notes, dividends and interest from investments, profit from the disposal of assets other than inventory, gain on foreign exchange, miscellaneous rent income. *See also* EXTRAORDINARY ITEM.

OTHER PEOPLE'S MONEY *see* OPM.

OUT-OF-FAVOR INDUSTRY OR STOCK industry or stock that is currently unpopular with investors. For example, the investing public may be disenchanted with an industry's poor earnings outlook. If interest rates were rising, interest-sensitive stocks such as banks and savings and loans would be out of favor because rising rates might harm these firms' profits. CONTRARIAN investors—those who consciously do the opposite of most other investors—tend to buy out-of-favor stocks because they can be bought cheaply. When the earnings of these stocks pick up, contrarians typically sell the stocks. Out-of-favor stocks tend to have a low PRICE/EARNINGS RATIO.

OUT OF LINE term describing a stock that is too high or too low in price in comparison with similar-quality stocks. A comparison of this sort is usually based on the PRICE/EARNINGS RATIO (PE), which measures how much investors are willing to pay for a firm's earnings prospects. If most computer industry stocks had PEs of 15, for instance, and XYZ Computers had a PE of only 10, analysts would say that XYZ's price is out of line with the rest of the industry.

OUT OF THE MONEY term used to describe an OPTION whose STRIKE PRICE for a stock is either higher than the current market value, in the case of a CALL, or lower, in the case of a PUT. For example, an XYZ December 60 CALL option would be out of the money when XYZ stock was selling for $55 a share. Similarly, an XYZ December 60 PUT OPTION would be out of the money when XYZ stock was selling for $65 a share.

Someone buying an out-of-the-money option hopes that the option will move IN THE MONEY, or at least in that direction. The buyer of the above XYZ call would want the stock to climb above $60 a share, whereas the put buyer would like the stock to drop below $60 a share.

OUTPERFORM to achieve a better RETURN than the relevant BENCHMARK. A PORTFOLIO MANAGER aims to outperform the Standard & Poor's 500 Stock Index, for example, or an investor will buy a mutual fund in the hope of outperforming the LIPPER MUTUAL FUND INDUSTRY AVERAGE or one of its subcategories. The term also used as a research opinion. *See also* BROKER RECOMMENDATIONS (OR OPINIONS OR RATINGS.)

OUTSIDE DIRECTOR member of a company's BOARD OF DIRECTORS who is not an employee of the company. Such directors are considered important because they are presumed to bring unbiased opinions to major corporate decisions and also can contribute diverse experience to the decision-making process. A retailing company may have outside directors with experience in finance and manufacturing, for instance. To avoid conflict of interest, outside directors never serve on the boards of two directly competing corporations. Directors receive fees from the company in return for their service, usually a set amount for each board meeting they attend. *See also* BOARD OF DIRECTORS.

OUTSOURCING contracting out to another manufacturer or supplier work that would otherwise be done by a company's own employees. Outsourcing by General Motors to avoid high wages paid to auto workers was a major issue in negotiations with the United Auto Workers union in the 1990s.

OUTSTANDING
1. unpaid; used of ACCOUNTS RECEIVABLE and debt obligations of all types.
2. not yet presented for payment, as a check or draft.
3. stock held by shareholders, shown on corporate balance sheets under the heading of CAPITAL STOCK issued and outstanding.

OUT THE WINDOW term describing the rapid way a very successful NEW ISSUE of securities is marketed to investors. An issue that goes out the window is also called a BLOWOUT. *See also* HOT ISSUE.

OVERALL MARKET PRICE COVERAGE total assets less intangibles divided by the total of (1) the MARKET VALUE of the security issue in question and (2) the BOOK VALUE of liabilities and issues having a prior claim. The answer indicates the extent to which the market value of a particular CLASS of securities is covered in the event of a company's liquidation.

OVERBOOKED *see* OVERSUBSCRIBED.

OVERBOUGHT description of a security or a market that has recently experienced an unexpectedly sharp price rise and is therefore vulnerable to a price drop (called a CORRECTION by technical analysts). When a stock has been overbought, there are fewer buyers left to drive the price up further. *See also* MOMENTUM INDICATORS; OVERSOLD.

OVERDRAFT extension of credit by a lending institution. An overdraft check for which there are not sufficient funds (NSF) available may be rejected (bounced) by the bank. A bounced-check charge will be assessed on the check writer's account. Alternatively, the bank customer may set up an overdraft loan account, which will cover NSF checks. While the customer's check will clear, the account will be charged overdraft check fees or interest on the outstanding balance of the loan starting immediately.

OVERHANG sizable block of securities or commodities contracts that, if released on the market, would put downward pressure on prices. Examples of overhang include shares held in a dealer's inventory, a large institutional holding, a secondary distribution still in registration, and a large commodity position about to be liquidated. Overhang inhibits buying activity that would otherwise translate into upward price movement.

OVERHEAD
1. costs of a business that are not directly associated with the production or sale of goods or services. Also called INDIRECT COST AND EXPENSE, *burden* and, in Great Britain, *on costs*.
2. sometimes used in a more limited sense, as in manufacturing or factory overhead.
   See also DIRECT OVERHEAD.

OVERHEATING term describing an economy that is expanding so rapidly that economists fear a rise in INFLATION. In an overheated economy, too much money is chasing too few goods, leading to price rises, and the productive capacity of a nation is usually nearing its limit. The remedies in the United

States are usually a tightening of the money supply by the Federal Reserve and curbs in federal government spending. *See also* MONETARY POLICY; OPTIMUM CAPACITY.

OVERISSUE shares of CAPITAL STOCK issued in excess of those authorized. Preventing overissue is the function of a corporation's REGISTRAR (usually a bank acting as agent), which works closely with the TRANSFER AGENT in canceling and reissuing certificates presented for transfer and in issuing new shares.

OVERLAPPING DEBT municipal accounting term referring to a municipality's share of the debt of its political subdivisions or the special districts sharing its geographical area. It is usually determined by the ratio of ASSESSED VALUATION of taxable property lying within the corporate limits of the municipality to the assessed valuation of each overlapping district. Overlapping debt is often greater than the direct debt of a municipality, and both must be taken into account in determining the debt burden carried by taxable real estate within a municipality when evaluating MUNICIPAL BOND investments.

OVERNIGHT POSITION broker-dealer's LONG POSITION or SHORT POSITION in a security at the end of a trading day.

OVERNIGHT REPO overnight REPURCHASE AGREEMENT; an arrangement whereby securities dealers and banks finance their inventories of Treasury bills, notes, and bonds. The dealer or bank sells securities to an investor with a temporary surplus of cash, agreeing to buy them back the next day. Such transactions are settled in immediately available FEDERAL FUNDS, usually at a rate below the federal funds rate (the rate charged by banks lending funds to each other).

OVERSHOOT to exceed a target figure, such as an economic goal or an earnings projection.

OVERSOLD description of a stock or market that has experienced an unexpectedly sharp price decline and is therefore due, according to some proponents of TECHNICAL ANALYSIS, for an imminent price rise. If all those who wanted to sell a stock have done so, there are no sellers left, and so the price will rise. *See also* MOMENTUM INDICATORS; OVERBOUGHT.

OVERSUBSCRIBED underwriting term describing a new stock issue for which there are more buyers than available shares. An oversubscribed, or *overbooked,* issue often will jump in price as soon as its shares go on the market, since the buyers who could not get shares will want to buy once the stock starts trading. In some cases, an issuer will increase the number of shares available if the issue is oversubscribed. *See also* GREEN SHOE; HOT ISSUE.

OVERSUBSCRIPTION PRIVILEGE in a rights issue, privilege given shareholders to apply for shares not purchased.

OVER THE COUNTER (OTC)
1. security that is not listed and traded on an organized exchange.
2. market in which securities transactions are conducted through a telephone and computer network connecting dealers in stocks and bonds, rather than on the floor of an exchange.

   Over-the-counter stocks are traditionally those of smaller companies that do not meet the LISTING REQUIREMENTS of the New York Stock Exchange or the American Stock Exchange. In recent years, however, many companies that qualify for listing have chosen to remain with over-the-counter trading, because they feel that the system of multiple trading by many dealers is preferable to the centralized trading approach of the New York Stock Exchange, where all trading in a stock has to go through the exchange SPE-CIALIST in that stock. The rules of over-the-counter stock trading are written and enforced largely by the FINANCIAL INDUSTRY REGULATORY AUTHORITY (FINRA), a self-regulatory group. Prices of over-the-counter stocks are published in daily newspapers. Other over-the-counter markets include those for government and municipal bonds. *See also* NASDAQ OMX.

OVERTRADING
Finance: practice of a firm that expands sales beyond levels that can be financed with normal WORKING CAPITAL. Continued overtrading leads to delinquent ACCOUNTS PAYABLE and ultimately to default on borrowings.

New issue underwriting: practice whereby a member of an underwriting group induces a brokerage client to buy a portion of a new issue by purchasing other securities from the client at a premium. The underwriter breaks even on the deal because the premium is offset by the UNDERWRITING SPREAD.

Securities: excessive buying and selling by a broker in a DISCRETIONARY ACCOUNT. *See also* CHURNING.

OVERVALUED description of a stock whose current price is not justified by the earnings outlook or the PRICE/EARNINGS RATIO. It is therefore expected that the stock will drop in price. Overvaluation may result from an emotional buying spurt, which inflates the market price of the stock, or from a deterioration of the company's financial strength. The opposite of overvalued is UNDERVALUED. *See also* FULLY VALUED.

OVERWITHHOLDING situation in which a taxpayer has too much federal, state, or local income tax withheld from salary. Because they have overwithheld, these taxpayers will usually be due income tax refunds after they file their tax returns by April 15. Overwithholding is not desirable for the taxpayer, because it is, in effect, granting the government an interest-free loan. To reduce overwithholding, a taxpayer must file a new W-4 form with his or her employer, increasing the number of dependents claimed, which will reduce the amount of tax withheld. *See also* UNDERWITHHOLDING.

OVERWRITING speculative practice by an OPTION WRITER who believes a security to be overpriced or underpriced and sells CALL OPTIONS or PUT OPTIONS on the security in quantity, assuming they will not be exercised. *See also* OPTION.

OWNER'S EQUITY PAID-IN CAPITAL, donated capital, and RETAINED EARN-INGS less the LIABILITIES of a corporation.

P

PAC BOND acronym for *planned amortization class bond,* PAC is a TRANCHE class offered by some COLLATERIZED MORTGAGE OBLIGATIONS (CMOs), which is unlike other CMO classes in that (1) it has a sinking fund schedule that is observed as long as the prepayments on underlying mortgages remain within a broad range of speeds and (2) its ability to make principal payments is not subordinated to other classes. PAC bonds thus offer certainty of cash flow except in extreme prepayment situations, and because of this they trade at a premium to comparable traditional CMOs. *See also* TAC BONDS.

PACIFIC EXCHANGE (PCX) founded in 1882 as the San Francisco Stock and Bond Exchange, a regional market for securities of companies formed during the California Gold Rush. It is now the fourth largest stock options exchange in the world, with average daily volume of more than 500,000 options contracts on more than 1,800 stocks. More than 95% of PCX options trades are handled electronically. Options trading hours: 9:30 A.M. to 4:02 P.M., Monday to Friday. In 2005 the PCX was bought by Archipelago Holdings, an ELECTRONIC COMMUNICATIONS NETWORK (ECN) and owner of the ArcaEx platform. In 2006 Archipelago was acquired by the New York Stock Exchange. The Pacific Exchange was the first U.S. exchange to demutualize, converting from a nonprofit membership organization into a for-profit corporation in 1999. *See also* SECURITIES AND COMMODITIES EXCHANGES; STOCK INDICES AND AVERAGES.

PACIFIC RIM Far Eastern countries and markets bordering the Pacific Ocean, including Hong Kong, South Korea, Singapore, Taiwan, China, Malaysia, Indonesia, the Philippines, New Zealand, and Australia. Japan, because of its singular economic importance, is not usually included in the definition. Previously termed an economic miracle, Pacific Rim markets collapsed in the late 1990s.

PACKAGE MORTGAGE mortgage on both a house and durable personal property in the house, such as appliances and furniture. The borrower therefore repays one mortgage loan instead of having to carry two loans. In construction lending, interim and takeout loans made by the same investor.

PAC-MAN STRATEGY technique used by a corporation that is the target of a takeover bid to defeat the acquirer's wishes. The TARGET COMPANY defends itself by threatening to take over the acquirer and begins buying its common shares. For instance, if company A moves to take over company B against the wishes of the management of company B, company B will begin buying shares in company A in order to thwart A's takeover attempt. The Pac-Man strategy is named after a popular video game of the early 1980s, in which each character that does not swallow its opponents is itself consumed. *See also* TAKEOVER; TENDER OFFER.

PAID-IN CAPITAL capital received from investors in exchange for stock, as distinguished from capital generated from earnings or donated. The paid-in capital account includes CAPITAL STOCK and contributions of stockholders credited to accounts other than capital stock, such as an excess over PAR value received from the sale or exchange of capital stock. It would also include surplus resulting from RECAPITALIZATION. Paid-in capital is sometimes classified more specifically as *additional paid-in capital, paid-in surplus,* or *capital surplus.* Such accounts are distinguished from RETAINED EARNINGS or its older variation, EARNED SURPLUS. *See also* DONATED STOCK.

PAID-IN SURPLUS *see* PAID-IN CAPITAL.

PAID UP a situation in which all payments due have been made. For example, if all premiums on a life insurance policy have been paid, it is known as a PAID-UP POLICY.

PAID-UP POLICY life insurance policy in which all premiums have been paid. Some policies require premium payments for a limited number of years, and if all premium payments have been made over those years, the policy is considered paid in full and requires no more premium payments. Such a policy remains in force until the insured person dies or cancels the policy.

PAINTING THE TAPE
1. illegal practice by manipulators who buy and sell a particular security among themselves to create artificial trading activity, causing a succession of trades to be reported on the CONSOLIDATED TAPE and luring unwary investors to the "action." After causing movement in the market price of the security, the manipulators hope to sell at a profit.
2. consecutive or frequent trading in a particular security, resulting in its repeated appearances on the ticker tape. Such activity is usually attributable to special investor interest in the security.

PAIRED SHARES common stocks of two companies under the same management that are sold as a unit, usually appearing as a single certificate printed front and back. Also called *Siamese shares* or *stapled stock.*

PAIRS TRADING *see* MARKET-NEUTRAL INVESTING

P & I abbreviations for *principal* and *interest* on bonds or mortgage-backed securities. A traditional debt instrument such as a bond makes periodic interest payments and returns bondholders' principal when the bond matures. But in many cases, the principal payment and each of the interest payments are separated from each other by brokerage firms and sold in pieces. When accomplished with Treasury bonds, each of the individual interest payments and the final principal payment is sold as a "stripped" zero-coupon bond known as a STRIP. In the case of a mortgage-backed security, each of the interest payments and principal repayments from mortgagees is packaged into a COLLATERALIZED MORTGAGE OBLIGATION. A security composed of only interest payments is known as an *interest-only* or *IO* security. A security composed of just principal repayments is known as a *principal-only* or PO security. Both IOs and POs are forms of DERIVATIVE SECURITIES.

P & L *see* PROFIT AND LOSS STATEMENT.

PANDA gold coin issued by Peoples Republic of China.

PANIC BUYING OR SELLING flurry of buying or selling accompanied by high volume done in anticipation of sharply rising or falling prices. A sudden news event will trigger panic buying or selling, leaving investors little time to evaluate the fundamentals of individual stocks or bonds. Panic buying may be caused by an unexpected cut in interest rates or outcome of a political election. Short sellers may initially add to the problem then later be forced into panic buying if stock prices start to rise quickly, and they have to cover their short positions to prevent further losses. Panic selling may be set off by an international crisis such as a war or currency devaluation, the assassination of a head of state, or other unforeseen event. If stock prices start to fall sharply, investors may start to panic sell because they fear prices will fall much farther. *See also* CIRCUIT BREAKERS.

PAPER shorthand for *short-term commercial paper,* which is an unsecured note issued by a corporation. The term is also more loosely used to refer to all debt issued by a company, as in "ABC has $100 million in short and long-term paper outstanding."

PAPER DEALER brokerage firm that buys COMMERCIAL PAPER at one rate of interest, usually discounted, and resells it at a lower rate to banks and other investors, making a profit on the difference.

PAPER PROFIT OR LOSS unrealized CAPITAL GAIN or CAPITAL LOSS in an investment or PORTFOLIO. Paper profits and losses are calculated by comparing the current market prices of all stocks, bonds, mutual funds, and commodities in a portfolio to the prices at which those assets were originally bought. These profits or losses become realized only when the securities are sold.

PAPER TRADING *see* MOCK TRADING.

PAR equal to the nominal or FACE VALUE of a security. A bond selling at par, for instance, is worth the same dollar amount it was issued for or at which it will be redeemed at maturity—typically, $1,000 per bond.

With COMMON STOCK, par value is set by the company issuing the stock. At one time, par value represented the original investment behind each share of stock in goods, cash, and services, but today this is rarely the case. Instead, it is an assigned amount (such as $1 a share) used to compute the dollar accounting value of the common shares on a company's balance sheet. Par value has no relation to MARKET VALUE, which is determined by such considerations as NET ASSET VALUE, YIELD, and investors' expectations of future earnings. Some companies issue NO-PAR VALUE STOCK. *See also* STATED VALUE.

Par value has more importance for bonds and PREFERRED STOCK. The interest paid on bonds is based on a percentage of a bond's par value—a 10% bond pays 10% of the bond's par value annually. Preferred dividends are normally stated as a percentage of the par value of the preferred stock issue.

PARADOX OF SAVINGS (or THRIFT) irony observed by John Maynard Keynes that the more people save, the less they consume, which increases the likelihood of recession, which causes incomes to fall with the result that national savings may be lower than when the process started. The idea got diminished attention as in recent years confidence grew in the ability of the modern Federal Reserve to engineer economic stability. It gained renewed relevance after events of 2007 revealed the limitations of the Fed. *See also* LIQUIDITY TRAP.

PAR BOND bond that is selling at PAR, the amount equal to its nominal value or FACE VALUE. A corporate bond redeemable at maturity for $1,000 is a par bond when it trades on the market for $1,000.

PARENT COMPANY company that owns or controls subsidiaries through the ownership of voting stock. A parent company is usually an operating company in its own right; where it has no business of its own, the term HOLDING COMPANY is often preferred.

PARETO'S LAW theory that the pattern of income distribution is constant, historically and geographically, regardless of taxation or welfare policies; also called *law of the trivial many and the critical few* or *80-20 law.* Thus, if 80% of a nation's income will benefit only 20% of the population, the only way to improve the economic lot of the poor is to increase overall output and income levels.

Other applications of the law include the idea that in most business activities a small percentage of the work force produces the major portion of output or that 20% of the customers account for 80% of the dollar volume of sales. The law is attributed to Vilfredo Pareto, an Italian-Swiss engineer and economist (1848–1923).

Pareto is also credited with the concept called *Paretian optimum* (or *optimality*) that resources are optimally distributed when an individual cannot move into a better position without putting someone else into a worse position.

PARITY *see* CONVERSION PARITY.

PARITY PRICE price for a commodity or service that is pegged to another price or to a composite average of prices based on a selected prior period. As the two sets of prices vary, they are reflected in an index number on a scale of 100. For example, U.S. farm prices are pegged to prices based on the purchasing power of farmers in the period from 1910 to 1914. If the parity ratio is below 100, reflecting a reduction in purchasing power to the extent indicated, the government compensates the farmer by paying a certain percentage of parity, either in the form of a direct cash payment, in the purchase of surplus crops, or in a NONRECOURSE LOAN.

The concept of parity is also widely applied in industrial wage contracts as a means of preserving the real value of wages.

PARKING placing assets in a safe investment while other investment alternatives are under consideration. For instance, an investor will park the proceeds of a stock or bond sale in an interest-bearing money market fund while considering what other stocks or bonds to purchase. Term also refers to an illegal practice whereby ownership of stock is concealed, and DISCLOSURE requirements circumvented, by holding stock in the name of a conspiring party.

PARTIAL DELIVERY term used when a broker does not deliver the full amount of a security or commodity called for by a contract. If 10,000 shares were to be delivered, for example, and only 7000 shares are transferred, it is called a partial delivery.

PARTICIPATING DIVIDEND dividend paid from PARTICIPATING PREFERRED STOCK.

PARTICIPATING LIFE INSURANCE POLICIES life insurance that pays dividends to policyholders. The policyholders participate in the success or failure of the company's underwriting and investment performance by having their dividends rise or fall. The fewer claims the company experiences and the better its investment performance, the higher the dividends. Policyholders have many choices in what they can do with the dividends. They can have them paid in cash, in which case the income is taxable in the year received; they can use them to reduce policy premiums; they can buy more paid-up insurance, either cash value or term; or they can put them in an account with the insurance company that earns interest. The opposite of a participating policy is a NONPARTICIPATING LIFE INSURANCE POLICY.

PARTICIPATING PREFERRED STOCK PREFERRED STOCK that, in addition to paying a stipulated dividend, gives the holder the right to participate with the common stockholder in additional distributions of earnings under specified conditions. One example would be an arrangement whereby preferred shareholders are paid $5 per share, then common shareholders are paid $5 per share, and then preferred and common shareholders share equally in further dividends up to $1 per share in any one year.

Participating preferred issues are rare. They are used when special measures are necessary to attract investors. Most preferred stock is *nonparticipating preferred stock,* paying only the stipulated dividends.

PARTICIPATION CERTIFICATE certificate representing an interest in a POOL of funds or in other instruments, such as a MORTGAGE POOL. The following quasi-governmental agencies issue and/or guarantee such certificates (also called PASS-THROUGH SECURITIES): FEDERAL HOME LOAN MORTGAGE CORPORATION, FEDERAL NATIONAL MORTGAGE ASSOCIATION, GOVERNMENT NATIONAL MORTGAGE ASSOCIATION, SALLIE MAE.

PARTICIPATION LOAN
Commercial lending: loan made by more than one lender and serviced (administered) by one of the participants, called the *lead bank* or *lead lender.* Participation loans make it possible for large borrowers to obtain bank financing when the amount involved exceeds the legal lending limit of an individual bank (approximately 10% of a bank's capital).
Real estate: mortgage loan, made by a lead lender, in which other lenders own an interest.

PARTNERSHIP contract between two or more people in a joint business who agree to pool their funds and talent and share in the profits and losses of the enterprise. Those who are responsible for the day-to-day management of the partnership's activities, whose individual acts are binding on the other partners, and who are personally liable for the partnership's total liabilities are called *general partners.* Those who contribute only money and are not involved in management decisions are called *limited partners;* their liability is limited to their investment.

Partnerships are a common form of organization for service professions such as accounting and law. Each accountant or lawyer made a partner earns a percentage of the firm's profits.

Limited partnerships are also sold to investors by brokerage firms, financial planners, and other registered representatives. These partnerships may be either public (meaning that a large number of investors will participate and the partnership's plans must be filed with the Securities and Exchange Commission) or private (meaning that only a limited number of investors may participate and the plan need not be filed with the SEC). Both public and private limited partnerships invest in real estate, oil and gas, research and development, and equipment leasing. Some of these partnerships are oriented towards offering tax advantages and capital gains to limited partners, while others are designed to provide mostly income and some capital gains.

See also GENERAL PARTNER; LIMITED PARTNERSHIP; OIL AND GAS LIMITED PARTNERSHIP; PRIVATE LIMITED PARTNERSHIP; PUBLIC LIMITED PARTNERSHIP.

PARTNERSHIP AGREEMENT written agreement among partners specifying the conduct of the partnership, including the division of earnings, procedures for dividing up assets if the partnership is dissolved, and steps to be followed when a partner becomes disabled or dies. Investors in LIMITED PARTNERSHIPS also receive partnership agreements, detailing their rights and responsibilities.

PAR VALUE *see* PAR.

PAR VALUE OF CURRENCY ratio of one nation's currency unit to that of another country, as defined by the official exchange rates between the two countries; also called *par of exchange* or *par exchange rate.* Since 1971, exchange rates have been allowed to float; that is, instead of official rates of exchange, currency values are being determined by the forces of supply and demand in combination with the buying and selling by countries of their own currencies in order to stabilize the market value, a form of PEGGING.

PASSBOOK book issued by a bank to record deposits, withdrawals, and interest earned in a savings account, usually known as a passbook savings account. The passbook lists the depositor's name and account number as well as all transactions. Passbook savings accounts, though usually offering low yields, are safe because deposits in them are insured up to $100,000 by the Federal Deposit Insurance Corporation. The basic limit on federal insurance coverage for all ownership categories was temporarily increased to $250,000 through at least 2013. There are many alternatives to passbooks today, including ATM machines, telephone banking services, and unlimited transfers.

PASSED DIVIDEND *see* OMITTED DIVIDEND; CUMULATIVE PREFERRED.

PASSIVE income or loss from activities in which a taxpayer does not materially participate, such as LIMITED PARTNERSHIPS, as distinguished from (1) income from wages and active trade or business or (2) *investment (or portfolio) income,* such as dividends and interest. Starting with the TAX REFORM ACT OF 1986, and after modification by the REVENUE RECONCILIATION ACT OF 1993, losses and credits from passive activities are deductible only against income and tax from passive activities, although one passive activity can offset another and unused passive losses can be carried forward until the earlier of (1) your realization of passive income to offset such losses; or (2) your sale of your entire interest in the activity, at which time suspended losses from that activity can be used without limitation. Under the 1986 Act, real estate rental activities were considered passive regardless of material participation. The 1993 Act liberalized that provision for tax years after 1993 by making an exception for professionals spending at least half their time or at least 750 hours involved in real property trade or services or for anyone, apparently including a landlord, meeting the same tests of material participation. Regular corporations (as opposed to S corporations) are exempt from passive activity rules unless they are closely held.

PASSIVE ACTIVITY LOSS (PAL) loss produced by PASSIVE investment activities. *See also* PASSIVE INCOME GENERATOR (PIG).

PASSIVE BOND BOND that yields no interest. Such bonds arise out of reorganizations or are used in NOT-FOR-PROFIT fund raising.

PASSIVE INCOME GENERATOR (PIG) investment whose main attraction is PASSIVE income. The most common example is an income-oriented real estate LIMITED PARTNERSHIP, especially an UNLEVERAGED PROGRAM. Since Tax Reform PASSIVE ACTIVITY LOSSES (PALs) are deductible to the limit of passive activity income, so an investor with excess PALs might buy a PIG as a source of tax-sheltered income.

PASSIVE INVESTING
1. putting money in an investment deemed *passive* by the Internal Revenue Service, such as a LIMITED PARTNERSHIP.
2. investing in a MUTUAL FUND that replicates a market index, such as the STANDARD & POOR'S INDEX, thus assuring investment performance no worse (or better) than the market as a whole. An INDEX FUND charges a much lower MANAGEMENT FEE than an ordinary mutual fund.

PASS THE BOOK system to transfer responsibility for a brokerage firm's trading account from one office to another around the world as trading ends in one place and begins in another. For example, a firm may start the day with the "book" of the firm's securities inventory controlled in London. As the London market closes, the book will be passed to New York, then Los Angeles, then Tokyo, then Singapore, and back to London. Passing the book is necessary because markets are now traded 24 hours a day. Customers wanting to trade at any time will often be referred to the office handling the book at that time.

PASS-THROUGH SECURITY security, representing pooled debt obligations repackaged as shares, that passes income from debtors through the intermediary to investors. The most common type of pass-through is a MORT-GAGE-BACKED CERTIFICATE, usually government-guaranteed, where homeowners' principal and interest payments pass from the originating bank or savings and loan through a government agency or investment bank to investors, net of service charges. Pass-throughs representing other types of assets, such as auto loan paper or student loans, are also widely marketed. *See also* CERTIFI-CATE OF AUTOMOBILE RECEIVABLES (CARS); COLLATERALIZED MORTGAGE OBLI-GATION; REMIC.

PATENT exclusive right to use a process or produce or sell a particular product for a designated period of time. In the United States the Patent and Trademarks Office issues design patents good for 14 years and plant and utility patents good for 20 years.

PATRIOT BOND special designation given the Series EE SAVINGS BOND after the September 11, 2001 World Trade Center terrorist attack.

PATTERN technical chart formation made by price movements of stocks, bonds, commodities, or mutual funds. Analysts use patterns to predict future price movements. Some examples of patterns include ASCENDING TOPS; DOUBLE BOTTOM; FLAG; HEAD AND SHOULDERS; RISING BOTTOMS; SAUCER; and TRIANGLE. *See also* TECHNICAL ANALYSIS.

PAWNBROKER individual or employee of a pawn shop who lends money at a high rate of interest to a borrower leaving COLLATERAL such as jewelry, furs, appliances, or other valuable items. If the loan is repaid, the borrower gets the collateral back. If the loan is not repaid, the pawnbroker keeps the collateral, and in many cases, sells it to the public. Borrowers who turn to pawnbrokers and pawn shops typically do not have access to credit from banks or other financial institutions because they are in poor financial condition.

PAY-AS-YOU-GO BASIS INCOME TAX payment option, whereby an employer deducts and remits to the Internal Revenue Service a portion of an employee's monthly salary. Also refers generally to any service that is paid for as it is used.

PAYBACK PERIOD in capital budgeting; the length of time needed to recoup the cost of a CAPITAL INVESTMENT. The payback period is the ratio of the initial investment (cash outlay) to the annual cash inflows for the recovery period. The major shortcoming of the payback period method is that it does not take into account cash flows after the payback period and is therefore not a measure of the profitability of an investment project. For this reason, analysts generally prefer the DISCOUNTED CASH FLOW methods of capital budgeting—namely, the INTERNAL RATE OF RETURN and the NET PRESENT VALUE methods.

PAYDOWN
Bonds: refunding by a company of an outstanding bond issue through a smaller new bond issue, usually to cut interest costs. For instance, a company that issued $100 million of 12% bonds a few years ago will pay down (refund) that debt with a new $80 million issue with an 8% yield. The amount of the net deduction is called the paydown.
Lending: repayment of principal short of full payment. *See also* ON ACCOUNT.

PAYEE person receiving payment through a check, bill, money order, promissory note, credit card, cash, or other payment method.

PAYER person making a payment to a PAYEE through a check, bill, money order, promissory note, cash, credit card, or other form of payment.

PAYING AGENT agent, usually a bank, that receives funds from an issuer of bonds or stock and in turn pays principal and interest to bondholders and dividends to stockholders, usually charging a fee for the service. Sometimes called *disbursing agent.*

PAYMENT DATE date on which a declared stock dividend or a bond interest payment is scheduled to be paid.

PAYMENT IN KIND payment for goods and services made in the form of other goods and services, not cash or other forms of money. Usually, payment in kind is made when the payee returns with the same kind of good or service. For example, if someone's tire blows out, the payee will buy another tire to replace the first one. In the securities world, PAYMENT-IN-KIND SECURITIES pay bondholders in more bonds instead of cash interest. Payment in kind is different from BARTER because the payer gets the same goods and services in return, not other goods or services of equivalent value, as is the case in barter.

PAYMENT-IN-KIND SECURITIES *see* PIK (PAYMENT-IN-KIND) SECURITIES.

PAYOUT RATIO percentage of a firm's profits that is paid out to shareholders in the form of dividends. Young, fast-growing companies reinvest most of their earnings in their business and usually do not pay dividends. Regulated electric, gas, and telephone utility companies have historically paid out larger proportions of their highly dependable earnings in dividends than have other industrial corporations. Since these utilities are limited to a specified return on assets and are thus not able to generate from internal operations the cash flow needed for expansion, they pay large dividends to keep their stock attractive to investors desiring yield and are able to finance growth through new securities offerings. *See also* RETENTION RATE.

PAYROLL WITHHOLDING *see* WITHHOLDING (under Taxes: 1).

PAY-TO-PLAY practice in the municipal bond underwriting business in which underwriters feel compelled to contribute to the political campaigns of elected officials who decide which underwriters are awarded the municipality's business. Rules curtailing the practice were promulgated by the MUNICIPAL SECURITIES RULEMAKING BOARD (MSRB), though underwriters still seek to gain influence with elected officials through other means.

PAY UP
1. situation when an investor who wants to buy a stock at a particular price hesitates and the stock begins to rise. Instead of letting the stock go, he "pays up" to buy the shares at the higher prevailing price.
2. when an investor buys shares in a high quality company at what is felt to be a high price. Such an investor will say "I realize that I am paying up for this stock, but it is worth it because it is such a fine company."

PBR abbreviation for price to BOOK VALUE ratio, which is the market value of a company's stock divided by its TANGIBLE NET WORTH. This ratio is especially significant to securities analysts where real estate not used in operations is a significant portion of assets, such as in the case of a typical Japanese company.

PC commonly used abbreviation for PARTICIPATION CERTIFICATE and, in brokerage parlance, for *plus commissions* (which are added to purchases and subtracted from sales).

PEACE DIVIDEND term used to describe the reallocation of spending from military purposes to peacetime priorities. After the end of World War II and at the end of the Cold War, government officials spoke of the peace dividend, which they presumed could be spent on housing, education, social initiatives, deficit reduction, and other programs instead of on maintaining the military establishment.

PEGGING stabilizing the price of a security, commodity, or currency by intervening in a market. For example, until 1971 governments pegged the price of gold at certain levels to stabilize their currencies and would therefore buy it when the price dropped and sell when the price rose. Since 1971, a FLOATING EXCHANGE RATE system has prevailed, in which countries use pegging—the buying or selling of their own currencies—simply to offset fluctuations in the exchange rate. The U.S. government uses pegging in another way to support the prices of agricultural commodities. *See also* PARITY PRICE.

    In floating new stock issues, the managing underwriter is authorized to try to peg the market price and stabilize the market in the issuer's stock by buying shares in the open market. With this one exception, securities price pegging is illegal and is regulated by the Securities and Exchange Commission. *See also* STABILIZATION.

PEG RATIO *see* PROSPECTIVE EARNINGS GROWTH RATIO.

PENALTY CLAUSE clause found in contracts, borrowing agreements, and savings instruments providing for penalties in the event a contract is not kept, a loan payment is late, or a withdrawal is made prematurely. *See also* PREPAYMENT PENALTY.

PENNANT technical chart pattern resembling a pointed flag, with the point facing to the right. Unlike a FLAG pattern, in which rallies and peaks occur in a uniform range, it is formed as the rallies and peaks that give it its shape become less pronounced. A pennant is also characterized by diminishing trade volume. With these differences, this pattern has essentially the same significance as a flag; that is, prices will rise or fall sharply once the pattern is complete.

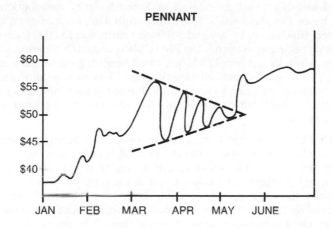

PENNANT

PENNY JUMPING (or PENNYING) *see* NEGATIVE OBLIGATION.

PENNY STOCK defined by the SEC as a security that sold for less than $5 per share and was not listed or authorized for quotation on a NASDAQ market exchange. Penny stocks are issued by companies with a short or erratic history of revenues and earnings, and therefore such stocks are more VOLATILE than those of large, well-established firms traded on the New York or American stock exchanges. Many brokerage houses therefore have special precautionary rules about trading in these stocks and the SECURITIES AND EXCHANGE COMMISSION (SEC) requires that brokers implement SUITABILITY RULES in writing and obtain written consent from investors.

All penny stocks are traded OVER-THE-COUNTER, many of them in the local markets of Denver, Vancouver, or Salt Lake City. These markets have had a history of boom and bust, with a speculative fervor for oil, gas, and gold-mining stocks in the Denver penny stock market in the late 1970s turning to bust by the early 1980s.

PENNY STOCK REFORM ACT OF 1990 congressional act to protect unsophisticated investors from unsuitable high-risk investments. It gave the SEC authority to regulate promoters, restrict BLANK CHECK OFFERINGS, require fuller disclosure by broker-dealers. and establish an electronic system providing quotations and last-sale information.

PENNY STOCK RULE *see* SECURITIES AND EXCHANGE COMMISSION RULES.

PENSION BENEFIT GUARANTY CORPORATION (PBGC) federal corporation established in 1974 under the EMPLOYEE RETIREMENT INCOME SECURITY ACT (ERISA) to guarantee basic pension benefits in covered plans by administering terminated plans and placing liens on corporate assets for certain unfunded pension liabilities. To be covered, a plan must promise clearly defined benefits to more than 25 employees. The PBGC is not funded by general tax revenues; it collects insurance premiums from pension plans, earns money from investments, and receives funds from pension plans it takes over to fund its operations. When PBGC terminates a pension plan, it pays benefits to pensioners according to the provisions of the plan up to PBGC maximum guarantees. This includes early retirement, disability, and survivor benefits. Under the single employer program, the PBGC limit is adjusted annually based on changes in Social Security contributions and benefit bases. For plans with a 2009 termination date, the maximum annual guarantee, which is set by law and adjusted yearly, was $54,000 for a single life annuity beginning at age 65. The PBGC also conducts a "Pension Search" program, which locates people who are owed benefits from terminated fully funded, PBGC-insured defined benefit plans. The agency also offers an "Early Warning" program to target underfunded plans posing the greatest risk of pension fund termination. *See also* PENSION FUND; RETIREMENT PROTECTION ACT OF 1994.

PENSION FUND fund set up by a corporation, labor union, governmental entity, or other organization to pay the pension benefits of retired workers. Pension funds invest billions of dollars annually in the stock and bond markets, and are therefore a major factor in the supply-demand balance of the markets. Earnings on the investment portfolios of pension funds are TAX DEFERRED. Fund managers make actuarial assumptions about how much they will be required to pay out to pensioners and then try to ensure that the RATE OF RETURN on their portfolios equals or exceeds that anticipated payout need. *See also* APPROVED LIST; EMPLOYEE RETIREMENT INCOME SECURITY ACT (ERISA); PRUDENT-MAN RULE; VESTING.

PENSION PARACHUTE pension agreement that specifies that in the event of a hostile takeover attempt, any excess assets in a company pension plan can be used for the benefit of pension plan participants, such as increasing pension payments. This prevents the raiding firm or individual from using the pension assets to finance the takeover, and therefore acts as an additional deterrent to help the firm ward off the acquisition. A pension parachute is a form of POISON PILL.

PENSION PLAN provides replacement for salary when a person is no longer working. In the case of a DEFINED BENEFIT PENSION PLAN, the employer or union contributes to the plan, which pays a predetermined benefit for the rest of the employee's life based on length of service and salary. Payments may be made either directly or through an annuity. Pension payments are taxable income to recipients in the year received. The employer or union has fiduciary responsibility to invest the pension funds in stocks, bonds, real estate, and other assets; earn a satisfactory rate of return; and make payments to retired workers. Pension funds holding trillions of dollars are one of the largest investment forces in the stock, bond, and real estate markets. If the employer defaults, pension plan payments are usually guaranteed by the PENSION BENEFIT GUARANTY CORPORATION (PBGC).

In the case of a DEFINED CONTRIBUTION PENSION PLAN, such as a 401(k) or 403(b) plan, employees choose whether or not to contribute to the plan offered by the employer, who may or may not match employee contributions. Pension benefits are determined by the amount of assets built up by the employee during his or her years of contributions. Self-employed individuals can also set up pension plans such as KEOGH PLANS. An INDIVIDUAL RETIREMENT ACCOUNT (IRA) is a form of pension plan. *See also* VESTING.

PENSION PROTECTION ACT OF 2006 Congressional pension reform legislation designed to encourage individual retirement savings and to make employer-funded plans subject to stricter regulation. Provisions also affected charitable contributions, long-term care, college savings plans, and assistance to employees in setting up 403(b) and 401(k) plans.

PENSION REVERSION procedure initiated by a company with an over-funded DEFINED BENEFIT PENSION PLAN to terminate the plan and reclaim the surplus assets for itself. Pension beneficiaries continue to receive their benefits because the company replaces the pension plan with a life insurance company-sponsored fixed annuity plan. In some cases, the company will offer current employees a DEFINED CONTRIBUTION PENSION PLAN to replace the terminated defined benefit plan. Employees are usually not pleased when their company carries out a pension reversion plan for two reasons: By replacing the pension plan backed by the company with a fixed annuity backed by an insurance company, pensioners are no longer covered by the guarantee of the Pension Benefit Guaranty Corporation; and pensioners lose the prospect for increased pension benefits that they might have enjoyed under the company's pension plan if it had achieved superior investment performance.

PENULTIMATE PROFIT PROSPECT (PPP) second lowest-priced of the ten highest-yielding stocks in the Dow Jones Industrial Average, identified (by co-authors of *Beating the Dow,* Michael B. O'Higgins and John Downes) as the single Dow stock with the greatest probability of outperforming the average as a whole.

PEOPLE PILL defensive tactic to ward off a hostile TAKEOVER. Management threatens that, in the event of a successful takeover, the entire management team will resign at once, leaving the company without experienced leadership. This is a version of the POISON PILL defense.

PER CAPITA in Latin translation, *per head.* In other words, *per person.*

PER CAPITA DEBT total bonded debt of a municipality, divided by its population. A more refined version, called *net per capita debt,* divides the total bonded debt less applicable sinking funds by the total population. The result of either ratio, compared with ratios of prior periods, reveals trends in a municipality's debt burden, which bond analysts evaluate, bearing in mind that, historically, defaults in times of recession have generally followed overexpansion of debts in prior booms.

PERCENTAGE-OF-COMPLETION (CAPITALIZED COST METHOD) *see* COMPLETED CONTRACT METHOD.

PERCENTAGE ORDER order to a securities broker to buy or sell a specified number of shares of a stock after a fixed number of these shares have been traded. It can be a LIMIT ORDER or a MARKET ORDER and usually applies to one trading day.

PERCENT HELD BY INSTITUTIONS *see* INSTITUTIONAL HOLDINGS.

PERCS acronym for *preferred equity—redemption cumulative stock*. A form of preferred stock that allows common shareholders to exchange common stock for preferred shares, thereby retaining a high dividend rate. PERCS usually have little appreciation potential, however.

PERFECT COMPETITION market condition wherein no buyer or seller has the power to alter the market price of a good or service. Characteristics of a perfectly competitive market are a large number of buyers and sellers, a homogeneous (similar) good or service, an equal awareness of prices and volume, an absence of discrimination in buying and selling, total mobility of productive resources, and complete freedom of entry. Perfect competition exists only as a theoretical ideal. Also called *pure competition*.

PERFECT HEDGE *see* HEDGE/HEDGING.

PERFORMANCE ATTRIBUTION ANALYSIS analysis of the performance results of a PORTFOLIO MANAGER to determine which elements of the strategy, such as market timing or security selection, were responsible for the results and why. *See also* BARRA'S PERFORMANCE ANALYSIS (PERFAN).

PERFORMANCE BOND surety bond given by one party to another, protecting the second party against loss in the event the terms of a contract are not fulfilled. The surety company is primarily liable with the principal (the contractor) for nonperformance. For example, a homeowner having a new kitchen put in may request a performance bond from the home improvement contractor so that the homeowner would receive cash compensation if the kitchen was not done satisfactorily within the agreed upon time.

PERFORMANCE FEE *see* INCENTIVE FEE.

PERFORMANCE FUND MUTUAL FUND designed for growth of capital. A performance fund invests in high-growth companies that do not pay dividends or that pay small dividends. Investors in such funds are willing to take higher-than-average risks in order to earn higher-than-average returns on their invested capital. *See also* GROWTH STOCK; PERFORMANCE STOCK.

PERFORMANCE STOCK high-growth stock that an investor feels will significantly rise in value. Also known as GROWTH STOCK, such a security tends to pay either a small dividend or no dividend at all. Companies whose stocks are in this category tend to retain earnings rather than pay dividends in order to finance their rapid growth. *See also* PERFORMANCE FUND.

PERIODIC PAYMENT PLAN plan to accumulate capital in a mutual fund by making regular investments on a monthly or quarterly basis. The plan has a set pay-in period, which may be 10 or 20 years, and a mechanism to withdraw funds from the plan after that time. Participants in periodic payment plans enjoy the advantages of DOLLAR COST AVERAGING and the diversification among stocks or bonds that is available through a mutual fund. Some plans also include completion insurance, which assures that all scheduled contributions to the plan will continue so that full benefits can be passed on to beneficiaries in the event the participant dies or is incapacitated.

PERIODIC PURCHASE DEFERRED CONTRACT ANNUITY contract for which fixed-amount payments, called *premiums,* are paid either monthly or quarterly and that does not begin paying out until a time elected by the holder (the *annuitant).* In some cases, premium payments may continue after payments from the annuity have begun. A periodic purchase deferred contract can be either fixed or variable. *See also* FIXED ANNUITY; VARIABLE ANNUITY.

PERIOD-CERTAIN ANNUITY annuity that guarantees payments to an ANNUITANT for a particular period of time. For example, a 10-year period-certain annuity will make annuity payments for 10 years and no more. If the annuitant dies before the 10 years have expired, the payments will continue to the policy's beneficiaries for the remaining term. The monthly payment rate for a period-certain annuity is generally higher than the rate for a LIFE ANNUITY because the insurance company knows its maximum liability in advance.

PERIOD OF DIGESTION time period after the release of a NEW ISSUE of stocks or bonds during which the trading price of the security is established in the marketplace. Particularly when an INITIAL PUBLIC OFFERING is released, the period of digestion may entail considerable VOLATILITY, as investors try to ascertain an appropriate price level for it.

PERMANENT FINANCING
Corporate finance: long-term financing by means of either debt (bonds or long-term notes) or equity (common or preferred stock),
Real estate: long-term mortgage loan or bond issue, usually with a 15-, 20-, or 30-year term, the proceeds of which are used to repay a CONSTRUCTION LOAN.

PERMANENT LIFE INSURANCE *see* WHOLE LIFE INSURANCE.

PERPENDICULAR SPREAD option strategy using options with similar expiration dates and different strike prices (the prices at which the options can be exercised). A perpendicular spread can be designed for either a bullish or a bearish outlook.

PERPETUAL BOND bond that has no maturity date, is not redeemable and pays a steady stream of interest indefinitely; also called *annuity bond.* The only notable perpetual bonds in existence are the consols first issued by the British Treasury to pay off smaller issues used to finance the Napoleonic Wars (1814). Some persons in the United States believe it would be more realistic to issue perpetual government bonds than constantly to refund portions of the national debt, as is the practice.

PERPETUAL INVENTORY inventory accounting system whereby book inventory is kept in continuous agreement with stock on hand; also called *continuous inventory.* A daily record is maintained of both the dollar amount and the physical quantity of inventory, and this is reconciled to actual physical counts at short intervals. Perpetual inventory contrasts with *periodic inventory.*

PERPETUAL WARRANT investment certificate giving the holder the right to buy a specified number of common shares of stock at a stipulated price with no expiration date. *See also* SUBSCRIPTION WARRANT.

PERQUISITE commonly known as a *perk*. A fringe benefit offered to an employee in addition to salary. Some examples of perquisites are reimbursement for educational expenses, legal services, vacation time, pension plans, life insurance coverage, company cars and aircraft, personal financial counseling, and employee assistance hotlines. In general, the higher an employee's position and the more valued he or she in a company, the more perks he or she receives.

PERSONAL ARTICLE FLOATER policy or an addition to a policy, used to cover personal valuables, such as jewelry and furs.

PERSONAL EXEMPTION amount of money a person can exclude from personal income in calculating federal and state income tax. Taxpayers can claim one exemption for every person in their household. The amount of the personal exemption is adjusted for inflation each year. In 2008 it was $3,500. Taxpayers can also claim additional exemptions for a spouse, a qualifying child, and a qualifying relative. Exemptions are phased out for certain high-income taxpayers. For a married couple filing jointly, exemptions begin to be phased out when adjusted gross income reaches $239,950. For singles, the phaseout starts when adjusted gross income reaches $159,950. For heads of household, the phaseout begins when adjusted gross income reaches $199,950. For married couples filing separately, the phaseout begins when adjusted gross income reaches $119,975. Taxpayers can lose no more than one-third of the dollar amount of an exemption. Thus each exemption cannot be reduced to less than $2,333.

PERSONAL INCOME income received by persons from all sources: from participation in production, from both government and business TRANSFER PAYMENTS and from government interest (which is treated like a transfer payment). "Persons" refers to individuals, nonprofit institutions that primarily serve individuals, private noninsured welfare funds, and private trust funds. Personal income is calculated as the sum of wages and salary disbursements, other labor income, proprietors' income with inventory valuation and capital consumption adjustment, rental income of persons, with capital consumption adjustment, personal dividend income, personal interest income, and transfer payments to persons, less personal contribution to Social Security.

PERSONAL INFLATION RATE rate of price increases as it affects a specific individual or couple. For example, a young couple with children who are buying and furnishing a home probably will have a much higher personal inflation rate than an elderly couple with their home paid off and self-supporting children, because the young couple needs to buy many more things that are likely to rise in price than the elderly couple. The personal inflation rate is far more relevant for most people than the general inflation rate tracked by the Labor Department's CONSUMER PRICE INDEX.

PERSONAL PROPERTY tangible and intangible assets other than real estate.

PER STIRPES formula for distributing the assets of a person who dies intestate (without a will) according to the "family tree." Under such a distribution, the estate is allocated according to the number of children the deceased had, and distributed accordingly to those surviving the decedent. If any children predeceased the decedent, the share allocated to them would be equally divided among their children and so on.

PETRODOLLARS dollars paid to oil-producing countries and deposited in Western banks. When the price of oil skyrocketed in the 1970s, Middle Eastern oil producers built up huge surpluses of petrodollars that the banks lent to oil-importing countries around the world. In the mid-1980s and 1990s, these surpluses had shrunk because oil prices fell and oil exporters spent a good deal of the money on development projects. By the mid-2000s, the sharp rise in oil prices had again filled the coffers of oil-producing countries, who reinvested billions of dollars back into the West. The flow of petrodollars, therefore, is very important in understanding the current world economic situation. Also called *petrocurrency* or *oil money*.

PETS *see* PREFERRED EQUITY TRADED BONDS.

PHANTOM INCOME LIMITED PARTNERSHIP income that arises from debt restructuring and creates taxability without generating cash flow. Phantom income typically occurs in a tax shelter created prior to the TAX REFORM ACT OF 1986 where real estate properties, having declined in market value, are refinanced; income arises from portions of the debt that are forgiven and recaptured.

PHANTOM STOCK PLAN executive incentive concept whereby an executive receives a bonus based on the market appreciation of the company's stock over a fixed period of time. The hypothetical (hence phantom) amount of shares involved in the case of a particular executive is proportionate to his or her salary level. The plan works on the same principle as a CALL OPTION (a right to purchase a fixed amount of stock at a set price by a particular date). Unlike a call option, however, the executive pays nothing for the option and therefore has nothing to lose.

PHILADELPHIA BOARD OF TRADE (PBOT) futures trading subsidiary of the Philadelphia Stock Exchange. The PBOT trades currency futures on the Australian dollar, British pound, Canadian dollar, Euro, Japanese yen, and Swiss franc and is adding additional non-currency futures products as well. *www.phlx.com.*

PHILADELPHIA STOCK EXCHANGE (PHLX) founded in 1790 as the first organized stock exchange in the United States, PHLX trades more than 2,000 stocks, 1,703 equity options, 26 proprietary industry sectors index options, a group of EXCHANGE-TRADED FUNDS, and currency options and currency futures on its Philadelphia Board of Trade (PBOT) subsidiary. Equity trading is conducted through floor brokers or the electronic order entry and execution system called PACE (Philadelphia Automated Communication and Execution System). In 2005 the Philadelphia Stock Exchange became the first floor-based exchange to trade all of its options and sector indexes electronically using PHLX XL, the exchange's electronic trading platform. The PHLX XL platform allows for market makers to enter quotes and trade from remote locations. In the Sector Index Option marketplace, the PHLX features many widely quoted and recognized industry benchmarks including the PHLX's Gold/Silver Sector (XAU), PHLX's Oil Service Sector (OSX), Semiconductor Sector (SOX), PHLX/KBW Bank Index (BKX), Housing

Sector (HGX), and Utility Sector (UTY). In 2004 the exchange demutualized, and it was acquired by NASDAQ OMX in 2008. In 1982 PHLX was the first exchange to trade options on currencies and was the first U.S. securities exchange to open international offices in overseas money centers. The PHLX pioneered evening trading in 1987 and 24-hour trading for currencies in 1990. Trading hours for equities are 9:30 A.M. to 4 P.M. with a post-primary session from 4 P.M. to 4:15 P.M. Equity options: 9:30 A.M. to 4:02 P.M. Index options: 9:30 A.M. to 4:02 P.M. (narrow-based); 9:30 A.M. to 4:15 P.M. (broad-based). Currency options: 2:30 A.M. to 2:30 P.M. *See also* SECURITIES AND COMMODITIES EXCHANGES.

PHILIPPINE STOCK EXCHANGE (PSE) operator of the primary stock exchange in the Philippines and founded in 1992. The exchange traces its roots to the Manila Stock Exchange, established in 1927, and the Makati Stock Exchange, established in 1963. It has two trading floors—the main one in Pasig City and another in Makati City. It uses the MakTrade trading system, a single-order-book system. The exchange began bond trading in 2001. *www.pse.com.ph.*

PHILLIPS CURVE chart curve showing that inflation tends to rise as the natural rate of unemployment declines.

PHYSICAL COMMODITY actual commodity that is delivered to the contract buyer at the expiration of a commodity contract in either the SPOT MARKET or the FUTURES MARKET. Some examples of physical commodities are corn, cotton, gold, oil, soybeans, and wheat. The quality specifications and quantity of the commodity to be delivered are specified by the exchange on which it is traded.

PHYSICAL INVENTORY *see* PHYSICAL VERIFICATION.

PHYSICAL VERIFICATION procedure by which an auditor actually inspects the assets of a firm, particularly inventory, to confirm their existence and value, rather than relying on written records. The auditor may use statistical sampling in the verification process.

PICKUP value gained in a bond swap. For example, bonds with identical coupon rates and maturities may have different market values, mainly because of a difference in quality, and thus in yields. The higher yield of the lower-quality bond received in such a swap compared with the yield of the higher-quality bond that was exchanged for it results in a net gain for the trader, called his or her pickup on the transaction.

PICKUP BOND bond that has a relatively high coupon (interest) rate and is close to the date at which it is callable—that is, can be paid off prior to maturity—by the issuer. If interest rates fall, the investor can look forward to picking up a redemption PREMIUM, since the bond will in all likelihood be called.

PICTURE Wall Street jargon used to request bid and asked prices and quantity information from a specialist or from a dealer regarding a particular security. For example, the question "What's the picture on XYZ?" might be answered, "$58\frac{3}{8}$ [best bid] to $\frac{3}{4}$ [best offer is $58\frac{3}{4}$], 1000 either way [there are both a buyer and a seller for 1000 shares]."

PIG *see* PASSIVE INCOME GENERATOR.

PIGGYBACKING illegal practice by a broker who buys or sells stocks or bonds in his personal account after a customer buys or sells the same security. The broker assumes that the customer is making the trade because of access to material, nonpublic information that will make the stock or bond rise or fall sharply. Trading following customer orders is a conflict of interest, and may be disciplined by the broker's firm or regulatory authorities if discovered.

PIGGYBACK LOANS second mortgage loans "piggybacked" onto first mortgages after home improvements have added value or, in a rapidly inflating housing market, to compensate for a small or nonexistent down payment and save the higher expense of PRIVATE MORTGAGE INSURANCE (PMI). The first and second loans, which close simultaneously, typically represent 80% and 10% of home value, respectively, with the remaining 10% a down payment, hence the term, *"80–10–10s."* Some lenders, however, will allow the piggyback loan to represent 20% and some will structure it as a HOMEOWNER'S EQUITY ACCOUNT.

PIGGYBACK REGISTRATION situation when a securities underwriter allows existing holdings of shares in a corporation to be sold in combination with an offering of new public shares. The prospectus in a piggyback registration will reveal the nature of such a public/private share offering and name the sellers of the private shares. *See also* PUBLIC OFFERING.

PIK (PAYMENT-IN-KIND) SECURITIES bonds or preferred stock that pay interest/dividends in the form of additional bonds or preferred. PIK securities have been used in takeover financing in lieu of cash and are highly speculative.

PINK SHEETS LLC name change of National Quotation Bureau, Cedar Grove, New Jersey, which provides daily bid and offer quotes from market makers on over-the-counter stocks (pink sheets) and bonds (yellow sheets) to subscribers. Its web site, *www.pinksheets.com*, provides electronic services.

PIN NUMBER acronym for *personal identification number.* Customers use PIN numbers to identify themselves, such as when performing transactions with a debit card at an automatic teller machine.

PIP smallest currency unit, a United States penny for example.

PIPELINE term referring to the underwriting process that involves securities being proposed for public distribution. The phrase used is "in the pipeline." The entire underwriting process, including registration with the Securities and Exchange Commission, must be completed before a security can be offered for public sale. Underwriters attempt to have several securities issues waiting in the pipeline so that the issues can be sold as soon as market conditions become favorable. In the municipal bond market, the pipeline is called the "Thirty Day Visible Supply" in the *Bond Buyer* newspaper.

PIPES *see* PRIVATE INVESTMENTS IN PUBLIC EQUITY SECURITIES (PIPES).

PIT location at a futures or options exchange in which trading takes place. Pits are usually shaped like rings, often with several levels of steps, so that a large number of traders can see and be seen by each other as they conduct business.

PITI acronym for *principal, interest, taxes and insurance,* the primary components of monthly mortgage payments. Many mortgage lenders, to ensure that property taxes and homeowner's insurance premiums are paid on schedule, require that borrowers include these amounts in their monthly payments. The funds are then placed in escrow until needed. When calculating how much a house will cost a borrower on a monthly basis, the payment is expressed for PITI.

PLACE to market new securities. The term applies to both public and private sales but is more often used with reference to direct sales to institutional investors, as in PRIVATE PLACEMENT. The terms FLOAT and *distribute* are preferred in the case of a PUBLIC OFFERING.

PLACEMENT AGENT intermediary hired by an investment management firm to gain access to large institutional asset pools such as state pension funds. Placement agents are usually politically well connected, thereby allowing money managers to capture business and management fees that they might not be able to line up on their own. Placement agents have been criticized by various attorneys general and the SEC as giving their clients an unfair advantage over other money managers who do not use placement agents to win pension business. *See also* PAY-TO-PLAY.

PLACEMENT RATIO ratio, compiled by the *Bond Buyer* as of the close of business every Thursday, indicating the percentage of the past week's new MUNICIPAL BOND offerings that have been bought from the underwriters. Only issues of $1 million or more are included.

PLANNED AMORTIZATION CLASS BONDS *see* PAC BOND.

PLAN PARTICIPANTS employees or former employees of a company, members of an employee organization or beneficiaries who may become eligible to receive benefits from an employee benefit plan. Participants are legally entitled to certain information about the plan and the benefits, including a summary annual report and summary plan description.

PLAN SPONSOR entity that establishes and maintains a pension or insurance plan. This may be a corporation, labor union, government agency, or nonprofit organization. Plan sponsors must follow government guidelines in the establishment and administration of these plans, including informing plan participants about the financial health of the plan and the benefits available.

PLANT assets comprising land, buildings, machinery, natural resources, furniture and fixtures, and all other equipment permanently employed. Synonymous with FIXED ASSET.

　　In a limited sense, the term is used to mean only buildings or only land and buildings: "property, plant, and equipment" and "plant and equipment."

PLASTIC BONDS *see* CARDS.

PLAYING THE MARKET unprofessional buying and selling of stocks, as distinguished from SPECULATION. Both players and speculators are seeking capital gains, but while playing the market is more akin to gambling, speculating is done by professionals taking calculated risks.

PLAZA ACCORD agreement in August of 1985 in which the finance ministers of the Group of 5—the United States, Great Britain, France, Germany, and Japan—met to reduce the value of the U.S. dollar against other major currencies. Though the dollar had already begun its decline months earlier, the Plaza Accord accelerated the move. The action was necessary because the dollar had become so strong that it was difficult for U.S. exporters to sell their products abroad, weakening the American economy.

PLC *see* a LIMITED COMPANY that offers shares or securities to the public whose name ends in p.l.c.

PLEDGING transferring property, such as securities or the CASH SURRENDER VALUE of life insurance, to a lender or creditor as COLLATERAL for an obligation. *Pledge* and *hypothecate* are synonymous, as they do not involve transfer of title. ASSIGN, although commonly used interchangeably with *pledge* and *hypothecate,* implies transfer of ownership or of the right to transfer ownership at a later date. *See also* HYPOTHECATION.

PLOW BACK to reinvest a company's earnings in the business rather than pay out those profits as dividends. Smaller, fast-growing companies usually plow back most or all earnings in their businesses, whereas more established firms pay out more of their profits as dividends.

PLUS

1. plus sign (+) that follows a price quotation on a Treasury note or bond, indicating that the price (normally quoted as a percentage of PAR value refined to 32ds) is refined to 64ths. Thus 95.16 + ($95^{16}/_{32}+$ or $95^{32}/_{64}+$) means $95^{33}/_{64}$.
2. plus sign after a transaction price in a listed security (for example, 39.50+), indicating that the trade was at a higher price than the previous REGULAR WAY transaction. *See also* PLUS TICK.
3. plus sign before the figure in the column labeled "Change" in the newspaper stock tables, meaning that the closing price of the stock was higher than the previous day's close by the amount stated in the "Change" column.

PLUS TICK expression used when a security has been traded at a higher price than the previous transaction in that security. A stock price listed as 28+ on the CONSOLIDATED TAPE has had a plus tick from 27.94 or below on previous trades. Also called *uptick. See also* MINUS TICK; TICK; SHORT-SALE RULE; ZERO-MINUS TICK.

POINT

Bonds: percentage change of the face value of a bond expressed as a point. For example, a change of 1% is a move of one point. For a bond with a $1,000 face value, each point is worth $10, and for a bond with a $5,000 face value, each point is $50.

Bond yields are quoted in basis points: 100 basis points make up 1% of yield. *See* BASIS POINT.

Futures/options: measure of price change equal to one one-hundredth of one cent in most futures traded in decimal units. In grains, it is one quarter of one cent; in Treasury bonds, it is 1% of par. *See also* TICK.

Real estate and other commercial lending: upfront fee charged by a lender, separate from interest but designed to increase the overall yield to the lender. A point is 1% of the total principal amount of the loan. For example, on a $100,000 mortgage loan, a charge of 3 points would equal $3,000. Since points are considered a form of prepaid mortgage interest, they are tax-deductible, usually over the term of the loan, but in some cases in a lump sum in the year they are paid.

Stocks: change of $1 in the market price of a stock. If a stock has risen 5 points, it has risen by $5 a share.

The movements of stock market averages, such as the Dow Jones Industrial Average, are also quoted in points. However, those points refer not to dollar amounts but to units of movement in the average, which is a composite of weighted dollar values. For example, a 20-point move in the Dow Jones Average from 8000 to 8020 does *not* mean the Dow now stands at $8,020.

POINT AND FIGURE CHART graphic technique used in TECHNICAL ANALYSIS to follow the up or down momentum in the price moves of a security or sector. Point and figure charting disregards the element of time and is solely used to record changes in price. Every time a price move is upward, an X is put on the graph above the previous point. Every time the price moves down, an O is placed one square down. When direction changes, the next column is used. The resulting lines of Xs and Os will indicate whether the security or sector being charted has maintained an up or a down momentum over a particular time period.

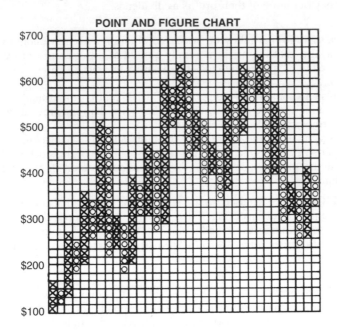

POINT AND FIGURE CHART

POISON PILL strategic move by a takeover-target company to make its stock less attractive to an acquirer. For instance, a firm may issue a new series of PREFERRED STOCK that gives shareholders the right to redeem it at a premium price after a TAKEOVER. Two variations: a *flip-in poison pill* allows all existing holders of target company shares except the acquirer to buy additional shares at a bargain price; a *flip-over poison pill* allows holders of common stock to buy (or holders of preferred stock to convert into) the acquirer's shares at a bargain price in the event of an unwelcome merger. Such measures raise the cost of an ACQUISITION, and cause DILUTION, hopefully deterring a takeover bid. A third type of poison pill, known as a PEOPLE PILL, is the threat that in the event of a successful takeover, the entire management team will resign at once, leaving the company without experienced leadership. *See also* PENSION PARACHUTE, POISON PUT, SUICIDE PILL.

POISON PUT provision in an INDENTURE giving bondholders the privilege of redemption at PAR if certain designated events occur, such as a hostile TAKE-OVER, the purchase of a big block of shares, or an excessively large dividend payout. Poison puts, or *superpoison puts* as the more stringent variations are called, are popular antitakeover devices because they create an onerous cash obligation for the acquirer. They also protect the bondholder from the deterioration of credit quality and RATING that might result from a LEVERAGED BUYOUT that added to the issuer's debt. *See also* EVENT RISK.

POLICYHOLDER owner of an INSURANCE contract (policy). Term is commonly used synonymously with *insured,* although the two can be different parties and *insured* is the preferred designation for the person indemnified by the insurance company.

POLICYHOLDER LOAN BONDS packaged policyholder loans. Life insurance policyholders borrow against the CASH SURRENDER VALUE of their policies. The policyholder loan will be repaid either by the policyholder while alive or from the proceeds of the insurance policy if the policyholder dies before repayment. These loans are packaged by a broker/dealer that offers these asset-backed securities as policyholder loan bonds.

POLICY LIMIT limit of coverage provided by an insurance policy, known as a *maximum lifetime benefit.* For coverage of individuals, roughly two-thirds of existing policies have a limit of $1 million or more; 21% have no limit. Most employee plans are based on maximum lifetime coverage.

POLICY LOAN loan from an insurance company secured by the CASH SUR-RENDER VALUE of a life insurance policy. The amount available for such a loan depends on the number of years the policy has been in effect, the insured's age when the policy was issued, and the size of the death benefit. Such loans are often made at below-market interest rates to policyholders, although more recent policies usually only allow borrowing at rates that fluctuate in line with money market rates. If the loan is not repaid by the insured, the death benefit of the life insurance policy will be reduced by the amount of the loan plus accrued interest.

PONZI SCHEME *see* PYRAMIDING.

POOL
Capital budgeting: as used in the phrase "pool of financing," the concept that investment projects are financed out of a pool of funds rather than out of bonds, preferred stock, and common stock individually. A weighted average cost of capital is thus used in analyses evaluating the return on investment projects. *See also* COST OF CAPITAL.
Industry: joining of companies to improve profits by reducing competition. Such poolings are generally outlawed in the United States by various ANTI-TRUST LAWS.
Insurance: association of insurers who share premiums and losses in order to spread risk and give small insurers an opportunity to compete with larger ones.

Investments:
1. combination of resources for a common purpose or benefit. For example, an INVESTMENT CLUB pools the funds of its members, giving them the opportunity to share in a PORTFOLIO offering greater diversification and the hope of a better return on their money than they could get individually. A *commodities pool* entrusts the funds of many investors to a trading professional and distributes profits and losses among participants in proportion to their interests.
2. group of investors joined together to use their combined power to manipulate security or commodity prices or to obtain control of a corporation. Such pools are outlawed by regulations governing securities and commodities trading.

See also MORTGAGE POOL.

POOLING OF INTERESTS accounting method used prior to June 30, 2001 in the combining or merging of companies following an acquisition, whereby the balance sheets (assets and liabilities) of the two companies were simply added together, item by item. This tax-free method contrasts with the PURCHASE ACQUISITION method, in which the buying company treats the acquired company as an investment and any PREMIUM paid over the FAIR MARKET VALUE of the assets is reflected on the buyer's balance sheet as GOODWILL. Because reported earnings are higher under the pooling of interests method, most companies preferred it to the purchase acquisition method, particularly when the amount of goodwill is sizable.

The pooling of interests accounting method was eliminated by actions of the Financial ACCOUNTING STANDARDS BOARD (FASB) on July 5, 2001. Statement 141 requires that the purchase method of accounting be used for all business combinations initiated after June 30, 2001. Statement 142 changed the accounting for goodwill from an amortization method to an impairment only approach. Thus, amortization of goodwill, including goodwill recorded in past business combinations, ceased upon adoption of that statement, which for companies on a calendar year basis was January 1, 2002. See also MERGER.

POOP AND SCOOP illegal scheme whereby unfavorable information about a stock is circulated, usually on the Internet, to drive down its price so it can be bought cheaply and later converted into a profit. In earlier years, BEAR RAIDS did essentially the same thing using SELLING SHORT instead of, or along with, negative publicity to drive down prices. The opposite of poop and scoop is *pump and dump*, a practice that had its pre-Internet counterparts in the BOILER ROOM and BUCKET SHOP.

PORCUPINE PROVISIONS see SHARK REPELLENTS.

PORTABILITY ability of employees to retain benefits from one employer to the next when switching jobs. The term is most frequently used in connection with pension and insurance coverage. Credits earned toward pension benefits in a DEFINED BENEFIT PENSION PLAN are rarely portable from one company to another. Conversely, accumulated assets in a DEFINED CONTRIBUTION PENSION PLAN may be transferable to the defined contribution plan of another employer through a rollover. Under the CONSOLIDATED OMNIBUS BUDGET RECONCILIATION ACT (COBRA), employees have the right to carry their group health insurance coverage with them to a new job for up to 18 months. An employee may wish to do so if the new employer's health plan is inferior to the previous employer's plan. Employees choosing to continue coverage with a previous employer's group plan under the COBRA provision pay the full premium, which is subject to change. Generally, this continued coverage costs considerably less than a policy at individual rates.

PORTFOLIO combined holding of more than one stock, bond, commodity, real estate investment, CASH EQUIVALENT, or other asset by an individual or institutional investor. The purpose of a portfolio is to reduce risk by diversification. *See also* PORTFOLIO BETA SCORE; PORTFOLIO THEORY.

PORTFOLIO BETA SCORE relative VOLATILITY of an individual securities portfolio, taken as a whole, as measured by BETA. Beta measures volatility relative to the market as a whole, as represented by an index such as Standard & Poor's 500 Stock Index. A beta of 1 means the stock or stock portfolio has about the same volatility as the market.

PORTFOLIO DEDICATION matching the returns on an investment portfolio with estimated liabilities. Related usually to a pension fund or insurance company portfolio. *See also* MATCHED MATURITIES.

PORTFOLIO DEPOSITARY RECEIPT one of two broad categories of EXCHANGE-TRADED FUNDS, based on four widely used indices: SPDRS, based on Standard & Poor's 500 Composite Stock Price Index; MidCap SPDRs, based on the S&P MidCap 400 Index; the Nasdaq-100 Index Tracking Stock SM; and DIAMONDS, based on the Dow Jones Industrial Averages. *See also* EXCHANGE-TRADED FUNDS; INDEX SHARES.

PORTFOLIO INCOME *see* INVESTMENT INCOME.

PORTFOLIO INSURANCE the use, by a PORTFOLIO MANAGER, of STOCK INDEX FUTURES to protect stock portfolios against market declines. Instead of selling actual stocks as they lose value, managers sell the index futures; if the drop continues, they repurchase the futures at a lower price, using the profit to offset losses in the stock portfolio. The inability of the markets on BLACK MONDAY to process such massive quantities of stock efficiently and the subsequent instituting of CIRCUIT BREAKERS all but eliminated portfolio insurance. *See also* PROGRAM TRADING.

PORTFOLIO MANAGER professional responsible for the securities PORTFOLIO of an individual or INSTITUTIONAL INVESTOR. Also called a *money manager* or, especially when personalized service is involved, an INVESTMENT COUNSEL. A portfolio manager may work for a mutual fund, pension fund, profit-sharing plan, bank trust department, or insurance company. In return for a fee, the manager has the fiduciary responsibility to manage the assets prudently and choose whether stocks, bonds, CASH EQUIVALENTS, real estate, or some other assets present the best opportunities for profit at any particular time. *See also* PORTFOLIO THEORY; PRUDENT-MAN RULE; SEPARATELY MANAGED ACCOUNTS.

PORTFOLIO THEORY more formally termed *modern portfolio theory* (MPT), a sophisticated investment decision approach that permits an investor to classify, estimate, and control both the kind and the amount of expected risk and return; also called *portfolio management theory*. Essential to portfolio theory are its quantification of the relationship between risk and return and the assumption that investors must be compensated for assuming risk. Portfolio theory departs from traditional security analysis in shifting emphasis from analyzing the characteristics of individual investments to determining the statistical relationships among the individual securities that comprise the overall portfolio. The portfolio theory approach has four basic steps: *security valuation*—describing a universe of assets in terms of expected return and expected risk; *asset allocation decision*—determining how assets are to be distributed among classes of investment, such as stocks or bonds; *portfolio optimization*—reconciling risk and return in selecting the securities to be included, such as determining which portfolio of stocks offers the best return for a given level of expected risk; and *performance measurement*— dividing each stock's performance (risk) into market-related (systematic) and industry/security-related (residual) classifications.

POSITION
Banking: bank's net balance in a foreign currency.
Finance: firm's financial condition.
Investments:
1. investor's stake in a particular security or market. A LONG POSITION equals the number of shares *owned;* a SHORT POSITION equals the number of shares *owed* by a dealer or an individual. The dealer's long positions are called his *inventory of securities.*
2. Used as a verb, to take on a long or a short position in a stock.

POSITION BUILDING process of buying shares to accumulate a LONG POSITION or of selling shares to accumulate a SHORT POSITION. Large institutional investors who want to build a large position in a particular security do so over time to avoid pushing up the price of the security.

POSITION LIMIT
Commodities trading: number of contracts that can be acquired in a specific commodity before a speculator is classified as a "large trader." Large traders are subject to special oversight by the COMMODITY FUTURES TRADING COMMISSION (CFTC) and the exchanges and are limited as to the number of contracts they can add to their positions. The position limit varies with the type of commodity.
Options trading: maximum number of exchange-listed OPTION contracts that can be owned or controlled by an individual holder, or by a group of holders acting jointly, in the same underlying security. The current limit is 2,000 contracts on the same side of the market (for example, long calls and short puts are one side of the market); the limit applies to all expiration dates.

POSITION TRADER commodities trader who takes a long-term approach— six months to a year or more—to the market. Usually possessing more than average experience, information, and capital, these traders ride through the ups and downs of price fluctuations until close to the delivery date, unless drastic adverse developments threaten. More like insurance underwriters than gamblers, they hope to achieve long-term profits from calculated risks as distinguished from pure speculation.

POSITIVE CARRY situation in which the cost of money borrowed to finance securities is lower than the yield on the securities. For example, if a fixed-income bond yielding 10% is purchased with a loan bearing 8% interest, the bond has positive carry. The opposite situation is called NEGATIVE CARRY.

POSITIVE YIELD CURVE situation in which interest rates are higher on long-term debt securities than on short-term debt securities of the same quality. For example, a positive yield curve exists when 20-year Treasury bonds yield 10% and 3-month Treasury bills yield 6%. Such a situation is common, since an investor who ties up his money for a longer time is taking more risk and is usually compensated by a higher yield. When short-term interest rates rise above long-term rates, there is called an INVERTED YIELD CURVE.

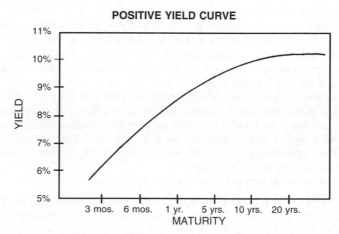

POSITIVE YIELD CURVE

POST

Accounting: to transfer from a journal of original entry detailed financial data, in the chronological order in which it was generated, into a ledger book. Banks post checking account deposits and withdrawals in a ledger, then summarize these transactions on the monthly bank statement.

Investments: horseshoe-shaped structure on the floor of the New York Stock Exchange where specialists trade specific securities. Video screens surround the post, displaying the bid and offer prices available for stocks traded at that location. Also called *trading post.*

POSTDATED CHECK check dated in the future. It is not negotiable until the date becomes current.

POSTING in bookkeeping terminology, the transfer of data from a journal to a ledger.

POSTPONING INCOME technique to delay receipt of income into a later year to reduce current tax liability. For example, if it seems likely that Congress or the state legislature may reduce income tax rates in the upcoming year, it may be advantageous to receive income in that year instead of in the current year when tax rates are higher. Salespeople can appeal to their managers to pay their commissions in the next year, and small business owners can send invoices after the first of the year so that they are paid in the next year. In addition to qualifying for a lower tax rate, the full tax on the income may be delayed until April 15 of the following year, unless the taxpayer receiving the income is required to file quarterly estimated tax payments. *See also* MANAGED EARNINGS.

POT securities underwriting term meaning the portion of a stock or bond issue returned to the MANAGING UNDERWRITER by the participating investment bankers to facilitate sales to INSTITUTIONAL INVESTORS. Institutions buying from the pot designate the firms to be credited with pot sales. *See also* RETENTION.

POT IS CLEAN MANAGING UNDERWRITER'S announcement to members of the underwriting group that the POT—the portion of the stock or bond issue withheld to facilitate institutional sales—has been sold.

POWER OF ATTORNEY

In general: written document that authorizes a particular person to perform certain acts on behalf of the one signing the document. The document, which must be witnessed by a notary public or some other public officer, may bestow either *full power of attorney* or *limited power of attorney.* It becomes void upon the death of the signer.

Investments: *full power of attorney* might, for instance, allow assets to be moved from one brokerage or bank account to another. A *limited power of attorney,* on the other hand, would only permit transactions within an existing account. A broker given a limited power of attorney, for instance, may buy and sell securities in an account but may not remove them. Such an account is called a DISCRETIONARY ACCOUNT.

See also DISCRETIONARY ORDER; PROXY; STOCK POWER.

PRAGUE STOCK EXCHANGE the main securities market in the Czech Republic and the second largest in Central and Eastern Europe. It was formed in November 1992 and began trading seven securities in April 1993. The exchange has two basic trading systems: SPAD for big and medium investors and trading modules auction, and continual for small investors. In May 2004 the U.S. Securities and Exchange Commission granted the exchange the status of a "designated offshore securities market" and included it on the list of offshore exchanges reliable for investors. *www.pse.cz.*

PREARRANGED TRADING questionable and probably fraudulent practice whereby commodities dealers arrange risk-free trades at predetermined prices, usually to gain tax advantages.

PREAUTHORIZED PAYMENT prearranged deductions from a bank account for the payment of a third party.

PRECEDENCE priority of one order over another on the floor of the exchanges, according to rules designed to protect the DOUBLE-AUCTION SYSTEM. The rules basically are that the highest bid and lowest offer have precedence over other bids and offers, that the first bid or first offer at a price has priority over other bids or offers at that price, and that the size of the order determines precedence thereafter, large orders having priority over smaller orders. Where two orders of equal size must compete for the same limited quantity after the first bid is filled, the impasse is resolved by a flip of the coin. *See also* MATCHED AND LOST. Exchange rules also require that public orders have precedence over trades for floor members' own accounts. *See also* OFF-FLOOR ORDER; ON-FLOOR ORDER.

PRECIOUS METALS gold, silver, platinum, and palladium. These metals are valued for their intrinsic value, backing world currencies, as well as their industrial applications. Fundamental issues of supply and demand are important factors in their prices, along with political and economic considerations, especially when producing countries are involved. Inflation fears will stimulate gold accumulation and higher prices, as will war and natural disaster, especially in major producing or consuming countries or regions. Precious metals are held by central banks and are considered a storehouse of value. While gold is often singled out, cultural factors assign different levels of significance to the metals. In the Far East, especially Japan, platinum traditionally is held in higher regard than gold, both in terms of physical metal and investment holdings, and for personal accumulation (e.g., jewelry and coins). Gold is favored in the West. In India and the Middle East, silver is highly prized, and the dowries of Indian women are replete with silver jewelry and coins. Investors can buy physical metal in bars, BULLION and NUMISMATIC COINS, and jewelry. There are numerous investment vehicles that do not involve physical delivery: futures and options contracts, mining company stocks, bonds, mutual funds, commodity indices, and commodity funds. The values of these investment vehicles are influenced by metal price volatility, with commodity funds and indices, and futures and options, more sensitive to daily price swings. Many metals analysts and advisors recommend that 5% to 15% of investor portfolios be held in some form of precious metals as a long-term hedge against inflation and political turmoil.

PRECOMPUTE in installment lending, methods of charging interest whereby the total amount of annual interest either is deducted from the face amount of the loan at the time the loan proceeds are disbursed or is added to the total amount to be repaid in equal installments. In both cases, the EFFECTIVE RATE to the borrower is higher than the stated annual rate used in the computation. "Truth in lending" laws require that the effective annual rate be expressed in SIMPLE INTEREST terms.

PREEMPTIVE RIGHT right giving existing stockholders the opportunity to purchase shares of a NEW ISSUE before it is offered to others. Its purpose is to protect shareholders from dilution of value and control when new shares are issued. Although 48 U.S. states have preemptive right statutes, most states also either permit corporations to pay stockholders to waive their preemptive rights or state in their statutes that the preemptive right is valid only if set forth in the corporate charter. As a result, preemptive rights are the exception rather than the rule. Where they do exist, the usual procedure is for each existing stockholder to receive, prior to a new issue, a SUBSCRIPTION WARRANT indicating how many new shares the holder is entitled to buy—normally, a proportion of the shares he or she already holds. Since the new shares would typically be priced below the market, a financial incentive exists to exercise the preemptive right. *See also* SUBSCRIPTION RIGHT.

PREFERENCE ITEM *see* TAX PREFERENCE ITEM.

PREFERENCE SHARES *see* PRIOR-PREFERRED STOCK.

PREFERRED DIVIDEND COVERAGE net income after interest and taxes (but before common stock dividends) divided by the dollar amount of preferred stock dividends. The result tells how many times over the preferred dividend requirement is covered by current earnings.

PREFERRED EQUITY TRADED BONDS (PETS) corporate bonds or bond-backed preferred shares that trade on exchanges like stocks in small lots, typically $25. They have the safety of bonds (90% are AAA or AA rated) with higher yields, and dividends/interest payments are typically monthly or quarterly, which tends to keep market prices stable. They are known by a variety of proprietary acronyms such as QUIBS (Morgan Stanley) and PINES (Smith Barney).

PREFERRED ORDINARY SHARES *see* ORDINARY SHARES.

PREFERRED STOCK class of CAPITAL STOCK that pays dividends at a specified rate and that has preference over common stock in the payment of dividends and the liquidation of assets. Preferred stock does not ordinarily carry voting rights.

Most preferred stock is *cumulative;* if dividends are passed (not paid for any reason), they accumulate and must be paid before common dividends. A PASSED DIVIDEND on *noncumulative preferred* stock is generally gone forever. PARTICIPATING PREFERRED STOCK entitles its holders to share in profits above and beyond the declared dividend, along with common shareholders, as distinguished from *nonparticipating preferred,* which is limited to the stipulated dividend. *Adjustable-rate preferred* stock pays a dividend that is adjustable, usually quarterly, based on changes in the Treasury bill rate or other money market rates. *Convertible preferred stock* is exchangeable for a given number of common shares and thus tends to be more VOLATILE than *nonconvertible preferred,* which behaves more like a fixed-income bond. *See also* CONVERTIBLE; CUMULATIVE PREFERRED; INCOME PREFERRED SECURITIES; PARTICIPATING PREFERRED; PIK (PAYMENT-IN-KIND) SECURITIES; PRIOR, PREFERRED STOCK.

PREFERRED STOCK RATIO PREFERRED STOCK at PAR value divided by total CAPITALIZATION; the result is the percentage of capitalization—bonds and net worth—represented by preferred stock.

PRELIMINARY PROSPECTUS first document released by an underwriter of a NEW ISSUE to prospective investors. The document offers financial details about the issue but does not contain all the information that will appear in the final or statutory prospectus, and parts of the document may be changed before the final prospectus is issued. Because portions of the cover page of the preliminary prospectus are printed in red ink, it is popularly called the *red herring.*

PREMIUM
In general: extra payment usually made as an incentive.
Bonds:
1. amount by which a bond sells above its face (PAR) value. For instance, a bond with a face value of $1,000 would sell for a $100 premium when it cost $1,100. The same meaning also applies to preferred stock. *See also* PREMIUM BOND; PREMIUM OVER BOND VALUE; PREMIUM OVER CONVERSION VALUE.
2. amount by which the REDEMPTION PRICE to the issuer exceeds the face value when a bond is called. *See also* CALL PREMIUM.
Closed-end and exchange-traded funds: amount by which the fund's share value exceeds net asset value.
Insurance: fee paid to an insurance company for insurance protection. Also, the single or multiple payments made to build an ANNUITY fund.
Options: price a put or call buyer must pay to a put or call seller (writer) for an option contract. The premium is determined by market supply and demand forces. *See also* OPTION; PREMIUM INCOME.

Stocks:

1. charge occasionally paid by a short seller when stock is borrowed to make delivery on a SHORT SALE.
2. amount by which a stock's price exceeds that of other stocks to which it is comparable. For instance, securities analysts might say that XYZ Foods is selling at a 15% premium to other food company stocks—an indication that the stock is more highly valued by investors than its industry peers. It does not necessarily mean that the stock is overpriced, however. Indeed, it may indicate that the investment public has only begun to recognize the stock's market potential and that the price will continue to rise. Similarly, analysts might say that the food industry is selling for a 20% premium to Standard & Poor's 500 index, indicating the relative price strength of the industry group to the stock market as a whole.
3. in new issues, amount by which the trading price of the shares exceeds the OFFERING PRICE.
4. amount over market value paid in an acquisition or promised in a *tender offer. See also* PREMIUM RAID.

PREMIUM BOND bond with a selling price above face or redemption value. A bond with a face value of $1,000, for instance, would be called a premium bond if it sold for $1,050. This price does not include any ACCRUED INTEREST due when the bond is bought. When a premium bond is called before scheduled maturity, bondholders are usually paid more than face value, though the amount may be less than the bond is selling for at the time of the CALL.

PREMIUM INCOME income received by an investor who sells a PUT OPTION or a CALL OPTION. An investor collects premium income by writing a COVERED OPTION, if he or she owns the underlying stock, or a NAKED OPTION, if he or she does not own the stock. An investor who sells options to collect premium income hopes that the underlying stock will not rise very much (in the case of a call) or fall very much (in the case of a put)

PREMIUM OVER BOND VALUE upward difference between the market value of a CONVERTIBLE bond and the price at which a straight bond of the same company would sell in the same open market. A convertible bond, eventually convertible to common stock, will normally sell at a PREMIUM over its bond value because investors place a value on the conversion feature. The higher the market price of the issuer's stock is relative to the price at which the bond is convertible, the greater the premium will be, reflecting the investor's tendency to view it more as a stock than as a bond. When the stock price falls near or below the conversion price, investors then tend to view the convertible as a bond and the premium narrows or even disappears. Other factors affecting the prices of convertible bonds generally include lower transaction costs on the convertibles than would be incurred in buying the stock outright, an attraction that exerts some upward pressure on the premium; the demand from life insurance companies and other institutional investors that are limited by law as to the common stock investments they can have and that gain their equity participation through convertibles; the duration period of the option to convert—the longer it is, the more valuable the future and the higher the premium; high dividends on the issuer's common stock, a factor increasing demand for the common versus the convertible, and therefore a downward pressure. *See also* PREMIUM OVER CONVERSION VALUE.

PREMIUM OVER CONVERSION VALUE amount by which the MARKET PRICE of a CONVERTIBLE preferred stock or convertible bond exceeds the price at which it is convertible. Convertibles (CVs) usually sell at a PREMIUM for two basic reasons: (1) if the convertible is a bond, the bond value—defined as the price at which a straight bond of the same company would sell in the same open market—is the lowest value the CV will reach; it thus represents DOWN-SIDE RISK protection, which is given a value in the marketplace, generally varying with the VOLATILITY of the common stock; (2) the conversion privilege is given a value by investors because they might find it profitable eventually to convert the securities.

At relatively high common-stock price levels, a convertible tends to sell for its common stock equivalent and the conversion value becomes negligible. This occurs because investors are viewing the security as a common stock, not as a bond, and because conversion would be preferable to redemption if the bond were called. On the other hand, when the market value of the convertible is close to its bond value, the conversion feature has little value and the security is valued more as a bond. It is here that the CONVER-SION PREMIUM is highest. The conversion premium is also influenced to some extent by transaction costs, insurance company investment restrictions, the duration of the conversion OPTION, and the size of common dividends. *See also* PREMIUM OVER BOND VALUE.

PREMIUM RAID surprise attempt to acquire a position in a company's stock by offering holders an amount—or premium—over the market value of their shares. The term *raid* assumes that the motive is control and not simply investment. Attempts to acquire control are regulated by federal laws that require disclosure of the intentions of those seeking shares. *See also* TENDER OFFER; WILLIAMS ACT.

PRENUPTIAL CONTRACT agreement between a future husband and wife that details how the couple's financial affairs are to be handled both during the marriage and in the event of divorce. The agreement may cover insurance protection, ownership of housing and securities, and inheritance rights. Such contracts may not be accepted in a court of law.

PREPACKAGED BANKRUPTCY a Chapter 11 BANKRUPTCY in which the terms of reorganization are agreed upon by creditors and owners prior to filing.

PREPAID INTEREST asset account representing interest paid in advance. The interest is expensed, that is, charged to the borrower's profit and loss statement (P & L), as it is earned by the lender. Synonymous with UNEARNED INTEREST, which is the preferred term when DISCOUNT is involved.

PREPAYMENT
In general: paying a debt obligation before it comes due.
Accounting: expenditure for a future benefit, which is recorded in a BALANCE SHEET asset account called a DEFERRED CHARGE, then written off in the period when the benefit is enjoyed. For example, prepaid rent is first recorded as an asset, then charged to expense as the rent becomes due on a monthly basis.
Banking: paying a loan before maturity. Some loans (particularly mortgages) have a prepayment clause that allows prepayment at any time without penalty, while others charge a fee if a loan is paid off before due.

Installment credit: making payments before they are due. *See also* RULE OF THE 78s.

Securities: paying a seller for a security before the settlement date.

Taxes: prepaying taxes, for example, to have the benefit of deducting state and local taxes from one's federal income tax return in the current calendar year rather than in the next year.

PREPAYMENT PENALTY fee paid by a borrower to a bank when a loan or mortgage that does not have a prepayment clause is repaid before its scheduled maturity. Prepayment penalties are prohibited in many states, and by FANNIE MAE and FREDDIE MAC. Also called *prepayment fee.*

PREREFUNDING procedure, called a *pre-re* on Wall Street, in which a bond issuer floats a second bond in order to pay off the first bond at the first CALL date. The proceeds from the sale of the second bond are safely invested, usually in Treasury securities, that will mature at the first call date of the first bond issue. Those first bonds are said to be prerefunded after this operation has taken place. Bond issuers prerefund bonds during periods of lower interest rates in order to lower their interest costs. *See also* ADVANCE REFUNDING; REFUNDING; REFUNDING ESCROW DEPOSITS (REDS).

PRESALE ORDER order to purchase part of a new MUNICIPAL BOND issue that is accepted by an underwriting SYNDICATE MANAGER before an announcement of the price or COUPON rate and before the official PUBLIC OFFERING. Municipals are exempt from registration requirements and other rules of the Securities and Exchange Commission, which forbids preoffering sales of corporate bond issues. *See also* PRESOLD ISSUE.

PRESENT VALUE value today of a future payment, or stream of payments, discounted at some appropriate compound interest or discount—rate. For example, the present value of $100 to be received 10 years from now is about $38.55, using a discount rate equal to 10% interest compounded annually.

The present value method, also called the DISCOUNTED CASH FLOW method, is widely used in corporate finance to measure the return on a CAPITAL INVESTMENT project. In security investments, the method is used to determine how much money should be invested today to result in a certain sum at a future time. Present value calculations are facilitated by present value tables, which are compound interest tables in reverse. Also called *time value of money.*

PRESIDENT highest-ranking officer in a corporation after the CHAIRMAN OF THE BOARD, unless the title CHIEF EXECUTIVE OFFICER (CEO) is used, in which case the president can outrank the chairman. The president is appointed by the BOARD OF DIRECTORS and usually reports directly to the board. In smaller companies the president is usually the CEO, having authority over all other officers in matters of day-to-day management and policy decision-making. In large corporations the CEO title is frequently held by the chairman of the board, leaving the president as CHIEF OPERATING OFFICER, responsible for personnel and administration on a daily basis.

PRESIDENTIAL ELECTION CYCLE THEORY hypothesis of investment advisers that major stock market moves can be predicted based on the four-year presidential election cycle. According to this theory, stocks decline soon after a president is elected, as the chief executive takes the harsh and unpopular steps necessary to bring inflation, government spending, and deficits under control. During the next two years or so, taxes may be raised and the economy may slip into a recession. About midway into the four-year cycle, stocks should start to rise in anticipation of the economic recovery that the incumbent president wants to be roaring at full steam by election day. The cycle then repeats itself with the election of a new president or the reelection of an incumbent.

PRESOLD ISSUE issue of MUNICIPAL BONDS or government bonds that is completely sold out before the price or yield is publicly announced. Corporate bond issues, which must be offered to the public with a Securities and Exchange Commission registration statement, cannot legally be presold. *See also* PRESALE ORDER.

PRETAX EARNINGS OR PROFITS NET INCOME (earnings or profits) before federal income taxes.

PRETAX RATE OF RETURN yield or capital gain on a particular security before taking into account an individual's tax situation. *See also* RATE OF RETURN.

PREVIOUS BALANCE METHOD method of charging credit card interest that uses the outstanding balance at the end of the previous month as the basis for the current month's interest computation. *See also* ADJUSTED BALANCE METHOD.

PRICE/BOOK RATIO ratio of a stock's price to its BOOK VALUE per share. This number is used by SECURITIES ANALYSTS and MONEY MANAGERS to judge whether a stock is undervalued or overvalued. A stock selling at a high price/book ratio, such as 3 or higher, may represent a popular GROWTH STOCK with minimal book value. A stock selling below its book value may attract value-oriented investors who think that the company's management may undertake steps, such as selling assets or restructuring the company, to unlock the hidden value on the company's BALANCE SHEET.

PRICE CHANGE net rise or fall of the price of a security at the close of a trading session, compared to the previous session's CLOSING PRICE. A stock that rose $2 in a day would have a +2 after its final price in the newspaper stock listings. A stock that fell $2 would have a –2. The average of the price changes for groups of securities, in indicators such as the Dow Jones Industrial Average and Standard & Poor's 500 Stock Index, is calculated by taking into account all the price changes in the components of the average or index.

PRICE DISCOVERY free market process by which an illiquid asset eventually attracts a buyer and discovers what price it will fetch.

PRICE/EARNINGS RATIO (P/E) price of a stock divided by its basic earnings per share. The P/E ratio may either use the reported earnings from the latest year (called a *trailing P/E*) or employ an analyst's forecast of next year's earnings (called a *forward P/E*). The trailing P/E is listed along with a stock's price and trading activity in the daily newspapers. For instance, a stock selling for $20 a share that earned $1 last year has a trailing P/E of 20. If the same stock has projected earnings of $2 next year, it will have a forward P/E of 10.

The price/earnings ratio, also known as the *multiple,* gives investors an idea of how much they are paying for a company's earning power. The higher the P/E, the more investors are paying, and therefore the more earnings growth they are expecting. High P/E stocks—those with multiples over 20— are typically young, fast-growing companies. They are far riskier to trade than low P/E stocks, since it is easier to miss high-growth expectations than low-growth predictions. Low P/E stocks tend to be in low-growth or mature industries, in stock groups that have fallen out of favor, or in old, established, BLUE-CHIP companies with long records of earnings stability and regular dividends. In general, low P/E stocks have higher yields than high P/E stocks, which often pay no dividends at all.

PRICE GAP term used when a stock's price either jumps or plummets from its last trading range without overlapping that trading range. For instance, a stock might shoot up from a closing price of $20 a share, marking the high point of an $18–$20 trading range for that day, and begin trading in a $22–$24 range the next day on the news of a takeover bid. Or a company that reports lower than expected earnings might drop from the $18–$20 range to the $13–$15 range without ever trading at intervening prices. Price gaps are considered significant movements by technical analysts, who note them on charts, because such gaps are often indications of an OVERBOUGHT or OVERSOLD position.

PRICE INDEXES indices that track levels of prices and rates of inflation. The two most common price indexes published by the government are the CONSUMER PRICE INDEX (CPI) and the PRODUCER PRICE INDEX (PPI).

PRICE LEADERSHIP establishment of a price by a leading producer of a product that becomes the price adopted by other producers.

PRICE LIMIT *see* LIMIT PRICE.

PRICE RANGE high/low range in which a stock has traded over a particular period of time. In the daily newspaper, a stock's 52-week price range is given. In most companies' annual reports, a stock's price range is shown for the FISCAL YEAR.

PRICE/SALES RATIO ratio of a stock's price to its per-share sales. This ratio is used by financial analysts to gauge whether a stock's current market price is expensive or cheap. Some analysts maintain that investors consistently buying stocks with low price/sales ratios will outperform those buying stocks with low price/book value, price/cash flow, or PRICE/EARNINGS RATIOS. Advocates of P/S ratio analysis say it works because it relates the popularity of a company's stock to the size of its business. Since sales are more difficult to manipulate than earnings, P/S ratios are less subject to accounting gimmickry. Sales are typically less volatile than earnings or cash flow, so P/S ratios work particularly well on companies that stumble temporarily. When profits decline, a stock's price/earnings ratio may increase, but the impact on the P/S ratio is usually dominated by the stock's price. Value investors will use this fact to identify good values among stocks with high P/E but low P/S ratios. Price/sales ratios vary widely among different industries. For instance, the P/S ratio of a retailer is usually much lower than the ratio of a high-technology company.

PRICE SPREAD OPTIONS strategy in which an investor simultaneously buys and sells two options covering the same security, with the same expiration months, but with different exercise prices. For example, an investor might buy an XYZ May 100 call and sell an XYZ May 90 call.

PRICE SUPPORT government-set price floor designed to aid farmers or other producers of goods. For instance, the government sets a minimum price for sugar that it guarantees to sugar growers. If the market price drops below that level, the government makes up the difference. *See also* PARITY PRICE.

PRICE-TO-CASH FLOW RATIO market capitalization divided by net earnings plus noncash charges, or market price per share divided by cash flow (earnings plus noncash charges) per share. (Both calculations yield the same ratio). Dividends are paid out of cash flow, not earnings.

PRICE-WEIGHTED INDEX index in which component stocks are weighted by their price. Higher-priced stocks therefore have a greater percentage impact on the index than lower-priced stocks. In recent years, the trend of using price-weighted indexes has given way to the use of MARKET-VALUE WEIGHTED INDEXES. The Dow Jones Industrial Average remains the most prominent example of a PRICE-WEIGHTED INDEX, although, strictly speaking, it is an average as distinguished from an index.

PRICEY term used of an unrealistically low bid price or unrealistically high offer price. If a stock is trading at $15, a pricey bid might be $10 a share, and a pricey offer $20 a share.

PRIMARY DEALER one of the three dozen or so banks and investment dealers authorized to buy and sell government securities in direct dealings with the FEDERAL RESERVE BANK of New York in its execution of Fed OPEN MARKET OPERATIONS. Such dealers must be qualified in terms of reputation, capacity, and adequacy of staff and facilities.

PRIMARY DISTRIBUTION sale of a new issue of stocks or bonds, as distinguished from a SECONDARY DISTRIBUTION, which involves previously issued stock. All issuances of bonds are primary distributions. Also called *primary offering,* but not to be confused with *initial public offering,* which refers to a corporation's *first* distribution of stock to the public.

PRIMARY EARNINGS PER (COMMON) SHARE earnings available to common stock (which is usually net earnings after taxes and preferred dividends) divided by the number of common shares outstanding. This figure, called *basic earnings per share* after 1998, contrasts with earnings per share after DILUTION, which assumes warrants, rights, and options have been exercised and convertibles have been converted. *See also* CONVERTIBLE; EARNINGS PER SHARE; FULLY DILUTED EARNINGS PER (COMMON) SHARE; SUBSCRIPTION WARRANT.

PRIMARY MARKET market for new issues of securities, as distinguished from the SECONDARY MARKET, where previously issued securities are bought and sold. A market is primary if the proceeds of sales go to the issuer of the securities sold. The term also applies to government securities auctions and to opening option and futures contract sales.

PRIME
Banking: PRIME RATE.
Investments: acronym for Prescribed Right to Income and Maximum Equity. PRIME was a UNIT INVESTMENT TRUST, sponsored by the Americus Share-

owner Service Corporation, which separated the income portion of a stock from its appreciation potential. The income-producing portion, called PRIME, and the appreciation potential, called SCORE (an acronym for Special Claim on Residual Equity) together made up a unit share investment trust, known by the acronym USIT. Both PRIME and SCORE were traded on the American Stock Exchange.

The first version of this unit came into existence with American Telephone and Telegraph stock in late 1983, as AT&T was under-going divestiture. PRIME units entitled their holders to the dividend income that a holder of one common share of the old AT&T would have gotten plus a proportionate share of the dividends of the seven regional operating companies split off from AT&T. PRIME holders also received all price APPRECIATION in the stock up to the equivalent of $75 a share. The trusts expired in 1988. SCORE holders received all appreciation over $75, but no dividend income.

This form of unit trust allows investors who want income from a stock to maximize that income, and investors who want capital gains to have increased leverage in achieving those gains. *See also* CAPITAL GAIN.

PRIME PAPER highest quality COMMERCIAL PAPER, as rated by Moody's Investor's Service and other rating agencies. Prime paper is considered INVESTMENT GRADE, and therefore institutions with FIDUCIARY responsibility can invest in it. Moody's has three ratings of prime paper:
P-1: Highest quality
P-2: Higher quality
P-3: High quality
Commercial paper below P-3 is not considered prime paper.

PRIME RATE base rate that banks use in pricing commercial loans to their best and most creditworthy customers. The rate is determined by the Federal Reserve's decision to raise or lower prevailing interest rates for short-term borrowing. Though some banks charge their best customers more and some less than the official prime rate, the rate tends to become standard across the banking industry when a major bank moves its prime up or down. The rate is a key interest rate, since loans to less-creditworthy customers are often tied to the prime rate. For example, a BLUE CHIP company may borrow at a prime rate of 5%, but a less-well-established small business may borrow from the same bank at prime plus 2, or 7%. Many consumer loans, such as home equity, automobile, mortgage, and credit card loans, are tied to the prime rate. Although the major bank prime rate is the definitive "best rate" reference point, many banks, particularly those in outlying regions, have a two-tier system, whereby smaller companies of top credit standing may borrow at an even lower rate.

PRIME RATE FUND *mutual fund* that buys portions of corporate loans from banks and passes along interest, which is designed to approximate the PRIME RATE, to shareholders, net of load charges and management fees. Although the bank loans are senior obligations and fully collateralized, they are subject to DEFAULT, particularly in recessions. Prime rate funds thus pay 2–3% more than the yield on one-year CERTIFICATES OF DEPOSIT (CDs), and management fees tend to be higher than those of other mutual funds. Another possible disadvantage is limited liquidity; the only way investors can get out is to sell back their shares to the funds once each quarter.

PRINCIPAL
In General:
1. major party to a transaction, acting as either a buyer or a seller. A principal buys and sells for his or her own account and risk.
2. owner of a privately held business.
Banking and Finance:
1. face amount of a debt instrument or deposit on which interest is either owed or earned.
2. balance of a debt, separate from interest. *See also* PRINCIPAL AMOUNT.
Investments: basic amount invested, exclusive of earnings.

PRINCIPAL AMOUNT FACE VALUE of an obligation (such as a bond or a loan) that must be repaid at maturity, as separate from the INTEREST.

PRINCIPAL EXCHANGE-RATED-LINKED SECURITIES (PERLS) *see* PERLS.

PRINCIPAL STOCKHOLDER stockholder who owns a significant number of shares in a corporation. Under Securities and Exchange Commission (SEC) rules, a principal stockholder owns 10% or more of the voting stock of a REGISTERED COMPANY. These stockholders are often on the board of directors and are considered insiders by SEC rules, so that they must report buying and selling transactions in the company's stock. *See also* AFFILIATED PERSON; CONTROL STOCK; INSIDER.

PRINCIPAL SUM
Finance: also used as a synonym for PRINCIPAL, in the sense of the obligation due under a debt instrument exclusive of interest. Synonymous with CORPUS. *See also* TRUST.
Insurance: amount specified as payable to the beneficiary under a policy, such as the death benefit.

PRINT MONEY strictly speaking, to engrave and produce physical currency. Connotatively, it means adding to the supply of money and credit for purposes of monetizing debt or stimulating spending, implicitly leading to inflation or, at worst, hyperinflation. Concept is also called the *quantitative easing*. *See also* MONETARY POLICY.

PRIORITY system used in an AUCTION MARKET, in which the first bid or offer price is executed before other bid and offer prices, even if subsequent orders are larger. Orders originating off the floor *(see* OFF-FLOOR ORDER) of an exchange also have priority over ON-FLOOR ORDERS. *See also* MATCHED AND LOST; PRECEDENCE.

PRIOR-LIEN BOND bond that has precedence over another bond of the same issuing company even though both classes of bonds are equally secured. Such bonds usually arise from REORGANIZATION. *See also* JUNIOR ISSUE.

PRIOR-PREFERRED STOCK PREFERRED STOCK that has a higher claim than other issues of preferred stock on dividends and assets in LIQUIDATION; also known as *preference shares*.

PRIVATE ACTIVITY BOND *see* PRIVATE PURPOSE BOND.

PRIVATE EQUITY FUND limited partnership controlled by a private equity firm that acts as the general partner and that gets specific dollar com-

mitments from QUALIFIED INSTITUTIONAL INVESTORS and individual ACCRED-
ITED INVESTORS. These passive limited partners fund *pro rata* portions of their
commitments when the general partner has identified an appropriate opportunity, which may be venture capital to finance new products and technologies, expanding working capital, making acquisitions, financing leveraged
buyouts (LBOs), and other investments in which the equity is not publicly
traded. A fund will typically make between 15 and 25 separate investments
over a ten-year life, with no single investment exceeding 10% of the total
commitment. Well-known examples of private equity funds are Blackstone
Group and Carlyle Group.

PRIVATE INVESTMENT IN PUBLIC EQUITY SECURITIES (PIPES)
deal, popular in the early 2000s with cash-strapped high-growth, small capitalization tech and telecom companies, in which investors, usually institutions, buy equity-linked securities of a company in a PRIVATE PLACEMENT,
typically at a discount of 5% to 15% from the current market price of the
company's common, with the understanding that the company will promptly
effect REGISTRATION of the security with the SEC. The company affords the
discount because it avoids the time and expense of a public offering and gets
immediate cash. The investor gets the discount and trades-off immediate
liquidity for a short period, typically 90 to 120 days. The initial experience
with PIPES was bad, giving rise to the term DEATH SPIRAL. By the mid-2000s,
with greater TRANSPARENCY and new rules controlling short selling and limiting potential dilution, PIPES experienced a revival. In 2008, 1,283 PIPES
transactions closed, with gross proceeds of $177.3 billion.

PRIVATE LABEL PASS-THROUGH *see* CONVENTIONAL PASS-THROUGH.

PRIVATE LETTER RULING Internal Revenue Service (IRS) response to
a request for interpretation of the tax law with respect to a specific question
or situation. Also called *letter ruling, revenue ruling*.

PRIVATE LIMITED PARTNERSHIP LIMITED PARTNERSHIP not registered
with the Securities and Exchange Commission (SEC) and having a maximum
of 35 limited partners. *See also* ACCREDITED INVESTOR.

PRIVATE MARKET VALUE (PMV) aggregate market value of a company
if each of its parts operated independently and had its own stock price. Also
called *breakup value* or *takeover value*. Analysts look for high PMV in relation to market value to identify bargains and potential TARGET COMPANIES.
PMV differs from LIQUIDATING VALUE, which excludes GOING CONCERN VALUE,
and BOOK VALUE, which is an accounting concept.

PRIVATE MORTGAGE INSURANCE (PMI) type of insurance available
from lenders that insures against loss resulting from a default on a mortgage
loan and can substitute for down payment money.

PRIVATE PLACEMENT sale of stocks, bonds, or other investments directly
to an institutional investor like an insurance company. A PRIVATE LIMITED
PARTNERSHIP is also considered a private placement. A private placement
does not have to be registered with the Securities and Exchange Commission, as a PUBLIC OFFERING does, if the securities are purchased for investment
as opposed to resale. *See also* LETTER SECURITY; PRIVATE INVESTMENT IN PUBLIC
EQUITY SECURITIES (PIPES).

PRIVATE PURPOSE BOND category of MUNICIPAL BOND distinguished from PUBLIC PURPOSE BOND in the TAX REFORM ACT OF 1986 because 10% or more of the bond's benefit goes to private activities or 5% of the proceeds (or $5 million if less) are used for loans to parties other than governmental units. Private purpose obligations, which are also called *private activity bonds* or *nonessential function bonds,* are taxable unless their use is specifically exempted. Even tax-exempt *permitted private activity bonds,* if issued after August 7, 1986, are TAX PREFERENCE ITEMS, except those issued for 501(c)(3) organizations (hospitals, colleges, universities). Private purpose bonds specifically *prohibited* from tax-exemption effective August 15, 1986, include those for sports, trade, and convention facilities and large-issue (over $1 million) INDUSTRIAL DEVELOPMENT BONDS. Permitted issues, except those for 501(c)(3) organizations, airports, docks, wharves, and government-owned solid-waste disposal facilities, are subject to volume caps. *See also* TAXABLE MUNICIPAL BOND.

PRIVATE SECURITIES LITIGATION REFORM ACT OF 1995 (PSLRA) law passed over presidential veto that discourages frivolous class-action lawsuits by disenchanted investors by raising the plead-ing standards for fraud action; introducing proportionate liability for defendants; making disclaimer cautionary language a protection against liability for unintentional errors in forecasting performance; limiting attorneys' fees and liberalizing the related Statute of Limitations; and creating new responsibilities for auditors. Main beneficiaries are syndicators in the high-technology sector, where fast-changing technology makes financial forecasting difficult.

PRIVATIZATION process of converting a publicly operated enterprise into a privately owned and operated entity. For example, many cities and states contract with private companies to run their prison facilities instead of managing them with municipal personnel. Many countries around the world have privatized formerly state-run enterprises such as banks, airlines, steel companies, utilities, phone systems, and large manufacturers. A wave of privatization swept through Russia and Eastern Europe after the fall of Communism in the 1990s, and through some Latin American countries such as Peru, as new, democratic governments were established. When a company is privatized, shares formerly owned by the government, as well as management control, are sold to the public. The theory behind privatization is that these enterprises run far more efficiently and offer better service to customers when owned by stockholders instead of the government.

PROBATE judicial process whereby the will of a deceased person is presented to a court and an EXECUTOR or ADMINISTRATOR is appointed to carry out the will's instructions.

PROCEEDS
1. funds given to a borrower after all costs and fees are deducted.
2. money received by the seller of an asset after commissions are deducted— for example, the amount a stockholder receives from the sale of shares, less broker's commission. *See also* PROCEEDS SALE.

PROCEEDS SALE OVER-THE-COUNTER (OTC) securities sale where the PRO-CEEDS are used to purchase another security. Under the FIVE PERCENT RULE of the FINANCIAL INDUSTRY REGULATORY AUTHORITY (FINRA), such a trade is considered one transaction and the FINRA member's total markup or commission is subject to the 5% guideline.

PRODUCER PRICE INDEX (PPI) measure of change in wholesale prices (formerly called the *wholesale price index),* as released monthly by the U.S. Bureau of Labor Statistics. The index is broken down into components by commodity, industry sector, and stage of processing. The PPI tracks prices of foods, metals, lumber, oil and gas, and many other commodities, but does not measure the price of services. Economists look at trends in the PPI as an accurate precursor to changes in the CPI, since upward or downward pressure on wholesale prices is usually passed through to consumer prices over time. The PPI, published by the Bureau of Labor Statistics in the Department of Labor, is based at 100 in 1982 and is released monthly. Economists also look at the PPI excluding the volatile food and energy components, which they call the "core" PPI. The consumer equivalent of this index is the CONSUMER PRICE INDEX.

PRODUCTION RATE coupon (interest) rate at which a PASS-THROUGH SECURITY guaranteed by the GOVERNMENT NATIONAL MORTGAGE ASSOCIATION (GNMA), popularly known as a Ginnie Mae, is issued. The rate is set a half percentage point under the prevailing Federal Housing Administration (FHA) rate, the maximum rate allowed on residential mortgages insured and guaranteed by the FHA and the Veterans Administration.

PRODUCTIVITY in labor and other areas of economics, the amount of output per unit of input, for example, the quantity of a product produced per hour of labor.

PROFIT

Finance: positive difference that results from selling products and services for more than the cost of producing these goods. *See also* NET PROFIT.

Investments: difference between the selling price and the purchase price of commodities or securities when the selling price is higher.

PROFITABILITY INDEX *see* CAPITAL RATIONING.

PROFIT AND LOSS STATEMENT (P & L) summary of the revenues, costs, and expenses of a company during an accounting period; also called INCOME STATEMENT, *operating statement, statement of profit and loss, income and expense statement.* Together with the BALANCE SHEET as of the end of the accounting period, it constitutes a company's financial statement. *See also* COST OF GOODS SOLD; NET INCOME; NET SALES.

PROFIT CENTER segment of a business organization that is responsible for producing profits on its own. A conglomerate with interests in hotels, food processing, and paper may consider each of these three businesses separate profit centers, for instance.

PROFIT FORECAST prediction of future levels of profitability by analysts following a company, as well as company officials. Investors base their buy and sell decisions on such earnings projections. Stock prices typically reflect analysts' profit expectations—companies expected to produce rapidly growing profits often have high price/earnings ratios. Conversely, projections of meager earnings result in lower P/E ratios. The company will often guide analysts so that their profit forecasts are not too high or too low, preventing unwelcome surprises. Analyst profit forecasts are tracked by the INSTITUTIONAL BROKERS ESTIMATE SYSTEM (I/B/E/S) and ZACKS ESTIMATE SYSTEM.

PROFIT MARGIN *see* MARGIN OF PROFIT.

PROFIT-SHARING PLAN agreement between a corporation and its employees that allows the employees to share in company profits. Annual contributions are made by the company, when it has profits, to a profit-sharing account for each employee, either in cash or in a deferred plan, which may be invested in stocks, bonds, or cash equivalents. The funds in a profit-sharing account generally accumulate tax deferred until the employee retires or leaves the company. Many plans allow employees to borrow against profit-sharing accounts for major expenditures such as purchasing a home or financing children's education. Because corporate profit-sharing plans have custody over billions of dollars, they are major institutional investors in the stock and bond markets.

PROFIT TAKING action by short-term securities or commodities traders to cash in on gains earned on a sharp market rise. Profit taking pushes down prices, but only temporarily; the term implies an upward market trend.

PRO FORMA Latin for "as a matter of form"; refers to a presentation of data, such as a BALANCE SHEET or INCOME STATEMENT, where certain amounts are hypothetical. For example, a pro forma balance sheet might show a debt issue that has been proposed but has not yet been consummated.

PROGRAM TRADING computer-driven buying (*buy program*) or selling (*sell program*) of baskets of 15 or more stocks by *index* ARBITRAGE specialists or institutional traders. "Program" refers to computer programs that constantly monitor stock, futures, and options markets, giving buy and sell signals when opportunities for arbitrage profits occur or when market conditions warrant portfolio accumulation or liquidation transactions. Program trading has been blamed for excessive volatility in the markets, especially on Black Monday in 1987, when PORTFOLIO INSURANCE—the since discredited use of index options and futures to hedge stock portfolios—was an important contributing factor.

PROGRESSIVE TAX income tax system in which those with higher incomes pay taxes at higher rates than those with lower incomes; also called *graduated tax*. The U.S. income tax system is based on the concept of progressivity. There are several tax brackets, based on the taxpayer's income, which determine the tax rate that applies to each taxpayer. *See also* CONSUMPTION TAX; FLAT TAX; REGRESSIVE TAX.

PROGRESS PAYMENTS
1. periodic payments to a supplier, contractor, or subcontractor for work satisfactorily performed to date. Such schedules are provided in contracts and can significantly reduce the amount of WORKING CAPITAL required by the performing party.
2. disbursements by lenders to contractors under construction loan arrangements. As construction progresses, bills and LIEN waivers are presented to the bank or savings and loan, which advances additional funds.

PROJECTED BENEFIT OBLIGATION (PBO) *see* ACCUMULATED BENEFIT OBLIGATION.

PROJECTION estimate of future performance made by economists, corporate planners, and credit and securities analysts with the help of available software. Economists use econometric models to project GROSS DOMESTIC PRODUCT (GDP), inflation, unemployment, and many other economic factors. Corporate financial planners project a company's operating results and CASH FLOW, using historical trends and making assumptions where necessary, in order to make budget decisions and to plan financing. Credit analysts use projections to forecast DEBT SERVICE ability. Securities analysts tend to focus their projections on earnings trends and cash flow per share in order to predict market values and dividend coverage. *See also* ECONOMETRICS.

PROJECT LINK econometric model linking all the economies in the world and forecasting the effects of changes in different economies on other economies. The project is identified with 1980 Nobel Memorial Prize in Economics winner Lawrence R. Klein. *See also* ECONOMETRICS.

PROJECT NOTE short-term debt issue of a municipal agency, usually a housing authority, to finance the construction of public housing. When the housing is finished, the notes are redeemed and the project is financed with long-term bonds. Both project notes and bonds usually pay tax-exempt interest to note- and bondholders, and both are also guaranteed by the U.S. Department of Housing and Urban Development.

PROMISSORY NOTE written promise committing the maker to pay the payee a specified sum of money either on demand or at a fixed or determinable future date, with or without interest. Instruments meeting these criteria are NEGOTIABLE. Often called, simply, a NOTE.

PROPERTY AND EQUIPMENT *see* FIXED ASSET.

PROPERTY INVENTORY personal finance term meaning a list of PERSONAL PROPERTY with cost and market values. A property inventory, which should be accompanied by photographs, is used to substantiate insurance claims and tax losses.

PROPERTY TAX tax assessed on property such as real estate. The tax is determined by several factors, including the use of the land (residential, commercial, or industrial), the assessed valuation of the property, and the tax rate, expressed in MILLS. Property taxes are usually assessed by county and local governments, school districts, and other special authorities such as for water and sewer service. Property taxes are usually deductible on federal income tax returns. If a mortgage lender requires that it pay all property taxes, borrowers must remit their property taxes as part of their monthly mortgage payments and the lender keeps the money in escrow until property taxes are due. *See also* AD VALOREM, PITI.

PROPORTIONAL REPRESENTATION method of stockholder voting, giving individual shareholders more power over the election of directors than they have under statutory voting, which, by allowing one vote per share per director, makes it possible for a majority shareholder to elect all the directors. The most familiar example of proportional representation is cumulative voting, under which a shareholder has as many votes as he has shares of stock, multiplied by the number of vacancies on the board, all of which can be cast for one director. This makes it possible for a minority shareholder or a group of small shareholders to gain at least some representation on the board. Another variety provides for the holders of specified classes of stock to elect a number of directors in certain circumstances.

PROPRIETARY TRADING trading by securities firms using their own, as opposed to client's, funds. Such trading, like hedge funds, involves higher risk and potentially greater returns than would be gained from commissions.

PROPRIETORSHIP unincorporated business owned by a single person and sometimes called a proprietorship. The individual proprietor has the right to all the profits from the business and also has responsibility for all the firm's liabilities. Since proprietors are considered self-employed, they are eligible for Keogh accounts for their retirement funds. *See also* KEOGH PLAN.

PRO RATA Latin for "according to the rate"; a method of proportionate allocation. For example, a pro rata property tax rebate might be divided proportionately (prorated) among taxpayers based on their original assessments, so that each gets the same percentage.

PROSPECTIVE EARNINGS GROWTH RATIO (PEG RATIO) projected one-year annual growth rate, determined by taking the consensus forecast of next year's earnings, less this year's earnings, and dividing the result by this year's earnings (sometimes seen as price-earning growth ratio).

PROSPECTUS formal written offer to sell securities that sets forth the plan for a proposed business enterprise or the facts concerning an existing one that an investor needs to make an informed decision. Prospectuses are also issued by MUTUAL FUNDS, describing the history, background of managers, fund objectives, a financial statement, and other essential data. A prospectus for a PUBLIC OFFERING must be filed with the Securities and Exchange Commission and given to prospective buyers of the offering. The prospectus contains financial information and a description of a company's business history, officers, operations, pending litigation (if any), and plans (including the use of the proceeds from the issue).

Before investors receive the final copy of the prospectus, called the *statutory prospectus,* they may receive a PRELIMINARY PROSPECTUS, commonly called a *red herring.* This document is not complete in all details, though most of the major facts of the offering are usually included. The final prospectus is also called the *offering circular.*

Offerings of limited partnerships are also accompanied by prospectuses. Real estate, oil and gas, equipment leasing, and other types of limited partnerships are described in detail, and pertinent financial information, the background of the general partners, and supporting legal opinions are also given.

PROTECTIONISM practice of protecting domestic goods and service industries from foreign competition with tariff and non-tariff barriers. Protectionism causes higher prices for consumers because domestic producers are not exposed to foreign competition, and can therefore keep prices high. But domestic exporters also may suffer, because foreign countries tend to retaliate against protectionism with tariffs and barriers of their own. Many economists say that the Depression of the 1930s was precipitated by the protectionist trade barriers erected by the United States under the Smoot-Hawley Act, which led to retaliation by many countries throughout the world. In more recent years, many protectionist trade barriers have fallen through the passage of GATT, the General Agreement on Tariffs and Trade, which went into effect in 1995, and the creation of the WORLD TRADE ORGANIZATION (WTO).

PROTECTIVE COVENANT *see* COVENANT.

PROVISION *see* ALLOWANCE.

PROVISIONAL CALL FEATURE provision found in convertible bonds that allows the issuer to call the bond during the period of call protection if the underlying common stock should trade at a specified multiple of the conversion price, called the PROVISIONAL CALL TRIGGER PRICE. A typical provisional call feature might be triggered when the stock trades at 150% of the conversion price for 30 consecutive days.

PROVISIONAL CALL TRIGGER PRICE *see* PROVISIONAL CALL FEATURE.

PROVISIONAL RATING *see* CONDITIONAL RATING.

PROVISION FOR INCOME TAXES item on a company's profit and loss statement (P & L) representing its estimated income tax liability for the year. Although taxes are actually paid according to a timetable determined by the Internal Revenue Service and a certain portion of the liability may be accrued, the provision gives an indication of the company's effective tax rate, which analysts compare to other companies as one measure of effective management and profitability. EARNINGS BEFORE TAXES is the net earnings figure before provision for income taxes.

PROXY
In general: person authorized to act or speak for another.
Business:
1. written POWER OF ATTORNEY given by shareholders of a corporation, authorizing a specific vote on their behalf at corporate meetings. Such proxies normally pertain to election of the BOARD OF DIRECTORS or to various resolutions submitted for shareholders' approval.
2. person authorized to vote on behalf of a stockholder of a corporation.

PROXY FIGHT technique used by an acquiring company to attempt to gain control of a TAKEOVER target. The acquirer tries to persuade the shareholders of the TARGET COMPANY that the present management of the firm should be ousted in favor of a slate of directors favorable to the acquirer. If the shareholders, through their PROXY votes, agree, the acquiring company can gain control of the company without paying a PREMIUM price for the firm.

PROXY STATEMENT information that the Securities and Exchange Commission requires must be provided to shareholders before they vote by proxy on company matters. The statement contains proposed members of the BOARD OF DIRECTORS, inside directors' salaries, and pertinent information regarding their bonus and option plans, as well as any resolutions of minority stockholders and of management.

PRUDENT-MAN RULE standard adopted by some U.S. states to guide those with responsibility for investing the money of others. Such fiduciaries (executors of wills, trustees, bank trust departments, and administrators of estates) must act as a prudent man or woman would be expected to act, with discretion and intelligence, to seek reasonable income, preserve capital, and, in general, avoid speculative investments. States not using the prudent-man system use the LEGAL LIST system, allowing fiduciaries to invest only in a restricted list of securities, called the *legal list.*

PSLRA *see* PRIVATE SECURITIES LITIGATION REFORM ACT OF 1995 (PSLRA).

PUBLIC COMPANY ACCOUNTING OVERSIGHT BOARD (PCAOB) private-sector nonprofit corporation created by the SARBANES-OXLEY ACT OF 2002 to oversee the auditors of public companies in order to protect the interests of investors and further the public interest in the preparation of informative, fair, and independent audit reports.

PUBLIC DEBT borrowings by governments to finance expenditures not covered by current tax revenues. *See also* AGENCY SECURITIES; MUNICIPAL BOND; TREASURIES.

PUBLIC HOUSING AUTHORITY BOND obligation of local public housing agencies, which is centrally marketed through competitive sealed-bid auctions conducted by the U.S. Department of Housing and Urban Development (HUD). These obligations are secured by an agreement between HUD and the local housing agency that provides that the federal government will loan the local authority a sufficient amount of money to pay PRINCIPAL and INTEREST to maturity.

   The proceeds of such bonds provide low-rent housing through new construction, rehabilitation of existing buildings, purchases from private builders or developers, and leasing from private owners. Under special provisions, low income families may also purchase such housing.

   The interest on such bonds is exempt from federal income taxes and may also be exempt from state and local income taxes.

PUBLIC LIMITED PARTNERSHIP real estate, oil and gas, equipment leasing, or other LIMITED PARTNERSHIP that is registered with the Securities and Exchange Commission and offered to the public through registered broker/dealers. Such partnerships may be oriented to producing income or capital gains, or, within PASSIVE income rules, to generating tax advantages for limited partners. The number of investors in such a partnership is limited only by the sponsor's desire to cap the funds raised. A public limited partnership, which does not have an active secondary market, is distinguished from a PRIVATE LIMITED PARTNERSHIP, which is limited to 35 limited partners plus ACCREDITED INVESTORS, and a MASTER LIMITED PARTNERSHIP (MLP) that is publicly traded, often on the major stock exchanges.

PUBLIC, THE term for individual investors, as opposed to professional investors. Wall Street analysts like to deride the public for constantly buying at the top of a bull market and selling at the bottom of a bear market. The public participates in stock and bond markets both by buying individual securities and through intermediaries such as mutual funds and insurance companies. The term *public* is also used to describe a security that is available to be bought and sold by individual investors (as opposed to just large institutions or wealthy people, in which case the offering is a private one). Stocks that offer shares to the public are known as *publicly held*, in contrast to *privately held* concerns in which shares are owned by founders, employees, and a few large investors.

PUBLICLY HELD company with shares outstanding that are held by public investors. A company converts from a privately held firm to a publicly held one through an INITIAL PUBLIC OFFERING (IPO) of stock.

PUBLICLY TRADED PUBLICLY HELD securities that are bought and sold in a public market, such as a stock market.

PUBLIC OFFERING

1. offering to the investment public, after registration requirements of the Securities and Exchange Commission (SEC) have been complied with, of new securities, usually by an investment banker or a syndicate made up of several investment bankers, at a public offering price agreed upon between the issuer and the investment bankers.

Public offering is distinguished from PRIVATE PLACEMENT of new securities, which is subject to different SEC regulations. *See also* REGISTERED NEW ISSUE; UNDERWRITE.

2. SECONDARY DISTRIBUTION of previously issued stock. *See also* SECONDARY OFFERING.

PUBLIC OFFERING PRICE price at which a NEW ISSUE of securities is offered to the public by underwriters. *See also* OFFERING PRICE; UNDERWRITE.

PUBLIC OWNERSHIP

Government: government ownership and operation of a productive facility for the purpose of providing some good or service to citizens. The government supplies the capital, controls management, sets prices, and generally absorbs all risks and reaps all profits—similar to a private enterprise. When public ownership displaces private ownership in a particular instance, it is called NATIONALIZATION.

Investments: publicly traded portion of a corporation's stock.

PUBLIC PRIVATE INVESTMENT PROGRAM (PPIP) program proposed by the Treasury department under President Obama to entice private institutional investors to buy up TOXIC ASSETS from banks at deep discounts from face value. The concept was to relieve banks of the burden of these defaulted and delinquent loans and provide private hedge funds and private equity funds an opportunity to profit by buying these assets at attractive prices.

PUBLIC PURPOSE BOND category of MUNICIPAL BOND, as defined in the TAX REFORM ACT OF 1986, which is exempt from federal income taxes as long as it provides no more than 10% benefit to private parties and no more than 5% of the proceeds or $5 million are used for loans to private parties; also called *public activity, traditional government purpose,* and *essential purpose* bond. Public purpose bonds include purposes such as roads, libraries, and government buildings.

PUBLIC SYNDICATE *see* PURCHASE GROUP.

PUBLIC UTILITY HOLDING COMPANY ACT OF 1935 major landmark in legislation regulating the securities industry, which reorganized the financial structures of HOLDING COMPANIES in the gas and electric utility industries and regulated their debt and dividend policies. Prior to the Act, abuses by holding companies were rampant, including WATERED STOCK, top-heavy capital structures with excessive fixed-debt burdens, and manipulation of the securities markets. In summary:

1. It requires holding companies operating interstate and persons exercising a controlling influence on utilities and holding companies to register with the Securities and Exchange Commission (SEC) and to provide information on the organizational structure, finances, and means of control.

2. It provides for SEC control of the operation and performance of registered holding companies and SEC approval of all new securities offerings, resulting in such reforms as the elimination of NONVOTING STOCK, the prevention of the milking of subsidiaries, and the outlawing of the upstreaming of dividends (payment of dividends by operating companies to holding companies).

3. It provides for uniform accounting standards, periodic administrative and financial reports, and reports on holdings by officers and directors, and for the end of interlocking directorates with banks or investment bankers.

4. It began the elimination of complex organizational structures by allowing only one intermediate company between the top holding company and its operating companies (the GRANDFATHER CLAUSE).

PULLBACK reversal of an upward price trend when a stock or market rises in price for several trading sessions and then declines in price.

PULLING IN THEIR HORNS move to defensive strategies on the part of investors. If the stock or bond market has experienced a sharp rise, investors may want to lock in profits by selling part of their positions or instituting hedging techniques to guard against a downturn. If stock prices fall after a steep runup, commentators will frequently say that "investors are pulling in their horns" to describe the reason for the downturn.

PUMP AND DUMP *see* POOP AND SCOOP.

PURCHASE ACQUISITION accounting method used in a business MERGER whereby the purchasing company treats the acquired company as an investment and adds the acquired company's assets to its own at their fair market value. Any premium paid over and above the FAIR MARKET VALUE of the acquired assets is reflected as GOODWILL on the buyer's BALANCE SHEET. Financial Accounting Standards Board (FASB) statements effective June 30, 2001 required that the purchase method of accounting be used for all business combinations (eliminating tax-free POOLING-OF-INTERESTS mergers) and that goodwill, previously amortizable under IRS rules, be subject to an impairment only accounting approach.

PURCHASE FUND provision in some PREFERRED STOCK contracts and BOND indentures requiring the issuer to use its best efforts to purchase a specified number of shares or bonds annually at a price not to exceed par value. Unlike SINKING FUND provisions, which require that a certain number of bonds be retired annually, purchase funds require only that a tender offer be made; if no securities are tendered, none are retired. Purchase fund issues benefit the investor in a period of rising rates when the redemption price is higher than the market price and the proceeds can be put to work at a higher return.

PURCHASE GROUP group of investment bankers that, operating under the AGREEMENT AMONG UNDERWRITERS, agrees to purchase a NEW ISSUE of securities from the issuer for resale to the investment public; also called the UNDERWRITING GROUP or *syndicate*. The purchase group is distinguished from the SELLING GROUP, which is organized by the purchase group and includes the members of the purchase group along with other investment bankers. The selling group's function is DISTRIBUTION.

The agreement among underwriters, also called the *purchase group agreement,* is distinguished from the underwriting or purchase agreement, which is between the underwriting group and the issuer. *See also* UNDERWRITE.

PURCHASE GROUP AGREEMENT *see* PURCHASE GROUP.

PURCHASE LOAN in consumer credit, a loan made at a rate of interest to finance a purchase.

PURCHASE-MONEY MORTGAGE MORTGAGE given by a buyer in lieu of cash for the purchase of property. Such mortgages make it possible to sell property when mortgage money is unavailable or when the only buyers are unqualified to borrow from commercial sources.

PURCHASE ORDER written authorization to a vendor to deliver specified goods or services at a stipulated price. Once accepted by the supplier, the purchase order becomes a legally binding purchase CONTRACT.

PURCHASING POWER
Economics: value of money as measured by the goods and services it can buy. For example, the PURCHASING POWER OF THE DOLLAR can be determined by comparing an index of consumer prices for a given base year to the present.
Investment: amount of credit available to a client in a brokerage account for the purchase of additional securities. Purchasing power is determined by the dollar amount of securities that can be margined. For instance, a client with purchasing power of $20,000 in his or her account could buy securities worth $40,000 under the Federal Reserve's currently effective 50% MARGIN REQUIRE-MENT. *See also* MARGIN SECURITY.

PURCHASING POWER OF THE DOLLAR measure of the amount of goods and services that a dollar can buy in a particular market, as compared with prior periods, assuming always an INFLATION or a DEFLATION factor and using an index of consumer prices. It might be reported, for instance, that one dollar in 1982 has 67 cents of purchasing power in the late 1990s because of the erosion caused by inflation. Deflation would increase the dollar's purchasing power.

PURCHASING POWER RISK the risk that inflation will have eroded the value of the currency in which a deal has been made. For example, a country may be willing to print the money necessary to satisfy a future payment, but if its currency is losing value to inflation, the creditor country has a purchas-ing power risk as opposed to a default risk.

PURE INDEX FUND index fund that is managed with the aim of exactly replicating the performance of a MARKET INDEX. Contrast with ENHANCED INDEXING.

PURE NO-LOAD FUND a MUTUAL FUND that has a MANAGEMENT FEE but no SALES CHARGE, REDEMPTION FEE or 12b-1 MUTUAL FUND fees.

PURE PLAY stock market jargon for a company that is virtually all devoted to one line of business. An investor who wants to invest in that line of business looks for such a pure play. For instance, Sears Roebuck may be considered a pure play in the retail business after spinning off its real estate and financial services businesses in the mid-1900s. Weyerhauser is a pure play in the forest products business. The opposite of a pure play is a widely diversified company, such as a CONGLOMERATE.

PURE MONOPOLY situation in which one firm controls the entire market for a product. This may occur because the firm has a patent on a product or a license from the government to be a monopoly. For example, an electric utility in a particular city may be a monopoly licensed by the city.

PURPOSE LOAN loan backed by securities and used to buy other securities under Federal Reserve Board MARGIN and credit regulations.

PURPOSE STATEMENT form filed by a borrower that details the purpose of a loan backed by securities. The borrower agrees not to use the loan proceeds to buy securities in violation of any Federal Reserve regulations. *See also* NONPURPOSE LOAN; REGULATION U.

PUT BOND bond that allows its holder to redeem the issue at specified intervals before maturity and receive full FACE VALUE. The bond-holders may be allowed to put bonds back to the issuer either only once during the lifetime of the issue or far more frequently. In return for this privilege, a bond buyer sacrifices some yield when choosing a put bond over a fixed-rate bond, which cannot be redeemed before maturity.

PUT-CALL PARITY principle that at any given underlying stock price, a CALL or PUT OPTION with the same expiration will have a static price relationship because variations will be eliminated by ARBITRAGE.

PUT-CALL RATIO ratio of trading volume in put options to the trading volume in call options. The ratio provides a quantitative measure of the bullishness or bearishness of investors. A high volume of puts relative to calls indicates investors are bearish, whereas a high ratio of calls to puts shows bullishness. Many market technicians find the put-call ratio to be a good contrary indicator, meaning that when the ratio is high, a market bottom is near and when the ratio is low, a market top is imminent. This reading assumes that the majority of options investors are making the wrong move.

PUT GUARANTEE LETTER letter from a bank certifying that the person writing a put option on an underlying security or index instrument has sufficient funds on deposit at the bank to cover the exercise price of the put if needed. On a short put, the obligation is to pay the aggregate exercise price. There are two forms, as required under New York Stock Exchange Rule 431: the *market index option deposit letter* for index options, and the *equity/Treasury option deposit letter* for security options.

PUT OPTION

   Bonds: bondholder's right to redeem a bond before maturity. *See also* PUT BOND.

   Options: contract that grants the right to sell at a specified price a specific number of shares by a certain date. The put option buyer gains this right in return for payment of an OPTION PREMIUM. The put option seller grants this right in return for receiving this premium. For instance, a buyer of an XYZ May 70 put has the right to sell 100 shares of XYZ at $70 to the put seller at any time until the contract expires in May. A put option buyer hopes the stock will drop in price, while the put option seller (called a *writer*) hopes the stock will remain stable, rise, or drop by an amount less than his or her profit on the premium.

PUT TO SELLER phrase used when a PUT OPTION is exercised. The OPTION WRITER is obligated to buy the underlying shares at the agreed upon price. If an XYZ June 40 put were "put to seller," for instance, the writer would have to buy 100 shares of XYZ at $40 a share from the put holder even though the current market price of XYZ may be far less than $40 a share.

PYRAMIDING

In general: practice using financial LEVERAGE to build expanded corporate structures.

Fraud: scheme that builds on nonexistent values, often in geometric progression, such as a chain letter, now outlawed by mail fraud legislation. Famous examples were the Ponzi scheme, perpetrated by Charles Ponzi in the late 1920s and the recent MADOFF SCANDAL. Investors were paid "earnings" out of money received from new investors until the scheme collapsed.

Investments: using unrealized profits from one securities or commodities POSITION as COLLATERAL to buy further positions with funds borrowed from a broker. This use of leverage creates increased profits in a BULL MARKET, and causes MARGIN CALLS and large losses in a BEAR MARKET.

Marketing: legal marketing strategy whereby additional distributorships are sold side-by-side with consumer products in order to multiply market reach and maximize profits to the sales organization.

Q

QQQQ *see* QUBES (QQQQ).

Q RATIO ratio of the market value of a firm's assets to their REPLACEMENT COST. Sometimes called *Tobin's Q ratio* after its inventor, the late James Tobin of Yale University.

Q-TIP TRUST qualified terminable interest property *trust,* which allows assets to be transferred between spouses. The grantor of a Q-tip trust directs income from the assets to his or her spouse for life but has the power to distribute the assets upon the death of the spouse. Such trusts qualify the grantor for the unlimited marital deduction if the spouse should die first.

A Q-tip trust is often used to provide for the welfare of a spouse while keeping the assets out of the estate of another (such as a future marriage partner) if the grantor dies first.

QUALIFICATION PERIOD period of time during which an insurance company will not reimburse a policyholder for a claim. The qualification period, which may be several weeks or months, gives the insurance company time to uncover fraud or deception in the policyholder's application for coverage. Such periods, which are stated in the insurance contract, are commonplace in health insurance plans.

QUALIFIED ENDORSEMENT endorsement (signature on the back of a check or other NEGOTIABLE INSTRUMENT transferring the amount to someone other than the one to whom it is payable) that contains wording designed to limit the endorser's liability. "Without recourse," the most frequently seen example, means that if the instrument is not honored, the endorser is not responsible. Where qualified endorsements are restrictive (such as "for deposit only") the term *restricted endorsement* is preferable.

QUALIFIED INSTITUTIONAL INVESTOR INSTITUTIONAL INVESTOR permitted by the SECURITIES AND EXCHANGE COMMISSION (SEC) to trade PRIVATE PLACEMENT securities with other qualified institutional investors without REGISTRATION.

QUALIFIED OPINION auditor's opinion accompanying financial statements that calls attention to limitations of the audit or exceptions the auditor takes to the statements. Typical reasons for qualified opinions: a pending lawsuit that, if lost, would materially affect the financial condition of the company; an indeterminable tax liability relating to an unusual transaction; inability to confirm a portion of the inventory because of inaccessible location. *See also* ACCOUNTANT'S OPINION.

QUALIFIED PLAN OR TRUST TAX-DEFERRED plan set up by an employer for employees under 1954 Internal Revenue Service rules. Such plans usually provide for employer contributions—for example, a profit-sharing or pension plan—and may also allow employee contributions. They build up savings, which are paid out at retirement or on termination of employment. The employees pay taxes only when they draw the money out. When employers make payments to such plans, they receive certain deductions and other tax benefits. *See also* 401(k) PLAN; SALARY REDUCTION PLAN.

QUALIFIED TUITION PROGRAM (529 PLAN) an investment vehicle created under the Small Business Job Protection Act of 1996 that allows individuals to make contributions to accounts that accumulate tax-free income if used to cover a beneficiary's qualified educational expenses. No tax is due on the distribution from a qualified tuition program unless the amount distributed is greater than the beneficiary's qualified educational expenses. Contributions to such a plan cannot be more than the amount necessary to provide for those expenses. There are two types of 529 plans: College Savings Plans that permit that establishment of an account for the purpose of paying the beneficiary's qualified educational expenses, and Prepaid Tuition Plans that allow savers to purchase credits at participating colleges, thereby locking in costs for future tuition and, in some cases, room and board. Investing in a 529 plan will generally reduce a student's eligibility to participate in need-based financial aid. *See also* COVERDELL EDUCATION SAVINGS ACCOUNT.

QUALIFYING ANNUITY ANNUITY that is purchased under, and forms the investment program for, a QUALIFIED PLAN OR TRUST, including pension and profit sharing plans, INDIVIDUAL RETIREMENT ACCOUNTS (IRAs), 403(b)s, and 457s. *See also* KEOGH PLAN.

QUALIFYING RATIOS ratios used by mortgage lenders to determine maximum mortgage amount for a particular home buyer.

QUALIFYING SHARE share of COMMON STOCK owned in order to qualify as a director of the issuing corporation.

QUALIFYING STOCK OPTION privilege granted to an employee of a corporation that permits the purchase, for a special price, of shares of its CAPITAL STOCK, under conditions sustained in the Internal Revenue Code. The law states (1) that the OPTION plan must be approved by the stockholders, (2) that the option is not transferable, (3) that the EXERCISE PRICE must not be less than the MARKET PRICE of the shares at the time the option is issued, and (4) that the grantee may not own stock having more than 10% of the company's voting power unless the option price equals 110% of the market price and the option is not exercisable more than 5 years after the grant. No income tax is payable by the employee either at the time of the grant or at the time the option is exercised. If the market price falls below the option price, another option with a lower exercise price can be issued. There is a $100,000 per employee limit on the value of stock covered by options that are exercisable in any one calendar year. *See also* INCENTIVE STOCK OPTION.

QUALITATIVE ANALYSIS
In general: analysis that evaluates important factors that cannot be precisely measured.
Securities and credit analysis: analysis that is concerned with such questions as the experience, character, and general caliber of management; employee morale; and the status of labor relations rather than with the actual financial data about a company. *See also* QUANTITATIVE ANALYSIS.

QUALITY CONTROL process of assuring that products are made to consistently high standards of quality. Inspection of goods at various points in their manufacture by either a person or a machine is usually an important part of the quality control process.

QUALITY COST cost resulting from imperfection in products, services, systems, or processes.

QUALITY OF EARNINGS phrase describing a corporation's earnings that are attributable to increased sales and cost controls, as distinguished from artificial profits created by inflated values in inventories or other assets. In a period of high inflation, the quality of earnings tends to suffer, since a large portion of a firm's profits is generated by the rising value of inventories. In a lower inflation period, a company that achieves higher sales and maintains lower costs produces a higher quality of earnings—a factor often appreciated by investors, who are frequently willing to pay more for a higher quality of earnings. In the wake of the Enron debacle in 2001, quality of earnings became an issue of high priority and a variety of accounting reforms were under consideration. *See also* FINANCIAL ACCOUNTING STANDARDS BOARD (FASB); OPERATING PROFIT (OR LOSS).

QUALITY SPREAD difference between yields (SPREAD) on Treasury securities and non-Treasury securities due to differences in quality or RATING, all other characteristics being identical.

QUANT person with mathematical and computer skills who provides numerical and analytical support services in the securities industry.

QUANTISE to denominate an asset or liability in a currency other than the one in which it usually trades.

QUANTITATIVE ANALYSIS analysis dealing with measurable factors as distinguished from such qualitative considerations as the character of management or the state of employee morale. In credit and securities analysis, examples of quantitative considerations are the value of assets; the cost of capital; the historical and projected patterns of sales, costs, and profitability and a wide range of considerations in the areas of economics; the money market; and the securities markets. Although quantitative and qualitative factors are distinguishable, they must be combined to arrive at sound business and financial judgments. *See also* QUALITATIVE ANALYSIS.

QUANTITATIVE EASING *see* PRINT MONEY.

QUANTITY THEORY OF MONEY *see* VELOCITY.

QUANTO OPTION option in one currency or interest rate that pays out in another. A quanto option can be used when an investor favors a foreign index, but is bearish on the outlook for that country's currency.

QUARTERLY
In general: every three months (one quarter of a year).
Securities: basis on which earnings reports to shareholders are made; also, usual time frame of dividend payments.

QUARTERLY INCOME CAPITAL SECURITIES (QUICS) *see* INCOME PREFERRED SECURITIES.

QUARTERLY INCOME DEBT SECURITIES (QUIDC) *see* INCOME PREFERRED SECURITIES.

QUARTER STOCK stock with a par value of $25 per share.

QUASI-PUBLIC CORPORATION corporation that is operated privately and often has its stock traded publicly, but that also has some sort of public mandate and often has the government's backing behind its direct debt obligations. Some examples: COMSAT (Communications Satellite Corporation), which was sponsored by the U.S. Congress to foster the development of space; the FEDERAL NATIONAL MORTGAGE ASSOCIATION (Fannie Mae), which was founded to encourage growth in the secondary mortgage market; and the STUDENT LOAN MARKETING ASSOCIATION (Sallie Mae), which was started to encourage the growth of a secondary market for student loans.

QUBES (QQQQ) EXCHANGE-TRADED FUND (ETF), whose ticker symbol is QQQQ, that tracks the technology-heavy NASDAQ 100 index and trades on the NASDAQ STOCK MARKET. Qubes are structured as UNIT INVESTMENT TRUSTS.

QUICK ASSETS cash, marketable securities, and accounts receivable. *See also* QUICK RATIO.

QUICK RATIO cash, MARKETABLE SECURITIES, and ACCOUNTS RECEIVABLE divided by current liabilities. By excluding inventory, this key LIQUIDITY ratio focuses on the firm's more LIQUID ASSETS, and helps answer the question "If sales stopped, could this firm meet its current obligations with the readily convertible assets on hand?" Assuming there is nothing happening to slow or prevent collections, a quick ratio of 1 to 1 or better is usually satisfactory. Also called *acid-test ratio, quick asset ratio.*

QUICK TURN purchase and sale of a security only briefly held, as in a DAY TRADE.

QUICS *see* INCOME PREFERRED SECURITIES.

QUID British slang for one pound currency unit.

QUID PRO QUO
In general: from the Latin, meaning "something for something." By mutual agreement, one party provides a good or service for which he or she gets another good or service in return.
Securities industry: arrangement by a firm using institutional research that it will execute all trades based on that research with the firm providing it, instead of directly paying for the research. This is known as paying in SOFT DOLLARS.

QUIET PERIOD period an ISSUER is "in registration" and subject to an SEC embargo on promotional publicity. It dates from the preunderwriting decision to 40 or 90 days after the EFFECTIVE DATE.

QUIPS *see* INCOME PREFERRED SECURITIES.

QUORUM minimum number of people who must be present at a meeting in order to make certain decisions go into effect. A quorum may be required at a board of directors, committee, shareholder, legislative, or other meeting for any decisions to have legal standing. A quorum may be achieved by providing a PROXY as well as appearance in person.

QUOTATION
Business: price estimate on a commercial project or transaction.
Investments: highest bid and lowest offer (asked) price currently available

on a security or a commodity. An investor who asks for a quotation ("quote") on XYZ might be told "60 to 60.50," meaning that the best bid price (the highest price any buyer wants to pay) is currently $60 a share and that the best offer (the lowest price any seller is willing to accept) is $60.50 at that time. Such quotes assume ROUND-LOT transactions—for example, 100 shares for stocks.

QUOTATION BOARD electronically controlled board at a brokerage firm that displays current price quotations and other financial data such as dividends, price ranges of stocks, and current volume of trading.

QUOTED PRICE price at which the last sale and purchase of a particular security or commodity took place. The terms quoted price and QUOTATION are, in practice, both shortened to "quote," which therefore connotes either or both.

R

RABBI TRUST an irrevocable trust used to fund deferred compensation benefits for key employees in the absence of a QUALIFIED PLAN OR TRUST. Name derives from an IRS letter ruling involving a rabbi whose congregation had made contributions to such a trust for his benefit. As a GRANTOR trust, income is taxed to the grantor or employer. The employer receives no deduction for payments of compensation to the trust, but receives a deduction when the trust pays the funds to the employee. The Rabbi Trust protects the employee's benefits from many company hazards, but not from insolvency or bankruptcy.

RACKETEER INFLUENCED AND CORRUPT ORGANIZATION ACT *see* RICO.

RADAR ALERT close monitoring of trading patterns in a company's stock by senior managers to uncover unusual buying activity that might signal a TAKEOVER attempt. *See also* SHARK WATCHER.

RAIDER individual or corporate investor who intends to take control of a company by buying a controlling interest in its stock and installing new management. Raiders who accumulate 5% or more of the outstanding shares in the TARGET COMPANY must report their purchases to the Securities and Exchange Commission, the exchange of listing, and the target itself. *See also* BEAR RAID; WILLIAMS ACT.

RAINMAKER individual who brings significant amounts of new business to a financial services organization. The rainmaker may bring in wealthy brokerage customers who generate a large dollar volume of commissions. Or he or she may be an investment banker who attracts corporate or municipal finance underwritings or merger and acquisition business. Because they are so important to the firm, rainmakers are usually given special PERQUISITES and bonus compensation.

RALLY marked rise in the price of a security, commodity future, or market after a period of decline or sideways movement.

R & D *see* RESEARCH AND DEVELOPMENT.

RANDOM WALK theory about the movement of stock and commodity futures prices hypothesizing that past prices are of no use in forecasting future price movements. According to the theory, stock prices reflect reactions to information coming to the market in random fashion, so they are no more predictable than the walking pattern of a drunken person. The random walk theory was first espoused in 1900 by the French mathematician Louis Bachelier and revived in the 1960s. It is hotly disputed by advocates of TECHNICAL ANALYSIS, who say that charts of past price movements enable them to predict future price movements. *See also* EFFICIENT MARKET.

RANGE high and low end of a security, commodity future, or market's price fluctuations over a period of time. Daily newspapers publish the 52-week high and low price range of stocks traded on the New York Stock Exchange, American Stock Exchange, and over-the-counter markets. Advocates of TECHNICAL ANALYSIS attach great importance to trading ranges because they consider it of great significance if a security breaks out of its trading range by going higher or lower. *See also* BREAKOUT.

RAPID IN AND OUT TRADING *see* MARKET TIMING 2.

RATE BASE value established for a utility by a regulatory body such as a Public Utility Commission on which the company is allowed to earn a particular rate of return. Generally the rate base includes the utility's operating costs but not the cost of constructing new facilities. Whether modernization costs should be included in the rate base, and thus passed on to customers, is a subject of continuing controversy. *See also* FAIR RATE OF RETURN.

RATE CAP *see* CAP.

RATE COVENANT provision in MUNICIPAL REVENUE BOND agreements or resolutions covering the rates, or methods of establishing rates, to be charged users of the facility being financed. The rate covenant usually promises that rates will be adjusted when necessary to cover the cost of repairs and maintenance while continuing to provide for the payment of bond interest and principal.

RATE OF EXCHANGE *see* EXCHANGE RATE; PAR VALUE OF CURRENCY.

RATE OF INFLATION *see* CONSUMER PRICE INDEX; INFLATION RATE; PRODUCER PRICE INDEX.

RATE OF RETURN
Fixed-income securities (bonds and preferred stock): CURRENT YIELD, that is, the coupon or contractual dividend rate divided by the purchase price. *See also* YIELD TO AVERAGE LIFE; YIELD TO CALL; YIELD TO MATURITY.
Common stock: (1) dividend yield, which is the annual dividend divided by the purchase price. (2) TOTAL RETURN rate, which is the dividend and other distributions plus capital appreciation.
Corporate finance: RETURN ON EQUITY or RETURN ON INVESTED CAPITAL.
Capital budgeting: INTERNAL RATE OF RETURN.
    See also FAIR RATE OF RETURN; HORIZON ANALYSIS; MEAN RETURN; REAL INTEREST RATE; REQUIRED RATE OF RETURN; RISK-ADJUSTED RETURNS; TOTAL RETURN; YIELD.

RATING
Credit and investments: evaluation of securities investment and credit risk by rating services such as FITCH RATINGS, MOODY'S INVESTORS SERVICE, MORNINGSTAR RATING SYSTEM, STANDARD & POOR'S CORPORATION, and VALUE LINE INVESTMENT SURVEY. *See also* CREDIT RATING; CREDIT RATING AGENCY REFORM ACT OF 2006; EVENT RISK; NOT RATED.
Insurance: using statistics, mortality tables, probability theory, experience, judgment, and mathematical analysis to establish the rates on which insurance premiums are based. There are three basic rating systems: *class rate*, applying to a homogeneous grouping of clients; *schedule system*, relating positive and negative factors in the case of a particular insured (for example, a smoker or nonsmoker in the case of a life policy) to a base figure; and *experience rating*, reflecting the historical loss experience of the particular insured. Also called *rate-making*.
    Insurance companies are also rated. *See also* BEST'S RATING.

LEADING BOND RATING SERVICES	RATING SERVICE		
Explanation of corporate/ municipal bond ratings	*Fitch*	*Moody's*	*Standard & Poor's*
Highest quality, "gilt edged" High quality Upper medium grade	AAA AA A	Aaa Aa A	AAA AA A
Medium grade Predominantly speculative Speculative, low grade	BBB BB B	Baa Ba B	BBB BB B
Poor to default Highest speculation Lowest quality, no interest	CCC CC C	Caa Ca C	CCC CC C
In default, in arrears, questionable value	{ DDD DD D		DDD DD D

Fitch and Standard & Poor's may use + or – to modify some ratings. Moody's uses the numerical modifiers 1 (highest), 2, and 3 in the range from Aa1 through Ca3.

RATING TRIGGER provision in a loan or indenture agreement that precipitates a specified action in the event of a downgrade of the borrower's credit rating.

RATIO ANALYSIS method of analysis, used in making credit and investment judgments, which utilizes the relationship of figures found in financial statements to determine values and evaluate risks and compares such ratios to those of prior periods and other companies to reveal trends and identify eccentricities. Ratio analysis is only one tool among many used by analysts. *See also* ACCOUNTS RECEIVABLE TURNOVER; ACID TEST RATIO; BOND RATIO; CAPITALIZATION RATIO; CAPITAL TURNOVER; CASH RATIO; COLLECTION PERIOD; COMMON STOCK RATIO; CURRENT RATIO; DEBT-TO-EQUITY RATIO; DIVIDEND PAYOUT RATIO; EARNINGS-PRICE RATIO; FIXED CHARGE COVERAGE; LEVERAGE; NET TANGIBLE ASSETS PER SHARE; OPERATING RATIO; PREFERRED STOCK RATIO; PRICE-EARNINGS RATIO; PROFIT MARGIN; QUICK RATIO; RETURN ON EQUITY; RETURN ON INVESTED CAPITAL; RETURN ON SALES; SHARE RATIO.

RATIO WRITER OPTIONS writer who sells more CALL contracts than he has underlying shares. For example, an investor who writes (sells) ten calls, five of them covered by 500 owned shares and the other five of them uncovered (or "naked"), has a 2 for 1 ratio write.

RAW LAND property in its natural state, prior to grading, construction, and subdividing. The property has no sewers, electricity, streets, buildings, water service, telephone service, or other amenities. Investors in raw land hope that the land's value will rise in the future if it is developed. While they wait, however, they must pay property taxes on the land's value.

RAW MATERIAL unfinished goods used in the manufacture of a product. For example, a steelmaker uses iron ore and other metals in producing steel. A publishing company uses paper and ink to create books, newspapers, and magazines. Raw materials are carried on a company's balance sheet as inventory in the current assets section.

REACTION drop in securities prices after a sustained period of advancing prices, perhaps as the result of PROFIT TAKING or adverse developments. *See also* CORRECTION.

READING THE TAPE judging the performance of stocks by monitoring changes in price as they are displayed on the TICKER tape. An analyst reads the tape to determine whether a stock is acting strongly or weakly, and therefore is likely to go up or down. An investor reads the tape to determine whether a stock trade is going with or against the flow of market action. *See also* DON'T FIGHT THE TAPE.

REAGANOMICS economic program followed by the administration of President Ronald Reagan beginning in 1980. Reaganomics stressed lower taxes, higher defense spending, and curtailed spending for social services. After a reduction of growth in the money supply by the Federal Reserve Board combined with Reaganomics to produce a severe recession in 1981–82, the Reagan years were characterized by huge budget deficits, low interest and inflation rates, and continuous economic growth.

REAL ESTATE piece of land and all physical property related to it, including houses, fences, landscaping, and all rights to the air above and earth below the property. Assets not directly associated with the land are considered *personal property.*

REAL ESTATE AGENT licensed salesperson working for a licensed broker. The agent may hold an individual REAL ESTATE BROKER's license.

REAL ESTATE APPRAISAL estimate of the value of property, usually required when a property is sold, financed, condemned, taxed, insured, or partitioned. An appraisal is not a determination of value. Three approaches are used. To produce an accurate resale price for a residence, appraisers compare the price of the property to the prices of similar nearby properties that have sold recently. For new construction and service properties such as churches and post offices, appraisers look at the reproduction or replacement cost of the improvements, less depreciation, plus the value of the land. For investment properties such as apartment buildings and shopping centers, an estimated value is based on the capitalization of net operating income from a property at an acceptable market rate.

REAL ESTATE BROKER person who arranges the purchase or sale of property for a buyer or seller in return for a commission. Brokers may help arrange financing of the purchase through contacts with banks, savings and loans, and mortgage bankers. Brokers must be licensed by the state to buy or sell real estate.

REAL ESTATE INVESTMENT TRUST (REIT) company, usually traded publicly, that manages a portfolio of real estate to earn profits for shareholders. Patterned after INVESTMENT COMPANIES, REITs make investments in a diverse array of real estate such as shopping centers, medical facilities, nursing homes, office buildings, apartment complexes, industrial warehouses, and hotels. Some REITs, called EQUITY REITS, take equity positions in real estate; shareholders receive income from the rents received and from the properties and receive capital gains as buildings are sold at a profit. Other REITs specialize in lending money to building developers; such MORTGAGE REITs pass interest income on to shareholders. Some REITs, called *hybrid REITs,* have a mix of equity and debt investments. To avoid taxation at the corporate level, 75% or more of the REIT's income must be from real property and 95% of its net earnings must be distributed to shareholders annually. Because REITs must distribute most of their earnings, they tend to pay high yields of 5% to 10% or more. *See also* NATIONAL ASSOCIATION OF REAL ESTATE INVESTMENT TRUSTS (NAREIT).

REAL ESTATE LIMITED PARTNERSHIP LIMITED PARTNERSHIP that invests in real estate. The partnership buys properties such as apartment or office buildings, shopping centers, industrial warehouses, and hotels and passes rental income through to limited partners. If the properties appreciate in value over time, they can be sold and the profit passed through to limited partners. A GENERAL PARTNER manages the partnership, deciding which properties to buy and sell and handling administrative duties, such as distributions to limited partners. In the early 1980s, many real estate partnerships were structured to reduce limited partners' tax liability, because operating losses, plus accelerated depreciation from real estate, could be used to offset other taxable income. But these deals were largely discontinued after the TAX REFORM ACT OF 1986 introduced the principle of PASSIVE LOSSES, meaning that investors could no longer use real estate partnership losses to offset their income from salaries and other investments. Since the mid-1980s, partnerships have been designed to produce high current income and long-term capital gains through appreciation in the underlying real estate, not tax benefits.

REAL ESTATE MORTGAGE INVESTMENT CONDUIT *see* REMIC.

REAL GAIN OR LOSS gain or loss adjusted for INFLATION. *See also* INFLATION ACCOUNTING.

REAL INCOME income of an individual, group, or country adjusted for changes in PURCHASING POWER caused by inflation. A price index is used to determine the difference between the purchasing power of a dollar in a base year and the purchasing power now. The resulting percentage factor, applied to total income, yields the value of that income in constant dollars, termed real income. For instance, if the cost of a market basket increases from $100 to $120 in ten years, reflecting a 20% decline in purchasing power, salaries must rise by 20% if real income is to be maintained.

REAL INTEREST RATE current interest rate minus inflation rate. The real interest rate may be calculated by comparing interest rates with present or, more frequently, with predicted inflation rates. The real interest rate gives investors in bonds and other fixed-rate instruments a way to see whether their interest will allow them to keep up with or beat the erosion in dollar values caused by inflation. With a bond yielding 10% and inflation of 3%, for instance, the real interest rate of 7% would bring a return high enough to beat inflation. If inflation were at 15%, however, the investor would fall behind as prices rise.

REALIZED PROFIT (OR LOSS) profit or loss resulting from the sale or other disposal of a security. Capital gains taxes may be due when profits are realized: realized losses can be used to offset realized gains for tax purposes. Such profits and losses differ from a PAPER PROFIT OR LOSS, which (except for OPTION AND FUTURES CONTRACTS) has no tax consequences.

REAL PROPERTY land and all property attached to the land, such as houses, trees, fences, and all improvements.

REAL RATE OF RETURN RETURN on an investment adjusted for inflation.

REAL TIME
1. said of historical data based on actual experience rather than BACK-TESTING.
2. quotation based on latest bid/offer information as opposed to a DELAYED QUOTE, which reports 15 or 20 minutes after a trade.

REALTOR registered trade name that can be used only by members of state and local real estate boards affiliated with the National Association of Realtors (NAR). A realtor-associate is trained and licensed to help clients buy and sell real estate. Realtors must follow a strict code of ethics and receive ongoing training from the NAR. Any complaints about a particular realtor are dealt with at the local real estate board affiliated with the NAR.

REBALANCE to buy and sell securities that have changed values in order to restore their original proportions in a portfolio.

REBATE
1. in lending, unearned interest refunded to a borrower if the loan is paid off before maturity.
2. in consumer marketing, payment made to a consumer after a purchase is completed, to induce purchase of a product. For instance, a customer who buys a television set for $500 may be entitled to a rebate of $50, which is received after sending a proof of purchase and a rebate form to the manufacturer. *See also* RULE OF THE 78s.

RECAPITALIZATION alteration of a corporation's CAPITAL STRUCTURE, such as an exchange of bonds for stock. BANKRUPTCY is a common reason for recapitalization; debentures might be exchanged for REORGANIZATION BONDS that pay interest only when earned. A healthy company might seek to save taxes by replacing preferred stock with bonds to gain interest deductibility. *See also* DEFEASANCE.

RECAPTURE
1. contract clause allowing one party to recover some degree of possession of an asset. In leases calling for a percentage of revenues, such as those for shopping centers, the recapture clause provides that the developer get a percentage of profits in addition to a fixed rent.
2. in the tax code, the reclamation by the government of tax benefits previously taken. For example, where a portion of the profit on the sale of a depreciable asset represented ACCELERATED DEPRECIATION or the INVESTMENT CREDIT, all or part of that gain would be "recaptured" and taxed as ORDINARY INCOME, with the balance subject to the favorable CAPITAL GAINS TAX. Recapture also has specialized applications in oil and other industries. Recapture

assumed a new meaning under the 1986 Act whereby banks with assets of $500 million or more were required to take into income the balance of their RESERVE FOR BAD DEBTS. The Act called for recapture of income at the rate of 10%, 20%, 30%, and 40% for the years 1987 through 1990, respectively.

RECEIVABLES *see* ACCOUNTS RECEIVABLE.

RECEIVER court-appointed person who takes possession of, but not title to, the assets and affairs of a business or estate that is in a form of BANKRUPTCY called *receivership* or is enmeshed in a legal dispute. The receiver collects rents and other income and generally manages the affairs of the entity for the benefit of its owners and creditors until a disposition is made by the court.

RECEIVER'S CERTIFICATE debt instrument issued by a RECEIVER, who uses the proceeds to finance continued operations or otherwise to protect assets in receivership. The certificates constitute a LIEN on the property, ranking ahead of all other secured or unsecured liabilities in LIQUIDATION.

RECEIVE VERSUS PAYMENT instruction accompanying sell orders by institutions that only cash will be accepted in exchange for delivery of the securities at the time of settlement. Institutions are generally required by law to accept only cash. Also called *receive against payment.*

RECESSION downturn in economic activity, defined by many economists as at least two consecutive quarters of decline in a country's GROSS DOMESTIC PRODUCT.

RECHARACTERIZATION treatment of an IRA contribution of one type as a contribution to another type, such as a conversion of assets from a traditional IRA to a ROTH IRA.

RECLAMATION
Banking: restoration or correction of a NEGOTIABLE INSTRUMENT—or the amount thereof—that has been incorrectly recorded by the *clearing house.*
Finance: restoration of an unproductive asset to productivity, such as by using landfill to make a swamp developable.
Securities: right of either party to a securities transaction to recover losses caused by *bad delivery* or other irregularities in the settlement process.

RECORD DATE *see* DATE OF RECORD; EX-DIVIDEND DATE; PAYMENT DATE.

RECOURSE legal ability the purchaser of a financial asset may have to fall back on the original creditor if the current debtor defaults. For example, an account receivable sold with recourse enables the buyer of the receivable to make claim on the seller if the account doesn't pay.

RECOURSE LOAN
1. loan for which an endorser or guarantor is liable for payment in the event the borrower defaults.
2. loan made to a DIRECT PARTICIPATION PROGRAM or LIMITED PARTNERSHIP whereby the lender, in addition to being secured by specific assets, has recourse against the general assets of the partnership. *See also* NONRECOURSE LOAN.

RECOVERY
Economics: period in a business cycle when economic activity picks up and

the GROSS NATIONAL PRODUCT grows, leading into the expansion phase of the cycle.

Finance: (1) absorption of cost through the allocation of DEPRECIATION; (2) collection of an ACCOUNT RECEIVABLE that had been written off as a bad debt; (3) residual cost, or salvage value, of a fixed asset after all allowable depreciation.

Investment: period of rising prices in a securities or commodities market after a period of falling prices.

RECOVERY PERIOD

Economics: period of time in which the economy is emerging from a recession or depression. The recovery period is marked by rising sales and production, improved consumer confidence, and in many cases, rising interest rates.

Stocks: period of time in which a stock that has fallen sharply in price begins to rise again, thereby recovering some of its value.

Taxation: period over which property is subject to depreciation for tax purposes following the ACCELERATED COST RECOVERY SYSTEM (ACRS). Different classes of assets are assigned different periods in which costs can be recovered.

REDEEMABLE BOND *see* CALLABLE.

REDEMPTION repayment of a debt security or preferred stock issue, at or before maturity, at PAR or at a premium price.

Mutual fund shares are redeemed at NET ASSET VALUE when a shareholder's holdings are liquidated.

REDEMPTION DATE date on which a bond is scheduled to mature or be redeemed. If a bond is CALLED AWAY before scheduled maturity, the redemption date is the day that the bond will be taken back.

REDEMPTION FEES fees charged by a mutual fund on shareholders who sell fund shares within a short period of time. The time limit and size of the fee vary among funds, but the redemption fee usually is a relatively small percentage (1% or 2% of the amount withdrawn). Some mutual funds charge a small flat redemption fee of $5 or $10 to cover administrative charges. The intent of the redemption fee is to discourage rapid-fire shifts from one fund to another in an attempt to "time" swings in the stock or bond market. This fee often is confused with the contingent deferred sales charge, or BACK END SALES CHARGE, typically a feature of the broker-sold fund. *See also* MUTUAL FUND SHARE CLASSES.

REDEMPTION PRICE *see* CALL PRICE.

RED HERRING *see* PRELIMINARY PROSPECTUS.

REDISCOUNT DISCOUNT short-term negotiable debt instruments, such as banker's ACCEPTANCES and COMMERCIAL PAPER, that have been *discounted* with a bank—in other words, exchanged for an amount of cash adjusted to reflect the current interest rate. The bank then discounts the paper a second time for its own benefit with another bank or with a Federal Reserve bank. Rediscounting was once the primary means by which banks borrowed additional reserves from the Fed. Today most banks do this by discounting their own notes secured by GOVERNMENT SECURITIES or other ELIGIBLE PAPER. But *redis-*

count rate is still used as a synonym for DISCOUNT RATE, the rate charged by the Fed for all bank borrowings.

REDLINING discrimination in the pattern of granting loans, insurance coverage, or other financial benefits. Lenders or insurers who practice redlining "draw a red line" around a troubled area of a city and vow not to lend or insure property in that neighborhood because of poor economic conditions and high default rates. Insurance companies withdraw from an area because of high claims experience and widespread fraud. With mortgage and business loans and insurance hard to obtain, redlining therefore tends to accelerate the decline of such neighborhoods. Redlining is illegal because it discriminates against residents of an area on the basis of where they live. Congress has enacted legislation such as the Community Reinvestment Act, which forces banks to lend to underprivileged areas, to combat redlining.

REDS *see* REFUNDING ESCROW DEPOSITS.

REDUCTION-OPTION LOAN (ROL) hybrid between a fixed-rate and adjustable mortgage and a cheaper alternative to refinancing, whereby the borrower has the one-time option from the second through the fifth year to match the current mortgage rate, which then becomes fixed for the rest of the term. The reduction is usually permitted if rates drop more than 2% in any one year.

REFCORP *see* RESOLUTION FUNDING CORPORATION (REFCORP).

REFERENCE INDEX *see* BENCHMARK.

REFINANCING
Banking: extending the maturity date, or increasing the amount of existing debt, or both.
Bonds: REFUNDING; retiring existing bonded debt by issuing new securities to reduce the interest rate, or to extend the maturity date, or both.
Personal finance: Replacing a debt obligation, typically a home mortgage, with another having more favorable terms, and sometimes releasing cash (called a cash out refi).

REFUND
Bonds: retirement of an existing bond issue through the sale of a new bond issue. When interest rates have fallen, issuers may want to exercise the CALL FEATURE of a bond and replace it with another debt instrument paying a lower interest rate. *See also* PREREFUNDING.
Commerce: return of merchandise for money. For example, a consumer who is not happy with a product has the right to return it for a refund of his money.
Taxes: *see* TAX REFUND.

REFUND ANNUITY also called *life income with refund annuity*, a contract that guarantees payments equal to the premiums paid, even if the annuitant dies.

REFUNDING
1. replacing an old debt with a new one, usually in order to lower the interest cost of the issuer. For instance, a corporation or municipality that has issued 10% bonds may want to refund them by issuing 7% bonds if interest rates have dropped. *See also* PREREFUNDING; REFINANCING.
2. in merchandising, returning money to the purchaser, e.g., to a consumer

who has paid for an appliance and is not happy with it.

REFUNDING ESCROW DEPOSITS (REDS) financial instruments used to circumvent 1984 tax restrictions on tax-exempt PREREFUNDINGS for certain kinds of state or local projects, such as airports, solid-waste disposal facilities, wharves, and convention centers. The object of prerefundings was to lock in a lower current rate in anticipation of maturing higher-rate issues. REDs accomplish this by way of a forward purchase contract obligating investors to buy bonds at a predetermined rate when they are issued at a future date. The future date coincides with the first optional call date on existing high-rate bonds. In the interim, investors' money is invested in Treasury bonds bought in the secondary market. The Treasuries are held in escrow, in effect securing the investor's deposit and paying taxable annual income. The Treasuries mature around the call date on the existing bonds, providing the money to buy the new issue and redeem the old one. Also called *municipal forwards.*

REGIONAL BANK bank that specializes in collecting deposits and making loans in one region of the country, as distinguished from a MONEY CENTER BANK, which operates nationally and internationally.

REGIONAL MUTUAL FUND mutual fund that buys securities from just one region of the country. There are regional mutual funds specializing in the Southwest, Southeast, Northwest, Midwest and other regions. Investors may be interested in such funds because they provide a PURE PLAY on the economic growth in a particular region. People living in these regions may also want to invest in nearby companies because of their firsthand experience with such firms.

Regional mutual funds also specialize in different regions of the world. There are funds limited to investments in Latin America, Europe, Asia, and other regions. Regional funds, whether domestic or international, tend to be more volatile than funds with more geographically diversified holdings. *See also* EXCHANGE-TRADED FUNDS (ETF).

REGIONAL STOCK EXCHANGES organized national securities exchanges located outside of New York City and registered with the SECURITIES AND EXCHANGE COMMISSION. They include the Boston, Chicago, National, Pacific, and Philadelphia stock exchanges. These exchanges list both regional issues and many of the securities listed on the New York exchanges. Companies listed on the NEW YORK STOCK EXCHANGE, the AMERICAN STOCK EXCHANGE, and THE NASDAQ STOCK MARKET broaden the market for regional exchanges' securities. Using the INTERMARKET TRADING SYSTEM (ITS), regional exchanges can see competing prices for the securities traded on video screens. Regional exchanges have increased their competitive positions by adopting electronic trading and clearing systems, demutualizing and adding products such as EXCHANGE-TRADED FUNDS. *See also* DUAL LISTING; GRADUATED SECURITY; SECURITIES AND COMMODITIES EXCHANGES.

REGISTERED BOND bond that is recorded in the name of the holder on the books of the issuer or the issuer's REGISTRAR and can be transferred to another owner only when ENDORSED by the registered owner. A bond registered for principal only, and not for interest, is called a *registered coupon bond.* One that is not registered is called a *bearer bond;* one issued with detachable coupons for presentation to the issuer or a paying agent when interest or principal payments are due is termed a COUPON BOND. Bearer bonds are NEGOTIABLE INSTRUMENTS payable to the holder and therefore do not legally require endorsement. Bearer bonds that may be changed to registered bonds are called *Interchangeable bonds.*

REGISTERED CHECK check issued by a bank for a customer who places funds aside in a special register. The customer writes in his name and the name of the payee and the amount of money to be transferred. The bank, which collects a fee for the service, then puts on the bank's name and the amount of the check and gives the check a special number. The check has two stubs, one for the customer and one for the bank. The registered check is similar to a money order for someone who does not have a checking account at the bank.

REGISTERED COMPANY company that has filed a REGISTRATION STATEMENT with the Securities and Exchange Commission in connection with a PUBLIC OFFERING of securities and must therefore comply with SEC DISCLOSURE requirements.

REGISTERED COMPETITIVE MARKET MAKER securities dealer registered with the FINANCIAL INDUSTRY REGULATORY AUTHORITY (FINRA) as a market maker in a particular OVER-THE-COUNTER stock—that is, one who maintains firm bid and offer prices in the stock by standing ready to buy or sell round lots. Such dealers must announce their quotes through NASDAQ, which requires that there be at least two market makers in each stock listed in the system; the bid and asked quotes are compared to ensure that the quote is a representative spread. *See also* MAKE A MARKET; MARKET MAKER.

REGISTERED COUPON BOND *see* REGISTERED BOND.

REGISTERED EQUITY MARKET MAKER AMERICAN STOCK EXCHANGE member firm registered as a trader for its own account. Such firms are expected to make stabilizing purchases and sales when necessary to correct imbalances in particular securities. *See also* REGISTERED COMPETITIVE MARKET MAKER.

REGISTERED INVESTMENT ADVISER investment adviser registered with the Securities and Exchange Commission. An RIA must fill out a form detailing educational and professional experience and pay an annual fee to the SEC. The Registered Investment Adviser (RIA) designation carries no endorsement from the SEC, which regulates RIAs' activities. RIAs may pick stocks, bonds, mutual funds, partnerships or other SEC-registered investments for clients. They may be paid on a fee-only or fee-plus-commission basis. Usually, fees are based on a fixed percentage of assets under management.

REGISTERED INVESTMENT COMPANY investment company, such as an open-end or closed-end MUTUAL FUND, which files a registration statement with the Securities and Exchange Commission and meets all the other requirements of the INVESTMENT COMPANY ACT OF 1940.

REGISTERED OPTIONS TRADER specialist on the floor of the AMERICAN STOCK EXCHANGE who is responsible for maintaining a fair and orderly market in an assigned group of options.

REGISTERED REPRESENTATIVE employee of a stock exchange member broker/dealer who acts as an ACCOUNT EXECUTIVE for clients. As such, the registered representative gives advice on which securities to buy and sell, and he collects a percentage of the commission income he generates as compensation. To qualify as a registered representative, a person must acquire a background in the securities business and pass a series of tests, including the General Securities Examination and state securities tests. "Registered" means licensed by the Securities and Exchange Commission and by the New York Stock Exchange. *See also* ACCOUNT EXECUTIVE; CORPORATE SECURITIES (LIMITED) REPRESENTATIVE; SERIES 7 REGISTERED; SERIES 6 REGISTERED; UNIFORM SECURITIES AGENT STATE LAW EXAMINATION.

REGISTERED RETIREMENT SAVINGS PLAN (RRSP) tax-deductible and tax-sheltered retirement plan for individuals in Canada, similar in concept to the INDIVIDUAL RETIREMENT PLAN (IRA) in the United States.

REGISTERED SECONDARY OFFERING offering, usually through investment bankers, of a large block of securities that were previously issued to the public, using the abbreviated Form S-16 of the Securities and Exchange Commission. Such offerings are usually made by major stockholders of mature companies who may be *control persons* or institutions who originally acquired the securities in a private placement. Form S-16 relies heavily on previously filed SEC documents such as the S-1, the 10-K, and quarterly filings. Where listed securities are concerned, permission to sell large blocks off the exchange must be obtained from the appropriate exchange. *See also* LETTER SECURITY; SECONDARY DISTRIBUTION; SECONDARY OFFERING; SHELF REGISTRATION.

REGISTERED SECURITY
1. security whose owner's name is recorded on the books of the issuer or the issuer's agent, called a *registrar*—for example, a REGISTERED BOND as opposed to a *bearer bond,* the former being transferable only by endorsement, the latter payable to the holder.
2. securities issue registered with the Securities and Exchange Commission as a new issue or as a SECONDARY OFFERING. *See also* REGISTERED SECONDARY OFFERING; REGISTRATION.

REGISTRAR agency responsible for keeping track of the owners of bonds and the issuance of stock. The registrar, working with the TRANSFER AGENT, keeps current files of the owners of a bond issue and the stockholders in a corporation. The registrar also makes sure that no more than the authorized amount of stock is in circulation. For bonds, the registrar certifies that a bond is a corporation's genuine debt obligation.

REGISTRATION process set up by the Securities Exchange Acts of 1933 and 1934 whereby securities that are to be sold to the public are reviewed by the Securities and Exchange Commission. The REGISTRATION STATEMENT details pertinent financial and operational information about the company, its management, and the purpose of the offering. Incorrect or incomplete information will delay the offering.

REGISTRATION FEE charge made by the Securities and Exchange Commission and paid by the issuer of a security when a public offering is recorded with the SEC.

REGISTRATION STATEMENT document detailing the purpose of a proposed public offering of securities. The statement outlines financial details, a history of the company's operations and management, and other facts of importance to potential buyers. *See also* REGISTRATION.

REGRESSION ANALYSIS statistical technique used to establish the relationship of a dependent variable, such as the sales of a company, and one or more independent variables, such as family formations, GROSS DOMESTIC PRODUCT, per capita income, and other ECONOMIC INDICATORS. By measuring exactly how large and significant each independent variable has historically been in its relation to the dependent variable, the future value of the dependent variable can be predicted. Essentially, regression analysis attempts to measure the degree of correlation between the dependent and independent variables, thereby establishing the latter's predictive value. For example, a manufacturer of baby food might want to determine the relationship between sales and housing starts as part of a sales forecast. Using a technique called a scatter graph, it might plot on the X and Y axes the historical sales for ten years and the historical annual housing starts for the same period. A line connecting the average dots, called the regression line, would reveal the degree of correlation between the two factors by showing the amount of unexplained variation—represented by the dots falling outside the line. Thus, if the regression line connected all the dots, it would demonstrate a direct relationship between baby food sales and housing starts, meaning that one could be predicted on the basis of the other. The proportion of dots scattered outside the regression line would indicate, on the other hand, the degree to which the relationship was less direct, a high enough degree of unexplained variation meaning there was no meaningful relationship and that housing starts have no predictive value in terms of baby food sales. This proportion of unexplained variations is termed the *coefficient of determination,* and its square root the CORRELATION COEFFICIENT. The correlation coefficient is the ultimate yardstick of regression analysis: a correlation coefficient of 1 means the relationship is direct—baby food and housing starts move together; –1 means there is a negative relationship—the more housing starts there are, the less baby food is sold; a coefficient of zero means there is no relationship between the two factors.

Regression analysis is also used in securities' markets analysis and in the risk-return analyses basic to PORTFOLIO THEORY.

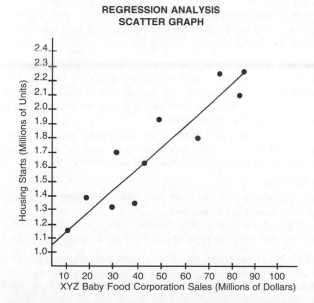

**REGRESSION ANALYSIS
SCATTER GRAPH**

Housing Starts (Millions of Units) vs. XYZ Baby Food Corporation Sales (Millions of Dollars)

REGRESSIVE TAX

1. system of taxation in which tax rates decline as the tax base rises. For example, a system that taxed values of $1,000 to $5,000 at 5%, $5,000 to $10,000 at 4% and so on would be regressive. A regressive tax is the opposite of a PROGRESSIVE TAX.

2. tax system that results in a higher tax for the poor than for the rich, in terms of percentage of income. In this sense, a sales tax is regressive even though the same rate is applied to all sales, because people with lower incomes tend to spend most of their incomes on goods and services. Similarly, payroll taxes are regressive because they are borne largely by wage earners and not by higher income groups. Local property taxes also tend to be regressive because poorer people spend more of their incomes on housing costs, which are directly affected by property taxes. *See also* FLAT TAX.

REGULAR WAY DELIVERY (AND SETTLEMENT) completion of securities transaction at the office of the purchasing broker on (but not before) the third full business day following the date of the transaction, as required by the NEW YORK STOCK EXCHANGE. Government transactions are an exception; for them, regular way means delivery and settlement the next business day following a transaction.

REGULATED COMMODITIES all commodity futures and options contracts traded on organized U.S. futures exchanges. *See also* COMMODITY FUTURES TRADING COMMISSION.

REGULATED INVESTMENT COMPANY MUTUAL FUND or UNIT INVESTMENT TRUST eligible under *Regulation M* of the Internal Revenue Service to pass capital gains, dividends, and interest earned on fund investments directly to its shareholders to be taxed at the personal level. The process, designed to avoid double taxation, is called the *conduit theory*. To qualify as a regulated investment company, the fund must meet such requirements as 90% minimum distribution of interest and dividends received on investments less expenses and 90% distribution of capital gain net income. To avoid a 4% excise tax, however, a regulated investment company must pay out 98% of its net investment income and capital gains. Shareholders must pay taxes even if they reinvest their distributions.

REGULATION A

1. Securities and Exchange Commission provision for simplified REGISTRATION of small issues of securities. A Regulation A issue requires a shorter form of PROSPECTUS and carries lesser liability for officers and directors for false or misleading statements.

2. Federal Reserve Board statement of the means and conditions under which Federal Reserve banks make loans to member and other banks at what is called the DISCOUNT WINDOW. *See also* REDISCOUNT.

REGULATION D

1. FEDERAL RESERVE BOARD rule pertaining to the amount of reserves banks must maintain relative to deposits.

2. SECURITIES AND EXCHANGE COMMISSION (SEC) rules concerning PRIVATE PLACEMENTS and defining related concepts such as ACCREDITED INVESTOR.

REGULATION FD Securities and Exchange Commission regulation requiring simultaneous disclosure to investors of material information and disclosure within 24 hours of material information released inadvertently.

REGULATION G Federal Reserve Board rule regulating lenders other than commercial banks, brokers or dealers who, in the ordinary course of business, extend credit to individuals to purchase or carry securities. Special provision is made for loans by corporations and credit unions to finance purchases under employee stock option and stock purchase plans.

REGULATION S Securities and Exchange Commission regulation that permits foreign sales to foreign investors by U.S. companies without REGISTRATION.

REGULATION SHO *see* SHORT-SALE RULE.

REGULATION T Federal Reserve Board regulation covering the extension of credit to customers by securities brokers, dealers, and members of the national securities exchanges. It establishes INITIAL MARGIN requirements and defines registered (eligible), unregistered (ineligible), and exempt securities. *See also* MARGIN REQUIREMENT; MARGIN SECURITIES.

REGULATION U Federal Reserve Board limit on the amount of credit a bank may extend a customer for purchasing and carrying MARGIN SECURITIES. *See also* NONPURPOSE LOAN.

REGULATION Z Federal Reserve Board regulation covering provisions of the CONSUMER CREDIT PROTECTION ACT OF 1968, known as the Truth in Lending Act.

REHYPOTHECATION pledging by brokers of securities in customers' MARGIN ACCOUNTS to banks as collateral for broker loans under a GENERAL LOAN AND COLLATERAL AGREEMENT. Broker loans cover the positions of brokers who have made margin loans to customers for margin purchases and SELLING SHORT. Margin loans are collateralized by the HYPOTHECATION of customers securities to the broker. Their rehypothecation is authorized when the customer originally signs a GENERAL ACCOUNT agreement.

REIMBURSEMENT paying someone back for out-of-pocket expenses. For example, a company reimburses employees for their out-of-pocket business-related expenses when employees file expense reports. Insurance companies reimburse policyholders for out-of-pocket expenses incurred paying medical bills (for health insurance) or for home repairs (homeowner's insurance).

REINSTATEMENT in INSURANCE, the restoration of coverage after a policy has lapsed because premium payments have not been made. Typically, life insurance can be reinstated within a three-year period if premiums are paid and subject to evidence of continued insurability.

REINSURANCE sharing of RISK among insurance companies. Part of the insurer's risk is assumed by other companies in return for a part of the premium fee paid by the insured. By spreading the risk, reinsurance allows an individual company to take on clients whose coverage would be too great a burden for one insurer to carry alone.

REINVESTMENT PRIVILEGE right of a shareholder to reinvest dividends in order to buy more shares in the company or MUTUAL FUND, usually at no additional sales charge.

REINVESTMENT RATE rate of return resulting from the reinvestment of the interest from a bond or other fixed-income security. The reinvestment rate on a ZERO-COUPON BOND is predictable and locked in, since no interest payments are ever made, and therefore all imputed interest is reinvested at the same rate. The reinvestment rate on coupon bonds is less predictable because it rises and falls with market interest rates.

REINVESTMENT RISK risk that rates will fall causing cash flows from an investment (dividends or interest), assuming reinvestment, to earn less than the original investment.

REIT *see* REAL ESTATE INVESTMENT TRUST.

REJECTION
Banking: refusal to grant credit to an applicant because of inadequate financial strength, a poor credit history, or some other reason.
Insurance: refusal to underwrite a risk, that is, to issue a policy.
Securities: refusal of a broker or a broker's customer to accept the security presented to complete a trade. This usually occurs because the security lacks the necessary endorsements. or because of other exceptions to the rules for GOOD DELIVERY.

RELATIVE STRENGTH rate at which a stock falls relative to other stocks in a falling market or rises relative to other stocks in a rising market. Analysts reason that a stock that holds value on the downside will be a strong performer on the upside and vice versa. Comparative relative strength, as the concept is more accurately called, compares a security's price performance with that of a "base security," which is often a market index. The security price is divided by the base security's price to get the ratio between the two, which is called the comparative relative strength indicator. When the indicator is moving up, the security is outperforming the base security and vice versa.

Comparative relative strength should not be confused with what technical analysts call the RELATIVE STRENGTH INDEX (RSI). The RSI is a MOMENTUM OSCILLATOR developed by J. Welles Wilder in the late 1970s and discussed in his book, *New Concepts in Technical Trading Systems*. The name relative strength index is somewhat misleading since it does not compare the relative strength of two securities, but rather the internal strength of a single security. The RSI measures the relative strength of the current price movement as increasing from 0 to 100. Although many variations are in use, Wilder favored the use of a 14-period measurement and set the significant levels of the indicator at 30 for oversold (signaling an imminent upturn) and 70 for overbought (signaling an imminent downturn). Thus the averages of up days and down days for 14-day periods would be plotted. If the security makes a new high but the RSI fails to surpass its previous high, this divergence is an indication of an impending reversal. When the RSI then turns down and falls below its most recent trough, it has completed a "failure swing" which confirms the impending reversal.

RELEASE CLAUSE provision in a MORTGAGE agreement allowing the freeing of pledged property after a proportionate amount of payment has been made.

REMAINDER remaining interest in a TRUST or ESTATE after expenses and after prior beneficiaries have been satisfied. *See also* CHARITABLE REMAINDER TRUST.

REMAINING MONTHLY BALANCE amount of debt remaining unpaid on a monthly statement. For example, a credit card customer may charge $300 worth of merchandise during a month, and pay $100, leaving a remaining monthly balance of $200, on which interest charges would accrue.

REMARGINING putting up additional cash or eligible securities to correct a deficiency in EQUITY deposited in a brokerage MARGIN ACCOUNT to meet MINIMUM MAINTENANCE REQUIREMENTS. Remargining usually is prompted by a MARGIN CALL.

REMIC acronym for *real estate mortgage investment conduit,* a pass-through vehicle created under the TAX REFORM ACT OF 1986 to issue multiclass mortgage-backed securities. REMICs may be organized as corporations, partnerships, or trusts, and those meeting qualifications are not subject to DOUBLE TAXATION. Interests in REMICs may be senior or junior, *regular* (debt instruments) or *residual* (equity interests). The practical meaning of REMICs has been that issuers have more flexibility than is afforded by the COLLATERALIZED MORTGAGE OBLIGATION (CMO) vehicle. Issuers can thus separate mortgage pools not only into different maturity classes but into different risk classes as well. Whereas CMOs normally have AAA bond ratings, REMICs represent a range of risk levels. *See also* RE-REMIC.

REMIT pay for purchased goods or services by cash, check, or electronic payment.

RENEWABLE TERM LIFE INSURANCE term life insurance policy offering the policyholder the option to renew for a specific period of time—frequently one year—for a particular length of time. Some term life policies stipulate a maximum age benefit. Some policies offer fixed premium rates for a certain number of years, usually ten, after which they are renewable at a higher premium rate. Other term policies are renewable every year, and charge escalating premium rates as the policyholder ages.

RENT payment from a tenant to a building owner for use of the specified property. For example, an apartment dweller must pay monthly rent to a landlord for the right to inhabit the apartment. A commercial tenant in an office or store must pay monthly rent to the building owner for the use of the commercial space.

RENT CONTROL state and local government regulation restricting the amount of rent landlords can charge their tenants. Rent control is used to regulate the quality of rental dwellings, with controls implemented only against those units that do not conform to building codes, as in New York City; or used across the board to deal with high rents resulting from a gross imbalance between housing supply and demand, as in Massachusetts and California. If a landlord violates rent control laws, the tenant may protest at the local housing authority charged with enforcing the law. While tenants may like rent control, landlords argue that it reduces their ability to earn a profit on their property, thereby discouraging them from investing any further to maintain or upgrade the property. In some cases, landlords argue that rent control encourages owners to abandon their property altogether since it will never be profitable to retain it.

R.E.O. designation for *real estate owned,* meaning property in foreclosure and owned by a bank. Homes can be bought at big discounts through agents handling R.E.O.s. Sales at prices below the mortgage balance are termed *short sales*.

REORGANIZATION financial restructuring of a firm in BANKRUPTCY. *See also* TRUSTEE IN BANKRUPTCY; VOTING TRUST CERTIFICATE.

REORGANIZATION BOND debt security issued by a company in REORGA-NIZATION proceedings. The bonds are generally issued to the company's creditors on a basis whereby interest is paid only if and when it is earned. *See also* ADJUSTMENT BOND; INCOME BOND.

REPATRIATION return of the financial assets of an organization or individual from a foreign country to the home country.

REPLACEMENT COST cost to replace an asset with another of similar utility at today's prices. Also called *current cost* and *replacement value. See also* BOOK VALUE, REPLACEMENT COST INSURANCE.

REPLACEMENT COST ACCOUNTING accounting method allowing additional DEPRECIATION on part of the difference between the original cost and current replacement cost of a depreciable asset.

REPLACEMENT COST INSURANCE property and casualty insurance that replaces damaged property. Replacement cost contents insurance pays the dollar amount needed to replace damaged personal property with items of like kind and quality, without deducting for depreciation. Replacement cost dwelling insurance pays the policyholder the cost of replacing the damaged property without deduction for depreciation, but limited by the maximum dollar amount indicated on the declarations page of the policy. *See also* REPLACEMENT COST.

REPURCHASE AGREEMENT (REPO; RP) agreement between a seller and a buyer, usually of U.S. government securities, whereby the seller agrees to repurchase the securities at an agreed upon price and, usually, at a stated time. Repos, also called RPs or buybacks, are widely used both as a money market investment vehicle and as an instrument of Federal Reserve MONE-TARY POLICY. Where a repurchase agreement is used as a short-term investment, a government securities dealer, usually a bank, borrows from an investor, typically a corporation with excess cash, to finance its inventory, using the securities as collateral. Such RPs may have a fixed maturity date or be OPEN REPOS, callable at any time. Rates are negotiated directly by the parties involved, but are generally lower than rates on collateralized loans made by New York banks. The attraction of repos to corporations, which also have the alternatives of COMMERCIAL PAPER, CERTIFICATES OF DEPOSIT, TREASURY BILLS and other short-term instruments, is the flexibility of maturities that makes them an ideal place to "park" funds on a very temporary basis. Dealers also arrange *reverse repurchase agreements,* whereby they agree to buy the securities and the investor agrees to repurchase them at a later date.

The FEDERAL RESERVE BANK also makes extensive use of repurchase agreements in its OPEN MARKET OPERATIONS as a method of fine tuning the MONEY SUPPLY. To temporarily expand the supply, the Fed arranges to buy securities from nonbank dealers who in turn deposit the proceeds in their commercial bank accounts thereby adding to reserves. Timed to coincide with whatever length of time the Fed needs to make the desired adjustment, usually 1 to 15 days, the dealer repurchases the securities. Such transactions are made at the Federal Reserve DISCOUNT RATE and accounts are credited in FEDERAL FUNDS. When it wishes to reduce the money supply temporarily, the Fed reverses the process. Using a procedure called the MATCHED SALE PURCHASE TRANSACTION, it sells securities to a nonbank dealer who either draws down bank balances directly or takes out a bank loan to make payment, thereby draining reserves.

In a third variation of the Repurchase agreement, banks and thrift institutions can raise temporary capital funds with a device called the *retail repurchase agreement*. Using pooled government securities to secure loans from individuals, they agree to repurchase the securities at a specified time at a price including interest. Despite its appearance of being a deposit secured by government securities, the investor has neither a special claim on the securities nor protection by the FEDERAL DEPOSIT INSURANCE CORPORATION in the event the bank is forced to liquidate.

See also OVERNIGHT REPO.

REQUIRED RATE OF RETURN return required by investors before they will commit money to an investment at a given level of risk. Unless the expected return exceeds the required return, an investment is unacceptable. *See also* HURDLE RATE; INTERNAL RATE OF RETURN; MEAN RETURN.

REQUIRED RESERVE RATE factor used to determine the amount of reserves a bank must maintain on its deposits.

RE-REMIC post-2008 Wall Street product that re-securitizes existing REMICS to create higher-rated ones.

RESCHEDULED LOANS bank loans that, as an alternative to DEFAULT, were restructured, usually by lengthening the maturity to make it easier for the borrower to meet repayment terms.

RESCIND cancel a contract agreement. The Truth in Lending Act confers the RIGHT OF RESCISSION, which allows the signer of a contract to nullify it within three business days without penalty and have any deposits refunded. Contracts may also be rescinded in cases of fraud, failure to comply with legal procedures, or misrepresentation. For example, a contract signed by a child under legal age may be rescinded, since children do not have the right to take on contractual obligations.

RESCISSION *see* RIGHT OF RESCISSION.

RESEARCH AND DEVELOPMENT (R&D) scientific and marketing evolution of a new product or service. Once such a product has been created in a laboratory or other research setting, marketing specialists attempt to define the market for the product. Then, steps are taken to manufacture the product to meet the needs of the market. Research and development spending is often listed as a separate item in a company's financial statements. In industries such as high-technology and pharmaceuticals, R&D spending is quite high, since products are outdated or attract competition quickly. Investors looking for companies in such fast-changing fields check on R&D spending as a percentage of sales because they consider this an important indicator of the company's prospects. *See also* RESEARCH AND DEVELOPMENT LIMITED PARTNERSHIP.

RESEARCH AND DEVELOPMENT LIMITED PARTNERSHIP plan whose investors put up money to finance new product RESEARCH AND DEVELOPMENT. In return, the investors get a percentage of the product's profits, if any, together with such benefits as DEPRECIATION of equipment. R&D partnerships may be offered publicly or privately, usually through brokerage firms. Those that are offered to the public must be registered with the Securities and Exchange Commission. *See also* LIMITED PARTNERSHIP.

RESEARCH DEPARTMENT division within a brokerage firm, investment company, bank trust department, insurance company, or other institutional investing organization that analyzes markets and securities. Research departments include analysts who focus on particular securities, commodities, and whole industries as well as generalists who forecast movements of the markets as a whole, using both FUNDAMENTAL ANALYSIS and TECHNICAL ANALYSIS. An analyst whose advice is followed by many investors can have a major impact on the prices of individual securities.

RESERVE
1. segregation of RETAINED EARNINGS to provide for such payouts as dividends, contingencies, improvements, or retirement of preferred stock.
2. VALUATION RESERVE, also called ALLOWANCE, for DEPRECIATION, BAD DEBT losses, shrinkage of receivables because of discounts taken, and other provisions created by charges to the PROFIT AND LOSS STATEMENT.
3. hidden reserves, represented by understatements of BALANCE SHEET values.
4. deposit maintained by a commercial bank in a FEDERAL RESERVE BANK to meet the Fed's RESERVE REQUIREMENT.

RESERVE REQUIREMENT FEDERAL RESERVE SYSTEM rule mandating the financial assets that member banks must keep in the form of cash and other liquid assets as a percentage of DEMAND DEPOSITS and TIME DEPOSITS. This money must be in the bank's own vaults or on deposit with the nearest regional FEDERAL RESERVE BANK. Reserve requirements, set by the Fed's Board of Governors, are one of the key tools in deciding how much money banks can lend, thus setting the pace at which the nation's money supply and economy grow. The higher the reserve requirement, the tighter the money— and therefore the slower the economic growth. *See also* MONETARY POLICY; MONEY SUPPLY; MULTIPLIER.

RESET BONDS bonds issued with a provision that on specified dates the initial interest rate must be adjusted so that the bonds trade at their original value. Although reset provisions can work in an issuer's favor by lowering rates should market rates fall or credit quality improve, they were designed as a protective feature for investors to enhance the marketability of JUNK BOND issues. Should market rates rise or credit quality decline (causing prices to decline), the interest rate would be increased to bring the bond price to PAR or above. The burden of increased interest payments on a weak issuer could prompt DEFAULT.

RESIDENTIAL ENERGY CREDIT tax credit granted to homeowners prior to 1986 by the federal government for improving the energy efficiency of their homes. Installation of storm windows and doors, insulation, or new fuel-saving heating systems before the end of 1985 meant a maximum federal credit on expenditures of $300. Equipping a home with renewable energy devices such as solar panels or windmills meant a maximum federal credit of $4,000. Many states offer incentives for installing such devices.

RESIDENTIAL MORTGAGE mortgage on a residential property. Interest on such mortgages is deductible for federal and state income tax purposes up to $1 million; for home equity loans, interest up to $100,000 is deductible.

RESIDENTIAL PROPERTY property zoned for single-family homes, townhouses, multifamily apartments, condominiums, and coops. Residential property falls under different zoning and taxation regulations than commercial property.

RESIDUAL SECURITY

1. SECURITY that has a potentially dilutive effect on earnings per common share. Warrants, rights, convertible bonds, and preferred stock are potentially dilutive because exercising or converting them into common stock would increase the number of common shares competing for the same earnings, and earnings per share would be reduced. *See also* DILUTION: FULLY DILUTED EARNINGS PER (COMMON) SHARE.

2. the term *residual* is also used informally to describe investments based on the excess cash flow generated by collateral pools. CMO REITs and the bottom tier of most COLLATERALIZED BOND OBLIGATIONS (CBOs) are examples of "residuals."

RESIDUAL VALUE

1. realizable value of a FIXED ASSET after costs associated with the sale.
2. amount remaining after all allowable DEPRECIATION charges have been subtracted from the original cost of a depreciable asset.
3. scrap value, which is the value to a junk dealer. Also called *salvage value.*
4. in automotive leasing, the contractual purchase price and the termination of the lease.

RESISTANCE LEVEL price ceiling at which technical analysts note persistent selling of a commodity or security. If XYZ's stock generally trades between a low of $50 and a high of $60 a share, $50 is called the SUPPORT LEVEL and $60 is called the resistance level. Technical analysts think it significant when the stock breaks through the resistance level because that means it usually will go on to new high prices. *See illustration on page 686. See also* BREAKOUT; TECHNICAL ANALYSIS.

RESOLUTION

1. in general, expression of desire or intent.
2. formal document representing an action of a corporation's BOARD OF DIRECTORS—perhaps a directive to management, such as in the declaration of a dividend, or a corporate expression of sentiment, such as acknowledging the services of a retiring officer. A *corporate resolution,* which defines the authority and powers of individual officers, is a document given to a bank.
3. legal order or contract by a government entity—called a *bond resolution*—authorizing a bond issue and spelling out the rights of bondholders and the obligations of the issuer.

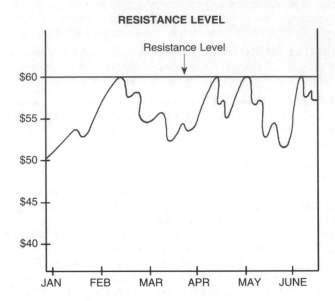

RESISTANCE LEVEL

RESOLUTION FUNDING CORPORATION (REFCORP) U.S. government agency created by Congress in 1989 to (1) issue BAILOUT BONDS and raise industry funds to finance activities of the RESOLUTION TRUST CORPORATION (RTC) and (2) merge or close sick institutions inherited from the disbanded FEDERAL SAVINGS AND LOAN INSURANCE CORPORATION (FSLIC). *See also* OFFICE OF THRIFT SUPERVISION (OTS).

RESOLUTION TRUST CORPORATION (RTC) U.S. government agency created by the 1989 bailout bill to merge or close savings and loan institutions becoming insolvent between 1989 and August 1992. The RTC was terminated in 1996 and its responsibilities were shifted to the SAVINGS ASSOCIATION INSURANCE FUND (SAIF), a unit of the FEDERAL DEPOSIT INSURANCE CORPORATION. The *Resolution Trust Corporation Oversight Board,* an arm of the executive branch, was charged with overseeing broad policy and the dispensing of funds to sick thrifts by RTC. *See also* OFFICE OF THRIFT SUPERVISION (OTS).

RESTATEMENT correction of a previously issued financial statement, usually because of an accounting irregularity or misrepresentation. Although restatement can result from honest error, the practice became notorious during the wave of corporate scandals in the early 2000s.

RESTRAINT OF TRADE interference with free market competition in violation of Federal Trade Commission regulations.

RESTRICTED said of stock brokered by a firm that is actively involved with the issuing company in nonpublic investment banking activities representing potential conflict of interest, such as a merger/acquisition defense or an underwriting. A firm can handle transactions in restricted stock only as an agent performing a brokerage function. It cannot trade for its own account, give INDICATIONS, or solicit orders with reference to restricted stock. Lists of restricted stock cannot be disclosed outside the trading area of the firm. *See also* LETTER SECURITY.

RESTRICTED ACCOUNT MARGIN ACCOUNT with a securities broker in which the EQUITY is less than the INITIAL MARGIN requirement set by the Federal Reserve Board's REGULATION T. A customer whose account is restricted may not make further purchases and must, in accordance with Regulation T's *retention requirement,* retain in the account a percentage of the proceeds of any sales so as to reduce the deficiency (debit balance). This retention requirement is currently set at 50%. *See also* MARGIN CALL.

RESTRICTED STOCK *see* RESTRICTED; LETTER SECURITY.

RESTRICTED STOCK AWARD plan whereby registered company stock is granted as compensation but ownership rights await VESTING.

RESTRICTED SURPLUS portion of RETAINED EARNINGS not legally available for the payment of dividends. Among the circumstances giving rise to such restriction: dividend arrearages in CUMULATIVE PREFERRED stock, a short-fall in the minimum WORKING CAPITAL ratio specified in an INDENTURE, or simply a vote by the BOARD OF DIRECTORS. Also called *restricted retained earnings.*

RESTRICTIVE COVENANT *see* COVENANT.

RESTRICTIVE ENDORSEMENT signature on the back of a check specifying the transfer of the amount of that check, under specific conditions. The most common type of restrictive endorsement is "for deposit only," meaning the check must be deposited in the payee's bank account and cannot be cashed.

RESTRUCTURING general term for major corporate changes aimed at greater efficiency and adaptation to changing markets. SPIN-OFFS, RECAPITAL-IZATIONS, STRATEGIC BUYOUTS, and major management realignments are all developments frequently associated with corporate restructurings. *See also* DOWNSIZING.

RESTRUCTURING CHARGE nonrecurring but not extraordinary (i.e., it must be deducted from current earnings) charge to earnings resulting from RESTRUCTURING. *See also* MANAGED EARNINGS.

RESYNDICATION LIMITED PARTNERSHIP partnership in which existing properties are sold to new limited partners, who can gain tax advantages that had been exhausted by the old partnership. For instance, a partnership with government subsidized housing may have given partners substantial tax benefits five years ago. Now the same housing development may be sold to a resyndication partnership, which will start the process of DEPRECIATION over again and claim additional tax benefits for its new limited partners. Resyndication partnerships are usually offered as PRIVATE PLACEMENTS through brokerage houses, although a few have been offered to the public.

RETAIL HOUSE brokerage firm that caters to retail investors instead of institutions. Such a firm may be a large national broker called a WIRE HOUSE, with a large RESEARCH DEPARTMENT and a wide variety of products and services for individuals, or it may be a small BOUTIQUE serving an exclusive clientele with specialized research or investment services.

RETAIL INVESTOR investor who buys securities and commodities futures on his own behalf, not for an organization. Retail investors typically buy shares of stock or commodity positions in much smaller quantities than institutions such as mutual funds, bank trust departments, and pension funds and therefore are usually charged commissions higher than those paid by the institutions. In recent years, market activity has increasingly been dominated by INSTITUTIONAL INVESTORS.

RETAIL PRICE price charged to retail customers for goods and services. Retailers buy goods from wholesalers, and increase the price to cover their costs, plus a profit. Manufacturers list suggested retail prices for their products; retailers may adhere to these prices or offer discounts from them.

RETAINED EARNINGS net profits kept to accumulate in a business after dividends are paid. Also called *undistributed profits* or *earned surplus*. Retained earnings are distinguished from *contributed capital*—capital received in exchange for stock, which is reflected in CAPITAL STOCK or CAPITAL SURPLUS and DONATED STOCK or DONATED SURPLUS. STOCK DIVIDENDS—the distribution of additional shares of capital stock with no cash payment— reduce retained earnings and increase capital stock. Retained earnings plus the total of all the capital accounts represent the NET WORTH of a firm. *See also* ACCUMULATED PROFITS TAX; PAID-IN CAPITAL.

RETAINED EARNINGS STATEMENT reconciliation of the beginning and ending balances in the RETAINED EARNINGS account on a company's BALANCE SHEET. It breaks down changes affecting the account, such as profits or losses from operations, dividends declared, and any other items charged or credited to retained earnings. A retained earnings statement is required by GENERALLY ACCEPTED ACCOUNTING PRINCIPLES whenever comparative balance sheets and income statements are presented. It may appear in the balance sheet, in a combined PROFIT AND LOSS STATEMENT and retained earnings statement, or as a separate schedule. It may also be called *statement of changes in earned surplus* (or *retained income*).

RETENTION in securities underwriting, the number of units allocated to a participating investment banker (SYNDICATE member) minus the units held back by the syndicate manager for facilitating institutional sales and for allocation to firms in the selling group that are not also members of the syndicate. *See also* UNDERWRITE.

RETENTION RATE percentage of after-tax profits credited to RETAINED EARNINGS. It is the opposite of the DIVIDEND PAYOUT RATIO.

RETENTION REQUIREMENT *see* RESTRICTED ACCOUNT.

RETIREMENT
1. cancellation of stock or bonds that have been reacquired or redeemed. *See also* CALLABLE; REDEMPTION.
2. removal from service after a fixed asset has reached the end of its useful life or has been sold and appropriate adjustments have been made to the asset and depreciation accounts.
3. repayment of a debt obligation.
4. permanent withdrawal of an employee from gainful employment in accordance with an employer's policies concerning length of service, age, or disability. A retired employee may have rights to a pension or other retirement provisions offered by the employer. Such benefits may in some circumstances supplement payments from an INDIVIDUAL RETIREMENT ARRANGEMENT (IRA) or KEOGH PLAN.

RETIREMENT AGE age at which employees no longer work. Though there is no longer any mandatory retirement age, many institutions do impose a retirement age. The federal government has a retirement age of 70. Many corporations have a retirement age of 65, although this has become more flexible and is no longer standard. Employees reaching age 62 may start to receive Social Security benefits, though the minimum age for receiving full Social Security benefits starts at age 65 and is gradually increasing to age 67. For example, for those born from 1943 through 1954, the age to receive full Social Security benefits is 66. For those born in 1960 or later, the age for full benefits rises to 67.

RETIREMENT PROTECTION ACT OF 1994 legislation designed to protect the pension benefits of American workers and retirees by increasing funding of underfunded pension plans and strengthening the pension insurance program administered by the PENSION BENEFIT GUARANTY CORPORATION (PBGC). Reinforcing the special requirement known as the Deficit Reduction Contribution (DRC) to fund underfunded pension plans, the act required severely underfunded plans to have enough cash and marketable securities to cover current benefit payments. The law also increased PBGC premiums for pension plans posing the greatest liquidation risk. It also required employers whose plans are less than 90% funded to provide a notice to their employees in simple language on the plan's funding and the limits of PBGC guarantees. The act also created the "Pension Search Program" which locates people who are owed benefits from fully funded, PBGC-insured defined benefit plans that terminate. *See also* PENSION BENEFIT GUARANTY CORPORATION (PBGC).

RETROCESSION *reinsurance* of REINSURANCE.

RETURN

Finance and investment: profit on a securities or capital investment, usually expressed as an annual percentage rate. *See also* RATE OF RETURN; RETURN ON EQUITY; RETURN ON INVESTED CAPITAL; RETURN ON SALES; TOTAL RETURN.

Retailing: exchange of previously sold merchandise for REFUND or CREDIT against future sales.

Taxes: form on which taxpayers submit information required by the government when they file with the INTERNAL REVENUE SERVICE. For example, Form 1040 is the tax return used by individual taxpayers.

Trade: physical return of merchandise for credit against an invoice.

RETURN OF CAPITAL distribution of cash resulting from DEPRECIATION tax savings, the sale of a CAPITAL ASSET or of securities in a portfolio, or any other transaction unrelated to RETAINED EARNINGS. Returns of capital are not directly taxable but may result in higher CAPITAL GAINS taxes later on if they reduce the acquisition cost base of the property involved. Also called *return of basis.*

RETURN ON COMMON EQUITY *see* RETURN ON EQUITY; RETURN ON INVESTED CAPITAL.

RETURN ON EQUITY amount, expressed as a percentage, earned on a company's common stock investment for a given period. It is calculated by dividing common stock equity (NET WORTH) at the beginning of the accounting period into NET INCOME for the period after preferred stock dividends but before common stock dividends. Return on equity tells common shareholders how effectually their money is being employed. Comparing percentages for current and prior periods reveals trends, and comparison with industry composites reveals how well a company is holding its own against its competitors.

RETURN ON INVESTED CAPITAL amount, expressed as a percentage, earned on a company's total capital—its common and preferred stock EQUITY plus its long-term FUNDED DEBT—calculated by dividing total capital into earnings before interest, taxes, and dividends. Return on invested capital, usually termed *return on investment,* or *ROI,* is a useful means of comparing companies, or corporate divisions, in terms of efficiency of management and viability of product lines.

RETURN ON SALES net pretax profits as a percentage of NET SALES—a useful measure of overall operational efficiency when compared with prior periods or with other companies in the same line of business. It is important to recognize, however, that return on sales varies widely from industry to industry. A supermarket chain with a 2% return on sales might be operating efficiently, for example, because it depends on high volume to generate an acceptable RETURN ON INVESTED CAPITAL. In contrast, a manufacturing enterprise is expected to average 4% to 5%, so a return on sales of 2% is likely to be considered highly inefficient.

REVALUATION change in the value of a country's currency relative to others that is based on the decision of authorities rather than on fluctuations in the market. Revaluation generally refers to an increase in the currency's value; DEVALUATION refers to a decrease. *See also* FLOATING EXCHANGE RATE; PAR VALUE OF CURRENCY.

REVENUE ANTICIPATION NOTE (RAN) short-term debt issue of a municipal entity that is to be repaid out of anticipated revenues such as sales taxes. When the taxes are collected, the RAN is paid off. Interest from the note is usually tax-free to RAN holders.

REVENUE BOND *see* MUNICIPAL REVENUE BOND.

REVENUE ENHANCEMENT a synonym for taxation, including such less-direct measures as eliminating tax credits and curtailing deductions.

REVENUE NEUTRAL guiding criterion in drafting the TAX REFORM ACT OF 1986 whereby provisions estimated to add revenue were offset by others estimated to reduce revenue, so that on paper the new bill would generate the same amount of revenue as the old tax laws. The concept, which has guided subsequent tax legislation, was theoretical rather than real, since estimates are subject to variation.

REVENUE RECONCILIATION ACT OF 1993 landmark legislation signed into law by President Clinton in August 1993 to reduce the federal budget deficit by curtailing spending and raising taxes. Among its major components:

Provisions Affecting Individuals
   1. added a fourth tax bracket of 36% to the existing 15%, 28%, and 31% brackets. Single taxpayers earning over $115,000 and married taxpayers filing jointly earning over $140,000 pay at the 36% marginal rate.
   2. added a 10% surtax on married couples filing jointly reporting more than $250,000 in taxable income, or on married couples filing separately with

taxable incomes of more than $125,000, creating, in effect, a fifth tax bracket at 39.6%.

3. kept capital gains tax rate at 28% for assets held at least a year.

4. created special tax break for investing in small companies. Investors buying newly issued stock in a small company with less than $50 million in gross assets who hold the stock for at least 5 years may exclude 50% of the profit from capital gains taxes. For each subsequent year the investor holds the stock, the tax rate declines 10% until there is no capital gains tax after 10 years.

5. gasoline taxes were increased from 14.1 cents to 18.4 cents a gallon.

6. taxes on Social Security benefits were raised. Couples with provisional income plus half their Social Security benefits totaling more than $44,000 owe tax on up to 85% of their Social Security benefits. For singles, the equivalent level is $34,000. Provisional income is defined as adjusted gross income, interest on tax-exempt bonds, and certain income from foreign sources. Previously, couples with taxable income over $32,000 and singles with income over $25,000 had to pay taxes on 50% of their Social Security benefits.

7. Medicare tax cap was eliminated. Before this Act, the Medicare tax of 1.45% on wages applied to the first $135,000 of wages.

8. phaseout of personal exemptions, which had been temporary, was made permanent. Personal exemptions begin to phase out for singles reporting adjusted gross incomes of $108,450. For married couples filing jointly, exemptions begin to phase out when adjusted gross income reaches $167,700. (These amounts are adjusted for inflation annually).

9. investment interest deductions were limited. Interest paid to finance the purchase of securities remain deductible from interest income earned from investments, but that interest can no longer be deducted against realized capital gains.

10. pension contributions were limited. The income limit for contributions to pension plans such as Keoghs and SEPs was lowered from $235,840 to $150,000.

11. earned income credit was expanded. For taxpayers with more than one child, a credit of up to 18.5% can be claimed for the first $7,750 of income, up to a maximum of $1,511. The credit rose to 36% in 1995 and 40% in 1996.

12. moving deductions were limited. Under the law, unreimbursed moving expenses for house-hunting, closing fees, broker's commissions, and food costs while living in temporary quarters are no longer deductible as they had been previously. In addition, moves must be 50 miles, up from 35 miles, from the previous home in order to qualify for tax benefits. Moving expenses were converted from an itemized deduction—available only to those who filed an itemized return—to an above-the-line deduction, similar to alimony.

13. estimated tax rules were changed. For married taxpayers filing jointly reporting more than $150,000 in taxable income, quarterly estimated taxes must be paid at 110% of the previous year's tax liability.

14. alternative minimum tax (AMT) rates were raised. The AMT tax rate on income exceeding $175,000 was raised from 24% to 28%.

15. estate tax rates were raised. The top rate on inheritance taxes was raised from 50% to 55% on estates worth more than $3 million.

16. luxury taxes were repealed. The 10% luxury tax on airplanes, boats, cars,

furs, and jewelry was repealed on all items except cars selling for more than $32,000.

17. rules governing donations of appreciated property were made permanent. Temporary rules allowing donors to deduct the full value of appreciated property such as art, real estate, and securities were made permanent. Such donations were also removed from calculations toward the alternative minimum tax (AMT).

Provisions Affecting Business

18. corporate tax rates were increased from 34% to 35%, for companies with taxable income of at least $10 million.

19. deductions for executive salaries exceeding $1 million were limited.

20. meal and entertainment deductions were lowered from 80% to 50% for business-related meal and entertainment expenses.

21. deductions were increased for small business purchases of equipment up to $17,500 a year, up from $10,000 previously.

22. tax breaks were reinstated for real estate professionals. Certified real estate professionals, defined as those working at least 750 hours a year in a real-estate-related line of work such as sales or construction, are allowed to deduct losses on rental property against any form of income. Previously, such passive losses could only be offset against passive income.

23. commercial real estate depreciation was lengthened from 31 years to 39 years.

24. club dues for country clubs; airline lounges; and social, athletic, and health clubs were made nondeductible.

25. standard period for depreciating goodwill when acquiring a business was set at 15 years.

26. expenses for lobbying Congress were made nondeductible.

27. restrictions on deductions for traveling spouses were imposed. Expenses for spouses traveling on a business trip were made nondeductible, unless the spouse is an employee of the company paying for the trip and has a business reason for going.

28. empowerment zones were created. Businesses that invest and create jobs in authorized empowerment zones in particular depressed communities qualify for tax incentives and special grants.

REVENUE RULING a letter from the Internal Revenue Service accepting a way of treating a transaction for tax purposes. Also called a *letter ruling.*

REVENUES in a general business sense, synonymous with sales except that "revenues" is often preferred where a service, such as a money loaned, is being exchanged as opposed to a tangible product. Large, diversified companies often report "sales and revenues," both on a gross and net basis. Receipts from taxes and government services are always called revenues.

REVENUE SHARING
Limited partnerships: percentage split between the general partner and limited partners of profits, losses, cash distributions, and other income or losses which result from the operation of a real estate, oil and gas, equipment leasing, or other partnership. *See also* LIMITED PARTNERSHIP.

Taxes: return of tax revenue to a unit of government by a larger unit, such as from a state to one of its municipalities. GENERAL REVENUE SHARING between the federal government and states, localities, and other subunits existed between 1972 and 1987.

REVERSAL change in direction in the stock or commodity futures markets, as charted by technical analysts. If the Dow Jones Industrial Average has been climbing steadily from 7400 to 7900, for instance, chartists would speak of a reversal if the average started a sustained fall back toward 7400.

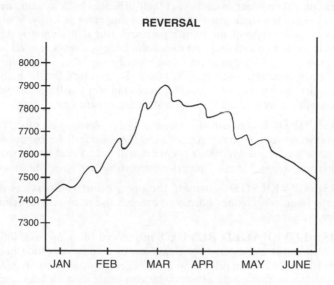

REVERSAL

REVERSE ANNUITY MORTGAGE (RAM) MORTGAGE instrument that allows an elderly person to live off the equity in a fully paid-for house. Such a homeowner would enter into a reverse annuity mortgage agreement with a financial institution such as a bank, which would guarantee a lifelong fixed monthly income in return for gradually giving up ownership of the house. The longer the payments continue, the less equity the elderly owner would retain. At the owner's death the bank gains title to the real estate, which it can sell to offset outstanding claims. The law also permits such arrangements between relatives, so that, for instance, a son or daughter might enter into a reverse annuity mortgage transaction with his or her retiring parents, thus providing the parents with cash to invest in income-yielding securities and the son or daughter with the depreciation and other tax benefits of real estate ownership. *See also* ARM'S LENGTH TRANSACTION; LIFETIME REVERSE MORTGAGE.

REVERSE A SWAP restore a bond portfolio to its former position following a swap of one bond for another to gain the advantage of a YIELD SPREAD or a tax loss. The reversal may mean that the yield differential has disappeared or that the investor, content with a short-term profit, wishes to stay with the original bond for the advantages that may be gained in the future. *See also* BOND SWAP.

REVERSE CONVERSION technique whereby brokerage firms earn interest on their customers' stock holdings. A typical reverse conversion would work like this: A brokerage firm sells short the stocks it holds in customers' margin accounts, then invests this money in short-term money market instruments. To protect against a sharp rise in the markets, the firm hedges its short position by buying CALL options and selling PUT options. To unwind the reverse conversion, the firms buys back the stocks, sells the call, and buys the put. *See also* MARGIN ACCOUNT; OPTION.

REVERSE CONVERTIBLES short-term bonds coupled to well-known stocks, often paying double-digit yields. When the notes mature, typically in three months to one year, investors get their principal back as with any other bond as long as the stock price of the underlying company stays where it is or rises from the time of the bond's issuance. But if the underlying stock plunges in value to a certain point called the knock-in level, usually at least 20% below the stock's price when the security was first issued, investors receive stock instead of their principal back. So in return for the high yield, investors are taking the risk that the underlying stock will not fall very far between when they buy the security and when it matures.

REVERSE HEDGE also called a *Chinese hedge,* owning a COMMON STOCK and SELLING SHORT a CONVERTIBLE with the same underlying common stock in the hope that the convertible's premium will fall. A real hedge would be the other way around, that is, long the convertible and short the stock.

REVERSE LEVERAGE situation, the opposite of FINANCIAL LEVERAGE, where the interest on money borrowed exceeds the return on investment of the borrowed funds.

REVERSE LEVERAGED BUYOUT process of bringing back into publicly traded status a company—or a division of a company—that had been publicly traded and taken private. In the 1980s, many public companies were taken private in LEVERAGED BUYOUTS by corporate raiders who borrowed against the companies' assets to finance the deal. When some or all of the debt incurred in the leveraged buyout was repaid, many of these companies were in sufficiently strong financial condition to go public again, enriching the private stockholders as well as the investment bankers who earned fees implementing these deals.

REVERSE MORTGAGE arrangement whereby a homeowner borrows against home equity and receives regular payments (tax-free) from the lender until the accumulated principal and interest reach the credit limit of equity; at that time, the lender either gets repayment in a lump sum or takes the house. Reverse mortgages are available privately and through the Federal Housing Administration (FHA). They are appropriate for cash-poor but house-rich older borrowers who want to stay in their homes and expect to live long enough to amortize high up-front fees but not so long that the lender winds up with the house. Lower income but greater security is provided by a variation, the REVERSE ANNUITY MORTGAGE (RAM).

REVERSE REPURCHASE AGREEMENT *see* REPURCHASE AGREEMENT.

REVERSE SPLIT procedure whereby a corporation reduces the number of shares outstanding. The total number of shares will have the same market value immediately after the reverse split as before it, but each share will be worth more. For example, if a firm with 10 million outstanding shares selling at $10 a share executes a reverse 1 for 10 split, the firm will end up with 1 million shares selling for $100 each. Such splits are usually initiated by companies wanting to raise the price of their outstanding shares because they think the price is too low to attract investors. Also called *split down. See also* SPLIT.

REVERSING TRADE offsetting options or futures transaction to CLOSE A POSITION.

REVISIONARY TRUST IRREVOCABLE TRUST that becomes a REVOCABLE TRUST after a specified period, usually over 10 years or upon the death of the GRANTOR.

REVOCABLE TRUST agreement whereby income-producing property is deeded to heirs. The provisions of such a TRUST may be altered as many times as the GRANTOR pleases, or the entire trust agreement can be canceled, unlike irrevocable trusts. The grantor receives income from the assets, but the property passes directly to the beneficiaries at the grantor's death, without having to go through PROBATE court proceedings. Since the assets are still part of the grantor's estate, however, estate taxes must be paid on this transfer. This kind of trust differs from an IRREVOCABLE TRUST, which permanently transfers assets from the estate during the grantor's lifetime and therefore escapes estate taxes.

REVOLVING CREDIT
Commercial banking: contractual agreement between a bank and its customer, usually a company, whereby the bank agrees to make loans up to a specified maximum for a specified period, usually a year or more. As the borrower repays a portion of the loan, an amount equal to the repayment can be borrowed again under the terms of the agreement. In addition to interest borne by notes, the bank charges a fee for the commitment to hold the funds available. A COMPENSATING BALANCE may be required in addition.
Consumer banking: loan account requiring monthly payments of less than the full amount due, and the balance carried forward is subject to a financial charge. Also, an arrangement whereby borrowings are permitted up to a specified limit and for a specified period, usually a year, with a fee charged for the commitment. Also called *open-end credit* or *revolving line of credit*.

REVOLVING LINE OF CREDIT *see* REVOLVING CREDIT.

RICH
1. term for a security whose price seems too high in light of its price history. For bonds, the term may also imply that the yield is too low.
2. term for rate of interest that seems too high in relation to the borrower's risk.
3. synonym for *wealthy*.

RICO acronym for *Racketeer Influenced and Corrupt Organization Act,* a federal law used to convict firms and individuals of INSIDER TRADING. Many critics have charged that the law was excessively enforced, and several indictments were dismissed for lack of evidence.

RIDER written form attached to an insurance policy that alters the policy's coverage, terms, or conditions. For example, after buying a diamond bracelet, a policyholder may want to add a rider to her homeowner's insurance policy to cover the jewelry. *See also* FLOATER.

RIEGLE-NEAL INTERSTATE BANKING AND BRANCHING EFFICIENCY ACT OF 1994 law allowing interstate banking in America. The legislation permitted banks to establish branches nationwide by eliminating all barriers to interstate banking at the state level. Before this legislation went into effect, banks had been required to set up separate subsidiaries in each state to conduct business and it was illegal for banks to accept deposits from customers out of their home states.

RIGGED MARKET situation in which the prices for a security are manipulated so as to lure unsuspecting buyers or sellers. *See also* MANIPULATION.

RIGHT *see* SUBSCRIPTION RIGHT.

RIGHT OF FIRST REFUSAL right of someone to be offered a right before it is offered to others. For example, a baseball team may have the right of first refusal on a ballplayer's contract, meaning that the club can make the first offer, or even match other offers, before the player plays for another team. A company may have the right of refusal to distribute or manufacture another company's product. A publishing company may have the right of refusal to publish a book proposed by one of its authors.

RIGHT OF REDEMPTION right to recover property transferred by a MORT-GAGE or other LIEN by paying off the debt either before or after foreclosure. Also called *equity of redemption.*

RIGHT OF RESCISSION right granted by the federal CONSUMER CREDIT PROTECTION ACT OF 1968 to void a contract within three business days with full refund of any down payment and without penalty. The right is designed to protect consumers from high-pressure door-to-door sales tactics and hastily made credit commitments which involve their homes as COLLATERAL, such as loans secured by second mortgages.

RIGHT OF SURVIVORSHIP right entitling one owner of property held jointly to take title to it when the other owner dies. *See also* JOINT TENANTS WITH RIGHT OF SURVIVORSHIP; TENANTS IN COMMON.

RIGHTS OFFERING offering of COMMON STOCK to existing shareholders who hold rights that entitle them to buy newly issued shares at a discount from the price at which shares will later be offered to the public. Rights offerings are usually handled by INVESTMENT BANKERS under what is called a STANDBY COMMITMENT, whereby the investment bankers agree to purchase any shares not subscribed to by the holders of rights. *See also* OVERSUBSCRIPTION PRIVILEGE; PREEMPTIVE RIGHT; SUBSCRIPTION RIGHT.

RING location on the floor of an exchange where trades are executed. The circular arrangement where traders can make bid and offer prices is also called a *pit,* particularly when commodities are traded.

RING FENCE strategy used to isolate an asset from outside risks, such as taxes, inflation, market fluctuations, and other factors. For example, a bank might use an OFFSHORE subsidiary to avoid onerous regulations that would otherwise threaten.

RISING BOTTOMS technical chart pattern showing a rising trend in the low prices of a security or commodity. As the range of prices is charted daily, the lows reveal an upward trend. Rising bottoms signify higher and higher basic SUPPORT LEVELS for a security or commodity. When combined with a series of ASCENDING TOPS, the pattern is one a follower of TECHNICAL ANALYSIS would call bullish.

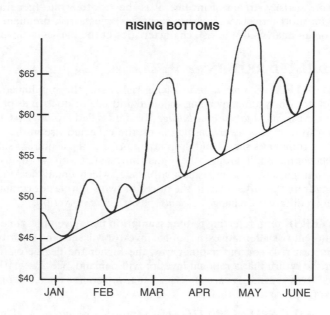

RISK

1. with reference to fluctuating market values of securities and portfolios, risk means exposure to uncertainty, which is manifest as variability (or, synonymously, volatility), and is measured by STANDARD DEVIATION.

2. in its stricter and narrower senses, risk means the potential for loss of value. Among the commonly encountered types of risk are these:

Actuarial risk: risk an insurance underwriter covers in exchange for premiums, such as the risk of premature death.

Exchange risk: chance of loss on foreign currency exchange.

Inflation risk: chance that the value of assets or of income will be eroded as inflation shrinks the value of a country's currency.

Interest rate risk: possibility that a fixed-rate debt instrument will decline in value as a result of a rise in interest rates.

Inventory risk: possibility that price changes, obsolescence, or other factors will shrink the value of INVENTORY.

Liquidity risk: possibility that an investor will not be able to buy or sell a commodity or security quickly enough or in sufficient quantities because buying or selling opportunities are limited.

Political risk: possibility of NATIONALIZATION or other unfavorable government action.

Repayment (credit) risk: chance that a borrower or trade debtor will not repay an obligation as promised.

Risk of principal: chance that invested capital will drop in value.

Underwriting risk: risk taken by an INVESTMENT BANKER that a new issue of securities purchased outright will not be bought by the public and/or that the market price will drop during the offering period.

RISK-ADJUSTED DISCOUNT RATE in PORTFOLIO THEORY and CAPITAL BUDGET analysis, the rate necessary to determine the PRESENT VALUE of an uncertain or risky stream of income; it is the risk-free rate (generally the return on short-term U.S. Treasury securities) plus a risk premium that is based on an analysis of the risk characteristics of the particular investment or project.

RISK-ADJUSTED RETURN *see* EXCESS RETURN.

RISK ARBITRAGE ARBITRAGE involving risk, as in the simultaneous purchase of stock in a company being acquired and sale of stock in its proposed acquirer. Also called *takeover arbitrage*. Traders called *arbitrageurs* attempt to profit from TAKEOVERS by cashing in on the expected rise in the price of the target company's shares and drop in the price of the acquirer's shares. If the takeover plans fall through, the traders may be left with enormous losses. Risk arbitrage differs from riskless arbitrage, which entails locking in or profiting from the differences in the prices of two securities or commodities trading on different exchanges. *See also* RISKLESS TRANSACTION.

RISK AVERSE term referring to the assumption that, given the same return and different risk alternatives, a rational investor will seek the security offering the least risk—or, put another way, the higher the degree of risk, the greater the return that a rational investor will demand. *See also* BEHAVIORAL FINANCE (OR INVESTING); CAPITAL ASSET PRICING MODEL; EFFICIENT PORTFOLIO; MEAN RETURN; PORTFOLIO THEORY.

RISK-BASED CAPITAL RATIO FIRREA-imposed requirement that banks maintain a minimum ratio of estimated total capital to estimated risk-weighted assets.

RISK CAPITAL *see* VENTURE CAPITAL.

RISK CATEGORY classification of risk elements used in analyzing MORTGAGES.

RISK-FREE RETURN YIELD on a risk-free investment. The 3-month Treasury bill is considered a riskless investment because it is a direct obligation of the U.S. government and its term is short enough to minimize the risks of inflation and market interest rate changes. The CAPITAL ASSET PRICING MODEL (CAPM) used in modern PORTFOLIO THEORY has the premise that the return on a security is equal to the risk-free return plus a RISK PREMIUM. *See also* EXCESS RETURN.

RISKLESS ARBITRAGE *see* ARBITRAGE; RISK ARBITRAGE.

RISKLESS TRANSACTION
1. trade guaranteeing a profit to the trader that initiates it. An arbitrageur may lock in a profit by trading on the difference in prices for the same security or commodity in different markets. For instance, if gold were selling for $927 an ounce in New York and $925 in London, a trader who acts quickly could buy a contract in London and sell it in New York for a riskless profit.
2. concept used in evaluating whether dealer MARKUPS and MARKDOWNS in OVER-THE-COUNTER transactions with customers are reasonable or excessive. In what is known as the FIVE PERCENT RULE, the FINANCIAL INDUSTRY REGULATORY AUTHORITY (FINRA) takes the position that markups (when the customer buys) and markdowns (when the customer sells) should not exceed 5%, the proper charge depending on the effort and risk of the dealer

in completing a trade. The maximum would be considered excessive for a riskless transaction, in which a security has high marketability and the dealer does not simply act as a broker and take a commission but trades from or for inventory and charges a markup or markdown. Where a dealer satisfies a buy order by making a purchase in the open market for inventory and then sells the security to the customer, the trade is called a simultaneous transaction. To avoid FINRA criticism, broker-dealers commonly disclose the markups and markdowns to customers in transactions where they act as dealers.

RISK PREMIUM in PORTFOLIO THEORY, the difference between the RISK-FREE RETURN and the TOTAL RETURN from a risky investment. In the CAPITAL ASSET PRICING MODEL (CAPM), the risk premium reflects market-related risk (SYSTEMATIC RISK) as measured by BETA. Other models also reflect specific risk as measured by ALPHA. *See also* EXCESS RETURN.

RISK-RETURN TRADE-OFF concept, basic in investment management, that RISK equals (varies with) RETURN; in other words, the higher the return the greater the risk and vice versa. In practice, it means that a speculative investment, such as stock in a newly formed company, can be expected to provide a higher potential return than a more conservative investment, such as BLUE CHIP or a BOND. Conversely, if you don't want the risk, don't expect the return. *See also* PORTFOLIO THEORY.

RISK TOLERANCE the extent to which an investor is RISK AVERSE. The concept is used by investment advisers and financial planners, who ask questions or administer tests attempting to determine an individual's risk comfort level, which involves emotional as well as rational factors. *See also* BEHAVIORAL FINANCE (OR INVESTING).

RISK TRANSFER shifting of risk, as with INSURANCE or the SECURITIZATION of debt.

ROAD SHOW presentation by an issuer of securities to potential buyers about the merits of the issue. Management of the company issuing stocks or bonds doing a road show travels around the country presenting financial information and an outlook for the company and answering the questions of analysts, fund managers, and other potential investors. Also known as a *dog and pony show.*

ROCKET SCIENTIST investment firm creator of innovative securities.

ROLL DOWN move from one OPTION position to another one having a lower EXERCISE PRICE. The term assumes that the position with the higher exercise price is closed out.

ROLL FORWARD move from one OPTION position to another with a later expiration date. The term assumes that the earlier position is closed out before the later one is established. If the new position involves a higher EXERCISE PRICE, it is called a *roll-up and forward;* if a lower exercise price, it is called a *roll-down and forward.* Also called *rolling over.*

ROLLING STOCK equipment that moves on wheels, used in the transportation industry. Examples include railroad cars and locomotives, tractor-trailers, and trucks.

ROLLOVER

1. movement of funds from one investment to another. For instance, an INDIVIDUAL RETIREMENT ARRANGEMENT may be rolled over when a person retires into an ANNUITY or other form of pension plan payout system. Balances in regular IRAs can be rolled over into ROTH IRAS, although income taxes will be due on untaxed earnings in the regular IRA account. When a BOND or CERTIFICATE OF DEPOSIT matures, the funds may be rolled over into another bond or certificate of deposit. A stock may be sold and the proceeds rolled over into the same stock, establishing a different cost basis for the shareholder. *See also* THIRTY-DAY WASH RULE.

2. term often used by banks when they allow a borrower to delay making a PRINCIPAL payment on a loan. Also, a country that has difficulty in meeting its debt payments may be granted a rollover by its creditors. With governments themselves, rollovers in the form of REFUNDINGS or REFINANCINGS are routine.

   See also CERTIFICATE OF DEPOSIT ROLLOVER.

ROLL UP move from one OPTION position to another having a higher EXERCISE PRICE. The term assumes that the earlier position is closed out before the new position is established. *See also* MASTER LIMITED PARTNERSHIP.

ROTATION *see* SECTOR ROTATION.

ROTH IRA INDIVIDUAL RETIREMENT ARRANGEMENTS created by the TAXPAYER RELIEF ACT OF 1997 permitting account holders to allow their capital to accumulate tax-free under certain conditions. The Roth IRA is named after Delaware Senator William V. Roth, Jr., who championed the idea of expanded IRAs. Individuals can invest up to $5,000 per year ($6,000 for those age 50 and older). There are income limitations on who can contribute to a Roth IRA. In 2008 a married couple filing jointly could make the full contribution if their modified adjustable gross income (MAGI) was less than $159,000. For a MAGI between $159,000 and $169,000, the amount they could contribute is reduced, and they could not contribute to a Roth IRA at all once their MAGI reached $169,000 or more. For singles, heads of household, and married couples filing separately, a full contribution could be made if their MAGI was less than $101,000. For a MAGI between $101,000 and $116,000, the amount they could contribute was reduced, and they could not contribute to a Roth IRA at all once their MAGI reached $116,000 or more. Assets inside Roth IRAs can be invested in stocks, bonds, mutual funds, bank instruments like CDs and money market accounts, precious metals, annuities, and real estate, like traditional IRAs. Roth IRA holders can withdraw the principal and earnings tax-free after age 59½, as long as the assets have remained in the account for at least 5 years after the first contribution. If the account holder dies before withdrawing from a Roth IRA, the proceeds are distributed to beneficiaries tax-free. Unlike traditional IRAs, participants do not have to take any distributions from Roth IRAs starting at age 70½, nor are they required to take any distributions at all during their lifetimes. They can also continue to contribute after reaching age 70½. Individuals with a traditional tax-deductible IRA can convert to a Roth IRA without the usual 10% early distribution penalty, although regular income taxes are due on untaxed earnings in the account. Determining whether or not it is advantageous to roll over or transfer assets from a traditional IRA to a Roth IRA is a complex decision and may require advice from a financial professional. *See also* ROLLOVER.

ROTH 401(K) PLAN type of retirement account, first introduced in 2006, allowing employees to designate part or all of their 401(k) contributions as Roth 401(k) contributions. As with a Roth IRA, these contributions will not be tax deductible, but all of the income and earnings that accumulate in the plan will be tax free when distributed. Participants have to meet the same requirements as the Roth IRA—5 years of participation, distributions taken after age 59½, and disability or use of up to $10,000 for a first-time home purchase.

ROUND LOT generally accepted unit of trading on a securities exchange. On the New York Stock Exchange, for example, a round lot is 100 shares for stock and $1,000 or $5,000 par value for bonds. In inactive stocks, the round lot is 10 shares. Increasingly, there seems to be recognition of a 500-share round lot for trading by institutions. Large denomination CERTIFICATES OF DEPOSIT trade on the OVER THE COUNTER market in units of $1 million. Investors who trade in round lots do not have to pay the DIFFERENTIAL charged on ODD LOT trades.

ROUND TRIP TRADE purchase and sale of a security or commodity within a short time. For example, a trader who continually is making short-term trades in a particular commodity is making round trip or *round turn* trades. Commissions for such a trader are likely to be quoted in terms of the total for a purchase and sale—$100 for the round trip, for instance. Excessive round trip trading is called CHURNING.

ROYALTY payment to the holder for the right to use property such as a patent, copyrighted material, or natural resources. For instance, inventors may be paid royalties when their inventions are produced and marketed. Authors may get royalties when books they have written are sold. Land owners leasing their property to an oil or mining company may receive royalties based on the amount of oil or minerals extracted from their land. Royalties are set in advance as a percentage of income arising from the commercialization of the owner's rights or property.

ROYALTY TRUST oil or gas company *spin-off* of oil reserves to a trust, which avoids DOUBLE TAXATION, eliminates the expense and risk of new drilling, and provides DEPLETION tax benefits to shareholders. In the mid-1980s, Mesa Royalty Trust, which pioneered the idea, led other trusts in converting to a MASTER LIMITED PARTNERSHIP form of organization, offering tax advantages along with greater flexibility and liquidity.

R-SQUARED MUTUAL FUND term that indicates, on a scale of 0 to 100, the percentage of a fund's performance that is explained by movements of its benchmark index. An S&P 500 index fund would thus have an R-squared at or close to 100. R-squared is useful in evaluating the significance of BETA. The higher the R-squared, the more meaningful the beta.

RUBBER CHECK check for which insufficient funds are available. It is called a rubber check because it bounces. *See also* OVERDRAFT.

RULE 405 New York Stock Exchange codification of an ethical concept recognized industry wide by those dealing with the investment public. These

KNOW YOUR CUSTOMER rules recognize that what is suitable for one investor may be less appropriate for another and require investment people to obtain pertinent facts about a customer's other security holdings, financial condition, and objectives. *See also* SUITABILITY RULES.

RULE OF 72 formula for approximating the time it will take for a given amount of money to double at a given COMPOUND INTEREST rate. The formula is simply 72 divided by the interest rate. In six years $100 will double at a compound annual rate of 12%, thus: 72 divided by 12 equals 6.

RULE OF THE 78s method of computing REBATES of interest on installment loans. It uses the SUM-OF-THE-YEAR'S-DIGITS basis in determining the interest earned by the FINANCE COMPANY for each month of a year, assuming equal monthly payments, and gets its name from the fact that the sum of the digits 1 through 12 is 78. Thus interest is equal to $^{12}/_{78}$ths of the total annual interest in the first month, $^{11}/_{78}$ths in the second month, and so on.

RULE 144 *see* INVESTMENT LETTER; SECURITIES AND EXCHANGE COMMISSION RULES.

RULES OF FAIR PRACTICE set of rules established by the FINANCIAL INDUSTRY REGULATORY AUTHORITY (FINRA), a self-regulatory organization comprising investment banking houses and firms dealing in the securities market. As summarized in the FINRA bylaws, the rules are designed to foster just and equitable principles of trade and business; high standards of commercial honor and integrity among members; the prevention of fraud and manipulative practices; safeguards against unreasonable profits, commissions, and other charges; and collaboration with governmental and other agencies to protect investors and the public interest in accordance with Section 15A of the MALONEY ACT. *See also* FIVE PERCENT RULE; IMMEDIATE FAMILY; KNOW YOUR CUSTOMER; MARKDOWN; RISKLESS TRANSACTION.

RUMORTRAGE stock traders' term, combining rumor and ARBITRAGE, for buying and selling based on rumor of a TAKEOVER. *See also* DEAL STOCK; GARBATRAGE.

RUN
Banking: demand for their money by many depositors all at once. If large enough, a run on a bank can cause it to fail, as hundreds of banks did in the Great Depression of the 1930s. Such a run is caused by a breach of confidence in the bank, perhaps as a result of large loan losses or fraud.
Securities:
1. list of available securities, along with current bid and asked prices, which a market maker is currently trading. For bonds the run may include the par value as well as current quotes.
2. when a security's price rises quickly, analysts say it had a quick run up, possibly because of a positive earnings report.

RUNDOWN
In general: status report or summary.
Municipal bonds: summary of the amounts available and the prices on units in a SERIAL BOND that has not yet been completely sold to the public.

RUNNING AHEAD illegal practice of buying or selling a security for a broker's personal account before placing a similar order for a customer, also called FRONT RUNNING. For example, when a firm's analyst issues a positive report on a company, the firm's brokers may not buy the stock for their own accounts before they have told their clients the news. Some firms prohibit brokers from making such trades for a specific period, such as two full days from the time of the recommendation.

RUNOFF printing of an exchange's closing prices on a TICKER tape after the market has closed. The runoff may take a long time when trading has been very heavy and the tape has fallen far behind the action.

RUSSELL INDICES float market-capitalization-weighted U.S. equity indices launched in 1984 by the Russell Investment Group of Tacoma, Washington, to measure market segments and better track the performance of investment managers. The Russell Indices are widely quoted on TV and radio and in newspapers, and are used as benchmarks for more than $2.5 trillion invested in mutual and pension funds. The company offers a family of 24 U.S. equity indices, all of them subsets of the Russell 3000 Index, a broad index that measures the performance of the 4,000 largest U.S. companies based on market capitalization, approximately 99% of the U.S. equity market. The stocks in the index have a market capitalization range of approximately $55 million to $387 billion, with a weighted average of $73.8 billion; the median market capitalization is approximately $540 million.

The Russell 1000 Index represents the highest-ranking 1,000 stocks in the Russell 3000 Index, comprising about 90% of the total market capitalization of that index. The Russell 1000 Index has a weighted average market capitalization of $81 billion; the median market capitalization is approximately $4.6 billion. The smallest company in the index has a market capitalization of $1.8 billion. The Russell 2000 Index measures performance of the 2,000 smallest companies in the Russell 3000 Index, about 9% of its total market capitalization. The weighted average capitalization is approximately $948.6 million; the median market capitalization is $539.5 million. The largest company in the index has an approximate market capitalization of $1.8 billion.

The Russell 2000 is a popular measure of the stock price performance of small companies.

The Russell Top 200 Index measures the performance of the 200 largest companies (63% of total market capitalization) in the Russell 1000, with weighted average market capitalization of $110.5 billion. The median capitalization is $24 billion; the smallest company in the index has an approximate capitalization of $14 billion.

The Russell Midcap Index measures performance of the 800 smallest companies (26% of total capitalization) in the Russell 1000, with weighted average market capitalization of approximately $6.7 billion, median capitalization of $3.6 billion, and market capitalization of the largest company $13.7 billion.

The Russell 2500 Index measures the performance of the 2,500 smallest companies in the Russell 3000 Index, or about 19% of its total capitalization. Weighted average capitalization is approximately $2 billion, and median capitalization is $705.8 million. The largest company in the index is $4.5 billion.

The Russell Small Cap Completeness Index measures the performance of the companies in the Russell 3000 excluding the companies in the Standard & Poor's 500 Index. It provides a performance standard for active money managers seeking a liquid extended benchmark and can be used for a passive investment strategy in the extended market. Weighted average market capitalization is approximately $5.7 billion; median market capitalization, $711.5 million. The index's largest company has a market capitalization of approximately $83.7 billion; the smallest, $182.6 million. Russell offers growth and value indices based on these equity indices. Growth indices measure performance of the respective companies with higher PRICE/BOOK RATIOS and higher forecasted growth values. Value indices measure the performance of those companies with lower price/book ratios and lower forecasted growth values. The company has licensed Barclays Global Investors the right to create exchange-traded funds based on 13 of the Russell indices. These exchange-traded funds, called ISHARES are managed by Barclays Global Fund Advisors. Russell 2000 Index MITTS, or Market Index Target-Term Securities, reflects the composite performance of the index. The CHICAGO BOARD OPTIONS EXCHANGE trades options on the Russell 2000 Index, the CHICAGO MERCANTILE EXCHANGE trades futures, options, and e-mini futures on the Russell 2000 Index and futures on the Russell 1000. The INTERCONTINENTAL EXCHANGE trades futures (three contract sizes) and options on the Russell 1000 Index, Russell 2000, Russell 2000 Growth, Russell 2000 Value, Russell 1000 Growth, Russell 1000 Value, and Russell 2500 indices. PHILADELPHIA STOCK EXCHANGE, PACIFIC EXCHANGE, INTERNATIONAL SECURITIES EXCHANGE, and AMEX offer options on Russell index-based ishares. Russell also offers indices and related products for the Japanese market with 15 Japan equity indices in association with Nomura Securities Co., Ltd. *www.russell.com*. *See also* STOCK INDICES AND AVERAGES.

RUSSIAN TRADING SYSTEM STOCK EXCHANGE (RTS) electronic system established in Russia in 1995, consolidating various regional trading floors into one exchange. Originally RTS was modeled on NASDAQ's trading and settlement software, but in 1998 it switched to an in-house product. The RTS Index is the main benchmark for the 50 most liquid and capitalized companies on the exchange. The RTS product line includes RTS Classic Market, the only trading platform in Russia that allows for settlement in both rubles and dollars; RTS T + O Market, securities trading for retail investors; RTS Board, for securities not listed on the exchange; and FORTS, for futures and options trading. *www.rts.ru*.

RUST BELT geographical area of the United States, mainly in Pennsylvania, West Virginia, and the industrial Midwest, where iron and steel is produced and where there is a concentration of industries that manufacture products using iron and steel. Term is used broadly to mean traditional American manufacturing with its largely unmodernized plants and facilities.

S

SAFE HARBOR

1. General: any recourse offering protection from threatened loss. For example, during the global financial debacle following the bankruptcy of Lehman Brothers in 2008, foreign investors bought U.S. treasury securities in the belief they were free of default risk and thus represented a safe harbor.
2. financial or accounting step that avoids legal or tax consequences. Commonly used in reference to *safe harbor leasing,* as permitted by the ECONOMIC RECOVERY TAX ACT OF 1981 (ERTA) and curtailed by provisions in the TAX EQUITY AND FISCAL RESPONSIBILITY ACT OF 1982 (TEFRA).
3. provision in a law that excuses liability if the attempt to comply in good faith can be demonstrated. For example, safe harbor provisions would protect management from liability under Securities and Exchange Commission rules for financial PROJECTIONS made in good faith.
4. form of SHARK REPELLENT whereby a TARGET COMPANY acquires a business so onerously regulated it makes the target less attractive, giving it, in effect, a safe harbor.

SAFEKEEPING storage and protection of a customer's financial assets, valuables, or documents, provided as a service by an institution serving as AGENT and, where control is delegated by the customer, also as custodian. An individual, corporate, or institutional investor might rely on a bank or a brokerage firm to hold stock certificates or bonds, keep track of trades, and provide periodic statements of changes in position. Investors who provide for their own safekeeping usually use a *safe deposit box,* provided by financial institutions for a fee. *See also* SELLING SHORT AGAINST THE BOX; STREET NAME.

SAFETY NET RETURN *see* CONTINGENT IMMUNIZATION.

SAIF *see* SAVINGS ASSOCIATION INSURANCE FUND (SAIF).

SALARY regular wages received by an employee from an employer on a weekly, biweekly, or monthly basis. Many salaries also include such employee benefits as health and life insurance, savings plans, and Social Security. Salary income is taxable by the federal, state, and local government, where applicable, through payroll withholding.

SALARY FREEZE cessation of increases in salary throughout a company for a period of time. Companies going through a business downturn will freeze salaries in order to reduce expenses. When business improves, salary increases are frequently reinstated.

SALARY REDUCTION PLAN plan allowing employees to contribute pretax compensation to a qualified TAX DEFERRED retirement plan. Until the TAX REFORM ACT OF 1986, the term was synonymous with 401(K) PLAN, but the 1986 act prohibited employees of state and local governments and tax-exempt organizations from establishing new 401(k) plans and added restrictions to existing government and tax-exempt unfunded deferred compensation arrangements and tax-sheltered annuity arrangements creating, in effect, a broadened definition of salary reduction plan.

Federal government employees are allowed salary deductions up to the limits for 401(k) plans. State and local governments and tax-exempt organizations other than churches may set up Section 457 deferred compensation plans allowing employees to defer annually up to $16,500, or 100% of any employee's total compensation, whichever is less. Tax-exempt and educational organizations can offer their employees 403(b) plans, also known as tax-sheltered annuities or TSA plans. These plans offer benefits and rules similar to those that apply to 457 and 401(k) plans. Employer plans must limit elective deferrals to an annual tax-free ceiling set by legislation or the plan could be disqualified. Under the ECONOMIC GROWTH AND TAX RELIEF RECONCILIATION ACT OF 2001, the salary reduction plan limit is $16,500 in 2009. For employees aged 50 and older, catch-up contributions of $5,500 can be made, meaning that up to $22,000 can be contributed annually. These limits also apply to 403(b) annuities, SEPs, and Sec. 457 governmental plans.

SALARY REDUCTION SIMPLIFIED EMPLOYEE PENSION PLAN (SARSEP) SIMPLIFIED EMPLOYEE PENSION PLAN (SEP) allowing employees to contribute pretax dollars through salary reduction. SARSEP is a simpler alternative to a 401(k) PLAN and is also known as a *408(k) Plan*.

SALE
In general: any exchange of goods or services for money. *Contrast with* BARTER.
Finance: income received in exchange for goods and services recorded for a given accounting period, either on a cash basis (as received) or on an accrual basis (as earned). *See also* GROSS SALES.
Securities: in securities trading, a sale is executed when a buyer and a seller have agreed on a price for the security.

SALE AND LEASEBACK form of LEASE arrangement in which a company sells an asset to another party—usually an insurance or finance company, a leasing company, a limited partnership, or an institutional investor—in exchange for cash, then contracts to lease the asset for a specified term. Typically, the asset is sold for its MARKET VALUE, so the lessee has really acquired capital that would otherwise have been tied up in a long-term asset. Such arrangements frequently have tax benefits for the lessee, although there is normally little difference in the effect on income between the lease payments and the interest payments that would have existed had the asset been purchased with borrowed money. A company generally opts for the sale and leaseback arrangement as an alternative to straight financing when the rate it would have to pay a lender is higher than the cost of rental or when it wishes to show less debt on its BALANCE SHEET (called *off-balance-sheet financing*). *See also* CAPITAL LEASE.

SALES CHARGE fee paid to a brokerage house by a buyer of shares in a load MUTUAL FUND or a LIMITED PARTNERSHIP. Normally, the sales charge for a mutual fund starts at 4.5% to 5% of the capital invested and decreases as the size of the investment increases. The sales charge for a limited partnership can be even higher—as much as 10%. In return for the sales charge, investors are entitled to investment advice from the broker on which fund or partnership is best for them. A fund that carries no sales charge is called a NO-LOAD FUND. *See also* BACK-END LOAD; FRONT-END LOAD; LETTER OF INTENT; LOAD FUND; REDEMPTION FEES; 12B-1 MUTUAL FUND. *See also* MUTUAL FUND SHARE CLAUSES.

SALES LITERATURE
In general: written material designed to help sell a product or a service.
Investments: written material issued by a securities brokerage firm, mutual fund, underwriter, or other institution selling a product that explains the advantages of the investment product. Such literature must be truthful and must comply with disclosure regulations issued by the Securities and Exchange Commission and state securities agencies.

SALES LOAD *see* SALES CHARGE.

SALES TAX
tax based on a percentage of the selling price of goods and services. State and local governments assess sales tax and decide what percentage to charge. The retail buyer pays the sales tax to the retailer, who passes it on to the sales tax collection agency of the government. For an item costing $1,000 in a state with a 5% sales tax, the buyer pays $50 in sales tax, for a total of $1,050. Individuals can deduct state and local general sales taxes, including compensating use taxes, instead of state and local income taxes on their federal income tax returns.

SALLIE MAE
publicly traded stock corporation, formally called the SLM Corporation, that guarantees student loans traded in the SECONDARY MARKET. It was created by Congress in 1972 to increase the availability of education loans to college and university students made under the federally sponsored Guaranteed Student Loan Program and the Health, Education Assistance Loan Program. Sallie Mae began privatizing in 1997 and at the end of 2004 terminated its GSE charter, cutting its ties to the federal government. Sallie Mae purchases student loans from originating financial institutions and provides financing to state student loan agencies.

SALVAGE VALUE *see* RESIDUAL VALUE.

SAME-DAY FUNDS SETTLEMENT (SDFS)
method of settlement in good-the-same-day FEDERAL FUNDS used by the DEPOSITORY TRUST COMPANY for transactions in U.S. government securities, short-term municipal notes, medium-term commercial paper notes, COLLATERALIZED MORTGAGE OBLIGATIONS (CMOs), DUTCH AUCTION PREFERRED STOCK, and other instruments when both parties to the trade are properly collateralized.

SAME-DAY SUBSTITUTION
offsetting changes in a MARGIN ACCOUNT in the course of one day, resulting in neither a MARGIN CALL nor a credit to the SPECIAL MISCELLANEOUS ACCOUNT. Examples: a purchase and a sale of equal value; a decline in the MARKET VALUE of some margin securities offset by an equal rise in the market value of others.

SAMURAI BONDS
bonds denominated in yen issued by non-Japanese companies for sale mostly in Japan. The bonds are not subject to Japanese withholding taxes, and therefore offer advantages to Japanese buyers.

SANDWICH GENERATION
middle-aged working people who feel squeezed by the financial pressures of supporting their aging parents, the costs of raising and educating their children, and the need to save for their own retirement.

SANTA CLAUS RALLY
rise in stock prices in the week between Christmas and New Year's Day. Also called the *year-end rally*. Some analysts attribute this rally to the anticipation of the JANUARY EFFECT, when stock prices rise in

the first few days of the year as pension funds add new money to their accounts.

SAO PAULO STOCK EXCHANGE *see* BOLSA DE VALORES DE SAO PAULO (BOVESPA).

S&P/ASX 200 Australia's premier large capitalization index, launched in April 2000. It has replaced the ALL ORDINARIES INDEX on the AUSTRALIAN STOCK EXCHANGE (ASX) as the leading indicator on the exchange. The index is made up of 200 stocks selected by the S&P/ASX Australian Index Committee, based on liquidity and size. The number of companies is always fixed at 200. When an index constituent is removed, it will be replaced immediately by a company in the S&P/ASX 300, but that is not in the S&P/ASX 200 index. The index's liquidity supports derivatives trading and fund composition, and it is sufficiently broad to attract international investors.

S&P 500 INDEX widely regarded as the best single gauge of the U.S. equities market; commonly known as the Standard & Poor's 500 (or S&P 500). This world-renowned index includes a representative sample of 500 leading companies in leading industries of the U.S. economy. Although the S&P 500 focuses on the large-cap segment of the market, with over 80% coverage of U.S. equities, it is also an ideal proxy for the total market. More than $4.85 trillion is benchmarked to S&P indices and approximately $1.7 trillion is directly tied to S&P indices. The selection of stocks, their relative weightings to reflect differences in the number of outstanding shares, and publication of the index itself are services of STANDARD & POOR'S. Stocks in the index are chosen for market size, liquidity, and industry group representation. Like all S&P indices, the S&P 500 is classified according to the Global Industry Classification System (GICS), which consists of 10 sectors—Energy, Materials, Industrials, Consumer Discretionary, Consumer Staples, Health Care, Financials, Information Technology, Telecommunications Services, and Utilities. In terms of market capitalization, the largest sectors in the S&P 500 are Financials, Information Technology, and Health Care. The composition of the 500 stocks is continuously updated, and the number of issues in each sector varies over time so that the index constantly reflects the sectoral makeup of the market and economy. Standard & Poor's also publishes several other important indices including the S&P MidCap 400, the S&P SmallCap 600, and the S&P 1500 Composite Index, which totals the S&P 500, 400, and 600 indices and which represents approximately 90% of the total market capitalization of stocks traded in the U.S. equity market. S&P also maintains more than 90 individual industry indices. *www.indices.standardandpoors.com. See also* S&P PHENOMENON; STANDARD & POOR'S CORPORATION; STOCK INDICES AND AVERAGES.

S&P/CITIGROUP GLOBAL EQUITY INDICES a comprehensive top-down, float capitalization-weighted index that includes shares of more than 9,000 companies in 52 countries. The index includes all companies with available market capitalization greater than $100 million. Each issue is weighted by the proportion of its available equity capital, its FLOAT, rather than by its total equity capital. The index is the successor to the Citigroup Global Equity Indices.

S&P GLOBAL 100 INDEX measures the performance of the world's largest 100 multinational companies whose business is global in nature and who derive a substantial portion of their operating income from multiple countries. It was jointly developed by Standard & Poor's and the NEW YORK STOCK EXCHANGE, and maintained by Standard & Poor's.

S&P GLOBAL 1200 INDEX the first real-time, free-float weighted world index, covering 29 countries and approximately 70% of global market capitalization. It is comprised of seven regional indices: the S&P 500; S&P/TSX 60 (Canada); the S&P Latin America 40 (Mexico, Brazil, Argentina, Chile); the S&P/TOPIX 150 (Japan); the S&P Asia 50 (Hong Kong, Korea, Singapore, Taiwan); the S&P/ASX 50 (Australia), and the S&P Europe 350. The European index is divided into three subindices: the S&P Euro, covering the Euro zone markets; the S&P Euro Plus, adding Denmark, Norway, Sweden, and Switzerland; and the S&P United Kingdom. Constituents of the S&P Global 1200 are selected to ensure sectoral and country balance. Constituent weights are determined by a company's free-float market capitalization: corporate cross-holdings, government ownership, strategic holders, and foreign investment restrictions are removed. The component indices are maintained by an index committee consisting of Standard & Poor's worldwide staff, using the same index governance and maintenance principles used by the S&P 500.

Standard & Poor's collaborates with the TORONTO STOCK EXCHANGE, the TOKYO STOCK EXCHANGE, and the AUSTRALIAN STOCK EXCHANGE on maintenance of the Canada, Japan, and Australia indices, respectively. Exchange-traded funds are available on the S&P 500, S&P Europe 350, S&P/TSX 60, S&P/ASX 50, and the S&P Latin America 40. Futures and options are traded on the S&P 500, the S&P/TSX 60, and the S&P/ASX 50. Like all S&P indices, the S&P Global 1200 is classified according to the Global Industry Classification System (GICS), which consists of 10 sectors—Energy, Materials, Industrials, Consumer Discretionary, Consumer Staples, Health Care, Financials, Information Technology, Telecommunications Services, and Utilities. In terms of market capitalization, the largest sectors in the S&P 500 are Financials, Information Technology, and Health Care. The largest, in terms of market capitalization, is Financials. Other top sectors represented are Consumer Discretionary, Health Care, and Information Technology. Among the smallest are Utilities, Materials, Telecommunications Services, and Energy. *www.indices.standardandpoors.com. See also* S&P/TSX 60 INDEX; STOCK INDICES AND AVERAGES; TORONTO STOCK EXCHANGE; TOKYO STOCK EXCHANGE.

S&P PHENOMENON tendency of stocks newly added to the STANDARD & POOR'S COMPOSITE INDEX to rise temporarily in price as S&P-related INDEX FUNDS adjust their portfolios, creating heavy buying activity.

S&P/TSX 60 INDEX a capitalization-weighted index of 60 large, liquid companies in Canada that trade on the TORONTO STOCK EXCHANGE (TSX). It was developed jointly by S&P and TSX and is a constituent index of the S&P Global 1200. The index is the underlying instrument for futures and options traded on the MONTREAL EXCHANGE/BOURSE DE MONTREAL. Like all S&P indices, the S&P/TSX 60 is classified according to the Global Industry Classification System (GICS), which consists of 10 sectors—Energy, Materials, Industrials, Consumer Discretionary, Consumer Staples, Health Care, Financials, Information Technology, Telecommunications Services, and Utilities.

SARBANES-OXLEY ACT OF 2002 (SOX) known also as the CORPORATE RESPONSIBILITY ACT OF 2002, signed July 30, 2002 in the wake of Enron and other accounting and corporate governance scandals, introducing radical reforms in four key areas:
Corporate Responsibility: Requires CEOs and CFOs to certify financial reports and forfeit profits and bonuses from earnings restated due to securi-

ties fraud; prohibits executives from selling company stock during blackout periods; requires insiders to report company stock trades within two days; prohibits company loans to executives not available to outsiders; requires immediate disclosure in "plain English" of material changes in company's financial condition.

New Criminal Penalties: Creates a new crime with 20-year prison term for destroying, altering, or fabricating records in federal investigations, or any "scheme or artifice" to defraud shareholders; raises maximum penalty for securities fraud to 25 years; increases CEO, CFO penalties for false statements to SEC or failing to certify financial reports to $5 million fine, 20-year prison term; requires key audit documents and e-mail be preserved for five years and creates a 10-year felony for destroying such documents; raises maximum penalties for mail, wire fraud to 20 years, for defrauding pension funds to 10 years.

Accounting Regulation: Establishes a five-member oversight board with investigative and disciplinary powers that is majority independent, funded by publicly held companies, and overseen by SEC; curtails consulting services by auditors to clients in nine categories; requires accounting firms to rotate lead or reviewing partners from client assignments every five years.

New Protections: Extends statute of limitations on securities fraud to five years, or two from discovery; liberalizes whistle-blowers' abilities to sue and prove retaliation; prohibits investment firms from retaliating against analysts who criticize firm's clients; directs civil penalties from SEC enforcement actions to accounts that benefit victimized investors; increases SEC budget by $776 million for fiscal 2003; prevents officials facing fraud judgements from taking refuge in bankruptcy.

SARSEP *see* SALARY REDUCTION SIMPLIFIED EMPLOYEE PENSION PLAN (SARSEP).

SATURDAY NIGHT SPECIAL surprise public TENDER OFFER, which was ended by the WILLIAMS ACT.

SAUCER technical chart pattern shaped like a saucer signaling that the price of a security or a commodity has formed a bottom and is moving up. An upside-down saucer shows a top in the security's price and signals a downturn. *See also* TECHNICAL ANALYSIS.

SAVING RATE ratio of personal saving to disposable personal income. Disposable personal income is personal income less personal tax and nontax payments. Personal saving is disposable personal income less personal outlays.

SAVINGS ACCOUNT deposit account at a commercial bank, savings bank, or savings and loan association that pays interest, usually on a day-of-deposit to day-of-withdrawal basis. Financial institutions can pay whatever rate they like on savings accounts, but this rate tends to be in relation to the actions of the money center banks in repricing their PRIME RATE. Traditionally, savings accounts offered PASSBOOKS, but in recent years alternatives such as ATMs, monthly account statements, and telephone banking services have been added to credit deposits and interest earned. Savings deposits are insured up to $100,000 per account if they are on deposit at banks insured by the BANK INSURANCE FUND (BIF) or a savings and loan insured by the SAVINGS ASSOCIATION INSURANCE FUND (SAIF). In 2005 Congress passed legislation merging the SAIF and BIF into the DEPOSIT INSURANCE FUND (DIF), administered by the FEDERAL DEPOSIT INSURANCE CORPORATION. The same law also raised the federal deposit insurance level from $100,000 to $250,000 on retirement accounts and gave the FDIC the option to increase insurance ceilings on regular bank accounts from $100,000 by $10,000 a year, based on inflation, every five years thereafter starting in 2010. In 2008 Congress passed the Emergency Economic Stabilization Act that temporarily increased the basic limit on deposit insurance for all ownership categories from $100,000 to $250,000. In the following year, Congress extended the expiration date on this temporary increase from 2010 to 2013.

SAVINGS AND LOAN ASSOCIATION depository financial institution, federally or state chartered, that obtains the bulk of its deposits from consumers and holds the majority of its assets as home mortgage loans. A few such specialized institutions were organized in the 19th century under state charters but with minimal regulation. Reacting to the crisis in the banking and home building industries precipitated by the Great Depression, Congress in 1932 passed the Federal Home Loan Bank Act, establishing the FEDERAL HOME LOAN BANK SYSTEM to supplement the lending resources of state-chartered savings and loans (S&Ls). The Home Owners' Loan Act of 1933 created a system for the federal chartering of S&Ls under the supervision of the Federal Home Loan Bank Board. Deposits in federal S&Ls were insured with the formation of the Federal Savings and Loan Insurance Corporation in 1934. A second wave of restructuring occurred in the 1980s. The DEPOSITORY INSTITUTIONS DEREGULATION AND MONETARY CONTROL ACT of 1980 set a six-year timetable for the removal of interest rate ceilings, including the S&Ls' quarter-point rate advantage over the commercial bank limit on personal savings accounts. The act also allowed S&Ls limited entry into some markets previously open only to commercial banks (commercial lending, nonmortgage consumer lending, trust services) and, in addition, permitted MUTUAL ASSOCIATIONS to issue INVESTMENT CERTIFICATES. In actual effect, interest rate parity was achieved by the end of 1982. The Garn-St Germain Depository Institutions Act of 1982 accelerated the pace of deregulation and gave the Federal Home Loan Bank Board wide latitude in shoring up the capital positions of S&Ls weakened by the impact of record-high interest rates on portfolios of old, fixed-rate mortgage loans. The 1982 act also encouraged the formation of stock savings and loans or the conversion of existing mutual (depositor-owned) associations to the stock form, which gave the associations another way to tap the capital markets and thereby to bolster their net worth.

In 1989, responding to a massive wave of insolvencies caused by mismanagement, corruption, and economic factors, Congress passed the FINANCIAL INSTITUTIONS REFORM, RECOVERY AND ENFORCEMENT ACT OF 1989 (FIRREA) that revamped the regulatory structure of the industry under a newly created agency, the OFFICE OF THRIFT SUPERVISION (OTS). Disbanding the FEDERAL SAVINGS AND LOAN INSURANCE CORPORATION (FSLIC), it created the SAVINGS ASSOCIATION INSURANCE FUND (SAIF), which later merged with the BANK INSURANCE FUND (BIF) to form the DEPOSIT INSURANCE FUND (DIF) under the administration of the FEDERAL DEPOSIT INSURANCE CORPORATION (FDIC). It also created the RESOLUTION TRUST CORPORATION (RTC) and RESOLUTION FUNDING CORPORATION (REFCORP) to deal with insolvent institutions and scheduled the consolidation of their activities with SAIF after 1996. The Federal Home Loan Bank Board was replaced by the Federal Housing Finance Board, which in 2008 was replaced by the FEDERAL HOUSING FINANCE AGENCY (FHFA). *See also* SAVINGS BANK.

SAVINGS ASSOCIATION INSURANCE FUND (SAIF) U.S. government entity created by Congress in 1989 as part of its SAVINGS AND LOAN ASSOCIATION bailout bill to replace the FEDERAL SAVINGS AND LOAN INSURANCE CORPORATION (FSLIC) as the provider of deposit insurance for thrift institutions. SAIF (rhymes with safe) was administered by the FEDERAL DEPOSIT INSURANCE CORPORATION (FDIC) separately from its bank insurance program, called the BANK INSURANCE FUND (BIF). In 2005 Congress passed legislation merging the SAIF and BIF into one insurance fund called the DEPOSIT INSURANCE FUND (DIF). The same law also raised the federal deposit insurance level from $100,000 to $250,000 on retirement accounts and gave the FDIC the option to increase insurance ceilings on regular bank accounts from $100,000 by $10,000 a year, based on inflation, every five years thereafter starting in 2010. In 2008 Congress passed the Emergency Economic Stabilization Act that temporarily increased the basic limit on deposit insurance for all ownership categories from $100,000 to $250,000. This temporary increase is set to expire in 2013. *See also* OFFICE OF THRIFT SUPERVISION (OTS).

SAVINGS BANK depository financial institution that primarily accepts consumer deposits and makes home mortgage loans. Historically, savings banks were of the mutual (depositor-owned) form and chartered in only 16 states; the majority of savings banks were located in the New England states, New York, and New Jersey. Prior to the passage of the Garn-St Germain Depository Institutions Act of 1982, state-chartered savings bank deposits were insured along with commercial bank deposits by the FEDERAL DEPOSIT INSURANCE CORPORATION (FDIC). The Garn-St Germain Act gave savings banks the options of a federal charter, mutual-to-stock conversion, supervision by the Federal Home Loan Bank Board, and insurance from the FEDERAL SAVINGS AND LOAN INSURANCE CORPORATION (FSLIC). In 1989 the Federal Home Loan Bank Board was replaced by the FEDERAL HOUSING FINANCE BOARD (FHFB), and the FSLIC by the newly created SAVINGS ASSOCIATION INSURANCE FUND (SAIF). The SAIF merged with the BANK INSURANCE FUND (BIF), the bank insurance program in 2005, and the FHFB was replaced by the FEDERAL HOUSING FINANCE AGENCY (FHFA) in 2008. *See also* MUTUAL SAVINGS BANK; SAVINGS AND LOAN ASSOCIATION.

SAVINGS BOND U.S. government bond issued in FACE VALUE denominations ranging from $50 to $10,000. From 1941 to 1979, the government issued SERIES E BONDS. Starting in 1980, Series EE and HH bonds were issued. Series EE bonds, issued at a discount of half their face value, range from $50 to $10,000; interest bearing Series HH bonds range from $500 to $10,000. Series EE bonds earn interest for 30 years; Series HH bonds earn interest for 20 years. Series EE bonds, if held for five years, pay 90% of the average yield on 5-year Treasury securities based on the previous six months. Series HH bonds are no longer issued. For many years, the government guaranteed a minimum yield on savings bonds. This yield decreased from 7.5% to 6% and then to 4%. The guaranteed minimum feature was dropped in May 1995, and bonds issued on May 1, 1997, or later and held for less than five years are now subject to a 3-month interest penalty. For example, a bond cashed in after 18 months would receive 15 months' worth of interest. Savings bond yields are readjusted every six months, on May 1 and November 1. Series I bonds provide a return that rises and falls with inflation. I bonds are issued in face amounts from $50 to $10,000. The interest on an I bond is determined by two rates. One, set by the Treasury department, remains constant for the life of the bond. The second is a variable inflation rate announced each May and November by the Treasury department to reflect changes in the Consumer Price Index reported by the Department of Labor. I bonds earn interest for 30 years and interest is added monthly and paid when the bond is redeemed. The interest from savings bonds is exempt from state and local taxes, and no federal tax on EE bonds is due until redemption. Taxpayers meeting income qualifications can buy EE bonds to save for higher education expenses and enjoy total or partial federal tax exemption. This applies to individuals with modified ADJUSTED GROSS INCOMES between $67,100 and $82,100 and married couples filing jointly with incomes between $100,650 and $130,650. Income levels are adjusted for inflation annually. *See also* I-BONDS.

SAVINGS DEPOSITS interest-earning cash balances that can be withdrawn on demand, kept for the purpose of savings, in commercial banks, savings banks, credit unions, and savings and loans. Passbook savings, statement savings, and money market accounts are examples of savings deposits.

SAVINGS ELEMENT cash value accumulated inside a life insurance policy. A cash value policy has two components: a death benefit paid to beneficiaries if the insured dies, and a savings element, which is the amount of premium paid in excess of the cost of protection. This excess is invested by the insurance company in stocks, bonds, real estate, and other ventures and the returns build up tax-deferred inside the policy. A policyholder can borrow against this cash value or take it out of the policy, at which point it becomes taxable income. Once a policyholder reaches retirement age, he or she can ANNUITIZE the accumulated cash value and receive a regular payment from the insurance company for life. Insurance companies encourage people to buy policies with a savings element because it provides a disciplined way to save.

SAVINGS INCENTIVE MATCH PLAN FOR EMPLOYEES (SIMPLE) a matching funds retirement plan for companies with fewer than 100 employees that can be structured either as an INDIVIDUAL RETIREMENT ARRANGEMENT (IRA) or a 401(k) PLAN. Also called SIMPLE IRA or *SIMPLE 401(k) Plan.*

SCALE
Labor: wage rate for specific types of employees. For example: "Union scale for carpenters is $15.60 per hour."
Production economics: amount of production, as in "economy or diseconomy of scale." *See also* MARGINAL COST.
Serial bonds: vital data for each of the scheduled maturities in a new SERIAL BOND issue, including the number of bonds, the date they mature, the COUPON rate, and the offering price.
    See also SCALE ORDER.

SCALE ORDER order for a specified number of shares that is to be executed in stages in order to average the price. Such an order might provide for the purchase of a total of 5,000 shares to be executed in lots of 500 shares at each quarter-point interval as the market declines. Since scale orders are clerically cumbersome, not all brokers will accept them.

SCALPER
In general: speculator who enters into quasi-legal or illegal transactions to turn a quick and sometimes unreasonable profit. For example, a scalper buys tickets at regular prices for a major event and when the event becomes a sellout, resells the tickets at the highest price possible.

Securities:
1. investment adviser who takes a position in a security before recommending it and then sells out after the price has risen as a result of the recommendation. *See also* INVESTMENT ADVISERS ACT.
2. market maker who, in violation of the RULES OF FAIR PRACTICE of the FINANCIAL INDUSTRY REGULATORY AUTHORITY (FINRA), adds an excessive markup or takes an excessive MARKDOWN on a transaction. *See also* FIVE PERCENT RULE.
3. commodity trader who trades for small gains, usually establishing and liquidating a position within one day.

SCHEDULE C common reference to a section of the bylaws of the FINANCIAL INDUSTRY REGULATORY AUTHORITY (FINRA) concerned with membership requirements and procedures.

SCHEDULE 13D form required under Section 13d of the SECURITIES ACT OF 1934 within ten business days of acquiring direct or BENEFICIAL OWNERSHIP of 5% or more of any class of equity securities in a PUBLICLY HELD corporation. In addition to filing with the Securities and Exchange Commission, the purchaser of such stock must also file the 13d with the stock exchange on which the shares are listed (if any) and with the company itself. Required information includes the way the shares were acquired, the purchaser's background, and future plans regarding the target company. The law is designed to protect against insidious TAKEOVER attempts and to keep the investing public aware of information that could affect the price of their stock. *See also* WILLIAMS ACT.

SCOR *see* SMALL CORPORATE OFFERING REGISTRATION.

SCORCHED-EARTH POLICY technique used by a company that has become the target of a TAKEOVER attempt to make itself unattractive to the acquirer. For example, it may agree to sell off the most attractive parts of its business, called the CROWN JEWELS, or it may schedule all debt to become due immediately after a MERGER. *See also* JONESTOWN DEFENSE; POISON PILL; SHARK REPELLENT.

SCORE acronym for *Special Claim on Residual Equity,* a certificate issued by the Americus Shareowner Service Corporation, a privately held company formed to market the product. A SCORE gave its holder the right to all the appreciation on an underlying security above a specified price, but none of the dividend income from the security. Its counterpart, called PRIME, passed all dividend income to its holders, who got the benefit of price appreciation up to the limit where SCORE began. PRIME and SCORE together formed a unit share investment trust (USIT), and both were listed on the American Stock Exchange. A buyer of a SCORE unit hoped that the underlying stock would rise steeply in value.

The first USIT was formed with the shares of American Telephone and Telegraph. PRIME holders got all dividends and price appreciation in AT&T up to $75 a share; SCORE holders received all appreciation above $75. The trusts expired in 1988.

S CORPORATION *see* SUBCHAPTER S.

SCREEN (STOCKS) to look for stocks that meet certain predetermined investment and financial criteria. Often, stocks are screened using a computer and a data base containing financial statistics on thousands of companies. For instance, an investor may want to screen for all those companies that have a PRICE/EARNINGS RATIO of less than 10, an earnings growth rate of more than 15%, and a dividend yield of more than 4%.

SCRIP
In general: receipt, certificate, or other representation of value recognized by both payer and payee. Scrip is not currency, but may be convertible into currency.
Securities: temporary document that is issued by a corporation and that represents a fractional share of stock resulting from a SPLIT, exchange of stock, or SPIN-OFF. Scrip certificates may be aggregated or applied toward the purchase of full shares. Scrip dividends have historically been paid in lieu of cash dividends by companies short of cash.

SCRIPOPHILY practice of collecting stock and bond certificates for their scarcity value, rather than for their worth as securities. The certificate's price rises with the beauty of the illustration on it and the importance of the issuer in world finance and economic development. Many old certificates, such as those issued by railroads in the 19th century or by Standard Oil before it was broken up in the early 20th century, have risen greatly in value since their issue, even though the issuing companies no longer exist.

SDR *see* SPECIAL DRAWING RIGHTS.

SEASONALITY variations in business or economic activity that recur with regularity as the result of changes in climate, holidays, and vacations. The retail toy business, with its steep sales buildup between Thanksgiving and Christmas and pronounced dropoff thereafter, is an example of seasonality in a dramatic form, though nearly all businesses have some degree of seasonal variation. It is often necessary to make allowances for seasonality when interpreting or projecting financial or economic data, a process economists call *seasonal adjustment.*

SEASONED securities that have been trading in the secondary market for a lengthy period of time, and have established a track record of significant trading volume and price stability. Many investors prefer buying only seasoned issues instead of new securities that have not stood the test of time.

SEASONED ISSUE securities (usually from established companies) that have gained a reputation for quality with the investing public and enjoy LIQUIDITY in the SECONDARY MARKET.

SEC *see* SECURITIES AND EXCHANGE COMMISSION.

SEC EDGAR known simply as EDGAR, the electronic data gathering, analysis, and retreival system that performs automated collection, validation, indexing, acceptance, and forwarding of submissions by companies and others who are required by law to file forms with the Securities and Exchange Commission. SEC documents can be read or downloaded from the web site *www.sec.gov.*

SEC FEE small (one cent per several hundred dollars) fee charged by the Securities and Exchange Commission (SEC) to sellers of EQUITY securities that are exchange traded.

SECONDARY DISTRIBUTION public sale of previously issued securities held by large investors, usually corporations, institutions, or other AFFILIATED PERSONS, as distinguished from a NEW ISSUE or PRIMARY DISTRIBUTION, where the seller is the issuing corporation. As with a primary offering, secondaries are usually handled by INVESTMENT BANKERS, acting alone or as a syndicate, who purchase the shares from the seller at an agreed price, then resell them, sometimes with the help of a SELLING GROUP, at a higher PUBLIC OFFERING PRICE, making their profit on the difference, called the SPREAD. Since the offering is registered with the Securities and Exchange Commission, the syndicate manager can legally stabilize—or peg—the market price by bidding for shares in the open market. Buyers of securities offered this way pay no commissions, since all costs are borne by the selling investor. If the securities involved are listed, the CONSOLIDATED TAPE will announce the offering during the trading day, although the offering is not made until after the market's close. Among the historically large secondary distributions were the Ford Foundation's offering of Ford Motor Company stock in 1956 (approximately $658 million) handled by 7 firms under a joint management agreement and the sale of Howard Hughes' TWA shares ($566 million) through Merrill Lynch, Pierce, Fenner & Smith in 1966.

A similar form of secondary distribution, called the SPECIAL OFFERING, is limited to members of the New York Stock Exchange and is completed in the course of the trading day. *See also* EXCHANGE DISTRIBUTION; REGISTERED SECONDARY OFFERING; SECURITIES AND EXCHANGE COMMISSION RULES 144 and 237.

SECONDARY MARKET

1. exchanges and over-the-counter markets where securities are bought and sold subsequent to original issuance, which took place in the PRIMARY MARKET. Proceeds of secondary market sales accrue to the selling dealers and investors, not to the companies that originally issued the securities.
2. market in which money-market instruments are traded among investors.

SECONDARY MORTGAGE MARKET
buying, selling, and trading of existing mortgage loans and mortgage-backed securities. Original lenders are thus able to sell loans in their portfolios in order to build LIQUIDITY to support additional lending. Mortgages originated by lenders are purchased by government agencies (such as the FEDERAL HOME LOAN MORTGAGE CORPORATION and the FEDERAL NATIONAL MORTGAGE ASSOCIATION) and by investment bankers. These agencies and bankers, in turn, create pools of mortgages, which they repackage as mortgage-backed securities, called PASS-THROUGH SECURITIES or PARTICIPATION CERTIFICATES, which are then sold to investors. The secondary mortgage market thus encompasses all activity beyond the PRIMARY MARKET, which is between the homebuyers and the originating mortgage lender.

SECONDARY OFFERING *see* SECONDARY DISTRIBUTION.

SECONDARY STOCKS
used in a general way to mean stocks having smaller MARKET CAPITALIZATION, less quality, and more risk than BLUE CHIP issues represented by the Dow Jones Industrial Average. Secondary stocks, which often behave differently than blue chips, are tracked by the Amex Market Value Index, the NASDAQ Composite Index, and broad indexes, such as the Standard & Poor's Index. Also called *second-tier stocks.*

SECOND MORTGAGE LENDING
advancing funds to a borrower that are secured by real estate previously pledged in a FIRST MORTGAGE loan. In the case of DEFAULT, the first mortgage has priority of claim over the second.

A variation on the second mortgage is the *home equity loan,* in which the loan is secured by independent appraisal of the property value. A home equity loan may also be in the form of a line of credit, which may be drawn down on by using a check or even a credit card. *See also* HOMEOWNER'S EQUITY ACCOUNT; RIGHT OF RESCISSION.

SECOND-PREFERRED STOCK preferred stock issue that ranks below another preferred issue in terms of priority of claim on dividends and on assets in liquidation. Second-preferred shares are often issued with a CONVERTIBLE feature or with a warrant to make them more attractive to investors. *See also* JUNIOR SECURITY; PREFERRED STOCK; PRIOR-PREFERRED STOCK; SUBSCRIPTION WARRANT.

SECOND ROUND intermediate stage of VENTURE CAPITAL financing, coming after the SEED MONEY (or START-UP) and *first round* stages and before the MEZZANINE LEVEL, when the company has matured to the point where it might consider a LEVERAGED BUYOUT by management or an INITIAL PUBLIC OFFERING (IPO).

SECOND-TO-DIE INSURANCE insurance policy that pays a death benefit upon the death of the spouse who dies last. Such insurance typically is purchased by a couple wanting to pass a large estate on to their heirs. When the first spouse dies, the couple's assets are passed tax-free to the second spouse under the MARITAL DEDUCTION. When the second spouse dies, the remaining estate could be subject to large estate taxes. The proceeds from the second-to-die insurance are designed to pay the estate taxes, leaving the remaining estate for the heirs. Such insurance is appropriate only for those facing large estate tax liabilities. Because the policy is based on the joint life expectancy of both husband and wife, premiums typically cost less than those on traditional cash value policies on both lives insured separately. Also called *survivorship life insurance.*

SECTION 31 FEE transaction fees self-regulatory organizations, such as the national securities exchanges, are required, under Section 31 of the Securities Exchange Act of 1934, to pay the Securities and Exchange Commission based on the volume of securities sold on their markets. Fees cover the SEC's costs for supervising and regulating the markets and securities professionals.

SECTOR *see* INDUSTRIAL SECTOR.

SECTOR FUND *see* SPECIALIZED MUTUAL FUND.

SECTOR NEUTRAL INDEXING type of ENHANCED INDEXING where sectors comprising an index are replicated but individual stocks are varied with the aim of outperformance.

SECTOR ROTATION stock investment strategy in which money is moved from one INDUSTRIAL SECTOR to another in an effort to catch respective upcycles and thus outperform the overall market. Also called GROUP ROTATION.

SECULAR long-term (10–50 years or more) as distinguished from seasonal or cyclical time frames.

SECURED BOND bond backed by the pledge of COLLATERAL, a MORTGAGE, or other LIEN. The exact nature of the security is spelled out in the INDEN-

TURE. Secured bonds are distinguished from unsecured bonds, called DEBENTURES.

SECURED DEBT debt guaranteed by the pledge of assets or other COLLATERAL. *See also* ASSIGN; HYPOTHECATION.

SECURED LEASE OBLIGATION BOND (SLOB) bonds, typically issued by electric utilities to finance power plants, where payments are made from an assigned lease. Some SLOBS are additionally secured by a lien on the facility.

SECURITIES ACT OF 1933 first law enacted by Congress to regulate the securities markets, approved May 26, 1933, as the Truth in Securities Act. It requires REGISTRATION of securities prior to public sale and adequate DISCLOSURE of pertinent financial and other data in a PROSPECTUS to permit informed analysis by potential investors. It also contains antifraud provisions prohibiting false representations and disclosures. Enforcement responsibilities were assigned to the SECURITIES AND EXCHANGE COMMISSION by the SECURITIES EXCHANGE ACT OF 1934. The 1933 act did not supplant BLUE SKY LAWS of the various states.

SECURITIES ACTS AMENDMENTS OF 1975 federal legislation enacted on June 4, 1975, to amend the SECURITIES EXCHANGE ACT OF 1934. The 1975 amendments directed the SECURITIES AND EXCHANGE COMMISSION to work with the industry toward establishing a NATIONAL MARKET SYSTEM together with a system for the nationwide clearance and settlement of securities transactions. Because of these provisions, the 1975 laws are sometimes called the National Exchange Market System Act. New regulations were also introduced to promote prompt and accurate securities handling, and clearing agencies were required to register with and report to the SEC. The 1975 amendments required TRANSFER AGENTS other than banks to register with the SEC and provided that authority with respect to bank transfer agents would be shared by the SEC and bank regulatory agencies. The Municipal Securities Rule-making Board was created to regulate brokers, dealers, and banks dealing in municipal securities, with rules subject to SEC approval and enforcement shared by the FINANCIAL INDUSTRY REGULATORY AUTHORITY (FINRA) and bank regulatory agencies. The law also required the registration of broker-dealers in municipals but preserved the exemption of issuers from REGISTRATION requirements. The amendments contained the prohibition of fixed commission rates, adopted earlier by the SEC in its Rule 19b-3.

SECURITIES ANALYST individual, usually employed by a stock brokerage house, bank, or investment institution, who performs investment research and examines the financial condition of a company or group of companies in an industry and in the context of the securities markets. Many analysts specialize in a single industry or SECTOR and make investment recommendations to buy, sell, or hold in that area. Among a corporation's financial indicators most closely followed by ANALYSTS are sales and earnings growth, CAPITAL STRUCTURE, stock price trend and PRICE/EARNINGS RATIO, DIVIDEND PAYOUTS, and RETURN ON INVESTED CAPITAL. Securities analysts promote corporate financial disclosure by sponsoring forums through associations, such as the ASSOCIATION FOR INVESTMENT MANAGEMENT AND RESEARCH and its member societies and chapters, such as the New York Society of Security Analysts.

See also FORECASTING; FUNDAMENTAL ANALYSIS; QUALITATIVE ANALYSIS; QUANTITATIVE ANALYSIS; TECHNICAL ANALYSIS.

SECURITIES AND COMMODITIES EXCHANGES organized, national exchanges where securities, options, and futures contracts are traded by members for their own accounts and for the accounts of customers. In the United States, the stock exchanges are registered with and regulated by the SECURITIES AND EXCHANGE COMMISSION (SEC); the commodities exchanges are registered with and regulated by the Commodity Futures Trading Commission (*see* REGULATED COMMODITIES); where options are traded on an exchange, such activity is regulated by the SEC.

STOCKS, BONDS, SUBSCRIPTION RIGHTS, SUBSCRIPTION WARRANTS, STOCK OPTIONS, INDEX OPTIONS, and other derivative products are traded on various stock exchanges in the United States as well as over the counter. COMMODITY FUTURES, FUTURES OPTIONS, and FINANCIAL FUTURES are traded on commodities exchanges and also over the counter.

Exchanges listing basic securities—stocks, bonds, rights, warrants, and options on individual stocks—are described in more detail under their respective entries. See below for a description of their futures and other options products:

American Stock Exchange (New York) *stock index options*: Airline Index, China Index, Defense Index, Gold Bugs Index, Test Symbol, Computer Technology, Consumer Index Opt., Cyclical Index Opt., Deutschebank Energy, Eurotop 100 Index, Hong Kong Index, Internet Index, Major Market Index, Min Nasdaq 100, Ms Commodities Index, Nasdaq Biotech Index, Nasdaq 100 Index, Natural Gas Index, Oil Index, Spade Defense Index, The Biotechnology Index, The Broker Dealer Index, The Disk Drive Index, The Japan Index, The Microcap Index, The Morgan Stanley Index, The Pharma Index.

Chicago Board of Trade (Chicago) *futures:* corn, oats, rough rice, soybeans, soybean oil, soybean meal, wheat, mini-sized corn, mini-sized soybeans, mini-sized wheat, South American soybeans; silver (1,000 ounces, 5,000 ounces), gold (33.2 ounces, 100 ounces); ethanol; U.S. Treasury Bonds, U.S. Treasury notes (10-year, 5-year, 2-year), 30-Day Fed Funds, 10-Year Municipal Note Index, Interest Rate Swaps (10-year, 5-year), mini-sized Eurodollars, Bund, Bobl, Schatz; Dow Jones Industrial Index, mini-sized Dow Jones Industrial Index, Total Market Index, Dow Jones-AIGCI. *Options:* corn, oats, rough rice, soybeans, soybean oil, soybean meal, wheat; U.S. Treasury bonds, U.S. Treasury notes (10-year, 5-year, 2-year), 30-Day Fed Funds, Flexible U.S. Treasury bonds, Flexible U.S. Treasury notes (10-year, 5-year, 2-year), Interest Rate Swaps (10-year, 5-year); Dow Jones Industrial IndexSM, mini-sized Dow Jones Industrial Index.

Chicago Board Options Exchange (Chicago): equity options, index options, EXCHANGE-TRADED FUND (ETF) options, interest rate options, structured product options, Long-Term Equity AnticiPation Securities (LEAPS), and Flexible Exchange (FLEX) options. CBOE trades options on approximately 1,700 equities, 44 indexes, 54 ETFs, and 4 interest rate products. CBOE introduced options and futures on 12 newly created sector indexes called "PowerPacksSM" in July 2005. The dozen individual sector indexes included in the family of CBOE PowerPacks are banks, biotechnology, gold, Internet, iron and steel, oil, oil services, pharmaceuticals, retail, semiconductor, technology, and telecom indexes. Among the most actively-traded options on indexes at CBOE are S&P 500 Index (SPX); S&P 100 Index (American-Style Exercise, OEX and European-Style Exercise, XEO); S&P Depositary Receipts (SPDRs); Dow Jones Industrial Average (DJX); DIAMONDS Trust, Series 1 (DIA); Nasdaq-100 Index; CBOE Mini-NDX Index (MNX); Nasdaq-100 Index Tracking Stock (QQQ), Russell 2000 Index (RUT), iShares Russell 2000 Index Fund (IWM); Semiconductor HOLDRs Trust (SMH) and iShares Lehman 20+Year Treasury Bond Fund (TLT). Products traded on the CBOE Futures Exchange include futures on: CBOE Volatility Index (VX), CBOE S&P 500 Three Month Variance (VT), CBOE China Index (CX), Mini-Russell 2000 Index (RT), Russell 1000 Index (RN), CBOE DJIA Volatility Index (DV), and CBOE PowerPacksSM Indices.

Chicago Mercantile Exchange (Chicago) *foreign currency futures and options:* Australian dollar, Brazilian real, British pound, Canadian dollar, Czech Koruna, U.S. dollar index, Euro, E-mini Euro, Hungarian forint, Japanese yen, E-mini Japanese yen, Mexican peso, New Zealand dollar, Norwegian Krone, Polish Zloty, Russian ruble, South African rand, Swedish Krona, Swiss franc. *Cross-rate futures and options:* Euro FX/Australian dollar, Euro FX/Canadian dollar, Euro FX/Hungarian Forint, Euro FX/Norwegian Krone, Euro FX/Swedish Krona, Australian dollar/Canadian dollar, Canadian dollar/Japanese yen, Australian dollar/Japanese yen, Australian dollar/New Zealand dollar, British pound/Japanese yen, British pound/Swiss franc, Swiss franc/Japanese yen, Euro FX/British pound, Euro FX/Czech Koruna, Euro FX/Japanese yen, Euro FX/Polish Zloty, Euro FX/Swiss franc. *Foreign currency-denominated interest rate futures and options:* Euroyen, 91-day CETES, 28-day TIIE. *Interest rate futures and options:* Eurodollar, Eurodollar FRA, 13-week U.S. Treasury bill, 1-month LIBOR (London Interbank Offer Rate), swap futures, turn rate futures, Japanese government bonds, CPI futures, mid-curve options. *Stock index futures and options:* Standard & Poor's 500, E-Mini S&P 500 Stock Price Index, Standard & Poor's MidCap 400, Nikkei 225 Stock Average, Goldman Sachs Commodity Index, Russell 2000 Stock Price Index, S&P 500/BARRA Growth Index, S&P 500 BARRA Value Index, NASDAQ 100 Index, E-mini NASDAQ Composite, S&P SmallCap 600, SPCTR Futures, X-Funds, Futures on ETFs E-mini NASDAQ-100, E-mini S&P 500 MidCap 400, E-mini Russell 1000, E-mini Russell 2000. *Alternative investment products:* U.S. monthly weather, U.S. seasonal weather, European monthly weather, European seasonal weather, Asia-Pacific monthly weather, Asia-Pacific seasonal weather, ethanol. *Agricultural futures and options:* live cattle, feeder cattle, lean hogs, frozen pork bellies, milk (Class III & IV), nonfat dry milk, butter, random-length butter, cheese, DAP, UAN, urea.

Kansas City Board of Trade (Kansas City) *futures and options:* wheat, Value Line Index. *Futures:* wheat, Value Line Index.

Minneapolis Grain Exchange (Minneapolis) *futures and options:* hard red spring wheat, Hard Red Winter Wheat Index (HRWI), Hard Red Spring Wheat Index (HRSI), Soft Red Winter Wheat Index (SRWI), National Corn Index (NCI), and National Soybean Index (NSI).

New York Board of Trade *agricultural futures and options contracts:* cocoa, Coffee "C," Cotton No. 2, ethanol, frozen concentrated orange juice (FCOJ), Sugar No. 11, Sugar No. 14, and pulp. *Index and currency marketplace:* futures and options on NYSE Composite Index, Reuters/Jefferies CRB Index, Russell 1000, 2000, and 3000 Indexes, the U.S. Dollar Index, and 32 cross-rate currency contracts.

New York Mercantile Exchange (New York) NYMEX Division: *futures and options:* light, sweet crude oil, New York Harbor unleaded gasoline, heating oil, Henry Hub natural gas, platinum. *Futures:* palladium. COMEX Division: *Futures and options:* gold, silver, copper, and aluminum.

Pacific Exchange (San Francisco) Options, LEAPS, and FLEX options on more than 1,800 stocks and ETFs.

Philadelphia Stock Exchange (Philadelphia): *currency options:* Australian dollar, British pound, Canadian dollar, Euro, Japanese yen, Mexican peso (customized contracts only), Swiss franc, U.S. dollar (customized contracts only); SPDR Options; *sector index options:* capital markets, insurance, mortgage finance, regional bank, defense, drug, Europe, gold and silver, housing, oil service, semiconductor, utility, media and entertainment, casino gaming, coal producers, footwear and athletic, investment managers, oil exploration and production, semiconductor capital equipment, semiconductor device, specialty retail, steel producers, Internet, bio-clinical trials; FLEX options, LEAPS, HOLDRS; currency futures.

SECURITIES AND EXCHANGE COMMISSION (SEC) federal agency created by the SECURITIES EXCHANGE ACT OF 1934 to administer that act and the SECURITIES ACT OF 1933, formerly carried out by the FEDERAL TRADE COMMISSION. The SEC is made up of five commissioners, appointed by the President of the United States on a rotating basis for five-year terms. The chairman is designated by the President and, to insure its independence, no more than three members of the commission may be of the same political party. The statutes administered by the SEC are designed to promote full public DISCLOSURE and protect the investing public against malpractice in the securities markets. All issues of securities offered in interstate commerce or through the mails must be registered with the SEC; all national securities exchanges and associations are under its supervision, as are INVESTMENT COMPANIES, investment counselors and advisers, OVER THE COUNTER brokers and dealers, and virtually all other individuals and firms operating in the investment field. In addition to the 1933 and 1934 securities acts, responsibilities of the SEC include the PUBLIC UTILITY HOLDING COMPANY ACT of 1935, the TRUST INDENTURE ACT of 1939, the INVESTMENT COMPANY ACT of 1940 and the INVESTMENT ADVISERS ACT of 1940. It also administers the SECURITIES ACTS AMENDMENTS OF 1975, which directed the SEC to facilitate the establishment of a NATIONAL MARKET SYSTEM and a nationwide system for clearance and settlement of transactions and established the Municipal Securities Rulemaking Board, a self-regulatory organization whose rules are subject to SEC approval. *See also* SECURITIES AND EXCHANGE COMMISSION RULES.

SECURITIES AND EXCHANGE COMMISSION RULES The following are some of the more commonly encountered rules of the SEC. The list highlights the most prominent features of the rules and is not intended as a legal interpretation. The rules are listed in numerical order.

Rule 3b-3: Definition of Short Sale defines short sale as one in which the seller does not own the SECURITY sold or which is consummated by delivery of a borrowed security; ownership is defined in terms of securities, CONVERTIBLES, OPTIONS, and SUBSCRIPTION WARRANTS.

Rule 10a-1: Short sales known as the SHORT SALE RULE, prohibits a short sale of securities below the price of the last regular trade and at that price unless it was higher than the last different price preceding it. In determining the price at which a short sale can be made after a security goes EX-DIVIDEND, EX-RIGHTS, or ex- any other distribution, all sales prices prior to the ex- date may be reduced by the amount of the distribution.

Rule 10b-2: Solicitation of purchases on an exchange to facilitate distribution of securities prohibits parties concerned with a PRIMARY DISTRIBUTION or a SECONDARY DISTRIBUTION of a security from soliciting orders for the issue other than through the offering circular or formal PROSPECTUS.

Rule 10b-4: Short tendering of securities prohibits a SHORT TENDER—the sale of borrowed securities (as in SELLING SHORT) to a person making a TENDER OFFER.

Rule 10b-6: Prohibitions against trading by persons interested in a distribution rule that prohibits issuers, underwriters, broker-dealers, or others involved in a DISTRIBUTION of securities from buying the issue, or rights to it, during the distribution. The section permits transactions between the issuer and the underwriters and among the participating underwriters as required to carry out a distribution. The law extends to a repurchase by the issuer or to a purchase by participants in a new issue of CONVERTIBLE securities already on the market and convertible into the securities being offered.

Rule 10b-7: Stabilizing to effect a distribution provisions governing market STABILIZATION activities by issuers or underwriters in securities offerings.

Rule 10b-8: Distributions through rights prohibits market price MANIPULATION by interested parties in a RIGHTS OFFERING.

Rule 10b-10: Confirmation of transactions sets minimum information and disclosure requirements for the written confirmations of sales or purchases that broker-dealers send to clients, including disclosure of whether a firm is acting as AGENT (broker) or as PRINCIPAL (dealer).

Rule 10b-13: Other purchases during tender offer or exchange offer prohibits a person making a cash tender offer or an offer to exchange one EQUITY security for another from taking a position in the security being tendered or in a security CONVERTIBLE into the security being tendered until the tender offer or exchange offer expires.

Rule 10b-16: Credit terms in margin transactions terms and conditions concerning the interest charges on MARGIN loans to brokerage customers and the broker's disclosure responsibilities to borrowers.

Rule 11A: Floor trading regulations rules governing floor trading by exchange members, including those concerning PRIORITY and PRECEDENCE of transactions, transactions for the accounts of persons associated with members, HEDGE transactions, exchange bond trading, transactions by REGISTERED COMPETITIVE MARKET MAKERS and REGISTERED EQUITY MARKET MAKERS, and transactions between members. Of current relevence to Nasdaq's SUPERMONTAGE is the Limit Order Display Rule, which is covered by **Rule 11Ac1–4**. Generally, this rule requires market makers to display the full size of customer orders that are priced at or above the market maker's bid or offer. New order execution and order-routing disclosure rules designed to enable investors to analyze and compare executions in different market centers, defined as exchange specialists, OTC market makers, and alternative trading systems.

Rule 12b-1: *see* 12b-1 MUTUAL FUND.

Rule 13d: Acquisition of beneficial interest disclosures required by any person who directly or indirectly acquires a beneficial interest of 5% or more of any class of a registered equity security. *See also* WILLIAMS ACT.

Rule 13e: Repurchase of shares by issuers prohibits purchase by an issuer of its own shares during a TENDER OFFER for its shares and regulates GOING PRIVATE transactions by issuers or their affiliates.

Rule 14a: Solicitation of proxies sets forth the information and documentation required with PROXY materials distributed to shareholders of a public corporation.

Rule 14d: Tender offers regulations and restrictions covering public TENDER OFFERS and related disclosure requirements. *See also* WILLIAMS ACT.

Rule 15c2-1: Hypothecation of customers' securities regulates a broker-dealer's SAFEKEEPING of customers securities in a MARGIN ACCOUNT, prohibiting the COMMINGLING of customers accounts without the consent of the respective customers and the commingling of customers' accounts with the securities of non-customers, and limiting broker borrowings secured by customers' collateral to the aggregate amount of customers' indebtedness. *See also* HYPOTHECATION.

Rule 15c3-1: Net capital requirements for brokers or dealers covers NET CAPITAL REQUIREMENTS relative to the aggregate indebtedness of brokers and dealers of different types.

Rule 15c3-2: Customers' free credit balances requires a broker-dealer to notify customers with credit balances in their accounts that such balances may be withdrawn on demand.

Rule 15c3-3: Customer-protection reserves and custody of securities regulates the handling of customers' fully paid securities and excess MARGIN securities (security value in excess of MARGIN REQUIREMENTS) with broker-dealers. Fully paid securities must be segregated, and the broker must make weekly deposits to a Special Reserve Bank Account for the Exclusive Benefit of Customers.

Rules 15g-2,-3,-5,-6,-9, and -100 set forth disclosure standards and sales practice requirements relative to the PENNY STOCK market.

Rule 17a-12 sets strict standards for accounting, auditing, and financial reporting of OTC Derivatives Dealers.

Rule 17f-1: Missing, lost, counterfeit, or stolen securities requires exchanges, broker-dealers, clearing agencies, banks and transfer agents to report promptly to both the SEC and the appropriate law enforcement agency any knowledge of missing, lost, counterfeit, or stolen securities and to check with the SEC whenever a security comes into their possession to make sure it has not been reported at large.

Rule 19b-3: Prohibiting fixing of rates of commission by exchanges prohibits fixed commissions on stock exchange transactions pursuant to the SECURITIES ACT AMENDMENTS OF 1975.

Rule 19c-3: Off-board trading by exchange members permits securities listed on an exchange after April 26, 1979, to be traded off the exchange by member firms, a step toward an experimental NATIONAL MARKET SYSTEM in compliance with the SECURITIES ACT AMENDMENTS OF 1975.

Rule 19c-4: One share, one vote prohibits U.S. exchanges and the NASD from listing or providing quotes for any issuer of stock with more voting power than other common shares of the same issuer.

Rule 36a1–2 Exempts OTC Derivatives Dealers from the provisions of the Securities Investor Protection Act of 1970, citing special requirements detailed in **Rule 15a-1**.

In the wake of the Enron bankruptcy, the SEC in mid-2002 was considering rule changes that would shorten the time companies have to issue earnings reports. Under proposed rules, quarterly reports would be required within 30 days of the end of the quarter rather than 45 days, and annual reports within 60 days of the end of the fiscal year, instead of 90 days.

Rule 144: Public sale of unregistered securities sets forth the conditions under which a holder of unregistered securities may make a public sale without filing a formal REGISTRATION STATEMENT. No LETTER SECURITY purchased through a PRIVATE PLACEMENT may be sold for at least two years after the date of purchase. Thereafter, during any three-month period, the following amounts may be sold: if listed securities, the greater of 1% of the amount outstanding or the average trading volume within the four preceding weeks; if unlisted, 1% of outstandings. Securities may be sold only in broker's transactions.

Rule 145: Securities acquired in recapitalization persons who acquire securities as a result of reclassification, MERGER, consolidation, or transfer of corporate assets may sell such securities without REGISTRATION under stipulated conditions.

Rule 156: Mutual fund sales literature forbids false and misleading sales materials promoting INVESTMENT COMPANY securities.

Rule 237: Public sale of unregistered securities expanding on Rule 144, provides that five years after full payment for the purchase of privately placed securities, the lesser of $50,000 of such securities or 1% of the securities outstanding in a particular CLASS may be sold within a one year period.

Rule 254: Registration of small issues provides for simplified registration of small issues ($1.5 million or less in the mid-1980s) including a short-form REGISTRATION STATEMENT and PROSPECTUS. *See also* REGULATION A.

Rule 415: Shelf registration permits corporations to file a REGISTRATION for securities they intend to issue in the future when market conditions are favorable. *See also* SHELF REGISTRATION.

Rule 419: Blank-check companies (companies that issue penny stock before operations have begun or before engaging in an acquisition or merger with an unspecified business entity) must put investors' funds in an escrow account for the benefit of the purchaser.

The full text of SEC rules, including four volumes of Exchange Act Rules and Regulations and alphabetical Regulations, including Regulation ATS (Alternative Trading Systems Rules 300 through 303) and Regulation S-T (Electronic Filings), can be accessed at *www.bowne.com. See also* HEDGE FUND; REGULATION A; REGULATION D; REGULATION FD; REGULATION S; SHORT SALE RULE.

SECURITIES ENFORCEMENT REMEDIES AND PENNY STOCK REFORM ACT OF 1990 act that empowered the SEC directly to impose civil penalties on violators of securities laws.

SECURITIES EXCHANGE ACT OF 1934 law governing the securities markets, enacted June 6, 1934. The act outlaws misrepresentation, MANIPULATION, and other abusive practices in the issuance of securities. It created the SECURITIES AND EXCHANGE COMMISSION (SEC) to enforce both the SECURITIES ACT OF 1933 and the Securities Exchange Act of 1934.

Principal requirements of the 1934 act are as follows:

1. REGISTRATION of all securities listed on stock exchanges, and periodic DISCLOSURES by issuers of financial status and changes in condition.
2. regular disclosures of holdings and transactions of "INSIDERS"—the offi-

cers and directors of a corporation and those who control at least 10% of equity securities.

3. solicitation of PROXIES enabling shareholders to vote for or against policy proposals.

4. registration with the SEC of stock exchanges and brokers and dealers to ensure their adherence to SEC rules through self-regulation.

5. surveillance by the SEC of trading practices on stock exchanges and over-the-counter markets to minimize the possibility of insolvency among brokers and dealers.

6. regulation of MARGIN REQUIREMENTS for securities purchased on credit; the FEDERAL RESERVE BOARD sets those requirements.

7. SEC subpoena power in investigations of possible violations and in enforcement actions.

The SECURITIES ACT AMENDMENTS OF 1975 ratified the system of free-market determination of brokers' commissions and gave the SEC authority to oversee development of a NATIONAL MARKET SYSTEM.

SECURITIES INDUSTRY AND FINANCIAL MARKETS ASSOCIATION (SIFMA) nonprofit trade group for participants in the global and financial markets, including more than 650 securities firms, banks, and asset managers. Formed in 2006 from the merger of the Bond Market Association and the Securities Industry Association, SIFMA represents the industry on regulatory and legislative issues and serves as a forum for training and investor education.

SECURITIES INDUSTRY AUTOMATION CORPORATION (SIAC) a subsidiary of the NEW YORK STOCK EXCHANGE (NYSE) that provides technical services for the exchanges, members, and other financial institutions. Established in 1972 by the NYSE, which owned two-thirds, and the AMERICAN STOCK EXCHANGE (AMEX), which owned one-third. The NYSE purchased the AMEX stake in 2006 and NYSE EURONEXT, its parent company, acquired the AMEX in 2008.

SECURITIES INDUSTRY COMMITTEE ON ARBITRATION (SICA) private body that applies its arbitration code in cases of customer complaints against securities firms.

SECURITIES INFORMATION CENTER (SIC) organization that operates the Securities and Exchange Commission Lost and Stolen Securities Program.

SECURITIES INVESTOR PROTECTION CORPORATION (SIPC) nonprofit corporation, established by Congress under the Securities Investor Protection Act of 1970, that insures the securities and cash in the customer accounts of member brokerage firms against the failure of those firms. All brokers and dealers registered with the Securities and Exchange Commission and with national stock exchanges are required to be members of SIPC. The Corporation acts similarly to the FEDERAL DEPOSIT INSURANCE CORPORATION (FDIC), which insures banks, and the SAVINGS ASSOCIATION INSURANCE FUND (SAIF), which insures savings and loans. When a brokerage firm fails, SIPC will first try to merge it into another brokerage firm. If this fails, SIPC will liquidate the firm's assets and pay off account holders up to an overall maximum of $500,000 per customer, with a limit of $100,000 on cash or cash equivalents. SIPC does not protect investors against market risks. *See also* SEPARATE CUSTOMER.

SECURITIES LAW ENFORCEMENT REMEDIES ACT OF 1990 act
amending the Securities Acts of 1933 and 1934, the Investment Company Act of 1940, and the Investment Advisers Act of 1940, to establish tiered civil money penalties and other enforcement measures relating to "unfit" officers and directors of securities-issuing entities.

SECURITIES LOAN
1. loan of securities by one broker to another, usually to cover a customer's short sale. The lending broker is secured by the cash proceeds of the sale.
2. in a more general sense, loan collateralized by MARKETABLE SECURITIES. These would include all customer loans made to purchase or carry securities by broker-dealers under Federal Reserve Board REGULATION T margin rules, as well as by banks under REGULATION U and other lenders under REGULATION G. Loans made by banks to brokers to cover customers' positions are also collateralized by securities, but such loans are called *broker's loans* or *call loans*. *See also* HYPOTHECATION; LENDING AT A PREMIUM; LENDING AT A RATE; LENDING SECURITIES; REHYPOTHECATION; SELLING SHORT.

SECURITIES MARKETS general term for markets in which securities are
traded, including both ORGANIZED SECURITIES EXCHANGES and OVER-THE-COUNTER (OTC) markets.

SECURITIZATION process of distributing risk by aggregating debt instru-
ments in a pool, then issuing new securities backed by the pool. *See also* ASSET-BACKED SECURITIES.

SECURITY
Finance: collateral offered by a debtor to a lender to secure a loan called *collateral security.* For instance, the security behind a mortgage loan is the real estate being purchased with the proceeds of the loan. If the debt is not repaid, the lender may seize the security and resell it.

Personal security refers to one person or firm's GUARANTEE of another's primary obligation.

Investment: instrument that signifies an ownership position in a corporation (a stock), a creditor relationship with a corporation or governmental body (a bond), or rights to ownership such as those represented by an OPTION, SUBSCRIPTION RIGHT, and SUBSCRIPTION WARRANT.

SECURITY DEPOSIT money paid in advance to protect the provider of a
product or service against damage or nonpayment by the buyer. For example, landlords require a security deposit of one month's rent when a tenant signs a lease, to cover the possibility that the tenant will move out without paying the last month's rent, or that the tenant will inflict substantial damage on the property while living there. In such a case, the money from the security deposit is used to cover repairs. Similarly, car leasing companies typically demand security deposits for the last month's lease payment to protect the leasing company against damage to the car or nonpayment of the lease. If all payments are made on time and there is no damage, security deposits must be returned to those who paid them.

SECURITY MARKET LINE relationship between the REQUIRED RATE OF
RETURN on an investment and its SYSTEMATIC RISK.

SECURITY RATINGS evaluations of the credit and investment risk of securities issues by commercial RATING agencies.

SEED MONEY venture capitalist's first contribution toward the financing or capital requirements of a START-UP business. It frequently takes the form of a loan, often SUBORDINATED, or an investment in convertible bonds or preferred stock. Seed money provides the basis for additional capitalization to accommodate growth. *See also* MEZZANINE LEVEL; SECOND ROUND; VENTURE CAPITAL.

SEEK A MARKET to look for a buyer (if a seller) or a seller (if a buyer) of securities.

SEGMENT REPORTING *see* BUSINESS SEGMENT REPORTING.

SEGREGATION OF SECURITIES Securities and Exchange Commission rules (8c and 15c2–1) designed to protect customers' securities used by broker-dealers to secure broker loans. Specifically, broker-dealers may not (1) commingle the securities of different customers without the written consent of each customer, (2) commingle a customer's securities with those of any person other than a bona-fide customer, or (3) borrow more against customers' securities than the customers, in the aggregate, owe the broker-dealer against the same securities. *See also* COMMINGLING; HYPOTHECATION; REHYPOTHECATION; SECURITIES AND EXCHANGE COMMISSION RULE 15c2–1.

SELECTED DEALER AGREEMENT agreement governing the SELLING GROUP in a securities underwriting and distribution. *See also* UNDERWRITE.

SELECTIVE DISCLOSURE practice, made illegal in 2000 by SEC Regulation FD, whereby a public company would disclose material information to selected groups of people, such as institutional investors, prior to making the information public. Selective disclosure provided opportunities for INSIDER TRADING.

SELF-AMORTIZING MORTGAGE mortgage in which all principal is paid off in a specified period of time through periodic interest and principal payments. The most common self-amortizing mortgages are for 15 and 30 years. Lenders will provide a table to borrowers showing how much principal and interest is being paid off each month until the loan is retired.

SELF-DIRECTED IRA INDIVIDUAL RETIREMENT ACCOUNT (IRA) that can be actively managed by the account holder, who designates a CUSTODIAN to carry out investment instructions. The account is subject to the same conditions and early withdrawal limitations as a regular IRA. Investors who withdraw money from a qualified IRA plan have 60 days in which to roll over the funds to another plan before they become liable for tax penalties. Most corporate and U.S. government securities, stocks, mutual funds, and metals such as gold, silver, platinum, and palladium are eligible to be held by a self-directed IRA. *See also* ROTH IRA.

SELF-DIRECTED PORTFOLIO investment product introduced experimentally in mid-2002 and called a *folio,* which consists of a basket of stocks professionally selected that an investor can modify. Folios have been described as a cross between EXCHANGE-TRADED FUNDS and customized portfolios.

SELF-EMPLOYED INCOME net taxable income of a self-employed person, as reported on Schedule C of IRS Form 1040. Self-employment income may be generated by freelance work, royalties, consulting, or income from sole proprietorship businesses. Social Security taxes must be paid on self-employment income.

SELF-EMPLOYED RETIREMENT PLAN *see* KEOGH PLAN.

SELF-EMPLOYMENT TAX tax paid by self-employed people to Social Security, qualifying them for receiving Social Security benefits at retirement. The tax is filed on Schedule SE of IRS Form 1040, which indicates the type of business generating self-employment income, net earnings, and the amount of self-employment tax.

SELF-REGULATORY ORGANIZATION (SRO) principal means contemplated by the federal securities laws for the enforcement of fair, ethical, and efficient practices in the securities and commodities futures industries. It is these organizations that are being referred to when "industry rules" are mentioned, as distinguished from the regulatory agencies such as the Securities and Exchange Commission or the Federal Reserve Board. The SROs include all the national SECURITIES AND COMMODITIES EXCHANGES and the Municipal Securities Rulemaking Board, created under the Securities Acts Amendments of 1975 to regulate brokers, dealers, and banks dealing in municipal securities.

SELF-SUPPORTING DEBT bonds sold for a project that will produce sufficient revenues to retire the debt. Such debt is usually issued by municipalities building a public structure (for example, a bridge or tunnel) that will be producing revenue through tolls or other charges. The bonds are not supported by the taxing power of the municipality issuing them. *See also* REVENUE BOND.

SELF-TENDER *see* SHARE REPURCHASE PLAN.

SELLER FINANCING financing provided by the owner/seller of real estate, who takes back a secured note. The buyer may be unable to qualify for a mortgage from a lending institution, or interest rates may have risen so high that the buyer is unwilling to take on a market-rate loan. In order to sell their property, sellers offer to lend the buyer the money needed, often at a below-market interest rate. The buyer takes full title to the property when the loan is fully repaid. If the buyer defaults on the loan, the seller can repossess the property. Also called *creative financing*.

SELLER'S MARKET situation in which there is more demand for a security or product than there is available supply. As a result, the prices tend to be rising, and the sellers can set both the prices and the terms of sale. It contrasts with a buyer's market, characterized by excess supply, low prices, and terms suited to the buyer's desires.

SELLER'S OPTION securities transaction in which the seller, instead of making REGULAR WAY DELIVERY, is given the right to deliver the security to the purchaser on the date the seller's option expires or before, provided written notification of the seller's intention to deliver is given to the buyer one full business day prior to delivery. Seller's option deliveries are normally not made before 6 business days following the transaction or after 60 days.

SELLING CLIMAX sudden plunge in security prices as those who hold stocks or bonds panic and decide to dump their holdings all at once. Technical analysts see a climax as both a dramatic increase in volume and a sharp drop in prices on a chart. To these analysts, such a pattern usually means that a short-term rally will soon follow since there are few sellers left after the climax. Sometimes, a selling climax can signal the bottom of a BEAR MARKET, meaning that after the climax the market will start to rise.

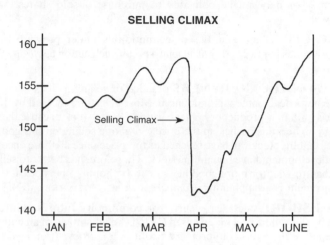

SELLING CONCESSION discount at which securities in a NEW ISSUE offering (or a SECONDARY DISTRIBUTION) are allocated to the members of a SELLING GROUP by the underwriters. Since the selling group cannot sell to the public at a price higher than the PUBLIC OFFERING PRICE, its compensation comes out of the difference between the price paid to the issuer by the underwriters and the public offering price, called the SPREAD. The selling group's portion, called the CONCESSION, is normally one half or more of the gross spread, expressed as a discount off the public offering price. *See also* FLOTATION COST; UNDERWRITE; UNDERWRITING SPREAD.

SELLING DIVIDENDS questionable practice by sales personnel dealing in MUTUAL FUNDS whereby a customer is induced to buy shares in a fund in order to get the benefit of a dividend scheduled in the near future. Since the dividend is already part of the NET ASSET VALUE of the fund and therefore part of the share price, the customer derives no real benefit.

SELLING, GENERAL, AND ADMINISTRATIVE (SG&A) EXPENSES grouping of expenses reported on a company's PROFIT AND LOSS STATEMENT between COST OF GOODS SOLD and INCOME DEDUCTIONS. Included are such items as salespersons' salaries and commissions, advertising and promotion, travel and entertainment, office payroll and expenses, and executives' salaries. SG&A expenses do not include such items as interest or amortization of INTANGIBLE ASSETS, which would be listed as income deductions. *See also* OPERATING PROFIT (OR LOSS).

SELLING GROUP group of dealers appointed by the syndicate manager of an UNDERWRITING GROUP, as AGENT for the other underwriters, to market a new or secondary issue to the public; also called *selling syndicate*. The selling group typically includes members of the underwriting group but varies in size with the size of the issue, sometimes running into several hundred dealers. The selling group is governed by the selling group agreement, also called the SELECTED DEALER AGREEMENT. It sets forth the terms of the relationship, establishes the commission (or SELLING CONCESSION, as it is called), and provides for the termination of the group, usually in 30 days. The selling group may or may not be obligated to purchase unsold shares. *See also* UNDERWRITE.

SELLING OFF selling securities or commodities under pressure to avoid further declines in prices. Technical analysts call such action a *sell-off*. *See also* DUMPING.

SELLING ON THE GOOD NEWS practice of selling a stock soon after a positive news development is announced. Most investors, cheered by the news of a successful new product or higher earnings, buy a stock because they think it will go higher: this pushes up the price. Someone selling on this good news believes that the stock will have reached its top price once all those encouraged by the development have bought the stock. Therefore, it is better to sell at this point than to wait for more good news or to be holding the stock if the next announcement is disappointing. *Compare with* BUYING ON THE BAD NEWS.

SELLING SHORT sale of a security or commodity futures contract not owned by the seller; a technique used (1) to take advantage of an anticipated decline in the price or (2) to protect a profit in a LONG POSITION (*see* SELLING SHORT AGAINST THE BOX).

An investor borrows stock certificates for delivery at the time of short sale. If the seller can buy that stock later at a lower price, a profit results; if the price rises, however, a loss results.

A commodity sold short represents a promise to deliver the commodity at a set price on a future date. Most commodity short sales are COVERED before the DELIVERY DATE.

Example of a short sale involving stock: An investor, anticipating a decline in the price of XYZ shares, instructs his or her broker to sell short 100 XYZ when XYZ is trading at $50. The broker then loans the investor 100 shares of XYZ, using either its own inventory, shares in the MARGIN ACCOUNT of another customer, or shares borrowed from another broker. These shares are used to make settlement with the buying broker within five days of the short sale transaction, and the proceeds are used to secure the loan. The investor now has what is known as a SHORT POSITION—that is, he or she still does not own the 100 XYZ and, at some point, must buy the shares to repay the lending broker. If the market price of XYZ drops to $40, the investor can buy the shares for $4,000, repay the lending broker, thus covering the short sale, and claim a profit of $1,000, or $10 a share.

Short selling is regulated by REGULATION T of the Federal Reserve Board. *See also* LENDING AT A RATE; LENDING AT A PREMIUM; LOANED FLAT; MARGIN REQUIREMENT; R.E.O. SHORT SALE RULE.

SELLING SHORT AGAINST THE BOX SELLING SHORT stock actually owned by the seller but held in SAFEKEEPING, called the BOX in Wall Street jargon. The motive for the practice, which assumes that the securities needed to COVER are borrowed as with any short sale, may be simply inaccessibility of the box or that the seller does not wish to disclose ownership. The main motive is to protect a CAPITAL GAIN in the shares that are owned, while deferring a LONG-TERM GAIN into another tax year. This technique was curtailed as a way to defer taxes by the TAXPAYER RELIEF ACT OF 1997. Under the law, shorting against the box after June 8, 1997 is considered a "constructive sale," resulting in capital gains liability.

SELLING THE SPREAD spread where the sold option is trading at a higher premium than the purchased option. For example, purchasing a shorter term option and selling a longer term option (assuming both options have the same EXERCISE PRICE) would usually result in a net credit. *See* CALENDAR SPREAD. Another example would be purchasing a call with a higher exercise price and selling a call with a lower exercise price, assuming both options have the same expiration date. *See also* CREDIT SPREAD.

SELL-OFF massive selling of stocks or bonds after a steep decline in prices. Traders sell quickly in order to avoid further losses.

SELL ORDER order by an investor to a broker to sell a particular stock, bond, option, future, mutual fund, or other holding. There are several kinds of sell orders, including DAY ORDERS, GOOD-TILL-CANCELED ORDERS (GTC), LIMIT ORDERS, MARKET-ON-CLOSE ORDERS, MARKET ORDERS, ON THE CLOSE ORDERS, ON THE OPENING ORDERS, STOP-LIMIT ORDERS, STOP LOSS ORDERS, and STOP ORDERS.

SELL OUT
1. liquidation of a MARGIN ACCOUNT by a broker after a MARGIN CALL has failed to produce additional equity to bring the margin to the required level. *See also* CLOSE A POSITION; MARGIN REQUIREMENT; MINIMUM MAINTENANCE.
2. action by a broker when a customer fails to pay for securities purchased and the securities received from the selling broker are sold to cover the transaction. Term also applies to commodities futures transactions.
3. expression used when all the securities in a NEW ISSUE underwriting have been distributed.

SELL PLUS sell order with instructions to execute only if the trading price in a security is higher than the last different preceding price. *See also* SHORT-SALE RULE.

SELL-SIDE ANALYST Contrast with BUY-SIDE ANALYST.

SELL SIGNAL opposite of BUY SIGNAL.

SELL-STOP ORDER *see* STOP ORDER.

SELL THE BOOK order to a broker by the holder of a large quantity of shares of a security to sell all that can be ABSORBED at the current bid price. The term derives from the SPECIALIST'S BOOK—the record of all the buy and sell orders members have placed in the stock he or she handles. In this scenario, the buyers potentially include those in the specialist's book, the specialist for his or her own account, and the broker-dealer CROWD.

SENAF the electronic trading platform for Spanish public debt bonds, part of the integrated Financial Markets Holding that includes the country's derivatives and fixed-income markets. The SENAF operates a blind bond-trading system and a single order book. Its main shareholders are the majority of the Spanish banks through the AIAF (Asociación de Intermediarios de Activos Financieros, or the Association of Financial Assets Intermediaries) and the four blind brokers officially authorized by the Bank of Spain. In addition to

Barcelona, Madrid, and Valencia, SENAF also has operative terminals in London, Paris, Frankfurt, and Milan. *www.senaf.net.*

SENIOR DEBT loans or DEBT SECURITIES that have claim prior to junior obligations and EQUITY on a corporation's assets in the event of LIQUIDATION. Senior debt commonly includes funds borrowed from banks, insurance companies, or other financial institutions, as well as notes, bonds, or debentures not expressly defined as junior or subordinated.

SENIOR MORTGAGE BOND bond with the highest claim on the assets of the issuer in case of bankruptcy or liquidation. Senior mortgage bondholders are paid off in full before any payments are made to junior bondholders.

SENIOR REFUNDING replacement of securities maturing in 5 to 12 years with issues having original maturities of 15 years or longer. The objectives may be to reduce the bond issuer's interest costs, to consolidate several issues into one, or to extend the maturity date.

SENIOR SECURITY security that has claim prior to a junior obligation and EQUITY on a corporation's assets and earnings. Senior securities are repaid before JUNIOR SECURITIES in the event of LIQUIDATION. Debt, including notes, bonds, and debentures, is senior to stock; first mortgage bonds are senior to second mortgage bonds; and all mortgage bonds are senior to debentures, which are unsecured.

SENSITIVE MARKET market easily swayed by good or bad news.

SENSITIVITY ANALYSIS study measuring the effect of a change in a variable (such as sales) on the risk or profitability of an investment.

SENTIMENT INDICATORS measures of the bullish or bearish mood of investors. Many technical analysts look at these indicators as contrary indicators—that is, when most investors are bullish, the market is about to drop, and when most are bearish, the market is about to rise. Some financial newsletters measure swings in investor sentiment by tabulating the number of INVESTMENT ADVISORY SERVICES that are bullish or bearish.

SEP *see* SIMPLIFIED EMPLOYEE PENSION (SEP) PLAN.

SEPARATE CUSTOMER concept used by the SECURITIES INVESTOR PROTECTION CORPORATION (SIPC) in allocating insurance coverage. If there is a difference in the way investment accounts are owned, each account is viewed as a separate customer entitled to the maximum protection; thus two accounts, one in the name of John Jones and the other in the name of John Jones and his wife Mary Jones, would be treated as separate accounts and separate persons. On the other hand, a CASH ACCOUNT, a MARGIN ACCOUNT, and a special convertible bond account all owned by John Jones are not treated as separate customer accounts but as one.

SEPARATELY MANAGED ACCOUNT (SMA) professionally managed portfolio of securities that uses pooled money to buy investments owned directly by the account holder. SMAs, also called *separate accounts, individually managed accounts*, or *managed accounts,* are usually marketed by broker-dealers, who select money managers, called subadvisors, for clients from a selected list. (An alternative to *subadvisor programs*, called *open architecture programs*, allows investors to choose from a much broader menu of managers with more flexible pricing arrangements.) A phenomenon of computer technology and mass affluence, SMAs offer customized professional management to clients with as little as $100,000 for fees of 2% or less. With assets of more than $1 trillion in 2005 and a 20% annual growth rate, they are challenging mutual funds' preeminence as wealth-management vehicles. The chief advantage of SMAs over mutual funds is direct ownership of securities in the portfolio. This permits customization (the investor can, for example, restrict investments in tobacco and gambling without having to buy a socially conscious fund), and provides individual COST BASIS for income tax purposes; the investor, unlike a mutual fund investor, thus has control of the tax consequences of the timing of purchases and REALIZED PROFIT OR LOSS. MORNINGSTAR RATING SYSTEM has started giving star ratings to SMAs through its *Morningstar Principia Separate Accounts* database. A variation, *ETF-SMAs*, which are separately managed accounts composed of EXCHANGE-TRADED FUNDS (ETFs), is a professionally run asset allocation service that is rapidly gaining popularity. IXIS Asset Management Advisors of Boston, for example, calls its product MEPs, for Managed ETF Portfolios.

SEPARATELY REPORTABLE SEGMENT *see* BUSINESS SEGMENT REPORTING.

SEPARATE TAX RETURNS tax returns filed by a married couple choosing the married, filing separately, status. Each person reports his or her own income, deductions, exemptions, and credits. Couples may choose to file separately instead of with a JOINT TAX RETURN for several reasons. A couple may choose to keep all of their financial affairs, including tax filing, separate. In some cases, a couple may find that the total amount of tax paid is less if they file separately than if they file jointly. This is usually the case when there is a wide disparity between the earnings of the husband and wife. However, because of the way the tax tables are designed, it is frequently more advantageous for a married couple to file a joint return than for them to file separate returns. *See also* FILING STATUS, HEAD OF HOUSEHOLD, MARRIAGE PENALTY.

SEQUENTIAL COMPARISON in financial analysis, comparing one period to the period immediately preceding it. Comparing the fourth quarter to the third quarter of the same year would be sequential, for example. In contrast, comparing the fourth quarter to the fourth quarter of the prior year would be called a year-to-year comparison.

SERIAL BOND bond issue, usually of a municipality, with various MATURITY DATES scheduled at regular intervals until the entire issue is retired. Each bond certificate in the series has an indicated REDEMPTION DATE. Serial bonds are distinguished from *term bonds*, where the bonds in an issue have the same maturity date, although municipalities will often issue a combination of both types.

SERIAL REDEMPTION redemption of a SERIAL BOND.

SERIES E BOND savings bond issued by the U.S. government from 1941 to 1979. The bonds were then replaced by Series EE and Series HH bonds. Outstanding Series E bonds, which may be exchanged for Series HH bonds, continue to pay interest for between 30 and 40 years from their issue date. Those issued from 1941 to November 1965 accrue interest for 40 years; those issued from December 1965 and later, for 30 years. Their interest is exempt from state and local income and personal property taxes. *See also* SAVINGS BOND.

SERIES EE BOND *see* SAVINGS BOND.

SERIES FUND a MUTUAL FUND with multiple portfolios.

SERIES HH BOND *see* SAVINGS BOND.

SERIES OF OPTION class of OPTION, either all CALL OPTIONS or all PUT OPTIONS, on the same underlying security, all of which have the same EXERCISE PRICE (strike price) and maturity date. For example, all XYZ May 50 calls would form a series of options.

SERIES 6 REGISTERED broker who has passed the Investment Company/ Variable Contracts Products Limited Representative Qualification Examination administered by the FINANCIAL INDUSTRY REGULATORY AUTHORITY (FINRA) and is licensed to trade redeemable securities of companies registered pursuant to the INVESTMENT COMPANY ACT OF 1940, securities of similarly registered CLOSED-END MANAGEMENT COMPANIES during the period of initial distribution only, and variable contracts and insurance premium funding programs and other contracts issued by an insurance company except EXEMPT SECURITIES. Series 6 registered brokers cannot trade corporate securities, direct participation programs, municipal securities, or options. *See also* CORPORATE SECURITIES (LIMITED) REPRESENTATIVE; SERIES 7 REGISTERED.

SERIES 63 REGISTERED *see* UNIFORM SECURITIES AGENT STATE LAW EXAMINATION.

SERIES 7 REGISTERED broker who has passed the General Securities Registered Representative Examination, commonly called the Series 7, and who is a REGISTERED REPRESENTATIVE. In addition to the Series 7, which is a six-hour multiple-choice test developed by the New York Stock Exchange (NYSE) and administered by the FINANCIAL INDUSTRY REGULATORY AUTHORITY (FINRA), many states require that registered representatives pass a UNIFORM SECURITIES AGENT STATE LAW EXAMINATION.

SESSION *see* TRADING SESSION.

SET-ASIDE percentage of a job set aside for bidding to minority contractors. In the securities business, many municipal and some corporate bond underwritings require that a certain percentage of the offering be handled by a minority-owned broker/ dealer underwriting firm. Other government and corporate contracts for products and services also stipulate that a certain percentage of the business must be handled by minority firms. Set-aside programs are designed to help minority firms become established more quickly than they might if they had to compete on an equal footing with entrenched competitors.

SETTLE
In general: to pay an obligation.
Estates: distribution of an estate's assets by an executor to beneficiaries after all legal procedures have been completed.
Law: (1) to resolve a legal dispute short of adjudication; (2) to arrange for disposition of property, such as between spouses or between parents and children, if there has been a dispute such as a divorce.
Securities: to complete a securities trade between brokers acting as AGENTS or between a broker and his customer. A trade is settled when the customer

has paid the broker for securities bought or when the customer delivers securities that have been sold and the customer receives the proceeds from the sale. *See also* CONTINUOUS NET SETTLEMENT.

SETTLEMENT in general, a resolution of differences among various parties. For example, a labor dispute resulting in a strike may finally be settled by a new contract, or a conflict between a landlord and tenant may be settled in a housing court.

Securities: conclusion of a securities transaction in which a broker/dealer pays for securities bought for a customer or delivers securities sold and receives payment from the buyer's broker. REGULAR WAY DELIVERY AND SETTLEMENT is completed on the third full business day following the date of the transaction for stocks, called the SETTLEMENT DATE. Government bonds and options trades are settled the next business day. *See also* CONTINUOUS NET SETTLEMENT.

Futures/Options: the final price, established by exchange rule, for the prices prevailing during the closing period and upon which futures contracts are marked to market.

SETTLEMENT DATE date by which an executed order must be settled, either by a buyer paying for the securities with cash or by a seller delivering the securities and receiving the proceeds of the sale for them. In a REGULAR-WAY DELIVERY of stocks and bonds, the settlement date is three business days after the trade was executed. For listed options and government securities, settlement is required by the next business day. *See also* SELLER'S OPTION.

SETTLEMENT OPTIONS options available to beneficiaries when a person insured by a life insurance policy dies. The DEATH BENEFIT may be paid in one lump sum, in several installments over a fixed period of time, or in the form of an ANNUITY for the rest of the beneficiary's life, among other options.

SETTLEMENT RISK the risk that the delivering party will not deliver or that the paying party will not pay. In foreign exchange trading the risk that either party to a contract will fail to perform is called *Herstatt risk.*

SETTLOR person who creates an INTER VIVOS TRUST as distinguished from a TESTAMENTARY TRUST. Also called *donor, grantor,* or *trustor.*

SEVERALLY BUT NOT JOINTLY form of agreement used to establish the responsibility for selling a portion of the securities in an underwriting. UNDERWRITING GROUP members agree to buy a certain portion of an issue (severally) but do not agree to joint liability for shares not sold by other members of the syndicate. In a less common form of underwriting arrangement, called a *several and joint agreement,* syndicate members agree to sell not only the shares allocated to them, but also any shares not sold by the rest of the group. *See also* UNDERWRITE.

SEVERANCE PAY money paid to an employee who has been laid off by an employer. The money may be paid in the form of a LUMP SUM, as an ANNUITY, or in the form of paychecks for a specified period of time. The size of the termination benefit is based on the length of service and job level of the employee, union contracts, and other factors. Also called *termination benefit.*

SG&A EXPENSES *see* SELLING, GENERAL, AND ADMINISTRATIVE EXPENSES.

SHADOW CALENDAR backlog of securities issues in REGISTRATION with the Securities and Exchange Commission for which no OFFERING DATE has been set pending clearance.

SHAKEOUT change in market conditions that results in the elimination of marginally financed participants in an industry. For example, if the market for microcomputers suddenly becomes glutted because there is more supply than demand, a shakeout will result, meaning that companies will fall by the wayside. In the securities markets, a shakeout occurs when speculators are forced by market events to sell their positions, usually at a loss.

SHAM transaction conducted for the purpose of avoiding taxation. Once discovered by tax authorities, it will be considered null and void, and the parties to the transaction will have to pay the taxes due. Some limited partnerships have been ruled to be "sham transactions" in the past, causing limited partners to owe back taxes, penalties, and interest to the Internal Revenue Service.

SHANGHAI STOCK EXCHANGE (SHSE) established in late 1990 as a nonprofit organization, regulated by the China Securities Regulatory Commission. A shares are restricted to domestic investors, while B shares are open to all investors. Bonds traded on the exchange include government, corporate, and convertible. Trading hours for B shares are 9:30 A.M. to 11:30 A.M. and 1 P.M. to 3 P.M., Monday through Friday. *www.sse.com.cn.*

SHADOW BANKING SYSTEM the miscellany of non-deposit-taking financial institutions that exist between investors and borrowers but are not subject to the reserve requirements and other disciplines that banks are. Examples include investment banks, hedge funds, SPECIAL INVESTMENT VEHI-CLES (SIVs), money market funds, insurance companies, and a host of other nonbank financial institutions and the complex world of DERIVATIVE products they produced. In total, as many dollars were available through the shadow banking system as were held by banks. Essentially the problem with the shadow banking system (in addition to its lack of regulation) was that it was borrowing on a highly leveraged basis from short-term investors and lending to institutions financing long-term, illiquid assets, such as collateralized debt obligations. When the mortgage market melted, short-term financing dried up and long-term obligations became writeoffs.

SHARE
1. unit of equity ownership in a corporation. This ownership is represented by a stock certificate, which names the company and the shareowner. The number of shares a corporation is authorized to issue is detailed in its corporate charter. Corporations usually do not issue the full number of AUTHORIZED SHARES.
2. unit of ownership in a mutual fund. *See also* INVESTMENT COMPANY.
3. interest, normally represented by a certificate, in a general or LIMITED PARTNERSHIP.

SHARE BROKER DISCOUNT BROKER whose charges are based on the number of shares traded. The more shares in a trade, the lower the per-share cost will be. Trading with a share broker is usually advantageous for those trading at least 500 shares, or for those trading in high-priced shares, who would otherwise pay a percentage of the dollar amount. Those trading in small numbers of shares, or lower-priced ones, may pay lower commissions with a VALUE BROKER, the other kind of discount brokerage firm.

SHARED APPRECIATION MORTGAGE (SAM) mortgage in which the borrower receives a below-market rate of interest in return for agreeing to share part of the appreciation in the value of the underlying property with the lender in a specified number of years. If the borrower does not want to sell at that time, he or she must pay the lender its share of the appreciation in cash. If the borrower does not have that amount of cash on hand, the lender may force the borrower to sell the property to satisfy their claim.

SHARE DRAFT instrument similar to a bank check that is used by credit unions to withdraw from interest-bearing share draft accounts.

SHAREHOLDER
1. owner of one or more shares of STOCK in a corporation. A common shareholder is normally entitled to four basic rights of ownership: (1) claim on a share of the company's undivided assets in proportion to number of shares held; (2) proportionate voting power in the election of DIRECTORS and other business conducted at shareholder meetings or by PROXY; (3) DIVIDENDS when earned and declared by the BOARD OF DIRECTORS; and (4) PREEMPTIVE RIGHT to subscribe to additional stock offerings before they are available to the general public except when overruled by the ARTICLES OF INCORPORATION or in special circumstances, such as where stock is issued to effect a merger.
2. owner of one or more shares or units in a MUTUAL FUND. Mutual fund investors have voting rights similar to those of stock owners.
    Shareholders' rights can vary according to the articles of incorporation or BYLAWS of the particular company.
    See also PREFERRED STOCK.

SHAREHOLDER DERIVATIVE SUIT *see* DERIVATIVE SUIT.

SHAREHOLDER REPORT *see* STOCKHOLDER'S REPORT.

SHAREHOLDER'S EQUITY total ASSETS minus total LIABILITIES of a corporation. Also called *stockholder's equity,* EQUITY, and NET WORTH.

SHARE REPURCHASE PLAN program by which a corporation buys back its own shares in the open market. It is usually done when shares are UNDERVALUED. Since it reduces the number of shares outstanding and thus increases EARNINGS PER SHARE, it tends to elevate the market value of the remaining shares held by stockholders. *See also* GOING PRIVATE; TREASURY STOCK.

SHARES AUTHORIZED number of shares of stock provided for in the ARTICLES OF INCORPORATION of a company. This figure is ordinarily indicated in the capital accounts section of a company's BALANCE SHEET and is usually well in excess of the shares ISSUED AND OUTSTANDING. A corporation cannot legally issue more shares than authorized. The number of authorized shares can be changed only by amendment to the corporate charter, with the approval of the shareholders. The most common reason for increasing authorized shares in a public company is to accommodate a stock SPLIT.

SHARES OUTSTANDING *see* ISSUED AND OUTSTANDING.

SHARK REPELLENT measure undertaken by a corporation to discourage unwanted TAKEOVER attempts. Also called *porcupine provision.*

For example:
(1) fair price provision requiring a bidder to pay the same price to all share-holders. This raises the stakes and discourages TENDER OFFERS designed to attract only those shareholders most eager to replace management.
(2) GOLDEN PARACHUTE contract with top executives that makes it prohibitively expensive to get rid of existing management.
(3) defensive merger, in which a TARGET COMPANY combines with another organization that would create antitrust or other regulatory problems if the original, unwanted takeover proposal was consummated. *See also* SAFE HARBOR.
(4) STAGGERED BOARD OF DIRECTORS, a way to make it more difficult for a corporate RAIDER to install a majority of directors sympathetic to his or her views.
(5) supermajority provision, which might increase from a simple majority to two-thirds or three-fourths the shareholder vote required to ratify a takeover by an outsider.
  See also POISON PILL; SCORCHED-EARTH POLICY.

SHARK WATCHER firm specializing in the early detection of TAKEOVER activity. Such a firm, whose primary business is usually the solicitation of proxies for client corporations, monitors trading patterns in a client's stock and attempts to determine the identity of parties accumulating shares.

SHARPE RATIO average return, less the RISK-FREE RETURN, divided by the STANDARD DEVIATION of return. The ratio measures the relationship of reward to risk in an investment strategy. The higher the ratio, the safer the strategy. *See also* INFORMATION RATIO.

SHELF REGISTRATION term used for SECURITIES AND EXCHANGE COMMISSION RULE 415 adopted in the 1980s, which allows a corporation to comply with REGISTRATION requirements up to two years prior to a PUBLIC OFFERING of securities. With the registration on the shelf, the corporation, by simply updating regularly filed annual, quarterly, and related reports to the SEC, can go to the market as conditions become favorable with a minimum of administrative preparation. The flexibility corporate issuers enjoy as the result of shelf registration translates into substantial savings of time and expense.

SHELL CORPORATION company that is incorporated but has no significant assets or operations. Such corporations may be formed to obtain financing prior to starting operations, in which case an investment in them is highly risky. The term is also used of corporations set up by fraudulent operators as fronts to conceal tax evasion schemes.

SHENZHEN STOCK EXCHANGE (SZSE) one of China's three stock exchanges and created in 1990 in the Shenzhen province of China. In 2004, the exchange launched the Small and Medium Enterprises Board, which is a market exclusively for small- and mid-caps. Trading hours are from 9:30 A.M. to 3 P.M., Monday through Friday. Settlement period is T + 1 for securities traded in local currency and T + 3 for B-shares. *www.szse.cn.*

SHERMAN ANTI-TRUST ACT OF 1890 *see* ANTITRUST LAWS.

SHOCK ABSORBERS *see* CIRCUIT BREAKERS.

SHOGUN SECURITY security issued and distributed exclusively in Japan by a non-Japanese company and denominated in a currency other than yen.

SHOP
1. area of a business location where production takes place, as distinguished from the office or warehouse areas.
2. factory work force of an employer, as in a "union shop."
3. office of a broker-dealer in securities.
4. the act of canvassing dealers for the most favorable price, as in shopping securities dealers for the best bid or offer.
5. a small retail establishment.

SHORT AGAINST THE BOX *see* SELLING SHORT AGAINST THE BOX.

SHORT BOND
1. bond with a short maturity; a somewhat subjective concept, but generally meaning two years or less. *See also* SHORT TERM.
2. bond repayable in one year or less and thus classified as a CURRENT LIABILITY in accordance with the accounting definition of SHORT-TERM DEBT.
3. SHORT COUPON bond.

SHORT COUPON
1. bond interest payment covering less than the conventional six-month period. A short coupon payment occurs when the original issue date is less than a half year from the first scheduled interest payment date. Depending on how short the coupon is, the ACCRUED INTEREST makes a difference in the value of the bond at the time of issue, which is reflected in the offering price.
2. bond with a relatively short maturity, usually two years or less.
    See also LONG COUPON.

SHORT COVERING actual purchase of securities by a short seller to replace those borrowed at the time of a short sale. *See also* LENDING SECURITIES; SELLING SHORT.

SHORT EXEMPT an order to sell short that is exempt from the SHORT-SALE RULE and its TICK TEST. Term has traditionally applied to special trading situations, such as that where the owners of a convertible security trading at parity can sell the equivalent amount of common short on a minus tick, assuming they have the firm intention to convert. Regulation SHO was adopted in 2005 to update short-sale regulation in light of numerous market developments since short sales were first regulated in 1938. In 2008 the SECURITIES AND EXCHANGE COMMISSION adopted amendments to Regulation SHO to eliminate an exception extending the delivery time for market makers in options.

SHORTFALL amount by which a financial objective has not been met. For example, a municipality expecting $100 million in tax revenue will say there is a $10 million shortfall if it collects only $90 million. For individual investors, a shortfall is the amount by which investment objectives have not been reached. For instance, investors execting to earn 15% a year will have a 5% shortfall if they earn 10% a year.

SHORT HEDGE transaction that limits or eliminates the risk of declining value in a security or commodity without entailing ownership.
Examples:

(1) SELLING SHORT AGAINST THE BOX leaves the owned securities untouched, possibly to gain in value, while protecting against a decline in value, since that would be offset by a profit on the short sale.

(2) purchasing a PUT OPTION to protect the value of a security that is owned limits loss to the cost of the option.

(3) buying a futures contract on raw materials at a specific price protects a manufacturer committed to sell a product at a certain price at a specified future time but who cannot buy the raw materials at the time of the commitment. Thus, if the price of the materials goes up, the manufacturer makes a profit on the contract; if the price goes down, he or she makes a profit on the product.

Compare with LONG HEDGE.

SHORT INTEREST total amount of shares of stock that have been sold short and have not yet been repurchased to close out SHORT POSITIONS. The short interest figure for the New York Stock Exchange, which is published monthly in newspapers, indicates how many investors think stock prices are about to fall. The Exchange reports all issues in which there are at least 5,000 shares sold short, and in which the short interest position had changed by at least 2,000 shares in the preceding month. The higher the short interest, the more people are expecting a downturn. Such short interest also represents potential buying pressure, however, since all short sales must eventually be covered by the purchase of shares. For this reason, a high short interest position is viewed as a bullish sign by many sophisticated market watchers. *See also* SELLING SHORT; SHORT INTEREST THEORY.

SHORT INTEREST THEORY theory that a large SHORT INTEREST in a stock presages a rise in the market price. It is based on the reasoning that even though short selling reflects a belief that prices will decline, the fact that short positions must eventually be covered is a source of upward price pressure. It is also called the CUSHION THEORY, since short sales can be viewed as a cushion of imminent buy orders. *See also* MEMBERS SHORT-SALE RATIO; ODD-LOT SHORT-SALE RATIO; SELLING SHORT; SPECIALIST'S SHORT-SALE RATIO.

SHORT POSITION

Commodities: contract in which a trader has agreed to sell a commodity at a future date for a specific price.

Stocks: stock shares that an individual has sold short (by delivery of borrowed certificates) and has not covered as of a particular date. *See also* COVER; SELLING SHORT.

SHORT SALE *see* SELLING SHORT.

SHORT-SALE RULE SECURITIES AND EXCHANGE COMMISSION rule requiring that short sales be made only in a rising market; also called PLUS TICK rule. Under the rule, first adopted in 1938, a short sale could be transacted only under these conditions: (1) if the last sale was at a higher price than the sale preceding it (called an UPTICK or PLUS TICK); (2) if the last sale price is unchanged but higher than the last preceding different sale (called a ZERO-PLUS TICK). But in 2007, the rule was abolished.

SHORT SQUEEZE situation when prices of a stock or commodity futures contract start to move up sharply and many traders with short positions are forced to buy stocks or commodities in order to COVER their positions and prevent losses. This sudden surge of buying leads to even higher prices, further aggravating the losses of short sellers who have not covered their positions. *See also* SELLING SHORT.

SHORT TENDER using borrowed stock to respond to a TENDER OFFER. The practice is prohibited by SECURITIES AND EXCHANGE COMMISSION RULE 10b-4.

SHORT TERM
Accounting: assets expected to be converted into cash within the normal operating cycle (usually one year), or liabilities coming due in one year or less. *See also* CURRENT ASSETS; CURRENT LIABILITY.
Investment: investment with a maturity of less than one year. This includes bonds, although in differentiating between short-, medium-, and long-term bonds, short-term often is stretched to mean two years or less. *See also* SHORT-TERM BOND FUND; SHORT-TERM DEBT; SHORT-TERM GAIN (OR LOSS).
Taxes: HOLDING PERIOD of less than 12 months, used to differentiate SHORT-TERM GAIN OR LOSS from LONG-TERM GAIN or LOSS. *See also* CAPITAL GAINS TAX.

SHORT-TERM BOND FUND bond mutual fund investing in short-to-intermediate term bonds. Such bonds, maturing in 3 to 5 years, typically pay higher yields than the shortest maturity bonds of 1 year or less, which are held by ULTRA-SHORT-TERM BOND FUNDS. Short-term bond funds also usually pay higher yields than money market mutual funds, which buy short-term commercial paper maturing in 90 days or less. However, short-term bond funds usually yield less than long-term bond funds holding bonds maturing in 10 to 30 years. Short-term bond funds, while yielding less than long-term bond funds, are also considerably less volatile, meaning that their value falls less when interest rates rise and rises less when interest rates fall. Many short-term bond funds offer checkwriting privileges, making them a source of easy liquidity. However, shareholders should remember than such checks will likely result in the realization of short- or long-term capital gains or losses.

SHORT-TERM DEBT all debt obligations coming due within one year; shown on a balance sheet as current liabilities. *See also* CURRENT LIABILITY.

SHORT-TERM GAIN (OR LOSS) for tax purposes, the profit or loss realized from the sale of securities or other capital assets held for less than 12 months. Short-term gains are taxable at ordinary income rates to the extent they are not reduced by offsetting capital losses. *See also* CAPITAL GAIN (OR LOSS).

SHORT-TERM INVESTMENT *see* SHORT-TERM.

SHOW STOPPER legal barrier erected to prevent a takeover attempt from becoming successful. For example, a target company may appeal to the state legislature to pass laws preventing the takeover. Or the company may embark on a SCORCHED-EARTH POLICY, making the company unappealing to the suitor. *See also* SHARK REPELLENT.

SHRINKAGE difference between the amount of inventory recorded in a firm's books and the actual amount of inventory on hand. Shrinkage may occur because of theft, deterioration, loss, clerical error, and other factors.

SIDE-BY-SIDE TRADING trading of a security and an OPTION on that security on the same exchange.

SIDEWAYS MARKET period in which prices trade within a narrow range, showing only small changes up or down. Also called HORIZONTAL PRICE MOVEMENT. *See also* FLAT MARKET.

SIFMA acronym for Securities Industry and Financial Markets Association, a 501 © (6) organization that represents participants in the global financial markets. Members include international securities firms, U.S.-registered broker-dealers, and asset managers. SIFMA represents the industry on regulatory and legislative issues and initiatives and also serves as a forum for outreach, training, education, and community involvement. It has offices in New York, Washington, D.C., London, and Hong Kong, where its sister organization, the Asia Securities and Financial Markets Association, is located.

SIGMA PRIME DERIVATIVE PRICING MODEL that measures effect of volatility. Used interchangeably with *vega* and also with KAPPA, OMEGA, and ZETA.

SIGNATURE GUARANTEE written confirmation by a financial institution such as a bank or brokerage firm that a customer's signature is valid. The institution will compare a new signature from a customer with the signature on file. Transfer agents require signature guarantees when transferring stocks, bonds, mutual funds, or other securities from one party to another to ensure that the transactions are legitimate.

SIGNATURE LOAN unsecured loan requiring only the borrower's signature on a loan application. The lender agrees to make the loan because the borrower has good credit standing. Collateral is not required. Also known as a *good-faith loan* or *character loan.*

SIGNIFICANT INFLUENCE holding of a large enough equity stake in a corporation to require accounting for it in financial statements. Usually, a company that holds at least 20% of the voting stock in another company is considered a holder of significant influence. A company with such a large holding is likely represented on the board of directors of the other firm. The company owning such a stake has to declare its equity holdings, and all dividends received from the position, in its financial reports.

SIGNIFICANT ORDER order to buy or sell securities that is significant enough to affect the price of the security. Many institutional investors, such as mutual funds, will try to spread out their significant buying or selling of a particular security over several days or weeks so they do not adversely affect the price at which they buy or sell.

SIGNIFICANT ORDER IMBALANCE large number of buy or sell orders for a stock, causing an unusually wide spread between bid and offer prices. Stock exchanges frequently halt trading of a stock with a significant order imbalance until more buyers or sellers appear and an orderly market can be reestablished. A significant order imbalance on the buying side can occur when there is an announcement of an impending takeover of the company, better-than-expected earnings, or other unexpected positive news. A significant order imbalance on the selling side can occur when a takeover offer has fallen through, a key executive has left the company, earnings came in far worse than expected, or there is other unexpected negative news.

SILENT PARTNER

1. limited partner in a DIRECT PARTICIPATION PROGRAM, such as real estate and oil and gas limited partnerships, in which CASH FLOW and tax benefits are passed directly through to shareholders. Such partners are called silent because, unlike general partners, they have no direct role in management and no liability beyond their individual investment.
2. general partner in a business who has no role in management but represents a sharing of the investment and liability. Silent partners of this type are often found in family businesses, where the intent is to distribute tax liability.

See also LIMITED PARTNERSHIP.

SILVER THURSDAY the day—March 27, 1980—when the extremely wealthy Hunt brothers of Texas failed to meet a MARGIN CALL by the brokerage firm of Bache Halsey Stuart Shields (which later became Prudential-Bache Securities and then Prudential Securities) for $100 million in silver futures contracts. Their position was later covered and Bache survived, but the effects on the commodities markets and the financial markets in general were traumatic.

SIMPLE COMPOUND GROWTH METHOD see COMPOUND ANNUAL RETURN.

SIMPLE 401(k) PLAN see SAVINGS INCENTIVE MATCH PLAN FOR EMPLOYEES (SIMPLE).

SIMPLE INTEREST interest calculation based only on the original principal amount. Simple interest contrasts with COMPOUND INTEREST, which is applied to principal plus accumulated interest. For example, $100 on deposit at 12% simple interest would yield $12 per year (12% of $100). The same $100 at 12% interest compounded annually would yield $12 interest only in the first year. The second year's interest would be 12% of the first year's accumulated interest and principal of $112, or $13.44. The third year's payment would be 12% of $125.44—the second year's principal plus interest—or $15.05. For computing interest on loans, simple interest is distinguished from various methods of calculating interest on a precomputed basis. See also PRECOMPUTE; CONSUMER CREDIT PROTECTION ACT OF 1968.

SIMPLE IRA form of SALARY REDUCTION PLAN that qualifying small employers may offer to their employees. SIMPLE stands for Savings Incentive Match Plans for Employees. Employers with no more than 100 employees earning $5,000 or more in a year who do not offer any other retirement plan can offer SIMPLE IRAs. Self-employed workers also are eligible to establish these accounts. Workers offered a SIMPLE IRA may contribute up to $10,500 per year into the account. Employees age 50 or older can contribute up to $13,000. Employee contributions are excluded from taxable pay on Form W-2 and are not subject to income tax withholding, although Social Security taxes are paid on those earnings. While the employer may pick the financial institution in which to deposit the simple IRA funds, employees have the right to transfer the funds to another financial institution of their choice without cost or penalty. Employers must make either a matching contribution or a fixed "nonelective" contribution to their employees' accounts each year. If the employer chooses matching contributions, the employer must match the amount the employee contributes up to 3% of compensation. Or the employer may make a nonelective contribution of 2% of wages for each eligible employee. Distributions from SIMPLE IRAs follow the same rules as regular IRAs, with one exception. If premature distributions are taken before the employee reaches age $59\frac{1}{2}$ and during the first two years after the employee starts participating in the plan, the penalty is 25%, not the usual 10%. After the first two years, the regular 10% penalty applies to pre-age $59\frac{1}{2}$ withdrawals. Withdrawals taken after age $59\frac{1}{2}$ are fully taxable at regular income tax rates, and mandatory withdrawals must begin at age $70\frac{1}{2}$, according to IRS life expectancy tables.

Assets inside SIMPLE IRAs can be invested like any other IRAs, in stocks, bonds, mutual funds, bank deposits, annuities, real estate, or precious metals. The SIMPLE IRA replaced the Salary Reduction Simplified Employee Pension plan (known as SARSEP) in 1997. SARSEPs may be continued only by employers who established them before 1997. *See also* SIMPLIFIED EMPLOYEE PENSION (SEP) PLAN.

SIMPLE RATE OF RETURN rate of return that results from dividing the income and capital gains from an investment by the amount of capital invested. For example, if a $1,000 investment produced $50 in income and $50 in capital appreciation in one year, the investment would have a 10% simple rate of return. This method of calculation does not factor in the effects of compounding.

SIMPLIFIED EMPLOYEE PENSION (SEP) PLAN pension plan in which both the employee and the employer contribute to an INDIVIDUAL RETIREMENT ARRANGEMENT (IRA). Under the TAX REFORM ACT OF 1986, employees (except those participating in SEPs of state or local governments) may elect to have employer contributions made to the SEP or paid to the employee in cash as with cash or deferred arrangements (401(k) PLANS). Elective contributions, which are excludable from earnings for income tax purposes but includable for employment tax (FICA and FUTA) purposes, are limited to 25% of net wages up to a certain maximum, which was $245,500 in 2009, or $49,000, whichever is less. SEPs are limited to small employers (25 or fewer employees) and at least 50% of employees must participate. Special provisions pertain to self-employed persons, the integration of SEP contributions and Social Security benefits, and limitations on tax deferrals for highly compensated individuals.

SINGAPORE EXCHANGE LIMITED (SGX) Asia-Pacific's first demutualized and integrated securities and derivatives exchange. The exchange was established on December 1, 1999, with the merger of the Stock Exchange of Singapore and the Singapore International Monetary Exchange. On November 23, 2000, SGX became the first exchange in the Asia-Pacific region to be listed via a public offering and a private placement. The stock is listed on its own exchange and is a component of benchmark indices such as the MSCI Singapore Free Index and the Straits Times Index. *www.sgx.com.*

SINGLE-COUNTRY MUTUAL FUNDS mutual funds investing in the securities of just one country. Such funds may be open-end, meaning they continue to create new shares as more money comes into the fund, or closed-end, meaning they issue a limited number of shares which then trade on the stock exchange at a premium or discount to net asset value. Single-country funds offer investors a PURE PLAY on the fortunes of securities in that country. This means that these funds typically are far more volatile than REGIONAL

MUTUAL FUNDS holding securities in a wider region, or GLOBAL MUTUAL FUNDS investing in markets around the world. There are many single-country funds, including funds for Argentina, Australia, Canada, China, France, Germany, Israel, Japan, Korea, Mexico, Spain, Switzerland, and the United Kingdom. *See also* ISHARES.

SINGLE OPTION term used to distinguish a PUT OPTION or a CALL OPTION from a SPREAD or a STRADDLE, each of which involves two or more put or call options. *See also* OPTION.

SINGLE-PREMIUM DEFERRED ANNUITY (SPDA) tax-deferred investment similar to an INDIVIDUAL RETIREMENT ACCOUNT, without many of the IRA restrictions. An investor makes a lump-sum payment to an insurance company or mutual fund selling the annuity. That lump sum can be invested in either a fixed-return instrument like a CD or a variable-return portfolio that can be switched among stocks, bonds, and money-market accounts. Proceeds are taxed only when distributions are taken. In contrast to an IRA, there is no limit to the amount that may be invested in an SPDA. Like the IRA, the tax penalty for withdrawals before age $59\frac{1}{2}$ is 10%.

SINGLE-PREMIUM LIFE INSURANCE WHOLE LIFE INSURANCE policy requiring one premium payment. Since this large, up-front payment begins accumulating cash value immediately, the policy holder will earn more than holders of policies paid up in installments. With its tax-free appreciation (assuming it remains in force); low or no net-cost; tax-free access to funds through POLICY LOANS; and tax-free proceeds to beneficiaries, this type of policy emerged as a popular TAX SHELTER under the TAX REFORM ACT OF 1986.

SINGLE-STATE MUNICIPAL BOND FUND MUTUAL FUND that invests entirely in tax-exempt obligations of governments and government agencies within a single state. Therefore, dividends paid on fund shares are not taxable to residents of that state when they file state tax returns although capital gains, if any, are taxable.

SINGLE STOCK FUTURE (SSF) only recently legalized in the United States, a FUTURES CONTRACT with one stock, basket of stocks, or NARROW-BASED INDEX as the UNDERLYING SECURITY. SSFs are traded in 100 share blocks. The holder gives up the rights and dividends that come with stock ownership, but gains a number of significant advantages: SSFs can be sold short without any of the restrictions of the SHORT-SALE RULE; MARGIN buying can be done on a 20% basis (vs. 50% for stocks) and with no interest costs; transaction costs are less; and cross-border transactions avoid the expense of foreign clearing systems.

SINKER bond on which interest and principal payments are made from the proceeds of a SINKING FUND.

SINKING FUND money accumulated on a regular basis in a separate custodial account that is used to redeem debt securities or preferred stock issues. A bond indenture or preferred stock charter may specify that payments be made to a sinking fund, thus assuring investors that the issues are safer than bonds (or preferred stocks) for which the issuer must make payment all at once, without the benefit of a sinking fund. *See also* PURCHASE FUND.

SIN TAX informal term for a tax on products considered vices, such as liquor or cigarettes. *See also* LUXURY TAX.

SIX GROUP owner of the SIX Swiss Exchange, Switzerland's principal stock exchange and formerly called the SWX Swiss Exchange. The group also holds financial interests in EUREX, the world's largest futures and derivatives exchange, as well as in STOXX, Europe's leading provider of securities market indices. The SIX Swiss Exchange has more than a 150-year-history and ranks among the world's most technologically advanced securities exchanges. In 1995 fully electronic trading replaced traditional floor trading at the stock exchanges of Geneva (founded in 1850), Zurich (founded in 1873), and Basel (founded in 1876). Another SIX Group subsidiary, SWX Europe, is a cross-border electronic exchange operating on the trading platform developed by the SIX Swiss Exchange. London-based SWX Europe has the status of an FSA "Recognized Investment Exchange" and is the home market for all constituent stocks of the capital-weighted Swiss Market Index (SMI), which comprises the largest and most liquid blue chip Swiss companies representing 80% of total market capitalization. *www.swx.com.* *See also* EUREX; STOXX.

SIZE
1. number of shares or bonds available for sale. A market maker will say, when asked for a quote, that a particular number of shares (the size) is available at a particular price.
2. term used when a large number of shares are for sale—a trader will say that "shares are available in size," for instance.

SKIP-PAYMENT PRIVILEGE
1. clause in some MORTGAGE contracts and installment loan agreements allowing borrowers to miss payments if ahead of schedule.
2. option offered some bank credit-card holders whereby they may defer the December payment on balances due.

SKYSCRAPER INDICATOR *see* ELLIOTT WAVE THEORY.

SLD LAST SALE indication, meaning "sold last sale," that appears on the CONSOLIDATED TAPE when a greater than normal change occurs between transactions in a security. The designation, which appears after the STOCK SYMBOL, is normally used when the change is a point or more on lower-priced issues (below $20) or two points or more on higher-priced issues.

SLEEPER stock in which there is little investor interest but which has significant potential to gain in price once its attractions are recognized. Sleepers are most easily recognized in retrospect, after they have already moved up in price.

SLEEPING BEAUTY potential TAKEOVER target that has not yet been approached by an acquirer. Such a company usually has particularly attractive features, such as a large amount of cash, or undervalued real estate or other assets.

SLIPPAGE
Securities:
1. price erosion between a QUOTED PRICE and an EXECUTION due to selling pressure.

2. higher than expected transaction costs.

Corporate finance: shortfall in projected revenues, sales, earnings, or other target figure.

United Kingdom: excess expenditure of investment capital (in U.S. called BURN RATE).

SLOB *see* SECURED LEASE OBLIGATION BOND (SLOB).

SLUMP short-term drop in performance. The economy may enter a slump when it goes into a RECESSION. An individual stock or mutual fund may be in a slump if its price falls over several weeks or months. A normally productive employee may go into a slump and be less productive if he or she is having financial or emotional difficulties. A slump is considered to be a temporary phenomenon, from which the economy, investment or employee will soon recover.

SMALL BUSINESS ADMINISTRATION (SBA) federal agency created in 1953 to provide financial assistance (through direct loans and loan guarantees) as well as management assistance to businesses that lack the access to CAPITAL MARKETS enjoyed by larger more creditworthy corporations. Further legislation authorized the SBA to contribute to the VENTURE CAPITAL requirements of START-UP companies by licensing and funding small business investment companies (SBICs), to maintain a loan fund for rehabilitation of property damaged by natural disasters (floods, hurricanes, etc.), and to provide loans, counseling and training for small businesses owned by minorities, the economically disadvantaged, and the disabled.

The SBA finances its activities through direct grants approved by Congress.

SMALL BUSINESS INVESTMENT COMPANY *see* SMALL BUSINESS ADMINISTRATION (SBA).

SMALL CAP shorthand for *small capitalization stocks* or mutual funds holding such stocks. Small cap stocks usually have a market capitalization (number of shares outstanding multiplied by the stock price) of $500 million or less. Those under $50 million in market cap are known as *microcap issues.* Small capitalization stocks represent companies that are less well established, but in many cases faster-growing than *mid-cap stocks* (from $500 million to $3 billion–$5 billion) or *large cap stocks* ($1 billion or more). (Ranges vary somewhat and may overlap, depending on the funds or indexer defining them.) Since they are less established, small cap stocks are usually more volatile than BLUE CHIPS.

SMALL CORPORATE OFFERING REGISTRATION *see* SMALL ISSUES EXEMPTION.

SMALL FIRM EFFECT tendency of stocks of smaller firms, defined by MARKET CAPITALIZATION, to outperform larger firms. Theories to explain this phenomenon vary, but include the following: (1) smaller companies tend to have more growth potential; (2) small capitalization groupings include more companies in financial difficulty; when fortunes recover, price gains are dramatic and lift the return of the group as a whole; (3) small firms are generally neglected by analysts and hence by institutions; once discovered, they become appropriately valued, registering dramatic gains in the process. The term is also used to describe the tendency of lower priced stocks to rise or fall in greater percentage increments than higher priced shares, market capitalization, and other factors being equal. *See also* ANKLE BITER.

SMALL INVESTOR individual investor who buys small amounts of stock or bonds, often in ODD LOT quantities; also called the RETAIL INVESTOR. Although there are millions of small investors, their total holdings are dwarfed by the share ownership of large institutions such as mutual funds and insurance companies. Together with the proliferation of mutual funds, recent developments in the brokerage industry and its diversification along full-service lines have brought new programs specifically designed to make investing more convenient for small investors. Thus, much cash traditionally kept in savings banks has found its way into the stock and bond markets. *See also* ODD-LOT SHORT-SALE RATIO; ODD-LOT THEORY.

SMALL ISSUES EXEMPTION securities issues under $1.5 million that qualify for simplified REGISTRATION under Securities and Exchange Commission REGULATION A.

SMALL ORDER ENTRY (OR EXECUTION) SYSTEM *see* SOES.

SMART MONEY investors who make profitable investment moves at the right time, no matter what the investing environment. In a bull market, such investors buy the stocks that go up the most. In bear markets, they sell stocks short that fall the most. Smart money investors also have access to information about companies, either positive or negative, in advance of when the typical small investor learns of it. The term is also used in a more general sense to convey what sophisticated investors are doing now. Analysts will say "the smart money is buying cyclical stocks now because the economy is improving," for example.

SMOKESTACK INDUSTRIES basic manufacturing industries, such as autos, chemicals, steel, paper, and rubber, which typically have smokestacks on their plants. The fate of these industries, when viewed by Wall Street analysts, is closely tied to the ups and downs of the economy—they are therefore called CYCLICAL stocks. Many smokestack industries are located in what is known as the RUST BELT.

SNOWBALLING process by which the activation of STOP ORDERS in a declining or advancing market causes further downward or upward pressure on prices, thus triggering more stop orders and more price pressure, and so on.

SOCIALISM political-economic doctrine that, unlike CAPITALISM, which is based on competition, seeks a cooperative society in which the means of production and distribution are owned by the government or collectively by the people.

SOCIALLY CONSCIOUS MUTUAL FUND mutual fund that is managed for capital appreciation while at the same time investing in securities of companies that do not conflict with certain social priorities. As a product of the social consciousness movements of the 60s and 70s, this type of mutual fund might not invest in companies that derive significant profits from defense contracts or whose activities cause environmental pollution, nor in companies with significant interests in countries with repressive or racist governments. *See also* GREEN INVESTING.

SOCIAL RESPONSIBILITY principle that businesses should actively contribute to the welfare of society and not only maximize profits. Most corporate annual reports will highlight what the company has done to further education, help minorities, give to the arts and social welfare agencies, and in general improve social conditions. The concept is also used by investors in picking companies that are fair to their employees, do not pollute or build weapons, and make beneficial products. *See also* SOCIALLY CONSCIOUS MUTUAL FUND.

SOCIAL SECURITY benefits provided under the Social Security Act (1935), financed by the SOCIAL SECURITY TAX authorized by the FEDERAL INSURANCE CONTRIBUTORS ACT (FICA), and administered by the Social Security Administration. Term usually refers to retirement income benefits, but other benefits include SOCIAL SECURITY DISABILITY INCOME INSURANCE; Aid to Families with Dependent Children (AFDC); the Food Stamp program; Unemployment Insurance; Medicare; Medicaid; Public Assistance for the Aged, Blind and Disabled; Veterans' Compensation and Pensions; Housing Subsidies and Public Housing; Nutritional Programs for Children; and Student Aid.

SOCIAL SECURITY DISABILITY INCOME INSURANCE insurance financed by the SOCIAL SECURITY TAX that provides lost income to qualifying employees whose disabilities are expected to last at least one year. Benefits are payable until death.

SOCIAL SECURITY TAX federal tax created by the Social Security Act (1935) that is shared equally by employers and their employees, is levied on annual income up to a maximum level, and is invested in Social Security trust funds. Employees then qualify for retirement benefits based on years worked, amounts paid into the fund, and retirement age.

SOCIETY FOR WORLDWIDE INTERBANK FINANCIAL TELE-COMMUNICATIONS (SWIFT) *See* SWIFT.

SOES acronym for the computerized *Small Order Entry (or Execution) System* used by NASDAQ, in which orders for under 1000 shares bypass brokers and are aggregated and executed against available firm quotes by market makers on the NASDAQ system. *See also* ORDER SPLITTING.

SOFT CURRENCY funds of a country that are not acceptable in exchange for the hard currencies of other countries. Soft currencies, such as Russia's ruble, are fixed at unrealistic exchange rates and are not backed by gold, so that countries with hard currencies, like U.S. dollars or British pounds, are reluctant to convert assets into them. *See also* HARD MONEY (HARD CURRENCY).

SOFT DOLLARS means of paying brokerage firms for their services through commission revenue, rather than through direct payments, known as *hard-dollar fees.* For example, a mutual fund may offer to pay for the research of a brokerage firm by executing trades generated by that research through that brokerage firm. The broker might agree to this arrangement if the fund manager promises to spend at least $100,000 in commissions with the broker that year. Otherwise, the fund would have to pay a hard-dollar fee of $50,000 for the research. Following the mutual fund scandals of the early 2000s, the INVESTMENT COMPANY INSTITUTE came out in favor of limiting soft dollars to proprietary research, and a number of large funds followed by curtailing soft money arrangements or eliminating them entirely. *Compare with* HARD DOLLARS.

SOFT GOODS consumer nondurables, such as textiles. *See also* DURABLE GOODS.

SOFT LANDING term used to describe a rate of growth sufficient to avoid recession but slow enough to prevent high inflation and interest rates. When the economy is growing very strongly, the Federal Reserve typically tries to engineer a soft landing by raising interest rates to head off inflation. If the economy threatens to fall into a recession, the Fed may lower rates to stimulate growth. *See also* GOLDILOCKS ECONOMY.

SOFT MARKET market characterized by an excess of supply over demand. A soft market in securities is marked by inactive trading, wide bid-offer spreads, and pronounced price drops in response to minimal selling pressure. Also called *buyer's market.*

SOFTS term used to refer to tropical commodities—coffee, sugar, and cocoa—but in a broader sense could include grains, oilseeds, cotton, and orange juice. Metals, financial futures, and livestock generally are excluded from this category.

SOFT SPOT weakness in selected stocks or stock groups in the face of a generally strong and advancing market.

SOLD-OUT MARKET commodities market term meaning that futures contracts in a particular commodity or maturity range are largely unavailable because of contract liquidations and limited offerings.

SOLE PROPRIETORSHIP *see* PROPRIETORSHIP.

SOLVENCY state of being able to meet maturing obligations as they come due. *See also* INSOLVENCY.

SOUR BOND bond in DEFAULT on its interest or principal payments. The issue will typically trade at a deep discount and have a low credit rating. Traders say that the bond has "gone sour" when it defaults.

SOURCES AND APPLICATIONS (or USES) OF FUNDS STATEMENT financial statement section that analyzed changes affecting WORKING CAPITAL (or, optionally, cash) and that appeared as part of the annual reports of the publicly held companies prior to 1988. In that year, the Financial Accounting Standards Board (FASB) supplanted this statement with the STATEMENT OF CASH FLOWS, which analyzes all changes affecting cash in the categories of operations, investment, and financing.

SOVEREIGN DEBT any debt obligation of, or guaranteed by, an autonomous government and therefore subject to SOVEREIGN RISK.

SOVEREIGN RISK risk that a foreign government will default on its loan or fail to honor other business commitments because of a change in national policy. A country asserting its prerogatives as an independent nation might prevent the REPATRIATION of a company or country's funds through limits on the flow of capital, tax impediments, or the nationalization of property. Sovereign risk became a factor in the growth of international debt that followed the oil price increases of the 1970s. Several developing countries that borrowed heavily from Western banks to finance trade deficits had difficulty later keeping to repayment schedules. Banks had to reschedule loans to such countries as Mexico and Argentina to keep them from defaulting. These loans ran the further risk of renunciation by political leaders, which also would have affected loans to private companies that had been guaranteed by previous governments. Beginning in the 1970s, banks and other multinational corporations developed sophisticated analytical tools to measure sovereign risk before committing to lend, invest, or begin operations in a given foreign country. Throughout periods of worldwide economic volatility, the United States has been able to attract foreign investment because of its perceived lack of sovereign risk. Also called *country risk* or *political risk*.

SOVEREIGN WEALTH FUNDS government-owned pools of investment funds in the currency of another sovereign entity. They are funded by foreign currency reserves—the currency that is accumulated when the fund holder runs current account surpluses—but they are managed separately from official currency reserves. The funds are often invested in foreign companies. Recent examples: China's $3 billion investment in 2007 in the Blackstone private equity group and Dubai's $7.5 billion investment in Citigroup, also in 2007. *See also* COMMITTEE ON FOREIGN INVESTMENT.

SPDR acronym for *Standard & Poor's Depositary Receipt*, traded on the American Stock Exchange under the ticker symbol "SPY." Called *spiders*, they are securities that represent ownership in a long-term UNIT INVESTMENT TRUST that holds a portfolio of common stocks designed to track the performance of the S&P 500 INDEX. A SPDR entitles a holder to receive proportionate quarterly cash distributions corresponding to the dividends that accrue to the S&P 500 stocks in the underlying portfolio, less trust expenses. Like a stock, SPDRs can be traded continuously throughout the trading day, or can be held for the long term. In contrast, S&P 500 index mutual funds are priced only once, at the end of each trading day. Amex also trades MidCap SPDRs, which track the S&P MidCap 400 Index. *See also* DIAMONDS; EXCHANGE TRADED FUNDS (ETFs).

SPECIAL ARBITRAGE ACCOUNT special MARGIN ACCOUNT with a broker reserved for transactions in which the customer's risk is hedged by an offsetting security transaction or position. The MARGIN REQUIREMENT on such a transaction is substantially less than in the case of stocks bought on credit and subject to price declines. *See also* HEDGE/HEDGING.

SPECIAL ASSESSMENT BOND municipal bond that is repaid from taxes imposed on those who benefit directly from the neighborhood-oriented public works project funded by the bond; also called *special assessment limited liability bond, special district bond, special purpose bond,* SPECIAL TAX BOND. For example, if a bond finances the construction of a sewer system, the homeowners and businesses hooked up to the sewer system pay a special levy that goes to repay the bonds. The interest from special assessment bonds is tax free to resident bondholders. These are not normally GENERAL OBLIGATION BONDS, and the FULL FAITH AND CREDIT of the municipality is not usually behind them. Where the full faith and credit does back such bonds, they are called general obligation special assessment bonds.

SPECIAL BID infrequently used method of purchasing a large block of stock on the New York Stock Exchange whereby a MEMBER FIRM, acting as a broker, matches the buy order of one client, usually an institution, with sell orders solicited from a number of other customers. It is the reverse of an EXCHANGE DISTRIBUTION. The member broker makes a fixed price offer, which is announced in advance on the CONSOLIDATED TAPE. The bid cannot be lower than the last sale or the current regular market bid. Sellers of the stock pay no commissions; the buying customer pays both the selling and buying commissions. The transaction is completed during regular trading hours.

SPECIAL BOND ACCOUNT special MARGIN ACCOUNT with a broker that is reserved for transactions in U.S. government bonds, municipals, and eligible listed and unlisted nonconvertible corporate bonds. The restrictions under which brokers may extend credit with margin securities of these types are generally more liberal than in the case of stocks.

SPECIAL CASH ACCOUNT same as CASH ACCOUNT.

SPECIAL DISTRICT BOND *see* SPECIAL ASSESSMENT BOND.

SPECIAL DIVIDEND *see* EXTRA DIVIDEND.

SPECIAL DRAWING RIGHTS (SDR) measure of a nation's reserve assets in the international monetary system; known informally as "paper gold." First issued by the INTERNATIONAL MONETARY FUND (IMF) in 1970, SDRs are designed to supplement the reserves of gold and convertible currencies (or hard currencies) used to maintain stability in the foreign exchange market. For example, if the U.S. Treasury sees that the British pound's value has fallen precipitously in relation to the dollar, it can use its store of SDRs to buy excess pounds on the foreign exchange market, thereby raising the value of the remaining supply of pounds.

This neutral unit of account was made necessary by the rapid growth in world trade during the 1960s. International monetary officials feared that the supply of the two principal reserve assets—gold and U.S. dollars—would fall short of demand, causing the value of the U.S. currency to rise disproportionately in relation to other reserve assets. (At the time SDRs were introduced, the price of gold was fixed at about $35 per ounce.)

The IMF allocates to each of its more than 140 member countries an amount of SDRs proportional to its predetermined quota in the fund, which in turn is based on its GROSS NATIONAL PRODUCT (GNP). Each member agrees to back its SDRs with the full faith and credit of its government, and to accept them in exchange for gold or convertible currencies.

Originally, the value of one SDR was fixed at one dollar and at the dollar equivalent of other key currencies on January 1, 1970. As world governments adopted the current system of FLOATING EXCHANGE RATES, the SDR's value fluctuated relative to the "basket" of major currencies. Increasing reliance on SDRs in settling international accounts coincided with a decline in the importance of gold as a reserve asset.

Because of its inherent equilibrium relative to any one currency, the SDR has been used to denominate or calculate the value of private contracts, international treaties, and securities on the EUROBOND market.

See also EUROPEAN CURRENCY UNIT (ECU).

SPECIALIST member of a stock exchange who maintains a fair and orderly market in one or more securities. A specialist or SPECIALIST UNIT performs two main functions: executing LIMIT ORDERS on behalf of other exchange members for a portion of the FLOOR BROKER'S commission, and buying or selling—sometimes SELLING SHORT—for the specialist's own account to counteract temporary imbalances in supply and demand and thus prevent wide swings in stock prices. The specialist is prohibited by exchange rules from buying for his own account when there is an unexecuted order for the same security at the same price in the SPECIALIST'S BOOK, the record kept of limit orders in each price category in the sequence in which they are received. Specialists must meet strict minimum capital requirements before receiving formal approval by the New York Stock Exchange. *See also* NEGATIVE OBLIGATIONS; SPECIALIST BLOCK PURCHASE AND SALE; SPECIALIST'S SHORT SALE RATIO.

SPECIALIST BLOCK PURCHASE AND SALE transaction whereby a SPECIALIST on a stock exchange buys a large block of securities either to sell for his own account or to try and place with another block buyer and seller, such as a FLOOR TRADER. Exchange rules require that such transactions be executed only when the securities cannot be ABSORBED in the regular market. *See also* NOT HELD.

SPECIALIST'S BOOK record maintained by a SPECIALIST that includes the specialist's own inventory of securities, market orders to sell short, and LIMIT ORDERS and STOP ORDERS that other stock exchange members have placed with the specialist. The orders are listed in chronological sequence. For example, for a stock trading at 57 a broker might ask for 500 shares when the price falls to 55. If successful at placing this limit order, the specialist notifies the member broker who entered the request, and collects a commission. The specialist is prohibited from buying the stock for his own account at a price for which he has previously agreed to execute a limit order.

SPECIALIST'S SHORT-SALE RATIO ratio of the amount of stock sold short by specialists on the floor of the New York Stock Exchange to total short sales. The ratio signals whether specialists are more or less bearish (expecting prices to decline) on the outlook for stock prices than other NYSE members and the public. Since specialists must constantly be selling stock short in order to provide for an orderly market in the stocks they trade, their short sales cannot be entirely regarded as an indication of how they perceive trends. Still, their overall short sales activity reflects knowledge, and technical analysts watch the specialist's short-sale ratio carefully for a clue to imminent upturns or downturns in stock prices. Traditionally, when the ratio rises above 60%, it is considered a bearish signal. A drop below 45% is seen as bullish and below 35% is considered extremely bullish. *See also* ODD-LOT SHORT-SALE RATIO; SELLING SHORT; SPECIALIST.

SPECIALIST UNIT stock exchange SPECIALIST (individual, partnership, corporation, or group of two or three firms) authorized by an exchange to deal as PRINCIPAL and AGENT for other brokers in maintaining a stable market in one or more particular stocks. A specialist unit on the New York Stock Exchange is required to have enough capital to buy at least 5000 shares of the common stock of a company it handles and 1000 shares of the company's CONVERTIBLE preferred stock.

SPECIALIZED MUTUAL FUND mutual fund concentrating on one industry. By so doing, shareholders have a PURE PLAY on the fortunes of that industry, for better or worse. Some of the many industries with specialized mutual funds include banking, biotechnology, chemicals, energy, environmental services, natural resources, precious metals, technology, telecommunications, and utilities. These funds tend to be more volatile than funds holding a diversified portfolio of stocks in many industries. Also called *sector funds* or *specialty funds*.

SPECIAL MISCELLANEOUS ACCOUNT (SMA) memorandum account of the funds in excess of the MARGIN REQUIREMENT. Such excess funds may arise from the proceeds of sales, appreciation of market values, dividends, or cash or securities put up in response to a MARGIN CALL. An SMA is not under the jurisdiction of REGULATION T of the Federal Reserve Board, as is the INITIAL MARGIN requirement, but this does not mean the customer is free to withdraw balances from it. The account is maintained essentially so that the broker can gauge how far the customer might be from a margin call. Any withdrawals require the broker's permission.

SPECIAL OFFERING method of selling a large block of stock that is similar to a SECONDARY DISTRIBUTION but is limited to New York Stock Exchange members and takes place during normal trading hours. The selling member announces the impending sale on the CONSOLIDATED TAPE, indicating a fixed price, which is usually based on the last transaction price in the regular market. All costs and commissions are borne by the seller. The buyers are member firms that may be buying for customer accounts or for their own inventory. Such offerings must have approval from the Securities and Exchange Commission.

SPECIAL PURPOSE ENTITY (SPE)

1. also known as *special purpose vehicles*, or *variable interest entities*, SPE's are finite life entities created by corporations, usually as subsidiaries but sometimes as partnerships, trusts, or other forms of unincorporated structures, for a single, well-defined, and narrow purpose, such as those (sometimes also called *derivative products companies*) established to issue INCOME PREFERRED SECURITIES. SPEs got a bad name when they were used by Enron to conduct illegal OFF-BALANCE-SHEET FINANCING activities. SPEs are subject to complicated accounting rules designed to assure that if any risks taken by SPEs expose the parent company, financial disclosure must be made on a consolidated basis.
2. structures, also called *bankruptcy remote vehicles*, devised by attorneys and investment bankers to circumvent the bankruptcy laws.

SPECIAL SITUATION

1. undervalued stock that should soon rise in value because of an imminent favorable turn of events. A special situation stock may be about to introduce a revolutionary new product or be undergoing a needed management change. Many securities analysts concentrate on looking for and analyzing special situation stocks.
2. stock that fluctuates widely in daily trading, often influencing market averages, because of a particular news development, such as the announcement of a TAKEOVER bid.

SPECIAL TAX BOND

1. MUNICIPAL REVENUE BOND that will be repaid through excise taxes on such purchases as gasoline, tobacco, and liquor. The bond is not backed by the ordinary taxing power of the municipality issuing it. The interest from these bonds is tax free to resident bondholders.
2. SPECIAL ASSESSMENT BOND.

SPECTAIL term for broker-dealer who is part retail broker but preponderantly dealer/speculator.

SPECULATION assumption of risk in anticipation of gain but recognizing a higher than average possibility of loss. Speculation is a necessary and productive activity. It can be profitable over the long term when engaged in by professionals, who often limit their losses through the use of various HEDGING techniques and devices, including OPTIONS trading, SELLING SHORT, STOP LOSS ORDERS, and transactions in FUTURES CONTRACTS. The term speculation implies that a business or investment risk can be analyzed and measured, and its distinction from the term INVESTMENT is one of degree of risk. It differs from gambling, which is based on random outcomes.

See also VENTURE CAPITAL.

SPECULATIVE GRADE see RATING.

SPECULATOR market participant who tries to profit from buying and selling futures and options contracts by anticipating future price movements. Speculators assume market price risk and add liquidity and capital to the futures markets. Speculators may purchase volatile stocks or mutual funds, and hold them for a short time in order to reap a profit. They may also sell stocks short and hope to cash in when the stock price drops quickly.

SPIDERS see SPDR.

SPINNING dubious investment banking practice whereby shares in an INITIAL PUBLIC OFFERING are allocated to senior managers of the issuing company to profit them personally and entice them to direct future business to the investment bank.

SPIN-OFF form of corporate DIVESTITURE that results in a subsidiary or division becoming an independent company. In a traditional spin-off, shares in the new entity are distributed to the parent corporation's shareholders of record on a PRO RATA basis. Spin-offs can also be accomplished through a LEVERAGED BUYOUT by the subsidiary or division's management, or through an EMPLOYEE STOCK OWNERSHIP PLAN (ESOP).

SPINS acronym for *Standard & Poor's 500 Index Subordinated Notes,* a Salomon Brothers' product combining features of debt, equity, and options.

SPLIT increase in a corporation's number of outstanding shares of stock without any change in the shareholders' EQUITY or the aggregate MARKET VALUE at the time of the split. In a split, also called a *split up,* the share price declines. If a stock at $100 par value splits 2-for-1, the number of authorized shares doubles (for example, from 10 million to 20 million) and the price per share drops by half, to $50. A holder of 50 shares before the split now has 100 shares at the lower price. If the same stock splits 4-for-1, the number of shares quadruples to 40 million and the share price falls to $25. Dividends per share also fall proportionally. Directors of a corporation will authorize a split to make ownership more affordable to a broader base of investors. Where stock splits require an increase in AUTHORIZED SHARES and/or a change in PAR VALUE of the stock, shareholders must approve an amendment of the corporate charter.

See also REVERSE SPLIT.

SPLIT COMMISSION commission divided between the securities broker who executes a trade and another person who brought the trade to the broker, such as an investment counselor or financial planner. Split commissions between brokers are also common in real estate transactions.

SPLIT COUPON BOND debt instrument that begins as a zero-coupon bond and converts to an interest-paying bond at a specified date in the future. These bonds, issued by corporations and municipalities, are advantageous to issuers because they do not have to pay out cash interest for several years. They are attractive to investors, particularly in tax-sheltered accounts like IRAs and Keoghs, because they have locked in a reinvestment rate for several years, and then can receive cash interest. For example, a 55-year-old investor may want a split coupon bond because it will appreciate in value for 10 years, and then pay interest when he is retired and needs regular income. Also known as ZERO-COUPON CONVERTIBLE SECURITY.

SPLIT DOWN *see* REVERSE SPLIT.

SPLIT OFFERING new municipal bond issue, part of which is represented by SERIAL BONDS and part by term maturity bonds.

SPLIT OFF IPO *see* EQUITY CARVE OUT.

SPLIT ORDER large transaction in securities that, to avoid unsettling the market and causing fluctuations in the market price, is broken down into smaller portions to be executed over a period of time.

SPLIT RATING situation in which two major rating agencies, such as Standard & Poor's and Moody's Investors Service, assign a different rating to the same security.

SPLIT UP *see* SPLIT.

SPONSOR

Limited partnerships: GENERAL PARTNER who organizes and sells a LIMITED PARTNERSHIP. Sponsors (also called *promoters*) rely on their reputation in past real estate, oil and gas, or other deals to attract limited partners to their new deals.

Mutual funds: investment company that offers shares in its funds. Also called the *underwriter.*

Stocks: important investor—typically, an institution, mutual fund, or other big trader—whose favorable opinion of a particular security influences other investors and creates additional demand for the security. Institutional investors often want to make sure a stock has wide sponsorship before they invest in it, since this should ensure that the stock will not fall dramatically.

SPONSORED ADRS *see* AMERICAN DEPOSITORY RECEIPTS (ADRs).

SPOT COMMODITY COMMODITY traded with the expectation that it will actually be delivered to the buyer, as contrasted to a FUTURES CONTRACT that will usually expire without any physical delivery taking place. Spot commodities are traded in the SPOT MARKET.

SPOT DELIVERY MONTH nearest month of those currently being traded in which a commodity could be delivered. In late January, therefore, the spot delivery month would be February for commodities with a February contract trade.

SPOT MARKET market in which commodities or currencies are sold for cash and delivered immediately. Trades that take place in FUTURES CONTRACTS expiring in the current month are also called *spot market trades.* The spot market tends to be conducted OVER-THE-COUNTER—that is, through telephone trading—rather than on the floor of an organized commodity exchange. Also called *actual market, cash market* or *physical market. See also* FUTURES MARKET.

SPOT PRICE current delivery price of a commodity traded in the SPOT MARKET. Also called *cash price.*

SPOUSAL IRA type of INDIVIDUAL RETIREMENT ARRANGEMENT that may be opened in the name of a nonworking spouse. The maximum annual IRA contribution for a married couple, only one of whom is employed, is $10,000 in 2008. The husband and wife can each contribute up to $5,000, as long as their combined compensation is at least that much. If one spouse is 50 or older, the couple can contribute as much as $11,000; if both are 50 or older, the couple can contribute as much as $12,000. Contributions are deductible only if both husband and wife are not actively participating in a qualified retirement plan.

SPOUSAL REMAINDER TRUST means used prior to the TAX REFORM ACT OF 1986 to shift income to a person taxable at a lower rate. Income-producing property, such as securities, is transferred by the grantor to the trust for a specific time, typically five years. Trust income is distributed to the beneficiary (or to a minor's CUSTODIAL ACCOUNT) to be used for expenses such as a child's college education. The income is therefore taxed at the beneficiary's lower tax rate. When the trust term expires, the property passes irrevocably to the grantor's spouse. The TAX REFORM ACT OF 1986 provided that effective for trusts established or contributions to trusts made after March 1, 1986, income must be taxed at the grantor's tax rate if the beneficiary is under age 14 and the property can revert to the grantor or the grantor's spouse.

SPREAD

Commodities: In futures trading, the difference in price between delivery months in the same market, or between different or related contracts. *See also* MOB SPREAD; NOB SPREAD; TED SPREAD.

Fixed-income securities: (1) difference between yields on securities of the same quality but different maturities. For example, the spread between 6% short-term Treasury bills and 10% long-term Treasury bonds is 4 percentage points. (2) difference between yields on securities of the same maturity but different quality. For instance, the spread between a 10% long-term Treasury bond and a 14% long-term bond of a B-rated corporation is 4 percentage points, since an investor's risk of default is so much less with the Treasury bond. *See also* YIELD SPREAD.

Foreign exchange: spreading one currency versus another, or multiple spreads within various currencies. An example would be a long position in the U.S. dollar versus a short position in the Japanese yen or the Euro. An example of an intermonth spread would be a long March spot position in Swiss francs versus a short March position in the same currency. Spreads are frequently done in cash and futures markets. Interest rate differentials often have significant impact.

Options: position usually consisting of one long call and one short call option, or one long put and one short put option, with each option representing one "leg" of the spread. The two legs, if taken independently, would profit from opposite directional price movements. Spreads usually have lower cost and lower profit potential than an outright long option. They are entered into to reduce risk, or to profit from the change in the relative prices of the options. *See also* BEAR SPREAD; BULL SPREAD; BUTTERFLY SPREAD; CALENDAR SPREAD; CREDIT SPREAD; DEBIT SPREAD; DIAGONAL SPREAD; OPTION; PRICE SPREAD; SELLING THE SPREAD; VERTICAL SPREAD.

Stocks and bonds: (1) difference between the bid and offer price. If a stock is bid at $45 and offered at $46, the spread is $1. This spread narrows or widens according to supply and demand for the security being traded. *See also* BID-ASKED SPREAD; DEALER SPREAD. (2) difference between the high and low price of a particular security over a given period.

Underwriting: difference between the proceeds an issuer of a new security receives and the price paid by the public for the issue. This spread is taken by the underwriting syndicate as payment for its services. A security issued at $100 may entail a spread of $2 for the underwriter, so the issuer receives $98 from the offering. *See also* UNDERWRITING SPREAD.

SPREADING practice of buying and selling OPTION contracts of the same CLASS on the same underlying security in order to profit from moves in the price of that security. *See also* SPREAD.

SPREAD OPTION SPREAD position involving the purchase of an OPTION at one EXERCISE PRICE and the simultaneous sale of another option on the same underlying security at a different exercise price and/or expiration date. *See also* DIAGONAL SPREAD; HORIZONTAL SPREAD; VERTICAL SPREAD.

SPREAD ORDER OPTIONS market term for an order designating the SERIES of LISTED OPTIONS the customer wishes to buy and sell, together with the desired SPREAD—or difference in option premiums (prices)—shown as a net debit or net credit. The transaction is completed if the FLOOR BROKER can execute the order at the requested spread.

SPREAD POSITION status of an account in which a SPREAD has been executed.

SPREADSHEET ledger sheet on which a company's financial statements, such as BALANCE SHEETS, INCOME STATEMENTS, and sales reports, are laid out in columns and rows. Spreadsheets are used by securities and credit analysts in researching companies and industries. Since the advent of personal computers, spreadsheets have come into wide use, because software makes them easy to use. In an electronic spreadsheet on a computer, any time one number is changed, all the other numbers are automatically adjusted according to the relationships the computer operator sets up. For instance, in a spreadsheet of a sales report of a company's many divisions, the updating of a single division's sales figure will automatically change the total sales for the company, as well as the percentage of total sales that division produced.

SPRINKLING TRUST trust under which no beneficiary has a right to receive any trust income. Instead, the trustee is given discretion to divide, or "sprinkle," the trust's income as the trustee sees fit among a designated group of persons. Sprinkling trusts can be created both by LIVING TRUST agreements and by WILLS.

SPX ticker symbol for the Standard & Poor's 500 stock index options traded on the Chicago Board Options Exchange. The European-style index options contract is settled in cash, and can be exercised only on the last business day before expiration. The SPX is one of the most heavily traded of all index options contracts.

SQUARZ *see* NEGATIVE INTEREST RATE.

SQUAWK BOX intercom system used by brokerage firms to communicate with brokers about current analysts' recommendations and other matters relating to the market, the firm's activities, and particular stocks. *Box* refers to the speaker typically located on a broker's or trader's desk.

SQUEEZE

Finance: (1) tight money period, when loan money is scarce and interest rates are high, making borrowing difficult and expensive—also called a *credit crunch;* (2) any situation where increased costs cannot be passed on to customers in the form of higher prices.

Investments: situation when stocks or commodities futures start to move up in price, and investors who have sold short are forced to COVER their short positions in order to avoid large losses. When done by many short sellers, this action is called a SHORT SQUEEZE. *See also* SELLING SHORT; SHORT POSITION.

SRO *see* SELF-REGULATORY ORGANIZATION.

SS1 speaker box that transmits sales communications to the regional trading and sales desks of INVESTMENT BANKERS.

STABILIZATION

Currency: buying and selling of a country's own currency to protect its exchange value, also called PEGGING.

Economics: leveling out of the business cycle, unemployment, and prices through fiscal and monetary policies.

Market trading: action taken by REGISTERED COMPETITIVE TRADERS on the New York Stock Exchange in accordance with an exchange requirement that 75% of their trades be stabilizing—in other words, that their sell orders follow a PLUS TICK and their buy orders a MINUS TICK.

New issues underwriting: intervention in the market by a managing underwriter in order to keep the market price from falling below the PUBLIC OFFERING PRICE during the offering period. The underwriter places orders to buy at a specific price, an action called PEGGING that, in any other circumstance, is a violation of laws prohibiting MANIPULATION in the securities and commodities markets.

STAG speculator who makes it a practice to get in and out of stocks for a fast profit, rather than to hold securities for investment.

STAGFLATION term coined by economists in the 1970s to describe the previously unprecedented combination of slow economic growth and high unemployment (stagnation) with rising prices (inflation). The principal factor was the fourfold increase in oil prices imposed by the Organization of Petroleum Exporting Countries (OPEC) cartel in 1973–74, which raised price levels throughout the economy while further slowing economic growth. As is characteristic of stagflation, fiscal and monetary policies aimed at stimulating the economy and reducing unemployment only exacerbated the inflationary effects.

STAGGERED BOARD OF DIRECTORS board of directors of a company in which a portion of the directors are elected each year, instead of all at once. A board is often staggered in order to thwart unfriendly TAKEOVER attempts, since potential acquirers would have to wait a longer time before they could take control of a company's board through the normal voting procedure. Normally, all directors are elected at the annual meeting.

STAGGERING MATURITIES technique used to lower risk by a bond investor. Since long-term bonds are more volatile than short-term ones, an investor can HEDGE against interest rate movements by buying short-, medium- and long-term bonds. If interest rates decline, the long-term bonds will rise faster in value than the shorter-term bonds. If rates rise, however, the shorter-term bonds will hold their value better than the long-term debt obligations, which could fall precipitously. Also called LADDERING; LIQUIDITY DIVERSIFICATION.

STAGNATION
Economics: period of no or slow economic growth or of economic decline, in real (inflation-adjusted) terms. Economic growth of 3% or less per year— as was the case in the late 1970s, measured according to increases in the U.S. gross national product—generally is taken to constitute stagnation.
Securities: period of low volume and inactive trading.

STAGS acronym for *Sterling Transferable Accruing Government Securities.* A British version of U.S. government STRIPS, STAGS are deep discount zero-coupon bonds backed by British Treasury securities. *See also* ZERO-COUPON SECURITY.

STAKEHOLDER any party having an interest in an enterprise. For example, stakeholders in the healthcare industry would include doctors, hospitals, medical employees, insurers, patients, drug companies, medical equipment manufacturers, governments, and many others, even including taxpayers.

STALKING HORSE in a bankruptcy auction sale, the lead bidder designated by the debtor to set the minimum price it will receive for its asset in the sale. The stalking horse bidder takes a risk that the auction will be disappointing and the asset sold at a lower price, and is usually given an incentive to take that risk.

STANDARD & POOR'S division of The McGraw-Hill Companies. Well known and trusted in the financial community for its independent credit ratings and indices, as well as risk evaluation, investment research, data, and valuations. The New York-based company, which has offices in 21 countries, was founded in 1860 and acquired by McGraw-Hill in 1966. Among other things, it compiles the globally known Standard & Poor's 500 Index as well as numerous other indices. *www.standardandpoors.com. See also* STANDARD & POOR'S RATING, STOCK INDICES AND AVERAGES.

STANDARD & POOR'S RATING Standard & Poor's opinion on the general creditworthiness of an obligor, or the creditworthiness of an obligor with respect to a particular debt security or other financial obligation. A Standard & Poor's long-term rating reflects a borrower's capacity to meet its financial commitments on a timely basis. Long-term ratings range from the highest category, AAA, to the lowest, D. Ratings from AA to CCC categories may also include a plus or minus sign to show relative standing within the category. A short-term rating is an assessment of the likelihood of timely repayment of obligations considered short-term in relevant markets. Short-term ratings are graded into several categories, ranging from A-1 for the highest quality obligations to D for the lowest. The A-1 rating may also be modified by a plus sign to distinguish the stronger credits in that category. In addition to long-term and short-term ratings, Standard & Poor's has specific rating definitions for preferred stock, money market funds, mutual bond funds, financial strength, and financial enhancement ratings of insurance companies and program ratings for derivative product companies.

STANDARD COST estimate, based on engineering and accounting studies, of what costs of production should be, assuming normal operating conditions. Standard costs differ from budgeted costs, which are forecasts based on expectations. Variances between standard costs and actual costs measure productive efficiency and are used in cost control.

STANDARD DEDUCTION individual taxpayer alternative to itemizing deductions. Current tax rules index the standard deduction to inflation, adjusting annually. For 2008 they were

Single Taxpayer	$5,450
Head of Household	$8,000
Married Filing Jointly	$10,900
Married Filing Separately	$5,450

STANDARD DEVIATION statistical measure of the degree to which an individual value in a probability distribution tends to vary from the mean of the distribution. It is widely applied in modern PORTFOLIO THEORY, for example, where the past performance of securities is used to determine the range of possible future performances and a probability is attached to each performance. Mutual fund analysts average the returns over three years, then determine the range in which returns have varied from that mean. So, if the mean return is 10% and the range has been +25% to −5%, standard deviation is 15. *See also* REGRESSION ANALYSIS; RISK.

STANDARD INDUSTRIAL CLASSIFICATION (SIC) SYSTEM federally designed standard numbering system identifying companies by industry and providing other information. Gradually being replaced by North American Industry Classification System (NAICS). Both are widely used by market researchers, securities analysts, and data bases.

STANDARD OF LIVING degree of prosperity in a nation, as measured by income levels, quality of housing and food, medical care, educational opportunities, transportation, communications, and other measures. The standard of living in different countries is frequently compared based on annual per capita income. On an individual level, the standard of living is a measure of the quality of life in such areas as housing, food, education, clothing, transportation, and employment opportunities.

STANDBY COMMITMENT

Securities: agreement between a corporation and an investment banking firm or group (the *standby underwriter*) whereby the latter contracts to purchase for resale, for a fee, any portion of a stock issue offered to current shareholders in a RIGHTS OFFERING that is not subscribed to during the two- to four-week standby period. A right, often issued to comply with laws guaranteeing the shareholder's PREEMPTIVE RIGHT, entitles its holder, either an existing shareholder or a person who has bought the right from a shareholder, to purchase a specified amount of shares before a PUBLIC OFFERING and usually at a price lower than the PUBLIC OFFERING PRICE.

The risk to the investment banker in a standby commitment is that the market price of shares will fall during the standby period. *See also* LAY OFF for a discussion of how standby underwriters protect themselves. *See also* FLOTATION COST; SUBSCRIPTION RIGHT; UNDERWRITE.

Lending: a bank commitment to loan money up to a specified amount for a specific period, to be used only in a certain contingency. The most common example would be a commitment to repay a construction lender in the event a permanent mortgage lender cannot be found. A COMMITMENT FEE is normally charged.

STANDBY UNDERWRITER *see* STANDBY COMMITMENT.

STANDSTILL AGREEMENT accord by a RAIDER to abstain from buying shares of a company for a specified period. *See also* GREENMAIL.

START-UP new business venture. In VENTURE CAPITAL parlance, start-up is the earliest stage at which a venture capital investor or investment pool will provide funds to an enterprise, usually on the basis of a business plan detailing the background of the management group along with market and financial PROJECTIONS. Investments or loans made at this stage are also called SEED MONEY.

STATE BANK bank organized under a charter granted by a regulatory authority in one of the 50 U.S. states, as distinguished from a NATIONAL BANK, which is federally chartered. The powers of a state-chartered commercial bank are generally consistent with those of national banks, since state laws tend to conform to federal initiatives and vice versa. State banks deposits are insured by the FEDERAL DEPOSIT INSURANCE CORPORATION. State banks have the option of joining the FEDERAL RESERVE SYSTEM, and even if they reject membership, they may purchase support services from the Fed, including check-processing and coin and currency services.

STATED INTEREST RATE
Banking: rate paid on savings instruments, such as PASSBOOK savings accounts and certificates of deposit. The stated interest rate does not take into account any compounding of interest.
Bonds: interest rate stated on a bond coupon. A bond with a 7% coupon has a 7% stated interest rate. This rate is applied to the face value of the bond, normally $1,000, so that bondholders will receive 7% annually for every $1,000 in face value of bonds they own.

STATED VALUE assigned value given to a corporation's stock for accounting purposes in lieu of par value. For example, the stated value may be set at $1 a share, so that if a company issued 10 million shares, the stated value of its stock would be $10 million. The stated value of the stock has no relation to its market price. It is, however, the amount per share that is credited to the CAPITAL STOCK account for each share outstanding and is therefore the legal capital of the corporation. Since state law generally prohibits a corporation from paying dividends or repurchasing shares when doing so would impair its legal capital, stated value does offer stockholders a measure of protection against loss of value.

STATEMENT
1. summary for customers of the transactions that occurred over the preceding month. A bank statement lists all deposits and withdrawals, as well as the running account balances. A brokerage statement shows all stock, bond, commodity futures, or options trades, interest and dividends received, margin debt outstanding, and other transactions, as well as a summary of the worth of the accounts at month end. A trade supplier provides a summary of open account transactions. *See also* ASSET MANAGEMENT ACCOUNT.
2. statement drawn up by businesses to show the status of their ASSETS and LIABILITIES and the results of their operations as of a certain date. *See also* FINANCIAL STATEMENT.

STATEMENT OF CASH FLOWS
analysis of CASH FLOW included as part of the financial statements in annual reports of publicly held companies as set forth in Statement 95 of the FINANCIAL ACCOUNTING STANDARDS BOARD (FASB). The statement shows how changes in balance sheet and income accounts affected cash and cash equivalents and breaks the analysis down according to operating, investing, and financing activities. As an analytical tool, the statement of cash flows reveals healthy or unhealthy trends and makes it possible to predict future cash requirements. It also shows how actual cash flow measured up to estimates and permits comparisons with other companies.

STATEMENT OF CONDITION
Banking: sworn accounting of a bank's resources, liabilities, and capital accounts as of a certain date, submitted in response to periodic "calls" by bank regulatory authorities.

Finance: summary of the status of assets, liabilities, and equity of a person or a business organization as of a certain date. *See also* BALANCE SHEET.

STATEMENT OF INCOME *see* PROFIT AND LOSS STATEMENT.

STATEMENT OF OPERATIONS *see* PROFIT AND LOSS STATEMENT.

STATUTE OF LIMITATIONS
statute describing the limitations on how many years can pass before someone gives up their right to sue for a wrongful action. For example, the INTERNAL REVENUE SERVICE has up to three years to assess back taxes from the time the return is filed, unless tax fraud is charged. Most states impose a statute of limitations of six years to challenge the violation of a written contract. Therefore, a suit claiming damages filed seven years after the alleged contract violation would be thrown out of court because the statute of limitations had run out.

STATUTORY INVESTMENT
investment specifically authorized by state law for use by a trustee administering a trust under that state's jurisdiction.

STATUTORY MERGER
legal combination of two or more corporations in which only one survives as a LEGAL ENTITY. It differs from *statutory consolidation,* in which all the companies in a combination cease to exist as legal entities and a new corporate entity is created. *See also* MERGER.

STATUTORY PROSPECTUS *see* PROSPECTUS.

STATUTORY VOTING
one-share, one-vote rule that governs voting procedures in most corporations. Shareholders may cast one vote per share either

for or against each nominee for the board of directors, but may not give more than one vote to one nominee. The result of statutory voting is that, in effect, those who control over 50% of the shares control the company by ensuring that the majority of the board will represent their interests. *Compare with* CUMULATIVE VOTING. *See also* PROPORTIONAL REPRESENTATION.

STAYING POWER ability of an investor to stay with (not sell) an investment that has fallen in value. For example, a commodity trader with staying power is able to meet margin calls as the commodities FUTURES CONTRACTS he has bought fall in price. He can afford to wait until the trade ultimately becomes profitable. In real estate, an investor with staying power is able to meet mortgage and maintenance payments on his or her properties and is therefore not harmed as interest rates rise or fall, or as the properties become temporarily difficult to sell.

STEENTH slang for 1/16 of a point. *See also* TEENYO.

STEP DOWN NOTE type of FLOATING RATE whose interest rate declines at specified times in the course of the loan.

STEP-LOCK OPTION Same as LADDER OPTION.

STEPPED-UP BASIS Internal Revenue Service provision that allowed the tax BASIS of securities left to heirs to be determined by the market value at the time of the benefactor's death rather than at the benefactor's original cost. The ECONOMIC GROWTH AND TAX RELIEF RECONCILIATION ACT OF 2001 ended the step-up provision for securities left to heirs in excess of the lifetime transfer exemption. Heirs must now calculate capital gains based on original cost.

STEP-UP NOTES bonds, usually callable, with a rate that applies for a specified period of time and a second, higher rate that applies after the initial period. Also called DUAL COUPON BOND; RISING COUPON SECURITY; STEPPED COUPON BOND; STEP-UP COUPON SECURITY.

STICKY DEAL new securities issue that the underwriter fears will be difficult to sell. Adverse market conditions, bad news about the issuing entity, or other factors may lead underwriters to say, "This will be a sticky deal at the price we have set." As a result, the price may be lowered or the offering withdrawn from the market.

STIMULUS PLAN federal government programs designed to counteract weak economic activity with stimulus in form of government spending on infrastructure and other initiatives, tax breaks, and subsidies. Central banks stimulate the economy with loose monetary policy, which drives down interest rates to encourage businesses and consumers to borrow and spend. In the late 2000s, governments around the world enacted aggressive fiscal and monetary stimulus plans to counteract the recession and financial crisis. *See also* AMERICAN RECOVERY AND REINVESTMENT ACT OF 2009.

STOCHASTICS INDEX computerized TECHNICAL ANALYSIS tool, or oscillator, that measures OVERBOUGHT and OVERSOLD conditions in a stock, using MOVING AVERAGES and RELATIVE STRENGTH techniques. In its simplest form, the stochastics index is expressed as a percentage of the difference between the low and high stock price during the stochastics period. For example, if the stochastics period is 14 days and the high in that period was 50 and the low

40, the difference would be 10. On the day it is calculated, the stochastics is the percentage of the difference that the current price represents. If the price at the time of calculation was 40, the stochastics reading would be zero. At a price of 50, the stochastics reading would be 100. At 45, the stochastics reading would be 50.

In practice, the stochastics index typically plots a five-day moving average of the stochastics. Lines drawn at the 25% and 75% levels on the graph represent overbought and oversold conditions. When the stochastics index falls below the 25% line, it generally indicates an oversold condition, and when the stochastics index goes above the 75% line it indicates an overbought condition. An upward reversal that breaks the 25% line is a positive BREAKOUT and a downward reversal that breaks the 75% line is a negative breakout, signaling new uptrends and downtrends respectively. *See also* MOMENTUM INDICATOR; MOVING AVERAGE CONVERGENCE/DIVERGENCE (MACD).

STOCK

1. ownership of a CORPORATION represented by shares that are a claim on the corporation's earnings and assets. COMMON STOCK usually entitles the shareholder to vote in the election of directors and other matters taken up at shareholder meetings or by proxy. PREFERRED STOCK generally does not confer voting rights but it has a prior claim on assets and earnings—dividends must be paid on preferred stock before any can be paid on common stock. A corporation can authorize additional classes of stock, each with its own set of contractual rights. *See also* ARTICLES OF INCORPORATION; AUTHORIZED SHARES; BLUE CHIP; BOOK VALUE; CAPITAL STOCK; CERTIFICATE; CLASS; CLASSIFIED STOCK; CLOSELY HELD; COMMON STOCK; COMMON STOCK EQUIVALENT; CONVERTIBLES; CONTROL STOCK; CORPORATION; CUMULATIVE PREFERRED; DIVIDEND; EARNINGS PER SHARE; EQUITY; FLOAT; FRACTIONAL SHARES; GOING PUBLIC; GROWTH STOCK; INACTIVE STOCK; INITIAL PUBLIC OFFERING; ISSUED AND OUTSTANDING; JOINT STOCK COMPANY; LETTER SECURITY; LISTED SECURITY; MARKET VALUE; NONVOTING STOCK; NO-PAR VALUE STOCK; OVER THE COUNTER; PAR VALUE; PARTICIPATING PREFERRED; PENNY STOCK; PREEMPTIVE RIGHT; PREFERENCE SHARES; PREFERRED STOCK; PRIOR PREFERRED STOCK; QUARTER STOCK; REGISTERED SECURITY; REGISTRAR; REVERSE SPLIT; SCRIP; SECURITY; SHARE; SHAREHOLDER; SPLIT; STATED VALUE; STOCK CERTIFICATE; STOCK DIVIDEND; STOCK EXCHANGE; STOCKHOLDER; STOCKHOLDER OF RECORD; STOCK MARKET; STOCK POWER; STOCK PURCHASE PLAN; STOCK SYMBOL; STOCK WATCHER; TRANSFER AGENT; TREASURY STOCK; VOTING STOCK; VOTING TRUST CERTIFICATE; WATERED STOCK.

2. inventories of accumulated goods in manufacturing and retailing businesses.

3. *see* ROLLING STOCK.

STOCK AHEAD situation in which two or more orders for a stock at a certain price arrive about the same time, and the exchange's PRIORITY rules take effect. New York Stock Exchange rules stipulate that the bid made first should be executed first or, if two bids came in at once, the bid for the larger number of shares receives priority. The bid that was not executed is then reported back to the broker, who informs the customer that the trade was not completed because there was stock ahead. *See also* MATCHED AND LOST.

STOCK BONUS PLAN plan established and maintained by an employer to provide benefits similar to those of a profit-sharing plan. Contributions by the employer, however, are not necessarily dependent on profits, and the benefits are distributed in shares of stock in the employer company. Stock bonus plans reward employee performance, and by giving employees a stake in the company they are used to help motivate them to perform at maximum efficiency.

STOCKBROKER *see* REGISTERED REPRESENTATIVE.

STOCK BUYBACK corporation's purchase of its own outstanding stock. A buyback may be financed by borrowings, sale of assets, or operating CASH FLOW. Its purpose is commonly to increase EARNINGS PER SHARE and thus the market price, often to discourage a TAKEOVER. When a buyback involves a PREMIUM paid to an acquirer in exchange for a promise to desist from take-over activity, the payment is called GREEN-MAIL. A buyback having a formula and schedule may also be called a SHARE REPURCHASE PLAN or SELF-TENDER. *See also* TREASURY STOCK.

STOCK BUYBACK PLAN *see* STOCK REPURCHASE PLAN (OR PROGRAM).

STOCK CERTIFICATE documentation of a shareholder's ownership in a corporation. Stock certificates are engraved intricately on heavy paper to deter forgery. They indicate the number of shares owned by an individual, their PAR VALUE (if any), the CLASS of stock (for example, common or pre-ferred), and attendant voting rights. To prevent theft, shareholders often store certificates in safe deposit boxes or take advantage of a broker's SAFE-KEEPING service. Stock certificates become negotiable when endorsed.

STOCK DIVIDEND payment of a corporate dividend in the form of stock rather than cash. The stock dividend may be additional shares in the company, or it may be shares in a SUBSIDIARY being spun off to shareholders. The divi-dend is usually expressed as a percentage of the shares held by a shareholder. For instance, a shareholder with 100 shares would receive 5 shares as the result of a 5% stock dividend. From the corporate point of view, stock divi-dends conserve cash needed to operate the business. From the stockholder point of view, the advantage is that additional stock is not taxed until sold, unlike a cash dividend, which is declarable as income in the year it is received.

STOCK EXCHANGE organized marketplace in which stocks, COMMON STOCK EQUIVALENTS, and bonds are traded by members of the exchange, acting both as agents (brokers) and as principals (dealers or traders). Most exchanges have a physical location where brokers and dealers meet to execute orders from institutional and individual investors to buy and sell securities. Each exchange sets its own requirements for membership; the New York Stock Exchange has the most stringent requirements. *See also* AMERICAN STOCK EXCHANGE; LISTING REQUIREMENTS; NEW YORK STOCK EXCHANGE; REGIONAL STOCK EXCHANGES; SECU-RITIES AND COMMODITIES EXCHANGES.

STOCK EXCHANGE OF THAILAND (SET) established in 1975 as the Securities Exchange of Thailand, it changed its name in 1991 to The Stock Exchange of Thailand. Major indices include the SET Index, a market capi-talization-weighted price index that compares the current market value of all listed common shares on the main board with its value on the base date of April 30, 1975, which was when the SET Index was established and set at 100 points. Trading is conducted through the ASSET automated electronic trading system Monday through Friday from 10 A.M. to 12:30 P.M., and 2 P.M. to 4:30 P.M. *www.set.or.th/th/index.html.*

STOCKHOLDER individual or organization with an ownership position in a corporation; also called a SHAREHOLDER or *shareowner.* Stockholders must own at least one share, and their ownership is confirmed by either a stock certificate or a record by their broker, if shares are in the broker's custody.

STOCKHOLDER DERIVATIVE SUIT *see* DERIVATIVE SUIT.

STOCKHOLDER OF RECORD common or preferred stockholder whose name is registered on the books of a corporation as owning shares as of a particular date. Dividends and other distributions are made only to shareholders of record. Common stockholders are usually the only ones entitled to vote for candidates for the board of directors or on other matters requiring shareholder approval.

STOCKHOLDER'S EQUITY *see* OWNER'S EQUITY.

STOCKHOLDER'S REPORT company's ANNUAL REPORT and supplementary quarterly reports giving financial results and usually containing an ACCOUNTANT'S OPINION. Special stockholder's reports are sometimes issued covering major corporate developments. Also called *shareholder's report. See also* DISCLOSURE.

STOCK INDEX FUTURE security that combines features of traditional commodity futures trading with securities trading using composite stock indices. Investors can speculate on general market performance or buy an index future contract to hedge a LONG POSITION or SHORT POSITION against a decline in value. Settlement is in cash, since it is obviously impossible to deliver an index of stocks to a futures buyer. Among the most popular stock index futures traded are the electronically traded E-mini S&P 500 contract as well as the NASDAQ 100 on the CHICAGO MERCANTILE EXCHANGE, the Dow Jones Industrial Average on the CHICAGO BOARD OF TRADE, the New York Stock Exchange Composite Index on the New York Board of Trade (NYBOT), and the Value Line Composite Index on the KANSAS CITY BOARD OF TRADE (KCBT). It is also possible to buy options on stock index futures. Unlike stock index futures or index options, however, futures options are not settled in cash; they are settled by delivery of the underlying stock index futures contracts. *See also* FUTURES CONTRACT; HEDGE/HEDGING; SECURITIES AND COMMODITIES EXCHANGES.

STOCK INDICES AND AVERAGES indicators used to measure and report value changes in representative stock groupings. Strictly speaking, an AVERAGE is simply the ARITHMETIC MEAN of a group of prices, whereas an INDEX is an average expressed in relation to an earlier established BASE MARKET VALUE. (In practice, the distinction between indices and averages is not always clear; the AMEX Major Market Index is an average, for example.) Indices and averages may be broad based—comprised of many stocks representative of the overall market—or narrowly based, meaning they are composed of a smaller number of stocks reflecting a particular industry or market SECTOR. Selected indices and averages are also used as the underlying value of stock index futures, index options, or options on index futures; these derivative instruments enable investors to hedge a position against general market movement at relatively low cost. An extensive number and variety of indices and averages exist. Among the best known and most widely used are

AMEX Composite Index (XAX): introduced in January 1997, it is a MARKET CAPITALIZATION-weighted, price appreciation index with a base level of 550 as of December 29, 1995. XAX reflects the aggregate market value of all of its components relative to their aggregate value on December 29, 1995. The index includes common stocks, or AMERICAN DEPOSITARY RECEIPTS of all AMEX-listed companies, REITs, master limited partnerships, and closed-end investment funds. Each component's market value is determined by multiplying its price by the number of shares outstanding. The day-to-day price change in each issue is weighted by its market value at the start of the day as a percent of the total market value for all components. The level of the index is not altered by stock splits, stock dividends, trading halts, new listings, additional issuances, delistings, or suspensions. *www.amex.com.*

AMEX Major Market Index (XMI): AMERICAN STOCK EXCHANGE'S price-weighted average of 20 BLUE CHIP industrial stocks representative of major U.S. corporations; several of the stocks are components of the DOW JONES INDUSTRIAL AVERAGE (DJIA). The index was established with a base value of 200.00 as of April 29, 1983. Futures on the XMI Index are traded on the CHICAGO BOARD OF TRADE. Options on the index are traded on Amex, and are traded under license on Euronext. *www.amex.com.*

Dow Jones Industrial Average: price-weighted average of 30 actively traded BLUE CHIP stocks, it is the oldest and most-quoted market indicator, first published on May 26, 1896. The Dow is prepared and published by Dow Jones Indexes, a unit of Dow Jones & Co. The Dow's components, which were once entirely industrial companies, have shifted with market dynamics and now represent a range of industries, including telecommunications, technology, consumer services, and financials. The components generally represent 20%–25% of the market value of U.S. stocks. The Dow is calculated by adding the trading prices of the component stocks and using a divisor adjusted for STOCK DIVIDENDS and SPLITS, CASH EQUIVALENT distributions equivalent to 10% or more of the closing prices of an issue, and substitutions and mergers. The average is quoted in points, not dollars. The Dow underlies a variety of investment products, inlcuding one of the largest U.S. exchange-traded funds, DIAMONDS, which are are traded on the AMERICAN STOCK EXCHANGE. Other averages similarly maintained by Dow Jones Indexes are the *Dow Jones Transportation Average*—20 stocks representative of the airline, trucking, railroad, and shipping businesses (*see also* DOW THEORY); and the *Dow Jones Utility Average*—15 geographically representative gas and electric utilities. The combination of the three averages encompasses 65 stocks and is known as the *Dow Jones Composite Average. www.djindexes.com.*

Dow Jones STOXX Indices: STOXX Ltd. is a joint venture of Deutsche Boerse AG, Dow Jones & Company, and the SWX Group the development, maintenance, distribution, and marketing of the Dow Jones STOXX indices. The cornerstone of the STOXX success story are the DJ STOXX BLUE CHIP indices. The DJ STOXX 50 (covering the largest sector leaders in Europe), the DJ EURO STOXX 50 (covering the largest sector leaders in the Euro-zone), the DJ STOXX EU Enlarged 15 (providing a representation of the largest companies in the ten new member states that joined the European Union in 2004) and the DJ STOXX NORDIC 30 (covering the largest sector leaders in the Nordic region).

The DJ STOXX blue chip indices are derived from the DJ STOXX 600 index (with the exception of the DJ STOXX EU Enlarged 15 Index), a broader market index that combines the DJ STOXX Large 200, Mid 200, and Small 200 size indices. The DJ STOXX 600 contains the 600 largest stocks of the DJ STOXX Total Market index. The DJ STOXX TMI and the DJ EURO STOXX TMI cover 95% of the free float market capitalization of the European and Eurozone markets and are further subdivided into Size and Style indices.

The DJ STOXX 600 is the European sub-index of the DJ STOXX Global 1800. The DJ STOXX Americas 600 and the DJ STOXX Asia/Pacific 600 are their complementary counterparts; in combination they create the DJ STOXX Global 1800. All three regional indices cover the largest stocks of the developed countries in their respective regions. Further regional subsets and sector indices of the DJ STOXX Global 1800 are also calculated. The DJ STOXX Global 1800 is directly derived from the DJ World Index, consisting of approximately 5,500 stocks and covering 95% of the world's free float market capitalization.

Dow Jones Titans Indices: blue chip indices representing various countries, regions, and sectors. The flagship index of the family, the Dow Jones Global Titans 50 Index, was created to reflect the globalization of international blue chip securities in the wake of mergers and the creation of mega-corporations. The components are large-cap companies with at least some of their operations outside of their domestic markets. *Dow Jones Sector Titans Indices* represent 18 global industries such as financial services, chemicals, health care, and technology. The Dow Jones Titans family also includes country and regional indices that track the biggest and most liquid stocks traded in individual countries and regions. Each index in the Dow Jones Titans family is contructed by selecting stocks from broad-based indices maintained by Dow Jones Indices. *www.djindexes.com.*

Dow Jones Wilshire 5000 is the broadest available measure of the U.S. stock market. It includes all stocks traded on the New York Stock Exchange, the American Stock Exchange, and Nasdaq with readily available prices. The index was created in the 1970s by Wilshire Associates and was originally called the Wilshire 5000. In 2004, Dow Jones Indices and Wilshire Associates teamed up to cobrand the index and create a float-adjusted version that reflects only those stock shares available to investors. Dow Jones and Wilshire also maintain a full complement of subindices representing various sectors and industries, investment styles (growth and value) and size segments (large-cap, mid-cap, small-cap, and micro-cap).

NASDAQ Composite Index: market value-weighted index that measures all domestic and non-U.S.-based securities—approximately 3,200 companies—listed on the NASDAQ Stock Market. The index was introduced on February 5, 1971, with a base value of 100. The market value—the last-sale price multiplied by total shares outstanding—is calculated through the trading day, and is related to the total value of the index. Each security in the Index is assigned to a NASDAQ subindex: Bank, Biotechnology, Computer, Health Care, Industrial, Insurance, Other Finance, Transportation, and Telecommunications. Values for the subindices began in February 1971, except for Biotechnology, Computer, and Telecommunications, which started November 1, 1993, and Health Care that started on July 12, 2005. *www.nasdaq.com.*

NASDAQ-100 Index: a MARKET CAPITALIZATION-weighted index representing the largest and non-financial domestic and international securities listed on The NASDAQ Stock Market. The index reflects companies across major industry groups including computer hardware and software, telecommunications, retail/wholesale trade, and biotechnology. Financial companies, including investment companies, are not included. The index is calculated under a modified capitalization-weighted methodology. The index was introduced on January 31, 1985, with a base of 250. On January 1, 1994, the Nasdaq-100 base was reset by division of a factor of 2 to 125. To be eligible, a security must have a minimum average daily trading volume of 200,000 shares and be listed on NASDAQ for at least two years among other criteria. Foreign securities must be eligible for listed options trading. A ranking review is performed annually in December. NASDAQ-100 futures and options on futures trade on the CHICAGO MERCANTILE EXCHANGE. The NASDAQ-100 option trade on CBOE, AMEX, and ISE, and is a European-style Option that can be exercised on its expiration date only. *www. nasdaq.com.*

The NYSE Composite Index (NYA): relaunched in January 2003 under a new methodology and recalculated to a base value of 5,000, outperformed all broad-based indices in 2004. Designed to measure the performance of all common stocks, ADRs, REITs, and tracking stocks listed on the NYSE, the index represents 77% of the total U.S. market capitalization and 64% of the total global market capitalization.

PSE/PCX 100 Index: price-weighted, broad-based index representing 100 listed and over-the-counter stocks from 15 different industries—including computer hardware, software, semiconductors, telecommunications, data storage and processing, electronics, and biotechnology. The index measures the performance of the technology sector of the U.S. equities market, and is considered the industry benchmark. It is used by mutual fund rating services and analysts to gauge the overall performance of the technology sector of the U.S. equities market. The PACIFIC EXCHANGE has maintained the index since 1982. Options are traded on the Pacific Exchange. *www.pacificex.com.*

Russell Indices: float MARKET CAPITALIZATION-weighted U.S. equity indices published by Russell Investment Group of Tacoma, Washington. The Russell 3000 Index measures the performance of the 3,000 largest U.S. companies based on market capitalization, representing about 99% of the investable U.S. equities market. The 1,000 highest-ranking stocks in this index comprise the Russell 1000® Index. The Russell 2000 Index consists of the 2,000 smallest companies in the Russell 3000 Index. The Russell Top 200® Index measures performance of the 200 largest companies in the Russell 1000, while the Russell 2500 Index measures performance of the 2,500 smallest companies in the Russell 3000 Index. Growth indices on the Russell Indices measure performance of the respective companies with higher PRICE/BOOK RATIOS and higher forecasted growth values. Value indices on the Russell Indices measure performance of those companies with lower price/book ratios and lower forecasted growth values. Futures and/or options on some of the indices or associated exchange-traded funds are traded on the CHICAGO BOARD OF TRADE, CHICAGO BOARD OPTIONS EXCHANGE, the NEW YORK BOARD OF TRADE, INTERNATIONAL SECURITIES EXCHANGE, EUREX US, AMERICAN STOCK EXCHANGE, CBOE FUTURES EXCHANGE, CHICAGO MERCANTILE EXCHANGE, PACIFIC STOCK EXCHANGE, and PHILADELPHIA STOCK EXCHANGE. *www.russell.com. See also* RUSSELL INDICES.

S&P 500 Index: widely regarded as the best single gauge of the U.S. equities market; commonly known as the *Standard & Poor's 500* (or *S&P 500*). This world-renowned index includes a representative sample of 500 leading companies in leading industries of the U.S. economy. Although the S&P 500 focuses on the large-cap segment of the market, with more than 80% coverage of U.S. equities, it is also an ideal proxy for the total market. More than $4 trillion is benchmarked against the S&P 500 and more than $1 trillion is directly invested in the index. The selection of stocks, their relative weightings to reflect differences in the number of outstanding shares, and publication of the index itself are services of STANDARD & POOR'S. Stocks in the index are chosen for market size, liquidity, and industry group representation. Like all S&P indices, the S&P 500 is classified according to the Global Industry Classification System (GICS), which consists of 10 sectors—Energy, Materials, Industrials, Consumer Discretionary, Consumer Staples, Health Care, Financials, Information Technology, Telecommunications Services, and Utilities. In terms of market capitalization, the largest sectors in the S&P 500 are Financials, Information Technology, and Health Care. The composition of the 500 stocks is continuously updated and the number of issues in each sector varies over time so that the index constantly reflects the sectoral makeup of the market and economy. Standard & Poor's also publishes several other important indices including the *S&P MidCap 400*, the *S&P SmallCap 600*, and the *S&P 1500 Composite Index*, which totals the S&P 500, 400, and 600 indices and which represent approximately 90% of the total market capitalization of stocks traded in the U.S. equity market. S&P also maintains more than 90 individual industry indices. *www.indices.standardandpoors.com.*

S&P Global 1200 Index: the first real-time, free-float weighted world index, covering 29 countries and approximately 70% of global market capitalization. It is comprised of seven regional indices: the S&P 500; S&P/TSX 60 (Canada); the S&P Latin America 40 (Mexico, Brazil, Argentina, Chile); the S&P/TOPIX 150 (Japan); the S&P Asia 50 (Hong Kong, Korea, Singapore, Taiwan); the S&P/ASX 50 (Australia) and the S&P Europe 350. The European index is divided into three subindices: the S&P Euro, covering the Euro zone markets; the S&P Euro Plus, adding Denmark, Norway, Sweden, and Switzerland; and the S&P United Kingdom. Constituents of the S&P Global 1200 are selected to ensure sectoral and country balance. Constituent weights are determined by a company's free-float market capitalization: corporate cross-holdings, government ownership, strategic holders, and foreign investment restrictions are removed. The component indices are maintained by an index committee consisting of Standard & Poor's worldwide staff, using the same index governance and maintenance principles used by the S&P 500. Standard & Poor's collaborates with the TORONTO STOCK EXCHANGE, the TOKYO STOCK EXCHANGE, and the AUSTRALIAN STOCK EXCHANGE on maintenance of the Canada, Japan, and Australia indices, respectively. Exchange-traded funds are available on the S&P 500, S&P Europe 350, S&P/TSX 60, S&P/ASX 50, and the S&P Latin America 40. Futures and options are traded on the S&P 500, the S&P/TSX 60, and the S&P/ASX 50. Like all S&P indices, the S&P Global 1200 is classified according to the Global Industry Classification System (GICS), which consists of 10 sectors—Energy, Materials, Industrials, Consumer Discretionary, Consumer Staples, Health Care, Financials, Information Technology, Telecommunications Services, and Utilities. In terms of market capitalization, the largest sectors in the S&P 500 are Financials, Information Technology, and Health Care. The largest, in terms of market capitalization, is Financials. Other top sectors represented are Consumer Discretionary, Health Care, and Information Technology. Among the smallest are Utilities, Materials, Telecommunications Services, and Energy. *www.indices.standardandpoors.com.*

Standard & Poor's 100 Index (OEX): market-capitalization-weighted index of 100 major, blue chip stocks across diverse industry groups. The index is a sub-set of the S&P 500 and measures large-company U.S. stock market performance. Options on the S&P 100 Index are listed on the CHICAGO BOARD OPTIONS EXCHANGE. Its components are mainly NYSE industrials, with some transportation, utility, and financial stocks. *www.indices.standardandpoors.com.*

Value Line Composite Averages: equally weighted arithmetic and geometric averages of approximately 1700 NYSE, AMEX, and NASDAQ stocks tracked by the VALUE LINE INVESTMENT SURVEY. The stocks cover more than 90 industries, the stock markets, and the economy. The averages use a base value of 100, established June 30, 1961; changes are expressed in index numbers rather than dollars and cents. Value Line also offers three sector indices: the Value Line Geometric Industrial Average, Value Line Geometric Rail Average, and Value Line Geometric Utilities Average. The KANSAS CITY BOARD OF TRADE trades Value Line Stock Index futures and options. *www.valueline.com.*

Many indices and averages track the performance of stock markets around the world. The major indices and exchanges that offer them include: ALL ORDINARIES INDEX; ATHENS STOCK EXCHANGE; BOLSA DE COMMERCIO DE SANTIAGO; BOLSA DE MADRID; BOLSA MEXICANA DE VELORES; BOVESPA; BORSA ITALIANA; CAC 40 INDEX; EAFE INDEX; EURONEXT; HANG SENG INDEX; JOHANNESBURG STOCK EXCHANGE; BURSA MALAYSIA; LONDON STOCK EXCHANGE; MORGAN STANLEY CAPITAL INTERNATIONAL INDICES; NEW ZEALAND STOCK EXCHANGE LIMITED; OMX; OSLO STOCK EXCHANGE; SINGAPORE EXCHANGE LIMITED; STOCK EXCHANGE OF THAILAND (SET); SWX SWISS EXCHANGE; TOKYO STOCK EXCHANGE; TEL AVIV STOCK EXCHANGE; TORONTO STOCK EXCHANGE (TSX); and WIENER BÖRSE AG. *See also* BARRON'S CONFIDENCE INDEX; BOND BUYER'S INDEX; COMMODITY INDICES; LIPPER MUTUAL FUND INDUSTRY AVERAGE; SECURITIES AND COMMODITIES EXCHANGES.

STOCK INSURANCE COMPANY insurance company that is owned by stockholders, as distinguished from a MUTUAL COMPANY that is owned by POLICYHOLDERS. Even in a stock company, however, policyholders interests are ahead of shareholder's dividends.

STOCK JOCKEY stockbroker who actively follows individual stocks and frequently buys and sells shares in his client's portfolios. If the broker does too much short-term trading in accounts over which he has discretion, he may be accused of CHURNING.

STOCK LIST function of the organized stock exchanges that is concerned with LISTING REQUIREMENTS and related investigations, the eligibility of unlisted companies for trading privileges, and the delisting of companies that have not complied with exchange regulations and listing requirements. The New York Stock Exchange department dealing with listing of securities is called the Department of Stock List.

STOCK MARKET general term referring to the organized trading of securities through the various physical and electronic exchanges and the OVER THE COUNTER market. The securities involved include COMMON STOCK, PREFERRED STOCK, BONDS, CONVERTIBLES, OPTIONS, rights, and warrants. The term may also encompass commodities when used in its most general sense, but more often than not the stock market and the commodities (or futures) market are distinguished. The query "How did the market do today?" is usually answered by a reference to the Dow Jones Industrial Average, comprised of stocks listed on the New York Stock Exchange. *See also* SECURITIES AND COMMODITIES EXCHANGES.

STOCK OPTION

1. right to purchase or sell a stock at a specified price within a stated period. OPTIONS are a popular investment medium, offering an opportunity to hedge positions in other securities, to speculate in stocks with relatively little investment, and to capitalize on changes in the MARKET VALUE of options contracts themselves through a variety of options strategies.

    See also CALL OPTION; PUT OPTION.

2. widely used form of employee incentive and compensation, usually for the executives of a corporation. The employee is given an OPTION to purchase its shares at a certain price (at or below the market price at the time the option is granted) for a specified period of years.

    See also INCENTIVE STOCK OPTION; QUALIFIED STOCK OPTION.

STOCK POWER power of attorney form transferring ownership of a REGIS- TERED SECURITY from the owner to another party. A separate piece of paper from the CERTIFICATE, it is attached to the latter when the security is sold or pledged to a brokerage firm, bank, or other lender as loan COLLATERAL. Technically, the stock power gives the owner's permission to another party (the TRANSFER AGENT) to transfer ownership of the certificate to a third party. Also called *stock/bond power.*

STOCK PURCHASE PLAN organized program for employees of a company to buy shares of its stock. The plan could take the form of compensation if the employer matches employee stock purchases. In some companies, employees are offered the chance to buy stock in the company at a discount. Also, a corporation can offer to reinvest dividends in additional shares as a service to shareholders, or it can set up a program of regular additional share purchases for participating shareholders who authorize periodic, automatic payments from their wages for this purpose. *See also* AUTOMATIC INVESTMENT PROGRAM.

Another form of stock purchase plan is the EMPLOYEE STOCK OWNERSHIP PLAN (ESOP), whereby employees regularly accumulate shares and may ultimately assume control of the company.

STOCK RATING evaluation by rating agencies of common stocks, usually in terms of expected price performance or safety. Standard & Poor's and Value Line's respective quality and timeliness ratings are among the most widely consulted.

STOCK RECORD control, usually in the form of a ledger card or computer report, used by brokerage films to keep track of securities held in inventory and their precise location within the firm. Securities are recorded by name and owner.

STOCK REPURCHASE PLAN (OR PROGRAM) action taken by a board of directors that authorizes but does not obligate corporate manage- ment to go into the open market and repurchase its own shares up to a specified limit within a specified period of time. Upon retirement of the shares repurchased, the company has a lesser number of issued and outstand- ing shares, thereby theoretically increasing its earnings per share. With higher earnings per share, the company's shares theoretically rise in value, giving shareholders long-term capital gains. Stock buybacks, which often fall short of the amount authorized and are announced partly for psychological effect to boost the stock price, have been a popular use of cash built up by companies that do not want to initiate mergers or acquisitions, reinvest in their businesses, or raise their dividends any further.

STOCK RIGHT *see* SUBSCRIPTION RIGHT.

STOCK SCREENING using computer programs, such as Telescan, to apply stock selection criteria to a data base of thousands of companies. Corporate financial and stock performance data, both fundamental and technical, are thus screened to exclude stocks that fail to match criteria, resulting in a handful of promising investment prospects. Stock screening is part of the nascent and quickly developing field called *cyber-investing*.

STOCK SPLIT *see* SPLIT.

STOCK SYMBOL letters used to identify listed companies on the securities exchanges on which they trade. These symbols, also called *trading symbols,* identify trades on the CONSOLIDATED TAPE and are used in other reports and documents whenever such shorthand is convenient. Symbols for stocks listed on the NEW YORK STOCK EXCHANGE and the AMERICAN STOCK EXCHANGE range from one to three letters. AT&T's symbol, for example is T; Alcoa's is AA; 3M Company's is MMM. A fourth letter indicates a special class or category. Over-the-counter stock symbols have four or five letters. A fifth letter indicates that the security has something special about it. The following is a guide: A = Class A; B = Class B; D = New; E = Delinquent in SEC filings; F = Foreign, except ADRs; G, H, I = Additional warrants of preferreds; J = Voting; K = Nonvoting; L = Miscellaneous situations, such as stubs, depositary receipts, additional warrants or preferred; M = Fourth preferred; N = Third preferred; O = Second preferred; P = First preferred; Q = bankruptcy; R = Rights; S = Beneficial interest; T = Delinquent in filing; U = Units; V = When-issued and when-distributed; W = Warrants; Y = ADRs; Z = Miscellaneous situations, similar to L. Stock symbols are not necessarily the same as abbreviations used to identify the same companies in the stock tables of newspapers. *See also* COMMITTEE ON UNIFORM SECURITIES IDENTIFICATION PROCEDURES (CUSIP).

STOCK-TRANSFER AGENT *see* TRANSFER AGENT.

STOCK WARRANT *see* SUBSCRIPTION WARRANT.

STOCK WATCH (NYSE) computerized service that monitors all trading activity and movement in stocks listed on the New York Stock Exchange. The system is set up to identify any unusual activity due to rumors or MANIPULA-TION or other illegal practices. The stock watch department of the NYSE is prepared to conduct investigations and to take appropriate action, such as issuing clarifying information or turning questions of legality over to the Securities and Exchange Commission. *See also* SURVEILLANCE DEPARTMENT OF EXCHANGES.

STOP-LIMIT ORDER order to a securities broker with instructions to buy or sell at a specified price or better (called the *stop-limit price*) but only after a given *stop price* has been reached or passed. It is a combination of a STOP ORDER and a LIMIT ORDER. For example, the instruction to the broker might be "buy 100 XYZ 55 STOP 56 LIMIT" meaning that if the MARKET PRICE reaches $55, the broker enters a limit order to be executed at $56 or a better (lower) price. A stop-limit order avoids some of the risks of a stop order, which becomes a MARKET ORDER when the stop price is reached; like all price-limit orders, however, it carries the risk of missing the market altogether, since the specified limit price or better may never occur. The American Stock Exchange prohibits stop-limit orders unless the stop and limit prices are equal.

STOP LOSS
Insurance: promise by a reinsurance company that it will cover losses incurred by the company it reinsures over and above an agreed-upon amount.
Stocks: customer order to a broker that sets the sell price of a stock below the current MARKET PRICE. A stop-loss order therefore will protect profits that have already been made or prevent further losses if the stock drops.

STOP ORDER order to a securities broker to buy or sell at the MARKET PRICE once the security has traded at a specified price called the *stop price.* A stop order may be a DAY ORDER, a GOOD-TILL-CANCELED ORDER, or any other form of time-limit order. A stop order to buy, always at a stop price above the current market price, is usually designed to protect a profit or to limit a loss on a short sale *(see* SELLING SHORT). A stop order to sell, always at a price below the current market price, is usually designed to protect a profit or to limit a loss on a security already purchased at a higher price. The risk of stop orders is that they may be triggered by temporary market movements or that they may be executed at prices several points higher or lower than the stop price because of market orders placed ahead of them. Also called *stop-loss order. See also* GATHER IN THE STOPS; STOP LIMIT ORDER; STOP LOSS (stocks).

STOP-OUT PRICE lowest dollar price at which Treasury bills are sold at a particular auction. This price and the beginning auction price are averaged to establish the price at which smaller purchasers may purchase bills under the NONCOMPETITIVE BID system. *See also* BILL; DUTCH AUCTION.

STOP PAYMENT revocation of payment on a check after the check has been sent or delivered to the payee. So long as the check has not been cashed, the writer has up to six months in which to request a stop payment. The stop payment right does not carry over to electronic funds transfers.

STOPPED OUT term used when a customer's order is executed under a STOP ORDER at the price predetermined by the customer, called the *stop price.* For instance, if a customer has entered a stop-loss order to sell XYZ at $30 when the stock is selling at $33, and the stock then falls to $30, his or her position will be stopped out. A customer may also be stopped out if the order is executed at a guaranteed price offered by a SPECIALIST. *See also* GATHER IN THE STOPS; STOPPED STOCK.

STOPPED STOCK guarantee by a SPECIALIST that an order placed by a FLOOR BROKER will be executed at the best bid or offer price then in the SPECIALIST'S BOOK unless it can be executed at a better price within a specified period of time.

STOP PRICE *see* STOP ORDER.

STORY STOCK/BOND security with values or features so complex that a "story" is required to persuade investors of its merits. Story stocks are frequently from companies with some unique product or service that is difficult for competitors to copy. In a less formal sense, term is used by news organizations to mean stocks most actively traded.

STOXX LIMITED a joint venture of Deutsche Boerse AG, Dow Jones & Company, and the SWX Group in the development, maintenance, distribution and marketing of the Dow Jones STOXX indices, a rules-based, transparent, and free-float weighted family of indices globally integrated into that of the Dow Jones Indices. Launched in 1998 in advance of European Monetary Union, the introduction of the Euro, and the creation of the Eurozone, the Dow Jones STOXX indices have become Europe's leading regional equity indices in a fast and impressive success story. STOXX Limited expanded its strategy beyond Europe by purposefully responding to market requirements. Today, STOXX Limited is a global index provider covering the world markets and providing investors with access to Europe, Asia/Pacific, and the Americas. STOXX Limited issues licences for the commercial use of the Dow Jones STOXX indices and has more than 350 licensees worldwide, selling more than 4,000 financial products based on the DJ STOXX indices. STOXX holds a 40% market share in the ETF segment and has a leading edge over all other index providers in Europe. STOXX has also held a very strong position in the derivatives segment. With 560 billion Euros in open interest for futures and options (as of July 2005), STOXX ranks first in Europe and second worldwide. *See also* STOCK INDICES AND AVERAGES.

STRADDLE strategy consisting of an equal number of PUT OPTIONS and CALL OPTIONS on the same underlying stock, stock index, or commodity future at the same STRIKE PRICE and maturity date. Each OPTION may be exercised separately, although the combination of options is usually bought and sold as a unit.

STRAIGHT-LINE DEPRECIATION method of depreciating a fixed asset whereby the asset's useful life is divided into the total cost less the estimated salvage value. The procedure is used to arrive at a uniform annual DEPRECIATION expense to be charged against income before figuring income taxes. Thus, if a new machine purchased for $1,200 was estimated to have a useful life of ten years and a salvage value of $200, annual depreciation under the straight-line method would be $100, charged at $100 a year. This is the oldest and simplest method of depreciation and is used by many companies for financial reporting purposes, although faster depreciation of some assets with greater tax benefits in the early years is allowed under the MODIFIED ACCELERATED COST RECOVERY SYSTEM (MACRS).

STRAIGHT TERM INSURANCE POLICY term life insurance policy for a specific number of years in which the death benefit remains unchanged. A level premium policy will charge the same premium for a number of years, usually ten, and then increase. An annual renewable term policy will charge slightly higher premiums each year.

STRAIGHT-THROUGH PROCESSING direct exchange of cash for securities, common with cross-border transactions where settlement is often costly.

STRANGLE sale or purchase of a put option and a call option on the same underlying instrument, with the same expiration, but at strike prices equally OUT OF THE MONEY. A strangle costs less than a STRADDLE because both options are out of the money, but profits are made only if the underlying instrument moves dramatically.

STRAP OPTION contract combining one PUT OPTION and two CALL OPTIONS of the same SERIES, which can be bought at a lower total premium than that of the three options bought individually. The put has the same features as the calls—same underlying security, exercise price, and maturity. Also called *triple option. Compare with* STRIP.

STRATEGIC BUYOUT ACQUISITION based on analysis of the operational benefits of consolidation. Implicitly contrasts with the type of TAKEOVER based on "paper values" that characterized the "merger mania" of the 1980s—undervalued stock bought using JUNK BONDS ultimately repayable from the liquidation of acquired assets and activities. A strategic buyout focuses on how companies fit together and anticipates enhanced long-term earning power. *See also* SYNERGY.

STREET short for Wall Street, referring to the financial community in New York City and elsewhere. It is common to hear "The Street likes XYZ." This means there is a national consensus among securities analysts that XYZ's prospects are favorable. *See also* STREET NAME.

STREET NAME phrase describing securities held in the name of a broker or another nominee instead of a customer. Since the securities are in the broker's custody, transfer of the shares at the time of sale is easier than if the stock were registered in the customer's name and physical certificates had to be transferred.

STRESS TEST requirement of the Obama administration's financial rescue plan announced in the Spring of 2009 that certain large banks undergo a series of tests to assess their ability to survive a protracted slump without requiring additional capital infusions from the government or private sources. Under the plan, banks must test the resilience of their portfolios and capital assuming a 3.3% contraction in gross domestic product in 2009 and home price declines of 22% in 2009 and 7% in 2010. The test also assumes an unemployment rate averaging 8.9% in 2009 and 10.3% in 2010.

STRETCH IRA an INDIVIDUAL RETIREMENT ARRANGEMENT (IRA) set up in a way that extends the period of tax deferred earnings beyond the lifetime of the owner, typically over several generations. The benefits of stretching IRAs can be maximized by leaving as much in the IRA to grow tax-deferred as is legal and by designating beneficiaries who are young enough to exhaust the maximum legal distribution period, defined as the original non-spouse beneficiary's life expectancy. For example: A 29-year-old contributes $2,000 a year to a traditional IRA for 40 years, taking no withdrawals and earning a compound annual return of 7%. That IRA owner dies at age 69 and his spouse, who is 20 years younger, now owns the IRA, which has grown to a value of $399,400. The spouse, again taking no withdrawals and watching the value grow at a compound annual rate of 7%, dies at 69, leaving an account worth $1,612,547. to a baby granddaughter. With 70 years of compounding, and earning the same 7%, the granddaughter would have $213,487,584 on her retirement. With contributions scheduled to rise to $5,000 in 2008, that value could be conservative, assuming the 7 percent return is realistic, inflation is minimal, the tax laws don't change, nobody takes any distributions, and the owners die before required minimum distributions kick in at age 70½.

STRIKE PRICE *see* EXERCISE PRICE.

STRIP
Bonds: brokerage-house practice of separating a bond into its CORPUS and COUPONS, which are then sold separately as ZERO-COUPON SECURITIES. The 1986 Tax Act permitted MUNICIPAL BOND strips. Some, such as Salomon

Brothers' tax-exempt M-CATS, represent PREREFUNDINGS backed by U.S. Treasury securities held in escrow. Other strips include Treasuries stripped by brokers, such as TIGERS, and stripped mortgage-backed securities of government-sponsored issuers like Fannie Mae. A variation known by the acronym STRIPS (Separate Trading of Registered Interest and Principal of Securities) is a prestripped zero-coupon bond that is a direct obligation of the U.S. Treasury.

Options: OPTION contract consisting of two PUT OPTIONS and one CALL OPTION on the same underlying stock or stock index with the same strike and expiration date. *Compare with* STRAP.

Stocks: to buy stocks with the intention of collecting their dividends. Also called *dividend stripping. See also* DIVIDEND ROLLOVER PLAN.

STRIPPED BOND bond separated into its two components: periodic interest payments and principal repayment. Each of the interest payments and the principal repayment are stripped apart by a brokerage firm and sold individually as ZERO-COUPON SECURITIES. Investors therefore have a wide choice of maturities to pick from when shopping for a zero-coupon bond. When a U.S. government bond is stripped, it is often called a STRIP, which stands for *separate trading of registered interest and principal of securities*. Such bonds are also called CATS AND TIGRS.

STRIPPED MORTGAGE-BACKED SECURITIES mortgage-backed certificates representing separated principal and interest components of the underlying mortgages.

STRONG DOLLAR dollar that can be exchanged for a large amount of a foreign currency. The dollar can gain strength in currency markets because the United States is considered a haven of political and economic stability, or because yields on American securities are attractive. A strong dollar is a blessing for American travelers going abroad, because they get more pounds, Euros, and yen and other currencies for their greenbacks. However, a strong dollar makes it difficult for American firms to export their goods to foreign countries because it raises the cost to foreigners of purchasing American products. In 1985, the dollar became so strong that the PLAZA ACCORD was signed to bring the dollar down. *See also* EXCHANGE RATE; WEAK DOLLAR.

STRUCTURED FINANCE financing using STRUCTURED NOTES or SECURITIZATION.

STRUCTURED INVESTMENT VEHICLE (SIV) type of investment fund that had a huge role in the building of the financial crisis but then self-destructed in 2008. Its modus operandi was to borrow money by issuing short-term securities, such as COMMERCIAL PAPER, at low rates and lending it out by buying long-term securities, such as COLLATERALIZED DEBT OBLIGATIONS (CDOs) and other ASSET BACKED SECURITIES, at higher rates, rewarding investors with the difference. Originated by Citigroup in 1988, SIVs were part of what was called the SHADOW BANKING SYSTEM. SIVs were dependent on a continuous source of short-term investment to fund their long-term exposure. When the credit crunch came, commercial paper and other short-term investors fled to the quality of bonds and government-guaranteed bank deposits. Forced as a result to sell long-term assets into a nonexistent market, the SIVs had to default.

STRUCTURED NOTE

1. derivative instrument based on the movement of an underlying index, stock price, interest rate benchmark, or other financial asset. For example, a structured note issued by a corporation may pay interest to noteholders based on the rise and fall of oil prices. This gives investors the opportunity to earn interest and profit from the change in price of a commodity at the same time.

2. complex debt instrument, usually a medium-term note, in which the issuer enters into one or more SWAP arrangements to change the cash flows it is required to make. A simple form utilizing interest-rate swaps might be, for example, a three-year FLOATING RATE NOTE paying the London Interbank Offered Rate (LIBOR) plus a premium semiannually. The issuer arranges a swap transaction whereby it agrees to pay a fixed semiannual rate for three years in exchange for the LIBOR. Since the floating rate payments (cash flows) offset each other, the issuer has synthetically created a fixed-rate note.

STRUCTURED PRODUCT name covering a broad range of novel investment products, many with proprietary names or acronyms, that combine two or more financial instruments, at least one of which must be a DERIVATIVE.

STRUCTURED SETTLEMENT agreement to pay a designated person a specified sum of money in periodic payments, usually for his or her lifetime, instead of in a single LUMP SUM payment. Structured settlements typically are used to pay court-ordered or privately-agreed upon damages to injured claimants or their survivors. Structured settlements are also used to pay lottery winners. In both cases, the settlement is funded with an ANNUITY.

STUB STOCK common stocks or instruments convertible to equity in a company that is overleveraged as the result of a BUYOUT or RECAPITALIZATION and may have DEFICIT NET WORTH. Stub stock is highly speculative and highly volatile but, unlike JUNK BONDS, has unlimited potential for gain if the company succeeds in restoring financial balance.

STYLE *see* INVESTMENT PHILOSOPHY.

STYLE BOX Morningstar's compact graphic representation of the two variables that comprise a mutual fund's or exchange-traded fund's holdings and risk: its investment methodology and the size of the companies in which the fund invests. The Domestic-Equity Style Box is a nine box grid resembling a tic-tac-toe square. The vertical boxes indicate whether the stocks the fund holds are small-, medium-, or large-capitalization. The horizontal boxes indicate whether the fund's investment methodology is value-based, growth-based, or a blend of value and growth. A fund's location on the matrix provides a quick take on the fund. The Style Box also helps an investor identify the different funds that meet his or her objectives. By going to the *www.morningstar.com* web site, an investor can simply click on a Style Box square to get a list of the funds meeting desired capitalization and methodology criteria. Morningstar also has an International-Equity Style Box and a Fixed-Income Style Box. The latter uses variables of interest-rate sensitivity (short, intermediate, and long duration) and credit quality (high, medium, low). *See also* MORNINGSTAR RATING SYSTEM.

STYLE DRIFT *see* INVESTMENT PHILOSOPHY.

SUBADVISOR in some mutual funds, the fund advisors, the company or companies that have primary responsibility for managing a fund, will hire another company, called the subadvisor, to handle the fund's day-to-day management. In such cases, the portfolio manager will report to the subadvisor, not the advisor.

SUBCHAPTER M Internal Revenue Service regulation dealing with what is commonly called the *conduit theory,* in which qualifying investment companies and real estate investment trusts avoid double taxation by passing interest and dividend income and capital gains directly through, without taxation, to shareholders, who are taxed as individuals. *See also* REAL ESTATE INVESTMENT TRUST; REGULATED INVESTMENT COMPANY.

SUBCHAPTER S section of the Internal Revenue Code giving a corporation that has 35 or fewer shareholders and meets certain other requirements the option of being taxed as if it were a PARTNERSHIP. Thus a small corporation candistribute its income directly to shareholders and avoid the corporate income tax while enjoying the other advantages of the corporate form. These companies are known as *Subchapter S corporations, tax-option corporations,* or *small business corporations.*

SUBINDEX an index representing a sector of a larger index. For example, the NASDAQ Telecommunications Index is one of 11 subindexes of the NASDAQ Composite Index. *See also* STOCK INDICES AND AVERAGES.

SUBJECT Wall Street term referring to a bid and/or offer that is negotiable—that is, a QUOTATION that is not firm. For example, a broker looking to place a sizable order might call several dealers with the question, "Can you give me a *subject quote* on 20,000 shares of XYZ?"

SUBJECT QUOTE *see* SUBJECT.

SUBJECT TO OPINION *see* QUALIFIED OPINION.

SUBORDINATED junior in claim on assets to other debt, that is, repayable only after other debts with a higher claim have been satisfied. Some subordinated debt may have less claim on assets than other subordinated debt; a *junior subordinated debenture* ranks below a subordinated DEBENTURE, for example.

It is also possible for unsubordinated (senior) debt to become subordinated at the request of a lender by means of a subordination agreement. For example, if an officer of a small company has made loans to the company instead of making a permanent investment in it, a bank might request the officer's loan be subordinated to its own loan as long as the latter is outstanding. This is accomplished by the company officer's signing a subordination agreement. *See also* EFFECTIVE NET WORTH; JUNIOR SECURITY.

SUBORDINATION CLAUSE clause in a MORTGAGE loan agreement that permits a mortgage recorded at a subsequent date to have preference over the original mortgage.

SUBPRIME having poor credit quality and descriptive of mortgages not meeting the standards of Fannie Mae and Freddie Mac but that were bought and securitized by Wall Street investment banks leading to the real estate crisis that began in 2006. *See also* ALT-A-LOAN.

SUBROGATION legal process by which an insurance company, after paying for a loss, seeks to recover the amount of the loss from another party who is legally liable for it.

SUBSCRIPTION agreement of intent to buy newly issued securities. *See also* NEW ISSUE; SUBSCRIPTION RIGHT; SUBSCRIPTION WARRANT.

SUBSCRIPTION AGREEMENT application submitted by an investor seeking to join a limited partnership. All prospective limited partners must be approved by the general partner before they are allowed to become limited partners.

SUBSCRIPTION PRICE price at which existing shareholders of a corporation are entitled to purchase common shares in a RIGHTS OFFERING or at which subscription warrants are exercisable. *See also* SUBSCRIPTION RIGHT; SUBSCRIPTION WARRANT.

SUBSCRIPTION PRIVILEGE right of existing shareholders of a corporation, or their transferees, to buy shares of a new issue of common stock before it is offered to the public. *See also* PREEMPTIVE RIGHT; SUBSCRIPTION RIGHT.

SUBSCRIPTION RATIO see SUBSCRIPTION RIGHT.

SUBSCRIPTION RIGHT privilege granted to existing shareholders of a corporation to subscribe to shares of a new issue of common stock before it is offered to the public; better known simply as a *right*. Such a right, which normally has a life of two to four weeks, is freely transferable and entitles the holder to buy the new common stock below the PUBLIC OFFERING PRICE. While in most cases one existing share entitles the stockholder to one right, the number of rights needed to buy a share of a new issue (called the *subscription ratio*) varies and is determined by a company in advance of an offering. To subscribe, the holder sends or delivers to the company or its agent the required number of rights plus the dollar price of the new shares.

Rights are sometimes granted to comply with state laws that guarantee the shareholders' PREEMPTIVE RIGHT—their right to maintain a proportionate share of ownership. It is common practice, however, for corporations to grant rights even when not required by law; protecting shareholders from the effects of DILUTION is seen simply as good business.

The actual certificate representing the subscription is technically called a SUBSCRIPTION WARRANT, giving rise to some confusion. The term *subscription warrant,* or simply *warrant,* is commonly understood in a related but different sense—as a separate entity with a longer life than a right—maybe 5, 10, or 20 years or even perpetual—and with a SUBSCRIPTION PRICE higher at the time of issue than the MARKET VALUE of the common stock.

Subscription rights are offered to shareholders in what is called a RIGHTS OFFERING, usually handled by underwriters under a STANDBY COMMITMENT.

SUBSCRIPTION WARRANT type of security, usually issued together with a BOND or PREFERRED STOCK, that entitles the holder to buy a proportionate amount of common stock at a specified price, usually higher than the market price at the time of issuance, for a period of years or to perpetuity; better known simply as a *warrant*. In contrast, rights, which also represent the right to buy common shares, normally have a subscription price lower than the current market value of the common stock and a life of two to four weeks.

A warrant is usually issued as a SWEETENER, to enhance the marketability of the accompanying fixed income securities. Warrants are freely transferable and are traded on the major exchanges. They are also called *stock-purchase warrants*. *See also* PERPETUAL WARRANT; SUBSCRIPTION RIGHT.

SUBSIDIARY company of which more than 50% of the voting shares are owned by another corporation, called the PARENT COMPANY. *See also* AFFILIATE.

SUBSTITUTION
Banking: replacement of COLLATERAL by other collateral.
Contracts: replacement of one party to a contract by another. *See also* NOVATION.
Economics: concept that, if one product or service can be replaced by another, their prices should be similar.
Law: replacement of one attorney by another in the exercise of stock powers relating to the purchase and sale of securities. *See also* STOCK POWER.
Securities:
1. exchange or SWAP of one security for another in a client's PORTFOLIO. Securities analysts often advise substituting a stock they currently favor for a stock in the same industry that they believe has less favorable prospects.
2. substitution of another security of equal value for a security acting as COLLATERAL for a MARGIN ACCOUNT. *See also* SAME-DAY-SUBSTITUTION.

SUICIDE PILL POISON PILL with potentially catastrophic implications for the company it is designed to protect. An example might be a poison pill providing for an exchange of stock for debt in the event of a *hostile takeover;* that would discourage an acquirer by making the TAKEOVER prohibitively expensive, but its implementation could put the TARGET COMPANY in danger of bankruptcy.

SUITABILITY RULES guidelines that those selling sophisticated and potentially risky financial products, such as limited partnerships or commodities futures contracts, must follow to ensure that investors have the financial means to assume the risks involved. Such rules are enforced through self-regulation administered by such organizations as the NATIONAL ASSOCIATION OF SECURITIES DEALERS, the SECURITIES AND COMMODITIES EXCHANGES, and other groups operating in the securities industry. Individual brokerage firms selling the products have their own guidelines and policies. They typically require the investor to have a certain level of NET WORTH and LIQUID ASSETS, so that he or she will not be irreparably harmed if the investment sours. A brokerage firm may be sued if it has allowed an unsuitable investor to buy an investment that goes sour. *See also* KNOW YOUR CUSTOMER.

SUM-OF-THE-YEARS'-DIGITS METHOD (SOYD) method of ACCELERATED DEPRECIATION that results in higher DEPRECIATION charges and greater tax savings in the earlier years of a FIXED ASSET'S useful life than the STRAIGHT-LINE DEPRECIATION method, where charges are uniform throughout. Sometimes called just *sum-of-digits method,* it allows depreciation based on an inverted scale of the total of digits for the years of useful life. Thus, for four years of life, the digits 4, 3, 2, and 1 are added to produce 10. The first year's rate becomes $\frac{4}{10}$ths of the depreciable cost of the asset (cost less salvage value), the second year's rate $\frac{3}{10}$ths, and so on. The effects of this method of accelerated depreciation are compared with the straight-line method in the following illustration, which assumes an asset with a total cost of $1000, a useful life of four years, and no salvage value:

YEAR	STRAIGHT LINE		SUM-OF-YEARS' DIGITS	
	Expense	Cumulative	Expense	Cumulative
1	$250	$250	$400	$400
2	$250	$500	$300	$700
3	$250	$750	$200	$900
4	$250	$1000	$100	$1000
	$1000		$1000	

See also MODIFIED ACCELERATED COST RECOVERY SYSTEM (MACRS).

SUNK COSTS costs already incurred in a project that cannot be changed by present or future actions. For example, if a company bought a piece of machinery five years ago, that amount of money has already been spent and cannot be recovered. It should also not affect the company's decision on whether or not to buy a new piece of machinery if the five-year old machinery has worn out.

SUNRISE INDUSTRIES figurative term for the emerging growth sectors that some believe will be the mainstays of the future economy, taking the place of declining *sunset industries.* Although the latter, including such mature industries as the automobile, steel, and other heavy manufacturing industries, will continue to be important, their lead role as employers of massive numbers of workers is expected to be superseded by the electronics and other computer-related high-technology, biotechnology, and genetic engineering sectors and by service industries.

SUNSET PROVISION condition in a law or regulation that specifies an expiration date unless reinstated by legislation. For examples a sunset provision in the TAX REFORM ACT OF 1986 prohibited tax-exempt single-family mortgage bonds after 1988.

SUNSHINE LAWS state or federal laws (also called *government in the sunshine laws)* that require most meetings of regulatory bodies to be held in public and most of their decisions and records to be disclosed. Many of these statutes were enacted in the 1970s because of concern about government abuses during the Watergate period. Most prominent is the federal Freedom of Information (FOI) Act, which makes it possible to obtain documents relating to most federal enforcement and rule-making agencies.

SUPER BOWL INDICATOR technical indicator that holds that if a team from the old American Football League pre-1970 wins the Super Bowl, the stock market will decline during the coming year. If a team from the old pre-1990 National Football League wins the Super Bowl, the stock market will end the coming year higher. The indicator has been a remarkably accurate predictor of stock market performance for many years.

SUPER DOT *see* DESIGNATED ORDER TURNAROUND (DOT).

SUPERMAJORITY AMENDMENT corporate AMENDMENT requiring that a substantial majority (usually 67% to 90%) of stockholders approve important transactions, such as mergers.

SUPER NOW ACCOUNT deregulated transaction account authorized for depository institutions in 1982. It paid interest higher than on a conventional NOW (NEGOTIABLE ORDER OF WITHDRAWAL) account but slightly lower than that on the MONEY MARKET DEPOSIT ACCOUNT (MMDA). With the deregulation of banking deposit accounts in 1986, however, banks are free to pay whatever rates they feel cost considerations and competitive conditions warrant. Although some banks continue to offer MMDA accounts which pay a slightly higher rate to compensate for the fact that checkwriting is limited to three checks a month, most banks now offer one transaction account with unlimited checkwriting.

SUPER SINKER BOND bond with long-term coupons (which might equal a 20-year-bond's yield) but with short maturity. Typically, super sinkers are HOUSING BONDS, which provide home financing. If homeowners move from their homes and prepay their mortgages, bondholders receive their principal back right away. Super sinkers may therefore have an actual life of as little as three to five years, even though their yield is about the same as bonds of much longer maturities. *See also* COUPON BOND.

SUPERVISORY ANALYST member firm research analyst who has passed a special New York Stock Exchange examination and is deemed qualified to approve publicly distributed research reports.

SUPPLEMENTAL AGREEMENT agreement that amends a previous agreement and contains additional conditions.

SUPPLEMENTAL SECURITY INCOME SOCIAL SECURITY program benefiting the blind, disabled, and indigent.

SUPPLEMENTARY FINANCING PROGRAM temporary program set up in 2008 by the Treasury department at the request of the Federal Reserve whereby the Treasury would sell special short-term "cash management bills" and put the proceeds in an account at the Fed for the purpose of financing crumbling U.S. financial institutions. The program was set up that way apparently to avoid the appearance of the Fed's printing money, although the program was reportedly being scaled back in 2009 because of fears that the Treasury would hit its $12.1 trillion debt ceiling adding to concerns about the size of the federal debt. At its peak, the program reached about $560 billion, mainly backing up commercial paper, its balance had dropped to $200 billion in 2009.

SUPPLY-SIDE ECONOMICS theory of economics contending that drastic reductions in tax rates will stimulate productive investment by corporations and wealthy individuals to the benefit of the entire society. Championed in the late 1970s by Professor Arthur Laffer *(see* LAFFER CURVE*)* and others, the theory held that MARGINAL TAX RATES had become so high (primarily as a result of big government) that major new private spending on plant, equipment, and other "engines of growth" was discouraged. Therefore, reducing the size of government, and hence its claim on earned income, would fuel economic expansion.

Supporters of the supply-side theory claimed they were vindicated in the first years of the administration of President Ronald W. Reagan, when marginal tax rates were cut just prior to a sustained economic recovery. However, members of the opposing KEYNESIAN ECONOMICS school maintained that the recovery was a classic example of "demand-side" economics—

growth was stimulated not by increasing the supply of goods, but by increasing consumer demand as disposable incomes rose. Also clashing with the supply-side theory were MONETARIST economists, who contended that the most effective way of regulating aggregate demand is for the Federal Reserve to control growth in the money supply. *See also* AGGREGATE SUPPLY.

SUPPORT LEVEL price level at which a security tends to stop falling because there is more demand than supply. Technical analysts identify support levels as prices at which a particular security or market has bottomed in the past. When a stock is falling towards its support level, these analysts say it is "testing its support," meaning that the stock should rebound as soon as it hits the support price. If the stock continues to drop through the support level, its outlook is considered very bearish. The opposite of a support level is a RESISTANCE LEVEL.

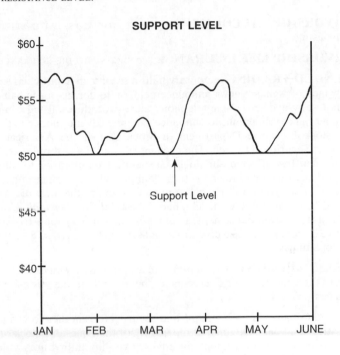

SUPPORT LEVEL

SURCHARGE charge added to a charge, cost added to a cost, or tax added to a tax. *See also* SURTAX.

SURETY individual or corporation, usually an insurance company, that guarantees the performance or faith of another. Term is also used to mean *surety bond,* which is a bond that backs the performance of the person bonded, such as a contractor, or that pays an employer if a bonded employee commits theft.

SURPLUS connotes either CAPITAL SURPLUS or EARNED SURPLUS. *See also* FEDERAL DEFICIT (SURPLUS); PAID-IN CAPITAL; RETAINED EARNINGS.

SURRENDER VALUE *see* CASH SURRENDER VALUE.

SURTAX tax applied to corporations or individuals who have earned a certain level of income. For example, the REVENUE RECONCILIATION ACT OF 1993 provided for a 10% surtax on adjusted gross incomes over $250,000.

SURVEILLANCE DEPARTMENT OF EXCHANGES division of a stock exchange that is constantly watching to detect unusual trading activity in stocks, which may be a tipoff to an illegal practice. These departments cooperate with the Securities and Exchange Commission in investigating misconduct. *See also* STOCK WATCHER.

SURVIVING SPOUSE spouse remaining alive when his or her spouse dies (in other words, the spouse who lives longer). In most states, the surviving spouse cannot be totally disinherited, but has a right to receive a share of the deceased spouse's estate, with the size of that share determined by state law.

SURVIVORSHIP ACCOUNT *see* JOINT TENANTS WITH RIGHT OF SURVIVORSHIP.

SURVIVORSHIP LIFE INSURANCE *see* SECOND-TO-DIE INSURANCE.

SUSPENDED TRADING temporary halt in trading in a particular security, in advance of a major news announcement or to correct an imbalance of orders to buy and sell. Using telephone alert procedures, listed companies with material developments to announce can give advance notice to the New York Stock Exchange Department of Stock List or the American Stock Exchange Securities Division. The exchanges can then determine if trading in the securities affected should be suspended temporarily to allow for orderly dissemination of the news to the public. Where advance notice is not possible, a *floor governor* may halt trading to stabilize the price of a security affected by a rumor or news development. Destabilizing developments might include a MERGER announcement, an unfavorable earnings report, or a major resource discovery. *See also* CIRCUIT BREAKER; DISCLOSURE; FORM 8-K; INVESTOR RELATIONS DEPARTMENT.

SUSPENSE ACCOUNT in accounting, an account used temporarily to carry receipts, disbursements, or discrepancies, pending their analysis and permanent classification.

SWAP traditionally, an exchange of one security for another to change the maturities of a bond PORTFOLIO or the quality of the issues in a stock or bond portfolio, or because investment objectives have shifted. Investors with bond portfolio losses often swap for other higher-yielding bonds to be able to increase the return on their portfolio and realize tax losses. Recent years have seen explosive growth in more complex *currency swaps,* used to link increasingly global capital markets, and in *interest-rate swaps,* used to reduce risk by synthetically matching the DURATION of assets and liabilities of financial institutions as interest rates got higher and more volatile. In a simple currency swap (swaps can be done with varying degrees of complexity), two parties sell each other a currency with a commitment to re-exchange the principal amount at the maturity of the deal. Originally done to get around the problems of exchange controls, currency swaps are widely used to tap new capital markets, in effect to borrow funds irrespective of whether the borrower requires funds within that market. The INTERNATIONAL BANK FOR RECONSTRUCTION AND DEVELOPMENT (WORLD BANK) has been an active participant in currency swaps with U.S. corporations.

An interest-rate swap is an arrangement whereby two parties (called counterparties) enter into an agreement to exchange periodic interest payments. The dollar amount the counterparties pay each other is an agreed-upon periodic interest rate multiplied by some predetermined dollar principal, called the *notational principal amount.* No principal (no notational amount) is exchanged between parties to the transaction; only interest is exchanged. In its most common and simplest variation, one party agrees to pay the other a fixed rate of interest in exchange for a floating rate. The benefit of interest-rate swaps, which can be used to synthetically extend or shorten the duration characteristics of an asset or liability, is that direct changes in the contractual characteristics of the assets or the liabilities become matters affecting only administrative, legal, and investment banking costs.

See also BOND SWAP; CREDIT DEFAULT SWAPS; SUBSTITUTION.

SWAP ORDER *see* CONTINGENT ORDER.

SWAPTION option to enter an interest rate swap. A *payer swaption* gives its purchaser the right, but not the obligation, to enter into an interest-rate swap at a preset rate within a specific period of time. The swaption buyer pays a premium to the seller for this right. A *receiver swaption* gives the purchaser the right to receive fixed payments. The seller agrees to provide the specified swap if called upon, though it is possible for him to hedge that risk with other offsetting transactions.

SWEAT EQUITY equity created in a property by the hard work of the owner. For example, a small business may be built up more on the efforts of its founders than on the capital raised to finance it.

SWEEP ACCOUNT bank or other depository account that provides for automatic overnight investment of all or a portion of idle balances. *See also* ASSET MANAGEMENT ACCOUNT.

SWEETENER feature added to a securities offering to make it more attractive to purchasers. A bond may have the sweetener of convertibility into common stock added, for instance. *See also* KICKER.

SWIFT acronym for *Society for Worldwide Interbank Financial Telecommunications,* an industry-owned cooperative supplying funds transfer messages via a dedicated computer network internationally to more than 7,000 financial institutions in 197 countries.

SWING TRADING short-term (one day to two week) trading guided by MOMENTUM INDICATORS.

SWISS OPTIONS AND FINANCIAL FUTURES EXCHANGE (SOFFEX) *see* EUREX ZURICH AG.

SWITCHING
Mutual funds: moving assets from one mutual fund to another, either within a FUND FAMILY or between different fund families. There is no charge for switching within a no-load family of mutual funds, which offer a variety of stock, bond, and money market funds. A sales charge might have to be paid when switching from one LOAD FUND to another. Customers of many discount brokerage firms can switch among fund families, sometimes at no fee and sometimes by paying a brokerage commission. Switching usually occurs at the

shareholder's initiative, as a result of changes in market conditions or investment objectives. Some investment advisers and investment advisory newsletters recommend when to switch into or out of different mutual funds. *See also* NO-LOAD FUND.

Securities: selling stocks or bonds to replace them with other stocks and bonds with better prospects for gain or higher yields. *See also* SWAP.

SWITCH ORDER *see* CONTINGENT ORDER.

SYSTEMIC RISK the risk that a sudden shock in an interlinked and interdependent financial industry will lead to a market seizure or a domino effect of failures that puts the entire financial system at risk. In testimony before Congress in July of 2009, the chairman of the Securities and Exchange Commission, Mary L. Shapiro, cited two types of systemic risk: (1) the risk of sudden, near-term systemic seizures or cascading failures and (2) the longer-term risk that our system will unintentionally favor large systemically important institutions over smaller, more nimble competitors, reducing the system's ability to innovate and adapt to change. She warned that efforts to protect the system from short-term systemic seizures could inadvertently result in long-term systemic imbalance. She urged improved regulation and market transparency, particularly with respect to over-the-counter derivatives and hedge funds as ways of reducing systemic risk. Systemic risk should not be confused with SYSTEMATIC RISK. *See also* DECOUPLING.

SYMBOL *see* STOCK SYMBOL; MUTUAL FUND SYMBOL.

SYNDICATE *see* PURCHASE GROUP.

SYNDICATE MANAGER *see* MANAGING UNDERWRITER.

SYNERGY ideal sought in corporate mergers and acquisitions that the performance of a combined enterprise will exceed that of its previously separate parts. For example, a MERGER of two oil companies, one with a superior distribution network and the other with more reserves, would have synergy and would be expected to result in higher earnings per share than previously. *See also* STRATEGIC BUYOUT.

SYNTHETIC ASSET value that is artificially created by using other assets, such as securities, in combination. For example, the simultaneous purchase of a CALL OPTION and sale of a PUT OPTION on the same stock creates *synthetic stock* having the same value, in terms of CAPITAL GAIN potential, as the underlying stock itself.

SYNTHETIC SECURITIES *see* STRUCTURED NOTE; SYNTHETIC ASSET.

SYSTEMATIC INVESTMENT PLAN plan in which investors make regular payments into a stock, bond, mutual fund, or other investment. This may be accomplished through an AUTOMATIC INVESTMENT PROGRAM, such as a salary reduction plan with an employer, a dividend reinvestment plan with a company or mutual fund, or an automatic investment plan in which a mutual fund withdraws a set amount from a bank checking or savings account on a regular basis. By investing systematically, investors are benefiting from the advantages of DOLLAR-COST AVERAGING.

SYSTEMATIC RISK that part of a security's risk that is common to all securities of the same general class (stocks and bonds) and thus cannot be eliminated by DIVERSIFICATION; also known as *market risk*. The measure of systematic risk in stocks is the BETA COEFFICIENT. *See also* NONSYSTEMATIC RISK; PORTFOLIO BETA SCORE; PORTFOLIO THEORY.

SYSTEMATIC WITHDRAWAL PLAN MUTUAL FUND option whereby the shareholder receives specified amounts at specified intervals.

T

TAC BONDS *see* TARGETED AMORTIZATION CLASS (TAC) BONDS.

TACTICAL ASSET ALLOCATION shifting percentages of portfolios among stocks, bonds, or cash, depending on the relative attractiveness of the respective markets. *See also* ASSET ALLOCATION.

TAFT-HARTLEY ACT federal law (in full, Labor Management Relations Act) enacted in 1947, which restored to management in unionized industries some of the bargaining power it had lost in prounion legislation prior to World War II. Taft-Hartley prohibited a union from
• refusing to bargain in good faith
• coercing employees to join a union
• imposing excessive or discriminatory dues and initiation fees
• forcing employers to hire union workers to perform unneeded or non-existent tasks (a practice known as *featherbedding*)
• striking to influence a bargaining unit's choice between two contesting unions (called a *jurisdictional strike*)
• engaging in secondary boycotts against businesses selling or handling non-union goods
• engaging in sympathy strikes in support of other unions
Taft-Hartley also
• imposed disclosure requirements to regulate union business dealings and uncover fraud and racketeering
• prohibited unions from directly making contributions to candidates running for federal offices
• authorized the President of the United States to postpone strikes in industries deemed essential to national economic health or national security by declaring an 80-day "cooling-off period"
• permitted states to enact right-to-work laws, which outlaw compulsory unionization.

TAIL
Insurance: interval between receipt of premium income and payment of claims. For example, REINSURANCE companies have a long tail as compared to CASUALTY INSURANCE companies.
Treasury auctions: spread in price between the lowest COMPETITIVE BID accepted by the U.S. Treasury for bills, bonds, and notes and the average bid by all those offering to buy such Treasury securities. *See also* TREASURIES.
Underwriting: decimal places following the round-dollar amount of a bid by a potential UNDERWRITER in a COMPETITIVE BID underwriting. For instance, in a bid of $97.3347 for a particular bond issue, the tail is .3347.

TAILGATING unethical practice of a broker who, after a customer has placed an order to buy or sell a certain security, places an order for the same security for his or her own account. The broker hopes to profit either because of information the customer is known or presumed to have or because the customer's purchase is of sufficient size to put pressure on the security price.

TAIWAN STOCK EXCHANGE CORPORATION (TSEC) founded in 1961 and located in Taipei. The *Taiwan Stock Exchange Capitalization Weighted Stock Index* is the oldest and most widely quoted of all TSEC indices, and is comparable to the STANDARD & POOR'S 500 INDEX in terms of its construction. In August 1985, the exchange's open trading floor was gradually replaced by a computer-aided trading system (CATS), which was eventually upgraded to a fully automated securities trading (FAST) system in 1993. The centralized market trading session is 9 A.M.-1:30 P.M., Monday through Friday. (Orders can be entered from 8:30 A.M. to 1:30 P.M.) The off-hour trading session is 2–2:30 P.M., Monday through Friday. *www.tse.com.tw/en.*

TAKE
In general:
1. profit realized from a transaction.
2. gross receipts of a lottery or gambling enterprise.
3. open to bribery, as in *being on the take.*
Law: to seize possession of property. When a debtor defaults on a debt backed by COLLATERAL, that property is taken back by the creditor.
Securities: act of accepting an OFFER price in a transaction between brokers or dealers.

TAKE A BATH to suffer a large loss on a SPECULATION or investment, as in "I took a bath on my XYZ stock when the market dropped last week."

TAKE A FLIER to speculate, that is, to buy securities with the knowledge that the investment is highly risky.

TAKE A POSITION
1. to buy stock in a company with the intent of holding for the long term or, possibly, of taking control of the company. An acquirer who takes a position of 5% or more of a company's outstanding stock must file information with the Securities and Exchange Commission, the exchange the TARGET COMPANY is listed on, and the target company itself.
2. phrase used when a broker/dealer holds stocks or bonds in inventory. A position may be either long or short. *See also* LONG POSITION; SHORT POSITION.

TAKEDOWN
1. each participating INVESTMENT BANKER'S proportionate share of the securities to be distributed in a new or a secondary offering.
2. price at which the securities are allocated to members of the UNDERWRITING GROUP, particularly in municipal offerings.
   See also UNDERWRITE.

TAKE-HOME PAY amount of salary remaining after all deductions have been taken out. Some of the most common deductions are for federal, state, and local income tax withholding; Social Security tax withholding; health care premiums, flexible spending account contributions; and contributions to salary reduction or other retirement savings plans.

TAKE OFF to rise sharply. For example, when positive news about a company's earnings is released, traders say that the stock takes off. The term is also used referring to the overall movement of stock prices, as in "When the Federal Reserve lowered interest rates, the stock market took off."

TAKE-OR-PAY CONTRACT agreement between a buyer and a seller that obligates the buyer to pay a minimum amount of money for a product or a service, even if the product or service is not delivered. These contracts are most often used in the utility industry to back bonds to finance new power plants. A take-or-pay contract stipulates that the prospective purchaser of the power will take the power from the bond issuer or, if construction is not completed, will repay bondholders the amount of their investment. Take-or-pay contracts are a common way to protect bondholders. In a precedent-setting case in 1983, however, the Washington State Supreme Court voided take-or-pay contracts that many utilities had signed to support the building of the Washington Public Power Supply System (known as WHOOPS) nuclear plants. This action caused WHOOPS to default on some of its bonds, putting a cloud over the validity of the take-or-pay concept.

TAKEOUT

Real estate finance: long-term mortgage loan made to refinance a short-term construction loan (INTERIM LOAN). *See also* STANDBY COMMITMENT.

Securities: withdrawal of cash from a brokerage account, usually after a sale and purchase has resulted in a net CREDIT BALANCE.

TAKEOVER change in the controlling interest of a corporation. A takeover may be a friendly acquisition or an unfriendly bid that the TARGET COMPANY may fight with SHARK REPELLENT techniques. A hostile takeover (aiming to replace existing management) is usually attempted through a public TENDER OFFER. Other approaches might be unsolicited merger proposals to directors, accumulations of shares in the open market, or PROXY FIGHTS that seek to install new directors. *See also* ANY-AND-ALL BID; ARBITRAGEUR; ASSET STRIPPER; BEAR HUG; BLITZKREIG TENDER OFFER; BUST-UP TAKEOVER; CRAM-DOWN DEAL; CROWN JEWELS; DAWN RAID; DEAL STOCK; FAIR-PRICE AMENDMENT; GAP OPENING; GARBATRAGE; GODFATHER OFFER; GOLDEN PARACHUTE; GOODBYE KISS; GREENMAIL; GREY KNIGHT; HIGHLY CONFIDENT LETTER; HIGHJACKING; HOSTILE TAKEOVER; IN PLAY; INSIDER TRADING; KILLER BEES; LADY MACBETH STRATEGY; LEVERAGED BUYOUT; LEVERAGED RECAPITALIZATION; LOCK-UP OPTION; MACARONI DEFENSE; MANAGEMENT BUYOUT; MATERIALITY; MERGER; PAC-MAN STRATEGY; PEOPLE PILL; POISON PILL; POISON PUT; RADAR ALERT; RAIDER; RISK ARBITRAGE; REVERSE LEVER-AGED BUYOUT; RUMORTRAGE; SAFE HARBOR; SATURDAY NIGHT SPECIAL; SCHEDULE 13D; SCORCHED EARTH POLICY; SHARK WATCHER; SHOW STOPPER; SLEEPING BEAUTY; STAGGERED BOARD OF DIRECTORS; STANDSTILL AGREEMENT; STOCK BUYBACK; STRA-TEGIC BUYOUT; SUICIDE PILL; SUPERMAJORITY AMENDMENT; TAKEOVER TARGET; TWO-TIER BID; WAR CHEST; WHITE KNIGHT; WHITEMAIL; WHITE SQUIRE; WILLIAMS ACT.

TAKEOVER ARBITRAGE *see* RISK ARBITRAGE.

TAKEOVER TARGET company that is the object of a takeover offer, whether the offer is friendly or unfriendly. In a HOSTILE TAKEOVER attempt, management tries to use various defensive strategies to repel the acquirer. In a friendly takeover situation, management cooperates with the acquirer, negotiating the best possible price, and recommends that shareholders vote to accept the final offer. *See also* TAKEOVER.

TAKING DELIVERY

In general: accepting receipt of goods from a common carrier or other shipper, usually documented by signing a bill of lading or other form of receipt.

Commodities: accepting physical delivery of a commodity under a FUTURES

CONTRACT or SPOT MARKET contract. Delivery requirements, such as the size of the contract and the necessary quality of the commodity, are established by the exchange on which the commodity is traded.

Securities: accepting receipt of stock or bond certificates that have recently been purchased or transferred from another account.

TANGIBLE ASSET any asset not meeting the definition of an INTANGIBLE ASSET, which is a nonphysical right to something presumed to represent an advantage in the marketplace, such as a trademark or patent. Thus tangible assets are clearly those having physical existence, like cash, real estate, or machinery. Yet in accounting, assets such as ACCOUNTS RECEIVABLE are considered tangible, even though they are no more physical than a license or a lease, both of which are considered intangible. In summary: if an asset has physical form it is tangible; if it doesn't, consult a list of what accountants have decided are intangible assets.

TANGIBLE COST oil and gas drilling term meaning the cost of items that can be used over a period of time, such as casings, well fittings, land, and tankage, as distinguished from intangible costs such as drilling, testing, and geologist's expenses. In the most widely used LIMITED PARTNERSHIP sharing arrangements, tangible costs are borne by the GENERAL PARTNER (manager) while intangible costs are borne by the limited partners (investors), usually to be taken as tax deductions. In the event of a dry hole, however, all costs become intangibles. *See also* INTANGIBLE COST.

TAKEUNDER offer to TAKE OVER a company at a price below the current market value of its stock. Such an offer might be attractive to shareholders when the stock is in a clear downward trend and they believe the lower price offered will be higher than the price at which they could get market orders successfully traded.

TANGIBLE COMMON EQUITY measure of capital used by banking regulators to judge the financial soundness of a bank. Tangible common equity places greater emphasis on liquid resources that a bank has at its disposal than more traditional TIER 1 AND TIER 2 capital. Tangible common equity is widely used in evaluating a bank's financial strength during a STRESS TEST.

TANGIBLE NET WORTH total ASSETS less INTANGIBLE ASSETS and total LIABILITIES; also called *net tangible assets*. Intangible assets include nonmaterial benefits such as goodwill, patents, copyrights, and trademarks.

TAPE

1. service that reports prices and size of transactions on major exchanges. Also called *composite tape* and *ticker tape* (because of the sound made by the machine that printed the tape before the process was computerized).

2. tape of Dow Jones and other news wires, usually called the BROAD TAPE. *See also* CONSOLIDATED TAPE.

TAPE IS LATE situation in which trading volume is so heavy that the consolidated tape is running more than a minute behind when the actual trades are taking place on the floor of the exchange. The tape will not run faster than 900 characters a minute because the human eye cannot take in information any faster. When trading volume is heavy and the tape is running late, some price digits will first be deleted, and then volume digits will be deleted.

TARGET COMPANY firm that has been chosen as attractive for TAKEOVER by a potential acquirer. The acquirer may buy up to 5% of the target's stock without public disclosure, but it must report all transactions and supply other information to the Securities and Exchange Commission, the exchange the target company is listed on, and the target company itself once 5% or more of the stock is acquired. *See also* TOEHOLD PURCHASE; SCHEDULE 13D; SLEEPING BEAUTY; TENDER OFFER; WILLIAMS ACT.

TARGETED AMORTIZATION CLASS (TAC) BONDS bonds offered as a tranche class of some COLLATERALIZED MORTGAGE OBLIGATIONS (CMOs). TACs are similar to PAC BONDS in that, unlike conventional CMO classes, they are based on a SINKING-FUND schedule. They differ from PAC bonds, however, in that whereas a PAC's amortization is guaranteed as long as prepayments on the underlying mortgages do not exceed certain limits, a TAC's schedule will be met at only one prepayment rate. At other prepayment rates, the TAC will experience either excesses or shortfalls. A TAC bond provides more cash flow stability than a regular CMO class but less than a PAC, and trades accordingly.

TARGET PRICE
Finance: price at which an acquirer aims to buy a company in a TAKEOVER.
Options: price of the underlying security after which a certain OPTION will become profitable to its buyer. For example, someone buying an XYZ 50 call for a PREMIUM of $200 could have a target price of 52, after which point the premium will be recouped and the CALL OPTION will result in a profit when exercised.
Stocks: price that an investor is hoping a stock he or she has just bought will rise to within a specified period of time. An investor may buy XYZ at $20, with a target price of $40 in one year's time, for instance. BROKER RECOMMENDATIONS are often accompanied by a target price predicated on research analysis.

TARGET RATE *see* FEDERAL FUNDS RATE.

TARIFF
1. federal tax on imports or exports usually imposed either to raise revenue (called a *revenue tariff*) or to protect domestic firms from import competition (called a *protective tariff*). A tariff may also be designed to correct an imbalance of payments. The money collected under tariffs is called DUTY or *customs duty.*
2. schedule of rates or charges, usually for freight.

TARP *see* TROUBLED ASSETS RELIEF PROGRAM.

TAXABLE ESTATE portion of an estate subject to the unified transfer tax of the federal government and to state taxes where applicable. The estate, not the recipients, is taxed on what remains after all expenses, contributions, transfers to a surviving spouse, debts, taxes, and losses. There is a federal EXCLUSION on property transferred by the person who died. According to the ECONOMIC GROWTH AND TAX RELIEF RECONCILIATION ACT OF 2001, the amount of assets that each person can exclude from federal taxes is $2 million from 2006 through 2008, rising to $3.5 million in 2009. In 2010, the estate tax is completely repealed, and in 2011 the estate tax law returns using 2001 rules, except that the exemption returns to $1 million. Any assets passed to beneficiaries over these limits that are not protected by TRUSTS are assessed estate taxes at a 46% rate, falling to 45% from 2007 through 2009.

TAXABLE EVENT occurrence with tax consequences. For example, if a stock or mutual fund is sold at a profit, CAPITAL GAINS TAXES may be due. Withdrawal of assets from a tax-deferred retirement account like an IRA, KEOGH, or SALARY REDUCTION PLAN is a taxable event because some or all of the proceeds may be considered TAXABLE INCOME in the year withdrawn. Proper TAX PLANNING can help taxpayers time taxable events to maximum advantage.

TAXABLE INCOME amount of income (after all allowable deductions and adjustments to income) subject to tax. On an individual's federal income tax return, taxable income is ADJUSTED GROSS INCOME (the sum of wages, salaries, dividends, interest, capital gains, business income, etc., less allowable adjustments that, in part, include INDIVIDUAL RETIREMENT ACCOUNT contributions, alimony payments, unreimbursed business expenses and CAPITAL LOSSES up to $3,000) less itemized or standard deductions and the total of personal exemptions. Once taxable income is known, the individual taxpayer finds the total income tax obligation for his or her TAX BRACKET by checking the Internal Revenue Service tax tables or by calculating the tax according to a rate schedule. TAX CREDITS reduce the tax liability dollar-for-dollar.

NET INCOME of a self-employed person (self-proprietorship) and distributions to members of a partnership are included in adjusted gross income, and hence taxable income, on an individual tax return.

Taxable income of an incorporated business, also called *net income before taxes,* consists of total revenues less cost of goods sold, selling and administrative expenses, interest, and extraordinary items.

TAXABLE MUNICIPAL BOND taxable debt obligation of a state or local government entity, an outgrowth of the TAX REFORM ACT OF 1986 (which restricted the issuance of traditional TAX-EXEMPT SECURITIES). Taxable MUNICIPAL BONDS are issued as PRIVATE PURPOSE BONDS to finance such prohibited projects as a sports stadium; as MUNICIPAL REVENUE BONDS where caps apply; or as PUBLIC PURPOSE BONDS where the 10% private use limitation has been exceeded.

TAX AND LOAN ACCOUNT account in a private-sector depository institution, held in the name of the district Federal Reserve Bank as fiscal agent of the United States, that serves as a repository for operating cash available to the U.S. Treasury. Withheld income taxes, employers' contributions to the Social Security fund, and payments for U.S. government securities routinely go into a tax and loan account.

TAX AMNESTY program by government to offer a period of amnesty to taxpayers who have not paid their taxes to come forward and volunteer to pay their back taxes without fear of prosecution. After the amnesty period expires, the state pursues the taxpayers and prosecutes them for tax fraud. This program is carried out on the state level and also on the federal level when the IRS offered a period of tax amnesty for Americans who had been hiding assets in tax havens such as Switzerland before it began to prosecute them.

TAX ANTICIPATION BILL (TAB) short-term obligation issued by the U.S. Treasury in competitive bidding at maturities ranging from 23 to 273 days. TABs typically come due within five to seven days after the quarterly due dates for corporate tax payments, but corporations can tender them at PAR value on those tax deadlines in payment of taxes without forfeiting interest income. Since 1975, TABs have been supplemented by cash management bills, due in 30 days or less, and issued in minimum $10 million blocks. These instruments, which are timed to coincide with the maturity of existing issues, provide the Treasury with additional cash management flexibility while giving large investors a safe place to park temporary funds.

TAX ANTICIPATION NOTE (TAN) short-term obligation of a state or municipal government to finance current expenditures pending receipt of expected tax payments. TAN debt evens out the cash flow and is retired once corporate and individual tax revenues are received.

TAX AUDIT audit by the INTERNAL REVENUE SERVICE (IRS), or state or local tax collecting agency, to determine if a taxpayer paid the correct amount of tax. Returns will be chosen for audits if they have suspiciously high claims for deductions or credits, or if reported income is suspiciously low, or if computer matching of income uncovers discrepancies. Audits may be done on a relatively superficial level, or in great depth. If the auditor finds a tax deficiency, the taxpayer may have to pay back-taxes, as well as interest and penalties. The taxpayer does have the right of appeal through the IRS appeals process and, if warranted, to the U.S. Tax Court and even the U.S. Supreme Court.

TAX AVOIDANCE strategy to pay the least amount of tax possible through legal means. For example, taxpayers may buy tax-free municipal bonds; shelter gains inside tax-deferred IRA, KEOGH accounts, SALARY REDUCTION PLANS or tax free ROTH IRA accounts; shift assets to children who need not pay taxes on part of their income; make legitimate charitable contributions to generate tax deductions; and establish trusts to avoid ESTATE TAXES. Illegal strategies to avoid paying taxes are called TAX EVASION.

TAX BASE total amount of taxable property, assets, and income that can be taxed within a specific jurisdiction. A town's tax base is the assessed value of the homes and apartments (minus exempted property), income from businesses, and other sources of taxable activity. If a business moves out of the town, the tax base shrinks, shifting the tax burden onto remaining homeowners and businesses.

TAX BASIS
Finance: original cost of an ASSET, less accumulated DEPRECIATION, that goes into the calculation of a gain or loss for tax purposes. Thus, a property acquired for $100,000 that has been depreciated by $40,000 has a tax basis of $60,000 assuming no other adjustments; sale of that property for $120,000 results in a taxable CAPITAL GAIN of $60,000. *See also* STEPPED-UP BASIS.
Investments: price at which a stock or bond was purchased, plus brokerage commission. The law requires that a PREMIUM paid on the purchase of an investment be amortized.

TAX BRACKET point on the income-tax rate schedules where TAXABLE INCOME falls; also called marginal tax bracket. It is expressed as a percentage applied to each additional dollar earned over the base amount for that bracket. Under a PROGRESSIVE TAX SYSTEM, increases in taxable income lead to higher marginal rates in the form of higher brackets. There are six tax brackets for individuals: 10%, 15%, 25%, 28%, 33%, and 35%. A DEDUCTION comes off the last marginal dollar earned; thus the 33% taxpayer would save $33 in taxes with each additional $100 of deductions until he worked his way back into the 28% bracket where each $100 deduction would save $28. (A deduction should not be confused with a tax credit.)

For corporations, there are six effective tax brackets. Firms with taxable incomes of $50,000 or less are subject to a 15% rate; incomes from $50,000 to $75,000 are taxed at 25%; incomes from $75,000 to $100,000 are taxed at 34%; incomes from $100,000 to $335,000 are taxed at 39%; incomes from $335,000 to $10 million are taxed at 34%; incomes from $10 million to $15 million are taxed at 35%; incomes from $15 million to $18.3 million are taxed at 38% and those with incomes over $18.3 million are taxed at 35%.

TAX COURT the United States Tax Court, a federal court whose sole jurisdiction is litigation involving individuals and the INTERNAL REVENUE SERVICE. It has locations in the different states and an Electronic (North) Courtroom in Washington, D.C. *www.ustaxcourt.gov/*.

TAX CREDIT direct, dollar-for-dollar reduction in tax liability, as distinguished from a TAX DEDUCTION, which reduces taxes only by the percentage of a taxpayer's TAX BRACKET. (A taxpayer in the 33% tax bracket would get a 33-cent benefit from each $1 deduction, for example.) In the case of a tax credit, a taxpayer owing $10,000 in tax would owe $9,000 if he took advantage of a $1,000 tax credit.

Under certain conditions, tax credits are allowed for:

1. taxpayers age 65 and older with adjusted gross incomes of less than $17,500 for a single or head of household, or $25,000 or less for married couples filing jointly.
2. earned income credit for married couples filing jointly with one child and income of $35,241 or less, with more than one child and income of $39,783 or less, and with no children and income of $14,590 or less.
3. child tax credit of $1,000 per child for those whose modified adjusted gross income is $110,000 or less for married couples filing jointly, or $75,000 or less for singles or heads of household.
4. people with disabilities, as proven by the fact that they are receiving disability income.
5. income tax paid to a foreign country (known as the foreign tax credit).
6. child care expenses up to $3,000 for one child or $6,000 for more than one child.
7. costs of adopting a child (up to $11,650).
8. a mortgage interest credit intended to help lower-income people afford home ownership.
9. a retirement savings contributions credit of up to $1,000 for a single person and $2,000 for a married couple filing jointly for making contributions to retirement plans, with adjusted gross income of up to $26,500 for a single and up to $53,000 for a couple.
10. the Hope Scholarship Credit, which can offset college tuition and related educational expenses for the first two years of post-secondary education, up to a maximum of $1,800, taken on Form 8863. This credit is available for those with modified adjusted gross income of $58,000 or less for singles and $116,000 or less for married couples filing jointly.

11. the Lifetime Learning Credit, which applies to tuition costs for undergraduates, graduates, and those improving their skills through a training program. The credit is worth up to 20% of up to $10,000 of qualified expenses, or $2,000 paid for qualified tuition and related expenses. The income limitations for the Lifetime Learning Credit are the same as those for the Hope Scholarship Credit.
12. electric vehicle credit of 10% of the cost of the car up to $2,500. Other credits are available for buying a fuel cell car, an advanced lean burn technology car, a hybrid car, and an alternative fuel motor vehicle.
13. residential energy efficient property, including solar panels, solar water heaters, and fuel cells (up to $500 for each 0.5 kilowatt of capacity).
14. health coverage credit of 65% of the premiums paid for health insurance for those who receive a pension benefit from the Pension Benefit Guaranty Corporation or Trade Adjustment Assistance. Businesses also qualify for various tax credits including:
1. making business investments.
2. rehabilitation of historic properties.
3. conducting research and development.
4. providing low-income housing.
5. providing jobs for economically disadvantaged people (the work opportunity credit and welfare-to-work credit).
6. small employers starting a pension plan.

TAX DEDUCTIBLE expense that generates a tax deduction. For individuals, some tax deductible items include charitable contributions, mortgage interest, investment interest, state, local and foreign taxes, casualty and theft losses, medical expenses, and unreimbursed business expenses. In some cases, taxpayers must meet a minimum threshold before an expense is deductible. For example, unreimbursed medical expenses are deductible if they exceed 7.5% of ADJUSTED GROSS INCOME (AGI) in a tax year, and casualty and theft losses must exceed 10% of AGI before they are deductible. In order to deduct miscellaneous expenses, they must total at least 2% of adjusted gross income. If that threshold is reached, such expenses as professional dues and subscriptions, employer-required equipment or uniforms, unreimbursed business travel and entertainment expenses, investment and tax advice, moving expenses, and some home office expenses are deductible. For businesses, the costs of doing business are generally tax deductible.

TAX DEDUCTION deductible expense that reduces taxable income for individuals or businesses. *See also* TAX DEDUCTIBLE for examples of legal tax deductions.

TAX DEFERRED term describing an investment whose accumulated earnings are free from taxation until the investor takes possession of them. For example, the holder of an INDIVIDUAL RETIREMENT ARRANGEMENT postpones paying taxes on interest, dividends, or capital appreciation if he or she waits until after age $59\frac{1}{2}$ to cash in those gains. Other examples of tax-deferred investment vehicles include KEOGH PLANS; ANNUITIES; VARIABLE LIFE INSURANCE, WHOLE LIFE INSURANCE, AND UNIVERSAL LIFE INSURANCE; STOCK PURCHASE or DIVIDEND REINVESTMENT PLANS; SIMPLE IRAS; SALARY REDUCTION PLANS and SERIES EE and SERIES HH U.S. SAVINGS BONDS.

TAX EQUITY AND FISCAL RESPONSIBILITY ACT OF 1982

(TEFRA) federal legislation to raise tax revenue, mainly through closing various loopholes and instituting tougher enforcement procedures. Among its major components:

1. penalties for noncompliance with tax laws were increased, and various steps were taken to facilitate the collection of taxes by the Internal Revenue Service (IRS).
2. ten percent of interest and dividends earned was required to be withheld from all bank and brokerage accounts and forwarded directly to the IRS. (This provision was later canceled by Congress after a major lobbying campaign to overturn it.)
3. TAX PREFERENCE ITEMS were added to the old add-on minimum tax to strengthen the ALTERNATIVE MINIMUM TAX.
4. the floor for medical expense deductions was raised from 3% to 5% of ADJUSTED GROSS INCOME (AGI).
5. casualty and theft losses were made deductible only if each loss exceeds $100 and the total excess losses exceed 10% of AGI.
6. deductions for original issue discount bonds were limited to the amount the issuer would deduct as interest if it issued bonds with a face amount equivalent to the actual proceeds and paying the market rate of interest. This amount must be reduced by the amount of the deductions for any actual interest.
7. more rapid rates for recovering costs under the ACCELERATED COST RECOVERY SYSTEM (ACRS), which had been scheduled to go into effect in 1985 and 1986, were repealed.
8. most of the rules providing for SAFE HARBOR leasing transactions authorized under ERTA were repealed.
9. excise taxes were raised to 3% on telephone use, to 16 cents a pack on cigarettes, and to 8% on airline tickets.
10. the Federal Unemployment Tax Act wage base and tax rate were increased.
11. numerous tax incentives for corporate mergers were reduced.
12. net extraction losses in foreign oil and gas operations in one country were allowed to offset net extraction income from such operations in other countries in the computation of oil and gas extraction taxes.
13. most bonds were required to be registered so that the government could ensure that bondholders are reporting interest.
14. As long as they are not prohibited by a Foreign Corrupt Practices Act, payments to foreign officials were authorized to be deducted as legitimate business expenses.
15. the basis of assets that generate tax INVESTMENT CREDITS was reduced by one-half the amount of the credit.
16. pension and profit-sharing qualified plans were curtailed with a series of new rules that restricted plan loans, required withholding on plan distributions, limited estate-tax exclusions on certain plan distributions, and restricted "top-heavy" plans, those tilted to benefit mostly the top-earning employees of a company.
17. changes were made in the way life insurance companies were taxed.

TAX-EQUIVALENT YIELD pretax yield that a taxable bond would have to pay to equal the tax-free yield of a municipal bond in an investor's tax bracket. To figure out the tax-equivalent yield, an investor must subtract his or her marginal tax bracket from 100, which results in the *tax bracket reciprocal*. This figure must then be divided by the yield of the tax-free municipal bond. The result is the yield that a taxable bond would have to pay to give the investor the same dollars in his or her pocket after all taxes were paid. For example, an investor in the 33% tax bracket would first take 33 from 100, producing 67 (the tax bracket reciprocal). To evaluate a 7% tax-free bond, the investor would divide 7% by 67, resulting in a 10.4% yield. Therefore, the investor would have to find a taxable bond paying 10.4% to end up with the same after-tax return as the 7% tax-free bond is offering. In general, the higher tax rates become, the more attractive tax-free income becomes, because it allows investors to escape more taxes than if tax rates were lower. *See also* YIELD EQUIVALENCE.

TAX EVASION illegal practice of intentionally evading taxes. Taxpayers who evade their true tax liability may underreport income, overstate deductions and exemptions, or participate in fraudulent tax shelters. If the taxpayer is caught, tax evasion is subject to criminal penalties, as well as payment of back taxes with interest, and civil penalties. Tax evasion is different from TAX AVOIDANCE, which is the legal use of the tax code to reduce tax liability.

TAX-EXEMPT free from tax liability. This status is granted to most municipal bonds, which pay interest that is totally free from federal taxes. Municipal bond interest is also usually tax-exempt to bondholders who are residents of the issuing state. However, other states may impose taxes on interest earned from out-of-state bonds. Certain organizations, such as registered charities, religious organizations, educational institutions, and nonprofit groups, also hold tax-exempt status, meaning they are exempt from federal, state, or local government taxes. Earnings on assets held for at least five years inside a ROTH IRA also accumulate tax-free, as long as they are withdrawn after the account holder reaches age 59½.

TAX-EXEMPT MONEY MARKET FUND MONEY MARKET FUND invested in short-term municipal securities that are tax-exempt and that thus distributes income tax-free to shareholders. Such funds pay lower income than taxable funds and should be evaluated on an AFTERTAX BASIS.

TAX-EXEMPT SECURITY obligation whose interest is exempt from taxation by federal, state, and/or local authorities. It is frequently called a MUNICIPAL BOND (or simply a *municipal),* even though it may have been issued by a state government or agency or by a county, town, or other political district or subdivision. The security is backed by the FULL FAITH AND CREDIT or by anticipated revenues of the issuing authority. Interest income from tax-exempt municipals is free from federal income taxation as well as from taxation in the jurisdiction where the securities have been issued. Thus, New York City obligations are TRIPLE TAX-EXEMPT to city residents whose income is taxed on the federal, state, and local levels. (A very few municipalities tax residents for their own otherwise tax-exempt issues.)

MUTUAL FUNDS that invest exclusively in tax-exempt securities confer the same tax advantages on their shareholders. However, while a fund's dividends would be entirely tax-exempt on a shareholder's federal tax return, they would be free from state income tax only in proportion to the amount of interest income derived from the taxpayer's home state, assuming no interstate reciprocity arrangements pertain.

The return to investors from a tax-exempt bond is less than that from a corporate bond, because the tax exemption provides extra compensation; the higher the TAX BRACKET of the investor, the more attractive the tax-free alternative becomes. Municipal bond yields vary according to local economic factors, the issuer's perceived ability to repay, and the security's quality RATING assigned by one of the bond-rating agencies. *See also* MORAL OBLIGATION BOND.

TAX-FREE EXCHANGE *see* 1031 TAX-FREE EXCHANGE.

TAX HAVEN country offering outside businesses and individuals an environment with little or no taxation. Several Caribbean islands, such as the Cayman Islands, have attracted billions of dollars in bank deposits by creating a tax haven. Depositors and businesses not only lower the tax burdens in their home countries, but also are subject to less regulation and increased privacy for their financial affairs.

TAX LIABILITY income, property, sales, or other taxes owed to a government entity. *See also* PROVISION FOR INCOME TAXES.

TAX LIEN statutory right obtained by a government to enforce a claim against the property of a person owing taxes until the debt is paid.

TAX LOSS CARRYBACK, CARRYFORWARD tax benefit that allows a company or individual to apply losses to reduce tax liability. A company may OFFSET the current year's NET OPERATING LOSSES against profits in the two immediately preceding years, with the earliest year first. After the carryback, it may carry forward (also called a *carryover*) net operating losses up to 20 years. By then it will presumably have regained financial health.

Individuals may carry over capital losses until they are used up for an unlimited number of years to offset capital gains. Unlike corporations, however, individuals generally cannot carry back losses to apply to prior years' tax returns. Capital losses left over beyond capital gains earned in one year can be used to reduce taxable income up to $3,000 per year.

TAXPAYER RELIEF ACT OF 1997 landmark legislation signed into law by President Clinton in August 1997 as part of a larger act designed to balance the federal budget. Some of the major provisions of the law:

1. **Tax credits for children:** Parents or grandparents supporting children under the age of 17 are allowed to claim a TAX CREDIT of $400 per child in 1998 and $500 per child in 1999 and every year thereafter. The credit can be used in addition to the existing deduction for each dependent. This tax credit is phased out for families reporting an ADJUSTED GROSS INCOME of $110,000 on a joint return, $55,000 for those married filing separately, and $75,000 for a single filer. The credit is reduced by $50 for each $1,000 of the threshold, and it disappears altogether for couples with incomes of $119,000 or more and singles with incomes of $85,000 or higher. A tax credit of $5,000 was also added for taxpayers who adopt children, with up to $6,000 for adoptions of "special needs" children.
2. **Estate tax exclusion raised:** The amount of ASSETS that individuals can exclude from estate taxes was boosted from $600,000 to $1 million, and up to $1.3 million for small businessmen and farmers. The increase in the universal estate tax exclusion is phased in over a 9-year period, with the limit rising to $625,000 in 1998, $650,000 in 1999, $675,000 in 2000 and 2001, $700,000 in 2002 and 2003, $850,000 in 2004, $950,000 in 2005, and topping out at $1 million in 2006 and later years. However, the $1.3 million limit

for farms and other small businesses went into effect fully on January 1, 1998. To qualify as a small business, an estate's business assets must represent at least 50% of its total assets. To preserve the tax break, heirs must also "materially participate" in running the business for at least five of the eight years within ten years of the owner's death. If heirs sell the business to nonfamily members within 10 years after the owner's death, they must pay some of the taxes from which they were originally exempt.

In the Tax Act, three other estate tax limits were indexed to inflation, rounded to the next lowest multiple of $10,000:

- the $1 million exemption from the generation-skipping transfer (GST) tax.
- the $750,000 maximum reduction in value on special use valuation of real property used in farming or a closely held business.
- the $1 million maximum value of a closely-held business eligible for a special 4% interest rate on estate tax installment payments.

3. **Gift tax limit indexed to inflation:** The $10,000 a year GIFT TAX limit was tied to the rate of inflation, and is adjustable in $1,000 increments starting on January 1, 1999.

4. **Lower capital gains tax rates:** The top tax rate on profits from the sale of assets like stocks, bonds, mutual funds and real estate was lowered from 28% to 20%. Before this law, those in the 15% and 28% income tax brackets paid the same tax rate on CAPITAL GAINS as on regular income. Only those in higher tax brackets benefited from the 28% capital gains tax rate cap. Under the 1997 law, those in the 28% bracket pay a maximum rate of 20%, while those in the 15% tax bracket pay a maximum of just 10% when they realize capital gains. The new rules apply to anyone selling assets after May 6, 1997, but do not apply to sales of hard assets like art, antiques, stamps, coins, gems and collectibles, for which the top capital gains tax rate remains 28%. These capital gains tax rates apply for ALTERNATIVE MINIMUM TAX (AMT) purposes as well as for regular federal taxes.

5. **New tax rate for property that received accelerated depreciation:** For those selling a business or investment real estate on which they took accelerated depreciation, the portion of the capital gain representing depreciation is eligible for a maximum tax rate of 25% if the asset is sold after May 6, 1997.

6. **Longer-term capital gains rates created:** For assets like stocks, bonds, and mutual funds purchased after January 1, 2000 and held for at least five years, the top capital gains rate was lowered to 18% for those in the 28% tax bracket or higher. The tax rate for holding assets for five years was lowered to 8% for those in the 15% tax bracket.

7. **Changed holding period for capital gains:** Previous law stated that assets had to be held for at least 12 months to qualify for long-term CAPITAL GAINS rates. Under the 1997 law, assets must be held for at least 18 months to qualify for the advantageous capital gains tax rates. Subsequently, the INTERNAL REVENUE SERVICE RESTRUCTURING AND REFORM ACT OF 1998, enacted into law in the summer of 1998, reduced the holding period back to 12 months.

8. **Expanded tax deductibility for individual retirement account contributions:** Under previous law, taxpayers could not fully deduct their contributions to INDIVIDUAL RETIREMENT ACCOUNTS if their adjusted gross income

exceeded $40,000 on a joint tax return or $25,000 for a single tax return. The law raised those income caps to $50,000 for a joint return and $30,000 for a single, starting in 1998. The caps gradually climb over ten years (by 2007) to $80,000 for a couple and $50,000 for a single. Over those limits, the deduction phases out for the next $10,000 in income. For singles, the deduction is phased out completely once income tops $40,000 in 1998, climbing to $60,000 in 2005. For married couples filing jointly, the deduction is phased out once income exceeds $60,000 in 1998, rising to $100,000 in 2007.

9. **Introduction of the Roth IRA:** A new kind of INDIVIDUAL RETIREMENT ACCOUNT was created called the ROTH IRA, which allows individuals to invest up to $2,000 in earnings a year, even after they reach age 70½. They can withdraw all the principal and earnings totally tax free after age 59½, as long as the assets have remained in the IRA for at least five years. Unlike regular IRAs, participants do not have to take distributions from a Roth IRA starting at age 70½. In fact, they do not have to take distributions at all in their lifetime if they prefer, allowing them to pass the assets in the Roth to their beneficiaries income-tax free. Contributions to Roth IRAs do not generate tax deductions.

Roth IRA rules also permit account holders to withdraw assets without the usual 10% early withdrawal penalty if they use the money for the purchase of a first home (withdrawals are limited to up to $10,000), for college expenses or if they become disabled.

Only married couples with adjusted gross incomes of $150,000 or less and singles with adjusted gross incomes of $95,000 or less can contribute the full amount to Roth IRAs. The amount they can contribute is phased out for incomes between $150,000 and $160,000 for married couples, and between $95,000 and $110,000 for singles. No contributions are allowed over those income limits.

For those with adjusted gross incomes of $100,000 or less, the law allows people to roll over existing deductible and nondeductible IRA balances into a Roth IRA without the normal 10% premature distribution penalty. When they do so, however, they must pay income tax on all previously untaxed contributions and earnings. For rollovers executed before January 1, 1999, the resulting tax bill is spread over four years. Starting in 1999, the rollover is fully taxable in the year it is completed.

10. **"Cash-out" threshold for 401(k) plans raised:** Under previous law, an employer could "cash out" any departing employee whose 401(k) balance was $3,500 or less. The employee could either take the money and pay taxes on it or roll it over into an IRA ROLLOVER ACCOUNT. The new tax law raised that limit to $5,000, meaning that more workers will be "cashed out" of their 401(k) plans than before.

11. **More investments allowed in IRAs:** Starting in 1998, IRA account holders can invest in metals such as gold, silver, platinum and palladium. Previously, such IRA investments were banned.

12. **Repeal of the "short-short" rule:** Under previous law, mutual funds lost their tax pass-through status if more than 30% of their gross income was generated from short-term investment gains under what was known as the "short-short" rule. As a result, fund managers were afraid to use trading strategies such as the use of options contracts, hedging, and short-selling that would generate short-term profits on holdings, even though

the fund manager wanted to do so for investment reasons. The tax bill repealed the "short-short" rule, freeing up managers to trade frequently without fear of losing their tax pass-through status. *See also* SHORT-SHORT RULE.

13. **Eliminated "short against the box" as a tax delay technique:** A popular way for some investors to delay paying taxes was "SELL SHORT AGAINST THE BOX." In this technique, an investor who owns a particular stock would sell borrowed shares of the stock rather than shares already owned. This tactic is similar to selling because the investor no longer owns an economic interest in the stock, but previous tax law did not treat it as a sale. Under the 1997 law, shorting against the box after June 8, 1997 is considered a "constructive sale," and will result in a CAPITAL GAINS TAX liability. In effect, this law change means it no longer makes sense to use this technique to delay paying taxes.

14. **Simplifies reporting of taxes on foreign investments:** Starting with 1998 tax-year returns, investors with holdings in foreign stocks, bonds, or mutual funds no longer need to fill out the complicated IRS Form 116 to claim the foreign tax credit. This applies to single investors who pay up to $300 a year in foreign taxes and for married couples filing jointly up to $600 a year. The amount of foreign earned income that taxpayers can exclude from taxation increases from $72,000 in 1998 to $74,000 in 1999, $76,000 in 2000, $78,000 in 2001 and $80,000 in 2002 and later years.

15. **Repeal of excess accumulation and excess distributions tax:** In earlier legislation, Congress imposed a 15% "excess accumulation tax" on LUMP SUM payouts of more than $800,000 from pension plans and a 15% "excess distributions tax" on payouts from INDIVIDUAL RETIREMENT ACCOUNTS of more than $160,000. All of these taxes were repealed for distributions made after December 31, 1996.

16. **New capital gains rules for home sales:** Under previous law, homeowners could avoid CAPITAL GAINS TAXES on the sale of their home only if they bought another home within two years and reinvested the proceeds into a home of the same or greater value. Those over age 55 could escape capital gains tax when selling their homes up to $125,000 once in their lifetime. The 1997 tax law allows people to avoid all capital gains taxes on profits up to $500,000 for married couples filing jointly and up to $250,000 for those filing singly. The rule which benefits anyone selling their home after May 6, 1997, only applies to a person's primary residence, defined as a home occupied for at least two of the five years prior to the sale. Individuals can claim the $500,000 capital gains tax exemption every two years. The old $125,000 exemption for those over 55 was superceded by the new law. In the past, someone with gains of more than $500,000 could avoid taxes by rolling the profits into a larger home. The 1997 law eliminates such a rollover. Capital gains taxes of up to 20% are due upon the sale of a home with profits over $500,000. One other twist affects real-estate investors who depreciate their property over time. When these investors sell the property, they must pay a maximum 25% capital gains tax for the part of their gain due to depreciation.

17. **Tax credits for college education:** The law created the "Hope Scholarship," a tax credit to help pay for the first two years of tuition and fees for students attending college or vocational school. The tax credit started at $1,500 in 1998 and rises to $2,000 in 2003. Starting on July 1, 1998, a yearly "Lifetime

Learning Credit" of up to $1,000 for 20% of tuition and school fees up to $5,000 is available for third- and fourth-year college students, graduate students, and people returning to school to sharpen job skills. This credit rises to 20% of $10,000, or a maximum of $2,000, in 2002. These tax credits are available only to married couples filing jointly with adjusted gross incomes of $80,000 or less, or singles with $40,000 or less. The credit is phased out for couples with incomes of $100,000 and singles earning over $50,000.

18. **Deductible education-related interest:** Starting in 1998, up to $1,000 in interest on student loans is deductible for taxpayers repaying loans for their own or a dependent's college or vocational school expenses. The interest is deductible only for the first 60 months (5 years) that the loan is outstanding. The $1,000 cap increases by $500 annually until it reaches a maximum of $2,500 in 2001. Taxpayers can get this deduction even if they don't file an itemized return. This deductible interest is fully available to married taxpayers with $60,000 or less in income if filing jointly or $40,000 or less for singles. The deduction phases out for couples with incomes between $60,000 and $75,000 and for singles with incomes between $40,000 and $55,000, and is not available for those with incomes over those thresholds. Income levels will be adjusted for inflation starting in 2003.

19. **Tax-free employer-paid education:** Employees are entitled to receive up to $5,250 per year from their employers for undergraduate classes without having to declare that money as taxable income. This rule applies to classes not directly related to their job. The tax break remains in effect for courses beginning before June 1, 2000. Reimbursement for schooling that is job-related remains tax-free without limitation.

20. **Creation of Education IRA:** A new type of account, similar to an INDI-VIDUAL RETIREMENT ACCOUNT, called the EDUCATION IRA, was created to allow parents to save up to $500 per year per child under age 18 to help pay educational expenses. The money invested does not generate a deduction when placed in the Education IRA, but the principal, income, and CAPITAL GAINS are completely tax-free when withdrawn to pay for college expenses such as tuition, fees, books and room and board. *See also* EDUCATION IRA.

21. **Tax relief for children:** In the past, children earning more than $650 a year in wages could not use their standard deduction to shelter investment income from taxes. Beginning in 1998, children can use the standard deduction to shelter both their job earnings plus up to $250 in investment income.

22. **Bigger deductions for health insurance premiums for the self-employed:** Under previous law, only a portion of health insurance premiums paid by the self-employed were deductible, while all premiums paid by larger companies were deductible. This inequity was phased out by the law. In 1997, 40% of the premium paid by the self-employed were deductible. In 1998 and 1999, it rose to 45%. In 2000 and 2001, it rises to 50%. In 2002 it is 60%. From 2003 through 2005, the deduction rises to 80%. In 2006 it is 90%. From 2007 and future years, the deduction is 100%.

23. **Creation of the Medical Savings Account (MSA):** People with high-deductible health plans may participate in a Medical Savings Account. They can deduct MSA contributions even if they do not itemize deductions. MSAs are generally available for the self-employed and small

employers with fewer than 50 workers.

24. **Social Security and Medicare taxes:** The maximum wages subject to Social Security tax (6.2%) was raised to $65,400. All wages are subject to the Medicare tax of 1.45%.

25. **Liberalization of the home office deduction:** For many years, the IRS rules and court decisions greatly restricted home office deductions. The 1997 tax law eased the rules and home office deductions are allowed starting in 1999 if the space used is essential to running or administering the business. No longer does the space have to be the only place where the taxpayer meets clients or conducts their work. However, taxpayers must use the home office space exclusively and regularly for business purposes.

26. **Higher exemption from filing quarterly estimated taxes:** Starting in 1998, the law exempts those expecting to pay less than $1,000 in taxes from having to make quarterly estimated tax payments. This doubles the previous limit of $500. In figuring estimated tax, however, taxpayers must include any expected employment taxes for household workers.

27. **Higher deduction for charitable use of your car:** The deduction for using an automobile to benefit a charity rose from 12 cents to 14 cents a mile, starting in 1998.

28. **Repeal of motorboat gas tax:** The 24.3 cent a gallon tax on diesel fuel for recreational motorboats was repealed.

29. **Paying taxes by credit card:** The bill authorized the Internal Revenue Service to accept payment of taxes by credit or debit card or electronic funds transfer, though the IRS is prohibited from paying fees to card issuers.

30. **Higher cigarette taxes:** The excise tax on cigarettes rose by 10 cents a pack to 34 cents in 2000 and by an additional 5 cents to 39 cents in 2002.

31. **Higher airline ticket taxes:** The excise tax on airline tickets rose from $6 to $12 on departures to international destinations, and a $12 per ticket fee was added on international arrivals. A $3 airport-to-airport segment tax was also added on all domestic flights. The airline ticket tax was gradually scaled back from 10% to 7.5%.

See also ECONOMIC GROWTH AND TAX RELIEF RECONCILIATION ACT OF 2001; INTERNAL REVENUE SERVICE RESTRUCTURING AND REFORM ACT OF 1998.

TAX PLANNING strategy of minimizing tax liability for an individual or company by analyzing the tax implications of various options throughout a tax year. Tax planning involves choosing a FILING STATUS, figuring out the most advantageous time to realize capital gains and losses, knowing when to accelerate deductions and postpone income or vice versa, setting up a proper estate plan to reduce estate taxes, and other legitimate tax-saving moves.

TAX PREFERENCE ITEM item specified by the tax law that a taxpayer must include when calculating the ALTERNATIVE MINIMUM TAX (AMT). Preference items include:

1. addition of personal exemptions.
2. addition of the standard deduction.
3. addition of itemized deductions claimed for state and local taxes, certain interest, most miscellaneous deductions, and part of medical expenses.
4. subtraction of any refund of state and local taxes included in gross income.

5. changes to accelerated depreciation of certain property.
6. difference between gain and loss on the sale of property reported for regular tax purposes and AMT purposes.
7. addition of certain income for incentive stock options.
8. change in passive activity loss deductions.
9. private activity bond interest.
10. addition of certain depletion that is more than the adjusted basis of the property.
11. addition of part of the deduction for certain intangible drilling costs.
12. addition of tax-exempt interest on certain private activity bonds.

Taxpayers may have to pay the alternative minimum tax if their taxable income for regular tax purposes, combined with these adjustments and tax preference items, is more than $58,000 for a married couple filing jointly, $40,250 for singles or heads of household, and $29,000 for married couples filing separately.

TAX PREPARATION SERVICES businesses that specialize in preparing tax returns. Such services may range from national tax preparation chains such as H&R Block to local tax preparers, enrolled agents, CPA accountants, and tax lawyers. Services normally charge based on the complexity of the tax return and the amount of time needed to fill it out correctly. Many services can arrange to file a tax return with the Internal Revenue Service electronically, which can result in a faster TAX REFUND.

TAX RATE percentage of tax paid on a certain level of income. The U.S. uses a system of marginal tax rates, meaning that the rates rise with taxable income. The top rate is paid only on the portion of income over the threshold. The federal government imposes six tax rates on individuals—10%, 15%, 25%, 28%, 33%, and 35%. It imposes six tax rates on corporations—15%, 25%, 34%, 35%, 38%, and 39%. *See also* TAX BRACKET.

TAX REFORM ACT OF 1976 federal legislation that tightened several provisions and benefits relating to taxation, beginning in the 1976 tax year. Among its major provisions:

1. extended the long-term CAPITAL GAINS holding period from six months to nine months in 1977 and to 12 months beginning in 1978.
2. instituted new rules on determining the TAX BASIS of inherited property.
3. set a new minimum capital gains tax on the sale of a house.
4. established, for homeowners over age 65, a once-in-a-lifetime exclusion of up to $35,000 in capital gains tax on the sale of a principal residence. (This amount was later raised by other tax bills, until it stood at $125,000 in the mid-1980s.)
5. increased the maximum net CAPITAL LOSS deduction from ordinary income on a personal income tax return to $3,000 beginning in 1978.
6. extended the period of tax loss carryforward from five years to seven; gave companies the option of carrying losses forward without having first to carry them back; and prohibited acquiring corporations from taking advantage of an acquired firm's loss carryovers unless it gave the acquired firm's stockholders continuing ownership in the combined company.
7. limited deductions for home-office expenses to cases where homes are used as principal business locations, or for meeting with clients.
8. disallowed owners who rent their vacation homes from reporting losses, deducting maintenance costs or taking depreciation on those rentals unless the owners themselves used the homes less than two weeks per

　　year, or less than 10% of total rental time.

9. instituted a deduction up to $3,000 for "indirect" moving costs if a new job is more than 35 miles from a previous job.

10. established a child-care tax credit of up to $400 for one child and up to $800 for more than one child.

11. allowed a divorced parent, if contributing at least $1200 in child support, to claim a child as a dependent deduction.

12. instituted a spousal INDIVIDUAL RETIREMENT ACCOUNT, which allowed non-working spouses to contribute up to $250.

13. disallowed losses on tax shelters financed through loans made without any obligation to pay, or where taxpayer's risk is limited by a form of guarantee, except for real estate investments.

14. treated the exercise of a STOCK OPTION as ordinary income rather than as a CAPITAL GAIN.

TAX REFORM ACT OF 1984 legislation enacted by Congress as part of the Deficit Reduction Act of 1984 to reduce the federal budget deficit. The following are highlights from the more than 100 provisions in the Act:

1. shortened the minimum holding period for assets to qualify for long-term capital gains treatment from one year to six months.

2. allowed contributions to be made to an INDIVIDUAL RETIREMENT ACCOUNT no later than April 15 after the tax year for which an IRA benefit is sought; previously the cut-off was the following October 15th.

3. allowed the Internal Revenue Service to tax the benefits of loans made on below-market, interest-free, or "gift" terms.

4. tightened INCOME AVERAGING requirements.

5. set a $150 per capita limit on the amount of INDUSTRIAL DEVELOPMENT BONDS that a state could issue in a year, and permitted interest to be tax-exempt only for certain "small issues."

6. retained the 15% minimum tax on corporate TAX PREFERENCE ITEMS as in the TAX REFORM ACT OF 1976, but increased from 15% to 20% the deduction allowed for a tax preference item.

7. restricted GOLDEN PARACHUTE payments to executives by eliminating the corporate tax deductibility of these payments and subjecting them to a nondeductible 20% excise tax.

8. required registration of TAX SHELTERS with the Internal Revenue Service and set penalties for failure to comply. Also set penalties for overvaluing assets used for depreciation in a tax shelter.

9. expanded rules in ERTA to cover additional types of stock and options transactions that make up TAX STRADDLES.

10. repealed the 30% withholding tax on interest, dividends, rents, and royalties paid to foreign investors by U.S. corporations and government agencies.

11. raised the liquor tax, reduced the cigarette tax, and extended the 3% telephone excise tax.

12. delayed to 1987 the scheduled decline in estate and gift taxes.

13. granted a specific tax exemption for many fringe benefits.

14. extended mortgage subsidy bonds through 1988.

15. required ALTERNATIVE MINIMUM TAX quarterly estimated payments.

16. changed the rules affecting taxation of life insurance companies.

17. disqualified from eligibility for long-term capital gains tax the appreciation of market discounts on newly issued ORIGINAL ISSUE DISCOUNT bonds.

18. real estate depreciation was lengthened from 15 to 18 years.
19. delayed implementation of new finance leasing rules until 1988.
20. restricted the sale of unused depreciation tax deductions by tax-exempt entities to companies that can use the deductions.
21. phased out the graduated corporate income tax on the first $100,000 of income for corporations with income over $1 million.
22. created Foreign Sales Corporations (FSCs) to provide American companies with tax deferral advantages to encourage exports.
23. limited tax breaks for luxury automobiles to a maximum writeoff of $16,000 in the first three years of ownership.
24. increased the earned income tax credit for lower-income taxpayers from 10% to a maximum of 11% of the first $5,000 of income.
25. eliminated the tax on property transfers in a divorce.
26. increased the standard automobile mileage rate from 9 cents a mile to 12 cents a mile for expenses incurred in volunteer charity work.
27. tightened rules and increased penalties for those who try to inflate deductions by overvaluing property donated to charity.

TAX REFORM ACT OF 1986 landmark federal legislation enacted that made comprehensive changes in the system of U.S. taxation. Among the law's major provisions:

Provisions Affecting Individuals
1. lowered maximum marginal tax rates from 50% to 28% beginning in 1988 and reduced the number of basic TAX BRACKETS from 15 to 2—28% and 15%. Also instituted a 5% rate surcharge for high-income taxpayers.
2. eliminated the preferential tax treatment of CAPITAL GAINS. Starting in 1988, all gains realized on asset sales were taxed at ordinary income rates, no matter how long the asset was held.
3. increased the personal exemption to $1,900 in 1987, $1,950 in 1988, and $2,000 in 1989. Phased out exemption for high-income taxpayers.
4. increased the STANDARD DEDUCTION, and indexed it to inflation starting in 1989.
5. repealed the deduction for two-earner married couples.
6. repealed income averaging for all taxpayers.
7. repealed the $100 ($200 for couples) dividend exclusion.
8. restricted the deductibility of IRA contributions.
9. mandated the phaseout of consumer interest deductibility by 1991.
10. allowed investment interest expense to be offset against investment income, dollar-for-dollar, without limitation.
11. limited unreimbursed medical expenses that could be deducted to amounts in excess of 7.5% of adjusted gross income.
12. limited the tax deductibility of interest on a first or second home mortgage to the purchase price of the house plus the cost of improvements and amounts used for medical or educational purposes.
13. repealed the deductibility of state and local sales taxes.
14. limited miscellaneous deductions to expenses exceeding 2% of adjusted gross income.
15. limited the deductibility of itemized charitable contributions.
16. strengthened the ALTERNATIVE MINIMUM TAX, and raised the rate to 21%.
17. tightened home office deductions.
18. lowered the deductibility of business entertainment and meal expenses from 100% to 80%.

19. eliminated the benefits of CLIFFORD TRUSTS and other income-shifting devices by taxing unearned income over $1,000 on gifts to children under 14 years old at the grantor's tax rate.
20. repealed the tax credit for political contributions.
21. limited the use of losses from PASSIVE activity to offsetting income from passive activity.
22. lowered the top rehabilitation tax credit from 25% to 20%.
23. made all unemployment compensation benefits taxable.
24. repealed the deduction for attending investment seminars.
25. eased the rules for exercise of INCENTIVE STOCK OPTIONS.
26. imposed new limitations on SALARY REDUCTION PLANS and SIMPLIFIED EMPLOYEE PENSION (SEP) PLANS.

Provisions Affecting Business

27. lowered the top corporate tax rate to 34% from 46%, and lowered the number of corporate tax brackets from five to three.
28. applied the ALTERNATIVE MINIMUM TAX (AMT) to corporations, and set a 20% rate.
29. repealed the investment tax credit for property placed in service after 1985.
30. altered the method of calculating DEPRECIATION.
31. limited the deductibility of charges to BAD DEBT reserves to financial institutions with less than $500 million in assets.
32. extended the research and development tax credit, but lowered the rate from 25% to 20%.
33. eliminated the deductibility of interest that banks pay to finance tax-exempt securities holdings.
34. eliminated the deductibility of GREENMAIL payments by companies warding off hostile takeover attempts.
35. restricted COMPLETED CONTRACT METHOD accounting for tax purposes.
36. limited the ability of a company acquiring more than 50% of another firm to use NET OPERATING LOSSES to offset taxes.
37. reduced the corporate DIVIDEND EXCLUSION from 85% to 80%.
38. limited cash and installment method accounting for tax purposes.
39. restricted tax-exemption on MUNICIPAL BONDS to PUBLIC PURPOSE BONDS and specified PRIVATE PURPOSE BONDS. Imposed caps on the dollar amount of permitted private purpose bonds. Limited PREREFUNDING. Made interest on certain private purpose bonds subject to the AMT.
40. amended the rules for qualifying as a REAL ESTATE INVESTMENT TRUST and the taxation of REITs.
41. set up tax rules for real estate mortgage investment conduits (REMICs).
42. changed many rules relating to taxation of foreign operations of U.S. multinational companies.
43. liberalized the requirements for employee VESTING rules in a company's qualified pension plan, and changed other rules affecting employee benefit plans.
44. enhanced benefit of SUBCHAPTER S corporation status.

TAX REFORM ACT OF 1993 *see* REVENUE RECONCILIATION ACT OF 1993.

TAX REFUND refund of overpaid taxes from the government to the taxpayer. Refunds are due when the taxpayer has been OVERWITHHOLDING, or has over-estimated income or underestimated deductions, exemptions, and credits. Though taxpayers may like the fact that they are getting a tax refund, in fact they are granting the government an interest-free loan for most of the year, which is not astute TAX PLANNING.

TAX SCHEDULES tax forms used in addition to the Form 1040 to report itemized deductions (Schedule A); dividend and interest income (Schedule B); profit or loss from business (Schedule C); capital gains and losses (Schedule D); supplemental income and loss (Schedule E); and Social Security Self-employment tax (Schedule SE).

TAX SELLING selling of securities, usually at year end, to realize losses in a PORTFOLIO, which can be used to OFFSET capital gains and thereby lower an investor's tax liability. *See also* LONG TERM GAIN; LONG TERM LOSS; SELLING SHORT AGAINST THE BOX; SHORT TERM GAIN OR LOSS; SWAP; THIRTY-DAY WASH RULE.

TAX SHELTER method used by investors to legally avoid or reduce tax liabilities. Legal shelters include those using DEPRECIATION of assets like real estate or equipment, or DEPLETION allowances for oil and gas exploration. LIMITED PARTNERSHIPS traditionally offered investors limited liability and tax benefits including "flow through" operating losses which offset income from other sources. The TAX REFORM ACT OF 1986 dealt a severe blow to such tax shelters by ruling that passive losses could only offset passive income, lengthening depreciation schedules, and extending AT RISK rules to include real estate investments. Vehicles that allow tax-deferred capital growth, such as INDIVIDUAL RETIREMENT ACCOUNTS (IRAs) and KEOGH PLANS (which also provide current tax deductions for qualified taxpayers), SALARY REDUCTION PLANS, SIMPLE IRAS, and LIFE INSURANCE, are also popular tax shelters as are tax-exempt MUNICIPAL BONDS. The ROTH IRA, created in the TAXPAYER RELIEF ACT OF 1997, allows tax free accumulation of earnings on assets held in the account for at least five years.

TAX SHIELD deductions that reduce tax liabilities. For example, mortgage interest, charitable contributions, unreimbursed business expenses, and medical expenses can be considered tax shields if a taxpayer qualifies for the deduction. The higher the marginal tax rate, the more the deduction is worth.

TAX SOFTWARE software that helps taxpayers plan for and prepare their tax returns. Software such as TurboTax and TaxCut helps taxpayers analyze their tax situation and take actions to minimize tax liability. Different versions of tax software are appropriate for large and small businesses, partnerships, individuals, and estates. The software also comes in state-specific versions to aid in preparation and planning for state taxes. When integrated with a personal finance software package, a taxpayer does not have to reenter data, which can easily be exchanged from the personal finance side into the tax preparation side of the package.

TAX STATUS ELECTION selection of filing status. Individuals may choose single, married filing jointly, married filing separately, or head of household. Businesses may elect C corporation, S corporation, limited partnership, limited liability corporation (LLC), or sole proprietorship status. Taxpayers may choose to figure their tax return under two filing status categories to find out which status is most advantageous.

TAX STRADDLE technique whereby OPTION or FUTURES CONTRACTS are used to eliminate economic risk while creating an advantageous tax position. In its most common use, an investor with a CAPITAL GAIN would take a position creating an offsetting "artificial" loss in the current tax year and postponing the gain until the next tax year. The ECONOMIC RECOVERY TAX ACT OF 1981 curtailed this practice by requiring traders to MARK TO THE MARKET at year-end and include unrealized gains in taxable income. The TAX REFORM ACT OF 1986 introduced a change whereby an exception for COVERED WRITERS of calls is denied if the taxpayer fails to hold the covered CALL OPTION for 30 days after the related stock is disposed of at a loss, if gain on the termination or disposition of the option is included in the next year.

TAX UMBRELLA tax loss carryforwards stemming from losses of a firm in past years, which shield profits earned in current and future years from taxes. *See also* TAX LOSS CARRYBACK, CARRYFORWARD.

TEAR SHEET sheet from one of a dozen loose-leaf books comprising Standard & Poor's Stock Reports, which provide essential background and financial data on several thousand companies. Brokers often tear and mail these sheets to customers (hence the name).

TEASER RATE introductory interest rate on an adjustable rate mortgage (ARM) designed to entice borrowers. The teaser rate may last for a few months, or as long as a year, before the rate returns to a market level. In a competitive mortgage market, some mortgage lenders may offer competing teaser rates to try to win over potential borrowers. In addition to the marketing rationale for teaser rates, lenders maintain that having a low initial rate makes it easier for homeowners to settle into a new home, with all the expenses entailed in moving in. Only portfolio lenders can offer teaser rates. Mortgage bankers cannot because they must comply with investor guidelines.

TECHNICAL ANALYSIS research into the demand and supply for securities, options, mutual funds, and commodities based on trading volume and price studies. Technical analysts use charts or computer programs to identify and project price trends in a market, security, fund, or futures contract. Most analysis is done for the short- or intermediate term, but some technicians also predict long-term cycles based on charts and other data. Unlike FUNDAMENTAL ANALYSIS, technical analysis is not concerned with the financial position of a company. *See also* ADVANCE/DECLINE (A/D); ASCENDING TOPS; BREAKOUT; CORRECTION; DEAD CAT BOUNCE; DESCENDING TOPS; DIP; DOUBLE BOTTOM; ELVES; FALL OUT OF BED; FLAG; FLURRY; GAP; GAP OPENING; HEAD AND SHOULDERS; HORIZONTAL PRICE MOVEMENT; MOMENTUM INDICATORS; MOVING AVERAGE; MOVING AVERAGE CONVERGENCE/DIVERGENCE (MACD); NEW HIGH/ NEW LOW; PENNANT; POINT AND FIGURE CHART; PUT-CALL RATIO; RELATIVE STRENGTH; RESISTANCE LEVEL; REVERSAL; RISING BOTTOMS; SAUCER; SELLING CLIMAX; STOCHASTICS INDEX; SUPPORT LEVEL; TRADING PATTERN; TRIANGLE; V FORMATION; VERTICAL LINE CHARTING; W FORMATION.

TECHNICAL RALLY short rise in securities or commodities futures prices within a general declining trend. Such a rally may result because investors are bargain-hunting or because analysts have noticed a particular SUPPORT LEVEL at which securities usually bounce up. Technical rallies do not last long, however, and soon after prices resume their declining pattern.

TECHNICAL RISK *see* SYSTEMATIC RISK.

TECHNICAL SIGN short-term trend that technical analysts can identify as significant in the price movement of a security or a commodity. *See also* TECHNICAL ANALYSIS.

TED SPREAD difference between interest rates on U.S. Treasury bills and Eurodollars. The term *Ted* refers to *Treasuries over Eurodollars.* Many traders in the futures markets actively trade the Ted spread, speculating that the difference between U.S. Treasuries and Eurodollars will widen or narrow. The Ted spread also is used as an indicator of confidence in the U.S. government and the general level of fear or confidence in the markets for private financing. A narrow spread indicates confidence in financial markets in general and the U.S. Government in particular. When the spread is wide, confidence is diminished. *See also* FLIGHT TO QUALITY.

TEENYO Wall Street slang for 1/16th of a point. Also called STEENTH.

TEFRA *see* TAX EQUITY AND FISCAL RESPONSIBILITY ACT OF 1982.

TEL-AVIV STOCK EXCHANGE (TASE) only stock exchange in Israel; equity trading is the primary business. The TASE trades 1,100 securities, including shares, warrants, and convertible bonds, government bonds and corporate bonds; and futures and options. Futures and options are traded on the TA 25 Index, and the shekel exchange rate vs. the U.S. dollar and Euro. The exchange trades six major indices measured by market capitalization. The TA 25 Index is comprised of the 25 largest companies traded on the exchange that account for more than 50% of the TASE's total market capitalization. The TA 100 Index, the exchange's BENCHMARK index, comprises the largest 100 shares that account for more than 60% of the exchange's total market capitalization. Weightings for the TA 75 Index, like the TA 100, are capped. Tel-Tech index reflects the performance of 50 listed companies from the electronics, computer, and life sciences sectors and publicly traded VENTURE CAPITAL funds, accounting for 10% of the TASE's total market capitalization. Tel-Tech-15 index covers the 15 largest high-tech shares. The TA Banking Index reflects the performance of the exchange's five largest commercial banks. All products are traded on the exchange's electronic TACT (Tel Aviv Continuous Trading) system, adapted from the system developed by the CHICAGO STOCK EXCHANGE. Trading is conducted Sunday through Thursday. Trading hours for equities, bonds, and Treasury bills run in four phases, from 8:30 A.M. to 5 P.M. Derivatives are traded continuously from 9:30 A.M. to 5 P.M. *www.tase.co.il.*

TELEPHONE SWITCHING process of shifting assets from one MUTUAL FUND or VARIABLE ANNUITY portfolio to another by telephone. Such a switch may be among the stock, bond, or money-market funds of a single FAMILY OF FUNDS, or it may be from a fund in one family to a fund in another. Transfers involving portfolios in annuity contracts do not trigger taxation of gains as do mutual fund switches.

TEMPORARY INVESTMENT investment designed to be held for a short period of time, typically a year or less. Some examples of temporary investments are money market mutual funds, money market deposit accounts, NOW checking accounts, Treasury bills, and short-term CDs. Investors shifting money into such investments may have sold stocks, bonds, or mutual funds, and are keeping their assets liquid while they decide which investments to buy next. They also may be fearful that securities prices are about to fall, and they want to keep their assets in temporary investments to sidestep such a downdraft. While their money is in temporary investments, it continues to earn interest at prevailing market interest rates. *See also* PARKING.

TEMPORARY LIQUIDITY GUARANTEE PROGRAM debt-guarantee program initiated by the FEDERAL DEPOSIT INSURANCE CORPORATION (FDIC) during the financial crisis of the late 2000s which allowed banks, for a fee, to issue new debt with government backing that protected investors in case of a collapse by the issuing bank. The program covered promissory notes, commercial paper, and unsecured portions of secured debt. Government officials believe that the program allowed banks access to short-term funding at a time when they would otherwise have been frozen out of the credit markets.

TENANCY AT WILL tenancy where a person holds or occupies real estate with the permission of the owner, for an unspecified term. A tenancy at will could occur when a lease is being negotiated, or under a valid oral lease or contract of sale. All the duties and obligations of a landlord-tenant relationship exist. Notice of termination is required by either party. The tenancy is not assignable.

TENANCY BY THE ENTIRETY (TBE) form of individual (versus corporate or partnership) co-ownership in which ownership passes automatically at the death of one co-owner to the surviving co-owner. The person with a TBE co-ownership interest lacks the power to freely dispose of that interest by WILL. In this respect, it is similar to JOINT TENANCY WITH RIGHT OF SURVIVORSHIP (JTWROS). Unlike JTWROS, however, the TBE ownership interests are limited to ownership by two persons who are husband and wife at the time the property is acquired. If the married couple then divorces, the form of ownership automatically changes to TENANCY IN COMMON (TIC). Generally, TBE ownership is limited to real estate, although about a dozen states permit TBE ownership of personal property.

TENANCY IN COMMON (TIC) ownership of real or personal property by two or more persons in which ownership at the death of one co-owner is part of the owner's disposable ESTATE, and does not pass to the co-owner(s). There is no limit to the number of persons who can acquire property as TIC, and those persons could be, but need not be married to each other.

TENANT
   Real Estate: (1) holder or possessor of real property; (2) lessee.
   Securities: part owner of a security.
      See also JOINT TENANTS WITH RIGHT OF SURVIVORSHIP; TENANCY IN COMMON.

TENBAGGER stock that grows in value by ten times. The term comes from baseball lingo, since a double is called a two-bagger because it earns the hitter the right to two bases, or bags. Similarly, a triple is a three-bagger and a home run a four-bagger. The term, as applied to investing, is also used in larger multiples, such as a twenty-bagger, for a stock that grows twenty-fold.

TENDER
   1. act of surrendering one's shares in a corporation in response to an offer to buy them at a set price. *See also* TENDER OFFER.

2. to submit a formal bid to buy a security, as in a U.S. Treasury bill auction. *See also* DUTCH AUCTION.

3. offer of money or goods in settlement of a prior debt or claim, as in the delivery of goods on the due date of a FUTURES CONTRACT.

4. agreed-upon medium for the settlement of financial transactions, such as U.S. currency, which is labeled "legal tender for all debts, public and private."

TENDER OFFER offer to buy shares of a corporation, usually at a PREMIUM above the shares' market price, for cash, securities, or both, often with the objective of taking control of the TARGET COMPANY. A tender offer may arise from friendly negotiations between the company and a corporate suitor or may be unsolicited and possibly unfriendly, resulting in countermeasures being taken by the target firm. The Securities and Exchange Commission requires any corporate suitor accumulating 5% or more of a target company to make disclosures to the SEC, the target company, and the relevant exchange. *See also* SCHEDULE 13D; TAKEOVER; TREASURY STOCK.

1040 EZ FORM simplified alternative to the 1040 FORM for taxpayers who (1) have single or "married filing jointly" status; (2) are under age 65; (3) are not blind; (4) claim no dependents; (5) have taxable income under $50,000; (6) have income only from salaries, wages, tips, taxable scholarship or fellowship grants, unemployment compensation and taxable interest income below $400; and (7) did not receive any advance EARNED INCOME CREDIT payments.

1040 FORM basic form issued by the INTERNAL REVENUE SERVICE for individual tax returns. *See also* TAX SCHEDULES.

10-K REPORT *see* FORM 10-K.

1099 annual statement sent to the Internal Revenue Service and to taxpayers by the payers of dividends (1099-DIV) and interest (1099-INT) and by issuers of taxable ORIGINAL ISSUE DISCOUNT securities (1099-OID).

TEN PERCENT GUIDELINE MUNICIPAL BOND analysts' guideline that funded debt over 10% of the ASSESSED VALUATION of taxable property in a municipality is excessive.

10-Q *see* FORM 10-Q.

1031 TAX-FREE EXCHANGE "like-kind" exchange of business or investment property that is free of capital gain taxation under Section 1031 of the Internal Revenue Code. Properties held for rental income, for business purposes, as investment property, or as vacation homes may be exchanged for qualifying like-kind property (a piece of land and a building can be traded because both are real estate), provided certain conditions are met: (1) the seller must identify the replacement property within 45 days after escrow on the old property and (2) the seller must take title to the new property within the earlier of 180 days of the old property's close of escrow or the seller's tax deadline. To the extent *boot,* meaning cash or additional property, is part of the exchange, the transaction is taxable.

TERM

1. period of time during which the conditions of a contract will be carried out. This may refer to the time in which loan payments must be made, or the time when interest payments will be made on a certificate of deposit or a bond. It also may refer to the length of time a life insurance policy is in force. *See also* TERM LIFE INSURANCE.

2. provision specifying the nature of an agreement or contract, as in *terms and conditions.*

3. period of time an official or board member is elected or appointed to serve. For example, Federal Reserve governors are appointed for 14-year terms.

TERM ASSET-BACKED SECURITIES LOAN FACILITY (TALF) funding facility under which the Federal Reserve Bank of New York will lend up to $200 billion on a nonrecourse basis to holders of certain AAA-rated ASSET BACKED SECURITIES (ABS) backed by newly and recently issued consumer and small business loans. On August 17, 2009, the Federal Reserve Board and the Treasury announced that to promote the flow of credit to businesses and households and to facilitate the financing of commercial properties, the TALF program would continue to provide loans against newly issued ABS and legacy commercial mortgage-backed securities (CMBS) through June 30, 2010. TARP guarantees $20 billion of TALF loans.

TERM AUCTION FACILITY temporary program instituted in December 2007 by the Federal Reserve whereby the Fed auctions a set amount of funds to depository institutions against the same wide range of collateral as it accepts for discount window loans.

TERM BONDS *see* SERIAL BOND.

TERM CERTIFICATE CERTIFICATE OF DEPOSIT with a longer-term maturity date. Such CDs can range in length from one year to ten years, though the most popular term certificates are those for one or two years. Certificate holders usually receive a fixed rate of interest, payable semiannually during the term, and are subject to costly EARLY WITHDRAWAL PENALTIES if the certificate is cashed in before the scheduled maturity.

TERMINATION BENEFIT *see* SEVERANCE PAY.

TERM LIFE INSURANCE form of life insurance, written for a specified period, that requires the policyholder to pay only for the cost of protection against death; that is, no cash value is built up as in WHOLE LIFE INSURANCE. Every time the policy is renewed, the premium is higher, since the insured is older and therefore statistically more likely to die. Term insurance is far cheaper than whole life, giving policyholders the alternative of using the savings to invest on their own.

TERM LOAN intermediate- to long-term (typically, two to ten years) secured credit granted to a company by a commercial bank, insurance company, or commercial finance company usually to finance capital equipment or provide working capital. The loan is amortized over a fixed period, sometimes ending with a BALLOON payment. Borrowers under term loan agreements are normally required to meet minimum WORKING CAPITAL and debt to net worth tests, to limit dividends, and to maintain continuity of management.

TERRITORY BOND debt instrument issued by a U.S. Territory (for instance, Guam). Interest is generally TRIPLE TAX EXEMPT in any state of the United States.

TEST

In general: examination to determine knowledge, competence, or qualifications.

Finance: criterion used to measure compliance with financial ratio requirements of indentures and other loan agreements (e.g., a current asset to current liability test or a debt to net worth test). *See also* QUICK RATIO.

Securities: term used in reference to a price movement that approaches a SUPPORT LEVEL or a RESISTANCE LEVEL established earlier by a commodity future, security, or market. A test is passed if the levels are not penetrated and is failed if prices go on to new lows or highs. Technical analysts say, for instance, that if the Dow Jones Industrials last formed a solid base at 11,000, and prices have been falling from 12,000, a period of testing is approaching. If prices rebound once the Dow hits 11,000 and go up further, the test is passed. If prices continue to drop below 11,000, however, the test is failed. *See also* TECHNICAL ANALYSIS.

TESTAMENT synonym for a WILL, a document that will dispose of property a person owns at his or her death. The testament is created by the TESTATOR or TESTATRIX, usually with the aid of an estate planning lawyer or will-writing software.

TESTAMENTARY TRUST trust created by a will, as distinguished from an INTER VIVOS TRUST created during the lifetime of the GRANTOR.

TESTATE having made and left a valid WILL; a person who dies with a will is said to die testate. A person who dies without a will is said to die INTESTATE.

TESTATOR/TESTATRIX a man/woman who has made and left a valid WILL at his/her death.

THEORETICAL FUTURES PRICE *see* FAIR VALUE.

THEORETICAL VALUE (OF A RIGHT) mathematically determined MARKET VALUE of a SUBSCRIPTION RIGHT after the offering is announced but before the stock goes EX-RIGHTS. The formula includes the current market value of the common stock, the subscription price, and the number of rights required to purchase a share of stock:

theoretical value of a right

$$= \frac{\text{market value of common stock} - \text{subscription price per share}}{\text{number of rights needed to buy 1 share} + 1}$$

Thus, if the common stock market price is $50 per share, the subscription price is $45 per share, and the subscription ratio is 4 to 1, the value of one right would be $1:

$$\frac{50 - 45}{4 + 1} = \frac{5}{5} = 1$$

THETA PRICING MODEL *see* DERIVATIVE PRICING MODELS.

THIN MARKET market in which there are few bids to buy and few offers to sell. A thin market may apply to an entire class of securities or commodities futures such as small OVER THE COUNTER stocks or the platinum market—or it may refer to a particular stock, whether exchange-listed or over-the-counter. Prices in thin markets are more volatile than in markets with great LIQUIDITY, since the few trades that take place can affect prices significantly. Institutional investors who buy and sell large blocks of stock tend to avoid thin markets, because it is difficult for them to get in or out of a POSITION without materially affecting the stock's price.

THIRD MARKET nonexchange-member broker/dealers and institutional investors trading OVER THE COUNTER in exchange-listed securities. The third market rose to importance in the 1950s when institutional investors began buying common stocks as an inflation hedge and fixed commission rates still prevailed on the exchanges. By trading large blocks with nonmember firms, they both saved commissions and avoided the unsettling effects on prices that large trades on the exchanges produced. After commission rates were deregulated in May 1975, a number of the firms active in the third market became member firms so they could deal with members as well as nonmembers. At the same time, member firms began increasingly to move large blocks of stock off the floor of the exchanges, in effect becoming participants in the third market. Before selling securities off the exchange to a nonmember, however, a member firm must satisfy all LIMIT ORDERS on the SPECIALIST'S BOOK at the same price or higher. *See also* OFF-FLOOR ORDER.

THIRD-PARTY CHECK
1. check negotiated through a bank, except one payable to the writer of the check (that is, a check written for cash). The *primary party* to a transaction is the bank on which a check is drawn. The *secondary party* is the drawer of the check against funds on deposit in the bank. The *third party* is the payee who endorses the check.
2. double-endorsed check. In this instance, the payee endorses the check by signing the back, then passes the check to a subsequent holder, who endorses it prior to cashing it. Recipients of checks with multiple endorsers are reluctant to accept them unless they can verify each endorser's signature.
3. payable-through drafts and other negotiable orders not directly serviced by the providing company. For example, a check written against a money market mutual fund is processed not by the mutual fund company but typically by a commercial bank that provides a "third-party" or "payable-through" service. Money orders, credit union share drafts, and checks drawn against a brokerage account are other examples of payable-through or third-party items.

THIRD WORLD name for the less-developed countries of Africa, Asia, and Latin America.

THIRTY-DAY VISIBLE SUPPLY total dollar volume of new MUNICIPAL BONDS carrying maturities of 13 months or more that are scheduled to reach the market within 30 days. The figure is supplied on Thursdays in the *BOND BUYER.*

THIRTY-DAY WASH RULE Internal Revenue Service rule stating that losses on a sale of stock may not be used as losses for tax purposes (that is, used to OFFSET gains) if equivalent stock is purchased within 30 days before or 30 after the date of sale.

THOMSON REUTERS established in 2008 as a worldwide provider of critical information to businesses and professionals by the merger of the Reuters Group, which dates back to 1851, and the Thomson Corporation, which traces its roots to 1934. Reuters, founded as a news and stock price information service in London, grew to include such services as financial information, text newswires, video, pictures, and graphics. Thomson, following its beginnings as a newspaper owner in Canada, expanded to become an integrated information provider in such fields as financial, legal, accounting science, and healthcare. Thomson Reuters is organized in two divisions: Markets, which includes such major brands as Lipper, First Call, Reuters Knowledge, Thomson ONE, and StreetEvents; and Professional, which includes such major brands as Westlaw, Sweet & Maxwell, Hubbard One, Checkpoint, and Web of Science. *www.thomsonreuters.com.*

THREE-PHASE DDM (DIVIDEND DISCOUNT MODEL) DIVIDEND DISCOUNT MODEL that uses a different expected dividend rate depending on whether a company is in a growth, transition, or maturity phase.

THREE STEPS AND A STUMBLE RULE rule holding that stock and bond prices will fall if the Federal Reserve raises the DISCOUNT RATE three times in a row. By raising interest rates, the Federal Reserve both raises the cost of borrowing for companies and makes alternative investments such as money market funds and CDs relatively more attractive than stocks and bonds. Many market historians have tracked this rule, and found it to be a good predictor of drops in stock and bond prices.

THRIFT INSTITUTION organization formed primarily as a depository for consumer savings, the most common varieties of which are the SAVINGS AND LOAN ASSOCIATION and the SAVINGS BANK. Traditionally, savings institutions have loaned most of their deposit funds in the residential mortgage market. Deregulation in the early 1980s expanded their range of depository services and allowed them to make commercial and consumer loans. Deregulation led to widespread abuse by savings and loans that used insured deposits to engage in speculative real estate lending. This resulted in the OFFICE OF THRIFT SUPERVISION (OTS), established in 1989 by the FINANCIAL INSTITUTIONS REFORM AND RECOVERY ACT (FIRREA), popularly known as the "bailout bill." CREDIT UNIONS are sometimes included in the thrift institution category, since their principal source of deposits is also personal savings, though they have traditionally made small consumer loans, not mortgage loans. *See also* DEPOSITORY INSTITUTIONS DEREGULATION AND MONETARY CONTROL ACT; MUTUAL ASSOCIATION; MUTUAL SAVINGS BANK.

TICK
1. upward or downward price movement in a security's trades. Technical analysts watch the tick of a stock's successive up or down moves to get a feel of the stock's trend. The term also applies to the overall market. In futures and options trading, a minimum change in price up or down.
2. market indicator representing the difference between the number of stocks whose last sale was on an up-tick and the number of stocks whose last sale was on a down-tick. A negative low tick, for example, would be a short-term technical signal of a weak market.
   See also CLOSING TICK; DOWNTICK; MINUS TICK; PLUS TICK; SHORT SALE RULE; TECHNICAL ANALYSIS; TRIN; UPTICK; ZERO-MINUS TICK; ZERO-PLUS TICK.

TICKER system that produces a running report of trading activity on the stock exchanges, called the TICKER TAPE. The name derives from machines that, in times past, printed information by punching holes in a paper tape, making an audible ticking sound as the tape was fed forth. Today's ticker tape is a computer screen and the term is used to refer both to the CONSOLIDATED TAPE, which shows the STOCK SYMBOL, latest price, and volume of trades on the exchanges, and to news ticker services. *See also* QUOTATION BOARD; TICKER TAPE.

TICKER SYMBOL *see* STOCK SYMBOL; TICKER TAPE.

TICKER TAPE device that relays the STOCK SYMBOL and the latest price and volume on securities as they are traded to investors around the world. Prior to the advent of computers, this machine had a loud printing device that made a ticking sound. Since 1975, the New York Stock Exchange and the American Stock Exchange have used a CONSOLIDATED TAPE that indicates the New York or REGIONAL STOCK EXCHANGE on which a trade originated. Other systems, known as news tickers, pass along the latest economic, financial and market news developments. See also TAPE. *See* illustration of consolidated tape, following.

MMM&P	IBM&T	XOM&C
110.50	4S100.25	2S41

Sample section of the consolidated tape.

Trades in Minnesota Mining & Manufacturing, IBM, and Exxon Mobil are shown. Letters following the ampersands in the upper line indicate the marketplace in which the trade took place. P signifies the Pacific Exchange, T the THIRD MARKET, C the Chicago Stock Exchange; no indication means the New York Stock Exchange. Other codes not illustrated are X for Philadelphia Stock Exchange, B for Boston Stock Exchange, O for other markets, including INSTINET. In the lower line, where a number precedes the letter S, a multiple of 100 shares is indicated. Thus, 100 shares of Minnesota Mining & Manufacturing were traded on the Pacific Exchange at 110.50, and so on.

TICKET short for ORDER TICKET.

TICK TEST a trading curb that permits only UPTICK and ZERO-PLUS TICK transactions in a falling market and DOWNTICK or ZERO-MINUS TICK transactions in a rising market. *See also* SHORT-SALE RULE.

TIE-IN AGREEMENT illegal investment banking practice in which investors who buy shares of an INITIAL PUBLIC OFFERING (IPO) are required to agree to buy shares in the AFTERMARKET to support the price.

TIER 1 AND TIER 2 in computing the capital adequacy of banks, Tier 1 refers to core capital, the sum of equity capital and disclosed reserves as adjusted, while Tier 2 refers to undisclosed reserves, revaluation reserves, general provisions and loan loss reserves, hybrid debt-equity instruments, and subordinated long-term debt.

TIGER acronym for Treasury Investors Growth Receipt, a form of ZERO-COUPON SECURITY first created by the brokerage firm of Merrill Lynch. TIGERs are U.S. government backed bonds that have been stripped of their COUPONS. Both the CORPUS (principal) of the bonds and the individual coupons are sold separately at a deep discount from their face value. Investors receive FACE VALUE for the TIGERs when the bonds mature but do not receive periodic interest payments. Under Internal Revenue Service rules, however, TIGER holders owe income taxes on the imputed interest they would have earned had the bond been a FULL COUPON BOND. To avoid having to pay taxes without having the benefit of the income to pay them from, most investors put TIGERs in Individual Retirement or Keogh accounts, or in other TAX DEFERRED plans. Also called TIGR.

TIGHT MARKET market in general or market for a particular security marked by active trading and narrow bid-offer price spreads. In contrast, inactive trading and wide spreads characterize a *slack market. See also* SPREAD.

TIGHT MONEY economic condition in which credit is difficult to secure, usually as the result of Federal Reserve action to restrict the MONEY SUPPLY. The opposite is *easy money. See also* MONETARY POLICY.

TIME DEPOSIT savings account or CERTIFICATE OF DEPOSIT held in a financial institution for a fixed term or with the understanding that the depositor can withdraw only by giving notice. While a bank is authorized to require 30 days' notice of withdrawal from savings accounts, passbook accounts are generally regarded as readily available funds. Certificates of deposit, on the other hand, are issued for a specified term of 30 days or more, and provide penalties for early withdrawal. Financial institutions are free to negotiate any maturity term a customer might desire on a time deposit or certificate, as long as the term is at least 30 days, and to pay interest rates as high or low as the market will bear. *See also* DEPOSITORY INSTITUTIONS DEREGULATION AND MONETARY CONTROL ACT; REGULATION Q.

TIME DRAFT DRAFT payable at a specified or determinable time in the future, as distinguished from a *sight draft,* which is payable on presentation and delivery.

TIMES FIXED CHARGES *see* FIXED-CHARGE COVERAGE.

TIME SHARING
Computers: practice of renting time on a central computer through a smaller computer, frequently through modems and phone lines. The user can upload or download files, access electronic mail, use computer programs on the central computer, and perform other tasks, for a fee based on usage.
Real estate: practice of sharing a piece of real estate, such as a condominium, apartment, or house, with other owners. Typically, a buyer will purchase a particular block of time for a vacation, such as the second week of February, during which the buyer will have exclusive use of the property. In return, the buyer must pay his share of annual maintenance charges, whether he uses the property or not. One condominium may therefore be sold to 52 different parties, each for one week per year. Time share owners have the benefit of changing their weeks with other owners around the world through one of the worldwide exchange companies. Time shares should be viewed as a

purchase of one's vacation, and not as a real estate investment.

TIMES INTEREST EARNED *see* FIXED-CHARGE COVERAGE.

TIME SPREAD OPTION strategy in which an investor buys and sells PUT OPTION and CALL OPTION contracts with the same EXERCISE PRICE but with different expiration dates. The purpose of this and other option strategies is to profit from the difference in OPTION PREMIUMS—the prices paid to buy the options. *See also* CALENDAR SPREAD; HORIZONTAL SPREAD; SPREAD.

TIME VALUE

In general: price put on the time an investor has to wait until an investment matures, as determined by calculating the PRESENT VALUE of the investment at maturity. *See also* YIELD TO MATURITY.

Options: that part of a stock option PREMIUM that reflects the time remaining on an option contract before expiration. The premium is composed of this time value and the INTRINSIC VALUE of the option.

Stocks: difference between the price at which a company is taken over and the price before the TAKEOVER occurs. For example, if XYZ Company is to be taken over at $30 a share in two months, XYZ shares might presently sell for $28.50. The $1.50 per share difference is the cost of the time value those owning XYZ must bear if they want to wait two months to get $30 a share. As the two months pass, the time value will shrink, until it disappears on the day of the takeover. The time that investors hold XYZ has a price because it could be used to invest in something else providing a higher return. *See also* OPPORTUNITY COST.

TIME-WEIGHTING OF RETURNS investment performance measurement method that eliminates distortions caused by additions and withdrawals of capital by subdividing reporting periods into smaller time frames that can be geometrically linked. Global Investment Performance Standards (GIPS) adopted February, 2005, require that TOTAL RETURNS be reported on a time-weighted basis, specifying that for periods beginning January 2005, firms use approximated rates of return that adjust for daily-weighted external cash flows. Beginning in January 1, 2010, firms must value portfolios on the date of all large external cash flows.

TIMING trying to pick the best time to make a decision. For example, MARKET TIMING involves the analysis of fundamental and technical data to decide when to buy or sell stocks, bonds, mutual funds or futures contracts. Timing is also important in making consumer decisions, such as when to make a major purchase. Consumers might want to time their purchase of real estate when prices and mortgage rates are especially attractive, or their purchase of a car when dealers are offering particularly good prices.

TIP

In general: payment over and above a formal cost or charge, ostensibly given in appreciation for extra service, to a waiter, bellhop, cabdriver, or other person engaged in service. Also called a *gratuity*.

Investments: information passed by one person to another as a basis for buy or sell action in a security. Such information is presumed to be of material value and not available to the general public. The Securities and Exchange Commission regulates the use of such information by so-called insiders, and court cases have established the liability of persons receiving and using or passing on such information (called tippees) in certain circumstances. *See also* INSIDER; INSIDE INFORMATION.

TIPS *see* TREASURY INFLATION PROTECTED SECURITIES (TIPS); TORONTO INDEX PARTICIPATION SECURITIES (TIPS).

TIPS SPREAD the difference between the nominal U.S. Treasury bond yield and the yield on TREASURY INFLATION PROTECTED SECURITIES (TIPS) having the same maturity, usually ten years. The greater the spread, the higher the expected inflation rate.

TITLE INSURANCE insurance policies, written by title insurance companies, protecting lenders against challenges to the title claim to a property. Title insurance protects a policyholder against loss from some occurrence that already has happened, such as a forged deed somewhere in the chain of title. If, for example, someone came along claiming that her parents formerly owned the house in question, and that, as beneficiary of her parents' estate, she now deserved to take possession of the property, the title insurance company would defend the present owner's title claim in court. Title insurance premiums are usually paid in one lump sum at the time the policy is issued, and the policy remains in force until the property is sold. Mortgage lenders normally require that borrowers obtain title insurance to protect the lenders' interest in the property. Property buyers also may purchase an owner's policy to protect their interest in the property.

TOEHOLD PURCHASE accumulation by an acquirer of less than 5% of the shares of a TARGET COMPANY. Once 5% is acquired, the acquirer is required to file with the Securities and Exchange Commission, the appropriate stock exchange, and the target company, explaining what is happening and what can be expected. *See also* SCHEDULE 13D; WILLIAMS ACT.

TOYKO COMMODITY EXCHANGE (TOCOM) established in 1984 through a merger of the Tokyo Textile Exchange (founded in 1951), the Tokyo Rubber Exchange (founded in 1952), and the Tokyo Gold Exchange (founded in 1982). Demutualized in 2008, TOCOM regulates trading of futures contracts and options products on all commodities in Japan. The market introduced a screen-based trading system for the precious metals market in 1991 and revamped its technology again in 2003. Products include gold futures and options, silver futures, platinum futures, palladium futures, aluminum futures, gasoline futures, kerosene futures, crude oil futures, and rubber futures. Trading of rubber is conducted on the floor starting at 9:45 A.M. An exchange official indicates a provisional price to members, who place bids. The official lowers or raises the price based on the number of orders. When the number of bids and offers becomes equal, all orders are executed at a single price. Precious metals, aluminum, and oil are traded in two sessions, from 9 A.M. to 11 A.M. and from 12:30 P.M. to 5:30 P.M. All orders for these products, which can be entered, modified, or removed from 8:30 A.M. to 9 A.M. and from 12:10 P.M. to 12:30 P.M., are matched at a single price at which they can be executed. After that, orders are continuously executed based on price and time priority. *www.tocom.or.jp*.

TOKYO FINANCIAL EXCHANGE (TFX) formerly known as the Tokyo International Financial Futures Exchange, or TIFFE. The exchange was established in 1989 to provide a financial futures market and conduct clearing services; it has since grown into a more comprehensive exchange that handles all financial products. Demutualized in 2004. Products include three-month Euroyen futures and Japanese yen-U.S. dollar currency futures. *www.tfx.co/jp/en*.

TOKYO GRAIN EXCHANGE (TGE) nonprofit membership organization trading futures and options on soybeans, Azuki Bean, corn, soybean meal, and coffee as well as raw and refined sugar products. The exchange began trading rice futures in 1730 at the Dojima Rice Market because clans asked rice traders to commercialize rice produced in their territories. In 1988 the TGE was the first Japanese exchange to convert completely to electronic trading. The exchange merged with the Tokyo Sugar Exchange in 1993, with the Hokkaido Grain Exchange in 1995, and with the Yokohama Commodity Exchange in 2006. The morning trading session for futures is from 9 A.M. to 11 A.M. and the afternoon session runs from 1 P.M. to 3:45 P.M. Trading for each session begins at the starting time, with each product trading in a slot within a particular sequence. Options also trade according to a set schedule. *www.tge.or.jp.*

TOKYO STOCK EXCHANGE (TSE) largest of six stock exchanges in Japan and one of the largest and most active global stock markets. Founded in 1878 and demutualized in 2001, the exchange is a unit of Tokyo Stock Exchange Group. TSE is a continuous, all-electronic market. Its trading floor was closed in April 1999 and renovated into TSE Arrows, a state-of-the-art market center. Trading takes place Monday through Friday in two daily sessions: 9 A.M. to 11 A.M. and 12:30 P.M. to 3 P.M. In 1998 the exchange introduced an off-hours trading system called ToSTNet to supplement its traditional trading hours. TSE listed shares settle on the third business day following the trade. TSE's principal index is the Tokyo Stock Price Index (TOPIX), a composite stock price index of all stocks listed on the TSE first section. TOPIX is supplemented by size-based indices that classify first section companies as small, medium, and large and by subindices for each of 33 industry groups. TSE's derivatives market is home to both bond and equity-based products. Japanese Government Bond (JGB) futures trading is the cornerstone of TSE's fixed-income derivatives market. The JGB futures contract is one of the most active long-term interest rate futures contracts in the world. The TOPIX futures contract, which is actively traded by institutional investors, is the leading stock index futures product in Japan, with the largest open interest among Japanese stock index futures products. TOPIX futures trading volume and open interest have grown dramatically since the mid-1990s. *www.tse.or.jp/english.*

TOKYO STOCK PRICE INDEX (TOPIX) *see* NIKKEI STOCK AVERAGE.

TOLL REVENUE BOND MUNICIPAL BOND supported by revenues from tolls paid by users of the public project built with the bond proceeds. Toll revenue bonds frequently are floated to build bridges, tunnels, and roads. *See also* REVENUE BOND.

TOMBSTONE advertisement placed in newspapers by investment bankers in a PUBLIC OFFERING of securities. It gives basic details about the issue and lists the UNDERWRITING GROUP members involved in the offering in alphabetically organized groupings according to the size of their participations. It is not "an offer to sell or a solicitation of an offer to buy," but rather it calls attention to the PROSPECTUS, sometimes called the *offering circular.* A tombstone may also be placed by an investment banking firm to announce its role in a PRIVATE PLACEMENT, corporate MERGER, or ACQUISITION; by a corporation to announce a major business or real estate deal; or by a firm in the financial community to announce a personnel development or a principal's death. *See also* MEZZANINE BRACKET.

TOM NEXT term used in foreign exchange on EURODOLLAR markets meaning that the delivery date is the next business day.

TON bond traders' jargon for $100 million.

TOO BIG TO FAIL said of an organization whose failure would pose SYSTEMIC RISK. During the months of 2008 and 2009 when government bailouts dominated the news, the phrase was used loosely to include General Motors and Chrysler, where the problem was not systemic risk but saving jobs. In its most significant sense, the phrase refers to global financial institutions, where the problem is interdependence more than size. Even there, however, the phrase lacks precision. The result of rescuing Bear Stearns and Merrill Lynch by combining them with behemoths like J. P. Morgan Chase and Bank of America, for example, was to make the latter companies even bigger and arguably more prone to failure. The too-big-to-fail issue will probably be resolved as a part of upcoming regulatory reform where the question will be at what point an organization is too big, or too complex, or too lacking in transparency to regulate.

TOP-DOWN APPROACH TO INVESTING method in which an investor first looks at trends in the general economy and next selects industries and then companies that should benefit from those trends. For example, an investor who thinks inflation will stay low might be attracted to the retailing industry, since consumers' spending power will be enhanced by low inflation. The investor then might look at Sears, Wal-Mart, Macy's, Target, and other retailers to see which company has the best earnings prospects in the near term. Or, an investor who thinks there will be rapid inflation may identify the mining industry as attractive, and then look at particular gold, copper, and other mining companies to see which would benefit most from a trend of rising prices. The opposite method is called the BOTTOM-UP APPROACH TO INVESTING.

TOPIX *see* NIKKEI STOCK AVERAGE.

TOPPING OUT term denoting a market or a security that is at the end of a period of rising prices and can now be expected to stay on a plateau or even to decline.

TOPr(S) *see* INCOME PREFERRED SECURITIES.

TORONTO INDEX PARTICIPATION SECURITIES (TIPS) UNIT INVESTMENT TRUSTS that replicate the Toronto 35 Index and trade on the TORONTO STOCK EXCHANGE. TIPS options also trade on the TSX.

TORONTO STOCK EXCHANGE (TMX) largest stock exchange in Canada, established in 1852 and listing about 4,000 companies that are traded electronically. The exchange is part of TMX Group, which includes the Montreal Exchange/Bourse de Montreal and the TMX Venture Exchange. In 1999 Canada's exchanges were reorganized along product lines, with the Toronto Stock Exchange handling trading in senior equities, TMX Venture Exchange—a merger of the Vancouver Stock Exchange and the Alberta Stock exchange—handling trading in junior equities, and the Montreal Exchange handling trading in derivatives. The TMX's BENCHMARK index is the S&P/TMX Composite Index; the exchange also offers a group of S&P/TMX Canadian sector indices for energy, information technology, financial services, consumer discretionary, consumer staples, industrials, telecommunications services, utilities, health care, materials, gold, diversified metals and mining, and real estate. Trading hours are 9:30 A.M. to 4 P.M., Monday through Friday. Settlement is the third day following the trade. *www.tsx.com*.

TOTAL CAPITALIZATION CAPITAL STRUCTURE of a company, including LONG-TERM DEBT and all forms of EQUITY.

TOTAL COST
Accounting: (usually pl.) sum of FIXED COSTS, semivariable costs, and VARIABLE COSTS.
Investments: contract price paid for a security plus the brokerage commission plus any ACCRUED INTEREST due the seller (if the security is a bond). The figure is not to be confused with the COST BASIS for the purpose of figuring the CAPITAL GAINS TAX, which may involve other factors such as amortization of bond premiums.

TOTAL DISABILITY injury or illness that is so serious that it prevents a worker from performing any functions for which he or she is educated and trained. Workers with total disability may qualify for DISABILITY INCOME INSURANCE, either though a private employer's plan or through Social Security's disability insurance program. There is normally a waiting period before disability insurance payments begin, to determine if the disability is long-term. Waiting periods vary, from a month to several months, and are determined by the plan and premium structure of the employer.

TOTAL RETURN annual return on an investment including appreciation, dividends, or interest, and other distributions. For bonds held to maturity, total return is YIELD TO MATURITY. For stocks, future appreciation is projected using the current PRICE/EARNINGS RATIO. In options trading, total return means dividends plus capital gains plus premium income.

TOTAL VOLUME total number of shares or contracts traded in a stock, bond, commodity future, or option on a particular day. For stocks and bonds, this is the aggregate of trades on national exchanges like the New York and American stock exchanges and on regional exchanges. For commodities futures and options, it represents the volume of trades executed around the world in one day. For over-the-counter securities, total volume is measured by the NASDAQ index.

TOTTEN TRUST a trust whose assets are designated for a beneficiary but the grantor retains control, including the right to reclaim the assets. When the grantor dies, the assets pass to the beneficiary but not until the assets have been taxed as part of the grantor's estate.

TOUT to promote a particular security aggressively, usually done by a corporate spokesman, public relations firm, broker, or analyst with a vested interest in promoting the stock. Touting a stock is unethical if it misleads investors. *See also* INVESTMENT ADVISERS ACT; INVESTOR RELATIONS DEPARTMENT.

TOXIC ASSETS nontechnical term that supplanted the less dramatic and urgent designation "troubled assets" used during 2007 and 2008 to describe mortgage-related loans and investments that had lost most if not all value in a market that was virtually not functioning. Carried on the books of banks and other financial institutions on a MARK-TO-MARKET basis, they were "poisoning" balance sheets and causing a wave of insolvencies. TARP was initially going to buy the toxic assets from the affected banks directly, but revised its approach in favor of infusing capital. In a later action, the FASB suspended mark-to-market accounting rules.

T-PLUS-THREE *see* DELIVERY DATE.

TRACKING also called *portfolio tracking*, monitoring the performance of a portfolio, usually to analyze the extent to which its price movements conform or deviate from those of a BENCHMARK. In an INDEXING strategy, it would be done by determining the STANDARD DEVIATION between the index and the portfolio designed to replicate it. There should be no deviation, so any significant dispersion would comprise a TRACKING ERROR.

TRACKING RISK the discrepancy between the actual performance of a security or index and the performance of the product TRACKING it.

TRACKING STOCK
1. category of common stock that pays a dividend based on the operating performance of a particular corporate segment. Tracking stock, which is sometimes informally called "designer stock," exists alongside the issuer's regular common shares, but, unlike the latter, usually has limited or no voting power and does not represent a legal claim on assets of the corporation. When identified with a letter, the stock is also called ALPHABET STOCK, but differs from CLASSIFIED STOCK.
2. a stock that has a high CORRELATION COEFFICIENT relative to another stock and can be used as a substitute in a HEDGING strategy.
3. *See* INDEX SHARES.

TRADE
In general:
1. buying or selling of goods and services among companies, states, or countries, called *commerce*. The amount of goods and services imported minus the amount exported makes up a country's BALANCE OF TRADE. *See also* TARIFF; TRADE DEFICIT.
2. those in the business of selling products are called *members of the trade*. As such, they receive DISCOUNTS from the price the public has to pay.
3. group of manufacturers who compete in the same market. These companies form trade associations and publish trade journals.
4. commercial companies that do business with each other. For example, ACCOUNTS PAYABLE to suppliers are called *trade accounts payable;* the term TRADE CREDIT is used to describe accounts payable as a source of WORKING CAPITAL financing. Companies paying their bills promptly receive *trade discounts* when available.
5. synonymous with BARTER, the exchange of goods and services without the use of money.
Securities: to carry out a transaction of buying or selling a stock, a bond, or a commodity future contract. A trade is consummated when a buyer and seller agree on a price at which the trade will be executed. A TRADER frequently buys and sells for his or her own account securities for short-term profits, as contrasted with an investor who holds his positions in hopes of long-term gains.

TRADE ASSOCIATION organization, usually a not-for-profit corporation, that is comprised of and supported by members engaged in a particular type of business and thus having common interests. Trade associations typically engage in advocacy activities, legislative and congressional lobbying, public and membership information services, research and education, and other functions promoting the interests of the particular industry group.

TRADE BALANCE *see* BALANCE OF TRADE.

TRADE BUST cancellation of a trade on an electronic exchange because the price, due to an error, was outside of normal ranges.

TRADE CREDIT open account arrangements with suppliers of goods and services, and a firm's record of payment with the suppliers. Trade liabilities comprise a company's ACCOUNTS PAYABLE. DUN & BRADSTREET is the largest compiler of trade credit information, rating commercial firms and supplying published reports. Trade credit data is also processed by MERCANTILE AGENCIES specializing in different industries.

Trade credit is an important external source of WORKING CAPITAL for a company, although such credit can be highly expensive. Terms of 2% 10 days, net 30 days (2% discount if paid in 10 days, the net [full] amount due in 30 days) translate into a 36% annual interest rate if not taken advantage of. On the other hand, the same terms translate into a borrowing rate of slightly over 15% if payment is made in 60 days instead of 30.

TRADE DATE day on which a security or a commodity future trade actually takes place. The SETTLEMENT DATE usually follows the trade date by three business days but varies depending on the transaction and method of delivery used. *See also* DELAYED DELIVERY; DELIVERY DATE; REGULAR-WAY DELIVERY (AND SETTLEMENT); SELLER'S OPTION.

TRADE DEFICIT OR SURPLUS excess of imports over exports *(trade deficit)* or of exports over imports *(trade surplus)*, resulting in a negative or positive BALANCE OF TRADE. The balance of trade is made up of transactions in merchandise and other movable goods and is only one factor comprising the larger *current account* (which includes services and tourism, transportation, and other *invisible items,* such as interest and profits earned abroad) in the overall BALANCE OF PAYMENTS. Factors influencing a country's balance of trade include the strength or weakness of its currency in relation to those of the countries with which it trades (a strong U.S. dollar, for example, makes goods produced in other countries relatively cheap for Americans), production advantages in key manufacturing areas (Japanese automobiles, for instance), or the domestic economy of a trading country where production may or may not be meeting demand.

TRADEMARK distinctive name, symbol, motto, or emblem that identifies a product, service, or firm. In the United States, trademark rights—the right to prevent competitors from using similar marks in selling or advertising—arise out of use; that is, registration is not essential to establish the legal existence of a mark. A trademark registered with the U.S. Patent and Trademark Office is good for 10 years, renewable as long as used. Products may be both patented and protected by trademark, the advantage being that when the patent runs out, exclusivity can be continued indefinitely with the trademark. A trademark is classified on a BALANCE SHEET as an INTANGIBLE ASSET.

Although, like land, trademarks have an indefinite life and cannot tech-

nically be amortized, in practice accountants do amortize trademarks over
their estimated life, not to exceed 40 years.

TRADER
In general: anyone who buys and sells goods or services for profit; a DEALER
or *merchant. See also* BARTER; TRADE.

Investments:
1. individual who buys and sells securities, such as STOCKS, BONDS, OPTIONS,
   or commodities, such as wheat, gold, or FOREIGN EXCHANGE, for his or her
   own account—that is, as a dealer or PRINCIPAL—rather than as a BROKER
   or AGENT.
2. individual who buys and sells securities or commodities for his or her own
   account on a short-term basis in anticipation of quick profits; a *speculator.
   See also* DAY TRADE; COMPETITIVE TRADER; FLOOR TRADER; REGISTERED COM-
   PETITIVE MARKET MAKER; REGISTERED COMPETITIVE TRADER; SPECULATION.

TRADE-THROUGH RULE New York Stock Exchange rule instituted in
1975 and extended to NASDAQ in 2005. Requires that trades, with few exceptions, be sent to whatever market has the best available price for immediate
execution electronically. Also known as Order Protection Rule. With this
rule, no exchange or broker can trade through—execute an order at a price
inferior to—a protected quote, wherever that quote resides.

TRADING AHEAD *see* NEGATIVE OBLIGATION.

TRADING AUTHORIZATION document giving a brokerage firm
employee acting as AGENT (BROKER) the POWER OF ATTORNEY in buy-sell transactions for a customer.

TRADING CURB *see* SUSPENDED TRADING.

TRADING DIVIDENDS technique of buying and selling stocks in other
firms by a corporation in order to maximize the number of DIVIDENDS it can
collect. This action is advantageous, because 80% of the dividend income it
receives from the stocks of other companies is not taxed, according to Internal Revenue Service regulations. *See also* DIVIDEND EXCLUSION.

TRADING HALT *see* SUSPENDED TRADING.

TRADING LIMIT *see* DAILY TRADING LIMIT; LIMIT UP, LIMIT DOWN.

TRADING PATTERN long-range direction of a security or commodity
future price. This pattern is charted by drawing a line connecting the highest
prices the security has reached and another line connecting the lowest prices
the security has traded at over the same time frame. These two lines will be
pointing either up or down, indicating the security's long-term trading
pattern. *See also* TECHNICAL ANALYSIS, TRENDLINE. See illustration next page.

TRADING POST physical location on a stock exchange floor where particu-
lar securities are bought and sold. It is here that the SPECIALIST in a particular
security performs his market-making functions and that the CROWD (floor
brokers with orders in that security) congregates. The New York Stock
Exchange, for example, has 17 trading posts. *See also* FLOOR BROKER; FLOOR
TRADER; MAKE A MARKET.

TRADING PROFIT profit earned based on short-term trades. For assets
such as stocks, bonds, futures contracts, and mutual funds held under a year,
such trading profits are taxed at regular income tax rates. In general com-

merce, *trading profit* refers to the difference between what a product is sold for by a retailer and what it costs to buy or produce at the wholesale or producer level.

TRADING RANGE

Commodities: trading limit set by a COMMODITIES futures exchange for a particular commodity. The price of a commodity future contract may not go higher or lower than that limit during one day's trading. *See also* LIMIT UP, LIMIT DOWN.

Securities: range between the highest and lowest prices at which a security or a market has traded. The trading range for XYZ Corporation might be $40 to $60 over the last two years, for example. If a security or a market seems to be stuck in a narrow price range, analysts say that it is a trading range market, which will eventually be followed by a significant up or down move. *See also* FLAG; PENNANT; TRIANGLE; WEDGE.

TRADING SESSION the hours an exchange or formal market is open for business. For example, a trading session at the NEW YORK STOCK EXCHANGE begins with the opening BELL at 9:30 A.M. EST and ends with the closing bell at 4 P.M. EST on a trading day.

TRADING UNIT number of SHARES, BONDS, or other securities that is generally accepted for ordinary trading purposes on the exchanges. *See also* ODD LOT; ROUND LOT; UNIT OF TRADING.

TRAILING historical as opposed to projected, usually referring to performance statistics measured in periods of a year. A trailing PRICE/EARNINGS RATIO (P/E), for example, would be the current price divided by the prior year's earnings, whereas a *forward P/E* would cover the projected 12-month period. In the case of a *trailing* STOP ORDER, the STOP PRICE is set at a fixed percentage below the market price and trails it; that is, it increases as the market price increases. It does not decrease, however, so if the market price drops and meets it, the STOP LOSS order is activated.

TRADING PATTERN

TRAILING STOP LOSS *see* TRAILING.

TRANCH CD *see* TRANCHES.

TRANCHES
1. risk, maturity, or other classes into which a multi-class security, such as a COLLATERALIZED MORTGAGE OBLIGATION (CMO) or a REMIC is split. For example, the typical CMO has A, B, C, and Z tranches, representing fast pay, medium pay, and slow pay bonds plus an issue (tranch) that bears no coupon but receives the cash flow from the collateral remaining after the other tranches are satisfied. More sophisticated CMO versions have multiple Z tranches and a Y tranch incorporating a sinking fund schedule.
2. in the United Kingdom, fixed-rate security issues are often prearranged by governments, local authorities, or corporations, then brought out in successive rounds, termed tranches. One thus speaks of new tranches of existing securities. A variation of the term, *tranchettes,* refers to small tranches of gilt-edged securities (government bonds) sold by the government to the Bank of England, which then sells them into the market at times it deems appropriate.
3. subunits of a large ($10–$30 million) Eurodollar certificate of deposit that are marketed to smaller investors in $10,000 denominations. Tranches are represented by separate certificates and have the same interest rate, issue date, interest payment date, and maturity of the original instrument, which is called a *tranch CD*.

TRANCHETTES *see* TRANCHES.

TRANSACTION
Accounting: event or condition recognized by an entry in the books of account.
Securities: execution of an order to buy or sell a security or commodity futures contract. After the buyer and seller have agreed on a price, the seller is obligated to deliver the security or commodity involved, and the buyer is obligated to accept it. *See also* TRADE.

TRANSACTION COSTS cost of buying or selling a security, which consists mainly of the *brokerage commission,* the dealer MARKDOWN or markup, or fee (as would be charged by a bank or broker-dealer to transact Treasuries, for example) but also includes direct taxes, such as the SEC FEE, any state-imposed TRANSFER TAXES, or other direct taxes.

TRANSACTION RISK (or EXPOSURE) the risk that changes in EXCHANGE RATES during the time it takes to settle a CROSS-BORDER contract will adversely affect the profit of a party to the transaction. Currency SWAPS and CURRENCY FUTURES are designed to reduce transaction risk. *See also* FOREIGN EXCHANGE.

TRANSFER exchange of ownership of property from one party to another. For example, a piece of real estate may be transferred from seller to buyer through the execution of a sales contract. Securities and mutual funds are typically transferred through a transfer agent, who electronically switches ownership of the securities. In banking, *transfer* refers to the movement of funds from one account to another, such as from a passbook account to a checking account.

TRANSFER AGENT agent, usually a commercial bank, appointed by a corporation, to maintain records of stock and bond owners, to cancel and issue certificates, and to resolve problems arising from lost, destroyed, or stolen certificates. (Preventing OVERISSUE of shares is the function of the REGISTRAR.) A corporation may also serve as its own transfer agent.

TRANSFER PAYMENTS money transferred to people from the government. Many payments under government benefit programs are considered transfer payments, including Social Security, disability payments, unemployment compensation, welfare, and veterans' benefits. A large portion of the federal government's yearly budget goes to make transfer payments.

TRANSFER PRICE price charged by individual entities in a multi-entity corporation on transactions among themselves; also termed *transfer cost.* This concept is used where each entity is managed as a PROFIT CENTER—that is, held responsible for its own RETURN ON INVESTED CAPITAL—and must therefore deal with the other internal parts of the corporation on an arm's-length (or market) basis. *See also* ARM'S LENGTH TRANSACTION.

TRANSFER TAX
1. combined federal tax on gifts and estates. *See* ESTATE TAX; GIFT TAX.
2. federal tax on the sale of all bonds (except obligations of the United States, foreign governments, states, and municipalities) and all stocks. The tax is paid by the seller at the time ownership is transferred and involves a few pennies per $100 of value.
3. tax levied by some state and local governments on the transfer of such documents as deeds to property, securities, or licenses. Such taxes are paid, usually with stamps, by the seller or donor and are determined by the location of the transfer agent. States with transfer taxes on stock transactions include New York, Florida, South Carolina, and Texas. New York bases its tax on selling price; the other states apply the tax to PAR value (giving NO-PAR-VALUE STOCK a value of $100). Bonds are not taxed at the state level.

TRANSMITTAL LETTER letter sent with a document, security, or shipment describing the contents and the purpose of the transaction.

TRANSPARENCY in financial reporting, ease of understanding, made possible by the full, clear, and timely disclosure of relevant information. In securities transactions, *price transparency* means access to information concerning the DEPTH OF THE MARKET that would enable detection of fraud or manipulation.

TRAVEL AND ENTERTAINMENT ACCOUNT separate account set up by an employer to track and reimburse employees' travel and entertainment expenses. Many employers give special credit cards to employees so that all travel and entertainment expenses can be tracked separately from personal expenses. Employers need to track travel and entertainment expenses carefully if they are to claim the appropriate tax deductions for these business expenses.

TRAVEL AND ENTERTAINMENT EXPENSE expense for travel and entertainment that may qualify for a tax deduction. Under current tax law, employers may deduct 50% of legitimate travel and entertainment expenses. Expenses are deductible if they are directly related to business. For example, a business meal must include a discussion that produces a direct business benefit.

TRAVELER'S CHECK check issued by a financial institution such as American Express, Visa, or Mastercard that allows travelers to carry travel funds in a more convenient way than cash. The traveler buys the checks, often for a nominal fee, with cash, a credit card, or a regular check at a bank or travel service office and then signs each traveler's check. The check can then be used virtually anywhere in the world once it has been countersigned with the same signature. The advantage to the traveler is that the traveler's check cannot be used by someone else if it is lost or stolen, and can be replaced usually anywhere in the world. Traveler's checks are also issued in many foreign currencies, allowing a traveler to lock in at a particular exchange rate before the trip begins. Many issuers of traveler's checks offer a type of check that enables two travelers to share the same travel funds. American Express was the first issuer to introduce this form of check. Institutions issuing traveler's checks profit from the FLOAT, earning interest on the money from the time the customer buys the check to the time they use the check.

TREASURER company officer responsible for the receipt, custody, investment, and disbursement of funds, for borrowings, and, if it is a public company, for the maintenance of a market for its securities. Depending on the size of the organization, the treasurer may also function as the CONTROLLER, with accounting and audit responsibilities. The laws of many states require that a corporation have a treasurer. *See also* CHIEF FINANCIAL OFFICER (CFO).

TREASURIES NEGOTIABLE debt obligations of the U.S. government, secured by its FULL FAITH AND CREDIT and issued at various schedules and maturities. The income from Treasury securities is exempt from state and local, but not federal, taxes.

1. *Treasury bills*—short-term securities with maturities of one year or less issued at a discount from FACE VALUE. Auctions of 91-day and 182-day BILLS take place weekly, and the yields are watched closely in the money markets for signs of interest rate trends. Many floating rate loans and variable-rate mortgages have interest rates tied to these bills. The Treasury also auctions 52-week bills once every four weeks. At times it also issues very short-term cash management bills, TAX ANTICIPATION BILLS, and treasury *certificates of indebtedness*. Treasury bills are issued in minimum denominations of $10,000, with $5,000 increments above $10,000 (except for cash management bills, which are sold in minimum $10 million blocks). Individual investors who do not submit a COMPETITIVE BID are sold bills at the average price of the winning competitive bids. Treasury bills are the primary instrument used by the Federal Reserve in its regulation of MONEY SUPPLY through OPEN MARKET OPERATIONS. *See also* DUTCH AUCTION-REPURCHASE AGREEMENT.

2. *Treasury bonds*—long-term debt instruments with maturities of 10 years or longer issued in minimum denominations of $1,000.

3. *Treasury notes*—intermediate securities with maturities of 1 to 10 years. Denominations range from $1,000 to $1 million or more. The notes are sold by cash subscription, in exchange for outstanding or maturing government issues, or at auction.

TREASURY BILL *see* BILL; TREASURIES.

TREASURY BOND *see* TREASURIES.

TREASURY DIRECT system through which an individual investor can make a NONCOMPETITIVE BID on U.S. Treasury securities (TREASURIES), thus bypassing middlemen like banks or broker-dealers and avoiding their fees.

The system works through FEDERAL RESERVE BANKS and branches, and the minimum purchase is $1,000. *www.publicdebt.treas.gov*

TREASURY INFLATION PROTECTED SECURITIES (TIPS) United States Treasury securities issued at a fixed rate of interest but with principal adjusted every six months based on changes in the CONSUMER PRICE INDEX. At maturity, TIPS, which are issued in January and July as 10-year and 30-year notes, and in October as 30-year bonds, are redeemable either at their inflation-adjusted principal or their face value, whichever is greater. TIPS sacrifice some yield as a tradeoff for the inflation protection and the inflation adjustment is federally taxable annually, although not paid out until maturity. *See also* I-BONDS; INFLATION-INDEXED SECURITIES.

TREASURY STOCK stock reacquired by the issuing company and available for RETIREMENT or resale. It is issued but not outstanding. It cannot be voted and it pays or accrues no dividends. It is not included in any of the ratios measuring values per common share. Among the reasons treasury stock is created are (1) to provide an alternative to paying taxable dividends, since the decreased amount of outstanding shares increases the per share value and often the market price; (2) to provide for the exercise of stock options and warrants and the conversion of convertible securities; (3) in countering a TENDER OFFER by a potential acquirer; (4) to alter the DEBT-TO-EQUITY RATIO by issuing bonds to finance the reacquisition of shares; (5) as a result of the STABILIZATION of the market price during a NEW ISSUE. Also called *reacquired stock* and *treasury shares*. *See also* ISSUED AND OUTSTANDING; UNISSUED STOCK.

TREND
In general: any general direction of movement. For example: "There is an upward (downward, level) trend in XYZ sales," or "There is a trend toward increased computerization of trading on Wall Street."
Securities: long-term price or trading volume movements either up, down, or sideways, which characterize a particular market, commodity or security. Also applies to interest rates and yields.

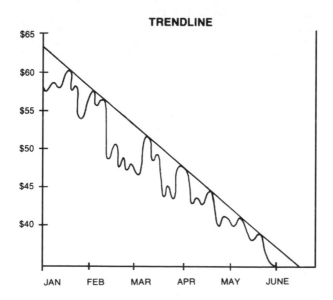

TRENDLINE

TRENDLINE line used by technical analysts to chart the past direction of a security or commodity future in order to help predict future price movements. The trendline is made by connecting the highest or lowest prices to which a security or commodity has risen or fallen within a particular time period. The angle of the resulting line will indicate if the security or commodity is in a downtrend or uptrend. If the price rises above a downward sloping trendline or drops below a rising uptrend line, technical analysts say that a new direction may be emerging. *See also* TECHNICAL ANALYSIS; TRADING PATTERN.

TREYNOR RATIO RISK-ADJUSTED return measure used to rate mutual funds and derived by dividing EXCESS RETURN by BETA. A fund with a high ratio has high historical returns relative to market-related risk.

TRIANGLE technical chart pattern that has two base points and a top point, formed by connecting a stock's price movements with a line. In a typical triangle pattern, the apex points to the right, although in reverse triangles the apex points to the left. In a typical triangle, there are a series of two or more rallies and price drops where each succeeding peak is lower than the preceding peak, and each bottom is higher than the preceding bottom. In a right-angled triangle, the sloping part of the formation often points in the direction of the breakout. Technical analysts find it significant when a security's price breaks out of the triangle formation, either up or down, because that usually means the security's price will continue in that direction. See chart below. *See also* PENNANT; TECHNICAL ANALYSIS; WEDGE.

TRICKLE DOWN theory that economic growth can best be achieved by letting businesses flourish, since their prosperity will ultimately trickle down to middle- and lower-income people, who will benefit by increased economic activity. Proponents say that it produces more long-term growth than direct welfare grants to the middle- and lower-income sectors. *See also* SUPPLY-SIDE ECONOMICS.

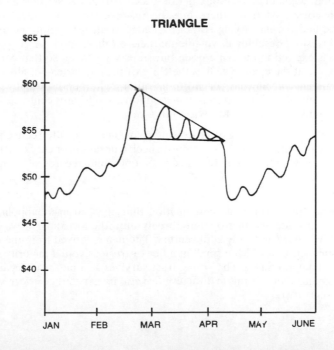

TRIANGLE

TRIN measure of stock market strength that relates the ADVANCE-DECLINE ratio (the number of issues that advanced in price divided by the number of issues that declined in price) to the advance volume-decline volume ratio (the total number of shares that advanced divided by the total number of shares that declined). For example, if 800 stocks advanced and 750 issues declined while a total of 68 million shares advanced and 56 million shares declined, the trin would be calculated as follows:

$$\frac{\text{Advances } 800 \div \text{Declines } 750}{\text{Advance volume } 68{,}000{,}000 \div \text{Decline volume } 56{,}000{,}000} = \frac{1.067}{1.214}$$

$$= 0.88$$

A trin of under 1.00 is considered bullish while a trin over 1.00 is considered bearish. The above trin of 0.88 is thus a bullish sign. A trin based on closing figures is called a *closing trin. See also* CLOSING TICK.

TRIPLE NET LEASE lease requiring tenants to pay all ongoing maintenance expenses such as utilities, taxes, insurance, and upkeep of the property. There are many LIMITED PARTNERSHIPS investing in triple net lease real estate deals. In such a deal, the limited partnership owns the property and collects rent, but the tenants pay most of the operating expenses. This results in higher returns for limited partners with lower risks, because tenants bear any increased costs for utilities, insurance, or taxes.

TRIPLE TAX EXEMPT feature of MUNICIPAL BONDS in which interest is exempt from federal, state, and local taxation for residents of the states and localities that issue them. Such bonds are particularly attractive in states with high income tax rates. Many municipal bond funds buy only triple tax exempt bonds and market them to residents of the state and city of the issuer. *See also* SINGLE-STATE MUNICIPAL BOND FUND.

TRIPLE WITCHING DAY third Friday in March, June, September, and December when OPTIONS, INDEX OPTIONS, AND FUTURES CONTRACTS all expire simultaneously. At times there may be massive trades in index futures, options, and the underlying stocks by hedge strategists, arbitrageurs, and other investors, resulting in volatile markets on those days. In the past, all contracts expired in the same hour, but steps were taken so that contracts now expire at the open as well as the close of the day instead of all at once. Smaller-scale witching days occur in the other eight months, usually on the third Friday, when other options, index options, and futures contracts expire concurrently. *See also* DOUBLE WITCHING DAY.

TRUNCATION shortening of processing steps, in an effort to reduce paperwork and operating costs. For example, check truncation, or check SAFEKEEPING, where the bank holds the checks or microfilm records of them in a central file.

TRUST
Business: type of corporate combination that engaged in monopolies and restraint of trade and that operated freely until the ANTITRUST LAWS of the late 19th century and early 20th century. The name derived from the use of the voting trust, in which a small number of trustees vote a majority of the shares of a corporation. The voting trust survives as a means of facilitating the reorganization of firms in difficulty. *See also* INVESTMENT COMPANY; VOTING TRUST CERTIFICATE.

Law: FIDUCIARY relationship in which a person, called a *trustee,* holds title to property for the benefit of another person, called a BENEFICIARY. The agreement that establishes the trust, contains its provisions, and sets forth the powers of the trustee is called the *trust indenture.* The person creating the trust is the *creator, settlor,* GRANTOR, or *donor;* the property itself is called the CORPUS, *trust res, trust fund,* or *trust estate,* which is distinguished from any income earned by it. If the trust is created while the donor is living, it is called a *living trust* or INTER VIVOS TRUST. A trust created by a will is called a TESTAMENTARY TRUST. The trustee is usually charged with investing trust property productively and, unless specifically limited, can sell, mortgage, or lease the property as he or she deems warranted. *See also* CHARITABLE REMAINDER TRUST; CLIFFORD TRUST; INVESTMENT TRUST; REVISIONARY TRUST; TRUST COMPANY; TRUSTEE IN BANKRUPTCY; TRUST INDENTURE ACT OF 1939.

TRUST COMPANY organization, usually combined with a commercial bank, which is engaged as a trustee, FIDUCIARY, or AGENT for individuals or businesses in the administration of TRUST funds, estates, custodial arrangements, stock transfer and registration, and other related services. Trust companies also engage in fiduciary investment management functions and estate planning. They are regulated by state law.

TRUSTEE *see* TRUST.

TRUSTEE IN BANKRUPTCY trustee appointed by a U.S. district court or by creditors to administer the affairs of a bankrupt company or individual. Under Chapter 7 of the U.S. BANKRUPTCY Code, the trustee has the responsibility for liquidating the property of the company and making distributions of liquidating dividends to creditors. Under the Chapter 11 provision, which provides for REORGANIZATION, a trustee may or may not be appointed. If one is, the trustee is responsible for seeing that a reorganization plan is filed and often assumes responsibility for the company.

TRUST FUND *see* TRUST.

TRUST INDENTURE ACT OF 1939 federal law requiring all corporate bonds and other debt securities to be issued under an INDENTURE agreement approved by the SECURITIES AND EXCHANGE COMMISSION (SEC) and providing for the appointment of a qualified trustee free of conflict of interest with the issuer. The Act provides that indentures contain protective clauses for bondholders, that bondholders receive semiannual financial reports, that periodic filings be made with the SEC showing compliance with indenture provisions, and that the issuer be liable for misleading statements. Securities exempted from regulation under the SECURITIES ACT OF 1933 are also exempted from the Trust Indenture Act, but some securities not requiring registration under the 1933 Act do fall under the provisions of the Trust Indenture Act, such as bonds issued in REORGANIZATION or RECAPITALIZATION.

TRUST-ISSUED RECEIPTS one of two major categories of EXCHANGE-TRADED FUNDS. Developed by Merrill Lynch under the name HOLDRs in conjunction with the AMERICAN STOCK EXCHANGE. HOLDRs trade only in round lots. They represent deposited shares of stock issued by a specific group of companies and are designed to enable investors to own companies in a particular industry sector or investment grouping through a single, exchange-traded security. The sectors include biotechnology, telecom, semiconductor, pharmaceutical, business-to-business, Internet, Internet architecture, Internet infrastructure, and broadband companies. *See also* EXCHANGE-TRADED FUNDS.

TRUST-ORIGINATED PREFERRED SECURITIES (TOPrS) *see* INCOME PREFERRED SECURITIES.

TRANSPARENCY paradigm covering clear and complete disclosure necessary to a layperson's understanding of a company and its finances, a financial product, or transaction, a market, a government program, or anything else that a stakeholder would need to evaluate a risk.

TROUBLED ASSETS RELIEF PROGRAM (TARP) U.S. Treasury program set up and funded with $700 billion by the EMERGENCY ECONOMIC STABILIZATION ACT OF 2008. Originally H.R. 1424, this was the ballyhooed "bailout bill," enacted October 2, 2008, when the credit markets were frozen and the American economy seemed to be on the brink of implosion. TARP's initial intention was to buy TOXIC ASSETS directly from ailing banks to restore their solvency and get them lending again. Within days, however, that plan was replaced by a *Capital Purchase Program* whereby instead of buying toxic assets, the Treasury would buy senior nonvoting preferred stock and equity warrants in the nine largest American banks reasoning that fattening their capitalization would spur a general unlocking of the credit freeze. Participants would agree to a series of strict restrictions on executive compensation. The Treasury would also use the first $250 billion of the allotment to bolster the capitalization of hundreds of smaller banks. Other plans for using the money to aid the recovery of financial institutions were announced within a period of two or three months. Secretary Paulson announced that reviving the securitization market for consumer credit would be a priority in the second allotment. (*See* TALF.) Paulson's successor, Timothy Geithner, announced March 23, 2009, the PUBLIC-PRIVATE INVESTMENT PROGRAM (P-PIP).

On December 19, 2008, President Bush had used his executive authority to extend TARP funds beyond financial institutions to cover any program he believed necessary to avert the financial crisis. That opened the way for the use of TARP funds to aid General Motors and Chrysler prior to their bankruptcy filings. Congressional Budget Office figures released in January 2009 reportedly indicated that through the calendar year 2008 transactions under TARP totaled $247 billion including $178 billion of shares and warrants purchased from 214 financial institutions, $40 billion of preferred stock in AIG, $25 billion of preferred stock in Citicorp, $15 billion in Bank of America, and $18.4 billion loaned to GM and Chrysler. Another $50 billion was earmarked for infrastructure rebuilding under a *City Fund*. In the course of 2009, there have been additional TARP investments in various financial and nonfinancial applications and repayments have been received from several large financial institutions.

The TARP bill established several oversight boards in the interest of oversight and transparency, notably the Congressional Oversight Panel (COP) (*cop.senate.gov/reports*); the Financial Stability Oversight Board (FSOB) (*financialstability.gov*); and the Special Inspector General For TARP (SIGTARP). Each is a source of specific information on specific programs (or an explanation of the difficulty of obtaining it) comprising a gargantuan program that is still feeling its way. Understandably, none yet answers clearly the question, "How's the TARP program working?" Of course, it has to be said that TARP brought us back from the abyss or at least bought us some time.

TRUTH IN LENDING LAW legislation stipulating that lenders must disclose to borrowers the true cost of loans and make the interest rate and terms of the loan simple to understand. *See also* CONSUMER CREDIT PROTECTION ACT OF 1968; RIGHT OF RESCISSION.

TULIPMANIA legendary speculative episode that occurred in Holland in the 1600s when at one point 12 acres of land were reportedly exchanged for one tulip bulb and the subsequent crash ruined many investors and had a major effect on Dutch commerce.

TURKEY disappointing investment. The term may be used with reference to a business deal that went awry, or to the purchase of a stock or bond that dropped in value sharply, or to a new securities issue that did not sell well or had to be sold at a loss.

TURNAROUND favorable reversal in the fortunes of a company, a market, or the economy at large. Stock market investors speculating that a poorly performing company is about to show a marked improvement in earnings might profit handsomely from its turnaround.

TURNKEY any project constructed or manufactured by a company that ultimately turns it over in finished form to the company that will use it, so that all the user has to do is turn the key, so to speak, and the project is underway. The term is used of housing projects that, after construction, are turned over to property managers. There are also turnkey computer systems, for which the user needs no special computer knowledge and which can therefore be put right to work once they are installed.

TURNOVER
Finance:
1. number of times a given asset is replaced during an accounting period, usually a year. *See also* ACCOUNTS RECEIVABLE TURNOVER; INVENTORY TAKEOVER.
2. ratio of annual sales of a company to its NET WORTH, measuring the extent to which a company can grow without additional capital investment when compared over a period. *See also* CAPITAL TURNOVER.
Great Britain: annual sales volume.
Industrial relations: total employment divided by the number of employees replaced during a given period.
Securities: volume of shares traded as a percentage of total shares listed on an exchange during a period, usually either a day or a year. The same ratio is applied to individual securities and the portfolios of individual or institutional investors.

12b-1 MUTUAL FUND MUTUAL FUND that assesses shareholders for some of its promotion expenses. Adopted by the Securities and Exchange Commission in 1980, Rule 12b-1 provides mutual funds and their shareholders with an asset-based alternative method of covering sales and marketing expenses. At least half of the more than 10,000 mutual funds in existence today have a 12b-1 fee typically ranging from .25%, in the case of "no-load" funds that use it to cover advertising and marketing costs, to as high as 8.5%, the maximum "front-end load" allowed under National Association of Securities Dealers (NASD) rules, in cases where annual 12b-1 "spread loads" replaced traditional front-end loads. The predominant use of 12b-1 fees is in funds sold through brokers, insurance agents, and financial planners.

Changes to 12b-1 that became effective July 7, 1993, aim to limit fees paid by most fund investors to the 8.5% limit on front-end loads. This is achieved by an annual limit and by a rolling cap placed on new sales. The annual limit is .85% of assets, with an additional .25% permitted as a service fee. The rolling cap on the total of all sales charges is 6.25% of new sales, plus interest, for funds that charge the service fee, and 7.25%, plus interest, for funds that do not. The new regulation also prohibits funds with front-end, deferred, and/or 12b-1 fees in excess of .25% from being called "no-load." *See also* MUTUAL FUND SHARE CLASSES; NO-LOAD FUND.

TWENTY BOND INDEX index tracking the yields on 20 general obligation municipal bonds with 20-year maturities and an average rating equivalent to A1. The index, published weekly by *The Bond Buyer* in the newspaper's Friday edition, serves as a benchmark for the general level of municipal bond yields. *See also* BOND BUYER'S INDEX; ELEVEN BOND INDEX.

TWENTY-DAY PERIOD period required by the Securities and Exchange Commission (SEC) after filing of the REGISTRATION STATEMENT and PRELIMINARY PROSPECTUS in a NEW ISSUE or SECONDARY DISTRIBUTION during which they are reviewed and, if necessary, modified. The end of the twenty-day period—also called the COOLING-OFF PERIOD—marks the EFFECTIVE DATE when the issue may be offered to the public. The period may be extended by the SEC if more time is needed to respond to a DEFICIENCY LETTER.

TWENTY-FIVE PERCENT RULE MUNICIPAL BOND analyst's guideline that bonded debt over 25% of a municipality's annual budget is excessive.

TWENTY-PERCENT CUSHION RULE guideline used by analysts of MUNICIPAL REVENUE BONDS that estimated revenues from the financed facility should exceed the operating budget plus maintenance costs and DEBT SERVICE by a 20% margin or "cushion" to allow for unanticipated expenses or error in estimating revenues.

TWISTING unethical practice of convincing a customer to trade unnecessarily, thereby generating a commission for the broker or salesperson. Examples: A broker may induce a customer to sell one mutual fund with a sales charge in order to buy another fund, also with a sales charge, thereby generating a commission. A life insurance salesperson may persuade a policyholder to cancel his or her policy or allow it to lapse, in order to sell the insured a new policy, which would be more costly but which would produce sizable commissions for the salesperson. Also called CHURNING.

TWO AND TWENTY typical formula for compensation of HEDGE FUND managers where 2% of total asset value is charged as a management fee and an additional 20% of profits is taken as a performance fee. *See also* GATE; HIGH WATER MARK.

TWO-DOLLAR BROKER FLOOR BROKER who executes orders for other brokers too busy to do it themselves; a "broker's broker." Such brokers once were paid two dollars for a ROUND LOT trade, hence the name. Today they receive a negotiated commission rate varying with the dollar value of the transaction. *See also* INDEPENDENT BROKER.

200-DAY MOVING AVERAGE indicator used in TECHNICAL ANALYSIS representing the average closing price of a stock over the most recent 200 days. It represents a long-term trend and is typically superimposed on a LINE CHART. A break above the 200-day moving average is a BUY SIGNAL and vice versa. *See also* MOVING AVERAGE; MOMENTUM INDICATORS.

200 PERCENT DECLINING BALANCE METHOD *see* DOUBLE DECLINING-BALANCE DEPRECIATION METHOD (DDB).

TWO-SIDED MARKET market in which both the BID AND ASKED sides are firm, such as that which a SPECIALIST and others who MAKE A MARKET are required to maintain. Both buyers and sellers are thus assured of their ability to complete transactions. Also called *two-way market.*

TWO-TIER BID TAKEOVER bid where the acquirer offers to pay more for the shares needed to gain control than for the remaining shares; contrasts with ANY-AND-ALL BID.

TWO-WAY TRADING in general, a contract feature that permits trading back and forth the two assets involved. Term is used in international finance to mean AMERICAN DEPOSITARY RECEIPTS (ADRs) or GLOBAL DEPOSITARY RECEIPTS (GDRs) that are interchangeable, respectively, with their underlying common shares. ADRs and GDRs that can be converted to related common shares and vice versa enjoy enhanced liquidity.

U

ULTRA-SHORT-TERM BOND FUND mutual fund buying bonds with maturities typically of one year or less. Such funds usually pay higher yields than money market mutual funds, but lower yields than SHORT-TERM BOND FUNDS. Their advantage to investors is that they offer more price stability than short-term bond funds, along with a yield that beats money funds. The NET ASSET VALUE of ultra-short-term bond funds does fluctuate, however, unlike the net asset value for money market mutual funds, which remains fixed at $1 a share. It is therefore possible to realize capital gains and losses with ultra-short-term bond funds.

ULTRA VIRES ACTIVITIES actions of a corporation that are not authorized by its charter and that may therefore lead to shareholder or third-party suits. *See also* ARTICLES OF INCORPORATION.

UMA *see* UNIFIED MANAGED ACCOUNT.

UMBRELLA PERSONAL LIABILITY POLICY liability insurance policy providing excess coverage beyond regular liability policies. For example, typical homeowner's policies offer $300,000 in liability coverage against lawsuits and other negligence claims. An umbrella policy may provide $1 million in liability coverage. An umbrella policy will begin to pay claims only after the underlying liability policy's coverage limits have been exceeded. People usually buy umbrella policies to protect themselves against the possibility of a large jury award in a lawsuit. An umbrella policy also protects in situations not covered by a standard liability policy found in homeowner's and automobile insurance, like slander and libel. An umbrella policy also links policies, raising the limits on underlying policies in a cost-effective manner.

UNAMORTIZED BOND DISCOUNT difference between the FACE VALUE (par value) of a bond and the proceeds received from the sale of the bond by the issuing company, less whatever portion has been amortized, that is, written off to expense as recorded periodically on the PROFIT AND LOSS STATEMENT. At the time of issue, a company has two alternatives: (1) it can immediately absorb as an expense the amount of discount plus costs related to the issue, such as legal, printing, REGISTRATION, and other similar expenses, or (2) it can decide to treat the total discount and expenses as a DEFERRED CHARGE, recorded as an ASSET to be written off over the life of the bonds or by any other schedule the company finds desirable. The amount still to be expensed at any point is the unamortized bond discount.

UNAMORTIZED PREMIUMS ON INVESTMENTS unexpensed portion of the amount by which the price paid for a security exceeded its PAR value (if a BOND or PREFERRED STOCK) or MARKET VALUE (if common stock). A PREMIUM paid in acquiring an investment is in the nature of an INTANGIBLE ASSET.

UNBUNDLING
1. separating a hybrid security or derivative into the components that were originally *bundled* to create it;
2. separating returns on an asset into classes or, in the case of the *unbundled stock unit* (developed in the late 1980s but never successfully marketed), decomposing a COMMON STOCK into three parts: a dividend claim, a zero coupon bond, and a stock appreciation right;

3. the process by which one Wall Street firm in the 1980s created what it called an *unbundled unit*, an antitakeover device packaged and sponsored by the investment bank comprising a 30-year bond, a preferred share, and a warrant; the unit was then exchangeable for a voting share of a client corporation's common stock;

4. in Great Britain, divesting a conglomerate of its noncore businesses.

UNCOLLECTED FUNDS portion of bank deposit made up of checks that have not yet been collected by the depository bank—that is, payment has not yet been acknowledged by the bank on which a check was drawn. A bank will usually not let a depositor draw on uncollected funds. *See also* FLOAT.

UNCOLLECTIBLE ACCOUNT customer account that cannot be collected because of the customer's unwillingness or inability to pay. A business normally writes off such a receivable as worthless after several attempts at collecting the funds.

UNCOVERED OPTION short option that is not fully collateralized. A short call position is uncovered if the writer does not have long stock to deliver or does not own another call on the same security with a lower or same strike price, and with a longer or same time of expiration. Also called NAKED OPTION. *See also* NAKED POSITION; COVERED OPTION; COVERED WRITER.

UNDERBANKED said of a NEW ISSUE underwriting when the originating INVESTMENT BANKER is having difficulty getting other firms to become members of the UNDERWRITING GROUP, or syndicate. *See also* UNDERWRITE.

UNDERBOOKED said of a NEW ISSUE of securities during the preoffering REGISTRATION period when brokers canvassing lists of prospective buyers report limited INDICATIONS OF INTEREST. The opposite of underbooked would be *fully circled*. *See also* CIRCLE.

UNDERCAPITALIZATION situation in which a business does not have enough capital to carry out its normal business functions. *See also* CAPITALIZATION; WORKING CAPITAL.

UNDERLYING DEBT MUNICIPAL BOND term referring to the debt of government entities within the jurisdiction of larger government entities and for which the larger entity has partial credit responsibility. For example, a township might share responsibility for the general obligations of a village within the township, the debt of the village being underlying debt from the township's standpoint. The term OVERLAPPING DEBT is also used to describe underlying debt, but overlapping debt can also exist with entities of equal rank where, for example, a school district crosses boundaries of two or more townships.

UNDERLYING FUTURES CONTRACT FUTURES CONTRACT that underlies an OPTION on that future. For example, the Chicago Board of Trade offers a U.S. Treasury bond futures option. The underlying future is the Treasury bond futures contract traded on the Board of Trade. If the option contract were exercised, delivery would be made in the underlying futures contract.

UNDERLYING SECURITY
Options: security that must be delivered if a PUT OPTION or CALL OPTION contract is exercised. Stock INDEX OPTIONS and STOCK INDEX FUTURES, however, are settled in cash, since it is not possible to deliver an index of stocks.
Securities: common stock that underlies certain types of securities issued by

corporations. This stock must be delivered if a SUBSCRIPTION WARRANT or SUBSCRIPTION RIGHT is exercised, if a CONVERTIBLE bond or PREFERRED STOCK is converted into common shares, or if an INCENTIVE STOCK OPTION is exercised.

UNDERMARGINED ACCOUNT MARGIN ACCOUNT that has fallen below MARGIN REQUIREMENTS or MINIMUM MAINTENANCE requirements. As a result, the broker must make a MARGIN CALL to the customer.

UNDERVALUED security selling below its LIQUIDATION value or the MARKET VALUE analysts believe it deserves. A company's stock may be undervalued because the industry is out of favor, because the company is not well known or has an erratic history of earnings, or for many other reasons. Fundamental analysts try to spot companies that are undervalued so their clients can buy before the stocks become FULLY VALUED. Undervalued companies are also frequently targets of TAKEOVER attempts, since acquirers can buy assets cheaply this way. *See also* FUNDAMENTAL ANALYSIS.

UNDERWATER
1. a loan balance that exceeds the underlying collateral. Since 2007, the term has been widely used to describe mortgage debt in excess of home value, as in UPSIDE-DOWN MORTGAGE.
2. OPTIONS are said to be underwater when the exercise price is higher than the market price of the underlying stock.
3. a portfolio of stocks or bonds that is losing value.

UNDERWATER OPTION OUT-OF-THE MONEY option. Being out of the money indicates the option has no intrinsic value; all of its value consists of time value. A call option is out of the money if its exercise price is higher than the current price of the underlying contract. A put option is out of the money if its exercise price is lower than the current price of the underlying contract.

UNDERWITHHOLDING situation in which taxpayers have too little federal, state, or local income tax withheld from their salaries. Because they have underwithheld, these taxpayers may owe income taxes when they file their tax returns. If the underwithholding is large enough, penalties and interest also may be due. To correct underwithholding, taxpayers must file a new W-4 form with their employers, decreasing the number of dependents claimed. *See also* OVERWITHHOLDING.

UNDERWRITE
Insurance: to assume risk in exchange for a PREMIUM.
Investments: to assume the risk of buying a NEW ISSUE of securities from the issuing corporation or government entity and reselling them to the public, either directly or through dealers. The UNDERWRITER makes a profit on the difference between the price paid to the issuer and the PUBLIC OFFERING PRICE, called the UNDERWRITING SPREAD.

Underwriting is the business of investment bankers, who usually form an UNDERWRITING GROUP (also called a PURCHASE GROUP or syndicate) to pool the risk and assure successful distribution of the issue. The syndicate operates under an AGREEMENT AMONG UNDERWRITERS, also termed a *syndicate contract* or PURCHASE GROUP contract.

The underwriting group appoints a MANAGING UNDERWRITER, also known as *lead underwriter, syndicate manager,* or simply *manager,* that is usually the *originating investment banker*—the firm that began working with the issuer months before to plan details of the issue and prepare the REGISTRATION materials to be filed with the SECURITIES AND EXCHANGE COMMISSION. The manager, acting as agent for the group, signs the UNDERWRITING AGREEMENT (or *purchase contract*) with the issuer. This agreement sets forth the terms and conditions of the arrangement and the responsibilities of both issuer and underwriter. During the offering period, it is the manager's responsibility to stabilize the MARKET PRICE of the issuer's shares by bidding in the open market, a process called PEGGING. The manager may also appoint a SELLING GROUP, comprised of dealers and the underwriters themselves, to assist in DISTRIBUTION of the issue.

Strictly speaking, *underwrite* is properly used only in a FIRM COMMITMENT underwriting, also known as a BOUGHT DEAL, where the securities are purchased outright from the issuer.

Other investment banking arrangements to which the term is sometimes loosely applied are BEST EFFORT, ALL OR NONE, and STANDBY COMMITMENTS; in each of these, the risk is shared between the issuer and the INVESTMENT BANKER.

The term is also sometimes used in connection with a REGISTERED SECONDARY OFFERING, which involves essentially the same process as a new issue, except that the proceeds go to the selling investor, not to the issuer. For these arrangements, the term *secondary offering* or SECONDARY DISTRIBUTION is preferable to *underwriting,* which is usually reserved for new, or primary, distributions.

There are two basic methods by which underwriters are chosen by issuers and underwriting spreads are determined: NEGOTIATED UNDERWRITINGS and COMPETITIVE BID underwritings. Generally, the negotiated method is used in corporate equity (stock) issues and most corporate debt (bond) issues, whereas the competitive bidding method is used by municipalities and public utilities. *See also* ALLOTMENT; BLOWOUT; FLOATING AN ISSUE; FLOTATION COST; HOT ISSUE; INITIAL PUBLIC OFFERING; PRESOLD ISSUE; PRIMARY MARKET; PUBLIC OFFERING; STANDBY UNDERWRITER.

UNDERWRITER

Insurance: company that assumes the cost risk of death, fire, theft, illness, etc., in exchange for payments, called *premiums.*

Securities: INVESTMENT BANKER who, singly or as a member of an UNDERWRITING GROUP or syndicate, agrees to purchase a NEW ISSUE of securities from an issuer and distribute it to investors, making a profit on the UNDERWRITING SPREAD. *See also* UNDERWRITE.

UNDERWRITING AGREEMENT agreement between a corporation

issuing new securities to be offered to the public and the MANAGING UNDERWRITER as agent for the UNDERWRITING GROUP. Also termed the *purchase agreement* or *purchase contract,* it represents the underwriters' commitment to purchase the securities, and it details the PUBLIC OFFERING PRICE, the UNDERWRITING SPREAD (including all discounts and commissions), the net proceeds to the issuer, and the SETTLEMENT DATE.

The issuer agrees to pay all expenses incurred in preparing the issue for resale, including the costs of REGISTRATION with the SECURITIES AND EXCHANGE COMMISSION (SEC) and of the PROSPECTUS, and agrees to supply the managing underwriter with sufficient copies of both the PRELIMINARY PROSPECTUS (red herring) and the final, statutory prospectus. The issuer guarantees (1) to make all required SEC filings and to comply fully with the provisions of the SECURITIES ACT OF 1933; (2) to assume responsibility for the completeness, accuracy, and proper certification of all information in the registration statement and prospectus; (3) to disclose all pending litigation; (4) to use the proceeds for the purposes stated; (5) to comply with state securities laws; (6) to work to get listed on the exchange agreed upon; and (7) to indemnify the underwriters for liability arising out of omissions or misrepresentations for which the issuer had responsibility.

The underwriters agree to proceed with the offering as soon as the registration is cleared by the SEC or at a specified date thereafter. The underwriters are authorized to make sales to members of a SELLING GROUP.

The underwriting agreement is not to be confused with the AGREEMENT AMONG UNDERWRITERS. *See also* BEST EFFORT; FIRM COMMITMENT; STANDBY COMMITMENT; UNDERWRITE.

UNDERWRITING GROUP temporary association of investment bankers, organized by the originating INVESTMENT BANKER in a NEW ISSUE of securities. Operating under an AGREEMENT AMONG UNDERWRITERS, it agrees to purchase securities from the issuing corporation at an agreed-upon price and to resell them at a PUBLIC OFFERING PRICE, the difference representing the UNDERWRITING SPREAD. The purpose of the underwriting group is to spread the risk and assure successful distribution of the offering. Most underwriting groups operate under a *divided syndicate contract,* meaning that the liability of members is limited to their individual participations. Also called DISTRIBUTING SYNDICATE, PURCHASE GROUP, *investment banking group,* or *syndicate. See also* FIRM COMMITMENT; UNDERWRITE; UNDERWRITING AGREEMENT.

UNDERWRITING SPREAD difference between the amount paid to an issuer of securities in a PRIMARY DISTRIBUTION and the PUBLIC OFFERING PRICE. The amount of SPREAD varies widely, depending on the size of the issue, the financial strength of the issuer, the type of security involved (stock, bonds, rights), the status of the security (senior, junior, secured, unsecured), and the type of commitment made by the investment bankers. The range may be from a fraction of 1% for a bond issue of a big utility company to 25% for the INITIAL PUBLIC OFFERING of a small company. The division of the spread between the MANAGING UNDERWRITER, the SELLING GROUP, and the participating underwriters also varies, but in a two-point spread the manager might typically get 0.25%, the selling group 1%, and the underwriters 0.75%. It is usual, though, for the underwriters also to be members of the selling group, thus picking up 1.75% of the spread, and for the manager to be in all three categories, thus picking up the full 2%. *See also* COMPETITIVE BID; FLOTATION COST; GROSS SPREAD; NEGOTIATED UNDERWRITING; SELLING CONCESSION; UNDERWRITE.

UNDIGESTED SECURITIES newly issued stocks and bonds that remain undistributed because there is insufficient public demand at the OFFERING PRICE. *See also* UNDERWRITE.

UNDISTRIBUTED PROFITS (EARNINGS, NET INCOME) *see* RETAINED EARNINGS.

UNDIVIDED PROFITS account shown on a bank's BALANCE SHEET representing profits that have neither been paid out as DIVIDENDS nor transferred to the bank's SURPLUS account. Current earnings are credited to the undivided profits account and are then either paid out in dividends or retained to build up total EQUITY. As the account grows, round amounts may be periodically transferred to the surplus account.

UNEARNED DISCOUNT account on the books of a lending institution recognizing interest deducted in advance and which will be taken into income as earned over the life of the loan. In accordance with accounting principles, such interest is initially recorded as a LIABILITY. Then, as months pass and it is gradually "earned," it is recognized as income, thus increasing the lender's profit and decreasing the corresponding liability. *See also* UNEARNED INCOME.

UNEARNED INCOME (REVENUE)
Accounting: income received but not yet earned, such as rent received in advance or other advances from customers. Unearned income is usually classified as a CURRENT LIABILITY on a company's BALANCE SHEET, assuming that it will be credited to income within the normal accounting cycle. *See also* DEFERRED CHARGE.
Income taxes: income from sources other than wages, salaries, tips, and other employee compensation—for example, DIVIDENDS, INTEREST, rent.

UNEARNED INTEREST interest that has already been collected on a loan by a financial institution, but that cannot yet be counted as part of earnings because the principal of the loan has not been outstanding long enough. Also called DISCOUNT and UNEARNED DISCOUNT.

UNEMPLOYED OR UNEMPLOYMENT condition of being out of work involuntarily. The federal-state unemployment insurance system makes cash payments directly to laid-off workers. Most states now pay a maximum of 26 weeks, a few extend duration somewhat farther. In periods of very high unemployment in individual states, benefits are payable for as many as 13 additional weeks. These "extended benefits" are funded on a shared basis, approximately half from state funds and half from federal sources. In general, to collect unemployment benefits a person must have previously held a job and must be actively seeking employment. Unemployed people apply for and collect unemployment compensation from their state's Department of Labor. Except in states where there are small employee payments, the system is financed by a payroll tax on employers.

UNEMPLOYMENT RATE percentage of the civilian labor force actively looking for work but unable to find jobs. The rate is compiled by the U.S. Department of Labor, in cooperation with the Labor Departments in all the states, and released to the public on the first Friday of every month. The unemployment rate is affected by the number of people entering the workforce as well as the number of unemployed people. An important part of the Labor Department's report is "Payroll Employment," which covers data on hours, earnings, and employment for non-farm industries nationally, by state and for major metropolitan areas. The unemployment report is one of the most closely watched of all government reports, because it gives the clearest indication of the direction of the economy. A rising unemployment rate will be seen by analysts and the Federal Reserve as a sign of a weakening economy, which might call for an easing of monetary policy by the Fed. On the other hand, a drop in the unemployment rate shows that the economy is growing, which may spark fears of higher inflation on the part of the Fed, which may raise interest rates as a result.

UNENCUMBERED property free and clear of all liens (creditors' claims). When a homeowner pays off his mortgage, for example, the house becomes unencumbered property. Securities bought with cash instead of on MARGIN are unencumbered.

UNFUNDED PENSION PLAN pension plan that is funded by the employer out of current income as funds are required by retirees or beneficiaries. Also known as a *pay-as-you-go* pension plan, or a plan using the *current disbursement funding approach*. This contrasts with an ADVANCE FUNDED PENSION PLAN, under which the employer puts aside money on a regular basis into a separate fund that is invested in stocks, bonds, real estate, and other assets.

UNIFIED CREDIT federal TAX CREDIT that may be applied against the gift tax, the estate tax, and, under specified conditions, the generation-skipping transfer tax.

UNIFIED MANAGED ACCOUNT (UMA) variation on the SEPARATELY MANAGED ACCOUNT (SMA) that handles an investor's stocks, bonds, managed accounts, and mutual funds in one diversified, customized, "umbrella" portfolio, designed to minimize the investor's taxes.

UNIFORM COMMERCIAL CODE (UCC) legal code adopted by most states that codifies various laws dealing with commercial transactions, primarily those involving the sale of goods, both tangible and intangible, and secured transactions. It was drafted by the National Conference of Commissioners of Uniform State Laws and covers bank deposits, bankruptcy, commercial letters of credit, commercial paper, warranties, and other commercial activities. Article 8 of the UCC applies to transactions in investment securities.

UNIFORM GIFTS TO MINORS ACT (UGMA) enacted to provide a simple way to transfer property to a minor without the complications of a formal trust, and without the restrictions applicable to the guardianship of a minor's property. In many states, gifts under the UGMA can be made both by lifetime gift and by the donor's WILL. Lifetime UGMA gifts quality for the $13,000 annual GIFT TAX exclusion. An UGMA property is managed by a CUSTODIAN appointed by the donor. If the donor names him/herself as custodian and dies before the property is turned over to the minor, the value of the custodial property at the donor–custodian's death is included in the donor–custodian's taxable estate even though the property belongs to the minor from the instant the UGMA gift is made. The custodial property must be turned over to the minor when the minor attains the age specified in the UGMA law of the state in which the gift is made. In most states, the age is 18, but in some states it is 21. In New York State it is 18 unless the donor, at the time the UGMA gift is made, specifies age 21. All 50 states also enacted a UNIFORM TRANSFER TO MINORS ACT (UTMA), which in some case supplements the UGMA, and in others replaces it.

UNIFORM PRACTICE CODE rules of the FINANCIAL INDUSTRY REGULATORY AUTHORITY (FINRA) concerned with standards and procedures for the operational handling of OVER THE COUNTER (OTC) securities transactions, such as delivery, SETTLEMENT DATE, EX-DIVIDEND DATE, and other ex-dates (such as EX-RIGHTS and EX-WARRANTS), and providing for the arbitration of disputes through Uniform Practice committees.

UNIFORM SECURITIES AGENT STATE LAW EXAMINATION Series 63 registered test required of prospective REGISTERED REPRESENTATIVES in many U.S. states. In addition to the examination requirements of states, all registered representatives, whether employees of member firms or OVER THE COUNTER (OTC) brokers, must pass the General Securities Representative Examination (also known as the Series 7 Examination), administered by the FINANCIAL INDUSTRY REGULATORY AUTHORITY (FINRA).

UNIFORM TRANSFERS TO MINORS ACT (UTMA) law adopted by all 50 states that is similar to the UNIFORM GIFTS TO MINORS ACT (UGMA) but different in that it extends the definition of GIFTS beyond cash and securities to include real estate, paintings, royalties, and patents. UTMA also prohibits the minor from taking control of the assets until age 21 (25 in California).

UNINSURED MOTORIST INSURANCE form of insurance that covers the policyholder and family members if injured by a hit-and-run motorist or driver who carries no liability insurance, assuming the driver is at fault. In most instances, reimbursements of costs of property damage and medical expenses resulting from the accident will be rewarded. The premiums for uninsured motorist coverage are usually rather modest, and are included as part of a regular auto insurance policy.

UNISSUED STOCK shares of a corporation's stock authorized in its charter but not issued. They are shown on the BALANCE SHEET along with shares ISSUED AND OUTSTANDING. Unissued stock may be issued by action of the board of directors, although shares needed for unexercised employee STOCK OPTIONS, rights, warrants, or convertible securities must not be issued while such obligations are outstanding. Unissued shares cannot pay dividends and cannot be voted. They are not to be confused with TREASURY STOCK, which is issued but not outstanding.

UNIT
In general: any division of quantity accepted as a standard of measurement or of exchange. For example, in the commodities markets, a unit of wheat is a bushel, a unit of coffee a pound, and a unit of shell eggs a dozen. The unit of U.S. currency is the dollar.
Banking: bank operating out of only one office, and with no branches, as required by states having unit banking laws.
Finance:
1. segment or subdivision (division or subsidiary, product line, or plant) of a company.
2. in sales or production, quantity rather than dollars. One might say, for example, "Unit volume declined but dollar volume increased after prices were raised."
Securities:
1. minimum amount of stocks, bonds, commodities, or other securities accepted for trading on an exchange. *See also* ODD LOT; ROUND LOT; UNIT OF TRADING.
2. group of specialists on a stock exchange, who maintain fair and orderly markets in particular securities. *See also* SPECIALIST; SPECIALIST UNIT.

3. more than one class of securities traded together; one common share and one SUBSCRIPTION WARRANT might sell as a unit, for example.
4. in primary and secondary distributions of securities, one share of stock or one bond.

UNITED STATES DOLLAR INDEX (USDX) index that compares variances in the U.S. dollar's value on a scale of 100 with a basket of currencies that includes the euro, the yen, the British pound sterling, the Canadian dollar, the Swedish krona, and the Swiss franc.

UNITED STATES GOVERNMENT SECURITIES direct GOVERNMENT OBLIGATIONS—that is, debt issues of the U.S. government, such as Treasury bills, notes, and bonds and SERIES EE and SERIES HH SAVINGS BONDS as distinguished from government-sponsored AGENCY issues. *See also* GOVERNMENT SECURITIES; TREASURIES.

UNIT INVESTMENT TRUST (UIT) investment vehicle registered with the SECURITIES AND EXCHANGE COMMISSION under the INVESTMENT COMPANY ACT OF 1940, that purchases a fixed PORTFOLIO of securities, such as corporate, municipal or government bonds, mortgage-backed securities, COMMON STOCK, or PREFERRED STOCK. Units in the trust, which usually cost at least $1,000 ($250 for IRAs), are sold to investors by brokers for a sales charge that is typically 4% for traditional municipal bond trusts and 1%–2% for equity trusts, which feature reduced sales charges when the trusts are rolled over. The trust expires when bonds mature or, in the case of some equity funds, at a specified future date. Unit holders receive an undivided interest in both the principal and the income portion of the portfolio in proportion to the amount of captial they invest.

Traditionally, the majority of UITs held municipal bonds. More recently, however, equity UITs have become predominant. Among the most popular variations were those holding high-yield stocks in the DOW JONES INDUSTRIAL AVERAGE (DOGS OF THE DOW) or the Standard & Poor's 500 Index and their counterparts on foreign exchanges. UITs are the legal vehicle for some EXCHANGE-TRADED FUNDS. *See also* DIAMONDS; SPDR; SPECIAL-PURPOSE ENTITIES (SPE); STRUCTURED RPODUCTS; UNIT SHARE INVESTMENT TRUST (USIT).

UNIT OF TRADING normal number of shares, bonds, or commodities comprising the minimum unit of trading on an exchange. For stocks, this is usually 100 shares, although inactive shares trade in 10-share units. For corporate bonds on the NYSE, the unit for exchange trading is $1,000 or $5,000 par value. Commodities futures units vary widely, according to the COMMODITY involved. *See also* BOARD LOT; FUTURES CONTRACT; ODD LOT; ROUND LOT.

UNIT SHARE INVESTMENT TRUST (USIT) specialized form of UNIT INVESTMENT TRUST comprising one unit of PRIME and one unit of SCORE.

UNIVERSAL DEFAULT practice in the credit card industry whereby a customer whose payment record with company A is good but who is penalized by that company because he or she has defaulted with company B.

UNIVERSAL LIFE INSURANCE form of life insurance, first marketed in the early 1980s, that combines the low-cost protection of TERM LIFE INSURANCE with a savings portion, which is invested in a tax-deferred account earning money-market rates of interest. The policy is flexible; that is, as age and income change, a policyholder can increase or decrease premium payments and coverage, or shift a certain portion of premiums into the savings account, without additional sales charges or complications. A new form of the policy; called *universal variable life insurance,* combines the flexibility of universal life with the growth potential of variable life. *See also* VARIABLE LIFE INSURANCE; WHOLE LIFE INSURANCE.

UNIVERSE OF SECURITIES group of stocks sharing a common characteristic. For example, one analyst may define a universe of securities as those with $100 to $500 million in outstanding market capitalization. Another may define it as stocks in a particular industry, such as communications, paper, or airlines. A mutual fund will often define itself to investors as limiting itself to a particular universe of securities, allowing investors to know in advance which kinds of securities that fund will buy and hold.

UNLEVERAGED PROGRAM LIMITED PARTNERSHIP whose use of borrowed funds to finance the acquisition of properties is 50% or less of the purchase price. In contrast, a *leveraged program* borrows 50% or more. Investors seeking to maximize income tend to favor unleveraged partnerships, where interest expense and other deductions from income are at a minimum. Investors looking for TAX SHELTERS might favor leveraged programs despite the higher risk because of the greater amount of property acquired with the borrowed money and the greater amount of tax deductible interest but the longer depreciation periods required by tax legislation have substantially reduced the tax benefits from real estate.

UNLIMITED MARITAL DEDUCTION *see* MARITAL DEDUCTION.

UNLIMITED TAX BOND MUNICIPAL BOND secured by the pledge to levy taxes at an unlimited rate until the bond is repaid.

UNLISTED SECURITY security that is not listed on an organized exchange, such as the NEW YORK STOCK EXCHANGE, the AMERICAN STOCK EXCHANGE, or the REGIONAL STOCK EXCHANGES, and is traded in the OVER THE COUNTER market.

UNLISTED TRADING trading of securities not listed on an organized exchange but traded on that exchange as an accommodation to its members. An exchange wishing to trade unlisted securities must file an application with the SECURITIES AND EXCHANGE COMMISSION and make the necessary information available to the investing public.

UNLOADING
Finance: selling off large quantities of merchandise inventory at below-market prices either to raise cash quickly or to depress the market in a particular product.
Investments: selling securities or commodities when prices are declining to preclude further loss.
See also PUMP; PROFIT TAKING; SELLING OFF.

UNMARGINED ACCOUNT brokerage CASH ACCOUNT.

UNPAID DIVIDEND dividend that has been declared by a corporation but has still not been paid. A company may declare a dividend on July 1, for example, payable on August 1. During July, the declared dividend is called an unpaid dividend. *See also* EX-DIVIDEND.

UNQUALIFIED OPINION independent auditor's opinion that a company's financial statements are fairly presented, in all material respects, in conformity with generally accepted accounting principles. The justification for the expression of the auditor's opinion rests on the conformity of his or her audit with generally accepted auditing standards and on his or her feelings. Materiality and audit risk underly the application of auditing standards. *See also* ACCOUNTANT'S OPINION; ADVERSE OPINION; QUALIFIED OPINION.

UNREALIZED PROFIT (OR LOSS) profit or loss that has not become actual. It becomes a REALIZED PROFIT (OR LOSS) when the security or commodity future contract in which there is a gain or loss is actually sold. Also called a *paper profit or loss.*

UNREGISTERED STOCK *see* LETTER SECURITY.

UNSECURED DEBT obligation not backed by the pledge of specific COLLATERAL.

UNSECURED LOAN loan without COLLATERAL.

UNWIND A TRADE to reverse a securities transaction through an offsetting transaction. *See also* OFFSET.

UPGRADING increase in the quality rating of a security. An analyst may upgrade a company's bond or stock rating if its finances improve, profitability is enhanced, and its debt level is reduced. For municipal bond issues, upgrading will occur if tax revenues increase and expenses are reduced. The upgrading of a stock or bond issue may in itself raise the price of the security because investors will feel more confident in the financial soundness of the issuer. The credit rating of issuers is constantly being evaluated, which may lead to further upgradings, or, if conditions deteriorate, downgradings. The term *upgrading* is also applied to an entire portfolio of securities. For example, a mutual fund manager who wants to improve the quality of his bond holdings will say that he is in the process of upgrading his portfolio.

UPSET PRICE term used in auctions that represents the minimum price at which a seller of property will entertain bids.

UPSIDE-DOWN MORTGAGE *see* UNDERWATER.

UPSIDE POTENTIAL amount of upward price movement an investor or an analyst expects of a particular stock, bond, or commodity. This opinion may result from either FUNDAMENTAL ANALYSIS or TECHNICAL ANALYSIS.

UPSTAIRS MARKET transaction completed within the broker-dealer's firm and without using the stock exchange. Securities and Exchange Commission and stock exchange rules exist to ensure that such trades do not occur at prices less favorable to the customer than those prevailing in the general market. *See also* OFF BOARD.

UPSTREAM opposite of DOWNSTREAM.

UPSWING upward movement in the price of a security or commodity after a period of falling prices. Analysts will say "that stock has bottomed out and now has started an upswing which should carry it to new highs." The term is also used to refer to the general condition of the economy. An economy that is recovering from a prolonged downturn or recession is said to be in an upswing.

UPTICK transaction executed at a price higher than the preceding transaction in that security; also called PLUS TICK. A plus sign is displayed throughout the day next to the last price of each stock that showed a higher price than the preceding transaction in that stock at the TRADING POST of the SPECIALIST on the floor of the New York Stock Exchange. *See also* SHORT-SALE RULE.

UPTICK RULE Securities and Exchange Commission rule that selling short may only be done on an UPTICK. In 1990 interpretation of the rule was extended to cover PROGRAM TRADING. In 2007 the uptick rule was repealed. *See also* SHORT-SALE RULE.

UPTREND upward direction in the price of a stock, bond, or commodity future contract or overall market. *See also* TRENDLINE.

USEFUL LIFE estimated period of time during which an asset subject to DEPRECIATION is judged to be productive in a business. Also called *depreciable life.* The MODIFIED ACCELERATED COST RECOVERY SYSTEM (MACRS) established useful lives for different property classes. *See also* RESIDUAL VALUE.

USES OF FUNDS *see* SOURCES AND APPLICATIONS (OR USES) OF FUNDS STATEMENT.

U.S. SAVINGS BOND *see* SAVINGS BOND.

U-SHAPED RECOVERY gradual recovery of economic growth in an economy as measured by decline and then a rebound in the Gross Domestic Product. *See also* V-SHAPED RECOVERY.

USURY LAWS state laws limiting excessive interest rates on loans.

UTILITY power company that owns or operates facilities used for the generation, transmission, or distribution of electric energy. Utilities provide electric, gas, and water to their customers. In the United States, utilities are regulated at the state and federal level. State public service and public utility commissions regulate retail rates. The Federal Energy Regulatory Commission (FERC) regulates wholesale rates, the sale, resale, and interstate commerce for approximately 200 investor-owned utilities. On a percentage and revenue basis, however, the states regulate most of the trade. Rates for the sale of power and its transmission to retail customers, as well as approval for the construction of new plants, are regulated at the state level. The electric utility industry came under government regulation in the 1920s because it was a virtual MONOPOLY, vertically integrated, producing energy and transmitting it to customers. The industry has evolved to include public power agencies and electricity cooperatives. DEREGULATION of the natural gas industry in recent years has served to open that market to more competition, although transmission pipelines still come under FERC jurisdiction. The electric utility industry is also undertaking a similar deregulation process.

Utility stocks usually offer above-average dividend yields to investors, but less capital appreciation potential than growth stocks. Utility stocks are also very sensitive to the direction of interest rates. Rising interest rates tend to harm the value of utility shares because higher rates provide a more attractive alternative to investors. In addition, utilities tend to be heavy borrowers, so higher interest rates add to their borrowing costs. Conversely, falling interest rates tend to buoy the value of utility stocks because utility dividends look more attractive and because the companies' borrowing costs will be reduced.

UTILITY REVENUE BOND MUNICIPAL BOND issued to finance the construction of electric generating plants, gas, water and sewer systems, among other types of public utility services. These bonds are repaid from the revenues the project produces once it is operating. Such bonds usually have a reserve fund that contains an amount equal to one year's DEBT SERVICE, which protects bondholders in case there is a temporary cash shortage or revenues are less than anticipated. *See also* REVENUE BOND.

UTP *see* UNLISTED TRADING PRIVILEGES.

V

VALUABLES *see* HIGH-TICKET ITEMS.

VALUATION placing a value or worth on an asset. Stock analysts determine the value of a company's stock based on the outlook for earnings and the market value of assets on the balance sheet. Stock valuation is normally expressed in terms of price/earnings (P/E) ratios. A company with a high P/E is said to have a high valuation, and a low P/E stock has a low valuation. Other assets, such as real estate and bonds, are given valuations by analysts who recommend whether the asset is worth buying or selling at the current price. Estates also go through the valuation process after someone has died.

VALUATION RESERVE reserve or allowance, created by a charge to expenses (and therefore, in effect, taken out of profits) in order to provide for changes in the value of a company's assets. Accumulated DEPRECIATION, allowance for BAD DEBTS, and UNAMORTIZED BOND DISCOUNT are three familiar examples of valuation reserves. Also called *valuation account.*

VALUE-ADDED TAX (VAT) a form of CONSUMPTION TAX levied on the value added to a product at each stage of its manufacturing cycle as well as at the time of purchase by the ultimate consumer. The value-added tax is a fixture in European countries and a major source of revenue for the EURO-PEAN UNION (EU). Advocates of a value-added tax for the U.S. contend that it would be the most efficient method of raising revenue and that the size of its receipts would permit a reduction in income tax rates. Opponents argue that in its pure form it would be the equivalent of a national sales tax and therefore unfair and regressive, putting the greatest burden on those who can least afford it. As an example, for each part that goes into the assembling of an automobile, the auto manufacturer would pay a value-added tax to the supplier, probably a percentage of the purchase price, as is the case with a sales tax. When the finished car is sold, the consumer pays a value-added tax on the cost of the finished product less the material and supply costs that were taxed at earlier stages. This avoids double taxation and thus differs from a flat sales tax based on the total cost of purchase.

VALUE BROKER DISCOUNT BROKER whose rates are based on a percentage of the dollar value of each transaction. It is usually advantageous to place orders through a value broker for trades of low-priced shares or small numbers of shares, since commissions will be relatively smaller than if a shareholder used a SHARE BROKER, another type of discount broker, who charges according to the number and the price of the shares traded.

VALUE CHANGE change in a stock price adjusted for the number of out-standing shares of that stock, so that a group of stocks adjusted this way are equally weighted. A unit of movement of the group—called an INDEX—is thus representative of the average performance.

VALUE DATE
Banking: official date when money is transferred, that is, becomes good funds to the depositor. The value date differs from the *entry date* when items are received from the depositor, since the items must then be forwarded to the paying bank or otherwise collected. The term is used mainly with reference to foreign accounts, either maintained in a domestic bank or maintained

by a domestic bank in foreign banks. *See also* FLOAT.

Eurodollar and foreign currency transactions: synonymous with SETTLEMENT DATE or DELIVERY DATE, which on spot transactions involving North American currencies (U.S. dollar, Canadian dollar, and Mexican peso) is one business day and on spot transactions involving other currencies, two business days. In the forward exchange market, value date is the maturity date of the contract plus one business day for North American currencies, two business days for other currencies. *See also* FORWARD EXCHANGE TRANSACTION; SPOT MARKET.

VALUE INVESTING INVESTMENT PHILOSOPHY that focuses on buying stocks that are trading at bargain prices based on FUNDAMENTAL ANALYSIS, then holding them until they become FULLY VALUED. Stocks with LOW PRICE/EARN-INGS RATIOS, low PRICE/BOOK RATIOS, or high DIVIDEND YIELD are likely to attract value investors.

VALUE LINE INVESTMENT SURVEY investment advisory service that ranks about 1,700 stocks for "timeliness" and safety. Using a computerized model based on earnings momentum, Value Line projects which stocks will have the best or worst relative price performance over the next 6 to 12 months. In addition, each stock is assigned a risk rating, which identifies the VOLATILITY of a stock's price behavior relative to the market average. The service also ranks all major industry groups for timeliness. Value Line's ranking system for both timeliness and safety of an individual stock is as follows:

    1—highest rank
    2—above average rank
    3—average rank
    4—below average rank
    5—lowest rank

The weekly writeups of companies that Value Line subscribers receive include detailed financial information about a company, as well as such data as corporate INSIDER buying and selling decisions and the percentage of a company's shares held by institutions.

Value Line offers several specialized financial surveys. The *Value Line Convertibles Survey* is a subscription service that evaluates convertible securities. The *Value Line Mutual Fund Survey* offers details on fund holdings and performance and ranks funds on expected returns. Value Line also sponsors its own family of mutual funds. Value Line also produces several stock indices and averages, the most important of which is the *Value Line Composite Average,* which tracks the stocks followed by the *Value Line Investment Survey.*

VA MORTGAGE *see* VETERANS ADMINISTRATION (VA) MORTGAGE.

VARIABILITY *see* VOLATILITY.

VARIABLE ANNUITY life insurance ANNUITY contract whose value fluctuates with that of an underlying securities PORTFOLIO or other INDEX of performance. The variable annuity contrasts with a conventional or FIXED ANNUITY, whose rate of return is constant and therefore vulnerable to the effects of inflation. Income on a variable annuity may be taken periodically, beginning immediately or at any future time. The annuity may be a single-premium or multiple-premium contract. The return to investors may be in the form of a periodic payment that varies with the MARKET VALUE of the portfolio or a fixed minimum payment with add-ons based on the rate of portfolio appreciation. *See also* SINGLE PREMIUM DEFERRED ANNUITY.

VARIABLE COST cost that changes directly with the amount of production—for example, direct material or direct labor needed to complete a product. *See also* FIXED COST.

VARIABLE INTEREST RATE interest rate on a loan that rises and falls based on the movement of an underlying index of interest rates. For example, many credit cards charge variable interest rates, based on a specific spread over the prime rate. Most home equity loans charge variable rates tied to the prime rate. Also called *adjustable interest rate.*

VARIABLE LIFE INSURANCE innovation in LIFE INSURANCE that allows policyholders to invest the cash value of the policy in stock, bond, or money market portfolios. Investors can elect to move from one portfolio to another or rely on the company's professional money managers to make such decisions for them. As in WHOLE LIFE INSURANCE, the annual premium is fixed, but part of it is earmarked for the investment PORTFOLIO. The policyholder bears the risk of securities investments, meaning that cash values and death benefits will rise if the underlying investments do well and fall if the investments drop in value. Some insurance companies guarantee a minimum death benefit for an extra premium. When portfolio investments rise substantially, policyholders can use a portion of the increased cash value to buy additional insurance coverage. Policyholders can borrow against the accumulated cash value or cash in the policy. As in an INDIVIDUAL RETIREMENT ARRANGEMENT, earnings from variable life policies are tax deferred until distributed. Income is then taxed only to the extent it exceeds the total premiums paid into the policy. Death benefits are not taxed as individual income but as taxable estate income, which carried an exclusion of $3.5 million in 2009. Variable life insurance is different from UNIVERAL LIFE INSURANCE. Universal life allows policyholders to increase or decrease premiums and change the death benefit. It also accrues interest at market-related rates on premiums over and above insurance charges and expenses.

VARIABLE RATE CERTIFICATE a CERTIFICATE OF DEPOSIT (CD) whose rate of interest is periodically adjusted in relation to some benchmark, such as the prime rate or a stock index.

VARIABLE-RATE DEMAND NOTE note representing borrowings (usually from a commercial bank) that is payable on demand and that bears interest tied to a money market rate, usually the bank PRIME RATE. The rate on the note is adjusted upward or downward each time the base rate changes.

VARIABLE RATE MORTGAGE (VRM) *see* ADJUSTABLE RATE MORTGAGE (ARM).

VARIABLE RATE PREFERRED STOCK *see* ADJUSTABLE RATE PREFERRED STOCK (ARP).

VARIANCE
Accounting: difference between actual cost and STANDARD COST in the categories of direct material, direct labor, and DIRECT OVERHEAD. A positive variation (when the actual cost is lower than the standard or anticipated cost) would translate into a higher profit unless offset by negative variances elsewhere.

Finance: (1) difference between corresponding items on a comparative BALANCE SHEET and PROFIT AND LOSS STATEMENT. (2) difference between actual experience and budgeted or projected experience in any financial category. For example, if sales were projected to be $2 million for a period and were actually $2.5 million, there would be a positive variance of $500,000 or 25%.
Real estate: allowed exception to zoning rules. If a particular neighborhood were zoned for residential use only, a person wanting to open a store would need to be granted a variance from the zoning board in order to proceed.
Statistics: measure of the dispersion of a distribution. It is the sum of the squares of the deviation from the mean. *See also* STANDARD DEVIATION.

VEGA PRICING MODEL *see* DERIVATIVE PRICING MODELS.

VELDA SUE acronym for *Venture Enhancement & Loan Development Administration for Smaller Undercapitalized Enterprises,* a federal agency that buys small business loans made by banks, pools them, then issues securities that are bought as investments by large institutions.

VELOCITY rate of spending, or turnover of money—in other words, how many times a dollar is spent in a given period of time. The more money turns over, the faster velocity is said to be. The concept of "income velocity of money" was first explained by the economist Irving Fisher in the 1920s as bearing a direct relationship to GROSS DOMESTIC PRODUCT (GDP). Velocity usually is measured as the ratio of GDP to the money supply. Velocity affects the amount of economic activity generated by a given money supply, which includes bank deposits and cash in circulation. Velocity is a factor in the Federal Reserve Board's management of MONETARY POLICY, because an increase in velocity may obviate the need for a stimulative increase in the money supply. Conversely, a decline in velocity might reflect dampened economic growth, even if the money supply holds steady. *See also* FISCAL POLICY.

VENDOR
1. supplier of goods or services of a commercial nature; may be a manufacturer, importer, or wholesale distributor. For example, one component of the Index of LEADING INDICATORS is vendor performance, meaning the rate at which suppliers of goods are making delivery to their commercial customers.
2. retailer of merchandise, especially one without an established place of business, as in *sidewalk vendor.*

VENTURE CAPITAL important source of financing for START-UP companies or others embarking on new or TURNAROUND ventures that entail some investment risk but offer the potential for above average future profits; also called *risk capital.* Sources of venture capital include wealthy individual investors; subsidiaries of banks and other corporations organized as small business investment companies (SBICs); groups of investment banks and other financing sources who pool investments in venture capital funds or VENTURE CAPITAL LIMITED PARTNERSHIPS. The SMALL BUSINESS ADMINISTRATION (SBA) promotes venture capital programs through the licensing and financing of SBICs. Venture capital financing supplements other personal or external funds that an ENTREPRENEUR is able to tap, or takes the place of loans of other funds that conventional financial institutions are unable or unwilling to risk. Some venture capital sources invest only at a certain stage of entrepreneurship, such as the start-up or SEED MONEY stage, the *first round* or SECOND ROUND phases that follow, or at the MEZZANINE LEVEL immediately preceding an INITIAL PUBLIC OFFERING. In return for taking an investment risk, venture capitalists are usually rewarded with some combination of PROFITS, PREFERRED STOCK, ROYALTIES on sales, and capital appreciation of common shares.

VENTURE CAPITAL LIMITED PARTNERSHIP investment vehicle organized by a brokerage firm or entrepreneurial company to raise capital for START-UP companies or those in the early processes of developing products and services. The partnership will usually take shares of stock in the company in return for capital supplied. Limited partners receive income from profits the company may earn. If the company is successful and goes public, limited partners' profits could be realized from the sale of formerly private stock to the public. This type of partnership differs from a RESEARCH AND DEVELOPMENT LIMITED PARTNERSHIP in that R&D deals receive revenue only from the particular products they UNDERWRITE, whereas a venture capital partnership participates in the profits of the company, no matter what product or service is sold. *See also* ENTREPRENEUR; LIMITED PARTNERSHIP; PRIVATE EQUITY FUND.

VERTICAL ANALYSIS *see* COMMON SIZE STATEMENT.

VERTICAL LINE CHARTING form of technical charting on which the high, low, and closing prices of a stock or a market are shown on one vertical line with the closing price indicated by a short horizontal mark. Each vertical line represents another day, and the chart shows the trend of a stock or a market over a period of days, weeks, months, or years. Technical analysts discern from these charts whether a stock or a market is continually closing at the high or low end of its trading range during a day. This is useful in understanding whether the market's action is strong or weak, and therefore whether prices will advance or decline in the near future. *See also* TECHNICAL ANALYSIS.

VERTICAL LINE CHARTING

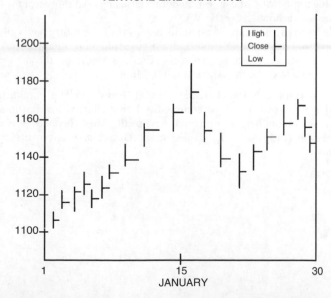

JANUARY

VERTICAL MERGER merger between a company that supplies goods and services and a company that buys those goods and services. For example, if a publishing company buys a paper producer, it is considered a vertical merger because the publisher buys large amounts of paper. In some cases, vertical mergers may be challenged by the government if they are found to violate ANTITRUST LAWS. *See also* MERGER.

VERTICAL SPREAD OPTION strategy that involves purchasing an option at one STRIKE PRICE while simultaneously selling another option of the same class at the next higher or lower strike price. Both options have the same expiration date. For example, a vertical spread is created by buying an XYZ May 30 call and selling an XYZ May 40 call. The investor who buys a vertical spread hopes to profit as the difference between the option premium on the two option positions widens or narrows. Also called a PRICE SPREAD. *See also* OPTION PREMIUM.

VESTED INTEREST in law, an interest in something that is certain to occur as opposed to being dependent on an event that might not happen. In general usage, an involvement having the element of personal gain. *See also* VESTING.

VESTING right an employee gradually acquires by length of service at a company to receive employer-contributed benefits, such as payments from a PENSION FUND, PROFIT-SHARING PLAN, or other QUALIFIED PLAN OR TRUST. Employees must be vested 100% after five years of service or at 20% a year starting in the third year and becoming 100% vested after seven years.

VETERANS AFFAIRS (VA) MORTGAGE home mortgage loan granted by a lending institution to qualified veterans of the U.S. armed forces or to their surviving spouses and guaranteed by the Department of Veterans Affairs (VA). The guarantee reduces risk to the lender for all or part of the purchase price on conventional homes, mobile homes, and condominiums. Because of this federal guarantee, banks and thrift institutions can afford to provide 30-year VA mortgages on favorable terms with a relatively low down payment even during periods of TIGHT MONEY. Interest rates on VA mortgages, formerly fixed by the Department of Housing and Urban Development together with those on Federal Housing Administration (FHA) mortgages, are now set by the VA.

VA mortgages comprise an important part of the mortgage pools packaged and sold as securities by such quasi-governmental organizations as the FEDERAL HOME MORTGAGE CORPORATION (Freddie Mac) and the GOVERNMENT NATIONAL MORTGAGE ASSOCIATION (Ginnie Mae).

V FORMATION technical chart pattern that forms a V. The V pattern indicates that the stock, bond, or commodity being charted has bottomed out and is now in a bullish (rising) trend. An upside-down (inverse) V is considered bearish (indicative of a falling market). *See also* BOTTOM; TECHNICAL ANALYSIS.

V FORMATION

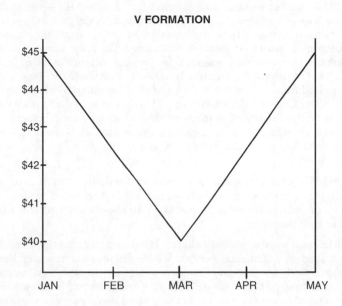

VIPER an EXCHANGE-TRADED FUND (ETF) whose underlying asset is one of the many INDEX FUNDS of the Vanguard Group. Acronym is Vanguard Index Participation Receipts. VIPERs are traded on the AMERICAN STOCK EXCHANGE.

VIRTUAL BANK a Web site that provides the consumer and business services available at a walk in bank.

VISIBLE SUPPLY dollar volume of municipal bonds scheduled to be issued over the coming month. Municipal bond investors, analysts, traders, and investment bankers watch the visible supply to determine whether the coming month might provide a good opportunity to buy bonds, sell bonds, or float a new bond issue. A large amount of new issues might depress bond prices and make it difficult to float a new issue. Conversely, a small amount of new issues may help bond prices and make it easier to float a new issue. The visible supply, also known as the calendar or the *30-day visible supply*, is compiled by *The Bond Buyer.*

VIX INDEX short for the CHICAGO BOARD OPTIONS EXCHANGE (CBOE) Volatility Index, which measures traders' expectations of volatility in the stock market by tracking bid/ask quotes on the Standard & Poor's 500 Stock Index. The VIX is determined by a complex formula based on the assumption that, other things being equal, options will trade at higher prices when expected VOLATILITY rises. The CBOE terms the VIX an "investor fear gauge." It has a mixed record of forecasting market trends, however, and some CONTRARIANS believe a high VIX reading presages a bull market and a low reading a bear market.

VOID deprived of legal force or effect, as a CONTRACT.

VOIDABLE contract that can be annulled by either party after it is signed because fraud, incompetence, or another illegality exists or because a RIGHT OF RESCISSION applies.

VOLATILE tending to rapid and extreme fluctuations. The term is used to describe the size and frequency of the fluctuations in the price of a particular stock, bond, or commodity. A stock may be volatile because the outlook for the company is particularly uncertain, because there are only a few shares outstanding (*see also* THIN MARKET), or because of various other reasons. Where the reasons for the variation have to do with the particular security as distinguished from market conditions, return is measured by a concept called ALPHA. A stock with an alpha factor of 1.25 is projected to rise in price by 25% in a year on the strength of its inherent values such as growth in earnings per share and regardless of the performance of the market as a whole. Market-related volatility, also called SYSTEMATIC RISK, is measured by BETA. *See also* DURATION.

VOLATILITY characteristic of a security, commodity, or market to rise or fall sharply in price within a short-term period. Also called VARIABILITY. A measure of the relative volatility of a stock to the overall market is its BETA. *See also* RISK; VOLATILE.

VOLUME total number of stock shares, bonds, or commodities futures contracts traded in a particular period. Volume figures are reported daily by exchanges, both for individual issues trading and for the total amount of trading executed on the exchange. Technical analysts place great emphasis on the amount of volume that occurs in the trading of a security or a commodity futures contract. A sharp rise in volume is believed to signify future sharp rises or falls in price, because it reflects increased investor interest in a security, commodity, or market. *See also* TECHNICAL ANALYSIS; TURNOVER.

VOLUME DELETED note appearing on the CONSOLIDATED TAPE, usually when the tape is running behind by two minutes or more because of heavy trading, that only the STOCK SYMBOL and the trading price will be displayed for transactions of less than 5000 shares.

VOLUME DISCOUNT any reduction in price based on the purchase of a large quantity.

VOLUME-WEIGHTED AVERAGE PRICE (VWAP) the price at which the majority of trading in a given stock took place on a given day. It multiplies the price by the shares traded for each transaction and divides the total transaction value by the total shares traded for the day. Pension plans managers reason that if the price of a buy trade is lower than the VWAP, it is a good trade, if higher, a bad trade.

VOLUNTARY ACCUMULATION PLAN plan subscribed to by a MUTUAL FUND shareholder to accumulate shares in that fund on a regular basis over time. The amount of money to be put into the fund and the intervals at which it is to be invested are at the discretion of the shareholder. A plan that invests a set amount on a regular schedule is called a dollar cost averaging plan or CONSTANT DOLLAR PLAN.

VOLUNTARY BANKRUPTCY legal proceeding that follows a petition of BANKRUPTCY filed by a debtor in the appropriate U.S. district court under the Bankruptcy Act. Petitions for voluntary bankruptcy can be filed by any insolvent business or individual, except a building and loan association or a municipal, railroad, insurance, or banking corporation. *See also* BANKRUPTCY ABUSE PREVENTION AND CONSUMER PROTECTION ACT OF 2005.

VOLUNTARY LIQUIDATION LIQUIDATION approved by a company's shareholders, as opposed to involuntary liquidation under Chapter 7 BANKRUPTCY. In the United Kingdom, a distinction is made between creditors' voluntary liquidation (or winding-up), which requires insolvency, and members' voluntary liquidation (or winding-up), which requires a declaration of solvency. *See also* VOLUNTARY BANKRUPTCY.

VOLUNTARY PLAN short for *voluntary deductible employee contribution plan*, a type of pension plan where the employee elects to have contributions (which, depending on the plan, may be before- or after-tax) deducted from each paycheck.

VOTING RIGHT right attending the ownership of most common stock to vote in person or by PROXY on corporate resolutions and the election of directors. *See also* NONVOTING STOCK.

VOTING STOCK shares in a corporation that entitle the shareholder to voting and PROXY rights. When a shareholder deposits such stock with a CUSTODIAN that acts as a voting TRUST, the shareholder retains rights to earnings and dividends but delegates voting rights to the trustee. *See also* COMMON STOCK; PROPORTIONAL REPRESENTATION; VOTING TRUST CERTIFICATE.

VOTING TRUST CERTIFICATE transferable certificate of beneficial interest in a *voting trust*, a limited-life trust set up to center control of a corporation in the hands of a few individuals, called *voting trustees*. The certificates, which are issued by the voting trust to stockholders in exchange for their common stock, represent all the rights of common stock except voting rights. The common stock is then registered on the books of the corporation in the names of the trustees. The usual purpose for such an arrangement is to facilitate REORGANIZATION of a corporation in financial difficulty by preventing interference with management. Voting trust certificates are limited to the five-year life of a TRUST but can be extended with the mutual consent of the holders and trustees.

V-SHAPED RECOVERY sharp rebound in economic activity as measured by a precipitous decline and then surging recovery in economy activity, as measured by the GROSS DOMESTIC PRODUCT (GDP). *See also* U-SHAPED RECOVERY.

VULTURE FUND type of LIMITED PARTNERSHIP that invests in depressed property, usually real estate, aiming to profit when prices rebound.

VWAP *see* VOLUME-WEIGHTED AVERAGE PRICE (VWAP).

W

WAGE ASSIGNMENT loan agreement provision, prohibited in some states, that authorizes the lender to deduct payments from an employee's wages in the event of DEFAULT.

WAGE GARNISHMENT *see* GARNISHMENT.

WAGE-PUSH INFLATION inflationary spiral caused by rapid increases in wages. *See also* COST-PUSH INFLATION; DEMAND-PULL INFLATION; INFLATION.

WAITING PERIOD period of time before something goes into effect. In securities, there is a waiting period between the filing of registration statements and the time when securities may be offered for sale to the public. This waiting period may be extended if the Securities and Exchange Commission requires revisions to the registration statement. In DISABILITY INCOME INSURANCE, there is a waiting period of several months from the time the disability occurs to the time when disability benefits are paid. For insurance claims, the waiting period is also known as the *elimination period.*

WAIVER OF PREMIUM clause in an insurance policy providing that all policy premiums will be waived if the policyholder becomes seriously ill or disabled, either permanently or temporarily, and therefore is unable to pay the premiums. Some policies include a waiver-of-premium clause automatically, while in other cases it is an optional feature that must be paid with additional premiums. During the waiver period, all policy benefits remain in force.

WALLFLOWER *see* ORPHAN STOCK.

WALLPAPER worthless securities. The implication of the term is that certificates of stocks and bonds that have gone bankrupt or defaulted have no other use than as wallpaper. However, there may be value in the worthless certificates themselves by collectors of such certificates, who prize rare or historically significant certificates. The practice of collecting such certificates is known as SCRIPOPHILY.

WALL STREET
1. common name for the financial district at the lower end of Manhattan in New York City, where the New York and American Stock Exchanges and numerous brokerage firms are headquartered. The New York Stock Exchange is actually located at the corner of Wall and Broad Streets.
2. investment community, such as in "Wall Street really likes the prospects for that company" or "Wall Street law firm," meaning a firm specializing in securities law and mergers. Also referred to as "the Street."

WALRASIAN MARKET also known as a *call market*, a market process that collects buy and sell orders, which are then analyzed to determine a clearing price that will decide the market price. Similar to the method used by New York Stock Exchange SPECIALISTS when they determine an opening price by analyzing all the orders for a stock and determining the price that will clear the greatest number of trades. Contrasts with a *continuous market*, which describes the way buy and sell orders are matched as they are received after the opening bell.

WANTED FOR CASH TICKER tape announcement that a bidder will pay cash the same day for a specified block of securities. Cash trades are executed for delivery and settlement at the time the transaction is made.

WAR BABIES jargon for the stocks and bonds of corporations engaged primarily as defense contractors. Also called *war brides*.

WAR CHEST fund of liquid assets (cash) set aside by a corporation to pay for a takeover or to defend against a takeover. Traders will say that a company has a war chest that it plans to use to take over another company. Or traders might say that a particular company will be difficult to take over because it has a large war chest that it can use to defend itself by buying back its stock, making an acquisition of its own, paying for legal fees to mount defenses, or taking other defensive measures. *See also* TAKEOVER.

WAREHOUSE RECEIPT document listing goods or commodities kept for SAFEKEEPING in a warehouse. The receipt can be used to transfer ownership of that commodity, instead of having to deliver the physical commodity. Warehouse receipts are used with many commodities, particularly precious metals like gold, silver, and platinum, which must be safeguarded against theft.

WARRANT *see* SUBSCRIPTION WARRANT.

WARRANTY contract between the seller and the buyer of a product specifying the conditions under which the seller will make repairs or remedy other problems that may arise, at no additional cost to the buyer. The warranty document describes how long the warranty remains in effect, and which specific repairs will be performed at no extra charge. Warranties usually cover workmanship or the failure of the product if used normally, but not negligence on the part of the user if the product is used in ways for which it was not designed. Warranties are commonly issued for automobiles, appliances, electronic gear, and most other products. In some cases, manufacturers will offer extended warranties for several years beyond the original warranty period, at an extra charge. Consumers should consult federal and state laws for more extensive applications or interpretations of warranties.

WARSAW STOCK EXCHANGE (WSE) exchange that traces its roots back to 1817, but that began activity in its present form on April 16, 1991. Since 2000, quotations on the Warsaw Stock Exchange take place in the WARSET system (WARsaw Stock Exchange Trading system). In 2002 the joint-stock company signed a cross-membership and cross-access agreement with EURONEXT. In 2003 it launched index options and the first foreign company was listed on the exchange. Products listed on the WSE include equities, bonds, options, subscription rights, and derivatives. Trading on the WSE also includes futures on three indices—the WIG20, TechWIG, and MIDWIG—as well as on individual stock futures and exchange rate futures on the U.S. dollar and the euro. The exchange is open for trading Monday through Friday from 9 A.M. to 4:30 P.M., while futures contracts are quoted from 8:30 A.M. to 4:30 P.M. All trading occurs in electronic form. *www.wse.com.pl.*

WASH SALE purchase and sale of a security either simultaneously or within a short period of time. It may be done by a single investor or (where MANIPULATION is involved) by two or more parties conspiring to create artificial market activity in order to profit from a rise in the security's price. Wash sales taking place within 30 days of the underlying purchase do not qualify as tax losses under Internal Revenue Service rules.

Under the TAX REFORM ACT OF 1984, wash sale rules were extended to all taxpayers except those trading in securities in the normal course of business, such as securities dealers. Prior to the 1984 Act, noncorporate taxpayers engaged in a trade or business were exempt from wash sale rules. The Act also extended the wash sale prohibition to closing short sales of substantially identical securities, or to instances where short sales are made within 30 days of closing. *See also* THIRTY-DAY WASH RULE.

WASTING ASSET
1. fixed asset, other than land, that has a limited useful life and is therefore subject to DEPRECIATION.
2. natural resource that diminishes in value because of extractions of oil, ores, or gas, or the removal of timber, or similar depletion and that is therefore subject to AMORTIZATION.
3. security with a value that expires at a particular time in the future. An OPTION contract, for instance, is a wasting asset, because the chances of a favorable move in the underlying stock diminish as the contract approaches expiration, thus reducing the value of the option.

WATCH LIST list of securities singled out for special surveillance by a brokerage firm or an exchange or other self-regulatory organization to spot irregularities. Firms on the watch list may be TAKEOVER candidates, companies about to issue new securities, or others that seem to have attracted an unusually heavy volume of trading activity. *See also* STOCK WATCHER; SURVEILLANCE DEPARTMENT OF EXCHANGES.

WATERED STOCK stock representing ownership of OVERVALUED assets, a condition of overcapitalized corporations, whose total worth is less than their invested capital. The condition may result from inflated accounting values, gifts of stock, operating losses, or excessive stock dividends. Among the negative features of watered stock from the shareholder's standpoint are inability to recoup full investment in LIQUIDATION, inadequate return on investment, possible liability exceeding the PAR value of shares, low MARKET VALUE because of poor dividends and possible adverse publicity, reduced ability of the firm to issue new stock or debt securities to capitalize on growth opportunity, and loss of competitive position because of the need to raise prices to provide a return acceptable to investors. To remedy the situation, a company must either increase its assets without increasing its OUTSTANDING shares or reduce outstanding shares without reducing assets. The alternatives are to increase RETAINED EARNINGS or to adjust the accounting values of assets or of stock.

WEAK DOLLAR dollar that has fallen in value against foreign currencies. This means that those holding dollars will get fewer pounds, yen, Euros, or other currencies in exchange for their dollars. A weak dollar makes it easier for U.S. companies to export their goods to other countries because foreigners' buying power is enhanced. The dollar may weaken because of loose U.S. monetary policy (creating too many dollars) and lack of confidence in the U.S. government, large trade and budget deficits, unattractive interest rates on dollar-denominated investments compared to investments denominated in other currencies, or other reasons.

WEAK MARKET market characterized by a preponderance of sellers over buyers and a general declining trend in prices.

WEALTH EFFECT in economics, the idea that as wealth increases or decreases, discretionary spending increases or decreases disproportionately. As paper profits increase during a BULL MARKET, some economists fear a wealth effect could cause stock speculation and other reckless forms of spending to gain momentum and cause dangerous inflation. Conversely, when there is a BEAR MARKET, investors tend to feel poorer and therefore reign in their spending, potentially causing falling prices and deflation.

WEBCRD *see* CENTRAL REGISTRATION DEPOSITORY (CRD).

WEBS (WORLD EQUITY BENCHMARK SHARES) *see* iSHARES.

WEDGE technical chart pattern similar to but varying slightly from a TRIANGLE. Two converging lines connect a series of peaks and troughs to form a wedge. These converging lines move in the same direction, unlike a triangle, in which one rises while the other falls or one rises or falls while the other line stays horizontal. Falling wedges usually occur as temporary interruptions of upward price rallies, rising wedges as interruptions of a falling price trend. *See also* TECHNICAL ANALYSIS.

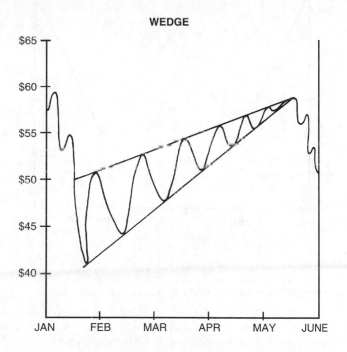

WEDGE

WEIGHTED AVERAGE MATURITY also called *average life* or *weighted average life* and used in mortgage-backed PASS-THROUGH SECURITIES meaning the weighted-average time to the return of a dollar of principal. It is arrived at by multiplying each portion of principal received by the time at which it is received, and then summing and dividing by the total amount of principal. Fabozzi's *Handbook of Fixed Income Securities* uses this example: Consider a simple annual-pay, four-year bond with a face value of $100 and principal payments of $40 the first year, $30 the second year, $20 the third year, and $10 the fourth year. The average life would be calculated as: Average life = .4 × 1 year + .3 × 2 years + .2 × 3 years + .1 × 4 years = 2 years. An alternative measure of investment life is DURATION.

WELLS NOTICE notification by the SECURITIES AND EXCHANGE COMMISSION that an investigation has found violations of the law and an enforcement action is being contemplated. The letter also gives the individual or company an opportunity to provide information arguing against the potential action.

W FORMATION technical chart pattern of the price of a stock, bond, or commodity that shows the price has hit a SUPPORT LEVEL two times and is moving up; also called a *double bottom.*

A reverse W is just the opposite; the price has hit a resistance level and is headed down. This is called a DOUBLE TOP.

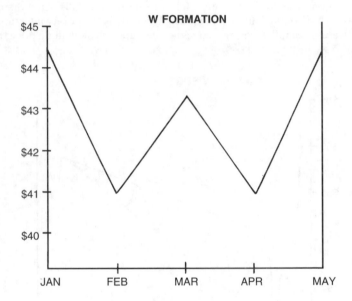

W-4 FORM tax form prepared by an employee for an employer indicating the employee's exemptions and Social Security number and enabling the employer to determine the amount of taxes to be withheld.

WHEN DISTRIBUTED transactions conditional on the SECONDARY DISTRIBUTION of shares ISSUED AND OUTSTANDING but CLOSELY HELD, as those of a wholly owned subsidiary, for example. *See also* WHEN ISSUED.

WHEN ISSUED short form of "when, as, and if issued." Term refers to a transaction made conditionally because a security, although authorized, has not yet been issued. NEW ISSUES of stocks and bonds, stocks that have SPLIT, and Treasury securities are all traded on a when issued basis. In a newspaper listing, a "WI" is placed next to the price of such a security. *See also* WHEN DISTRIBUTED.

WHIPSAWED caught in VOLATILE price movements while making losing trades as prices rise and fall. A trader is whipsawed if he or she buys just before prices fall and sells just before prices rise. A variation of this term is also used in TECHNICAL ANALYSIS referring to misleading signals, called *whip-saws* or *chatter,* in the chart trends of markets or particular securities.

WHISPER NUMBER unofficial earnings estimates made by security analysts. If an analyst is more optimistic about a company's earnings prospects than his official profit estimate reveals, he may speak of a "whisper number" to his clients that is higher than his published numbers. The opposite can be true on the downside. Investors and the media sometimes start to count on "whisper numbers" when earnings are announced. While a company may report profits in line with official estimates, those companies that do not meet their "whisper numbers," disappoint investors, which drives stock prices down.

WHISPER STOCK stock that is rumored to be a takeover target. Speculators, arbitrageurs, and other investors may buy shares in the company hoping that the "whispers" they have heard are true, allowing them to reap huge profits when the takeover is officially announced. Whisper stocks may trade in heavier-than-usual volume once the rumors about the takeover spread widely. Investing in whisper stocks is risky, however, because the takeover rumors may prove to be inaccurate.

WHISTLE BLOWER employee or other person with inside knowledge of wrongdoing inside a company or government agency. The employee is supposed to be protected from retribution by the employer by several federal laws protecting whistle blowers, though whistle blowers frequently are punished for revealing wrongdoing by their employer. Several employees who disclosed illegal billing practices by defense contractors were demoted or fired, for example. In securities, under the Insider Trading and Securities Fraud Enforcement Act of 1988, whistle blowers who provide the SEC with information about illegal insider trading or other illegal activity that leads to a conviction may qualify for bounties.

WHITE COLLAR WORKER office worker in professional, managerial, or administrative position. Such workers typically wear shirts with white collars. Those working in factories or doing manual labor typically wear blue collars, and are therefore called *blue-collar workers.*

WHITE KNIGHT friendly acquirer sought by the target of an unfriendly TAKEOVER.

WHITEMAIL anti-TAKEOVER device whereby a vulnerable company sells a large amount of stock to a friendly party at below-market prices. This puts a potential raider in a position where it must buy a sizable amount of stock at inflated prices to get control and thus helps perpetuate existing management.

WHITE SHEETS list of prices published by the NATIONAL QUOTATION BUREAU for market makers in OVER-THE-COUNTER stocks traded in Chicago, Los Angeles, and San Francisco.

WHITE-SHOE FIRM anachronistic characterization of certain broker-dealers as venerable, "upper-crust" and "above" such practices as participating in hostile takeovers. Derives from the '50s culture of Ivy League colleges, where white buck shoes were *de rigueur* in elite fraternities and clubs.

WHITE SQUIRE WHITE KNIGHT who buys less than a majority interest.

WHITE'S RATING White's Tax-Exempt Bond Rating Service's classification of municipal securities, which is based on market factors rather than credit considerations and which attempts to determine appropriate yields. *See also* MUNICIPAL BOND.

WHOLE LIFE INSURANCE form of life insurance policy that offers protection in case the insured dies and also builds up cash value. The policy stays in force for the lifetime of the insured, unless the policy is canceled or lapses. The policyholder usually pays a level PREMIUM for whole life, which does not rise as the person grows older (as in the case of TERM INSURANCE). The earnings on the cash value in the policy accumulate tax-deferred, and can be borrowed against in the form of a POLICY LOAN. The death benefit is reduced by the amount of the loan, plus interest, if the loan is not repaid.

Traditionally, life insurance companies invest insurance premiums conservatively in bonds, stocks, and real estate in order to generate increases in cash value for policyholders. Policyholders have no input into the investment decision-making process in a whole life insurance policy. Other forms of cash value policies, such as UNIVERSAL LIFE INSURANCE and VARIABLE LIFE INSURANCE give policyholders more options, such as stock, bond, and money market accounts, to choose from in investing their premiums. Whole life insurance is also known as *ordinary life, permanent life, or straight life insurance. See also* ADEQUACY OF COVERAGE; ANNUAL EXCLUSION; CASH VALUE INSURANCE; CONTINGENT BENEFICIARY; CONVERTIBILITY; DEATH BENEFIT; EXPERIENCE RATING; FINANCIAL NEEDS APPROACH; FIXED PREMIUM; FULLY PAID POLICY; GUARANTEED INSURABILITY; HIDDEN LOAD; INCOME EXCLUSION RULE; INSURABILITY; INSURABLE INTEREST; INSURANCE AGENT; INSURANCE CLAIM; INSURANCE DIVIDEND; INSURANCE POLICY; INSURANCE PREMIUM; INSURANCE SETTLEMENT; INSURED; LAPSE; LIFE INSURANCE; LIFE INSURANCE POLICY; LIVING BENEFITS; LUMP SUM; MORTALITY RISK; NONCONTESTABILITY CLAUSE; NONPARTICIPATING LIFE INSURANCE POLICY; PAID UP; PAID UP POLICY; PARTICIPATING DIVIDENDS; PARTICIPATING INSURANCE; SAVINGS ELEMENT; SECOND-TO-DIE INSURANCE; SETTLEMENT OPTIONS; SINGLE-PREMIUM LIFE INSURANCE; SURRENDER VALUE.

WHOLE LOAN SECONDARY MORTGAGE MARKET term that distinguishes an investment representing an original residential mortgage loan (whole loan) from a loan representing a participation with one or more lenders or a PASS-THROUGH SECURITY representing a pool of mortgages.

WHOLESALE PRICE INDEX *see* PRODUCER PRICE INDEX.

WHOLESALER
In general: middleman or DISTRIBUTOR who sells mainly to retailers, JOBBERS, other merchants, and industrial, commercial, and institutional users as distinguished from consumers. *See also* VENDOR.
Securities:
1. INVESTMENT BANKER acting as an UNDERWRITER in a NEW ISSUE or as a distributor in a secondary offering of securities. *See also* SECONDARY DISTRIBUTION.
2. broker-dealer who trades with other broker-dealers, rather than with the retail investor, and receives discounts and selling commissions.
3. SPONSOR of a MUTUAL FUND.

WHOLLY OWNED SUBSIDIARY SUBSIDIARY whose common stock is virtually 100%-owned by the PARENT COMPANY.

WIDE OPENING abnormally large SPREAD between the BID AND ASKED prices of a security at the OPENING of a trading session.

WIDGET symbolic American gadget, used wherever a hypothetical product is needed to illustrate a manufacturing or selling concept.

WIDOW-AND-ORPHAN STOCK stock that pays high dividends and is very safe. It usually has a low BETA COEFFICIENT and is involved in a noncyclical business. For years American Telephone and Telegraph was considered a widow-and-orphan stock, but it lost that status after the breakup of the Bell System in 1984. High-quality electric utility stocks are still considered widow-and-orphan stocks by and large.

WIENER BÖRSE AG (VIENNA STOCK EXCHANGE) founded in 1771 by Maria Theresa, Wiener Börse is the only securities exchange and listing authority in Austria. Early on, the exchange was primarily a marketplace for trading bonds, bills of exchange, and foreign currencies; shares were traded for the first time in 1818. Today, the market segments are equity market (stocks), bond market (bonds), OTOB market (derivatives), structured products (certificates, warrants), and other listings (containing all securities that cannot be allocated to any other segment). All trading on Wiener Börse is operated by the fully electronic trading system EQOS (Electronic Quote and Order-Driven System). This system guarantees the greatest possible transparency as well as fast and efficient execution of market transactions. Futures and options are traded on the OTOB (Osterreichische Termin-und Optionborse). The ATX (Austrian Traded Index), representing the continuously traded stocks on the prime market with the highest liquidity and market capitalization, is the largest stock market index on the exchange. The WBI (Wiener Börse index) represents the performance of all Austrian stocks admitted to listing on the Official Market. The Vienna Dynamic Index (ViDX) includes growth- and technology-oriented companies listed at the Wiener Börse. The CECE indices track the most attractive companies listed on Central and East European stock exchanges. Trading at Wiener Börse is conducted Monday through Friday from 9:15 A.M. to 5:35 P.M. The Wiener Börse Information Products department supplies professionally compiled real-time price data and market depth data to data vendors and private investors. As a special service, Wiener Börse computes and disseminates 19 stock indices in real time, which have become established as benchmarks for the domestic and Central and East European markets. *www.wienerborse.at.*

WILDCAT DRILLING exploring for oil or gas in an unproven area. A wildcat OIL AND GAS LIMITED PARTNERSHIP is structured so that investors take high risks but can reap substantial rewards if oil or gas is found in commercial quantities.

WILL document, also called a *testament,* that, when signed and witnessed, gives legal effect to the wishes of a person, called a *testator,* with respect to disposal of property upon death.

WILLIAMS ACT federal legislation enacted in 1968 that imposes requirements with respect to public TENDER OFFERS. It was inspired by a wave of unannounced TAKEOVERS in the 1960s, which caught managers unawares and confronted stockholders with decisions they were ill prepared to make, The Williams Act and amendments now comprise Sections 13(d) and 14(d) of the SECURITIES EXCHANGE ACT OF 1934. The law requires the bidder opening a tender to file with both the SECURITIES AND EXCHANGE COMMISSION and the TARGET COMPANY a statement detailing the terms of the offer, the bidder's background, the cash source, and his or her plans for the company if there is a takeover. The same information is required within 10 days from any person or company acquiring 5% or more of another company. The law mandates a minimum offering period of 20 days and gives tendering share-holders 15 days to change their minds. If only a limited number of shares are accepted, they must be prorated among the tendering stockholders. *See also* SATURDAY NIGHT SPECIAL.

WILSHIRE INDICES performance measurement indices developed by Wilshire Associates, Inc., of Santa Monica, California. The Wilshire 5000 Total Market Index, named after the nearly 5,000 stocks it contained when it was originally created, is the most widely followed index; it is published in national daily newspapers and is carried by the Associated Press. It measures the performance of all U.S. equity securities with readily available price data; as of June 30, 2009, 4,241 capitalization-weighted security returns were included in the index. The Wilshire 5000 base is its December 31, 1980, capi-talization of $1,404.596; its capitalization is approximately 77.5% NEW YORK STOCK EXCHANGE (NYSE), 0.3% NYSE Amex Equities (AMEX), and 22.2% NATIONAL ASSOCIATION OF DEALERS AUTOMATED QUOTATIONS (NASDAQ). Equity issues include common stocks and REITs. Additions to the index are made monthly, after the third Friday's close. INITIAL PUBLIC OFFERINGS (IPOs) are generally added with the monthly adds. The Wilshire 4500 Equity Index is the Wilshire 5000 less the STANDARD & POOR'S 500 COMPOSITE INDEX; current capitalization is about 62.4% NYSE, 1.3% AMEX, and 36.3% NASDAQ. The Wilshire Small Cap Index consists of 250 companies with an average market capitalization of $1,207 million and is designed to meet the need for derivative trading instruments reflecting the true character of the small cap market. Ten individual style indices (such as growth and value) and three real estate securities indices are derived from the Wilshire 5000. *See also* STOCK INDICES AND AVERAGES.

WINDFALL PROFIT profit that occurs suddenly as a result of an event not controlled by the person or company profiting from the event. For example, oil companies profited in the 1970s from an explosion in the price of oil brought about by the Arab oil embargo and the price increases demanded by the Organization of Petroleum Exporting Countries. *See also* WINDFALL PROFITS TAX.

WINDFALL PROFITS TAX tax on profits that result from a sudden windfall to a particular company or industry. In 1980, federal legislation was passed that levied such a tax on oil companies because of the profits they earned as a result of the sharp increase in oil prices in the 1970s. Since then, the tax has not been reenacted.

WINDOW
  1. limited time during which an opportunity should be seized, or it will be lost. For example, a period when new stock issues are welcomed by the public only lasts for a few months, or maybe as long as a year—that time is called the *window of opportunity.*

2. DISCOUNT WINDOW of a Federal Reserve bank.
3. cashier department of a brokerage firm, where delivery and settlement of securities transactions takes place.

WINDOW DRESSING
1. trading activity near the end of a quarter or fiscal year that is designed to dress up a PORTFOLIO to be presented to clients or shareholders. For example, a fund manager may sell losing positions in his portfolio so he can display only positions that have gained in value.
2. accounting gimmickry designed to make a FINANCIAL STATEMENT show a more favorable condition than actually exists—for example by omitting certain expenses, by concealing liabilities, by delaying WRITE-OFFS, by anticipating sales, or by other such actions, which may or may not be fraudulent.

WIRE HOUSE national or international brokerage firm whose branch offices are linked by a communications system that permits the rapid dissemination of prices, information, and research relating to financial markets and individual securities. Although smaller retail and regional brokers currently have access to similar data, the designation of a firm as a wire house dates back to the time when only the largest organizations had access to high-speed communications. Therefore, *wire house* still is used to refer to the biggest brokerage houses.

WIRELESS TRADING *see* ON-LINE TRADING.

WIRE ROOM operating department of a brokerage firm that receives customers' orders from the REGISTERED REPRESENTATIVE and transmits the vital data to the exchange floor, where a FLOOR TICKET is prepared, or to the firm's trading department for execution. The wire room also receives notices of executed trades and relays them to the appropriate registered representatives. Also called *order department, order room,* or *wire and order.*

WIRE TRANSFER *see* ELECTRONIC FUNDS TRANSFER (EFT).

WITCHING HOUR *see* TRIPLE WITCHING HOUR.

WITHDRAWAL PLAN program available through most open-end MUTUAL FUND companies in which shareholders can receive fixed payments of income or CAPITAL GAINS (or both) on a regular basis, usually monthly or quarterly.

WITHHOLDING
Securities: violation of the RULES OF FAIR PRACTICE of the FINANCIAL INDUSTRY REGULATORY AUTHORITY (FINRA) whereby a participant in a PUBLIC OFFERING fails to make a bona fide public offering at the PUBLIC OFFERING PRICE—for example, by withholding shares for his or her own account or selling shares to a family member, an employee of the dealer firm, or another broker-dealer—in order to profit from the higher market price of a HOT ISSUE. *See also* IMMEDIATE FAMILY; INVESTMENT HISTORY.
Taxes:
1. deduction from salary payments and other compensation to provide for an individual's tax liability. Federal income taxes and Social Security contributions are withheld from paychecks and are deposited in a Treasury TAX AND LOAN ACCOUNT with a bank. The yearly amount of withholding is reported on an income statement (form W-2), which must be submitted

with the federal, state, and local tax returns. Liability not provided for by withholding must be paid in four ESTIMATED TAX payments.

2. withholding by corporations and financial institutions of a flat 10% of interest and dividend payments due securities holders, as required under the TAX EQUITY AND FISCAL RESPONSIBILITY ACT OF 1982. The purpose was to levy a tax on people whose earnings escaped tracking by the Internal Revenue Service. The 10% withholding requirement was repealed in 1983. As a compromise, "backup withholding" was instituted, whereby, using Social Security numbers, payments can be reported to the IRS and matched against the actual income reported.

3. withholdings from pension and annuity distributions, sick pay, tips, and sizeable gambling winnings, as stipulated by law.

4. 30% withholding requirement on income from U.S. securities owned by foreigners—repealed by the TAX REFORM ACT OF 1984.

WORKERS COMPENSATION INSURANCE INSURANCE that pays benefits on behalf of an insured employer to employees or their families in the case of injury, disability, or death resulting from occupational hazards.

WORKING CAPITAL funds invested in a company's cash, ACCOUNTS RECEIVABLE, INVENTORY, and other CURRENT ASSETS *(gross working capital);* usually refers to *net working capital*—that is, current assets minus CURRENT LIABILITIES. Working capital finances the CASH CONVERSION CYCLE of a business—the time required to convert raw materials into finished goods, finished goods into sales, and accounts receivable into cash. These factors vary with the type of industry and the scale of production, which varies in turn with seasonality and with sales expansion and contraction. Internal sources of working capital include RETAINED EARNINGS, savings achieved through operating efficiencies and the allocation of CASH FLOW from sources like DEPRECIATION or deferred taxes to working capital. External sources include bank and other short-term borrowings, TRADE CREDIT, and term debt and EQUITY FINANCING not channeled into long-term assets. *See also* CURRENT RATIO; NET CURRENT ASSETS.

WORKING CONTROL effective control of a corporation by a shareholder or shareholders with less than 51% voting interest. Working control by a minority holder, or by two or more minority holders working in concert, is possible when share ownership of a firm is otherwise widely dispersed. *See also* MINORITY INTEREST.

WORKING FAMILIES TAX RELIEF ACT OF 2004 legislation designed to extend a variety of tax breaks for individuals and businesses and simplify certain parts of the tax code. Some of the most important provisions of the law include:

1. **Continuing the child tax credit at $1,000 for 2005 through 2009.**

2. **Full marriage penalty relief for the basic standard deduction.** In 2005 through 2008, the basic standard deduction amount for married joint filers is double the standard deduction for single taxpayers. Also, full marriage penalty relief for those in the 15% tax bracket.

3. **Repeal of the reduction in the 10% tax bracket for 2005 through 2010.** The 10% bracket applies to the first $7,000 of taxable income for singles and the first $14,000 of taxable income for married couples filing jointly, and the first $10,000 of taxable income for those filing as heads of household.

4. **No rollback in 2005 AMT exemptions for individuals.** The Alternative

Minimum Tax exemption amount for individuals is increased to $58,000 for married couples filing jointly and $40,250 for singles.

5. **Uniform definition of a child.** In the past, there were many definitions of a child for various tax purposes that were all unified into one definition based on a test of residency, relationship, and age. This applies for the purpose of the dependency exemption, child credits, earned income credits, dependent care credits, and head of household filing status.

6. **Research credit extended through 2005.**

7. **Work opportunity and welfare-to-work tax credits extended through 2005.**

8. **Energy incentives extended through 2005.** This applies to credits for electric vehicles, clean fuel properties, and production of electricity from renewable resources such as wind and biomass.

WORKING INTEREST direct participation with unlimited liability, as distinguished from passive LIMITED PARTNERSHIP shares. The TAX REFORM ACT OF 1986 let investors with working interests in drilling ventures, such as GENERAL PARTNERS, offset losses against all types of income.

WORK-IN-PROCESS *see* INVENTORY.

WORKOUT situation, such as a bad loan or troubled firm, where remedial measures are being taken.

WORKSHEET computerized page allowing the user to manipulate many columns and rows of numbers. The worksheet can contain formulas so that if one number is changed, the entire worksheet is automatically updated, based on those formulas. Analysts, investors, and accountants track a company's financial statements, balance sheets, and other data on worksheets.

WORLD BANK *see* INTERNATIONAL BANK FOR RECONSTRUCTION AND DEVELOPMENT.

WORLD TRADE ORGANIZATION (WTO) independent multilateral agency administering world trade agreements. WTO, headquartered in Geneva, Switzerland, resulted from the Uruguay round of GENERAL AGREEMENT ON TRADE AND TARIFFS (GATT) concluded in 1995. WTO's tasks include fostering trade relations among its members, resolving disputes, and serving as a forum for future multilateral trade negotiations.

WRAP ACCOUNT investment consulting relationship in which a client's funds are placed with one or more money managers, and all administrative and management fees, along with commissions, are wrapped into one comprehensive fee, which is paid quarterly. The wrap fee varies, but usually ranges from 1% to 3% of the value of the assets in the account. Wrap accounts usually require a minimum initial investment of anywhere from $25,000 to $10 million for individual accounts. The term *wrap* has been expanded to involve mutual fund asset allocation programs. Technically, these are not wrap programs because they are not "all inclusive." Transaction commissions in these programs on mutual funds are still a variable and they are pooled accounts as distinguished from individual accounts. From the customer's point of view, a wrap account provides access to top investment managers. The broker overseeing the account is paid an ongoing fee to monitor the performance of the money managers. Although brokers may switch assets to other managers within the program if one manager consistently starts to underperform, most sponsors of wrap programs suggest a three- to five-year time horizon to reach investment goals.

WRAPAROUND ANNUITY ANNUITY contract allowing an annuitant discretion in the choice of underlying investments. Wraparound refers to the protection the annuity vehicle provides through its TAX-DEFERRED status, which becomes precarious when the annuity vehicle is being used as a technical way to avoid tax payment. The tax courts have ruled against tax deferment where money can be allocated by an annuity owner to a portfolio managed by an annuitant and where the annuitant can switch among funds of the sponsoring insurance company that are also marketed independently of annuities. On the other hand, the IRS has upheld tax deferral where an individual could not buy such funds without also buying the annuity. In any event, the insurer must legally own the annuity money.

WRAPAROUND MORTGAGE second mortgage that increases a borrower's indebtedness while leaving the original mortgage contract in force. The wraparound mortgage becomes the JUNIOR MORTGAGE and is held by the lending institution as security for the total mortgage debt. The borrower makes payments on both loans to the wraparound lender, who in turn makes scheduled installment payments on the original *senior mortgage.* It is a convenient way for a property owner to obtain additional credit without having first to pay off an existing mortgage.

WRINKLE novel feature that may attract a buyer for a new product or a security. For example, ZERO COUPON SECURITIES were a new wrinkle when they were introduced but soon thereafter became quite commonplace.

WRITE-OFF charging an ASSET amount to expense or loss. The effect of a write-off is to reduce or eliminate the value of the asset and reduce profits. Write-offs are systematically taken in accordance with allowable tax DEPRECIATION of a FIXED ASSET, and with the AMORTIZATION of certain other assets, such as an INTANGIBLE ASSET and a capitalized cost (like premiums paid on investments). Write-offs are also taken when assets are, for whatever reason, deemed worthless, the most common example being uncollectible ACCOUNTS RECEIVABLE. Where such write-offs can be anticipated and therefore estimated, the usual practice has been to charge income regularly in amounts needed to maintain a RESERVE, the actual losses then being charged to the reserve. The TAX REFORM ACT OF 1986 required that BAD DEBT write-offs be charged directly to income by taxpayers other than small banks and thrift institutions. *See also* EXTRAORDINARY ITEM; NONRECURRING CHARGE.

WRITE OUT procedure followed when a SPECIALIST on an exchange makes a trade involving his own inventory, on one hand, and an order he is holding for a FLOOR BROKER, on the other. Exchange rules require a two-part transaction: the broker first completes a trade with the specialist, who then completes the transaction by a separate trade with the customer. The write out involves no charge other than the normal broker's commission.

WRITER
1. person who sells PUT OPTION and CALL OPTION contracts, and therefore collects PREMIUM INCOME. The writer of a put option is obligated to buy (and the writer of a call option is obligated to sell) the UNDERLYING SECURITY at a predetermined price by a particular date if the OPTION is exercised. *See also* COVERED CALL; NAKED OPTION; WRITING NAKED.
2. insurance UNDERWRITER.

WRITE UP/WRITE DOWN upward or downward adjustment of the accounting value of an asset according to GENERALLY ACCEPTED ACCOUNTING PRINCIPLES (GAAP). *See also* WRITE-OFF.

WRITING CASH-SECURED PUTS OPTION strategy that a trader who wants to sell PUT OPTIONS uses to avoid having to use a MARGIN ACCOUNT. Rather than depositing MARGIN with a broker, a put WRITER can deposit cash equal to the option EXERCISE PRICE. With this strategy, the put option writer is not subject to additional margin requirements in the event of changes in the underlying stock's price. The put writer can also be earning money by investing the PREMIUM he or she receives in MONEY MARKET instruments.

WRITING NAKED strategy used by an OPTION seller in which the trader does not own the UNDERLYING SECURITY. This strategy can lead to large profits if the stock moves in the hoped-for direction, but it can lead to large losses if the stock moves in the other direction, since the trader will have to go into the marketplace to buy the stock in order to deliver it to the option buyer. *See also* NAKED OPTION.

WRITING PUTS TO ACQUIRE STOCK strategy used by an OPTION writer (seller) who believes a stock is going to decline and that its purchase at a given price would represent a good investment. By writing a PUT OPTION exercisable at that price, the writer cannot lose. If the stock, contrary to his expectation, goes up, the option will not be exercised and he is at least ahead the amount of the PREMIUM he received. If, as expected, the stock goes down and the option is exercised, he has bought the stock at what he had earlier decided was a good buy, and he has the premium income in addition.

WRITTEN-DOWN VALUE BOOK VALUE of an asset after DEPRECIATION or other AMORTIZATION; also called *net book value.* For example, if the original cost of a piece of equipment was $1,000 and accumulated depreciation charges totaled $400, the written-down value would be $600. *See also* INTANGIBLE ASSET.

WRONG WAY RISK *see* COUNTERPARTY RISK.

WT abbreviation for *warrant. See also* SUBSCRIPTION WARRANT.

W-2 FORM tax form prepared by an employer for an employee to enclose with the 1040 FORM, summarizing wages earned for the year, federal and state taxes withheld, and SOCIAL SECURITY tax information.

X Y Z

X or XD symbol used in newspapers to signify that a stock is trading EX-DIV-IDEND, that is, without dividend. The symbol X is also used in bond tables to signify without interest.

XR symbol used in newspapers to signify that a stock is trading EX-RIGHTS, that is, without rights attached. *See also* SUBSCRIPTION RIGHT.

XW symbol used in newspapers to signify that a stock is trading EX-WARRANTS, that is, without warrants attached. *See also* SUBSCRIPTION WARRANT.

YANKEE BOND MARKET dollar-denominated bonds issued in the U.S. by foreign banks and corporations. The bonds are issued in the U.S. when market conditions there are more favorable than on the EUROBOND market or in domestic markets overseas. Similarly, Yankee CERTIFICATES OF DEPOSIT are negotiable CDs issued in the U.S. by branches and agencies of foreign banks.

YARD one billion currency units, usually yen.

YEAR-END BONUS bonus payment given to employees at the end of a year, based on the employee's performance and the performance of the company. Most securities firms operate on a bonus system, providing employees with huge bonuses in highly profitable years. Many salespeople also operate on a year-end bonus system, in which they receive bonuses if they met or exceeded certain sales goals during the year.

YEAR-END DIVIDEND an additional or special DIVIDEND declared based on a company's profits during the fiscal year.

YEAR-TO-DATE (YTD) period from the beginning of the calendar year (or FISCAL YEAR (FY) if so indicated) to the reporting date. For example third-quarterly results of a company would be reported for the quarter alone and for the year-to-date, which would be nine months.

YEAR-TO-YEAR COMPARISON Contrast with SEQUENTIAL COMPARISON.

YELLOW SHEETS daily publication of Pink Sheets LLC that details the BID AND ASKED prices and firms that MAKE A MARKET in CORPORATE BONDS traded in the OVER THE COUNTER (OTC) market. Much of this information is not available in the daily OTC newspaper listings. The sheets are named for their color. OTC equity issues are covered separately on PINK SHEETS and regional OTC issues of both classes are listed on white sheets.

YEN BOND in general terms, any bond issue denominated in Japanese yen. International bankers using the term are usually referring to yen-denominated bonds issued or held outside Japan.

YIELD
In general: RETURN on an investor's CAPITAL INVESTMENT. A piece of real estate may yield a certain return, or a business deal may offer a particular yield. *See also* RETURN ON INVESTED CAPITAL.
Agriculture: agricultural output in terms of quantity of a crop.
Bonds:
1. COUPON rate of interest divided by the purchase price, called CURRENT YIELD. For example, a bond selling for $1,000 with a 10% coupon offers a

10% current yield. If that same bond were selling for $500, however, it would offer a 20% yield to an investor who bought it for $500. (As a bond's price falls, its yield rises and vice versa.)

2. rate of return on a bond, taking into account the total of annual interest payments, the purchase price, the redemption value, and the amount of time remaining until maturity; called *maturity yield* or YIELD TO MATURITY. *See also* DURATION; YIELD TO AVERAGE LIFE; YIELD TO CALL.

Lending: total money earned on a loan—that is, the ANNUAL PERCENTAGE RATE of interest multiplied by the term of the loan.

Stocks: percentage rate of return paid on a common or preferred stock in dividends. For example, a stock that sells for $20 and pays an annual dividend of $2 per share has a yield, also called a *dividend yield,* of 10%.

Taxes: amount of revenue received by a governmental entity as a result of a tax.

YIELD ADVANTAGE extra amount of return an investor will earn if he or she purchases a CONVERTIBLE security instead of the common stock of the same issuing corporation. If an XYZ Corporation convertible yields 10% and an XYZ common share yields 5%, the yield advantage is 5%. *See also* YIELD SPREAD.

YIELD BURNING MUNICIPAL BOND financing practice whereby underwriters in ADVANCE REFUNDINGS (PREREFUNDING) slap excessive MARKUPS on U.S. Treasury bonds bought and held in escrow to compensate investors during the time between issuance of the new bonds and repayment of the old ones. Since bond prices and yields move in opposite directions, when underwriters mark up the bonds, they "burn down" the yield, violating federal tax rules and costing the government tax revenues. Under IRS regulations, municipalities, not the underwriters, incur the tax liability. The SEC, which conducted a wide-ranging probe of alleged yield-burning abuses by Wall Street firms in the late 1990s, favors making the underwriters responsible, not the municipalities.

YIELD CURVE graph showing the term structure of interest rates by plotting the yields of all bonds of the same quality with maturities ranging from the shortest to the longest available. The resulting curve shows if short-term interest rates are higher or lower than long-term rates. If short-term rates are lower, it is called a POSITIVE YIELD CURVE. If short-term rates are higher, it is called a NEGATIVE (or INVERTED) YIELD CURVE. If there is little difference between short-term and long-term rates, it is called a *flat yield* curve. For the most part, the yield curve is positive, since investors who are willing to tie up their money for a longer period of time usually are compensated for the extra risk they are taking by receiving a higher yield. The most common version of the yield curve graph plots Treasury securities, showing the range of yields from a three-month TREASURY BILL to a 20- or 30-year TREASURY BOND.

Fixed-income analysts study the yield curve carefully in order to make judgments about the direction of interest rates. *See also* DURATION.

YIELD EQUIVALENCE the rate of interest at which a tax-exempt bond and a taxable security of similar quality provide the same return. To calculate the yield that must be provided by a taxable security to equal that of a tax-exempt bond for investors in different tax brackets, the tax exempt yield is divided by the reciprocal of the tax bracket (100 less 28%, for example) to arrive at the taxable yield. Thus, a person in the 28% tax bracket who wished to figure the taxable equivalent of a 10% tax free municipal bond would divide 10% by 72% (100 minus 28%) to get 13.9%—the yield a corporate taxable bond would have to provide to be equivalent, after taxes, to the 10% municipal bond. To convert a taxable yield to a tax-exempt yield, the formula is reversed—that is, the tax exempt yield is equal to the taxable yield multiplied by the reciprocal of the tax bracket. *See also* TAX-EQUIVALENT YIELD.

YIELD SPREAD difference in YIELD between various issues of securities. In comparing bonds, it usually refers to issues of different credit quality since issues of the same maturity and quality would normally have the same yields, as with Treasury securities, for example. Yield spread also refers to the differential between dividend yield on stocks and the CURRENT YIELD on bonds. The comparison might be made, for example, between the STANDARD & POOR'S INDEX (of 500 stocks) dividend yield and the current yield of an index of corporate bonds. A significant difference in bond and stock yields, assuming similar quality, is known as a *yield gap*.

YIELD TO AVERAGE LIFE yield calculation used, in lieu of YIELD TO MATURITY or YIELD TO CALL, where bonds are retired systematically during the life of the issue, as in the case of a SINKING FUND with contractual requirements. Because the issuer will buy its own bonds on the open market to satisfy its sinking fund requirements if the bonds are trading below PAR, there is to that extent automatic price support for such bonds; they therefore tend to trade on a yield-to-average-life basis.

YIELD TO CALL yield on a bond assuming the bond will be redeemed by the issuer at the first CALL date specified in the INDENTURE agreement. The same calculations are used to calculate yield to call as YIELD TO MATURITY except that the principal value at maturity is replaced by the first CALL PRICE and the maturity date is replaced by the first call date. Assuming the issuer will put the interest of the company before the interest of the investor and will call the bonds if it is favorable to do so, the lower of the yield to call and the yield to maturity can be viewed as the more realistic rate of return to the investor. *See also* DURATION.

YIELD TO MATURITY (YTM) concept used to determine the rate of return an investor will receive if a long-term, interest-bearing investment, such as a bond, is held to its MATURITY DATE. It takes into account purchase price, REDEMPTION value, time to maturity, COUPON yield, and the time between interest payments. Recognizing time value of money, it is the DISCOUNT RATE at which the PRESENT VALUE of all future payments would equal the present price of the bond, also known as INTERNAL RATE OF RETURN. It is implicitly assumed that coupons are reinvested at the YTM rate. YTM can be approximated using a bond value table (also called a bond yield table) or can be determined using a programmable calculator equipped for bond mathematics calculations. *See also* DURATION; HORIZON ANALYSIS; YIELD TO AVERAGE LIFE, YIELD TO CALL.

YIELD TO WORST bond yield assuming worst-case scenario, that is, earliest redemption possible under terms of the INDENTURE. *See also* YIELD TO CALL; YIELD TO MATURITY.

YO-YO STOCK stock that fluctuates in a VOLATILE manner, rising and falling quickly like a yo-yo.

ZACKS ESTIMATE SYSTEM service offer by Zacks Investment Research of Chicago compiling earnings estimates and brokerage buy/hold/sell recommendations from more than 200 Wall Street research firms, covering more than 4,500 stocks. Zacks tracks the number of analysts following each stock, how many analysts have raised or lowered their estimates, and the high, low, and average earnings estimate for each quarter and fiscal year. Zacks offers a multiple selection of databases, print reports, and software for institutional and individual investors. *See also* THOMSON REUTERS.

Z-BOND the fourth (Z) TRANCHE of bonds in the structure of a typical COLLATERALIZED MORTGAGE OBLIGATION (CMO). Combining features of ZERO-COUPON SECURITIES and mortgage PASS-THROUGH SECURITIES, Z bonds receive no coupon payments until the earlier A (fast-pay), B (medium-pay), and C (slow-pay) classes have been paid off. Z holders then receive all the remaining cash flow, although interest has been added to principal as cash was used to repay earlier tranches. Some CMOs have been issued with multiple Z and Y tranches, incorporating SINKING-FUND schedules.

ZERO-BASE BUDGETING (ZBB) method of setting budgets for corporations and government agencies that requires a justification of all expenditures, not only those that exceed the prior year's allocations. Thus all budget lines are said to begin at a zero base and are funded according to merit rather than according to the level approved for the preceding year, when circumstances probably differed.

ZERO-BRACKET AMOUNT until the TAX REFORM ACT OF 1986, the STANDARD DEDUCTION, that is, the income automatically not subject to federal income tax for taxpayers choosing not to itemize deductions. The zero-bracket amount was built into the tax tables and schedules used to compute tax. The 1986 Act replaced the zero-bracket amount with an increased standard deduction, which was subtracted from income before computing taxes rather than being part of the rate tables. Current (*see* REVENUE RECONCILIATION ACT OF 1993) law indexes the standard deduction to inflation and contains special provisions for the blind and elderly.

ZERO-COUPON CONVERTIBLE SECURITY
1. Zero-coupon BOND convertible into the common stock of the issuing company when the stock reaches a predetermined price. Introduced as Liquid Yield Option Notes (LYONS), these securities have a PUT OPTION that permits holders to redeem the bonds within three years after the initial offering. They tend to trade at a small PREMIUM OVER CONVERSION VALUE and provide a lower YIELD TO MATURITY than their nonconvertible counterparts.
2. Zero-coupon bond, usually a MUNICIPAL BOND, convertible into an interest bearing bond at some time before maturity. For example, a zero-coupon (tax-free) municipal bond would automatically accumulate and compound interest for its first 15 years at which time it would convert to a regular income-paying bond. Thus, an investor is able to lock in a current interest rate with a small initial investment. Varieties are marketed under the acronyms GAINS (Growth and Income Securities) and FIGS (Future Income and Growth Securities).

ZERO-COUPON SECURITY security that makes no periodic interest payments but instead is sold at a deep discount from its face value. The buyer of such a bond receives the rate of return by the gradual APPRECIATION of the security, which is redeemed at FACE VALUE on a specified maturity date. For tax purposes, the Internal Revenue Service maintains that the holder of a zero-coupon bond owes income tax on the interest that has accrued each year, even though the bondholder does not actually receive the cash until maturity. The IRS calls this interest *imputed interest*. Because of this interpretation, many financial advisers recommend that zero-coupon securities be used in INDIVIDUAL RETIREMENT ACCOUNTS or KEOGH ACCOUNTS, where they remain tax-sheltered.

There are many kinds of zero-coupon securities. The most commonly known is the zero-coupon bond, which either may be issued at a deep discount by a corporation or government entity or may be created by a brokerage firm when it strips the coupons off a bond and sells the CORPUS and the coupons separately. This technique is used frequently with Treasury bonds, and the zero-coupon issue is marketed under such names as CATS (CERTIFICATE OF ACCRUAL ON TREASURY SECURITIES), TIGER (Treasury Investors Growth Receipt) or STRIPS (separate trading of registered interest and principal of securities). Zero-coupon bonds are also issued by municipalities. Buying a municipal zero frees its purchaser of the worry about paying taxes on imputed interest, since the interest is tax-exempt. Zero-coupon certificates of deposit and zero mortgages also exist; they work on the same principle as zero-coupon bonds—the CD holder or mortgage holder receives face value at maturity, and no payments until then. Zero-coupon securities based on COLLATERALIZED MORTGAGE OBLIGATION bonds are called *Z-tranche bonds*. Some mutual funds buy exclusively zero-coupon securities, offering shareholders a diversified portfolio that will mature in a particular year.

Zero-coupon securities are frequently used to plan for a specific investment goal. For example, parents knowing their child will enter college in 10 years can buy a zero that will mature in 10 years, and thus be assured of having money available for tuition. People planning for retirement in 20 years can buy 20-year zeros, assuring them that they will get the money when they need it.

Because zero-coupon securities bear no interest, they are the most VOLATILE of all fixed-income securities. Since zero-coupon bondholders do not receive interest payments, zeros fall more dramatically than bonds paying out interest on a current basis when interest rates rise. However, when interest rates fall, zero-coupon securities rise more rapidly in value than full-coupon bonds, because the bonds have locked in a particular rate of reinvestment that becomes more attractive the further rates fall. The greater the number of years that a zero-coupon security has until maturity, the less an investor has to pay for it, and the more LEVERAGE is at work for him. For instance, a bond maturing in 5 years may double, but one maturing in 25 years may increase in value 10 times, depending on the interest rate of the bond. *See also* ACCRUAL BONDS; COUPON BOND; DEEP DISCOUNT BOND, SPLIT-COUPON BONDS; STAGS; STRIPPED BOND; ZERO-COUPON CONVERTIBLE SECURITY.

ZERO-MINUS TICK sale that takes place at the same price as the previous sale, but at a lower price than the last different price; also called a *zero downtick*. For instance, stock trades may be executed consecutively at prices of $52, $51, and $51. The final trade at $51 was made at a zero-minus tick, because it was made at the same price as the previous trade, but at a lower price than the last different price.

ZERO-PLUS TICK securities trade that takes place at the same price as the previous transaction but at a higher price than the last different price; also called zero uptick. For instance, with trades executed consecutively at $51,

$52, and $52, the last trade at $52 was made at a zero-plus tick—the same price as the previous trade but a higher price than the last different price. *See also* SHORT-SALE RULE.

ZERO-SUM GAME situation in which the gains of the winners are matched by the losses of the losers. For example, futures and options trading are zero-sum games because for every investor holding a profitable contract, there is another investor on the other side of the trade who is losing money. The total amount of wealth held by all the traders in a zero-sum game remains the same, but the wealth is shifted from some traders to others.

ZETA DERIVATIVE PRICING MODEL that measures the effect of volatility. Used interchangeably with *vega* and also with KAPPA, OMEGA, and SIGMA prime.

ZOMBIES companies that continue to operate even though they are insolvent and bankrupt. For example, during the savings and loan industry bailout, many savings and loans that had lost millions of dollars in bad real estate loans continued to function, awaiting merger into another financial institution or closure by the RESOLUTION TRUST CORPORATION. In the financial crisis of the late 2000s, many banks became zombies because of their huge load of TOXIC ASSETS and had to be supported by a federal government bailout. Such companies, in addition to being called zombies, are called *brain dead* or *living dead*.

ZONING LAWS municipal ordinances that authorize the establishment of zoning boards to administer regulations concerning the use of property and buildings in designated areas.

PART V

Finance and Investment
Ready Reference

INTRODUCTION

In today's complex world of finance and investment, it's crucial not only to know *how* different investments work, but also *where* to find the information essential to making wise decisions about those investments.

In the following pages you will find an enormous wealth of information concerning finance and investment. In some cases, the data presented is designed mainly to help you tap the many sophisticated sources available to investors. In other cases, we present well-organized data that can offer important insight into the workings of finance and investment. *In all cases, you are given information you can use.* The address, telephone number, and, if available, Web site address is given for just about every institution, organization, and firm listed, and you are encouraged to make direct contact in order to obtain the data required to make a well-informed investment decision.

The section is divided into the following principal parts:

Sources of Information and Assistance Public and private agencies, associations that help investors and consumers, and major financial publications, online databases, and Web sites are listed.

Major Financial Institutions In this part are listed the names, addresses, and phone numbers of commercial banks, thrift institutions, life insurance companies, brokerage firms, accounting firms, and major stock and futures exchanges around the world.

Mutual Funds Both open-end and closed-end funds are presented.

Futures and Options Contracts Detailed specifications of each contract are presented in tabular form, along with a list of where each contract is traded.

Historical Data This section provides graphs and tabular matter showing important longer-term financial and economic trends. Dow Jones and other indexes are included.

Publicly Traded Companies Hundreds of corporations are listed, according to the place where the shares trade: NYSE and Nasdaq. Listings include name, stock symbol, address, phone number, line of business, option availability, and whether the firm offers a dividend reinvestment plan.

1. SOURCES OF INFORMATION AND ASSISTANCE

When trying to make decisions and keep up to date in the increasingly complex world of finance and investment, it is often necessary to turn to others. This section of the *Handbook* is designed to guide you to the organizations that can help you.

Since the financial markets are so heavily regulated by the government today, it is important to know which federal and state regulators can be of assistance. The first part of this section gives a brief description of major federal, state, and provincial regulatory agencies in the United States and Canada, and how to contact them.

A government agency sometimes is not the best place to turn. Private associations, trade groups, and self-regulatory organizations are often well equipped to deal with problems or questions related to finance and investment. The second part of this section lists many of these private groups.

For advice on where to invest and how to manage your financial affairs, there is an enormous pool of advice available in finance and investment publications. The third part of this section gives you the information you need to contact a great number of worthy publications that contain such advice.

To tap information about financial markets in an even speedier fashion, you can use computer databases and Web sites, which are listed in the fourth section.

FEDERAL REGULATORY ORGANIZATIONS IN THE UNITED STATES AND CANADA

This is a list of the major governmental agencies that regulate the finance and investment markets in the United States and Canada. Each agency's address, telephone number, and Web site is accompanied by a brief description of its major responsibilities. These agencies primarily oversee the fairness and efficiency of finance and investment markets. In that role, consumers and investors can complain to them about perceived abuses or illegalities in the marketplace. Many of the agencies are discussed in more detail in the Dictionary section of the *Handbook*, along with the legislation that created the agency. The regulatory aspect of some of the agencies is less important than other functions.

Agencies of the United States Government

Bureau of Economic Analysis
1441 L Street, NW
Washington, D.C. 20230
(202) 606-9900
www.bea.gov
Compiles, analyzes, and publishes data on economic activity, including gross domestic product, personal income, corporate profits, and other economic indicators.

Bureau of Labor Statistics
2 Massachusetts Avenue, NE
Washington, D.C. 20212-0001
(202) 691-5200
www.bls.gov
Compiles, analyzes, and publishes data on labor activity such as unemployment, consumer price index, producer price index, and wages.

The Centers for Medicare and Medicaid Services
7500 Security Boulevard
Baltimore, Maryland 21244
(410) 786-3000
www.cms.hhs.gov
Oversees the Medicare and Medicaid health insurance system.

Commerce Department
1401 Constitution Avenue, NW
Washington, D.C. 20230
(202) 482-2000
www.commerce.gov
Promotes domestic and international commerce and helps American businesses expand in a variety of ways. Publishes a large amount of data about the U.S. economy.

Commodity Futures Trading Commission
Three Lafayette Centre
1155 21st Street, NW
Washington, D.C. 20581
(202) 418-5000
www.cftc.gov
Regulates U.S. futures and options markets. Investigates charges of fraud against commodity dealers and approves all new contracts that exchanges want to trade.

Comptroller of the Currency
250 E Street, SW
Washington, D.C. 20219
(202) 874-5000
www.occ.treas.gov
Charters, regulates, and supervises all national banks in the United States and supervises the federal branches and agencies of foreign banks. Handles consumer complaints against those banks.

Consumer Product Safety Commission
4330 East West Highway
Bethesda, Maryland 20814
(301) 504-7923
www.cpsc.gov
Regulates and monitors the safety of consumer products. Provides information to the public on, and develops manufacturing standards for, consumer goods.

Council of Economic Advisers
The White House
1600 Pennsylvania Avenue, NW
Washington, D.C. 20500
(202) 456-1414
www.whitehouse.gov/cea
Monitors and analyzes the economy and advises the president on economic developments, trends, and policies. Also prepares the economic reports of the president to Congress.

Farm Credit Administration
1501 Farm Credit Drive
McLean, Virginia 22102-5090
(703) 883-4056
www.fca.gov
Supervises and regulates lending activities of the Farm Credit System, which provides funding for farmers, ranchers, and agricultural and rural utility cooperatives.

Federal Deposit Insurance
  Corporation
550 17th Street, NW
Washington, D.C. 20429-9990
(202) 898-7021
www.fdic.gov
Insures deposits in banks and thrift institutions for up to $250,000 per depositor. Also examines and supervises banks and responds when a bank or thrift fails.

Federal Home Loan Mortgage
  Corporation
8200 Jones Branch Drive
McLean, Virginia 22102-3110
(703) 903-2000
www.freddiemac.com
Freddie Mac, as it is known, encourages the growth of the secondary mortgage market by buying mortgages from lenders, packaging and guaranteeing them, and reselling them as mortgage-backed securities.

Federal Housing Finance Agency
1700 G Street, NW, 4th Floor
Washington, D.C. 20552
(866) 796-5595
www.fhfb.gov
Supervises the 12 regional Federal Home Loan Banks that bolster the supply of funds to local mortgage lenders. Also regulates Fannie Mae and Freddie Mac.

Federal National Mortgage
  Association
3900 Wisconsin Avenue, NW
Washington, D.C. 20016
(202) 752-7000
www.fanniemae.com
Creates a secondary market in mortgage-backed securities. Called Fannie Mae, the agency offers a wide variety of tools and resources about real estate.

Federal Reserve System
20th Street and Constitution
  Avenue, NW
Washington, D.C. 20551
(202) 452-3946
www.federalreserve.gov
The central bank of the United States. Regulates national money supply, supervises and regulates the country's banking and financial system, and conducts monetary policy.

Federal Trade Commission
600 Pennsylvania Avenue, NW
Washington, D.C. 20580
(202) 326-2222
www.ftc.gov
Enforces antitrust laws and consumer protection legislation.

Internal Revenue Service
1111 Constitution Avenue, NW
Washington, D.C. 20224
(800) 829-1040
www.irs.ustreas.gov
Collects personal and corporate taxes for the federal government and administers rules and regulations of the Treasury Department.

International Trade
  Administration
1401 Constitution Avenue, NW
Room 3416
Washington, D.C. 20230
(800) 872-8723
www.trade.gov
Regulates and promotes nonagricultural trade between the United States and its trading partners. Also develops global policies to expand U.S. exports.

National Credit Union
  Administration
1775 Duke Street
Alexandria, Virginia 22314-3428
(703) 518-6300
www.ncua.gov
Charters and regulates federally chartered credit unions and handles consumer complaints.

Office of Thrift Supervision
1700 G Street, NW
Washington, D.C. 20552
(202) 906-6000
www.ots.treas.gov
Primary regulator of all federally
chartered and many state-chartered
thrift institutions, which include savings banks and savings and loan associations.

Pension Benefit Guaranty
   Corporation
1200 K Street, NW
Washington, D.C. 20005
(202) 326-4000
www.pbgc.gov
Insures corporate pension plans to
make sure that covered pensioners
receive the money due them.

Securities and Exchange Commission
100 F Street, NE
Washington, D.C. 20549
(202) 942-8088
www.sec.gov
Regulates the securities industry. Registers issues of securities; investigates
fraud and insider trading; supervises
public companies, securities brokers
and dealers, securities exchanges, investment advisors, and mutual funds.

Securities Investor Protection
   Corporation
805 15th Street, NW, Suite 800
Washington, D.C. 20005-2215
(202) 371-8300
www.sipc.org
Helps customers of brokerage firms
to recover cash, stock, and other securities when a firm closes due to
financial difficulty or bankruptcy. Insures brokerage customers' holdings
up to $500,000 per customer, with a
limit of $100,000 on claims for cash.

Small Business Administration
409 3rd Street, SW
Washington, D.C. 20416
(800) 827-5722
www.sba.gov
Offers advice and guarantees loans
to small businesses. Assists families
and small businesses in recovering
from natural disasters.

Social Security Administration
6401 Security Boulevard
Baltimore, Maryland 21235
(800) 772-1213
www.ssa.gov
Regulates eligibility and payments
of social security benefits to workers after they retire or become
disabled. Also administers supplemental income programs for the
aged, blind, and dependents.

Treasury Department
1500 Pennsylvania Avenue, NW
Washington, D.C. 20220
(202) 622-2000
www.treas.gov
Regulates the issuance of government debt (Treasury bills, bonds,
and notes) in coordination with the
Federal Reserve and issues savings
bonds. Plays a large role in coordinating economic and financial issues
with foreign governments.

United States International Trade
   Commission
500 E Street, SW
Washington, D.C. 20436
(202) 205-2000
www.usitc.gov
Investigates the effects of subsidized
imports on domestic industries. Also
provides technical advice on trade
and tariffs for government and private policy makers.

United States Tax Court
400 Second Street, NW
Washington, D.C. 20217
(202) 521-0700
www.ustaxcourt.gov
Hears cases involving disputes between the IRS and taxpayers.

Federal Government Agencies of Canada

Bank of Canada
234 Wellington Street
Ottawa, Ontario K1A 0G9
(800) 303-1282
www.bankofcanada.ca
Regulates Canada's money supply.
It is the central bank of Canada.

The Business Development Bank
  of Canada
BDC Building
5 Place Ville Marie, Suite 400
Montreal, Quebec H3B 5E7
(877) 232-2269   www.bdc.ca
Wholly owned by the Canadian government, the BDC delivers financial
and consulting services to Canadian
small businesses, with a focus on
technology and exporting.

Canada Deposit Insurance
  Corporation
50 O'Connor Street, 17th Floor
P.O. Box 2340, Station D
Ottawa, Ontario K1P 5W5
(800) 461-2342   www.cdic.ca
Insures deposits up to $100,000
(Canadian) per depositor in mem-
ber institutions.

Canada Mortgage and Housing
  Corporation
700 Montreal Road
Ottawa, Ontario K1A 0P7
(613) 748-2000   www.cmhc.ca
Provides mortgage loan insurance, mortgage-backed securities,
housing policy and programs, and
housing research.

Canada Revenue Agency
555 MacKenzie Avenue
Ottawa, Ontario K1A 0L5
(800) 959-8281   www.cra-arc.gc.ca
Administers tax laws for the federal
government and most provinces and
territories.

Department of Finance Canada
19th Floor, East Tower
140 O'Connor Street
Ottawa, Ontario K1A 0G5
(613) 992-1573   www.fin.gc.ca

Conducts the financial affairs and
economic planning for the Canadian
government.

Export Development Canada
151 O'Connor Street
Ottawa, Ontario K1A 1K3
(613) 598-2500   www.edc.ca
Provides trade finance and risk management services to Canadian exporters and investors in developing
markets.

Foreign Affairs and International
  Trade Canada
125 Sussex Drive
Ottawa, Ontario K1A 0G2
(800) 267-8376
www.dfait-maeci.gc.ca
Supports Canadians abroad and
represents Canada through a network of embassies and trade and
diplomatic offices.

Office of the Superintendent of
  Financial Institutions Canada
255 Albert Street
Ottawa, Ontario K1A 0H2
(613) 990-7788
www.osfi-bsif.gc.ca
Regulates institutions and pension
plans.

Statistics Canada
150 Tunney's Pasture Driveway
Ottawa, Ontario K1A 0T6
(800) 263-1136
www.statcan.ca
Compiles economic and financial
statistics for the government.

Treasury Board of Canada
  Secretariat
L'Esplanade Laurier, 9th Floor,
  East Tower
140 O'Connor Street
Ottawa, Ontario K1A 0R5
(613) 957-2400
www.tbs-sct.gc.ca
The administrative arm of the Treasury Board. Provides advice on
policies governing the government's
resources.

U.S. STATE ATTORNEYS GENERAL OFFICES

The office of the attorney general in each state is the place to go for a wide variety of consumer complaints. Stopping fraud is a particular concern, and frequently several attorneys general will coordinate their efforts to stop a multistate fraudulent business. Those who suspect a solicitation to be fraudulent should contact their state attorney general on this list before handing over any money or personal financial information. The attorney general's office also will assist a consumer in a credit complaint with a credit ratings agency that cannot be resolved through normal channels. In such personal matters, the involvement of the attorney general's office will expedite complaints that otherwise could be tangled in bureaucratic red tape.

Besides taking consumer complaints, the attorney general's office promulgates rules and regulations that promote fair business practices. Areas within its jurisdiction include deceptive advertising and contract law. When appropriate, the attorney general appeals to legislative bodies to pass new consumer protection laws. To enforce these laws, the attorney general pursues both civil and criminal prosecutions of violators.

Your state attorney general's office also may be the source of help when you are considering a purchase. Through its consumer affairs division, the office usually publishes helpful publications giving consumer protection tips on such issues as what to avoid in entering certain kinds of sales contracts. Even if one is unsure where to turn for help for a particular consumer problem, the attorney general is a good place to start.

ALABAMA
Attorney General
500 Dexter Avenue
Montgomery, Alabama 36130
(334) 242-7300
www.ago.state.al.us

ALASKA
Attorney General
Diamond Courthouse
Juneau, Alaska 99811-0300
(907) 465-3600
www.law.state.ak.us

ARIZONA
Attorney General
1275 West Washington Street
Phoenix, Arizona 85007
(602) 542-4266
www.azag.gov

ARKANSAS
Attorney General
200 Tower Building
323 Center Street
Little Rock, Arkansas 72201-2610
(800) 482-8982
www.ag.arkansas.gov

CALIFORNIA
Attorney General
1300 I Street, Suite 1740
Sacramento, California 95814
(916) 445-9555
www.ag.ca.gov

COLORADO
Attorney General
1525 Sherman Street
Denver, Colorado 80203
(303) 866-4500
www.ago.state.co.us

CONNECTICUT
Attorney General
55 Elm Street
Hartford, Connecticut 06141-0120
(860) 808-5318
www.ct.gov/ag

DELAWARE
Attorney General
Carvel State Office Building
820 North French Street
Wilmington, Delaware 19801
(302) 577-8338
www.attorneygeneral.delaware.gov

DISTRICT OF COLUMBIA
Attorney General
John A. Wilson Building
1350 Pennsylvania Avenue, NW,
    Suite 409
Washington, D.C. 20009
(202) 727-3400
http://occ.dc.gov

FLORIDA
Attorney General
The Capitol, PL-01
Tallahassee, Florida 32399-1050
(850) 414-3300
www.myfloridalegal.com

GEORGIA
Attorney General
40 Capitol Square, SW
Atlanta, Georgia 30334-1300
(404) 656-3300
www.law.ga.gov

HAWAII
Attorney General
425 Queen Street
Honolulu, Hawaii 96813
(808) 586-1500
www.hawaii.gov.ag

IDAHO
Attorney General
State House
Boise, Idaho 83720-1000
(208) 334-2400
www.state.id.us/ag

ILLINOIS
Attorney General
James R. Thompson Center
100 West Randolph Street
Chicago, Illinois 60601
(312) 814-3000
www.illinoisattorneygeneral.gov

INDIANA
Attorney General
Indiana Government Center South
402 West Washington Street,
    5th Floor
Indianapolis, Indiana 46204
(317) 232-6201
www.in.gov/attorneygeneral

IOWA
Attorney General
Hoover State Office Building
1305 East Walnut
Des Moines, Iowa 50319
(515) 281-5164
www.IowaAttorneyGeneral.org

KANSAS
Attorney General
120 Southwest 10th Avenue,
    2nd Floor
Topeka, Kansas 66612-1597
(785) 296-2215
www.ksag,org

KENTUCKY
Attorney General
Capitol Building
700 Capitol Avenue, Suite 118
Frankfort, Kentucky 40601-3449
(502) 696-5300
www.ag.ky.gov

LOUISIANA
Attorney General
P.O. Box 94095
Baton Rouge, Louisiana 70804 4095
(225) 326-6000
www.ag.state.la.us

MAINE
Attorney General
State House Station 6
Augusta, Maine 04333
(207) 626-8800
www.state.me.us/ag

MARYLAND
Attorney General
200 St. Paul Place
Baltimore, Maryland 21202-2202
(410) 576-6300
www.oag.state.md.us

MASSACHUSETTS
Attorney General
1 Ashburton Place
Boston, Massachusetts 02108-1698
(617) 727-2200
www.mass.gov/ago

MICHIGAN
Attorney General
525 West Ottawa Street
Lansing, Michigan 48909-0212
(517) 373-1110
www.michigan.gov/ag

MINNESOTA
Attorney General
State Capitol, Suite 102
St. Paul, Minnesota 55155
(651) 296-3353
www.ag.state.mn.us

MISSISSIPPI
Attorney General
P.O. Box 220
Jackson, Mississippi 37205-0220
(601) 359-3680
www.ago.state.ms.us

MISSOURI
Attorney General
Supreme Court Building
207 West High Street
Jefferson City, Missouri 65101
(573) 751-3321
www.ago.mo.gov

MONTANA
Attorney General
Justice Building
215 North Sanders
Helena, Montana 59620-1401
(406) 444-2026
www.doj.mt.gov

NEBRASKA
Attorney General
P.O. Box 98920
Lincoln, Nebraska 68509-8920
(402) 471-2682
www.ago.state.ne.us

NEVADA
Attorney General
Old Supreme Court Building
100 North Carson Street
Carson City, Nevada 89701
(775) 684-1100
www.ag.state.nv.us

NEW HAMPSHIRE
Attorney General
State House Annex
33 Capitol Street
Concord, New Hampshire 03301-6397
(603) 271-3658
www.state.nh.us/nhdoj

NEW JERSEY
Attorney General
Richard J. Hughes Justice Complex
25 Market Street, CN 080
Trenton, New Jersey 08625
(609) 292-8740
www.state.nj.us/lps

NEW MEXICO
Attorney General
P.O. Drawer 1508
Santa Fe, New Mexico 87504-1508
(505) 827-6000
www.nmag.gov

NEW YORK
Attorney General
The Capitol, 2nd Floor
Albany, New York 12224
(518) 474-7330
www.oag.state.ny.us

NORTH CAROLINA
Attorney General
P.O. Box 629
Raleigh, North Carolina 27602-0629
(919) 716-6400
www.ncdoj.com

NORTH DAKOTA
Attorney General
State Capitol
600 East Boulevard Avenue
Bismarck, North Dakota 58505-0040
(701) 328-2210
www.ag.state.nd.us

OHIO
Attorney General
State Office Tower
30 East Broad Street
Columbus, Ohio 43266-0410
(614) 466-4320
www.ohioattorneygeneral.gov

OKLAHOMA
Attorney General
313 NE 21st Street
Oklahoma City, Oklahoma 73105
(405) 521-3921
www.oag.state.ok.us

OREGON
Attorney General
Justice Building
1162 Court Street, NE
Salem, Oregon 97301
(503) 378-4732
www.doj.state.or.us

PENNSYLVANIA
Attorney General
1600 Strawberry Square
Harrisburg, Pennsylvania 17120
(717) 787-3391
www.attorneygeneral.gov

RHODE ISLAND
Attorney General
150 South Main Street
Providence, Rhode Island 02903
(401) 274-4400
www.riag.state.ri.us

SOUTH CAROLINA
Attorney General
Rembert C. Dennis Office Building
P.O. Box 11549
Columbia, South Carolina 29211-
1549
(803) 734-3970
www.scattorneygeneral.org

SOUTH DAKOTA
Attorney General
1302 East Highway 14, Suite 1
Pierre, South Dakota 57501-8501
(605) 773-3215
www.state.sd.us/attorney

TENNESSEE
Attorney General
500 Charlotte Avenue
Nashville, Tennessee 37243
(615) 741-5860
www.attorneygeneral.state.tn.us

TEXAS
Attorney General
Capitol Station
P.O. Box 12548
Austin, Texas 78711-2548
(512) 463-2100
www.oag.state.tx.us

UTAH
Attorney General
State Capitol, Room 236
Salt Lake City, Utah 84114-0810
(801) 538-9600
www.attorneygeneral.utah.gov

VERMONT
Attorney General
109 State Street
Montpelier, Vermont 05609-1001
(802) 828-3173
www.atg.state.vt.us

VIRGINIA
Attorney General
900 East Main Street
Richmond, Virginia 23219
(804) 786-2071
www.oag.state.va.us

WASHINGTON
Attorney General
1125 Washington Street, SE
Olympia, Washington 98504-0100
(360) 753-6200
www.atg.wa.gov

WEST VIRGINIA
Attorney General
State Capitol
1900 Kanawha Boulevard E
Charleston, West Virginia 25305
(304) 558-2021
www.wvago.us

WISCONSIN
Attorney General
State Capitol, Suite 114 East
Madison, Wisconsin 53707-7857
(608) 266-1221
www.doj.state.wi.us

WYOMING
Attorney General
State Capitol Building
Cheyenne, Wyoming 82002
(307) 777-7841
www.attorneygeneral.state.wy.us

U.S. STATE BANKING REGULATORS

The regulators listed here are charged with supervising the activities of state-chartered banks. These are banks not regulated at the national level, where the Comptroller of the Currency and Federal Reserve Board do the supervision. Depending on the state, state-chartered banks may have more or fewer powers than federally regulated banks. For example, the amount of money state banks can lend to customers as a percent of deposits varies widely from state to state. State banking regulators also oversee the financial soundness of the banks in their jurisdictions and help to merge failing banks into healthy ones. These regulators do not insure state bank deposits; that usually is done by the Federal Deposit Insurance Corporation.

State bank regulators also pursue consumer complaints against banks in their state. For example, it would be appropriate to contact a regulator if a state bank was preventing checks from clearing within a reasonable time or if fees were excessive. Complaints about deceptive advertising or promotional materials by banks can be addressed to these agencies. These regulators also handle questions about credit, and the denial of credit privileges.

State banking agencies are helpful when shopping for a bank. They may publish helpful literature about banks and bank services. Do not expect these agencies to do comparisons of yields paid on bank accounts or interest rates charged on loans. These numbers change too frequently for the agencies to track them.

ALABAMA
State Banking Department
401 Adams Avenue, Suite 680
Montgomery, Alabama 36104
(334) 242-3452
www.banking.alabama.gov

ALASKA
Division of Banking and Securities
Department of Commerce
P.O. Box 110807
Juneau, Alaska 99811-0807
(907) 465-2521
www.commerce.state.ak.us/bsc/
   home.htm

ARIZONA
Arizona Department of Financial
   Institutions
2910 North 44th Street, Suite 310
Phoenix, Arizona 85018
(602) 771-2800
http://azdfi.gov

ARKANSAS
Arkansas State Bank Department
400 Hardin Road, Suite 100
Little Rock, Arkansas 72211
(501) 324-9019
www.accessarkansas.org/bank

CALIFORNIA
California Department of
   Financial Institutions
45 Fremont Street, Suite 1700
San Francisco, California 94105-2219
(415) 263-8500
www.dfi.ca.gov

COLORADO
Colorado Division of Banking
1560 Broadway, Suite 975
Denver, Colorado 80202
(303) 894-7575
www.dora.state.co.us/banking

CONNECTICUT
Connecticut Department of Banking
260 Constitution Plaza
Hartford, Connecticut 06103-1800
(860) 240-8299
www.ct.gov/dob

DELAWARE
Office of the State Bank
   Commissioner
555 East Loockerman Street,
   Suite 210
Dover, Delaware 19901
(302) 739-4235
www.state.de.us/bank

DISTRICT OF COLUMBIA
Department of Insurance,
    Securities and Banking
810 First Street NE, Suite 701
Washington, D.C. 20551
(202) 727-8000
http://disb.dc.gov/disr

FLORIDA
Office of Financial Regulation
200 East Gaines Street
Tallahassee, Florida 32399-0371
(850) 413-9800
www.fldfs.com

GEORGIA
Department of Banking and
    Finance
2990 Brandywine Road, Suite 200
Atlanta, Georgia 30341-5565
(770) 986-1633
www.ganet.org/dbf

HAWAII
Division of Financial Institutions
King Kalakaua Building
335 Merchant Street, Room 221
Honolulu, Hawaii 96813
(808) 586-2820
www.hawaii.gov/dcca/areas/dfi

IDAHO
Department of Finance
700 West State Street, 2nd Floor
Boise, Idaho 83720-0031
(208) 332-8000
http://finance.idaho.gov

ILLINOIS
Division of Banking
Department of Financial
    Professional Regulation
320 West Washington Street
Springfield, Illinois 62786
(217) 785-2900
www.idfpr.com

INDIANA
Department of Financial
    Institutions
30 South Meridian Street, Suite 300
Indianapolis, Indiana 46204
(317) 232-3955
www.in.gov/dfi

IOWA
Iowa Division of Banking
200 East Grand Avenue, Suite 300
Des Moines, Iowa 50309-1827
(515) 281-4014
www.idob.state.ia.us

KANSAS
Office of the State Bank
    Commissioner
700 SW Jackson, Suite 300
Topeka, Kansas 66603
(785) 296-2266
www.osbckansas.org

KENTUCKY
Division of Financial Institutions
1025 Capital Center Drive
Frankfort, Kentucky 40601
(502) 573-3390
www.kfi.ky.gov

LOUISIANA
Office of Financial Institutions
8660 United Plaza Boulevard
Baton Rouge, Louisiana 70804-9095
(225) 925-4660
www.ofi.state.la.us

MAINE
Bureau of Financial Institutions
36 State House Station
Augusta, Maine 04333-0036
(207) 624-8570
www.state.me.us/pfr/bkg/bkg_
    index.htm

MARYLAND
Office of Financial Regulation
500 North Calvert Street, Room 402
Baltimore, Maryland 21202
(410) 230-6100
www.dllr.state.md.us/finance

MASSACHUSETTS
Division of Banks
One South Station
Boston, Massachusetts 02110
(617) 956-1500
www.mass.gov/dob

MICHIGAN
Office of Financial and Insurance
   Regulation
611 West Ottawa Street
Lansing, Michigan 48909-7220
(517) 373-6350
www.michigan.gov/ofis

MINNESOTA
Minnestota Department of
   Commerce
85 7th Place East, Suite 500
St. Paul, Minnesota 55101-2298
(651) 296-2135
www.commerce.state.mn.us

MISSISSIPPI
Department of Banking and
   Consumer Finance
501 N. West Street
901 Woolfolk Building, Suite A
Jackson, Mississippi 39225-3729
(601) 359-1031
www.dbcf.state.ms.us

MISSOURI
Division of Finance
301 West High Street
Jefferson City, Missouri 65102
(573) 751-3242
www.missouri-finance.org

MONTANA
Division of Banking and Financial
   Institutions
301 South Park, Suite 316
Helena, Montana 59620-0546
(406) 841-2920
http://banking.mt.gov

NEBRASKA
Department of Banking and
   Finance
Commerce Court
1230 O Street
Lincoln, Nebraska 68509-5006
(402) 471-2171
www.ndbf.org

NEVADA
Financial Institutions Division
2785 East Desert Inn Road, Suite 180
Las Vegas, Nevada 89121
(702) 486-4120
www.fid.state.nv.us

NEW HAMPSHIRE
New Hampshire Banking
   Department
53 Regional Drive, Suite 200
Concord, New Hampshire 03301
(603) 271-3561
www.nh.gov/banking

NEW JERSEY
Department of Banking and
   Insurance
20 West State Street
Trenton, New Jersey 08625
(609) 292-3420
www.njdobi.org

NEW MEXICO
Financial Institutions Division
2550 Cerrillos Road, 3rd Floor
Santa Fe, New Mexico 87504
(505) 476-4885
www.rld.state.nm.us/FID

NEW YORK
New York State Banking
   Department
One State Street Plaza, Sixth Floor
New York, New York 10004-1417
(212) 709-3501
www.banking.state.ny.us

NORTH CAROLINA
Office of the Commissioner
   of Banks
316 West Edenton Street
Raleigh, North Carolina 27699-4309
(919) 733-3016
www.nccob.com

NORTH DAKOTA
Banking Division
Department of Financial
   Institutions
2000 Schafer Street, Suite G
Bismarck, North Dakota 58501-1204
(701) 328-9933
www.state.nd.us/dfi

OHIO
Division of Financial Institutions
77 South High Street, 21st Floor
Columbus, Ohio 43215-6120
(614) 728-8400
www.com.state.oh.us/dfi

OKLAHOMA
State Banking Department
2900 N. Lincoln Boulevard
Oklahoma City, Oklahoma 73105
(405) 521-2782
www.osbd.state.ok.us

OREGON
Division of Finance and Corporate
  Securities
350 Winter Street NE, Room 410
Salem, Oregon 97309-0405
(503) 378-4140
www.oregondfcs.org

PENNSYLVANIA
Department of Banking
17 North Second Street, Suite 1300
Harrisburg, Pennsylvania 17101-2290
(717) 787-2665
www.banking.state.pa.us

RHODE ISLAND
Department of Business Regulation
1511 Pontiac Avenue, Building 69-2
Cranston, Rhode Island 02920
(401) 462-9503
www.dbr.state.ri.us

SOUTH CAROLINA
State Board of Financial Institutions
1205 Pendleton Street, Suite 305
Columbia, South Carolina 29201
(803) 734-2001

SOUTH DAKOTA
South Dakota Division of Banking
217 ½ West Missouri Avenue
Pierre, South Dakota 57501-4590
(605) 773-3421
www.state.sd.us/banking

TENNESSEE
Tennessee Department of
  Financial Institutions
Bank of America Building
414 Union Street, Suite 1000
Nashville, Tennessee 37219
(615) 741-2236
www.tennessee.gov/tdfi

TEXAS
Texas Department of Banking
2601 North Lamar Boulevard
Austin, Texas 78705-4294
(877) 276-5554
www.banking.state.tx.us

UTAH
Department of Financial Institutions
324 South State Street, Suite 201
Salt Lake City, Utah 84114-6800
(801) 538-8830
www.dfi.utah.gov

VERMONT
Department of Banking and
  Insurance
89 Main Street
Montpelier, Vermont 05620-3101
(802) 828-3307
www.bishca.state.vt.us

VIRGINIA
Bureau of Financial Institutions
Tyler Building
1300 East Main Street
Richmond, Virginia 23218-0640
(804) 371-9957
www.scc.virginia.gov

WASHINGTON
Department of Financial Institutions
P.O. Box 41200
Olympia, Washington 98504-1200
(360) 902-8704
www.dfi.wa.gov

WEST VIRGINIA
Division of Banking
One Players Club Drive, Suite 300
Charleston, West Virginia 25311-
  1638
(304) 558-2294
www.wvdob.org

WISCONSIN
Department of Financial
  Institutions
345 West Washington Avenue
Madison, Wisconsin 53707-8861
(608) 264-7800
www.wdfi.org

WYOMING
Division of Banking
Herschler Building, 3rd Floor East
122 West 25th Street
Cheyenne, Wyoming 82002
(307) 777-7797
http://audit.state.wy.us/banking

U.S. STATE INSURANCE REGULATORS

Every state has its own laws and regulations that govern all types of insurance. Unlike most other areas in the financial services field, there is very little regulation of the insurance industry at the federal level. The state agencies listed here enforce all state insurance laws. Insurance commissioners must approve the sale of all life, health, automobile, and homeowners' insurance products in their states. Some states, such as New York and California, are particularly rigorous in approving any new product for sale to state residents. If a product has been approved for sale in one of those states, it is often approved elsewhere as well.

When there are problems with an insurance company, these regulators step in. For example, they oversee the process of merging failing insurance companies into strong ones. They also protect policyholders by assuring that insurance companies keep adequate reserves. In the case of an insurance company failure, they see to it that policyholders' interests are protected as much as possible. State insurance offices also respond to consumer complaints against insurance companies on such issues as unfair pricing, denial of insurance claims, and deceptive advertising practices. Before bringing a complaint to one of these agencies, however, it is important to complain to the insurance company first. If the problem has not been resolved at that level, then these agencies should be consulted.

These insurance regulators also offer assistance to those looking to purchase insurance coverage. They may provide helpful literature about the kinds of insurance policies being offered, and also be able to inform buyers about patterns of complaints against particular companies.

ALABAMA
Alabama Department of Insurance
201 Monroe Street, Suite 1700
Montgomery, Alabama 36104
(334) 269-3550
www.aldoi.gov

ALASKA
Department of Commerce,
   Community and Economic
   Development
Division of Insurance
550 West 7th Avenue, Suite 1560
Anchorage, Alaska 99501-3567
(907) 269-7900
www.dced.state.ak.us/insurance

ARIZONA
Arizona Department of Insurance
2910 North 44th Street, Suite 210
Phoenix, Arizona 85018-7256
(602) 364-1000
www.id.state.az.us

ARKANSAS
Arkansas Insurance Department
1200 West 3rd Street
Little Rock, Arkansas 72201-1904
(501) 371-2600
http://insurance.arkansas.gov

CALIFORNIA
Department of Insurance
300 Capital Mall, Suite 1700
Sacramento, California 95814
(916) 492-3500
www.insurance.ca.gov

COLORADO
Division of Insurance
1560 Broadway, Suite 850
Denver, Colorado 80202
(303) 894-7499
www.dora.state.co.us/insurance

CONNECTICUT
Connecticut Insurance Department
153 Market Street, 7th Floor
Hartford, Connecticut 06142-0816
(860) 297-3800
www.ct.gov/cid

DELAWARE
Delaware Department of Insurance
Rodney Building
841 Silver Lake Boulevard
Dover, Delaware 19904
(302) 674-7300
www.state.de.us/inscom

DISTRICT OF COLUMBIA
Department of Insurance,
  Securities and Banking
810 First Street, NE, Suite 701
Washington, D.C. 20002
(202) 727-8000
http://disr.washingtondc.gov/disr

FLORIDA
Florida Department of Financial
  Services
State Capitol
Plaza Level Eleven
Tallahassee, Florida 32399-0300
(850) 413-2850
www.floir.com

GEORGIA
Office of Insurance and Safety
  Fire Commissioner
2 Martin Luther King, Jr. Drive
Floyd Memorial Building
704 West Tower
Atlanta, Georgia 30334
(404) 656-2056
www.gainsurance.org

HAWAII
Department of Commerce and
  Consumer Affairs
335 Merchant Street, Room 213
Honolulu, Hawaii 96813
(808) 586-2790
www.hawaii.gov/dcca

IDAHO
Department of Insurance
700 West State Street, 3rd Floor
Boise, Idaho 83720-0043
(208) 334-4250
www.doi.idaho.gov

ILLINOIS
Illinois Division of Insurance
320 West Washington Street,
  4th Floor
Springfield, Illinois 62767-0001
(217) 785-4515
www.idfpr.com

INDIANA
Department of Insurance
311 West Washington Street, Suite 300
Indianapolis, Indiana 46204-2787
(317) 232-2385
www.ai.org/idoi

IOWA
Iowa Insurance Division
330 East Maple Street
Des Moines, Iowa 50319
(515) 281-5705
www.iid.state.ia.us

KANSAS
Kansas Insurance Department
420 Southwest Ninth Street
Topeka, Kansas 66612-1678
(785) 296-3071
www.ksinsurance.org

KENTUCKY
Department of Insurance
215 West Main Street
Frankfort, Kentucky 40601
(502) 564-3630
http://doi.ppr.ky.gov/kentucky

LOUISIANA
Department of Insurance
1702 North Third Street
Baton Rouge, Louisiana 70802
(225) 342-5423
www.ldi.state.la.us

MAINE
Department of Professional and
  Financial Regulation
34 State House Station
Augusta, Maine 04333-0034
(207) 624-8475
 www.state.me.us/pfr

MARYLAND
Maryland Insurance Administration
200 St. Paul Place, Suite 2700
Baltimore, Maryland 21202
(410) 468-2090
www.mdinsurance.state.md.us

MASSACHUSETTS
Division of Insurance
One South Station, 5th Floor
Boston, Massachusetts 02110-2208
(617) 521-7794
www.mass.gov/doi

MICHIGAN
Office of Financial and Insurance
  Regulation
Ottawa Building, 3rd Floor
611 West Ottawa
Lansing, Michigan 48933
(517) 373-0220
www.michigan.gov/cis

MINNESOTA
Minnesota Department of
    Commerce
85 7th Place East, Suite 500
St. Paul, Minnesota 55101-2198
(651) 296-4026
www.commerce.state.mn.us

MISSISSIPPI
Mississippi Insurance Department
501 North West Street
Woolfolk State Office Building,
    10th Floor
Jackson, Mississippi 39201
(601) 359-3569
www.doi.state.ms.us

MISSOURI
Missouri Department of Insurance
301 West High Street, Suite 530
Jefferson City, Missouri 65101
(573) 751-4126
www.insurance.mo.gov

MONTANA
Commissioner of Securities and
    Insurance
840 Helena Avenue
Helena, Montana 59601
(406) 444-2040
http://sao.mt.gov

NEBRASKA
Nebraska Department of Insurance
Terminal Building, Suite 400
941 O Street
Lincoln, Nebraska 68508
(402) 471-2201
www.doi.ne.gov

NEVADA
Nevada Division of Insurance
788 Fairview Drive, Suite 300
Carson City, Nevada 89701
(775) 687-4270
http://doi.state.nv.us

NEW HAMPSHIRE
New Hampshire Insurance
    Department
21 South Fruit Street, Suite 14
Concord, New Hampshire 03301
(603) 271-2261
www.nh.gov/insurance

NEW JERSEY
Department of Banking and
    Insurance
20 West State Street
Trenton, New Jersey 08625-0325
(609) 292-7272
www.state.nj.us/dobi

NEW MEXICO
Division of Insurance
PERA Building
1120 Paseo de Peralta
Santa Fe, New Mexico 87501
(505) 827-4601
www.nmprc.state.nm.us/
    insurance/inshm.htm

NEW YORK
New York State Insurance
    Department
25 Beaver Street
New York, New York 10004-2319
(212) 480-2301
www.ins.state.ny.us

NORTH CAROLINA
Department of Insurance
Dobbs Building
430 North Salisbury Street
Raleigh, North Carolina 27603
(919) 733-3058
www.ncdoi.com

NORTH DAKOTA
North Dakota Insurance Department
600 East Boulevard Avenue,
    5th Floor
Bismarck, North Dakota 58505-0320
(701) 328-2440
www.state.nd.us/ndins

OHIO
Department of Insurance
50 West Town Street, Suite 300
Columbus, Ohio 43215
(614) 644-2658
www.ohioinsurance.gov

OKLAHOMA
Oklahoma Insurance Department
2401 Northwest 23rd Street, Suite 28
Oklahoma City, Oklahoma 73107
(405) 521-2828
www.oid.state.ok.us

OREGON
Oregon Insurance Division
350 Winter Street NE, Room 440
Salem, Oregon 97301-3883
(503) 947-7980
www.cbs.state.or.us/ins

PENNSYLVANIA
Insurance Department
1326 Strawberry Square,
    13th Floor
Harrisburg, Pennsylvania 17120
(717) 783-0442
www.ins.state.pa.us/ins

RHODE ISLAND
Division of Insurance
1511 Pontiac Avenue, Building 69-2
Cranston, Rhode Island 02920
(401) 462-9520
www.dbr.state.ri.us

SOUTH CAROLINA
Department of Insurance
Capitol Center
1201 Main Street, Suite 1000
Columbia, South Carolina 29201
(803) 737-6805
www.doi.sc.gov

SOUTH DAKOTA
Division of Insurance
445 East Capitol Avenue
Pierre, South Dakota 57501-3185
(605) 773-3563
www.state.sd.us/insurance

TENNESSEE
Department of Commerce and
    Insurance
Davy Crockett Tower
500 James Robertson Parkway,
    5th Floor
Nashville, Tennessee 37243-0565
(615) 741-2241
www.state.tn.us/commerce

TEXAS
Department of Insurance
333 Guadalupe Street
Austin, Texas 78701
(512) 463-6169
www.tdi.state.tx.us

UTAH
Utah Insurance Department
3110 State Office Building
Salt Lake City, Utah 84114
(801) 538-3890
www.insurance.utah.gov

VERMONT
Division of Insurance
89 Main Street
Montpelier, Vermont 05620-3101
(802) 828-3301
www.bishca.state.vt.us

VIRGINIA
Bureau of Insurance
1300 East Main Street
Richmond, Virginia 23219
(804) 371-9741
www.scc.virginia.gov/division/boi

WASHINGTON
Office of the Insurance
    Commissioner
5000 Capitol Way
Tumwater, Washington 98501
(360) 725-7000
www.insurance.wa.gov

WEST VIRGINIA
Offices of the Insurance
    Commissioner
1124 Smith Street
Charleston, West Virginia 25301
(304) 558-3354
www.wvinsurance.gov

WISCONSIN
Office of the Commissioner of
    Insurance
125 South Webster Street
GEF III, 2nd Floor
Madison, Wisconsin 53703-3474
(608) 266-3585
http://oci.wi.gov

WYOMING
Wyoming Insurance Department
106 East 6th Avenue
Cheyenne, Wyoming 82002-0440
(307) 777-7401
http://insurance.state.wy.us

U.S. STATE SECURITIES REGULATORS

Anyone dealing with the potential purchase or sale of securities might want to consult with the state regulators listed here. Brokerage firms and financial planners selling securities must pass tests administered by state securities departments. In the event of any malfeasance on the part of those with a license to sell securities, the state securities department will look into the complaint, and possibly revoke the license, if such action is required.

These regulators protect buyers of securities sold in their states in another way:

They screen all securities offering documents such as prospectuses to ensure that adequate information has been disclosed and that the deal is not fraudulent. The securities office will not judge each deal on its investment potential, but it will reject offerings that it deems abusive. This prescreening process is commonly called the blue-sky process, because a judge once asserted that a particular offering had as much value as a patch of blue sky. It is important to ask these state securities regulators, therefore, if a particular security, such as a mutual fund or limited partnership, has passed the blue-sky process in one's state. If it has not, state residents are not allowed to buy it.

Besides watching over the securities industry in their states and screening new securities offerings, state securities offices can be helpful in explaining the pros and cons of various kinds of securities. They often have helpful literature describing what investors should watch for in making good investments and avoiding bad ones. In general, these offices will be one of the best places to contact about any question that might come up regarding a security sold in one's state.

ALABAMA
Securities Commission
401 Adams Avenue, Second Floor
Montgomery, Alabama 36130
(334) 242-2984
www.asc.state.al.us

ALASKA
Division of Banking, Securities
   and Corporations
150 Third Street, Room 217
Juneau, Alaska 99811-0807
(907) 465-2521
www.dced.state.ak.us/bsc/secur.htm

ARIZONA
Arizona Corporation Commission
   Securities Division
1300 West Washington, Third Floor
Phoenix, Arizona 85007
(602) 542-4242
www.ccsd.cc.state.az.us

ARKANSAS
Securities Department
Heritage West Building
201 East Markham, Room 300
Little Rock, Arkansas 72201-1692
(501) 324-9260
www.securities.arkansas.gov

CALIFORNIA
Department of Corporations
1515 K Street, Suite 200
Sacramento, California 95814
(916) 445-7205
www.corp.ca.gov

COLORADO
Division of Securities
1560 Broadway, Suite 900
Denver, Colorado 80202
(303) 894-2320
www.dora.state.co.us/securities

CONNECTICUT
Department of Banking
260 Constitution Plaza
Hartford, Connecticut 06103-1800
(860) 240-8230
www.ct.gov/dob

DELAWARE
Division of Securities
Carvel State Office Building
820 North French Street, 5th Floor
Wilmington, Delaware 19801
(302) 577-8424
www.state.de.us/securities

DISTRICT OF COLUMBIA
Department of Insurance and
  Securities Regulation
801 First Street, NE, Suite 701
Washington, D.C. 20002
(202) 442-7800

FLORIDA
Office of Financial Regulation
The Fletcher Building
200 East Gaines Street
Tallahassee, Florida 32399-0372
(850) 410-9500
www.flofr.com

GEORGIA
Division of Business Services and
  Regulation
2 Martin Luther King, Jr. Drive, SE
802 West Tower
Atlanta, Georgia 30334
(404) 656-3920
www.sos.state.ga.us/securities

HAWAII
Division of Business Regulation
335 Merchant Street, Room 203
Honolulu, Hawaii 96813
(808) 586-2744
www.hawaii.gov/dcca/areas/scc

IDAHO
Department of Finance
800 Park Boulevard, Suite 200
Boise, Idaho 83712
(208) 332-8004
http://finance.idaho.gov

ILLINOIS
Securities Department
69 West Washington Street,
  Suite 1220
Chicago, Illinois 60602
(312) 793-3384
www.cyberdriveillinois.com/
  departments/securities

INDIANA
Securities Division
302 West Washington
Room E-111
Indianapolis, Indiana 46204
(317) 232-6681
www.in.gov/sos/securities/index.html

IOWA
Securities Bureau
340 East Maple Street
Des Moines, Iowa 50319-0066
(515) 281-4441
www.iid.state.ia.us

KANSAS
Office of the Securities
  Commissioner
618 South Kansas Avenue
Topeka, Kansas 66603-3804
(785) 296-3307
www.securities.state.ks.us

KENTUCKY
Department of Financial
  Institutions
1025 Capital Center Drive,
  Suite 200
Frankfort, Kentucky 40601
(502) 573-3390
www.kfi.ky.gov

LOUISIANA
Securities Commission
8660 United Plaza Boulevard,
  Second Floor
Baton Rouge, Louisiana 70809-7024
(225) 925-4512
www.ofi.state.la.us/securit.htm

MAINE
Securities Division
State House Station 121
Augusta, Maine 04333
(207) 624-8551
www.state.me.us/pfr/sec/
  sec_index.htm

MARYLAND
Division of Securities
200 St. Paul Place
Baltimore, Maryland 21202-2020
(410) 576-6360
www.oag.state.md.us/securities/
  index.htm

MASSACHUSETTS
Securities Division
One Ashburton Place, Room 1701
Boston, Massachusetts 02108
(617) 727-3548
www.state.ma.us/sec/sct

MICHIGAN
Office of Financial and Insurance
    Services
611 West Ottawa Street, Third Floor
Lansing, Michigan 48933
(877) 999-6442
www.michigan.gov/ofis

MINNESOTA
Department of Commerce
85 East Seventh Place, Suite 500
St. Paul, Minnesota 55101
(651) 296-4026
www.commerce.state.mn.us

MISSISSIPPI
Business Regulation and
    Enforcement Division
700 North Street
Jackson, Mississippi 39202
(601) 359-9055
www.sos.state.ms.us

MISSOURI
Office of the Secretary of State
600 West Main Street
Jefferson City, Missouri 65101
(573) 751-4136
www.sos.mo.gov/securities

MONTANA
Securities Department
840 Helena Avenue
Helena, Montana 59601
(406) 444-2040
www.state.mt.us/sao

NEBRASKA
Nebraska Department of Banking
    and Finance
Commerce Court
P.O. Box 95006
1230 O Street, Suite 400
Lincoln, Nebraska 68509-5006
(402) 471-3445
www.ndbf.org

NEVADA
Securities Division
555 East Washington Avenue,
    Suite 5200
Las Vegas, Nevada 89101
(702) 486-2440
www.sos.state.nv.us/securities

NEW HAMPSHIRE
Bureau of Securities Regulation
P.O. Box 3715
Suite 317A
Concord, New Hampshire 03302-3715
(603) 271-1463
http://www.sos.nh.gov/securities

NEW JERSEY
Bureau of Securities
153 Halsey Street, 6th Floor
Newark, New Jersey 07102
(973) 504-3600
www.state.nj.us/lps/ca/bos.htm

NEW MEXICO
Securities Division
2550 Cerrillos Road
Santa Fe, New Mexico 87505
(505) 476-4580
www.rld.state.nm.us/securities

NEW YORK
Investor Protection and Securities
    Bureau
120 Broadway, 23rd Floor
New York, New York 10271
(212) 416-8222
www.oag.state.ny.us/investors/
    investors.html

NORTH CAROLINA
Securities Division
Old Revenue Complex
2 South Salisbury Street
Raleigh, North Carolina 27601
(919) 733-3924
www.secretary.state.nc.us/sec

NORTH DAKOTA
Securities Commission
State Capitol
600 East Boulevard, 5th Floor
Bismarck, North Dakota 58505-0510
(701) 328-2910
www.state.nd.us/securities

OHIO
Division of Securities
77 South High Street, 22nd Floor
Columbus, Ohio 43215
(614) 644-7381
www.securities.state.oh.us

OKLAHOMA
Department of Securities
First National Center
120 North Robinson, Suite 860
Oklahoma City, Oklahoma 73102
(405) 280-7700
www.securities.state.ok.us

OREGON
Division of Finance and Corporate
　Securities
350 Winter Street, NE, Suite 410
Salem, Oregon 97301-3881
(503) 378-4140
www.cbs.state.or.us/external/dfcs

PENNSYLVANIA
Securities Commission
Eastgate Office Building
1010 North Seventh Street,
　2nd Floor
Harrisburg, Pennsylvania 17102-
　1410
(717) 787-8061
www.psc.state.pa.us

RHODE ISLAND
Department of Business Regulation
John O. Pastore Complex,
　Building 6901
1511 Pontiac Avenue
Providence, Rhode Island 02903-
　4232
(401) 462-9527
www.dbr.state.ri.us

SOUTH CAROLINA
Securities Division
Rembert C. Dennis Office Building
1000 Assembly Street
Columbia, South Carolina 29201
(803) 734-4731
www.scsecurities.com

SOUTH DAKOTA
Division of Securities
445 East Capitol Avenue
Pierre, South Dakota 57501-2000
(605) 773-4823
www.state.sd.us/drr2/reg/
　securities/index.htm

TENNESSEE
Securities Division
Davy Crockett Tower
500 James Robertson Parkway,
　Suite 680
Nashville, Tennessee 37243-0575
(615) 741-2947
www.state.tn.us/commerce/securities

TEXAS
State Securities Board
208 East 10th Street, 5th Floor
Austin, Texas 78701
(512) 305-8300
www.ssb.state.tx.us

UTAH
Division of Securities
160 East 300 South, 2nd Floor
Salt Lake City, Utah 84111
(801) 530-6600
www.securities.utah.gov

VERMONT
Department of Banking, Insurance,
　Securities and Health Care
　Administration
89 Main Street, Drawer 20
Montpelier, Vermont 05620-3101
(802) 828-3420
www.bishca.state.vt.us

VIRGINIA
Division of Securities and Retail
　Franchising
1300 East Main Street, 9th Floor
Richmond, Virginia 23219
(804) 371-9051
www.scc.virginia.gov/division/srf

WASHINGTON
Securities Division
150 Israel Road, SW
Tumwater, Washington 98501
(360) 902-8760
www.dfi.wa.gov/sd

WEST VIRGINIA
Securities Division
Building 1
Room W-100
Charleston, West Virginia 25305-0230
(304) 558-2257
www.wvauditor.com/securities

WISCONSIN
Division of Securities
345 West Washington Avenue,
    4th Floor
Madison, Wisconsin 53703
(608) 266-1064
www.wdfi.org/fi/securities

WYOMING
Securities Division
State Capitol
200 West 24th Street, Room 109
Cheyenne, Wyoming 82002-0020
(307) 777-7370
http://soswy.state.wy.us/securiti/
    securiti.htm

CANADIAN PROVINCIAL AGENCIES

These provincial and territorial agencies have many of the same powers as state regulators in the United States. Where available, we have listed the two major finance and investment agencies in each province. Consumer and Corporate Affairs agencies and departments regulate such areas as consumer protection, mortgages, insurance, credit, and securities. The Finance Departments of each province run the financial affairs of government and collect taxes. In some cases, some of these functions are part of a province's Justice Department or attorney general's office.

ALBERTA
Alberta Finance and Enterprise
Terrace Building, Room 426
9515 107th Street
Edmonton, Alberta T5K 2C3
(780) 427-3035
www.finance.gov.ab.ca

Alberta Securities Commission
300 Fifth Avenue, SW, Suite 400
Calgary, Alberta T2P 3C4
(403) 297-6454
www.albertasecurities.com

BRITISH COLUMBIA
British Columbia Securities
    Commission
701 West Georgia Street
Vancouver, British Columbia V7Y 1L2
(604) 899-6500
www.bcsc.bc.ca

Ministry of Finance
701 West Georgia Street
Vancouver, British Columbia V7Y 1L2
(604) 660-2421
www.gov.bc.ca

MANITOBA
Manitoba Finance
350-363 Broadway
Winnipeg, Manitoba R3C 3N9
(204) 945-3744
www.gov.mb.ca/finance

Manitoba Securities Commission
400 St. Mary Avenue, Suite 500
Winnipeg, Manitoba R3C 4K5
(204) 945-2548
www.msc.gov.mb.ca

NEW BRUNSWICK
Department of Finance
Centennial Building
670 King Street
Fredericton, New Brunswick E3B 1G1
(506) 453-2451
www.gnb.ca

New Brunswick Securities
    Commission
85 Charlotte Street, Suite 300
Saint John, New Brunswick E2L 2J2
(505) 658-3060
www.nbsc-cvmnb.ca

NEWFOUNDLAND and
    LABRADOR
Department of Finance
P.O. Box 8700
St. John's, Newfoundland A1B 4J6
(709) 729-3255
www.gov.nl.ca/fin

Department of Government
    Services
P.O. Box 8700
St. John's, Newfoundland A1B 4J6
(709) 729-4189
www.gov.nl.ca/gs

NORTHWEST TERRITORIES
Department of Finance
P.O. Box 1320
Yellowknife, Northwest Territories
  X1A 2L9
(867) 873-7117
www.fin.gov.nt.ca

Office of the Superintendent
  of Securities
Government of the Northwest
  Territories
P.O. Box 1320
Ycllowknife, NT X1A 2L9
(867) 920-3318
www.justice.gov.nt.ca/Securities
  Registry

NOVA SCOTIA
Department of Finance
1723 Hollis Street
Halifax, Nova Scotia B3J 2N3
(902) 424-5554
www.gov.ns.ca/fina

Nova Scotia Securities Commission
Joseph Howe Building
1690 Hollis Street, 2nd Floor
Halifax, Nova Scotia B3J 3J9
(902) 424-7768
www.gov.ns.ca/nssc

NUNAVUT
Department of Finance
P.O. Box 1000, Station 330
Iqaluit, Nunavut X0A 0H0
(867) 975-5800
www.gov.nu.ca/finance

Office of the Superintendent
  of Securities
P.O. Box 1000, Station 570
Iqaluit, Nunavut X0A 0H0
(867) 975-6590
www.justice.nov.nu.ca/i8n/english/
  legreg/sr_index.shtm

ONTARIO
Ministry of Finance
Frost Building North, 3rd Floor
95 Grosvenor Street
Toronto, Ontario M7A 1Z1
(800) 263-7965
www.fin.gov.on.ca

Ontario Securities Commission
20 Queen Street West, Suite 1903
Toronto, Ontario M5II 3S8
(416) 593-8314
www.osc.gov.on.ca

PRINCE EDWARD ISLAND
Securities Office
Office of the Attorney General
95 Rochford Street
Charlottetown, Prince Edward
  Island C1A 7N8
(902) 368-4569
www.gov.pe.ca/securities

Department of the Provincial
  Treasury
2nd Floor South, Shaw Building
95 Rochford Street
P.O. Box 2000
Charlottetown, Prince Edward
  Island C1A 7N8
(902) 368-4050
www.gov.pe.ca/pt

QUEBEC
Autorité des Marchés Financiers
800, Square Victoria, 22e etage
Montreal, Quebec H4Z 1G3
(514) 395-0337
www.lautorite.qc.ca

Ministère des Finances
12, rue Saint-Louis
Québec, Québec G1R 5L3
(418) 528-9323
www.finances.gouv.qc.ca

SASKATCHEWAN
Sasketchewan Financial Services
  Commission
1919 Saskatchewan Drive, 6th Floor
Regina, Saskatchewan S4P 3V7
(306) 787-5645
www.sfsc.gov.sk.ca

Ministry of Finance
2350 Albert Street
Regina, Saskatchewan S4P 4A6
(306) 787-6768
www.finance.gov.sk.ca

YUKON
Department of Finance
Yukon Government Administration
  Building
2071 Second Avenue, 3rd Floor
P.O. Box 2703
Whitehorse, Yukon Y1A 2C6
(867) 667-5343
www.finance.gov.yk.ca

Superintendent of Securities
Box 2703
Whitehorse, Yukon Y1A 3C6
(867) 667-5225
www.community.gov.yk.ca/corp/
  secureinvest.html

FINANCE AND INVESTMENT ORGANIZATIONS

These organizations are the most important in the finance and investment field. The listing includes trade associations that educate the public about their industries and lobby for their political positions in Congress; self-regulatory organizations that regulate the conduct of the marketplace under the supervision of a federal regulatory agency; and consumer and investor organizations that educate consumers and investors and help them resolve problems.

America's Health Insurance Plans
601 Pennsylvania Avenue, NW
South Building, Suite 500
Washington, D.C. 20004
(202) 778-3200
www.ahip.org
Represents health, dental, and long-term care insurance companies in lobbying efforts, and educates the public about health insurance.

American Arbitration Association
1633 Broadway, 10th Floor
New York, New York 10019
(212) 716-5800
www.adr.org
Sets the rules for arbitration proceedings and supplies arbitrators to resolve disputes.

American Association of Individual
  Investors
625 North Michigan Avenue
Chicago, Illinois 60611
(312) 280-0170
www.aaii.org
Nonprofit organization that educates individual investors about opportunities in stocks, bonds, and mutual funds. Conducts seminars, workshops, offers home study courses and education on its Web site.

American Bankers Association
1120 Connecticut Avenue, NW
Washington, D.C. 20036
(202) 663-5000
www.aba.com
Represents commercial banks in legislative and regulatory activities and legal action. Also educates the public about banking.

American College of Trust
  and Estate Counsel
3415 South Sepulveda Boulevard,
  Suite 330
Los Angeles, California 90034
(310) 398-1888
www.actec.org
Professional organization of trust and estate lawyers; provides written referrals upon request.

American Council of Life Insurers
101 Constitution Avenue, NW,
  Suite 700
Washington, D.C. 20001-2133
(202) 624-2000
www.acli.com
Represents life insurance companies in lobbying life insurance-related issues; educates the public about insurance.

American Financial Services
 Association
919 18th Street, NW, Suite 300
Washington, D.C. 20006
(202) 296-5544
www.americanfinsvcs.com
Represents companies that lend to consumers and small businesses. Lobbies on issues related to consumer lending, and also educates the public about credit and budgeting issues.

American Institute of Certified
 Public Accountants
1211 Avenue of the Americas,
 19th Floor
New York, New York 10036
(212) 575-6436
www.aicpa.org
Professional society of certified public accountants; establishes auditing and reporting standards and prepares the Uniform CPA Examination for state licensing bodies.

American Insurance Association
2101 L Street, NW, Suite 400
Washington, D.C. 20037
(202) 828-7100
www.aiadc.org
Represents property and liability insurance companies in lobbying on insurance-related issues. Educates the public about safety issues and suggests codes to governments on such areas as industrial safety and fire prevention.

American Management Association
1601 Broadway
New York, New York 10019
(212) 586-8100
www.amanet.org
Nonprofit educational organization working to improve management skills in government and industry.

American Numismatic Association
818 North Cascade Avenue
Colorado Springs, Colorado
 80903-3279
(719) 632-2646
www.money.org
Nonprofit educational organization promoting the study and collection of money, including coins, tokens, medals, and paper currency. Offers research and education through its library, museum, and publications.

Appraisers Association of America
386 Park Avenue South, Suite 2000
New York, New York 10016
(212) 889-5404
www.appraisersassoc.org
Professional association that sets standards for appraisers of personal property.

Association for Advanced Life
 Underwriting
2901 Telestar Court
Falls Church, Virginia 22042
(703) 641-9400
www.aalu.org
Professional society of planners specializing in life insurance, retirement, and estate planning.

Association of Financial Guaranty
 Insurers
139 Lancaster Street
Albany, New York 12210-1003
(518) 449-4698
www.afgi.org
Represents issuance companies that insure municipal bonds against default.

BAI Inc.
1 North Franklin, Suite 1000
Chicago, Illinois 60606
(312) 553-4600
www.bai.org
Conducts research, sponsors developmental programs, and serves as the financial services industry's major resource in management, administrative, and technical specialties.

CSI
200 Wellington Street West,
   15th Floor
Toronto, Ontario M5V 3C7 Canada
(416) 364-9130
www.csi.ca
Provides investment education to
Canadian financial industry professionals.

CCIM Institute
430 North Michigan Avenue,
   8th Floor
Chicago, Illinois 60611-4092
(312) 321-4460
www.ccim.com
Education and certification program
in commercial real estate and investment real estate for brokers, developers, mortgage bankers, and other
professionals.

Canadian Society of Technical
   Analysts
157 Adelaide Street West, Suite 436
Toronto, Ontario M5H4E7
(519) 620-9339
www.csta.org
Offers courses and seminars on technical analysis.

Certified Financial Planner Board
   of Standards
1425 K Street, Suite 500
Washington, D.C. 20005
(202) 379-2300
www.cfp-board.org
Administers the Certified Financial
Planner examinations and licenses
individuals to use the CFP designation.

CFA Institute
560 Ray C. Hunt Drive
Charlottesville, Virginia 22903-2981
(434) 951-5499
www.cfainstitute.org
Certifies and educates investment
management professionals who are
known as Chartered Financial Analysts once they are admitted to membership.

Chartered Property Casualty
   Underwriters (CPCU) Society
720 Providence Road
Malvern, Pennsylvania 19355
(800) 932-2728
www.cpcusociety.org
Professional association of agents
selling property and casualty insurance and risk management services.

Closed-End Fund Association
P.O. Box 28037
Kansas City, Missouri 64188
(816) 413-8900
www.closed-endfunds.com
Represents closed-end mutual funds
to the public.

Consumer Bankers Association
1000 Wilson Boulevard, Suite 2500
Arlington, Virginia 22209-3912
(703) 276-1750
www.cbanet.org
Represents commercial banks, savings and loans, and credit unions, and
educates the public about banking.

Consumer Data Industry
   Association
1090 Vermont Avenue, NW,
   Suite 200
Washington, D.C. 20005-4905
(202) 371- 0134
www.cdiaonline.org
Trade association for consumer information companies; it is involved
in government relations, public affairs, and education.

Consumer Federation of America
1620 I Street, NW, Suite 200
Washington, D.C. 20006
(202) 387-6121
www.consumerfed.org
Organization representing consumer
interests in several fields, including
banking, insurance, and government
regulation.

Council of Better Business Bureaus
4200 Wilson Boulevard, Suite 800
Arlington, Virginia 22203-1838
(703) 276-0100
www.bbb.org
Umbrella organization for the Better Business Bureau system. Mediates disputes between consumers and businesses and promotes ethical business standards.

Council of Institutional Investors
888 17th Street, NW, Suite 500
Washington, D.C. 20000
(202) 822-0800
www.cii.org
Represents trustees from public, union, and corporate pension funds and nonprofit endowment or foundations.

Credit Union National Association
    Inc.
5710 Mineral Point Road
Madison, Wisconsin 53705-4454
(800) 356-9655
www.cuna.org
Represents credit unions in lobbying on issues related to credit unions. Promotes credit union membership and the formation of new credit unions, and educates the public about credit unions and personal finance.

Electronic Funds Transfer
    Association
11350 Random Hills Road, Suite 800
Fairfax, Virginia 22030
(703) 934-6052
www.efta.org
Provides a forum for financial institutions, retailers, telecommunications companies, and other businesses involved in electronic payment systems and commerce.

Employee Benefit Research
    Institute
1100 13th Street, NW, Suite 878
Washington, D.C. 20005
(202) 659-0670
www.ebri.org
A group of trade associations, banks, insurance companies, and other corporations concerned with employee benefit programs.

ESOP Association
1726 M Street, NW, Suite 501
Washington, D.C. 20036
(202) 293-2971
www.esopassociation.org
Association of companies offering Employee Stock Ownership Plans; promotes wider use of these plans.

Financial Accounting Standards
    Board
401 Merritt 7
P.O. Box 5116
Norwalk, Connecticut 06856-5116
(203) 847-0700
www.fasb.org
Sets financial accounting and reporting standards for private-sector organizations. Its sister organization, the Governmental Accounting Standards Board, sets standards for state and local governments.

Financial Industry Regulatory
    Authority
1735 K Street
Washington, D.C. 20006
(301) 590-6500
www.finra.org
Regulator for securities firms doing business in the United States.

The Financial Planning Association
4100 East Mississippi Avenue,
    Suite 400
Denver, Colorado 80246-3053
(800) 322-4237
www.fpanet.org
Represents financial planners who have earned the CFP (Certified Financial Planner) designation. Provides continuing education for planners, and refers consumers who inquire about CFPs in their area.

Futures Industry Association
2001 Pennsylvania Avenue, NW,
    Suite 600
Washington, D.C. 20006
(202) 466-5460
www.futuresindustry.org
Represents brokerage firms and brokers that deal in futures and options, and lobbies on issues related to the futures industry.

Independent Community Bankers
   of America
1615 L Street, NW, Suite 900
Washington, D.C. 20036
(800) 422-8439
www.ibaa.org
Represents community banks. Provides products and services that promote the profitability and competitiveness of community banks.

Industry Council for Tangible Assets
P.O. Box 1365
Severna Park, Maryland 21146-8365
(410) 626-7005
www.ictaonline.org
National trade association for rare coins, precious metals, and the tangible assets industry.

Insurance Information Institute
110 William Street
New York, New York 10038
(212) 346-5500
www.iii.org
Represents property and casualty insurance companies. Provides information about insurance to the public.

Insurance Institute of America
720 Providence Road, Suite 100
Malvern, Pennsylvania 19355-3423
(800) 644-2101
www.aicpcu.org
The educational arm of the American Institute for Chartered Property Casualty Underwriters, offering professional certification to people in the property and liability insurance businesses.

International Association of
   Registered Financial Consultants
The Financial Planning Building
2507 North Verity Parkway
P.O. Box 42506
Middletown, Ohio 45042
(800) 532-9060
www.iarfc.org
Association of consultants who provide overall financial planning.

International Bond and Share
   Society
P.O. Box 430
Hackensack, New Jersey 07602-0430
(201) 489-2440
www.scripophily.org
Society for promoting the hobby of scripophily, the collection and study of antique stock and bond certificates.

International Franchise Association
1501 K Street, NW, Suite 350
Washington, D.C. 20005
(202) 628-8000
www.franchise.org
Represents franchisors, franchisees, and suppliers of many different kinds of businesses by lobbying Congress on issues of concern to the industry. Gives advice to those wanting to evaluate franchise opportunities.

International Swaps and Derivatives
   Association
360 Madison Avenue, 16th Floor
New York, New York 10017
(212) 901-6000
www.isda.org
Identifies sources of risk in the derivatives and risk management business.

Investment Adviser Association
1050 17th Street, NW, Suite 725
Washington, D.C. 20036-5503
(202) 293-4222
www.icaa.org
Represents investment adviser firms that select and manage investments for individuals and institutional clients such as pension plans, trusts, and nonprofit organizations.

Investment Company Institute
1401 H Street, NW, Suite 1200
Washington, D.C. 20005
(202) 326-5800
www.ici.org
Represents companies that offer mutual funds, closed-end funds, exchange-traded funds, and unit investment trusts. Lobbies on mutual fund issues in Congress and educates the public about the uses of mutual funds.

Investment Management
Consultants Association
5619 DTC Parkway, Suite 500
Greenwood Village, Colorado 80111
(303) 770-3377
www.imca.org
Represents consultants who supervise the performance of money managers on behalf of individual and institutional investors.

Investment Programs Association
445 Park Avenue, 9th Floor
New York, New York 10022
(212) 812-9799
www.ipaonline.org
Trade association that represents interests of investors of nontraded investment programs, including partnerships, REITS, and limited liability companies.

Investors Alliance
P.O. Box 10136
Pompano Beach, Florida 33061-9951
(866) 627-9090
www.powerinvestor.com
Enhances industry skills through research, education, and training.

IRRC Institute
1 Chase Manhattan Plaza, 44th Floor
New York, New York 10005
(646) 778-4193
www.irrcinstitute.org
Provides objective information on corporate governance and social responsibility for corporations and institutional investors that vote proxies independently.

LIMRA International
300 Day Hill Road
Windsor, Connecticut 06095
(860) 688-3358
www.limra.com
Conducts research and operates seminars and professional development programs for companies in the annuity, disability, life insurance, mutual fund, and retirement savings industries.

Managed Funds Association
2025 M Street, NW, Suite 800
Washington, D.C. 20036-3309
(202) 367-1140
www.mfainfo.org
Represents hedge funds.

Market Technicians Association
61 Broadway, Suite 514
New York, New York 10006
(646) 652-3300
www.mta.org
Establishes and maintains standards of professional competence in technical analysis.

Mortgage Bankers Association
1331 L Street, NW
Washington, D.C. 20006
(202) 557-2700
www.mbaa.org
Represents mortgage lenders such as mortgage bankers, commercial banks, savings and loans, and insurance companies. The MBAA lobbies on housing finance issues before Congress and conducts continuing education seminars for members of the industry.

Municipal Securities Rulemaking
Board
1900 Duke Street, Suite 600
Alexandria, Virginia 22314
(703) 797-6600
www.msrb.org
A self-regulatory agency for municipal securities brokers and dealers, overseen by the Securities and Exchange Commission, that sets standards for the municipal securities industry.

Mutual Fund Education Alliance
100 Northwest Englewood Road,
Suite 130
Kansas City, Missouri 64118
(816) 454-9422
www.mfea.com
Represents the mutual fund industry and provides information to consumers on investing and the name, telephone numbers, and kinds of funds available.

National Association for Business
Economics
1233 20th Street, NW, Suite 505
Washington, D.C. 20036
(202) 463-6223
www.nabe.com
Society composed of corporate and
governmental economists, and those
with an active interest in applied,
practical economics.

National Association of Insurance
and Financial Advisors
2901 Telestar Court
Falls Church, VA 22042-1205
(703) 770-8100
www.naifa.org
Association of insurance and financial agents and brokers. Educates the
public on how to work with insurance
agents and brokers.

National Association of Investment
Companies
1300 Pennsylvania Avenue NW,
Suite 700
Washington, D.C. 20004
(202) 204-3001
www.naicvc.com
Provides technical assistance and
monitors legislation for investment
companies supplying capital to
minority-owned businesses.

National Association of Investors
Corporation
711 West 13 Mile Road
Madison Heights, Michigan 48071
(248) 583-6242
www.betterinvesting.org
Promotes growth of investment
clubs. Helps people set up these clubs
and monitors their performance.

National Association of
Manufacturers
1331 Pennsylvania Avenue, NW
Washington, D.C. 20004-1790
(202) 637-3000
www.nam.org
Represents views to government of
manufacturing companies. Also reviews legislation, administrative rulings, and judicial decisions affecting
industry.

National Association of Personal
Financial Advisors
3250 North Arlington Heights
Road, Suite 109
Arlington Heights, Illinois 60004
(847) 483-5400
www.napfa.org
Represents financial planners who
work on a fee-only basis and do not
take commissions for selling products.

National Association of Real
Estate Investment Trusts
1875 I Street, NW, Suite 600
Washington, D.C. 20006
(202) 739-9400
www.nareit.org
National association for real estate
investment trusts and publicly traded
real estate companies. Represents
REITs before Congress and educates
the public about REITs.

National Association of Realtors
430 North Michigan Avenue
Chicago, Illinois 60611-4087
(800) 874-6500
www.realtor.org
Trade group representing real estate
agents.

National Association of Small
Business Investment Companies
1100 G Street, NW, Suite 750
Washington, D.C. 20015
(202) 628-5055
www.nasbic.org
Represents small business investment
companies (SBICs) that are publicly
traded or private companies that invest in private small businesses. The
Association lobbies Congress on issues related to the industry and educates the public about SBICs.

National Association of Women
Business Owners
601 Pennsylvania Avenue, Suite 900
Washington, D.C. 20004
(800) 556-2926
www.nawbo.org
Provides technical assistance, management training, and business and
economic information to women business owners, and represents members
in legislative and lobbying efforts.

National Bankers Association
1513 P Street NW
Washington, D.C. 20005
(202) 588-5432
www.nationalbankers.org
Represents minority and women-owned financial institutions. Provides counseling, consulting, and technical assistance to member banks.

National Foundation for Credit
  Counseling
801 Roeder Road, Suite 900
Silver Spring, Maryland 20910
(800) 388-2227
www.nfcc.org
Aids consumers who have taken on too much debt. Helps consumers restructure their debt through local consumer credit counseling service centers throughout the United States.

National Futures Association
300 South Riverside Plaza,
  Suite 1800
Chicago, Illinois 60606-6615
(312) 781-1300
www.nfa.futures.org
Represents firms that trade futures and options. Resolves disputes between its members and customers with complaints against those members.

National Investor Relations
  Institute
8020 Towers Crescent Drive,
  Suite 250
Vienna, Virginia 22182
(703) 506-3570
www.niri.org
Represents executives in the investor relations and financial communications fields. Conducts continuing education programs for members.

National Venture Capital
  Association
1655 North Fort Myer Drive,
  Suite 850
Arlington, Virginia 22209
(703) 524-2549
www.nvca.org
Represents venture capitalists seeking to invest money in growing enterprises.

New York Society of Security
  Analysts
1177 Avenue of the Americas,
  2nd Floor
New York, New York 10036-2714
(212) 541-4530
www.nyssa.org
Promotes awareness and understanding of securities analysis, investing, and the operation of the securities markets. The largest society of the CFA Institute.

North American Securities
  Administrators Association
750 First Street, NE, Suite 1140
Washington, D.C. 20002
(202) 737-0900
www.nasaa.org
Represents the securities regulators of the United States, the District of Columbia, Puerto Rico, Canada, and Mexico. Provides grassroots investor protection.

Options Industry Council
One North Wacker Drive, Suite 500
Chicago, Illinois 60606
(312) 463-6193
www.888options.com
Educates the investing public and brokers about exchange-traded equity options.

Overseas Private Investment
  Corporation
1100 New York Avenue, NW
Washington, D.C. 20527
(202) 336-8400
www.opic.gov
Established as a development agency of the U.S. government. Supports and assists qualified U.S. investors in private ventures in emerging markets and supports U.S. foreign policy.

Pension Rights Center
1350 Connecticut Avenue, NW,
  Suite 206
Washington, D.C. 20036
(202) 296-3776
www.pensionrights.org
Educates the public about pension issues. Offers a legal referral service for pension-related problems.

Professional Numismatists Guild
3950 Concordia Lane
Fallbrook, California 92028
(760) 728-1300
www.pngdealers.com
Organization of professional coin/
paper money dealers. The Guild offers binding arbitration services for
consumer disputes with coin dealers.

Profit-Sharing/401(k) Council
  of America
20 North Wacker Drive, Suite 3700
Chicago, Illinois 60606
(312) 419-1863
www.psca.org
Devoted to explaining and promoting the use of profit-sharing, 401(k)
plans and related defined contribution programs.

Securities Industry and Financial
  Markets Association
120 Broadway, 35th Floor
New York, New York 10271-0080
(212) 313-1200
www.sifma.org
Represents securities broker/dealers,
mutual fund companies, and investment bankers in lobbying Congress
on issues of concern to the securities
industry. Educates the public about
the securities industry.

United States Chamber of
  Commerce
1615 H Street, NW
Washington, D.C. 20062-2000
(202) 659-6000
www.uschamber.com
Represents the business community's views on business, the economy,
and other issues at the federal, state,
and local level. Sponsors educational
programs and maintains a business
forecast and survey center.

World Gold Council
424 Madison Avenue
New York, New York 10017
(212) 317-3800
www.gold.org
Represents gold mining companies
and offers research and analysis about
market trends, supply and demand,
and other data useful for investing in
gold or gold-mining companies.

FINANCE AND INVESTMENT PUBLICATIONS

The following major publications can help keep you informed about the fast-changing world of finance and investment, from mass circulation business magazines to investment newsletters that reach a select number of subscribers. The publications cover a wide variety of topics, from investment advice about stocks, bonds, derivatives, money market instruments and commodities to mutual funds, taxation, entrepreneurship, and corporate finance. Other subjects include international investing, banking, precious metals, collectibles, management trends, economic forecasting, socially conscious investing, estate planning, venture capital, insider trading, and real estate. The title of each newsletter will often give you a clue to its subject matter.

Almost all the publications are available for a subscription charge; some also require that you join the organization that publishes it. Many will send you a sample either free or for a nominal charge.

Before subscribing to a newsletter or magazine, you must assess your needs and level of sophistication. Some newsletters are designed for the novice investor with a relatively small amount of money to put into stocks or mutual funds. Other publications are aimed at a highly sophisticated audience that is knowledgeable about technical analysis, commodity trading, or some other specialty. In general, the more complex the publication, the higher the subscription fee.

Whichever publications you read, employ an appropriate amount of caution before following specific investment recommendations. Despite many advisors' claims, no one calls every move in the complex financial markets right every time. You should be satisfied if you find a few newsletters that offer a style with which you are comfortable and have a solid track record of spotting unfolding investment trends.

AAII Journal
AAII Tax Guide
Computerized Investing
Individual Investor
Mutual funds guides
Stock Superstars Report
American Association of
   Individual Investors
625 North Michigan Avenue
Chicago, Illinois 60611
(312) 280-0170
www.aaii.org

AI Stock Forecast
P.O. Box 1835
Medina, Oregon 44258
(330) 764-4927
www.idmresearch.com

The Aden Forecast
P.O. Box 025216
Miami, Florida 33102
(305) 395-6141
www.adenforecast.com

Alcosta Growth Report
111 Deerwood Road, Suite 193
San Roman, California 94583
(888) 267-6729
www.alcostacapital.com

All Star Fund Trader
P.O. Box 203427
Austin, Texas 78720
(800) 299-4223
www.allstarinvestor.com

AlphaProfit Sector Investors'
   Newsletter
2803 Arrowhead Drive
Sugarland, Texas 77479
(281) 565-6963
www.alphaprofit.com

Barron's
1211 Avenue of the Americas
New York, New York 10036
(212) 416-2000
www.barrons.com

Bernie Schaeffer's Option Advisor
1259 Kemper Meadow Drive
Cincinnati, Ohio 45240
(800) 327-8833
www.schaefferresearch.com

Better Investing
National Association of Investors
   Corporation
711 West 13 Mile Road
Madison Heights, Michigan 48071
(248) 583-6242
www.betterinvesting.org

BI Research
P.O. Box 133
Redding, Connecticut 06875
www.biresearch.com

Bloomberg Markets Magazine
110 East 59th Street
New York, New York 10022
(212) 318-2000
www.bloomberg.com

The Blue Chip Investor
575 Anton Road, Suite 500
Costa Mesa, California 92626
(800) 710-5777
www.checkcapital.com

Daily Tax Report
Bureau of National Affairs
1801 South Bell Street
Arlington, Virginia 23202
(800) 372-1033
www.bna.com

Boardroom, Inc. publications:
Bottom Line Personal
Bottom Line Retirement
Bottom Line Wealth
281 Tresser Boulevard
Stamford, Connecticut 06901
(203) 973-5900
www.bottomlinesecrets.com

Bob Brinker's Marketimer
858 Happy Canyon Road, Suite 255
Castle Rock, Colorado 80108
(303) 660-8686
www.bobbrinker.com

Bob Carlson's Retirement Watch
P.O. Box 970
Oxon Hill, Maryland 20750
(800) 552-1152
www.retirementwatch.com

The Bowser Report
P.O. Box 6278
Newport News, Virginia 23606
(757) 877-5979
www.thebowserreport.com

Brinker Fixed Income Advisor
858 Happy Canyon Road, Suite 255
Castle Rock, Colorado 80108
(303) 688-2555
www.brinkeradvisor.com

The Buyback Letter
15415 Sunset Boulevard, Suite 200-D
Pacific Palisades, California 90272
(888) 289-2225
www.buybackletter.com

Business Week Magazine
1221 Avenue of the Americas
New York, New York 10020
(212) 512-2511
www.businessweek.com

CSIN Aggressive Educated
   Risk Taker
578 Richards Road
Wayne, Pennsylvania 19087
(610) 783-0980
www.csi-newsletter.com

The Cabot Market Letter
176 North Street
Salem, Massachusetts 01970
(978) 745-5532
www.cabot.net

ChangeWave Investing
700 Indian Springs Drive
Lancaster, Pennsylvania 17601
(888) 225-9373
www.changewave.com

The Chartist
The Chartist Mutual Fund Letter
P.O. Box 758
Seal Beach, California 90740
(800) 942-4278
www.thechartist.com

COINage Magazine
Miller Magazines Inc.
290 Maple Court, Suite 232
Ventura, California 93003
(805) 644-3824
www.coinagemag.com

Coin World
Ames Hobby Publishing
P.O. Box 926
Sidney, Ohio 45365
(937) 498-0800
www.coinworld.com

The Complete Investor
6 West 40th Street, 19th Floor
New York, New York 10018
(866) 833-2070
www.completeinvestor.com

The Contrarian's View
132 Moreland Street
Worcester, Massachusetts 01609
www.onashi.org

*Coolcat Explosive Small Cap
   Growth Stock Report*
P.O. Box 8
Sanger, California 93657
(559) 875-0613
www.coolcatreport.com

Crain Communications:
Advertising Age
AutoWeek
Automotive News
BtoB
Business Insurance
Crain's Chicago Business
Crain's Cleveland Business
Crain's Detroit Business
Crain's New York Business
Creativity
Investment News
Modern Healthcare
Pensions and Investments
Rubber & Plastics News
Television Week
Waste News & Recycling
Workforce Management
Crain Communications, Inc.
1155 Gratiot Avenue
Detroit, Michigan 48207
(313) 446-6000
www.crain.com

Crawford Perspectives
6890 East Sunrise Drive, Suite 70
Tucson, Arizona 85750
(520) 577-1158
www.crawfordperspectives.com

*CRB Commodity Yearbook
Futures Market Service*
Commodity Research Bureau
330 South Wells Street, Suite 612
Chicago, Illinois 60606
(312) 939-4135
www.crbtrader.com

*Cycles Research Early Warning
   Service*
511 6th Avenue, Suite 550
New York, New York 10011
www.cyclesresearch.com

*Daily Deal
The Deal*
105 Madison Avenue
New York, New York 10016
(212) 313-9200
www.thedeal.com

The Dines Letter
P.O. Box 22
Belvedere, California 94920
(800) 845-8259
www.dinesletter.com

Dividend Genius
8955 Katy Freeway, Suite 310
Houston, Texas 77024
(888) 853-1456
www.dividendgenius.com

Dow Jones Newsletters:
Daily Bankruptcy Review
DBR Small Cap
DBR Corporate Governance
DBR High Yield
1211 Avenue of the Americas
New York, New York 10036
(212) 416-2000
www.dowjones.com

Dow Theory Forecasts
Horizon Publishing Company
7412 Calumet Avenue
Hammond, Indiana 46324
(219) 852-3200
www.dowtheory.com

Dow Theory Letters
P.O. Box 1759
La Jolla, California 92038
(858) 454-0481
www.dowtheoryletters.com

The Economist
111 West 57th Street
New York, New York 10019
(212) 541-0500
www.economist.com

ETF Trader
201 California Street
San Francisco, California 94111
www.marketwatch.com

The Elliott Wave Financial Forecast
P.O. Box 1618
Gainesville, Georgia 30503
(800) 336-1618
www.elliottwave.com

Equities Magazine
439 North Canon Drive
Beverly Hills, California 90210
(310) 271-1700
www.equitiesmagazine.com

Equities Special Situations
2118 Wilshire Boulevard, Suite 722
Santa Monica, California 90403
(800) 709-7005
www.equitiesmagazine.com

Eric Dany's Stock Prospector
P.O. Box 1081
Moline, Illinois 61265
(866) 541-5299
www.ericdany.com

Eric Kobren's Fidelity Insight
20 William Street
Wellesley Hills, Massachusetts 02481
(800) 444-6342
www.fidelityinsight.com

The FXC Newsletter
2408 Richmond Road
Staten Island, New York 10306
(800) 392-0992
www.fxcnewsletter.com

Fabian's Successful Investing
1 Massachusetts Avenue, NW
Washington, D.C. 20001
(800) 950-8765
www.fabian.com

Fidelity Independent Adviser
25 Main Street
Williamstown, Massachusetts 01267
(800) 548-3797
www.fidelityadviser.com

Fidelity Investor
P.O. Box 920477
Needham, Massachusetts 02492
(800) 572-7907
www.fidelityinvestor.com

Fidelity Monitor
P.O. Box 1270
Rocklin, California 95677
(800) 397-3094
www.fidelitymonitor.com

Fidelity Navigator
1207 Route 9, Suite 10
Wappingers Falls, New York 12590
(877) 585-2785
www.fidelitynavigator.com

Financial Times
1330 Avenue of the Americas,
   Suite 1600
New York, New York 10019
(212) 641-6500
www.ft.com

Forbes
60 Fifth Avenue
New York, New York 10011
(800) 295-0893
www.forbes.com

Forbes Newsletters
Forbes Growth Investor
Forbes Special Situation Survey
Forbes Wireless Stock Watch
Forbes/Wolf Emerging Tech Report
60 Fifth Avenue
New York, New York 10011
(800) 295-0893
www.forbes.com

Fortune
Time & Life Building
Rockefeller Center
New York, New York 10020
(212) 522-8263
www.fortune.com

Fosback's Fund Forecaster
528 Alexander Palm Road
Boca Raton, Florida 33432
www.fosback.com

FredHager.com
3241 Main Street
Stratford, Connecticut 06614
(866) 319-3733
www.fredhager.com

FundAdvice.com
800 Fifth Avenue, Suite 2900
Seattle, Washington 98104
www.fundadvice.com

Futures Industry Magazine
Futures Industry Association
2001 Pennsylvania Avenue, NW,
    Suite 600
Washington, D.C. 20006
(202) 466 5460
www.futuresindustry.org

Futures Magazine
222 South Riverside Plaza, Suite 620
Chicago, Illinois 60606
(312) 846-4600
www.futuresmag.com

Global Investing
1040 First Avenue, Suite 305
New York, New York 10022
(800) 388-4237
www.global-investing.com

Good Fortune
P.O. Box 1500
Woodland, California 95776
(530) 661-7394
www.fundsystem.com

Grant's Interest Rate Observer
Two Wall Street
New York, New York 10005
(212) 809-7994
www.grantspub.com

The Granville Market Letter
P.O. Box 413006
Kansas City, Missouri 64141
(800) 876-5388
www.granvilleletter.com

Growth Fund Guide
P.O. Box 6600
Rapid City, South Dakota 57709
(800) 621-8322

Growth Stock Outlook
P.O. Box 15381
Chevy Chase, Maryland 20825

The Harley Market Letter
P.O. Box 1062
Thousand Oaks, California 91358
(805) 558-3590
www.harleymarketletter.com

Hidden Values Alert
P.O. Box 290708
Brooklyn, New York 11229
(800) 524-4832
www.hiddenvaluesalert.com

Inc. Magazine
7 World Trade Center
New York, New York 10007
(212) 389-3377
www.inc.com

*Independent Adviser for Vanguard
    Investors*
Fund Family Shareholder
    Association
2420A Gehman Lane
Lancaster, Pennsylvania 17602
(800) 211-7641
www.adviseronline.com

Index Rx
P.O. Box 34452
San Antonio, Texas 78265
(877) 374-6339
www.indexrx.com

Inevitable Wealth
P.O. Box 290708
Brooklyn, New York 11229
(800) 524-4832
www.hiddenvaluesalert.com

Institutional Investor Publications:
Alpha Magazine
Euromoney Magazine
Institutional Investor Magazine
Journal of Alternative Investments
Journal of Derivatives
Journal of Fixed Income
Journal of Investing
Journal of Portfolio Management
Journal of Private Equity
Journal of Strategic and Project
   Financing
Journal of Trading
Journal of Wealth Management
225 Park Avenue South
New York, New York 10003
(212) 224-3300
www.institutionalinvestor.com

International Harry Schultz Letter
P.O. Box 622
Lausanne, Switzerland
(866) 725-3724
www.hsletter.com

InvesTech Research Portfolio Strategy
2472 Birch Glen
Whitefish, Montana 59937
(406) 862-7777
www.investech.com

Investment Quality Trends
2888 Loker Avenue East, Suite 116
Carlsbad, California 92010
(866) 927-5250
www.iqtrends.com

The Investor's Guide to Closed-End
   Funds
Thomas J. Herzfeld Advisors
P.O. Box 161465
Miami, Florida 33116
(305) 271-1900
www.herzfeldresearch.com

Investors Business Daily
12655 Beatrice Street
Los Angeles, California 90066
(310) 448-6700
www.investors.com

Investors Intelligence
30 Church Street
New Rochelle, New York 10802
(914) 632-0422
www.investorsintelligence.com

Jack Adamo's Insiders PLUS
59 Beaver Brook Road, Suite 203-B
Lincoln Park, New Jersey 07035
(973) 202-7344
www.jackadamo.com

John Dessauer's Investor's World
9201 Corporate Boulevard
Rockville, Maryland 20850
(800) 804-0943
www.dessauerinvestorsworld.com

The Journal of Financial Planning
Financial Planning Association
4100 E. Mississippi Avenue, Suite 400
Denver, Colorado 80246
(800) 322-4237
www.fpanet.org/journal

Kiplinger's Personal Finance
   Magazine
The Kiplinger Letter
The Kiplinger Biofuels Market Alert
The Kiplinger Agriculture Letter
Kiplinger's Retirement Report
The Kiplinger Tax Letter
1729 H Street, NW
Washington, D.C. 20006
(800) 544-0155

Linde Equity Report
9-1301 Johnston Street
Vancouver, British Columbia
   V6H 3R9
(604) 738-5600
www.lindeequity.com

Louis Navellier's Blue Chip
   Growth Letter
700 Indian Springs Drive
Lancaster, Pennsylvania 17601
(800) 718-8289
www.bluechipgrowth.com

Louis Navellier's Emerging Growth
700 Indian Springs Drive
Lancaster, Pennsylvania 17601
(800) 219-8592
www.navelliergrowth.investor
   place.com

Lowry On Demand-Investor
1201 U.S. Highway One, Suite 250
North Palm Beach, Florida 33408
(561) 799-1889
www.lowryondemand.com

*Mark Skousen's Forecasts &
Strategies*
One Massachusetts Avenue, NW
Washington, D.C. 20001
(800) 211-7661
www.markskousen.com

Market Forecast
9420 Bonita Beach Road, Suite 201
Bonita Springs, Florida 34135
(239) 947-6068

Martin Weiss' Safe Money Report
15430 Endeavour Drive
Jupiter, Florida 33478
(800) 236-0407

Medical Technology Stock Letter
P.O. Box 40460
Berkeley, California 94704
(510) 843-1857
www.bioinvest.com

*Michael Murphy's New World
Investor*
700 Indian Springs Drive
Lancaster, Pennsylvania 17601
www.newworldinvestor.com

Moneyletter
479 Washington Street
Holliston, Massachusetts 01746
(800) 890-9670
www.moneyletter.com

Money Magazine
Time & Life Building
Rockefeller Center
New York, New York 10020
(212) 522-8263
www.money.cnn.com

Moneypaper newsletters:
The Moneypaper
Guide to Direct Investment Plans
DirectInvesting
555 Theodore Fremd Avenue,
Suite B-103
Rye, New York 10580
(914) 925-0022
www.directinvesting.com

Morningstar newsletters:
*Morningstar American Funds
Family Report*
*Morningstar Fidelity Fund Family
Report*
Morningstar Dividend Investor
MorningstarFund Investor
Morningstar Mutual Funds

Morningstar Opportunistic Investor
Morningstar StockInvestor
*Morningstar Vanguard Fund
Family Report*
225 West Wacker Drive
Chicago, Illinois 60606
(312) 696-6000
www.morningstar.com

Motley Fool newsletters:
Motley Fool Champion Funds
Motley Fool Hidden Gems
Motley Fool Income Investor
Motley Fool Inside Value
Motley Fool Rule Breakers
123 North Pitt Street
Alexandria, Virginia 22314
(888) 665-3665
www.fool.com

Mutual Fund Prospector
P.O. Box 1081
Moline, Illinois 61266
(866) 541-5299
www.prospectornewsletters.com

The Mutual Fund Strategist
P.O. Box 755
Shelburne, Vermont 05482
(800) 355-3863
www.mutualfundstrategist.com

Nate's Notes
P.O. Box 667
Healdsburg, California 95448
(707) 433-7903
www.natesnotes.com

The National Investor
W4265 4th Avenue
Spooner, Wisconsin 54801
(800) 771-2147
www.nationalinvestor.com

National Trendlines
14001 Berryville Road
North Potomac, Maryland 20874
(800) 521-1585
www.nationalinvestment.com

The New York Times
620 8th Avenue
New York, New York 10018
(212) 556-1234
www.nytimes.com

Nicholas Vardy's Global Stock
*   Investor*
One Massachusetts Avenue, NW
Washington, D.C. 20001
(800) 211-4774
www.globalstockinvestor.com

No-Load Fund Analyst
4 Orinda Way, Suite 200-D
Orinda, California 94563
(800) 776-9555
www.nlfa.com

No-Load Fund X
235 Montgomery Street, Suite 1049
San Francisco, California 94104
(800) 763-8639
www.fundx.com

No-Load Fund Investor
P.O. Box 3029
Brentwood, Tennessee 37024
(800) 706-6364
www.sheldonjacobs.com

No-Load Mutual Fund Selections
*   & Timing Newsletter*
100 North Central Expressway,
   Suite 1112
Richardson, Texas 75080
(800) 800-6563
www.investmentst.com

No-Load Navigator
1207 Route 9, Suite 10
Wappingers Falls, New York 12590
(877) 585-2785
www.noloadnavigator.com

No-Load Portfolios
8635 West Sahara, Suite 420
The Lakes, Nevada 89117

The Oberweis Report
3333 Warrenville Road, Suite 500
Lisle, Illinois 60532
(800) 323-6166
www.oberweis.net

On The Money
100 West Canyon Crest Road,
   Suite 200
Alpine, Utah 84004
(800) 772-5789
www.onthemoney.com

Outstanding Investments
808 St. Paul Street
Baltimore, Maryland 21202
(888) 696-4483
www.agorafinancialpublications.com

The Oxford Club
105 West Monument Street
Baltimore, Maryland 21201
(800) 992-0205
www.oxfordclub.com

The PAD System Report
502 Sea Isle Drive
San Diego, California 92154
(619) 594-5323
www.padsystemreport.com

Personal Finance
7600A Leesburg Pike
Falls Church, Virginia 22043
(703) 394-4931
www.pfnewsletter.com

The Peter Dag Portfolio Strategy
*   and Management*
65 Lakefront Drive
Akron, Ohio 44319
(800) 833-2782
www.peterdag.com

Peter Eliades' StockMarket Cycles
P.O. Box 751060
Petaluma, California 94975
(800) 888-4351
www.stockmarketcycles.com

Professional Timing Service
P.O. Box 7483
Missoula, Montana 59807
(888) 891-4326
www.protiming.com

The Prudent Speculator
32392 Coast Highway, Suite 260
Laguna Beach, California 92651
(877) 817-4394
www.alfrank.com

Real Wealth Report
15430 Endeavour Drive
Jupiter, Florida 33478
(800) 604-3649
www.larryedeson.com

Research Institute of America
   Publications:
All States Tax Handbook
Guide to Sales and Use Taxes
Federal Tax Handbook
Federal Tax Regulations
Internal Auditing Manual
Internal Revenue Code
Payroll Guide
Practical Guide to Corporate
   Governance & Accounting
Thomson Reuters Tax and
   Accounting
195 Broadway
New York, New York 10007
(800) 950-1216
www.ria.thomsonreuters.com

Richard E. Band's Profitable
   Investing
9201 Corporate Boulevard
Rockville, Maryland 20850
(800) 211-8566
www.rband.com

Richard Schmidt's Stellar
   Stock Alert
P.O. Box 110597
Naples, Florida 34108
(866) 478-3552
www.stellarstockreport.com

Richard C. Young's Intelligence
   Report
9201 Corporate Boulevard
Rockville, Maryland 20850
(800) 301-8968
www.intelligencereport.com

Roger Conrad's Utility Forecaster
7600A Leesburg Pike
Falls Church, Virginia 22043
(800) 832-2330
www.utilityforecaster.com

The Ruff Times
P.O. Box 545
Ithaca, New York 14851
(877) 665-6818
www.rufftimes.com

Sector Navigator
1207 Route 9
Wappingers Falls, New York 12590
(877) 585-2785
www.sectornavigator.com

Smart Money Magazine
1755 Broadway, 2nd Floor
New York, New York 10019
(800) 925-0485
www.smartmoney.com

Sound Advice
939 Hartz Way, Suite 210
Danville, California 94526
(800) 825-7007
www.soundadvice-newsletter.com

Source Media publications:
Accounting Today
American Banker
The Bond Buyer
Financial Planning Magazine
Investment Dealers Digest
National Mortgage News
One State Street Plaza, 27th Floor
New York, New York 10004
(212) 803-8200
www.sourcemedia.com

The Spear Report
45 Wintonbury Avenue
Bloomfield, Connecticut 06002
(800) 491-7119
www.spearreport.com

Standard & Poor's Outlook
Standard & Poor's
55 Water Street
New York, New York 10041
(212) 438-1000
www2.standardandpoors.com

Stock Market Leaders
501 Silverside Road, Suite 105
Wilmington, Delaware 19809
www.123wealthquest.com

Stock Trader's Almanac Investor
　Newsletter
111 River Street
Hoboken, New Jersey 07030
(800) 762-2974
www.stocktradersalmanac.com

The Street.com Insider Insights
132 East 43rd Street
New York, New York 10017
(212) 784-6860
www.insiderinsights.com

The Successful Investor
6021 Yonge Street, Suite 977
Toronto, Ontario M2M 3W2
(888) 292-0296
www.thesuccessfulinvestor.com

Superstock Investor
925 South Federal Highway, Suite 500
Boca Raton, Florida 33432
(800) 894-3424
www.superstockinvestor.com

Sy Harding's Street Smart Report
505 East New York Avenue, Suite 9
DeLand, Florida 32724
(888) 427-3464
www.streetsmartreport.com

Systems and Forecasts
150 Great Neck Road, Suite 301
Great Neck, New York 11021
(800) 829-6229
www.signalert.com

Timer Digest
P.O. Box 1688
Greenwich, Connecticut 06836
(800) 356-2527
www.timerdigest.com

TimingCube
P.O. Box 500032
Austin, Texas 78750
www.timingcube.com

Todd Market Forecast
P.O. Box 4131
Crestline, California 92325
(909) 338-8354
www.toddmarketforecast.com

The Turnaround Letter
225 Friend Street, Suite 801
Boston, Massachusetts 02114
(800) 468-3810
www.turnarounds.com

TurnerTrends
10002 Glencarrie Lane, Suite 1000
Austin, Texas 78750
(512) 577-2810
www.turnertrends.com

2 or 1 Stock Split Newsletter
140 O'Connor Street
Menlo Park, California 94025
(888) 775-4824
www.2-for-1.com

U.S. Investment Report
65 Chapel Road
New Hope, Pennsylvania 18938
(215) 862-1313
www.usinvestmentreport.com

USA Today
Gannett Co., Inc.
7950 Jones Branch Drive
McLean, Virginia 22107
(800) 872-0001
www.usatoday.com

Upside
7412 Calumet Avenue
Hammond, Indiana 46324
(800) 233-5922
www.upsidestocs.com

Value Line publications:
Value Line Convertibles Survey
Value Line Investment Survey
Value Line Investment Survey and
　Mid-Cap Edition
Value Line Mutual Fund Survey
Value Line Options Survey
Value Line Special Situations
　Service
75 Broad Street
New York, New York 10004
(212) 785-4086
www.valueline.com

Vickers Weekly Insider Report
61 Broadway
New York, New York 10006
(800) 645-5043
www.vickers-stock.com

Wall Street Stock Forecaster
6021 Yonge Street
Toronto, Ontario M2M 3W2
(888) 292-0296
www.wssf.us

The Wall Street Digest
8830 South Tamiami Trail, Suite 110
Sarasota, Florida 34238
(941) 954-5500
www.wallstreetdigest.com

Wall Street Transcript
48 West 37th Street
New York, New York 10018
(212) 952-7400
www.twst.com

The Wall Street Journal
1211 Avenue of the Americas
New York, New York 10036
(212) 416-2000
www.wsj.com

The Yamamoto Forecast
P.O. Box 573
Kahului, Hawaii 96733
(808) 292-0296

Zacks Elite
111 North Canal Street
Chicago, Illinois 60606
(800) 767-3771
www.zacksadvisor.com

Wall Street Letter
225 Park Avenue South
New York, New York 10003
(212) 224-3300
www.wallstreetletter.com

DATABASES, SOFTWARE, AND ONLINE SERVICES FOR INVESTING AND FINANCIAL PLANNING

The growth of the World Wide Web has opened up a wealth of opportunities for people who want to learn more about investing and, ultimately, to invest and manage their portfolios online. Supporting this phenomenon as an educational tool are a number of databases that have been selected for their comprehensive approach to investing and ease of learning about the financial markets. Investors can follow price movements with up-to-the-second accuracy and tap into these data banks to download current and historical information. Many of these products include significant research about industries and companies, economic information, breaking news, and, in most cases, real-time market prices.

Most of these sites are free to the public, although enhancements and special features often carry an additional cost. Some sites or products linked to financial publications may charge a fee related to the publication's subscription price: Subscribe, and you get a better deal. Online services are continually being enhanced by new bells and whistles. Trade execution, once an electronic marvel, is commonplace.

The databases and online services listed below provide comprehensive services covering the range of investor interests.

A separate section, ONLINE SERVICES FOR INVESTING AND FINANCIAL PLANNING, follows, divided into key application categories.

Throughout this book, Web sites have been provided to assist in gathering information. This listing of databases and online services, therefore, does not include banks and brokerages that offer broad-based online services from trading and portfolio management to paying one's bills.

The final online section, INVESTMENT WEB SITES, lists a broad variety of sites by name, Web address, and primary function.

We wish to thank the American Association of Individual Investors (625 North Michigan Avenue, Chicago, Illinois 60611, (312) 280-0170, www.aaii.com) for its assistance in preparing these listings.

Business Week Online
Bloomberg L.P.
www.businessweek.com

CNBC on MSN Money
CNBC/Microsoft, Inc.
www.moneycental.msn.com/
investor

GainsKeeper
Wolters Kluwer Financial Services
www.gainskeeper.com

Kiplinger.com
Kiplinger's Personal Finance
magazine
www.kiplinger.com

MarketWatch
MarketWatch.com
www.marketwatch.com

Morningstar.com
Morningstar
www.morningstar.com

Quicken.com
Intuit, Inc.
www.quicken.com

SmartMoney.com
Smart Money magazine
www.smartmoney.com

Yahoo! Finance
Yahoo!, Inc.
www.finance.yahoo.com

ONLINE SERVICES FOR INVESTING AND FINANCIAL PLANNING

From listening to a CEO defend his or her company's performance to screening out the handful of mutual funds that are right for you from the thousands on the market, technology has put the individual investor in the driver's seat. Webcasts of annual meetings, stock charting and technical analysis, portfolio management, stock screening, personal finance—these are among the options available to investors through online services. These tools can help investors to make better decisions, improve recordkeeping, and adjust and respond quickly to shifting economic trends, as well as perform personal financial planning tasks such as evaluating home equity financing and planning for college educations. The Web sites listed here were selected from the American Association of Individual Investors' guides to top investment Web sites.

Comprehensive sites were featured in the previous section. Group 1 lists the Web sites in the AAII guide that offer the best comprehensive services in terms of asset allocation, stocks, bonds, mutual funds, technical analysis, and other key features listed in this section. Since these sites are cited in many of the groups in this section, special features are highlighted to provide assistance.

Group 2 programs offer pricing on certain bonds, including Treasuries, municipals, and corporates. Compared to online services for stocks, however, the offerings are slim, and tend to focus on the general market and individual issues, along with market commentary and educational information. The U.S. government's TreasuryDirect system allows individuals to buy newly issued Treasuries directly from the Treasury without paying commission.

Group 3 focuses on personal finance and retirement planning. These sites offer information on personal loans, mortgages, credit cards, certificates of deposit, money market accounts, and insurance. They include calculators and planning tools to track investments, formulate tax strategies, and develop retirement and estate options.

The programs and services in Group 4 allow users to screen lists of stocks to isolate the companies that meet certain fundamental investment criteria.

Group 5 programs enable users to track their investment portfolios. Once stocks, bonds, and other instruments are entered into the computer, the value of the portfolio can be updated easily by tapping into a database. These programs also reveal the tax implications of potential investment moves.

Technical analysis services featured in Group 6 have become more popular with individual investors as their levels of sophistication about their own investment strategies grow, another benefit of these products. These services pick stocks, derivatives, and mutual funds based on technical considerations, such as price movements and volume. There are usually several charting choices available for investors to isolate financial products with technical indicators thought to point to a good buying or selling opportunity.

Group 7, mutual fund screening, helps investors pick the best mutual funds for their portfolios that meet personal risk, return, and management style needs.

Several futures and options sites are featured in Group 8. All are free. The Futures Industry Association offers a wealth of information about these derivative products, as well as a host of links to Web sites of U.S. and international exchanges that trade financial and commodity instruments.

1. Comprehensive Investment Sites

Kiplinger Online
www.kiplinger.com
The free site offers portfolio management, quotes, news, stock and mutual fund data, screening tools, and investment education.

MSN Money
www.moneycentral.msn.com
The combined Web site of Microsoft and CNBC offers news stories from multiple sources, charts, educational articles, stock and mutual fund research, and portfolio tracking.

SmartMoney.com
www.smartmoney.com
SmartMoney.com provides access to its magazine's articles and helpful investment tools such as stock and mutual fund screeners and a portfolio tracker.

Yahoo! Finance
www.finance.yahoo.com
Offers an unsophisticated set of financial tools, but it is a good site for portfolio tracking, fund and stock screening, and reading current market news.

2. Bonds

FINRA Bond Market Date
www.finra.org/marketdata

InvestinginBonds.com
www.investinginbonds.com

Treasury Direct
www.treasurydirect.gov

3. Personal Finance and Retirement Planning

Bankrate.com
www.bankrate.com

Yahoo! Finance
www.finance.yahoo.com

CNN/Money
www.money.cnn.com

T. Rowe Price
www.troweprice.com

MSN Money
www.moneycentral.msn.com

Vanguard
www.vanguard.com

SmartMoney.com
www.smartmoney.com

4. Stock Screening Systems

Morningstar.com
www.morningstar.com

SmartMoney.com
www.smartmoney.com

MSN Money (Deluxe Screener)
www.moneycental.msn.com/investor

5. Portfolio Management

Morningstar.com
www.morningstar.com

RiskGrades
www.riskgrades.com

MSN Money
www.moneycentral.msn.com/
   investor

SmartMoney.com
www.smartmoney.com

6. Technical Analysis

FreeStockCharts.com
www.freestockcharts.com

StockCharts.com
www.stockcharts.com

Prophet.Net
www.prophet.net

7. Mutual Funds Screening

Morningstar.com
www.morningstar.com

SmartMoney.com
www.smartmoney.com

MSN Money
www.moneycentral.msn.com/investor

Yahoo! Finance
www.finance.yahoo.com

8. Futures and Options

*Chicago Board Options Exchange
   (CBOE)*
www.cboe.com

Options Industry Council
www.888options.com

*Commodity Futures Trading
   Commission (CFTC)*
www.cftc.gov

INVESTMENT WEB SITES

Keeping up with investment related Web sites can be as challenging as monitoring the financial markets. Each section of the *Handbook* presents Web sites for each listing where available, but there are many sites that fall into a broader information basket or offer unique perspectives on these topics. To that end, this listing runs a gamut of key sites, from real-time news and price information providers, such as Dow Jones, Reuters, and Bloomberg News, to analysts' estimates, technical charting, tax information, and fraud. Many of these sites supply information to other investing sites that are reported in this book. Sites offering online trading or sales of products and services are not included, nor are most U.S. government agencies, trade associations, or stock and futures exchanges. Some of these sites are available only with a subscription.

Site Name	Site Address	Primary Focus
Allstarstocks.com	www.allstarstocks.com	research, news
AnnualReports.com	www.annualreports.com	company annual reports
AOL Money & Finance	www.money.aol.com	stock quotes, news
Bank Rate	www.bankrate.com	mortgage calculators
Barron's	www.barrons.com	financial news, analysis
BigCharts	www.bigcharts.com	stock charts
Bloomberg News	www.bloomberg.com	financial news, analysis
Bondtrac.com	www.bondtrac.com	bond offerings
Bradynet Inc.	www.bradynet.com	bond information
Briefing.com	www.briefing.com	news, analysis
Bureau of Public Debt	www.publicdebt.treas.gov	Treasury securities
Business Week	www.businessweek.com	financial news, analysis
CNN Money	http://money.cnn.com	financial news, analysis
Daily Stocks	www.dailystocks.com	stock/fund quotes
Dick Davis Publishing	www.dickdavis.com	advisory services
Dow Jones	www.dowjones.com	financial news, analysis
DTN.IQ	www.dtniq.com	real-time stock quotes
EarningsWhispers.com	www.earningswhispers.com	estimates, warnings
Edgar	www.sec.gov	securities filings
Emuni.com	www.emuni.com	municipal bonds
The Economist	www.economist.com	financial news, analysis
Emerging Market Companion	www.emgmkts.com	foreign investing
Financial Planning Magazine	www.fponline.com	financial planning
Financial Times	www.ft.com	financial news, analysis
FINRA	www.finra.org	securities regulations
Forex News	www.forexnews.com	foreign exchange analysis
Fortune Magazine	www.fortune.com	finance news, analysis
GainsKeeper	www.gainskeeper.com	portfolio tracking
Global Financial Data	www.globalfinancialdata.com	historical market data
Google Finance	http://finance.google.com	stock quotes, news
H&R Block	www.hrblock.com	tax information
Hoover's	www.hoovers.com	company profiles, news
InvesTools	www.investools.com	portfolio tracking
Investor Guide	www.investorguide.com	investment links, news
Investor Home	www.investorhome.com	investment web links
Investor's Business Daily	www.investors.com	financial news, analysis
Investors Edge	www.investorsedge.com	portfolio tracking

Site Name	Site Address	Primary Focus
Kiplinger Online	www.kiplinger.com	financial news, analysis
Marketwatch	www.marketwatch.com	financial news, information
MoneyAnswers	www.moneyanswers.com	personal finance
Moneypages	www.moneypages.com	investment Web links
Moody's Investors Service	www.moodys.com	bond ratings
Morningstar.com	www.morningstar.com	research, mutual fund ratings
Morningstar Document Research	www.10k wizard.com	search regulatory filings
Motley Fool	www.fool.com	stock data, analysis
MSN Money	www.moneycentral.msn.com	stock quotes, news, message board
NAREIT Online	www.nareit.com	REIT news, information
National Fraud Information Center	www.fraud.org	investment fraud
Nikkei Net (English version)	www.nni.nikkei.co.jp	foreign investing
PR Newswire	www.prnewswire.com	financial news releases
PRS Online	www.countrydata.com	foreign investing
Public Register's Annual Report Service (PRARS)	www.prars.com	company reports
Quote.Com	www.quote.com	stock data, analysis
Raging Bull	www.ragingbull.com	news groups
Research Magazine	www.researchxtra.com	investment information
Reuters	www.reuters.com	financial news, company info
Schaeffer's Investment Research	www.schaeffersresearch.com	investment information
SEC Law.com	www.seclaw.com	regulations
Securities Fraud & Investor Protection	www.securitieslaw.com	securities fraud
Silicon Investor	www.siliconinvestor.com	technology stocks
Smallcapcenter.com	www.smallcapcenter.com	small, microcap stocks
Smart Money	www.smartmoney.com	financial news, analysis
Standard & Poor's	standardandpoors.com	credit data, research
Stat-USA	www.stat-usa.gov	trade, economic data
StockMaster	www.stockmaster.com	stock/fund data
StockWiz	www.stockwiz.com	mathematical stock data
1040.com	www.1040.com	tax information
TheStreet.com	www.thestreet.com	stock/fund quotes, analysis
Value Line.com	www.valueline.com	stock research, analysis
Wall Street On Demand	www.wallst.com	research
Wall Street Journal Digital Network	www.wsj.com	financial news, analysis
WWQuote	www.wwquote.com	stock quotes
Yahoo! Finance	www.finance.yahoo.com	stock quotes, news, message board
Zacks Investment Research	www.zacks.com	stock quotes, research

2. MAJOR FINANCIAL INSTITUTIONS

This section of the *Finance and Investment Handbook* provides listings of major financial institutions, such as banks, life insurance companies, brokerages, limited partnership sponsors, and securities and commodities exchanges. All provide vital financial services. Personal investors deal directly with most of the institutions, and at least indirectly with all. Introductions to the lists provide background information on the types of institutions covered; for additional information it is best to contact an institution directly.

The first part of this section provides lists of the major institutions of the banking system. The 12 banks and the 24 branches that make up the Federal Reserve System and the 12 banks that comprise the Federal Home Loan Bank System are listed. Then follows a list of the primary dealers in government securities, which interact with the Federal Reserve banks. Next is a compilation of the 100 largest commercial banks in the United States and the commercial banks of Canada, followed by a listing of the 100 largest thrift institutions (savings and loans and savings banks) in the United States and the trust and loans of Canada.

The second part of this section provides a listing of the top 100 life-insurance companies in the United States and Canada. Insurance companies are important not only because of the protection they provide to policyholders, but also because they are major institutional investors.

A listing of the top 100 full-service and discount brokerage firms follow. Full-service brokers play a key role in raising capital for corporations and government bodies, and distributing securities and a wide array of financial services to individual and institutional investors. Investors can save on commissions by dealing with discount brokers.

Next is a listing of the 25 leading accounting firms. These firms, which in the past generally restricted their activities to auditing and accounting, have diversified recently into a variety of financial services. The final part of this section presents stock and commodity exchanges around the world. As financial markets have grown and become more interdependent, foreign exchanges have become more important to North Americans looking for investment opportunities.

FEDERAL RESERVE BANKS

The Federal Reserve System is comprised of 12 banks and 24 branch banks that supervise the activities of commercial banks and savings banks in their regions. Each branch is associated with one of the 12 Federal Reserve banks; in the listing of branch banks, the parent bank is noted in parentheses. Nationally chartered banks must join the Federal Reserve System; state-chartered banks join on a voluntary basis. The Fed banks ensure that the banks they supervise adhere to Federal Reserve rules and provide member banks with access to emergency funds through the discount window. Each regional bank is owned by the member banks in its region. The listings include locations, telephone numbers, and Web sites for the 12 Fed banks. Additional information can be found through the Federal Reserve site, www.federalreserve.gov.

The Federal Reserve System was set up by Congress in 1913 to regulate the U.S. monetary and banking system. The System regulates the nation's money supply by buying and selling government securities on the open market, setting reserve requirements for member banks, setting the discount rate at which it lends funds to member banks, supervising printing of the currency at the mint, acting as a clearinghouse for the transfer of funds throughout the banking system, and examining member banks to ensure that they meet Federal Reserve regulations.

Members of the top policy-making body of the Federal Reserve—the Board of Governors—are appointed by the President of the United States with the consent of the Senate. However, in conducting monetary policy, the Fed is designed to operate independently, so that the rate of growth of the money supply is not directly controlled by Congress or the President. To assure independence, members of the Board of Governors of the Federal Reserve are appointed to 14-year terms. Statements by members of the Board of Governors—especially the Chairman—often have much influence in the finance and investment community.

Depositors and borrowers can complain to the Federal Reserve about practices of member banks considered unfair or abusive. The Fed has jurisdiction over consumer credit, for instance, so consumers can bring complaints about problems with bank lending policies, credit cards, or advertising. In addition, consumers wanting to buy U.S. Treasury and government agency securities without the fees that banks and brokers usually charge can buy them directly through any of the Federal Reserve banks or branches on this list. Several years ago the Federal Reserve reorganized its U.S. Savings Bond sales operation. Now, only the Kansas City bank actually issues savings bonds. Private banks, which used to keep a supply of bonds for sale to customers, only process applications. An application is forwarded to the Kansas City Federal Reserve with a check for the appropriate amount, and the bond is sent to the purchaser within several weeks. Investors may also directly contact the Kansas City Fed to buy savings bonds. Also, Federal Reserve banks publish a variety of economic reports and studies that can be helpful to an investor.

Board of Governors

Board of Governors of the Federal
Reserve System
20th Street and Constitution
Avenue, NW
Washington, D.C. 20551
(800) 337-0429
www.federalreserve.gov

Federal Reserve Banks

ATLANTA
Federal Reserve Bank of Atlanta
1000 Peachtree Street, NE
Atlanta, Georgia 30309-4470
(404) 498-8500
www.frbatlanta.org

BOSTON
Federal Reserve Bank of Boston
600 Atlantic Avenue
Boston, Massachusetts 02210
(617) 973-3000
www.bos.frb.org

CHICAGO
Federal Reserve Bank of Chicago
230 South LaSalle Street
Chicago, Illinois 60604-1413
(312) 322-5322
www.chicagofed.org

CLEVELAND
Federal Reserve Bank of Cleveland
P.O. Box 6387
Cleveland, Ohio 44101-1387
(216) 579-2000
www.clevelandfed.org

DALLAS
Federal Reserve Bank of Dallas
2200 North Pearl Street
Dallas, Texas 75201
(214) 922-6000
www.dallasfed.org

KANSAS CITY
Federal Reserve Bank of
  Kansas City
1 Memorial Drive
Kansas City, Missouri 64198-0001
(816) 333-1010
www.kansascityfed.org

MINNEAPOLIS
Federal Reserve Bank of
  Minneapolis
90 Hennepin Avenue
Minneapolis, Minnesota 55401
(612) 204-5000
www.minneapolisfed.org

NEW YORK
Federal Reserve Bank of New York
33 Liberty Street
New York, New York 10045
(212) 720-5000
www.newyorkfed.org

PHILADELPHIA
Federal Reserve Bank of Philadelphia
Ten Independence Mall
Philadelphia, Pennsylvania
  19106-1574
(215) 574-6000
www.philadelphiafed.org

RICHMOND
Federal Reserve Bank of
  Richmond
P.O. Box 27622
Richmond, Virginia 23261
(804) 697-8000
www.richmondfed.org

ST. LOUIS
Federal Reserve Bank of St. Louis
One Federal Reserve Bank Plaza
Broadway and Locust Streets
St. Louis, Missouri 63166-0442
(314) 444-8444
www.stlouisfed.org

SAN FRANCISCO
Federal Reserve Bank of
  San Francisco
101 Market Street
San Francisco, California 94105
(415) 974-2000
www.frbsf.org

Federal Reserve Branch Banks
BALTIMORE (Richmond)
502 South Sharp Street
Baltimore, Maryland 21201
(410) 576-3300

BIRMINGHAM (Atlanta)
524 Liberty Parkway
Birmingham, Alabama 35242
(205) 968-6700

CHARLOTTE (Richmond)
530 Trade Street
Charlotte, North Carolina 28202
(704) 358-2100

CINCINNATI (Cleveland)
150 East Fourth Street
Cincinnati, Ohio 45202
(513) 721-4787

DENVER (Kansas City)
1020 16th Street
Denver, Colorado 80202
(303) 572-2300

DETROIT (Chicago)
1600 East Warren Avenue
Detroit, Michigan 48207-1063
(313) 961-6880

EL PASO (Dallas)
301 East Main Street
El Paso, Texas 79901
(915) 521-5200

HELENA (Minneapolis)
100 Neill Avenue
Helena, Montana 59601
(406) 447-3800

HOUSTON (Dallas)
1801 Allen Parkway
Houston, Texas 77019
(713) 659-4433

JACKSONVILLE (Atlanta)
800 Water Street
Jacksonville, Florida 32204
(904) 632-1000

LITTLE ROCK (St. Louis)
Stephens Building
111 Center Street, Suite 1000
Little Rock, Arkansas 72201
(501) 324-8300

LOS ANGELES (San Francisco)
950 South Grand Avenue
Los Angeles, California 90015
(213) 683-2300

LOUISVILLE (St. Louis)
National City Tower
101 South Fifth Street
Louisville, Kentucky 40202
(502) 568-9200

MEMPHIS (St. Louis)
200 North Main Street
Memphis, Tennessee 38103
(901) 523-7171

MIAMI (Atlanta)
9100 Northwest 36th Street
Miami, Florida 33178
(305) 591-2065

NASHVILLE (Atlanta)
301 Rosa L. Parks Boulevard
Nashville, Tennessee 37203-4407
(615) 251-7100

NEW ORLEANS (Atlanta)
525 St. Charles Avenue
New Orleans, Louisiana 70130
(504) 593-3200

OKLAHOMA CITY (Kansas City)
226 Dean A. McGee Avenue
Oklahoma City, Oklahoma 73102
(405) 270-8400

OMAHA (Kansas City)
2201 Farnam Street
Omaha, Nebraska 68102
(402) 221-5500

PITTSBURGH (Cleveland)
717 Grant Street
Pittsburgh, Pennsylvania 15219
(412) 261-7800

PORTLAND (San Francisco)
1500 SW First Avenue
Portland, Oregon 97201
(503) 276-3000

SALT LAKE CITY (San Francisco)
120 South State Street
Salt Lake City, Utah 84111
(801) 322-7900

SAN ANTONIO (Dallas)
126 East Nueva Street
San Antonio, Texas 78204
(210) 224-2141

SEATTLE (San Francisco)
2700 Naches Avenue SW
Renton, Washington 98057
(425) 203-0800

PRIMARY GOVERNMENT SECURITIES DEALERS

The following banks and brokerage firms act as primary government securities dealers, reporting to the Federal Reserve Bank of New York. In this role, they facilitate the Fed's open market operations by buying and selling Treasury securities directly through the New York Fed's Securities Department, commonly called The Desk. These dealers are key players in the execution of Federal Reserve policy, as set down by the Federal Open Market Committee, which decides to tighten or loosen the money supply to combat inflation or to ease the money supply to stimulate economic growth. When the Fed wants to tighten the money supply, it sells government securities to the primary dealers. The dollars the dealers use to pay for the securities are taken out of circulation, and the money supply contracts. When the Fed wants to expand the money supply, it buys government securities from the dealers. The proceeds from these sales go into the economy, and the money supply increases.

When the government issues new Treasury securities, these primary dealers also play a key role, because they are among other large dealers and investors making competitive bids for the securities. Under the competitive bid system, also known as a Dutch auction, bidders offer higher prices for the securities, and the highest prices are accepted. Most individual investors do not participate in this auction. Rather than risk losing out to a higher bidder, they buy Treasury securities with noncompetitive bids, for which the investor accepts whatever price is determined by the competitive auction.

In order to become a primary dealer, a firm must show the Federal Reserve that the company has an excellent reputation, large capacity for trading in government securities, and adequate staff and facilities. It is considered to be very prestigious to be accepted into the inner circle of primary government securities dealers.

Banc of America Securities, LLC
One Bryant Park, 3rd Floor
New York, New York 10036
(800) 432-1000
www.bankamerica.com

Deutsche Bank Securities Inc.
60 Wall Street
New York, New York 10005
(212) 250-2500
www.db.com

Barclays Capital, Inc.
200 Park Avenue
New York, NY 10166
(212) 412-4000
www.barcap.com

Goldman, Sachs & Company
85 Broad Street, 17th Floor
New York, New York 10004
(212) 902-0300
www.gs.com

BNP Paribas Securities Corporation
787 Seventh Avenue
New York, New York 10019
(212) 841-2000
www.bnpparibas.com

HSBC Securities (USA), Inc.
26525 North Riverwoods Boulevard
Mettawa, Illinois 60045
(800) 975-4722
www.hsbc.com

Cantor Fitzgerald & Co.
499 Park Avenue
New York, New York 10022
(212) 938-5000
www.cantor.com

Jefferies & Company Inc.
520 Madison Avenue, 16th Floor
New York, New York 10022
(212) 284-2300
www.jefferies.com

Citigroup Global Markets, Inc.
399 Park Avenue
New York, New York 10022
(212) 723-9150
www.citigroup.com

J.P. Morgan Securities, Inc.
277 Park Avenue
New York, New York 10017
(212) 623-0572
www.jpmorganchase.com

Credit Suisse Securities (USA) LLC
11 Madison Avenue
New York, New York 10010-3629
(212) 325-2000
www.credit-suisse.com

Mizuho Securities USA Inc.
1251 Avenue of the Americas
New York, New York 10020
(212) 282-3000
www.mizuhosecurities.com

Daiwa Securities America, Inc.
32 Old Slip
One Financial Square
New York, New York 10005-3538
(212) 612-7000
www.daiwausa.com

Morgan Stanley & Co., Inc.
1585 Broadway
New York, New York 10036
(212) 761-4000
www.morganstanley.com

Nomura Securities International, Inc.
2 World Financial Center, Building B
New York, New York 10281-1198
(212) 667-9300
www.nomura.com

RBS Securities Inc.
101 Park Avenue, 10th Floor
New York, New York 10178
(212) 401-3200
www.rbs.com

RBC Capital Markets Corporation
165 Broadway
New York, New York 10006-1404
(212) 858-7000
www.rbccm.com

UBS Securities LLC
1285 Avenue of the Americas
New York, New York 10019
(212) 713-2000
www.ubs.com

FEDERAL HOME LOAN BANKS

The following are the names, addresses, and telephone numbers of the 12 banks of the Federal Home Loan Bank System. The Federal Home Loan Bank System, established by Congress in 1932 after the collapse of the banking system during the Great Depression, raises money by issuing notes and bonds and lends money to savings and loans and other mortgage lenders based on the amount of collateral the borrowing institution can provide. The Federal Home Loan Banks supply credit reserves to federally and state-chartered savings and loans, cooperative banks, and other mortgage lenders in their regions. Each Home Loan Bank is owned by the member financial institutions in its region.

Prior to the Thrift Bailout Bill of 1989, the Federal Home Loan Banks were supervised by the Federal Home Loan Bank Board. With the bailout, however, the FHLBB was eliminated and was replaced by two organizations: the Office of Thrift Supervision and the Federal Housing Finance Board. The Office of Thrift Supervision regulates federal- and state-chartered thrifts. The Federal Housing Finance Agency, which replaced the Federal Housing Finance Board, supervises the 12 Federal Home Loan Banks.

National Headquarters
Federal Housing Finance Agency
1700 G Street, NW, 4th Floor
Washington, D.C. 20552
(866) 796-5595
www.fhfa.gov

Office of Thrift Supervision
1700 G Street, NW
Washington, D.C. 20552
(202) 906-6000
www.ots.treas.gov

Federal Home Loan Banks
ATLANTA
Federal Home Loan Bank of Atlanta
1475 Peachtree Street, NE
Atlanta, Georgia 30309
(404) 888-8000

BOSTON
Federal Home Loan Bank of Boston
111 Huntington Avenue, 24th Floor
Boston, Massachusetts 02199-7614
(617) 292-9600

CHICAGO
Federal Home Loan Bank of Chicago
200 East Randolph Drive
Chicago, Illinois 60601
(312) 565-5700

CINCINNATI
Federal Home Loan Bank
   of Cincinnati
221 East Fourth Street,
   1000 Atrium Two
Cincinnati, Ohio 45202
(513) 852-7500

DALLAS
Federal Home Loan Bank of Dallas
P.O. Box 619026
Dallas, Texas 75261-9026
(214) 441-8500

DES MOINES
Federal Home Loan Bank
of Des Moines
801 Walnut Street, Suite 200
Des Moines, Iowa 50309-3513
(515) 281-1000

INDIANAPOLIS
Federal Home Loan Bank
of Indianapolis
8250 Woodfield Crossing Boulevard
Indianapolis, Indiana 46240
(317) 465-0200

NEW YORK
Federal Home Loan Bank
of New York
101 Park Avenue
New York, New York 10178-0599
(212) 681-6000

PITTSBURGH
Federal Home Loan Bank
of Pittsburgh
601 Grant Street
Pittsburgh, Pennsylvania 15219-4455
(412) 288-3400

SAN FRANCISCO
Federal Home Loan Bank
of San Francisco
600 California Street
San Francisco, California 94108
(415) 616-1000

SEATTLE
Federal Home Loan Bank
of Seattle
1501 4th Avenue, Suite 1800
Seattle, Washington 98101
(800) 973-6223

TOPEKA
Federal Home Loan Bank of Topeka
1 Security Benefit Place, Suite 100
Topeka, Kansas 66606
(785) 233-0507

COMMERCIAL BANKS

The following is an alphabetical listing of the 100 largest commercial banks in the United States, based on total assets. Banks also can be ranked by the amount of permanent capital. This capital has been built over the years by offerings of stock to the public and by retained earnings. This method of ranking would not result in significant change from the method employed here.

Most banks listed here are national banks, which are chartered by the federal government. Although there are some 14,000 banks in the United States, assets and capital are highly concentrated in the largest banks. The two largest banks in this listing, Bank of America and JPMorgan Chase, have total assets of $2.3 trillion and $2.0 trillion, respectively. Each of the banks in the top 10 has assets of more than $200 billion. Each in the top one-third has assets in excess of $37 billion. By contrast, the banks that rank near number 100 have assets of about $7 billion.

Bank mergers dominated the 1980s and 1990s, as these institutions sought to compete more effectively in the less regulated environment brought about primarily by the Depository Institutions Deregulation and Monetary Control Act of 1980. Some large banks operate newly acquired banks as separate subsidiaries.

This list, current as of October 20, 2009, was provided by SNL Financial LLC, One SNL Plaza, P.O. Box 2124, Charlottesville, Virginia 22902 (434-977-1600, www.snl.com).

Ally Bank
6985 Union Park Center
Midvale, Utah 64047
(801) 790-5000
www.ally.com

American Express Centurion Bank
4315 South 2700 West
Salt Lake City, Utah 84184
(801) 945-5000
www.americanexpress.com

Arvest Bank Group, Inc.
125 West Central Avenue, Suite 218
Bentonville, Arkansas 72712
(918) 631-1067
(501) 374-7777
www.arvest.com/bob/corporate/

Associated Banc-Corp
1200 Hansen Road
Green Bay, Wisconsin 54304
(920) 491-7000
www.associatedbank.com

BancorpSouth, Inc.
One Mississippi Plaza
201 South Spring Street
Tupelo, Mississippi 38804
(662) 680-2000
www.bancorpsouth.com

BancWest Corporation
180 Montgomery Street
San Francisco, California 94104
(808) 525-7000
www.bancwestcorp.com

Bank of America Corporation
100 North Tryon Street, 25th Floor
Charlotte, North Carolina 28255
(704) 386-5681
www.bankofamerica.com

Bank of Hawaii Corporation
130 Merchant Street
Honolulu, Hawaii 96813
(888) 643-3888
www.boh.com

Bank of New York Mellon
   Corporation
One Wall Street. 10th Floor
New York, New York 10286
(212) 495-1784
www.bnymellon.com

Barclays Group US Inc.
100 South West Street
Wilmington, Delaware 19801
(302) 888-1400
www.quietlyconquering.com

BB&T Corporation
200 West Second Street
Winston-Salem, North Carolina
   27101
(336) 733-2000
www.bbt.com

BBVA USA Bancshares, Inc.
200 Kirby Drive, Suite 661
Houston, Texas 77019
(713) 831-5625
www.bbvacompass.com

BOK Financial Corporation
Bank of Oklahoma Tower
Tulsa, Oklahoma 74192
(918) 588-6000
www.bokf.com

Boston Private Financial
   Holdings, Inc.
Ten Post Office Square
Boston, Massachusetts 02109
(617) 912-1900
www.bostonprivate.com

Bremer Financial Corporation
445 Minnesota Street, Suite 2000
Saint Paul, Minnesota 55101
(651) 227-7621
www.bremer.com

Capital One Financial Corporation
1680 Capital One Drive
McLean, Virginia 22102
(703) 720-1000
www.capitalone.com

CapitalSource Inc.
4445 Willard Avenue, 12th Floor
Chevy Chase, Maryland 20815
(301) 841-2700
www.capitalsource.com

Capmark Bank
6955 Union Park, Suite 330
Midvale, Utah 84047
(801) 304-2900
www.capmarkbank.com

Cathay General Bancorp
9650 Flair Drive
El Monte, California 91731
(626) 279-3286
www.cathaygeneralbancorp.com

Central Bancompany, Inc.
238 Madison Street
Jefferson City, Missouri 65101
(573) 634-1234
www.centralbank.net

CIT Bank
2180 South 1300 East, Suite 250
Salt Lake City, Utah 84106
(801) 412-6800
www.cit.com

Citigroup, Inc.
399 Park Avenue
New York, New York 10043
(212) 559-1000
www.citigroup.com

Citizens Banking Corporation
328 South Saginaw Street
Flint, Michigan 48502
(810) 766-7500
www.citizensbanking.com

City National Corporation
555 South Flower Street
Los Angeles, California 90071
(800) 773-7100
www.cnb.com

Comerica Incorporated
1717 Main Street
Dallas, Texas 75201
(248) 371-5000
www.comerica.com

Commerce Bancshares, Inc.
1000 Walnut
Kansas City, Missouri 64106
(816) 234-2000
www.commercebank.com

Cullen/Frost Bankers, Inc.
100 West Houston Street
San Antonio, Texas 78205
(210) 220-4011
www.frostbank.com

Discount Bancorp, Inc.
511 Fifth Avenue
New York, New York 10017
(212) 551-8500
www.idbny.com

Discover Bank
502 East Market Street
Greenwood, Delaware 19950
(302) 349-4512
www.discoverbank.com

Doral Financial Corporation
1451 Franklin D. Roosevelt Avenue
San Juan, Puerto Rico 00920
(787) 474-6700
www.doralfinancial.com

East West Bancorp, Inc.
135 North Los Robles Avenue,
   7th Floor
Pasadena, California 91101
(626) 768-6000
www.eastwestbank.com

F.N.B. Corporation
One F.N.B. Boulevard
Hermitage, Pennsylvania 16148
(724) 961-6000
www.fnbcorporation.com

FBOP Corporation
11 West Madison Street
Oak Park, Illinois 60302
(708) 386-5000
www.fbopcorporation.com

Fifth Third Bancorp
38 Fountain Square Plaza
Cincinnati, Ohio 45263
(513) 579-5353
www.53.com

First BanCorp
1519 Ponce de Leon Avenue
Stop 23-Box 9146
San Juan, Puerto Rico 00908
(787) 729-8200
www.firstbankpr.com

First Banks, Inc.
35 North Meramec
Clayton, Missouri 63105
(314) 854-4600
www.firstbanks.com

First Citizens Bankcorporation, Inc.
1230 Main Street
Columbia, South Carolina 29201
(803) 733-2020
www.firstcitizensonline.com

First Citizens BancShares, Inc.
4300 Six Forks Road
Raleigh, North Carolina 27609
(919) 716-7000
www.firstcitizens.com

First Horizon National Corporation
165 Madison Avenue
Memphis, Tennessee 38103
(901) 523-4444
www.fhnc.com

First Midwest Bancorp, Inc.
One Pierce Place, Suite 1500
Itasca, Illinois 60143
(630) 875-7450
www.firstmidwest.com

First National of Nebraska, Inc.
One First National Center
Omaha, Nebraska 68197
(402) 341-0500
www.firstnational.com

FirstBank Holding Company
12345 West Colfax Avenue
Lakewood, Colorado 80215
(303) 232-3000
www.efirstbank.com

FirstMerit Corporation
III Cascade Plaza, 7th Floor
Akron, Ohio 44308
(330) 996-6300
www.firstmerit.com

Fulton Financial Corporation
One Penn Square
Lancaster, Pennsylvania 17604
(717) 291-2411
www.fult.com

GE Capital Financial Inc.
6510 Milrock Drive
Holladay, Utah 84121
(801) 733-2820
www.ge.com

Goldman Sachs Bank USA
85 Broad Street
New York, New York 10004
(212) 902-1000
www.gs.com

Hancock Holding Company
2510 14th Street
Gulfport, Mississippi 39501
(228) 868-4000
www.hancockbank.com

Harris Financial Corp.
21209 Orange Street
Wilmington, Delaware 19801
(312) 461-2121
www.harrisbank.com

HSBC North America Holdings, Inc.
26525 North Riverwoods Boulevard
Mettawa, Illinois 60045
(224) 544-2000
www.hsbc.com

Huntington Bancshares Incorporated
41 South High Street
Columbus, Ohio 43287
(614) 480-8300
www.huntington.com

International Bancshares
  Corporation
1200 San Bernardo Avenue
Laredo, Texas 78040
(956) 722-7611
www.ibc.com

Investors Bancorp, MHC
101 JFK Parkway
Short Hills, New Jersey 07078
(973) 376-5100
www.isbnj.com

JPMorgan Chase & Co.
270 Park Avenue, 38th Floor
New York, New York 10017
(212) 270-6000
www.jpmorganchase.com

KeyCorp
127 Public Square
Cleveland, Ohio 44114
(216) 689-6300
www.key.com

M&T Bank Corporation
One M&T Plaza
Buffalo, New York 14203
(716) 842-5445
www.mtb.com

Marshall & Ilsley Corporation
770 North Water Street
Milwaukee, Wisconsin 53202
(414) 765-7801
www.micorp.com

MB Financial, Inc.
800 West Madison Street
Chicago, Illinois 60607
(888) 422-6562
www.mbfinancial.com

Met Life Bank, National
    Association
501 Route 22 West, Floor One W
Bridgewater, New Jersey 08807
(908) 253-2800
www.metlifebank.com

Morgan Stanley Bank, National
    Association
201 South Main Street, Fifth Floor
Salt Lake City, Utah 84111
(801) 566-4161
www.morganstanley.com

National Penn Bancshares, Inc.
P.O. Box 547
Boyertown, Pennsylvania 19512
(800) 822-3321
www.nationalpennbancshares.com

Northern Trust Corporation
50 South LaSalle Street
Chicago, Illinois 60603
(312) 630-6000
www.northerntrust.com

Old National Bancorp
1 Main Street
Evansville, Indiana 47708
(812) 464-1294
www.oldnational.com

Pacific Capital Bancorp
1021 Anacapa Street, Third Floor
Santa Barbara, California 93101
(805) 564-6405
www.pcbancorp.com

PNC Financial Services Group, Inc.
249 Fifth Avenue
Pittsburgh, Pennsylvania 15222
(412) 762-2000
www.pnc.com

Popular, Inc.
209 Muñoz Rivera Avenue
Hato Rey, Puerto Rico 00918
(787) 765-9800
www.popular.com

PrivateBancorp, Inc.
129 South LaSalle Street, Suite 400
Chicago, Illinois 60603
(312) 564-2000
www.theprivatebank.com

Prosperity Bancshares, Inc.
4295 San Felipe
Houston, Texas 77027
(713) 693-9300
www.prosperitybanktx.com

RBC Bancorporation (USA)
301 Fayetteville Street, Suite 1100
Raleigh, North Carolina 27601
(919) 839-4400
www.rbcbankusa.com

Regions Financial Corporation
1900 Fifth Avenue North
Birmingham, Alabama 35203
(205) 944-1300
www.regions.com

Sallie Mae Bank
5217 South State Street, Suite 210
Murray, Utah 84107
(801) 281-1423
www.salliemaebank.com

Santander BanCorp
Tabonucco Street B 7, 18th Floor
San Patricio
Guaunabo, Puerto Rico 00968
(787) 777-4100
www.santandernet.com

Signature Bank
565 Fifth Avenue
New York, New York 10017
(646) 822-1500
www.signatureny.com

South Financial Group, Inc.
102 South Main Street, Pointsett
   Plaza, 10th Floor
Greenville, South Carolina 29601
(864) 255-7900
www.thesouthgroup.com

State Street Corporation
One Lincoln Street
Boston, Massachusetts 02111
(617) 786-3000
www.statestreet.com

Sterling Financial Corporation
111 North Wall Street
Spokane, Washington 99201
(509) 458-3711
www.sterlingfinancialcorporation-
   spokane.com/

SunTrust Banks, Inc.
303 Peachtree Street NE
Atlanta, Georgia 30308
(404) 588-7711
www.suntrust.com

Susquehanna Bancshares, Inc.
26 North Cedar Street
Lititz, Pennsylvania 17543
(717) 626-4721
www.ssquehanna.net

SVB Financial Group
3003 Tasman Drive
Santa Clara, California 95054
(408) 654-7400
www.svb.com

Synovus Financial Corp.
1111 Bay Avenue, Suite 500
Columbus, Georgia 31901
(706) 649-2311
www.synovus.com

Taunus Corporation
60 Wall Street
New York, New York 10005
(212) 250-2500
www.db.com

TCF Financial Corporation
200 Lake Street East
Mail Code EX0-03-A
Wayzata, Minnesota 55391
(952) 475-7926
www.tcfbank.com

TD Banknorth, Inc.
2 Portland Square
Portland, Maine 04112
(207) 761-8500
www.tdbank.com

Trustmark Corporation
248 East Capitol Street
Jackson, Mississippi 39201
(601) 208-5111
www.trustmark.com

UBS Bank USA
299 South Main Street, Suite 2275
Salt Lake City, Utah 84111
(801) 741-0310
www.bankusa.ubs.com/UBK

UCBH Holdings, Inc.
555 Montgomery Street, 14th Floor
San Francisco, California 94111
(415) 315-2800
www.ucbh.com

UMB Financial Corporation
1010 Grand Boulevard
Kansas City, Missouri 64106
(816) 860-7000
www.umb.com

Umpqua Holdings Corporation
One SW Columbia Street,
   Suite 1200
Portland, Oregon 97258
(503) 727-4100
www.umpquabank.com

UnionBanCal Corporation
400 California Street, Ninth Floor
San Francisco, California 94104
(415) 765-2969
www.unionbank.com

United Bankshares, Inc.
500 Virginia Street, East
Charleston, West Virginia 25301
(304) 424-8800
www.ubai-inc.com

United Community Banks, Inc.
63 Highway 515
Blairsville, Georgia 30512
(706) 781-2265
www.ucbi.com

U.S. Bankcorp
800 Nicollet Mall
Minneapolis, Minnesota 55402
(651) 466-3000
www.usbank.com

Utrecht-America Holdings, Inc.
245 Park Avenue
New York, New York 10167
(212) 808-6940
www.rabobank.com

Valley National Bancorp
1455 Valley Road
Wayne, New Jersey 07470
(973) 305-8800
www.valleynationalbank.com

W Holding Company, Inc.
19 West McKinley Street
Mayagüez, Puerto Rico 00680
(787) 834-8000
www.wbpr.com/WBPortal

Webster Financial Corporation
145 Bank Street
Waterbury, Connecticut 06702
(203) 465-4364
www.websteronline.com

Wells Fargo & Company
420 Montgomery Street
San Francisco, California 94104
(866) 249-3302
www.wellsfargo.com

Whitney Holding Corporation
228 St. Charles Avenue
New Orleans, Louisiana 70130
(504) 586-7272
www.whitneybank.com

Wilmington Trust Corporation
1100 North Market Street
Wilmington, Delaware 19890
(302) 651-1000
www.wilmingtontrust.com

Wintrust Financial Corporation
727 North Bank Lane
Lake Forest, Illinois 60045
(847) 615-4096
www.wintrust.com

Zions Bancorporation
One South Main Street, Suite 1500
Salt Lake City, Utah 84133
(801) 524-4787
www.zionsbancorporation.com

CANADIAN BANKS

The following is a list of the chartered banks of Canada. Unlike the United States, Canadian banking is highly concentrated into a few large institutions that provide the full range of banking services to consumers and institutions. These banks are regulated at the federal and provincial levels in a similar way to American banks. Deposits are insured to $100,000 (Canadian).

BMO Bank of Montreal
First Bank Tower
First Canadian Place
Toronto, Ontario M5X 1A1
(416) 867-5000

Bank West
1010-24 Street SE
High River, Alberta T1V 2A7
(403) 652-2107

Bridgewater Bank
10310 G.A. MacDonald
   (39A) Avenue
Edmonton, Alberta T6H 5X9
(888) 837-2326

CIBC
Commerce Court West, 56th Floor
Toronto, Ontario M5L 1A2
(416) 980-2211

Canadian Tire Bank
555 Prince Charles Drive
Welland, Ontario L3C 6B5
(905) 735-3131

Canadian Western Bank
2300-10303 Jasper Avenue
Edmonton, Alberta T5J 3X6
(780) 423-8888

Citizens Bank of Canada
401-815 West Hastings Street
Vancouver, British Columbia
  V6C 1B4
(604) 708-7800

CS Alterna Bank
165 Attwell Drive
Toronto, Ontario M9W 5Y5
(877) 560-0160

DirectCash Bank
1420 28th Street North East, Bay #6
Calgary, Alberta T2A 7W6
(888) 466-4043

Dundee Bank of Canada
44 King Street West
Toronto, Ontario M5H 1H1
(888) 884-3434

First Nations Bank of Canada
224 Fourth Avenue South
Saskatoon, Saskatchewan S7K 5M5
(888) 454-3622

General Bank of Canada
#006, 11523 100th Avenue
LeMarchand Mansion
Edmonton, Alberta T5K 0J8
(877) 443-5620

Jameson Bank
200 Front Street West, Suite 2203
Toronto, Ontario M5V 3K2
(800) 363-7363

Laurentian Bank of Canada
1981 McGill College Avenue
Montreal, Quebec H3A 3K3
(514) 522-1846

Manulife Bank of Canada
500 King Street North
Waterloo, Ontario N2J 4C6
(877) 765-2265

National Bank of Canada
600 rue de la Gauchetière West
Montreal, Quebec H3B 4L2
(514) 394-4000

Pacific & Western Bank of Canada
140 Fullarton Street, Suite 2002
London, Ontario N6A 5P2
(519) 645-1919

President's Choice Bank
439 King Street West, 5th Floor
Toronto, Ontario M5V 1K4
(888) 872-4724

RBC Financial Group
Royal Bank Plaza
200 Bay Street, 8th Floor,
  South Tower
Toronto, Ontario M5J 2J5
(416) 974-5151

Scotiabank (The Bank of
  Nova Scotia)
Scotia Plaza
40 King Street West, 7th Floor
Toronto, Ontario M5H 1H1
(416) 866-6161

TD Bank Financial Group
Toronto-Dominion Centre
55 King Street West
Toronto, Ontario M5K 1A2
(866) 222-3456

THRIFT INSTITUTIONS

The following is an alphabetical listing of the names, addresses, telephone numbers and websites of the 100 largest savings and loans and savings banks in the United States based on total assets. The list, current as of October 20, 2009, is based on both GAAP and regulatory filings and was provided by SNL Financial LLC, One SNL Plaza, P.O. Box 2124, Charlottesville, Virginia 22902 (434-977-1600, www.snl.com).

Savings and loans were initially founded predominantly in the western states, particularly California, as a mechanism for pioneer settlers in the 19th century to finance the construction of homes. They were largely regulated by state authorities until 1932, when the Federal Home Loan Bank Board was set up in reaction to the crisis of the banking and home-building industries during the Great Depression. Savings and loans are now regulated at both the federal and state levels and most deposits are insured by the Savings Association Insurance Fund.

Savings banks were initially found mainly on the East Coast, where, like savings and loans, they catered to consumers and made home loans. They are chartered and regulated both by state authorities and the Federal Reserve Board, as well as the Office of Thrift Supervision in some cases. Most deposits are insured by the Federal Deposit Insurance Corporation (FDIC). Over the years, the few distinctions between savings banks and savings and loans have largely faded away.

Historically, both types of thrifts have been distinguished from commercial banks in that they obtained most of their deposits from consumers, and lent that money out in the form of fixed-rate mortgages to homebuyers. To give them an edge in attracting deposits, they were allowed (under Regulation Q) to pay 1/4% more interest on passbook savings accounts than commercial banks. Starting in the late 1970s, when the general level of interest rates started to rise dramatically, many thrifts ran into financial trouble, because their income from mortgages was fixed at low rates, while they had to pay out higher rates on unregulated certificates of deposit to retain depositors. The pressure from this predicament ultimately led to the Depository Institutions Deregulation and Monetary Control Act of 1980 and the Garn-St. Germain Act of 1982, which mandated the gradual phase-out of control on interest rates on all deposits, and permitted thrifts to offer adjustable-rate mortgages. They were also allowed to enter businesses from which they had previously been banned, such as commercial lending, issuing credit cards, and providing trust services.

By the mid-1980s, thrifts played a prominent and highly competitive role in providing financial services. Many institutions went after consumer dollars by paying among the highest interest rates in the country on money-market deposits and certificates of deposit. These savings and loans and savings banks often arranged to take deposits over the phone. They sometimes brought in millions of dollars by allying with a securities brokerage firm that sells certificates of deposit. With the ability to bring in large amounts of money quickly, many thrifts became aggressive lenders as well.

By the late 1980s and early 1990s, many thrifts had gotten into severe financial trouble because they had taken excessive risks or because of fraud. A federal bailout had to be arranged to merge failed institutions into healthy ones. The bailout bill created a new regulatory structure for the industry by replacing the Federal Savings and Loan Insurance Corporation with the Savings Association Insurance Fund. The Federal Home Loan Bank Board became the Office of Thrift Supervision, and a new agency, the Resolution

Trust Corporation, was formed to dispose of thrift assets. The RTC was dissolved in 1996 and its responsibilities were shifted to the Savings Association Insurance Fund. By the end of the 1990s, the thrifts that remained were generally financially healthy and operating profitably.

American Savings Bank, FSB
1001 Bishop Street, Suite 100
Honolulu, Hawaii 96813
(808) 627-6900
www.asbhawaii.com

Ameriprise Bank, FSB
834 Ameriprise Financial Center
Minneapolis, Minnesota 55474
(612) 678-1744
www. ameriprise.com

AmTrust Financial Corporation
1801 East Ninth Street, Suite 200
Cleveland, Ohio 44114
(216) 736-3480
www.amtrust.com

Anchor BanCorp Wisconsin, Inc.
25 West Main Street
Madison, Wisconsin 53703
(608) 252-8781
www.anchorbank.com

Apple Financial Holdings, Inc.
122 East 42nd Street, Ninth Floor
New York, New York 10168
(212) 224-8400
www.theapplebank.com

Astoria Financial Corporation
One Astoria Federal Plaza
Lake Success, New York 11042
(516) 327-3000
www.astoriafederal.com

Aurora Bank FSB
1000 North West Street, Suite 200
Wilmington, Delaware 19801
(888) 522-9295
www.aurorabankfsb.com

Bangor Bancorp, MHC
3 State Street
Bangor, Maine 04401
(207) 942-5211
www.bangor.com

Bank Mutual Corporation
4949 West Brown Deer Road
Milwaukee, Wisconsin 53223
(414) 354-1500
www.bankmutualcorp.com

BankAtlantic Bancorp, Inc.
2100 West Cypress Creek Road
Fort Lauderdale, Florida 33309
(954) 940-5000
www.bankatlanticbancorp.com

BankFinancial Corporation
15W060 North Frontage Road
Burr Ridge, Illinois 60527
(800) 894-6900
www.bankfinancial.com

BankUnited
255 Alhambra Circle
Coral Gables, Florida 33134
(305) 569-2000
www.bankunited.com

Beal Bank
6000 Legacy Drive
Plano, Texas 75024
(469) 467-5000
www.bealbank.com

Beneficial Mutual Bancorp, Inc.
  (MHC)
530 Walnut Street
Philadelphia, Pennsylvania 19106
(215) 864-6730
www.thebeneficial.com

Berkshire Hills Bancorp, Inc.
24 North Street
Pittsfield, Massachusetts 01201
(413) 443-5601
www.berkshirebank.com

BFC Financial Corporation
2100 West Cyprus Creek Road
Fort Lauderdale, Florida 33309
(954) 940-4900
www.bfcfinancial.com

Brookline Bancorp, Inc.
160 Washington Street
Brookline, Massachusetts 02447
(617) 730-3500
www.brooklinebank.com

Cambridge Financial Group, Inc.
1374 Massachusetts Avenue
Cambridge, Massachusetts 02138
(617) 864-8700
www.cambridgesavings.com

Cape Cod Five Cents Savings Bank
Main Street
Harwich Port, Massachusetts 02646
(508) 240-0555
www.capecodfive.com

Capitol Federal Financial (MHC)
700 Kansas Avenue
Topeka, Kansas 66603
(785) 235-1341
www.capfed.com

Charles Schwab Bank
5190 Neil Road, Suite 100
Reno, Nevada 89502
(775) 689-6800
www.schwabbank.com

Citizens Financial Group, Inc.
One Citizens Plaza
Providence, Rhode Island 02903
(401) 456-7570
www.citizensbank.com

Citizens First Bancorp, Inc.
525 Water Street
Port Huron, Michigan 48060
(810) 987-8300
www.cfsbank.com

Columbia Bank (MHC)
19-01 Route 208 North
Fair Lawn, New Jersey 07410
(201) 794-5840
www.columbiabankonline.com

Danvers Bancorp, Inc.
One Conant Street
Danvers, Massachusetts 01923
(978) 777-2200
www.danversbank.com

Dime Community Bancshares, Inc.
209 Havemeyer Street
Brooklyn, New York 11211
(718) 782-6200
www.dime.com

Dollar Bank, Federal Savings Bank
401 Liberty Avenue
Pittsburgh, Pennsylvania 15222
(412) 261-3098
www.dollarbank.com

E*TRADE Bank
671 North Glebe Road, 16th Floor
Arlington, Virginia 22203
(646) 531-4322
www.bankus.etrade.com/e/t/bank/
home

Eastern Bank Corporation
265 Franklin Street
Boston, Massachusetts 02110
(617) 897-1008
www.easternbank.com

El Dorado Savings Bank, FSB
404 El Dorado Road
Placerville, California 95667
(530) 622-1492
www.eldoradosavingsbank.com

ESB Financial Corporation
600 Lawrence Avenue
Ellwood City, Pennsylvania 16117
(724) 758-5584
www.esbbank.com

EverBank
501 Riverside Avenue
Jacksonville, Florida 32202
(904) 281-6000
www.everbank.com

Fairfield County Bank
150 Danbury Road
Ridgefield, Connecticut 06877
(203) 438-6518
www.fairfieldcountybank.com

Fidelity Bank
100 East English Street
Wichita, Kansas 67202
(316) 265-2261
www.fidelitybank.com

First Defiance Financial Corporation
601 Clinton Street
Defiance, Ohio 43512
(419) 782-5051
www.fdef.com

First Financial Holdings, Inc.
34 Broad Street
Charleston, South Carolina 29401
(843) 529-5933
www.firstfinancialholdings.com

First Niagara Financial Group, Inc.
6950 South Transit Road
Lockport, New York 14095
(716) 625-7500
www.fnfg.com

First Place Financial Corp.
185 East Market Street
Warren, Ohio 44481
(330) 373-1221
www.firstplacebank.com

FirstFed Financial Corp.
12555 West Jefferson Boulevard
Los Angeles, California 90066
(310) 319-6000
www.firstfedca.com

Firstrust Savings Bank
15 East Ridge Pike
Conshohocken, Pennsylvania 19428
(610) 238-5000
www.firsttrust.com

Flagstar Bancorp, Inc.
5151 Corporate Drive
Troy, Michigan 48098
(248) 312-2000
www.flagstar.com

Flushing Financial Corporation
1979 Marcus Avenue, Suite E140
Lake Success, New York 11042
(718) 961-5400
www.flushingsavings.com

FPC Financial, FSB
8402 Excelsior Drive
Madison, Wisconsin 53717
(608) 821-5862
www.deere.com

GE Money Bank
170 West Election Road, Suite 125
Draper, Utah 84020
(801) 517-5035
www.gemoney.com

Home Federal Bank of Tennessee
515 Market Street
Knoxville, Tennessee 37902
(865) 546-0330
www.homefederalbanktn.com

HomeStreet Bank
601 Union Street
Seattle, Washington 98101
(206) 623-3050
www.homestreetbank.com

Hudson City Bancorp, Inc.
West 80 Century Road
Paramus, New Jersey 07652
(201) 967-1900
www.hcbk.com

ING Bank, FSB
1 South Orange Street
Wilmington, Delaware 19801
(302) 658-2200
www.ingdirect.com

Investors Bancorp, Inc. (MHC)
101 JFK Parkway
Short Hills, New Jersey 07078
(973) 924-5100
www.isbnj.com

Kearny Financial Corp. (MHC)
120 Passaic Avenue
Fairfield, New Jersey 07004
(973) 244-4500
www.kearnyfederalsavings.com

La Jolla Bank, FSB
6134 La Granada
Rancho Santa Fe, California 92067
(858) 756-7888
www.ljbank.com

Liberty Bank
315 Main Street
Middletown, Connecticut 06457
(860) 638-2922
www.liberty-bank.com

Luther Burbank Savings
804 Fourth Street
Santa Rosa, California 95404
(707) 578-9216
www.lutherburbanksavings.com

Lydian Private Bank
180 Royal Palm Way
Palm Beach, Florida 33480
(561) 514-4900
www.lydianbank.com

Middlesex Bancorp, MHC
6 Main Street
Natick, Massachusetts 01760
(508) 653-0300
www.middlesexbank.com

Midfirst Bank
501 N.W. Grand Boulevard
Oklahoma City, Oklahoma 73118
(405) 767-7000
www.midfirst.com

Mutual of Omaha Bank
3333 Farnam Street
Omaha, Nebraska 68131
(402) 351-8000
www.mutualofomahabank.com

NASB Financial, Inc.
12498 South 71 Highway
Grandview, Missouri 64030
(816) 765-2200
www.nasb.com

National Consumer Cooperative
  Bank
601 Pennsylvania Avenue, NW,
  Suite 750
Washington, D.C. 20004
(202) 349-7444
www.ncb.com

Nationwide Bank
One Nationwide Plaza
Columbus, Ohio 43215
(614) 249-7111
www.nationwide.com

NCB, FSB
139 South High Street
Hillsboro, Ohio 45133
(937) 393-4246
www.ncb.coop

New South Federal Savings Bank
1900 Crestwood Boulevard
Birmingham, Alabama 35210
(205) 951-4000
www.newsouthfederal.com

New York Community Bancorp, Inc.
615 Merrick Avenue
Westbury, New York 11590
(516) 683-4100
www.myNYCB.com

New York Private Bank & Trust
  Corporation
Five East 42nd Street
New York, N.Y. 10017
(212) 850-4000
www.emigrant.com

NewAlliance Bancshares, Inc.
195 Church Street
New Haven, Connecticut 06510
(203) 789-2767
www.newalliancebank.com

North Shore Bank, FSB
15700 West Bluemound Road
Brookfield, Wisconsin 53005
(262) 797-3858
www.northshorebank.com

Northfield Bancorp, Inc. (MIIC)
1410 St. Georges Avenue
Avanel, New Jersey 07001
(732) 499-7200
www.enorthfield.com

Northwest Bancorp, Inc. (MHC)
100 Liberty Street
Warren, Pennsylvania 16365
(814) 728-2140
www.northwestsavingsbank.com

OceanFirst Financial Corp.
975 Hooper Avenue
Toms River, New Jersey 08753
(732) 240-4500
www.oceanfirst.com

OneWest Bank, FSB
888 East Walnut Street
Pasadena, California 91101
(626) 535-4870
www.owb.com

Oritani Financial Corp. (MHC)
370 Pascack Road
Township of Washington,
   New Jersey 07676
(201) 664-5400
www.oritani.com

Parkvale Financial Corporation
4220 William Penn Highway
Monroeville, Pennsylvania 15146
(412) 373-7200
www.parkvale.com

Peoples First Community Bank
1022 West 23rd Street
Panama City, Florida 32405
(850) 770-7000
www.peoplesfirstonline2.com

People's United Financial, Inc.
850 Main Street
Bridgeport, Connecticut 06604
(203) 338-7171
www.peoples.com

Principal Bank
711 High Street
Des Moines, Iowa 50392
(800) 672-3343
www.principal.com

Provident Financial Holdings, Inc.
3756 Central Avenue
Riverside, California 92506
(951) 686-6060
www.myprovident.com

Provident Financial Services, Inc.
830 Bergen Avenue
Jersey City, New Jersey 07306
(201) 333-1000
www.providentbanknj.com

Provident New York Bancorp
400 Rella Boulevard
Montebello, New York 10901
(845) 369-8040
www.providentbanking.com

Prudential Bank & Trust, FSB
280 Trumbull Street
Hartford, Connecticut 06103
(888) 244-6295
www.prudential.com

Raymond James Bank, FSB
710 Carillon Parkway
Saint Petersburg, Florida 33716
(727) 567-8000
www.raymondjamesbank.com

Ridgewood Savings Bank
71-02 Forest Avenue
Ridgewood, New York 11385
(718) 240-4800
www.ridgewoodbank.com

Salem Five Bancorp
210 Essex Street
Salem, Massachusetts 01970
(978) 745-5555
www.salemfive.com

Scottrade Bank
12800 Corporate Hill Drive
Des Peres, Missouri 63131
(314) 965-1555
www.scottrade.com

Southwest Securities, FSB
1201 Elm Street
Dallas, Texas 75270
(469) 941-1200
www.southwestsecuritiesfsb.com

Sovereign Bancorp, Inc.
75 State Street
Boston, Massachusetts 02109
(617) 346-7200
www.sovereignbank.com

Spencer Savings Bank, SLA
611 River Drive
Elmwood Park, New Jersey 07407
(201) 703-3800
www.spencersavings.com

State Farm Bank, FSB
One State Farm Plaza, E6
Bloomington, Illinois 61710
(309) 766-2311
www.statefarm.com/bank/bank.asp

Superior Bancorp
17 North 20th Street
Birmingham, Alabama 35203
(205) 327-1400
www.superiorbank.com

TFS Financial Corporation (MHC)
7007 Broadway Avenue
Cleveland, Ohio 44105
(216) 441-6000
www.thirdfederal.com

TierOne Corporation
1235 N Street
Lincoln, Nebraska 68508
(402) 475-0521
www.tieronebank.com

TrustCo Bank Corp NY
Five Sarnowski Drive
Glenville, New York 12302
(518) 377-3311
www.trustcobank.com

Union Savings Bank
226 Main Street
Danbury, Connecticut 06810
(203) 830-4200
www.unionsavings.com

United Community Financial Corp.
275 West Federal Street
Youngstown, Ohio 44503
(330) 742-0500
www.ucfconline.com

United Western Bancorp, Inc.
700 17th Street, Suite 2100
Denver, Colorado 80202
(303) 595-9898
www.uwbancorp.com

USAA Federal Savings Bank
10750 McDermott Freeway
San Antonio, Texas 78284
(210) 498-2265
www.usaa.com

ViewPoint Financial Group (MHC)
1309 West 15th Street
Plano, Texas 75075
(972) 578-5000
www.viewpointbank.com

Washington Federal, Inc.
425 Pike Street
Seattle, Washington 98101
(206) 624-7930
www.washingtonfederal.com

Waterstone Financial, Inc. (MHC)
11200 West Plank Street
Wauwatosa, Wisconsin 53226
(414) 761-1000
www.wsbonling.com

WSFS Financial Corporation
500 Delaware Avenue
Wilmington, Delaware 19801
(302) 792-6000
www.wsfsbank.com

Yakima Federal Savings & Loan
  Association
118 East Yakima Avenue
Yakima, Washington 98901
(509) 248-2634
www.yakimafed.com/

CANADIAN TRUSTS AND LOANS

These financial institutions are the equivalent of the U.S. savings and loan. They operate under either provincial or federal legislation and conduct activities similar to a bank. Because of a trust company's fiduciary role, it can administer estates, trusts, pension plans, and agency contracts, which banks are not permitted to administer. Trust companies serve as transfer agents, registrars, and bond trustees for corporations, take deposits that are invested in fixed-term instruments, offer unit investment trusts, and offer mortgage loans, mostly to residential home buyers. The following institutions are regulated under Canada's Federal Trust and Loan Companies Act by the Office of the Superintendent of Financial Institutions. They are authorized to accept deposits, which may be eligible for deposit insurance provided by the Canada Deposit Insurance Corporation. This list includes the trusts and loans that are federally regulated.

AGF Trust Company
66 Wellington Street West, 31st Floor
Toronto, Ontario M5K 1E9

B2B Trust
130 Adelaide Street West, 2nd Floor
Toronto, Ontario M5K 3P5

The Bank of Nova Scotia Trust Co.
44 King Street West
Toronto, Ontario M5C 2W5

BMO Mortgage Corporation
2609 Granville Street, Suite 301
Vancouver, British Columbia
   V6H 4M7

BMO Trust Company
First Canadian Place
100 King Street West, 49th Floor
Toronto, Ontario M5X 1H3

BNY Trust Company of Canada
4 King Street West, 11th Floor
Toronto, Ontario M5N 1K9

Caledon Trust Company
130 Adelaide Street West, Suite 3402
Toronto, Ontario M5H 3P5

The Canada Trust Company
P.O. Box 1, TD Centre
Toronto, Ontario M5K 1A2

Canadian Western Trust Company
10303 Jasper Avenue, Suite 2300
Edmonton, Alberta T5J 3X6

CIBC Mellon Trust Corporation
320 Bay Street, 5th Floor
Toronto, Ontario M5H 4A6

CIBC Mortgages Inc.
33 Yonge Street, Suite 700
Toronto, Ontario M5E 1G4

CIBC Trust Corporation
55 Yonge Street, 10th Floor
Toronto, Ontario M5E 1J4

Citi Trust Company Canada
2920 Matheson Blvd. East
Mississauga, Ontario L4W 5J4

Citizens Trust Company
401-815 West Hastings Street
Vancouver, British Columbia
   V6C 1B4

Community Trust Company
2271 Bloor Street West
Toronto, Ontario M6S 1P1

Computershare Trust Company
   of Canada
100 University Avenue, 11th Floor
Toronto, Ontario M5J 2Y1

Concentra Trust
333 Third Avenue North
Saskatoon, Saskatchewan S7K 2M2

Desjardins Trust Inc.
1 Complexe Desjardins
South Tower, 14th Floor
Montreal, Quebec H5B 1E4

The Effort Trust Company
242 Main Street East
Hamilton, Ontario L8N 1H5

The Equitable Trust Company
30 St. Clair Avenue West, Suite 700
Toronto, Ontario M4V 3A1

Equity Transfer & Trust Company
200 University Avenue, Suite 400
Toronto, Ontario M5H 4H1

Fiduciary Trust Company of Canada
200 King Street West, Suite 1500
Toronto, Ontario M5H 3T4

First Data Loan Company, Canada
132 Coldstream Avenue
Toronto, Ontario M5N 1X9

Home Trust Company
145 King Street West, Suite 2300
Toronto, Ontario M5H 1J8

Household Trust Company
3381 Steeles Avenue East, Suite 300
Toronto, Ontario M2H 3S7

HSBC Loan Corporation (Canada)
885 West Georgia Street, 4th Floor
Vancouver, British Columbia
   V6C 3E8

HSBC Mortgage Corporation
(Canada)
885 West Georgia Street, Suite 300
Vancouver, British Columbia
V6C 3E9

HSBC Trust Company (Canada)
70 York Street, 6th Floor
Toronto, Ontario M5J 1S9

Industrial Alliance Trust Inc.
1080 Grand Allee West
Quebec, Quebec G1K 7M3

Investors Group Trust Co. Ltd.
One Canada Centre
447 Portage Avenue
Winnipeg, Manitoba R3C 3B6

Laurentian Trust of Canada Inc.
1981 McGill College Avenue,
15th Floor
Montreal, Quebec H3A 3K3

LBC Trust
130 Adelaide Street West
Toronto, Ontario M5H 3P5

League Savings and Mortgage
Company
6074 Lady Hammond Road,
3rd Floor
Halifax, Nova Scotia B3K 5M5

Legacy Private Trust
1 Toronto Street, Suite 800
P.O. Box 1
Toronto, Ontario M5C 2V6

M.R.S. Trust Company
777 Bay Street, Suite 2100
Toronto, Ontario M5G 2N4

Maple Trust Company
79 Wellington Street West, Suite 3400
Toronto, Ontario M5K 1K7

MCAN Mortgage Corporation
200 King Street West, Suite 400
Toronto, Ontario M5H 3T4

MD Private Trust Company
1870 Alta Vista Drive
Ottawa, Ontario K1G 6R7

Montreal Trust Company of Canada
44 King Street West
Toronto, Ontario M5H 1H1

Natcan Trust Company
1100 University Street, 12th Floor
Montreal, Quebec H3B 2G7

National Trust Company
44 King Street West
Toronto, Ontario M5H 1H1

The Northern Trust Company,
Canada
145 King Street West, Suite 1910
Toronto, Ontario M5H 1J8

Oak Trust Company
2410-255 Queens Street
London, Ontario N6A 5R8

Peace Hills Trust Company
10011 109th Street, 10th Floor
Edmonton, Alberta T5J 3S8

Peoples Trust Company
888 Dunsmuir Street, Suite 1400
Vancouver, British Columbia
V6C 3K4

RBC Dexia Investor Services Trust
77 King Street West, 10th Floor
Toronto, Ontario M5W 1P9

ResMor Trust Company
3250 Bloor Street West
East Tower, Suite 1400
Etobicoke, Ontario M8X 2X9

Royal Bank Mortgage Corporation
1 Place Ville Marie
8th Floor, East Wing
Montreal, Quebec H3C 3A9

The Royal Trust Company
200 Bay Street, 8th Floor
Toronto, Ontario M5J 2J5

Royal Trust Corporation of Canada
200 Bay Street, 8th Floor
Toronto, Ontario M5J 2J5

Scotia Mortgage Corporation
79 Wellington Street West, Suite 3400
Toronto, Ontario M5K 1K7

Services Hypothécaires CIBC Inc.
161 Bay Street, 11th Floor
Toronto, Ontario M5J 2S8

TD Mortgage Corporation
P.O. Box 1, TD Centre
Toronto, Ontario M5K 1A2

Standard Life Trust Company
1245 Sherbrooke Street West,
   15th Floor
Montreal, Quebec H3G 1G3

TD Pacific Mortgage Corporation
700 West Georgia Street, 3rd Floor
Vancouver, British Columbia
   V7Y 1A2

State Street Trust Company Canada
7 Governors Road
Toronto, Ontario M4W 2E9

Valiant Trust Company
10303 Jasper Avenue, Suite 2300
Edmonton, Alberta T5J 3X6

Sun Life Financial Trust Inc.
227 King Street South
Waterloo, Ontario N2J 4C5

LIFE INSURANCE COMPANIES

The following is an alphabetical list of the names, addresses, telephone numbers and websites of the 100 largest life insurance companies in the United States based on assets. The list is compiled and published by A.M. Best Company, Ambest Road, Oldwick, New Jersey 08858 (908-439-2200), which rates the financial stability of life insurance companies.

Life insurance companies are ranked in three ways: by net admitted assets, by life insurance in force, or by net premiums written. Most of these companies would be included in rankings using any of these methods. Admitted assets provide the most direct indication of a company's importance in the finance and investment markets. These assets include all the assets a life insurance company has accumulated over the years, including investments in real estate, mortgages, stocks, and bonds. Because of the enormous size of these assets, insurance companies have become extremely important institutional investors. The other two methods of ranking these companies, by life insurance in force and by net premiums written, show the amount of coverage insurance companies are providing and the dollar amount of their sales. These also are important figures by which to judge a company.

The life insurance industry is characterized by a few giant firms with a high concentration of the industry's total assets and a large number of smaller companies. Assets of the top two firms, Metropolitan Life Insurance Company and Prudential Insurance Company of America, were $289.6 billion and $237.5 billion, respectively. The third-ranking firm, Teachers Insurance & Annuity Association of America, had assets of $195.2 billion. The 25th-ranked company, John Hancock Life Insurance Company, had assets of $62.9 billion, while the 50th, Minnesota Life Insurance Company, posted assets of $19.7 billion. The 100th-ranked firm, Provident Life and Accident Insurance Company, reported $7.7 billion.

The companies on this list represent two distinct types of insurance company. One is owned by stockholders, and its stock or that of its parent company is traded on the New York Stock Exchange, the American Stock Exchange, or the Nasdaq Stock Market. This type of company is in business to write life insurance policies and invest premiums — and a portion of the difference between investment income and insurance claims and expenses ultimately reaches shareholders as dividends or increases in shareholder equity. The other type of company, called a mutual life insurance company (the word mutual is usually in the name), is owned by policyholders, who receive a portion of the profits the company may earn through policyholder dividends. Stock is not traded in mutual companies.

As in other areas of the financial services industry, competition has been increasing among life insurers. In the early 1980s, the advent of universal life insurance, which ties cash value buildup to money-market rates, put additional pressure on all insurers to make policies more competitive. By the 1990s, the life insurance industry had produced a panoply of products that allow policyholders a wide range of flexibility in paying premiums, building cash value, and buying insurance protection. In addition to traditional whole life and term policies, companies now offer universal life, variable life (where the policyholder chooses between stock, bond, and money-market investments), variable universal life, and a range of annuity and Individual Retirement Account products. Many insurers also offer financial planning services.

In addition to their role as insurers of lives, life insurance companies have become an important source of capital for world capital markets. Insurance companies are a major force in the stock market; in the municipal, corporate, and government bond markets; in real estate, both as owners and lenders; and as providers of venture capital. Some insurance companies have expanded their offerings by acquiring brokerage and money management firms.

Aetna Life Insurance Company
151 Farmington Avenue
Hartford, Connecticut 06156
(860) 273-0123
www.aetna.com

AIG Life Insurance Company
One ALICO Plaza
Wilmington, Delaware 19801
(713) 522-1111
www.aigag.com

AGC Life Insurance Company
222 Monroe Street
Jefferson City, Missouri 65101
(615) 749-1000
www.aigag.com

Allianz Life Insurance Company
of North America
5701 Golden Hills Drive
Minneapolis, Minnesota 55416
(763) 765-6500
www.allianzlife.com

Allstate Life Insurance Company
3100 Sanders Road
Northbrook, Illinois 60062
(847) 402-5000
www.allstate.com

American Equity Investment Life
Insurance Company
5000 Westown Parkway, Suite 440
West Des Moines, Iowa 50266
(515) 221-0002
www.american-equity.com

American Family Life Assurance
Company of Columbus (AFLAC)
10306 Regency Parkway Drive
Omaha, Nebraska 68114
(706) 323-3431
www.aflac.com

American General Life and
Accident Insurance Company
American General Center
Nashville, Tennessee 37250
(615) 749-1000
www.agla.com

American General Life Insurance
Company
2727-A Allen Parkway
Houston, Texas 77019
(713) 522-1111
www.aglife.com

American Investors Life
  Insurance Company
555 South Kansas Avenue
Topeka, Kansas 66603
(800) 255-2405
www.avivausa.com

American Life Insurance Company
One ALICO Plaza
Wilmington, Delaware 19801
(302) 594-2000

American National Insurance
  Company
One Moody Plaza
Galveston, Texas 77550
(409) 763-4661
www.anico.com

American United Life Insurance
  Company
One American Square
Indianapolis, Indiana 46282
(317) 285-1877
www.oneamerica.com

Aviva Life and Annuity Company
611 Fifth Avenue
Des Moines, Iowa 50309
(800) 800-9882
www.avivausa.com

AXA Equitable Life Insurance
  Company
1290 Avenue of the Americas,
  16th Floor
New York, New York 10104
(212) 554-1234
www.axa-equitable.com

Bankers Life and Casualty Company
600 West Chicago Avenue
Chicago, Illinois 60654
(312) 396-6000
www.bankers.com

Connecticut General Life
  Insurance Co.
900 Cottage Grove Road
Bloomfield, Connecticut 06152
(860) 226-6000
www.cigna.com

CUNA Mutual Insurance Society
2000 Heritage Way
Waverly, Iowa 50677
(608) 238-5851
www.cunamutual.com

Employers Reassurance Corporation
5700 Broadmoor, Suite 1000
Mission, Kansas 66201
(913) 982-3700

EquiTrust Life Insurance Company
5400 University Avenue
West Des Moines, Iowa 50266
(877) 249-3694
www.equitrust.com

Fidelity Investments Life
  Insurance Co.
49 North 400 West, 6th Floor
Salt Lake City, Utah 84101
(801) 537-2070
www.fidelity.com

General American Life Insurance
  Company
13045 Tesson Ferry Road
St. Louis, Missouri 63128
(314) 843-8700
www.metlife.com

Genworth Life and Annuity
  Insurance Company
6610 West Broad Street
Richmond, Virginia 23230
(804) 662-2400
www.genworth.com

Genworth Life Insurance Company
2711 Centerville Road, Suite 400
Wilmington, Delaware 19808
(888) 322-4629
www.genworth.com

Great American Life Insurance
  Company
580 Walnut Street
Cincinnati, Ohio 45202
(513) 357-3300
www.gafri.com

Great-West Life & Annuity
  Insurance Co.
8515 East Orchard Road
Greenwood Village, Colorado 80111
(303) 737-3000
www.greatwest.com

Guardian Life Insurance Company
  of America
7 Hanover Square
New York, New York 10004
(212) 598-8000
www.guardianlife.com

Hartford Life and Accident
  Insurance Company
200 Hopmeadow Street
Simsbury, Connecticut 06089
(860) 525-8555
www.thehartford.com

Hartford Life and Annuity
  Insurance Company
200 Hopmeadow Street
Simsbury, Connecticut 06089
(860) 525-8555
www.thehartford.com

Hartford Life Insurance Company
200 Hopmeadow Street
Simsbury, Connecticut 06089
(860) 525-8555
www.thehartford.com

ING Life Insurance and Annuity
  Company
One Orange Way
Windsor, Connecticut 06095
(860) 580-4646
www.ing-usa.com

ING USA Annuity and Life
  Insurance Company
909 Locust Street
Des Moines, Iowa 50309
(515) 698-7000
www.ing-usa.com

Jackson National Life Insurance
  Company
1 Corporate Way
Lansing, Michigan 48951
(517) 381-5500
www.jackson.com

John Hancock Life Insurance
  Company
John Hancock Plaza
Boston, Massachusetts 02117
(617) 572-6000
www.jhancock.com

John Hancock Life Insurance
  Company USA
38500 Woodward Avenue
Bloomfield Hills, Michigan 48304
(617) 854-4300
www.johnhancock.com

John Hancock Variable Life
  Insurance Company
197 Clarendon Street
Boston, Massachusetts 02117
(617) 572-6000
www.johnhancock.com

Kemper Investors Life Insurance
  Company
1400 American Lane
Schaumburg, Illinois 60196
(425) 577-5100
www.kibenefits.com

Knights of Columbus
1 Columbus Plaza
New Haven, Connecticut 06510
(203) 752-4000
www.kofc.org

Liberty Life Assurance Company
  of Boston
175 Berkeley Street
Boston, Massachusetts 02117
(617) 357-9500
www.libertymutual.com

Lincoln Life and Annuity
  Company of New York
100 Madison Street, Suite 1860
Syracuse, New York 13202
(603) 226-5000
www.lfg.com

Lincoln National Life Insurance
  Company
1300 South Clinton Street
Fort Wayne, Indiana 46802
(260) 455-2000
www.lfg.com

Massachusetts Mutual Life
  Insurance Company
1295 State Street
Springfield, Massachusetts 01111
(413) 788-8411
www.massmutual.com

Merrill Lynch Life Insurance
  Company
425 West Capital Avenue, Suite 1800
Little Rock, Arkansas 72201
(319) 355-8511
www.aegonins.com

Met Life Insurance Company
  of Connecticut
1300 Hall Boulevard
Bloomfield, Connecticut 06002
(860) 308-1000
www.metlife.com

Met Life Investors Insurance
  Company
13045 Tesson Ferry Road
St. Louis, Missouri 63028
(949) 717-6536
www.metlife.com

Met Life Investors USA Insurance
  Company
222 Delaware Avenue, Suite 900
Wilmington, Delaware 19899
(949) 717-6536
www.metlife.com

Metropolitan Life Insurance
  Company
200 Park Avenue
New York, New York 10166
(212) 579-2211
www.metlife.com

Midland National Life Insurance
  Company
4601 Westown Parkway, Suite 300
West Des Moines, Iowa 50266
(605) 335-5700
www.mnlife.com

Minnesota Life Insurance Company
400 Robert Street North
St. Paul, Minnesota 55101
(651) 665-3500
www.minnesotalife.com

Modern Woodmen of America
1701 First Avenue
Rock Island, Illinois 61201
(309) 786-6481
www.modern-woodmen.org

Monumental Life Insurance
  Company
4333 Edgewood Road N.E.
Cedar Rapids, Iowa 52499
(319) 355-8511
www.aegonins.com

MONY Life Insurance Company
1290 Avenue of the Americas,
  16th Floor
New York, New York 10104
(212) 554-1234
www.axa-equitable.com

Mutual of America Life Insurance
  Company
320 Park Avenue
New York, New York 10022
(212) 224-1600
www.mutualofamerica.com

National Life Insurance Company
1 National Life Drive
Montpelier, Vermont 05604
(802) 229-3333
www.nationallife.com

Nationwide Life Insurance
  Company
1 Nationwide Plaza
Columbus, Ohio 43215
(614) 249-7111
www.nationwidefinancial.com

New England Life Insurance
  Company
501 Boylston Street
Boston, Massachusetts 02116
(617) 578-2000
www.nef.com

New York Life Insurance Company
51 Madison Avenue
New York, New York 10010
(212) 576-7000
www.newyorklife.com

New York Life Insurance and
  Annuity Corporation
200 Continental Drive
Newark, Delaware 19713
(212) 576-7000
www.newyorklife.com

North American Company for
  Life and Health Insurance
4601 Westown Parkway, Suite 300
West Des Moines, Iowa 50266
(605) 373-8560
www.nacolah.com

Northwestern Mutual Life
  Insurance Company
720 East Wisconsin Avenue
Milwaukee, Wisconsin 53202
(414) 271-1444
www.nmfn.com

Ohio National Life Insurance
  Company
One Financial Way
Cincinnati, Ohio 45242
(513) 794-6100
www.ohionational.com

OM Financial Life Insurance
  Company
1001 Fleet Street
Baltimore, Maryland 21202
(410) 895-0100
www.omfn.com

Pacific Life Insurance Company
1299 Farnam Street
Omaha, Nebraska 68102
(949) 219-3011
www.pacificlife.com

Penn Mutual Life Insurance
  Company
600 Dresher Road
Horsham, Pennsylvania 19044
(215) 956-8000
www.pennmutual.com

Phoenix Life Insurance Company
31 Tech Valley Drive
East Greenbush, New York 12061
(860) 403-5000
www.phoenixwm.com

Principal Life Insurance Company
711 High Street
Des Moines, Iowa 50392
(515) 247-5111
www.principal.com

Protective Life Insurance Company
1620 Westgate Circle, Suite 200
Brentwood, Tennessee 37027
(205) 268-1000
www.protective.com

Provident Life and Accident
  Insurance Company
1 Fountain Square
Chattanooga, Tennessee 37402
(423) 294-1011
www.unum.com

Pruco Life Insurance Company
2999 North 44th Street, Suite 250
Phoenix, Arizona 85018
877-301-1212
www.prudential.com

Prudential Annuities Life
  Assurance Corporation
One Corporate Drive
Shelton, Connecticut 06484
(800) 628-6039
www.prudential.com

Prudential Insurance Company
  of America
751 Broad Street, 23rd Floor
Newark, New Jersey 07102
(973) 802-6000
www.prudential.com

Prudential Retirement and
  Annuity Company
280 Trumbull Street
Hartford, Connecticut 06103
(215) 761-1000
www.prudential.com

Reassure America Life Insurance
  Company
1700 Magnavox Way
Fort Wayne, Indiana 46804
(877) 794-7773
www.swissre.com

ReliaStar Life Insurance Company
20 Washington Avenue South
Minneapolis, Minnesota 55401
(612) 372-5432
www.ing-usa.com

RGA Reinsurance Company
1370 Timberlake Manor Parkway
Chesterfield, Missouri 63017
(636) 736-7000
www.rgare.com

RiverSource Life Insurance
  Company
227 Ameriprise Financial Center
Minneapolis, Minnesota 55474
(612) 671-3131
www.ameriprise.com

Security Benefit Life Insurance
  Company
One Security Benefit Place
Topeka, Kansas 66636
(785) 438-3000
www.securitybenefit.com

Security Life of Denver Insurance
  Company
1290 Broadway
Denver, Colorado 80203
(303) 860-1290
www.ing-usa.com

Southern Farm Bureau Life
  Insurance Company
1401 Livingston Lane
Jackson, Mississippi 39213
(601) 981-7422
www.sfbli.com

Standard Insurance Company
1100 S.W. Sixth Avenue
Portland, Oregon 97204
(971) 321-7000
www.standard.com

State Farm Life Insurance Company
One State Farm Plaza
Bloomington, Illinois 61710
(309) 766-2311
www.statefarm.com

Sun Life Assurance Company
  of CA (US)
1209 Orange Street
Wilmington, Delaware 19801
(781) 237-6030
www.sunlife.com

Sun Life Assurance Co. of
  Canada USB
150 King Street West
Toronto, Ontario, Canada M5H 1J9
(781) 237-6030

SunAmerica Annuity and Life
  Assurance Company
2999 North 44th Street, Suite 250
Phoenix, Arizona 85018
(310) 772-6000
www.sunamerica.com

SunAmerica Life Insurance
  Company
2999 North 44th Street, Suite 250
Phoenix, Arizona 85018
(310) 772-6000
www.sunamerica.com

Swiss Re Life & Health America,
  Inc.
One Commercial Plaza
Hartford, Connecticut 06103
(877) 794-7773
www.swissre.com

Symetra Life Insurance Company
777 108th Avenue NE, Suite 1200
Bellevue, Washington 98004
(425) 256-8000
www.symetra.com

Teachers Insurance & Annuity
  Association (TIAA)
730 Third Avenue
New York, New York 10017
(212) 490-9000
www.tiaa-cref.org

Thrivent Financial for Lutherans
4321 North Ballard Road
Appleton, Wisconsin 54919
(800) 847-4836
www.thrivent.com

Transamerica Financial Life
   Insurance Company
4 Manhattanville Road
Purchase, New York 10577
(319) 355-8511
www.aegonins.com

Transamerica Life Insurance
   Company
4333 Edgewood Road N.E.
Cedar Rapids, Iowa 52499
(319) 355-8511
www.aegonins.com

Union Fidelity Life Insurance
   Company
200 North Martingale Road
Schaumburg, Illinois 60173
(215) 542-4590

United Healthcare Insurance
   Company
450 Columbus Boulevard
Hartford, Connecticut 06103
(877) 832-7734
www.unitedhealthgroup.com

United of Omaha Life Insurance
   Company
Mutual of Omaha Plaza
Omaha, Nebraska 68175
(402) 342-7600
www.mutualofomaha.com

Unum Life Insurance Company
   of America
2211 Congress Street
Portland, Maine 04122
(207) 575-2211
www.unum.com

USAA Life Insurance Company
9800 Fredericksburg Road
San Antonio, Texas 78288
(210) 498-8000
www.usaa.com

Variable Annuity Life Insurance
   Company
2929 Allen Parkway
Houston, Texas 77019
(713) 522-1111
www.aigretirement.com

Western National Life Insurance
   Company
205 SE 10th Avenue
Amarillo, Texas 79101
(806) 345-7400
www.aigannuity.com

Western Reserve Life Assurance
   Company of Ohio
366 East Broad Street
Columbus, Ohio 43215
(319) 355-8511
www.aegonins.com

Western-Southern Life Assurance
   Company
400 Broadway
Cincinnati, Ohio 45202
(513) 629-1800
www.westernsouthernlife.com

BROKERAGE FIRMS

Traditionally, brokers sold mostly stocks and bonds to their customers, who were primarily persons of substantial means. Today, these firms allow customers to buy and sell stocks, bonds, commodities, options, mutual funds, bank certificates of deposit, limited partnerships, and many other financial products. Brokers also offer asset management accounts, which combine holdings of assets such as stocks and bonds with a money-market fund that provides check-writing and credit-card features. Most brokers in addition offer individualized financial planning services. As a result of this wide range of products, brokers today have a much more diverse clientele, ranging from young persons just starting to invest to wealthy, retired people who are experienced investors.

On May 1, 1975, known as May Day in the brokerage industry, the era of fixed commissions ended. This move brought much more competition within the industry and ushered in a new breed of broker—the discounter. These brokers specialize in executing buy and sell orders for stocks, bonds, and options. As a rule, they charge commissions far lower than full-service brokers. Discounters do not give advice about which securities to buy or sell, however, so investors who use them generally are more experienced and knowledgeable.

Within the full-service brokerage firm category, two varieties exist. The largest firms are known as wire houses, because they have a large network of offices nationally linked by advanced communications equipment. National wire house firms also tend to have an important presence overseas. In contrast, regional brokerage firms concentrate on serving customers in a particular area of the country. Such firms typically do not offer as wide an array of financial products, although they usually provide all the basics. Regional firms tend to concentrate on finding investment opportunities not yet discovered by large national firms.

In addition to providing services to individuals, brokers who also engage in investment banking play an important role in raising capital for federal, state, and local governments and for corporations. Such firms underwrite new issues of debt securities for governments and equity and debt issues for corporations and distribute them to both institutional and individual investors. In addition, brokers act as advisers to corporations involved in merger and acquisition activity and other areas of corporate finance. Increasingly, brokerage firms are expanding their operations internationally, to facilitate trading of foreign currencies, and foreign debt and equity securities.

This alphabetical list contains the top 100 brokerage firms as measured by the amount of capital. (Capital is the sum of long-term borrowings and ownership equity.) Capital is crucial to a brokerage firm because it must constantly be put at risk in underwriting and trading securities. Most of these brokerage firms were originally formed as partnerships, but in recent years, many incorporated and a number offered shares of stock in their companies to the public. Such public offerings are often the best way for a brokerage firm to raise the additional capital it needs to be competitive.

Today, the lines are blurring in the full-service sector. Many brokerage firms, such as Charles Schwab, which made its reputation as a discount broker, offer full-service brokerage features. The discount brokerage business has expanded dramatically, adding a range of services while keeping brokerage fees relatively low. Moreover, online brokerage services have given the business a new dimension. Online brokerages listed here include sophisticated businesses such as Schwab and E*Trade Financial that also offer banking, insurance, and other financial services, as well as true discounters.

The listing of the top 100 full-service brokerage firms is courtesy of the Securities Industry and Financial Markets Association, 120 Broadway, New York, NY 10271-0080; (212) 608-1500.

Brokerage Firms
ABN AMRO, Inc.
540 West Madison, Suite 2514
Chicago, Illinois 60661
(312) 855-7600
www.abnamro.com

A.G. Edwards & Sons, Inc.
1 North Jefferson Avenue
St. Louis, Missouri 63103
(314) 955-3000
www.agedwards.com

Alexandra & James Co.
521 Fifth Avenue
New York, New York 10175
(212) 425-6006
www.lebenthal.com/aj/

Ameriprise Financial Services, Inc.
70100 Ameriprise Financial Center
Minneapolis, Minnesota 55474
(800) 862-7919
www.ameriprise.com

Banca IMI Securities Corporation
One William Street
New York, New York 10004
(212) 326-1100
www.bancaimi.it

BMO Capital Markets Corp.
1 First Canadian Place
Toronto, Ontario, Canada M5X 1H3
(416) 359-4000
www.bmonesbittburns.com

BNY ConvergEx Executive
Solutions LLC
100 Wall Street
New York, New York 10005
(800) 367-8998
www.bnybrokerage.com

Butler, Wick & Co., Inc.
100 Federal Plaza East
Youngstown, Ohio 44503
(330) 744-4351
www.butlerwick.com

Calyon Securities (USA), Inc.
1301 Avenue of the Americas
New York, New York 10019
(212) 261-7000
www.calyon.com

Canaccord Capital Corporation
2200-609 Granville Street
Vancouver, British Columbia,
Canada V7Y 1H2
(604) 643-7300
www.canaccord.com

The Charles Schwab Corporation
211 Main Street
San Francisco, California 94105
(415) 636-7000
www.schwab.com

CIBC World Markets Corporation
300 Madison Avenue
New York, New York 10017
(212) 856-4000
www.cibcwm.com

Citigroup Global Markets
Holdings, Inc.
388 Greenwich Street
New York, New York 10013
(212) 816-6000
www.citigroup.com

City Securities Corporation
30 South Meridian Street, Suite 600
Indianapolis, Indiana 46204
(317) 634-4400
www.citysecurities.com

G.X. Clarke & Co.
10 Exchange Place, Suite 1005
Jersey City, New Jersey 07302
(201) 200-3600
www.gxecute.com

Credit Suisse
11 Madison Avenue
New York, New York 10010
(212) 325-2000
www.credit-suisse.com

Crowell, Weedon & Company
1 Wilshire Boulevard, 26th Floor
Los Angeles, California 90017
(213) 620-1850
www.crowellweedon.com

Davenport & Company LLC
One James Center, Suite 1100
901 East Cary Street
Richmond, Virginia 23219
(800) 846-6666
www.davenportllc.com

D.A. Davidson & Company
8 Third Street North
Great Falls, Montana 59401
(406) 727-4200
www.davidsoncompanies.com

Daiwa Securities America, Inc.
32 Old Slip
New York, New York 10005
(212) 612-7000
www.daiwausa.com

Deltec Asset Management LLC
623 Fifth Avenue
New York, New York 10022
(212) 546-6200
www.deltec-ny.com

Deutsche Bank Securities, Inc.
60 Wall Street
New York, New York 10005
(212) 250-2500
www.db.com

Dresdner, Kleinwort Securities LLC
2 World Financial Center, 31st Floor
New York, New York 10281
(212) 703-4000
www.commerzbank.com

E*Trade Brokerage Holdings, Inc.
135 East 57th Street
New York, New York 10022
(646) 521-4300
http://www.etrade.com

Edward Jones
2731 South Jefferson Avenue
St. Louis, Missouri 63118
(314) 577-0167
www.edwardjones.com

Ferris, Baker Watts, Inc.
100 Light Street
Baltimore, Maryland 21202
(410) 685-2500
www.rbcwm.com

Fidelity Brokerage Services LLC
44 Mall Road
Burlington, Massachusetts 01803
(781) 272-3600
www.fidelity.com

Fifth Third Securities Inc.
38 Fountain Square Plaza
Cincinnati, Ohio 45202
(513) 534-8888
www.53.com

First Albany Capital, Inc.
30 South Pearl Street, Suite 100
Albany, New York 12207
(518) 447-8500
www.bpsg.com

First Southwest Company
325 North St. Paul Street, Suite 800
Dallas, Texas 75201
(214) 953-4000
www.firstsouthwest.com

Folger Nolan Fleming Douglas, Inc.
725 15th Street NW
Washington, D.C. 20005
(202) 783-5252
www.fnfd.com

Friedman, Billings, Ramsey &
   Co., Inc.
1001 Nineteenth Street North
Arlington, Virginia 22209
(703) 312-9500
www.fbrcapitalmarkets.com

Griffin, Kubik, Stephens &
   Thompson, Inc.
111 West Monroe
Chicago, Illinois 60606
(312) 441-2500
www.gkst.com

The Goldman Sachs Group, Inc.
85 Broad Street
New York, New York 10004
(212) 902-1000
www.gs.com

H&R Block Financial Advisors, Inc.
One H&R Block Way
Kansas City, Missouri 64105
(888) 687-4722
www.hrblock.com

H.D. Vest Investment Services
6333 North State Highway 161,
   Fourth Floor
Irving, Texas 75038
(972) 870-6000
www.hdvest.com

Howe Barnes Hoefer & Arnet Inc.
222 South Riverside Plaza, 7th Floor
Chicago, Illinois 60607
(800) 800-4693
www.howebarnes.com

Hudson Securities Inc.
111 Town Square Place
Jersey City, New Jersey 07310
(201) 216-0100
www.hudsonsecurities.com

ING Financial Markets LLC
One Orange Way
Windsor, Connecticut 06095
(860) 580-4640
www.ingfinancialadvisers.com

Intersecurities Inc.
570 Carillon Parkway
St. Petersburg, Florida 33716
(800) 322-7161
www.tfa.transamerica.com

Janney Montgomery Scott LLC
1801 Market Street
Philadelphia, Pennsylvania 19103
(215) 665-6000
www.janneys.com

Jefferies Group, Inc.
520 Madison Avenue, 10th Floor
New York, New York 10022
(212) 284-2300
www.jefferies.com

J.J.B. Hilliard, W.L. Lyons, Inc.
500 West Jefferson Street
Louisville, Kentucky 40202
(502) 588-8400
www.hilliard.com

JPMorgan Securities, Inc.
270 Park Avenue
New York, New York 10017
(212) 270-4435
www.jpmorgan.com

KBC Financial Products USA, Inc.
140 East 45th Street, 42nd Floor
New York, New York 10017
(212) 845-2000
www.kbcfp.com

C.L. King & Associates Inc.
9 Elk Street
Albany, New York 12207
(518) 431-3500
www.clking.com

Knight Equity Markets LP
525 Washington Boulevard
Jersey City, New Jersey 07310
(201) 557-6853
www.knight.com

Linsco/Private Ledger Corp.
9785 Towne Center Drive
San Diego, California 92121
(619) 450-9606
www.lpl.com

Merrill Lynch & Company, Inc.
4 World Financial Center
New York, New York 10080
(212) 449-1000
www.ml.com

Mesirow Financial Holdings, Inc.
350 North Clark Street
Chicago, Illinois 60654
(312) 595-6000
www.mesirowfinancial.com

MML Investors Services Inc.
1295 State Street
Springfield, Massachusetts 01111
(800) 542-8767
www.massmutual.com

Morgan Keegan & Company, Inc.
50 North Front Street
Memphis, Tennessee 38103
(901) 524-4100
www.morgankeegan.com

Morgan Stanley
1585 Broadway
New York, New York 10036
(212) 761-4000
www.morganstanley.com

NatCity Investments, Inc.
National City Center
1900 East Ninth Street
Cleveland, Ohio 44114
(216) 222-2000
http://wealth.nationalcity.com/natcity

Natexis Bleichroeder, Inc.
1345 Avenue of the Americas
New York, New York 10105-4300
(212) 698-3000
www.natexisblr.com

National Bank Financial, Inc.
1155 Metcalfe Street, 5th floor
Montreal, Quebec H3B 4S9 Canada
(514) 879-2222
www.nbfinancial.com

Needham & Company, LLC
445 Park Avenue
New York, New York 10022
(212) 371-8300
www.needhamco.com

NFP Securities, Inc.
340 Madison Avenue
New York, New York 10173
(212) 301-4000
www.nfp.com

Nomura Securities International, Inc.
2 World Financial Center, Building B
New York, New York 10281-1198
(212) 667-9300
www.nomura.com

Northwestern Mutual Investment
   Services LLC
720 East Wisconsin Avenue
Milwaukee, Wisconsin 53202
(414) 271-1444
www.nmfn.com

NYFIX Clearing Corporation
333 Ludlow Street
Stamford, Connecticut 06902
(203) 425-8000
www.nyfix.com

Oppenheimer & Company, Inc.
125 Broad Street
New York, New York 10004
(212) 668-8000
www.opco.com

Pacific Crest Securities Inc.
111 SW Fifth Avenue, 42nd Floor
Portland, Oregon 97204
(503) 248-0721
www.pacificcrest.com

Park Avenue Securities LLC
954 Ridgebrook Road, Suite 300
Sparks, Maryland 21152
(410) 828-5400
www.glc.com

Pension Financial Services Inc.
330 West 42nd Street
New York, New York 10036
(212) 502-4401
www.bellsouth.com

Pershing LLC
1 Pershing Plaza
Jersey City, New Jersey 07399
(201) 413-2000
www.pershing.com

Piper Jaffray & Co.
800 Nicollet Mall, Suite 800
Minneapolis, Minnesota 55402
(612) 303-6000
www.piperjaffray.com

PNC Capital Markets LLC
800 Grant Street
Pittsburgh, Pennsylvania 15219
(888) 762-2265
www.pnc.com

T. Rowe Price Investment
   Services, Inc.
500 East Pratt Street
Baltimore, Maryland 21202
(410) 345-2000
www.troweprice.com

Raymond James Financial, Inc.
880 Carillon Parkway
St. Petersburg, Florida 33716
(727) 567-1000
www.raymondjames.com

RBC Dain Rauscher Inc.
60 South 6th Street
Minneapolis, Minnesota 55402
(612) 371-2811
www.rbcwm-usa.com

RBS Greenwich Capital
1 Washington Boulevard
Stamford, Connecticut 06901
(203) 356-9540
www.rbsgc.com

Ridge Clearing & Outsourcing
  Solutions Inc.
1981 Marcus Avenue
Lake Success, New York 11042
(201) 793-9304
www.ridgeclearing.com

Robert W. Baird & Company, Inc.
777 East Wisconsin Avenue
Milwaukee, Wisconsin 53202
(800) 792-2473
www.rwbaird.com

Sandler O'Neill & Partners LP
919 Third Avenue
New York, New York 10022
(212) 466-7800
www.sandleroneill.com

Scotia Capital (USA), Inc.
One Liberty Plaza
165 Broadway, 26th Floor
New York, New York 10006
(212) 225-5000
www.scotiacapital.com

Southeast Securities Inc.
1201 Elm Street, Suite 3500
Dallas, Texas 75270
(214) 859-1800
www.swst.com

Seattle-Northwest Securities Corp.
1420 Fifth Avenue, Suite 4300
Seattle, Washington 98101
(206) 628-2882
www.seattlenorthwest.com

Scott & Stringfellow, Inc.
909 East Main Street
Richmond, Virginia 23219
(804) 643-1811
www.scottstringfellow.com

Sovereign Securities Corporation
  LLC
P.O. Box 12646
Reading, Pennsylvania 19612
(877) 768-2265
www.sovereignbank.com

State Farm VP Management Corp.
One State Farm Plaza
Bloomington, Illinois 61710
(877) 734-2265
www.statefarm.com

Stifel, Nicolaus & Company, Inc.
501 North Broadway
St. Louis, Missouri 63102
(314) 342-2000
www.stifel.com

Stone & Youngberg LLC
One Ferry Building
San Francisco, California 94111
www.syllc.com

TD Ameritrade Holding
  Corporation
1005 North Ameritrade Place
Bellevue, Nebraska 68005
(402) 970-5805
www.tdameritrade.com

UBS Securities LLC
1285 Avenue of the Americas
New York, New York 10019
(212) 713-2000
www.ubs.com

Vining Sparks
775 Ridge Lake Boulevard
Memphis, Tennessee 38120
(901) 766-3000
www.viningsparks.com

Wachovia Capital Markets LLC
1 Wachovia Center
Charlotte, North Carolina 28288
(704) 715-5320
www.wachovia.com

Wayne Hummer Investments LLC
222 South Riverside Plaza, 28th Floor
Chicago, Illinois 60606
(312) 431-1700
www.whummer.com

Wells Fargo Investments LLC
420 Montgomery Street
San Francisco, California 94104
(415) 396-0318
www.wellsfargo.com

WestLB Securities, Inc.
1211 Avenue of the Americas
New York, New York 10036
(212) 852-6000
www.westlb.de

William Blair & Company LLC
222 West Adams Street
Chicago, Illinois 60606
(312) 236-1600
www.williamblair.com

Zions First National Bank
One South Main Street
Salt Lake City, Utah 84133
(801) 524-4787
www.zionsbank.com

The Ziegler Companies, Inc.
250 East Wisconsin Avenue,
   Suite 1900
Milwaukee, Wisconsin 53202
(414) 978-6400
www.ziegler.com

ACCOUNTING FIRMS

Following is a list of the names, addresses, telephone numbers and websites of the headquarters of the 25 largest U.S. certified public accounting firms, based on fiscal year 2008 net billings. These firms are organized as partnerships of the certified public accountants who work in them. CPAs, who must pass examinations to earn their licenses, mainly do corporate accounting and auditing and prepare tax returns.

Mergers and the closure of Arthur Anderson have reduced the Big Five to the Big Four. Deloitte & Touche LLP, with 2008 net billings of $11 billion, was the largest U.S. firm, followed by Ernst & Young at $8.1 billion. PricewaterhouseCoopers ranked third at $7.6 billion, followed by KPMG at $5.7 billion.

Most major corporations do business with the Big Four; their billings and revenue far outpace other accounting firms. The seventh-ranked firm, BDO Seidman, posted net billings of $620 million. The 25th-ranked firm, Amper Politziner & Mattia, reported net billings of $119.9 million.

Diversification has played a key role in the consolidation trend. Accounting firms are branching out beyond traditional auditing and accounting functions into business services such as management consulting. A number of these firms offer specialized advice for clients in financial services, health care, and telecommunications.

This list was provided by Bowman Communications, publisher of FirstAlert, Bowman's Accounting Report, 323 Wilcrest Drive SW, Atlanta, Georgia 30044 (770-972-0783) www.bowmancomm.com.

Amper Politziner & Mattia
2015 Lincoln Highway
Edison, New Jersey 08818
(732) 287-1000
www.amper.com

BKD
901 East St. Louis Street
Springfield, Missouri 65801
(417) 831-7283
www.bkd.com

Baker Tilly Virchow Krause
Ten Terrace Court
Madison, Wisconsin 53707
(608) 249-6622
www.bakertilly.com

CBiz/Mayer Hoffman McCann
6480 Rockside Woods Boulevard
   South, Suite 330
Cleveland, Ohio 44131
(216) 447-9000
www.cbiz.com

BDO Seidman
130 East Randolph Avenue, Suite 2800
Chicago, Illinois 60601
(312) 240-1236
www.bdo.com

Clifton Gunderson
1001 Innovation Drive, Suite 201
Milwaukee, Wisconsin 53226
(414) 476-1880
www.cliftoncpa.com

Crowe Horwath
One Mid-America Plaza, Suite 700
Oak Brook Terrace, Illinois 60522
(630) 574-7878
www.crowehorwath.com

Deloitte & Touche
1633 Broadway
New York, New York 10019
(212) 492-4169
www.deloitte.com

Dixon Hughes
500 Ridgefield Court
High Point, North Carolina 28802
(828) 254-2254
www.dixon-hughes.com

Eide Bailly
4310 17th Avenue South
Fargo, North Dakota 58103
(701) 239-8500
www.eidebailly.com

Eisner
750 Third Avenue
New York, New York 10017
(212) 949-8700
www.eisnerllp.com

Ernst & Young
787 Seventh Avenue
New York, New York 10019
(212) 773-1300
www.ey.com

Grant Thornton
175 West Jackson Boulevard
Chicago, Illinois 60604
(312) 602-8007
www.gt.com

J.H. Cohn
4 Becker Farm Road
Roseland, New Jersey 07068
(973) 228-3500
www.jhcohn.com

KPMG
345 Park Avenue
New York, New York 10154
(212) 758-9700
www.kpmg.com

LarsonAllen
220 South Sixth Street, Suite 300
Minneapolis, Minnesota 55402
(612) 376-4500
www.larsonallen.com

Marcum
750 Third Avenue
Melville, New York 10017
(212) 981-3000
www.marcumllp.com

Moss Adams
999 Third Avenue, Suite 3300
Seattle, Washington 98104
(206) 302-6800
www.mossadams.com

Plante & Moran
27400 Northwestern Highway
Southfield, Michigan 48037
(248) 352-2500
www.plantemoran.com

PricewaterhouseCoopers
300 Madison Avenue
New York, New York 10017
(646) 471-4000
www.pwc.com

Reznick Group
7700 Old Georgetown Road,
   Suite 400
Bethesda, Maryland 20814
(301) 652-9100
www.reznickgroup.com

Rothstein Kass & Co.
4 Becker Farm Road
Roseland, New Jersey 07068
(973) 994-6666
www.rkco.com

RSM/McGladrey & Puilen
3600 West 80th Street, Suite 500
Bloomington, Minnesota 55431
(612) 921-7724
www.mcgladrey.com

UHY Advisors
30 South Wacker Drive, Suite 2580
Chicago, Illinois 60606
(312) 578-9600
www.uhy-us.com

Weiser
135 West 50th Street
New York, New York 10020
(212) 812-7000
www.weiserllp.com

SECURITIES AND DERIVATIVES
EXCHANGES AROUND THE WORLD

These exchanges are listed alphabetically by country. Telephone numbers
and Web sites are provided for exchanges in North America and major South
American, European, Asia-Pacific, and African locations. Traded products
are listed for the most active exchanges, especially for those with a dominant
role in a particular market. For more detail about the leading exchanges, refer
to the *Dictionary* section of this book, and the exchange Web sites. Contact
information is from the World Federation of Exchanges or the exchange Web
sites.

The most active financial markets are those in the industrialized countries
of North America, Western Europe, and Japan. In these countries, there is
more regulation of securities markets, and companies have to disclose more
about their financial status; the regulation and disclosure requirements of U.S.
exchanges are by far the strictest. The more active markets are more competitive and, therefore, are characterized by narrower spreads between bid and
asked prices.

The stock markets of the less-industrialized countries offer both greater
rewards and greater risks to investors. Regulation of these markets tends to
be looser and financial disclosure rules less stringent. With less trading activity, the spreads between bid and asked prices tend to be wide. In some cases,
investment by non-nationals of the country is banned or strictly limited. Many
of these markets provide rich opportunities to participate in some of the
world's fastest growing economies, such as Taiwan and Singapore.

The growth of mutual offset agreements that allow exchanges to trade
each other's products during their respective trading hours has served to
tighten regulations where they may have been less stringent. These agreements are especially prevalent in the futures and options markets. To participate on a U.S. futures exchange, for example, a small foreign exchange would
be required to meet the regulations of the U.S. Commodity Futures Trading
Commission.

The shares of some prominent companies listed on these and other
exchanges are also traded in the United States as American Depositary
Receipts (ADRs). For investors who are interested in participating in these
foreign markets, but do not have the time or expertise to do so directly, there
are a number of mutual funds, both closed-end and open-end, specializing in
buying securities in markets around the world.

Argentina
Bolsa de Comercio de Buenos Aires
(54) 11 4316 7000
www.bcba.sba.com.ar

Armenia
NASDAQ OMX – Armenia
(374) 1 54 3324
www.nasdaqomx.am

Australia
Australian Securities Exchange
 (ASX)
(61) 2 9338 000
www.asx.com.au
*Equities, derivatives, fixed income
securities*

Austria
Wiener Börse AG
(43) 1 531 65 0
www.wienerboerse.at
Stocks, indices, futures and options

Belgium
Euronext-Brussels
(32) 2 509 1211
www.euronext.com
*Stocks, stock options, index futures/
options*

Bermuda
Bermuda Stock Exchange
(441) 292 7212
www.bsx.com

Brazil
BM&FBovespa S.A.
(55) 11 2565 4000
www.bmfbovespa.com.br
*Agricultural futures/options; gold
futures; index, exchange rate and
interest rate futures; flexible options;
swaps*

Canada
Bourse de Montreal (TMX Group)
(514) 514 871 2424
www.m-x.ca
*Equity options, interest rate deriva-
tives, index derivatives*

Toronto Stock Exchange
  (TMX Group)
(416) 947-4670
www.tsx.com
*Senior equities; emerging companies;
natural gas and electricity contracts*

Chile
Bolsa de Comercio de Santiago
(56) 2 399 3000
www.bolsadesantiago.com
*Stocks, bonds, equity futures/options,
currency and precious metals*

China
Shanghai Stock Exchange
(86) 21 6880 8888
www.sse.com.cn
Stocks

Shenzhen Stock Exchange
(86) 755 2591 8545
www.szsc.org.cn
Stocks

Colombia
Bolsa de Valores de Colombia
  (BVC)
(57) 1 313 9800
www.bvc.com.co
*Stocks, foreign exchange, derivative
and fixed income*

Cyprus
Cyprus Stock Exchange (CSE)
(357) 22 71 2300
www.cse.com.cy

Denmark
NASDAQ OMX – Copenhagen
(45) 3393 3366
www.nasdaqomx.com

Egypt
The Egyptian Exchange (EGX)
(20) 2 2392 1447
www.zawya.com

Estonia
NASDAQ OMX – Tallinn
(372) 640-8800
www.nasdaqomx.com

Finland
Helsinki Stock Exchange
(358) 9 616 671
www.hex.com
Securities, derivatives

France
Euronext-Paris
(33) 1 49 27 10 00
www.euronext.com
Stocks, derivatives

Germany
Deutsche Börse AG
(49) 69 2111 1670
www.deutsche-boerse.com
Securities and derivatives

Greece
Athens Exchange S.A.
(30) 210 336 6800
www.ase.gr
Stocks and derivatives

Hong Kong
Hong Kong Exchanges & Clearing
(852) 2522 1122
www.hkex.com.hk
Stocks, bonds, stock and index
futures/options, interest rate, and
fixed income

Hungary
Budapest Stock Exchange
(361) 429-6700
www.bse.hu

Iceland
NASDAQ OMX – Iceland
(354) 525 2800
www.nasdaqomx.com

India
Bombay Stock Exchange Ltd.
(91) 22 227 21233
www.bseindia.com
Stocks, debt instruments, derivatives

National Stock Exchange
    of India Ltd.
(91) 22 2659 8100 8114
www.nseindia.com
Equities, derivatives, ETFs

Indonesia
Indonesia Stock Exchange
(62) 21 515 0515
www.idy.co.id

Iran
Stock Exchange of Tehran
(98) 21 667 19535
www.tse.ir

Ireland
Irish Stock Exchange
(353) 1 617 4200
www.ise.ie

Israel
Tel Aviv Stock Exchange
(972) 3 567 7411
www.tase.co.il

Italy
Borsa Italiana SpA
(39) 02 724 261
www.borsaitaliana.it
Stocks, fixed income products,
derivatives

Japan
Osaka Securities Exchange
(81) 6 4706 0800
www.ose.or.jp
Stocks and derivatives

Tokyo Stock Exchange Group
(81) 3 3666 0141
www.tse.or.jp
Stocks, bonds, futures and options

Jordan
Amman Stock Exchange
(962) 6 566 4109
www.ase.com.jo

Korea
Korea Exchange
(82) 51 662 2000
www.krx.co.kr
Stocks, bonds, financial futures/
options, currency and gold futures

Latvia
NASDAQ OMX – Riga
(371) 6 721 2431
www.nasdaqomx.com

Lithuania
NASDAQ OMX – Vilnius
(370) 5 272 3871
www.nasdaqomx.com

Luxembourg
Bourse de Luxembourg
(352) 47 79 36-1
www.bourse.lu

Malaysia
Bursa Malaysia
(603) 2034 7000
www.klse.com.my

Malta
Malta Stock Exchange
(356) 2124 4051
www.borzamalta.com.mt

Mauritius
The Stock Exchange of Mauritius
(230) 212 9541
www.stockexchangeofmauritius.com

Mexico
Bolsa Mexicana de Valores
(52) 555 726 6600
www.bmv.com.mx

Netherlands
Euronext-Amsterdam
(31) 20 550 4444
www.euronext.com
Stocks, derivatives

New Zealand
New Zealand Exchange Ltd.
(64) 4 472 7599
www.nzx.com

Norway
Oslo Bors
(47) 22 341 700
www.oslobors.no

Peru
Bolsa de Valores de Lima
(51) 1 619 3333
www.bvl.com.pe

Philippines
Philippine Stock Exchange
(632) 688-7600
www.pse.com.ph

Poland
Warsaw Stock Exchange
(48) 22 628 3232
www.wse.com.pl

Portugal
Euronext-Lisbon
(351) 21 790 00 00
www.euronext.com

Russia
Moscow Interbank Currency
  Exchange (MICEX)
(7 095) 234 48 11
www.micex.com
*Foreign exchange, government
bonds, equities, corporate bonds,
derivatives and commodities*

Saudi Arabia
Saudi Stock Exchange
(966) 2 664 1264
www.gulfbase.com

Singapore
Singapore Exchange (SGX)
(65) 6236 8888
www.sgx.com
Securities, derivatives

Slovenia
Ljubljana Stock Exchange
(386) 1 471 0211
www.ljse.si

South Africa
JSE Ltd.
(27 11) 520 7314
www.jse.co.za

Spain
Bolsas y Mercados Españoles
(34) 91 709 5000
www.bolsasymercados.es
*Also operates Bolsa de Barcelona,
Bolsa de Bilbao, Bolsa de Madrid,
and Bolsa de Valencia*

Sri Lanka
Colombo Stock Exchange
(941) 1244 6581
www.cse.lk

Switzerland
SIX Swiss Exchange
(41) 58 854 5454
www.six-swiss-exchange.com
*Stocks, bonds, ETFs, repurchase
agreements*

Taiwan
Taiwan Stock Exchange
(886) 2 8101 3101
www.tse.com.tw

Thailand
Stock Exchange of Thailand
(0) 2229 2222
www.set.or.th

Turkey
Istanbul Stock Exchange
(90 212) 298 21 00
www.ise.org

United Kingdom
London Stock Exchange
(44) 20 7797 1000
www.londonstockexchange.com

United States of America
American Stock Exchange (AMEX)
11 Wall Street
New York, New York 10005
(212) 656-3000
www.nyse.com
Equities, options, ETFs, HOLDRs,
structured products

.Boston Options Exchange
100 Franklin Street
Boston, Massachusetts 02110
(866) 768-8845
www.bostonoptions.com

Chicago Board Options Exchange
  (CBOE)
400 South LaSalle Street
Chicago, Illinois 60605
(312) 786-5600
www.cboe.com
Options: equity, index, ETFs,
HOLDRs, interest rates; indices,
LEAPs, FLEX

Chicago Mercantile Exchange (CME)
20 South Wacker Drive
Chicago, Illinois 60606
(312) 930-1000
www.cmegroup.com
Interest rate, equity, foreign
exchange, agricultural commodity
and alternative investment futures
and options on futures

Chicago Stock Exchange (CHX)
One Financial Place
440 South LaSalle Street
Chicago, Illinois 60605
(312) 663-2222
www.chx.com
Equities

Kansas City Board of Trade
  (KCBT)
4800 Main Street, Suite 303
Kansas City, Missouri 64112
(816) 753-7500
www.kcbt.com
Wheat futures and options

Minneapolis Grain Exchange (MGE)
130 Grain Exchange Building
400 South Fourth Street
Minneapolis, Minnesota 55415
(612) 321-7101
www.mgex.com
Wheat futures and options; cash
grain market

NASDAQ OMX
One Liberty Plaza
165 Broadway
New York, New York 10006
(212) 401-8700
www.nasdaqomx.com
Stocks, derivatives, debt, commodities

National Stock Exchange (formerly
  Cincinnati Stock Exchange)
101 Hudson Street
Jersey City, New Jersey 07302
(201) 499-3700
www.nsx.com
Equities

Intercontinental Exchange
2 World Financial Center
New York, New York 10282
(212) 618-2100
www.theice.com
Cocoa, sugar, coffee, cotton, ethanol,
pulp; currency pairs, US dollar index,
cross-rate currency futures/options

International Securities Exchange
65 Broad Street
New York, New York 10004
(212) 943-2400
www.ise.com
Options, ETFs

New York Stock Exchange (NYSE)
11 Wall Street
New York, New York 10005
(212) 656-3000
www.nyse.com
Stocks, bonds, indices, options

3. MUTUAL FUNDS AND ETFs

MUTUAL FUNDS

The following is a list of the names, addresses, telephone numbers and web sites of American mutual fund families. Most families offer more than one fund. In order to obtain information about the individual funds offered by a fund family, consult your local newspaper listings, which should group together all of the funds in a fund family.

The mutual fund families on this list are both open- and closed-end. The difference between open- and closed-end fund families is that the former create new shares of their funds whenever customers add money to those funds, while the latter issue a fixed number of shares per fund.

AARP Financial Inc. (open-end)
Two Highland Drive, Suite 202
Tewksbury, MA 01876
(800) 958-6457
www.aarpfunds.com

Aberdeen Asset Management, Inc.
 (open-end and closed-end)
1735 Market Street, 30th Floor
Philadelphia, Pennsylvania 19103
(800) 667-9231
www.aberdeen-asset.com

Absolute Investment Advisors LLC
 (open-end)
350 Lincoln Street, Suite 216
Hingham, Massachusetts 02043
(888) 992-2765

Abundance Technologies Inc.
 (open-end)
5955 Deerfield Boulevard
Mason, Ohio 454040
(866) 780-0357

Academy Asset Management LLC
 (open-end)
1735 Market Street
Philadelphia, Pennsylvania 19103
(877) 386-3890

Acadian Asset Management Inc.
 (open-end)
One Post Office Square, 20th Floor
Boston, Massachusetts 02109
(866) 226-6161
www.acadian-asset.com

Accrued Equities Inc. (open-end)
150 Broadhollow Road
Melville, New York 11747
(631) 423-7373

Adams Asset Investors LLC
 (open-end)
8150 North Central Expressway,
 Suite 101
Dallas, Texas 75206
(800) 704-6072

Adams Express Company
 (closed-end)
Seven St. Paul Street, Suite 1140
Baltimore, MD 21202
(410) 752-5900
www.adamsexpress.com

Adirondack Research &
 Management (open-end)
26 Vly Road
Albany, New York 12205
(518) 690-0470

Advance Capital Management Inc.
 (open-end)
One Towne Square, Suite 444
Southfield, MI 48076
(800) 345-4783
www.advancecapitalonline.com

Advent Capital Management LLC
(closed-end)
1065 Avenue of the Americas,
31st Floor
New York, New York 10018
(212) 482-1600
www.adventcap.com

AdvisorOne Funds (open-end)
4020 South 147th Street
Omaha, NE 68137
(866) 811-0225
www.advisoronefunds.com

AdvisorShares Investments LLC
(open-end)
3 Bethesda Metro Center, Suite 700
Bethesda, Maryland 20814
(877) 843-3831

Aegis Financial Corporation
(open-end)
1100 North Glebe Road, Suite 1040
Arlington, VA 22201
(800) 528-3780
www.aegisfunds.com

**AFBA 5 Star Investment
Management Company**
(open-end)
900 North Washington Street
Alexandria, Virginia 22314
(800) 243-9865
www.afbafivestarfunds.com

AH Lisante Capital Growth LLC
(open-end)
608 Fifth Avenue, Suite 301
New York, New York 10020
(800) 441-7031

**AIG Global Investment
Corporation** (open-end)
70 Pine Street, 20th Floor
New York, New York 10270
(610) 254-1000

Akre Capital Management LLC
(open-end)
2 West Marshall Street
Middleburg, Virginia 20117
(877) 862-9556

Akros Capital LLC (open-end)
230 Park Avenue, Suite 453
New York, New York 10169
(877) 257-6748

Al Frank Asset Management Inc.
(open-end)
32392 Coast Highway, Suite 260
Laguna Beach, California 92651
(888) 263-6443
www.alfrankfund.com

Allegiant Funds (open-end)
200 Public Square, 5th Floor
Cleveland, Ohio 44114
(800) 622-3863
www.allegiantfunds.com

AllianceBernstein LP (open-end
and closed-end)
1345 Avenue of the Americas
New York, New York 10105
(800) 221-5672
www.alliancebernstein.com

**Allianz Global Investment Fund
Management LLC**
(open-end and closed-end)
1345 Avenue of the Americas
New York, New York 10105
(800) 426-0107
www.allianzinvestors.com

Allied Asset Investors Inc.
(open-end)
745 McClintock Drive, Suite 314
Burr Ridge, Illinois 60527
(630) 789-0453

AlphaMark Advisors LLC
(open-end)
250 Grandview Drive, Suite 175
Fort Mitchell, Kentucky 41017
(866) 420-3350

AlphaStream Portfolios Inc.
(open-end)
2625 Cumberland Parkway, Suite 220
Atlanta, Georgia 30339
(877) 900-6565

Alpine Woods Capital Investors Inc.
(open-end and closed-end)
1625 Broadway, Suite 2200
Denver, Colorado 80202
(800) 617-7610
www.alpinecef.com

ALPS Advisors Inc. (open-end and
closed-end)
1290 Broadway, Suite 1100
Denver, Colorado 80203
(800) 241-1850
www.all-starfunds.com

**Ambassador Capital Management
LLC** (open-end)
500 Griswold Street, Suite 2800
Detroit, Michigan 48226
(800) 992-0444

American Beacon Advisors Inc.
(open-end)
4151 Amon Carter Road
Fort Worth, Texas 76155
(800) 658-5811
www.aafunds.com

**American Century Investment
Management Inc.** (open-end)
4500 Main Street
Kansas City, MO 64111
(800) 345-2021
www.americancentury.com

American Funds (open-end)
333 South Hope Street, 52nd Floor
Los Angeles, CA 90071
(800) 421-0180
www.americanfunds.com

**American Independence Financial
Services LLC** (open-end)
335 Madison Avenue
New York, New York 10017
(888) 266-8787

**American Money Management
LLC** (open-end)
14249 Rancho Santa Fe Farms Road
Rancho Santa Fe, California 92097
(866) 663-8023

**American Trust Investment
Advisors** (open-end)
One Court Street
Lebanon, NH 03766
(603) 448-6415
www.amertrust.com

Amerisrael Capital Management
(open-end)
207 East 83rd Street
New York, New York 10028
(866) 745-5955

Ameristock Corporation
(open-end)
1320 Harbor Bay Parkway, Suite 145
Alameda, CA 94502
(925) 376-3490
www.ameristock.com

Ameritor Financial Corporation
(open-end)
4400 Macarthur Boulevard NW,
Suite 301
Washington, D.C. 20007
(202) 625-6000

**America First Capital Management
LLC** (open-end)
8150 Sierra College Boulevard,
Suite 290
Roseville, California 95661
(877) 217-8363

Analytic Investors LLC
(open-end)
500 South Grand Avenue, 23rd Floor
Los Angeles, CA 90071
(610) 254-1000
www.aninvestor.com

**Anchor Capital Management Group
LLC** (open-end)
16140 Sand Canyon Avenue,
Suite 101
Irvine, California 92618
(800) 797-9577

Ancora Advisors LLC (open-end)
200 Auburn Drive, Suite 300
Cleveland, Ohio 44122
(866) 626-2672

**Appleton Group Wealth
Management** (open-end)
100 West Lawrence Street,
Third Floor
Appleton, Wisconsin 54911
(866) 993-7767
www.appletongroupfunds.com

AQ Johnson & Co. Inc.
(open-end)
7855 Ivanhoe Avenue, Suite 210
La Jolla, California 92037
(800) 595-2877

AQR Capital Management LLC
  (open-end)
Two Greenwich Plaza, 3rd Floor
Greenwich, Connecticut 06830
(866) 290-2688

Aquila Investment Management
  (open-end)
380 Madison Avenue, Suite 2300
New York, NY 10017
(800) 437-1020
www.aquilafunds.com

Archer Investment Corporation
  (open-end)
9000 Keystone Crossing, Suite 630
Indianapolis, IN 46240
(800) 238-7701
www.thearcherfunds.com

Ariel Investments LLC (open-end)
200 East Randolph Drive
Chicago, Illinois 60601
(800) 292-7435
www.arielmutualfunds.com

Arnold Investment Counsel Inc.
  (open-end)
700 North Water Street
Milwaukee, Wisconsin 53202
(800) 443-6544

Arrow Investment Advisors LP
  (open-end)
2943 Olney-Sandy Spring Road,
  Suite A
Olney, Maryland 20832
(877) 277-6933

Artio Global Management LLC
  (open-end)
330 Madison Avenue
New York, New York 10017
(800) 387-6977

Artisan Partners LP (open-end)
875 East Wisconsin Avenue,
  Suite 800
Milwaukee, Wisconsin 53202
(800) 344-1770
www.artisanfunds.com

ASA Limited (closed-end)
11 Summer Street
Buffalo, New York 14209
(973) 377-3535
www.asaltd.com

Ascentia Capital Partners LLC
  (open-end)
9408 Double R Boulevard, Suite B
Reno, Nevada 89521
(866) 506-7390

**Asset Management Group of Bank
  of Hawaii** (open-end)
130 Merchant Street
Honolulu, Hawaii 96073
(212) 697-6666

**Aster Investment Management
  Company Inc.** (open-end)
60 East Sir Francis Drake Boulevard
Larkspur, California 94939
(800) 446-6662

**Aston Asset Management
  Company** (open-end)
120 North LaSalle Street, 25th Floor
Chicago, Illinois 60602
(800) 992-8151

Auxier Asset Management LLC
  (open-end)
5285 Meadows Road, Suite 333
Lake Oswego, Oregon 97035
(877) 328-9437
www.auxierfunds.com

Aviemore Asset Management LLC
  (open-end)
20 Phelps Road
Old Chatham, New York 12136
(800) 239-9136

Azzad Asset Management Inc.
  (open-end)
3141 Fairview Park Drive, Suite 460
Falls Church, VA 22042
(888) 350-3369
www.azzadfund.com

Babson Capital Management LLC
  (closed-end)
1500 Main Street
Springfield, Massachusetts 01115
(413) 226-1516
www.babsoncapital.com/mci

BAMCO Inc. (open-end)
767 Fifth Avenue, 49th Floor
New York, New York 10153
(212) 583-2100

Barclays Global Fund Advisors
(open-end)
400 Howard Street
San Francisco, CA 94105
(877) 244-1544
www.barclaysglobal.com

Baring Asset Management (Asia)
(closed-end)
15 Queens Road Central
Hong Kong
+852 2841 1411
www.asiapacificfund.com

Barrett Associates Inc. (open-end)
90 Park Avenue
New York, New York 10016
(877) 363-6333
www.barrettassociates.com

Baxter Financial Corporation
(open-end)
1200 North Federal Highway,
Suite 424
Boca Raton, Florida 33432
(800) 749-9933

BB&T Asset Management Inc.
(open-end)
434 Fayetteville Street
Raleigh, North Carolina 27601
(800) 228-1872
www.bbtfunds.com

Becker Capital Management Inc.
(open-end)
1211 SW 5th Avenue, Suite 2185
Portland, OR 97204
(800) 551-3998
www.beckervaluefunds.com

Beck Mack & Oliver LLC
(open-end)
360 Madison Avenue
New York, New York 10179
(207) 879-0001

Bell Investment Advisors Inc.
(open-end)
1111 Broadway, Suite 1630
Oakland, California 94607
(888) 592-2355

Berkshire Capital Holdings Inc.
(open-end)
475 Milan Drive
San Jose, California 95134
(877) 526-0707
www.berkshirefunds.com

Bertolet Capital LLC (open-end)
1414 Sixth Avenue, Suite 900
New York, New York 10019
(877) 369-3705

Bessemer Investment Management
LLC (open-end)
630 Fifth Avenue
New York, New York 10111
(800) 607-2200

Bhirud Associates Inc. (open-end)
6 Thorndal Circle, Suite 205
Darien, Connecticut 06820
(203) 977-1521

Biondo Investment Advisors
(open-end)
544 Routes 6 & 209
Milford, Pennsylvania 18337
(800) 672-9152

Birmiwal Asset Management Inc.
(open-end)
5270 Highland Drive
Bellevue, WA 98006
(800) 417-5525
www.birmiwal.com

Bishop Street Capital Management
(open-end)
999 Bishop Street
Honolulu, Hawaii 96813
(800) 262-9565
www.bishopstreetfunds.com

BlackRock Advisors (open-end and
closed-end)
40 East 52nd Street
New York, New York 10022
(800) 441-7762
www.blackrock.com

Blackstone Asia Advisors LLC
(closed-end)
345 Park Avenue, 32nd Floor
New York, New York 10154
(866) 800-8933
www.blackstone.com

Blue Chip Value Fund (closed-end)
1225 17th Street, 26th Floor
Denver, CO 80202
(800) 624-4190
www.blu.com

Bogle Investment Management LP
(open-end)
2310 Washington Street, Suite 310
Newton Lowe, Massachusetts 02462
(877) 264-5346
www.boglefunds.com

**Boston Trust Investment
Management Inc.** (open-end)
One Beacon Street, 23rd Floor
Boston, MA 02108
(800) 282-8782
www.bostontrust.com

Boulder Investment Advisors LLC
(closed-end)
2344 Spruce Street, Suite A
Boulder, CO 80302
(303) 444-0426
www.boulderfunds.net

Boyar Asset Management Inc.
(open-end)
35 East 21st Street
New York, New York 10010
(513) 629-2050

Bragg Financial Advisors Inc.
(open-end)
1031 South Caldwell Street,
Suite 200
Charlotte, North Carolina 28203
(440) 922-0066

Brandes Investment Partners LP
(open-end)
11988 El Camino Road, Suite 500
San Diego, California 92130
(800) 331-2979
www.brandes.com

Brazos Capital Management LP
(open-end)
5949 Sherry Lane
Dallas, Texas 75225
(800) 426-9157
www.brazosfund.com

Brick Asset Management Inc.
(open-end)
1700 California Street, Suite 335
San Francisco, California 94109
(888) 463-3957

**Bridges Investment Management
Inc.** (open-end)
8401 West Dodge Road
Omaha, NE 68114
(402) 397-4700
www.bridgesfund.com

**Bridgeway Capital Management
Inc.** (open-end)
5815 Kirby Drive, Suite 518
Houston, Texas 77005
(713) 661-3500
www.bridgewayfund.com

Brown Brothers Harriman
(open-end)
140 Broadway
New York, New York 10005
(800) 625-5759

Bruce & Company Inc. (open-end)
20 North Wacker Drive, Suite 2414
Chicago, Illinois 60606
(800) 872-7823
www.thebrucefund.com

Bryce Capital Management LLC
(open-end)
2 Thornell Road
Pittsford, New York 14534
(866) 622-7923

Buffalo Mutual Funds (open-end)
615 East Michigan Street
Milwaukee, Wisconsin 53202
(800) 492-8332
www.buffalofunds.com

Bull Path Capital Management LLC
(open-end)
150 East 52nd Street, 31st Floor
New York, New York 10022
(888) 899-2726

Bullfinch open-end)
1370 Pittsford Mendon Road
Mendon, New York 14506
(888) 285-5346
www.bullfinchfund.com

Burnham Asset Management Corporation (open-end)
1325 Avenue of the Americas
New York, New York 10019
(212) 262-3100
www.burnhamfunds.com

C & O Funds Advisor Inc.
(open-end)
5185 Peachtree Parkway, Suite 3270
Norcross, Georgia 30092
(678) 533-7850

Calamos Advisors LLC (closed-end)
2020 Calamos Court
Naperville, IL 60563
(800) 582-6959
www.calamos.com

California Investment Funds
(open-end)
44 Montgomery Street, Suite 2100
San Francisco, California 94104
(800) 225-8778
www.caltrust.com

Callahan Credit Union Financial Services (open-end)
1001 Connecticut Avenue
Washington, D.C. 20036
(212) 902-0800

Calvert Funds (open-end)
4550 Montgomery Avenue,
Suite 1000 North
Bethesda, MD 20814
(800) 368-2748
www.calvert.com

Cambiar Investors LLC (open-end)
2401 East Second Avenue
Denver, CO 80206
(866) 777-8227
www.cambiar.com

Capital Management Associates Inc.
(open-end)
140 Broadway
New York, New York 10005
(252) 972-9922

Capital Southwest Corporation
(closed-end)
12900 Preston Road, Suite 700
Dallas, Texas 75230
(972) 233-8242
www.capitalsouthwest.com

Capstone Asset Management Company (open-end)
5847 San Felipe, Suite 4100
Houston, Texas 77057
(800) 262-6631
www.capstonefinancial.com

Catalyst Funds (open-end)
630 Fitzwatertown Road
Willow Grove, Pennsylvania 19090
(866) 447-4228

Causeway Capital Management LLC (open-end)
1111 Santa Monica Boulevard
Los Angeles, California 90025
(866) 947-7000
www.causewayfunds.com

Cavanal Hill Funds (open-end)
One Williams Center
Tulsa, Oklahoma 74192
(800) 762-7085

CEF Advisors Inc. (closed-end)
11 Hanover Square, 12th Floor
New York, New York 10005
(212) 344-6316
www.foxbycorp.com

Central Securities Corporation
(closed-end)
630 Fifth Avenue, Suite 820
New York, New York 10111
(212) 698-2020
www.centralsecurities.com

Century Capital Management
(open-end)
100 Federal Street, 29th Floor
Boston, MA 02110
(800) 321-1928
www.centuryfunds.com

Champlain Investment Partners LLC (open-end)
346 Shelburne Road
Burlington, Vermont 05401
(866) 773-3238
www.cipvt.com

Changing Parameters LLC (open-end)
250 Oak Grove Avenue, Suite A
Menlo Park, California 94025
(866) 618-3456

Charles Schwab Investment Management Inc. (open-end)
101 Montgomery Street
San Francisco, California 94104
(800) 435-4000

Chartwell Investment Partners LLP
(closed-end)
1235 Westlakes Drive, Suite 400
Berwyn, PA 19312
(610) 296-1400
www.chartwellip.com

Chase Investment Counsel Corporation
300 Preston Avenue, Suite 403
Charlottesville, Virginia 22902
(888) 861-7556
www.chaseinv.com

Check Capital Management Inc.
(open-end)
575 Anton Boulevard, Suite 570
Costa Mesa, California 92626
(877) 593-8637

Cheswold Lane Asset Management LLC (open-end)
100 Front Street, Suite 960
West Conshohocken, Pennsylvania 19428
(800) 771-4701

City National Asset Management Inc. (open-end)
400 North Roxbury Drive
Beverly Hills, California 90210
(312) 444-6200

Claremont Investment Partners LLC (open-end)
104 Summit Avenue
Summit, New Jersey 07902
(908) 273-5440

Claymore Advisors LLC
(open-end and closed-end)
2455 Corporate West Drive
Lisle, IL 60532
(800) 345-7999
www.adventclaymore.com

Clipper Funds (open-end)
2949 East Elvira Road
Tucson, Arizona 85706
(800) 432-2504
www.clipperfund.com

Clough Capital Partners LP
(closed-end)
1290 Broadway, Suite 1100
Denver, CO 80203
(877) 256-8445
www.cloughglobal.com

CMG Capital Management Group Inc. (open-end)
150 North Radnor-Chester Road, Suite A150
Radnor, Pennsylvania 19087
(866) 264-9456

CNL Fund Advisors Company
(open-end)
450 South Orange Avenue, 10th Floor
Orlando, Florida 32801
(888) 890-8934

Cohen & Steers Capital Management Inc.
(open-end and closed-end)
280 Park Avenue
New York, NY 10017
(212) 832-3232
www.cohenandsteers.com

Columbia Funds (open-end)
One Financial Center
Boston, Massachusetts 02111
(800) 345-6611
www.columbiafunds.com

Commerce Investment Advisors
(open-end)
8000 Forsyth Boulevard
St. Louis, Missouri 63105
(800) 995-6365
www.commercefunds.com

Commonwealth Capital Management LLC (open-end)
8730 Stony Point Parkway
Richmond, Virginia 22235
(804) 285-8211
www.commonwealthfunds.com

Community Capital Management LLC (open-end)
2500 Weston Road, Suite 101
Weston, Florida 33331
(877) 272-1977

Compass Advisory Group LLC
(open-end)
213 Overlook Circle, Suite A-1
Brentwood, Tennessee 37027
(888) 934-4367

Concorde Investment Management
(open-end)
5430 LBJ Freeway
Dallas, TX 75240
(800) 294-1699

Conestoga Capital Advisors LLC
(open-end)
259 North Radnor-Chester Road
Radnor, PA 19087
(800) 320-7790
www.conestogacapital.com

**Congress Asset Management
Company** (open-end)
2 Seaport Lane
Boston, Massachusetts 02210
(888) 688-1299

**Congressional Effect Management
LLC** (open-end)
420 Lexington Avenue, Suite 601
New York, New York 10170
(888) 333-4233

**Consulting Group Cap Market
Funds** (open-end)
388 Greenwich Street, 22nd Floor
New York, New York 10013
(212) 816-6000

**Cook & Bynum Capital
Management LLC** (open-end)
2204 Lakeshore Drive, Suite 218
Birmingham, Alabama 35209
(877) 839-2629

Cookson Pierce & Company
(open-end)
555 Grand Street, Suite 380
Pittsburgh, Pennsylvania 15219
(866) 412-2673

Copley Financial Services Inc.
(open-end)
P.O. Box 3287
Fall River, Massachusetts 02722
(508) 674-8459

**Corbyn Investment Management
Inc.** (open-end)
2330 West Joppa Road
Lutherville, Maryland 21093
(410) 823-5353

CornerCap Investment Counsel Inc.
(open-end)
1355 Peachtree Street NE
Atlanta, Georgia 30309
(888) 813-8637
www.cornercap.com

Country Trust Bank (open-end)
1705 North Towanda Avenue
Bloomington, Illinois 61702
(800) 245-2100
www.countryinvestment.com

Cramer Rosenthal Moglynn LLC
(open-end)
520 Madison Avenue
New York, New York 10022
(800) 276-2883

Crawford Investment Counsel Inc.
(open-end)
100 Galleria Parkway, Suite 980
Atlanta, Georgia 30339
(800) 431-1716

**Credit Suisse Asset Management
LLC** (open-end and closed-end)
466 Lexington Avenue
New York, NY 10017
(800) 222-8977
www.credit-suisse.com

Critical Math Advisors LLC
(open-end)
29 Emmons Drive, Suite A-20
Princeton, New Jersey 08540
(866) 263-9260

Croft-Leominster Inc. (open-end)
300 Water Street
Baltimore, MD 21202
(440) 922-0066
www.croftleo.com

CSI Capital Management Inc.
(open-end)
600 California Street, 18th Floor
San Francisco, California 94108
(804) 285-8211

CS Mckee LP (open-end)
One Gateway Center
Pittsburgh, Pennsylvania 15222
(610) 254-1000

Cullen Capital Management LLC
(open-end)
645 Fifth Avenue
New York, NY 10022
(877) 485-8586
www.cullenfunds.com

CUNA (open-end)
2000 Heritage Way
Waverly, Iowa 50677
(212) 632-6400

Cutler Investment Counsel LLC
(open-end)
525 East Bigham Knoll, Suite 100
Jacksonville, Oregon 97530
(888) 288-5374
www.cutler.com

Dai Investment Company LLC
(open-end)
235 Montgomery Street, Suite 1-49
San Francisco, California 94104
(866) 455-3863

Daiwa Securities Trust Company
(closed-end)
One Evertrust Plaza, 9th Floor
Jersey City, NJ 07302
(201) 333-7300
www.daiwast.com

Dalton Granier Hartman Maher &
Co. LLC (open-end)
565 Fifth Avenue, Suite 2101
New York, New York 10017
(800) 653-2839

Davenport & Company (open-end)
901 East Cary Street
Richmond, Virginia 23219
(800) 281-3217
www.davenportllc.com

Davidson Investment Advisors Inc.
(open-end)
8 Third Street North
Great Falls, Montana 59401
(877) 332-0529

Davis Selected Advisors LP
(open-end)
2949 East Elvira Road, Suite 101
Tucson, Arizona 85756
(800) 243-1575

DB Commodity Services LLC
(open-end)
60 Wall Street
New York, New York 10005
(877) 369-4617

Dean Investment Associates LLC
(open-end)
2480 Kettering Tower
Dayton, OH 45423
(888) 899-8343
www.chdean.com

Delaware Investments (open-end
and closed-end)
2005 Market Street
Philadelphia, PA 19103
(800) 523-1918
(800) 362-FUND
www.delawarefunds.com

Denver Advisors Inc. (closed-end)
1225 17th Street
Denver, Colorado 80202
(303) 312-5100
www.blu.com

Destination Capital Management
(open-end)
200 North Main Street
Walnut Creek, Oregon 94596
(866) 738-1128

D.F. Dent and Company Inc.
(open-end)
2 East Read Street, Floor Six
Baltimore, Maryland 21202
(866) 233-3368

Diamond Hill Capital Management
(closed-end)
315 John H. McConnell Boulevard,
Suite 200
Columbus, OH 43215
(614) 255-3333
www.diamond-hill.com

Dimensional Fund Advisers LP
1299 Ocean Avenue, 11th Floor
Santa Monica, California 90401
(310) 395-8005

**Dinsmore Capital Management
Company** (closed-end)
15 Madison Avenue
Morristown, New Jersey 07960
(973) 631-1177
www.bancroftfund.com

Dividend Capital Investments LLC
(closed-end)
518 17th Street, 17th Floor
Suite 1700
Denver, CO 80202
(866) 324-7348
www.dividendcapital.com

Dividend Growth Advisors LLC
(open-end)
58 Riverwalk Boulevard
Ridgeland, South Carolina 29936
(317) 917-7000
www.dividendgrowthadvisors.com

Dodge & Cox (open-end)
555 California Street
San Francisco, California 94104
(800) 621-3979
www.dodgeandcox.com

Domini Social Investments LLC
(open-end)
536 Broadway, 7th Floor
New York, New York 10012
(800) 582-6757
www.domini.com

Dreman Value Management LLC
(open-end)
Harborside Financial Plaza 10,
Suite 880
Jersey City, New Jersey 07311
(800) 247-1014

Dreyfus Corporation (closed-end)
200 Park Avenue
New York, New York 10166
(800) 645-6561
www.dreyfus.com

Driehaus Capital Management LLC
(open-end)
5 East Erie Street
Chicago, Illinois 60611
(800) 560-6111
www.driehaus.com

**Duff & Phelps Investment
Management Company**
(closed-end)
200 South Wacker Drive
Chicago, Illinois 60606
(800) 864-0629
www.ducfund.com

DSM Capital Partners LLC
320 East Main Street
Mount Kisco, New York 10549
(877) 862-9555

DundeeWealth US LP
1160 West Swedesford Road,
Suite 140
Berwyn, Pennsylvania 19312
(888) 572-0968

**Dunham & Associates Investment
Counsel Inc.** (open-end)
10251 Vista Sorrento Parkway,
Suite 200
San Diego, California 92121
(888) 338-6426
www.dunham.com

Dupree & Company Inc.
(open-end)
125 South Mill Street
Lexington, Kentucky 40567
(859) 254-7741
www.dupree-funds.com

DWS Investments (open-end)
222 South Riverside Plaza
Chicago, Illinois 60606
(800) 621-1048
www.dws-scudder.com

Eagle Asset Management Inc.
(open-end)
880 Carillon Parkway
St. Petersburg, Florida 33716
(727) 573-8193
www.philadelphiafund.com

Earnest Partners Inc. (open-end)
1180 Peachtree Street NE
Atlanta, Georgia 30309
(800) 525-3863
www.earnestpartners.com

Eaton Vance Management
 (open-end and closed-end)
255 State Street
Boston, Massachusetts
(800) 262-1122
www.eatonvance.com

Edgemoor Capital Management Inc.
 (open-end)
1900 M Street NW, Suite 600
Washington, D.C. 20036
(866) 884-5968

Edgewood Management LLC
 (open-end)
350 Park Avenue, 18th Floor
New York, New York 10022
(800) 791-4226

Emerald Research Corporation
 (open-end)
2160 Highway 88
Brick, New Jersey 08724
(732) 842-3465

Emerging Global Shares
 (open-end)
1290 Broadway, Suite 1100
Denver, Colorado 80203
(888) 800-4347

Epoch Investment Partners Inc.
 (open-end)
640 Fifth Avenue, 18th Floor
New York, New York 10019
(800) 527-9525

EquiTrust Investment Management
 Service (open-end)
5400 University Avenue
West Des Moines, Iowa 50266
(877) 860-2904
www.equitrust.com

Equus Capital Management
 Corporation (closed-end)
2727 Allen Parkway
Houston, Texas 77019
(713) 529-0900
www.equuscap.com

Evergreen Investment Services Inc.
 (open-end and closed-end)
P.O. Box 8400
Boston, Massachusetts 02266
(800) 343-2898
www.evergreeninvestments.com

Eulav Asset Management LLC
 (open-end)
220 East 42nd Street
New York, New York 10017
(212) 907-1500

Fairholme Asset Management LLC
 (open-end)
4400 Biscayne Boulevard, 9th Floor
Miami, Florida 3137
(440) 922-0066

FAF Advisors Inc. (open-end and
 closed-end)
800 Nicollet Mall
Minneapolis, Minnesota 55402
(800) 677-3863
www.firstamericanfunds.com

FBR Fund Advisors Inc. (open-end)
1001 Nineteenth Street North
Pittsburgh, Pennsylvania 15222
(888) 341-7400
www.fbrdirect.com/funds

FCA Corporation (open-end)
5847 San Felipe, Suite 850
Houston, Texas 77057
(888) 345-1898

Federated Investors Funds
 (closed-end)
1001 Liberty Avenue
Pittsburgh, Pennsylvania 15222
(800) 341-7400
www.federatedinvestors.com

Fenimore Asset Management Inc.
 (open-end)
384 North Grand Street
Cobleskill, New York 12043
(518) 234-7400

Fidelity Management & Research
 Company (open-end)
82 Devonshire Street
Boston, Massachusetts 02109
(800) 544-8544
www.fidelity.com

Fiduciary Management Inc.
(open-end)
100 East Wisconsin Avenue
Milwaukee, Wisconsin 53202
(414) 765-4124

Fifth Third Asset Management Inc.
(open-end)
38 Fountain Square Plaza
Cincinnati, Ohio 45263
(800) 282-5706
www.53.com

Financial Counselors Inc.
(open-end)
442 West 47th Street
Kansas City, Missouri 64112
(877) 627-8504

**First Associated Investment
Advisors Inc.** (open-end)
5161 Miller Trunk Highway
Duluth, Minnesota 55811
(866) 209-1964

First Eagle Funds (open-end)
1345 Avenue of the Americas
New York, NY 10105
(800) 334-2143
www.firsteaglefunds.com

First Financial Capital Advisors
(open-end)
9120 Union Center Boulevard
West Chester, Ohio 45069
(888) 494-8510

Firsthand Capital Management Inc.
(open-end)
125 South Market Street, Suite 1200
San Jose, California 95113
(888) 884-2675

**First Investors Management
Company** (open-end)
110 Wall Street, 4th Floor
New York, New York 10005
(800) 423-4026
www.firstinvestors.com

First Manhattan Company
(open-end)
437 Madison Avenue, Floor 31
New York, New York 10022
(610) 254-1000

First Pacific Advisors
(open-end and closed-end)
11400 West Olympic Boulevard
Los Angeles, California 90064
(310) 473-0225
www.fpafunds.com

First Trust Advisors L.P.
(open-end and closed-end)
120 East Liberty Drive
Wheaton, Illinois 60187
(630) 241-4141
www.ftportfolios.com

Fischer Investments (open-end)
13100 Skyline Boulevard
Woodside, California 94062
(650) 571-5800

Flaherty & Crumrine (closed-end)
301 East Colorado Boulevard,
 Suite 720
Pasadena, CA 91101
(626) 795-7300
www.preferredcome.com

Flippin Bruce & Porter Inc.
(open-end)
800 Main Street
Lynchburg, Virginia 24504
(513) 587-3443

FolioMetrix LLC (open-end)
9940 SW Aborcrest Way
Portland, Oregon 97225
(800) 773-3863

Foresight Asset Management LLC
24695 Deer Ridge Lane
Athens, Alabama 35613
(877) 378-3863

Forester Capital Management Inc.
(open-end)
400 East Cook Avenue, Suite 201
Libertyville, Illinois 60048
(800) 388-0365
www.forestervalue.com

Fort Pitt Capital Group Inc.
(open-end)
680 Anderson Drive
Pittsburgh, Pennsylvania 15220
(866) 688-8775

Forward Management LLC
  (open-end)
433 California Street
San Francisco, California 94104
(800) 999-6809
www.forwardfunds.com

Foxhall Capital Management Inc.
  (open-end)
1630 Duke Street, Suite 200
Alexandria, Virginia 22314
(708) 683-8575

Frank Capital Partners LLC
  (open-end)
6 Stacy Court
Parsippany, New Jersey 07054
(866) 706-9790

Franklin Templeton Investments
  (open-end and closed-end)
One Franklin Parkway
San Mateo, California 94403
(650) 212-3200
www.franklintempleton.com

Fred Alger Management Inc.
  (open-end)
111 Fifth Avenue
New York, New York 10003
(201) 547-3600

Freedom Funds Management
  Company (open-end)
1200 17th Street, Suite 850
Denver, Colorado 80202
(303) 572-6990

Freiss Associates LLC (open-end)
3711 Kennett Pike
Greenville, Delaware 19807
(414) 765-4124

Frontegra Asset Management Inc.
  (open-end)
400 Skokie Boulevard, Suite 500
Northbrook, Illinois 60062
(888) 825-2100
www.frontegra.com

Frontier Investment Management
  Company (open-end)
8401 North Central Expressway
Dallas, Texas 75225
(866) 653-4626

Frost Investment Advisors LLC
  (open-end)
100 West Houston, 15th Floor Tower
San Antonio, Texas 78205
(877) 713-7678

FundQuest Inc. (open-end)
125 High Street
Boston, Massachusetts 02110
(877) 273-8635

Gabelli Inc. (open-end and
  closed-end)
One Corporate Center
Rye, NY 10580-1422
(800) 422-3554
www.gabelli.com

Gardner Lewis Asset Management
  LP (open-end)
285 Wilmington-WestChester Pike
Chadds Ford, Pennsylvania 19317
(252) 972-9922

Gateway Investment Advisors LLC
  (open-end)
3805 Edwards Road, Suite 600
Cincinnati, OH 45209
(617) 449-2000
www.gatewayfund.com

GE Asset Management Inc.
  (open-end)
3001 Summer Street
Stamford, Connecticut 06904
(800) 242-0134
www.gefunds.com

General American Investors
  Company Inc. (closed-end)
100 Park Avenue, 35th Floor
New York, New York 10017
(212) 916-8400
www.generalamericaninvestors.com

Genworth Financial Wealth
  Management Inc. (open-end)
2300 Contra Costa Boulevard,
  Suite 800
Pleasant Hill, California 94523
(309) 821-4600

Giordano Asset Management
(open-end)
135 Gorman Street
Annapolis, Maryland 21401
(800) 773-3863

**Glenmede Investment Management
LP** (open-end)
1650 Market Street, Suite 1200
Philadelphia, Pennsylvania 19103
(215) 419-6024
www.glenmede.com

Glickenhaus & Company
(open-end)
6 East 43rd Street, 10th Floor
New York, New York 10017
(800) 847-5886

**Global X Management Company
LLC** (open-end)
220 Fifth Avenue, 20th Floor
New York, New York 10001
(888) 493-8631

Goldman Sachs & Company
(open-end)
32 Old Slip, 23rd Floor
New York, New York 10005
(212) 902-0800
www.gs.com

Golub Group LLC (open-end)
2929 Campus Drive, Suite 145
San Mateo, California 94403
(866) 954-6682

Gould Investment Partners LLC
(open-end)
1235 Westlakes Drive, Suite 280
Berwyn, Pennsylvania 19312
(309) 821-4600

Grail Advisors LLC (open-end)
One Ferry Building, Suite 255
San Francisco, California 94111
(415) 677-5870

Gratio Capital (open-end)
28 West 44th Street, Suite 1200
New York, New York 10036
(877) 254-7284

**Green Century Capital
Management** (open-end)
114 State Street, Suite 200
Boston, Massachusetts 02109
(800) 934-7336
www.greencentury.com

**Greenhaven Commodity Services
LLC** (open-end)
3840 Peachtree Road, Suite 1900
Atlanta, Georgia 30326
(866) 501-7704

Greenwich Advisors LLC
(open-end)
330 Railroad Avenue
Greenwich, Connecticut 06830
(866) 667-8733

Grisanti Brown & Partners
(open-end)
45 Rockefeller Plaza, 17th Floor
New York, New York 10111
(866) 775-8439

GRT Capital Management LLC
(open-end)
50 Milk Street, 21st Floor
Boston, Massachusetts 02109
(877) 478-4478

**Grubb & Ellis Alesco Global
Advisors** (open-end)
400 South El Camino Real,
Suite 1250
San Mateo, California 94402
(877) 404-7822

GuideStone Funds Trust (open-end)
2401 Cedar Springs Road
Dallas, TX 75201
(888) 984-8433
www.guidestone.org

**Guinness Atkinson Asset
Management Inc.** (open-end)
21550 Oxnard Street, Suite 750
Woodland Hills, California 91367
(800) 915-6566
www.gafunds.com

**Hambrecht & Quist Capital
Management** (closed-end)
2 Liberty Square, 9th Floor
Boston, Massachusetts 02109
(617) 772-8500
www.hqcm.com

Hancock Horizon Funds (open-end)
2600 Citiplace Drive Suite 100
Baton Rouge, LA 70808
(610) 254-1000
www.hancockhorizonfunds.com

Hansberger Global Investors Inc.
(open-end)
401 East Las Olas Boulevard,
Suite 1700
Ft. Lauderdale, FL 33301
(800) 414-6927
www.hansberger.com

Harbor Capital Advisors Inc.
(open-end)
111 South Wacker Drive, 34th Floor
Chicago, Illinois 60606
(800) 422-1050
www.harborfund.com

Harding Loevner Management LP
(open-end)
50 Division Street, Suite 401
Somerville, NJ 08876
(877) 435-8105
www.hardingloevner.com

Hartford Life Investment Advisors
(open-end)
P.O. Box 2161
Hartford, Connecticut 06145
(800) 862-6668
www.hartfordinvestor.com

**Hatteras Alternative Mutual Funds
LLC** (open-end)
600 Mamaroneck Avenue, Suite 400
Harrison, New York 10528
(877) 569-2382

Haverford Financial Services Inc.
(open-end)
Three Radnor Corporate Center
Radnor, Pennsylvania 19087
(866) 301-7212
haverfordfunds.com

Heartland Advisors Inc. (open-end)
789 North Water Street, Suite 500
Milwaukee, Wisconsin 53202
(800) 432-7856
www.heartlandfunds.com

Henderson Global Investors Inc.
(open-end)
737 North Michigan Avenue,
Suite 1700
Chicago, Illinois 60611
(866) 443-6337
www.hendersonglobalfunds.com

**Hennessy Management Company
LP** (open-end)
7250 Redwood Boulevard, Suite 200
Novato, CA 94945
(800) 422-2760
www.hennessyfunds.com

**Hennion & Walsh Asset
Management Inc.** (open-end)
2001 Route 46
Parsippany, New Jersey 07054
(888) 465-5722

Henssler Equity Fund (open-end)
3735 Cherokee Street
Kennesaw, Georgia 30144
(800) 936-3863
www.henssler.com

Thomas J. Herzfeld Advisors Inc.
(closed-end)
P.O. Box 161465
Miami, FL 33116
(305) 271-1900
www.herzfeld.com

HGK Asset Management
(open-end)
525 Washington Boulevard
Jersey City, New Jersey 07310
(877) 342-5445
www.hgk.com

Highland Capital Management
(open-end and closed-end)
13455 Noel Road, Suite 800
Dallas, TX 75240
(877) 665-1287
www.highlandfunds.com

HighMark Capital Management Inc.
(open-end)
350 California Street
San Francisco, California 94104
(800) 433-6884
www.highmarkfunds.com

Hilliard Lyons Research Advisors
(open-end)
500 West Jefferson Street
Louisville, Kentucky 40202
(502) 588-8400
www.hilliard.com

Hillman Capital Management
(open-end)
7600 Wisconsin Avenue
Bethesda, Maryland 20814
(800) 773-3863
www.hillmancapital.com

HM Payson & Company
(open-end)
One Portland Square
Portland, Maine 04112
(207) 879-0001

Hodges Capital Management Inc.
(open-end)
2905 Maple Avenue
Dallas, Texas 75201
(866) 811-0224
www.hodgesfund.com

Holland & Company LLC
(open-end)
375 Park Avenue
New York, New York 10152
(800) 304-6552
www.thehollandfund.com

Hotchkis & Wiley Capital Management LLC (open-end)
725 South Figueroa Street, 39th Floor
Los Angeles, California 90017
(866) 493-8607
www.hwcm.com

Hottinger Capital Corporation
(closed-end)
1270 Avenue of the Americas
New York, New York 10020
(888) 794-7700
www.swz.com

HSBC Global Asset Management (USA) (open-end)
452 Fifth Avenue
New York, New York 10018
(800) 782-8183
www.investorfunds.us.hsbc.com

Huber Capital Management LLC
(open-end)
10940 Wilshire Boulevard, Suite 925
Los Angeles, California 90024
(888) 482-3726

Huntington Asset Advisors Inc.
(open-end)
41 South High Street
Columbus, Ohio 43287
(800) 253-0412
www.huntingtonfunds.com

Hussman Econometrics Advisors
(open-end)
5736 Dorsey Hall Drive
Ellicott City, Maryland 21042
(800) 487-7626
www.hussmanfunds.com

Hyperion Brookfield Inc
(closed-end)
200 Vesey Street, 10th Floor
New York, New York 10281
(800) 497-3746
www.hyperionbrookfield.com

ICON Funds (open-end)
5299 DTC Boulevard, Suite 1200
Greenwood Village, CO 80111
(800) 764-0442
www.iconfunds.com

IMS Capital Management Inc.
(open-end)
8995 SE Otty Road
Portland, OR 97086
(800) 934-s5550
www.imscapital.com

Incline Capital LLC (open-end)
4741 Caughlin Parkway, Suite 2
Reno, Nevada 89519
(866) 994-5729

IndexIQ Advisors LLC (open-end)
800 Westchester Avenue, Suite N611
Rye Brook, New York 10573
(877) 474-6339

ING Investments (open-end and closed-end)
7337 East Doubletree Ranch Road
Scottsdale, Arizona 85258
(480) 477-3000
www.ingfunds.com

Integrity Asset Management LLC
  (open-end)
9900 Corporate Campus Drive
Louisville, Kentucky 40223
(866) 896-9292
www.integritymf.com

IQI Investment Advisors LLC
  (closed-end)
P.O. Box 9011
Princeton, New Jersey 08543
(877) 449-4742
www.iqiafunds.com

International Value Advisors LLC
  (open-end)
645 Madison Avenue, 12th Floor
New York, New York 10022
(866) 941-4482

Intrepid Capital Management Inc.
  (open-end)
3652 South Third Street, Suite 200
Jacksonville Beach, Florida 32250
(866) 996-3863

Invesco AIM (open-end)
11 Greenway Plaza, Suite 100
Houston, Texas 77046
(713) 626-1919

Investment Research Corporation
  (open-end)
110 Sixteenth Street, Suite 1400
Denver, Colorado 80202
(303) 626-0600

Iron Financial Management Inc.
  (open-end)
630 Dundee Road, Suite 200
Northbrook, Illinois 60062
(877) 322-0575

**Ivy Investment Management
  Company** (open-end)
6300 Lamar Avenue
Shawnee Mission, Kansas 66202
(800) 777-6472
www.ivyfunds.com

Jacobs & Company (open-end)
300 Summers Street, Suite 970
Charleston, West Virginia 25301
(304) 342-3535

James Investment Research Inc.
  (open-end)
1349 Fairgrounds Road
Xenia, Ohio 45385
(513) 629-2050

Janus Capital Management LLC
  (open-end)
151 Detroit Street
Denver, Colorado 80206
(303) 333-3863
www.janus.com

**Javelin Investment Management
  LLC** (open-end)
33 West Thompson Street, Suite 218
Princeton, New Jersey 08542
(866) 528-0029

JennisonDryden Funds (open-end)
P.O. Box 8098
Philadelphia, Pennsylvania 19101
(800) 225-1852
www.jennisondryden.com

**Jensen Investment Management
  Inc.** (open-end)
5300 Meadows Road, Suite 250
Lake Oswego, Oregon 97035
(800) 992-4144

JJB Hilliard WL Lyons Inc.
  (open-end)
Hilliard Lyons Center
Louisville, Kentucky 40202
(502) 588-8400

John Hancock Group (open-end
  and closed-end)
601 Congress Street
Boston, Massachusetts 02210
(800) 225-5291
www.jhfunds.com

Johnson Investment Counsel Inc.
  (open-end)
3777 West Fork Road
Cincinnati, Ohio 45247
(800) 541-0170
www.johnsonfamilyfunds.com

**Jones Villalta Asset Management
  Inc.** (open-end)
805 Las Cimas Parkway, Suite 125
Austin, Texas 78746
(866) 950-5863

JPMorgan Funds (open-end)
522 Fifth Avenue, 18th Floor
New York, New York 10036
(800) 480-4111
www.jpmorganfunds.com

Juruka Mills & Kiefer LLC
(open-end)
2101 Webster Street, Suite 1550
Oakland, California 94612
(866) 544-2737

Kalmar Investment Advisors
(open-end)
3701 Kennett Pike
Wilmington, Delaware 19807
(800) 282-2319
www.kalmarinvestments.com

KA Fund Advisors LLC
(closed-end)
1800 Avenue of the Stars, 2nd Floor
Los Angeles, CA 90067
(877) 657-3863
www.kaynemlp.com

KCO Investments Inc. (open-end)
3717 Buchanan Street, Suite 200
San Francisco, California 94123
(800) 595-3166

**Keeley Asset Management
Corporation** (open-end)
401 South LaSalle Street, Suite 1201
Chicago, IL 60605
(888) 933-5391
www.keeleyfunds.com

Kerns Capital Management Inc.
(open-end)
5075 Westheimer Road, Suite 1177
Houston, Texas 77056
(877) 275-5599

Killen Group Inc. (open-end)
1189 Lancaster Avenue
Berwyn, Pennsylvania 19312
(800) 992-6757

Kinetics Asset Management Inc.
(open-end)
16 New Broadway
Sleepy Hollow, New York 10591
(800) 930-3828
www.kineticsfunds.com

King Investment Advisors
(open-end)
980 Post Oak Boulevard, Suite 2400
Houston, Texas 77056
(207) 879-1001

Kirr, Marbach Company LLC
(open-end)
621 Washington Street
Columbus, Indiana 47201
(812) 376-9444
www.kmpartnersfunds.com

Lacerte Capital Advisors LLC
(open-end)
2811 McKinney Avenue, Suite 206
Dallas, Texas 75204
(877) 738-9888

Lateef Investment Management LP
(open-end)
300 Drakes Landing Road, Suite 100
Greenbrae, California 94904
(866) 499-2151

Lazard Asset Management LLC
(open-end and closed-end)
30 Rockefeller Plaza, 59th Floor
New York, New York 10112
(800) 823-6300
www.lazardnet.com

Leader Capital Corporation
(open-end)
121 SW Morrison Street
Portland, Oregon 97204
(800) 711-9164
www.leadercapital.com

Leeb Capital Management Inc.
(open-end)
8 West 40th Street, 19th Floor
New York, New York 10018
(866) 400-5332

Lee Financial Group (open-end)
2756 Woodlawn Drive, Suite 6-201
Honolulu, Hawaii 96822
(808) 988-8088

Legg Mason (open-end and
closed-end)
100 Light Street
Baltimore, Maryland 21202
(800) 451-2010
www.leggmason.com/cef

Leigh Baldwin & Company LLC
(open-end)
112 Albany Street
Cazenovia, New York 13035
(800) 659-8044

Lend Lease Real Estate
Investments (open-end)
3424 Peachtree Road NE, Suite 800
Atlanta, Georgia 30326
(877) 563-5327

Leuthold Weeden Capital
Management (open-end)
33 South Sixth Street, Suite 4600
Minneapolis, Minnesota 55402
(309) 821-4600
www.leutholdfunds.com

Liberty Street Advisors Inc.
(closed-end)
125 Maiden Lane, 6th Floor
New York, New York 10038
(800) 207-7108
www.all-starfunds.com

Litman/Gregory Fund Advisors
LLC (open-end)
4 Orinda Way, Suite 230D
Orinda, California 94563
(800) 960-0188

Longleaf Partners (open-end)
6075 Poplar Avenue
Memphis, Tennessee 38119
(800) 445-9469
www.longleafpartners.com

Loomis & Company LP (open-end)
One Financial Center
Boston, Massachusetts 02111
(617) 449-2000
www.loomissayles.com

Lord Abbett & Company LLC
(open-end)
90 Hudson Street, 10th Floor
Jersey City, New Jersey 07302
(201) 395-2000
www.lordabbett.com

Lowry Hill Investment Advisors
Inc. (open-end)
90 South Seventh Street, Suite 5300
Minneapolis, Minnesota 55402
(877) 333-0246

Luther King Capital Management
Corporation (open-end)
301 Commerce Street, Suite 1600
Fort Worth, Texas 76102
(800) 688-5526

Macquarie Capital Investment
(closed-end)
120 West 55th Street
New York, New York 10019
(800) 910-1434
www.macquarie.com

Macromarkets LLC (open-end)
14 Main Street, Suite 100
Madison, New Jersey 07940
(800) 345-7999

Madison Mosaic (open-end and
closed-end)
550 Science Drive
Madison, WI 53711
(608) 274-0300
www.madisonfunds.com

Mainstay Funds (open-end)
51 Madison Avenue
New York, New York 10010
(800) 624-6782
www.mainstayfunds.com

Mairs and Power Inc. (open-end)
322 Minnesota Street
St. Paul, Minnesota 55101
(651) 222-8478
www.mairsandpower.com

Managers Investment Group LLC
(open-end)
333 West Wacker Drive
Chicago, Illinois 60606
(800) 548-4539
www.managersinvest.com

Manarin Investment Counsel
(open-end)
15858 West Dodge Road, Suite 310
Omaha, Nebraska 68118
(888) 339-4230

Marketfield Asset Management
LLC (open-end)
292 Madison Avenue, 14th Floor
New York, New York 10017
(888) 236-4298

Marketocracy Funds (open-end)
1200 Park Place, Suite 100
San Mateo, California 94403
(888) 884-8482

Marsico Capital Management LLC
  (open-end)
200 17th Street, Suite 1600
Denver, Colorado 80202
(888) 860-8686
www.marsicofunds.com

Martin Currie Global Investors
(closed-end)
1250 Avenue of the Americas
New York, New York 10019
(888) CHN-CALL
www.chinafundinc.com

**Massachusetts Financial Services
  Company** (open-end and
  closed-end)
P.O. Box 55824
Boston, Massachusetts 02205
(800) 637-2304
www.mfs.com

**MassMutual Life Insurance
  Company** (open-end)
1295 State Street
Springfield, MA 01111
(888) 309-3539
www.massmutual.com

Matrix Asset Advisors Inc.
  (open-end)
747 Third Avenue, 31st Floor
New York, New York 10017
(212) 486-2004

**Matthew 25 Management
  Corporation** (open-end)
605 West Avenue
Jenkintown, Pennsylvania 19046
(215) 884-4458
www.matthew25fund.com

**Matthews International Capital
  Management LLC** (open-end)
Four Embarcadero Center,
  Suite 550
San Francisco, California 94111
(800) 789-2742
www.matthewsfunds.com

**MBIA Capital Management
  Corporation** (closed-end)
113 King Street
Armonk, New York 10504
(914) 273-4545
www.mbiaam.com

McCarthy Group Advisors LLC
  (open-end)
1125 South 103rd Street, Suite 250
Omaha, Nebraska 68124
(866) 811-0228

McConnell Asset Management LLC
  (open-end)
6075 Roswell Road, Suite 450
Atlanta, Georgia 30328
(800) 595-4922

McCormick Asset Management Inc.
  (open-end)
1325 Fourth Avenue, Suite 2144
Seattle, Washington 98101
(206) 624-5863

Meeder Asset Management Inc.
  (open-end)
6125 Memorial Drive
Dublin, Ohio 43017
(614) 766-7000

Mercer Global Investments Inc.
  (open-end)
200 Clarendon Street
Boston, Massachusetts 02116
(866) 658-9896

Merk Investments LLC (open-end)
555 Bryant Street, Suite 455
Palo Alto, California 94301
(866) 637-5386

Merrill Lynch HOLDRS
  (open-end)
250 Vesey Street
New York, New York 10281
(800) MERRILL
www.mlim.ml.com

**Metropolitan West Asset
  Management LLC** (open-end)
11766 Wilshire Boulevard,
  Suite 1580
Los Angeles, California 90025
(800) 241-4671
www.mwamllc.com

Metzler/Payden LLC (open-end)
333 South Grand Avenue
Los Angeles, California 90071
(800) 572-9336
www.metzlerpayden.com

MH Investment Management Inc.
(open-end)
220 Russell Avenue
Rahway, New Jersey 07065
(800) 318-7969

Midas Management Corporation
(open-end)
11 Hanover Square
New York, New York 10005
(800) 400-6432
www.midasfunds.com

Milestone Capital Management
(open-end)
115 East Putnam Avenue
Greenwich, Connecticut 06830
(914) 964-5355

Mirzam Asset Management LLC
(open-end)
1 Main Street, Suite 200
Tequesta, Florida 33469
(888) 693-8056

MMA Capital Management
(open-end)
1110 North Main Street
Goshen, Indiana 46528
(800) 977-2947
www.mmapraxis.com

Mohawk Asset Management Inc.
(open-end)
1292 Gower Road
Scotia, New York 12302
(518) 370-0289

Monetta Financial Services
(open-end)
1776-A South Naperville Road,
Suite 207
Wheaton, Illinois 60187
(630) 462-9800

Montebello Partners LLC
(open-end)
75 Montebello Road
Suffern, New York 10901
(877) 464-3111

**Morgan Stanley Investment
Advisors Inc.** (closed-end)
522 Fifth Avenue
New York, New York 10036
(800) 869-6397
www.morganstanley.com/im

Morris Capital Advisors Inc.
(open-end)
15 Chester Commons Street
Malvern, Pennsylvania 19355
(610) 722-0900

MTB Investment Advisors Inc.
(open-end)
100 East Pratt Street, 17th Floor
Baltimore, Maryland 21202
(301) 657-1517
www.mtbfunds.com

Muhlenkamp & Company
(open-end)
5000 Stonewood Drive, Suite 300
Wexford, Pennsylvania 15090
(800) 860-3863
www.muhlenkamp.com

Munder Capital Management
(open-end)
480 Pierce Street
Birmingham, Michigan 48009
(800) 438-5789
www.munderfunds.com

**Mutual of America Capital
Management Corporation**
(open-end)
320 Park Avenue
New York, New York 10022
(800) 914-8716
www.mutualofamerica.com

Mutuals.com (open-end)
615 East Michigan Street
Milwaukee, Wisconsin 53202
(866) 264-8783
www.mutuals.com

Nakoma Capital Management LLC
(open-end)
8040 Excelsior Drive, Suite 401
Madison, Wisconsin 53717
(866) 662-5662

**Nanking Road Capital
Management** (closed-end)
111 Gillett Street
Hartford, Connecticut 06105
(212) 681-9600
www.taiwangreaterchinafund.com

Nashville-Capital Corporation
(open-end)
209 Tenth Avenue South, Suite 332
Nashville, Tennessee 37203
(888) 263-5593

Nationwide Fund Advisors
(open-end)
1000 Continental Drive, Suite 400
King of Prussia, Pennsylvania 19406
(800) 848-0920

**Natixis Asset Management
Advisors LP** (open-end)
399 Boylston Street
Boston, Massachusetts 02116
(617) 449-2000

Navellier & Associates Inc.
(open-end)
1 East Liberty, Third Floor
Reno, Nevada 89501
(775) 785-2300
www.navellier.com

NCM Capital Advisors Inc.
(open-end)
2634 Durham-Chapel Hill
Boulevard, Suite 206
Durham, North Carolina 27707
(866) 515-4626

**Needham Investment Management
LLC** (open-end)
445 Park Avenue
New York, New York 10022
(800) 625-7071
www.needhamfunds.com

Neiman Capital Management
(open-end)
6325 La Valle Plateada
Rancho Santa Fe, California 92067
(877) 385-2720

**Neuberger Berman Management
LLC** (open-end and closed-end)
605 Third Avenue, 2nd Floor
New York, New York 10158
(212) 476-8800
www.nb.com

New America High Income Fund
(closed-end)
100 East Pratt Street
Baltimore, Maryland 21202
(301) 470-7447
www.newamerica-hyb.com

Newgate Capital Management LLC
(open-end)
One Soundshore Drive
Greenwich, Connecticut 06830
(888) 963-9428

New Ireland Fund (closed-end)
4400 Computer Drive
Westborough, Massachusetts 01581
(302) 791-1700
www.newirelandfund.com

**New Provident Capital
Management** (open-end)
2859 Paces Ferry Road, Suite 2125
Atlanta, Georgia 30339
(252) 972-9922

**Nicholas-Applegate Capital
Management** (open-end)
600 West Broadway, Suite 2900
San Diego, California 92101
(800) 581-8043
www.nacm.com

Nicholas Company Inc. (open-end)
700 North Water Street, Suite 1010
Milwaukee, Wisconsin 53202
(800) 544-6547
www.nicholasfunds.com

**Nomura Asset Management USA
Inc.** (open-end and closed-end)
535 Madison Avenue
New York, New York 10022
(212) 667-1414
www.nomura.com

NorthCoast Asset Management LLC (open-end)
6 Glenville Street
Greenwich, Connecticut 06831
(800) 558-9105

Northeast Management & Research Company Inc. (open-end)
150 Federal Street
Boston, Massachusetts 02110
(617) 523-3588

Northern Trust Investments
(open-end)
50 South LaSalle Street
Chicago, Illinois 6-0603
(800) 637-1380
www.northernfunds.com

Nuveen Asset Management
(open-end and closed-end)
333 West Wacker Drive
Chicago, Illinois 60606
(800) 257-8787
www.nuveen.com

Oak Associates Ltd (open-end)
3875 Embassy Parkway, Suite 250
Akron, Ohio 44333
(888) 462-5386
www.oakfunds.com

Oakmark Family of Funds
(open-end)
Two North LaSalle Street, Suite 500
Chicago, Illinois 50502
(800) 625-6275
www.oakmark.com

Oak Value Capital Management Inc. (open-end)
3100 Tower Boulevard, Suite 700
Durham, North Carolina 27707
(800) 622-2474
www.oakvaluefund.com

Oberweis Asset Management Inc.
(open-end)
3333 Warrenville Road, Suite 500
Lisle, Illinois 60532
(800) 245-7311
www.oberweisfunds.com

Old Mutual Capital Inc. (open-end)
4643 South Ulster Street, Suite 600
Denver, Colorado 80237
(888) 772- 2888
www.omfunds.com

Olstein Capital Management LP
(open-end)
4 Manhattanville Road, Suite 102
Purchase, New York 10577
(800) 799-2113
www.olsteinfunds.com

One Compass Advisors (open-end)
200 East Twelfth Street
Jeffersonville, Indiana 47130
(877) 835-4531

Oppenheimer Funds Inc.
(open-end)
225 Liberty Street, 11th Floor
New York, New York 10281
(303) 763-3200
www.oppenheimerfunds.com

Oxford Private Client Group LLC
(open-end)
1900 LaSalle Avenue North
Minneapolis, Minnesota 55403
(877) 350-8668

Pacific Financial Group (open-end)
10900 NE 8th Street
Bellevue, California 91203
(888) 451-8734
www.pacificadvisorsfund.com

Pacific Global Investment Management Group (open-end)
101 North Brand Boulevard
Glendale, California 91203
(800) 282-6693
www.pacificcapitalfunds.com

Pacific Life Insurance Company
(open-end)
700 Newport Center Drive
Newport Beach, California 92660
(800) 722-2333
www.pacificlife.com

Palantir Capital Management Ltd.
(open-end)
3355 West Alabama, Suite 1025
Houston, Texas 77098
(866) 977-2549

Paradigm Capital Management Inc.
 (open-end)
Nine Elk Street
Albany, New York 12207
(800) 239-0732

Parnassus Investments (open-end)
One Market—Stewart Tower,
 Suite 1600
San Francisco, CA 94105
(800) 999-3505
www.parnassus.com

Parr Financial Group LLC
 (open-end)
5100 Poplar Avenue, Suite 3117
Memphis, Tennessee 38137
(877) 244-6235

Pax World Management
 Corporation (open-end)
30 Penhallow Street, Suite 400
Portsmouth, New Hampshire 03801
(800) 767-1729
www.paxfund.com

Payden & Rygel (open-end)
333 South Grand Avenue,
 32nd Floor
Los Angeles, California 90071
(800) 572-9336
www.paydenfunds.com

Peak Wealth Opportunities LLC
 (open-end)
10225 Ulmerton Road, Suite 3D
Largo, Florida 33771
(800) 494-2755

Pearl Management Company
 (open-end)
2610 Park Avenue
Muscatine, Iowa 52761
(563) 288-2773
www.pearlfunds.com

Pennsylvania Avenue Advisors
 (open-end)
4201 Massachusetts
Washington, D.C. 20016
(888) 642-6393

Perimeter Capital Partners LLC
 (open-end)
5 Concourse Parkway, Suite 2725
Atlanta, Georgia 30328
(888) 968-4964

Perkins Capital Management Inc.
 (open-end)
730 East Lake Street
Wayzata, Minnesota 55391
(800) 998-3190

Permanent Portfolio Family of
 Funds (open-end)
600 Montgomery Street
San Francisco, California 94111
(707) 778-1000

Perritt Capital Management
 (open-end)
300 South Wacker Drive, Suite 2880
Chicago, Illinois 60606
(312) 669-1650
www.perrittmutualfunds.com

Petroleum & Resources
 Corporation (closed-end)
Seven St. Paul Street, Suite 1140
Baltimore, Maryland 21202
(800) 638-3479
www.peteres.com

PFM Asset Management LLC
 (open-end)
One Keystone Plaza, Suite 300
Harrisburg, Pennsylvania 17101
(800) 338-3383

Phocas Financial Corporation
 (open-end)
980 Atlantic Avenue, Suite 106
Alameda, California 94501
(866) 746-2271

PIA Mutual Fund (open-end)
1299 Ocean Avenue, Suite 210
Santa Monica, California 90401
(310) 899-1935
www.pacificincome.com

PIMCO (open-end and closed-end)
840 Newport Center Drive,
 Suite 300
Newport Beach, California 92660
(800) 927-4648
www.allianzinvestors.com

Pinnacle Advisors Inc. (open-end)
507 Plum Street
Syracuse, New York 13204
(573) 587-3443
www.pinnaclevaluefund.com

Pioneer Investment Management
(open-end and closed-end)
60 State Street
Boston, Massachusetts 02109
(800) 225-6292
www.pioneerfunds.com

PNC Funds (open-end)
Two Hopkins Plaza
Baltimore, Maryland 21201
(800) 551-2145

Polaris Capital Management Inc.
(open-end)
125 Summer Street, Floor 14
Boston, Massachusetts 02110
(888) 263-5594
www.polarisfunds.com

Portfolios Inc. (open-end)
750 North St. Paul, Suite 1300
Dallas, Texas 75201
(214) 720-9101

Potkul Capital Management LLC
(open-end)
3633 Hill Road, 3rd Floor
Parsippany, New Jersey 07054
(973) 331-1000

Primecap Management Company
(open-end)
225 South Lake Street, Suite 400
Pasadena, California 91101
(800) 729-2307
www.odysseyfunds.com

**Principal Management
Corporation** (open-end)
711 High Street
Des Moines, Iowa 50392
(800) 222-5852
www.principal.com

Profit Investment Management
(open-end)
8401 Colesville Road, Suite 320
Silver Spring, Maryland 20910
(888) 744-2337
www.profitfunds.com

ProFunds Group (open-end)
7501 Wisconsin Avenue,
  Suite 1000
Bethesda, Maryland 20814
(888) 776-3637
www.profunds.com

**Progressive Investment Management
Corporation** (open-end)
721 NW Ninth Avenue. Suite 250
Portland, Oregon 97209
(978) 772-0052

**Prospector Partners Asset
Management LLC** (open-end)
370 Church Street
Guilford, Connecticut 06437
(877) 734-7862

Prudential Investments LLC
(open-end)
100 Mulberry Street
Newark, New Jersey 07102
(201) 367-7420
www.prudential.com

**Putnam Investment Management
LLC** (open-end and closed-end)
One Post Office Square
Boston, Massachusetts 02109
(617) 292-1000
www.putnam.com

Quaker Funds (open-end)
309 Technology Drive
Malvern, Pennsylvania 19355
(800) 220-8888
www.quakerfunds.com

**Quantitative Investment Advisors
Inc.** (open-end)
55 Old Bedford Road
Lincoln, Massachusetts 01773
(800) 326-2151
www.quantfunds.com

Rady Asset Management LLC
(open-end)
1020 Prospect Street, Suite 312
La Jolla, California 92037
(877) 839-7239

Rafferty Asset Management LLC
(open-end)
33 Whitehall Street, 10th Floor
New York, New York 10004
(800) 851-0511

**Rainier Investment Management
Inc.** (open-end)
601 Union Street
Seattle, Washington 98101
(800) 248-6314
www.rainierfunds.com

RCM Capital Management LLC
(closed-end)
4 Embarcadero Center
San Francisco, California 94111
(212) 739-3371
www.thekoreafund.com

RE Advisors Corporation
(open-end)
4301 Wilson Boulevard
Arlington, Virginia 22209
(800) 258-3030

**Real Estate Management Services
LLC** (open-end)
1100 Fifth Avenue South, Suite 301
Naples, Florida 34102
(800) 527-9525

W.H. Reaves & Company
(open-end and closed-end)
10 Exchange Place
Jersey City, New Jersey 07302
(866) 342-7058
www.whreaves.com

Reich & Tang Asset Management
(open-end)
600 Fifth Avenue
New York, New York 10020
(212) 830-5220

Renaissance Capital Corporation
(open-end and closed-end)
2 Greenwich Place
Greenwich, Connecticut 06830
(214) 891-8294
www.rencapital.com

Reserve Management Company Inc.
(open-end)
1250 Broadway
New York, New York 10001
(800) 637-1700

Reynolds Capital Management
(open-end)
80 East Sir Francis Drake
  Boulevard
Larkspur, California 94939
(800) 773-9665
www.reynoldsfunds.com

Riazzi Asset Management LLC
(open-end)
2331 Far Hills Avenue, Suite 200
Dayton, Ohio 45419
(888) 884-8099

Rice Hall James & Associates LLC
(open-end)
600 West Broadway, Suite 1000
San Diego, California 92101
(610) 254-1000

Ridgeworth Funds (open-end)
50 Hurt Plaza, Suite 1400
Atlanta, Georgia 30303
(888) 784-3863

Rigel Capital LLC (open-end)
601 Union Street, Suite 3930
Seattle, Washington 98101
(866) 977-4435

RMR Advisors Inc. (closed-end)
400 Centre Street
Newton, Massachusetts 02458
(617) 332-9530
www.rmrfund.com

**Rivernorth Capital Management
Inc.** (open-end)
325 North LaSalle Street, Suite 645
Chicago, Illinois 60654
(888) 848-7569

RiverSource Investment LLC
(open-end)
200 Ameriprise Financial Center
Minneapolis, Minnesota 55474
(800) 791-3380
www.performance.riversource.com

RNC Capital Management
(open-end)
11601 Wilshire Boulevard
Los Angeles, California 90025
(800) 877-7624

Robeco Investment Funds
(open-end)
909 Third Avenue, 31st Floor
New York, New York 10022
(212) 908-9500
www.robecoinvest.com

Robert W. Baird & Company Inc.
(open-end)
777 East Wisconsin Avenue,
  Suite 2700
Milwaukee, Wisconsin 53202
(866) 442-2473

Rochdale Investment Management
  LLC (open-end)
570 Lexington Avenue
New York, New York 10022
(800) 245-9888
www.rochdale.com

Roosevelt Investment Group
(open-end)
317 Madison Avenue, Suite 1004
New York, New York 10017
(877) 322-0576

Roxbury Capital Management LLC
(open-end)
100 Wilshire Boulevard, Suite 1000
Santa Monica, California 90401
(800) 497-2960

Royce & Associates LLC
(open-end and closed-end)
1414 Avenue of the Americas
New York, New York 10019
(800) 221-4268
www.roycefunds.com

RS Investment Management
  Company LLC (open-end)
388 Market Street, Suite 1700
San Francisco, California 94111
(800) 766-3863
www.rsinvestments.com

Ruane Cuniff & Goldfarb Inc.
(open-end)
767 Fifth Avenue, Suite 4701
New York, New York 10153
(800) 686-6884

Russell Investment Group (open-end)
909 "A" Street
Tacoma, Washington 98402
(253) 627-7001
www.russell.com

RW Roge & Company (open-end)
630 Johnson Avenue
Bohemia, New York 11716
(888) 800-7643

Rydex Investments (open-end)
9601 Blackwell Road, Suite 500
Rockville, Maryland 20850
(800) 820-0888
www.rydexfunds.com

Sarasota Capital Strategies Inc.
(open-end)
460 South Tamiami Trail
Osprey, Florida 34229
(888) 898-4784

Saratoga Capital Management LLC
(open-end)
1101 Stewart Avenue, Suite 207
Garden City, New York 11530
(800) 807-3863
www.saratogacap.com

Satuit Capital Management LLC
(open-end)
2807 Gaston Gate
Mount Pleasant, South Carolina 29466
(866) 972-8848

Saturna Capital Corporation
(open-end)
1300 North State Street
Bellingham, Washington 98225
(360) 734-9900
www.saturna.com

SBAuer Funds LLC (open-end)
10401 North Meridian Street, Suite 100
Indianapolis, Indiana 46290
(888) 711-2837

SBG Capital Management Inc.
(open-end)
15 South Raymond Avenue,
  Suite 200
Pasadena, California 91105
(626) 844-1440

Schneider Capital Management LP
(open-end)
460 East Swedesford Road, Suite 1080
Wayne, Pennsylvania 19087
(302) 791-1196

Schooner Investment Group LLC
(open-end)
150 North Radnor Chester Road,
  Suite E-200
Radnor, Pennsylvania 19087
(866) 724-5997

**Schroder Investment Management
North America** (open-end)
875 Third Avenue, 34th Floor
New York, New York 10022
(800) 464-3108
www.schroderfunds.com

Schwartz Investment Counsel Inc.
(open-end)
3707 West Maple Road, Suite 100
Bloomfield Hills, Michigan 48301
(888) 726-0753
www.schwartzinvest.com

Scout Investment Advisors Inc.
(open-end)
1010 Grand Boulevard
Kansas City, Missouri 64141
(816) 860-7000

**Securities Management & Research
Inc.** (open-end)
2450 South Shore Boulevard, Suite 400
League City, Texas 77573
(281) 334-2469

Security Investors LLC (open-end)
One Security Benefit Place
Topeka, Kansas 66636
(800) 888-2461
www.securitybenefit.com

SEI Group (open-end)
One Freedom Valley Drive
Oaks, Pennsylvania 19456
(800) 342-5734
www.seic.com

Seligman Funds (open-end)
100 Park Avenue
New York, New York 10017
(212) 850-1864
www.seligman.com

Sentinel Asset Management
(open-end)
National Life Drive
Montpelier, Vermont 05604
(800) 282-3863
www.sentinelfunds.com

SGM Fund Management LLC
(open-end)
1165 Park Avenue, Suite 12B
New York, New York 10128
(877) 743-7820

Shay Assets Management Inc.
(open-end)
230 West Monroe Street, Suite 2810
Chicago, Illinois 60606
(800) 982-1846

**Sheets Smith Wealth Management
Inc.** (open-end)
120 Club Oaks Court, Suite 200
Winston-Salem, North Carolina
27104
(800) 773-3863

**Sherwood Forest Capital
Management LLC** (open-end)
1649 Brandywine Drive
Charlottesville, Virginia 22901
(800) 673-0550

Sims Capital Management
(closed-end)
205 East Wisconsin Avenue,
Suite 120
Milwaukee, Wisconsin 53202
(414) 765-1107
www.eaglecapitalgrowthfund.com

SIT Investment Associates Inc.
(open-end)
80 South Eighth Street
Minneapolis, Minnesota 55400
(800) 332-5580
www.sitfunds.com

SiVest Group Inc. (open-end)
469 El Camino Real, Suite 227
Santa Clara, California 95050
(888) 884-2675

Smead Capital Management Inc.
(open-end)
1420 Fifth Avenue, Suite 2625
Seattle, Washington 98101
(877) 807-4122

SMI Advisory Services LLC
(open-end)
422 Washington Street
Columbus, Indiana 47201
(877) 764-3863

**Smith Barney Fund Management
LLC** (open-end)
399 Park Avenue
New York, New York 10022
(800) 451-2010
www.citigroupam.com

Snow Capital Management LP
(open-end)
2100 Georgetowne Drive, Suite 400
Sewickley, Pennsylvania 15143
(877) 766-9363

Sound Shore Management Inc.
(open-end)
8 Sound Shore Drive
Greenwich, Connecticut 06836
(207) 879-1900

**Southernsun Asset Management
Inc.** (open-end)
6000 Poplar Avenue, Suite 220
Memphis, Tennessee 38119
(866) 672-3863

Sparrow Capital Management Inc.
(open-end)
11330 Olive Boulevard, Suite 230
St. Louis, Missouri 63141
(888) 727-3301

Spears Abacus Advisors LLC
(open-end)
147 East 48th Street
New York, New York 10017
(866) 684-4915

Spectrum Advisory Services Inc.
(open-end)
1050 Crown Pointe Parkway,
Suite 750
Atlanta, Georgia 30336
(800) 788-6086

**Spirit of America Management
Company** (open-end)
477 Jericho Turnpike
Syosset, New York 11791
(800) 452-4892

Staar Invesment Trust (open-end)
604 McNight Park Drive
Pittsburgh, Pennsylvania 15237
(440) 922-0066

Stadion Money Management Inc.
(open-end)
1061 Cliff Dawson Road
Watkinsville, Georgia 30677
(866) 383-7636

**State Farm Investment
Management Group** (open-end)
Three State Farm Plaza
Bloomington, Illinois 61710
(800) 450-0740
www.statefarm.com

**State Street Bank & Trust
Company** (open-end)
225 Franklin Street
Boston, Massachusetts 02110
(253) 572-9500

St. Denis J Villere & Company LLC
(open-end)
601 Poydras Street, Suite 1808
New Orleans, Louisiana 70130
(866) 209-1129

**Stephens Investment Management
Group LLC** (open-end)
111 Center Street
Little Rock, Arkansas 72201
(866) 735-7464

Sterling Capital Management LLC
(open-end)
Two Morrowcroft Center
Charlotte, North Carolina 28211
(866) 450-3722
www.sterling-capital.com

Stewart Capital Advisors
(open-end)
800 Philadelphia Street
Indiana, Pennsylvania 15701
(877) 420-4440

**Stone Harbor Investment
Partners LP** (open-end)
31 West 52nd Street, 16th Floor
New York, New York 10019
(866) 699-8125

**Stonebridge Capital Management
Inc.** (open-end)
1801 Century Park East, Suite 1800
Los Angeles, California 90067
(303) 623-2577

Stralem & Company Inc.
(open-end)
645 Madison Avenue
New York, New York 10022
(212) 888-8123

Stratton Management Company
(open-end)
610 West Germantown Pike,
Suite 300
Plymouth Meeting, Pennsylvania
19462
(800) 634-5726
www.strattonmgt.com

**Structured Investment
Management Inc.** (open-end)
245 Park Avenue, 39th Floor
New York, New York 10167

Summit Portfolio Advisors LLC
(open-end)
12606 Julian Street
Broomfield, Colorado 80020
(888) 526-5527
www.summitfunds.com

**SunAmerica Asset Management
Corporation** (open-end and
closed-end))
Harborside Financial Center
3200 Plaza 5
Jersey City, New Jersey 07311
(800) 858-8850
www.sunamericafunds.com

Swank Energy Income Advisors
(closed-end)
3300 Oak Lawn Avenue
Dallas, Texas 75219
(214) 692-6334
www.swankcapital.com

Sycuan Capital Management Inc.
(open-end)
307 Dehesa Road
El Cajon, California 92019
(888) 899-8344

Symons Capital Management
(open-end)
650 Washington Road, Suite 800
Pittsburgh, Pennsylvania 15228
(877) 679-6667

Tanaka Capital Management Inc.
(open-end)
369 Lexington Avenue
New York, New York 10017
(877) 482-6252

**TCW Investment Management
Company** (open-end and
closed-end)
865 South Figueroa Street,
Suite 1800
Los Angeles, California 90017
(213) 244-0456
www.tcw.com

TD Asset Management USA Inc.
(open-end)
100 Wall Street, Floor 29
New York, New York 10005
(800) 669-3900

Templeton Asset Management Ltd.
(open-end and closed-end)
Seven Tamasek Boulevard
Singapore
65-6338-7177
www.franklintempleton.com.ag

TFS Capital LLC (open-end)
1800 Bayberry Court, Suite 103
Richmond, Virginia 23226
(888) 534-2001

Third Avenue Management LLC
(open-end)
622 Third Avenue, 5th Floor
New York, New York 10017
(800) 443-1021
www.thirdave.com

**Third Milenium Investment
Advisors LLC** (open-end)
1185 Avenue of the Americas
New York, New York 10036
(804) 285-8211

Thomas White International Ltd.
(open-end)
440 South LaSalle Street, Suite 3900
Chicago, Illinois 60605
(800) 811-0535
www.thomaswhite.com

Thompson Plumb Funds
(open-end)
1200 John O. Hammons Drive
Madison, Wisconsin 53717
(800) 999-0887
www.thompsonplumb.com

Thompson, Siegel & Walmsley
  (closed-end)
6806 Paragon Place
Richmond, Virginia 23230
(610) 254-1000
www.tswinvest.com

**Thornburg Investment
  Management LLC** (open-end)
2300 North Ridgetop Road
Santa Fe, New Mexico 87506
(800) 847-0200
www.thornburg.com

Three G Financial LLC (open-end)
5940 South Rainbow Boulevard
Las Vegas, Nevada 89118
(877) 238-2406

Thrivent Financial for Lutherans
  (open-end)
625 Fourth Avenue South
Minneapolis, Minnesota 55415
(800) 847-4836
www.thrivent.com

Thunderstorm Mutual Funds LLC
  (open-end)
101 Federal Street, Suite 1900
Boston, Massachusetts 02110
(877) 374-3888

TIAA-CREF (open-end)
730 Third Avenue
New York, New York 10017
(212) 490-9000
www.tiaa-cref.com

Timothy Partners Ltd. (open-end)
1055 Maitland Center Commons
  Boulevard
Maitland, Florida 32701
(800) 846-7526
www.timothyplan.com

T Leavell & Associates Inc.
  (open-end)
150 Government Street, Suite 3000
Mobile, Alabama 36633
(513) 587-3443

Tocqueville Asset Management LP
  (open-end)
40 West 57th Street, 19th Floor
New York, New York 10019
(800) 697-3863
www.tocqueville.com

Toews Corporation (open-end)
1201 New Road, Suite 111
Linwood, New Jersey 08221
(877) 558-6397

Tokarz Group Advisors LLC
  (closed-end)
287 Bowman Avenue, 2nd Floor
Purchase, New York 10577
(914) 701-0310
www.myccapital.com

TOP Fund Management Inc.
  (open-end)
1819 South Dobson Road, Suite 207
Mesa, Arizona 85202
(800) 651-8228

Toreador Research & Trading LLC
  (open-end)
7493 North Ingram, Suite 104
Fresno, California 93711
(800) 343-5902

Torray LLC (open-end)
7501 Wisconsin Avenue, Suite 1100
Bethesda, Maryland 20814
(301) 493-4600

Tortoise Capital Advisors LLC
  (closed-end)
11550 Ash Street
Leawood, Kansas 66211
(913) 981-1020
www.tortoiseavisors.com

Touchstone Advisors Inc.
  (open-end)
303 Broadway, Suite 1100
Cincinnati, Ohio 45202
(800) 543-0407
www.touchstonefunds.com

**Transamerica Asset Management
  Inc.** (open-end and closed-end)
570 Carillon Parkway
St. Petersburg, Florida 33716
(800) 755-5801
www.transamerica.com

Trinity Fiduciary Partners LLC
  (open-end)
306 West 7th Street, Suite 616
Fort Worth, Texas 76102
(800) 320-2185

T. Rowe Price Associates Inc.
(open-end)
100 East Pratt Street
Baltimore, Maryland 21202
(800) 638-5660
www.troweprice.com

Trustmark Investment Advisors Inc.
(open-end)
1701 Lakeland Drive
Jackson, Mississippi 39216
(800) 737-3676

T2 Partners Management LP
(open-end)
145 East 57th Street, 10th Floor
New York, New York 10022
(888) 484-5766

Turner Investment Partners Inc.
(open-end)
1205 Westlakes Drive, Suite 100
Berwyn, Pennsylvania 19312
(800) 224-6312
www.turner-invest.com

Tweedy Browne Company LLC
(open-end)
350 Park Avenue, 9th Floor
New York, New York 10022
(212) 916-0600
www.tweedy.com

Tygh Capital Management
(open-end)
1211 SW 5th Avenue, Suite 2100
Portland, Oregon 97204
(800) 536-3230

UBS Global Asset Management
(open-end and closed-end)
51 West 52nd Street
New York, New York 10019
(800) 647-1568
www.ubs.com/globalam-us

Union Investment Advisors
(open-end)
6801 South 27th Street
Lincoln, Nebraska 68512
(402) 476-3000

United Association of Pipe Fitters
(open-end)
370 17th Street, Suite 3100
Denver, Colorado 80202
(888) 766-8043
www.uafund.com

**United States Commodity Funds
LLC** (open-end)
1320 Harbor Bay Parkway, Suite 145
Alameda, California 94502
(800) 920-0259

Upright Financial Corporation
(open-end)
615 West Mount Pleasant Avenue,
Floor 12
Livingston, New Jersey 07039
(973) 533-1818

**USAA Investment Management
Company** (open-end)
9800 Fredericksburg Road
San Antonio, Texas 78288
(800) 531-8722
www.usaa.com

U.S. Global Investors Funds
(open-end)
7900 Callaghan Road
San Antonio, Texas 78229
(210) 308-1234
www.usfunds.com

**Valley Forge Management
Corporation** (open-end)
1375 Anthony Wayne Drive
Wayne, Pennsylvania
(610) 688-6839
www.vfam.com

**Value Trend Capital Management
LP** (open-end)
480 North Magnolia Avenue,
Suite 103
El Cajon, California 92020
(800) 590-0898

Van Den Berg Management Inc.
(open-end)
805 Las Cimas Parkway, Suite 430
Austin, Texas 78746
(888) 859-5856

Van Eck Associates Corporation
(open-end)
99 Park Avenue
New York, New York 10016
(800) 826-1115
www.vaneck.com

Vanguard Group Inc. (open-end)
100 Vanguard Boulevard
Malvern, Pennsylvania 19355
(800) 662-7447
www.vanguard.com

Van Kampen Asset Management
(open-end and closed-end)
522 Fifth Avenue
New York, New York 10016
(800) 847-2424
www.vankampen.com

**Vantagepoint Investment Advisors
LLC** (open-end)
777 North Capital Street NE,
Suite 600
Washington, D.C. 20002
(202) 962-4600
www.icmarc.org

Van Wagoner Capital Management
(open-end)
Three Embarcadero Center,
Suite 1120
San Francisco, California 94111
(800) 228-2121

Victoria 1522 Investments LP
(open-end)
244 California Street, Suite 610
San Francisco, California 94111
(888) 819-1522

Victory Capital Management Inc.
(open-end)
127 Public Square
Cleveland, Ohio 44114
(800) 539-3863
www.victoryfunds.com

Viking Fund Management LLC
(open-end)
1400 14th Avenue SW
Minot, North Dakota 58701
(800) 933-8413

Virtus Investment Partners
(open-end)
56 Prospect Street
Hartford, Connecticut 06115
(800) 243-1574

Volumetric Advisors Inc.
(open-end)
87 Violet Drive
Pearl River, New York 10965
(845) 623-7637
www.volumetric.com

Voyageur Asset Management Inc.
(open-end)
100 South Fifth Street, Suite 2300
Minneapolis, Minnesota 55402
(800) 422-2766

VTL Associates LLC (open-end)
2005 Market Street, Suite 2020
Philadelphia, Pennsylvania 19103
(877) 738-8870

**Waddell & Reed Investment
Management Company**
(open-end)
6300 Lamar Avenue
Shawnee Mission, Kansas 66202
(888) 923-3355
www.waddell.com

Wallace R. Weitz & Company
(open-end)
1125 South 103rd Street, Suite 600
Omaha, Nebraska 68124
(402) 391-1980

**Wall Street Management
Corporation** (open-end)
230 Park Avenue, Suite 1635
New York, New York 10169
(212) 856-8200

Walthausen & Company LLC
(open-end)
9 Executive Park Drive, Suite B
Clifton Park, New York 12065
(888) 925-8428

Wasatch Advisors Inc. (open-end)
150 Social Hall Avenue
Salt Lake City, Utah 84111
(800) 551-1700
www.wasatchfunds.com

Water Island Capital LLC
(open-end)
41 Madison Avenue, 28th Floor
New York, New York 10010
(309) 821-4600

**Wayne Hummer Management
Company** (open-end)
300 South Wacker Drive, Suite 1500
Chicago, Illinois 60606
(877) 942-8434
www.whummer.com

WB Capital Mutual Funds
(open-end)
2203 Grand Avenue
Des Moines, Iowa 50312
(515) 244-5426

Wegener LLC (open-end)
5575 Vincent Gate Terrace,
Suite 1248
Alexandria, Virginia 23312
(800) 595-4077

Weiss Capital Management Inc.
(open-end)
7111 Fairway Drive, Suite 102
Palm Beach Gardens, Florida 33418
(800) 430-9617

Wellesley Investment Advisors Inc.
(open-end)
20 William Street
Wellesley, Massachusetts 02481
(877) 441-4434

Wells Asset Management Inc.
(open-end)
6200 The Corners Parkway, Suite 102
Atlanta, Georgia 33418
(800) 222-1581

Wells Fargo Fund Management
(open-end)
525 Market Street, 12th Floor
San Francisco, California 94105
(800) 222-8222
www.wellsfargoadvantagefunds.com

Wentworth Hauser & Violich Inc.
(open-end)
301 Battery Street, Suite 400
San Francisco, California 94111
(888) 948-4685

**Wertz York Capital Management
Group LLC** (open-end)
3434 Colwell Avenue, Suite 100
Tampa, Florida 33614
(866) 329-2673

Wesbanco Bank Wheeling
(open-end)
One Bank Plaza
Wheeling, West Virginia 26003
(800) 864-1013
www.wesmarkfunds.com

**Westchester Capital Management
Inc.** (open-end)
100 Summit Lake Drive
Valhalla, New York 10595
(800) 343-8959

Westcore Funds (open-end)
370 17th Street, Suite 3100
Denver, Colorado 80202
(800) 392-2673
www.westcore.com

**Western Asset Management
Company** (closed-end)
385 East Colorado Boulevard
Pasadena, California 91101
(888) 777-0102
www.leggmason.com/cef

Weston Financial Group (open-end)
40 William Street, Suite 100
Wellesley, Massachusetts 02481
(781) 239-0445

Westport Advisors LLC (open-end)
53 Riverside Avenue
Westport, Connecticut 06880
(888) 593-7878
www.westportfunds.com

Westwood Management Group
(open-end)
200 Crescent Court, Suite 1200
Dallas, Texas 75201
(877) 386-3944

William Blair & Company
(open-end)
222 West Adams Street
Chicago, Illinois 60606
(312) 364-8000
www.williamblairfunds.com

Willis Group Inc. (open-end)
128 South Tejon Street, Suite 150
Colorado Springs, Colorado 80903
(888) 544-2685

Wilmington Funds (open-end)
P.O. Box 9828
Providence, Rhode Island 02940
(800) 336-9970
www.wilmingtontrust.com

Wilshire Target Funds (open-end)
1299 Ocean Avenue, Suite 700
Santa Monica, California 90401
(888) 200-6796

Winans International Inc.
 (open-end)
330 Ignacio Boulevard, Suite 203
Novato, California 94949
(866) 722-1677

Windowpane Advisors LLC
 (open-end)
600 West Broadway, Suite 1225
San Diego, California 92101
(800) 441-7013

**Winslow Management Company
 LLC** (open-end)
99 High Street, 12th Floor
Boston, Massachusetts 02110
(888) 314-9049
www.winslowgreen.com

Wintergreen Advisors LLC
 (open-end)
333 Route 46 West
Mountain Lakes, New Jersey 07046
(888) 468-6473

**Wisdom Tree Asset Management
 Inc.** (open-end)
380 Madison Avenue, 21st Floor
New York, New York 10017
(866) 909-9473

WP Stewart & Company Inc.
 (open-end)
527 Madison Avenue, Floor 20
New York, New York 10022
(212) 750-8585

Wright Management LLC (open-end)
3420 Ocean Park Boulevard,
 Suite 3080
Santa Monica, California 90405
(866) 738-4363
www.wisi.com

Xshares Advisors LLC (open-end)
420 Lexington Avenue, Suite 2550
New York, New York 10170
(800) 925-2870

**Yacktman Asset Management
 Company** (open-end)
6300 Bridgepoint Parkway
Austin, Texas 78730
(800) 525-8258
www.yacktman.com

Yieldquest Advisors LLC
 (open-end)
3280 Peachtree Road, Suite 2600
Atlanta, Georgia 30305
(877) 497-3534

**Yorktown Management & Research
 Inc.** (open-end)
2303 Yorktown Avenue
Lynchburg, Virginia 24501
(804) 846-1361

Zacks Investment Management Inc.
 (open-end)
100 North Riverside Plaza, Suite 2200
Chicago, Illinois 60606
(800) 453-4003

Zweig Advisors LLC (closed-end)
900 Third Avenue
New York, New York 10022
(800) 272-2700
www.virtus.com

ETFs

ETFs, or exchange-traded funds, are baskets of securities that trade continuously on stock exchanges, like any stock. In contrast, mutual funds are priced once at the end of each trading day. ETFs can consist of stocks, bonds, commodities or currencies and can track either a particular index, a single country, a sector or an industry. Operating costs are generally low, but trades require a commission or fee.

The following is a list of the names, addresses, telephone numbers and web sites of the companies offering ETFs. Most of these companies offer more than one ETF. Current information about these exchange-traded portfolios appears each week in *Barron's* magazine.

BlackRock, Inc.
52 East 52nd Street
New York, New York 10055
(212) 810-5300
www.blackrock.com

BNY Mellon Asset Management
One Wall Street
New York, New York 10286
(212) 495-1784
www.bnymellon.com

Charles Schwab Corporation
120 Kearny Street
San Francisco, California 94108
(415) 636-7000
www.schwab.com

Claymore Advisors LLC
2455 Corporate West Drive
Lisle, Illinois 60532
(630) 505-3700
www.claymore.com

**Cohen and Steers Capital
  Management Inc.**
280 Park Avenue
New York, New York 10017
(800) 330-7348
www.cohenandsteers.com

DB Commodity Services LLC
60 Wall Street
New York, New York 10005
(212) 250-5883
www.dbfunds.db.com

**Fidelity Management and Research
  Company**
82 Devonshire Street
Boston, Massachusetts 02109
(617) 563-7000
www.fidelity.com

First Trust Advisors LP
120 East Liberty Drive, Suite 400
Wheaton, Illinois 60187
(630) 765-8000
www.ftportfolio.com

Focusshares LLC
210 Summit Avenue, Suite C 11
Montvale, New Jersey 07645
(201) 930-8500
www.focusshares.com

**Greenhaven Commodity Services
  LLC**
1290 Broadway, Suite 1100
Denver, Colorado 80203
(866) 501-7704
www.greenhavenfunds.com

**Invesco Powershares Capital
  Management LLC**
1555 Peachtree Street N.E.,
  Suite 1800
Atlanta, Georgia 30304
(404) 479-1095
www.invesco.com

J.P. Morgan Funds
P.O. Box 8528
Boston, Massachusetts 02266
(800) 480-4111
www.jpmorganfunds.com

Macromarkets LLC
14 Main Street
Madison, New Jersey 07940
(973) 889-1973
www.macromarkets.com

Merrill Lynch HOLDRs
4 World Financial Center
New York, New York 10080
(212) 449-1000
www.ml.com

Northern Trust Investments NA
50 South LaSalle Street
Chicago, Illinois 60603
(877) 651-9156
www.northerntrust.com

PDR Services LLC
11 Wall Street
New York, New York 10005
(212) 656-3000
www.nyse.com

Proshare Advisors LLC
7501 Wisconsin Avenue, Suite 1000
Bethesda, Maryland 20814
(866) 776-5125
www.proshares.com

Rafferty Asset Management LLC
33 Whitehall Street, 10th Floor
New York, New York 10004
(646) 572-3390
www.direxionfunds.com

Rydex Investments
9601 Blackwell Road, Suite 500
Rockville, Maryland 20850
(800) 717-7776
www.rydex-sgi.com

SPA ETF Inc.
4 Triton Square
Regent's Place
London NW1 3NG United Kingdom
+44 207 396-3270
www.spa-etf.com

State Street Global Advisors
One Lincoln Street
Boston, Massachusetts 02111
(617) 786-3000
www.statestreet.com

**United States Commodity Funds
  LLC**
1290 Broadway, Suite 1100
Denver, Colorado 80203
(800) 920-0259
www.unitedstatescommodityfunds.
  com

Van Eck Associates Corporation
335 Madison Avenue, 19th Floor
New York, New York 10017
(212) 293-2000
www.vaneck.com

Vanguard Group Inc.
400 Devon Park Drive
Wayne, Pennsylvania 19087
(877) 662-7447
www.vanguard.com

VTL Associates LLC
2005 Market Street, Suite 2020
Philadelphia, Pennsylvania 19103
(215) 854-8181
www.vtlassoc.com

Wisdom Tree Asset Management Inc.
380 Madison Avenue, 21st Floor
New York, New York 10017
(866) 909-9473
www.wisdomtree.com

Xshares Advisors LLC
420 Lexington Avenue, Suite 2550
New York, New York 10170
(800) 925-2870
www.xsharesadvisors.com

Ziegler Capital Management LLC
250 East Wisconsin Avenue,
  Suite 1900
Milwaukee, Wisconsin 53202
(414) 978-6400
www.ziegler.com

4. HISTORICAL DATA

This section of the *Handbook* allows you to follow the major ups and downs of the financial markets and the United States economy during the 20th century and into the early 21st century. Although history never repeats itself exactly, it is important to understand historical market cycles if you are to understand where the markets and economy stand today, as well as where they might be going in the future.

The historical section is presented with graphs accompanied by tabular data and explanations of what the information signifies to you as an investor. Graphs are based on end-of-month closing stock index values; municipal bond yields compiled the first week of each month; month-end London afternoon fix prices of gold; monthly average discount, prime, and federal funds rates; and monthly or monthly average government economic statistics.

The tabular data show annual highs, lows, and year-end figures on the same monthly bases as the above with these exceptions: stock indexes are based on daily closing figures; the consumer and producer price indexes and money supply (M-1) statistics are annual percentage changes (for instance, December 2005 vs. December 2004); gold prices are daily London afternoon fixings; and the discount and prime rates are day-end figures.

Note that the month-end data points on which the stock index graphs are based may reflect different highs and lows than the daily closing data. The month-end data plot long-term trends with a minimum of aberrations caused by PROGRAM TRADES and other NOISE, while the daily data are more subject to short-term fluctuations. The graphs showing trends of the discount and prime rates, because they are based on monthly averages, will also differ from the accompanying tables, which are based on day-end rates.

The sources of the data and related charts have been credited.

AMEX COMPOSITE INDEX

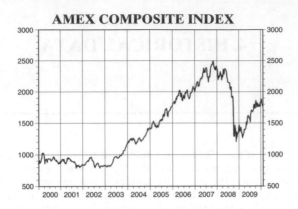

Source: Thomson Reuters Datastream

The AMEX Composite (symbol XAX) is a capitalization-weighted, price appreciation index that measures the performance of about 800 issues, including the common shares and American Depositary Receipts of all Amex-listed companies, REITs, master limited partnership, and closed-end investment vehicles. The companies listed on the American Stock Exchange tend to be medium-sized and smaller growth firms. The AMEX Composite Index replaced the AMEX Market Value Index (XAM) on January 2, 1997. The Market Value Index had been calculated on a total return basis to include reinvestment of dividends and price change. The AMEX Composite's capitalization method is the same as most other major market indices.

Year	High	Low	Close
1970	58.60	36.10	49.21
1971	60.86	49.09	58.49
1972	69.18	58.55	64.53
1973	65.24	42.61	45.17
1974	51.46	29.13	30.16
1975	48.43	31.10	41.74
1976	54.92	42.16	54.92
1977	63.95	54.81	63.95
1978	88.44	59.87	75.28
1979	123.54	76.02	123.54
1980	185.38	107.85	174.50
1981	190.18	138.38	160.32
1982	170.93	118.65	170.30
1983	254.33	169.61	223.01
1984	227.73	187.16	203.24
1985	246.13	201.93	246.13
1986	285.19	240.30	263.27
1987	365.01	231.90	260.35
1988	309.59	262.76	306.00
1989	397.29	304.60	377.72
1990	383.32	286.93	308.11
1991	395.06	295.80	395.05

Year	High	Low	Close
1992	419.18	361.72	399.23
1993	484.59	394.97	477.15
1994	488.00	419.43	433.67
1995	553.96	432.20	548.23
1996	616.32	510.98	583.28
1997	723.03	541.02	684.61
1998	753.67	563.75	688.99
1999	876.97	683.61	876.97
2000	1036.40	846.59	897.75
2001	958.75	780.46	847.61
2002	992.69	771.81	824.38
2003	1175.19	803.54	1173.55
2004	1434.34	1160.18	1434.34
2005	1766.99	1385.85	1759.08
2006	2085.15	1781.62	2053.48
2007	2538.91	1999.60	2409.62
2008	2419.04	1157.44	1397.53
2009	1878.84	1246.46	1824.95

BOND BUYER INDEX (20 BONDS)

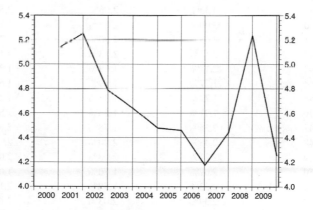

Source: Thomson Reuters Datastream

This graph shows the movement of the *Bond Buyer* Index of 20 bonds. The *Bond Buyer* is a daily newspaper covering the municipal bond market. This index is made up of the yields of 20 newly issued general obligation municipal bonds with an average maturity of 20 years, rated from Baa to AAA, thus including all those of investment grade, and selling at par. The issuers of these bonds are among the most creditworthy of all those issuing bonds in the municipal market.

Year	High	Low	Close
1917	4.56%	3.92%	4.62%
1918	4.72%	4.40%	4.44%
1919	4.55%	4.44%	4.56%
1920	5.27%	4.56%	5.06%
1921	5.26%	4.50%	5.06%
1922	4.41%	4.09%	4.16%
1923	4.40%	4.11%	4.37%
1924	4.37%	4.11%	4.16%
1925	4.26%	3.99%	4.23%
1926	4.23%	4.10%	4.13%
1927	4.13%	3.93%	3.87%
1928	4.18%	3.87%	4.17%
1929	4.49%	4.17%	4.23%
1930	4.29%	3.97%	4.12%
1931	4.45%	3.74%	4.87%
1932	5.09%	4.57%	4.61%
1933	5.69%	4.48%	5.48%
1934	5.48%	3.89%	3.81%
1935	3.8%	3.23%	3.25%
1936	3.25%	2.69%	2.62%
1937	3.17%	2.62%	3.16%
1938	3.19%	2.83%	2.78%
1939	3.30%	2.66%	2.59%
1940	3.00%	2.18%	2.14%
1941	2.43%	1.90%	2.24%
1942	2.51%	2.13%	2.17%
1943	2.17%	1.69%	1.77%
1944	1.77%	1.59%	1.62%
1945	1.72%	1.35%	1.42%
1946	1.91%	1.29%	1.85%
1947	2.35%	1.78%	2.36%
1948	2.48%	2.20%	2.19%
1949	2.21%	2.08%	2.07%
1950	2.07%	1.70%	1.06%
1951	2.23%	1.58%	2.11%
1952	2.39%	2.03%	2.40%
1953	3.09%	2.40%	2.54%
1954	2.54%	2.26%	2.38%
1955	2.63%	2.37%	2.56%
1956	3.24%	2.42%	3.23%
1957	3.57%	2.96%	2.97%
1958	3.59%	2.85%	3.40%
1959	3.81%	3.26%	3.78%
1960	3.78%	3.27%	3.39%
1961	3.55%	3.26%	3.37%
1962	3.37%	2.98%	3.05%
1963	3.31%	3.01%	3.26%
1964	3.32%	3.12%	3.07%

Year	High	Low	Close
1965	3.56%	3.04%	3.53%
1966	4.24%	3.51%	3.76%
1967	4.45%	3.40%	4.38%
1968	4.85%	4.07%	4.85%
1969	6.90%	4.82%	6.61%
1970	7.12%	5.33%	5.74%
1971	6.23%	4.97%	5.03%
1972	5.54%	4.96%	5.08%
1973	5.59%	4.99%	5.18%
1974	7.15%	5.16%	7.08%
1975	7.67%	6.27%	7.13%
1976	7.13%	5.83%	5.83%
1977	5.93%	5.45%	5.66%
1978	6.67%	5.58%	6.61%
1979	7.38%	6.08%	7.23%
1980	10.56%	7.11%	9.76%
1981	13.30%	9.49%	13.30%
1982	13.44%	9.25%	9.56%
1983	10.04%	8.78%	9.76%
1984	11.07%	9.51%	9.91%
1985	9.87%	8.36%	8.36%
1986	8.33%	6.77%	6.83%
1987	9.17%	6.54%	7.86%
1988	7.97%	7.33%	7.50%
1989	7.72%	6.86%	6.97%
1990	7.53%	7.08%	7.14%
1991	7.14%	6.58%	6.58%
1992	6.77%	5.89%	6.17%
1993	6.10%	5.28%	5.28%
1994	7.03%	5.28%	6.71%
1995	6.66%	5.35%	5.44%
1996	6.12%	5.33%	5.66%
1997	5.88%	5.17%	5.17%
1998	5.32%	4.82%	5.03%
1999	6.00%	4.96%	6.00%
2000	6.11%	5.14%	5.14%
2001	5.34%	4.91%	5.26%
2002	5.34%	4.66%	4.79%
2003	5.10%	4.33%	4.64%
2004	5.07%	4.41%	4.48%
2005	4.57%	4.23%	4.46%
2006	4.71%	4.03%	4.17%
2007	4.81%	4.08%	4.44%
2008	6.01%	4.15%	5.24%
2009	5.16%	3.94%	4.25%

DOW JONES INDUSTRIAL AVERAGE

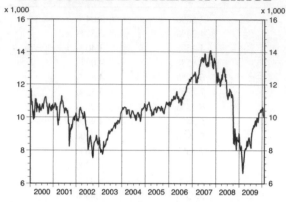

Source: Thomson Reuters Datastream

The graph above shows the movement of the Dow Jones Industrial Average, the oldest and most widely used of all stock market indicators. When people ask "What did the market do today?" they usually expect to hear whether this average was up or down for the day. The price-weighted average is comprised of the stocks of 30 blue-chip firms. The components, which change from time to time, represent between 15% and 20% of the market value of all NYSE stocks. The Dow, as it is known, is calculated by adding the closing prices of the component stocks and using a divisor that adjusts for splits and stock dividends equal to 10% or more of the market issue as well as for mergers and changes in the components of the list. The Dow Jones 65 Composite Stock Average is composed of the Dow Jones 30 industrials, the Dow Jones 20 transportations, and the Dow Jones 15 utilities.

The components of the Dow Jones Industrial Average (DJIA) are

    3M Company
    Alcoa, Inc.
    American Express Company
    AT&T, Inc.
    Bank of America
    The Boeing Company
    Caterpillar, Inc.
    Chevron
    Cisco Systems
    Coca-Cola Company
    E.I. Dupont de Nemours and Company
    ExxonMobil Corporation
    General Electric Company
    Hewlett-Packard Company
    Home Depot, Inc.
    Intel Corporation
    International Business Machines Corporation
    Johnson & Johnson Company
    J.P. Morgan Chase & Company, Inc.
    Kraft Foods
    McDonald's Corporation

Merck & Company
Microsoft Corporation
Pfizer, Inc.
The Procter & Gamble Company
Travelers Companies
United Technologies Corporation
Verizon Communications, Inc.
Wal-Mart Stores, Inc.
The Walt Disney Company

Year	High	Low	Close
1897	55.82	38.49	49.41
1898	60.97	42.00	60.52
1899	77.61	58.27	66.08
1900	71.04	52.96	70.71
1901	78.26	61.52	64.56
1902	68.44	59.57	64.29
1903	67.70	42.15	49.11
1904	73.23	46.41	69.61
1905	96.56	68.76	96.20
1906	103.00	85.18	93.63
1907	96.37	53.00	58.75
1908	88.38	58.62	86.15
1909	100.53	79.91	99.05
1910	98.34	73.62	81.36
1911	87.06	72.94	81.68
1912	94.15	80.15	87.87
1913	88.57	72.11	78.78
1914	83.43	53.17	53.17
1915	99.21	54.22	99.15
1916	110.15	84.96	95.00
1917	99.18	65.95	74.38
1918	89.07	73.38	82.20
1919	119.62	79.15	107.23
1920	109.88	66.75	71.95
1921	81.50	63.90	81.10
1922	103.43	78.59	98.73
1923	105.38	85.76	95.52
1924	120.51	88.33	120.51
1925	159.39	115.00	156.66
1926	166.64	135.20	157.20
1927	202.40	152.73	202.40
1928	300.00	191.33	300.00
1929	381.17	198.69	248.48
1930	294.07	157.51	164.58
1931	194.36	73.79	77.90
1932	88.78	41.22	59.93
1933	108.67	50.16	99.90

Year	High	Low	Close
1934	110.74	85.51	104.04
1935	148.44	96.71	144.13
1936	184.90	143.11	179.90
1937	194.40	113.64	120.85
1938	158.41	98.95	154.76
1939	155.92	121.44	150.24
1940	152.80	111.84	131.13
1941	133.59	106.34	110.96
1942	119.71	92.92	119.40
1943	145.82	119.26	135.89
1944	152.53	134.22	152.32
1945	195.82	151.35	192.91
1946	212.50	163.12	177.20
1947	186.85	163.21	181.16
1948	193.16	165.39	177.30
1949	200.52	161.60	200.13
1950	235.47	196.81	235.41
1951	276.37	238.99	269.23
1952	292.00	256.35	291.90
1953	293.79	255.49	280.90
1954	404.39	279.87	404.39
1955	488.40	388.20	488.40
1956	521.05	462.35	499.47
1957	520.77	419.79	435.69
1958	583.65	436.89	583.65
1959	679.36	574.46	679.36
1960	685.47	566.05	615.89
1961	734.91	610.25	731.14
1962	726.01	535.76	652.10
1963	767.21	646.79	762.95
1964	891.71	766.08	874.13
1965	969.26	840.59	969.26
1966	995.15	744.32	785.69
1967	943.08	786.41	905.11
1968	985.21	825.13	943.75
1969	968.85	769.93	800.36
1970	842.00	631.16	838.92
1971	950.82	797.97	890.20
1972	1036.27	889.15	1020.02
1973	1051.70	788.31	850.86
1974	891.66	577.60	616.24
1975	881.81	632.04	852.41
1976	1014.79	858.71	1004.65
1977	999.75	800.85	831.17
1978	907.74	742.12	805.01
1979	897.61	796.67	838.74

Year	High	Low	Close
1980	1000.17	759.13	963.99
1981	1024.05	824.01	875.00
1982	1070.55	776.92	1046.55
1983	1287.20	1027.04	1258.64
1984	1286.64	1086.57	1211.57
1985	1553.10	1184.96	1546.67
1986	1955.57	1502.29	1895.95
1987	2722.42	1738.74	1938.83
1988	2183.50	1879.14	2168.57
1989	2791.41	2144.64	2753.20
1990	3024.26	2344.31	2633.66
1991	3204.61	2447.03	3168.83
1992	3435.24	3087.41	3301.11
1993	3818.92	3219.25	3754.09
1994	4002.84	3520.80	3834.44
1995	5266.69	3794.40	5117.12
1996	6607.81	5000.07	6560.91
1997	8340.14	6315.84	7679.31
1998	9374.27	7539.06	9181.42
1999	11497.12	9120.69	11497.12
2000	11722.98	9796.04	10786.85
2001	11337.92	8235.81	10021.50
2002	10635.25	7286.27	8341.63
2003	10453.92	7524.06	10453.92
2004	10854.54	9749.99	10783.01
2005	10940.55	10012.36	10717.50
2006	12501.52	10688.77	12501.52
2007	14164.53	12050.41	13254.82
2008	13058.20	7552.29	8776.39
2009	10548.51	6547.05	10428.05

DOW JONES TRANSPORTATION STOCK AVERAGE

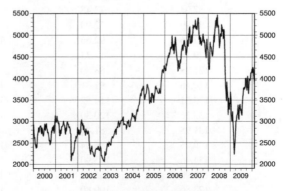

Source: Thomson Reuters Datastream

This graph shows the movement of the Dow Jones Transportation Stock Average. This price-weighted average consists of the stocks of the 20 large companies in the transportation business, which includes airlines, railroads, and trucking. The index is important not only in that it tracks the movement of a major segment of American industry, but also because it is watched by the proponents of the Dow Theory, which maintains that a significant trend is not confirmed until both the Dow Jones Industrial Average and Transportation Average reach new highs or lows; if they don't, the market will fall back to its former trading range, according to this theory. From 1897 to 1969, this average was called the Dow Jones Railroad Average. The Dow Jones 65 Composite Average is composed of the Dow Jones 20 Transportation Stock Average, as well as the Dow Jones 30 Industrials and the Dow Jones 15 Utilities.

The components of the Dow Jones Transportation Average are

Alexander & Baldwin, Inc.
AMR Corporation
CH Robinson Worldwide, Inc.
Continental Airlines, Inc.
Con-Way, Inc.
CSX Corporation
Delta Air Lines Inc.
Expeditors International of Washington, Inc.
Fedex Corporation
GATX Corporation
Hunt (J.B.) Transport Services, Inc.
JetBlue Airways Corporation
Kansas City Southern
Landstar System, Inc.
Norfolk Southern Corporation
Overseas Shipholding Group
Ryder System, Inc.
Southwest Airlines Company
Union Pacific Corporation
United Parcel Service

Year	High	Low	Close
1897	67.23	48.12	62.29
1898	74.99	55.89	74.99
1899	87.04	72.48	77.73
1900	94.99	72.99	94.99
1901	117.86	92.66	114.85
1902	129.36	111.73	118.98
1903	121.28	88.80	98.33
1904	119.46	91.31	117.43
1905	133.51	114.52	133.26
1906	138.36	120.30	129.80
1907	131.95	81.41	88.77
1908	120.05	86.04	120.05
1909	134.46	113.90	130.41
1910	129.90	105.59	114.06
1911	123.86	109.80	116.83
1912	124.35	114.92	116.84

Year	High	Low	Close
1913	118.10	100.50	103.72
1914	109.43	87.40	88.53
1915	108.28	87.85	108.05
1916	112.28	99.11	105.15
1917	105.76	70.75	79.73
1918	92.91	77.21	84.32
1919	91.13	73.63	75.30
1920	85.37	67.83	75.96
1921	77.56	65.52	74.27
1922	93.99	73.43	86.11
1923	90.63	76.78	80.86
1924	99.50	80.23	98.33
1925	112.93	92.98	112.93
1926	123.33	102.41	120.86
1927	144.82	119.29	140.30
1928	152.70	132.60	151.14
1929	189.11	128.07	144.72
1930	157.94	91.65	96.58
1931	111.58	31.42	33.63
1932	41.30	13.23	25.90
1933	56.53	23.43	40.80
1934	52.97	33.19	36.44
1935	41.84	27.31	40.48
1936	59.89	40.66	53.63
1937	64.46	28.91	29.46
1938	33.98	19.00	33.98
1939	35.90	24.14	31.83
1940	32.67	22.14	28.13
1941	30.88	24.25	25.42
1942	29.28	23.31	27.39
1943	38.30	27.59	33.56
1944	48.40	33.45	48.40
1945	64.89	47.03	62.80
1946	68.31	44.69	51.13
1947	53.42	41.16	52.48
1948	64.95	48.13	52.86
1949	54.29	41.03	52.76
1950	77.89	51.24	77.64
1951	90.08	72.39	81.70
1952	112.53	82.03	111.27
1953	112.21	90.56	94.03
1954	146.23	94.84	145.86
1955	167.83	137.84	163.29
1956	181.23	150.44	153.23
1957	157.67	95.67	96.96
1958	157.91	99.89	157.65
1959	173.56	146.65	154.05

Year	High	Low	Close
1960	160.43	123.37	130.85
1961	152.93	131.06	143.84
1962	149.83	114.86	141.04
1963	179.46	142.03	178.54
1964	224.91	178.81	205.34
1965	249.55	187.29	247.48
1966	271.72	184.34	202.97
1967	274.49	205.16	233.24
1968	279.48	214.58	271.60
1969	279.88	169.03	176.34
1970	183.31	116.69	171.52
1971	248.33	169.70	243.72
1972	275.71	212.24	227.17
1973	228.10	151.97	196.19
1974	202.45	125.93	143.44
1975	174.57	146.47	172.65
1976	237.03	175.69	237.03
1977	246.64	199.60	217.18
1978	261.49	199.31	206.56
1979	271.77	205.78	252.39
1980	425.68	233.69	398.10
1981	447.38	335.48	380.30
1982	464.55	292.12	448.38
1983	612.57	434.24	598.59
1984	612.63	444.03	558.13
1985	723.31	553.03	708.21
1986	866.74	686.97	807.17
1987	1101.16	661.00	748.86
1988	973.61	737.57	969.84
1989	1532.01	959.95	1177.81
1990	1225.18	809.73	910.23
1991	1368.27	882.22	1358.00
1992	1481.88	1196.35	1449.21
1993	1789.47	1441.15	1762.32
1994	1874.87	1353.96	1455.03
1995	2105.19	1443.62	1981.00
1996	2336.43	1858.88	2287.69
1997	3391.26	2203.27	3101.69
1998	3686.02	2345.00	3149.30
1999	3783.50	2808.44	2977.20
2000	2980.50	2263.59	2946.60
2001	3145.65	2033.86	2639.99
2002	3049.96	2013.02	2309.96
2003	3038.15	1942.19	3007.05
2004	3811.62	2750.80	3798.05
2005	4266.75	3382.89	4196.03
2006	4998.94	4148.37	4586.21

Year	High	Low	Close
2007	5446.49	4366.60	4570.55
2008	5492.95	2988.99	3537.15
2009	4188.16	2146.89	4099.63

DOW JONES UTILITY AVERAGE

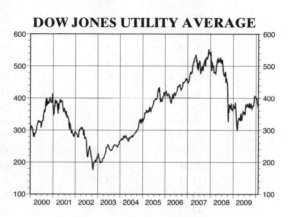

Source: Thomson Reuters Datastream

This price-weighted average is composed of 15 geographically representative and well-established gas and electric utility companies. Since utilities are heavy borrowers, their stock prices are inversely affected by the ups and downs of interest rates. The Dow Jones 65-stock Composite Average is composed of the 15 Dow Jones utilities, the 30 Dow Jones industrials, and the 20 Dow Jones transportation stocks.

The components of the Dow Jones Utility Average are

AES Corporation
American Electric Power, Inc.
CenterPoint Energy, Inc.
Consolidated Edison, Inc.
Dominion Resources
Duke Energy Corporation
Edison International
Exelon Corporation
FirstEnergy Corporation
Nextera Energy Inc.
NiSource, Inc.
PG&E Corporation
Public Service Enterprise Group, Inc.
Southern Company
Williams Companies

Year	High	Low	Close
1929	144.61	64.72	88.27
1930	108.62	55.14	60.80
1931	73.40	30.55	31.41
1932	36.11	16.53	27.50
1933	37.73	19.33	23.29

Year	High	Low	Close
1934	31.03	16.83	17.80
1935	29.78	14.46	29.55
1936	36.08	28.63	34.83
1937	37.54	19.65	20.35
1938	25.19	15.14	23.02
1939	27.10	20.71	25.58
1940	26.45	18.03	19.85
1941	20.65	13.51	14.02
1942	14.94	10.58	14.54
1943	22.30	14.69	21.87
1944	26.37	21.74	26.37
1945	39.15	26.15	38.13
1946	43.74	33.20	37.27
1947	37.55	32.28	33.40
1948	36.04	31.65	33.55
1949	41.31	33.36	41.29
1950	44.26	37.40	40.98
1951	47.22	41.47	47.22
1952	52.64	47.53	52.60
1953	53.88	47.87	52.04
1954	62.47	52.22	62.47
1955	66.68	61.39	64.16
1956	71.17	63.03	68.54
1957	74.61	62.10	68.58
1958	91.00	68.94	91.00
1959	94.70	85.05	87.83
1960	100.07	85.02	100.02
1961	135.90	99.75	129.16
1962	130.85	103.11	129.23
1963	144.37	129.19	138.99
1964	155.71	137.30	155.17
1965	163.32	149.84	152.63
1966	152.39	118.96	136.18
1967	140.43	120.97	127.91
1968	141.30	119.79	137.17
1969	139.95	106.31	110.08
1970	121.84	95.86	121.84
1971	128.39	108.03	117.75
1972	124.14	105.06	119.50
1973	120.72	84.42	89.37
1974	95.09	57.93	68.76
1975	87.07	72.02	83.65
1976	108.38	84.52	108.38
1977	118.67	104.97	111.28
1978	110.98	96.35	98.24
1979	109.74	98.24	106.60
1980	117.34	96.04	114.42
1981	117.81	101.28	109.02

Year	High	Low	Close
1982	122.83	103.22	119.46
1983	140.70	119.51	131.84
1984	149.93	122.25	149.52
1985	174.96	146.54	174.81
1986	219.15	169.47	206.01
1987	227.83	160.98	175.08
1988	190.02	167.08	186.28
1989	235.98	181.84	235.04
1990	236.98	187.94	209.70
1991	226.53	194.54	226.15
1992	226.46	199.67	221.02
1993	257.58	215.82	229.30
1994	229.77	172.03	181.52
1995	226.66	180.79	225.40
1996	239.59	202.84	235.95
1997	270.81	207.80	267.60
1998	320.51	262.66	312.30
1999	333.45	269.20	283.36
2000	416.11	274.12	412.16
2001	412.16	275.10	293.94
2002	310.75	167.57	215.18
2003	267.70	190.22	266.90
2004	336.86	261.89	334.95
2005	437.63	324.68	405.11
2006	462.19	382.49	458.00
2007	552.74	445.16	532.53
2008	550.06	324.57	370.76
2009	406.72	290.68	398.01

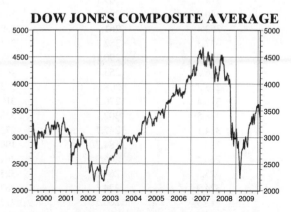

DOW JONES COMPOSITE AVERAGE

Source: Thomson Reuters Datastream

This average, also known as the 65 Stock Average, is made up of the 30 stocks in the Dow Jones Industrial Average, the 20 stocks in the Dow Jones Transportation Average, and the 15 stocks in the Dow Jones Utility Average. The average therefore is significant because it combines the three blue-chip averages and thus gives a good indication of the overall direction of the largest, most established companies.

Year	High	Low	Close
1939	53.0	40.4	50.6
1940	51.7	37.2	44.0
1941	44.9	35.5	39.4
1942	39.6	31.5	39.6
1943	50.9	39.8	47.1
1944	56.6	47.0	56.6
1945	73.5	55.9	73.5
1946	79.4	58.5	65.4
1947	67.1	57.3	65.1
1948	71.9	59.9	64.7
1949	71.9	57.8	71.9
1950	87.2	70.3	87.2
1951	100.0	86.9	97.4
1952	113.6	96.1	113.6
1953	114.0	98.2	108.0
1954	150.2	106.0	150.2
1955	174.2	137.8	174.2
1956	184.1	164.3	174.2
1957	179.9	142.8	149.4
1958	202.4	147.4	202.4
1959	233.5	200.1	219.5
1960	222.6	190.4	206.1
1961	251.4	204.8	249.6
1962	245.8	187.4	228.9
1963	269.1	228.7	269.1
1964	314.2	269.1	307.5
1965	340.9	290.4	340.9
1966	352.4	261.3	290.3
1967	337.3	282.7	314.1
1968	353.1	290.1	352.7
1969	346.2	253.0	268.3
1970	273.2	208.7	273.2
1971	318.4	270.2	310.1
1972	338.5	302.1	338.5
1973	334.1	247.7	272.5
1974	282.5	184.2	199.7
1975	268.2	205.3	261.7
1976	325.5	264.5	325.5
1977	324.9	274.3	287.2
1978	315.3	260.7	272.2
1979	315.1	274.3	298.3
1980	388.9	271.7	373.4
1981	394.6	320.6	347.8
1982	416.3	299.4	409.2
1983	515.1	401.0	502.9

Year	High	Low	Close
1984	514.0	421.4	489.9
1985	619.4	480.9	616.5
1986	767.9	602.8	736.8
1987	992.2	653.7	714.2
1988	830.2	700.7	825.9
1989	1115.1	816.9	1035.1
1990	1073.82	830.62	920.61
1991	1167.02	869.42	1156.82
1992	1222.29	1092.09	1204.55
1993	1402.07	1188.85	1381.03
1994	1457.25	1207.50	1274.41
1995	1748.95	1265.28	1693.21
1996	2078.55	1642.43	2058.78
1997	2669.31	1984.65	2520.94
1998	2960.80	2411.00	2870.83
1999	3366.13	2831.53	3214.38
2000	3323.74	2751.55	3317.61
2001	3392.23	2489.27	2892.23
2002	3093.84	2033.44	2374.96
2003	3008.18	2108.95	3000.75
2004	3412.44	2852.12	3395.82
2005	3696.50	3211.74	3638.06
2006	4172.73	3658.44	4136.72
2007	4731.10	4107.53	4394.05
2008	4569.16	2669.51	3086.07
2009	3619.61	2195.30	3566.68

GOLD (London Afternoon Fix Price)

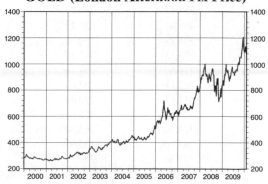

Source: Thomson Reuters Datastream

This graph shows the movement of the per troy ounce gold price, according to the month-end afternoon fixings in London. Twice each business day (at 10:30 A.M. and 3:30 P.M.), five major metals dealers meet in London to fix a benchmark price for gold, after assessing supply and demand at that time. Gold has traditionally been considered a store of value against both the erosion through inflation of a currency's purchasing power and political instability or turmoil. From the 1930s until the early 1970s, gold was fixed at $35 an ounce in the United States. When trading in the metal resumed, gold at first rose to about $200 an ounce, then fell to about $100, then rose again modestly in the mid-1970s. In the late 1970s and early 1980s, with inflation driven by rising oil prices, compounded by Middle East tensions, the gold price soared to $850. It then dropped precipitously and after a period of relative stability in the mid-1980s began falling as a reflection of disinflation. Gold prices fell for the most part in the 1990s to a low of about $250. Starting in the 2000s, gold rebounded sharply to well over $500. By 2010, gold broke through the $1,000 barrier.

Year	High	Low	Close
1975	185.25	128.75	140.25
1976	140.35	103.50	134.50
1977	167.95	121.00	164.95
1978	242.75	160.90	226.00
1979	512.00	216.85	512.00
1980	850.00	481.50	589.75
1981	599.25	391.25	397.50
1982	481.00	296.75	456.90
1983	509.25	374.50	382.40
1984	405.85	307.50	309.00
1985	340.90	284.25	326.80
1986	438.10	326.30	396.13
1987	499.75	390.00	484.10
1988	483.90	395.30	410.25
1989	415.80	355.75	398.60
1990	423.75	345.85	386.20
1991	403.00	344.25	353.20
1992	359.60	330.25	332.90
1993	405.60	326.10	391.75
1994	396.25	369.65	383.25
1995	395.55	372.40	387.00
1996	414.80	367.40	369.25
1997	362.15	283.00	290.20
1998	313.15	273.40	287.80
1999	325.50	252.80	290.25
2000	312.70	263.80	274.45
2001	293.25	255.95	276.50
2002	349.30	277.75	347.20
2003	417.25	320.00	417.25
2004	452.85	375.00	438.10
2005	537.10	412.10	512.55
2006	568.50	547.80	548.15
2007	665.70	657.20	663.55
2008	926.90	916.35	920.80
2009	946.20	911.90	942.30

NASDAQ COMPOSITE INDEX

Source: Thomson Reuters Datastream

This market-value weighted index is composed of all the stocks traded on the Nasdaq Stock Market. The companies in this index are smaller growth companies, many of them in high technology and financial services. The direction of the index is used by analysts to gauge investor interest in more speculative stocks. In times of enthusiasm for small stocks, this index will rise dramatically, and it will fall just as much when investors opt for safety instead of risk.

Year	High	Low	Close
1971	114.12	99.68	114.12
1972	135.15	113.65	133.73
1973	136.84	88.67	92.19
1974	96.53	54.87	59.82
1975	88.00	60.70	77.62
1976	97.88	78.06	97.88
1977	105.05	93.66	105.05
1978	139.25	99.09	117.98
1979	152.29	117.84	151.14
1980	208.15	124.09	202.34
1981	223.47	175.03	195.84
1982	240.70	159.14	232.41
1983	328.91	230.59	278.60
1984	287.90	225.30	247.35
1985	325.22	245.91	325.22
1986	411.16	323.01	348.83
1987	455.26	291.88	330.47
1988	396.11	331.97	381.38
1989	485.73	378.56	454.82
1990	469.60	325.44	373.84
1991	586.34	355.75	586.34
1992	676.95	547.84	676.95
1993	787.42	645.87	776.80
1994	803.93	693.79	751.96
1995	1069.79	743.58	1052.13
1996	1316.27	988.57	1291.03

Year	High	Low	Close
1997	1745.85	1201.00	1570.35
1998	2192.69	1419.12	2192.69
1999	4069.31	2208.05	4069.31
2000	5048.62	2332.78	2470.52
2001	2859.15	1423.19	1950.40
2002	2059.38	1114.11	1335.51
2003	2009.88	1271.47	2003.37
2004	2178.34	1752.49	2175.44
2005	2273.37	1904.18	2205.32
2006	2465.98	2020.39	2425.57
2007	2859.12	2340.68	2652.28
2008	1577.03	2609.63	1316.12
2009	2291.28	1268.64	2269.15

NYSE COMPOSITE INDEX

Source: Thomson Reuters Datastream

The New York Stock Exchange Composite Index is a market-value weighted index that provides a broader measure of the performance of the New York Stock Exchange than the more widely quoted Dow Jones Industrial Average. Stock index futures and options on the NYSE Composite are traded on the New York Futures Exchange, a subsidiary of the New York Board of Trade. The NYSE Composite was recalculated as of December 31, 2002, so index figures after this date are not comparable to earlier periods.

Year	High	Low	Close
1968	61.27	48.70	58.90
1969	59.32	49.31	51.53
1970	52.36	37.69	50.23
1971	57.76	49.60	56.43
1972	65.14	56.23	64.48
1973	65.48	49.05	51.82
1974	53.37	32.89	36.13
1975	51.24	37.06	47.64
1976	57.88	48.04	57.88
1977	57.69	49.78	52.50

Year	High	Low	Close
1978	60.38	48.37	53.62
1979	63.39	53.88	61.95
1980	81.02	55.30	77.86
1981	79.14	64.96	71.41
1982	82.35	58.80	81.03
1983	99.63	79.79	95.18
1984	98.12	85.13	96.38
1985	121.90	94.60	121.58
1986	145.75	117.75	138.58
1987	187.99	125.91	138.23
1988	159.42	136.72	156.26
1989	199.34	154.98	195.04
1990	201.55	161.76	180.49
1991	229.85	169.74	229.44
1992	242.76	216.86	240.21
1993	261.16	235.15	259.08
1994	267.78	241.79	250.94
1995	331.73	249.86	329.51
1996	401.08	320.90	398.10
1997	515.24	386.36	493.60
1998	600.75	477.20	595.80
1999	663.12	576.16	650.29
2000	677.58	576.42	656.87
2001	666.57	504.21	589.80
2002	609.53	421.09	473.87
2003	6443.60	4486.70	6440.30
2004	7253.56	6217.06	7250.06
2005	7852.18	6935.31	7753.95
2006	9172.76	7719.77	9172.76
2007	10311.61	8837.97	9740.32
2008	9656.00	4651.21	5757.05
2009	7261.24	4226.31	7184.96

S&P 500 STOCK INDEX

Source: Thomson Reuters Datastream

The Standard & Poor's 500 Stock Index is a market-value weighted index composed of mainly large-cap companies. Most of the stocks in the S&P 500 are found on the New York Stock Exchange, though there are a few from the American Stock Exchange and the Nasdaq Stock Market. The index represents about 80 percent of the market value of all U.S. equities. The S&P is commonly considered the benchmark against which the performance of individual stocks or stock groups is measured. It is a far broader measure of market activity than the Dow Jones Industrial Average, even though the DJIA is quoted more widely. There are mutual funds, called index funds, which aim to mirror the performance of the S&P 500. Such funds appeal to investors who wish to match the general performance of the stock market. Stock index futures and options are also traded on the S&P 500 and its smaller version, the S&P 100, on the Chicago Mercantile Exchange and the Chicago Board Options Exchange.

Year	High	Low	Close
1930	25.92	14.44	15.34
1931	18.17	7.72	8.12
1932	9.31	4.40	6.89
1933	12.20	5.53	10.10
1934	11.82	8.36	9.50
1935	13.46	8.06	13.43
1936	17.69	13.40	17.18
1937	18.68	10.17	10.55
1938	13.79	8.50	13.21
1939	13.23	10.18	12.49
1940	12.77	8.99	10.58
1941	10.86	8.37	8.69
1942	9.77	7.47	9.77
1943	12.64	9.84	11.67
1944	13.29	11.56	13.28
1945	17.68	13.21	17.36
1946	19.25	14.12	15.30
1947	16.20	13.71	15.30
1948	17.06	13.84	15.20
1949	16.79	13.55	16.76
1950	20.43	16.65	20.41
1951	23.85	20.69	23.77
1952	26.59	23.09	26.57
1953	26.66	22.71	24.81
1954	35.98	24.80	35.98
1955	46.41	34.58	45.48
1956	49.74	43.11	46.67
1957	49.13	38.98	39.99
1958	55.21	40.33	55.21
1959	60.71	53.58	59.89
1960	60.39	52.30	58.11
1961	72.64	57.57	71.55
1962	71.13	52.32	63.10
1963	75.02	62.69	75.02
1964	86.28	75.43	84.75

Year	High	Low	Close
1965	92.63	81.60	92.43
1966	94.06	73.20	80.33
1967	97.59	80.38	96.47
1968	108.37	87.72	103.86
1969	106.16	89.20	92.06
1970	93.46	69.29	92.15
1971	104.77	90.16	102.09
1972	119.12	101.67	118.05
1973	120.24	92.16	97.55
1974	99.80	62.28	68.56
1975	95.61	70.04	90.19
1976	107.83	90.90	107.46
1977	107.97	90.71	95.10
1978	106.99	86.90	96.11
1979	111.27	96.13	107.94
1980	140.52	98.22	135.76
1981	138.12	112.77	122.55
1982	143.02	102.42	140.64
1983	172.65	138.34	164.93
1984	170.41	147.82	167.24
1985	212.02	163.68	211.28
1986	254.00	203.49	242.17
1987	336.77	223.92	247.08
1988	283.66	276.83	277.72
1989	359.80	275.31	353.40
1990	369.78	294.51	330.22
1991	418.32	309.35	417.09
1992	442.65	392.41	435.71
1993	471.29	426.88	466.45
1994	482.85	435.86	459.27
1995	622.88	457.20	615.93
1996	762.12	597.29	756.80
1997	986.24	729.56	936.46
1998	1241.81	927.69	1229.23
1999	1469.25	1212.19	1469.25
2000	1527.46	1264.74	1320.28
2001	1373.73	965.80	1148.08
2002	1172.51	776.76	879.82
2003	1111.92	800.73	1111.92
2004	1213.55	1063.23	1211.92
2005	1272.74	1137.50	1248.29
2006	1424.73	1223.69	1424.73
2007	1565.15	1374.12	1468.36
2008	1447.16	752.44	903.25
2009	1127.78	676.53	1115.10

S&P/TSX COMPOSITE INDEX

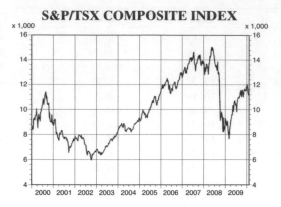

Source: Thomson Reuters Datastream

This graph shows the movement of the S&P/TSX Composite Index, formerly known as the TSE 300 Composite Stock Index. This is the major index for Canadian stocks, because most of the stock market trading in Canada takes place in Toronto. Stock index futures are traded on the Montreal Exchange.

Year	High	Low	Close
1971	1036.09	879.80	990.54
1972	1226.58	990.54	1226.58
1973	1319.26	1122.34	1187.78
1974	1276.81	821.10	835.42
1975	1081.96	862.74	942.94
1976	1100.55	931.17	1011.52
1977	1067.35	961.04	1059.59
1978	1332.71	998.19	1309.99
1979	1813.17	1315.82	1813.17
1980	2402.23	1702.51	2268.70
1981	2390.50	1812.48	1954.24
1982	1958.08	1346.35	1958.08
1983	2598.26	1949.81	2552.35
1984	2585.73	2079.69	2400.33
1985	2900.60	2348.55	2900.60
1986	3129.20	2754.06	3066.18
1987	4112.89	2837.90	3160.10
1988	3465.40	2978.00	3390.00
1989	3985.11	3350.50	3969.79
1990	4020.86	3007.80	3256.75
1991	3604.09	3150.88	3512.36
1992	3672.58	3149.97	3350.44
1993	4330.01	3263.19	4321.43
1994	4609.93	3935.66	4213.61
1995	4740.56	4042.82	4713.54

Year	High	Low	Close
1996	6016.64	4753.00	5902.60
1997	7110.40	5683.64	6539.48
1995	4740.56	4042.82	4713.54
1996	6016.64	4753.00	5902.60
1997	7110.40	5683.64	6539.48
1998	7822.25	5336.15	6485.94
1999	8472.58	6180.34	8413.75
2000	11388.82	8114.24	8933.68
2001	9348.36	6513.10	7688.41
2002	7958.10	5695.33	6617.55
2003	8260.54	6228.63	8220.89
2004	9287.40	8123.50	9246.65
2005	11296.29	9006.22	11272.26
2006	12899.58	10904.34	12909.54
2007	14625.00	12459.55	13833.06
2008	14984.20	7724.76	8987.70
2009	11746.11	7566.94	11746.11

TREASURY BILL (3-MONTH) YIELDS

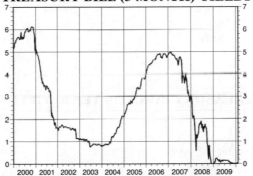

Source: Thomson Reuters Datastream

This graph shows the movement of the yields of 3-month U.S. Treasury bills. These yields are considered the most important yardsticks of short-term interest rates, and they are therefore watched closely by credit market analysts for signs that rates might be rising or falling. Many floating-rate loans and variable-rate mortgages are tied to the Treasury bill rate. The minimum purchase amount of a Treasury bill is $10,000. Auctions for Treasury bills are held weekly. Individual investors who do not submit a competitive bid are sold bills at the average price of the winning competitive bids. Treasury bills are the primary instrument used by the Federal Reserve in its regulation of the money supply through open market operations. Futures on Treasury bills are traded on the Chicago Mercantile Exchange.

Year	Average Rates	Year	Average Rates
1965	4.37%	1988	6.68%
1966	4.96%	1989	8.11%
1967	4.96%	1990	7.50%
1968	5.94%	1991	5.39%
1969	7.81%	1992	3.44%
1970	4.87%	1993	3.00%
1971	4.01%	1994	4.26%
1972	5.07%	1995	5.52%
1973	7.45%	1996	5.01%
1974	7.15%	1997	5.05%
1975	5.44%	1998	4.78%
1976	4.35%	1999	4.64%
1977	6.07%	2000	5.82%
1978	9.08%	2001	3.40%
1979	12.04%	2002	1.61%
1980	11.50%	2003	1.01%
1981	14.07%	2004	1.37%
1982	10.68%	2005	3.15%
1983	8.63%	2006	4.42%
1984	9.58%	2007	5.02%
1985	7.49%	2008	2.25%
1986	5.97%	2009	0.30%
1987	5.82%		

TREASURY BOND (10-YEAR) YIELDS

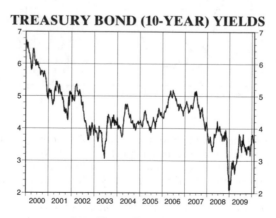

Source: Thomson Reuters Datastream

This graph shows the movement of the yields of 10-year Treasury bonds. Treasury-bond yields are considered the most important yardsticks of long-term interest rates, and they are therefore watched closely by credit market analysts for signs that rates might be rising or falling. The minimum denomination of a Treasury bond is $1000 and maturities range from 10 to 30 years. In the 1990s the 30-year Treasury bond became widely used. In the 2000s, the treasury stopped issuing new 30-year T-bonds, so the 10-year T-bond became more of a benchmark. Futures on Treasury bonds are traded on the Chicago Board of Trade and the MidAmerica Commodity Exchange. Futures options on T-bonds are traded on the Chicago Board of Trade, and interest rate options and LEAPS on T-bonds are traded on the Chicago Board Options Exchange.

Year	High	Low	Close
1980	12.84%	9.78%	12.84%
1981	15.32%	12.57%	13.72%
1982	14.59%	10.54%	10.54%
1983	11.85%	10.38%	11.83%
1984	13.56%	11.50%	11.50%
1985	11.86%	9.26%	9.26%
1986	9.19%	7.11%	7.11%
1987	9.52%	7.08%	8.99%
1988	9.26%	8.21%	9.11%
1989	9.36%	7.84%	7.84%
1990	8.89%	8.08%	8.08%
1991	8.28%	7.09%	7.09%
1992	7.54%	6.42%	6.77%
1993	6.60%	5.33%	5.77%
1994	7.96%	5.75%	7.81%
1995	7.78%	5.71%	5.71%
1996	6.91%	5.65%	6.30%
1997	6.89%	5.81%	5.81%
1998	5.65%	4.53%	4.65%
1999	6.28%	4.72%	6.28%
2000	6.66%	5.24%	5.24%
2001	5.39%	4.57%	5.09%
2002	5.28%	3.87%	4.03%
2003	4.45%	3.33%	4.27%
2004	4.73%	3.83%	4.23%
2005	4.54%	4.00%	4.47%
2006	4.54%	4.33%	4.58%
2007	4.89%	4.62%	4.78%
2008	4.03%	3.42%	3.61%
2009	3.93%	2.20%	2.76%

WILSHIRE 5000 TOTAL MARKET

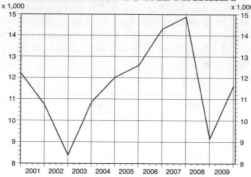

Source: Wilshire Associates

This graph shows the movement of the Dow Jones Wilshire 5000 Total Market. This is the broadest of all the averages, and represents the value, in billions of dollars, of all New York Stock Exchange, American Stock Exchange, and Nasdaq stocks. The index is used as a measure of how all stocks are doing as a group, as opposed to a particular segment of the market. Two versions of the index are calculated: one weighted by full market capitalization and the other weighted by float-adjusted market capitalization.

Year	High	Low	Close
1971	955	871	949
1972	1090	976	1090
1973	1059	854	861
1974	863	550	590
1975	840	675	784
1976	954	879	954
1977	919	851	887
1978	1004	822	922
1979	1101	935	1100
1980	1466	1026	1404
1981	1415	1208	1286
1982	1451	1099	1451
1983	1791	1508	1723
1984	1702	1536	1702
1985	2164	1845	2164
1986	2598	2109	2434
1987	3299	2188	2434
1988	2794	2398	2738
1989	3523	2718	3419
1990	3448	2834	3101
1991	4041	3245	4041
1992	4290	3930	4290
1993	4673	4316	4658
1994	4798	4395	4541

Year	High	Low	Close
1995	6057	4546	6057
1996	7292	5897	7288
1997	9407	7059	8976
1998	11317.59	8620.80	11317.59
1999	13812.67	11146.59	13812.67
2000	14751.64	11570.29	12175.88
2001	12719.22	8900.45	10707.68
2002	10953.64	7342.86	8343.19
2003	10799.63	7610.47	10799.63
2004	11987.82	10293.52	11971.14
2005	12755.58	11217.81	12517.69
2006	14356.88	12296.92	14257.55
2007	15806.69	13896.55	14819.58
2008	14613.57	7471.44	9087.17
2009	11678.47	6858.43	11561.72

CONSUMER PRICE INDEX

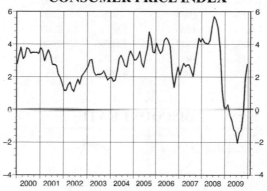

Source: Thomson Reuters Datastream

This graph shows the movement of the Consumer Price Index. The line represents the rolling 12-month average of changes in consumer prices—a method that best shows the ups and downs of the inflation rate. Each month, the U.S. Bureau of Labor Statistics shops a fixed market basket of goods and services available to an average urban wage earner. The market basket of goods is updated every few years. The major groups included in the CPI are food, shelter, fuels, transportation costs, medical care, entertainment, services, and commodities. The CPI is important because many pension and employment contracts are tied to changes in it. The inflationary spike of the 1970s did much damage to the world economy and had profound consequences, including the strongly anti-inflationary monetary policies from the middle 1980s to the present.

Year	Annual Change in CPI	Year	Annual Change in CPI	Year	Annual Change in CPI
1948	7.70%	1969	5.40%	1990	5.40%
1949	–1.00%	1970	5.90%	1991	4.20%
1950	1.10%	1971	4.20%	1992	3.00%
1951	7.90%	1972	3.30%	1993	3.00%
1952	2.30%	1973	6.30%	1994	2.60%
1953	0.80%	1974	11.00%	1995	2.80%
1954	0.40%	1975	9.10%	1996	2.90%
1955	–0.30%	1976	5.80%	1997	2.30%
1956	1.50%	1977	6.50%	1998	1.50%
1957	3.40%	1978	7.60%	1999	2.20%
1958	2.70%	1979	11.30%	2000	3.40%
1959	0.90%	1980	13.50%	2001	2.80%
1960	1.50%	1981	10.40%	2002	1.60%
1961	1.10%	1982	6.20%	2003	2.30%
1962	1.20%	1983	3.20%	2004	2.70%
1963	1.30%	1984	4.40%	2005	3.40%
1964	1.30%	1985	3.50%	2006	3.24%
1965	1.60%	1986	1.90%	2007	2.85%
1966	3.00%	1987	3.60%	2008	3.85%
1967	2.80%	1988	4.10%	2009	–0.34%
1968	4.20%	1989	4.80%		

DISCOUNT RATE

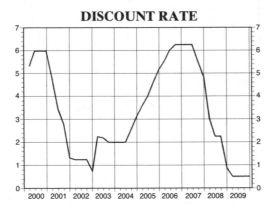

Source: Thomson Reuters Datastream

This graph shows the movement of the discount rate, which is the rate the Federal Reserve charges depository institutions on overnight loans. Credit market analysts watch the Fed's discount rate moves very carefully, because changes in the rate are a major indication of whether the Fed wants to ease or tighten the money supply. When the Fed wants to ease the money supply to stimulate the economy, it cuts the discount rate. When the Fed wants to tighten the money supply to slow the economy and thereby to try to lower the inflation rate, it raises the discount rate. The discount rate acts as a floor

on interest rates, because banks set their loan rates, such as the prime rate, a
notch above the discount rate.

Year	High	Low	Close
1914	6.00%	5.00%	6.00%
1915	5.00%	4.00%	4.00%
1916	4.00%	3.00%	3.00%
1917	3.50%	3.00%	3.00%
1918	3.50%	4.00%	4.00%
1919	4.75%	4.00%	4.75%
1920	7.00%	4.75%	7.00%
1921	7.00%	4.50%	4.50%
1922	4.50%	4.00%	4.00%
1923	4.50%	4.00%	4.50%
1924	4.50%	3.00%	3.00%
1925	3.50%	3.00%	3.50%
1926	4.00%	3.50%	4.00%
1927	4.00%	3.50%	4.00%
1928	5.00%	3.50%	5.00%
1929	6.00%	4.50%	4.50%
1930	4.50%	2.00%	2.00%
1931	3.50%	1.50%	3.50%
1932	3.50%	2.50%	2.50%
1933	3.50%	2.00%	2.00%
1934	2.00%	1.50%	1.50%
1935	1.50%	1.50%	1.50%
1936	1.50%	1.50%	1.50%
1937	1.50%	1.00%	1.00%
1938	1.00%	1.00%	1.00%
1939	1.00%	1.00%	1.00%
1940	1.00%	1.00%	1.00%
1941	1.00%	1.00%	1.00%
1942	1.00%	0.50%	0.50%
1943	1.00%	0.50%	0.50%
1944	1.00%	0.50%	0.50%
1945	1.00%	0.50%	0.50%
1946	1.00%	0.50%	0.50%
1947	1.00%	1.00%	1.00%
1948	1.50%	1.00%	1.50%
1949	1.50%	1.50%	1.50%
1950	1.75%	1.50%	1.75%
1951	1.75%	1.75%	1.75%
1952	1.75%	1.75%	1.75%
1953	2.00%	1.75%	2.00%
1954	2.00%	1.50%	2.00%
1955	2.50%	1.50%	2.50%
1956	3.00%	2.50%	3.00%
1957	3.50%	3.00%	3.00%
1958	3.00%	1.75%	3.00%

Year	High	Low	Close
1959	4.00%	2.50%	4.00%
1960	4.00%	3.00%	3.00%
1961	3.00%	3.00%	3.00%
1962	3.00%	3.00%	3.00%
1963	3.50%	3.00%	3.50%
1964	4.00%	3.50%	4.00%
1965	4.50%	4.00%	4.50%
1966	4.50%	4.50%	4.50%
1967	4.50%	4.00%	4.50%
1968	5.50%	4.50%	5.50%
1969	6.00%	5.50%	6.00%
1970	6.00%	5.50%	5.50%
1971	5.00%	4.50%	4.50%
1972	4.50%	4.50%	4.50%
1973	7.50%	4.50%	7.50%
1974	8.00%	7.75%	7.75%
1975	7.75%	6.00%	6.00%
1976	6.00%	5.25%	5.25%
1977	6.00%	5.25%	6.00%
1978	9.50%	6.00%	9.50%
1979	12.00%	9.50%	12.00%
1980	10.00%	13.00%	13.00%
1981	14.00%	12.00%	12.00%
1982	12.00%	8.50%	8.50%
1983	8.50%	8.50%	8.50%
1984	9.00%	8.00%	8.00%
1985	8.00%	7.50%	7.50%
1986	7.50%	5.50%	5.50%
1987	7.00%	5.50%	6.00%
1988	6.50%	6.00%	6.50%
1989	7.00%	6.50%	7.00%
1990	7.00%	6.80%	6.80%
1991	6.50%	4.10%	4.10%
1992	3.50%	3.00%	3.00%
1993	3.00%	3.00%	3.00%
1994	4.75%	3.00%	4.75%
1995	5.25%	4.75%	5.25%
1996	5.25%	5.00%	5.00%
1997	5.00%	5.00%	5.00%
1998	5.00%	4.50%	4.50%
1999	5.00%	4.50%	5.00%
2000	6.00%	5.00%	6.00%
2001	6.00%	1.25%	1.25%
2002	1.25%	0.75%	0.75%
2003	2.25%	0.75%	2.00%
2004	3.25%	2.00%	3.25%
2005	5.25%	3.25%	5.25%

Year	High	Low	Close
2006	5.54%	5.54%	6.25%
2007	6.25%	6.25%	4.83%
2008	3.04%	3.04%	0.86%
2009	0.50%	0.50%	0.50%

FEDERAL FUNDS RATE

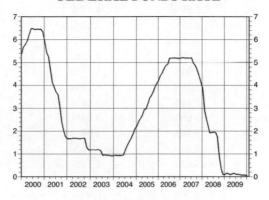

Source: Thomson Reuters Datastream

This graph shows the movement of the Federal Funds Rate, which is the rate at which banks with excess reserves lend to banks needing overnight loans to meet reserve requirements. The Fed Funds Rate is the most sensitive of all short-term interest rates, and therefore it is carefully watched by credit market analysts as a precursor of moves in other interest rates. For instance, when the Fed Funds Rate consistently stays below the discount rate, analysts often anticipate that the Federal Reserve will cut the discount rate.

Year	High	Low	Close
1968	6.12%	4.6%	6.02%
1969	9.19%	6.3%	8.97%
1970	8.98%	4.9%	4.9%
1971	5.57%	3.71%	4.14%
1972	5.33%	3.29%	5.33%
1973	10.78%	5.94%	9.95%
1974	12.92%	8.53%	8.53%
1975	7.13%	5.20%	5.20%
1976	5.48%	4.65%	4.65%
1977	6.56%	4.61%	7.75%
1978	10.03%	6.70%	10.03%
1979	13.78%	10.01%	13.78%
1980	18.90%	9.03%	18.90%
1981	19.08%	12.37%	12.37%
1982	14.94%	8.95%	8.95%
1983	9.56%	8.51%	9.47%
1984	11.64%	8.38%	8.38%

Year	High	Low	Close
1985	8.58%	7.53%	8.27%
1986	8.14%	5.85%	6.91%
1987	7.29%	6.10%	6.77%
1988	8.76%	6.58%	8.76%
1989	9.95%	8.46%	8.52%
1990	8.29%	7.31%	7.31%
1991	6.91%	4.43%	4.43%
1992	4.06%	2.92%	2.92%
1993	3.09%	2.96%	2.96%
1994	5.50%	3.05%	5.50%
1995	6.05%	5.53%	5.60%
1996	5.56%	5.22%	5.29%
1997	5.56%	5.19%	5.50%
1998	7.06%	4.07%	4.07%
1999	5.76%	3.99%	3.99%
2000	7.03%	5.36%	5.41%
2001	6.67%	1.19%	1.52%
2002	1.92%	1.15%	1.16%
2003	1.26%	0.98%	0.98%
2004	2.16%	1.00%	2.16%
2005	4.16%	2.28%	4.16%
2006	4.29%	4.29%	4.96%
2007	5.25%	5.25%	5.02%
2008	3.94%	3.94%	1.93%
2009	0.22%	0.15%	0.16%

INDEX OF LEADING ECONOMIC INDICATORS

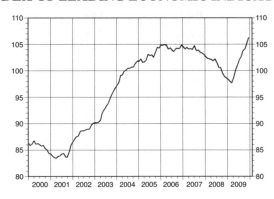

Source: Thomson Reuters Datastream

This graph shows the movement of the Index of Leading Economic Indicators. This composite of 10 economic indicators (adjusted for inflation) is designed to forecast whether the economy will gain or lose strength, and is therefore an important tool for economists and others doing business planning. On the whole, it has been an accurate barometer of future economic activity. The 10 components of the Index are: average workweek of production workers; average weekly claims for state unemployment insurance; manufacturers' new orders for consumer goods and materials; vendor performance (companies receiving slower deliveries from suppliers); contracts and orders for plant and equipment; new building permits; interest rate spread between the 10-year Treasury bond versus the Federal Funds rate; stock prices as measured by the Standard & Poor's 500 index; money supply as measured by M-2; and index of consumer expectations. The index is released monthly and is based at 100 in 1996.

Year	High	Low	Last
1959	58.40	56.80	57.90
1960	57.60	56.50	56.70
1961	60.90	57.00	60.90
1962	61.80	60.40	61.80
1963	64.50	62.10	64.50
1964	67.60	64.90	67.60
1965	70.80	68.10	70.80
1966	71.30	68.80	68.80
1967	72.30	68.90	72.30
1968	74.10	72.10	74.10
1969	74.50	72.10	72.10
1970	71.70	69.80	71.70
1971	76.40	72.40	76.40
1972	81.40	77.00	81.40
1973	81.60	77.90	77.90
1974	77.60	69.90	69.90
1975	75.90	69.70	75.90
1976	80.60	77.30	80.60
1977	81.80	80.50	81.80
1978	82.40	81.00	81.10
1979	81.30	78.00	78.00
1980	79.40	74.10	78.30
1981	79.50	76.80	77.00
1982	79.90	76.50	79.90
1983	86.80	81.20	86.80
1984	88.00	87.10	88.00
1985	90.60	88.60	90.60
1986	93.60	90.60	93.60
1987	95.30	93.50	94.00
1988	95.80	94.10	95.80
1989	95.80	94.20	95.60
1990	95.70	91.50	91.90
1991	95.00	91.40	93.50
1992	97.10	94.20	97.10
1993	97.50	95.30	97.50
1994	98.00	97.10	98.00

Year	High	Low	Last
1995	98.50	96.80	98.50
1996	101.20	97.60	101.10
1997	104.30	101.40	104.10
1998	107.00	104.30	107.00
1999	110.60	107.40	110.60
2000	110.90	108.70	108.70
2001	111.30	108.40	111.30
2002	112.30	111.40	112.30
2003	129.40	120.60	129.40
2004	136.10	130.30	136.10
2005	138.60	135.40	138.60
2006	105.00	105.00	104.50
2007	104.60	104.60	104.07
2008	102.70	102.70	101.19
2009	106.40	98.50	101.59

MONEY SUPPLY (M-1)

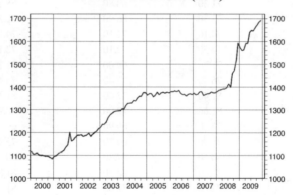

Source: Thomson Reuters Datastream

This graph shows the movement of changes in the money supply in the United States, as measured by M-1. The percentage change in the table is calculated by comparing, for example, the December 2009 figure with the December 2008 figure. This method best shows the ups and downs of the growth of the amount of money circulating in the economy. The rate of change in the money supply is important because it has an important bearing on how quickly or slowly the economy will be growing in the future. Monetarist economists believe changes in the money supply are the key to economic ups and downs. When the Federal Reserve, which strongly influences the money supply through its conduct of open market operations and by setting bank reserve requirements and the discount rate, wants the economy to expand, it eases the money supply. When the Fed is concerned that inflation may be accelerating, it will slow the economy by tightening the money supply. The components of the M-1 measure of the money supply are: currency in circulation; commercial and mutual savings bank demand

deposits; NOW and ATS (automatic transfer from savings) accounts; credit
union share drafts; and nonbank travelers checks.

Year	High	Low	Last
1960	0.79%	–1.13%	0.50%
1961	3.20%	0.79%	3.20%
1962	3.03%	1.73%	1.79%
1963	4.34%	2.13%	3.72%
1964	4.57%	3.26%	4.57%
1965	4.68%	3.74%	4.68%
1966	6.05%	2.50%	2.50%
1967	6.57%	1.40%	6.57%
1968	7.69%	6.12%	7.69%
1969	7.90%	3.29%	3.29%
1970	5.10%	2.81%	5.10%
1971	8.17%	4.46%	6.49%
1972	9.16%	5.90%	9.16%
1973	9.26%	5.46%	5.46%
1974	5.96%	4.30%	4.30%
1975	5.42%	3.33%	4.67%
1976	6.71%	4.78%	6.66%
1977	8.30%	6.84%	8.04%
1978	8.81%	7.33%	7.99%
1979	8.49%	6.86%	6.86%
1980	8.37%	4.11%	7.00%
1981	11.37%	4.74%	6.89%
1982	9.33%	4.64%	8.73%
1983	13.34%	7.80%	9.80%
1984	10.01%	5.16%	5.84%
1985	12.32%	5.97%	12.32%
1986	16.94%	10.95%	16.94%
1987	17.54%	3.51%	3.51%
1988	5.13%	3.26%	4.90%
1989	3.89%	–0.63%	0.76%
1990	5.01%	1.22%	4.04%
1991	8.75%	4.00%	8.75%
1992	14.45%	10.14%	14.26%
1993	13.22%	10.26%	10.26%
1994	9.97%	1.82%	1.82%
1995	1.65%	–2.02%	–2.02%
1996	–2.11%	–4.63%	–4.21%
1997	–0.64%	–5.31%	–0.64%
1998	2.32%	–0.60%	2.27%
1999	2.54%	1.48%	2.54%
2000	2.23%	–3.16%	–3.16%
2001	9.17%	–2.22%	8.30%
2002	7.95%	–0.73%	3.17%
2003	9.15%	3.04%	6.99%

Year	High	Low	Last
2004	7.37%	4.13%	5.21%
2005	4.68%	–0.28%	–0.24%
2006	1.38%	1.38%	1.37%
2007	1.37%	1.37%	1.37%
2008	1.38%	1.38%	1.43%
2009	1.69%	1.57%	1.63%

PRIME RATE

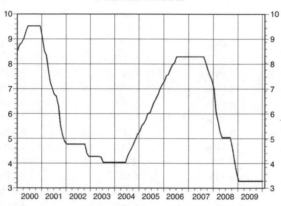

Source: Thomson Reuters Datastream

This graph shows the movement of the prime rate, which is the interest rate banks charge their most creditworthy customers. The rate is determined by market forces affecting a bank's cost of funds and the rates borrowers will accept. The prime rate often moves up or down in concert with the Federal Reserve discount rate. The prime rate tends to become standard across the banking industry when a major bank moves its rate up or down. The rate is a key interest rate, because loans to less creditworthy customers are often tied to the prime.

Year	High	Low	Close
1968	6.75%	6%	6.75%
1969	8.5%	6.75%	8.5%
1970	8.5%	6.75%	6.75%
1971	6.75%	5.25%	5.25%
1972	6%	5%	6%
1973	10%	6%	10%
1974	12%	8.75%	10.5%
1975	10.5%	7%	7%
1976	7.25%	6.25%	6.25%
1977	7.75%	6.5%	7.75%
1978	11.75%	7.75%	11.75%
1979	15.75%	11.5%	15%

Year	High	Low	Close
1980	21.50%	10.75%	21.50%
1981	20.5%	15.75%	15.75%
1982	17%	11.5%	11.5%
1983	11.5%	10.5%	11%
1984	13%	10.75%	10.75
1985	10.75%	9.5%	9.5%
1986	9.5%	7.5%	7.5%
1987	9.25%	7.5%	8.75%
1988	10.5%	8.5%	10.5%
1989	11.5%	10.5%	10.5%
1990	10.1%	10.0%	10.0%
1991	9.5%	7.2%	7.2%
1992	6.5%	6.0%	6.0%
1993	6.0%	6.0%	6.0%
1994	8.5%	6.0%	8.5%
1995	9.00%	8.50%	8.65%
1996	8.50%	8.25%	8.25%
1997	8.50%	8.25%	8.50%
1998	8.50%	7.75%	7.75%
1999	8.50%	7.75%	8.50%
2000	9.50%	8.50%	9.50%
2001	9.50%	4.75%	4.75%
2002	4.75%	4.25%	4.25%
2003	4.25%	4.00%	4.00%
2004	5.15%	4.00%	5.15%
2005	7.15%	5.25%	7.15%
2006	7.26%	7.26%	7.96%
2007	8.25%	8.25%	8.05%
2008	6.98%	6.98%	5.09%
2009	3.25%	3.25%	3.25%

PRODUCER PRICE INDEX

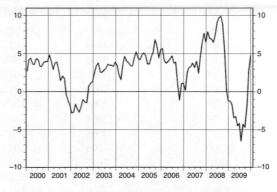

Source: Thomson Reuters Datastream

This graph shows the movement of the Producer Price Index. The line represents the rolling 12-month average of changes in producer prices, a method that best shows the ups and downs of the wholesale inflation rate. Each month, the U.S. Bureau of Labor Statistics measures changes in the prices of all commodities, at all stages of processing, produced for sale in primary markets in the United States. The prices are generally the first significant large-volume commercial transaction for each commodity—either the manufacturer's selling price or the selling price from an organized commodity exchange. The major commodity groups that are represented in the PPI are: farm products; processed food and feed; textiles and apparel; hides, skins and leather; fuels; chemicals; rubber and plastic products; lumber and wood products; pulp and paper products; metals and metal products; machinery and equipment; furniture and household durables; nonmetallic mineral products; and transportation equipment. The PPI is important not only because it is a good gauge of what is happening in the industrial economy, but also because it gives an indication of the future trend in consumer prices.

Year	Annual Change	Year	Annual Change
1949	–2.80%	1980	13.50%
1950	1.90%	1981	9.30%
1951	9.40%	1982	4.00%
1952	–0.60%	1983	1.60%
1953	–1.00%	1984	2.10%
1954	0.20%	1985	0.90%
1955	0.20%	1986	–1.30%
1956	2.80%	1987	2.10%
1957	3.70%	1988	2.50%
1958	2.20%	1989	5.10%
1959	–0.20%	1990	4.90%
1960	0.80%	1991	2.20%
1961	0.00%	1992	1.20%
1962	0.30%	1993	1.20%
1963	–0.30%	1994	0.60%
1964	0.40%	1995	1.90%
1965	1.80%	1996	2.60%
1966	3.10%	1997	0.40%
1967	1.20%	1998	–0.80%
1968	2.90%	1999	1.80%
1969	3.70%	2000	3.80%
1970	3.50%	2001	2.00%
1971	3.00%	2002	–1.38%
1972	3.10%	2003	3.20%
1973	9.20%	2004	3.60%
1974	15.30%	2005	4.80%
1975	10.80%	2006	2.94%
1976	4.40%	2007	3.92%
1977	6.50%	2008	6.37%
1978	7.80%	2009	–2.45%
1979	11.10%		

UNEMPLOYMENT RATE (CIVILIAN)

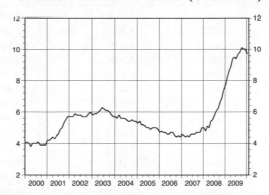

Source: Thomson Reuters Datastream

This graph shows the movement of the unemployment rate. This is the rate of civilians, 16 years of age and older, who were not employed, and who made specific efforts to find a job within the previous four weeks and who were available for work. Persons on layoff from a job or waiting to report to a new job within 30 days are also classified as unemployed. The unemployment rate is a lagging indicator—that is, it rises months after business has already slowed down, and it falls months after business has picked up.

Year	High	Low	Last
1948	4.00%	3.40%	4.00%
1949	7.90%	4.30%	6.60%
1950	6.50%	4.20%	4.30%
1951	3.70%	3.00%	3.10%
1952	3.40%	2.70%	2.70%
1953	4.50%	2.50%	4.50%
1954	6.10%	4.90%	5.00%
1955	4.90%	4.00%	4.20%
1956	4.40%	3.90%	4.20%
1957	5.20%	3.70%	5.20%
1958	7.50%	5.80%	6.20%
1959	6.00%	5.00%	5.30%
1960	6.60%	4.80%	6.60%
1961	7.10%	6.00%	6.00%
1962	5.80%	5.40%	5.50%
1963	5.90%	5.40%	5.50%
1964	5.60%	4.80%	5.00%
1965	5.10%	4.00%	4.00%
1966	4.00%	3.60%	3.80%
1967	4.00%	3.80%	3.80%
1968	3.80%	3.40%	3.40%
1969	3.70%	3.40%	3.50%
1970	6.10%	3.90%	6.10%

Year	High	Low	Last
1971	6.10%	5.80%	6.00%
1972	5.80%	5.20%	5.20%
1973	5.00%	4.60%	4.90%
1974	7.20%	5.10%	7.20%
1975	9.00%	8.10%	8.20%
1976	7.90%	7.40%	7.80%
1977	7.60%	6.40%	6.40%
1978	6.40%	5.80%	6.00%
1979	6.00%	5.60%	6.00%
1980	7.80%	6.30%	7.20%
1981	8.50%	7.20%	8.50%
1982	10.80%	8.60%	10.80%
1983	10.40%	8.30%	8.30%
1984	8.00%	7.20%	7.30%
1985	7.40%	7.00%	7.00%
1986	7.20%	6.60%	6.60%
1987	6.60%	5.70%	5.70%
1988	5.70%	5.30%	5.30%
1989	5.40%	5.00%	5.40%
1990	6.30%	5.20%	6.30%
1991	7.30%	6.40%	7.30%
1992	7.80%	7.30%	7.40%
1993	7.30%	6.50%	6.50%
1994	6.60%	5.50%	5.50%
1995	5.80%	5.40%	5.60%
1996	5.60%	5.10%	5.40%
1997	5.30%	4.60%	4.70%
1998	4.70%	4.40%	4.40%
1999	4.40%	4.10%	4.10%
2000	4.10%	3.90%	4.00%
2001	5.80%	4.20%	5.80%
2002	6.00%	5.50%	6.00%
2003	6.30%	5.70%	5.70%
2004	5.70%	5.40%	5.40%
2005	5.40%	4.90%	4.90%
2006	4.70%	4.70%	4.60%
2007	4.60%	4.60%	4.60%
2008	5.00%	5.00%	5.80%
2009	10.10%	7.70%	9.30%

5. PUBLICLY TRADED COMPANIES

On the following pages you will find lists of the 500 largest (by market capitalization) companies listed on the New York Stock Exchange and the 100 companies comprising the Nasdaq 100 Index. The Nasdaq 100 includes the largest and most actively traded nonfinancial United States and foreign equities listed on the Nasdaq Stock Market.

The New York Stock Exchange is the home of many of the largest, most-established public companies, though many smaller growth companies are traded there as well. The NYSE operates with a specialist system of trading, where buyers and sellers are brought together by a specialist on the floor of the Exchange. The specialist steps in to buy or sell shares if there is an imbalance of orders on one side of the market or the other. The requirements the NYSE imposes for being listed on the exchange are the most stringent of all the places where stocks are traded in the United States. Two of the most important requirements are that a corporation must have (1) a minimum aggregate market value of $40 million and (2) annual net income topping $2.5 million before federal income taxes.

The Nasdaq Stock Market is home to many of the nation's largest high-technology companies as well as a majority of its emerging growth companies. Many of these growth companies don't pay dividends since they plow their earnings back into their businesses. Unlike the NYSE, trading on The Nasdaq Stock Market is executed by hundreds of competing market makers who are linked by a network of Nasdaq computer terminals. The Nasdaq Stock Market has two tiers, the SmallCap market, for smaller emerging companies, and the National Market, where the larger issues trade. Listing standards vary for Nasdaq's two tiers, but they are more stringent for Nasdaq's National Market, and to be accepted a company must have either $6 million in tangible assets with pre-tax income of $1 million and a public share float value of $8 million, or tangible assets of $18 million, a public share float value of $18 million with no income requirement.

Each listing includes eight elements: the company's name, stock symbol, address, telephone number, website, line of business, if it has a dividend reinvestment plan, and whether options are traded on the stock.

Company Name: We have used each company's full corporate name as it is listed in filings to the Securities and Exchange Commission.

Stock Symbol: The stock symbol—usually three or four capital letters—follows each company's name. When asking a broker to look up the price or other information about a stock, it is usually necessary to provide the stock symbol. The symbol is then entered into a computer terminal, which retrieves data about the company. The stock symbol is not the same abbreviation as one sees in newspaper stock tables, however.

Address: The street address or post office box listed refers to the executive office at the headquarters of the company. In the case of foreign companies, the home address of the company usually is listed, though the address of a contact office in the United States may be given.

Telephone Number: The phone number generally is that of the executive offices at the company's headquarters. If you require further information about the company because you are considering whether to invest in it, you should ask for the investor relations department, which will send annual and quarterly financial reports and other data about the firm.

Website: The website generally is that of the executive offices at the company's headquarters.

Line of Business: This is a brief description of the main business of the company. Some companies specialize in a narrow field—in this case, the description is quite specific to its line of business. Other companies engage in diverse activities, and for them, we have listed the largest segments of their business, or when no business is dominant, we have labeled the company a conglomerate. To find out each company's exact product line, you must call or write the firm's investor relations department.

Dividend Reinvestment Plan: If the letters "DRP" are on the final line of an entry for a company, this means that shareholders can use a company plan to reinvest cash dividends into more of the company's stock, instead of receiving a cash payment. Usually, there will be little or no commission cost to the shareholder who participates in a plan. Many companies also allow shareholders to make cash payments in addition to reinvesting dividends to buy more shares, usually at no commission charge.

Some companies offer an extra bonus in their dividend reinvestment plan. Companies on the list with a 5% following the DRP listing offer a 5% discount on the purchase price of newly issued stock for the amount of reinvested dividends. Thus, a shareholder who reinvested $100 of dividends would be credited with purchasing $105 worth of stock. Some companies allow the 5% discount on both dividends reinvested as well as additional cash put up by the shareholder.

Most companies allow shareholders to participate in a dividend reinvestment plan while owning as little as one share. If the dividend is not sufficient to purchase a full share, a shareholder's account is credited with the appropriate fractional share.

The information on dividend reinvestment plans was compiled by the Moneypaper Newsletter, which maintains a directory of DRIP plans. Its address is 555 Theodore Fremd Avenue, Suite B-103, Rye, New York 10580. Its phone number is (914) 925-0022 or (800) 388-9993, and its Web site is www.directinvesting.com.

Options: Also on the final line of a company entry is a notation of whether options are traded on the company's stock. This is signified with the letter "O." Stock options may be traded on the American Stock Exchange, the Chicago Board Options Exchange, the Pacific Stock Exchange or the Philadelphia Stock Exchange. Options of larger companies may trade on more than one of these exchanges simultaneously. Stock options can be used by an investor to make a speculative bet on a stock going up or down. Other investors use options to increase their income or hedge the value of their stock holdings.

In today's fast-moving world of finance and investment, a company may merge with another, add or drop a line of business, change its address or telephone number, move from one exchange to another, or even go out of business. Despite such changes, this list will remain an indispensable resource for investors and others in the finance and investment community.

NEW YORK STOCK EXCHANGE 500

3M Company MMM
3M Center
St. Paul, Minnesota 55144
651-733-1110
www.3m.com
Conglomerate O DRP

ABB Ltd
PO Box 8131
Zurich, 8050 Switzerland
(41) 43-3177111
www.abb.com
Electronic instruments and controls O

Abbott Laboratories ABT
100 Abbott Park Road
Abbott Park, Illinois 60064
847-937-6100
www.abbott.com
Pharmaceuticals O DRP

Accenture Plc ACN
1 Grand Canal Square
Grand Canal Harbour
Dublin, 2 Ireland
(353) 1-6462000
www.accenture.com
Management consulting, technology
  services, and outsourcing O

Ace, Ltd. ACE
17 Woodbourne Avenue
Hamilton HM 08, Bermuda
441-295-5200
www.acelimited.com
Insurance and reinsurance holding
  company O

Advanced Micro Devices, Inc.
  AMD
P.O. Box 3453
Sunnyvale, California 94088
408-749-4000
www.amd.com
Semiconductors O

Aegon NV AEG
P.O. Box 85
The Hague, 2501 CB Netherlands
www.aegon.com
Life insurance O

AES Corporation AES
4300 Wilson Boulevard, Suite 1100
Arlington, Virginia 22203
703-522-1315
www.aes.com
Electric utility O

Aetna, Inc. AET
151 Farmington Avenue
Hartford, Connecticut 06156
860-273-0123
www.actna.com
Healthcare benefits O DRP

Aflac, Inc. AFL
1932 Wynnton Road
Columbus, Georgia 31999
706-323-3431
www.aflac.com
Supplemental health and life
  insurance O DRP

Agilent Technologies, Inc. A
5301 Stevens Creek Boulevard
Santa Clara, California 95051
408-553-7777
www.home.agilent.com
Electronic and bioanalytical
  measurement O

Agnico-Eagle Mines Ltd. AEM
145 King Street East, Suite 400
Toronto, ON M5C 2Y7 Canada
416-947-1212
www.agnico-eagle.com
Gold production O DRP

Agrium Inc. AGU
13131 Lake Forest Drive SE
Calgary, AB T2J 7E8 Canada
403-225-7000
www.agrium.com
Agricultural products O

Air Products and Chemicals, Inc.
  APD
7201 Hamilton Boulevard
Allentown, Pennsylvania 18195
610-481-4911
www.airproducts.com
Chemical manufacturing O DRP

Alcatel-Lucent ALU
54 Rue La Boetie
Paris, 75008 France
(33) 1-40761010
www.alcatel-lucent.com
Communications equipment O

Alcoa, Inc. AA
201 Isabella Street
Pittsburgh, Pennsylvania 15212
412-553-4545
www.alcoa.com
Aluminum O DRP

Alcon, Inc. ACL
Bösch 69
Hüenenberg, 6331 Switzerland
(41) 41-7858888
www.alcon.com
Eyecare O

Allergan, Inc. AGN
2525 Dupont Drive
Irvine, California 92612
714-246-4500
www.allergan.com
Biotechnology and drugs O DRP

Allstate Corporation ALL
2775 Sanders Road
Northbrook, Illinois 60062
847-402-5000
www.allstate.com
Insurance O DRP

Altria Group, Inc. MO
6601 West Broad Street
Richmond, Virginia 23230
804-274-2200
www.altria.com
Tobacco O DRP

Aluminum Corp. of China Ltd.
  ACH
No. 62 North Xizhimen Street
Haidian District
Beijing, 100082 China
(86) 10-82298103
www.chalco.com.cn
Aluminum mining O

Ameren Corporation AEE
1901 Chouteau Avenue
St. Louis, Missouri 63103
314-621-3222
www.ameren.com
Electric and gas utility holding
  company O DRP

America Movil S.A.B. De C.V.
  AMX
Lago Alberto 366, Colonia
  Anahuac
Mexico City, 11320 Mexico
781-575-4328
www.americamovil.com
Wireless communications
  services O DRP

American Electric Power
  Company, Inc. AEP
1 Riverside Plaza
Columbus, Ohio 43215
614-716-1000
Electric power holding
  company O DRP

American Express Company AXP
World Financial Center
200 Vesey Street
New York, New York 10285
212-640-2000
www.home.americanexpress.com
Global payments and
  travel O DRP

American International Group, Inc.
  AIG
70 Pine Street
New York, New York 10270
212-770-7000
www.aigcorporate.com
Insurance holding company O

American Tower Corporation AMT
116 Huntington Avenue
Boston, Massachusetts 02116
617-375-7500
www.americantower.com
Wireless and broadcast
  communications infrastructure O

Ameriprise Financial, Inc. AMP
55 Ameriprise Financial Center
Minneapolis, Minnesota 55474
612-671-3131
www.ameriprise.com
Investment services O DRP

Amerisourcebergen Corporation
  ABC
1300 Morris Drive, Suite 100
Chesterbrook, Pennsylvania 19087
610-727-7000
www.amerisourcebergen.com
Pharmaceutical services O

Amphenol Corp. APH
358 Hall Avenue
Wallingford, Connecticut 06492
203-265-8900
www.amphenol.com
Electronic instruments and controls
  O

Anadarko Petroleum Corporation
  APC
1201 Lake Robbins Drive
The Woodlands, Texas 77380
832-636-1000
www.anadarko.com
Oil and gas exploration and
  production O DRP

Analog Devices, Inc. ADI
One Technology Way
Norwood, Massachusetts 02062
781-329-4700
www.analog.com
Semiconductors O

AngloGold Ashanti Ltd. AU
PO Box 62117, Marshalltown
Johannesburg, 2107 South Africa
(27) 11-637-6000
www.anglogoldashanti.com
Gold production O

Anheuser-Busch InBev N.V. BUD
Grand Place/Grote Markt 1
Brussels, 1000 Belgium
(32) 16-247111
www.ab-inbev.com
Beer and consumer
  products O DRP

Annaly Capital Management Inc.
  NLY
1211 Avenue of the Americas,
  Suite 2892
New York, New York 10036
212-696-0100
www.annaly.com
Real estate investment trust O DRP

AON Corporation AON
200 East Randolph Street
Chicago, Illinois 60601
312-381-1000
www.aon.com
Insurance O DRP

Apache Corporation APA
2000 Post Oak Boulevard,
  Suite 100
Houston, Texas 77056
713-296-6000
www.apachecorp.com
Oil and gas operations O DRP

ArcelorMittal SA MT
19 avenue de la Liberté
L-2390
Luxembourg, L-2390 Luxembourg
(352) 10-47921
www.arcelormittal.com
Steel O DRP

Archer Daniels Midland Company
  ADM
4666 Faries Parkway
Decatur, Illinois 62526
217-424-5200
www.adm.com
Agricultural commodities and
  products O DRP

AstraZeneca PLC AZN
15 Stanhope Gate
London, W1K 1LN England
(44) 20-73045000
www.astrazeneca.com
Pharmaceuticals O DRP

AT&T Inc. T
208 South Akard Street
Dallas, Texas 75202
210-821-4105
www.att.com
Communications holding company
  O DRP

AU Optronics Corp. AUO
No. 1, Li-Hsin Rd 2
Hsinchu Science Park
Hsin-Chu, Taiwan
(886) 3-5632899
www.auo.com
Flat panel displays O

Autozone, Inc. AZO
123 South Front Street
Memphis, Tennessee 38103
901-495-6500
www.autozone.com
Retail automotive replacement parts
   and accessories O

AvalonBay Communities Inc. AVB
2900 Eisenhower Avenue, Suite 300
Alexandria, Virginia 22314
703-329-6300
www.avalonbay.com
Apartments real estate investment
   trust O DRP

Aviva PLC AV

Avon Products, Inc. AVP
1345 Avenue of the Americas
New York, New York 10105
212-282-5000
www.avon.com
Personal and household
   products O DRP

AXA S.A. AXA
25, avenue Matignon
Paris, 75008 France
(33) 1-40755700
www.axa.com
Insurance holding company O

Baker Hughes Inc. BHI
2929 Allen Parkway, Suite 2100
Houston, Texas 77019
713-439-8600
www.bakerhughes.com
Oilfield services O DRP

Banco Bilbao Vizcaya Argentaria
   S.A. BBVA
Plaza de San Nicholas 4
Bilbao, VIZ 48005 Spain
(34) 94-4876000
www.bbva.com
Banking O

Banco Bradesco S/A BBD
Cidade de Deus
Vila Yara
Osasco-SP, 06029-900 Brazil
(55) 11-36843702
www.bradescori.com
Banking O

Banco de Chile BCH
Agustinas 975
Piso 5
Santiago, Chile
(56) 2-6533239
www.bancochile.com
Banking

Banco Santander Brazil S.A. BSBR
Rua Amador Bueno, 474
Sao Paulo, 04752-005 Brazil
(55) 11-388654
www.santander.com.br
Banking O

Banco Santander S.A. STD
Ciudad Grupo Santander
Av. De Cantabria
Boadilla Del Monte
Madrid, MAD 28660 Spain
(34) 91-2596514
www.santander.com
Bank holding company O DRP

Banco Santander-Chile SAN
Agustinas 1065
Piso 2
Santiago, Chile
(56) 2-3202000
www.santander.cl
Banking O

BanColombia S.A. CIB
Calle 50 No. 51-66, Piso 7
Medellin, Colombia
574-5108866
www.grupobancolombia.com
Banking O

Bank of America Corporation BAC
100 North Tryon Street, 18th Floor
Charlotte, North Carolina 28255
704-386-5681
www.bankofamerica.com
Bank holding company O DRP

Bank of Montreal BMO
100 King Street West, 21st Floor
Toronto, ON M5X 1A1 Canada
416-867-5000
www.bmo.com
Banking O DRP

Bank of New York Mellon
  Corporation BK
One Wall Street
New York, New York 10286
212-495-1784
Financial services O DRP

Bank of Nova Scotia BNS
44 King Street West, 9th Floor
Toronto ON M5H 1H1 Canada
416-856-4862
www.scotiabank.com
Banking O

Barclays PLC BCS
1 Churchill Place
London E14 SHP England
(44) 20-7116100
www.group.barclays.com
Financial services O DRP

Barrick Gold Corporation ABX
161 Bay Street, Suite 3700
Toronto, ON M5J 2S1 Canada
416-861-9911
www.barrick.com
Gold production O

Baxter International, Inc. BAX
One Baxter Parkway
Deerfield, Illinois 60015
847-948-2000
www.baxter.com
Medical equipment and
  supplies O DRP

BB&T Corporation BBT
200 West Second Street
Winston-Salem, North Carolina
  27101
336-733-2000
www.bbt.com
Financial holding company O DRP

BCE Inc. BCE
1 Carrefour, 8th Floor
Verdun, QC H3E 3B3 Canada
888-932-6666
www.bce.ca
Communications services O

Becton, Dickinson & Company BDX
One Becton Drive
Franklin Lakes, New Jersey 07417
201-847-6800
www.bd.com
Medical equipment and supplies
  O DRP

Berkshire Hathaway, Inc. BRKA
3555 Farnam Street
Omaha, Nebraska 68131
402-346-1400
www.berkshirehathaway.com
Holding company for insurance and
  reinsurance

Best Buy Co., Inc. BBY
7601 Penn Avenue South
Richfield, Minnesota 55423
612-291-1000
www.bestbuy.com
Consumer electronics
  retailer O DRP

BHP Billiton Ltd. BHP
180 Lonsdale Street
Melbourne, VIC 3000 Australia
(61) 1300-554757
www.bhpbilliton.com
Natural resources. O DRP

BHP Billiton PLC BBL
Neathouse Place, Victoria
London, SW1V 1BH England
(44) 20-78024000
www.bhpbilliton.com
Natural resources O DRP

Blackrock Inc. BLK
40 East 52nd Street
New York, New York 10022
212-810-5300
www.blackrock.com
Investment management O

Blackstone Group L.P. BX
345 Park Avenue
New York, New York 10154
212-583-5000
www.blackstone.com
Investment services O

Boeing Company BA
100 N. Riverside Plaza
Chicago, Illinois 60606
312-544-2000
www.boeing.com
Aerospace and defense O DRP

Boston Properties, Inc. BXP
111 Huntington Avenue, Suite 300
Boston, Massachusetts 02199
617-236-3300
www.bostonproperties.com
Office properties and real estate
  investment trust O DRP

Boston Scientific Corporation BSX
One Boston Scientific Place
Natick, Massachusetts 01760
508-650-8000
www.bostonscientific.com
Medical devices O

BP PLC BP
1 St. James's Square
London, SW1Y 4PD England
800-638-5672
www.bp.com
Integrated oil and gas O DRP

BRF-Brazil Foods S/A BRFS
P.O. Box 358035
Pittsburgh, Pennsylvania 15252
888-269-2377
Food processing DRP

Bristol-Myers Squibb Company
  BMY
345 Park Avenue
New York, New York 10154
212-546-4000
www.bms.com
Pharmaceutical and nutritional
  products O DRP

British Sky Broadcasting Group
  PLC BSY
Grant Way, Isleworth
Middlesex, TW7 5QD England
(44) 870-2403000
www.corporate.sky.com
Broadcasting and cable television

Brookfield Asset Management Inc.
  BAM
181 Bay Street, Suite 300
Toronto, ON M5J 2T3 Canada
416-363-9491
www.brookfield.com
Real estate O

BT Group PLC BT
81 NewGate Street
London, EC1A 7AJ England
(44) 20-73565000
www.btplc.com
Communications services

Bunge Ltd. BG
50 Main Street
White Plains, New York 10606
914-684-2800
www.bunge.com
Food processing O

C.R. Bard Inc. BCR
730 Central Avenue
Murray Hill, New Jersey 07974
908-277-8000
www.crbard.com
Medical equipment and supplies O
  DRP

Cablevision Systems Corporation
  CVC
1111 Stewart Avenue
Bethpage, New York 11714
516-803-2300
www.cablevision.com
Cable operator O

Cadbury PLC CBY
Sanderson Road, Uxbridge
Middlesex, UB8 1DH England
(44) 1895-615000
www.cadbury.com
Confectionary O

Cameco Corp. CCJ
2121 11th Street West
Saskatoon, SK S7M 1J3 Canada
306-956-6200
www.cameco.com
Metal mining O

Cameron International Corp. CAM
1333 West Loop South, Suite 1700
Houston, Texas 77027
713-513-3300
www.c-a-m.com
Oil well services and equipment O

Campbell Soup Company CPB
One Campbell Place
Camden, New Jersey 08103
856-342-4800
www.campbellsoupcompany.com
Food products O DRP

Canadian Imperial Bank of
  Commerce CM
199 Bay Street, 44th Floor
Toronto, ON M5L 1A2 Canada
416-980-3096
www.cibc.com
Global financial institution O

Canadian National Railway
  Company CNI
935 de la Gauchetiere Street West
Montreal, Quebec H3B 2M9
  Canada
514-399-7212
www.cn.ca
Railroad O

Canadian Natural Resources, Ltd.
  CNQ
2500, 855 2nd Street, SW
Calgary, AB T2P 4J8 Canada
403-517-7345
www.cnrl.com
Crude oil and natural gas O

Canadian Pacific Railway Ltd. CP
401 9th Avenue SW, Suite 500
Calgary, AB T2P 4Z4 Canada
403-319-7000
www.cpr.ca
Railroad holding company O

Canon Inc. CAJ
3-30-2 Shimomaruko
Ohta-ku TKY 146-8501 Japan
(81) 3-37582111
www.canon.com
Computer peripherals O

Capital One Financial Corporation
  COF
1680 Capital One Drive, Suite 1400
McLean, Virginia 22102
703-720-1000
www.capitalone.com
Consumer financial
  services O DRP

Cardinal Health, Inc. CAH
7000 Cardinal Place
Dublin, Ohio 43017
614-757-5000
www.cardinal.com
Health care products and services O

Carnival Corporation CCL
3655 N.W. 87th Avenue
Miami, Florida 33178
305-599-2600
www.phx.corporate.com
Recreational activities O

Carnival PLC CUK
5 Gainsford Street
London, SE1 2NE England
(44) 20-79405381
www.phx,corporate.ir
Cruises and vacations O

Caterpillar, Inc. CAT
100 NE Adams Street
Peoria, Illinois 61629
309-675-1000
www/cat/com
Construction and agricultural
  machinery O DRP

CBS Corp. CBS
51 West 52nd Street, 35th Floor
New York, New York 10019
212-975-4321
www.cbscorporation.com
Mass media O DRP

Cemex S.A.B. de C.V. CX
Avenida Ricardo Margain Zozaya
 #325
Colonia Valle del Campestre
San Pedro Garza Garcia
Monterrey, 66265 Mexico
(52) 81-88888888
www.cemex.com
Cement O DRP
Construction holding company O
 DRP

Centrais Eletricas Brasileiras S/A
 EBR
Scn-Quadra 4-BL-B-N 100, sala 203
Asa Norte
Brasilia, 70714-900 Brazil
(55) 61-33297300
www.eletrobras.com
Electric power holding company O

CenturyTel Inc. CTL
100 CenturyTel Drive
Monroe, Louisiana 71203
318-388-9000
www.centurylink.com
Communications services O

Chesapeake Energy Corporation
 CHK
6100 North Western Avenue
Oklahoma City, Oklahoma 73118
405-848-8000
www.chk.com
Oil and gas operations O

Chevron Corporation CVX
6001 Bollinger Canyon Road
San Ramon, California 94583
925-842-1000
www.chevron.com
Integrated oil and gas O DRP

China Eastern Airlines Corp. Ltd.
 CEA
2550 Hongqiao Road
Shanghai, 200335 China
(86) 216-2686268
www.ce-air.com
Air carrier

China Life Insurance Co. Ltd. LFC
16 Chaowai Avenue
Chaoyang District
Beijing, 100020 China
(86) 10-85659999
www.e-chinalife.com
Life insurance O DRP

China Mobile Ltd. CHL
99 Queen's Road Central
Hong Kong, China
(86) 852-31218888
www.chinamobileltd.com
Mobile telecommunications services
 O

China Petroleum & Chemical Corp.
 SNP
6A, Huixindong Road
Chaoyang District
Beijing BEJ 100029 China
(86) 10-64990060
www.english.sinopec.com
Oil, gas and chemicals O

China Telecom Corp. Ltd. CHA
31 Jinrong Street
Xicheng, BEJ 100040 China
(86) 10-66428166
www.chinatelecom-h.com
Communications services O

China Unicom (Hong Kong) Ltd.
 CHU
99 Queen's Road, Central
Hong Kong, China
(852) null-null
www.chinaunicom.com.hk
Telecommunications services O

Chubb Corporation CB
15 Mountain View Road
Warren, New Jersey 07059
908-903-2000
www.chubb.com
Property and casualty insurance
 holding company O DRP

Chunghwa Telecom Co., Ltd. CHT
21-3 Hsinyi Road, Section 1
Taipei 100
Taipei, Taiwan
(886) 2-23444239
www.cht.com.tw
Telecommunications services O

CIGNA Corp. CI
1601 Chestnut Street
Philadelphia, Pennsylvania 19192
215-761-1000
www.cigna.com
Health services O DRP

Citigroup C
399 Park Avenue
New York, New York 10043
212-559-1000
www.citigroup.com
Banking DRP

Clorox Company CLX
1221 Broadway
Oakland, California 94612
510-271-7000
www.thecloroxcompany.com
Consumer products O DRP

CNA Financial Corporation CNA
333 South Wabash
Chicago, Illinois 60604
312-822-5000
www.cna.com
Insurance holding company O

CNOOC Ltd. CEO
One Garden Road
Central
Hong Kong, China
(852)
www.cnoocltd.com
Oil and gas operations O DRP

Coach, Inc. COH
516 West 34th Street
New York, New York 10001
212-594-1850
www.coach.com
Retail accessories and gifts O

The Coca-Cola Company KO
One Coca-Cola Plaza
Atlanta, Georgia 30313
404-676-2121
www.thecoca-colacompany.com
Beverages O DRP

Coca-Cola Enterprises, Inc. CCE
2500 Windy Ridge Parkway,
  Suite 700
Atlanta, Georgia 30339
770-989-3000
www.cokecce.com
Beverage bottling O DRP

Coca-Cola Femsa S.A.B. de C.V.
  KOF
Guillermo Gonzalez Camarena,
  No. 600
Col. Centro De Ciudad Santa Fe
DF, 01210 Mexico
212-688-6840
www.coca-colafemsa.com
Latin American beverage bottler

Coca-Cola Hellenic Bottling S.A.
  CCH
9, Frangoklissias Street
Marousi
Athens, 15125 Greece
(30) 210-6183100
www.coca-colahellenic.com
Non-alcoholic beverages

Colgate-Palmolive Company CL
300 Park Avenue
New York, New York 10022
212-310-2000
www.colgate.com
Consumer products O DRP

Companhia Brasileira de
  Distribuicao Grupo Pao de Acucar
  CBD
Av. Brigadeiro Luis Antonio,
  No. 3,142
Sao Paulo-SP, 01402-000 Brazil
(55) 11-38860421
www.grupopaodeacucar.com.br
Retail grocery chain

Companhia de Bebidas das
  Americas ABV
Rua Dr. Renato Paes de Barros
1017 – 4s andar
Sao Paulo-SP, 04530-001 Brazil
(55) 11-21221200
www.ambev-ir.com
Beverages O DRP

Companhia Energetica de Minas
  Gerais-CEMIG CIG
Av. Barbacena, 1200 Ed. Julio
  Soares
Santo Agostinho
Belo Horizonte, 30190-131 Brazil
(55) 31-35064900
www.cemig.com.br
Electric energy O

Companhia Siderurgica Nacional
  SID
Av. Brigadeiro Faria Lima 3,400,
  20th Floor
Sao Paulo-SP, 20010-020 Brazil
(55) 11-30497100
www.csn.com.br
Steel production O

Compania de Minas Buenaventura
  S.A. BVN
Carlos Villaran 790
Santa Catalina, 13
Lima, Peru
212-688-6840
www.buenaventura.com
Precious metals O

Computer Sciences Corporation
  CSC
3170 Fairview Park Drive
Falls Church, Virginia 22042
703-876-1000
www.csc.com
Computer services O

ConAgra Foods, Inc. CAG
One ConAgra Drive
Omaha, Nebraska 68102
402-595-4000
www.conagrafoods.com
Food processing O DRP

ConocoPhillips COP
600 North Dairy Ashford
Houston, Texas 77079
281-293-1000
www.conocophillips.com
Energy O DRP

Consol Energy Inc. CNX
1000 CONSOL Energy Drive
Canonsburg, Pennsylvania 15317
724-485-4000
www.consolenergy.com
Coal and gas O

Consolidated Edison Inc. ED
4 Irving Place
New York, New York 10003
212-460-4600
Holding company for electric
  utilities O DRP

Constellation Energy Group Inc.
  CEG
750 East Pratt Street
Baltimore, Maryland 21202
410-783-2800
www.constellation.com
Energy O DRP

Continental Resources Inc.
  Oklahoma CLR
302 N. Independence, Suite 1500
Enid, Oklahoma 73701
580-233-8955
www.contres.com
Oil and gas operations O

Cooper Industries, PLC CBE
600 Travis, Suite 5600
Houston, Texas 77002
713-209-8400
www.cooperindustries.com
Electric products and tools O DRP

Corning, Inc. GLW
1 Riverfront Plaza
Corning, New York 14831
607-974-9000
www.corning.com
Technology O DRP

Covidien PLC COV
Block G, First Floor
Cherrywood Business Park
Co. Dublin, Ireland
(353) null-null
www.covidien.com
Healthcare products O

CPFL Energia S.A. CPL
Rua Gomes de Carvalho 1540
14 Andar/cj 02
Sao Paulo-SP, 04547-005 Brazil
(55) 019-37568018
www.cpfl.com.br
Electric utility holding company

Credit Suisse Group CS
Paradeplatz 8
P.O. Box 1
Zurich, 8070 Switzerland
(41) 44-2121616
www.credit-suisse.com
Financial services O DRP

CRH PLC CRH
Belgard Castle
Clondalkin
Dublin, 22 Ireland
(353) 1-4041000
www.crh.com
Building materials

Crown Castle International
   Corporation CCI
1220 Augusta, Suite 500
Houston, Texas 77057
713-570-3147
www.crowncastle.com
Wireless communication towers O

CSX Corporation CSX
500 Water Street, 15th Floor
Jacksonville, Florida 32202
904-359-3200
www.csx.com
Rail-based transportation
   services O DRP

Cummins Inc. CMI
500 Jackson Street
Columbus, Indiana 47202
812-377-5000
www.cummins.com
Capital goods O DRP

CVS Caremark Corp. CVS
One CVS Drive
Woonsocket, Rhode Island 02895
401-765-1500
www.cvscaremark.com
Retail drugs O DRP

Daimler AG DAI
Mercedesstrasse 137
Stuttgart, 70327 Germany
(49) 711-170
www.daimler.com
Cars, trucks, vans and buses O DRP

Danaher Corp. DHR
2099 Pennsylvania Avenue N.W.,
   12th Floor
Washington, D.C. 20006
202-828-0850
www.danaher.com
Scientific and technical
   instruments O

Deere & Co. DE
One John Deere Place
Moline, Illinois 61265
309-765-8000
www.johndeere.com
Construction and agricultural
   machinery O DRP

Delhaize Group DEG
Square Marie Curie 40
Brussels, 1070 Belgium
(32) 2-4122211
www.delhaizegroup.com
Food supermarkets DRP

Delta Air Lines Inc. DAL
P.O. Box 20706
Atlanta, Georgia 30320
404-715-2600
www.delta.com
Airline O

Deutsche Bank AG DB
Theodor-Heuss-Allee 70
Frankfurt, 60262 Germany
(49) 69-91000
www.db.com
Investment services O

Deutsche Telekom AG DT
Friedrich-Ebert-Allee 140
Bonn, 53113 Germany
(49) 228-1814949
www.deutschetelekom.de
Telecommunications and
  information technology O

Devon Energy Corporation DVN
20 North Broadway, Suite 1500
Oklahoma City, Oklahoma 73102
405-235-3611
www.devonenergy.com
Oil and gas operations O

Diageo PLC DEO
8 Henrietta Place
London W1G 0NB England
(44) 20-79275200
www.diageo.com
Alcoholic beverages O

Diamond Offshore Drilling, Inc. DO
15415 Katy Freeway
Houston, Texas 77094
281-492-5300
www.diamondoffshore.com
Offshore oil and gas drilling O

Discover Financial Services DFS
2500 Lake Cook Road
Riverwoods, Illinois 60015
224-405-0900
www.discoverfinancial.com
Consumer financial services O DRP

Dollar General Corporation DG
100 Mission Ridge
Goodlettsville, Tennessee 37072
615-855-4000
www.dollargeneral.com
Discount retailer O

Dominion Resources, Inc. D
120 Tredegar Street
Richmond, Virginia 23219
804-819-2000
Energy O DRP

Dover Corp. DOV
280 Park Avenue
New York, New York 10017
212-922-1640
www.dovercorporation.com
Capital goods O DRP

Dow Chemical Company DOW
2030 Dow Center
Midland, Michigan 48674
989-636-1000
ww.dow.com
Chemicals, plastics and
  rubber O DRP

Dr Pepper Snapple Group Inc. DPS
5301 Legacy Drive
Plano, Texas 75024
972-673-7000
www.drpeppersnapplegroup.com
Non-alcoholic beverages O DRP

DTE Energy Company DTE
2000 Second Avenue
Detroit, Michigan 48226
313-235-4000
www.dteenergy.com
Energy O DRP

Duke Energy Corporation DUK
526 South Church Street
Charlotte, North Carolina 28202
704-594-6200
www.duke-energy.com
Energy O DRP

E.I. DuPont de Nemours & Co. DD
1007 Market Street
Wilmington, Delaware 19898
302-774-1000
www.dupont.com
Chemicals manufacturing O DRP

Eaton Corp. ETN
1111 Superior Avenue
Cleveland, Ohio 44114
216-523-5000
www.eaton.com
Electronic instruments and controls
  O DRP

Ecolab, Inc. ECL
370 Wabasha Street North
St. Paul, Minnesota 55102
651-292-2233
www.ecolab.com
Personal and household products O
 DRP

Ecopetrol S.A. EC
Carrera 7 No. 37-69
Bogota, Colombia
(57) 1-2344000
www.ecopetrol.com.co
Oil and gas operations

Edison International EIX
2244 Walnut Grove Avenue
Rosemead, California 91770
626-302-2222
www.edison.com
Electric utility holding company O
 DRP

El Paso Corporation EP
1001 Louisiana Street
Houston, Texas 77002
713-420-2600
www.elpaso.com
Energy O DRP

Eldorado Gold Corp. EGO
350 Burrard Street, Suite 1188
Vancouver, BC V6C 2B5 Canada
604-687-4018
www.eldoradogold.com
Gold production O

Eli Lilly and Co. LLY
Lilly Corporate Center
Indianapolis, Indiana 46285
317-276-2000
www.lilly.com
Pharmaceuticals O DRP

EMC Corp. EMC
176 South Street
Hopkinton, Massachusetts 01748
508-435-1000
www.emc.com
Computer storage devices O

Emerson Electric Co. EMR
8000 West Florissant Avenue
St. Louis, Missouri 63136
314-553-2000
www.emerson.com
Scientific and technical
 instruments O DRP

Empresa Nacional de Electricidad
 S.A. EOC
Santa Rosa 76
Santiago, 6510207 Chile
(56) 2-63090009
www.endesa.cl
Electric utility

Enbridge Energy Partners L.P. EEP
1100 Louisiana, Suite 3300
Houston, Texas 77002
713-821-2000
www.enbridgepartners.com
Oil well services and equipment O

Enbridge Inc. ENB
425 1st Street S.W.
Calgary, AB T2P 3L8 Canada
403- 231-3900
www.enbridge.com
Energy delivery O DRP 5%

EnCana Corp. ECA
1800-855 2nd Street S.W.
Calgary, AB T2P 2S5 Canada
403-645-2000
www.cncana.com
Natural gas O

Energy Transfer Equity L.P. ETE
3738 Oak Lawn Avenue
Dallas, Texas 75219
214-981-0700
www.energytransfer.com
Natural gas and retail propane O

Energy Transfer Partners L.P. ETP
3738 Oak Lawn Avenue
Dallas, Texas 75219
214-981-0700
www.energytransfer.com
Natural gas O

Enersis S.A. ENI
Avenida Santa Rosa 76
Santiago, Chile
(56) 2-353-4400
www.enersis.cl
Electric utility holding company O

ENI S.p.A. E
Piazzale Enrico Mattei 1
Rome, 00144 Italy
(39) 06-59821
www.eni.com
Integrated oil and gas

Entergy Corporation ETR
639 Loyola Avenue
New Orleans, Louisiana 70113
504-576-4000
www.entergy.com
Energy O DRP

Enterprise Products Partners L.P.
  EPD
1100 Louisiana Street, 10th Floor
Houston, Texas 77002
713-381-6500
www.epplp.com
Energy O

EOG Resources, Inc. EOG
1111 Bagby, Sky Lobby 2
Houston, Texas 77002
713-651-7000
www.eogresources.com
Oil and gas operations O

Equity Residential EQR
Two North Riverside Plaza,
  Suite 400
Chicago, Illinois 60606
312-474-1300
www.equityapartments.com
Apartment real estate investment
  trust O DRP 5%

Estée Lauder Companies EL
767 Fifth Avenue
New York, New York 10153
212-572-4200
www.elcompanies.com
Cosmetics and fragrances O DRP

Exelon Corporation EXC
10 South Dearborn Street,
  48th Floor
Chicago, Illinois 60680
312-394-7398
www.exeloncorp.com
Electric utility holding
  company O DRP

Exxon Mobil Corporation XOM
5959 Las Colinas Boulevard
Irving, Texas 75039
972-444-1000
www.exxonmobil.com
Integrated oil and gas O DRP

Fannie Mae FNM
3900 Wisconsin Avenue, NW
Washington, DC 20016
202-752-7000
www.fanniemae.com
Mortgage financing O

FedEx Corp. FDX
942 South Shady Grove Road
Memphis, Tennessee 38120
901-818-7500
www.fedex.com
Express transportation O DRP

Fibria Celulose S.A. FBR
Alameda Santos, 1357-6 andar
Cerqueira Cesar
Sao Paulo-SP, 01419-908 Brazil
(55) 011-2138400
www.vcp.com.br
Paper products O

Fidelity National Information
  Services Inc. FIS
601 Riverside Avenue
Jacksonville, Florida 32204
904-854-8100
www.fisglobal.com
Consumer financial services O

FirstEnergy Corp. FE
76 South Main Street
Akron, Ohio 44308
800-736-3402
www.firstenergycorp.com
Electric utility holding company O

Fluor Corp. FLR
6700 Las Colinas Boulevard
Irving, Texas 75039
469-398-7000
www.fluor.com
Engineering, procurement and
  construction management O

FMC Technologies Inc. FTI
1803 Gears Road
Houston, Texas 77067
281-591-4000
www.fmctechnologies.com
Oil well services and equipment O

Fomento Economico Mexicano
  S.A.B. de C.V. FMX
General Anaya 601 Poniente
Colonia Bella Vista
Monterrey, Nuevo Leon, 64410
  Mexico
(52) 818-3286167
www.femsa.com
Non-alcoholic beverage holding
  company

Ford Motor Company F
1 American Road, Suite 1026
Dearborn, Michigan 48126
313-322-3000
www.ford.com
Automobiles and trucks O DRP

Forest Laboratories, Inc. FRX
909 Third Avenue
New York, New York 10022
212-421-7850
www.frx.com
Biotechnology and drugs O

Fortune Brands, Inc. FO
520 Lake Cook Road
Deerfield, Illinois 60015
847-484-4400
www.fortunebrands.com
Alcoholic beverage holding
  company O DRP

FPL Group, Inc. FPL
700 Universe Boulevard
Juno Beach, Florida 33408
561-694-4000
www.fplgroup.com
Electric utility O DRP

France Telecom FTE
6, place d'Alleray
Paris, 75505 France
(33) 1-44442222
www.francetelecom.com
Communications services DRP

Franklin Resources, Inc. BEN
One Franklin Parkway
San Mateo, California 94403
650-312-2000
www.franklinresources.com
Investment management holding
  company O DRP

Freeport-McMoRan Copper &
  Gold, Inc. FCX
One North Central Avenue
Phoenix, Arizona 85004
602-366-8100
www.fcx.com
Copper and gold mining

Fresenius Medical Care AG & Co.
  KGaA FMS
Else-Kroner Strasse 1
Bad Momburg, 61346 Germany
(49) 781-4029000
www.fmc-ag.com
Dialysis products and services O

Gap, Inc. GPS
Two Folsom Street
San Francisco, California 94105
650-952-4400
www.gapinc.com
Specialty retailer O

General Dynamics Corporation GD
2941 Fairview Park Drive, Suite 100
Falls Church, Virginia 22042
703-876-3000
www.generaldynamics.com
Aerospace and defense O

General Electric Company GE
3135 Easton Turnpike
Fairfield, Connecticut 06828
203-373-2211
www.ge.com
Conglomerate O DRP

General Mills, Inc. GIS
Number One General Mills
  Boulevard
Minneapolis, Minnesota 55426
763-764-7600
www.generalmills.com
Food processing O DRP

Gerdau S.A. GGB
Av. Farrapos 1811
Porto Alegre
Rio Grande do Sul, 90220-005 Brazil
(55) 51-33232000
www.gerdau.com.br
Steel producer O

GlaxoSmithKline PLC GSK
980 Great West Road
Brentford, Middlesex, TW8 9GS
  England
(44) 20-80475000
www.gsk.com
Pharmaceutical products O DRP

Gold Fields Ltd. GFI
24 St. Andrews Road
Parktown
Johannesburg, 2193 South Africa
(27) 11-644-2400
www.goldfields.co.za
Gold producer O

Goldcorp Inc. GG
666 Burrard Street, Suite 3400
Park Place
Vancouver, BC V6C 2X8 Canada
604-696-3000
www.goldcorp.com
Gold, silver and copper producer O

Goldman Sachs Group, Inc. GS
85 Broad Street
New York, New York 10004
212-902-0300
www2.goldmansachs.com
Investment services O

Goodrich Corporation GR
2730 West Tyvola Road
Charlotte, North Carolina 28217
704-423-7000
www.goodrich.com
Aerospace and defense O DRP

Grupo Televisa S.A. de C.V. TV
Avenida Vasco de Quiroga No. 2000
Colonia Santa Fe
Mexico D.F., 01210 Mexico
(52) 55-52612000
www.esmas.com
Broadcasting and cable television O

H&R Block, Inc. HRB
One H&R Block Way
Kansas City, Missouri 64105
816-854-3000
www.hrblock.com
Personal services O

H.J. Heinz Co. HNZ
One PPG Place
Pittsburgh, Pennsylvania 15222
412-456-5700
www.heinz.com
Food processing O DRP

Halliburton Company HAL
1401 McKinney, Suite 2400
Houston, Texas 77010
713-759-2600
www.halliburton.com
Oil well services and equipment
  O DRP

Harris Corporation HRS
1025 West NASA Boulevard
Melbourne, Florida 32919
321-727-9100
www.harris.com
Communications
  equipment O DRP

Hartford Financial Services Group,
  Inc. HIG
One Hartford Plaza
Hartford, Connecticut 06115
860-547-5000
www.thehartford.com
Insurance and financial
  services O DRP

HCP, Inc. HCP
3760 Kilroy Airport Way, Suite 300
Long Beach, California 90806
562-733-5100
www.hcpi.com
Real estate investment trust O DRP

HDFC Bank Ltd. HDB
Senapati Bapat Marg
Lower Parel
Mumbai, 400 013 India
(91) 22-56521000
www.hdfcbank.com
Financial services O DRP

Hellenic Telecommunications
  Organization S.A. OTE
99 Kifissias Avenue
Amaroussion
Athens, GR 15181 Greece
212-815-2248
www.ote.gr
Communications services DRP

Hershey Company HSY
100 Crystal A Drive
Hershey, Pennsylvania 17033
717-534-4200
www.hersheys.com
Chocolate and confectionery
  products O DRP

Hess Corp. HES
1185 Avenue of the Americas
New York, New York 10036
212-997-8500
www.hess.com
Energy O DRP

Hewlett-Packard Company HPQ
3000 Hanover Street
Palo Alto, California 94304
650-857-1501
www.hp.com
Computer hardware O DRP

Hitachi Ltd. HIT
1-6-6 Marunouchi
Chiyoda-ku
Tokyo 100-8280 Japan
(81) 3-32581111
www.hitachi.com
Electronic instruments and controls O

Home Depot, Inc. HD
2455 Paces Ferry Road N.W.
Atlanta, Georgia 30339
770-433-8211
Home improvement
  retailer O DRP

Honda Motor Co. Ltd. HMC
1-1 Minami-Aoyama, 2-Chrome
Minato ku
Tokyo 1078556 Japan
www.world.honda.com
Automobiles and trucks O DRP

Honeywell International Inc. HON
101 Columbia Road
Morris Town, New Jersey 07962
973-455-2000
Aerospace and defense O DRP

Hospira Inc. HSP
275 North Field Drive
Lake Forest, Illinois 60045
224-212-2000
Pharmaceuticals and medication
  delivery O

Host Hotels and Resorts Inc. HST
6903 Rockledge Drive, Suite 1500
Bethesda, Maryland 20817
240-744-1000
Hotel real estate investment trust O

HSBC Holdings PLC HBC
8 Canada Square
London, E14 5HQ England
(44) 20-79918888
www.hsbc.com
Banking and financial
  services O DRP

Huaneng Power International Inc.
  HNP
2C, Fuxingmennan Street
Xicheng District
Beijing 100031 China
(86) 10-66491999
www.hpi.com.cn
Electric utility power plants O

Humana, Inc. HUM
500 West Main Street
Louisville, Kentucky 40202
502-580-1000
www.humana.com
Health and supplemental benefits O

ICICI Bank Ltd. IBN
ICICI Bank Towers
Bandra-Kurla Complex
Mumbai, 400 051 India
(91) 022-26531414
www.icicibank.com
Banking O DRP

Illinois Tool Works Inc. ITW
3600 West Lake Avenue
Glenview, Illinois 60026
847-724-7500
www.itw.com
Industrial products and
  equipment O DRP

ING Groep N.V. ING
Amstelveenseweg 500
Amsterdam, 1081 KL Netherlands
(31) 20-5415411
www.ing.com
Life insurance O

Ingersoll-Rand Plc IR
170/175 Lakeview Drive
Swords
Dublin, Ireland
(353) 01-8707400
www.company.ingersollrand.com
Capital goods O

Intercontinental Exchange Inc. ICE
2100 Riveredge Parkway, Suite 500
Atlanta, Georgia 30328
770-857-4700
www.theice.com
Investment services O

International Business Machines
  Corp. IBM
One New Orchard Road
Armonk, New York 10504
914-499-1900
www.ibm.com
Information technology O DRP

International Paper Co. IP
6400 Poplar Avenue
Memphis, Tennessee 38197
901-419-7000
www.internationalpaper.com
Paper and packaging O DRP

INVESCO Ltd. IVZ
1555 Peachtree Street N.E.,
  Suite 1800
Atlanta, Georgia 30309
404-479-1095
www.invesco.com
Investment management O DRP

Itau Unibanco Holding S/A ITUB
Praca Alfredo E.S. Aranha 100
Pq. Jabaquara
Sao Paulo, 04344-902 Brazil
(55) 11-50191122
www.itau.com
Private banking O DRP

ITT Corp. ITT
1133 Westchester Avenue
White Plains, New York 10604
914-641-2000
www.itt.com
Conglomerate O DRP

J.C. Penney Co., Inc. JCP
6501 Legacy Drive
Plano, Texas 75024
972-431-1000
www.jcpenney.net
Department stores O DRP

J.M. Smucker Co. SJM
One Strawberry Lane
Orrville, Ohio 44667
330-692-3000
www.smuckers.com
Food processing O DRP

Johnson & Johnson JNJ
One Johnson & Johnson Plaza
New Brunswick, New Jersey 08933
732-524-0400
www.jnj.com
Healthcare products O DRP

Johnson Controls Inc. JCI
5757 North Green Bay Avenue
Milwaukee, Wisconsin 53209
414-524-1200
www.johnsoncontrols.com
Building controls, automotive
  interiors and batteries O DRP

JPMorgan Chase & Co. JPM
270 Park Avenue
New York, New York 10017
212-270-6000
www.jpmorganchase.com
Financial holding company O DRP

Juniper Networks Inc. JNPR
1194 North Mathilda Avenue
Sunnyvale, California 94089
408-745-2000
www.juniper.net
Communications equipment O

KB Financial Group Inc. KB
9-1 Namdaemunno 2-Ga
Jung-Gu
Seoul, 100-092 South Korea
(82) 2-20732869
www.kbfng.com
Financial holding company O DRP

Kellogg Company K
One Kellogg Square
Battle Creek, Michigan 49016
269-961-2000
www.kelloggcompany.com
Cereal and convenience
  foods O DRP

Kimberly-Clark Corp. KMB
P.O. Box 619100
Dallas, Texas 75261
972-281-1200
www.kimberly-clark.com
Paper and paper products O DRP

Kinder Morgan Energy Partners
  L.P. KMP
500 Dallas Street, Suite 1000
Houston, Texas 77002
713-369-9000
www.kne.com
Pipeline transportation and energy
  storage O

Kinross Gold Corp. KGC
40 King Street West, 52nd Floor
Toronto, ON M5H 3Y2 Canada
416-365-5123
www.kinross.com
Gold mining O

Kohl's Corp. KSS
N56 W17000 Ridgewood Drive
Menomonee Falls, Wisconsin 53051
262-703-7000
www.kohls.com
Department stores O

Koninklijke Philips Electronics N.V.
  PHG
Amstelplein 2
Amsterdam, 1096 Netherlands
(31) 20-5977777
www.philips.co.uk
Audio and video equipment O DRP

Korea Electric Power Corp. KEP
411 Youngdong-Daero
Gangnam-Gu
Seoul, 135-791 South Korea
(82) 2-34564264
www.kepco.co.kr
Electric utility O DRP

Kraft Foods Inc. KFT
Three Lakes Drive
Northfield, Illinois 60093
847-646-2000
www.kraftfoodscompany.com
Packaged foods products O DRP

Kroger Company KR
1014 Vine Street
Cincinnati, Ohio 45202
513-762-4000
www.kroger.com
Food retailer O

KT Corp. KTC

Kubota Corporation KUB
1-2-47, Shikitsuhigashi
Naniwa-ku
Osaka 556-8601 Japan
(81) 6-66482622
www.kubota.co
Construction and agricultural
  machinery

Kyocera Corp. KYO
6 Takeda Tobadono-cho
Fushimi-ku
Kyoto 612-8501 Japan
(81) 75-6043500
www.global.kyocera.com
Semiconductors

L-3 Communications Holdings Inc.
  LLL
600 Third Avenue, 34th Floor
New York, New York 10016
212-697-1111
www.l-3com.com
Aerospace and defense O

Laboratory Corp. of America
  Holdings LH
358 South Main Street
Burlington, North Carolina 27215
336-229-1127
www.labcorp.com
Clinical laboratories O

Las Vegas Sands Corp. LVS
3355 Las Vegas Boulevard South
Las Vegas, Nevada 89109
702-414-1000
www.lasvegassands.com
Hotels and casinos O

LG Display Co. Ltd LPL
18F West Wing, LG Twin-Tower
Yeongdeungpo-Gu
Seoul, 150-721 South Korea
(82) 2-37771665
www.lgdisplay.com
Electronic instruments and controls O

Lincoln National Corporation LNC
150 North Radnor Chester Road,
  Suite A305
Radnor, Pennsylvania 19087
484-583-1400
www.lincolnfinancial.com
Life insurance holding
  company O DRP

Lloyds Banking Group PLC LYG
25 Gresham Street, 5th Floor
London, EC2V 7HN England
(44) 20-76261500
www.lloydsbankinggroup.com
Financial services O

Lockheed Martin Corp. LMT
6801 Rockledge Drive
Bethesda, Maryland 20817
301-897-6000
www.lockheedmartin.com
Technology systems and
  products O DRP

Loews Corporation L
667 Madison Avenue
New York, New York 10065
212-521-2000
www.loews.com
Insurance, oil and gas, hotels O

Lorillard Inc. LO
P.O. Box 10529
Greensboro, North Carolina 27404
877-703-0386
www.lorillard.com
Cigarettes O

Lowe's Companies LOW
1000 Lowe's Boulevard
Mooresville, North Carolina 28117
704-758-1000
www.lowes.com
Home improvement
  retailer O DRP

Luxottica Group S.p.A. LUX
Via Cantu 2
Milan, 20123 Italy
(39) 02-863341
www.luxottica.com
Eyewear manufacturer and retailer
  O DRP

M&T Bank Corp. MTB
One M&T Plaza
Buffalo, New York 14203
716-842-5445
www.mtb.com
Bank holding company O DRP

Macy's, Inc. M
7 West Seventh Street
Cincinnati, Ohio 45202
513-579-7000
www.macysinc.com
Retailer O DRP

Manulife Financial Corp. MFC
200 Bloor Street East
Toronto, Ontario, M4W 1E5
  Canada
416-926-3000
www.manulife.com
Life insurance holding company O
  DRP

Marathon Oil Corp. MRO
5555 San Felipe Road
Houston, Texas 77056
713-629-6600
www.marathon.com
Integrated oil and gas O DRP

Marriott International Inc. MAR
10400 Fernwood Road
Bethesda, Maryland 20817
301-380-3000
www.marriott.com
Hotels and lodging O DRP

Marsh & McLennan Companies
  MMC
1166 Avenue of the Americas
New York, New York 10036
212-345-5000
www.mmc.com
Insurance broker and
  consultant O DRP

MasterCard Inc. MA
2000 Purchase Street
Purchase, New York 10577
914-249-2000
www.mastercard.com
Consumer financial services O

McAfee, Inc. MFE
3965 Freedom Circle
Santa Clara, California 95054
408-988-3832
www.mcafee.com
Computer security O

McDonald's Corp. MCD
One McDonald's Plaza
Oak Brook, Illinois 60523
630-623-3000
www.mcdonalds.com
Food service O DRP

McGraw-Hill Companies MHP
1221 Avenue of the Americas
New York, New York 10020
212-512-2000
www.mcgraw-hill.com
Information services O DRP

McKesson Corp. MCK
One Post Street
San Francisco, California 94104
415-983-8300
www.mckesson.com
Drug distribution and
  technology O DRP

Mead Johnson Nutrition Co. MJN
2701 Patriot Boulevard,
  Fourth Floor
Glenview, Illinois 60026
847-832-2420
www.mjn.com
Pediatric nutrition O

Mechel OAO MTL
Ul. Krasnoarmeyskaya 1
Moscow, 125993 Russia
(7) 495-2218888
www.mechel.com
Iron and steel O

Medco Health Solutions Inc. MHS
100 Parsons Pond Drive
Franklin Lakes, New Jersey 07417
201-269-3400
www.medcohealth.com
Pharmacy services O

Medtronic Inc. MDT
710 Medtronic Parkway, LC-480
Minneapolis, Minnesota 55432
763-505-2692
www.medtronic.com
Medical devices O DRP

Merck & Co. Inc. MRK
2000 Galloping Hill Road
Kenilworth, New Jersey 07033
908-298-4000
www.merck.com
Pharmaceuticals O DRP

MetLife, Inc. MET
200 Park Avenue
New York, New York 10166
212-578-2211
www.metlife.com
Insurance and financial services O

Mitsubishi UFJ Financial Group
  Inc. MTU
7-1 Marunouchi, 2-chrome
Chiyoda-ku
Tokyo 100-8330 Japan
(81) 3-32408111
www.mufg.jp
Bank holding company O DRP

Mizuho Financial Group Inc. MFG
5-1 Marunouchi, 2-Chome
Chiyoda-ku
Tokyo 100-8330 Japan
(81) 3-52241111
www.mizuho-fg.co.jp
Financial services O

Mobile TeleSystems MBT
Ul. Marksistskaya 4
Moscow, 109147 Russia
(7) 495-9116565
www.mtsgsm.com
Mobile cellular communications O

Molson Coors Brewing Co. TAP
1225 17th Street
Denver, Colorado 80202
303-279-6565
www.molsoncoors.com
Brewers holding company O

Monsanto Co. MON
800 North Lindbergh Boulevard
St. Louis, Missouri 63167
314-694-1000
www.monsanto.com
Agricultural products O DRP

Moody's Corp. MCO
250 Greenwich Street
New York, New York 10007
212-553-0300
www.moodys.com
Credit ratings O

Morgan Stanley MS
1585 Broadway
New York, New York 10036
212-761-4000
www.morganstanley.com
Financial services O DRP

Mosaic Co. MOS
3033 Campus Drive, Suite E490
Plymouth, Minnesota 55441
800-918-8270
www.mosaicco.com
Crop nutrients O

Motorola, Inc. MOT
1303 East Algonquin Road
Schaumburg, Illinois 60196
847-576-5000
www.motorola.com
Communications equipment
  O DRP

Murphy Oil Corp. MUR
200 Peach Street
El Dorado, Arkansas 71731
870-862-6411
www.murphyoilcorp.com
Oil and gas exploration and
  production O

National Bank of Greece S.A. NBG
86 Eolou Street
Athens, 102 32 Greece
(30) 210-3342310
www.nbg.gr
Banking O DRP

National Grid PLC NGG
1-3 Strand
London WC2N 5EH England
(44) 20-70043000
www.nationalgrid.com
Electric and gas utility DRP

National Oilwell Varco, Inc. NOV
10000 Richmond Avenue, 4th Floor
Houston, Texas 77042
713-346-7500
www.nov.com
Oil well services and equipment O

Newfield Exploration Company
  NFX
363 N. Sam Houston Parkway East,
  Suite 2020
Houston, Texas 77060
281-847-6000
Oil and gas exploration and
  development O

Newmont Mining Corporation
  NEM
6363 South Fiddlers Green Circle
Greenwood Village, Colorado 80111
303-863-7414
www.newmont.com
Gold and copper production O

Nexen Inc. NXY
801 Seventh Avenue S.W.
Calgary, AB T2P 3P7 Canada
403-699-4000
www.nexeninc.com
Energy O

Nidec Corp. NJ
338 Tonoshiro-cho
Kuze Minami-ku
Kyoto 601-8205 Japan
(81) 75-9356140
www.nidec.co.jp
Electronic instruments and controls

Nike, Inc. NKE
One Bowerman Drive
Beaverton, Oregon 97005
503-671-6453
www.nike.com
Athletic and apparel O DRP

Nippon Telegraph & Telephone
  Corp. NTT
2-3-1 Otemachi
Chiyoda-ku
Tokyo 100-8116 Japan
(81) 3-52055581
www.ntt.co.jp
Communications services O DRP

Noble Corp. NE
Dorfstrasse 19A
Baar, Texas 64300
141-761-6555
www.noblecorp.com
Offshore drilling contractor O

Noble Energy, Inc. NBL
100 Glenborough Drive, Suite 100
Houston, Texas 77067
281-872-3100
www.nobleenergyinc.com
Energy O

Nokia Corp. NOK
Keilalahdentie 2-4
Espoo, 02150 Finland
(358) 7180-08000
www.nokia.com
Communications equipment
  O DRP

Nomura Holdings Inc. NMR
1-9-1 Nihonbashi
Chuo-ku
Tokyo 103-8645 Japan
(81) 3-52551000
www.nomura.com
Financial services O

Nordstrom, Inc. JWN
1617 Sixth Avenue, 6th Floor
Seattle, Washington 98101
206-628-2111
www.nordstrom.com
Retail apparel, shoes, cosmetics and
  accessories O

Norfolk Southern Corp. NSC
Three Commercial Place
Norfolk, Virginia 23510
757-823-5567
www.nscorp.com
Rail transportation O DRP

Northrop Grumman Corp. NOC
1840 Century Park East
Los Angeles, California 90067
310-553-6262
www.northropgrumman.com
Aerospace and defense O DRP

Novartis AG NVS
Lichtstrasse 35
Basel, 4022 Switzerland
www.novartis.com
Healthcare products O DRP

Novo Nordisk A/S NVO
Nova Alle
Bagsvaerd, 2880 Denmark
(45) 44-448888
www.novonordisk.com
Healthcare products O

NTT DoCoMo Inc. DCM
11-1 Nagata-cho, 2-chome
Chiyoda-ku
Tokyo 100-6150 Japan
(81) 3-51561111
www.nttdocomo.com
Mobile telecommunications O DRP

Nucor Corp. NUE
1915 Rexford Road
Charlotte, North Carolina 28211
704-366-7000
www.nucor
Iron and steel O DRP

NYSE Euronext NYX
11 Wall Street
New York, New York 10005
212-656-3000
www.nyse.com
Exchange group O

Occidental Petroleum Corporation
  OXY
10889 Wilshire Boulevard
Los Angeles, California 90024
310-208-8800
www.oxy.com
Oil and gas exploration and
  chemicals O DRP

Omnicom Group, Inc. OMC
437 Madison Avenue
New York, New York 10022
212-415-3600
www.omnicomgroup.com
Advertising, marketing,
  communications O DRP

Orix Corp. IX
4-1-23 Shiba
Minato-ku
Tokyo 108-0014 Japan
(81) 3-54195000
www.orix.co.jp
Rental and leasing

Panasonic Corp. PC
1006 Oaza Kadoma-shi
Kadoma
Osaka 571-8508 Japan
(81) 6-69081121
www.panasonic.net
Audio and video equipment O DRP

Parker-Hannifin Corp. PH
6035 Parkland Boulevard
Cleveland, Ohio 44124
216-896-3000
www.parker.com
Motion and control
  products O DRP

Peabody Energy Corp. BTU
701 Market Street
St. Louis, Missouri 63101
314-342-3400
www.peabodyenergy.com
Coal O DRP

Pearson PLC PSO
80 Strand
London WC2R 0RL England
(44) 20-70102000
www.pearson.com
Media and education

Penn West Energy Trust PWE
425 First Street S.W., Suite 2200
Calgary, Alberta T2P 3L8 Canada
403-777-2500
www.pennwest.com
Oil and gas operations O

Pepsi Bottling Group Inc. PBG
One Pepsi Way
Somers, New York 10589
914-767-6000
www.pbg.com
Soft drink distribution O DRP

PepsiCo, Inc. PEP
700 Anderson Hill Road
Purchase, New York 10577
914-253-2000
www.pepsico.com
Foods, snacks and
  beverages O DRP

Petrobras Petróleo Brasileiro PBR
Avenida República do Chile 65, 24s
  Andar
Centro
Rio de Janeiro, 20031-912 Brazil
(55) 21-32242040
www.petrobras.com.br
Integrated oil and gas O

PetroChina Company Ltd. PTR
9 Dongzhimen North Street
Dongcheng District
Beijing, 100007 China
212-815-2345
www.petrochina.com.cn
Integrated oil and gas O DRP

Petrohawk Energy Corp. HK
1000 Louisiana, Suite 5600
Houston, Texas 77002
832-204-2700
www.petrohawk.com
Oil and natural gas O

Pfizer, Inc. PFE
235 East 42nd Street
New York, New York 10017
212-573-2323
www.pfizer.com
Biopharmaceuticals O DRP

PG&E Corporation PCG
One Market, Spear Tower,
  Suite 2400
San Francisco, California 94105
415-267-7000
www.pgecorp.com
Utility holding company O DRP

Philip Morris International Inc. PM
120 Park Avenue
New York, New York 100117
917-663-2000
www.philipmorrisinternational.com
Cigarettes O DRP

Philippine Long Distance
  Telephone Co. PHI
Ramon Cojuangco Building, Makati
  Avenue
Makati City, Philippines
632-816-8556
www.pldt.com.ph
Telecommunications O

Plains All-American Pipeline L.P.
  PAA
333 Clay Street, Suite 1600
Houston, Texas 77002
713-646-4100
www.paalp.com
Oil and gas operation

PNC Financial Services Group, Inc.
  PNC
249 Fifth Avenue
Pittsburgh, Pennsylvania 15222
412-762-2000
www.pnc.com
Financial service O DRP

Polo Ralph Lauren Corp. RL
650 Madison Avenue
New York, New York 10022
212-318-7000
www.ralphlauren.com
Apparel and accessories O

Portugal Telecom SGPS S/A PT
Av. Fontes Pereira de Melo, 40
Lisbon, 1069-300 Portugal
(351) 21-5001701
www.telecom.pt
Telecommunications

POSCO PKX
1, Goidong-Dong
Nam-Gu
Pohang-Si, Kyongsahnbuk-Do, 790-
  785 South Korea
(82) 54-2200114
www.posco.com
Iron and steel O

Potash Corp. of Saskatchewan Inc.
  POT
1211 First Avenue South, Suite 500
Saskatoon, Saskatchewan S7K 7G3
  Canada
306-933-8500
www.potashcorp.com
Fertilizers O

PPG Industries, Inc. PPG
One PPG Place
Pittsburgh, Pennsylvania 15272
412-434-3131
www.ppg.com
Coatings O DRP

PPL Corporation PPL
Two North Ninth Street
Allentown, Pennsylvania 18101
610-774-5151
www.pplweb.com
Energy O DRP

Praxair, Inc. PX
39 Old Ridgebury Road
Danbury, Connecticut 06810
203-837-2000
Industrial gases supplier O DRP

Precision Castparts Corp. PCP
4650 SW Macadam Avenue,
  Suite 440
Portland, Oregon 97239
503-417-4800
Manufacturer of metal components
  and products O

Principal Financial Group Inc. PFG
711 High Street
Des Moines, Iowa 50392
515-247-5111
www.principal.com
Retirement savings, investment and
  insurance products and services O

Procter & Gamble Company PG
One Procter & Gamble Plaza
Cincinnati, Ohio 45202
513-983-1100
www.pg.com
Consumer packaged goods O DRP

Progress Energy Inc. PGN
410 South Wilmington Street
Raleigh, North Carolina 27601
919-546-6111
www.progress-energy.com
Electric utility holding
  company O DRP

Progressive Corporation PGR
6300 Wilson Mills Road
Mayfield Village, Ohio 44143
440-461-5000
www.progressive.com
Insurance holding company.
  com.y O

ProLogis PLD
4545 Airport Way
Denver, Colorado 80239
303-567-5000
www.prologis.com
Real estate investment
  trust O DRP 5%

Prudential Financial, Inc. PRU
751 Broad Street
Newark, New Jersey 07102
973-802-6000
www.prudential.com
Financial services O

Prudential PLC PUK
Laurence Pountney Hill
London EC4R 0HH England
(44) 20-72207588
www.prudential.co.uk
Financial services O DRP

Public Service Enterprise Group
  Inc. PEG
80 Park Place
Newark, New Jersey 07101
973-430-7000
www.pseg.com
Energy O DRP
Electric utility holding company O
  DRP

Public Storage, Inc. PSA
701 Western Avenue
Glendale, California 91201
818-244-8080
www.publicstorage.com
Self-storage real estate investment
  trust O

Quest Diagnostics, Inc. DGX
3 Giralda Farms
Madison, New Jersey 07940
201-393-5000
www.questdiagnostics.com
Diagnostic laboratory, information
  and services O

Questar Corp. STR
180 East 100 South Street
Salt Lake City, Utah 84145
801-324-5000
www.questar.com
Energy O DRP

Qwest Communications
  International, Inc. Q
1801 California Street
Denver, Colorado 80202
303-992-1400
www.qwest.com
Communications services O DRP

Range Resources Corp. RRC
100 Throckmorton Street,
  Suite 1200
Fort Worth, Texas 76102
817-870-2601
www.rangeresources.com
Natural gas O

Raytheon Company RTN
870 Winter Street
Waltham, Massachusetts 02451
781-522-3000
www.raytheon.com
Defense O DRP

Reed Elsevier N.V. ENL
Radarweg 29
Amsterdam, 1043 Netherlands
(31) 20-4852222
www.reedelsevier.com
Publisher and information provider

Reed Elsevier PLC RUK
1-3 Strand
London WC2N 5JR England
(44) 20-79307077
www.reedelsevier.com
Publisher and information provider

Regions Financial Corporation RF
1900 Fifth Avenue North
Birmingham, Alabama 35203
205-944-1300
www.regions.com
Financial holding company O DRP

Repsol YPF S.A. REP
Paseo de la Castellana 278-280
Madrid, 28046 Spain
(34) 91-3488100
www.repsol.com
Integrated oil and gas O

Republic Services Inc. RSG
18500 North Allied Way
Phoenix, Arizona 85054
480-627-2700
www.republicservices.com
Waste management services O

Reynolds American, Inc. RAI
401 North Main Street
Winston-Salem, North Carolina
  27101
336-741-2000
www.reynoldsamerican.com
Tobacco holding company O DRP

Rio Tinto PLC RTP
5 Aldermanbury Square
London, EC2V 7HR England
(44) 20-7812000
www.riotinto.com
Mining and exploration O DRP

Rockwell Automation Inc. ROK
1201 South Street
Milwaukee, Wisconsin 53204
414-382-2000
www.rockwellautomation.com
Automation power, control and
  information O DRP

Rockwell Collins Inc. COL
400 Collins Road NE
Cedar Rapids, Iowa 52498
319-295-1000
www.rockwellcollins.com
Communications and aviation
  electronics O DRP

Rogers Communications Inc. RCI
333 Bloor Street East, 10th Floor
Toronto, Ontario M4W 1G9 Canada
416-935-7777
www.rogers.com
Communications and media O

Royal Bank of Canada RY
200 Bay Street
Toronto, Ontario M5J 2J5 Canada
416-974-5151
www.rbc.com
Financial services O

Royal Bank of Scotland Group PLC
  RBS
36 St. Andrews Square
Edinburgh, EH2 2YB Scotland
(44) 131-5568555
www.rbs.com
Banking and financial services
  holding company O

Royal Dutch Shell PLC (Cl A)
RDSA
30, Carel van Bylandtlaan
The Hague, 2596 HR Netherlands
(31) 70-3779111
www.shell.com
Integrated oil and gas holding
company O DRP

Royal Dutch Shell PLC RDSB
30, Carel van Bylandtlaan
The Hague, 2596 HR Netherlands
(31) 70-3779111
www.shell.com
Integrated oil and gas holding
company O

Safeway, Inc. SWY
5918 Stoneridge Mall Road
Pleasanton, California 94588
925-467-3000
www.safeway.com
Food and drug retailer O DRP

SAIC, Inc. SAI
10260 Campus Point Drive
San Diego, California 92121
858-826-6000
www.saic.com
Software and programming O

Salesforce.com, Inc. CRM
The Landmark @ One Market,
Suite 300
San Francisco, California 94105
415-901-7000
www.salesforce.com
Customer relationship management O

Sanofi-Aventis S.A. SNY
174 avenue de France
Paris, 75635 France
(33) 1-53774000
www.sanofi-aventis.com
Pharmaceuticals and human
vaccines O DRP

SAP AG SAP
Dietmar-Hopp-Allee 16
Walldorf, 69190 Germany
(49) 622-7747474
www.sap.com
Software and programming O DRP

Sara Lee Corp. SLE
3500 Lacey Road
Downers Grove, Illinois 60515
630-598-6000
www.saralee.com
Food processing O DRP

Sasol Ltd. SSL
1 Sturdee Avenue
Rosebank
Johannesburg, 2196 South Africa
(27) 11-4413111
www.sasol.com
Energy and chemicals O

Schlumberger, Ltd. SLB
5599 San Felipe, 17th Floor
Houston, Texas 77056
713-513-2000
www.slb.com
Oil well services and equipment O

Scripps Networks Interactive Inc.
SNI
312 Walnut Street
Cincinnati, Ohio 45202
(513) 977-3000
www.scrippsnetworksinteractive.com
Media and interactive O DRP

Sempra Energy SRE
101 Ash Street
San Diego, California 92101
619-696-2034
www.sempra.com
Energy services holding company
O DRP

Shaw Communications Inc. SJR
630 Third Avenue S.W., Suite 900
Calgary, Alberta T2P 4L4 Canada
403-750-4500
www.shaw.ca
Communications

Sherwin-Williams Co. SHW
101 Prospect Avenue, N.W.
Cleveland, Ohio 44115
216-566-2000
www.sherwin-williams.com
Paints and coatings O DRP

Shinhan Financial Group Co. Ltd.
  SHG
120, Taepyungro-2 Ga
Joong-Gu
Seoul, 100-865 South Korea
(82) 2-63603000
www.shinhangroup.co.kr
Financial holding company

Siemens AG SI
Wittelsbacherplatz 2
Munich, 80333 Germany
(49) 89-63600
www.siemens.com
Technology O DRP

Simon Property Group Inc. SPG
225 West Washington Street
Indianapolis, Indiana 46204
317-636-1600
www.simon.com
Real estate investment trust
  O DRP

SINOPEC Shanghai Petrochemical
  Company Ltd. SHI
No. 48 Jinyl Road
Jinshin District
Shanghai, 20050 China
215-794-3143
www.spc.com.cn
Petrochemicals O DRP

SK Telecom Co. SKM
11, Eujiro-2ga
Choong-Gu
Seoul, 110-110 South Korea
(82) 2-61002114
www.sktelecom.com
Wireless telecommunications O

Smith & Nephew PLC SNN
15 Adam Street
London WC2N 6LA England
978-749-1000
www.smith-nephew.com
Medical devices O

Smith International Inc. SII
411 North Sam Houston Parkway,
  Suite 600
Houston, Texas 77060
281-443-3370
www.smith.com
Oil well services and equipment O

Sociedad Quimica y Minera de
  Chile S.A. SQM
El Trovador 4285, 6th Floor
Santiago, Chile
212-815-2296
www.sqm.com
Specialty plant nutrients and
  chemicals O DRP

Sony Corporation SNE
1-7-1 Konan
Minato-ku,
Tokyo, 108-0075 Japan
(81) 3-67482111
www.sony.net
Electronic equipment, instruments
  and devices O DRP

Southern Company SO
30 Ivan Allen Jr. Boulevard N.W.
Atlanta, Georgia 30308
404-506-5000
www.southerncompany.com
Public utility holding
  company O DRP

Southern Copper Corp. PCU
11811 North Tatum Boulevard,
  Suite 2500
Phoenix, Arizona 85028
602-494-5328
www.southernperu.com
Copper mining O DRP

Southwest Airlines Company LUV
P.O. Box 36611
Dallas, Texas 75235
214-792-4000
www.southwest.com
Airline O DRP

Southwestern Energy Company SWN
2350 North Sam Houston Parkway
  East, Suite 125
Houston, Texas 77032
281-618-4700
www.swn.com
Energy O DRP

Spectra Energy Corp. SE
5400 Westheimer Court
Houston, Texas 77056
713-627-5400
www.spectraenergy.com
Energy O DRP

Sprint Nextel Corp. S
6200 Sprint Parkway
Overland Park, Kansas 66251
703-433-4000
www.sprint.com
Communications services holding
  company O DRP

St. Jude Medical Inc. STJ
One Lillehei Plaza
St. Paul, Minnesota 55117
651-483-2000
www.sjm.com
Cardiac medical devices O

Starwood Hotels & Resorts
  Worldwide, Inc. HOT
1111 Westchester Avenue
White Plains, New York 10604
914-640-8100
www.starwoodhotels.com
Hotels and leisure O

State Street Corp. STT
One Lincoln Street
Boston, Massachusetts 02111
617-786-3000
www.statestreet.com
Financial holding company O DRP

Statoil ASA STO
Forusbeen 50
Stavanger, 4035 Norway
(47) 51-990000
www.statoil.com.en
Integrated oil and gas O DRP

Sterlite Industriesn (India) Ltd., SLT
SIPCOT Industrial Complex
Madural By Pass Road
T V Puram P.O.
Tuticorin, 628 002 India
(91) 11-24366023
www.sterlite-industries.com
Non-ferrous metals and mining O

STMicroelectronics N.V. STM
39, Chemin du Champ-Filles
Plan-les-Quates
Geneva, 1228 Switzerland
(41) 22-9292929
www.st.com
Semiconductors O

Stryker Corp. SYK
2825 Airview Boulevard
Kalamazoo, Michigan 49002
269-385-2600
www.stryker.com
Medical technology O

Sun Life Financial Inc. SLF
150 King Street West. 6th Floor
Toronto, Ontario M5H 1J9 Canada
416-979-9966
www.sunlife.com
Financial services O

Suncor Energy Inc. SU
112 4th Avenue S.W.
Calgary, Alberta T2P 2V5 Canada
403-269-8100
www.suncor.com
Energy O DRP

SunTrust Banks Inc. STI
303 Peachtree Street N.E.
Atlanta, Georgia 30308
404-588-7711
www.suntrust.com
Financial services holding
  company O DRP

Syngenta AG SYT
Schwarzwaldalee 215
Basel, 4002 Switzerland
(41) 61-323-1111
www.syngenta.com
Agribusiness O

Sysco Corp. SYY
1390 Enclave Parkway
Houston, Texas 77077
281-584-1390
www.sysco.com
Foodservice distributor O DRP

Taiwan Semiconductor
  Manufacturing Co. Ltd. TSM
No. 8, Li-Hsin Road 6
Hsinchu Science Park
Hsinchu, Taiwan
(866) 3-5636688
www/tsmc.com
Integrated circuits O

Talisman Energy Inc. TLM
3400-888 Third Street S.W.
Calgary, Alberta T2P 5C5 Canada
403-237-1234
www.talisman-energy.com
Oil and gas O

Target Corporation TGT
1000 Nicollet Mall
Minneapolis, Minnesota 55403
612-304-6073
www.target.com
General merchandise
  retailer O DRP

Tata Motors Ltd. TTM
24 Homi Mody Street
Mumbai, 400 100 India
(91) 22-66658282
www.tatamotors.com
Automotive vehicles O

Teck Resources Ltd. TCK
550 Burrard Street, Suite 3300
Bentall 5
Vancouver, British Columbia V6C
  0B3 Canada
604-699-4000
www.teck.com
Natural resources O

Tele Norte Leste Participacoes S/A
  TNE
Rua Humberto de Cacmpos 425, 8
  degree andar
Lebion
Rio de Janeiro, 2240-190 Brazil
212-815-2921
www.oi.com.br
Telecommunication service O

Telecom Italia S.p.A. TI
Piazza degil Affari 2
Milan, 20123 Italy
(39) 125-5200
www.new.telecomitalia.it
Telecommunications

Telecom Italia S.p.A. (Rep. 10
  Savings Shares) TIA
Piazza degli Affari 2
Milan, 20123 Italy
(39) 125-5200
www.new.telecomitalia.it
Telecommunications

Telecomunicacoes de Sao Paulo S/A
  TSP
Rua Martiniano de Carvalho
851 Bela Vista
São Paulo, 01321-001 Brazil
(55) 11 35497030
www.telefonica.com.br
Telecommunications DRP

Telefonica S.A. TEF
Edificio Central Pl 2
C/Ronda de la Comunicacion s/n
Madrid, 28050 Spain
(34) 91-4828700
www.telefonica.com
Communications services O

Teléfonos de México S.A.B. de C.V.
  TMX
Parqué Vía 190
Colonia Cuauhtémoc
Mexico City, 06599 Mexico
800-997-8970
www.telmex.com/mx
Telecommunications O DRP

Telekomunikasi Indonesia TLK
Japan Road No. 1
Bandung, 40133 Indonesia
(62) 22-4521510
www.telecom.co.id
Communications services O

Telmex International S.A.B. de
  C.V. TII
Avenida delos Insurgentes 3500
Colonia Pena Pobre
Delegacion Tialpan
Mexico, 14060 Mexico
(52) 55-52233200
www.telmexusa.com/us
Communications services holding
  company O

TELUS Corp. TU
3777 Kingsway, 21st Floor
Burnaby, British Columbia
  V5H 3Z7 Canada
800-667-4871
www.telus.com
Telecommunications DRP

Tenaris S.A. TS
46a, Avenue John F. Kennedy
Luxembourg, 1855 Luxembourg
(54) 11-40184020
www.tenaris.com
Construction holding company O

TERNIUM S.A. TX
46a, John F. Kennedy, 2nd Floor
Luxembourg, L-1855 Luxembourg
(352) 46-61113815
www.ternium.com
Iron and steel O

Texas Instruments Inc. TXN
12500 TI Boulevard
Dallas, Texas 75266
972-995-3773
www.ti.com
Semiconductors O DRP

Thermo Fisher Scientific Inc. TMO
81 Wyman Street
Waltham, Massachusetts 02454
781-622-1000
www.thermofisher.com
Scientific and technical
  instruments O

Thomson Reuters Corporation TRI
3 Times Square
New York, New York 10036
646-223-4000
www.thomsonreuters.com
Information provider O

TIM Participacoes S/A TSU
Av das Americas, 3434
Bloco 1-7 Andar parte
Barra da Tijuca
Rio de Janeiro, 22640-102 Brazil
(55) 21-40093742
www.tim.riweb.com.br
Mobile cellular holding company O

Time Warner Cable Inc. TWC
60 Columbus Circle
New York, New York 10023
212-364-8200
www.timewarnercable.com
Cable operator O

Time Warner, Inc. TWX
One Time Warner Center
New York, New York 10019
212-484-8000
www.timewarner.com
Media and entertainment O

TJX Companies, Inc. TJX
770 Cochituate Road
Framingham, Massachusetts 01701
508-390-1000
www.tjx.com
Off-price apparel and home fashions
  retailer O

Toronto-Dominion Bank TD
Toronto-Dominion Center
Toronto, Ontario M5K 1A2 Canada
416-308-6963
www.td.com
Financial services O

Total S.A. TOT
2, place Jean Miller
La Défense 6
Courbevoie, 92400 France
(33) 01-47444546
www.total.com
Oil and gas O DRP

Toyota Motor Corp. TM
1 Toyota-cho
Toyota-shi, 471-8571 Japan
(81) 565-282121
www.toyota.jp
Automotive O DRP

TransCanada Corp. TRP
450 First Street SW
Calgary, Alberta T2P 5H1 Canada
403-920-2000
www.transcanada.com
Pipelines and energy O DRP

Transocean Ltd. RIG
Building F, 7th Floor
Chemin de Blandonnet
Vernier, 1214 Switzerland
(41) 229-309000
www.deepwater.com
Offshore contract drilling
  services O DRP

Travelers Companies Inc. TRV
385 Washington Street
St. Paul, Minnesota 55102
651-310-7911
www.travelers.com
Property and casualty insurance
  holding company O DRP

Turkcell Iletisim Hizmetieri A.S.
  TKC
Mesrutiyet Caddesi, No. 71
Tepebasi
Istanbul, 80050 Turkey
(90) 12-3131000
www.turkcell.com.tr
Mobile services O

Tyco Electronics Ltd. TEL
Rheinstrasse 20, CH-8200
Schaffhausen, Switzerland
(41) 52-6336661
www.tycoelectronics.com
Electronic instruments and controls O

Tyco International Ltd. TYC
Freier Platz 10, CH-8200
Schaffhausen, 8200 Switzerland
(41) 52-6330244
www.tyco.com
Conglomerate O

U.S. Bancorp USB
800 Nicollet Mall
Minneapolis, Minnesota 55402
651-466-3000
www.usbank.com
Financial services holding company
  O DRP

UBS Ag UBS
Bahnhofstrasse 45
Zurich, 8001 Switzerland
212-821-3000
www.ubs.com
Financial services O

Ultra Petroleum Corp. UPL
363 North Sam Houston Parkway,
  Suite 1200
Houston, Texas 77060
281-876-0120
www.ultrapetroleum.com
Oil and natural gas O

Ultrapar Participacoes S/A UGP
Av. Brigadeiro Luiz Antonio, 1343,
  9s
Bela Vista
Sao Paulo, 01317-910 Brazil
(55) 11 31776513
www.ultra.com.br
Oil and gas

Unilever N.V. UN
Weena 455, 3013 AL
Rotterdam, 3000 DK Netherlands
(31) 10-2174000
www.unilever.com
Consumer goods O DRP

Unilever PLC UL
Unilever House
Blackfriers
London EC4Y 0DY England
(44) 20-78225252
www.unilever.com
Consumer goods O DRP

Union Pacific Corp. UNP
1400 Douglas Street
Omaha, Nebraska 68179
402-544-5000
www.up.com
Rail transportation O DRP

United Microelectronics Corp. UMC
No. 3, Li-Shin Road, 11
Hsinchu Science Park
Hsinchu, Taiwan
(886) 2-27006999
www.umc.com
Semiconductors O

United Parcel Service, Inc. UPS
55 Glenlake Parkway, N.E.
Atlanta, Georgia 30328
440-828-6000
www.ups.com
Package delivery O DRP

United States Steel Corp. X
600 Grant Street
Pittsburgh, Pennsylvania 15219
412-433-1121
www.ussteel.com
Steel producer O DRP

United Technologies Corp. UTX
One Financial Plaza
Hartford, Connecticut 06103
860-728-7000
www.utc.com
Capital goods O DRP

UnitedHealth Group Inc. UNH
9990 Bren Road East
Minnetonka, Minnesota 55343
952-936-1300
www.unitedhealthgroup.com
Health benefits O

Unum Group UNM
1 Fountain Square
Chattanooga, Tennessee 37402
423-294-1011
www.unum.com
Insurance O DRP

Vale S.A. VALE
Avenida Graca Aranha, Ns 26
Castelo
Rio de Janeiro, 20030-900 Brazil
(55) 21-38149631
www.vale.com
Metals and mining O

Valero Energy Corp. VLO
One Valero Way
San Antonio, Texas 78249
210-345-2000
www.valero.com
Oil and gas O

Ventas Inc. VTR
111 South Wacker Drive, Suite 4800
Chicago, Illinois 60606
877-483-6827
www.ventasreit.com
Real estate investment trust O DRP

Veolia Environnement VE
36-38 Avenue Kleber
Paris, 75116 France
(33) 1-71750000
www.veolia.com
Environmental management
  services O

Verizon Communications, Inc. VZ
140 West Street
New York, New York 10007
212-395-1000
www.verizon.com
Communications services O DRP

VF Corporation VFC
105 Corporate Center Boulevard
Greensboro, North Carolina 27408
336-424-6000
www.vfc.com
Apparel O DRP

Viacom, Inc. (Cl A) VIA
1515 Broadway
New York, New York 10036
212-258-6000
www.viacom.com
Media networks and filmed
  entertainment O

Viacom, Inc. (Cl B) VIAB
1515 Broadway
New York, New York 10036
212-258-6000
www.viacom.com
Media networks and filmed
  entertainment O

Vimpel Communications VIP
Ul 8-Marta, 10
Building 14
Moscow, 127083 Russia
(7) 495-7250700
www.vimpelcom.com
Telecommunications services O
  DRP

Visa Inc. V
P.O. Box 8999
San Francisco, California 94128
415-932-2100
www.visa.com
Consumer financial services O

Vivo Participacoes S/A VIV
Av. Roque Petroni Junior 1464
Morumbi.
Sao Paulo, 04707-000 Brazil
(55) 11-74201172
www.vivo.com.br
Telecommunications O

VMware Inc. VMW
3401 Hillview Avenue
Palo Alto, California 94304
650-427-5000
www.vmware.com
Software and programming O

Vornado Realty Trust VNO
888 Seventh Avenue
New York, New York 10019
212-894-7000
www.vno.com
Real estate investment trust O

Vulcan Materials Company VMC
1200 Urban Center Drive
Birmingham, Alabama 35242
205-298-3000
www.vulcanmaterials.com
Construction materials O DRP

W.W. Granger Inc. GWW
100 Granger Parkway
Lake Forest, Illinois 60045
847-535-1000
www.granger.com
Capital goods O

Walgreen Company WAG
200 Wilmot Road
Deerfield, Illinois 60015
847-914-2500
www.walgreens.com
Drug retailer O DRP

Wal-Mart Stores Inc. WMT
702 Southwest 8th Street
Bentonville, Arkansas 72716
479-273-4000
www.walmartstores.com
Retail stores O DRP

Walt Disney Company DIS
500 South Buena Vista Street
Burbank, California 91521
818-560-1000
www.disney.com
Entertainment O DRP

Waste Management Inc. WM
1001 Fannin Street, Suite 4000
Houston, Texas 77002
713-512-6200
www.wm.com
Waste management
  services O DRP

Weatherford International Ltd.
  WFT
Alpenstrasse 15
Zug, 6300 Switzerland
(41) 713-6934000
www.weatherford.com
Oil well services and equipment O

WellPoint, Inc. WLP
120 Monument Circle
Indianapolis, Indiana 46204
317-532-6000
www.wellpoint.com
Health benefits O

Wells Fargo & Company WFC
420 Montgomery Street
San Francisco, California 94163
866-249-3302
www.wellsfargo.com
Financial services O DRP

Western Digital Corp. WDC
20511 Lake Forest Drive
Lake Forest, California 92630
949-672-7000
www.westerndigital.com
Computer storage devices O

Western Union Company WU
12500 East Belford Avenue
Englewood, Colorado 80112
866-405-5012
www.westernunion.com
Money transfers and payment
  services O

Westpac Banking Corp. WBK
275, Kent Street
Sydney, NSW 2000 Australia
(61) 2-92263143
www.westpac.com.au
Banking and financial services

Weyerhaeuser Company WY
33663 Weyerhaeuser Way South
Federal Way, Washington 98063
253-924-2345
www.weyerhauser.com
Forest products O DRP

Williams Companies WMB
One Williams Center
Tulsa, Oklahoma 74172
918-573-2000
www.williams.com
Natural gas O DRP

Wipro Ltd. WIT
Doddakannelli
Sarjapur Road
Bangalore, 560 035 India
(91) 80-28440079
www.wipro.com
Information technology services O
  DRP

Woon Finance Holdings Company
  Ltd. WF
203, Hoehyeon-dong 1-ga
Chung-gu
Seoul, 100-792 South Korea
(82) 2-21252001
www.woonfg.com
Financial holding company

Xcel Energy Inc. XEL
414 Nicollet Mall
Minneapolis, Minnesota 55401
612-330-5500
www.xcelenergy.com
Electric utility holding company
  O DRP

Xerox Corporation XRX
45 Glover Avenue
Norwalk, Connecticut 06856
203-968-3000
www.xerox.com
Office equipment O DRP

XL Capital, Ltd. XL
1 Bermudiana Road
Hamilton, HM 11 Bermuda
441-292-8515
www.xlcapital.com
Insurance and reinsurance O DRP

XTO Energy Inc. XTO
810 Houston Street, Suite 2000
Fort Worth, Texas 76102
817-870-2800
www.xtoenergy.com
Oil and natural gas O DRP

Yamana Gold Inc. AUY
150 York Street, Suite 1102
Toronto, Ontario M5H 3S5 Canada
416-815-0220
www.yamana.com

Gold production O

Yanzhou Coal Mining Company
  Ltd. YZC
298 Fushan South Road
Zoucheng, SDG 273500 China
(86) 537-5382319
www.yanzhoucoal.com.cn
Coal O

YPF S.A. YPF
Avda. Pte. Roque Sáenz Peña 777
Buenos Aires, 1364 Argentina
(54) 11-43292000
www.ypf.com
Energy

YUM! Brands Inc. YUM
1441 Gardiner Lane
Louisville, Kentucky 40213
502-874-8300
www.yum.com
Quick service restaurants O DRP

Zimmer Holdings, Inc. ZMH
345 East Main Street
Warsaw, Indiana 46580
574-267-6131
Medical equipment and supplies O

NASDAQ 100

Activision Blizzard, Inc. ATVI
3100 Ocean Park Boulevard
Santa Monica, California 90405
310-255-2000
www.activisionblizzard.com
Game publisher O

Apple Computer, Inc. AAPL
1 Infinite Loop
Cupertino, California 95014
408-996-1010
www.apple.com
Computer hardware O

Adobe Systems, Incorporated ADBE
345 Park Avenue
San Jose, California 95110
408-536-6000
www.adobe.com
Software O

Applied Materials, Inc. AMAT
3050 Bowers Avenue
Santa Clara, California 95054
408-727-5555
www.appliedmaterials.com
Semiconductors O

Altera Corporation ALTR
101 Innovation Drive
San Jose, California 95134
408-544-7000
www.altera.com
Programmable semiconductors O

Autodesk, Inc. ADSK
111 McInnis Parkway
San Rafael, California 94903
415-507-5000
www.autodesk.com
Design software and services O

Amazon.com, Inc. AMZN
1200 12th Avenue South
Suite 1200
Seattle, Washington 98144
206-266-1000
www.amazon.com
Online retailer O

Automatic Data Processing, Inc. ADP
One ADP Boulevard
Roseland, New Jersey 07068
973-974-5000
www.adp.com
Business outsourcing O

Amgen, Inc. AMGN
One Amgen Center Drive
Thousand Oaks, California 91320
805-447-1000
www.amgen.com
Biotechnology O

Baidu, Inc. BIDU
12/F Ideal International Plaza
No. 58 West-North 4th Ring
Beijing, BEJ 100080 China
(86) 10-82621188
www.baidu.com
Internet search O

Apollo Group, Inc. APOL
4025 S. Riverpoint Parkway
Phoenix, Arizona 85040
480-966-5394
www.apollogrp.edu
Private education O

Bed Bath & Beyond, Inc. BBBY
650 Liberty Avenue
Union, New Jersey 07083
908-688-0888
www.bedbathandbeyond.com
Domestics and home furnishings O

Biogen Idec, Inc. BIIB
14 Cambridge Center
Cambridge, Massachusetts 02142
617-679-2000
www.biogenidec.com
Biotechnology and drugs O

BMC Software, Inc. BMC
2101 CityWest Boulevard
Houston, Texas 77042
713-918-8800
www.bmc.com
Software O

Broadcom Corporation, BRCM
5300 California Avenue
Irvine, California 92617
949-926-5000
www.broadcom.com
Communications semiconductors O

C.H. Robinson Worldwide, Inc.
 CHRW
14701 Charlson Road
Eden Prairie, Minnesota 55344
952-937-8500
www.chrobinson.com
Freight transportation O

CA Inc.
One CA Plaza
Islandia, New York 11749
800-225-5224
www.ca.com/us
Information technology O DRP

Celgene Corporation CELG
86 Morris Avenue
Summit, New Jersey 07901
908-673-9000
www.celgene.com
Biopharmaceutical O

Cephalon, Inc. CEPH
41 Moores Road
P.O. Box 4011
Frazer, Pennsylvania 19355
610-344-0200
www.cephalon.com
Biopharmaceutical O

Cerner Corporation CERN
2800 Rockcreek Parkway
North Kansas City, Missouri 64117
816-221-1024
www.cerner.com
Healthcare O

Check Point Software
 Technologies, Ltd. CHKP
5 Ha'solelim Street
Tel Aviv, Israel 52520
650-628-2000
Internet technology security O

Cintas Corporation CTAS
6800 Cintas Boulevard
P.O. Box 625737
Cincinnati, Ohio 45262
513-459-1200
www.cintas.com
Corporate identity uniforms O

Cisco Systems, Inc. CSCO
170 West Tasman Drive
San Jose, California 95134
408-526- 4000
www.cisco.com
Networking products O

Citrix Systems, Inc. CTXS
851 West Cypress Creek Road
Fort Lauderdale, Florida 33309
954-267-3000
www.citrix.com
Technology solutions O

Cognizant Technology Solutions
 Corporation CTSH
Glenpointe Centre West
500 Frank W. Burr Boulevard
Teaneck, New Jersey 07666
201-801-0233
www.cognizant.com
Information technology O

Comcast Corporation CMCSA
One Comcast Center
Philadelphia, Pennsylvania 19103
215-665-1700
www.comcast.com
Cable services O DRP

Costco Wholesale Corporation
  COST
999 Lake Drive
Issaquah, Washington 98027
425-313-8100
www.costco.com
Membership warehouses O DRP

Dell, Inc. DELL
One Dell Way
Round Rock, Texas 78682
512-338-4400
www.dell.com
Computer hardware O DRP

DENTSPLY International, Inc.
  XRAY
221 West Philadelphia Street
York, Pennsylvania 17405
717-845-7511
www.dentsply.com
Dental products O

DIRECTV DTV
2230 East Imperial Highway
El Segundo, California 90245
310-964-5000
www.directv.com
Digital entertainment O

DISH Network Corporation DISH
9601 South Meridian Boulevard
Englewood, Colorado 80112
303-723-1000
www.dishnetwork.com
Pay television O

eBay, Inc. EBAY
2145 Hamilton Avenue
San Jose, California 95125
408-376-7400
www.ebayinc.com
Online marketplace O

Electronic Arts, Inc. ERTS
209 Redwood Shores Parkway
Redwood City, California 94065
650-628-1500
www.ea.com
Video game software O

Expedia, Inc. EXPE
3150 139th Avenue SE
Bellevue, Washington 98005
425-679-7200
www.expediainc.com
Online travel O

Expeditors International of
  Washington, Inc. EXPD
1015 Third Avenue, 12th Floor
Seattle, Washington 98104
206-674-3400
www.expeditors.com
Logistics services O

Express Scripts, Inc. ESRX
One Express Way
St. Louis, Missouri 63121
314-996-0900
www.express-scripts.com
Pharmacy benefit manager O

Fastenal Company FAST
2001 Theurer Boulevard
Winona, Minnesota 55987
507-454-5374
Industrial and construction supplies
  O

First Solar, Inc. FSLR
350 West Washington Street,
  Suite 600
Tempe, Arizona 85281
602-414-9300
www.firstsolar.com
Solar modules O

Fiserv, Inc. FISV
255 Fiserv Drive
Brookfield, Wisconsin 53045
262-879-5000
Information management O

Flextronics International, Ltd.
  FLEX
2 Changi South Lane
Singapore, 486123 Singapore
(65) null-null
www.flextronics.com
Electronics manufacturing services
  O

FLIR Systems, Inc. FLIR
27700A SW Parkway Avenue
Wilsonville, Oregon 97070
503-498-3547
www.flir.com
Thermal imaging O

Foster Wheeler A.G. FWLT
Perryville Corporate Park
Service Road East 173
Clinton, New Jersey 08809
908-730-4000
www.fwc.com
Construction services O

Garmin, Ltd. GRMN
P.O. Box 10670
Grand Cayman, KY1-1006
  Cayman Islands
345-640-9050
www.garmin.com
Scientific and technical instruments
  O

Genzyme Corporation GENZ
500 Kendall Street
Cambridge, Massachusetts 02142
617-252-7500
www.genzyme.com
Biotechnology O

Gilead Sciences, Inc. GILD
333 Lakeside Drive
Foster City, California 94404
650-574-3000
Biopharmaceutical O

Google, Inc. GOOG
1600 Amphitheatre Parkway
Mountain View, California 94043
650-253-0000
ww.google.com
Search engine O

Henry Schein, Inc. HSIC
135 Duryea Road
Melville, New York 11747
631-843-5500
www.henryschein.com
Healthcare products. O

Hologic, Inc. HOLX
35 Crosby Drive
Bedford, Massachusetts 01730
781-999-7300
www.hologic.com
Medical imaging O

Illumina, Inc. ILMN
9885 Towne Center Drive
San Diego, California 92121
858-202-4500
www.illumina.com
Scientific and technical instruments
  O

Infosys Technologies Limited
  INFY
Plot No. 44 & 97A
Electronic City
Bangalore, 560 100 India
(91) 80-28520261
www.infosys.com
Technology services O DRP

Intel Corporation INTC
2200 Mission College Boulevard
Santa Clara, California 95054
408-765-8080
www.intel.com
Semiconductor chips O DRP

Intuit, Inc. INTU
2700 Coast Avenue
Mountain View, California 94043
650-944-6000
www.intuit.com
Software and programming O

Intuitive Surgical, Inc. ISRG
9LPBA50 Kifer Road
Sunnyvale, California 94086
408-523-2100
www.intuitivesurgical.com
Medical equipment and supplies O

J.B. Hunt Transport Services, Inc.
  JBHT
615 J.B. Hunt Corporate Drive
Lowell, Arizona 72745
479-820-0000
www.jbhunt.com
Transportation services O

Joy Global, Inc. JOYG
100 East Wisconsin Avenue,
Suite 2780
Milwaukee, Wisconsin 53202
414-319-8500
Mining equipment O

KLA-Tencor Corporation KLAC
160 Rio Robles
San Jose, California 95134
408-875-3000
www.kla-tencor.com
Semiconductor services O

Lam Research Corporation LRCX
4650 Cushing Parkway
Fremont, California 94538
510-572-0200
www.lamrc.com
Semiconductors O

Liberty Media Corporation LSTZA
12300 Liberty Boulevard
Englewood, Colorado 80112
720-875-5400
www.libertymedia.com
Broadcasting and cable TV O

Life Technologies Corporation
LIFE
5791 Van Allen Way
P.O. Box 6482
Carlsbad, California 92008
www.invitrogen
Biotechnology tools O

Linear Technology Corporation
LLTC
1630 McCarthy Boulevard
Milpitas, California 95035
408-432-1900
www.linear.com
Integrated circuits O

Logitech International S.A. LOGI
6505 Kaiser Drive
Fremont, California 94555
510-795-8500
www.logitech.com
Computer peripherals O

Marvell Technology Group, Ltd.
MRVL
Canon's Court, 22 Victoria Street
Hamilton, HM 12, Bermuda
441-296-6395
www.marvell.com
Seminconductors O

Mattel, Inc. MAT
333 Continental Boulevard
El Segundo, California 90245
310-252-2000
www.mattel.com
Toys O DRP

Maxim Integrated Products, Inc.
MXIM
120 San Gabriel Drive
Sunnyvale, California 94086
408-737-7600
www.maxim-ic.com
Analog circuits O

Microchip Technology Incorporated
MCHP
2355 West Chandler Boulevard
Chandler, Arizona 85224
480-792-7200
www.microchip.com
Semiconductors O

Microsoft Corporation MSFT
One Microsoft Way
Redmond, Washington 98052
425-882-8080
www.microsoft.com
Software O DRP

Millicom International Cellular S.A.
MICC
75 Route de Longwy
Bertrange, Luxembourg
www.millicom.com
Mobile telecommunications O

Mylan, Inc. MYL
1500 Corporate Drive, Suite 400
Canonsburg, Pennsylvania 15317
724-514-1800
www.mylan.com
Pharamaceuticals O

NetApp, Inc. NTAP
495 East Java Drive
Sunnyvale, California 94089
408-822-6000
www.netapp.com
Data storage O

News Corporation NWSA
1211 Avenue of the Americas
New York, New York 10036
212-852-7017
www.newscorp.com
Media O

NII Holdings, Inc. NIHD
10700 Parkridge Boulevard,
   Suite 600
Reston, Virginia 20191
703-390-5100
www.nii.com
Wireless communications O

NVIDIA Corporation NVDA
2701 San Tomas Expressway
Santa Clara, California 95050
408-486-2000
www.nvidia.com
Visual computing technologies O

O'Reilly Automotive, Inc. ORLY
233 South Patterson
Springfield, Missouri 65802
www.oreillyauto.com
Automotive retailer O

Oracle Corporation ORCL
500 Oracle Parkway
Redwood Shores, California 94065
650-506-7000
www.oracle.com
Enterprise software O

PACCAR, Inc. PCAR
777 106th Avenue NE
Bellevue, Washington 98004
425-468-7400
www.paccar.com
Truck manufacturing, finance and
   leasing O

Patterson Companies, Inc. PDCO
1031 Mendota Heights Road
St. Paul, Minnesota 55120
651-686-1600
www.pattersoncompanies.com
Medical equipment and supplies
   distributor O

Paychex, Inc. PAYX
911 Panorama Trail South
Rochester, New York 14625
585-385-6666
Business services O DRP

Priceline.com Incorporated PCLN
800 Connecticut Avenue
Norwalk, Connecticut 06854
203-299-8000
www.priceline.com
Online travel O

Qiagen N.V. QGEN
Spoorstraat 50
Vento, 5911 KJ Netherlands
(31) 77-3208400
www1.qiagen.com
Scientific and technical instruments O

Qualcomm Incorporated QCOM
5775 Morehouse Drive
San Diego, California 92121
858-587-1121
www/qualcomm.com
Wireless telecommunications O DRP

Research In Motion Limited RIMM
295 Phillip Street
Waterloo, ON N2L 3W8 Canada
519-888-7465
Wireless mobile communications O

Ross Stores, Inc. ROST
4440 Rosewood Drive
Pleasanton, California 94588
925-965-4400
Off-Price Retail Apparel O

SanDisk Corporation SNDK
601 McCarthy Boulevard
Milpitas, California 95035
408-801-1000
www.sandisk.com
Computer storage devices O

Seagate Technology STX
PO Box 309, Ugland House
South Church Street, George Tow
Grand Cayman, Cayman Islands
831-438-6550
www.seagate.com
Hard disc drives O

Sears Holdings Corporation SHLD
3333 Beverly Road
Hoffman Estates, Illinois 60179
847-286-2500
www.searsholdings.com
Retailer O

Sigma-Aldrich Corporation SIAL
3050 Spruce Street
St. Louis, Missouri 63103
314-771-5765
www.sigmaaldrich.com
Chemical manufacturing O

Staples, Inc. SPLS
Five Hundred Staples Drive
Framingham, Massachusetts 01702
508-253-5000
www.staples.com
Office products O DRP

Starbucks Corporation SBUX
2401 Utah Avenue South
Seattle, Washington 98134
206-447-1575
www.starbucks.com
Specialty coffee O

Stericycle, Inc. SRCL
28161 North Keith Drive
Lake Forest, Illinois 60045
847-367-5910
www.stericycle.com
Waste management O

Symantec Corporation SYMC
20330 Stevens Creek Boulevard
Cupertino, California 95014
408-517-8000
Information security O

Teva Pharmaceutical Industries
  Limited TEVA
5 Basel Street
Petach Tikva, 49131 Israel
(972)-3-9267267
www.tevapharm.com
Generic drugs O DRP

Urban Outfitters, Inc. URBN
5000 South Broad Street
Philadelphia, Pennsylvania 19112
215-454-5500
www.urbanoutfittersinc.com
Specialty retail O

VeriSign, Inc. VRSN
487 East Middlefield Road
Mountain View, California 94043
650-961-7500
www.verisign.com
Internet infrastructure services O

Vertex Pharmaceuticals
  Incorporated VRTX
130 Waverly Street
Cambridge, Massachusetts 02139
www.vrtx.com
Small molecule drugs O

Virgin Media, Inc. VMED
909 Third Avenue, Suite 2863
New York, New York 10022
212-906-8440
www.virginmedia.com
Communications services O

Vodafone Group plc VOD
P.O. Box 358035
Pittsburgh, Pennsylvania 15252
888-269-2377
www.vodafone.com
International mobile
  telecommunications DRP

Warner Chilcott Plc WCRX
Lincoln House, Lincoln Place
Dublin, 2 Ireland
(353) 1-6624962
www.wcrx.com
Specialty pharmaceutical O

Wynn Resorts, Limited WYNN
3131 Las Vegas Boulevard South
Las Vegas, Nevada 89109
702-770-7555
www.wynnresorts.com
Casino resorts O

Xilinx, Inc. XLNX
2100 Logic Drive
San Jose, California 95124
408-559-7778
www.xilinx.com
Semiconductors O

YAHOO!, Inc. YHOO
701 First Avenue
Sunnyvale, California 94089
408-349-3300
www.yahoo.com
Internet services O DRP

Appendix

SELECTED FURTHER READING

Economics

Keynes, John Maynard. *The General Theory of Employment, Interest and Money.* Orlando, FL: Harcourt.

The definitive work of the British economist and government advisor, whose influential theories advocating government intervention (fiscal policy) as a solution to economic problems have become known as Keynesian economics.

Lewis, Michael. *The Big Short. Inside the Doomsday Machine.* New York: Norton

A lucid and entertaining analysis of the 2008 financial crisis as seen through the eyes of Wall Street operatives who saw it coming and profited from an undrstanding of what derivatives were really about.

McConnell, Campbell R. and Stanley L. Brue. Economics: *Principles, Problems, and Policies.* 15th ed. New York: McGraw-Hill.

A highly regarded introduction to the fundamental problems and principles of economics and the policy alternatives available to countries, both from a national and international perspective.

Samuelson, Paul A. and W. Nordhaus. *Economics,* 18th ed. New York: McGraw-Hill.

This famous and widely used introductory economics text has been thoroughly revised and updated. It takes students from fundamental to sophisticated levels of understanding of income and production factors including international trade and finance and current economic problems.

Shlaes, Amity *The Forgotten Man.* New York: Harper Collins

A critical revision of conventional wisdom about the Great Depression and the roles of Herbert Hoover and FDR. A poignant history of America in the 1930s.

Smith, Adam. *An Inquiry into the Nature and Causes of the Wealth of Nations.* New York: Bantam Dell.

The definitive work, first published in 1776, of the most famous of the classical economists, who held that economies function best under a laissez-faire system in which market forces are free to operate without government interference.

The Economist Staff, *The Economist, Guide to Economic Indicators,* New York: Wiley.

Covering some 100 indicators, including GDP, population, exchange rates, disposable income, public expenditure, and bond yields, this practical resource explains clearly what they are, why they are significant, where and when they are published, and how reliable they are.

Global Economics, Finance, and Investment

Friedman, Thomas L. *The Lexus and the Olive Tree.* New York: Anchor Books.

A best-seller by the widely read *New York Times* Middle East expert. *Foreign Affairs* said, "Readers in search of a window into the problems of the cyberspace-driven virtual world economy of the 21st century are unlikely to find a better place to start."

Kreitler, Robert P., *Getting Started in Global Investing,* New York: Wiley.

Suggesting individual investors think of themselves as residents of a small island rather than as citizens of the United States, this readable book by a disciple of John Templeton puts a formidable subject in perspective and is an excellent introduction to methods and strategies.

Salvatore, Dominick, *International Economics*, 8th Edition, New York: Wiley.

Covers the major international economic (trade and financial) problems facing the United States and the world. Chapters include links to important Internet sites and data sources.

Money and Banking

Cecchetti, Stephen G., *Money, Banking and, Financial Markets*, New York: McGraw-Hill/Irwin.

New (2005), fresh, and student-friendly, by a former vice president of the Federal Reserve Bank of New York. Well-written, clear, relevant, and interesting.

Ritter, Lawrence S. and William L Silber. *Principles of Money, Banking and Financial Markets.* 11th ed. New York: Addison-Wesley.

A comprehensive introductory text that covers money and banking fundamentals; banks and other intermediaries; central banking; monetary theory; financial markets and interest rates; and international finance.

Updegrave, Walter. *How to Keep Your Savings Safe: Protecting the Money You Can't Afford to Lose.* New York: Crown Publishers.

How to find the strongest banks, insurance companies, and money market mutual funds. Lists of safe U.S. banks, insurers, savings and loan institutions, and money funds are provided.

Bond and Money Markets

Fabozzi, Frank J., editor. *The Handbook of Fixed Income Securities,* 6th ed. New York: McGraw-Hill.

Includes 47 chapters, each by an expert, covering general investment information; securities and instruments; bond investment management; interest rates and rate forecasting.

Faerber, Esme. *Fundamentals of the Bond Market.* New York: McGraw-Hill.

Plain English analyses and explanations combine with checklists, charts, and graphs to provide a guide to understanding the ins and outs of today's surprisingly versatile bond marketplace.

Stigum, Marcia. *The Money Market,* 3rd ed. New York: McGraw-Hill.

A comprehensive guide, by a working professional, to the U.S. money market. It covers the various instruments traded, how yields are calculated, and the role of the Federal Reserve; the major participants, including Eurobanks; and particular markets, such as those for commercial paper, Treasury bills, and CDs. Includes financial futures.

Corporate Finance

Altman, Edward I., *Handbook of Corporate Finance*, New York: Wiley.
Clear and comprehensive, with chapters by leading contributors on financial forecasting, planning and control, sources of funds, capital budgeting, mergers, bankruptcies, multinational finance, and more.

Brealey, Richard A. and Stewart C. Myers, *Corporate Finance: Capital Investment and Risk Management,* New York: McGraw-Hill/Irwin.
Written in a dynamic and often humorous style by two influential finance figures for practicing professionals. Offers a comprehensive look at how corporations balance financing and risk. Covers hedging, leveraging, securities markets, dividend policy, and more.

Groppelli, A.A. and Ehsan Nikbakht, *Finance,* 5th Edition, Hauppauge, New York: Barron's Educational Series.
A well-written, quick study in corporate finance.

Mutual Funds

Bogle, John, *Common Sense on Mutual Funds*: *New Imperatives for the Intelligent Investor,* New York: Wiley.
Fun to read, and possibly the best book ever on mutual funds, by the founder of Vanguard Group.

Taylor, John H. *Building Wealth with Mutual Funds.* New York: McGraw-Hill.
A step-by-step guide to investing in mutual funds, including international investing, index funds, variable annuity funds, and socially responsible funds.

Securities Markets, Securities Analysis, and Portfolio Management

Brown, David L. and Kassandra Bentley. *Cyber-Investing, Cracking Wall Street with Your Personal Computer.* New York: Wiley.
Using computer programs and data bases to sort for stock opportunities and to time purchases and sales.

Dreman, David, *Contrarian Investment Strategies in the Next Generation,* New York: Simon & Schuster.
The high priest of contrarian investing follows up on his classics, *The New Contrarian Investment Strategy* and *Contrarian Investment Strategy,* with insights and advice for the 21st-century investor.

Graham, Benjamin with commentary by Jason Zweig, *The Intelligent Investor: The Definitive Book on Value Investing, Revised Edition* (Paperback), New York: Harper Collins.

Graham, Benjamin, Sidney Cottle, and David L. Dodd. *Securities Analysis,* 3rd Edition. New York: McGraw-Hill.
This classic work remains the bible for students of the fundamentalist approach to securities analysis. It comprises six parts: survey and approach;

analysis of financial statements; fixed-income securities; the valuation of common stocks; senior securities with speculative features; and other aspects of security analysis.

Lynch, Peter. *One Up on Wall Street.* New York: Simon & Schuster.
Down-to-earth investment advice from the legendary former manager of Fidelity's Magellan Fund.

Malkiel, Burton G., *A Random Walk Down Wall Street: Completely Revised and Updated,* Eighth Edition, New York: W.W. Norton & Company.
Professor Malkiel's definitive classic on efficient market theory, revised and updated.

O'Shaughnessy, James P. *What Works on Wall Street.* New York: McGraw-Hill.
Investment tools and stock selection strategies are quantitatively tested over a 40-year period and the results discussed in a clear and readable fashion.

Pring, Martin. *Introduction to Technical Analysis.* New York: McGraw-Hill.
An introduction to the basics of technical analysis by the author of the classic *Technical Analysis Explained,* this chart-filled book explains traditional techniques as well as new analytical tools, such as momentum indicators, made possible by computers.

Schwager, Jack D. *The New Market Wizards; Conversations with America's Top Traders.* New York: Wiley.
A distinguished group of money managers discuss their secrets and methodologies.

Siegel, Jeremy J., *Stocks for the Long Run: The Definitive Guide to Financial Market Returns and Long-Term Investment Strategies,* 4th Edition, New York: McGraw-Hill/Irwin.
Wharton Professor Siegel's modern classic, revised and updated in which he argues that stocks are safer than bonds over the long run.

Teweles, Richard J. and Edward S. Bradley. *The Stock Market.* 7th ed. New York: Wiley.
A revision of a work originally authored by George L. Leffler in 1951. It examines the stock market in five sections dealing with fundamental information, the exchanges, securities houses, regulations, investing practices, and special instruments.

Train, John, *Money Masters of Our Time*, New York: Harper Collins.
Interesting stories, by the author of *The Money Masters* and *The New Money Masters*, about the investment philosophies and strategies of 17 great investors, with commentary on their methods and personalities.

Commodity and Financial Futures Markets

Kaufman, Perry J. *The New Commodity Trading Systems & Methods.* New York: Wiley.
An extensive reference guide dealing with individual commodities, including financial futures, and covering markets, forecasting, hedging, risk and money management, along with other technical aspects.

Kleinman, George, *Trading Commodities and Financial Futures: A Step by Step Guide to Mastering the Markets,* 3rd Edition, Englewood Cliffs, NJ: Financial Times Prentice Hall.

A user-friendly but very comprehensive guide to markets and trading strategies for the beginner as well as the professional reader.

Lass, John P. and Sol Waksman. *Managed Futures Portfolio Strategies; Investment Analysis and the Evaluation and Selection of Commodity Trading Advisors.* New York: McGraw-Hill.

How to evaluate, select, and track the performance of a commodity trading advisor.

Powers, Mark J. *Starting Out in Futures Trading.* 6th ed. New York: McGraw-Hill.

A combination of theory and practical information for the beginner; includes history, exchanges, choosing a broker, trading programs, hedging, and forecasting. Covers financial futures.

Rogers, Jim. *Hot Commodities; How Anyone Can Invest Profitably in the World's Best Market.* New York: Random House Trade Paperbacks.

A highly readable primer on commodities investing and a compelling argument for getting into a long-term commodities bull market still in its early stages. Rogers is a legendary investor and colorfully explains the countertrend relationship of stocks and commodities and how average investors can profit without undue risk.

Schwager, Jack D. *A Complete Guide to the Futures Markets: Fundamental Analysis, Technical Analysis, Trading, Spreads and Options.* New York: Wiley.

Assumes a basic familiarity with futures trading, but otherwise provides a nontechnical discussion of various analytical techniques, including regression analysis and chart analysis. Has sample charts and a section on trading guidelines.

Siegel, Daniel R. and Diane F. Siegel. *The Futures Markets.* New York: Harcourt Brace.

A comprehensive study of the futures markets. Emphasizing the mechanics of futures trading; the theory of futures pricing; futures trading stretegies used for arbitrage, hedging, and speculation; and descriptions of all the major futures contracts.

Options and Other Derivatives

Fabozzi, Frank J. *Mortgage-Backed Securities: Products, Structuring and Analytical Techniques.* Hoboken, New Jersey: Wiley

A timely and scholarly text on how mortgage-backed securities are structured and how to analyze them, related options strategies. Illustrated.

Hull, John C., *Options, Futures and Other Derivatives*, 6th Edition, Englewood Cliffs: Prentice Hall.

A best-selling book that carefully and extensively covers its subject and the related mathematics.

McMillan, Lawrence G. *Options as a Strategic Investment.* 4th ed. Englewood Cliffs: Prentice-Hall.

An advanced discussion of option strategies, focusing on which ones work where and why. Includes chapters on arbitrage, mathematical applications, and tax ramifications.

Roth, Harrison. *LEAPS (Long-Term Equity AnticiPation Securities).* New York: McGraw-Hill.

Written in easy-to-understand English with examples and summaries, this book covers the history, the risks, and the strategies possible with long-term options, a 1990s innovation.

Satyajit, Das. *Derivative Products and Pricing: The Swaps & Financial Derivatives Library,* 3rd Edition Revised, New York: Wiley.

Four parts divided into 16 chapters on the role and function of derivatives, basic derivative instruments (exchange-traded products, futures, and options on futures) and over-the-counter products (forwards, options, and swaps), the pricing and valuation of derivative instruments, derivative trading and portfolio management.

Other Securities and General Investor Information

Amerman, Daniel R. *Mortgage Securities: The High-Yield Alternative to CDs, the Low-Risk Alternative to Stocks.* New York: McGraw-Hill.

How to invest in mortgage securities, which are the highest yielding of all government-issued securities. Covers mortgage-backed securities mutual funds, buying and selling individual mortgage-backed bonds; how prepayment risk is factored into bond prices, differences among Fannie Mae, Ginnie Mae, and other issuers of mortgage-backed securities.

Calamos, John P. *Investing in Convertible Securities: Your Complete Guide to the Risk and Rewards.* Chicago: Dearborn Financial Publishing.

A clearly written guide through the sometimes bewildering world of convertible securities.

Goodman, Jordan E. *Everyone's Money Book.* New York: Kaplan.

A friendly, readable reference covering virtually every aspect of personal finance, with illustrations and recommended resources.

Quinn, Jane Bryant *Making the Most of Your Money Now.* New York: Simon & Schuster.

A best-selling classic completely revised for the post-2008 economy by eminent columnist and personal finance expert. Witty, clear, and thorough.

Strachman, Daniel A., *Getting Started in Hedge Funds*, 2nd Edition, New York: Wiley.

A complete and comprehensive introduction to the world of hedge funds, one of the fastest growing areas of 21st-century investing.

Zabulake, Laura A, *The Complete Guide to Convertible Securities Worldwide*, New York: Wiley.

Covers U.S. dollar-denominated and international convertible securities, foreign exchange, hedging, risk profile, and rate of return.

CURRENCIES OF THE WORLD

Currency-issuing countries are listed alphabetically, with the name of the currency, the currency's symbol in parentheses, and the denomination into which that currency is broken down. For example, the United States currency is the dollar, its symbol is $ and it is made up of 100 cents. This listing should be useful to anyone traveling or doing business in any of these countries.

The values of these currencies relative to the U.S. dollar change constantly; the major foreign exchange rates change daily. For current exchange rates of the currencies of most major countries, one must consult the financial tables of newspapers such as *The Wall Street Journal* or London's *Financial Times*.

On January 1, 1999, the Euro was introduced at the institutional level as the official currency of the member countries of the European Union for the issuance of public debt issues, for trade among corporations, and for stock market trading. On January 1, 2002, Euro bank notes and coins went into general circulation and by July 1, 2002, all national notes and coins were withdrawn from circulation and replaced by Euros. The Euro is denominated in cents, with 8 different coins from 1 cent to 2 Euros. Euronotes are issued in denominations of 5, 10, 20, 50, 100, 200, and 500 Euros.

This changeover also affects the former colonies and dependencies of European states that had been using national currencies such as francs, marks, and pesetas.

Afghanistan 1 afghani (Af) = 100 puls

Albania 1 lek (L) = 100 qintars

Algeria 1 dinar (DA) = 100 centimes

American Samoa 1 U.S. dollar (US$) = 100 cents

Andorra 1 Euro (E) = 100 euro-cents

Angola 1 new kwanza (Kz) = 100 lwei

Anguilla 1 Euro (E) = 100 euro-cents

Antartica Each Antartic base uses the currency of its home country

Antigua & Barbuda 1 Euro = 100 euro-cents

Argentina 1 austral (AA) = 100 centavos

Armenia 1 dram (Ar)= 100 luma

Aruba 1 Aruban guilder (also known as florin or gulden) (Af.) = 100 cents

Australia 1 Australian dollar (A$) = 100 cents

Austria 1 Euro (E) = 100 euro-cents

Azerbaijan 1 manat = 100 gopık

Bahamas 1 Bahamian dollar (B$) = 100 cents

Bahrain 1 dinar (BD) = 1,000 fils

Bangladesh 1 taka (Tk) = 100 paisa (poisha)

Barbados 1 Barbadian dollar (Bds$) = 100 cents

Belarus Balarusian rubel (BR)

Belgium 1 Euro (E) = 100 euro-cents

Belize 1 Belizean dollar (BZ$) = 100 cents

Benin 1 Euro (E) = 100 euro-cents

Bermuda 1 Bermudian dollar (Bd$) = 100 cents

Bhutan 1 ngultrum (Nu) = 100 chetrum; Indian currency also legal tender

Bolivia 1 boliviano (Bs) = 100 centavos

Bosnia-Herzegovina 1 B.H. dinar = 100 para

Botswana 1 pula (P) = 100 thebe

Brazil 1 real (R$) = 100 centavos

British Virgin Islands 1 U.S. dollar (US$) = 100 cents

Brunei 1 ringgit, a.k.a. Bruneian dollar (B$) = 100 sen or cents

Bulgaria 1 lev (Lv) = 100 stotinki

Burkina Faso 1 Euro (E) = 100 euro-cents

Burma (see Myanmar)

Burundi 1 Burundi franc (FBu) = 100 centimes

Cambodia 1 new riel (CR) = 100 sen

Cameroon 1 Euro (E) = 100 euro-cents

Canada 1 Canadian dollar (Can$) = 100 cents

Cape Verde Islands 1 Cape Verdean escudo (C.V. Esc) = 100 centavos

Cayman Islands 1 Caymanian dollar (CI$) = 100 cents

Central African Republic 1 Euro (E) = 100 euro-cents

Chad 1 Euro (E) = 100 euro-cents

Chile 1 peso (Ch$) = 100 centavos

China 1 yuan renminbi (Y) = 10 fen

Christmas Island 1 Australian dollar (A$) = 100 cents

Cocos (Keeling) Islands 1 Australian dollar (A$) = 100 cents

Colombia 1 peso (Col$) = 100 centavos

Comoros 1 Euro (E) = 100 euro-cents

Congo, Democratic Republic of, 1 Euro (E) = 100 euro-cents

Cook Islands 1 New Zealand dollar (NZ$) = 100 cents

Costa Rica 1 colon (C) = 100 centimos

Cote d'Ivoire 1 Euro (E) = 100 euro-cents

Croatia 1 Croatian kuna (HRK) = 100 lipas

Cuba 1 peso (Cu$) = 100 centavos

Cyprus 1 Euro (E) = 100 euro-cents; Northern Cyprus = 1 Turkish lira (TL) = 100 kurus

Czech Republic 1 koruna (Kc with hacek on the c) = 100 halers

Denmark 1 Danish krone (DKr) = 100 øre

Djibouti 1 Djibouti franc (DF) = 100 centimes

Dominica 1 Euro = 100 euro-cents

Dominican Republic 1 peso (RD$) = 100 centavos

Ecuador 1 dollar = 100 centavos

Egypt 1 Egyptian pound (£E) = 100 piasters or 1,000 milliemes

El Salvador 1 colon (c) = 100 centavos

Equatorial Guinea 1 Euro (E) = 100 euro-cents

Eritrea 1 birr (Br) = 100 cents

Estonia 1 Estonian kroon (KR) = 100 senti

Ethiopia 1 birr (Br) = 100 cents

European Union 1 Euro = 100 euro-cents

Faeroe Islands 1 Danish krone (DKr) = 100 ore

Falkland Islands 1 Falkland pound (£F) = 100 pence

Fiji 1 Fijian dollar (F$) = 100 cents

Finland 1 Euro = 100 euro-cents

France 1 Euro = 100 euro-cents

French Guiana 1 Euro = 100 euro-cents

French Polynesia 1 Euro = 100 euro-cents

Gabon 1 Euro = 100 euro-cents

Gambia 1 dalasi (D) = 100 bututs

Gaza 1 Israeli shekel (NIS) = 100 agorot
1 *Jordanian* dinar (JD) =1,000 fils

Georgia 1 lari (Gl) =100 tetri

Germany 1 Euro (E) = 100 euro-cents

Ghana 1 cedi (c) = 100 pesewas

Gibraltar 1 Gibraltar pound (£G) = 100 pence

Great Britain 1 pound (£)=100 pence

Greece 1 Euro (E) = 100 euro-cents

Greenland 1 Danish krone (DKr) = 100 ore

Grenada 1 Euro (E) = 100 euro-cents

Guadeloupe 1 Euro (E) = 100 euro-cents

Guam 1 U.S. dollar (US$) = 100 cents

Guatemala 1 quetzal (Q) = 100 centavos

Guernsey 1 pound (£) = 100 pence

Guinea 1 franc=100 centimes

Guinea-Bissau 1 Euro (E) = 100 euro-cents

Guyana 1 Guyanese dollar (G$) = 100 cents

Haiti 1 gourde (G) = 100 centimes

Holy See 1 Euro (E) = 100 euro-cents

Honduras 1 lempira (L) = 100 centavos

Hong Kong 1 Hong Kong dollar (HK$) = 100 cents

Hungary 1 forint (Ft) = 100 filler

Iceland 1 króna (Kr) = 100 aurar

India 1 rupee (Rs) = 100 paise

Indonesia 1 rupiah (Rp) = 100 sen

Iran 1 rial (Rls) = 100 dinars = 0.1 toman

Iraq 1 dinar (ID) = 1,000 fils

Ireland 1 Euro (E) = 100 euro-cents

Israel 1 shekel (NIS) – 100 agorot

Italy 1 Euro (E) = 100 euro-cents

Jamaica 1 Jamaican dollar (J$) = 100 cents

Japan 1 yen (Y) =100 sen

Jersey 1 pound (£) = 100 pence

Jordan 1 dinar (JD) = 1,000 fils

Kazakhstan 1 tenge (KZT) = 100 tiyn

Kenya 1 Kenyan shilling (KSh) = 100 cents

Kiribati 1 Australian dollar (A$) = 100 cents

Korea, North 1 North Korean won (Wn) = 100 chon

Korea, South 1 South Korean won (W) = 100 chon

Kosovo 1 Euro (E) = 100 euro-cents

Kuwait 1 dinar (KD) = 1,000 fils

Kyrgyzstan 1 som= 100 tyyn

Laos 1 new kip (NK) = 100 at

Latvia 1 lat (Ls) = 100 santims

Lebanon 1 Lebanese pound (£L) = 100 piastres

Lesotho 1 loti (L) = 100 lisente

Liberia 1 Liberian dollar (L$) = 100 cents

Libya 1 Libyan dinar (LD) = 1,000 dirhams

Liechtenstein 1 Swiss franc (SwF) = 100 centimes

Lithuania 1 litas (L) = 100 centu

Luxembourg 1 Euro (E) = 100 euro-cents

Macau 1 pataca (P) = 100 avos

Macedonia 1 denar (MKD) = 100 deni

Madagascar 1 Malagasy franc (FMG) = 100 centimes

Malawi 1 kwacha (MK) = 100 tambala

Malaysia 1 ringgit (RM) = 100 sen

Maldives 1 rufiyaa (Rf) = 100 laari

Mali 1 Euro (E) = 100 euro-cents

Malta 1 Euro (E) = 100 euro-cents

Man, Isle of 1 pound (£M) = 100 pence

Marshall Islands 1 U.S. dollar (US$) = 100 cents

Martinique 1 Euro (E) – 100 euro-cents

Mauritania 1 ouguiya (UM) = 5 khoums

Mauritius 1 Mauritian rupee (MauR) = 100 cents

Mayotte 1 Euro (E) = 100 euro-cents

Mexico 1 peso (MEX$) = 100 centavos

Micronesia, Federated States of, 1 U.S. dollar (US$) = 100 cents

Moldova 1 leu = 100 bani

Monaco 1 Euro (E) = 100 euro-cents

Mongolia 1 tugrik (Tug) = 100 mongos

Montenegro 1 Euro (E) = 100 cents

Montserrat 1 Euro (E) = 100 euro-cents

Morocco 1 dirham (DH) = 100 centimes

Mozambique 1 metical (Mt) = 100 centavos

Myanmar 1 kyat (K)=100 pyas

Namibia 1 Namibian dollar (N$) = 100 cents

Nauru 1 Australian dollar (A$) = 100 cents

Nepal 1 Nepalese rupee (NRs) = 100 paisa

Netherlands 1 Euro (E) = 100 euro-cents

Netherlands Antilles 1 Euro (E) = 100 euro-cents

New Caledonia 1 Euro (E) = 100 euro-cents

New Zealand 1 New Zealand dollar (NZ$) = 100 cents

Nicaragua 1 cordoba (C$) = 100 centavos

Niger 1 Euro (E) = 100 euro-cents

Nigeria 1 naira (N) = 100 kobo

Niue 1 New Zealand dollar (NZ$) = 100 cents

Norfolk Island 1 Australian dollar (A$) = 100 cents

Northern Mariana Islands 1 U.S. dollar (US$) = 100 cents

Norway 1 krone (NKr) = 100 øre

Oman 1 Omani rial (RO) = 1,000 baiza

Pacific Islands, Trust Territory of the 1 U.S. dollar (US$) = 100 cents

Pakistan 1 Pakistani rupee (Rs) = 100 paisa

Panama 1 balboa (B) = 100 centesimos

Papua New Guinea 1 kina (K) = 100 toeas

Paraguay 1 guarani (G) = 100 centimos

Peru 1 new sol (S/.) = 100 centimos

Philippines 1 peso (P) = 100 centavos

Pitcairn Islands 1 New Zealand dollar (NZ$) = 100 cents

Poland 1 zloty (Zl) = 100 groszy

Portugal 1 Euro (E) = 100 euro-cents

Puerto Rico 1 U.S. dollar (US$) = 100 cents

Qatar 1 riyal (QR) = 100 dirhams

Reunion 1 Euro (E) = 100 euro-cents

Romania 1 leu (L) = 100 bani

Russia 1 ruble (R) = 100 kopeks

Rwanda 1 Euro (E) = 100 euro-cents

Saint Pierre & Miquelon 1 Euro (E) = 100 euro-cents

Saint Vincent & the Grenadines 1 Euro (E) = 100 euro-cents

Samoa, Western 1 tala (WS$) = 100 sene

San Marino 1 Euro (E) = 100 euro-cents

Sao Tome & Principe 1 dobra (Db) = 100 centimos

Saudi Arabia 1 riyal (SRls) = 100 dirhams

Senegal 1 Euro (E) = 100 euro-cents

Serbia 1 dinar (D) = 100 paras

Seychelles 1 Seychelles rupee (SR) = 100 cents

Sierra Leone 1 leone (Le) = 100 cents

Singapore 1 Singapore dollar (S$) = 100 cents

Slovakia 1 Euro (E) = 100 euro-cents

Slovenia 1 Euro (E) = 100 euro-cents

Solomon Islands 1 Solomon Islands dollar (SI$) = 100 cents

Somalia 1 Somali shilling (So.Sh.) = 100 centesimi

South Africa 1 rand (R) = 100 cents

Spain 1 Euro (E) = 100 euro-cents

Sri Lanka 1 Sri Lankan rupee (SLRs) = 100 cents

St. Helena 1 pound (£S)= 100 new pence

St. Kitts and Nevis 1 Euro = 100 euro-cents

St. Lucia 1 Euro = 100 euro-cents

Sudan 1 dinar = 100 piastres

Suriname 1 Euro (E) = 100 euro-cents

Svalbard and Jan Mayen Islands 1 Norwegian krone (NKr) = 100 ore

Swaziland 1 lilangeni (L) = 100 cents

Sweden 1 krona (SK) = 100 ore

Switzerland 1 franc (SwF) = 100 centimes or rappen

Syria 1 pound (£S) = 100 piasters

Tahiti 1 Euro (E) = 100 euro-cents

Taiwan 1 New Taiwan dollar (NT$) = 100 cents

Tajikistan 1 ruble (R) = 100 kopeks

Tanzania 1 Tanzanian shilling (TSh) = 100 cents

Thailand 1 baht (Bht) = 100 satangs

Togo 1 Euro (E) = 100 euro-cents

Tokelau 1 New Zealand dollar (NZ$) = 100 cents

Tonga 1 pa'anga (T$) = 100 seniti

Trinidad & Tobago 1 Trinidad & Tobago dollar (TT$) = 100 cents

Tunisia 1 Tunisian dinar (TD) = 1,000 millimes

Turkey 1 Turkish lira (TL) = 100 kurus

Turkmenistan 1 manat (Tm) =100 tenga

Turks & Caicos Islands 1 U.S. dollar (US$) = 100 cents

Tuvalu 1 Tuvaluan dollar ($T) or 1 Australian dollar (A$) = 100 cents

Uganda 1 Ugandan shilling (USh) = 100 cents

Ukraine 1 Hryvnia (H) = 100 kopiykas

United Arab Emirates 1 dirham (Dh) = 1,000 fils

United Kingdom 1 pound (£) = 100 pence

United States of America 1 U.S. dollar (US$) = 100 cents

Uruguay 1 peso ($U) = 100 centésimos

Uzbekistan 1som (Us)= 100 tiyin

Vanuatu 1 vatu (VT) = 100 centimes

Vatican 1 (see Holy See)

Venezuela 1 bolivar (Bs) = 100 centimos

Vietnam 1 dong (D) = 100 xu or 100 hao

Virgin Islands 1 U.S. dollar (US$) = 100 cents

Wake Island 1 U.S. dollar (US$) =100 cents

Wallis & Futuna Islands 1 Euro (E) = 100 euro-cents

Western Sahara 1 Moroccan dirham (DH) = 100 centimes

Yemen 1 Yemeni rial (YRls) =100 fils

Zambia 1 kwacha (ZK) – 100 ngwee

Zimbabwe 1 Zimbabwean dollar (Z$) = 100 cents

ABBREVIATIONS AND ACRONYMS

A

A Includes Extra (or Extras) (in stock listings of newspapers)

AAII American Association of Individual Investors

AB Aktiebolag (Swedish stock company)

ABA American Bankers Association

ABA American Bar Association

ABC American Business Conference

ABLA American Business Law Association

ABO Accumulated Benefit Obligation

ABS Automated Bond System

ABWA American Business Women's Association

ACAT Automated Customer Account Transfer

ACE AMEX Commodities Exchange

ACES Advance Computerized Execution System

ACH Automated Clearing House

ACRS Accelerated Cost Recovery System

ACT Automated Confirmation Transaction

ACU Asian Currency Units

A-D Advance-Decline Line

ADB Adjusted Debit Balance

ADB Asian Development Bank

ADR American Depositary Receipt

ADR Automatic Dividend Reinvestment

ADRS Asset Depreciation Range System

ADS American Depositary Shares

ADS Advanced Detection System

AE Account Executive

AE ISO Code for United Arab Emirates

AED ISO Code for United Arab Emirates Dirham

AEX Amsterdam Exchanges

AF ISO Code for Afghanistan

AFA ISO Code for Afghan Afghani

AFL-CIO American Federation of Labor-Congress of Industrial Organizations

AFM Amman Financial Market

AG Aktiengesellschaft (West German stock company)

AG ISO Code for Antigua and Barbudaag

AGI Adjusted Gross Income

AI ISO Code for Anguillaai

AIAF Association of Financial Assets Intermediaries (Spain)

AIBD Association of International Bond Dealers

AICPA American Institute of Certified Public Accountants

AID Agency for International Development

AIM American Institute for Management

AIP Automatic Investment Program

AL ISO Code for Albania

ALL ISO Code for Albanian Lek

ALT Alternative Trading System

AM Allied Member

AM ISO Code for Armenia

AMA American Management Association

AMA Asset Management Account

AMBAC American Municipal Bond Assurance Corporation

AMD ISO Code for Armenian Dram

AMEX American Stock Exchange

AMPS Auction Market Preferred Stock

AMT Alternative Minimum Tax

AN ISO Code for Netherlands Antilles

ANG ISO Code for Netherlands Antilles Guilder

AO ISO Code for Angola

AON All or None
AOR ISO Code for Angolan Reajuustado Kwanza
AOS Automated Order System
APB Accounting Principles Board
APR Annual Percentage Rate
APS Auction Preferred Stock
APT Arbitrage Pricing Theory
APT Automated Pit Trading
APY Annual Percentage Yield
AQ ISO Code for Antarctica
AR ISO Code for Argentina
AR Auto-Regressive
ARB Airport Revenue Bond
ARCH Auto-Regressive Conditional Heteroskedasticity
Arb Arbitrageur
ARF American Retail Federation
ARM Adjustable Rate Mortgage
ARPS Adjustable Rate Preferred Stock
ARPS Auction Rate Preferred Stock
ARR Average Rate of Return
ARS ISO Code Argentinian Peso
ART Annual Renewable Term (insurance)
AS ISO Code for American Samoa
ASAP As Soon as Possible
ASE American Stock Exchange
ASE Amsterdam Stock Exchange
ASE Athens Stock Exchange
ASPIRIN Australian Stock Price Riskless Indexed Notes
ASX Australia Stock Exchange
AT ISO Code for Austria
ATM Automatic Teller Machine
ATP Arbitrage Trading Program
ATS Alternative Trading Systems
ATS ISO Code for Austrian Schilling
AU ISO Code for Australia
AUD ISO Code for Australian Dollar
AW ISO Code for Aruba
AWC Letter of Acceptance, Waiver, and Consent (Nasdaq)
AWG ISO Code for Aruban Guilder
AZ ISO Code for Azerbaijan
AZM ISO Code for Azerbaijan Manat

B

B Annual Rate Plus Stock Dividend (in stock listings of newspapers)
B2B Business to Business

B2C Business to Consumer
BA ISO Code for Bosnia and Herzegovina
BAC Business Advisory Council
BAM ISO Code for Boznia and Herzegovinan Convertible Mark
BAN Bond Anticipation Note
BB ISO Code for Barbados
BBB Better Business Bureau
BBD ISO Code for Barbadian Dollar
BD ISO Code for Bangladesh
BD Bank Draft
BD Bills Discounted
BDT ISO Code for Bangladeshi Taka
B/D Broker-Dealer
BE ISO Code for Belgium
BE Bill of Exchange
BEACON Boston Exchange Automated Communication Order-routing Network
BEARS Bond Enabling Annual Retirement Savings
BF ISO Code for Burkina Faso
BF Brought Forward
BFP Basic Formula Price (milk)
BG ISO Code for Bulgaria
BGN ISO Code for Bulgarian Lev
BH ISO Code for Bahrain
BHD ISO Code for Bahranian Dinar
BI ISO Code for Burundi
BIC Bank Investment Contract
BIF Bank Insurance Fund
BIF ISO Code for Burundian Franc
BIPS Basis Points
BIS Bank for International Settlements
BBJ ISO Code for Benin
BL Bill of Lading
BLS Bureau of Labor Statistics
BM ISO Code for Bermuda
BMA Bond Market Association
BM&F Bolsa de Mercadorias & Futuros
BMD IOS Code for Bermudian Dollar
BMV Bolsa Mexicana de Valores
BN ISO Code for Brunei Darussalam
BND ISO Code for Brunei Darussalam Dollar
BO ISO Code for Bolivia
BO Branch Office

BO Buyer's Option

BOB ISO Code for Bolivian Boliviano

BOM Beginning of the Month

BOP Balance of Payments

BOT Balance of Trade

BOT Bought

BOT Board of Trustees

BOT Build Own Transfer

BOVESPA Bolsa de Valores de Sao Paulo

BPS Basis Points

BPW Business and Professional Women's Foundation

BR Bills Receivable

BR ISO Code for Brazil

BRIC Brazil, Russia, India, China

BRL ISO Code for Brazilian Real

BS ISO Code for Bahamas

BS Balance Sheet

BS Bill of Sale

BS Bureau of Standards

BSD ISO Code for Bahamian Dollar

BSE Boston Stock Exchange

BSE Brussels Stock Exchange

BT ISO Code for Bhutan

BTCI Bankers Trust Commodity Index

BTM Book to Market

BTN ISO Code for Bhutan Ngultrum

BV ISO Code for Bouvet Island

BVRJ Bolsa de Valores de Rio de Janiero

BW Bid Wanted

BW ISO Code for Botswana

BWP ISO Code for Botswanan Pula

BY ISO Code for Belarus

BYB ISO Code for Belarus Rouble

BZ ISO Code for Belize

BZD ISO Code for Belize Dollar

C

C Liquidating Dividend (in stock listings of newspapers)

C&F Cost and Freight

C2C Consumer to Consumer

CA ISO Code for Canada

CA Capital Account

CA Chartered Accountant

CA Commercial Agent

CA Credit Account

CA Current Account

CACM Central American Common Market

CAD Cash Against Documents

CAD ISO Code for Canadian Dollar

CADS Cash Available for Debt Service

CAES Computer-Assisted Execution System (Nasdaq)

CAF Cost Assurance and Freight

CAGR Compound Annual Growth Rate

CAMPS Cumulative Auction Market Preferred Stocks

Capex Capital Expenditures

CAPM Capital Asset Pricing Model

CAPS Convertible Adjustable Preferred Stock

CARs Certificate for Automobile Receivables

CARDS Certificates for Amortizing Revolving Debts

CATS Certificate of Accrual on Treasury Securities

CATV Community Antenna Television

CAX ISO Code for Canadian Cent

CBA Capital Builder Account

CBA Cost Benefit Analysis

CBD Cash Before Delivery

CBO Collateralized Bond Obligation

CBOE Chicago Board Options Exchange

CBOT Chicago Board of Trade

CC Chamber of Commerce

CC ISO Code for Cocos (Keeling Islands)

CCH Commerce Clearing House

CD Certificate of Deposit

CD Commercial Dock

CD ISO Code for Congo

CDN Canadian Dealing Network

CDNX Canadian Ventures Exchange

CDO Collateralized Debt Obligation

CEA Council of Economic Advisors

CEC Commodities Exchange Center

CEO Chief Executive Officer

CF ISO Code for Central African Republic

CF Certificates (in bond listings of newspapers)

CF Carried Forward
CFA Chartered Financial Analyst
CFAT Cash Flow after Taxes
CFC Chartered Financial Counselor
CFC Consolidated Freight Classification
CFC Controlled Foreign Corporation
CFI Cost, Freight, and Insurance
CFO Chief Financial Officer
CFP Certified Financial Planner
CFR Cost and Freight
CFTC Commodities Futures Trading Commission
CG ISO Code for The Congo
CH ISO Code for Switzerland
CH Clearing House
CH Custom House
CHAP Clearing House Automated Payments System
CHESS Clearing House Electronic Subregister System
CHF ISO Code for Swiss Franc
ChFC Chartered Financial Consultant
CHIPS Clearing House Interbank Payments System
CHX Chicago Stock Exchange
CI ISO Code for Ivory Coast
Cía Compañía (Spanish company)
CIC Chartered Investment Counsel
Cie Compagnie (French company)
CIF Corporate Income Fund
CIF Cost, Insurance, and Freight
CIPs Cash Index Participations
CK ISO Code for Cook Islands
CL ISO Code for Chile
CLD Called (in stock listings of newspapers)
CLF ISO Code for Chilean Unidades de Fomento
CLN Construction Loan Note
CLO Collateralized Loan Obligation
CLOB Central Limit Order Book
CLP ISO Code for Chilean Peso
CLU Chartered Life Underwriter
CM ISO Code for Cameroon
CMBS Commercial Mortgage-Backed Securities
CME Chicago Mercantile Exchange
CMI Commercial Markets Index
CML Capital Market Line

CMO Collateralized Mortgage Obligation
CMTA Clearing Member Trade Agreement
CMV Current Market Value
CN ISO Code for China
CN Consignment Note
CN Credit Note
CNS Continuous Net Settlement
CNY ISO Code for Chinese Yuan
CO Cash Order
CO Certificate of Origin
CO ISO Code for Colombia
Co. Company
COB Close of Business (with date)
COBRA Consolidated Omnibus Budget Reconciliation Act
COCO Contingent Convertible
COD Cash on Delivery
COD Collect on Delivery
CODA Cash or Deferred Arrangement
COFI Cost of Funds Index
COLA Cost-of-Living Adjustment
COLTS Continuously Offered Longer-Term Securities
COMEX Commodity Exchange (New York)
COMMEX MALAYSIA Commodity and Monetary Exchange of Malaysia
COMSAT Communications Satellite Corporation
CONNIE LEE College Construction Loan Insurance Association
COO Chief Operating Officer
COP ISO Code for Colombian Peso
CPA Certified Public Accountant
CPCI Chase Physical Commodity Index
CPD Commissioner of Public Debt
CPPF Cast Plus Fixed Fee
CPI Consumer Price Index
CPM Cost per Thousand
CPPC Cost plus a Percentage of Cost
CQS Consolidated Quotation System
CR Carrier's Risk
CR Class Rate
CR Company's Risk
CR ISO Code for Costa Rica
CR Current Rate

CRA Community Reinvestment Act
CRB Commodity Research Bureau
CRC ISO Code for Costa Rican Colon
CRD Central Registration Depository
CROP Compliance Registered Options Principal
CRT Charitable Remainder Trust
CS Corporate Securities (Limited) Representative
CSCE Coffee, Sugar and Coca Exchange
CSE Cincinnati Stock Exchange
CSE Copenhagen Stock Exchange
CSVLI Cash Surrender Value of Life Insurance
CTA Commodity Trading Adviser
CTA Consolidated Tape Association
CTA Cumulative Translation Adjustment
CTCI Computer-to-Computer Interface (Nasdaq)
CU ISO Code for Cuba
CUBS Calls Underwritten by Swanbrook
CUNA Credit Union National Association
CUP ISO Code for Cuban Peso
CUSIP Committee on Uniform Securities Identification Procedures
CV ISO Code for Cape Verde Islands
CV Convertible Security (in bond and stock listings of newspapers)
CVE ISO Code for Cape Verde Islands Escudo
CWO Cash with Order
CX ISO Code for Christmas Island
CY ISO Code for Cyprus
CYP ISO Code for Cyprus Pound
CZ ISO Code for Czech Republic
CZK ISO Code for Czech Republic Koruna

D

DA Deposit Account
DA Documents Against Acceptance
DAC Delivery Against Cost
DAF Defined Asset Fund
D&B Dun and Bradstreet
DAPS Dutch Auction Preferred Stock

DATS Direct Access Trading Systems
DBA Doing Business As
DBCC District Business Conduct Committee (Nasdaq)
DC Deep Discount Issue (in bond listings of newspapers)
DCF Disounted Cash Flows
DCFM Discounted Cash Flow Method
DDB Double-Declining-Balance Depreciation Method
DDM Dividend Discount Model
DENKS Dual-Employed, No Kids
DEWKS Dual-Employed, With Kids
DE ISO Code for Germany
DEM ISO Code for Deutschemark
DEQ Delivered Ex Quay (Incoterm)
DES Delivered ex-Ship
DIDC Depository Institutions Deregulatory Committee
DIF Deposit Insurance Fund
DIFF Euro-rate Differential
DINKS Dual-Income, No Kids
DIS/CHIPS Digital Interface Service/Character Interface Presentation Server (Nasdaq)
DISC Domestic International Sales Corporation
DITM Deep In the Money
DJ ISO Code for Djibouti
DJF ISO Code for Djibouti Franc
DJIA Dow Jones Industrial Average
DJTA Dow Jones Transportation Average
DJUA Dow Jones Utility Average
DK ISO Code for Denmark
DK Don't Know
DKK ISO Code for Danish Krone
DM ISO Code for Dominica
DN Debit Note
DNI Do Not Increase
DNR Do Not Reduce
D/O Delivery Order
DO ISO Code for Dominican Republic
DOP ISO Code for Dominican Republic Peso
DOT Designated Order Turnaround
DOTM Deep Out of the Money

DP Documents Against Payment
DPI Disposable Personal Income
DPP Direct Participation Programs
DRIP Dividend Reinvestment Plan
DS Days After Sight
DSCR Debt Service Coverage Ratio
DTB Deutsche Terminbourse
DTC Depository Transfer Check
DTC Depository Trust Company
DTCC Depository Trust & Clearing Corporation
DUNS Data Universal Numbering System (Dun's Number)
DVP Delivery Versus Payment
DZ ISO Code for Algeria
DZD ISO Code for Algerian Dinar

E

E Declared or Paid in the Preceding 12 Months (in stock listings of newspapers)
EAFE Europe and Australasia, Far East Equity Index
E&OE Errors and Omissions Excepted
EASD European Association of Securities Dealers
EBIAT Earnings Before Interest After Taxes
EBIT Earnings Before Interest and Taxes
EBITD Earnings Before Interest, Taxes, and Depreciation
EBITDA Earnings Before Interest, Taxes, Depreciation, and Amortization
EBRD European Bank for Reconstruction and Development
EBS Electronic Blue Sheet
EBS Swiss Electronic Bourse
EBT Earnings Before Taxes
EC ISO Code for Ecuador
EC European Community
ECA Export Credit Agency
ECB European Central Bank
ECGD Export Credit Guarantee Department
ECI Employment Cost Index
ECM Emerging Company Marketplace
ECM European Common Market
ECN Electronic Communications Network
ECOA Equal Credit Opportunity Act

ECS ISO Code for Ecuadorian Sucre
ECT Estimated Completion Time
ECU European Currency Unit
EDC Export Development Corp.
EDD Estimated Delivery Date
EDGAR (SEC's) Electronic Data Gathering, Analysis, and Retreival
EDI Electronic Data Interchange
EDR European Depositary Receipts
EE ISO Code for Estonia
EEC European Economic Community
EEK ISO Code for the Estonian Kroon
EEOC Equal Employment Opportunity Commission
EFIC Export Finance Insurance Corp.
EFT Electronic Funds Transfer
EFTPOS Electronic Funds Transfer at Point of Sale
EG ISO Code for Egypt
EGP ISO Code for Egyptian Pound
EGTRRA Economic Growth and Tax Relief Reconciliation Act of 2001
EH ISO Code for Western Sahara
EIS Enhanced Income Security
EITF Emerging Issues Task Force
EM Effective Margin
EMF INDEX Emerging Market Free Index
EMP End-of-Month Payment
EMS European Monetary System
EMTA Emerging Market Traders Association
ENMET Energy and Metals Index
EOA Effective On or About
EOD Every Other Day (advertising)
EOE European Options Exchange
EOM End of Month
EOQ Economic Order Quantity
EPR Earnings Price Ratio
EPS Earnings Per Share
ER ISO Code for Eritrea
ERISA Employee Retirement Income Security Act of 1974
ERM Exchange Rate Mechanism
ERTA Economic Recovery Tax Act of 1981

ES ISO Code for Spain
ESOP Employee Stock Ownership Plan
ESP ISO Code for Spanish Peseta
ESP Exchange Stock Portfolio
ESPP Employee Stock Purchase Plan
ET ISO Code for Ethiopia
ETA Estimated Time of Arrival
ETB ISO Code for Ethiopian Birr
ETD Estimated Time of Departure
ETF Exchange-Traded Fund
ETLT Equal To or Less Than
ETM Escrowed to Maturity
ETS Energy Trading System (on the International Petroleum Exchange)
EU European Union
EUREX European Derivatives Exchange
EURIBOR Eurozone Interbank Offer Rates
EXIMBANK Export-Import Bank

F

F Dealt in Flat (in bond listings in newspapers)
FA Foreign Associate (Nasdaq)
FA Free Alongside
FAC Federal Advisory Council
FACT Factor Analysis Chart Technique
FACTA Fair and Accurate Credit Transactions Act of 2003
FAQ Frequently Asked Questions
FAQS Firm Access and Query System (Nasdaq)
FAS Free Alongside Ship
FASAC Financial Accounting Standards Advisory Council
FASB Financial Accounting Standards Board
FAT Fixed Asset Transfer
FAX Facsimile
FB Freight Bill
FC Foreign Currency Options Representative (Nasdaq)
FCA Fellow of the Institute of Chartered Accountants
FCA Free Carrier
FCBA Fair Credit Billing Act
FCC Federal Communications Commission
FCFAC Federal Credit Financial Assistance Corporation

FCIA Foreign Credit Insurance Association
FCM Futures Commission Merchant
FCRA Fair Credit Reporting Act
FCUA Federal Credit Union Administration
FDI Foreign Direct Investment
FDIC Federal Deposit Insurance Corporation
Fed Federal Reserve System
FET Federal Excise Tax
F&F Furniture and Fixtures
FFB Federal Financing Bank
FFCS Federal Farm Credit System
FFO Funds from Operations
FGIC Financial Guaranty Insurance Corporation
FHA Farmers Home Administration
FHA Federal Housing Administration
FHFB Federal Housing Finance Board
FHLBB Federal Home Loan Bank Board
FHLMC Federal Home Loan Mortgage Corporation (Freddie Mac)
FI ISO Code for Finland
FIBOR Frankfurt Interbank Offered Rate
FIBV Federation Internationale des Bourses de Valeurs
FICA Federal Insurance Contributions Act
FICB Federal Intermediate Credit Bank
FICO Fair Issac and Company (Credit Scoring)
FICO Financing Corporation
FIFO First In, First Out
FIM ISO Code for Finnish Markka
FIN Federal ID Number
FINEX Financial Derivatives Division of New York Cotton Exchange
FINRA Financial Industry Regulatory Authority
FIPS Fixed Income Pricing System
FIRREA Financial Institutions Reform and Recovery Act
FIT Federal Income Tax
FITW Federal Income Tax Withholding
FJ ISO Code for Fiji

FJD ISO Code for Fijian Dollar
FK ISO Code for Falkland Islands (Malvinas)
FKP ISO Code for Falkland Islands Pound
FLB Federal Land Bank
FLEX Flexible Exchange Options
FM ISO Code for Micronesia
FMAN February, May, August, November Cycle
FMC Federal Maritime Commission
FN Financial and Operations Principal (Nasdaq)
FNMA Federal National Mortgage Association (Fannie Mae)
FO ISO Code for Faroe Islands
FOB Free on Board
FOC Free of Charge
FOCUS Financial and Operations Combined Uniform Single Report
FOI Freedom of Information Act
FOK Fill or Kill
FOMC Federal Open Market Committee
FOOTSIE Financial Times-SE 100 Index of U.K. Stocks
FOR Free on Rail (or Road)
FOREX Foreign Exchange
FOT Free on Truck
FOX Finnish Options Index
FP Floating Policy
FP Fully Paid
FPA Free of Particular Average
FPM Fixed-Payment Mortgage
FQC Firm Quote Compliance System (Nasdaq)
FR ISO Code for France
FRA Federal Reserve Act
FRA Forward Rate Agreement
FRB Federal Reserve Bank
FRB Federal Reserve Board
FRD Federal Reserve District
FREDDIE MAC Federal Home Loan Mortgage Corporation
FREIT Finite Life REIT
FRF ISO Code for French Franc
FRN Floating Rate Note
FRS Federal Reserve System
FS Final Settlement
FSA Flexible Spending Account
FSC Foreign Sales Corporation
FSE Frankfurt Stock Exchange
FSLIC Federal Savings and Loan Insurance Corporation

FSMA Financial Services Modernization Act of 1999
FTC Federal Trade Commission
FTI Federal Tax Included
FUTA Federal Unemployment Tax Act
FVO For Valuation Only
FX Foreign
FY Fiscal Year
FYA For Your Attention
FYI For Your Information

G

G Dividends and Earnings in Canadian Dollars (in stock listings of newspapers)
GA ISO Code for Gabon
GAAP Generally Accepted Accounting Principles
GAAS Generally Accepted Auditing Standards
GAI Guaranteed Annual Income
GAO General Accounting Office
GARP Growth at a Reasonable Price
GATT General Agreement on Tariffs and Trade
GB ISO Code for Great Britain (United Kingdom)
GBT ISO Code for Pound Sterling Currency
GD ISO Code for Grenada
GDP Gross Domestic Product
GDR Global Depositary Receipt
GE ISO Code for Georgia
G-8 Group of Eight Finance Ministers
GEM Growing Equity Mortgage
GF ISO Code for French Guiana
GH ISO Code for Ghana
GI ISO Code for Gibraltar
GIC Guaranteed Investment Contract
GINNIE MAE Government National Mortgage Association
GIPS Global Investment Performance Standards
GIT Guaranteed Income (or Investment) Contract
GL ISO Code for Greenland
GM ISO Code for Gambia
GM General Manager
GmbH Gesellschaft mit beschränkter Haftung (West German limited liability company)

GMC Guaranteed Mortgage Certificate

GN ISO Code for Guinea

GNMA Government National Mortgage Association

GNP Gross National Product

GO General Obligation Bond

GOX (CBOE) Gold Index

GP General Partner

GP ISO Code for Guadeloupe

GPM Graduated Payment Mortgage

GR ISO Code for Greece

GRIT Grantor Retained Income Trust

GS ISO Code for South Georgia and the South Sandwich Islands

GSA General Services Administration

GSCC Government Securities Clearing Corporation

GSCI Goldman Sachs Commodity Index

GSE Government Sponsored Entity

GT ISO Code for Guatemala

GTC Good Till Canceled

GTM Good This Month

GTW Good This Week

GU ISO Code for Guam

GULP Group Universal Life Policy

GW ISO Code for Guinea-Bissau

GY ISO Code for Guyana

HKFE Hong Kong Futures Exchange

HLT Highly Leveraged Transaction

HM ISO Code for Heard Island and McDonald Islands

HMDA Home Mortgage Disclosure Act

HMI Housing Market Index

HN ISO Code for Honduras

HNL ISO Code for Honduran Lempira

HO Home Owner's Insurance Policy

HOLDRs Holding Company Depositary Receipts (Merrill Lynch)

HQ Headquarters

HR ISO Code for Croatia

HR U.S. House of Representatives

HR U.S. House of Representatives Bill (with number)

HRK ISO Code for Croatian Kuna

HSA Health Savings Account

HT ISO Code for Haiti

HTG ISO Code for Haitian Gourde

HU ISO Code for Hungary

HUD Department of Housing and Urban Development

HUF ISO Code for Hungarian Forint

HUI Basket of Unhedged Gold Stocks (BUGS index)

H

H Declared or Paid After Stock Dividend or Split-Up (in stock listings of newspapers)

HAB House Air Waybill

HECM Home Equity Conversion Mortgage

HEL Home Equity Loan

HELOC Home Equity Line of Credit

HEX Helsinki Stock and Derivatives Exchange

H/F Held For

HFR Hold For Release

HIBOR Hong Kong Interbank Offered Rate

HK ISO Code for Hong Kong

HKD ISO Code for Hong Kong Dollar

HKEx Hong Kong Exchanges and Clearing Ltd.

I

I Paid This Year, Dividend Omitted, Deferred, or No Action Taken at Last Dividend Meeting (in stock listings of newspapers)

IAFP International Association for Financial Planning

IBES Institutional Brokers Estimate System

IBF International Banking Facility

I-Bonds Inflation-indexed Savings Bonds

IBRD International Bank for Reconstruction and Development (World Bank)

IC Information Coefficient

ICAA Investment Counsel Association of America

ICC International Chamber of Commerce

ICC Interstate Commerce Commission

ICFP Institute of Certified Financial Planners

ICFTU International Confederation of Free Trade Unions

ICI Investable Commodity Index

ICI Investment Company Institute

ICMA Institute of Cost and Management Accountants

ICSD International Councils of Securities Dealers

ID ISO Code for Indonesia

IDB Industrial Development Bond

IDC Interest During Construction

IET Interest Equalization Tax

IDEM Italian Derivatives Market

IDR ISO Code for Indonesian Rupiah

IDR International (Global) Depositary Receipt

IDS Income Deposit Security

IE ISO Code for Ireland

IEP ISO Code for Irish Punt

IET Interest Equalization Tax

IFC International Finance Corporation

IL ISO Code for Israel

ILA International Longshoremen's Association

ILGWU International Ladies' Garment Workers' Union

ILO International Labor Organization

ILS ISO Code for Israeli Shekel

IMAB International Markets Advisory Board (Nasdaq)

IMF International Monetary Fund

IMM International Monetary Market of the Chicago Mercantile Exchange

Inc. Incorporated

IN ISO Code for India

INCOTERM International Chamber of Commerce Trade Terms

INR ISO Code for Indian Rupee

INS Institute for Supply Management

INSTINET Institutional Networks Corporation (now Instinet Group Incorporated)

IO ISO Code for British Indian Ocean Territory

IO Interest Only

IOC Immediate or Canceled Order

IOM Index and Option Market

IOSCO International Organization of Securities Commissions

IOU I Owe You

IPE International Petroleum Exchange

IPL Investment Product Line

IPO Initial Public Offering

IPS Income Participating Security

IPS Income Preferred Securities

IQ ISO Code for Iraq

IQD ISO Code for Iraqi Dinar

IR Investor Relations

IR ISO Code for Iran

IRA Individual Retirement Arrangement

IRB Industrial Revenue Bond

IRC Internal Revenue Code

IRR Internal Rate of Return

IRR ISO Code for Iranian Rial

IRS Internal Revenue Service

IRX 13-week Treasury Bill Index

ISBN International Standard Book Number

IS ISO Code for Iceland

ISE International Securities Exchange

ISE International Stock Exchange of the United Kingdom and the Republic of Ireland

ISE Irish Stock Exchange

ISE Italian Stock Exchange

ISG Intermarket Surveillance Group (Nasdaq)

ISIS Industry Support Information Services

ISIS Intermarket Surveillance Information System

ISK ISO Code for Icelandic Krona

ISM Institute for Supply Management

ISMA International Securities Market Association

ISO Incentive Stock Option

ISO Internationally Standardized Country (2 characters) and Currency (3 characters) Code

ISRO International Securities Regulatory Organization

ISS Institutional Shareholder Services

ISSN International Standard Serial Number

IT ISO Code for Italy
ITC Investment Tax Credit
ITL ISO Code for Italian Lira
ITM In The Money
ITS Intermarket Trading System
ITS/CAES Intermarket Trading System/Computer-Assisted Execution System

J

JA Joint Account
JAJO January, April, July, October Cycle
JASDAQ Japanese Association of Securities Dealers Automated Quotation System
Jeep Graduated Payment Mortgage
JM ISO Code for Jamaica
JMD ISO Code for Jamaican Dollar
JO ISO Code for Jordan
JOD ISO Code for Jordanian Dinar
JP ISO Code for Japan
JPMCI J.P. Morgan Commity Index
JPY ISO Code for Japanese Yen
JSE Johannesburg Stock Exchange
JTWROS Joint Tenancy with Right of Survivorship

K

K Declared or Paid This Year on a Cumulative Issue with Dividends in Arrears (in stock listings of newspapers)
K Kilo- (prefix meaning multiplied by one thousand)
KCBT Kansas City Board of Trade
KD Knocked Down (disassembled)
KES ISO Code for Kenyan Shilling
KG ISO Code for Kyrgyzstan
KGS ISO Code for Kyrgyzstan Som
KH ISO Code for Cambodia
KHR ISO Code for Cambodian Riel
KI ISO Code for Kiribati
KIBOR Kuala Lumpur Interbank Offered Rate
KK Kabushiki-Kaisha (Japanese stock company)
KLCE Kuala Lumpur Commodities Exchange
KLOFFE Kuala Lumpur Options & Financial Futures Exchange Barhad

KLSE Kuala Lumpur Stock Exchange
KM ISO Code for Comoros
KMF ISO Code for Comoros Franc
KN ISO Code for Saint Kitts and Nevis
KP ISO Code for Korea, Democratic People's Republic of
KPW ISO Code for North Korean Won
KR ISO Code for Korea, Republic of
KRW ISO Code for South Korean Won
KW Kilowatt
KW ISO Code for Kuwait
KWD ISO Code for Kuwait Dinar
KY ISO Code for Cayman Islands
KYD ISO Code for Cayman Islands Dollar
KWH Kilowatt-hour
KYC Know Your Customer Rule
KZ ISO Code for Kazakhstan
KZT ISO Code for Kazakhstan Tenge

L

L Listed (securities)
LA ISO Code for Lao People's Democratic Republic
LAK ISO Code for Laos New Kip
LB ISO Code for Lebanon
LBO Leveraged Buyout
LBP ISO Code for Lebanese Pound
L/C Letter of Credit
LC ISO Code for Saint Lucia
LCE London Commodity Exchange
LCL Less-Than-Carload Lot
LCM Least Common Multiple (mathematics)
LDC Less Developed Country
LEAPS Long-Term Equity AnticiPation Securities
LEI Leading Economic Indicators
LESOP Leveraged Employee Stock Ownership Plan
L/I Letter of Intent
LI ISO Code for Liechtenstein
LIBOR London Interbank Offered Rate
LIFFE London International Financial Futures and Options Exchange

LIFO Last In, First Out
LISBOR Lisbon Interbank Offered Rate
LK ISO Code for Sri Lanka
LKR ISO Code for Sri Lankan Rupee
LLC Limited Liability Company
LME London Metal Exchange
LMRA Labor-Management Relations Act
LOC Letter of Credit
LP Limited Partnership
LR ISO Code for Liberia
LRD ISO Code for Liberian Dollar
LS ISO Code for Lesotho
LSE Lisbon Stock Exchange
LSE London Stock Exchange
LSL ISO Code for Lesotho Loti
LT ISO Code for Lithuania
Ltd Limited (British Corporation)
LTL ISO Code for Lithuanian Litas
LTV Loan To Value
LU ISO Code for Luxembourg
LUF ISO Code for Luxembourg Franc
LV ISO Code for Latvia
LVL ISO Code for Latvian Lats
LY ISO Code for Libya
LYD ISO Code for Libyian Dinar
LYONS Liquid Yield Option Notes

M

M Matured Bonds (in bond listings in newspapers)
M Milli- (prefix meaning divided by one thousand)
M Mega- (prefix meaning multiplied by one million)
M One Thousand (Roman Numeral)
MA ISO Code for Morocco
MAB Master Air Waybill
MACD Moving Average Convergence/Divergence
MACRS Modified Accelerated Cost Recovery System
MAD ISO Code for Moroccan Dirham
MATIF Marche a Terme International de France
M&L Matched And Lost
Max Maximum
MBA Master of Business Administration

MBARS Municipal Bond Acceptance and Reconciliation Service
MBIA Municipal Bond Insurance Association
MBO Management Buyout
MBO Management By Objective
MBS Mortgage-Backed Security
MBSCC Mortgage-Backed Securities Clearing Corporation
MC Marginal Credit
MC ISO Code for Monaco
MCAMP Municipal Bond Check a Month Portfolio (Morgan Stanley)
M-CATS Municipal Certificates of Accrual on Tax-exempt Securities
MCE Malaysia Commodity Exchange
MD Months After Date
MD ISO Code for Moldova, Republic of
MD&A Management's Discussion and Analysis
MDA Multiple Discriminant Analysis
MDL ISO Code for Moldovan Leu
ME Montreal Exchange/Bourse de Montreal
MERC Chicago Mercantile Exchange
MFN Most Favored Nation (tariff regulations)
MG ISO Code for Madagascar
MGF ISO Code for Madagascar Franc
MGM Milligram
MH ISO Code for Marshall Islands
MHR Member of the U.S. House of Representatives
MHS Manufactured Housing Securities
MIBOR Madrid Interbank Offered Rate
MICEX Moscow Interbank Currency
MIDAS Market Information Data Access System (Nasdaq)
MIF Mercato Italiano Futures Exchange
MIG-1 Moody's Investment Grade
MIMC Member of the Institute of Management Consultants
Min Minimum

MIP Monthly Income Preferred
Security
MIS Management Information
System
Misc Miscellaneous
MIT Market If Touched
MIT Municipal Investment Trust
MITTS Market Index Target Term
Securities
MJSD March, June, September,
December Cycle
MK ISO Code for Macedonia
MKD ISO Code for Macedonian
Denar
ML ISO Code for Mali
MLP Master Limited Partnership
MLR Minimum Lending Rate
MM ISO Code for Myanmar
MM Millimeter (metric unit)
MMDA Money Market Deposit (or
Demand) Account
MMK ISO Code for Myanmar
Kyat
MN ISO Code for Mongolia
MNC Multinational Corporation
MNT ISO Code for Mongolian
Tugrik
MO Money Order
MO ISO Code for Macau
MOB Municipals Over Bonds
MOC Market-On-Close Order
MONEP Marche des Options
Negociables de Paris
MOP ISO Code for Macau Pataca
MP ISO Code for Northern
Mariana Islands
MPC Market Performance
Committee
MQ ISO Code for Martinique
MR ISO Code for Mauritania
MRO ISO Code for Mauritanian
Ouguiya
MRQ Most Recent Quarter
MS ISO Code for Montserrat
MSA Medical Savings Account
MSB Mutual Savings Bank
MSCI Morgan Stanley Capital
International
MSE Madrid Stock Exchange
(Bolsa de Madrid)
MSE Mexican Stock Exchange
MSRB Municipal Securities
Rulemaking Board
MT ISO Code for Malta

MTL ISO Code for Maltese Lira
MTN Medium-term Note
MTU Metric Units
MU ISO Code for Mauritius
MUD Municipal Utility District
MUNI Municipal Security
MUR ISO Code for Mauritius
Rupee
MV ISO Code for Maldives
MVR ISO Code for Makdive
Rufiyaa
MW ISO Code for Malawi
MWK ISO Code for Malawian
Kwacha
MY ISO Code for Malaysia
MYR ISO Code for Malaysian
Ringgit
MX ISO Code for Mexico
MXN ISO Code for Mexican Peso
MZ ISO Code for Mozambique
MZM ISO Code for Mozambique
Metical

N

N New Issue (in stock listings of
newspapers)
NA ISO Code for Namibia
NA National Association (National
Bank)
NAC National Adjudicatory
Council (Nasdaq)
NAD ISO Code for Namibian
Dollar
NAFTA North American Free
Trade Agreement
NAHB National Association of
Home Builders
NAIC National Association of
Investors Corporation
NAICS North American Industry
Classification System
NAM National Association of
Manufacturers
NAPA National Association of
Purchasing Agents
NAPFA National Association of
Personal Financial Advisors
NAPM National Association of
Purchasing Management
NAR National Association of
Realtors
NAREIT National Association of
Real Estate Investment Trusts

NASA National Aeronautics and Space Administration

NASAA North American Securities Administrators Association

NASAA National Association of Securities Administrators Association, Inc.

NASD National Association of Securities Dealers

NASDAQ National Association of Securities Dealers Automated Quotation

NASDR NASD Regulation, Inc. (subsidiary of NASD)

NATO North Atlantic Treaty Organization

NAV Net Asset Value

NBCC National Business Conduct Committee (Nasdaq)

NBI Narrow-Based Index

NBS National Bureau of Standards

NC ISO Code for New Caledonia

NC No Charge

NCUA National Credit Union Administration

NCV No Commercial Value

ND Next Day Delivery (in stock listings of newspapers)

NDF Nondeliverable Forward

NE ISO Code for Niger

NEMS National Exchange Market System

NEO Nonequity Options

NF ISO Code for Norfolk Island

NFA National Futures Association

NFCC National Foundation for Credit Counseling

NG ISO Code for Nigeria

NGN ISO Code for Nigerian Naira

NH Not Held

NI ISO Code for Nicaragua

NIC Net Interest Cost

NICS Newly Industrialized Countries

NIF Note Issuance Facility

NIO ISO Code for Nicaraguan Cordoba Oro

NIP Normal Investment Practice

NIRF NASD Information Request Form

NIRI National Investor Relations Institute

NIT Negative Income Tax

NL No Load

NL ISO Code for Netherlands

NLG ISO Code for the Dutch Guilder

NLRA National Labor Relations Act

NLRB National Labor Relations Board

NMAB National Market Advisory Board

NMB National Mediation Board

NMS National Market System

NMS Normal Market Size

NNP Net National Product

NO ISO Code for Norway

NOB Notes Over Bonds

NOK ISO Code for Norwegian Krone

NOL Net Operating Loss

NOREX Nordic Exchanges

NOW National Organization for Women

NOW Negotiable Order Of Withdrawal

NP No Protest (banking)

NP ISO Code for Nepal

NP Notary Public

N/P Notes Payable

NPR ISO Code for the Nepalese Rupee

NPV Net Present Value

NPV No Par Value

NQ No Quote

NQB National Quotation Bureau

NQB No Qualified Bidders

NQDS Nasdaq Quotation Dissemination Service

NR ISO Code for Nauru

NR Not Rated

NSBA National Small Business Association

NSCC National Securities Clearing Corporation

NSE National Stock Exchange (India)

NSF Not Sufficient Funds (banking)

NSTS National Securities Trading System

NSX National Stock Exchange

NTE Not to Exceed

NTU Normal Trading Unit

NU ISO Code for Niueo

NV Naamloze Vennootschap (Dutch corporation)

NYBOT New York Board of Trade
NYCE New York Cotton Exchange
NYCSCE New York Coffee, Sugar and Cocoa Exchange
NYFE New York Futures Exchange
NYMEX New York Mercantile Exchange
NYSE New York Stock Exchange
NZFOE New Zealand Futures and Options Exchange
NZSE New Zealand Stock Exchange

O

O Old (in options listing of newspapers)
OAPEC Organization of Arab Petroleum Exporting Countries
OAS Option Adjusted Spread
OATS Order Audit Trail System (Nasdaq)
OB Or Better
OBV On-Balance Volume
OCC Option Clearing Corporation
OD Overdraft, Overdrawn
ODE Oporto Derivatives Exchange (Bolsa de Derivados de Oporto) in Portugal
OECD Organization for Economic Cooperation and Development
OEX Standard & Poor's 100 Stock Index
OID Original Issue Discount
OM ISO Code for Oman
OMB Office of Management and Budget
OMLX London Securities and Derivatives Exchange
OMR ISO Code for Oman Rial
OPD Delayed Opening
OPEC Organization of Petroleum Exporting Countries
OPM Options Pricing Model
OPM Other People's Money
OPRA Options Prices Reporting Authority (Nasdaq)
OSE Oslo Stock Exchange
OSE Osaka Securities Exchange
OSJ Office of Supervisory Jurisdiction (Nasdaq)
O/T Overtime
OTC Over The Counter
OTCBB OTC Bulletin Board
OTS Office of Thrift Supervision
OW Offer Wanted

P

P Paid This Year (in stock listings of newspapers)
P Put (in options listings of newspapers)
PA ISO Code for Panama
PA Power of Attorney
PA Public Accountant
PA Purchasing Agent
PAB ISO Code for Panamanian Balboa
PAC Planned Amortization Class
PAC Preauthorized checks
PAC Put and Call (options market)
PACE Philadelphia Automated Communication and Execution System
PAD Preauthorized Electronic Debits
PAL Passive Activity Loss
PAYE Pay As You Earn
PBGC Pension Benefit Guaranty Corporation
PBO Projected Benefit Obligation
PBOT Philadelphia Board of Trade
PBR Price-to-Book Value Ratio
PC Participation Certificates
PC Plus Commissions
PC Price to Cash Flow Ratio
PCAOB Public Company Accounting Oversight Board
PCX Pacific Exchange
PE Price Earnings Ratio (in stock listings of newspapers)
PE ISO Code for Peru
PEFC Private Export Funding Corporation
PEG Prospective Earnings Growth
PEN ISO Code for Peruvian Nuevo Sol
PER Price Earnings Ratio
PERCS Preferred Equity Redemption Cumulative Stock
PERFAN Barra's Performance Analysis
PERLS Principal Exchange-Rate-Linked Securities
PF ISO Code for French Polynesia
PFD Preferred Stock
PG ISO Code for Papua New Guinea
PGK ISO Code for Papua New Guinea Kina
PH ISO Code for Philippines

PHLX Philadelphia Stock Exchange
PHP ISO Code for Philippines Peso
P&I Principal and Interest
PIBOR Paris Interbank Offer Rate
PIG Passive Income Generator
PIIG Portugal, Ireland, Italy, Greece
PIK Payment-In-Kind
PIN Personal Identification Number
PIP Smallest currency unit—e.g., one U.S. penny.
PIPES Private Investment in Public Equity Securities
PITI Principal, Interest, Taxes, and Insurance
P&L Profit and Loss Statement
PK ISO Code for Pakistan
PK Pink Sheets
PKR ISO Code for Pakistani Rupee
PL ISO Code for Poland
PL Price List
PLC Public Liability Company
PLC (British) Public Limited Company
PLC Project Loan Certificate
PLN ISO Code for Polish Zlotny
PM ISO Code for Saint Pierre and Miquelon
PMI Private Mortgage Insurance
PMV Private Market Value
PN ISO Code for Pitcairn
PN Project Note
PN Promissory Note
PO Principal Only
POA Power of Attorney
POD Pay on Delivery
POE Port of Embarkation
POE Port of Entry
POR Pay on Return
PPI Producer Price Index
PPP Penultimate Profit Prospect
PPP Purchasing Power Parity
PPS Prior Preferred Stock
PR ISO Code for Puerto Rico
PR Public Relations
PRE-RE Pre-refunded Municipal Note
PRI Political Risk Insurance
PRIME Prescribed Right to Income and Maximum Equity
PROCTOR Professional Certification Testing Organization (Nasdaq)

Prop Proprietor
P/S Price to Sales Ratio
PS ISO Code for Palestine Territory, Occupied
PSA Public Securities Association
PSE Philippine Stock Exchange
PSLRA Private Securities Litigation Reform Act of 1995
PSR Price/Sales Ratio
PT ISO Code for Portugal
PTE ISO Code for Portugese Escudo
PUC Public Utilities Commission
PUHCA Public Utility Holding Company Act of 1935
PV Present Value
PVBR Price Value of a Basis Point
PVR Profit/Volume Ratio
PW ISO Code for Palau
PY ISO Code for Paraguay
PYG ISO Code for the Paraguay Guarani

Q

QA ISO Code for Qatar
QAR ISO Code for Qatar Rial
QB Qualified Buyers
QC Quality Control
QDS Quote Dissemination System (Nasdaq)
QI Quarterly Index
QQQQ Qubes
QT Questioned Trade
QTC Quote Trade Comparison System (Nasdaq)
QTIP Qualified Terminable Interest Property Trust

R

R Declared or Paid in the Preceding 12 Months plus Stock Dividend (in stock listings of newspapers)
R Option Not Traded (in option listings in newspapers)
RADAR Research and Data Analysis Repository System (Nasdaq)
RAM Reverse Annuity Mortgage
RAN Revenue Anticipation Note
RAP Regulatory Accounting Procedures
R&D Research and Development

RCIA Retail Credit Institute of America

RCMM Registered Competitive Market Maker

RE ISO Code for Reunion

REA Rural Electrification Administration

REDs Refunding Escrow Deposits

REFCORP Resolution Funding Corporation

REIT Real Estate Investment Trust

RELP Real Estate Limited Partnership

REMIC Real Estate Mortgage Investment Conduit

REMM Registered Equity Market Maker

Repo Repurchase Agreement

RIA Registered Investment Adviser

RICO Racketeer Influenced and Corrupt Organization Act

RO ISO Code for Romania

ROA Return on Assets

ROA Right of Accumulation

ROC Return on Capital

ROE Return on Equity

ROI Return on Investment (Return on Invested Capital)

ROL ISO Code for Romanian Leu

ROL Reduction-Option Loan

ROP Registered Options Principal

ROS Return on Sales

RP Repurchase Agreement

RPA Retirement Protection Act of 1994

RPPP Relative Purchasing Power Parity

RRP Reverse Repurchase Agreement

RRSP Registered Retirement Savings Plan

RSI Relative Strength Index

RT Royalty Trust

RTC Resolution Trust Corporation

RTS Russian Trading System

RTW Right to Work

RU ISO Code for Russian Federation

RUB ISO Code for Russian Rouble

RW ISO Code for Rwanda

RWF ISO Code for Rwanda Franc

S

S No Option Offered (in option listings of newspapers)

S Signed (before signature on typed copy of a document, original of which was signed)

S Split or Stock Dividend (in stock listings of newspapers)

S&L Sale and Leaseback

S&L Savings and Loan

S&P Standard & Poor's

SA Sociedad Anónima (Spanish corporation)

SA Société Anonyme (French corporation)

SA ISO Code for Saudi Arabia

SAA Special Arbitrage Account

SAB Special Assessment Bond

SAIF Savings Association Insurance Fund

SAFEX South African Futures Exchange

SAIF Savings Association Insurance Fund

SALLIE MAE Student Loan Marketing Association (now SLM Corp.)

SAM Shared Appreciation Mortgage

SAR ISO Code for Saudi Arabian Riyal

SARSEP Salary Reduction Simplified Employee Pension Plan

SATURNS Structured Asset Trust Unit Repackagings

SAX Stockholm Automatic Exchange

SB Savings Bond

SB ISO Code for Solomon Islands

SB U.S. Senate Bill (with number)

SB Short Bill

SBA Small Business Administration

SBD ISO Code for Solomon Islands Dollar

SBIC Small Business Investment Corporation

SBLI Savings Bank Life Insurance

SBWEI Salomon Brothers World Equity Index

SC ISO Code for Seychelles

SCOR Small Corporate Offerings Registration

SCORE Special Claim on Residual Equity

SCR ISO Code for Seychelles Rupee

SD ISO Code for Sudan

SD Standard Deduction

SDB Special District Bond

SDBL Sight Draft, Bill of Lading Attached

SDD SO Code for Sudanese Dinar

SDFS Same Day Funds Settlement

SDRs Special Drawing Rights

SE Shareholders' Equity

SE ISO Code for Sweden

SEAQ Stock Exchange Automated Quotations

SEC Securities and Exchange Commission

SED Shipper's Export Declaration

SEHK Stock Exchange of Hong Kong

SEK ISO Code for Swedish Krona

Sen Senator

SEP Simplified Employee Pension Plan

SES Stock Exchange of Singapore

SET Securities Exchange of Thailand

SET Stock Exchange of Thailand

SF Sinking Fund

SFE Sydney Futures Exchange

SG ISO Code for Singapore

SG&A Selling, General and Administrative Expenses

SGD ISO Code for Singapore Dollar

SH ISO Code for Saint Helena

SHO SEC Regulation affecting Short Sale Rule

SHP ISO Code for Saint Helena Pound

SHSE Shanghai Securities Exchange

SI ISO Code for Slovenia

SIA Securities Industry Association

SIAC Securities Industry Automation Corporation

SIBE Spanish Stock Market Interconnection System

SIC Securities Information Center

SIC Standard Industrial Classification

SICA Securities Industry Committee on Arbitration

SIMEX Singapore International Monetary Exchange

SIMPLE IRA Savings Incentive Match Plan for Employees Individual Retirement Account

SIPC Securities Investor Protection Corporation

SIT ISO Code for Slovenian Tolar

SJ ISO Code for Svalbard and Jan Mayen

SK ISO Code for Slovakia

SKK ISO Code for Slovakian Koruna

SL ISO Code for Sierra Leone

SLD Sld

SLD Sold

SLL ISO Code for Sierra Leone Leone

SLMA Student Loan Marketing Association (Sallie Mae)

SLO Stop-Limit Order, Stop-Loss Order

SLOB Secured Lease Obligation Bond

SM ISO Code for San Marino

SMA Separately Managed Account

SMA Society of Management Accountants

SMA Special Miscellaneous Account

SMART Securities Market Automated Regulated Trading Architecture (Nasdaq)

SMBS Stripped Mortgage-Backed Securities

SN Stock Number

SN ISO Code for Senegal

SO ISO Code for Somalia

SOES Small Order Entry (or Execution) System

SOFFEX Swiss Options and Financial Futures Exchange

SOP Standard Operating Procedure

SOS ISO Code for Somalian Shilling

SOX Sarbanes-Oxley Act of 2002

SOYD Sum of the Years' Digits Method

SpA Società per Azioni (Italian corporation)

SPDA Single Premium Deferred Annuity

SPDR Standard & Poor's Depository Receipt

SPE Special Purpose Entity

SPINS Standard & Poor's 500 Index Subordinated Notes

SPLI Single Premium Life Insurance

SPQR Small Profits, Quick Returns

SPRI Société de Personnes a Responsabilité Limitée (Belgian corporation)

SPX Standard & Poor's 500 Stock Index

SR ISO Code for Suriname

Sr Senior

SRG ISO Code for Suriname Guilder

SRO Self-Regulatory Organization

SRP Salary Reduction Plan

SRT Spousal Remainder Trust

SS Social Security

SSA Social Security Administration

SSE Bolsa de Commercio de Santiago Chile

SSE Stockholm Stock Exchange

SSF Single Stock Future

ST ISO Code for Sao Tome and Principe

STAGS Sterling Transferable Accruing Government Securities

STB Special Tax Bond

STD ISO Code for Sao Tome and Principe Dobra

STRIPS Separate Trading of Registered Interest and Principal of Securities

SU Set Up (freight)

SV ISO Code for El Salvador

SVC ISO Code for El Salvadore Colon

SWAT StockWatch Automated Tracking System (Nasdaq)

SWIFT Society for Worldwide Interbank Financial Telecommunications

SY ISO Code for Syrian Arab Republic

SYP ISO Code for Syrian Pound

SZ ISO Code for Swaziland

SZL ISO Code for Swaziland Lilangeni

SZSE Shenzhen Stock Exchange

T

T- Treasury (as in T-bill, T-bond, T-note)

T&E Travel and Entertainment Expenses

TA Trade Acceptance

TA Transfer Agent

TAA Tactical Asset Allocation

TAB Tax Anticipation Bill

TAC Targeted Amortization Class (TAC)

TALF Term Asset-Backed Securities Loan Facilities

TAN Tax Anticipation Note

TARS Trade Acceptance and Reconciliation Service

TARP Troubled Asset Relief Program

TASE Tel Aviv Stock Exchange

TBA To Be Announced

TBE Tenancy by the Entirety

TBMA Bond Market Association, The

TC ISO Code for Turks and Caicos Islands

TC Tax Court of the United States

TD ISO Code for Chad

TD Time Deposit

TED Spread Treasury Bills Versus Eurodollar Futures

TEFRA Tax Equity and Fiscal Responsibility Act of 1982

TF ISO Code for French Southern Territories

TFE Toronto Futures Exchange

TG ISO Code for Togo

TGE Tokyo Grain Exchange

TH ISO Code for Thailand

THB ISO Code for Thai Baht

TIIS Treasury Inflation-Indexed Securities

TIC Tenancy in Common

TIFFE Tokyo International Financial Futures Exchange

TIGER Treasury Investors Growth Receipt

TIMES Trust Issued Mandatory Exchange Securities

TIP To Insure Promptness

TIPS Toronto Index Participation Securities

TIPS Treasury Inflation Protected Securities

TITAL Transaction Insured Trade Acceptance Locator

TJ ISO Code for Tajikistan

TJR ISO Code for the Tajikistan Rouble

TK ISO Code for Tokelau

TL Trade-Last

TM ISO Code for Turkmenistan

TM Trademark

TMM ISO Code for Turkmenistan Manet

TMTR Third Market Trade Reporting

TN ISO Code for Tunisia

TND ISO Code for Tunisian Dinar

TO ISO Code for Tonga

TOCOM Tokyo Commodity Exchange

TOP ISO Code for Tonga Pa'anga

TOPIX Tokyo Stock Price Index

TP ISO Code for East Timor

TR ISO Code for Turkey

TRA Taxpayer Relief Act of 1997

TRACES Trust Automatic Common Exchange Securities

TRL ISO Code for Turkish Lira

TSE Taiwan Stock Exchange

TSE Tokyo Stock Exchange

TSX Toronto Stock Exchange

TT Testamentary Trust

TT ISO Code for Trinidad and Tobago

TTD ISO Code for Trinidad and Tobago Dollar

TTM Trailing Twelve Months

TV ISO Code for Tuvalu

TVA Tennessee Valley Authority

TW ISO Code for Taiwan

TWD ISO Code for Taiwan Dollar

TYX Thirty-Year Treasury Bond Index

TZ ISO Code for Tanzania

TZS ISO Code for Tanzania Shilling

T+3 Settlement date for securities transactions (3 days following trade date)

U

UA ISO Code for Ukraine

UAH ISO Code for Ukraine Hryvnia

UAW United Automobile Workers

UBTI Unrelated Business Tax Income

UCC Uniform Commercial Code

UCOM United Currency Options Market

UG ISO Code for Uganda

UGMA Uniform Gifts To Minors Act

UGX ISO Code for Uganda Shilling

UIT Unit Investment Trust

UL Underwriters' Laboratories

ULC Underwriter's Laboratories of Canada

ULI Underwriter's Laboratories, Inc.

UM ISO Code for U.S. Minor Outlying Islands

UMA Unified Managed Account

UMW United Mine Workers

UN United Nations

UPC Uniform Practice Code

US ISO Code for United States

USA United States of America

USBS United States Bureau of Standards

USC United States Code

USCC United States Chamber of Commerce

USD ISO Code for United States Dollar

USIT Unit Share Investment Trust

USJCC United States Junior Chamber of Commerce (JAYCEES)

USS United States Senate

USS United States Ship

UTMA Uniform Transfer to Minors Act

UTP Unlisted Trading Privileges

UW Underwriter

UY ISO Code for Uruguay

UYU ISO Code for Uruguay Peso

UZ ISO Code for Uzbekistan

UZS ISO Code for Uzbekistan Sum

V

VA Veterans Administration

VA ISO Code for Holy See (Vatican City State)

VaR Value at Risk

VAT Value Added Tax

VC ISO Code for Saint Vincent and The Grenadines

VD Volume Deleted

VE ISO Code for Venezuela

VEB ISO Code for Venezuelan Bolivar

Veep Vice President

VELDA SUE Venture Enhancement & Loan Development Administration for Smaller Undercapitalized Enterprises

VG ISO Code for British Virgin Islands

VI ISO Code for United States Virgin Islands

VI In bankruptcy or receivership; being reorganized under the Bankruptcy Act; securities assumed by such companies (in bond and stock listings of newspapers)

VIP Very Important Person

VIPER Vanguard Index Participation Receipts

VIX Volatility Index of CBOE

VL Value Line Investment Survey

VN ISO Code for Viet Nam

VND ISO Code for Vietnamese Dong

VOL Volume

VP Vice President

VRDB Variable-Rate Demand Bond

VRM Variable Rate Mortgage

VSE Vancouver Stock Exchange

VSE Vienna Stock Exchange

VTC Voting Trust Certificate

VUV ISO Code for the Vanuatu Vatu

VWAP Volume-Weighted Average Price

W

WACC Weighted Average Cost of Capital

WAM Weighted Average Maturity

WB Waybill

WCA Workmen's Compensation Act

WCE Winnipeg Commodity Exchange

WD When Distributed (in stock listings of newspapers)

WebCRD Web Central Registration Depository (Nasdaq)

WEBS World Equity Benchmark Shares

WF ISO Code for Wallis and Futuna

WHOOPS Washington Public Power Supply System

WI When Issued (in stock listings of newspapers)

WR Warehouse Receipt

WS ISO Code for Samoa

WSE Warsaw Stock Exchange

WSJ Wall Street Journal

WST ISO Code for Samoa Tala

WT Warrant (in stock listings of newspapers)

W/Tax Withholding Tax

WTO World Trade Organization

WW With Warrants (in bond and stock listings of newspapers)

X

X Ex-Interest (in bond listings of newspapers)

XAF ISO Code for the CFA (Communaute Financiere Africaine BEAC) Franc

XAM AMEX Market Value Index

XAX Amex Composite Index

XBA ISO Code for the European Composite Unit (EURCO)

XBB ISO Code for the European Monetary Unit (EMU)

XCD ISO Code for the East Caribbean Dollar

XD Ex-Dividend (in stock listings of newspapers)

X-Dis Ex-Distribution (in stock listings of newspapers)

XDR ISO Code for Special Drawing Rights (SDR)

XEU ISO Code for European Currency Unit (ECU)

XMI AMEX Major Market Index

XOF ISO Code for the CFA (Communaute Financiere Africaine BCEAO) Franc

XPF ISO Code for the CFP (Comptois Francais du Pacifique) Franc

XR Ex-Rights (in stock listings of newspapers)

XW Ex-Warrants (in bond and stock listings of newspapers)

Y

Y Ex-Dividend and Sales in Full (in stock listings of newspapers)

YE ISO Code for Yemen

YER ISO Code for Yemen Rial

YLD Yield (in stock listings of newspapers)

YT ISO Code for Mayotte

YTB Yield to Broker

YTC Yield to Call

YTD Year to Date

YTM Yield to Maturity

Z

Z Zero

ZA ISO Code for South Africa

ZAR ISO Code for South African Rand

ZBA Zero Bracket Amount

ZBB Zero-Based Budgeting

ZM ISO Code for Zambia

ZMK ISO Code for Zambian Kwacha

ZR Zero Coupon Issue (Security) (in bond listings of newspapers)

ZRN ISO Code for the Zaire New Zaire

ZW ISO Code for Zimbabwe

ZWD ISO Code for Zimbabwe Dollar

INDEX

BARRON'S
Means Business!

Dictionary of Accounting Terms, 5th Ed.
978-0-7641-4310-6, $14.99, Can$17.99

Dictionary of Banking Terms, 5th Ed.
978-0-7641-3263-6, $14.99, Can$17.99

Dictionary of Business Terms, 4th Ed.
978-0-7641-3534-7, $14.99, Can$17.99

Dictionary of Computer and Internet Terms, 10th Ed.
978-0-7641-4105-8, $14.99, Can$17.99

Dictionary of Finance & Investment Terms, 8th Ed.
978-0-7641-4304-5, $14.99, Can$17.99

Dictionary of Insurance Terms, 5th Ed.
978-0-7641-3884-3, $14.99, Can$17.99

Dictionary of International Business Terms, 3rd Ed.
978-0-7641-2445-7, $16.99, Can$19.99

Dictionary of Marketing Terms, 4th Ed.
978-0-7641-3935-2, $14.99, Can$17.99

Dictionary of Real Estate Terms, 7th Ed.
978-0-7641-3936-9, $13.99, Can$16.99

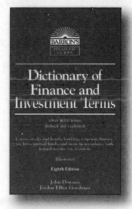

Prices subject to change without notice.

Barron's Educational Series, Inc.
250 Wireless Boulevard, Hauppauge, NY 11788
Order toll-free: 1-800-645-3476
Order by fax: 1-631-434-3217

In Canada: Georgetown Book Warehouse
34 Armstrong Ave., Georgetown, Ontario L7G 4R9
Canadian orders: 1-800-247-7160
Order by fax: 1-800-887-1594

To order visit us at **www.barronseduc.com**
or your local book store

(#12) R 4/10

BARRON'S BUSINESS KEYS
Take the Mystery Out of Doing Business

Each "key" explains approximately 50 concepts and provides a glossary and index. Each book: Paperback, approx. 176–224 pp., 5 1/4" x 8 1/4"

Keys to Buying Foreclosed and Bargain Homes, 3rd Edition
(978-0-7641-3883-6) $8.99, Can$10.99

Keys to Investing in Common Stocks, 4th Edition
(978-0-7641-2447-1) $7.95, Can$9.50

Keys to Investing in Options and Futures, 4th Edition
(978-0-7641-2905-6) $7.99, Can$9.50

Keys to Investing in Real Estate, 5th Edition
(978-0-7641-4329-8) $7.99, Can$9.50

Keys to Mortgage Financing and Refinancing, 4th Edition
(978-0-7641-3531-6) $7.99, Can$9.50

Keys to Reading an Annual Report, 4th Edition
(978-0-7641-3915-4) $8.99, Can$10.99

——————— To order ———————
Available at your local book store
or visit **www.barronseduc.com**

Barron's Educational Series, Inc.
250 Wireless Blvd.
Hauppauge, N.Y. 11788
Order toll-free: 1-800-645-3476
Order by fax: 1-631-434-3217

In Canada:
Georgetown Book Warehouse
34 Armstrong Ave.
Georgetown, Ontario L7G 4R9
Canadian orders: 1-800-247-7160
Order by fax: 1-800-887-1594

(#10) R 7/10   Prices subject to change without notice.

The More You Know About Barron's—
The Greater Your Opportunities for Success

BARRON'S ACCOUNTING HANDBOOK, 5th ED.
Joel G. Siegel and Jae K. Shim
Provides accounting rules, guidelines, formulas and techniques, etc. to help students
and business professionals work out accounting problems.
ISBN 978-0-7641-6270-1, 1040 pages, $39.99, Can$47.99

REAL ESTATE HANDBOOK, 7th ED.
Jack P. Friedman, Jack C. Harris, and Barry A. Diskin
A dictionary/reference for everyone in real estate. Defines approximately 2000 legal,
financial, and architectural terms.
ISBN 978-0-7641-6110-0, 784 pages, $39.99, Can$47.99

REAL ESTATE LICENSING EXAMS: SALESPERSON, BROKER,
APPRAISER, 8th ED.
J. Bruce Lindeman and Jack P. Friedman
Reviews current exam topics and features updated model exams and supplemental
exams, all with explained answers.
ISBN 978-0-7641-4237-6, 504 pages, $16.99, Can$19.99

BARRON'S FINANCE AND INVESTMENT HANDBOOK, 8th ED.
John Downes and Jordan Elliot Goodman
This hard-working handbook of essential information defines more than 3000 key
terms, and explores 30 basic investment opportunities. The investment information
is thoroughly up-to-date.
ISBN 978-0-7641-6269-5, 1232 pages, $39.99, Can$47.99

DICTIONARY OF REAL ESTATE TERMS, 7th ED.
Jack P. Friedman, Jack C. Harris, and J. Bruce Lindeman
This valuable handbook for home buyers and sellers defines and explains approximately
3000 real estate terms related to mortgages and financing, brokerage law, architecture,
rentals and leases, property insurance, and much more.
ISBN 978-0-7641-3936-9, 560 pages, $13.99, Can$16.99

Barron's Educational Series, Inc.
250 Wireless Blvd.
Hauppauge, N.Y. 11788
Order toll-free: 1-800-645-3476

In Canada:
Georgetown Book Warehouse
34 Armstrong Ave.
Georgetown, Ontario L7G 4R9
Canadian orders: 1-800-247-7160

Prices subject to change without notice.

To order visit **www.barronseduc.com** or your local book store   (#11) R4/10

Barron's helps you succeed in today's Business World

Business Review Series

Accounting, 5th Ed.
Peter J. Eisen
ISBN 978-0-7641-3547-7
456 pp., $18.99, Can$22.99

Finance, 5th Ed.
A. A. Groppelli and E. Nikbakht
ISBN 978-0-7641-3420-3
624 pp., $18.99, Can$22.99

Business Law, 5th Ed.
R. W. Emerson
ISBN 978-0-7641-4240-6
768 pp., $18.99, Can$22.99

Management, 4th Ed.
P. J. Montana and B. H. Charnov
ISBN 978-0-7641-3931-4
552 pp., $18.99, Can$22.99

Business Statistics, 5th Ed.
D. Downing and J. Clark
ISBN 978-0-7641-4239-0
560 pp., $18.99, Can$22.99

Marketing, 4th Ed.
Richard L. Sandhusen
ISBN 978-0-7641-3932-1
624 pp., $18.99, Can$22.99

Economics, 4th Ed.
Walter J. Wessels
ISBN 978-0-7641-3419-7
656 pp., $18.99, Can$22.99

Operations Management
J. K. Shim and J. G. Siegel
ISBN 978-0-7641-0510-4
496 pp., $18.99, Can$22.99

Barron's Educational Series, Inc.
250 Wireless Blvd.
Hauppauge, NY 11788
Order toll-free: 1-800-645-3476
Order by fax: 1-631-434-3217

In Canada:
Georgetown Book Warehouse
34 Armstrong Ave.
Georgetown, Ont. L7G 4R9
Canadian orders: 1-800-247-7160
Order by fax: 1-800-887-1594

Prices subject to change without notice.

(#88) R 7/10

——— To order ———
Available at your local book store
or visit **www.barronseduc.com**